GAMAGE'S

CHRISTMAS BAZAAR 1913

being a facsimile reprint
of the 1913 Christmas catalogue
of A. W. Gamage Ltd of Holborn, London,
with some pages from
the 1911 General Catalogue

Introduced by Alison Adburgham

DAVID & CHARLES REPRINTS

0 7153 6608 4

Library of Congress Catalog Card Number 74–83319

Printed in Great Britain
by Redwood Burn Ltd Trowbridge and Esher
for David & Charles (Holdings) Limited
South Devon House Newton Abbot Devon

Published in the United States of America
by David & Charles Inc North Pomfret
Vermont 05053 USA

Published in Canada
by Douglas David & Charles Limited
3645 McKechnie Drive West Vancouver BC

Introduction

TALL OAKS FROM LITTLE ACORNS GROW was the favourite motto of Arthur Walter Gamage, a Herefordshire farmer's son apprenticed to a draper in the City of London. In 1878 he set up shop for himself in Holborn, and hung his motto up above the counter. He was only twenty years old at the time, a very tender age to start in business on one's own; but Gamage did not come of tender stock. He saw the tiny shop with its five foot frontage as his little acorn, and sure enough it grew into a vast emporium, a conglomeration of Victorian buildings behind a grandoise neo-Gothic facade.

He had heard of the vacant property by chance one lunch hour when he took a watch to be mended by a Holborn watchmaker. In conversation, the watchmaker mentioned that the next door premises were empty and that what Holborn needed was a hosiery shop. Gamage's ambition was fired. The story, as told in a Gamage advertisement of some 25 years later, continues: 'The following Sunday, while attending service at Chapel, his business instincts prompted him to make the venture.' No suggestion that a voice from on high said 'Go forward Gamage'; no suggestion that he prayed for divine guidance. It was his business instincts, equally alive on the Sabbath as on every other day, that guided him from Chapel that Sunday to become a millionaire.

The rent was £220 a year, with a premium of £80 for the lease. Gamage had only £40 saved from his wages. But a friend named Frank Spain was persuaded to join the venture, and between them they managed to raise £150. £50 went on account for the premium; fittings cost £8 and they slept in the back room of the shop, reckoning 14s a week for living expenses. Their most pressing problem was to find wholesalers willing to allow credit to a couple of young men starting business with no backing. One wholesaler they approached, a friend of Gamage's former employer, advised Gamage to go back, saying the employer would repay the capital already spent. But Gamage was determined to go on, and the wholesaler was so impressed by his self-confidence that he promised them credit for a few months. The first week's total of trade was £24; the second week it dropped to £21; but in the third it jumped to £40, and by the end of the first year had reached £1,632. Frank Spain, however, was a less confident character than Arthur Walter Gamage; and when he became engaged to be married he was afraid the business would not support two families. He asked Arthur Walter to buy him out. This Gamage did, for £425.

Their most sensational sales scoop of those early days was when there was a sudden craze for hair brushes with wire bristles set in rubber. These brushes were selling everywhere for 2s 6d. Gamage filled his entire window with identical brushes at 1s 9d, and customers poured in. It was a good augury for the policy he had decided to pursue: that of selling good quality merchandise at lower prices than offered elsewhere. In fact, he worked on a 33⅓ per cent less profit margin than most other retailers. Understandably this did not endear him to his rivals in trade, and after the firm became a public company in 1897 Gamage was in continuous conflict. There were several law suits, and because of his price-cutting many manufacturers refused to supply him, so that it became necessary to concentrate mainly upon non-branded goods. Unlike Harrod's and the Army and Navy

5

Stores (which were both reaching great heights of prosperity at this period), Gamage never went in for manufacturing any of his own lines. Instead, by making direct contracts with small manufacturers to make large orders of goods exclusive to Gamage's, he was able to offer prices with which other retailers could not compete. In an interview he was reported as saying, 'I am quite content to be the best-hated man in the retail trade;' and declared that although he was attacked on many different pretexts, the real reason for all the attacks was that he undermined price monopolies.

Of those goods made especially for Gamage's, the Gamage bicycle was the most famous. The huge 900-page mail order catalogue of 1911 devotes no less than 49 pages to bicycles and equipment, headed by a CHEAP BICYCLE WARNING:

> The unprecedented success of the Gamage £3.19.9 machine has brought about the usual crop of imitators. These gentry attempt to foist upon the public an ALLEGED BICYCLE at a few pence under the price of our world-famed machine. In the majority of instances their products are simply a collection of cheap foreign parts and tubing carelessly assembled, and bearing a well-known name as to tyre or a single part, in order to give them the appearance of reliability. Such machines should be avoided as the plague. Another 'trap for the unwary' is that of selling the machine minus many parts. These parts are supplied at a high price after you get your machine.

After reading this self-righteous tirade, it is interesting to note that Gamage's world-famed machines are pictured in the catalogue without several essential accessories: no bells, no pumps, no saddle-bags for tool-kits.

Gamage's were appointed official Scouts' outfitters, and it was a great place for all kinds of camping equipment – the Jaeger sleeping bag, the Gamage explorer's table, mosquito curtaining, the military hammock chair with glass holder for whisky, the collapsible rubber urinal for travelling. A reputation for sports equipment was quickly built up as the opportunities for playing games became available to more people of all classes instead of being mainly confined to those with plenty of leisure. Naturally Lillywhites, founded in 1863 by the great cricketing family and specialising in sports equipment only, had greater prestige than a shop that styled itself 'the People's Emporium'; but Gamage's did well with sports associations, clubs and schools. Lillywhites were well ahead with winter sports equipment, having been right in at the beginning when ski-ing became a sport in the last years of the nineteenth century, and when Europe was opened up to holidaymakers after the 1914–18 war, they established themselves as *the* winter sports experts. Nevertheless, Gamage's were selling a certain amount of winter sports equipment before the era of cheap ski-ing holidays began in the 1920s. In their catalogue of 1911 there is a page devoted to sleighs, toboggans, and skis imported from Switzerland. A romantic drawing depicts a lady in long full skirt to the ankles, ski-ing arm in arm with a gallant gentleman down a perilous slope, one pair of ski sticks between them.

Arctic equipment was required for the unpredictable hazards of motoring in Edwardian days, and Gamage's sold motor cars and 'Everything for the automobilist': fur-lined overboots, leggings, gaiters, motoring headgear, goggles, klaxon horns, oil lamps, fire extinguishers. The automobile itself could be cossetted by the Gamage stove especially designed for the Motor-house. The Gamage 3 hp Motor Cycle was first sold in 1902, and by 1905 was claiming to have 'beaten the flower of both English and foreign makes of often double the hp'. Indeed, the Motoring Department must have been Arthur Walter's joy and pride, for when he died in 1930 he lay in state in the Motoring Department, with members of the staff mounting guard at the catafalque day and night. So goes the story, too nice to disbelieve; but whether this lying in state was by his own will we know not. It seems unlikely, because Arthur Walter Gamage was not a showman in the sense of personal presentation as was Gordon Selfridge, nor yet a colourful character like William Whiteley, the self-styled 'Universal Provider of Westbourne Grove'. Whiteley all his life had a genius for free editorial publicity, including two spectacular fires. Even in death he achieved maximum press coverage by being murdered by pistol shot in his own shop during the January sales of 1907, by a young man claiming to be his illegitimate son.

With so much free publicity, Mr Whiteley had been able to boast that he never spent a penny on advertising, whereas most of the big stores considered it essential to their business. As early as 1894 Mr Harrod had taken a full page in the *Daily Telegraph*, and two years later Swan & Edgar took space on the front page of the first issue of the *Daily Mail*. Gamage's claimed to have been the first store to take all of this most rewarding front page – on July 12, 1904, when the *Daily Mail* boasted 'A daily circulation five times as large as any penny London journal'. Gamage's front page had no illustrations of goods for sale. It was a prestige advertisement headed by the motto 'Tall oaks from little acorns grow', and carrying pictures of the original Gamage shop, the little acorn, and of the immense building into which it had grown. It announced that Holborn was going to 'be beautified by further extensions to the People's Popular Emporium', which already had more than two acres of floor space for the display of goods, and twice as much space again in unseen departments of administration, stockrooms, staff rooms, kitchens and canteens, and the mail order operation that dealt with a very large part of the Gamage trade. Everything that Gamage's sold (and they claimed to sell everything) could be ordered by post – to be exact, not quite everything, for the catalogues carried a warning: Please note, ammunition and explosives cannot be sent by post.

The property to be torn down for these beautifying extensions in 1904 included three public houses, and the licence of one of these was to be used for a 'First Class Restaurant at Gamage Prices' in the basement. One has to admit that Gamage's lacked style. But then there should be nothing posh or off-putting about a People's Popular Emporium, as there was about the West End department stores at that time, catering for the carriage trade. The West End and Kensington High Street stores were different, also, in that their policy was mainly directed towards attracting women shoppers, whereas Mr Gamage never made any particular efforts to woo the ladies. No doubt this was chiefly due to the position of his store, convenient for the City and Fleet Street, where there were few women workers before 1914. Gamage's was the great place for bank clerks, office workers and messenger boys to spend their lunch hour, a great place for 'the home handyman' sixty years before the term 'do-it-yourself' was coined. It was the great place for any man with a hobby, a sport, a half hour to spare.

Of course many of these lunch hour customers had wives and children, homes and gardens. Many lived in Essex towns such as Brentford and Romford, and in the growing villages along the Thames estuary. For them, Gamage's was the nearest place for important purchases such as furniture, carpets, kitchen equipment, greenhouses, perambulators. Thus Saturdays were very much family shopping days at Gamage's, a day in paradise for the children when they were old enough to be left in the toy and hobby departments, or in the pets department where Barney, the resident Mynah bird – one of the staff so to speak – spoke to the customers in a constant chatter of cheerio phrases. Clothes for the family would also be bought on these expeditions: no fashionable flim-flammery, but good, sensible, necessary, long-wearing clothes, clothes that father had to approve of as well as pay for.

Fathers were at home in Gamage's. Even the smell of the place was male – wood floors and brown linoleum, tools and fertilisers, paint, paraffin, mowing machines. There was also a smell of animals emanating from 'The largest and most complete zoological department in London'. No exaggerated boast that, when you see the list of items in pre-1914 catalogues, and no surprise about the smell either: male Abyssinian goats with long black hair and outstanding horns; Congo masked pigs; Civet cats, tree porcupines, chimpanzee (male) perfectly tame; Mexican coaiti; flying foxes; Indian mongoose, wild; Indian mongoose, tame. About forty species of reptiles were listed, and some pets were described as especially suitable for ladies: Lion-faced marmosets, Japanese newts (very pretty), skinks (no description), hedgehogs, 12″ Nile alligators, fancy rats, Japanese waltzing mice. 'Common pretty kittens' were from 3s 6d, which seems expensive when you think how common kittens are. One avairy list started lyrically with Hartz Mountain singing cock canaries, gas or daylight songsters, in full rolling song. If your hobby did not happen to be keeping birds or animals but stuffing them, you could buy a taxidermist's companion; and if your livelihood was farming, there were bull rings, cattle leaders, pig ringers, nigger collars. Rather oddly placed on the same page there is a sinister list of Asylum Requisites: lunatic locks, heavy warders' key chains, belts and fittings. It was perfectly true, you could find anything you could conceivably have read of at Gamage's.

Blessedly, however, there have always been more children than lunatics; and from quite early days Mr Gamage specialised in unusual toys. There are legendary tales of his travels in search of them: of being confronted by a blizzard in the wilds of Michigan when looking for the makers of an ingenious toy gun; of having his ears frostbitten when travelling to a trade fair in Chicago; of searching two days off the beaten track in Austria to find the maker of a toy he had seen in a Vienna shop. He visited Frau Steiff's doll and soft toy factory in the Black Forest, and became the largest British importer of her famous stuffed animals – four whole pages of them in this catalogue. 'Most of the Steiff animals have a *real animal voice*. The lamb bleats, the cat mews, the dog barks, the pig grunts, the bear growls.' Frau Steiff was the maker of the original teddy bear, named after Teddy Roosevelt. By 1907, Teddy had become the best seller of all stuffed animals, and he has ever since held his especial place in the heart's affections of every generation of children.

Arthur Walter's son Eric was a genuine acorn of the old Gamage oak. He went into the business straight from school, worked through most of the departments, and then took charge of the administrative sections. He was Managing Director for twenty years before his father died. And like his father, he was mad about toys. It was he who introduced the live Christmas attractions. One year it was a real live circus. In the year of this catalogue it was the Wonderful Fire Brigade Scene '*real* water is used, numbers of peasants are watching the conflagration'. There is also the Great Red Indian Encampment, and the Great Military Moving Model, and all the Marvels of Wireless Telegraphy being demonstrated. For Gamage's were always abreast of the times with toys, if not a little ahead. In their 1911 catalogue they wrote, rightly, that 'the problem of scientists today is a toy for the child tomorrow; and indeed the scientific toy has become an absolute necessity to the education of modern youth'.

In spite of extensions and modernisation at various times, it always seemed that the little old properties on each side of the original A. W. Gamage shop gradually acquired as their leases fell in, were just left as they were behind that red-brick neo-Gothic facade. Perhaps not – but everyone's memory of Gamage's is of a labyrinth of passages, of rooms joined to other rooms by sudden flights of steps, or by disconcerting ramps – everything on different levels, illogical juxtapositions of absurdly unrelated merchandise, a maze that bemused and misled the most seasoned Gamage customer. Of course, the rabbit warren principle may have been subtle salesmanship – the longer a customer took to find the department he wanted, the more likely he was to be distracted by an unrepeatable bargain he did not want, something he had no possible use for, had no place to put, but something that, as a Gamage salesman might point out, was so inexpensive that he simply could not afford not to buy it.

Yet no faithful Gamage customer would ever have wished a fresh wind of modern retailers to blow through that confusing conglomeration. And when in 1970 the Sterling Guarantee Trust acquired the property for a £20 million redevelopment scheme of shops and offices, it was no consolation to be told that one of the shops in the complex would be a bright new open-plan Gamage's; no consolation, either, to be told later that the name of A. W. Gamage was to be kept alive meanwhile by trading in the Oxford Street building vacated by Waring & Gillow when they moved to Oxford Street. The name might be kept alive, but the Gamage's we knew would be dead. A pillar of the establishment was to be pulled down. We had often laughed at it, but it was a very British thing. And when the closing down sale in Holborn took place in March 1972, a farewell excursion train was run from the Midlands, and nostalgia poured onto the pages of national newspapers. Journalists wrote as they might have written at the death of a national personality who had outlived his time – quirky, eccentric, a little seedy and down at heel, unlovely to look at but lovable through long association.

And nostalgia must inevitably be stirred up once more by the re-issue of this Christmas Bazaar. No need for me to describe its delights, for they are here for the browsing. But do not, I beg of you, miss the splendid pages of Masks, Noses, Wigs, Moustaches, and Beards; and do not skip too quickly through those 15 pages of Tricks, Jokes, and Puzzles. Study the 'Mirth Makers', which include surprise water cameras, plate lifters, whistling niggers, and Harry Lauder singing tie-pins. Find the skulls with electrical eyes, and the electrical tattoo-ing machine. Indeed, Gamage's supplied everything you could possibly require for hilarious Christmas parties, including the hire of Mr Henry Houston from Maskelyne and Devants, unrivalled manipulator of cards, coins and mystical creations.

Any Christmas of long ago, as we look back on it, is imbued with a certain sentimental melancholy; but there is an especial poignancy about Christmas 1913. Those who, all over England, spent happy hours with this catalogue choosing presents for the whole family, had no idea that next Christmas many fathers and brothers, uncles and cousins, would not be there. As they decided upon the crackers and decorations for New Year parties, there was no fear of what 1914 held in store. As they lit the candles on the tree, they did not know it would be the last Christmas before the lamps went out all over Europe.

ALISON ADBURGHAM

Daily Mail.

Daily Circulation Five Times as Large as That of Any Penny London Morning Journal.

TUESDAY, JULY 12, 1904.

ONE HALFPENNY.

"TALL OAKS FROM LITTLE ACORNS GROW."

ROMANCE OF THE HOUSE OF GAMAGE.

Holborn Being Beautified by the Extensions to the People's Popular Emporium.

ROMANCE OF THE HOUSE OF GAMAGE.

The Whole World's Mart which has Always Kept Its Future In Front.

THE LITTLE ACORN.

Gamage's 25 years ago.

THE TALL OAK WHICH FROM THE LITTLE ACORN GREW.

GAMAGE'S OF TO-DAY WITH ITS WHOLE FUTURE STILL TO COME.

A. W. GAMAGE, LTD.,
The World's Largest Sport and Athletic Outfitters.

HOLBORN, LONDON, E.C.

Some pages from

Gamage's 1911 General Catalogue

GAMAGES
DELIVERY OF GOODS.

PROMPT SURE and SWIFT

Special attention is directed to the arrangements that are now in operation in regard to Free Carriage and Delivery Terms.

LONDON AND SUBURBS.	Orders of 5/- and over, Free Delivery by L.P.D. Co. If within the Radius of our Express Motor Van Service, orders of any amount and description of goods Delivered Free, except goods sent direct from growers or manufacturers.
COUNTRY ORDERS.	Orders of 20/- and over (unless otherwise stated), sent carriage paid to any Goods Station in England and Wales. Half Rate charged (or allowed) to any Port or Goods Station in Scotland or Ireland. Should customers elect to have goods sent by Fast or Passenger Trains, the difference in Carriage will be charged.
PARCEL POST.	Postage paid on goods of the value of 20/- and over to any part of England, Scotland, Wales, Ireland and the Channel Islands, not exceeding 11 lbs. in weight. Liquids, Ammunition, Calcium Carbide, Rubber Solution, Fireworks, or any Explosives, cannot be sent by post.
PACKING ARRANGEMENTS.	We strongly recommend that when toys or goods of a fragile and breakable nature, are ordered to be sent by rail or boat, they should be packed in strong returnable crates or cases, full amount (paid) allowed when returned. When returning, reverse label and advise by post. Please add 6d., 1/- or larger amount according to the size of the article ordered.
EXPORT ORDERS.	We give special attention to this Branch of our business, all orders received being executed with the utmost despatch. We carry large stocks of goods suitable for the export trade, and every care is taken in the fulfilment of customers' commands. Orders should be accompanied with a remittance sufficient to cover the cost of the goods together

with the expenses of special cases, shipping charges, insurance, etc. Orders of £2 and over delivered free to any of the London, Southampton, Hull, Liverpool or Glasgow Docks.

EXPORT PARCEL POST.	Customers are specially requested to enquire at their Post Office for rates, as the Inland English Postal Rates do not apply to the Colonies or British Dominions beyond the seas, or to foreign countries. To assist customers as to weight of articles listed, the English Inland Postage Rate is :— 3d. the first lb., 2 lbs. 4d., 3 lbs. 5d., 5 lbs. 6d., 7 lbs. 7d., 8 lbs. 8d., 9 lbs. 9d., 10 lbs. 10d., 11 lbs. 11d.

Customers will please bear in mind that they must add the cost of a lb. or lbs. to their remittance, but when small articles are ordered, several will go to the lb. weight.

REMITTANCES may be made by Banker's Draft, Post Office Orders, or through a Commission House in England. Foreign stamps cannot be accepted in payment.

CATALOGUE
OF ANY
DEPARTMENT
POST FREE.

We issue Specially Illustrated Departmental Catalogues of the following departments, any of which may be obtained free on application.

Sports and Games.

Horticultural, Poultry Appliances,
and Live Stock.

Guns and Fishing Tackle,
Taxidermy, and everything for the Naturalist.

Tools, Lamps,
Gas and Electric Fittings.

Cycles, Cycle Accessories,
Cycle Clothing, &c.

Motor Clothing and Accessories.

Bags and Trunks
and all Travelling and Camping Equipment.

Baby Carriages, Cots,
Chairs, and Kindergarten Furniture.

Toys and Musical Instruments.

Jewellery, Fancy Goods,
Stationery, Books, &c.

Drugs and Toilet Requisites.

Cigars, Tobacco, Pipes, &c.

Furniture, China and Glass,
and Household Requisites.

Fitted Luncheon Baskets, &c.

Photography, Magic Lanterns
and Optical Goods.

Conjuring and Magic.

Sale Lists (Twice Yearly).

'Xmas Presents List.

GENTLEMEN'S OUTFITTING.

Tailoring, Hats and Caps, Waterproofs, Athletic Clothing, Boots and Shoes, Hosiery, Shirts, Collars, Ties, Umbrellas, Sticks, &c.

HOW TO GET TO GAMAGES BY 'BUS.

NORTH AND NORTH WESTERN DISTRICTS.

District.	Enter Service No.	Change 'Buses at	Enter Service No.
Brondesbury	1 or 16	Oxford Street	7, 8 or 12
Camden Town	5	High Holborn	do.
Canonbury	19	Gray's Inn Road	81
Child's Hill	2 or 24	Oxford Street	7, 8 or 12
Cricklewood	1 or 16	Do.	do.
Euston (L. & N.W.R.)	81	..	..
Golders Green	24	Oxford Street	7, 8 or 12
Hampstead	5	High Holborn	do.
Harringay	13	Oxford Circus	do.
Harlesden	39	Marble Arch	do.
Highbury	19	Gray's Inn Road	81
Highgate	91 or 92	Oxford Street	7, 8 or 12
Kilburn	1 or 16	Do.	do.
King's Cross (G.N.R.)	81	..	..
Muswell Hill	79	Oxford Street	7, 8 or 12
North Finchley	24	Do.	do.
St. Pancras (Mid. R.)	81	..	..
St. John's Wood	2 or 24	Oxford Street	7, 8 or 12
Tollington Park	80	Do.	do.
Willesden	50	Marble Arch	do

EAST AND NORTH EASTERN DISTRICTS.

District.	Enter Service No.	Change 'Buses at	Enter Service No.
Clapton	9 or 22	Liverpool Street	7 or 18
East Ham	17	..	..
Hackney	9	Liverpool Street	7 or 12
Ilford	8	..	..
Liverpool St. (G.E.R.)	7 or 12	..	..
Leyton	9 or 22	Liverpool Street	7 or 12
Leytonstone	10	Aldgate	17
Stamford Hill	57	..	..
Stratford	8	..	..

WEST AND SOUTH WESTERN DISTRICTS.

District.	Enter Service No.	Change 'Buses at	Enter Service No.
Acton	17	..	..
Barnes	9 or 25	Piccadilly Circus	85
Brompton	85	..	..
Chelsea	19	Oxford Street	7, 8 or 12
Chiswick	12	..	..
Ealing	17	..	..
Fulham	85	..	..
Hammersmith	9 or 25	Piccadilly Circus	85
Kensington	9 or 25	Do.	85
Marylebone (G.C.R.)	81	..	..
Mortlake	9 or 25	Piccadilly Circus	85
Paddington (G.W.R.)	7 or 65	..	..
Putney	14	Piccadilly Circus	81
Shepherd's Bush	12 or 17	..	..
Victoria	2 or 24	Marble Arch	7, 8 or 12
Waterloo	5	High Holborn	7, 8 or 12

SOUTH AND SOUTH EASTERN DISTRICTS.

District.	Enter Service No.	Change 'Buses at	Enter Service No.
Battersea	19	New Oxford St.	7, 8 or 12
Brixton	81	..	..
Camberwell	13 or 21	Elephant & Castle	81
Croydon	3	Kennington Park	81
Eltham	21	Elephant & Castle	81
Lee	21	Do.	do.
New Cross	21	Do.	do.
Norwood (West)	20	Charing Cross	57
Peckham	13 or 21	Elephant & Castle	81
Sidcup	21	Do.	do.
Streatham	3	Kennington Park	do.
Tulse Hill	20	Charing Cross	57
West Dulwich	20	Do.	do.

RAILWAY STATIONS.

Farringdon Street, Met. and District	**4** mins.	Snow Hill	**3** mins.	St Paul's	**10** mins.
P.O., Tube Station	**10** ,,	Cannon Street	**12** mins. 'Bus.	Holborn Viaduct	**3** ,,
Chancery Lane Tube Station	**3** ,,	Ludgate Hill	**5** mins.	London Bridge	**15** mins. 'Bus.

ALL ROADS LEAD TO GAMAGES.

OUR VANS deliver in the following districts every day. Those marked * twice a day.

LOOK OUT FOR OUR VANS, OUR CARMEN HAVE INSTRUCTIONS TO TAKE ORDERS.

Aberdeen Park
Acton
Acton Green
Alexandra Park
Alexandra Palace
Anerley

Balham
Balham Hill
*Balls Pond
Barking Road
Barnsbury
Battersea
*Bayswater
Beckenham
*Belgravia
Belsize Park
Bermondsey
Bethnal Green
*Blackfriars
Blackheath
Blackwall
*Borough
Bounds Green
Bow
Bowes Park
Brentford
Brixton
Brockley
Bromley
*Brompton
Brondesbury
*Brook Green
Brownswood Park
Burgess Hill, N.W.

Camberwell
Cambridge Heath
*Camden Town
Canning Town
Canonbury
Catford Bridge
Champion Hill
*Charing Cross
*Chelsea
Child's Hill
Chiswick
*City
Clapham
Clapham Common
Clapham Park
Clapton
Clapton, Upper
Clapton, Lower
*Clerkenwell
Clissold Park
College Park
Colney Hatch
Cricklewood
Crofton Park
Crouch End
Crystal Palace

Dalston
Denmark Hill
Dockhead
Docks (London)
Drayton Park
Dulwich, E. and W.
Dulwich Wood Park

Ealing
Ealing Dean
*Earl's Court
Earlsfield
East Ham
*Edgware Road

Finchley
Finchley, Church End
Finchley, East End
Finchley, Fortis Green
Finchley, North End
*Finsbury
Finsbury Park
Forest Gate
Forest Hill
Fortune Green
Frognal
*Fulham

Gipsy Hill
Golder's Green
Goodmayes
Goose Green
*Gospel Oak
Green Lanes
Grosvenor Park
Grove Park, S. E. & W.
Gunnersbury

Hackney, South & West
Hackney Wick
Haggerston
*Hammersmith
Hampstead
Hanwell
Harlesden
Harringay
Harrow Green
Hatcham
Haverstock Hill
Hendon
Hendon, The Hyde
Herne Hill
Highbury
Highgate
Hither Green
Holloway
*Holland Park
Homerton
Honor Oak
Hornsey
Hornsey Rise

*Horsleydown
Hounslow
*Hoxton
*Hurlingham
*Hyde Park

Ilford
Isleworth
*Islington

*Kennington
*Kennington Park
Kensal Green
Kensal Rise
Kent House
*Kentish Town
Kensington—
    N., S.W. and W.
Kew
Kilburn
*King's Cross
Kingsland
*Knightsbridge

Ladywell
Lambeth
Laurie Park
Lavender Hill
Lea Bridge Road
Lee
Lewisham
Leyton
Leytonstone
Limehouse
Little Ealing
Little Ilford
London Fields
Lordship Park
Loughboro' Park
Lower Sydenham
Lower Norwood

Maida Hill
Maida Vale
Maitland Park
Manor Park
Maryland Point
*Marylebone
*Mayfair
Mildmay Park
Mile End
Millwall
Muswell Hill

New Cross
Newington Green
*Newington Butts
*Newington Causeway
New Kent Road
Newlands Park
New Wanstead
Nine Elms
Norbury Hill
Norwood
*Notting Hill
Nunhead

Oakhill Park
Osterley Park
Old Ford
Old Kent Road

*Paddington
Palmer's Green
Parsons Green
Peckham
Peckham Rye
Penge
*Pentonville
Perry Vale
*Pimlico
Plaistow
Poplar
Primrose Hill
Putney Heath
Putney Vale

Queen's Park

Railways (All)
Ravenscourt Park
Ravenscroft Park
*Regent's Park
Rushey Green

Seven Kings
Seven Sisters Road
Shadwell
*Shepherd's Bush
South Ealing
Somers Town
Southgate, New and Old
South Hill Park
*Southwark
South Penge Park
Stamford Hill
*Starch Green
Stepney
*St. James
St. Johns, S.E.

*St. Peter's Park
Stockwell
Stoke Newington
Stonebridge Park
Strand on the Green
Stratford
Stratford New Town
Streatham
Streatham Hill
Streatham Common
Stroud Green
Sydenham

Tollington Park
Tooting,
    Upper & Lower
Torrington Park
Tufnell Park
Tulse Hill
Turnham Green

Upper Norwood
Upper Tulse Hill
Upton Manor
Upton Park

Vauxhall
*Victoria
Victoria Park

*Walham Green
Walthamstow
Walworth
Wandsworth
Wanstead
*Westbourne Grove
*Westbourne Park
Westcombe Park
West Dulwich
West Ham
*West Hampstead
*Westminster
Whipps Cross
Whitechapel
Whitehall Park
Willesden Green
Willesden Junction
Wimbledon
Wimbledon Park
Wimbledon Common
Wimbledon, South
Winchmore Hill
Wood Green
Woodside Park
Wormwood Scrubbs

GAMAGES OF HOLBORN.

Clockwork Motor, "Jollyboy," etc.

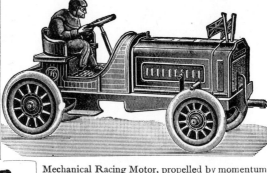

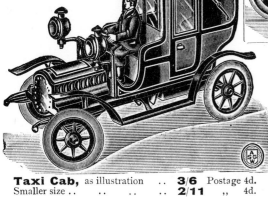

Taxi Cab, as illustration .. **3/6** Postage 4d.
Smaller size .. .. .. **2/11** ,, 4d.

Mechanical Racing Motor, propelled by momentum
of wheel—cannot get out of order. **10½d.** Post 3d.
Do., do., larger, as illustration .. **1/9** ,, 3d.

BENETFINKS OF CHEAPSIDE.

Clockwork Motor, as illustration ... **2/4½**
Postage 3d.

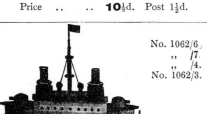

No. 141/3. Clockwork Wriggling Snake,
as illustration.

Price .. .. **10½d.** Post 1½d.

No. 30234. Fine Model Clockwork Motor 'Bus, as illustration.
Price ... ... **2/11** Postage 4d.

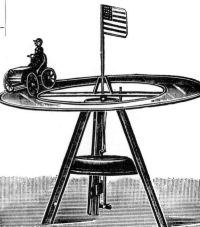

No. 7395. Great Novelty. Brooklands Motor
Track. Large size, **1/10½** Postage 3d.

No. 1062/6	Clockwork Man of War and 5 Boats, as illustration..	..	..	..	..	**2/9**	Postage 4d
,, /7.	Ditto, ditto, 6 ,,	..	..	..	..	**3/3**	,, 4d
,, /4.	Ditto, ditto, 3 ,,	..	..	..	..	**2/3**	,, 3d
No. 1062/3.	Clockwork Battleship, with 2 Boats	..	..	..	..	**1/9**	,, 3d

The Celebrated "Miss Plankfirst" the Dancing Suffragette.
She will dance a "two steps" Highland Fling, execute the most difficult
steps at ease. Operated by merely striking board. Strongly made of
wood. Cannot get out of order. Price **2/-** Postage 3d.

The Wonderful Dancing Man will execute any step with the utmost ease.
With a little practise the operator can produce most astonishing results,
must be seen to be appreciated. Strongly made of wood.
Price .. **1/10½** Postage 3d.

D 3

Humpty Dumpty Circus.

These figures are made of solid wood, leather, rubber, etc., jointed similar to a doll, but on a new principle. They are very neat and attractive in appearance, and are almost unbreakable. Their heads, arms and legs are movable, so that the figures can be set in an endless variety of positions, producing the most fascinating and grotesque results. The donkey and elephant can be stood on one leg, made to sit up or lie down; in fact, almost anything but talk. The clowns can be set in the most ridiculous positions, and made to imitate any variety of tricks on the ladder in mid-air. The numerous results attainable are most astonishing and amusing, not only to children but to grown persons as well.

N.B.—Each of the sets, except the No. 15/1, is accompanied with an elegant book of illustrations and rhymes, containing 150 photographic views, showing the different tricks that can be done with these toys. Set No. 15/1 is accompanied with an illustrated sheet showing 13 different tricks.

No. 15/1. Set of 4 pieces, **2/-**. Postage 3d.

No. 20/1. Set of 3 pieces, **3/11** Postage 4d.

No: 20/26. Set of 16 pieces, **14/-** Postage 9d.

No. 20/3. Set of 7 pieces, **4/3** Postage 5d.   No. 20/7. Set of 5 pieces, **5/6** Post 5d.

No. 20/70. **Farmer's Set** Set of 8 pieces,

Packed in Fancy Pasteboard Box, 20¼ by 12 by 3⅓ in. Weight per set 3 lbs.

Price .. **13/-** Postage 8d.

No. 20/31. Set of 22 pieces, **24/-**

No. 20/16. Set of 7 pieces, **8/-** Postage 6d.

Set No. 20/62. **Mary had a Little Lamb.**

A Toy for little girls,

Price .. **6/6** Postage 6d.

EXTRA ANIMALS AND PARTS.

11/2	Elephant	..	**2/9**
11/4	Donkey	..	**2/-**
11/5	Horse	..	**2/9**
11/6	Poodle	..	**3/-**
11/8	Goat	..	**2/-**
10/7	Horse with Bridle	..	**3/-**

Postage 3d. each.

11/26	Cow	..	**2/9**	11/20	Alligator	..	**2/9**	11/15	Giraffe	..	**3/6**	10/1	Clown	..	**1/2**
11/27	Sheep	..	**2/3**	11/21	Ostrich	..	**2/-**	11/16	Camel	..	**2/9**	10/3	Hobo	..	**1/9**
11/28	Bulldog	..	**2/-**	11/22	Monkey	..	**2/-**	11/9	Pig	..	**2/-**	10/4	Negro Dude		**2/3**
11/29	Cat	..	**2/-**	11/32	Burro	..	**2/-**	11/23	Polar Bear	..	**2/-**	10/5	Lady Circus Rider		
11/30	Wolf	..	**2/-**	11/11	Lion	..	**3/6**	11/24	Sea Lion	..	**2/-**				**2/-**
11/17	Zebra	..	**2/9**	11/12	Camel	..	**3/6**	11/25	Kangaroo		**2/9**	10/6	Ring Master		**2/3**
11/18	Buffalo	..	**3/6**	11/13	Leopard	..	**3/6**					10/12	Max	..	**2/-**
11/19	Bear	..	**2/-**	11/14	Hippo'tamus		**2/9**		Postage, 3d. each.			10/13	Moritz	..	**2/-**

10/8	Lady Acrobat	**2/-**	12/1	Ladder	..	**3**d.
10/9	Gentleman do.	**2/-**	12/2	Chair	..	**3**d.
10/11	Chinaman	**2/-**	12/3	Tub	..	**4**d.
			12/4	Barrel	..	**3**d.
			12/6	Hoop	..	**1**d.
			12/13A	Pedestal table		**3**d.
			12/11	Pedestal	..	**6**d.
			12/19	Wheelbarrow		**9**d.
			12/22	Weights	..	**2**d.
			12/23	,,	..	**3**d.
			12/24	,,	..	**4**d.

Postage, 3d. each.   Postage, 3d. each.   10/7 Lion Tamer **2/3**   Postage, 3d. each.   Postage 3d. each.

No. 30/5

Complete Collapsible Tent. With ring, and fitted with trapeze and rings, decorated with flags of all nations, as described in No. 20/45. Size 24 by 36 by 36 in., **13/9**

No. 30/4. **Circus Ring.** Size, 24¼ by 24¼ by 1¼ in., **4/-**

"Joiboy" Jointed Toys.

Life-like representations of Animals.

Made of 3-ply wood, so that they will not easily break.

Hunting Set (consisting of huntsman, horse, two hounds and a fowl **2/6**

Postage 4d.

Latest Clockwork Flying Machines, "Flip Flaps," etc.

Latest Flying Novelty!

With moving wings, can be attached to any electrolier or gasolier and will fly in a circle over the table.

Complete with instructions, **1/4½** Post 3d.

☞ **NOVELTY!**

The Flying Cupid.

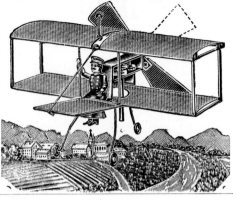

Clockwork ☞ Flying Machine.

Price .. **10½d.**

Postage 3d.

Acrobats on the Spiral Wire.

Clever self-acting toy.

Price **10½d.** Post extra.

370. Clockwork Clown and Balancing Chairs. Price **1/-** Postage 3d.

New "Nulli Secundus" Clockwork Air Ship **10½d.** Post 3d.

Write for Complete Model List.

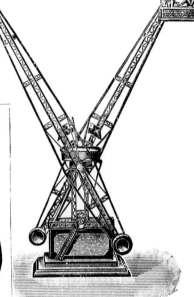

"FLIP-FLAP."

1982/246. Clockwork "Flip Flap."
1/4½ Postage 3d.

1982/250. Do., larger, **3/3** Postage 3

1982/251. Do., larger, **5/11** ,, 4

Special quality "Flip-Flap."
2/9 Postage 3d.

☞ **No. 952.** Model Clockwork **Aeroplane** Runs along suspended from Cord.
4/11
Pos. 4d.

The Wonderful Avernus Wheel. The sensation of the Earl's Court Exhibition.

This is a really splendid model.

No. 1, **1/10½** Post 3d.   No. 2, **3/6** Post 6d.

No. 951. Mechanical **Balloon,** as illustration.
Price **3/9** Post 3d.

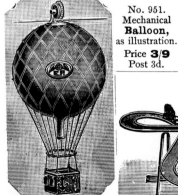

No. 425. Loop the Loop, as illustration.

Price .. .. **1/9** Post 3d.

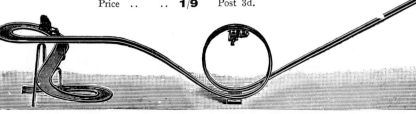

GRAMOPHONES AND PHONOGRAPHS.

This Machine outdistances anything on the market at the price, it being a superior machine in every way. Fitted with good reproducing diaphragm, trumpet, regulator, and levelling screw. Will take any Standard size cylinder record. Wonderfully effective. **3/6** Post 4d.

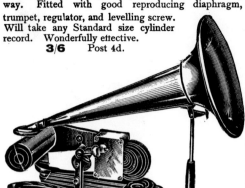

The Edison "Gem."
Price **52/-**

Height 8¾ in. Base 9¾ by 7¾ in. Weight 13 lbs. EQUIPMENT—Model C Reproducer, Flower horn, with crane, winding key, carrying cover, camel's hair brush.

The Edison "Standard."

Plays the Standard Size Records. Size— Height 10½ in. Base 12¾ by 8¾ in. Weight 20 lbs. EQUIPMENT—Model C Reproducer, Flower horn, camel's hair chip brush, winding crank, oak carrying case. Complete with Flower horn & crane Price **£4 15 0** Carriage paid.

The Gamage "Dreadnought" Disc Machine.

Oak cabinet, 12 in. by 11½ in. by 6 in.

Flower horn, new design, tapered arm and genuine Exhibition sound box, special new noiseless motor, plays two 10¾ in. Records at one winding.

As illustration but with plain Cabinet.

Has speed dial indicator.

Price   ..   **£2 10 0**

This is an entirely new machine, and gives a really good reproduction. All parts are finished in best style, and highly nickelled, except horn, which is of seamless aluminium. Will play any standard size cylinder record. Complete with highly polished cabinet with cover. **8/9** Carriage 9d.

Gamage's 1909 Model Disc Machine.

SPECIAL VALUE.

Polished imitation Rosewood body, strong motor (side-key wind), flower horn and concerto sound box, will run one 10 in. or two 7 in. records at one winding. Cabinet, 8¼ by 8¼ by 4¼ in. Horn, 11¼ by 10¼ in.

Price, **15/6**

Carriage 9d.

Similar machine to above without Tone Arm. Sound Box fixed direct to Trumpet.   Price **10/6**

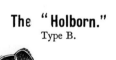

The "Holborn." Type B.

Cabinet. Oak, 11½ in. sq., 5½ in. high.

Horn. Shaded, 20 by 15 in. This machine plays two large records at a wind. Patent Soundbox, 9 in. Turntable.

This machine is very fine value, and is really a musical instrument. **33/9**

The "Cecil" Zonophone.

Specification. 10 in. turntable, tapered arm, strong single spring motor, spiral drive, flower horn, red, green or black, special new type sound box, movable horn, handsome stained walnut cabinet, **42/-**

The "Holborn." Type S.

Cabinet. Walnut, 12 in. sq., 6 in. high.

Horn. Shaded 21 by 18 in. This machine runs for five minutes at a wind. Patent Soundbox, 10 in. Turntable. **43/9**

THE FINEST SELECTION OF GRAMOPHONES IN LONDON.

"Monarch Junior" Gramophone.

Mahogany Cabinet, **£5 15 0**

Ditto, Oak Cabinet, tapered arm, 10 in. turntable, side wind, can be wound while playing, exhibition sound box, flower horn. 200 needles.

Oak Cabinet   Price **£5 10 0**

"Monarch Senior" Gramophone.

Mahogany Cabinet, **£11 0 0**

Do., Oak Cabinet .. **£11**

Handsomely finished quartered oak Cabinet (large size), with hinged top to open, triple spring motor, worm gear, 12in. turntable, plays 3 10 in. or 6 7 in. Records with 1 winding, and can be wound while playing.

This Machine is fitted with new patent speed dial, specially advantageous for pianoforte accompaniment. Exhibition sound box, 26 in. horn, 200 needles.

The "Intermediate Monarch" Gramophone

£4 10 0

SPECIFICATION.
Cabinet—Quartered oak, fine finish.
Motor—Special worm gear.
Turntable—10 in., will play any size of Record.
Taper Arm—Medium.
Horn—Morning Glory, in colours.
Sound Box—Exhibition.

The "INTERMEDIATE MONARCH" meets the demand for a Genuine Gramophone at a low price. It is a most reliable Single Spring Instrument, bearing the Gramophone Company's trade mark of excellence.

"Victor" Gramophone.

£3 10 0

SPECIFICATION.—Cabinet — Quartered oak, excellent finish. Motor—Special worm gear. Turntable—10 in., will play 10 in. or 12 in. Records. Taper Arm—Small. Sound Box—Exhibition (latest pattern). Horn — Morning Glory pattern, in colours.

A reliable and capable instrument. Sure to give satisfaction.

The "Pigmy" Grand.

WEIGHS **20** lbs. NO HORN TO CARRY.

Its compactness, lightness, and portability make the "Pigmy" Grand specially suitable for Pic-nics and Boating Parties. The complete outfit can be carried with ease on the luggage carrier of an ordinary bicycle.

Price .. .. **£5 10 0.**

In leather case, as illustrated **£7 0 0**

The Monarch Gramophone.

Tapered arm, 10 in. turntable, side wind, can be wound while playing, exhibition sound box, highly finished, polished oak hinged cabinet, with flower horn and 200 needles. **£7 10 0**

Record Carrying Cases, Pedestals, Horns and Baskets.

Case to carry Monarch Gramophone.
Strongly made wooden Case, covered stout canvas, with partitions for Records, sound box and tapered arm, fitted with lock and key, and straps. Price **17/6** Post 9d.

Disc Record Carrying Case.
Imitation brown Cowhide, neatly stitched, with lock and key, to hold 18 10-in. Records .. **5/11**   Postage 4d.

Imitation Brown Cowhide Stitched Record Carrying Case.

To hold 2 doz. 10-in. Disc Records, with carrying handle and straps, **4/11** Post 4d.
Ditto to carry 2 doz. 12-in. Disc Records, **5/11**   Postage 4d.

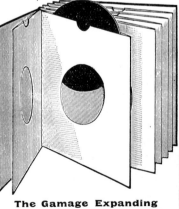

The Gamage Expanding Disc Record Albums.

With expanding back and thick manilla pockets, strongly bound in embossed cloth (various colours). To hold 12 10-in. Records.
Special Gamage, **1/10½** Postage 3d.
Also to hold 12 12-in., **2/11**
Ditto, 12 10¾ in. **2/3**

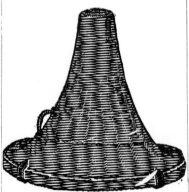

Trumpet Baskets.

Best quality.   Waterproof Lined.

24 in., **5/6**   31 in., **7/6**   42 in., **9/11**

Large best quality basket, lined green baize, for Gramophone Flower Horn, **16/6**

The Gamage Index Disc Record Case.

With strap and catch, as illust. Made stout wood, covered leatherette, to hold 10 in. discs **2**
Ditto, to hold 50 10 in. discs ... **2/1**
Very superior quality, cloth covered, to hold 25 10¾ in. discs **2**
Ditto, to hold 25 12 in. discs ... **2**
Ditto, to hold 50 12 in. discs ...**3/1**
Superior quality, covered with American cloth to hold 25 10 in. Records   ... **2**
To hold 50 10 in. discs ... **3/9** To hold 12 10 in. **1/**

A Special Range of the Latest China Novelties.

SUITABLE FOR
BOOBY WHIST PRIZES, &c.

We have many others similar to those shown. All thoroughly well finished.

China Boy Scout Figures.

Produced under license from the Boy Scout Head-quarters.

In natural colours, 7 in. high, price **6**d. ea. Postage 2d.

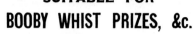

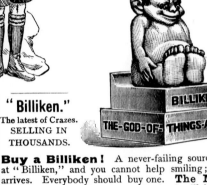

Life-like Pictures in China
of the well-known Companion Pictures

**"The Hope of his side"
and "Out first ball."**

Well-executed Models. Forms an As or Pin Tray. Matches stuck in form th wicket. Height 4½ in. Coloured after original, **6**d. Postage & Packing 3d.

"Billiken."
The latest of Crazes.
SELLING IN THOUSANDS.

"Billiken."
"The god of things as they ought to be."

Buy a Billiken! A never-failing source of Fun and Merriment. Look at "Billiken," and you cannot help smiling; dull care flies when "Billiken" arrives. Everybody should buy one. **The Mascot of Luck.** the Curer of Care and Maker of Laughter. England will be "Merrie England" once again now we have Billiken, with his never-failing smile. Price **1/6** Post 4d. Packed in a strong box.

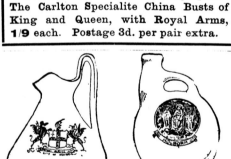

"Bulldog" Mascot of the 6th City of London Rifles. In Terra-cotta, **1/9** In Metal, **1/-** In metal miniature, **6**d. each. Post extra.

The Genuine CARLTON Heraldic China, in Latest and Quaintest Designs and Shapes. All London Boroughs. Prices from 6d. to **2/6** per large pairs. The Carlton Specialite China Busts of King and Queen, with Royal Arms, **1/9** each. Postage 3d. per pair extra.

Menu (Duck).

3 in. high, in China. Splendid Model. Suitable for holding Menus, Xmas Cards, Photos, etc. 1 duck is sufficient. Price **1/-** each. Postage 3d. Postage on pr. 4d.

THE SAUCY SUFFRAGETTE

China Cat Figure. The Newest Novelties. With Card, as illustrati An unique figure with Suffragette colou 6 in. and 8 in. high. Packed in neat b Price **1/6** Cheaper quality **1/-** Post

EGYPTIAN HERALDIC WARE
in great variety.

For Coloured Illustrations of same, see Special List. Post free.

The "GRAFTON" Transparent Ivory China Heraldic Ware.

No. 7. Jug, with City Arms. Price **9**d. Postage 1d.

No. 8. Quaint shaped Vase with Holborn Arms. Price **10½**d. Post 1d.

No. 5. 3-handled Loving Cup with Westminster Arms. Price **10½**d. Postage 1d. Various other shapes.

No. 6. Vase. Price **6**d. Postage 1d.

No. 9. Quaint Teapot with City Arms, from **10½**d. Post 1¾d

The following Arms we hold a big stock of :
City of London, City of Westminster, Borough of Holborn etc.

The above can be had in any of these.

Hundreds of various Shapes, etc.

ILLUSTRATIONS ONLY DEPICT A FEW.

Prices : Approximate sizes, 1½ to 1¾ in., **6**d. 1¾ to 2¼ in., **7½**d. 2¼ to 2¾ in., **9**d. A splendid range of 1/- size for **10½**d. 2¾ to 3in. Cheaper quality China, various Shapes and Arms, **2**d. each SPECIAL CHEAP LINE.

No. 3. Bowl with The Holborn Arms. Price **7½**d. Postage 1d. Various other shapes at same price.

No. 4. Price **10½**d. Postage 1

No. 1. Price **6**d. each. Postage 1d. Illustration displays The City Arms. Various other shapes same price.

No. 2. Price **10½**d. Postage

'Ruskin" Flower Pot, in Plain Colours. Red, Blue, Green. Yellow, Turquoise.

No. 1.	Size 12 in.	Price **2/4½**
,, 2.	,, 10½ ,,	,, **1/4½**
,, 3.	,, 9 ,,	,, **1/-**

The "Korea" Flower Pot

In Artistic Colours.

Carriage and Packing extra.

	Height.	Width	
1	9½in.	9in.	**3/6**
2	8½in.	8in.	**2/3**
3	7½in.	7in.	**1/6**
4	7in.	6½in.	**1/-**
5	5in.	4¾in.	**7½d.**
6	4½in.	4in.	**5½d.**

The "Flaxman" Flower Pot.

Height 8 in. by 7½ in. diameter.

Hundreds of various Pattern Flower Pots from **3½d.**

Printed in Dark Blue.

Price .. **2 11½**

Ditto, Burnished Gold edge.

Price .. **3/11**

Carriage & Packing extra

The "Ruskin" Flower Pot. New Decoration. Dark brown ground, shaded gold, with Flowers and Birds. Unique style.

No. 1.	Size 12 in.	Price ... **3/6**
,, 2.	,, 10½ ,,	,, ... **2/9**
,, 3.	,, 9 ,,	,, ... **2/6**

Packing Extra on all Pots. Dozens of various Pattern Flower Pots in all Sizes and Styles of Decoration.

The "Burlington" Flower Pot. Plain colours. Red. Blue, Green, Yellow, Turquoise.

No. 1.	No. 2.	No. 3.	No. 4.	No. 5.	No. 6.
11½	10	9	8	7	5½ in.
1/11½	**1/4½**	**11½d.**	**9½d.**	**6½d.**	**4½d.**

The "Burlington" with Imperial Decorations. Picked out by hand in various colours.

No. 1 **3/3** No. 2 **2/3** No. 3 **1/9** No. 4 **1/4½**

All Flower Pots Carriage forward, except with Goods to value of 20/- and over, when Carriage is Paid.

The "Lion" Flower Pot.

Pure Ground Gold Shaded. Decorated wit Rose Clusters.

No. 1.	Size 10½ in.	Price **4/6**
,, 2.	,, 9½ ,,	,, **2/11**
,, 3.	,, 7½ ,,	,, **2/6**

The "Roosevelt."

Pot and Pedestal, 35¼ in, high.
Plain colours, **10/6** Cyprian ditto, **11/6** Imperial Colours, **15/6**

Packing on Pots and Pedestals **1/-** to **1/6** extra Carriage forward.

The "Venus."

Pot and Pedestal, 28½ in. high.

Plain colours	**6/11**
Cyprian colours	**7/6**
Imperial colours ..	**9/6**

The Vulcan Pot & Pedestal

Height 43 in. 14 in. inside pot. Very Massive; bold design; very fine work. Exceptional value. Plain colours, **21/6**
Cyprian (3 assorted colours) ... **23/6**
Imperial (picked out in various colours) **25/6**

The "Lotus."

Pot and Pedestal, 38 in. high.
Plain colours, **12/6** Assorted ditto, **13 6**
Imperial colours **18/6**

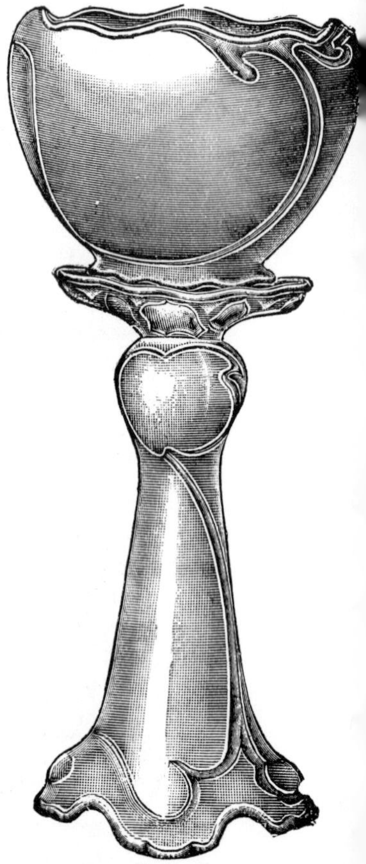

The "Melbourne."

Pot & Pedestal, 38 in. high. Plain colou
12/6 Cyprian ditto .. **13/**
Imperial Colours, ... **18/**
In light colours with hand-painted daisies and gold **28/**

Table and Hall Oil Lamps.

No. 22. Latest Design Table Reading Lamp. Heavy wrought iron and copper stand, with 50 candle power Veritas burner. Price **37/6** complete.

No. 7. Polished Brass Reading Lamp. With 7¼ in. white shade. Price **3/9** complete.

No. 9. Table Lamp. Polished Brass, with Duplex burner. Price **3/9** complete with globe.

No. 14. Table Lamp. Polished Brass, with Duplex burner and tinted shade. Price **13/6** complete.

No. 10. Table Lamp. Polished Brass, with Duplex burner and tinted globe. Price **10/9** complete.

No. 24. Good Value. Reading Lamp. Polished Brass, with 7½ in. opal shade. Price **2/6** complete.

Reading Lamp. Best quality. 35 candle power, with 9¼ in. opal shade. Price **6/9** complete.

No. 17. Table Lamp Polished Brass Pillar on black base, with Duplex burner and globe. Price **13/6** complete.

No. 8. Table Lamp Polished Brass, with Veritas burner and tinted shade Price **16/3** complete.

No. 11. Very handsome Pillar Lamp. Polished Brass, with best Duplex burner and tinted shade Price **23/6** complete.

No. 15. SPECIAL LINE. Table Lamp. Polished Brass, with Duplex burner and tinted globe. Price **7/11** complete.

No. 23. Best quality. Table Lamp. Heavy polished Brass. New Design. With 50 candle power Veritas burner. Price **37/6** complete.

No. 12. SPECIAL LINE Polished Brass, with Duplex burner and tinted globe. Price **15/11** complete.

No. 20. Table Lamp. Handsome design. Oxydised copper finish stand, with 50 candle power Veritas burner. Price **23/6** complete.

No. 19. Best quality Table Lamp. Polished Brass, with 50 candle power Veritas burner. Price **27/6** complete.

No. 7. **Oil Hall Lamp.** With ¾-in. burner. Best quality. Price **12/9**.

No. 6. **Oil Hall Lamp.** With leaded panels, 6 in. square. Bottom can be pulled down for lighting. Price **10/6** complete.

Package and Carriage extra on all Lamps and Gas Fittings.

No. 16. Table Lamp. Handsome Design. Brass and Copper Stand with Copper Fount and Duplex burner. Price **21/-** complete.

No. 21. SPECIAL LINE. Table Lamp. Imitation Onyx Pillar, with Gilt Mount. Brass Container. Fitted with 50 candle power Veritas burner. Price **16/6** complete.

Use "White Rose" Oil for all Lamps.

GAMAGES OF HOLBORN.

HANGING LAMPS FOR OIL.

BENETFINKS OF CHEAPSIDE.

No. 23.
Hanging Lamp,
Wrought iron and copper,
with 11 in. opal shade.
Copper front
and duplex burner.
Price .. **15/6** complete.

No. 11.
Hanging Lamp,
With 18 in. japanned Reflector,
fitted with brass fount and
duplex burner.
Price **6/3**
including chimney.

No. 20.
Hanging Lamp,
Bronzed finish,
with
central
draught
burner.
Small size,
Price **6/3**
complete.

No. 12.
Hanging Lamp,
With 18 in. japanned Reflector,
50 candle-power burner.
Price .. **9/3**
Do., with 22 in. Reflector and
100 candle-power burner,
Price .. **12/9**

No. 13.
Harp Hanging Lamp,
Twisted brass tube,
with
opal shade, brass container,
and duplex burner.
Price .. **8/6**

No. 24.
Hanging Lamp.
Wrought iron and copper, with 13 in.
opal shade, and 50 candle-power
burner.
Price .. **24/6** complete.

No. 21.
Hanging Lamp.
Cast iron bronzed finish.
Can be fitted together without
screws or nuts.
With 50 candle-power burner.
Price .. **15/9** complete.

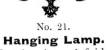
Use "White Rose" Oil.

No. 22.
Hanging Lamp.
Cast iron bronzed finish,
with 50 candle-power burner, and 12 in.
opal shade.
Price .. **17/6** complete.
Best for Lamps.

No. 25.
Hanging Lamp.
Cast iron electro brassed.
Can be fitted together without screws
or nuts.
with 50 candle-power burner.
Price .. **23/9** complete.

OIL LAMP AND CANDLE SHADES.

1644

China Material, Fluted Lace Flounce.

15 in. diameter	..	..	..	..	**4/11**
18 ,, ,,	..	..	..	..	**6/6**
21 ,, ,,	..	..	..	..	**8/9**

Postage 6d.

609.

Candle Shade, Crepe Paper, with paper lace lining.
Price **1½d.** each. Postage 1d.

2382.

Candle Shade, Crepe Paper.
Price **4½d.** each.
Postage 1d.

2107

China material with lace flounce.

15 in. square	..	..	..	..	**7/3**
18 ,, ,,	..	..	..	..	**9/6**
21 ,, ,,	..	..	..	..	**11/9**

Postage 6d.

1501

Candle Shade.

Goffered linen top and silk and lace flounce.

10½d. each.
Postage 1d.

Best Silk, Fluted, three rows Silk Flounce.

15 in. diameter	..	..	..	..	**15/-**
18 ,, ,,	..	..	..	..	**18/9**
21 ,,	..	..	..	..	**23/6**

2233

Embroidered Silk Handkerchief with Lace Coronet.

18 in. diameter	..	..	..	**28/6**
21 ,, ,,	..	..	..	**33/-**

2073.

Silk leaves on crepe Paper Lining.
10¾d. each.   Post 1d.

2295

China Material, Empire Shade.

15 in. diameter	..	..	..	..	**9/6**
18 ,, ,,	..	..	..	..	**13/6**
21 ,, ,,	..	..	..	..	**17/6**

Postage 6d.

2417.

Goffered Linen and Gauze Ruching.
6d. each.

2126

Best Silk, Fluted, two rows Flounce.

15 in. diameter	..	..	..	..	**17/6**
18 ,, ,,	..	..	..	..	**21/6**
21 ,, ,,	..	..	..	..	**25/6**

GAS AND ELECTRIC LIGHT SHADES.

201

Electric Shade, China material with lace flounce.

9 in., with 1⅛ in. fitting.. .. .. **3/6**

10 in. ditto **3/9**

Postage 3d.

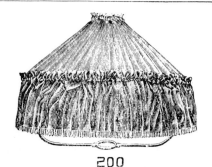

200

Electric Shade, suitable for Table Standards, with gimbal fitting. Can be tilted to any angle. 1⅛ in. fitting.

Best silk, lined with white silk.

8 in. diameter	..	..	**3/9** each
9 in. ,,	..	..	**4/3** ,,
10 in. ,,	..	..	**4/6** ,,

Ditto, Florentine silk, lined white

8 in. diameter	..	..	**3/3** each
9 in. ,,	..	..	**3/9** ,,
10 in. ,,	..	..	**4/3** ,,

Postage 3d.

State colour required when ordering.

273

Electric Shade. Pagoda shape, 5 in. diameter, 1⅛ top hole, Florentine silk, with bead gimp and 4 in. gold or silver bead fringe.

3/9 each. Postage 3d.

State colour required when ordering.

Electric Light Shade. Best Sarsnet with gimp trimming.

Size 4 in. by 3 in., Clip inside.

1/11 each. Postage 1d.

1575

Leaf Shade, for Electric Bulbs.

Crinkled paper. Complete with clip. **9**d. each. Post 1d. Colours—Red, Green, Pink and Yellow.

Leaf Shade, for Electric Bulbs. Embossed silk and sateen leaves. Complete with clip.

Price.. .. **1/-** each.

Postage 1d.

Please state colour required when ordering.

1987

Leaf Shade. for Electric Bulb. Embossed silk leaves.

Price.. .. **1/6** each.

Postage 1d.

State colour required when ordering.

1815

Leaf Shade. for Electric Bulbs. Embossed silk and velvet leaves.

Price .. **1/3** each

Postage 1d.

State colour required when ordering.

2037

Electric Bulb Screen. Best Sarsnet stretched with gimp edging. Complete with clip.

Price .. .. **1/9** each.

With white silk lining, 6d. extra.

Postage 1d.

235

Electric Bulb Screen with clip. Best Sarsnet, stretched silk gimp trimming, lined white silk.

Price.. .. .. **2/3** each

Postage 1d.

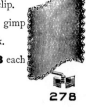

278

12

Inverted Incandescent Gas Shade. Best silk, two rows, silk flounce, 8 in. diameter.

Price **4/6**

Postage 3d.

14

Inverted Incandescent Gas Shade. China material, fluted and lace flounce. 9 in. diameter.

Price.. .. **3/9** each.

Postage 3d.

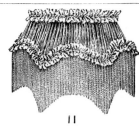

11

Inverted Incandescent Gas Shade. Best silk, fluted and rucked with 3 in. gold or silver coloured beads. 9 in. diameter.

Price .. .. .. **5/9** each.

Ditto, small size, for Bijou Burners, **3/-** ,,

Postage 3d.

Inverted Incandescent Gas Shade, 6 in. diam Oxydized or gilt band with 4 in. silver or gold coloured beads, **4/6** each

Ditto, small size, for Bijou Burners, **2/3**

Postage 3d.

5

Inverted Incandescent Gas Shade. Silk rucked collar, 6½ in. diameter, with 4 in. gold or silver bead fringe.

Price **3/9** each

Ditto, small size, for Bijou Burners, **2/3**

Postage 3d.

4

State colour of Collar required when ordering

First Class Lamps at Low Prices.

You are Invited to inspect our Show Rooms. Great Variety at all Prices.

We List only a few of the many Handsome Design in Stock. Splendid Selection.

All these Lamps are of First Class Materials and Workmanship throughout

No. 1. Floor Lamp, wrought Iron and Copper, with Duplex Burner. Price **10/6**

No. 2. Floor Lamp, wrought Iron and Copper, with Coppered Table and Duplex Burner. Price **21/-** Ditto, with 50 c.p. central draught burner. Price **27/6**

No. 3. Very Handsome Design wrought Iron and Copper, with Duplex Burner Price **22/6** Ditto, with 50 c.p. central draught burner. Price **27/6**

No. 4. Floor Lamp, wrought Iron and Copper, with Duplex Burner. Price **24/6** Ditto, with 50 c.p. central draught burner. Price **29/6**

No. 5. Floor Lamp, wrought Iron and Copper, with Duplex Burner. Price **27/6** Ditto, with 50 c.p. central draught burner Price **32/9**

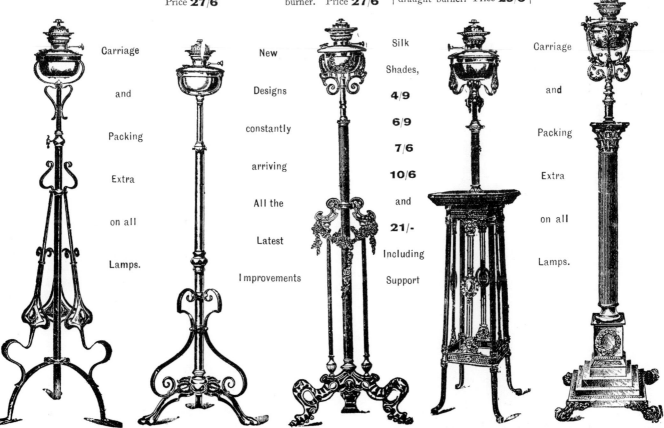

Carriage and Packing Extra on all Lamps.

New Designs constantly arriving All the Latest Improvements

Silk Shades, **4/9** **6/9** **7/6** **10/6** and **21/-** Including Support

Carriage and Packing Extra on all Lamps.

No. 6. Floor Lamp, Latest Design wrought Iron and Copper with Duplex Burner, Price **31/6**. Ditto with 50 c.p. Central Draught Burner. Price **37/6**

No. 7. Floor Lamp, Polished Brass with Duplex Burner. Price **39/6** Ditto with 50 c.p. Central Draught Burner. Price **45/6**

No. 8. Floor Lamp, very handsome Design. Cast Brass, polished, with Duplex Burner. Price **£5/5/-** Ditto, Oxidized Silver Finish. Price **£5/19/6**

No. 9. Floor Lamp, very handsome Cast Brass, polished and relieved, with real Onyx Table and best 50 c.p Central Draught Burner, Price **£6/17/6**

No. 9. Floor Lamp, very massive Cast Brass Corinthian Pillar, fitted with best quality 50 c.p. Burner. Price **£8/15/6**

CANDLE & OIL READING LAMPS.

The Holborn Candle Reading Lamp, Nickel Plated. Price **3/11** Post 4d. Candles 1/- box

The Viaduct Candle Reading Lamp, Nickel Plated Price **5/9** Post 4d. Candles 1/- box.

The Improved Candle Reading Lamp with Eye Screen, Nickel Plated. Price **6/3** Postage 4d. Candles 1/- box.

The Study Telescope Candle Reading Lamp, Nickel Plated. Price **7/3** Post 4d. Candles 1/- box.

The Cambridge Telescopic Candle Reading Lamp, Nickel Plated. Price **7/6** Post 4d. Candles 1/- box.

No. P42638

Plated Pocket Railway Lamp.

Price **5/9** each.

Postage 3d.

The University Reading Lamp, burns paraffin with round burner very good light. Price, nickel plated, **7/6** Carriage 6d.

The A.W.G. Reading Lamp, burns paraffin, very powerful light, nickel plated Price **10/6** Ditto with larger burner Price **11/6** Carriage 9d.

Improved Patent Oil Cabinet. No. I.

The Cabinet is made of tinned Steel with galvanized iron bottom and is of the very best finish and workmanship throughout.

It shuts up and is dustproof, and owing to its double lid is entirely free from smell.

There is a hinged inside lid on which lamps, etc., can stand when being filled; this lid is perforated, so that any overflow runs back into the Cabinet.

The pump is made of polished brass, simple in its construction and cannot get out of order.

It is screwed into its place, and can easily be taken out for filling the cabinet from a barrel.

Its action is so easy that it can be worked with one finger.

It will fill a one-gallon measure in twelve seconds.

The Oil can be obtained without stooping down.

If the measure or vessel be pumped too full the overflow runs back into the well of the Cabinet.

The amount of Oil contained in the Cabinet can be seen by a glance at the Measuring Rod.

A lamp may be filled direct from the Pump by using a funnel, tapered union, or hose and union.

Capacity—6 gallons		Price **28/-**
„ 12 „		„ **33/-**
„ 20 „		„ **40/-**

Carriage paid to any railway station in England and Wales.

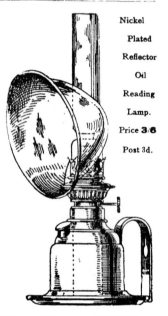

Nickel Plated Reflector Oil Reading Lamp.

Price **3/6** Post 3d.

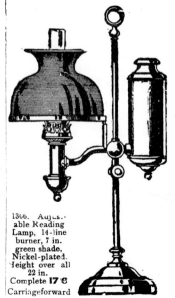

1366. Adjustable Reading Lamp, 14-line burner, 7 in. green shade, Nickel-plated. Height over all 22 in. Complete **17/6** Carriage forward

The Dripless Oil Drum.

A perfect system for keeping oil in small quantities for daily use, mess and overflow impossible. No tap sticking out to leak and get damaged. Size 1 to hold 5 gallons, Price **7/6** Size 2 to hold 10 gallons Price **9/-** Carriage forward.

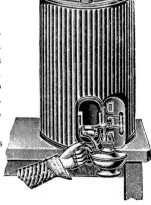

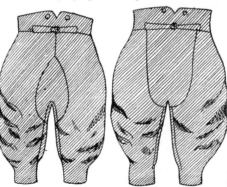

Waterproof Cycling Ponchos and Capes for Ladies and Gentlemen.

The "REFEREE" Cape or Poncho with deep turn down collar, all seams taped, sewn and cemented
Guaranteed Waterproof.   Full size and shape.

| | Gent' Ponchos. | | | Ladies' Ponchos & Cap | | |
	33 in.	36 in.	39 in.	33 in. Poncho.	33 in. Capes.	33 in. Capes with Golf Straps.
No. 1 Black Proof	4/11	5/6	5/11	4/11	5/11	6/11
„ 1A „ „ Ventilated	5/11	6/6	6/11	5/11	6/11	7/11
„ 2 Grey Electric Gossamer	5/6	5/11	6/6	5/6	6/6	7/6
„ 2A „ „ „ Ventil'd	6/6	6/11	7/6	6/6	7/6	8/6
„ 3 to 6 Navy blue, black, fawn and grey twill, ventilated	5/11	6/6	6/11	5/11	6/11	7/11
„ 8 to 12 Navy blue, dark and light grey, light brown and black tweed, very strong, ventilated	7/11	8/11	9/11	7/11	8/11	9/11
„ 15 to 17 Best quality, superfine navy blue and black cashmere, supr. proofing	9/6	10/6	11/6	9/6	10/6	11/6
„ 13 to 14 The 'Featherweight' grey or fawn, very light	11/6	12/6	13/6	11/6	12/6	13/6
„ 7 The celebrated 'Litanproof' fawn, ventilated	7/6	8/6	9/6	7/6	8/6	9/6

Lady's Cape.

Size 36 in. 1/- extra.   39 in. 2/- extra.

Gent's Capes to open down the Front, 1/- extra on all above prices.   Special sizes made to measure in 2 days from 1/- to 3/- extra.

Special Value.   Gents' Cycling Ponchos, Tunic Collar.   Black Proof or Grey Silkoline.   Price   ..   **3/3**   Postage 3d.

Gents' 36-in. full length sewn seams, ditto.   Black, Navy or Fawn Twill.   Price   **4/6**   Postage 3d.

Special Quality.   Gents' 36-in. full length sewn and taped seams, ditto.   In Black, Navy or Fawn Twill.   Price **5/11**   Post 3d.

The New Waterproof Jacket and Leggings.

Fig. 12 W.

Suitable for Cycling, Shooting, Golfing, Fishing,
Walking, &c.   Fitted with Wind Cuffs.

Stock Size.	Jackets. Chest 42 Length 36.	Leggings
Nos. 1 & 2, Black Proof or Silkoline	13/6	4/3
„ 3 to 6, Black, Fawn, Grey and Navy Blue Twill	14/6	4/11
„ 8 to 12, Navy Blue, Dark & Light Grey or Fawn Tweeds	16/11	5/11
„ 13 & 14, Grey and Fawn Featherweight	23/6	7/11
„ 15 to 17, Best Quality Superfine Cashmere, Fawn, Navy or Black	21/-	6/11
„ „, Drab, Litanproof	16/6	5/11
Range 1. Double Textures Cashmeres and Coverts	24/6	10/11
Range 2. Covert Coatings	28/6	12/11
Special Measures	1/- to 3/- extra.	

Waterproof Cap Covering.

As Illustration.

Nos. 1 and 2. Black Proof or Grey Electric Gossamer	2/6
„ 3 to 6. Twill	3/6
„ 8 to 12. Tweeds	3/11
„ 15 to 17. Superfine Cashmeres	4/6
„ 13 and 14. Featherweights	4/11
„ 7. Litanproof	3/11

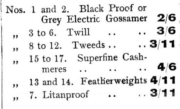

New Waterproof Case.
With Straps attached.

In Two Sizes.

Strong Black Patent Cloth.

Price **1/-** each.

Cases and Leather Straps for Waterproof on Cycles.

Waterproof Tops.

Length 30 in. outside
18 in. inside.

Nos. 1 & 2. Black Proof or Grey Electric Gossamer, **2/11**

Nos. 3 to 6. Navy, Black, Fawn, & Grey Twill, **3/6**

Nos. 8 to 12. Navy, Black, Light Brown, Light and Dark Grey Tweeds, **3/9**

Nos. 15 to 17. Superfine Cashmere, Navy, Black and Fawn, **3/11**

No. 7. Drab Litanproof, **3/9**

Nos. 13 and 14. Grey or Fawn Featherweight **4/11**

Waterproof Leggings & Overalls

	Leggings to button up side of leg, as illustn. Per pair.	Overalls suitable to wear with trousers. Per pair.
Nos. 1 & 2. Black Proof or Grey Electric Gossamer	4/3	4/3
Nos. 3 to 6. Black Navy, Fawn and Grey Twill	4/11	4/11
No. 7. Drab Litanproof	5/11	5/11
Nos. 8 to 12. Navy Blue Black, Dark and Light Grey Fawn Tweeds	5/11	5/11
Nos. 15 to 17. Superfine Cashmeres	6/11	6/11
Nos. 13 & 14. Featherweight	7/11	7/11

Stock sizes, inside leg 29 in. outside leg 45 in. to top button. Special measures 1/- to 3/-

American Cloth Cases .. **5**d.   Large size **9**d.
Same Material as Garment, **9**d.   .. „ **1/-**
Straps Extra, **4½**d. and **6**d. per pair.
Postage 3d.

Set of Straps only, **4½**d.   Superior quality **6**d.

Gamage's Christmas Bazaar 1913

GAMAGES

Heartily wish You

A MERRY CHRISTMAS
AND
A HAPPY NEW YEAR.

SPECIAL NOTICE.

In presenting this Great Bazaar Catalogue, we wish to say a word on the necessity to

SHOP EARLY !

We recognize that in many cases it is impossible to purchase Presents and Toys until near Christmas, but there will be tremendous pressure upon our organisation during the whole of December, and CUSTOMERS WILL GREATLY BENEFIT THEM-SELVES, AS WELL AS HELP US, BY SHOPPING AS EARLY AS THEY POSSIBLY CAN. If, for instance, those who are in a position to make their purchases by December 1st, would do so, it follows that the selection available will be greater, the delivery prompter, and subsequent congestion very much relieved. We earnestly appeal to our Customers to make every effort to help us as suggested.

GAMAGES OF HOLBORN.   BENETFINKS OF CHEAPSIDE.

MAIL ORDER DEPARTMENT. POINTS TO REMEMBER WHEN ORDERING BY POST.

A WELL ORGANIZED DEPARTMENT.	We have a well-organized department for Mail Orders, and give them special care. We make immediate despatch of all goods in our Catalogue and will gladly secure for our customers any article not listed herein, which will be charged at the lowest market rate, but is Not Returnable.
TERMS CASH.	To avoid the multiplication of accounts and loss from bad debts, the Proprietors find it absolutely necessary to make it a rule that all orders be accompanied with cash sufficient to cover the price of goods desired, and, if they are to be sent by post, an extra amount added for postage (but if over 10/-, for the United Kingdom, post free), EXCEPT WHERE OTHERWISE STATED. Any surplus will be returned or placed to your credit on the books of the establishment. Strict compliance with the above rules is absolutely necessary, as profits would be wiped out by book-keeping and the collecting of accounts.
HOW TO ORDER.	In ordering please give full description of goods wanted ; leave nothing to be guessed. Don't order : "Just like the last," but send full particulars with every order. Address your letters carefully. Write your name in full, and be careful to give name of street, city or town. The rank or conditions of the writer should be added to the signature of the writer.
TELEGRAPHIC ORDERS.	TELEGRAMS.—The only address needed for telegrams (inland and foreign) sent to the Company is "GAMAGE, HOLBORN, LONDON." For the Cheapside Branch, "BENETFINK, LONDON." Orders by telegram can only be executed for customers having a Deposit Account (to which reference should be made), or where the money is remitted by telegram. When money is remitted by Telegraphic Money Order customers must inform the Company of the fact by telegram, as no intimation is given to the payee by the Post Office authorities. Money should be telegraphed to P.O., Hatton Garden.
HOW TO REMIT.	Avoid enclosing coin in letters as it is liable to drop out, and double registration fees are enforced. English Postage stamps for small amounts will be accepted. THE SAFEST PLAN IS BY POST OFFICE OR POSTAL ORDER. Fill in the name "A. W. GAMAGE, Limited, payable at Hatton Garden," and cross same, "Lloyd's Bank." Take the number of the Orders for in case of loss the money can be claimed from the postal authorities, if not previously paid. Responsibility for money sent through the Post and lost in transit cannot be acknowledged. If the loss is occasioned by our employee we will be responsible. Customers abroad can remit by Bankers' Draft, Post Office Orders, or through a Commission House in England. Foreign Stamps cannot be accepted in payment.
DEPOSIT ACCOUNTS.	To save the trouble and expense of sending money through the Post, Deposit Accounts may be opened with the Company for sums of not less than £2. The Deposit Account will be debited with the amount of each order and balanced half-yearly, but on application to the Secretary it will be balanced at any time, and the amount due, if any, returned within a week. Deposit Accounts cannot be overdrawn. Orders to be paid for out of Deposit Account should be so marked. At the close of each half-year interest will be credited at the rate of 5 per cent. per annum on the minimum balance for each month during which it has not fallen below £1. No interest will be allowed for fractions of a pound, or for a less period than a complete month.
GOODS BY LETTER POST.	We cannot be responsible for goods sent by Letter Post. We strongly advise our patrons to order by Parcel Post ;—the lowest rate is 3d., but in case of loss the value can be recovered, and we will be responsible; and any article that may not be approved of will be readily exchanged or cash returned (less amount of carriage), except goods made to order.
ORDER FORMS.	Purchasers are requested to use the printed Order Forms, and to obviate crowding and inconvenience to make out their Orders, when practicable, at home. Order Forms will be supplied on application.
LETTERS OF ENQUIRY.	Letters enquiring for orders delayed, or goods not received, *should always mention the date of order, the description of goods, and the Department concerned,* and also state whether the order was given personally or by post, and whether on Deposit Order Account or not. Letters referring to goods already received should be accompanied by the invoice. **When replying to letters received from the Firm the reference number on the Company's letter or invoice should be quoted.** Customers are specially requested, when telegraphing respecting orders, to quote name of Department concerned, and the nature of goods referred to, as, owing to the omission of these, it is often impossible to trace the transaction. It is of the greatest importance that in sending telegrams or giving telephone messages, customers should quote the reference number of the order referred to.
HOW TO BE FORWARDED.	Please state how goods are to be despatched, whether by Passenger or Lug. Rail, Parcel Post or by Letter Post. (If by Mail include Postage.) If sent by Rail, minimum Carriage on Fireworks is 5/- ; Rubber Solution, 8d. ; Calcium Carbide, 1/-. Calcium Carbide can only be sent by rail, and not by steamer.
GOODS RETURNED.	If through any fault of ours a mistake has been made in goods sent you, please notify us first, and we will give instructions to have them returned at our expense. If the fault is yours return to us with invoice and full particulars ENCLOSED IN THE PARCEL, all charges prepaid, and we will exchange or credit you with amount. Goods which we do not Catalogue, but procure to your special order from others, are not returnable.
GOODS FOR REPAIR.	**Goods left with the Company for Repair, Alteration or otherwise.** Every care is taken of such articles, but the Company will not hold itself responsible for any damage done to very fragile goods, provided due care has been taken in the repair ; or for any damage or loss to articles left for repair, alteration or otherwise, if not taken away within three months.

ALL PREVIOUS LISTS CANCELLED.   PRICES SUBJECT TO FLUCTUATIONS OF THE MARKET.

Chief Depot: A. W. GAMAGE, Ltd., HOLBORN, LONDON, E.C.	**City Depot:** BENETFINK & Co., Ltd., CHEAPSIDE, LONDON, E.C.

CHRISTMAS PARCELS FOR ABROAD.

There are many thousands of Englishmen scattered throughout the Empire and in foreign countries, to whom friends and relatives at home send regularly each Christmas some gift or remembrance to remind them of the Old Country. In the nature of things there must always be a huge army of Englishmen permanently engaged abroad in the administration and commerce of our Colonies, and to those Britons out on the fringe of the Empire it is becoming established custom to send presents each year at this time.

For the convenience of those who intend to send such gifts we publish the following lists, showing the dates upon which mails are despatched to various places to arrive in time for Christmas or the New Year, and rates of postage.

It must be specially understood that the dates given are the dates of the actual despatch of mails from England, and that parcels must be posted some days previously in order to be included.

The tables show the latest dates of despatch from LONDON and NOT dates of posting. For latest dates and times of posting enquire at the Local Post Office.

M., against a date shows that the mail is made up in the morning, **E.,** evening.

Rates of Postage (subject to alteration.)

Colony or Country.	Rates of Postage.			Date of Despatch to secure arrival about (See footnote).	
	3 lbs.	7 lbs.	11 lbs.	Xmas day.	New Years day
Abyssinia	4/6	4/6	4/6	—	—
Aden, including Perim ..	1/-	2/	3/-	E. 3 Dec.	E. 10 Dec.
Algeria	1/9	2/2	2/7	—	—
Argentine Republic ..	2/-	3/-	4/-	M. 28 Nov.	M. 5 Dec.
Ascension	1/-	2/-	3/-	—	—
Austria-Hungary	1/4	1/8	2/-	—	
Australia (Commonwealth, i.e., States of New South Wales, Queensland, South Australia, Tasmania, Victoria, and Western Australia), Papua (British New Guinea) and Norfolk Island, not over 1 lb. **1/-** For each additional lb., up to 11 lbs. **6d.**				—	—
Azores	1/4	1/8	2/-	E. 28 Nov.	E. 12 Dec.
Bahamas	1/-	2/-	3/-	—	—
Bechuanaland Protectorate	1/-		—		
Belgian Congo ..	1/7	2/3	2/7	E. 25 Nov.	E. 25 Nov.
Belgium	1/-	1/4	1/9	—	—
Benadir	2/9	3/1	3/5	—	
Bermuda	1/-	2/-	3/-	E. 5 Dec.	E. 12 Dec.
Beyrout		..		M. 10 Dec.	M. 17 Dec.
Ditto, Long sea route (Parcels only) ..				E. 3 Dec.	E. 10 Dec.
Bolivia (**3/6** per parcel up to 7 los.) ..		..		M. 14 Nov.	M. 21 Nov.
Borneo and Sarawak ..	1/-	2/-	3/-	—	E. 12 Nov.
Brazil, limit of weigh, 6½ lbs.	3/6	4/-	—	M. 5 Dec.	M. 5 Dec.
British East Africa & Uganda	1/-	2/-	3/-	E. 26 Nov.	E. 26 Nov.
British Guiana ..	1/-	2/-	3/-	E. 2 Dec.	E. 2 Dec.
British Honduras ..	1/-	2/-	3/-	E. 7 Nov.	E. 7 Nov.
British Somaliland ..	1/-	2/-	3/-	—	
Bulgaria	2/4	2/8	3/-	—	—
Cameroons	2/2	2/6	2/10	—	
Canada	1/-	2/-	3/-	M. 9 Dec.	E. 16 Dec.
Manitoba ..		..		E. 2 Dec.	M. 9 Dec.
British Columbia ..		..		E. 2 Dec.	M. 9 Dec.
Cape of Good Hope— (Cape Town) ..	2/3	5/3	8/3	M. 6 Dec.	M. 13 Dec.
Cape Verde ..	2/2	2/6	2/10	M. 28 Nov.	M. 5 Dec.
Caroline Islands ..	2/2	3/3	3/7	—	—
Ceylon	1/-	2/-	3/-	E. 26 Nov.	E. 3 Dec.
Chili	2/-	3/-	4/-	E. 12 Nov.	E. 12 Nov.
Ditto (via the Andes) ..		..		M. 21 Nov.	M. 28 Nov.

Colony or Country.	Rates of Postage.			Date of Despatch to secure arrival about (See footnote).	
	3 lbs.	7 lbs.	11 lbs.	Xmas day.	New Years day
China—British Agencies ..	1/-	2/-	3/-	—	—
Chinese Agencies ..	2/-	3/-	4/-	—	—
German Agencies ..	2/2	3/3	3/7	—	—
Russian Agencies, **5/-** any weight up to 11 lbs.					
Colombia Republic ..	2/-	3/-	4/-	E. 2 Dec.	E. 2 Dec.
Corsica	1/9	2/2	2/7	—	
Costa Rica	2/-	3/-	4/-	M. 1 Dec.	M. 8 Dec.
Crete	1/11	2/3	2/7	—	
Cuba	2/2	2/11	3/3	E. 22 Nov.	E. 29 Nov.
Cyprus	1/-	2/-	3/-	E. 3 Dec.	E. 10 Dec.
Danish West Indies ..	2/-	3/-	4/-	—	
Dahomey	2/2	2/6	2/10	—	
Denmark, including Greenland	1/-	1/4	1/7	—	—
Dominican Republic ..	3/-	4/-	5/-	—	—
Dutch East Indies ..	2/6	3/3	4/-	—	
Dutch Guiana ..	2/-	3/-	4/-	—	
Dutch West Indies ..	3/6	4/-	4/6	E. 18 Nov.	E. 18 Nov.
Ecuador	2/-	3/-	4/-	—	—
Egygt, including Soudan ..	1/-	1/9	2/6		
Via Italy	2/-	2/6	3/-	E. 3 Dec.	E. 10 Dec.
Falkland Islands ..	1/-	2/-	3/-	E. 12 Nov.	E. 12 Nov.
Fiji Islands ..	1/8	3/4	5/-	E. 7 Nov.	E. 7 Nov.
France and Corsica..	1/4	1/9	2/2	—	
Gambia	1/-	2/-	3/-	E. 9 Dec.	E. 9 Dec.
Germany	1/-	1/4	1/7	—	—
Gibraltar	1/-	2/-	3/-	E. 17 Dec.	E. 22 Dec.
Gold Coast ..	1/-	2/-	3/-	E. 1 Dec.	E. 8 Dec.
Greece	2/4	2/8	3/-		
Guatemala				E. 7 Nov.	E. 7 Nov.
Holland	10d.	1/2	1/6	—	—
Hong Kong..	1/-	2/-	3/-	M. 19 Nov.	M. 19 Nov.
Ditto, Long sea route (Parcels only) ..		..		E. 12 Nov.	E. 12 Nov.
India, including the Andaman Islands and Burma; also the following places on the Persian Gulf and in Turkish Arabia:— Bagdad, Bahrain, Bandar Abas, Bushia, Busrah, Guadur, Jask, Linga, Mohammerah and Muscat ..	1/-	2/-	3/-	E. 26 Nov.	E. 3 Dec.
Via Italy	2/-	3/-	4/-	—	—

RATES OF POSTAGE—continued.

Colony or Country.	Rates of Postage.			Date of Despatch to secure arrival about (*See footnote*).	
	3 lbs.	7 lbs.	11 lbs.	Xmas day.	New Years day
Italy	1/6	1/10	2/2	—	
Japan, including Formosa and Corea	2/-	3/-	4/-	E. 18 Nov.	E. 18 Nov.
Ditto (via Siberia) ..	..			E. 28 Nov.	E. 5 Dec.
Java	..			E. 12 Nov.	E. 26 Nov.
Leeward Islands, including Antigua, Nevis, St. Kitts, Tortola, and Montserrat	1/-	2/-	3/-		
Liberia				E. 25 Nov.	E. 1 Dec.
Montenegro	2/2	2/6	2/10	—	—
Madagascar	2/6	3/-	3/6	E. 22 Nov.	E. 29 Nov.
Madeira	1/4	1/8	2/-	M. 20 Dec.	M. 27 Dec.
Malay States, including Negri Sembilan, Pahang, Perak, Selangor, Johore	1/-	2/-	3/-	—	—
Malta	1/-	2/-	3/-	M. 12 Dec.	M. 19 Dec.
Mauritius	1/-	2/-	3/-	E. 12 Nov.	E. 12 Nov.
Mexico	1/-	2/6	3/6	E. 21 Nov.	E. 21 Nov.
Morocco, including Casablanca, Mazagan, Mogador, Larache, Rabat, Saffi, Tangier, and Tetuan ..	1/-	2/-	3/-	—	—
Natal	2/3	5/3	8/3	M. 29 Nov.	M. 6 Dec.
Newfoundland and Labrador	1/-	2/-	3/-	E. 5 Dec.	E. 5 Dec.
New South Wales	..			E. 5 Nov.	E. 12 Nov.
New Zealand, including— Fanning Island, Cook Islands, Danger, Pukapuka, Manahiki, Palmerston, Rakaanga, Avarua, Penrhyn, Tongareva, Savage (Niue) & Suwarrow Islands, for parcels not exceeding 4 feet in length and girth combined ..	1/-	2/-	3/-	M. 5 Nov.	M. 5 Nov.
For parcels over 4 feet and not exceeding 6 feet in length and girth combined	2/-	3/-	4/-	—	—
Nicaragua	..			E. 18 Nov.	E. 2 Dec.
Nigeria, including Southern and Northern Lagos	1/-	2/-	3/-	E. 24 Nov.	E. 1 Dec.
Norway	1/-	1/4	1/7	—	—
Nyasaland	3/-	4/-	5/-	—	M. 14 Nov.
Ditto via Aden and Chinde	..			E. 4 Nov.	E. 25 Nov.
Orange Free State ..	2/3	5/3	8/3	M. 29 Nov.	M. 6 Dec.
Panama, Republic of (Colon)	..			E. 2 Dec.	E. 2 Dec.
Paraguay	..			M. 7 Nov.	M. 14 Nov.
Persia, North	3/9	4/1	4/5	E. 12 Nov.	E. 19 Nov.
Persia, South	2/-	3/-	4/-	—	—
Peru	2/-	3/-	4/-	—	—
Philippine Islands	..			E. 21 Nov.	E. 28 Nov.
Portugal	1/4	1/8	2/-	—	—
Queensland	..			—	E. 5 Nov.
Rhodesia, via Cape Town, 1/9 per lb. up to 11 lbs.	..				
Rhodesia, via Beira ..	3/6	5/-	7/6	E. 4 Nov.	E. 25 Nov.
Rhodesia, via France and Aden	4/6	6/-	8/6		
Roumania	1/11	2/3	2/7	—	—
Russia, including Finland	1/11	2/3	2/7	—	—
Russia in Asia	2/11	3/3	3/7	—	—
St. Helena	..			M. 6 Dec.	M. 6 Dec.
Salvador	..			E. 18 Nov.	E. 2 Dec.
Seychelles	..			M. 25 Nov.	M. 25 Nov.
Shanghai	..			E. 12 Nov.	E. 12 Nov.
Siam	2/-	3/3	4/6	E. 12 Nov.	E. 12 Nov.

Colony or Country.	Rates of Postage.			Date of Despatch to secure arrival about (*See footnote*).	
	3 lbs.	7 lbs.	11 lbs.	Xmas day.	New Years day
Sierra Leone	1/-	2/-	3/-	E. 1 Dec.	E. 8 Dec.
Servia	1/9	2/1	2/5	—	—
Spain	1/6	1/10	2/2	—	—
South Australia	..			E. 12 Nov.	E. 19 Nov.
Straits Settlements— Labuan, Malacca, Penang, Province Wellesley and Singapore	1/-	2/-	3/-	E. 12 Nov.	E. 26 Nov.
Via Italy	2/-	3/-	4/-	—	—
Sweden	1/6	1/10	2/2	—	—
Switzerland	1/4	1/8	2/-	—	—
Tasmania	..			E. 5 Nov	E. 12 Nov.
Transvaal	2/3	5/3	8/3	M. 29 Nov.	M. 6 Dec.
Turkey—British Agency or Austrian Agency should form part of the address. Ottoman Post Offices in Europe—Poste Ottoman should form part the of address.				—	—
Beyrout	1/-	2/-	3/-	—	—
Constantinople and Smyrna	1/-	1/4	1/8	—	—
Austrian Agency.. ..	1/11	2/3	2/7	—	—
Ottoman Agency ..	2/4	2/8	3/-	—	—
Offices in Europe and Asia	2/6	2/10	3/2		
United States— New York	..			E. 12 Dec.	E. 19 Dec.
San Francisco	..			E. 9 Dec.	E. 12 Dec.
United States of America Official Service, including Philippine Islands, Porto Rica, Alaska, Panama ..	1/3	2/3	3/3	—	—
Semi-official Service all places except New York City	3/6	4/6	5/6	—	—
Brooklyn, Jersey City or Hoboken	2/6	3/6	4/6	—	—
Parcels addressed to New York State are subject to the higher rate.	..			—	—
Uruguay— Canelones, Durazno, Florida, Fray Bentos, Mercedes, Minas, Monte Video, Paysandu, Salto, San José	2/-	3/-	4/-	M. 28 Nov.	M. 5 Dec.
Venezuela	2/6	3/3	4/-	E. 18 Nov.	E. 2 Dec.
Victoria	..		..	E. 12 Nov.	E. 19 Nov.
Western Australia ..	..		.	E. 12 Nov.	E. 19 Nov.
West Indies (British), Barbados					E. 16 Dec.
Antigua					E. 2 Dec.
Montserrat					E. 2 Dec.
Nevis					E. 2 Dec.
St. Kitts					E. 2 Dec.
Demerara					E. 2 Dec.
Dominica	1/-	2/-	3/-	E. 2 Dec.	E. 2 Dec.
Grenada					E. 16 Dec.
St. Lucia					E. 2 Dec.
St. Vincent					E. 16 Dec.
Tobago					E. 2 Dec.
Trinidad					E. 16 Dec.
Jamaica				Dates	uncertain
Zanzibar	1/-	2/-	3/-	E. 12 Nov.	E. 26 Nov.
Via France and Italy ..	2/-	3 -	4/-	—	—
Via Marseilles	2/-	3/-	4 -	—	—

Letters, parcels, etc., for distant or outlying places in Australia, India, South Africa, and other large Countries should be posted in time for earlier mails.

Please note Ammunition or Explosives cannot be sent by Post.

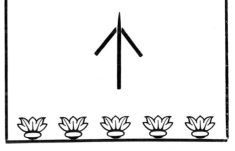

ALPHABETICAL INDEX.

A

	PAGE
ABC Blocks	127
Accessories, Golf	231
Accordions	252
Accumulators	47, 62
Adamant Metal Ware	422
Address Books	310
Aerial Wires	62
Aeroplanes	84-86
Aeroplane Accessories	87, 88
,, Engines	43, 45
Air Pistols	358
,, Rifles	358
Albums	312
,, Music	257
,, Postcard	315
,, Song	257
Alpine Ropes	235
Aneroid Barometers	273
Animals, Toy, facing page	132
,, Whitewood	133
Antimony, Japanese	404-406
Antiques Reproduced	423, 424
Aprons, Muslin	468
Armour, Toy	110
Arrows, Scout	114
Artists' Outfits	319
Ash Tray	420
Attache Writing Cases	382
Autograph Books	310
Automatic Gas Stove	336
,, Slot Machine	236
Aviation Models	84-86
Aviaries	441

B

	PAGE
Baby Dolls	143, 144
,, Walkers	153
Badminton Rackets	230
Bagatelle Balls	192
,, Boards	191
,, Cues	192
,, Tables	195
Bagpipes	111
,, Golf	231
,, Hand	363
,, School	365
Bags & Trunks Dept.	363-365
Baker's Barrow	152
Balances	320
Balls	115
Balls, Bagatelle	192
,, Golf	231
,, Pool	192
,, Punch	232
,, Pyramid	192
Bamboo Poles	62
Band Instruments	251
Banjo Cases	247
Banjos	247
Banks	115
Barometers	272
Barrows, Elm	155
,, Painted	155

	PAGE
Barry Sculler	79
Bass Drums	250
Bath Room Slippers	355
Batteries	47, 48, 62
Batteries, Pocket	48
Battleship Building Blocks	128
,, Hulls	73-75
Beads	162
Bead Curtains	409
Beards, Moustache	182
Bedroom Slippers	355
Bells, Dumb	232
Belt Buckle, Silver	375
Benares Tumblers	403
Bibles	327
Bicycles	345
Billiard Cues	192
,, Rests	193
,, Sundries	192, 193
,, Table	189, 191
Binocular	272
Birds' Egg Cabinets	361
Biscuit Barrels	418
Blackboard and Easel	122
Blotting Pads	308
Blow Lamps	34
Boats	69-80
Boat Engines	42, 43
,, Fittings	82
,, Motors	46
Boiler Fittings	38
Boilers	34
,, Marine	33, 34
Bombardons	251
Bookcases	428
Book Department	275-299
Book Trough	428
Books for Boys and Girls	293
,, ,, ,,	291
,, ,, ,,	275, 288
,, ,, ,,	292
,, Children	295
Books, Magical	178
,, Painting	299
,, of Poems	326
,, Rag	298
Boomerangs	359
Boot and Shoe Dept.	355-356
Boot Rack	428
Botanical Cases	361
Bows and Arrows, Toy	110
Boxing Gloves	232
Boxers, Toy	131
Boy Scouts' Dept.	254
Boy Scouts' Games	216
,, Note Book	303
Boys' and Girls' Books	292
,, Books	275-288
,, Clothing	353
,, Outfitting	353
,, Umbrellas	342
,, Walking Sticks	342
Bracelets	370
Brake Rails	18
Bottles, Brass	403
Brass Bottles	403
Bread Board and Knife, Toy	131
,, Boards	443
,, Carts, Toy	151
,, Knives	443
Bricks, Wood	127
Bridges, Electric	13
,, Railway	21

	PAGE
Bridge Arches	21
,, Sets	198
British Cavalry Horses	150
Brooches	371
Brush Set	444
,, Tray	416
Bubble Blowers, Rubber	124
Buffers, Railway	23
,, Model	23
Bugles	249
Building Bricks, Richters' facing page	126
Bureaux	427
Burlington Bricks	127
Butchers' Shops	132
Butter Dishes	386
,, Shapers	442
,, Workers, Toy	131
Buttonholes, Electric	48

C

	PAGE
Cabinets	320
Cake Basket	395
,, Stands	417
Calenders	300, 302, 305, 306
Cameras	116, 271
Campbell Kids Dolls	142
Canary Cages	441
Candle Clips for Xmas Trees	163
Candles for Xmas Trees	163
Candlesticks	406, 418
Candy Stores	162
Cane Chairs	469, 470
Cannon	105
Card Case	374
,, Games	197, 198, 206-208
Cards, Christmas	304-305
Cargo Steamers	74
Cartridge Bags	359
Carpet Sweepers	429
Cases, Cue	192
Castings, Petrol	43
Catches and Jokes	177
Cells, Dry	47
,, Wet	47
Chairs, Cane	469, 470
,, Children's	469
,, Kindergarten	426
Chalk Holders	193
Cheese Dish	396
Chemical Cabinet	66-68
Chessman	201
Chests, Tools	328, 329
Chest of Drawers, Dolls	140
Child's Bracelet	370
Children's Books	289-299
,, Chairs	425, 469
,, Frocks	467
,, Gift Books	294
,, Pinafores	467
Children's Playground	153
,, Playhouse	142
Chimes (Toy)	113
China Figures, Grotesque	412
,, Novelties	412

ALPHABETICAL INDEX—*continued.*

	PAGE
Chip-Carving Knives	434
Chocolates	164
Christmas Books	289
,, Cards	304, 305
,, Puddings	400
,, Stationery	307
Chronos, Clock	366
Cigar Boxes	389, 405
,, Cutter	375
Cigars	450
Cigarette Boxes	405
,, Holders	448
,, Cases, Silver	374
Cigarettes	448
Cinematograph Films	267
,, Machine	261-263
,, and Photograph Dept.	261
Circular Saw	333
Claret Jugs	398
Clarionets	249
Clocks	366
,, Electric	334
Clockmaking	125
Clockmaking Locomotives	4-6
Clockwork Model Fire Engine	29
,, Pond	80
,, Toys	90
,, Trains	1, 2
,, Trams	3
Cloth Brushes	444
Clothes Airer	442
Clubs, Golf	231
Coasters	235
Coal Scoop	421
,, Trolley	152
Coffee Machines	414
Collar Box	385
Collector's Gun	357
Coloured Lithographic Slides	268
Combs, Fancy	377
Comic Songs	258
Companion Pipe Sets	451
Concertinas	252
Condenser Foil	63
Conductors' Sets (Toy)	113
Confetti, Coloured	163
Confectionery	164
Conjuring Dept.	165-188
Coney Seal Tie	462
Construction Clock	125
Constructional Models	130
,, Model Steamers	128
,, Toys, facing page	26, 32, 118, 128
Controllers, Electric	13
Coon Songs	253
Copper Tea Kettles and Stands	415
Cord, Hemp	62
Cornets	251
Cots, Dolls	141
Counting Frames, Toy	124
Cowboy Suits	106
Crackers	158-161
Cradles, Dolls	141
Crane Builder	118
Crane Engine, Steam	29
Cranes, Electric	13
,, Wood	130
Crayon Sets	317
Crib Boards	202
Cross Rails, Toy	18
Crossing Gates, Railway	23
Croquet Table	225
Cruiser Hulls	75
Crumb Sets	443
,, Trays	416
Cubes, Picture	127
,, Embossed	127
Cues, Bagatelle	192
,, Billiard	192
,, Cases	192
,, Rests	192, 193
,, Stands	194
,, Tip Fastener	193

	PAGE
Curtains, Bead	409
Cutlery Dept.	394
Cuttings, Railway	21
Cut-outs, Electric	13
Cycle and Cycle Accessory Dept.	345-348
Cycle Car Speed Indicator	349
Cyclometer	348
Cycle Lamps	347
Cymbals	250

D

	PAGE
Dairy Cart, Giant	153
,, Cart	151
,, Set, Toy	131
Damascus Furniture	402
,, Music Stand	402
Darts	227
Date Stands	319
Designs in Wood Carving	438
Desks	425
Diaries	301
Dice	202
,, Watches	210
Dictionaries	311
Dinner Sets, Toy	139
Dish Covers	442
Dissected Puzzles	127
Dissected Puzzles, Geographical	127
District Electric Trains	11
Divers	80
Dolls	142-145
,, facing page	132
,, Bassinette	141
,, Chatelaine Sets	162
,, Chest of Drawers	140
,, Cots	141
,, Cradles	141
,, Dresser	142
,, Furniture	140
,, Houses	134, 135
,, Kitchen Sets	142
,, Prams	136, 137
,, Trousseau	141
,, Trunks, Fitted	141
,, Undressed	143
,, Wardrobe	140
,, Washing Sets	138
Donkey Engine, Steam	29
Dominoes	202
Drapery Department	461
Draughts	201, 202
Draughtmen's Sets	319
Drawing Room Scenery	187
,, Slates	118
Drawings for Model Power Boats	73
Drawings for Model Yachts	72
Dreadnought, Miniature	80
,, Blocks	129
Dress Shoes	355
Drug Department	444-447
Drums	106, 111, 250
Drum Sticks	250
Dry Fly Boxes	360
Dulcephones	241
Dulcet Gongs	419
Dumb Bells	282
Dutch Design Vase	412
,, Sabots	355
Duck Mechanical	80
,, Swimming	80
Dying Toys	116
Dynamos	45, 46
Dynamograph	264

E

	PAGE
Ear Rings	372
Ears, Electric	48
Easy Chair	426
Eau de Cologne	447
Ebonite Tube	63
Egg Boiler	415
,, Frame and Spoons	395
Elastic	87
Electric Boat Motors	46
,, Bridges	13
,, Buttonholes	48
,, Clocks	334
,, Controllers	13
,, Cranes	13
,, Cut-outs	13
,, Ears	48
,, Generating Plant	29
,, Haulers	10
,, Lamps	13, 335
,, Lighting Plants, Model	26-28
,, Lighting Sets	49
,, Locomotives	10, 11
,, Motors	45, 46
,, Noses	48
,, Novelties	334
,, Resistances	13
,, Switches	13, 14
,, Table Decorations	336
,, Tank Locomotive	11
,, Torches	335
,, Trains	12
,, Underground Locos	10
Electrical Experiment Sets	48
,, Novelties	48
,, Tie Pins	48
Electro Medical Machines	65
Embossed Cubes	127
Embossing Press	288
Embroideries, Oriental	401
Enamel Tea Sets, Toy	139
Engagement Calendars	312
,, Tablets	308
Engine Builder	128
,, Castings	43
,, Fittings	38-41
,, Shed, Railway	25
,, Sheds	14
,, Turntables	14
Engines, Clockwork	4-6
,, Marine	33-34
,, Sheds, Model	25
,, Wooden	154, 156
Enlargers	266
Enlarging Accessories	266
Epergnes	413
Euphoniums	251
Evening Scarves	409
Express Waggon	155

F

	PAGE
Face Powder	185
Fairy Dolls	145
Fancy Combs	377
,, Department	366-399
,, Stationery Boxes	307
Fans	402
,, Japanese	409
Farmyards	133
Father Xmas	163
Felt Toys facing page	132
Fern Pots	421
Fi Fi Cat	132
Fiddles, Japanese	248
Fire Engine, clockwork	29
,, Escape, constructional	128

ALPHABETICAL INDEX—*continued*.

	PAGE
Fish Knives	394
„ Servers	394
Fishing Dept.	360-362
Fishing Rods	360
Fittings, Boiler	38-41
„ Engine	38-41
Flags, Model	82
Flasks	389, 364
Flask Cases	364
Flat Compendiums	203
Flower Perfume	446
„ Stands	399, 413
„ Vases	399, 350
Flutes	249
Floor Gongs	419
Folding Tray Stands	402
Foll, Condenser	63
Footballs	230
Foot Muffs	350
„ Warmers	350
Foreign Stamps	316
Forts	104
Fountain Pens	314
Fountains, Table	362
Frames, Photo	379
Fretsaws	333
Fretwork Machines	333
„ Tools	332
Frocks, Children's	467
Frog, Swimming	80
Fruit Dishes and Stands	418
Fruits, Imitation	186
Fruit in Syrup	400
Fruits in Tins	400
Fur Caps	344
„ Rugs	352
„ Sets	461
Furniture	401, 440
„ Damascus	402
„ Dolls	140

G

	PAGE
Galloping Scooter, The	152
Games for Boy Scouts	216
Games, Card	197-200, 206-208
Games Dept.	189-235
„ Race	209
„ Table	211-228
Garden Roller, Toy	151
Garlands	163
Gas Engines	44
„ Stove, Automatic	336
Gauges	36
„ Pressure	38
Generating Plants	42
Gent's Gloves	454
„ Motor Coats	351
„ „ Gloves	456-458
„ Purses	386
„ Toilet Cases	381
„ Umbrellas	337
„ Walking Sticks	338, 339
„ Watches	368
Gig Horses	153
Gift Books	275-289
Girls' Books	275—288
„ Bracelets	370
„ Umbrellas	342
Gladstone Bags	363
Glass Ornaments for Xmas Trees	163
Glasses, Theatre	272
G.P.O. Barrow	152
Guitars	246
Glove Department	452

	PAGE
Gloves, Gent's	454
„ Ladies'	452-454
„ Motor	457
Gold Brooches	371
„ Necklets	370
„ Pencils	375
„ Rings	371
Golf Bags	231
„ Balls	231
„ Clubs	231
Gongs	419
Goods Rolling Stock	16, 17
„ Shed, Railway	25
„ Siding „	20
„ Station „	21
Gramophones	238, 239
„ Hornless	240
Gramophone Sundries	242
Grease Paints..	183
Grocery Dept.	400
Grocer's Shops	132
Grotesque facing page	132
„ China Figures	412
Gun Department	357-359
Guns	105
„ Toy	110
Gymnastic Sets, Home	229
Gyroscope Tops	98, 99

H

	PAGE
Haberdashery	463
Hair Brushes	373
„ Pin Boxes	377, 405
Hall Brush Sets	443
Hamper, Xmas	400
Hand Bags	363
„ Carts	155
„ Mirrors	445
„ Propelled Cars	148
Handle Bar Baskets	348
Handkerchiefs	465
„ Boxes	411
„ Case	384
Handsmobile	148
Harmless Shooting Sets	108
Harmoniums	255
Harps	248
Hat Pin Boxes	405
„ Stands	375
Hay Waggons	157
Hymn Books	325
Hide Attache Cases	364
Hobby Horses	153
Home Gymnastic Sets	229
Home Puff	231
Horizontal Engine to construct	130
Horses, Skin	132
„ Pole	150
„ Push	150
„ Swing	149
„ and Carts	151
Horse Rocking Chair	154
Horizontal Steam Engines	26-32
Hornless Gramaphones	240
Hot Air Engines, Model	30
„ Water Bottles	446
„ Jugs	416
Household Dept.	441-443
Humorous Songs	258
Hunting Crops	344

I

	PAGE
Ice Creepers	235
„ Skates	234
Icing Pipes	442
„ Syringe	442
Imitation Fruits	186
Indians' Camp	125
Indian Play Suits	107
„ Sandalwood	407
Indicator, Polarity	45
„ Toy	23
Inkstands	320, 404
Inlaid Stool	402
Insulating Rails	18
Instrument Cases	249
Interlocking Building Bricks	129
Ironmongery Dept.	328-336
Island Towers	80

J

	PAGE
Japanesee Antimony	404-406
„ Dolls	142
„ Fans	409
„ Fiddles	248
„ Lacquer Work	407
„ Tea Caddies	407
„ „ Cosies	409
Jardinieres	421
Jewel Cases	384
Jewellery Dept.	370
„ Paste	372
Jig Saw Puzzle	204-205
Jokes	48, 116
„ and Catches	177
Joiboy Toys	157
Jolly Joe	131
Jugs, Hammered	416
Juvenile Cycles	345

K

	PAGE
Kaleidoscopes	114
Kettle and Stand	415
Kimonos Silk	409
Kindergarten Chairs	426
Kit Bags	363
Kites	89
Kite Accessories	89
Kitchen Sets	140
„ Toys	117-124
Kinoscope	262
Kliptiko	128
Knife and Fork Basket, Toys	145
„ Cleaner	442
„ Rests	397
Knives, Pocket	391
„ Tea	394
Knitting Machine, Toy	131
Kodaks	271

ALPHABETICAL INDEX—*continued*.

L

	PAGE
Ladies' Bangle Tassels	34
,, Bureau	427
,, Court Shoes	355
,, Dressing Case	363
,, Gloves	452-454
,, Handkerchief	465
,, ,, Boxes	464
,, Hat Case	354
,, Ideal Comb	444
,, Motor Coats	351
,, Neckwear	466
,, Purses	386
,, Silver Bag	375
,, Slippers	355
,, Toilet Cases	380
,, Umbrellas	340, 341
,, Wrist Cases	355
Lady Swimmer	80
Lamps	49
,, Cycle	347
,, Electric	13, 335
Lamp (Railway Goods), Yard	23
,, Street	23
Lantern Slides	269
,, ,, Mechanical	270
Lanterns, Postcard	264
Lathe, Toy	130
Launches, Electric or Steam	74
Lawn Games	211, 228
,, Mower, Toy	154
Leather Cushions	363
Letter Case	385
,, Opener	310
,, Rack	420
Life Boats	71
Lighting Plants	42
,, Sets	46, 49
Live Hemp	62
Liners, Model	74
Literary Stands	428
Locomotives, Clockwork	4-6
,, Electric	10, 11
,, Steam	7-9
Log Boxes	420
Lyre Music Desks	249

M

	PAGE
Machines, Automatic	236
,, Fretwork	333
Magical Books	178
Magic Lanterns	265
Magneto Machines	65
Make Ups	183, 184
Mandolines	246
Manicure Sets	378
Map Cases	348
Marble Clocks	367
Marine Engines	33, 34
Marmalade Jars	396
Marking Boards	194
Masks and Noses	180
Masts, Bamboo	62
Match Boxes	404
Materials for Model Yachts	72
,, ,, Motor Boats, etc.	73
Mathematical Instrument Sets	324
Meccano	facing page 26
Mechanical Duck	80
,, Lantern Slides	270
,, Toys	90-97

	PAGE
Medical Coils	65
Memos	312
Menagerie	133
Metal Ware, Adamant	422
Microscopes	274
Miniature Billiard Tables	190-195
,, Dreadnoughts	80
,, Ocean Liner	80
Mincer	442
Mince Meat	400
Military Hair Brushes	444
Milk, Floats	152
Mirroscope	264
Mr. Jollyboy	131
Model Boilers	34
,, Coaches	15
,, Buffers	23
,, Crane Engine, Steam	29
,, Cranes	13
Model Department	1-49
Model Electric Generating Plant	29
,, ,, Lighting Plants	26-28
,, Engines	33, 34
,, Engine Sheds	25
,, Goods Rolling Stock	16
,, ,, Shed	25
,, Hot Air Engines	30
,, Locomotives	7-9
,, Motor Boats	74
,, Railway Points	18
,, Rolling Stock	17
,, Scaffolding	131
,, Signals	22
,, Signal Boxes	25
,, Star Switches	18
,, Steam Donkey Engine	29
,, Steam Engines	26-32
,, ,, Rollers	29
,, Street Lamp	23
,, Switchboards	18
,, Ticket Box	23
,, Three Way Switches	18
,, Track Simpull	19
,, Trucks	17
,, Turntable	23
,, Vertical Steam Engines	27, 28, 31, 32
Models, Working	35, 36
Money Boxes	115
Morse Dictating Machines	64
Monologues	258
Monoscopes	274
Mosaic Cubes	121, 127
Motor Tip Waggons	157
Moustaches and Beards	182
Mouth Organs	254
Motors	45
,, Water	42
Motor Boats	74
Motor ,, Hulls	75
,, Cars, Toy	146, 147
,, ,, (Wood)	156
,, Coats, Gent's	351
,, ,, Ladies'	351
Motor Cycle and Motor Accessories Dept.	349, 350
Motor Cycles	349
,, Lamp	349
,, Gloves	456-458
,, Lorry, Wooden	154
,, Mail Van, Wood	154
,, Maker (Constructional)	128
Music	237, 260
,, Cases	245, 365
Music Deptmt.	237
Music Racks	417
,, Rolls	255
,, Sheet	256
,, Stands	245
,, Waltz	260
Musical Boxes	253
,, Instruments, Toy	111-113
,, Tobacco Jar	253
Musettes	249
Mutes	245

N

	PAGE
Nail File	445
Necklets	370
Neckwear	466
Needle Boxes	242
,, Cases	388
Noah's Arks	133
North American Indian Novelties	410
Noses, Electric	48
,, and Masks	180
Note Books	303
Novelty Calendars	302
Novelties, Electric	334
,, Electrical	48
,, from the East	403
Nursery Skittles	117

O

	PAGE
Oak Tray	443
Ocean Liner, Miniature	80
Oil Painting Boxes	322
Oriental Embroideries	401
,, Novelties	403
Organs	255
Organ Cart	154
Outfits for Scouts	354

P

	PAGE
Paint Box	120
Painting Books	299
Paints, Grease	183
Paintings, Replicas of Oil Paintings	430
Paper Bells	163
,, Racks	417
,, Weight	310
Paraffin Blow Lamps	34
,, Wax	63
Parallel Switch Railway	18
,, Toy	18
Parlour Games	211-228
Parrot Cages	441
Passenger Bridges, Railway	20
Paste, Jewellery	372
Pen Painting Outfits	321
Pencils, Silver and Gold	375
Pens, Fountain	314
Penny Toys	163
Penwiper	319
Perfumed Soap	446
Perfume Sprays	447
Perfumery	447
Permodelle	126
Petrol Engines	42, 43
,, Engine, Castings	43, 44
Pewter, Modelling	438
,, Relief Modelling	439-440
Phonographs	243
Phonograph Sundries	242
Photo Frames	379, 406
Piano Albums	257
,, Player	255
Pianoforte Solos	257
Pianos	111, 255
Piccolos	249
Picture Cubes	127
Picnic Baskets, Toy	140
Pickford's Lorry	151
Pictorial Card Games	206-208
Picture Making	307

ALPHABETICAL INDEX—*continued*.

	PAGE
Pinafores, Children's ..	467
Ping Tung Building Blocks ..	129
Pipe Covers ..	410
,, Sets, Companion ..	451
Pipes ..	449
Pistols ..	105
,, Toy ..	110
Plasticine facing page	188
Playgrounds, Children's ..	153
Playing Cards ..	196
Play Carts ..	155
Playhouse, Children's ..	142
Pocket Batteries ..	48
,, Books ..	313
,, Brush and Comb Case	444
,, Cases ..	313
,, Diary Book ..	303
,, Knives ..	391
,, Lamps ..	335
Poker Points and Sundries ..	433
,, Work ..	432
,, Work, Whitewood Articles	435-437
Pole Carts Express ..	155
Poles, Bamboo ..	62
Polarity Indicator ..	45
Pond, clockwork ..	80
Pool Balls ..	192
,, Baskets ..	193
,, Marker ..	194
Pop Guns ..	105
Post Card Lanterns ..	264
,, ,, Albums ..	315
,, Horns ..	249
Pot Pourri Boxes ..	404
Potters Wheels ..	130
Poultry Keeper's Note Book	303
Powder Boxes ..	377
Prams, Dolls'	136-137
Prayer Books ..	325
Preserved Stew Ginger ..	400
Preserve Jar ..	396
Pressure Gauges ..	36, 38
Projection Post Cards ..	268
Puff Boxes ..	445
Pulley Blocks ..	62
Punch and Judy Show ..	125
,, Balls ..	232
Pumps, Steam ..	36
,, Rotary ..	36
Purses ..	386
Puzzles, Dissected ..	127
Pyramid Cubes ..	127
,, Balls ..	192

R

	PAGE
Race Games ..	209
Racks, Music ..	417
,, Paper ..	417
,, Toast ..	397
,, Tool ..	330
Rackets, Badminton ..	230
Ragtime Songs ..	260
Rag Books ..	298
Rails, Railway ..	14
,, Insulating ..	18
,, Toys ..	18
Railway Bridges, Electric ..	13
,, ,, ..	21
,, Buffers ..	23
,, Carriages ..	15
,, Crossings ..	18
,, ,, Gates ..	23
,, Cross Rails ..	18
,, Engine Shed ..	25
,, Footbridge with Signals	20

	PAGE
Railway Goods Siding ..	21
,, ,, Station ..	21
,, ,, Yard Lamp ..	23
,, Indicator ..	23
,, Lines ..	14
,, Passenger Bridges ..	20
,, Points ..	18
,, Rolling Stock ..	16
,, Signals ..	22
,, Signal Boxes ..	25
,, Stations ..	24
,, Stop Rails ..	18
. Switches ..	18
,, Switchboards ..	18
,, Ticket Box ..	23
,, Turntables	14, 23
,, Tunnels ..	23
,, Van ..	151
Railways, Clockwork ..	3
,, Toy ..	1
Razors ..	392
Rear Carriers ..	348
,, Lamps ..	347
Recitations ..	253
Record Holder ..	242
Reels, Fishing ..	360
Reflectors ..	49
Reins ..	113
Reproductions in Brass	423-424
Resistances, Electric	13-14
Rests, Knife ..	397
Reversible Billiard Tables ..	190
Rhyme Books ..	258
Richter's Building Bricks, facing page	126
Rickshaws ..	155
Riding Whips ..	344
Rifle Covers ..	359
Rings ..	371
Ring Games ..	227
Road Rollers, Steam ..	29
Roasters ..	442
Rocking Boats, Wood ..	157
,, Horses ..	149
Roller Skates ..	353
Rollikins ..	131
Rolling Pin and Board, Toy ..	140
,, Stock, Model ..	15
Rouges ..	185
Roulette ..	210
,, Watches ..	210
Rose Bowls ..	406
Russian Made Handkerchief Box ..	411
Russian Novelties ..	411
Rubber Strip ..	87
,, Toys ..	116

S

	PAGE
Sachets ..	464
Saddles ..	348
Safety Razors ..	392
,, Scooter, The ..	148
Safes ..	115
Sailing Yachts ..	69-72
Salad Bowl Servers ..	395
Santa Claus Stockings ..	161
Saxhorns ..	251
Scales ..	442
,, Toy ..	162
Scarves, Evening ..	409
Scenery ..	187
School Bags ..	365
Scissors, Silver ..	375
,, Steel ..	388
Scout Axes ..	354
Scout Dept. ..	351
Scout Outfits ..	109

	PAGE
Scouts' Jerseys ..	354
,, Water ..	354
Sculler (Barry) ..	79
Sealskin Caps ..	344
Seaplane ..	79
Seaplanes ..	85, 86
Seat Sticks ..	342
See Saws ..	156
Serviette Rings ..	403
Setting Houses ..	361
Sewing Companions ..	388
,, Machines ..	421
,, ,, Toy ..	138
Shadow Pictures ..	125
Shaving Brushes ..	444
,, Mirror ..	385
,, Stand ..	392
Sheds, Engine ..	14
Shepherds' Crook ..	342
Ship Fittings ..	82
Shocking Coils ..	65
Shoe Dept.	355, 356
Shoe Lifts ..	445
Shooting Cart ..	152
,, Sets (Harmless) ..	108
Shopping Lists ..	308
Shuttlecocks ..	114
Side Drums ..	250
Signal Boxes, Railway ..	25
,, ,, Model ..	25
,, Model ..	22
,, Railway ..	22
Silk, Kimonos ..	409
Silver Bags, Ladies' ..	375
,, Belt Buckle ..	375
,, Card Cases ..	374
,, Cigar Cutter ..	374
,, Cigarette Case ..	374
,, Cruet Frame ..	395
,, Fruit Knives ..	375
,, Hair Brushes ..	372
,, Hat Pin Stands ..	375
,, Inkstands ..	375
,, Pencils ..	375
,, Scissors ..	375
,, Smelling Salts, Bottle..	375
,, Tea Sets ..	393
,, Toothpick ..	374
,, Vanity Case ..	375
,, Vases ..	375
Simpull Electric Switches ..	19
,, Rails ..	19
,, ,, Electric ..	19
,, Switches, Railway ..	19
,, Truck Railways ..	19
Syphon Stands ..	398
Syrens ..	348
Skates, Ice ..	234
,, Roller ..	233
Sketch Books ..	309
Skipping Ropes ..	114
Skis ..	235
Ski-ing Sundries ..	235
Skittles ..	114
Sleighs ..	234
Slippers, Ladies' ..	355
Smokers' Cabinets ..	389
,, Set ..	420
Snooker Marker ..	194
Soap, perfumed ..	445
Soldering Sets ..	328
Soldiers	100-104
Soldier Uniforms ..	109
Song Albums	257-258
Songs ..	259
Sound Boxes ..	242
Sovereign Purse ..	374
Spelling Boards ..	118
Spirit Flask ..	398
,, Frames ..	389
,, Level ..	193
,, Stove ..	414
Sporting Guns ..	357
Sprays, Perfume ..	447
Stables, Toy ..	132

ALPHABETICAL INDEX—*continued.*

	PAGE
Stage Scenery ..	187
Stamps, Foreign ..	316
Stationery Dept.	299-327
Stations, Model ..	24
,, Railway ..	24
Steam Cooker ..	442
,, Engines ..	33-34
,, ,, Horizontal ..	26-32
,, ,, Model ..	26-32
,, ,, Vertical	27-28, 31-32
,, Locomotive Parts ..	7
,, Locomotives ..	7-9
,, Rollers, Model ..	29
Steel Scissors ..	388
Steiff's Toys facing page	122
Stencil Outfits ..	431
Step Mats ..	350
Stereoscopes ..	274
Sticks, Seat ..	342
Stock Caps ..	344
Stool Horses ..	150
,, Inlaid ..	402
Stoves, Toy ..	140
String Holder ..	319
Strip Woodwork ..	331
Structator facing page	32
Stuffed Toys ,, ,,	132
Sugar Bowls ..	397
Suits, Cowboy ..	106
,, Indian ..	107
Swan, Swimming ..	80
Sweepers, Carpet ..	429
Sweet Stalls ..	132
Swimming Duck ..	80
,, Frog ..	80
,, Lady ..	80
,, Swan ..	80
Switchbacks ..	156
Switchboards, Model Railways	18
,, Railway	18
Switches ..	49, 63
,, Electric	13, 14
,, Railway	14
Swords, Toy ..	110

T

	PAGE
Table Bell ..	422
,, Billiards ..	191
Tables, Billiard ..	189
Table, Croquet ..	225
,, Decoration, Electric ..	336
,, Fountains ..	362
,, Games	211-228
,, Gong ..	419
,, Heaters ..	414
Tailoring Dept.	351-353
Tally-ho Horses ..	152
Tambourines ..	248
Tattooing Machines ..	48
Tea ..	400
,, Caddies, Japanese ..	407
,, Knives ..	394
,, Sets ..	138
,, ,, China, Toy ..	138
,, ,, Enamelled Toy ..	139
,, ,, Silver ..	393
Teddy Bears facing page	132
Telegram Case ..	310
Telescopes ..	274
Tents, Soldier ..	103
,, Indian ..	107
Terminals ..	49, 63
Theatre Glasses ..	272
Theatres ..	125
The Wobbling Goblin ..	153
Three Way Switches, Model	18
Tie Case ..	385
,, Coney Seal ..	462
,, Pins Electrical ..	48

	PAGE
Ticket Box Railway ..	23
,, Sets, Toy ..	113
Timber Van, Toy ..	151
Tinsel Strings ..	163
Toast Racks ..	397
Tobacco Jars ..	449
Tobacco & Cigarette Department.	448-451
Tobacco Pouches ..	449
Toboggans ..	235
Toilet Brush Ware ..	445
,, Cases, Gents' ..	381
,, ,, Ladies ..	380
,, Requisites ..	373
,, Sets, Toy ..	139
Tool Cabinets ..	330
,, Chests	328, 329
,, Pads ..	329
,, Racks ..	330
Tops ..	98, 99
Tormentum	204, 205
Torpedo Destroyers ..	75
,, Hulls ..	75
Toys, Constructional, facing pages	26, 32
Toy Cranes ..	13
,, Dinner Sets, Enamelled ..	139
,, Enamelled Toilet Sets ..	139
,, Garden Set ..	140
,, Locomotives ..	4-9
,, Motor Cars	146, 147
,, Passenger Bridges ..	20
,, Rails ..	18
,, Railway Cuttings ..	21
,, ,, Switches ..	18
,, Sewing Machines ..	138
,, Spoon Set ..	145
,, Stoves ..	140
,, Trains ..	2, 3
,, Trams ..	1, 3
,, Trucks ..	17
Toys, Stuffed facing page	132
Trains (Clockwork) ..	1, 2
,, Electric ..	12
,, Toy ..	3
,, Wood ..	157
Trams, Wooden ..	154
Trays, Crumb ..	416
Tricycle Horses ..	150
Tricycles ..	346
Trinket Boxes ..	404
,, Case ..	385
Trouser Presses ..	390
Trout Fly Boo ..	360
Trucks, Model ..	17
,, Toys ..	17
Trumpets ..	249
Trumpet Cases ..	242
Tubing, Aluminium ..	87
Tubby Dog ..	132
Tudor Stone Bricks ..	127
Tumblers, Benares ..	403
Tunnels, Model ..	23
,, Railway ..	23
Turntables, Railway ..	14, 23
Turntable, Model ..	23
Typewriters ..	318

U

	PAGE
Umbrella and Stick Dept.	337-344
Umbrellas, Boys' ..	342
,, Gents' ..	337
,, Girls' ..	342
,, Ladies'	340-341
Underground Electric Locos	10
,, ,, Trains	11
Uniforms, Toy ..	109

V

	PAGE
Vacuum Shooting Sets ..	108
Vanity Case, Silver ..	375
Vase, Dutch Design ..	412
Vases	408, 412, 413, 420
,, Silver ..	375
Vertical steam Engines	27, 28, 31, 32
Vinegar Bottles ..	397
Violin Bows ..	245
,, Cases ..	244
,, Resin ..	245
,, Strings ..	245
Violins ..	244
Violoncellos ..	246
Vortex Fun Wheel ..	96

W

	PAGE
Waggons, American ..	155
,, Hardwood ..	155
Walking Sticks, Boys' ..	342
,, ,, Gents'	338, 339
,, and Talking Dolls ..	145
Waltz Music ..	260
Wardrobe, Doll's ..	140
,, Trunk ..	364
Washstands, Doll's ..	138
Watches, Wrist ..	369
Water Cart and Horse ..	154
,, Colours ..	323
,, Colour Boxes ..	321
,, Motors ..	42
Waterplanes ..	85, 86
Wax Paraffin ..	63
Wet Batteries ..	47
Wheel Barrows ..	155
Wheelboy ..	130
Whiskers and Wigs ..	18
Wigwams ..	107
Wigs and Whiskers ..	181
Wild Bird Cages ..	441
Wire ..	62
Wireless Apparatus ..	50-64
Wireless Dept. ..	50-66
Wood Bricks ..	127
,, Cannon ..	130
,, Carving Tools ..	434
Wooden Crane ..	130
Wood Carving	435-437
,, Engines ..	154
Woodwork Strip ..	331
Work Basket ..	387
,, Stand ..	387
Working Models ..	35, 37
Wraps, Squirrel ..	462
Wrist Cases, Ladies' ..	365
,, Watches ..	369
Writing Cases ..	383
,, Sets ..	317
,, Tablets ..	300

X

	PAGE
Xmas Decorations ..	163
,, Hampers ..	400
,, Stockings ..	161

Y

	PAGE
Yachts ..	69-72
Young Engine Builder ..	128
Youths' Clothing ..	353

Z

	PAGE
Zillograph ..	125
Zonophones ..	237
Zoological Dept.	459-460
Zoological Gardens ..	125

GAMAGES
Grand Xmas Bazaar

The Village Inn is on fire with flames blazing out through the roof. Numbers of peasants are watching the conflagration and the efforts of the **Village Fire Brigade,** who are endeavouring with their fire engine to extinguish the blaze. Real water is used, together with ladders and all the usual fire-fighting details.

Persons are being rescued from the burning house, and barrels of beer are being carefully salved.

This is easily the most exciting, as well as amusing, of the show pieces seen in Gamages Bazaar in recent years

See the Great Red Indian Encampment
WIGWAMS — CHIEFS — BRAVES — SQUAWS — COWBOYS — WAR WEAPONS — PIPES OF PEACE — ORNAMENTS

See the Great Military Moving Model

See the Marvels of Wireless Telegraphy demonstrated

Midland, Great Northern, and London & North Western Clockwork Trains.

As will be seen from the illustrations (which are from photographs of the actual models) these trains are most realistic in appearance. The mechanism and finish throughout is of the best, and the complete train with rails is packed in a strong cardboard box.

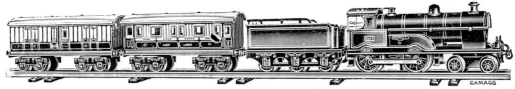

No. SD. Gauge 0. L.N.W.R. Clockwork Trains, consisting of Scale Model George V. loco. and tender fitted with brake and reversing gear, 1 Carriage, 1 guard's van with bogie wheels, complete with oval set of 16 wide radii rails. Len. 31 in. Carriage 10d. Price with box **17/6**

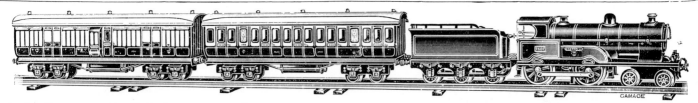

No. IAO. Gauge I. L.N.W.R. Passenger Express Train, consisting of Scale Model George V. loco. and tender, with brake and reversing gear, 2 speeds, 1 carriage, 1 guard's van, complete with oval set of 20 wide radii rails. Length 58 in. Carriage paid. Price with box **59/6**

No. GOA. Gauge O. L.N.W.R. Passenger Express Loco., consisting of ditto engine and tender, with brake and reversing gear, carriage and guard's van, mounted on bogie wheels, complete with oval track of 16 wide radii rails. Length 41 in. Carriage free **20/-**

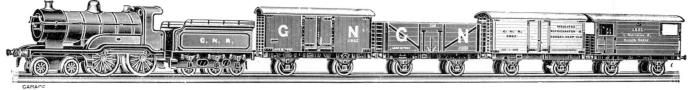

No. TZ. Gauge I. Scale Model G.N.R. Goods Train, consisting of loco. and tender, fitted with 2 speeds, brake and reversing gear, 1 open truck, 1 refrigerator van, 1 goods van, 1 goods guard's van, complete with oval set of 20 wide radii rails. Length 58 in. Carriage free. Price with box **63/-**

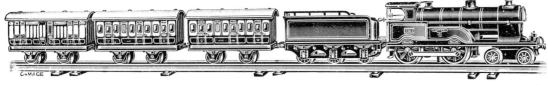

Gauge 0. 1¼ in.

Clockwork Train.

16/6

Postage 10d.

No. SI. Consisting of Scale Model "George the Fifth" Loco. and Tender, with brake and reversing gear, 2 Carriages and Guard's Van with doors to open, Oval Track of 16 wide radii rails.

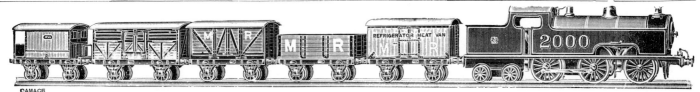

No. IL. Gauge I. Scale Model Midland Railway Goods Train, consisting of clockwork tank loco., fitted with 2 speeds reversing gear and brake, all worked from cab, 1 open truck, 1 goods van, 1 refrigerator van, 1 cattle truck, 1 goods guard's van, complete with oval set of 20 wide radii rails. Length 58 in. Carriage free .. .. Price with box **55/-**

No. GA. Gauge O. Latest Type M.R. Co. Tank Loco., with correct English pattern trucks, as illustration, a really first-class train, complete with oval of 16 wide radii rails. Length 38 in. .. Carriage free .. .. Price **28/6**

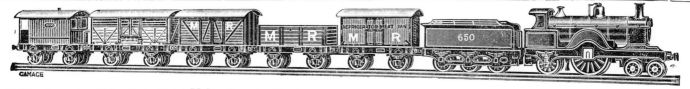

No. GAY. Gauge 0. 1¼ in. Scale Model M.R. Goods Train, consisting of Locomotive and Tender with brake and reversing gear, Open Truck, 1 Refrigerator Van, 1 Covered Goods Truck, 1 Cattle Truck, 1 Guard's Van, Oval Track of 12 Straight and 6 Curved Rails. Complete in Box—
22/6 Carriage free.

A

Scale Model Clockwork Train Sets.
(Packed in Strong Cardboard Boxes with Divisions.)

Gauge 0. 1¼ in. **Clockwork Train.**

As illustration, but with clockwork locomotive, No. 281, p. 4.

Consisting of Loco. and Tender, fitted with brake and reversing gear, 1 Carriage, 1 Guard's Van **with doors to open.** Oval Track of 8 rails.

Price .. **7/11** Postage 8d.

As illustration, but with locomotive No. 281, page 4.

Consisting of Loco. and Tender, fitted with Brake and Reversing Gear, 2 Carriages, 1 Guard's Van **with doors to open** Complete with Oval Track of 16 wide Radii Rails.

Price **11/9** Postage 6d.

0 Gauge. **G.N.R. & L.N.W.R.** **Passenger Train.**

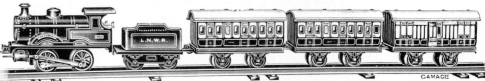

Gauge 0. 1¼ in. Scale Model **Clockwork Train.** Complete in Box, **15/-** Post 10d.

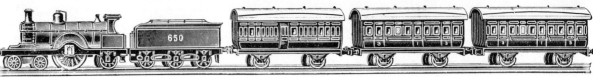

Consisting of Midland Locomotive and Tender, "Princess Beatrice" type, fitted with brake and reversing gear, 2 Carriages, 1 Guard's Van with doors to open, Oval Set of 12 small radii rails.

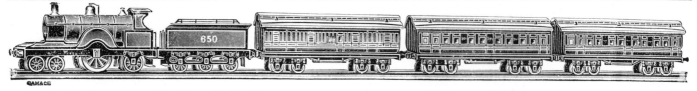

Gauge 0. 1¼ in. Scale Model **Clockwork Train** consisting of Midland Loco. and Tender, fitted with brake and reversing gear, 2 Carriages on Bogie Wheels, 1 Guard's Van Oval Track of 16 wide radii rails. Complete in Box .. .. **27/6** Carriage free.

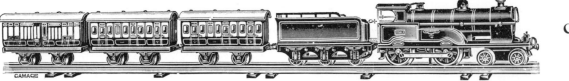

Gauge 0. 1¼ in.

Clockwork Train **25/6** Carriage free.

Consisting of Scale Model "George the Fifth" Loco. and Tender, with brake and reversing gear, 2 Carriages and Guard's Van, with doors to open, Oval Track of 16 wide radii rails.

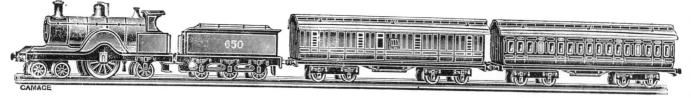

Gauge 0. 1¼ in. Scale Model **Clockwork Train** with Midland Locomotive and Tender, 1 Carriage on Bogie Wheels, 1 Guard's Van, 1 pair of Switches, 28 wide radii rails. Complete in Box— **27/6** Carriage free.

Gauge 0. 1¼ in. Scale Model **M.R. Goods Train,** consisting of Locomotive and Tender with brake and reversing gear, Open Truck 1 Refrigerator Van, 1 Covered Goods Truck, 1 Cattle Truck, 1 Guard's Van, Oval Track of 12 Straight and 6 Curved Rails. Complete in Box— **20/-** Carriage free

CLOCKWORK TRAINS and TRAMS.

his is a perfect model of a **L. & N.W.R. Express** on a very small scale.   Length of loco. with tender, 5⅛ in.   Length of carriage, 3¾ in.
Length of entire train, 21 in

The Train consists of locomotive, tender, **4 passenger carriages and 1 guard's van**   It is a perfect replica of the well-known
L. & N.W.R. Express from Euston to Birmingham, Liverpool, Glasgow, etc. ..   ..   Postage 2d.   **10½d**

---

0 Gauge. Clockwork Train. As illust.
Consisting of Locomotive with strong clockwork,
patent regulator, with brake to be worked from the
rail or from the cab; tender and two passenger cars,
japanned and lettered in the exact colours of the
respective railway companies, with oval set of 6 rails,
including brake rail (4 curved and 2 short straight
rails).   Length of complete train 18¾ in.

Price .. **I/II** Postage 4d.

Supplied in G.W.R., M.R., L. & N.W.R., Lancashire and Yorkshire Railway colours.

Supplied in Great Western, and London and North-Western Railway colours.

Clockwork Train.

Consisting of Locomotive with strong clockwork and **patent
regulator**, with brake to be worked from the cab, tender
with imitation coal, and **two** passenger cars, japanned and
lettered in the exact colours of the respective railway companies, with oval set of 6 rails.

Length of complete train 19½ in.

Price ..   ..   .. **3/6** Postage 4d.

---

0 Gauge. Clockwork Train.

Consisting of Locomotive with strong clockwork
and regulator, automatic brake to be worked from
the rail or from the cab, and *reversing gear;*
tender with imitation coal, and two passenger
cars, japanned and lettered in the exact colours
of the respective railway companies, with oval
set of rails = 6 rails including brake rail.   Length
of complete train 19½ in.

Price .. **4/II** Postage 6d.

Supplied in Midland, London and North-Western and Great Northern Railway Colours.

Clockwork Whistling Train.

Gauge 0 = 1¼ in.

Fine model Whistling Train, consisting of loco. and tender, carriage, and
guard's van, with circular track.   By an ingenious contrivance, the engine
whistles in a most realistic manner while the train is in motion.

Price .. **2/11**   Postage 4d.

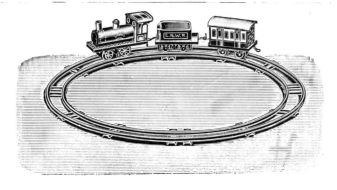

L.C.C. Clockwork Tram.   As illustration.

Complete with circular track.   The tram is fitted with best clockwork
motor and the finish throughout is good.

Price .. **3/6**   Postage 6d.

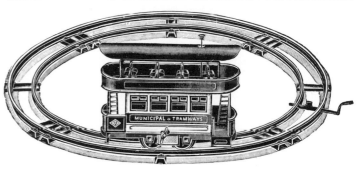

Clockwork Train.   Similar to illustration.

With one passenger car and circular track.   Length of train, 12 in.
Supplied in Great Western, Midland, and London & North Western Railway colours.

Price .. **10½d.**   Postage 3d.

A ..

Clockwork Locomotives.

Gauge 0=1¼ in.

Clockwork Tank Locomotive with extra strong clockwork with superforce movement and patent regulator with brake worked from, the rail or cab **reversing gear.** Nicely japanned with nickel fittings, 5¾ in. long. Price **3/11** Post 3d.

Gauge 0=1¼ in. **Midland Railway Clockwork Locomotive and Tender** (as illustration). With very powerful clockwork motor with patent speed regulator, fitted with automatic brake and reversing gear which can be operated from either cab or rail, beautifully enamelled in correct colours. 10¾ in. long. Price **5/6** Postage 4d.
Also supplied in L.N.W.R. and G.N.R. colours.

Gauge 0=1¼ in.

Clockwork Locomotive and Tender.

Fitted with brake and reversing gear, both worked from cab or rail.

Extra strong clockwork motor fitted with patent regulator. Length 9½ in.

Price **4/6** Postage 3d.

Also supplied in L.N.W.R. and M.R. colours.

SPECIAL VALUE. Gauge 0 1¼ in. Scale Model **Great Northern Railway,** 4-4-0, D.I. Class Clockwork Locomotive and Tender, fitted with automatic reversing motion and brake, which can be operated either from cab or rail. The clockwork movement is of the latest design and best make and finish throughout, enamelled and lined in correct G.N.R. colours
This Loco. will run either on small or large radii rails. 16 in. long. Price .. .. .. **8/11** Postage 4d.

Gauge I=1¾ in.

Scale Model L.N.W.R. Tank Loco.

with

powerful clockwork movement, fitted automatic brake and reversing gear, operated either from cab or rail, 2 speed lever for fast or slow running, spring buffers, and is enamelled and lined in the correct colours.

Length 17 in.

Price **47/6**

Ditto. Gauge 0=1¼ in. Without 2-speed gear. 12 in. long. These Locos. require our large radii rails.

Price .. **27/6**

Clockwork Locomotives.

Gauge 1=1¾ in.

LONDON & NORTH WESTERN

Clockwork Loco. and Tender

as illustration.

Fitted with automatic brake and reversing gear which can be operated either from cab or rail.

Extra powerful clockwork motor with patent speed regulator, enamelled and lined in correct colours.

Price **15/-**   Postage 5d.

Also supplied in G.N.R. and M.R. colours.

Midland Passenger Express Locomotive.

Gauge 1= 1¾ in., ⅜ in. scale, with extra powerful long running motor, reversing gear operated from the cab, new type governor, hand enamelled, lined and numbered in correct colours.

Length over all, 19½ in.	Price ..	**25/6**	Post free.
Also supplied in G.N.R. colours ..		**26/6**	Post free.
L.N.W. colours		**25/6**	Post free.

L. & N.W.R. Passenger Express Loco. "Achilles."

Gauge 0=1¼ in. This Locomotive is one of the latest famous "Precursor" Class, and is a replica of its prototype. It is fitted with the best quality long running motor with centrifugal governor, automatic brake and reversing gear, operated from the cab, and is a most handsome model. Length over all

14 in. **21/-**   Post 6d.

Also supplied in Midland colours.

N.B.—This Loco. requires our large radii Rails.

Great Northern Passenger Express Locomotive.

ATLANTIC TYPE. Gauge 0=1¼ in.

This is, without question, the most imposing Clockwork Locomotive produced. The motor is the very best, fitted with patent regulator, automatic brake and reversing gear, operated from the cab.

Length over all, 16 in.

Price .. .. **22/6** Post 6d.

N.B.—These Locos require our large radii Rail.

Midland Railway Tank Locomotive.

2,000 class (Improved Model).
This is the latest type Tank Locomotive in Great Britain, and the most powerful. It is a replica of its prototype except that the forward coupling rods have been omitted owing to the length of fixed wheel base. The loco. is fitted with the best quality motor with centrifugal governor **Brake and Reversing Gear**, and is enamelled, lined and numbered in correct colours. A powerful Locomotive.

Gauge 0. Length over all 16 in. .. **21/-**
.. 1. .. ,, 17 in. .. **32/6**
Post free.

N.B.—This Loco. requires our large radii rail

Scale Model Clockwork Locomotives.

Gauge 0 = 1¼ in. **Scale Model. Midland Railway.** "Single Wheeler." "**Princess Beatrice**" type.

Clockwork Locomotive and Tender, fitted with automatic brake and reversing gear, which can either be worked from cab or rail; very powerful clockwork motor. Enamelled and lined in correct Midland colours. Length over all 15 in. This Locomotive will run on either small or large radii rails.

It is only after considerable experiment that we are able to offer our customers a Clockwork-propelled Locomotive with **single driving wheels.** The results obtained have been highly successful, and we recommend this Locomotive with confidence and as a FINE EXAMPLE OF GAMAGE'S VALUE.

PRICE .. .. .. **8/6**   Postage 4d.

Gauge 0 = 1¼ in. **Scale Model. L.N.W.R. Experiment, Clockwork Locomotive and Tender,** as illustration.
Fitted with automatic brake and reversing gear, enamelled and lined in correct L.N.W.R. colours. Very powerful long running Clockwork Motor.

Length 15¾ in.   PRICE .. **32/6**   Post free.

Gauge 1 = 1¾ in. Ditto, but fitted with two-speed gear. Length over all 23¼ in.   PRICE .. .. .. **55/-**   Carriage paid.

These Locos. require our large Radii Rails.

Gauge I. = 1¾ in. **Scale Model. Great Northern Railway,** 4—4—0, D 1 Class, **Clockwork Locomotive and Tender.**

Fitted with automatic reversing motion and brake with 2-speed gear for fast or slow running. Reversing gear and brake can be operated from cab or rail. The clockwork movement is of the latest design and best make and finish throughout; the carcase enamelled and lined in correct G.N.R. colours. Will run on either small or large radii rails.

PRICE .. .. .. **45/-**   Post free.

STEAM LOCOMOTIVES.

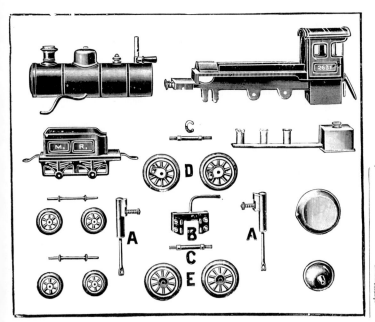

Gauge 0=1¼ in.

Constructional Steam Locomotives. Complete Set of Finished Parts for Constructing a Steam Locomotive.

Set complete as illustration, consisting of all the parts as shown, when fitted up complete makes a splendid Model Steam Locomotive and Tender, packed in strong red cardboard box, assorted in M.R. and L.N.W.R. colours with explicit instructions how to put together

Price .. .. **8/11** Postage 6d.

Gauge 0=1¼ in.

Steam Locomotive with oscillating brass cylinder and cog-wheel gear to increase the power, nicely japanned, with stamped frame, polished brass boiler and safety valve.

Length 7½ in. Price **2/3** Post 3d.

Supplied in Midland Railway or London and North Western Railway colours.

Gauge 0=1¼ in.

Improved Steam Locomotive with Tender.

With japanned brass boiler, 2 oscillating cylinders, steam dome, hand rails, steam whistle, flame guard, safety valve and 4 large driving wheels and connecting rods.
Length, including Tender, 13¼ in

Also Supplied in G.W.R. and L. & N.W.R. colours.

Price **10/6** Post 6d.

Enamelled, Lined and Lettered in the correct colours of the respective Railway Companies.

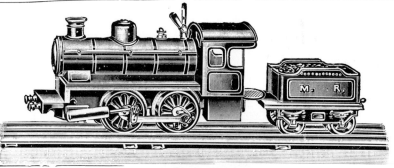

Gauge 0=1¼ in.
G.N.R. Steam Locomotive and Tender.
Improved new model, as illustration, safety valve, steam dome, oxydised brass boiler, oscillating cylinders. 12 in. long.
Enamelled and lined in correct colours .. **7/11** Post 6d.

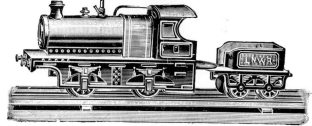

Gauge 0=1¼ in.
Steam Locomotive with oscillating brass cylinder.
Safety valve. An excellent working model.
Length, including Tender, 11¼ in. Price **4/6** Postage 4d.
Can be supplied in Midland Railway or London & North Western Railway Colours.

Gauge 0=1¼ in. **Midland Railway Steam Locomotive and Tender.** New Model, as illustration, fitted with safety valve, steam dome, oxydised brass boiler, oscillating cylinders. 12 in. long.
Enamelled and lined in correct colours .. .. **7/11** Post 6d.

Gauge 0. **L.N.W.R Steam Locomotive and Tender.**
Fitted with safety valve, steam dome, oscillating cylinders, oxydised brass boiler, as illustration. 12 in. long.
Enamelled and lined in correct colours .. .. **7/11** Post 6d.

Gauge 0 = 1¼ in. **Express Steam Locomotive and Tender,** 4—4—0 type, with two slide-valve cylinders and **slip eccentric reversing motion,** solid brass domed boiler. safety valve and whistle. Cylinders fitted with lubricators, stove enamelled, lined and lettered in correct colours Total length 13¾ in. Supplied in Midland, L.N.W. and G.N.R. colours. Price .. **19/6** Postage 6d.

Gauge 1=1¾ in. **Steam Locomotive with Tender.**

Excellent working model with **2** oscillating cylinders, finely japanned brass boiler and best fittings, steam dome, steam whistle, flame guard, safety valve and japanned flanged wheels ; including Tender 14⅜ in. long.

Enamelled, lined and lettered in the correct colours of the **M.R., G.W.R.** and **L. & N.W.R.**

Price .. **10/9** Postage 6d.

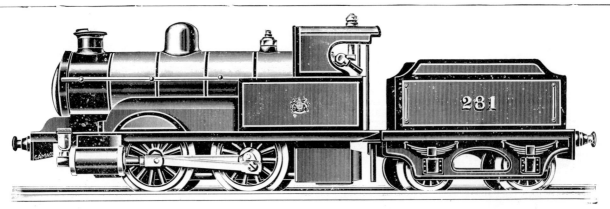

Gauge I. = 1¾ in. **Steam Locomotive and Tender,** with slide-valve cylinders, fitted with lubricators and **slip eccentric reversing motion,** solid brass domed boiler, with whistle and safety valve, stove enamelled and lined in correct colours. Supplied in Midland, Great Northern, and London and North-Western colours. Length 16½ in. Price .. **19/6** Postage 6d.

Improved, highly finished **Steam Locomotive with Tender** with automatic reversing gear, with 2 fixed slide valve cylinders with tubular slide valves, finely japanned brass boiler, highly nickelled flanged wheels, steam dome, bell steam whistle, starting tap, safety valve, hand rails and improved lubricating device built in the smoke box. All fittings accurately finished. Loco. with new **gas generating lamp,** flame guard, **exhaust steam passing through the funnel.** Including Tender 18¾ in long. Supplied in L. & N.W.R. and G.N.R. colours .. **25/9** Post free

SCALE MODEL STEAM LOCO.

With Slip Eccentric Reversing Gear.

Gauge 0=1¼ in. Scale Model **London and North Western Passenger Express Steam Locomotive** George I. These models are the first of their kind and are a great improvement on the outside Cylinder Engines. They work particularly well outdoors as well as indoors. The heating is by means of a vapour spirit lamp, the flame being carried through a central flue in the boiler. This arrangement allows of the best possible results, there being little or no heat lost. The placing of the **Cylinders inside the Frames** also prevents the cooling of the steam as it enters the Cylinders. Finished throughout in the very best style with stoved wireproof enamel. Very powerful Loco. Price **32/6** Post free.

Gauge I Do. do. .. .. ,, **63 -** ,,

Gauge 1=1¾ in. **Great Northern Mixed Traffic Steam Locomotive 1630.** This is a high-class scale model of the latest 2—6—0 Great Northern Locomotive, with six coupled driving wheels driven from two slide valve cylinders placed outside the frames with reversing gear and single two-wheeled leading bogie. A magnificent model, **exceedingly powerful and long running.** Painted, lined and lettered in correct colours and **stove enamelled.** Price **£4 4 0** Carriage free.

With Slip Eccentric Reversing Gear.

Gauge 0=1¼ in. **Midland Passenger Express Locomotive.** This is an exceedingly fine model of the latest 999 class of inside Cylinder Engine. The placing of the **Cylinders inside the Frames** materially assists the hauling power as the steam is not chilled when it enters the steam chests as with outside Cylinder Engines. The firing is by a vapour spirit lamp, the flames passing from the firebox through a central flue in the boiler, thereby preventing loss of heat. The Loco is a particularly good hauler and will work outdoors or indoors. Price **32/6** Post free.

Gauge I=1¾ in. Do. do. .. .. ,, **63/-** ,,

Gauge 1. First-class Scale Model **North British Railway Steam Locomotive.** 4—4—2. Fitted with water gauge, whistle, starting lever, brake and reversing lever which can be operated from Cab or Rail, head lights, spring buffers, outside cylinders, and four coupled driving wheels. Total length of Engine and Tender complete, 24 in. This Loco. requires our wide Radii Rails. Price **75/-** Carr. free.

ELECTRIC LOCOMOTIVES.

Gauge 0=1¼ in. **Electric Locomotive**
for low current. Will run from any 4-volt Battery.
Consumption, 1·25 amperes. Price .. **3/9** Postage 3d.
Length over all, 9¾ in.
Switch for Reversing .. **1/-** Postage 2d.

Gauge 1=1¾ in. **Metropolitan Locomotive.**
Fitted with reversing motor and headlight. Length over all, 13½ in.

Price **25/6** Post free. Requires 4 volt current.

Gauge 0=1¼ in. **Metropolitan Locomotive.**
Fitted with reversing motor and headlight. Length over all, 11 in.

Price **18/9** Post 6d. Requires 4 volt current.

Gauge 0=1¼ in.
Reversing Electric Underground Locomotive
for low current with electric headlight.
6¾ in. long,
Price .. **6/11** Post 4d.

Gauge 1=1¾ in. Ditto, 8¾ in. long.
Price .. **9/11** Post 6d.

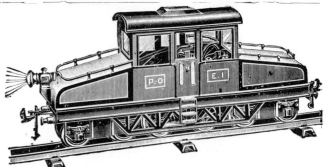

Gauge 0=1¼ in.
London and North Western Four-coupled Bogie Electric Locomotive.
For 4 volt current to be used with large radii rails.
With 2 electric headlights. Hand-made and hand-painted.
Length with tender, 14 in.
Price .. **25/-** Postage 6d.
Also supplied in M.R. colours.
These Locomotives require our large radii rails.

Gauge 0=1¼ in. **Scale Model Midland Railway Electric Locomotive** (Princess Beatrice Class) for 4-volt current.
The Motor is of the permanent magnet type which can be automatically reversed from track. Enamelled and lined in correct M.R. colours.
This Locomotive will run either on small or large radii rails. Total length 15 in. Price .. **10/9** Postage 6d.

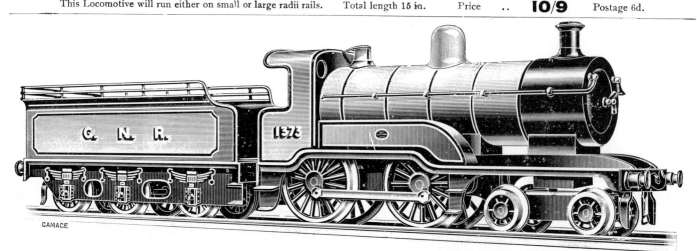

Gauge 0=1¼ in. **Scale Model Great Northern Railway 4-4-0 D.I. Class Electrically Driven Locomotive and Tender** for 4-volt current. The motor is of the permanent magnet type which can be automatically reversed from track.
Enamelled and lined in correct G.N.R. colours. This Locomotive will run either on small or large radii rails. Price **10/9** Postage 6d.

Electric Trains and Locomotives.

Electric Metropolitan Train.

Gauge 0=1¼ in.
As illustration, with 2 electric headlights, metal filament lamps, extra car with light inside, oval track (6 curved and 4 straight rails, including connecting rail). Total length 15 in.

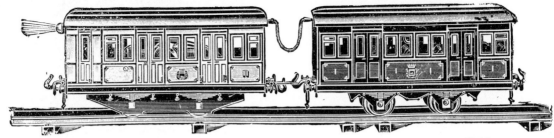

Price .. .. **16/6**   Post free.   Gauge 1=1¾ i   Ditto, with 8 curved and 4 straight rails.   Price .. .. **21/-**   Post free.
Accumulators for driving above trains (see index).   Reversing Commutators .. **1/-**   Post 2d.

Gauge 0=1¼ in

Great Northern "Atlantic" Type Electric Locomotive.

For 4-volt current and large radii rails.

With electric headlight.

Hand-made and hand-painted.

Length with tender, 16 in.

Price .. **26/6** Post free.

This Loco. requires our large radii rails.

Gauge 1=1¾ in.

Four-coupled Midland Passenger Express Locomotives.

With Reversing Model to work from a four-volt current and run on large radii rails.

Hand-finished and enamelled. Length over all 19 in.

Price .. **30/-**

Also supplied in L.N.W.R. and G.N.R. Colours

Something Particularly Good.

Gauge 0.   Scale Model **London & North Western Tank Locomotive.**
Electrically propelled, solid brass shell enamelled, lined and lettered in correct colours. This Loco. has tremendous haulage power for its size, and will negotiate a gradient with a load. The motor is of the best English make, and is so constructed that the Loco. will run on the ordinary wide radii *non-electrified* rails.
The accumulator can be carried in a Truck or Guard's Van.

Length 11 in., height 4 in.

Price   **35/-**   Complete with accumulator.

Scale Model Electrically Driven Locomotive "Precursor."

Gauge 1=1¾ in.   ⅜ in. scale.   Price, complete with Reversing Gear.. .. .. **55/-**
Special 6-volt 15 ampere Accumulator for use with this Locomotive. Price .. **16/6**   Carriage 7d.
6-volt 30 amperes .. **22/6**   Carriage paid.

This Locomotive is a very handsome Scale Model, and will appeal to every enthusiast. The Carcase is built from heavy Brass Plate beautifully hand enamelled, lined and lettered in correct colours; it is also fitted with Spring Buffers, Electric Head-light, Dummy Vacuum Tubes and Sand Pipes, as well as an Automatic Reversing Switch fitted into the Cab. Total length, Engine and Tender, 20 in. The Current required is 6 volts, which is obtained from an accumulator connected to the rails.

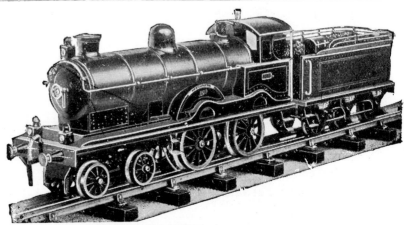

Accumulators for Driving above Locomotives, see Index.

ELECTRIC TRAINS.

All the undermentioned Electric Trains, with the exception of No. 179/7/00, will run successfully from any 4 volt wet battery.
There is not the slightest danger, and a young child can operate them.

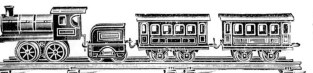

No. 179/7/00. Gauge 1⅛ in.

Electric Train, comprising locomotive, with tender, **two** passenger carriages and circular track (four rails). This train **can** be worked from a pocket battery or a 2-volt accumulator, and **can** be reversed by use of a special reversing switch. Length of Train 15¾ in.

Price, Train and Rails .. **2/6** Postage 4d.

Battery extra, **5**d. Post 2d. Reversing Switch, **1/-** Post 2d.

Gauge 0=1¼ in.

Electric Railway, fitted for Reversing, consisting of Locomotive, tender, two long passenger cars, with oval set of rails including connecting rail (four curved and two straight rails); length of train, 2 1¼ in. for a current of 3·5—5 volt and about 0·7 amps.

Price, without Battery and Reversing Switch **6/6**
Post 6d.

Switch for Reversing .. **1/-** Postage 2d.

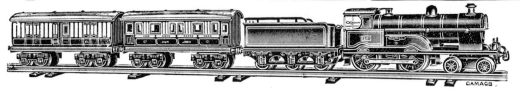

Without Head Lights.

Gauge 0. **Electric Railway.** Fitted for **Reversing,** consisting of Locomotive with Connecting Rods and Electric Head Light (Metallic Filament Lamp), Tender, Two Carriages and Guard's Van with Set of Rails (six curved and two straight rails including connecting rail).
Length of train 24¾ in. Reversing Switch .. **1/-** Post 2d. Price .. .. .. **10/6** Postage 6d.

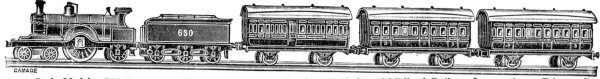

Gauge 0. **L.N.W.R. Electric Train,** consisting of Scale Model George V. Loco. and Tender, 1 Carriage, 1 Guard's Van with bogie wheels complete with oval set of 16 wide Radii Rails. Length 31 in. Carriage paid. Price with partitioned box .. **21/6** Carriage free.

Gauge 0. Scale Model. **Midland Railway Electric Train,** consisting of Midland Railway Locomotive, "Princess Beatrice" Type, 2 Carriages, 1 Guard's Van with doors to open, oval set of 8 Rails, complete with terminal rail. Price .. .. **17/6** Post 1/-

Gauge 0. Scale Model.
**L. & N.W.R.,
"George the Fifth,"
Electric Loco and
Tender,**
2 Carriages, 1 Guard's Van
WITH DOORS TO OPEN,
Oval Track of 8 small Radii
Rails including Connecting Rail
and Reversing Switch. Packed

in strong partitioned cardboard box .. .. **17/6** Postage 9d.

Gauge 0. **Scale Model Electric Train,** consisting of Midland Railway Locomotive, 1 Carriage, 1 Guard's Van on Bogie Wheels, oval set of wide radii Rails. complete with Terminal Rail .. .. Post free. Price **26/6**

Gauge 0. **Scale Model Electric Train,** consisting of Midland Railway Loco. and Tender, 2 Carriages, 1 Guard's Van, on Bogie Wheels, complete with oval set of 16 wide radii Rails including Terminal Rail, complete in partitioned box .. Post free. Price **25/-**

Gauge 0. **Scale Model Midland Railway Electric Goods Train,** consisting of Midland Loco. and Tender, 1 Open Truck, 1 Goods Guard's Van, 1 Covered Waggon, 1 Refrigerator Truck, 1 Cattle Truck, complete with oval set of 8 Rails, including Terminal Rail .. .. Post free. Price **21/6**

Electric Bridges, Switches, Cut Outs and Carnes.

Gauge 0 = 1¼ in. **Railway Bridge.**

For Electric Trains. Most Realistic Finish. With effective painting, arch in imitation ironwork 32 in. long, 5⅝ in. wide, price **3,6** Postage 6d.

Gauge 1 = 1¼ in. Ditto, 32 in. long, 5¾ in. wide. **4/6** Postage 8d.

Regulating Resistance.

For Low Current (maximum 4 amperes), mounted on wooden board, 3½ in. diameter.
If this apparatus is fitted between the accumulator or battery and the electric motor train, etc., a change of speed can be effected by pushing the lever either to the right or to the left.

Price **1/-** Postage 2d.

Switch for Low Current.

For use with all electric trains, having magnet motors for reversing and switching off current entirely, with four nickelled connecting clamps, 3½ in. long, 2¾ in. wide.

Price .. .. **1/-** Postage 2d.

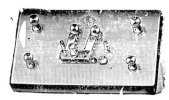

Switch or Commutator.

For Low Current.

For use with all electric trains having magnet motors (for reversing or switching off current entirely), with four nickelled connecting clamps, mounted on wooden board 4 in. long, 2¼ in. wide.

Price .. **2 3** Postage 3d.

Automatic Cut Out.

For automatically disconnecting the current in case of short circuit. Can be used in conjunction with our electric trains. Size 3½ in. by 1¾ in.

Price .. .. **2/-** Post 2d.

Electric Street Lamp.

For Low Current, with 6 in. flexible Wire Nicke Fittings.

7¾ in. high.

Price **2/3**

Post 3d.

Electric Controller.

For use in conjunction with Electric Trams, Trains, etc.

Will stop, start and reverse.

Price **2/9**

Postage 4d.

ELECTRIC -CRANE

(For 4-volt current).

NEW, VERY ORIGINAL AND INSTRUCTIVE TOY.

With Switch and Electro-magnet for lifting metal objects (iron pieces, railway trucks, etc.)

Lifting capacity, 2 lbs.

Electric Switchboard, for the lifting, lowering, and turning of crane in every direction worked by bichromate batteries or accumulators; the whole set, ready for connection, mounted on polished wooden base.

17¼ in. high, without accumulator.

Price **15/6** Postage 6d.

Accumulators extra, see index.

Electric Rails, Points, &c.

Small Radii, Straight or Curved Rails.

Gauge 0=1¼ in. ... ... **3¾d.** each. Post 5d. doz
Gauge 1=1¾ in. ... ... **5½d.** each. Post 5d. doz.
Large Radii, gauge 0 ... ... **4½d.** each. Post 6d. doz.
Gauge 1 ... **5½d.** each. 6d. doz.

Straight or Curved Rails, with 2 pole clamps for connection with the current supply (battery, etc.)

Small Radii. Gauge 0=1¼ in., **1/3** Gauge 1=1¾ in., **1/6** each.
Large ,, ,, ,, **1/3** ,, ,, **1/6**
Post 2d.

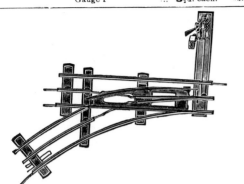

Left Hand Points.

(Heavy make.)

Gauge 0=1¼ in.

3/6 each, Post 4d.

Ditto, Large Radii, **4/6** ea. Post 6d.

Gauge 1=1¾ in.

4/6 each, Post 5d.

Ditto, Large Radii, **5/-** each. Post 7d.

Right Hand Points.

(Heavy make.)

Gauge 0=1¼ in.

3/6 each, Post 4d.

Ditto, Large Radii **4/6** each. Post 6d.

Gauge 1=1¾ in.

4/6 each. Post 5d.

Ditto, Large Radii ... **5/-** Post 7d.

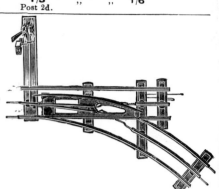

Electric Parallel Symmetrical Points.

With 1 lever and 1 turning lantern.
Small Radii.
Gauge 0=1¼ in. **5/6** ea. Post 4d.
Gauge 1=1¾ in. **6/11** ea. Post 5d.

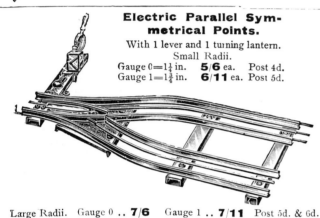

Large Radii. Gauge 0 .. **7/6** Gauge 1 .. **7/11** Post 5d. & 6d.

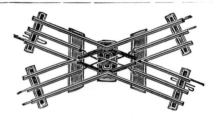

Acute Angle Crossing.

Small Radii Large Radii.

Gauge 0=1¼ in. .. Price **2/6** .. **2/9** each.
Postage 4d.

Gauge 1=1¾ in. Price, heavy make **3/-** .. **3/3** each.
Postage 5d.

Regulating Resistance.

For Low Current (maximum 4 amperes), mounted on wooden board, 3½ in. diameter.

If this apparatus is fitted between the accumulator or battery and the electric motor train, &c., a change of speed can be effected by pushing the lever either to the right or to the left. Price **1/-** Post 2d.

Switch for Low Current.

For use with all electric trains, having magnet motors for reversing and switching off current entirely, with four nickel connecting clamps, 3½ in. long, 2¾ in. wide.

Price .. .. **1/.** Post 2d.

Switch for Commutator.

For Low Current.

For use with all electric trains having magnet motors (for reversing or switching off current entirely), with four nickelled connecting clamps mounted on wooden board 4 in. long, 2¼ in. wide.

Price .. .. **2/3** Post 3d.

Gauge 0.
Electric Engine Shed.

With centre rail for electric

Price **10/6** Post 6d.

Gauge 1. Ditto.

Price **15/6** Post 9d.

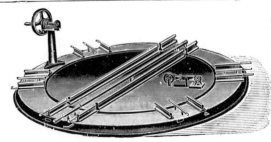

Turn Table for Electric Railways.

With mechanism for turning with rail attachments

Gauge 0 = 1¼ in. Price .. **7/11** each.
Post 5d.

Gauge 1 = 1¾ in. Price .. **11/3** each.
Post 6d.

Scale Model Passenger Rolling Stock.

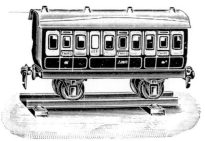

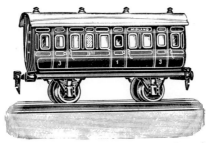

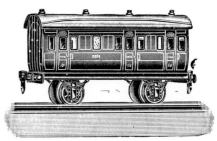

London and North Western 4-wheel Passenger Coach. With Doors to open.
Gauge 0, 1¼ in.   Length, 5½ in.
Price .. .. **1/3** Postage 3d.
Gauge 1, 1¾ in.   Length, 8¾ in.
Price .. .. **2/11** Postage 3d.
Guards Brake Van to match, same price as Coaches.

Midland 4-wheel Passenger Coach. With Doors to open
Gauge 0, 1¼ in.   Length, 5½ in.
Price .. .. **1/3** Postage 3d.
Gauge 1, 1¾ in.   Length, 8¾ in.
Price .. .. **2/11** Postage 3d.
Guards Brake Van to match, same price as Coaches.

Great Northern 4-wheel Passenger. Coach. With Doors to open.
Gauge 0, 1¼ in.   Length, 5½ in.
Price .. .. **1/3** Postage 3d.
Gauge 1, 1¾ in.   Length, 8¾ in.
Price .. .. **2/11** Postage 3d.
Guards Brake Van to match same price as Coaches.

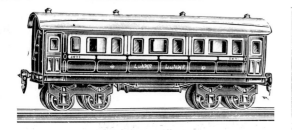

London and North Western Bogie Passenger Coach.
Gauge 0, 1¼ in.   Length, 7½ in.   Price .. **2/11** Post 3d.
Guards Brake Vans to match Coaches **2/11** Post 3d.

London and Great Northern and Midland

Scale Model Passenger Coaches, and Brake Vans.

Prepared from the Companies' Official Drawings. Beautifully finished and the most perfect Models on the market. Great care has been taken to obtain the correct shades of colour.

NOTE.— The illustrations are from Photographs of the Actual Models.

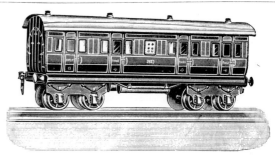

Great Northern Bogie Passenger Coach.
Gauge 0, 1¼ in.   Length, 7½ in.   Price .. **2/11** Postage 3d.
Guards Break Vans to match **2/11** each.   Post 3d.

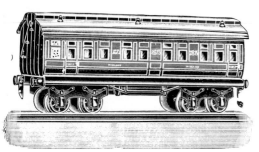

Midland Railway Express Passenger Coach, mounted on Bogies.
0 Gauge=1¼ in., length 7½ in.   Price .. **2/11** Post 3d.
Postage 3d.
Guards Brake Vans to match Coaches **2/11** Post 3d.

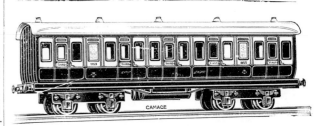

SCALE MODEL.
London & North Western Express Passenger Coach.
0 gauge=1¼ in.   Length, not including buffers, 11½ in.
Price .. **3/6** Post 4d.
1 gauge=1¾ in.   Length, not including buffers, 15¾ in.
Price .. **5/9** Post 5d.
Guards Break Vans to match Coaches, same price.

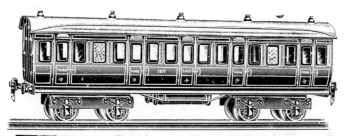

Great Northern Express Passenger Coach.
Mounted on Bogies
0 gauge=1¼ in.   Length 11½ in.   Postage 4d.   Price .. **4/11**
1 „ 1¾ in. „ 15¾ in. „ 5d. „ .. **7/-**
Guards Brake Vans to match Coaches, same price.

Midland Railway Express Passenger Coach.
Mounted on Bogies.
0 gauge=1¼ in.   Length 11½ in.   Postage 4d.   Price **4/11**
1 „ 1¾ in. „ 15¾ in. „ 5d. „ .. **7/-**
Guards Brake Vans to match Coaches, same price.

GOODS ROLLING STOCK.

The Waggons illustrated hereon have been produced to meet the demand for a Cheap Article, and although they cannot be compared with OUR Scale Model Goods Rolling Stock they are nevertheless fairly correct in detail and dimensions and exceedingly

GOOD VALUE.

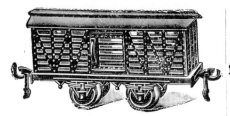

Cattle Truck with Sliding Doors.

Gauge 0. 5 in. long. Price **6**d. Post 2d.

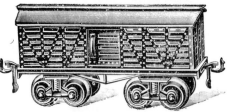

Bogie Truck with Sliding Doors, for Fast Traffic.

Gauge 0. 6¾ in. long. Price .. **1/-** Post 3d.

Working Model.

Crane Truck.

As illustration.

Gauge 0.

Price .. **9**d.

Post 3d.

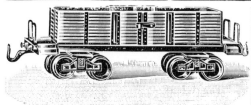

Long Goods Truck on Bogie Wheels. With doors to open.

Gauge 0. .. .. **1/-** Post 2d.

Petroleum Waggon. As illus·

Gauge 0. 4¾ in. long. **6**d. Post 1½d.

., 1. Price .. **1/-** ,, 3d.

Bogie Timber Truck.

Gauge 0 6½ in long, **1/3** Post 2d. Gauge 1. 15 in. **2/3** Post 3d·

Gauge 0. **Motor Car Truck.** 4½ in. long

Price .. .. **1/-** Post 3d.

Cement Truck. As illus. With top to open. Gauge 0 .. **10½**d. Post 3d.

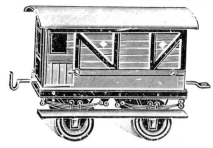

Goods Brake Van. As illus. Gauge 0 3½ in. long Price **6**d. Post 2d. Gauge 1. 5 in. long ... **1/-** Post 3d.

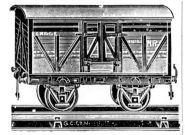

Gauge 0. **M.R. Cattle Truck.**

Length 5 in. Price .. **9**d. Post 2d.

Gauge 0.
L. & N.W.R. Covered Truck.

Length 5 in. Price **9**d. Post 2d.

L. & N.W.R Refrigerator.

Length 5 in. Price .. **9**d. Post 2d.

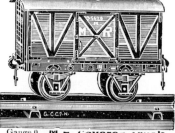

Gauge 0. **M.R. Covered Truck**

Length 5 in. Price ... **9**d. Post 2d.

Gauge 0. **G.N.R. Covered Truck**

Length 5 in. Price .. **9**d. Pos 2d.

G.N.R. Open Truck.

Length 5 n. Price .. **6**d. Post 2d.

M.R. Open Truck.

Gauge 0. Length 5 in. Price .. **6**d. Post 2d.

L. & N.W.R. Open Truck

Gauge 0. Length 5 in. Price **6**d. Post 4d.

SCALE MODEL ROLLING STOCK.

THE UNDERMENTIONED WAGGON BODIES AND UNDERFRAMES are made from tinned steel-plate lithographed in correct colours and pressed out by powerful machine tools. By this method perfect accuracy in detail and colour is obtained. THE INITIAL OUTLAY however is a VERY HEAVY ONE, and the final cost of each Waggon depends largely upon the quantity turned out. In order to produce at the minimum cost

We Manufactured Tens of Thousands,

Which enables us to Sell the Finest Metal Rolling Stock Made at what may appear to be impossible prices.

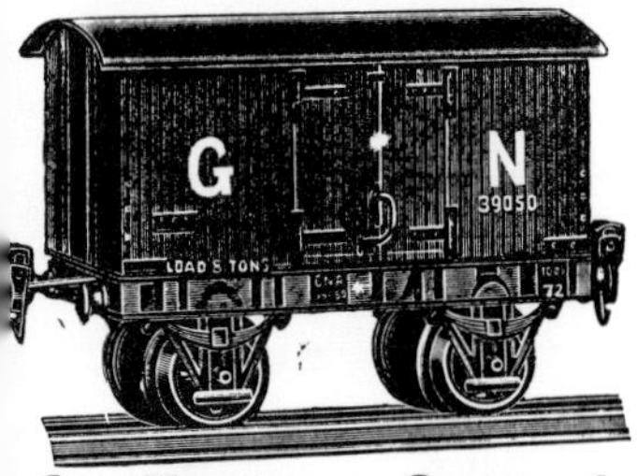

Gt. Northern Covered Goods Van.

Gauge 0=1¼ in. Length 5½ in... **1/9**
,, 1=1¾ in. ,, 8¼ in.. **2/11**

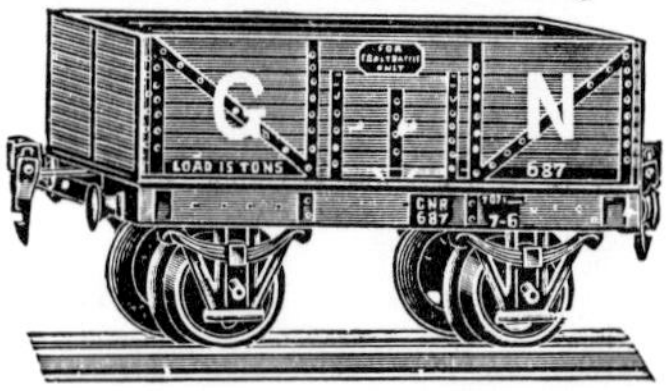

G.N. Open Goods Waggon

Gauge 0=1¼ in. Length 5¼ in... **1/9**
,, 1=1¾ in. ,, 8¼ in... **2/6**

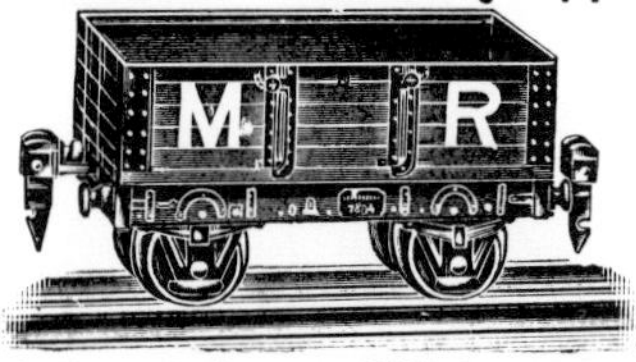

Midland 8-ton High-sided Waggon.

Gauge 0=1¼ in. Length 5¼ in... **1/6**
,, 1=1¾ in. ,, 8¼ in... **2/-**

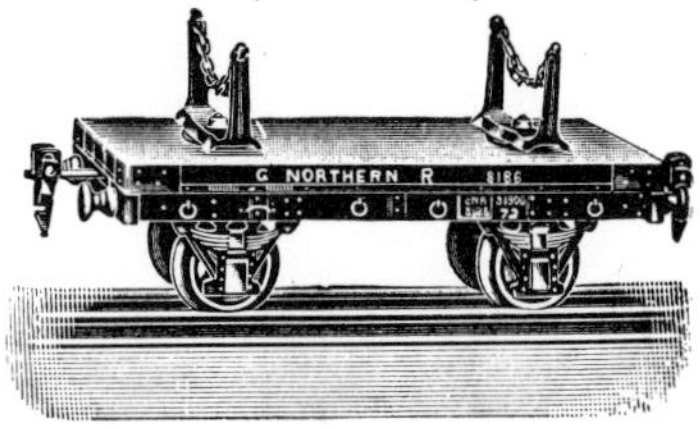

Great Northern Timber Truck.

Gauge 0=1¼ in. Length 6½ in... **1/9**
,, 1=1¾ in. ,, 8½ in... **2/11**

POSTAGE

— ON —

0 Gauge Trucks .. 2d. each.
1 Gauge Trucks .. 3d. ,,

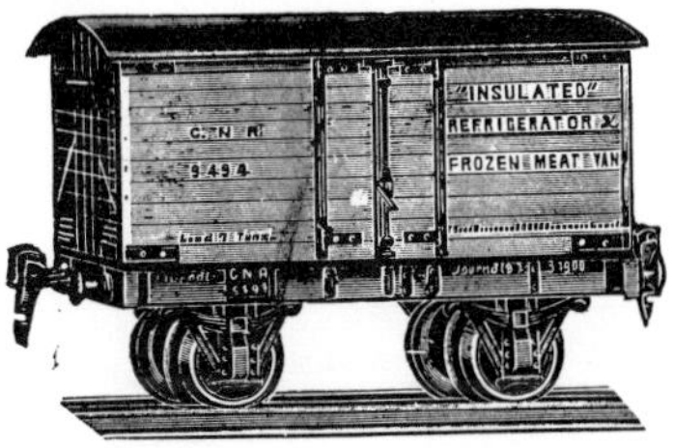

Gt. Northern Refrigerator Van.

Gauge 0 = 1¼ in. Length 5½ in. .. **1/9**
,, 1 = 1¾ in. ,, 8¼ in. .. **2/11**

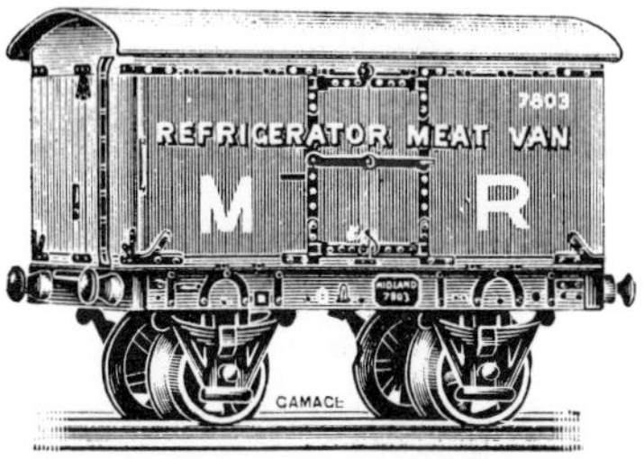

Midland Refrigerator Meat Van.

Gauge 0 = 1¼ in. Length 4½ in. .. **1/9**
,, 1 = 1¾ in. ,, 6½ in. .. **2/6**

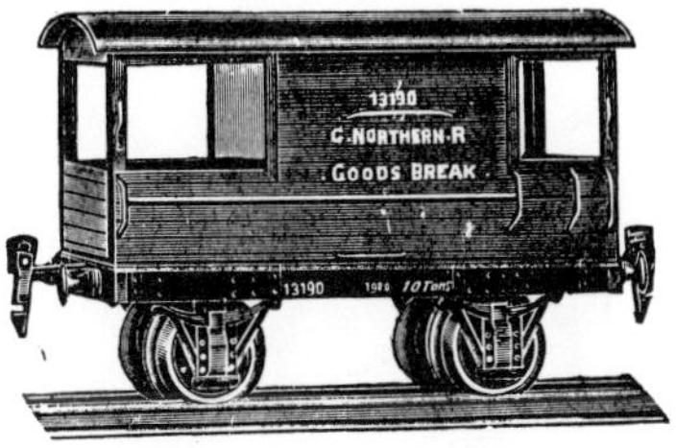

Gt. Northern Goods Brake Van.

Gauge 0=1¼ in. Length 5¼ in. **2/-**
,, 1=1¾ in. ,, 8¼ in. **2/11**

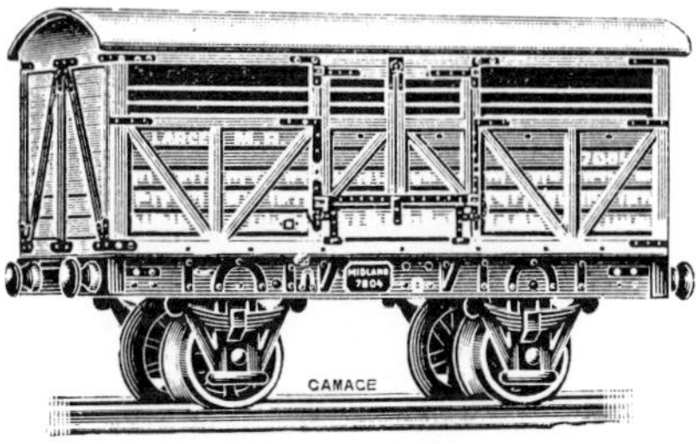

Midland Long Cattle Waggon.

Gauge 0 = 1¼ in. Length 5¼ in. .. **1/11**
,, 1 = 1¾ in. ,, 7½ in. .. **2/11**

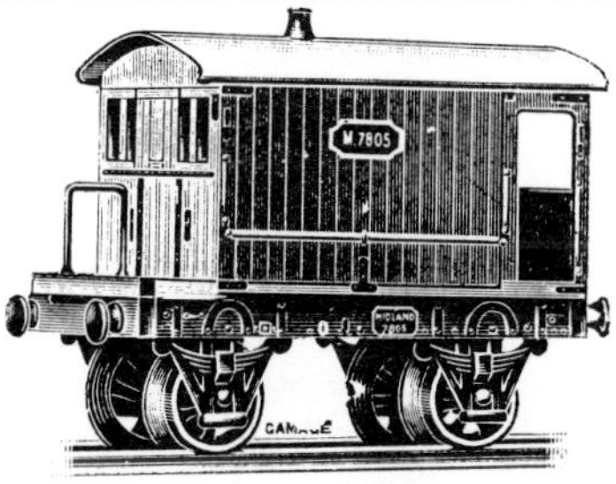

Midland Goods Brake Van.

Gauge 0 = 1¼ in. Length 5¼ in. .. **2/-**
,, 1 = 1¾ in. ,, 8¼ in. .. **2/11**

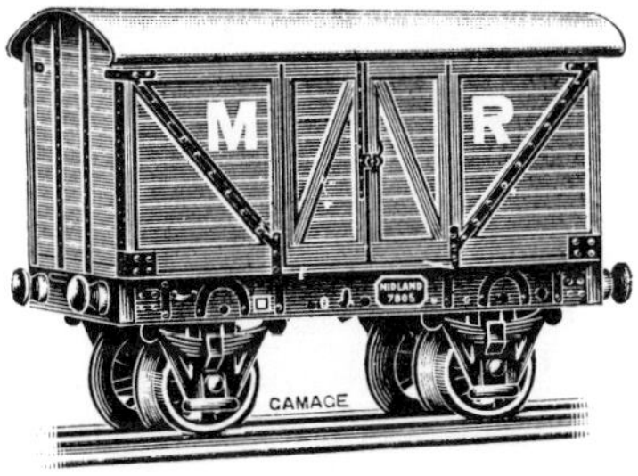

Midland Covered Goods Van.

Gauge 0 = 1¼ in. Length 4½ in. .. **1/9**
,, 1 = 1¾ in. ,, 6½ in. .. **2/6**

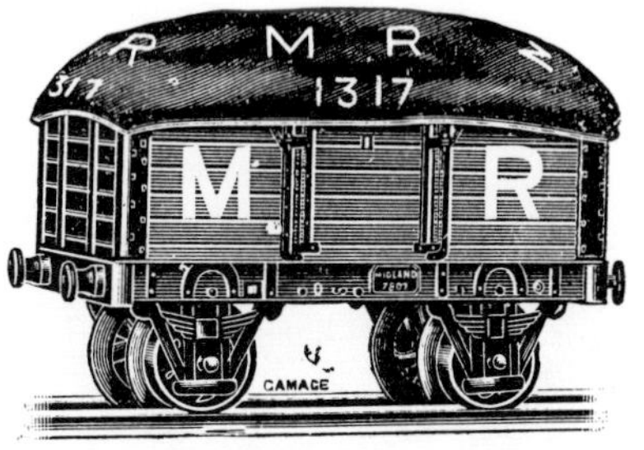

M.R. Truck, fitted with Tarpaulin, as illus.

Gauge 0. Length 5¼ in. **1/6**
,, 1. ,, 8¼ in. **2/-**

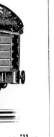

Crane Truck. As illustration.

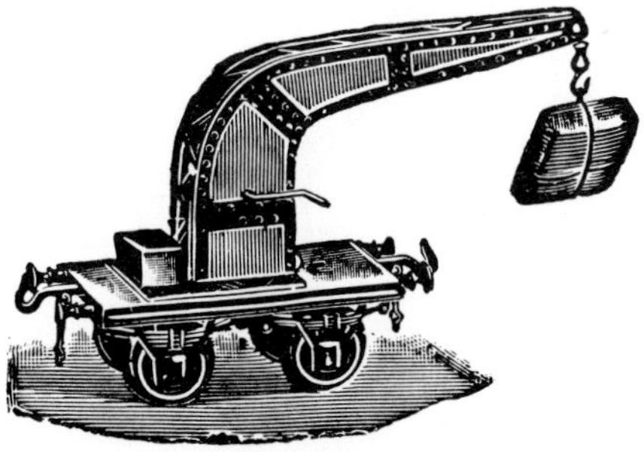

Gauge 0, **2/-** Post 3d. Gauge 1, **3/3** Post 4d.

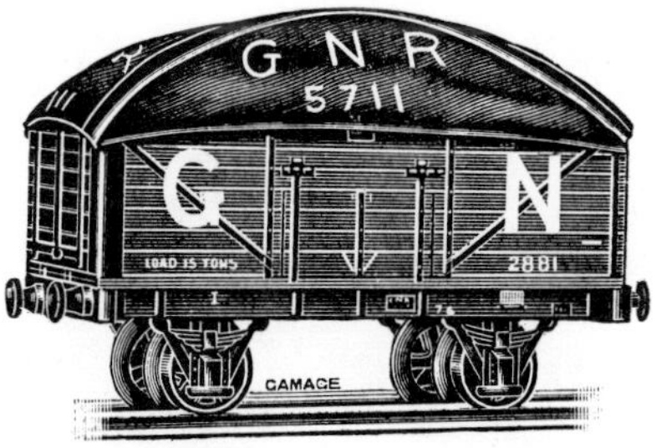

G.N.R. Truck, fitted with Tarpaulin, as illus.

Gauge 0. Length 5¼ in. **1/9**
,, 1. ,, 8¼ in. **2/6**

Rails and Switches.

No Fitting required.

SINGLE CENTRE RAILS.
For converting ordinary Rails into Electric Rails ☛

Merely Snapped into position.

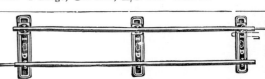

Straight or Curved Insulating Rails for converting the ordinary Rails into Electric Rails.

Straight or Curved. 0 Gauge, **2**d. each, **1/9** doz. Post 3d.   Straight or Curved. 1 Gauge, **3**d. each, **2/9** doz. Post 3d.

Curved Rails (Small Radii.)

Fitted with Patent Catches. 1¼ in. gauge 0, 10 in. long, 2 ft. diameter circle. 6 to circle, **2**d. per piece, Post 5d. doz.
1¾ in. gauge 1, 14 in. long, 3 ft. diameter circle. 8 to circle, **2½**d. per piece.   Post 5d. doz.

Large Radii.

1¼ in. gauge 0, 12¾ in. long, 4 ft. diameter circle. 12 to circle, **2½**d. per piece.   Post 5d. doz.
1¾ in. gauge 1, 14 in. long, 6 ft. diameter circle. 16 to circle, **3**d. per piece.   Post 5d. doz.

Acute Angle Crossings.

Small Radii.
1¼ in. gauge 0, **1/3** each. 1¾ in. gauge 1, **1 6** each.

Large Radii.
1¼ in. gauge 0, **1/6** 1¾ in. gauge 1, **1/9**   Post 3d.

☛ **Small Radii Points.** ☛
1¼ in. Gauge 0, **2/-** 1¾ in. Gauge 1, **2/3**   Post 3d.

Large Radii Points.
1¼ in. Gauge 0, **2/6** 1¾ in. Gauge 1, **2 9**   Post 3d.

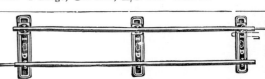

Small Radii Straight Rails.

Fitted with Patent Catches.
1¼ in. Gauge 0, 10 in. long, **2**d. per piece,
1¾ in. ,, 1, 14 ,, **2½**d. ,,

For Large Radii. Fitted with Patent Catches

1¼ in. Gauge 0, 14½ in. long, **2½**d. per piece,
1¾ in. ,, 1, 14½ ,, **2½**d. ,,

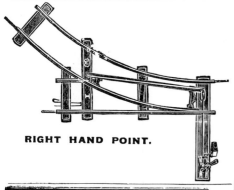

RIGHT HAND POINT.

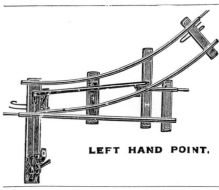

LEFT HAND POINT.

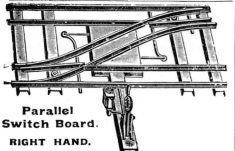

Parallel Switch Board.

RIGHT HAND.

Small Radii.
0 Gauge **4/6** Post 4d.   1 Gauge **5/6** Post 5d.

Large Radii.
0 Gauge **5/6** Post 5d.   1 Gauge **6/6** Post 6d.

Straight Automatic Brake Rails.

With arrangement to work the brake of the locomotive as well as the automatic reversing gear.

Gauge 0, 1¼ in. **7½**d.   Gauge 1, 1¾ in. **1/-**
Post 2d.   Post 2½d.

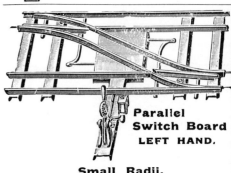

Parallel Switch Board
LEFT HAND.

Small Radii.
0 Gauge **4/6** Post 4d.   1 Gauge **5/6** Post 5d.

Large Radii.
0 Gauge **5/6** Post 5d.   1 Gauge **6/6** Post 6d.

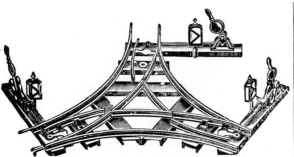

STAR SWITCH (Small Radii)

0 Gauge, **3/11** Post 4d.   1 Gauge, **5/11** Post 5d.

Wide Radii.

0 Gauge, **6/11** Post 5d.   1 Gauge, **7/11** Post 6d.

Brake Rails.

With arrangement to work the brake of the locomotive. Can be inserted without disturbing the rail formation.
Gauge 0, 1¼ in. **4**d.
Post 1d.
Gauge 1, 1¾ in. **6**d.
Post 1½d.

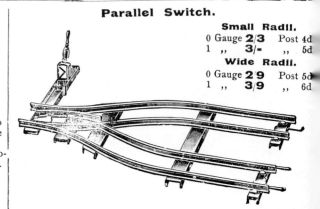

Parallel Switch.

Small Radii.
0 Gauge **2/3** Post 4d
1 ,, **3/-** ,, 5d

Wide Radii.
0 Gauge **2 9** Post 5d
1 ,, **3/9** ,, 6d

TRACK FOR MODEL RAILWAYS.

"Simpull" Track

For nearly two decades the model enthusiast has been waiting for a more satisfactory yet inexpensive railway for his locomotives.

The Old and Unsatisfactory System.

He has had to be content with a wobbley, flimsey, tin-plate track having quite a "tin-canny" sound as the trains rolled over it. In comparison with his locomotives and rolling stock, he has been ashamed of it. Some screw or nail it down after packing the sleepers somewhere near level with chips of wood. Others have painted the tin sleepers black, or entirely hidden them with sand or ballast. Anything to get a more even, smooth-running, and realistic track at little cost.

No. 0 Gauge (1¼ in.) Length of rail 12¼ in. 1 circle of 12 pieces, 4 ft. dia., mounted on 3 wood sleepers to each piece of rail. Straight rail mounted on wood sleepers .. **3/6** doz. Post 6d.
Curved ditto, ditto **4/-** ,, ,, 6d.
A Complete Circle **4/-** each. ,, 6d.
Switches for 4 ft. dia. Circle, left or right .. **4/-** each. ,, 3d.
Crossings, acute angle **3/-** ,, 3d.

Strength, Rigidity, Realism, Cheapness.

With the new patent "Simpull" track subterfuges are no longer necessary. The "Simpull" revolutionises model railway construction. It makes an excellent portable track, and quite as good a permanent one.

For Electric Systems "Simpull" Track costs less than Tinplate.

For electric traction "Simpull" track provides the model railway maker with a first-class method of fixing and insulating the conductor rail; and though it is in every way more satisfactory it actually costs less than tinplate track. It allows the scale enthusiast to add extra sleepers to a length of track in a few moments at an absurdly small additional cost, and in this way the track may be made to look as well when ballasted up, as the most expensive model permanent-way systems.

LOOSE RAIL and LOOSE SLEEPERS
NOT MADE UP.

Single pieces of Straight Rail only for 0 Gauge, 12¼ in. long **12/-** per 100, or **1/6** doz.
Ditto, 1 Gauge, 14 in. long— **12/6** per 100, or **1/8** doz.
Post 3d.

Sleepers, Cut for rail to slide in, Creosoted, 0 Gauge— **3/-** per 100, or **4½d.** doz.
Ditto. 1 Gauge— **3/3** per 100, or **5d.** doz.
Ditto, for ELECTRIC rail— 0 Gauge **3/3** 100, **5d.** doz.
1 ,, **3/6** ,, **6d.** ,,
Post 2d.

Sleepers fitted with Terminals
0 Gauge .. .. **3**d. each
1 ,, ... **4**d. ,,
Post 1d.

Hard Wooden Sleepers

The locomotive owner always needs large quantities of track. The "Simpull" is cheap. He demands wooden sleepers. The "Simpull" provides these without the attendant trouble and expense of fitting chairs, spikes and keys.

The model railway must be level, firm and noiseless. "Simpull" track is strong, lays flat, is quiet running, and as its name implies, is simple to make up or take apart.

No. 1 Gauge (1¾ in.) Length of rail 14 in. 1 Circle of 16 pieces, 6 ft. dia. 3 wood sleepers to each piece.
Straight Rail .. **4/6** doz. Post 6d.
Curved ,, .. **5/6** ,, ,, 6d.
Complete Circle .. **7/4** each. ,, 7d.
Switches, right and left **5/-** ,, 4d.
Crossings, acute .. **4/-** ,, 4d.

"Simpull" may be used to extend a Tinplate Railway.

Special lay-outs are quite easy to make from the patent "Simpull" track material. The rail may be easily bent to the correct radius required, and pushed into the sleepers fixed down on to the base-board or battens.

The standard curve length may also be easily adjusted to a new radius to fit into a special place. This is not possible with the tinplate rail. "Simpull" rail is of the same standard section as tinplate rail, therefore one or more lengths of "Simpull" track, a "Simpull" switch, or a "Simpull" crossing, may be added to a model railway system already laid with all tinplate rail.

The "Simpull" Track revolutionises Model Railway construction.

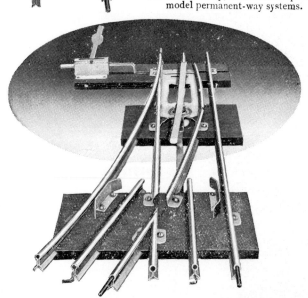

0 Gauge (1¼ in.) **Electric Rail** with centre rail mounted on wood sleepers and 1 terminal sleeper.
Straight, 12¼ in. lengths .. **6/-** doz. Post 5d.
Curved for 4 ft. dia. circle .. **6/-** ,, ,, 5d.
Switches, 4ft. dia. circle, left or right **5/** ea. ,, 4d.
Crossings, Acute angle .. .. **5/-** ,, ,, 4d.

1 Gauge Electric, mounted on wood sleepers and 1 terminal sleeper.
Straight, 14 in. lengths .. .. **7/-** doz. Post 6d.
Curved, for 6 ft. dia. circle .. **7/-** ,, ,, 6d.
Switches, right and left .. **5/6** ea. ,, 4d.
Crossings, acute .. .. **5/6** ,, ,, 4d.

B ..

PASSENGER BRIDGES.

Footbridge with Signals

In Fine Polychrome Japanning, with two Signals.

Height of Bridge, including signal, 10⅜ in. long, 16½ in.
Price   ..   ..   **10½d.**   Post. 3d.
Ditto, Larger, 28 in. long, 8¼ in. high to top of bridge.
Price   ..   **2/11**   Post 4d.

Footbridge,

As Illustration.

12 in. high, 18 in. long.

Price **1/6**

Postage 4d.

Footbridge with Signals,

As Illustration.

14 in. high, 28 in. long.

Price **3/11**

Postage 4d.

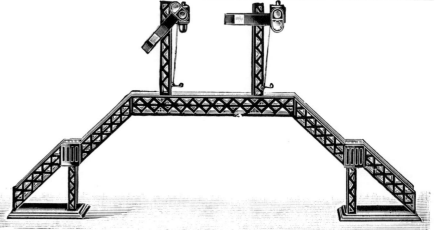

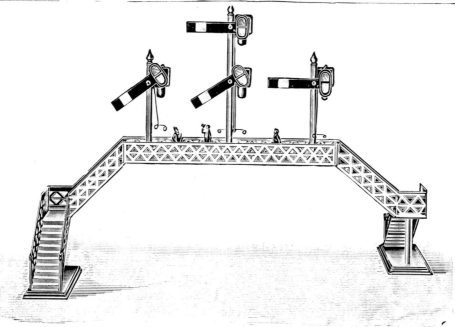

Fine Model Footbridge with Signals,

As Illustration.

16 in. high, 24½ long.

Price **6/11**

Post 6d.

Railway Bridges, Cutting, Goods Siding.

Railway Bridge.

Complete with Rails. Realistic finish. Middle piece with large arch as shown.

Gauge 0. 31 in. long, 4½ in. wide .. .. Price **2/4½** Post 3d.

Gauge 1. 31 ,, 5¼ ,, ... ,, **2/11** ,, 4d.

Bridge Arch.

Single arches to lengthen existing bridges or to form one long bridge consisting of any desired number of these arches.

Gauge 0. 10½ in. long .. Price **1/6** Post 3d.

Gauge 1 10½ ,, ... ,, **2/-** ,, 4d.

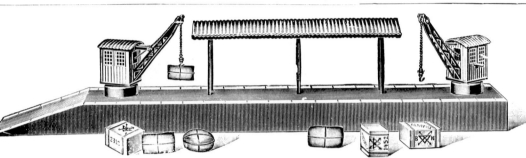

Goods Station or Goods Siding.

Shed with corrugated roof on 3 girder work supports, 2 revolving cranes on either side, incline at one end, 6 pieces of luggage (3 sacks, 3 cases). Realistic colouring.

27¾ in. long, 6 in. high, 4¼ in. wide.

Price .. **3/11**

Post 6d.

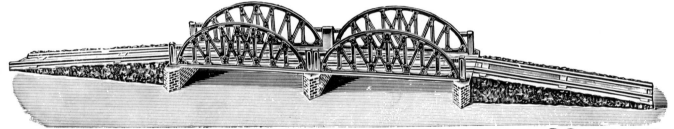

Gauge 0=1¾ in. **Double Span Railway Bridge** as illustration. 42 in. long. 5¾ in. wide. Price **3/6** Postage 7d.

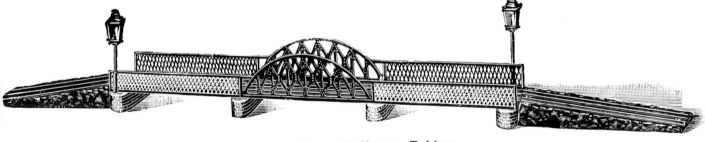

Three Span Railway Bridge.

As illustration. Finely japanned, plastically stamped, with lanterns fitted for lighting. Can be taken to pieces.

Gauge 0. 52 in. long, 5⅛ in. wide .. .. Price **8/11** Post 6d.

Gauge 1. 59 in. long, 5⅞ in. wide .. .. ,, **10/9** ,, 8d.

Cutting with Rails.

Strongly made and very realistic.

Gauge 0. Length 20 in.

Price **2/11**

Postage 8d

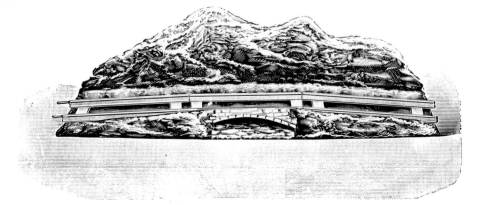

SCALE MODEL SIGNALS.
Fitted with Transparent Coloured Spectacles.

These Scale Model Signals are without question the best of their kind obtainable; all parts are of Metal, Stove Enamelled in the Correct Colours. Bases are fitted (not shown in the illustrations) which enables them to be nailed or screwed to a table or board. When used outdoors the base can be covered with earth.

This is the first occasion that Signals of this class have been obtainable at such low prices.

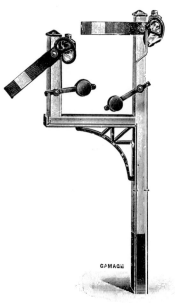

No. 1.

Two-arm Bracket Signal .. **1/6**

Post 2d.

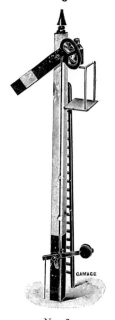

No. 2.

Single arm Signal, **1/-**

Post 1½d.

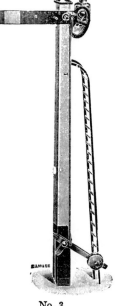

No. 3

Single arm Signal, **1/-**

Post 1½d.

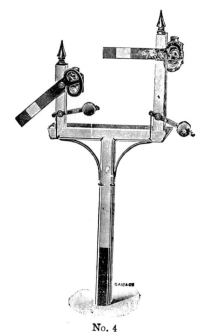

No. 4

Two-arm Bracket Signal .. **1/6**

Post 2d.

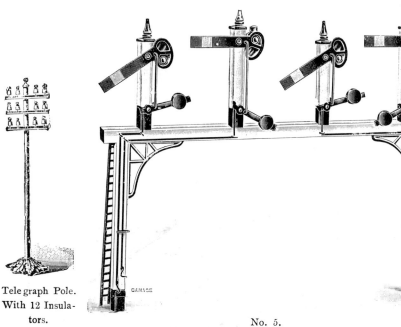
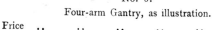

Telegraph Pole. With 12 Insulators.
10¾ in. high.
Price .. **10½d.**
Post 2d.

No. 5.
Four-arm Gantry, as illustration.

Price **4/6**

Post 4d.

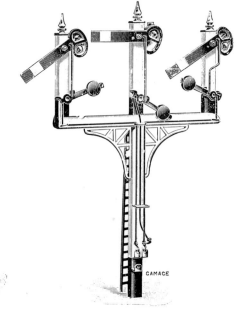

No. 6.
Three-arm Bracket Signal.

Price **2/11**

Post 3d.

Buffers, Turntables, Tunnels, Crossings, &c.

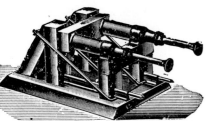

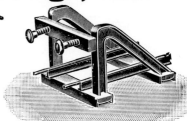

Buffers. Plain Finish, Spring Buffers.

Gauge 0 = 1¼ in. .. .. **8**d. each, Post 2d.
,, 1 = 1¾ in. .. .. .. **10½**d. each, ,, 2d.

Buffers. Very strong finish, fine grey iron japanning with nickle spring buffers (imitation hydraulic).

Gauge 0 = 1¼ in. .. .. **2 4½** each. Post 3d.
,, 1 = 1¾ in. .. .. **2 11** ,, ,, 3d.

Indicator.
Good finish, finely japanned, with 4 movable arms and 4 exchangeable boards, each indicating particulars of train and destination.
4 in. long, 7½ in. high.
10½d. Post 2d.

Railway Goods Yard Lamp.
As Illustration.
To light up. Finely japanned.
10½ in. high.
Price .. **1/6** Post 3d.

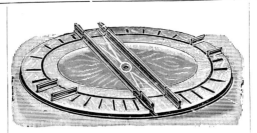

TURNTABLE.
As Illustration.
In fine polychrome japanning.

Gauge 0 .. Price **1/-** Post 3d.
,, 1 .. ,, **2/-** Post 4d.

Street Lamp.
As Illustration.
To light up.
Nickelled fittings, enamelled blue.
7¾ in. high.
Price **10½**d. Post 4d.

Automatic Ticket Box.
Finely japanned.
With 24 Tickets.
7 in. high.
Price **1/-**
Post 2d.

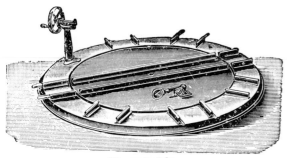

Turntable.
With mechanism for turning, 6 rail attachments in fine polychrome japanning.
Gauge 0. Price **3/6** Post 4d.   Gauge 1. Price **6/6** Post 6d.
Extra Large to take scale Model Locomotive and Tender.
Gauge 0. Price **7/6** Post 4d.   Gauge 1. Price **10/6** Post 5d.

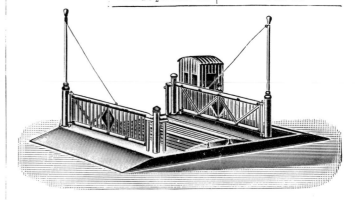

Railway Crossing Gates. (To open and close).
Gauge 0. 15 in. long .. .. .. **3/6** Post 3d.
,, 1. 17 in. ,, ... **4/11** ,, 4d.

Tunnel. (As Illustration).
With wooden slopes, imitation stonework, very realistic.
Gauge 0. Size 13¾ by 11½ by 8½ ins. Price **3/6**
Gauge 1. ,, 13¾ ,, 15½ ,, 11 ins. Price **4/6**
Postage 6d.

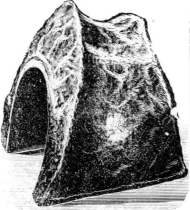

Tunnel. (As Illustration).
Gauge 0. Locomotives 8 in high 7½ in. long.
Price **1/-** Post 3d.
Ditto, Gauge 1. 11 in. high 10 in. long.
Price **2/-** Post 4d.

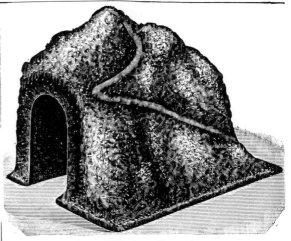

Tunnel. (As Illustration).
15¾ in. long. 13½ in. high. Price **4/11** Post 6d.

Model Railway Stations.

Fine Model Wayside Station,

As illustration. Imitation embossed slates and bricks, Japanned in five colours.

Wonderful Value!

Price .. .. **2/6** Post 4d.

Model Railway Station,

As illustration.

Embossed imitation brick walls, 4 door entrances, 3 platforms, with benches, passengers, restaurant, sign boards, double track.

22 in. long, 16¼ in. wide, 11 in. high.

Price .. .. **35/-** Post free.

Realistic Model English Railway Station

in fine polychrome japanning with advertisements in correct colours. 22 in. long .. **3/11**

Postage 5d.

Ditto, ditto. 26 in. long, with doors to open, **5/11**

Postage 7d.

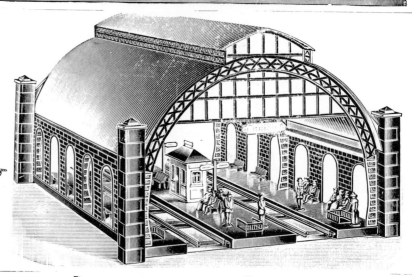

Fine Model
Wayside Station.

As illustration.

Neatly japanned in colours with removable roof and end pieces. 23 in. long.

Price **1/3**

Post 3d.

Correct Model of English Station as illustration.

Finely enamelled with movable Lamps and Signs.

One of the most correct Models ever produced. 25½ in. long.

Price **8/11** Postage 9d.

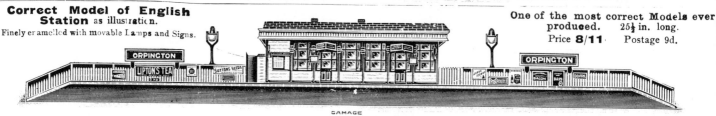

Scale Model Station.

Reproduced from drawing by Mr. HENRY GREENLY, *Model Railways*.

The Station is beautifully hand enamelled and accurately finished with doors to open and removable station signs and barriers. Platform of enamelled wood, station and barriers of metal.

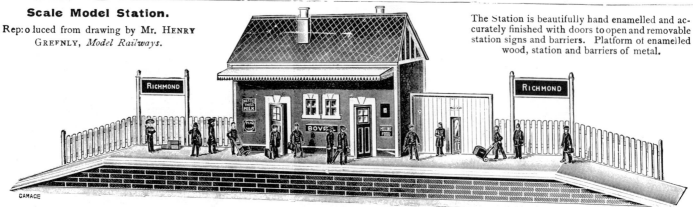

Complete with Station Master, Porters, Guards, Passengers, etc.

Ty. 1.	Suitable for 0 Gauge Scale Model Carriages and ordinary 1 Gauge Carriages.					33 in. long.	7 in. deep.	8½ in. high.	Price **13/6**	Postage 9d.
,, 2.	Do.	1	do.	do.	do.	do.	39½ ,, ,,	8½ ,, ,,	10 ,, ,,	,, **18/6**	,, 10d.
,, 3.	Do.	1	do.	do.	do.	do.	47 ,, ,,	8½ ,, ,,	11½ ,, ,,	,, **22/6**	,, Free.

Signal Boxes and Engine Shed.

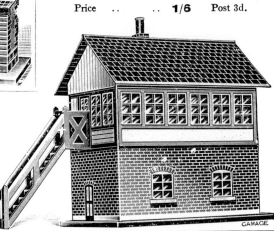

Scale Model **Signal Box.** As illustration.
6¾ in. high, 4¼ in. wide.

Price .. .. **1/6** Post 3d.

Signal Box.

Fine polychrome japanned with stamped roof (imitation tiles), with cut-out windows, 5½ in. long, 4 in. wide, 6 in. high.

Price .. .. **10½d.**

Postage 3d.

Goods Station.

With sliding door and loading platform, fine polychrome japanning.

10¼ in. long, 3½ in. wide, 3½ in. high.

Price .. .. **10½d.** Postage 3d.

Fine Model Goods Shed.

Door to open, as illustration.

10½ in. long. 6 in. wide. 6 in. high.

Price **2/6** Postage 3d.

Engine Shed.

For 2 Locomotives, fine polychrome japanning, plastically stamped.

Gauge 0. 8½ in. high, 9 in. long, 9½ in. wide.

Price .. **3/6**

Postage 4d.

Ditto, Gauge 1.
10¼ in. high, 17 in. long, 12 in. wide.

Price .. **6/6** Postage 6d.

Correct Model of an Up-to-date Signal Box, with Working Levers.

Nicely hand enamelled. No. 1. 8½ in. long, 2¾ in. deep, 7½ in. high. Price .. .. **6/11** Postage 4d.

No. 2. 12½ in. long, 4 in. deep, 10 in. high **8/6**
Postage 5d.

Engine Shed for 2 Locomotives.

Gauge 1=1¾ in.

Stamped (imitation brickwork) and finely japanned, with large swing doors, corrugated roof and symmetrical switch with brake arrangement on each door.

Shed 11 in. wide, 15¾ in. long, 9 in. high Price **12/9**

Postage 11d.

Ditto for Gauge 0, 9½ in. long, 7 in. high, 8 in. wide.

Price **6/6** Postage 6d.

Steam Engines and Lighting Plants.

Horizontal Steam Engine (Reversing).

This is an exceptionally fine engine with a fixed cylinder, ¾ bore and patent circular valve gear. The material and workmanship being of the very best. Boiler of extra stout burnished brass with steam dome, CENTRE FLUE, lever safety valve, starting cock, whistle, filling plug, water gauge, and PUMP for filling boiler worked from engine. Powerful spirit vapour lamp. Mounted on heavy japanned iron base.

Over-all measurements—
Length 10½ in.
Breadth 10½ in.
Height 14 in.
Diam. of flywheel 4 in.

PRICE **35/-**
Post free.

Electric Lighting Plant.

Improved Twin-Cylinder Horizontal Engine.

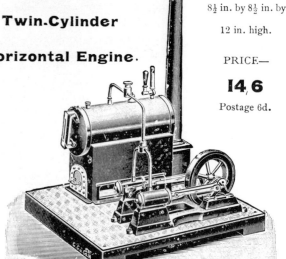

SIZE—
8½ in. by 8½ in. by 12 in. high.

PRICE—
14/6
Postage 6d.

With **oxydised** brass boiler with water gauge, spring safety valve, whistle, steampipe with lubricator, two fixed double-action patent slide valve cylinders, with patent eccentric reversing motion, engine and boiler mounted on strong wooden base with tiled metal covering.

Steam Engine Electric Lighting Plant.

With blue oxydised brass boiler, water gauge and steam whistle, oscillating cylinder, with **Dynamo**, which can be disconnected and allowing engine to run alone.

Electric lamp (4 volt) with mignon thread on nickelled stand, mounted on fine wooden base with coloured metal plate (imitation tiles). Capacity of dynamo 4 volt 0.25 ampère if 4,000 rev per minute are made. Base, 9¾ in. long, 4½ in. wide. Boiler, 6½ in. high, 2½ in. diam. Total height, 10¾ in.
Price .. **15/-** Post 6d.

With superior quality oxydised brass boiler, fixed slide value cylinder, reliable dynamo with device for connecting or disconnecting to and from engine with 4-volt electric lamp. On nickel stand with switch and two terminals on wood base with metal plate to represent tile floor.
Output of dynamo, 4 volt, 0.25 ampères.
Height, including chimney 15 in. Length of boiler 7 in. Diam. 2¾ in. Base, 12 by 11 in.
Price .. **25/-**
Carriage paid.

ELECTRIC LIGHTING PLANT.

VERTICAL AND HORIZONTAL ENGINES.

New Model
Vertical Engine,

With Reversing Gear, Oxydised Brass Boiler, Oscillating Nickelled Brass Cylinder, Safety Valve and Steam Whistle. Mounted on cast-iron bed plate.

10 in. high, diam. of boiler 2⅛ in.

3/11   Post 5d.

New Model
Steam Engine,

With brass boiler, oscillating brass cylinder, filling plug and whistle. Mounted on metal base, nicely japanned.

9 in. high.   Price **1/-**

Postage 4d.

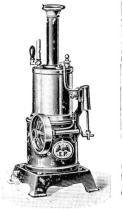

Vertical Steam Engine

as illustration.

Oxydised Brass Boiler, oscillating cylinder, whistle. safety valve.

Height 9½ inches.

Price **2 6**   Post 4d.

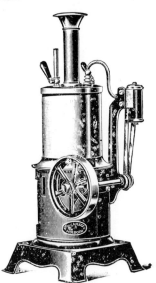

Vertica Steam Engine

as illustration.

Polished brass boiler, slide valve cylinder, slip eccentric reversing gear, steam whistle, safety valve, starting tap.

Diam. of fly wheel, 2¼ in.

10½ in. high.

Mounted on enamelled metal base 4 in. by 4 in. —

Price .. **3 11**

Postage 4d.

Horizontal Steam Engine.

Oxydised brass boiler, oscillating cylinder, safety valve, governors, mounted on metal base 5½ by 5¼ in.

Total height 8 in.

Price .. **3/3**

Postage 3d.

Particularly solid construction, burnished brass boiler, slide valve cylinder with lubricator & arranged to reverse ; exhaust pipe, safety valve and whistle. Mounted on japanned heavy cast iron bedplate.

Total height, 11½ in.
Diam. of flywheel, 2⅜ in.
Diam. of base, 4 by 4 in.

6/6

Post 6d.

New Model Vertical Engine.

New Model Steam Engine.

FACTORY TYPE.

No. 1.   NEW MODEL
With Oxydised Brass Boiler, fixed slide valve cylinder, with special lubricator, and safety valve.
7 in. high. Base 10½ in. long. 5½ in. wide. Boiler and Engine mounted on strong wooden base, with metal imitation tile bed.

Price .. **7/11**   Post 5d.

No. 2.   NEW MODEL
With Oxydised Brass Boiler, whistle, safety valve, pressure gauge, fixed slide valve cylinder, and special lubricator.
14¾ in. high.   Length of base 13½ in.   Width 6½ in.
Engine and Boiler mounted on strong wooden base, with metal imitation tile base-plate.

Price .. **10/9**   Postage 6d.

No. 3.   NEW MODEL.
With Oxydised Boiler, fixed slide valve cylinder special lubricator, whistle, safety valve and pressure gauge.
16¾ in. high.   Base 15 in. long.   7 in. wide.
Boiler and Engine mounted on strong wooden base, with metal imitation tile bed.

Price .. **15/6**   Postage 7d.

Horizontal and Vertical Steam Engine and Lighting Plant.

Massive
Vertical Steam Engine

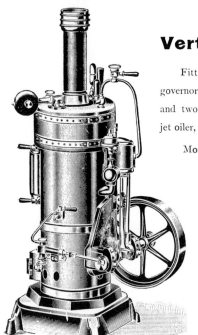

Fitted with powerful slide-valve cylinder and governors, oxydised brass boiler with water gauge and two taps, lever safety valve, whistle, steam jet oiler, feed pump, fire door, vapour spirit lamp.

Mounted on heavy cast iron foundation.

Total length $11\frac{3}{4}$ in.
Diam. of boiler $2\frac{1}{2}$ in.
Diam. of flywheel $3\frac{1}{8}$ in.

Price ... 17/6

Postage 6d.

Horizontal
Steam Engine.

As illustration.

Polished brass boiler, starting tap, **water gauge**, steam whistle, safety valve, slide valve cylinder, with **slip eccentric reversing motion.**

Mounted on metal base.

Diam. of boiler, $1\frac{1}{2}$ in.
Flywheel, $2\frac{1}{2}$ in.
Base, $6\frac{3}{4}$ by $6\frac{3}{4}$ in.
Height over all, $12\frac{1}{2}$ in.

Price - 4/11

Postage 4d.

Steam Electric Lighting Plant.

With steel burnished brass boiler and brazed firebox, nickel fittings, lever safety valve, steam whistle and feed tap, water gauge, **slide-valve cylinder** $\frac{3}{8}$ in. bore with lubricator, **governors**, slip eccentric reversing gear and feed pump.

Mounted on japanned iron foundation and imitation granite base with **dynamo and two arc lamps** of $2\frac{1}{2}$ volts.

Base, $13\frac{3}{4}$ by $13\frac{3}{4}$ in.　Diam. of Boiler, $2\frac{3}{4}$ in.
Total height, $16\frac{1}{2}$ in.　Diam. of flywheel, 4 in.

Price ... 49/6

Horizontal
Steam Engine,
as illustration,
WITHOUT DYNAMO, **27/6**
Exceptional Value.

Base .. $12\frac{1}{2}$ by $12\frac{1}{2}$ in.
Height .. .. 16 in.
Boiler .. .. $2\frac{3}{16}$ in.

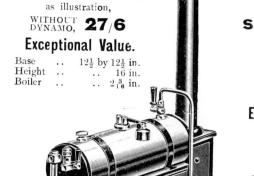

Horizontal
Steam Engine,
WITH DYNAMO.
as illustration,
37/6
Exceptional Value.

Massive Horizontal Steam Engine

With steel burnished brass boiler and brazed firebox, nickel fittings, safety valve, steam whistle, feed tap, water gauge, **slide valve cylinder** $\frac{3}{8}$ in. bore, **slip eccentric reversing gear,** pump and dynamo. Mounted on imitation granite foundation of enamelled iron. Diam. of boiler $2\frac{3}{4}$ in. Diam. of flywheel 4in. Size $13\frac{3}{4}$ by $13\frac{3}{4}$ by $16\frac{1}{2}$in. high.

With Dynamo, **37/6**

Steam Rollers and Fire Engines.

New Model Steam Rollers.

Latest pattern.   Correct type.

Superior quality and strictly reliable with oxydised brass boiler, oscillating brass cylinders, reversing gear, safety valve, steam whistle, improved flame guard, heavy solid flywheel, japanned red.

No. 1.   Height including chimney.
6½ in.   Length 9½ in.   Width 4 in.
Price **9/9**   Postage 5d.

No. 2.   Height.   Length.   Width.
7½ in.   10½ in.   5 in.
Price **12/9**   Postage 6d.

Latest Type
Motor Fire Engine.

Superior Clockwork movement, fitted with change over gear, which will either run car or work the pump with water reservoir complete pump gear, hose, bell, rubber tyres, front axle adjustable for straight or circular runs, fitted with brake, bell rings when running.

12 in. long.   4½ in. wide.   6¼ in. high.
Price **16/6**   Postage 6d.

Donkey Engine.

With Slide Valve Cylinder and slip eccentric reversing gear, with safety valve whistle.

Highly polished copper boiler, steel flywheel, two-speed pulley, starting cock and outlet tap.

8¼ in. high.   As illustration.
Price **10/9**   Postage 4d.

Electric Generating Station.

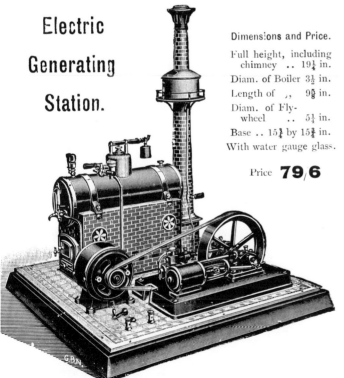

Dimensions and Price.

Full height, including chimney .. 19½ in.
Diam. of Boiler 3½ in.
Length of ,, 9⅝ in.
Diam. of Fly-
wheel .. 5¼ in.
Base .. 15¼ by 15¾ in.
With water gauge glass.

Price **79/6**

With powerful Engine with improved slide valve cylinders, oxydised brass boiler with complete fittings, correct steam pressure gauge, dynamo in superior finish, mechanical parts of the engine all finely polished, base, etc., mat black japanned, with driving belt connecting engine and dynamo, with switch and pole clamps for conducting the electric current produced by the dynamo.   All fittings highly nickelled. Boiler house and chimney stamped (imitation brickwork), with feed pump, three-way cock, lever safety valve, bell steam whistle, steam jet oiler, steam dome, fire door, vapour spirit lamp, with heater for feed water on chimney, exhaust steam passes through chimney.   Mounted on strong wooden base with finely japanned metal plate.

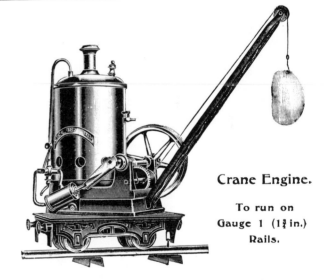

Crane Engine.

To run on Gauge 1 (1¾ in.) Rails.

Crane Engine with Slide Valve Cylinder.

Crane engine with throw-off lever to convert into donkey engine.

Base of enamelled cast-iron.   Boiler of polished brass, and constructed on improved lines, ensuring protection from accident, with safety valve, &c.   Engine has **powerful slide valve cylinder with steam reversing lever** to raise and lower, gear and pinion wheels, throw-off lever when crane not required, girder jib with pulley wheel complete with cord. Revolving platform, with movement controlled by worm wheel revolving the complete engine.   The whole mounted on 4 wheels to run on rails or any smooth surface.

Price .. .. .. **17/6**   Postage 6d.

Hot Air Engine.

With one deplacer and one working cylinder fitted into each other. Base 8¾ in. long, 3¼ in. wide, 7½ in. high.

PRICE .. **3/9** Postage 4d.

Improved Twin-Cylinder Horizontal Engine.

9/11

Hot Air Engine,

Similar to illustration.

WITH TWO DEPLACERS and TWO WORKING CYLINDERS fitted into each other.

WITH COOLING BOX.

Base 8¾ in. long, 3¼ in. wide, 9½ in. high.

PRICE .. **5/11** Post 4d.

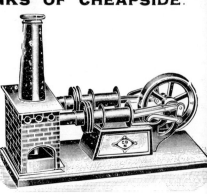

Horizontal Steam Engine with Slide Valve Cylinder and Slip Eccentric Reversing Gear.

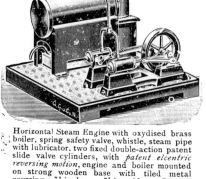

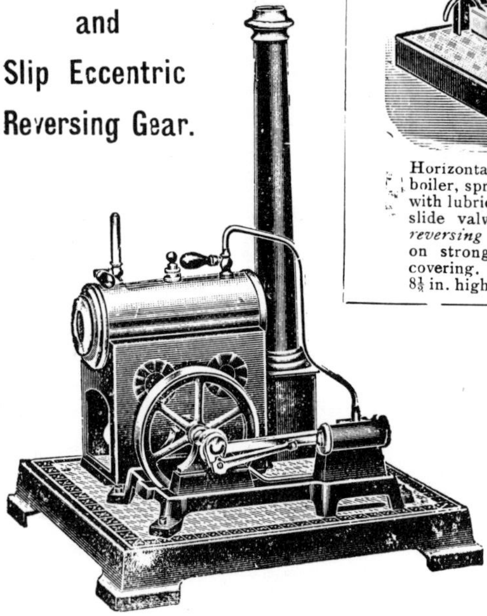

Horizontal Steam Engine with oxydised brass boiler, spring safety valve, whistle, steam pipe with lubricator, two fixed double-action patent slide valve cylinders, with *patent elcentric reversing motion*, engine and boiler mounted on strong wooden base with tiled metal covering. 7½ in long, 7½ in. wide, 8¾ in. high. Post 6d. Price **9/11**

Horizontal Hot Air Engine.

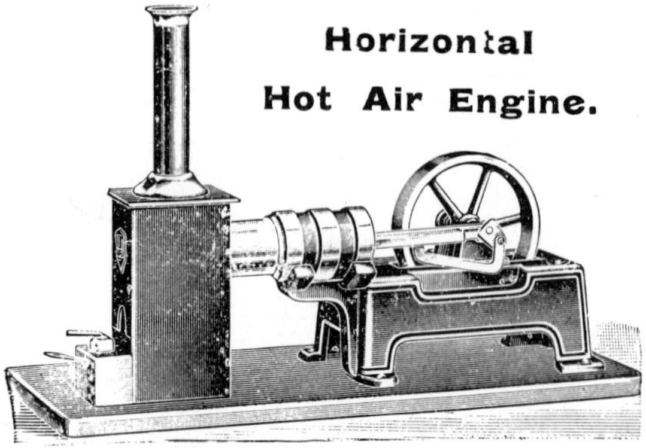

NOISELESS. Working 3—4 hours.

Working Cylinder arranged inside the Air-escaping Cylinde the latter fitted with cooling surface. and heated in separa casing by spirit lamp.

Can be used for small Fountains, Venti lators, Show Pieces & other light Models

IMPROVED CONSTRUCTION.
GREAT EFFICIENCY.

	No. 1.	2.	3.
Fly-wheel, diam., ins.	3	3¾	4⅛
Stroke of Piston ,,	⅜	7/16	½
Total size, ins.	11 by 5¼ by 8	11¾ by 6¼ by 9¾	16¼ by 6¼ by 1
PRICE ..	**8/11**	**13/6**	**18/9**
Postage	5d.	8d.	9d.

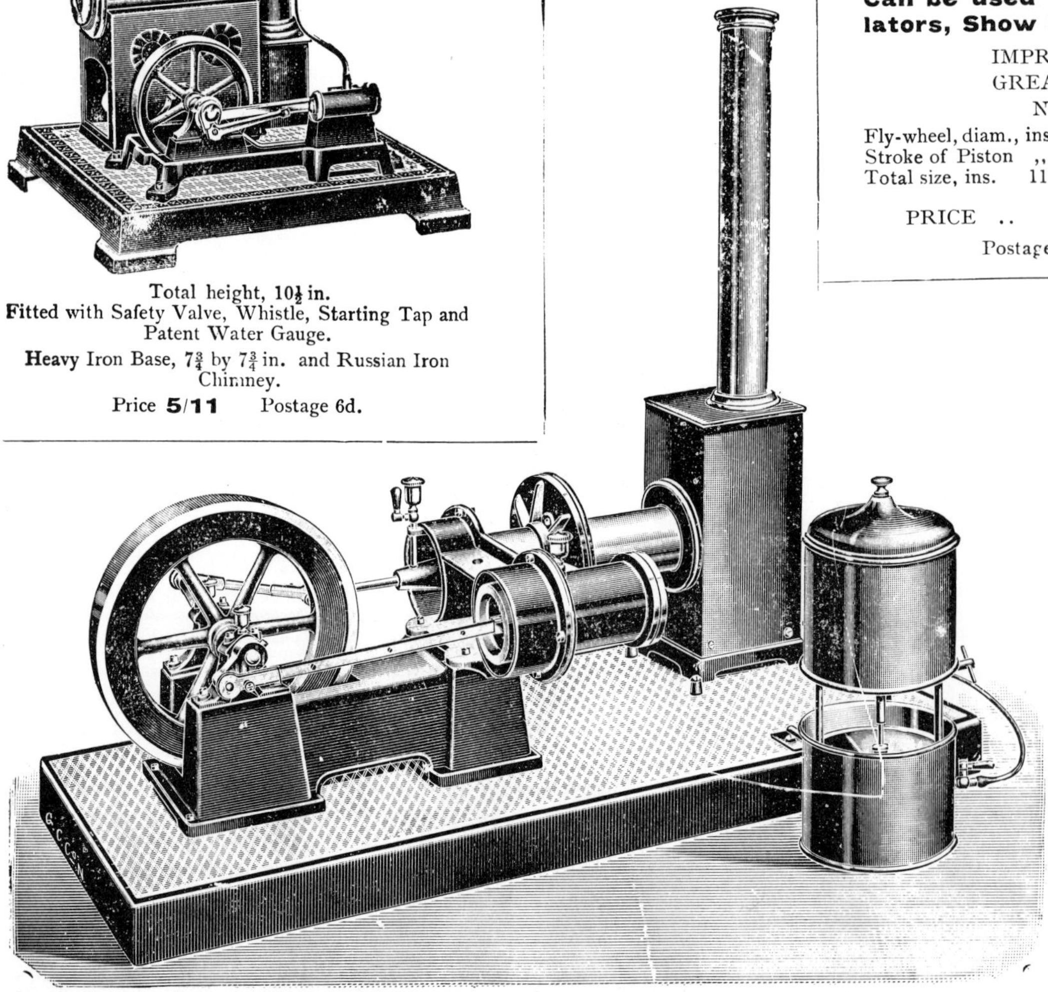

Total height, 10½ in.
Fitted with Safety Valve, Whistle, Starting Tap and Patent Water Gauge.
Heavy Iron Base, 7⅜ by 7¾ in. and Russian Iron Chimney.
Price **5/11** Postage 6d.

New Model Horizontal Hot Air Engine.

In handsome and technical design, wi spirit lamp giving about a 5 hours' co tinuous run without refilling.

This Hot Air Engine can be worked Gas Heating by using the Gas Bur specially made for it.

The Engine is a great imp ov ment on the older types,

both in the power developed and also the odourless continuous running a extremely small wear on the working par due to the patent ball joints.

Mounted on highly polished wooden b ornamented with tiled tin-plate fa 2 ft. long, 10 in. wide, 22 in. high.

PRICE **75/-**

Carriage free.

High-class English-made Steam Engines.

Stationary Steam Engines.

SPECIAL VALUE.

A VERY POPULAR MODEL.

FITTED COMPLETE WITH BOILER
as illustration.

Horizontal double-action slide valve cylinder, with trunk guide, steel connecting rod and crank shaft, disc crank, heavy flywheel and 3-speed grooved driving pulley for round belt. All working parts arranged for lubrication. Bright brass foundation plate, mounted on strong enamelled box, the engine and boiler then being mounted on a polished hard wood base.

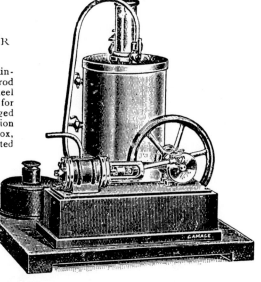

The Holborn Horizontal Engine (with Boiler).

No 1. ⅝ in. bore by ⅝ in. stroke .. **35/6**   No. 3. ⅞ in. bore by ⅞ in. stroke .. **59/6**
,, 2. ¾ in. bore by ¾ in. stroke .. **47/6**   ,, 4. 1 in. bore by 1 in. stroke .. **75/-**

Compound Cylinder Engines and Boilers.

No 1. ⅝ by ⅞ by ⅝ in. stroke .. **67/6**   No 2. ¾ by 1 by ¾ in stroke .. **85/-**

Engines only, mounted on bed-plate, as illustration. No. 1. .. **35/6**   No 2. **47/6**

Carriage Free.

The 'Compactum' Vertical or Portable Engine.

A very compact and workmanlike Engine.

Fitted complete with Boiler, as illustration.

It has an inverted double-action slide valve cylinder, trunk guide, steel connecting rod and crank shaft, disc crank, heavy flywheel and 3-speed driving pulley for round belt. All working parts arranged for lubrication. Mounted on polished hard wood base.

No. 1. ⅝ in. bore, ⅝ in. stroke **33/9**
,, 2. ¾ in. bore, ¾ in. stroke **45/-**
,, 3. ⅞ in. bore, ⅞ in. stroke **57/6**
,, 4. 1 in. bore, 1 in. stroke **72/-**

Carriage free.

Horizontal and Vertical Steam Engines.

Massive Vertical STEAM ENGINE.

With Burnished Brass Boiler, Slide Valve Cylinder, ⅝ in. bore, fitted with Lubricator and arranged for Reversing, Pressure Gauge with Tap to turn off steam when required, Water Gauge with Tap, Safety Valve and new Automatic Injector to replenish water supply when engine is running.

Engine can be kept working any length of time without interruption by means of automatic feeding apparatus.

Mounted on heavy Japanned Cast-iron Base

Total height 15¼ in.

Diameter of Boiler 4 in.

Diameter of Fly-wheel 4 in.

Diameter of Base 6 by 6 in. by 15⅛ in.

Price .. **27/6**

Postage free.

Horizontal Slide Valve Engine.

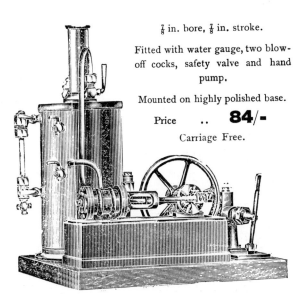

⅞ in. bore, ⅞ in. stroke.

Fitted with water gauge, two blow-off cocks, safety valve and hand pump.

Mounted on highly polished base.

Price .. **84/-**

Carriage Free.

This Engine is beautifully finished throughout

and with fair use will last for years

High Class English Made Steam Engines.

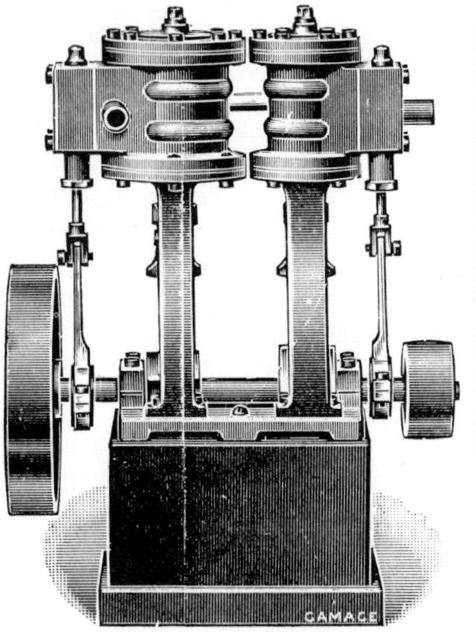

VERTICAL COMPOUND HIGH SPEED

Stationary Engine.

High pressure cylinder ⅝ in. bore, low pressure cylinder, ⅞ in. bore by ⅝ in. stroke, trunk guides, steel connecting rods, forged steel crank shaft, heavy fly wheel, also driving pulley for flat belt. All parts arranged for lubrication. Bright brass foundation plate mounted on heavy enamelled base ... **33/9**

No. 2. High pressure cylinder ¾ in. bore, low pressure cylinder, 1 in bore by ¾ in. stroke ... **45/-**

Fitted with bright brass vertical boilers and spirit lamp ... ... No. 1, **65/-** No. 2, **85/-**

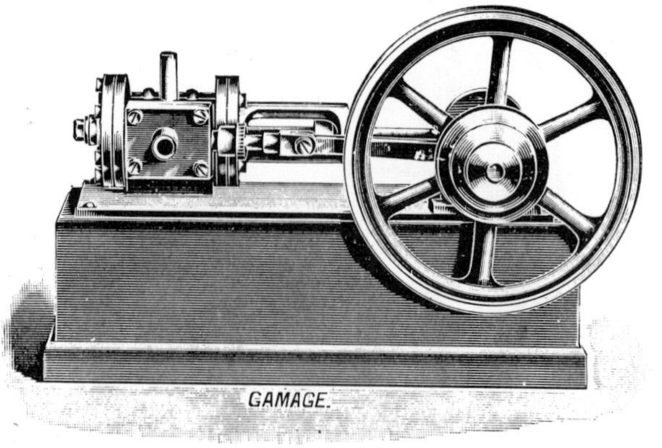

The Holborn Horizontal Steam Engine.

OUR OWN MAKE. SPECIAL VALUE

Horizontal double-action slide valve cylinder, trunk guide, steel connecting rod and crank shaft, disc crank, heavy fly-wheel, and 3-speed grooved driving pulley for round belt. All working parts arranged for lubrication. Bright brass foundation plate, mounted on strong enamelled base.

No. 1.	⅝ in. bore, ⅝ in. stroke	.. price	**17/6**	Post 6d.
,, 2.	¾ in. bore, ¾ in. stroke	.. ,,	**23/9**	Post free.
,, 3.	⅞ in. bore, ⅞ in. stroke	.. ,,	**29/6**	,, ,,
,, 4.	1 in. bore, 1 in. stroke	.. ,,	**35/-**	,, ,,

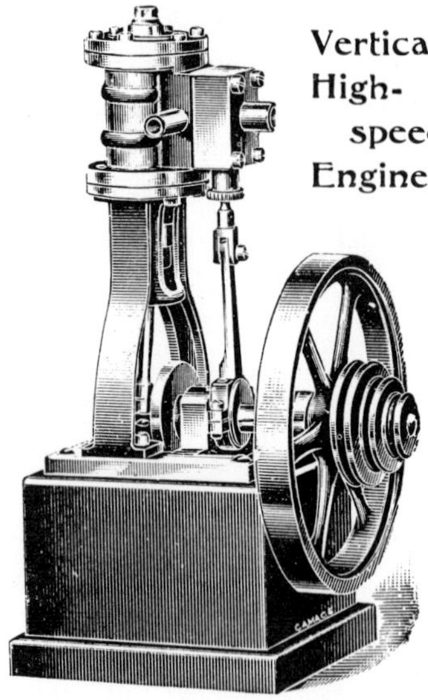

Vertical High-speed Engine

(As illustration). Fitted with double-action slide valve cylinder, trunk guide, steel connecting rod and crank shaft, disc crank and very massive fly-wheel, 3-speed pulley for round belt. All parts arranged for lubrication. The bed-plate is of solid brass and extra heavy, and is mounted on a stout wooden block.

No. 1.	⅝ in. bore, ⅝ in. stroke ...	**16/9**	Post 4d.
,, 2.	¾ in. bore, ¾ in. stroke ...	**22/6**	Post free
,, 3.	⅞ in. bore, ⅞ in. stroke ...	**28/9**	,,
,, 4.	1 in. bore, 1 in. stroke	**34/6**	,,

If fitted with boiler, lamp, etc.,

No. 1, **32/6** No. 2, **45/-** No. 3, **57/6** No. 4 **69/6**

This Model was awarded a Diploma at the "Model Engineer" Exhibition.

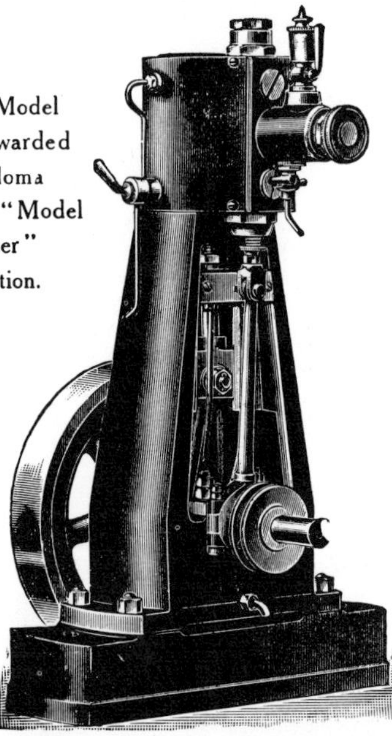

High-speed Vertical Steam Engine.

HIGHEST QUALITY WORKMANSHIP.

1½ in. bore, 1½ in. stroke.

Designed for 100 lbs. per square inch steam pressure at 1,000 revolutions per minute. Tested under steam at the works. Finished engine, fitted up complete as illustration, including stop valve, lubricator, oil boxes and pipes, drains and pulleys.

Price complete, as illustration	**£5 12 6**
Fitted with Reversing Gear, extra ...	**2 0 0**
Fitted with Couplings and Bolts... ..	**0 5 6**

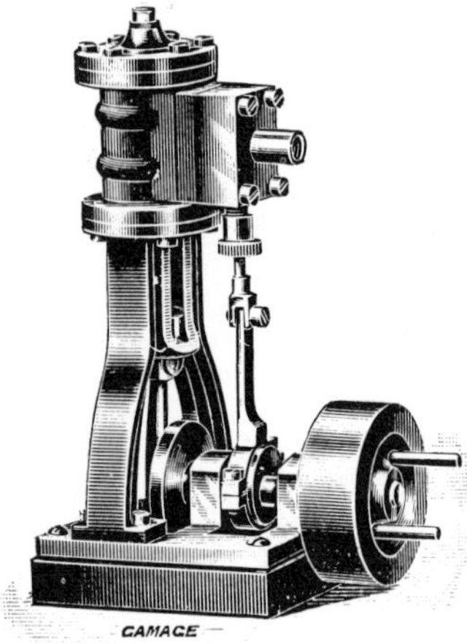

Special Value Launch Engine.

With double action slide valve cylinder, ⅝ in. bore, ⅝ in. stroke, trunk guide steel connecting rod and crank shaft, disc crank, heavy fly wheel with coupling. All working parts arranged for lubrication. Mounted on brass foundation plate, with stern tube and stuffing box, 3 blade propellor and shaft, with coupling complete.

Ty. 1. ⅝ in. bore, ⅝ in stroke For 3 ft boat ... **17/6**
Postage 4d.

Ty. 2. ¾ in. bore, ¾ in. stroke For 3 ft 6 in. boat **23/9**
Postage free.

Ty. 3. ⅞ in. bore ⅞ in. stroke. For 4 ft. boat ... **29/6**
Postage free.

Ty 4. 1 in. bore, 1 in. stroke. From 4 ft. to 5 ft. boat
Postage free. **35/-**

If fitted with bright horizontal copper boilers and spirit lamp, the whole mounted on wooden base.

Ty. 1.	... ...	**32/6**
Ty. 2.	... ...	**45/-**
Ty. 3.	... ...	**57/6**
Ty. 4.	... ...	**69/6**

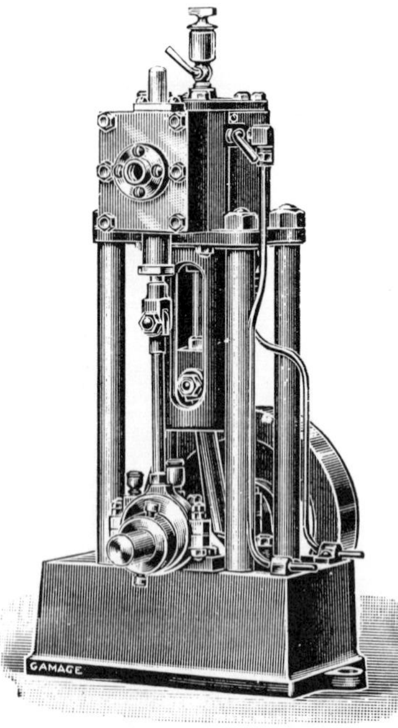

Very Massive Vertical High-speed Engine

For Electric Lighting and other purposes, strongly built of cast iron and steel. Cylinder 1⅜ in. bore by 1¼ in. stroke, piston fitted with cast iron packing rings, blue steel lagging, drain cocks with union and pipes, also lubricator. Trunk guide to piston rod, finished bright phosphor bronze slipper and connecting rod, forged steel crankshaft, heavy bronze bearings, heavy counter-balanced polished flywheel, cylinder supported on our brght steel columns to polished cast-iron base plate. engine fitted with nuts and bolts throughout, **£5 17 6**

Marine Engines, Boilers, etc.

ENGLISH MAKE.

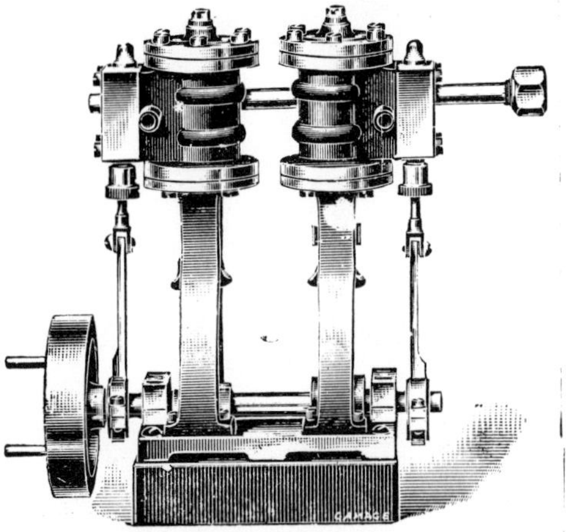

DOUBLE CYLINDER SLIDE VALVE

Launch Engine.

⅝-in. bore by ⅝-in. stroke, trunk guides, steel connecting rods and forged steel crank shaft, heavy fly-wheel with coupling, all working parts arranged for lubrication, mounted on bright brass foundation plate, stern tube and stuffing box, 3-blade propellor shaft and coupling complete.

No. 1.	⅝ in. bore by ⅝ in. stroke	**29/6**
No. 2.	¾ in. bore by ¾ in. stroke	**42/-**
No. 3.	⅞ in. bore by ⅞ in. stroke	**55/-**
No. 4.	1 in. bore by 1 in. stroke	**66/-**

If fitted with bright horizontal copper boiler and spirit lamp the whole mounted on wooden base.

No. 1 ...	**57/6**	No. 3. ...	**105/-**
No. 2 ...	**90/-**	No. 4. ...	**130/-**

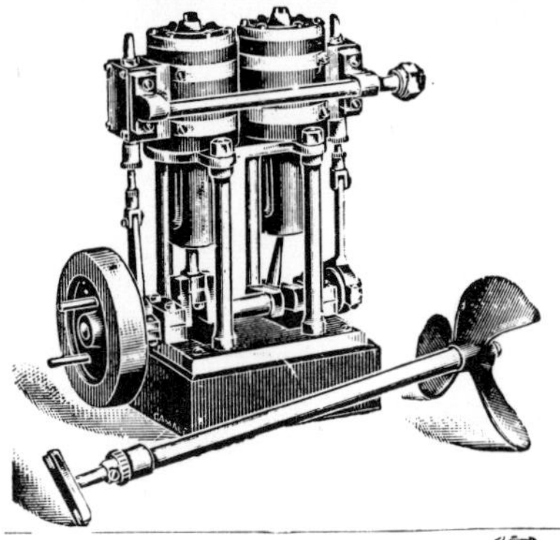

English made, **exhibition quality, fine model double cylinder**

Marine Engine.

As illustration.

¾ in. bore, ¾ in. stroke

59/-

⅞ in. bore, ⅞ in. stroke

72/-

Including propeller & shaft. Post free.

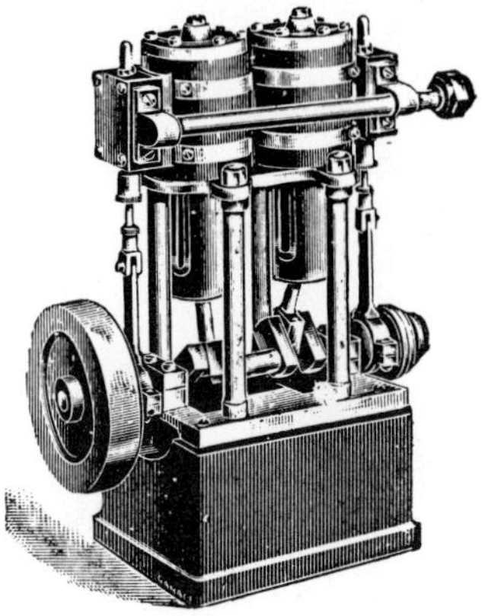

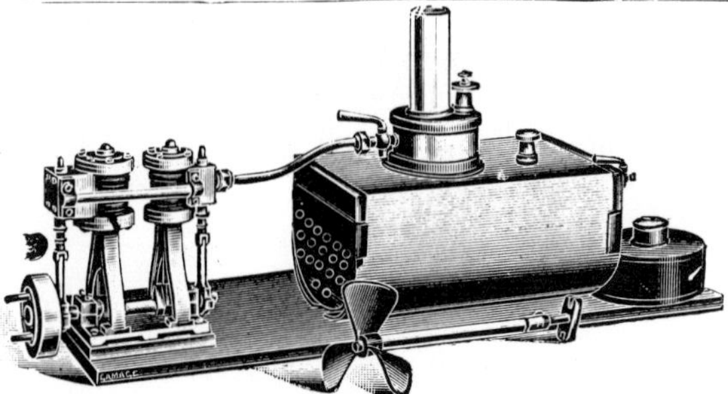

Compound Marine Engine and Boiler.

Engine same Specification as Compound Marine Engines, see p.

Boiler of polished copper, very high quality work.

No. 1. High pressure cylinder, ⅝ in. bore, low pressure cylinder, ⅞ in. bore, ⅝ in. stroke **65/-**

No. 2. H.P. cylinder, ¾ bore, L.P. cylinder, 1in. bore, ¾ stroke **85/-**

Double Cylinder Marine Engine and Boiler, same quantity and specification.

No. 1. ⅝in. l ore, ⅝in. stroke **57/6** 3. ⅞in. bore, ⅞ stroke, **105/-**

,, 2. ¾ ,, ,, **90/-** 4. ,, 1 ,, **130/-**

Gamage's English made, exhibition quality,

Vertical Engine.

With three-speed pulley mounted on wooden base

Fly-wheel 3 in. diameter, steel crank, cylinders lagged with copper.

Height over all 7 in. Width 5 in.

Bore ⅞ in., stroke ⅞ in.

Price **72/6**

Postage free.

Single Cylinder Marine Engine.

With slide valve cylinder fitted with lubricators, polished brass boiler, safety valve, water gauge, filling plug, lamp, &c., ready to fit into boat.

Price **14/6** Post 4d.

Boiler ... length 6 in.
,, diam. 2⅜ in.
Length ... 10 in.
Ht. without chimney 5½ in.
Breadth ... 3⅜ in.

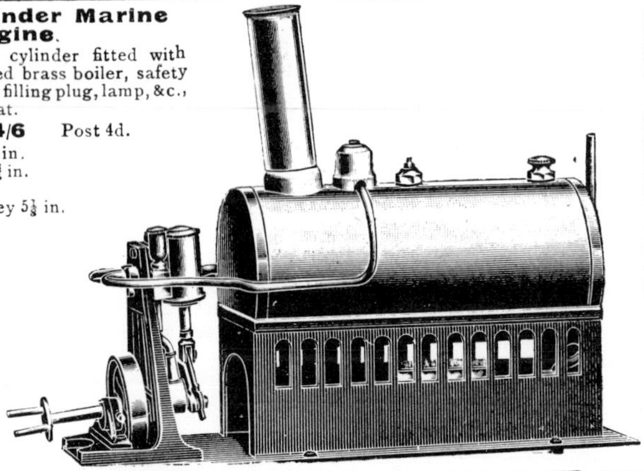

A new model of exceptionally good value.

Polished Brass Boiler with oscillating brass cylinders, safety valve and filling plug, complete with lamp.

Total length, 6¼in.
Height, 4¼ in.
Width, 2 in.
Weight, 8 ozs.

Price **3/11**

Postage 4d.

Marine Engine and Boiler.

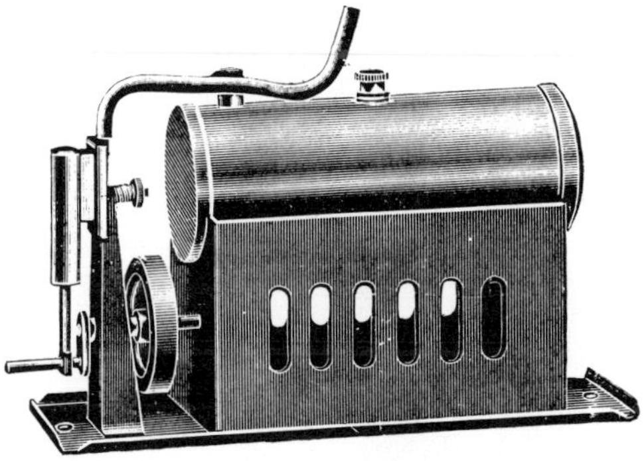

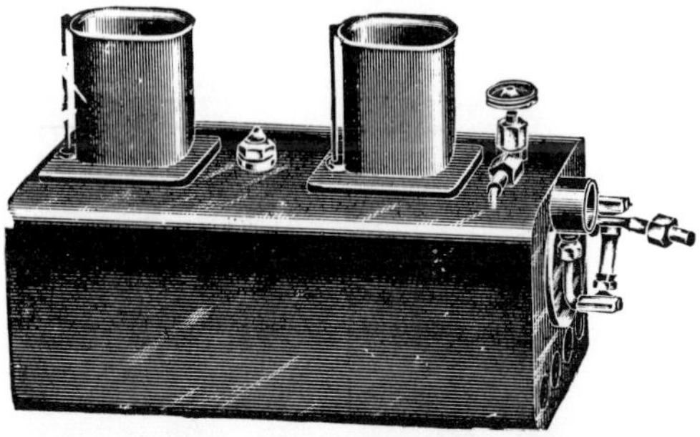

Brazed Water Tube Marine Boilers.

The specification of this boiler is similar to the one opposite except that it is fitted with **four brazed-in water tubes,** is larger and has more fittings.

Length of Boiler, 8½ in. with fitting. Height 3¾ in. Width 3⅜ in.

Weight (including lamp) 1 lb. 14 oz.

Price, complete, with screw-down stop valve, safety valve, filling plug, water gauge, pressure gauge and union, as illustration,

Complete with lamp, **27/6** Post free.

Brazed Water Tube Marine Boiler.

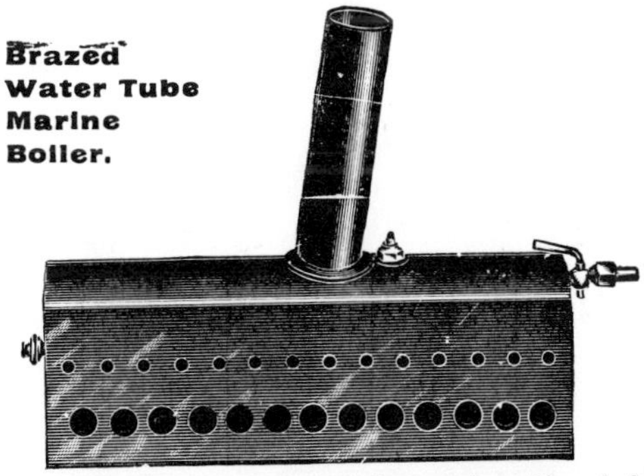

These boilers are a distinct improvement on similar articles on the market, the weight being considerably reduced, making it really possible to fit them into quite small craft, and also enables a good head of steam to be maintained without excessive heat. In spite of the reduction in weight, the strength is all that can be desired, the boiler being of the best drawn tube, with ends & **water tubes brazed in.** The boiler is enclosed in a Russian iron casing, and is complete with funnel, safety valve, steam cock and union and a blow-off cock.

Weight (including lamp) 1¼ lb., length 12 in. including union, width 2¼ in., height of boiler 3½ in, height to top of funnel 7 in.

Price complete, as illustration, with lamp, 15/- Postage 4d.

O

Vertical Model Marine Engine. Type A 1.

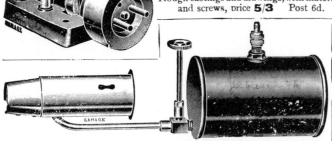

These Engines are designed to be used with flash boilers or the ordinary type. The cylinder is cast-iron, and is fitted with steel piston and valve. The balanced crank shaft is of steel and brazed up. They are very strong and rigid to suit high pressure and speed, and are an ideal engine for a racing metre boat. $\frac{3}{4}$-in. bore, $\frac{5}{8}$-in. stroke.

Finished engine, as illus., **30/-** Post 6d.

Machined sets, with materials and screws, that require no lathe to finish, Price **18/9** Post 6d.

Rough castings and drawings, with materials and screws, price **5/3** Post 6d.

Oscillating Cylinder Engines.

Marine Type.

These are suitable for small steamboats and other purposes where an inexpensive engine is required. In Gun-metal, German Silver piston rods. Cylinder $\frac{1}{2}$-in. diam., stroke $\frac{1}{2}$ in. Height 2$\frac{1}{4}$ in.

No. 1 .. **3/11** Post 4d.

Cylinder $\frac{3}{4}$ in. diam., stroke $\frac{3}{4}$ in. Height 3 in.

No. 2 .. **9/6** Post 4d.

Paraffin Blow Lamp.

Fitted with needle valve for regulating flow of oil. The air valve can be used with any ordinary cycle pump. This lamp is strongly made, very light, and gives 6-in. flame. Weight 8 oz., length 10 in., width 2$\frac{1}{2}$ in., height over all 3$\frac{1}{2}$ in. Price .. **13/6** Post 3d.

Flash Boiler for Model Boats.

These are exceptionally well made of steel tube brazed, strongly packed with asbestos and fitted with connections to take a No. 3 check valve. Length over all 10$\frac{1}{2}$ in., width 3 in., weight 2 lbs. 13 oz. Price .. .. **22/6** Post 4d.

Marine Engine and Boiler.

As illustration, but fitted with

A 1 Engine, as above.

Brazed brass boiler with four brazed tubes, steam cock and union, safety valve, vapour lamp, with regulating cock and union.

$\frac{3}{4}$-in. bore, $\frac{5}{8}$-in. stroke, Length 8$\frac{1}{4}$ in. by 3 in. wide.

Price .. **60/-**

Vertical Steel Centre Tube Boilers. (For Solid Fuel.)

SPECIFICATION.—Vertical boilers made of mild steel, riveted with steel rivets, all rivet holes drilled after plates are bent to shape. Internal firebox Water space all round fire. Centre flue or uptake. Cast iron door and frame. Firebars. Any of these Boilers can be fitted with cast iron foundations at 3 per cent. on prices; also can be had without brass fittings. Manholes can be made in Nos. 1 to 8 at extra charge of 2/6. Any Boilers can be made in copper, if required. Chimneys extra, according to height required; prices 6d. per foot to No. 10 size, and 1/- per foot other sizes; this includes $\frac{1}{2}$-round ring at top. Any sizes from 8 to 20 can be fitted with Buffalo injector, with copper pipes, steam valves, etc. Complete for **44/-** Hand force pumps, **21/-** to **40/-**, complete with pipes. Tubular boilers, without internal firebox, for gas firing, same prices as for centre flues, including gas burner complete. Nos. 2 to 20 are fitted with manholes, and Nos. 14 to 20 with mudholes.

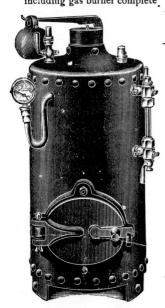

No.	Diameter.	Height.	Height of Firebox.	Thickness of Plate.	Tested in lbs.	Boiler only (no fittings)			Boiler with all fittings, as illustration.		
	Inches	Inches	Inches	Inches	lbs.	£	s.	d.	£	s.	d.
1	4	8	4$\frac{1}{2}$	$\frac{1}{8}$ bare	100	1	6	6	1	19	0
2	5	10	5$\frac{1}{2}$	$\frac{5}{8}$ bare	100	1	7	6	2	2	0
3	6	12	6$\frac{1}{2}$	$\frac{5}{8}$	100	1	9	0	2	9	6
4	7	14	8	$\frac{5}{8}$	100	1	18	0	2	17	6
5	9	18	10	$\frac{1}{8}$ full	100	2	12	6	3	9	6
6	10	20	11	$\frac{1}{8}$ full	100	2	16	0	3	17	6
7	11$\frac{1}{2}$	24	12	$\frac{3}{16}$	100	3	5	0	4	4	6
8	11$\frac{1}{2}$	24	12	$\frac{3}{16}$	140	3	12	0	4	17	6
9	12	30	18	$\frac{3}{16}$	140	5	10	0	6	15	0
10	12	30	18	$\frac{1}{4}$	200	6	17	6	8	8	0
11	14	24	12	$\frac{3}{16}$	120	5	10	0	7	5	0
12	14	30	18	$\frac{1}{4}$	200	6	17	6	9	5	0
13	16	30	18	$\frac{1}{4}$	170	7	17	6	9	5	0
14	18	30	18	$\frac{1}{4}$	160	9	5	0			
15	18	36	24	$\frac{1}{4}$	160	10	0	0	All Boilers		
16	18	42	24	$\frac{1}{4}$	160	10	15	0			
17	20	42	24	$\frac{1}{4}$	160	11	10	0	carriage		
18	22$\frac{1}{2}$	42	24	$\frac{1}{4}$	140	11	15	0			
19	22$\frac{1}{2}$	48	24	$\frac{1}{4}$	130	12	10	0	forward.		
20	22$\frac{1}{2}$	48	24	$\frac{5}{16}$	170	13	10	0			

Other sizes to order. Intermediate sizes charged next size larger.

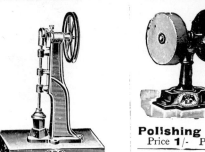

Hammer as illustration.
4¾ in. high. Price **1/-** Post 2d.

Polishing Bobs.
Price **1/-** Post 2d.

Lathe.
Price **1/-** Post 2d.

Circular Saw
as illustration.
3¼ in. long, 2¼ in. wide,
2¾ in. high.
Price **1/-** Post 2d.

Model Drill as illustration.
5 in. high.
Price **1/-** Post 2d.

Grindstone as illustration.
4 in. high. Price **1/-** Post 2d.
Superior Grindstone. **4/-** Post 3d.

Lathe, with 3-speed pulley, mandrel fitted inside, adjustable
head stock with mandrel and rest, oilers in bearings, wooden
table, exact finish.
5⅞ in. high, 8¾ in. long. Price ... **7/9** Post 3d.

Double Hammer
as illustration.
3¼ in. long, 2¼ in. wide,
3¼ in. high.
Price **1/-** Post 2d.

Model Fan as illustration.
Price **1/-** Post 2d.

Polishing Machines.
With 2-speed Pulleys
⅜ in. high, diam. of disc 2 in.
Price .. **2/6** Postage 3d.
Grinding and polishing Machine
with polishing bob and emery
wheel, 4 in. high, **4/-** Post 3d.

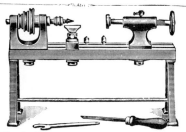

Model Lathe with 3 speed cone and
table for tools. Fine enamelled iron frame
ground and nickelled garniture mandrel,
fitted with elastic chuck, head stock, sliding
puppet, all adjustable. Height 3⅜ in.
Price **2/11** Post 3d.
Ditto, 4⅜ in. high. Price **5/11** Post 4d.
Larger, **9/11** Post 5d.

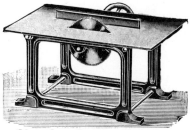

Circular Saw as illustration.
Fine enamelled frame of iron polished and
nickelled hinged plate with adjustable fence.
Price **2/11** Post 2d.
Circular Saw, similar, **3/-** Post 3d.

Punch. 6 in high.
Price **2/-** Post 2d.
Do. smaller, **1/-** Post 2d.

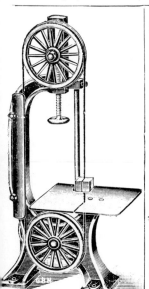

Band Saw with guide
wheels, screw, adjustable wheels,
and tension attachment.
7¾ in. high.
Price **5/-** Post 5d.

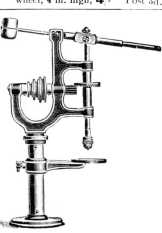

Drilling Machine.

Finely enamelled frame of iron
with stop pulley and firm plate
adjustable chuck, movable parts.
Highly polished and ground.
6⅝ in. high.

Best quality. Price **3/11** Post 3d.
Ditto, larger ,, **6/11** ,, 4d.

Press with cog wheels, with piston for
cutting out paper, cardboard and tin.
Price **8/6** Post 4d.

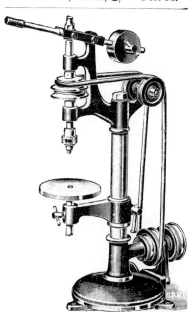

Sensitive Drills with conical speed
pulley, 9 in. high. Price **8/9** Post 6d.

C ..

MODEL PUMPS, CRANES, etc.

Aluminium Rotary Pump.

As illustration. Weight 2 ozs.. Inlet ⅜ in.
Price .. **4/6** Post 2d.

Model Grindstone.

Special heavy English made Grindstone with real stone wheel, 2 in. diam. and ¾ in. wide.
Price .. **1/6**
Postage 4d.
Do., with Hood **1/9**
Postage 4d.

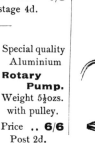

Special quality Aluminium **Rotary Pump.**
Weight 5½ozs. with pulley.
Price .. **6/6**
Post 2d.

Polished Brass Pressure Gauge.

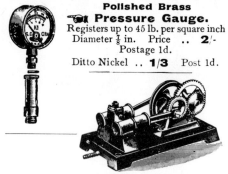

Registers up to 45 lb. per square inch
Diameter ⅞ in. Price .. **2/-**
Postage 1d.
Ditto Nickel .. **1/3** Post 1d.

Strongly made **Feed Pump.**
Best finish Price .. **8/9** Post 4d.

New Model Feed Pump.

Highly finished, cast iron stand, pump solid brass, 5½ in. high.
Price .. **4/9**
Postage 3d.

Model Steam Pump

Complete with eccentric and connections for attaching to Boiler.
Height 3⅜ in.
Cylinder ₁⁶₆ Bore.
Pumps ½ pint in 5 minutes.
Price **7/9** Post 3d.

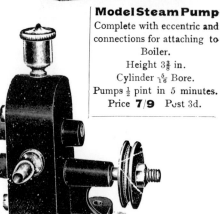

High-class Solid Brass **Gear Pump.**
Fitted with lubricator, as illustration. Height 2½ in., width 2⅛ in., weight 4½ ozs.
Price .. .. .. **3/6** Postage 2d.

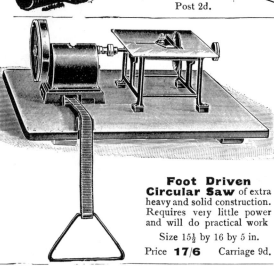

Foot Driven Circular Saw of extra heavy and solid construction. Requires very little power and will do practical work
Size 15½ by 16 by 5 in.
Price **17/6** Carriage 9d.

Dynamobil or Momentum Motor. Complete with Hammer and Motor, as illustration. The power and duration of this motor is really wonderful. The cheapest and most lasting source of power. Price **2/6** Postage 3d.

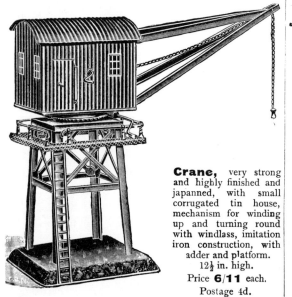

Crane, very strong and highly finished and japanned, with small corrugated tin house, mechanism for winding up and turning round with windlass, imitation iron construction, with ladder and platform.
12½ in. high.
Price **6/11** each.
Postage 4d.

Coffee Roaster (Working Model).

With Roasting Barrel and Spirit Lamp.
6¾ in. long. 4 in. wide. 4 in. high.
Price **1/6** Postage 3d.

You can Phone your orders by ringing 2700 HOLBORN.

Crane on Stamped Base (imitation Brickwork), with double action, one action to raise or to lower the load and the other to turn the crane round, with disconnecting lever. 8¼ in. high.
Price .. **3/11** Postage 4d.

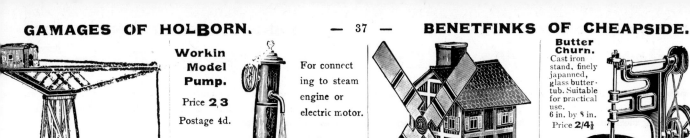

Workin Model Pump.

Price **2 3**

Postage 4d.

For connecting to steam engine or electric motor.

Butter Churn.

Cast iron stand, finely japanned, glass butter-tub. Suitable for practical use.
6 in. by 8 in.
Price **2/4½**

Model Overhead Crane.
As illustration.
Price **2/6**   Postage 5d.

Fountain

As illustration.
6¼ in. high,
7½ in. wide.

Price **2/-**

Post 3d.

Windmill,
As illustration.
Finely japanned,
with Sandmill.
10⅝ in. high.
4/11   Post 6d.

Cream Separator.
7 in high.
Price **3/6** Post 3d.
Ditto, smaller **2/3**

Model Dynamobil. Does work by momentum, will not get out of order, will drive several models.   Price ... **10½d.** Post 2d.

6½ in. diam.

3½ in. high.

1/-

Post 3d.

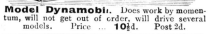

Fountain, as illustration, to be worked by model steam engine or electric motor. Finely japanned, 7¾ in. square. Price **3/11** Ditto, larger, 9½ in., **4/11** Post 3d. and 4d.

Shafting,
as illustration.
3 groove
Pulley Wheel.
4½ in. long,
2¾ in. wide,
3¼ in. high.
Price .. **1/-**
Postage 2d.

Model Swing.
To be worked from steam engine or electric motor,
Price .. **10½d.**
Post 3d.

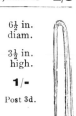

Travelling and Swivelling Harbour Crane, with handles, to run on rails (without rails)
Price **2/11** Post 3d.

Workshop Shafting.

with 2 strong cast pillars and 4 pulley wheels mounted on strong wooden base. 10 by 8 in.

1/6 Post 2d.

Shafting,
as illustration.

15¾ in. long,
3 in. wide,
3 in. high.

Price ... **3/6**
Postage 4d.

Model Shafting. With 3 cast iron columns adjustable pulley wheels, fastened with wedges. in. long, 4¾ in. high. Price **8/9** Post 6d.

High-class Model Engine and Boiler Fittings.

IN drawing special attention to the undermentioned fittings, we beg to point out that they are all of one quality only, **The best.** They are well known for their distinctive finish and design, the key of every cock being carefully ground and **fitted with a square hole washer,** and a long thread nut. They can be used in the highest class Model work with every confidence, as there is nothing better made.

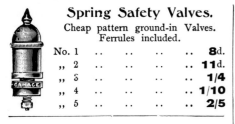

Spring Safety Valves.

Cheap pattern ground-in Valves. Ferrules included.

No. 1	..	..	..	..	**8**d.
,, 2	..	..	..	..	**11**d.
,, 3	..	..	..	..	**1/4**
,, 4	..	..	..	..	**1/10**
,, 5	..	..	..	..	**2/5**

Double-action Slide-valve Cylinders.

Fitted with Valve Head and Screws supplied fix them on to the Bed-plate.

No. 1	$\frac{7}{16}$ in. bore,	1 in. stroke	..	..	**4/9**
,, 2	$\frac{1}{2}$,,	1 ,,	..	..	**5/9**
,, 3	$\frac{5}{8}$,,	$1\frac{1}{4}$,,	..	..	**7/-**
,, 4	$\frac{3}{4}$,,	$1\frac{1}{2}$,,	..	..	**8/9**
,, 5	$\frac{7}{8}$,,	$1\frac{3}{4}$,,	..	..	**10/9**
,, 6	1 ,,	2 ,,	..	..	**12/3**
,, 7	$1\frac{1}{4}$,,	$2\frac{1}{2}$,,	..	..	**17/6**
,, 8	$1\frac{1}{2}$,,	3 ,,	..	..	**23/-**
,, 9	$1\frac{3}{4}$,,	$3\frac{1}{2}$,,	..	..	**29/-**
,, 10	2 ,,	4 ,,	..	..	**37/6**

NOTES.—Nos. 8, 9, and 10 Cylinders are fitted with bolts instead of ordinary screws. All other parts of engines to fit these sizes are also fitted with bolts to correspond.

All the Cylinders are made right-hand. Should a left-hand one be required, it can be made by reversing the covers and jacket.

Check Valves.

Fitted with ground-in Linings and Ball Valves.

Without cock, square, machined bodies. To take same size union.

No. 1	Union to take $\frac{1}{8}$ in. pipe	..	**1/7**
,, 2	,, $\frac{5}{32}$,,	..	**1/11**
,, 3	,, $\frac{3}{16}$,,	..	**2/4**
,, 4	,, $\frac{1}{4}$,,	..	**3/3**
,, 5	,, $\frac{5}{16}$,,	..	**3/10**
,, 6	,, $\frac{3}{8}$,,	..	**5/3**

Balls, for above, Brass or Bronze. Per dozen.

Inches	$\frac{1}{8}$	$\frac{5}{32}$	$\frac{3}{16}$	$\frac{7}{32}$	$\frac{9}{32}$	$\frac{5}{16}$	$\frac{11}{32}$	$\frac{3}{8}$ in.
	4d	**5**d	**6**d	**7**d	**9**d	**11**d	**1/-**	**1/2**

Check Valves.

Fitted with ground-in Linings and Ball Valves. With Cocks and Ferrules,

No.	Union to take Pipe.	Price.	No.	Union to take Pipe.	Price.
1	$\frac{1}{8}$	**2/8**	4	$\frac{1}{4}$	**4/3**
2	$\frac{5}{32}$	**3/3**	5	$\frac{5}{16}$	**5/3**
3	$\frac{3}{16}$	**3/10**	6	$\frac{3}{8}$	**6/3**

Regulators.

Non-leaking No stuffing. box required. Self-contained. Ready to screw into boiler.

With standard pattern handle, or long handle to come through cab root.

No. 0	$\frac{7}{16}$ in. scale	..	..	..	**2/10**
,, 1	$\frac{1}{2}$,,	..	..	..	**3/4**
,, 2	$\frac{5}{8}$,,	..	..	..	**4/3**
,, 3	$\frac{3}{4}$,,	..	..	..	**5/4**

Special Spring Safety Valves.

With two pillars.

The pressure of the spring acts *below* the seating of the valve. They are screwed standard sizes, and ferrules are not supplied unless specially ordered.

No.			
1	$\frac{3}{16}$ in. bore	..	**2/10**
2	$\frac{1}{4}$,,	..	**3/6**
3	$\frac{5}{16}$,,	..	**4/6**
4	$\frac{3}{8}$,,	..	**6/-**

Diagonal Force Pump,

With Eccentric.

Nos.	1	2	3	4	5	6
Plunger	3/16	$\frac{1}{4}$	5/16	$\frac{3}{8}$	7/16	$\frac{1}{2}$ in.
Price	**2/9**	**5/9**	**7/4**	**9/3**	**12/-**	**15/-**

Gun Metal Vertical Force Pumps.

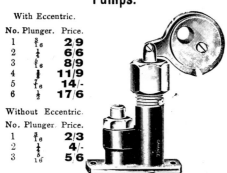

With Eccentric.

No.	Plunger.	Price.
1	$\frac{3}{16}$	**2/9**
2	$\frac{1}{4}$	**6/6**
3	$\frac{5}{16}$	**8/9**
4	$\frac{3}{8}$	**11/9**
5	$\frac{7}{16}$	**14/-**
6	$\frac{1}{2}$	**17/6**

Without Eccentric.

No.	Plunger.	Price.
1	$\frac{3}{16}$	**2/3**
2	$\frac{1}{4}$	**4/-**
3	$\frac{5}{16}$	**5/6**

Horizontal Force Pumps.

No.	Plunger.	Without Eccentric.	With Eccentric.
1	$\frac{3}{16}$	**2/3**	**2/9**
2	$\frac{1}{4}$	**4/-**	**5/9**
3	$\frac{5}{16}$	**5/6**	**7/6**
4	$\frac{3}{8}$	**7/6**	**9/6**
5	$\frac{7}{16}$	**9/6**	**12/6**
6	$\frac{1}{2}$	**12/6**	**15/-**

Hand Pumps.

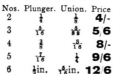

With plain screwed connection.

No. 1 $\frac{3}{16}$ in. plunger.
Price **2/-**

With Union.

Nos.	Plunger.	Union.	Price
2	$\frac{1}{4}$	$\frac{1}{8}$	**4/-**
3	$\frac{5}{16}$	$\frac{5}{32}$	**5/6**
4	$\frac{3}{8}$	$\frac{5}{16}$	**8/6**
5	$\frac{7}{16}$	$\frac{1}{4}$	**9/6**
6	$\frac{1}{2}$ in.	$\frac{5}{16}$ in.	**12/6**

High-class Brass Horizontal Hand Force Pump.

$\frac{3}{8}$ in. Trunk Plunger. Union to take 3/16 in.

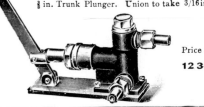

Price

12/3

Schaffer & Budenberg Pressure Gauges.

These are a special quality Pressure Gauge, and are suitable for those who require a reliable article. When used with steam must be furnished with an efficient syphon to keep them cool.

$\frac{3}{4}$ in. diameter, complete with nut and tail pipe,

7/-

1in. dia., **5/3** Post 2d.

Steam Pressure Gauges.

Bourdon Pattern.

To register up to 45 lbs. Perfectly accurate. Polished and lacquered brass case and enamelled back. Complete with nut and tail pipe. $\frac{3}{4}$ and 1 in. diam., **4/-** Post 2d. These gauges are thoroughly well made and are of similar appearance to a Schaffer gauge.

Postage extra on all fittings.

High-class Model Engines and Boiler Fittings.

Funnels.

Turned and Finished.

Scale—

Type	No. 0 $\frac{1}{16}$ in.	1 $\frac{1}{2}$ in.	2 $\frac{5}{8}$ in.	3 $\frac{3}{4}$ in.
North-Eastern Rly.	1/-	1/6	2/-	3/-
Midland Railway	1/-	1/6	2/-	3/-
Gt. Northern Rly.	1/-	1/6	2/-	3/-

Domes.

	No. 0 $\frac{1}{16}$ in.	1 $\frac{1}{2}$ in.	2 $\frac{5}{8}$ in.	3 $\frac{3}{4}$ in.
Type. Scale				
North-Eastern Railway	1/-	1/6	2/-	3/-
Midland Railway	1/-	1/6	2/-	3/-
Great Northern Rlwy.	1/-	1/6	2/-	3/-

Filling Plugs.

Screwed.

No. 1. With $\frac{3}{8}$ in. ferrule .. **9d**
,, 2 With $\frac{1}{4}$ in. iron gas ferrule **1/-**
,, 3 With $\frac{3}{8}$ in. ,, ,, **1/5**

Brass Bed Plates.

With all holes drilled and screws supplied to suit the different parts.

1	2	3	4	5	6	7	8
3/-	3/-	4/-	4/6	6/-	7/6	14/6	19/-

Bib Cocks.

In drawn Brass, with bent noses, and ferrules fitted.

No. 1 $\frac{1}{4}$ in. diameter body, bored $\frac{1}{16}$ in. **1/2**
No. 2 $\frac{5}{16}$ in. diameter body, bored $\frac{6}{64}$ in. **1/3**
No. 3 $\frac{3}{8}$ in. diameter body, bored $\frac{3}{32}$ in. **1/7**
,, 4 $\frac{7}{16}$ in. ,, ,, ,, $\frac{6}{64}$ in. **1/10**
,, 5 $\frac{1}{2}$ in. ,, ,, ,, $\frac{1}{8}$ in. **2/3**

Blow-off Cocks.

Straight noses.

Fitted with ferrules.

No. 1 Diam. of body $\frac{1}{4}$ in., bored $\frac{1}{16}$ in. **1/1**
,, 2 ,, ,, $\frac{5}{16}$,, ,, $\frac{6}{64}$,, **1/2**
,, 3 ,, ,, $\frac{3}{8}$,, ,, $\frac{3}{32}$,, **1/5**
,, 4 ,, ,, $\frac{7}{16}$,, ,, $\frac{6}{64}$,, **1/10**
,, 6 ,, ,, $\frac{1}{2}$,, ,, $\frac{1}{8}$,, **2/2**

Lever Safety Valves.

With German Silver Levers, and polished weights

Nos. ..	1	2	3	4	5	6
Bore ..	$\frac{5}{64}$	$\frac{6}{64}$	$\frac{1}{8}$	$\frac{5}{32}$	$\frac{3}{16}$	$\frac{7}{16}$ inch
Price ..	**2/4**	**3/-**	**4/3**	**5/3**	**6/6**	**8/9**

Loose Union.

With Union nut, ring and threaded piece.

No. 1	2	3	4	5	6
For $\frac{1}{8}$	5/32	3/16	$\frac{1}{4}$	5/16	$\frac{3}{8}$ in. pipe.
3d.	**4d.**	**5d.**	**6d.**	**7d.**	**9d.**

Double Union Cock.

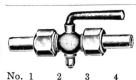

Fitted with two Unions.

No. 1	2	3	4	5	6
$\frac{1}{8}$	5/32	3/16	$\frac{1}{4}$	5/16	$\frac{3}{8}$ in. inside
1/5	**1/9**	**1/10**	**2/6**	**3/3**	**3/9** Union

Brass Locomotive Whistles.

No 1. $\frac{1}{16}$ in. dia. bell **2/7**
,, 2. $\frac{3}{8}$,, ,, **2/11**
,, 3. $\frac{7}{16}$,, ,, **3/9**
,, 4. $\frac{1}{2}$,, ,, **4/9**
,, 5. $\frac{5}{8}$,, .. **6/6**

Scale Model Buffers.

Conical Body, circular flange, with enclosed spring and screwed shank.

Nos.	0	1	2	3	4
Scale	$\frac{7}{16}$	$\frac{1}{2}$	$\frac{5}{8}$	$\frac{3}{4}$	1 in.
Price	**8d.**	**1/-**	**1/3**	**1/6**	**1/9**

Cylinder Lubricators.

Gun Metal. With 2 Cocks and Hollow Chamber.

No. 0 .. .. **2/2**
,, 1 .. .. **2/3**
,, 2 .. .. **2/5**
,, 3 .. .. **3/3**
,, 4 .. .. **4/6**
,, 5 .. .. **6/6**

Cylinder Lubricator.

Gun-metal.

With 1 Cock and Screw Lid

No.	Price
1	**1/1**
2	**1/3**
3	**1/6**
4	**1/6**
5	**2/-**

Gun Metal Elbows.

Screwed inside.

Turned and polished—

No. 0	1	2	3	4	5	6
$\frac{3}{32}$	$\frac{1}{8}$	$\frac{5}{32}$	$\frac{3}{16}$	$\frac{1}{4}$	$\frac{5}{16}$	$\frac{3}{8}$ in.
5d	**5d**	**6d**	**6d**	**6d**	**7d**	**11d**

With Male End and polished—

— **6d.** **7d.** **7d.** **8d.** **9d.** **1/3**

Gun Metal Tees.

Turned and polished.

Screwed inside.

Nos. 0	1	2	3	4	5	6
$\frac{3}{32}$	$\frac{1}{8}$	$\frac{5}{32}$	$\frac{3}{16}$	$\frac{1}{4}$	$\frac{5}{16}$	$\frac{3}{8}$ in.
Price **5d.**	**d.**	**7d.**	**7d.**	**8d.**	**9d.**	**1/-**

Gun Metal Syphons

For Schaffer Pressure Gauges

N.B.—When ordering Syphon for gauge, please state for what class of gauge they are required, so as threads can be made to suit. Complete with Cock Bushing and Union. As illustrated.

No. 1 Suitable for Gauges up to 1 in. dia. **2/10**
,, 2 Do. 1$\frac{1}{2}$,, **4/3**
,, 3 Do. for 2 in. to 2$\frac{1}{2}$ dia. **6/-**

Special short pattern for Loco. work, for gauges up to 1 in. diameter .. **3/-**

Double-Action Oscillating Cylinders.

With steam block and pivot.

No. 1. $\frac{7}{8}$ in. bore, 1 in. stroke,	**4/3**	No. 6. 1 in. bore 2 in. stroke,	**10/9**
,, 2. $\frac{1}{2}$,, ,, 1 ,,	**4/9**	,, 7. 1$\frac{1}{4}$,, ,, 2$\frac{1}{2}$,,	**15/6**
,, 3. $\frac{5}{8}$,, ,, 1$\frac{1}{4}$,,	**6/3**	,, 8. 1$\frac{1}{2}$,, ,, 3 ,,	**19/6**
,, 4. $\frac{3}{4}$,, ,, 1$\frac{1}{2}$,,	**7/6**	,, 9. 1$\frac{3}{4}$,, ,, 3$\frac{1}{2}$,,	**24/-**
,, 5. $\frac{7}{8}$,, ,, 1$\frac{3}{4}$,,	**9/-**	,, 10. 2 ,, ,, 4 ,,	**31/6**

Cheap Pattern Check Valve.

As illustration complete with union. Body not machined.

No. 1.	2	3
For $\frac{1}{8}$	5/32	3/16
1/-	**1/3**	**1/6**
4.	5.	6.
$\frac{1}{4}$	5/16	$\frac{3}{8}$ in. pipe.
2/-	**2/6**	**4/-**

Water Gauges.

GUN METAL. With 3 Cocks, Clearing Screws, and Ferrules.

No. 1	$\frac{3}{16}$ in. glass ..	**4/9**
,, 2	$\frac{3}{16}$,, ,, ..	**5/9**
,, 3	$\frac{1}{4}$,, ,, ..	**6/6**
,, 4	$\frac{5}{16}$,, ,, ..	**8/3**
,, 5	$\frac{3}{8}$,, ..	**10/5**

Water Gauges.

GUN METAL. With 1 Cock.

No. 1 ..	$\frac{3}{16}$ in. ..	**2/8**
,, 2 ..	$\frac{3}{16}$,, ..	**3/10**
,, 3 ..	$\frac{1}{4}$,, ..	**4/10**
,, 4 ..	$\frac{5}{16}$,, ..	**5/10**
,, 5 ..	$\frac{3}{8}$,, ..	**6/9**

Postage extra on all Fittings.

High-class Engine and Boiler Fittings.

Small Drain Cocks for Cylinders.

No. 0 Straight nose, screwed, $\frac{5}{32}$ in. .. **I/-**
Larger sizes, same as Blow-off Cocks, but without ferrules.
No. 0 Straight nose, screwed, $\frac{5}{32}$ in., with union .. **I/5**

Union Cocks.

With Ground Unions.
Ordinary pattern with Ferrule.
With union tor :—

Nos.	1	2	3	4	5	6
Pipe	$\frac{1}{8}$	$\frac{3}{32}$	$\frac{1}{8}$	$\frac{1}{8}$	$\frac{1}{8}$	in.
Price	I/3	I/7	I/9	2/2	2/7	3/5

With Hexagon, to take same Pipe as Union Lining
With lining to take—

No. 1 $\frac{1}{8}$ in. pipe ..	I/3	No. 4 $\frac{1}{4}$ in. pipe ..	2/3
,, 2 $\frac{3}{32}$,, ..	I/6	,, 5 $\frac{5}{16}$,, ..	2/9
,, 3 $\frac{3}{16}$,, ..	I/II	,, 6 $\frac{3}{8}$,, ..	3/5

Oil Cups.

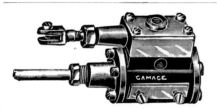

With Hexagon Base.
Without Lid.

No.	Diam.	With Lid.	No.	Diam.	Without Lid
1	$\frac{3}{16}$ in. ..	5d.	1	$\frac{3}{8}$ in. ..	3d.
2	$\frac{1}{4}$ in. ..	6d.	2	$\frac{1}{4}$ in. ..	4d.
3	$\frac{5}{16}$ in. ..	7d.	3	$\frac{5}{16}$ in. ..	5d.
4	$\frac{3}{8}$ in. ..	8d.	4	$\frac{3}{8}$ in. ..	6d.
5	$\frac{7}{16}$ in. ..	9d.	5	$\frac{7}{16}$ in. ..	7d.
6	$\frac{1}{2}$ in. ..	I/-	6	$\frac{1}{2}$ in. ..	8d.

With Lid and Syphon for Cotton.
No. 4, $\frac{3}{8}$ in. diam. 9d. 5, $\frac{7}{16}$ in., I/I 6, $\frac{1}{2}$ in., I/4

Small Bent Drain Cocks.

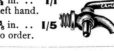

No. 1 Screwed, $\frac{3}{32}$ in. .. **I/I**
Bent right or left hand.
No. 2 Screwed, $\frac{3}{16}$ in. .. **I/5**
Larger sizes to order.

Pulley Wheels.

Three speeds; turned bright all over.

	Largest				Largest	
1.	diam.	$\frac{3}{4}$ in.	5d.	6.	diam. 2 in.	I/10
2.	,,	$\frac{7}{8}$	7d.	7.	,, 2$\frac{1}{2}$	2/8
3.	,,	1	8d.	8.	,, 2$\frac{3}{4}$	3/3
4.	,,	1$\frac{1}{4}$	9d.	9.	,, 3	4/-
5.	,,	1$\frac{1}{2}$	I/3	10.	,, 3$\frac{1}{4}$	4/9

Turned Brass Supporting Columns.

Complete with screws tor fixing. Set of 4 columns.

No.	1	2	3	4	5	6
	I/4	I/9	2/4	2/9	3/9	4/6

Injectors.

For Locomotives and Small Power Boilers.

These injectors work from 20/60 lbs. pressure per square inch, but can be made to suit higher or lower pressures to order.

No.		suitable for		Price.
1.	3/16 in.	1/16 to $\frac{1}{4}$ H.P.		15/-
2.	$\frac{1}{4}$ in.	$\frac{1}{4}$-$\frac{1}{2}$,, $\frac{3}{4}$		18/-
3.	$\frac{3}{8}$ in.	$\frac{1}{2}$-1 ,, $\frac{3}{4}$		19/-

ENGINE FITTINGS.

Unions.
With Ground Coned Linings. Plain.

No.	0	With lining to take $\frac{3}{32}$ in. pipe ..	7d.
,,	1	,, ,, ,, $\frac{1}{8}$,,	7d.
,,	2	,, ,, ,, $\frac{5}{32}$,,	8d.
,,	3	,, ,, ,, $\frac{3}{16}$,,	9d.
,,	4	,, ,, ,, $\frac{1}{4}$,,	10d.
,,	5	,, ,, ,, $\frac{5}{16}$,,	IId.
,,	6	,, ,, ,, $\frac{3}{8}$,,	I/-
,,	7	,, ,, ,, $\frac{7}{16}$,,	I/9
,,	8	,, ,, ,, $\frac{1}{2}$,,	3/-

With Hexagon Male End.

No.	0	With lining to take $\frac{3}{32}$ in. pipe ..	10d.
,,	1	,, ,, ,, $\frac{1}{8}$,,	10d.
		,, right-angle flange ..	I/2
,,	2	,, lining to take $\frac{5}{32}$ in. pipe ..	I/-
		,, right-angle flange ..	I/6
,,	3	,, lining to take $\frac{3}{16}$ in. pipe ..	I/3
		,, right-angle flange ..	I/8
,,	4	,, lining to take $\frac{1}{4}$ in. pipe ..	I/6
		,, right-angle flange ..	2/2
,,	5	,, lining to take $\frac{5}{16}$ in. pipe ..	I/9
		,, right-angle flange ..	2/4
,,	6	,, lining to take $\frac{3}{8}$ in. pipe ..	2/4

Silver-steel Rod.
In 12-in. Lengths.

NOTE PRICES.				NOTE PRICES.		
$\frac{1}{32}$	$\frac{3}{64}$	$\frac{1}{16}$	$\frac{3}{32}$	$\frac{1}{8}$	$\frac{3}{16}$	in. diam.
6d.	6d.	6d.	1/-	1/6	1/6	3/- doz.

Tubing and Steam Piping.
In 12 or 18 in. Lengths.

No.	Approx. diam.	$\frac{1}{8}$	5/32	3/16	$\frac{1}{4}$ in.
163 F.	Brazed brass	2d.	2$\frac{1}{4}$d.	3d.	3$\frac{1}{2}$d. ft.
163 C.	Brazed copper	3d.	3$\frac{1}{4}$d.	3$\frac{1}{2}$d.	4$\frac{1}{4}$d. ,,
163 S.	Solid drawn seamless brass	4d.	4$\frac{1}{2}$d.	6d.	

Lever Safety Valves
With Spring Balances

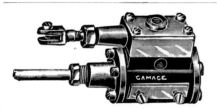

No. ..	1	2	3	4	5	6
Bore. Inch	$\frac{5}{32}$	$\frac{3}{16}$	$\frac{1}{4}$	$\frac{5}{16}$	$\frac{3}{8}$	$\frac{7}{16}$
Price ..	4/3	5/6	7/3	9/9	11/3	14/3

Short-stroke Cylinders for Loco. and Marine Work.

No.	Bore.	Stroke.	Price.	No.	Bore.	Stroke.	Price.
1	$\frac{7}{16}$	$\frac{3}{4}$	4/10	4	$\frac{3}{4}$	1$\frac{1}{4}$	8/9
2	$\frac{1}{2}$	$\frac{3}{4}$	5/10	5	$\frac{7}{8}$	1$\frac{1}{4}$	9/6
3	$\frac{5}{8}$	1	7/-				

Handrail Knobs.

Price .. .. 2d. each

Model Displacement Lubricator.

Screwed $\frac{3}{32}$ in. with drain valve, and polished all over **1/9**

Needle Valves.

With ground coned union, polished all over.

No. ..	1	2	3	4	5
Inches. For	$\frac{1}{8}$	$\frac{3}{32}$	$\frac{1}{8}$	$\frac{1}{4}$	$\frac{1}{8}$
Price ..	3/-	3/6	4/-	5/-	6/9

Safety Valves.

NORTH-EASTERN TYPE.—Spring Satety Valve, with hexagon base and loose casing, turned and polished.

No. 0	$\frac{1}{16}$ in. scale	..	..	3/-
,, 1	$\frac{1}{8}$,,		..	4/-
,, 2	$\frac{5}{8}$,,	..	..	5/-

RAMSBOTTOM TYPE.—Spring Safety Valve, with hexagon base, and Ramsbottom pattern casing.

No. 0	$\frac{1}{16}$ in. scale..	..	..	3/-
,, 1	$\frac{1}{8}$,,	..	..	4/-
,, 3	$\frac{5}{8}$,,	..	..	5/-

Ramsbottom Safety Valves.

With German Silver Levers, Steel Springs.

No. 1	$\frac{1}{4}$ in. approximate scale..	..	8/-
,, 1A	$\frac{3}{8}$ in. ,, ,,	..	10/3
,, 2	$\frac{3}{4}$ in. ,, ,,	..	11/6
,, 3	1 in. ,, ,,	..	14/9
,, 4	1$\frac{1}{2}$ in. ,, ,,	..	19/-

Inside Loco. Cylinders.

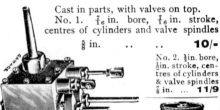

Cast in parts, with valves on top.
No. 1. $\frac{7}{16}$ in. bore, $\frac{7}{16}$ in. stroke, centres of cylinders and valve spindles $\frac{5}{8}$ in. **10/-**

No. 2. $\frac{1}{2}$ in. bore, $\frac{1}{2}$ in. stroke, centres of cylinders & valve spindles $\frac{7}{8}$ in. **11/9**

Globe Valves.

With machined hexagons.
Polished all over. Screwed.

No. 0	$\frac{3}{16}$ in. inside ..	3/2
,, 01	$\frac{7}{32}$,,	3/4
,, 1	$\frac{1}{4}$,,	3/8
,, 2	$\frac{5}{16}$,,	4/3
,, 3	$\frac{3}{8}$,,	4/9

Postage extra on all Fittings.

HIGH CLASS ENGINE FITTINGS—*continued.*

Best Forged and Turned

Whole-Crank Shafts.

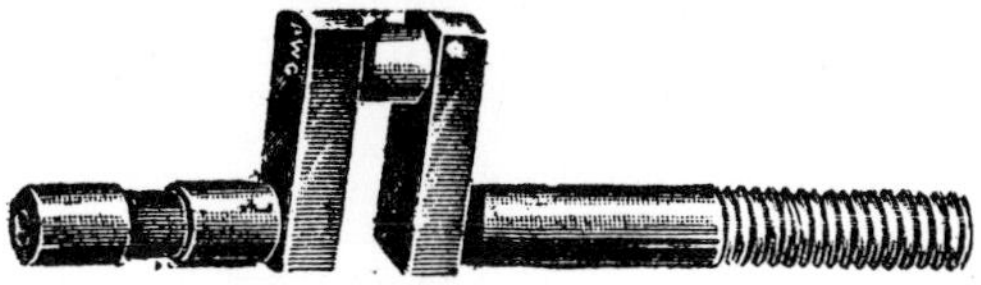

No. 1. $\frac{1}{2}$in. throw, 1in. stroke,	**3/9**	No. 6. 1in. throw, 2in. stroke,	**6/9**
,, 2. $\frac{1}{2}$in. ,, 1 ,,	**4/-**	,, 7. $1\frac{1}{4}$,, $2\frac{1}{2}$,,	**7/9**
,, 3. $\frac{5}{8}$in. ,, $1\frac{1}{4}$,,	**4/9**	,, 8. $1\frac{1}{2}$,, 3 ,,	**9/-**
,, 4. $\frac{3}{4}$in. ,, $1\frac{1}{2}$,,	**5/-**	,, 9. $1\frac{3}{4}$,, $3\frac{1}{2}$,,	**11/9**
,, 5. $\frac{7}{8}$in. ,, $1\frac{3}{4}$,,	**5/9**	,, 10. 2 ,, 4 ,,	**16/-**

Loose Collars are not required with these whole Cranks.

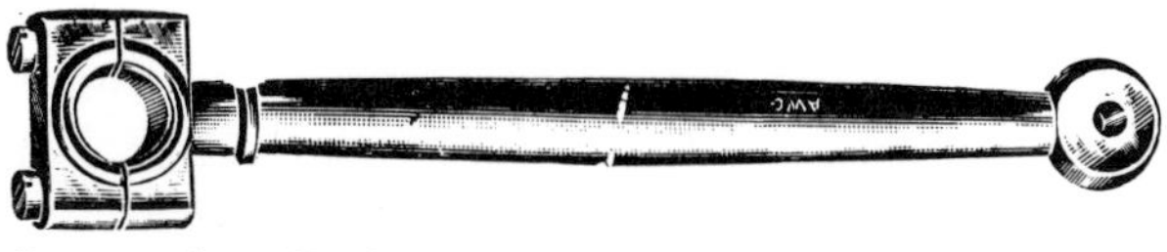

Connecting Rods and Heads, with Polished Steel Rod.

No. 1 **3/-** 2 **3/-** 3 **3/3** 4 **3/3** 5 **4/-** each.
,, 6 **4/9** 7 **5/6** 8 **6/6** 9 **7/6** 10 **9/-** ,,

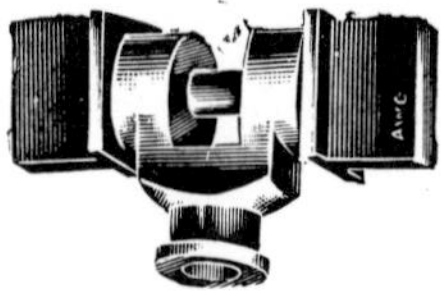

Cross Heads.

With pair of Gun Metal Slide Blocks and Pins.

No. 1	2	3	4	5	
2/6	**2/6**	**3/3**	**3/6**	**3/6**	each.
No. 6	7	8	9	10	
4/3	**5/-**	**5/-**	**5/6**	**7/-**	each.

Parallel Guide Bars.

No. 1	2	3	4	
3/6	**3/6**	**4/-**	**4/9**	pair
No. 5	6	7	8	
6/3	**7/-**	**8/9**	**10/6**	,,
No. 9	10			
13/-	**17/-**			,,

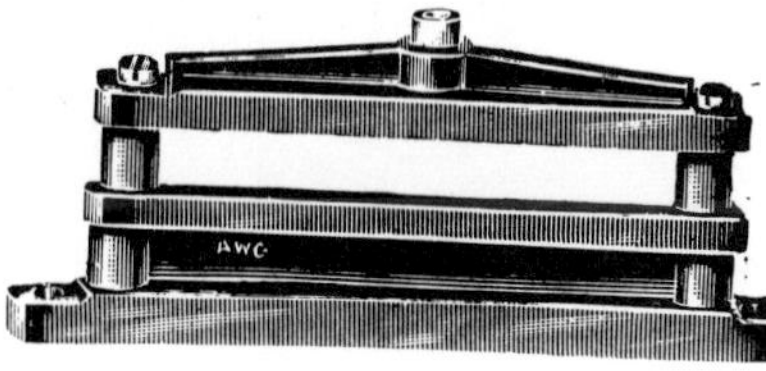

Eccentrics. Complete with Band and Rod to suit Slide valve Cylinders.

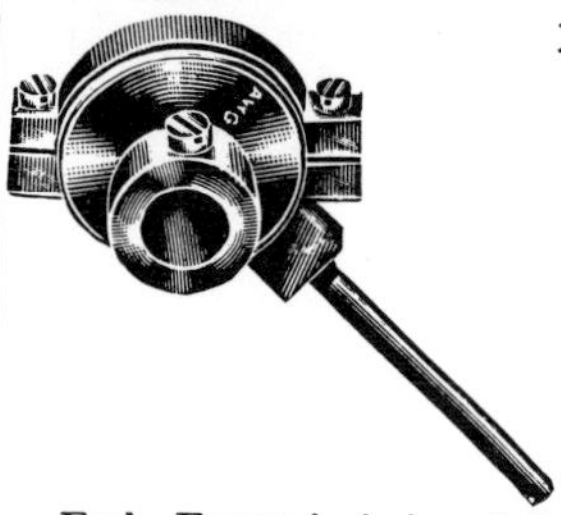

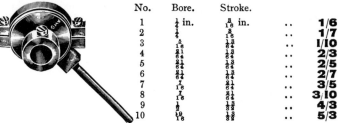

No.	Bore.	Stroke.		
1	$\frac{1}{4}$ in.	$\frac{3}{16}$ in.	..	**1/6**
2	$\frac{1}{4}$	$\frac{3}{16}$	..	**1/7**
3	$\frac{5}{16}$	$\frac{13}{64}$	..	**1/10**
4	$\frac{21}{64}$	$\frac{13}{64}$	..	**2/3**
5	$\frac{21}{64}$	$\frac{13}{64}$	..	**2/5**
6	$\frac{21}{64}$	$\frac{13}{64}$	..	**2/7**
7	$\frac{7}{16}$	$\frac{21}{64}$	..	**3/5**
8	$\frac{7}{16}$	$\frac{21}{64}$	..	**3/10**
9	$\frac{1}{2}$	$\frac{13}{32}$	..	**4/3**
10	$\frac{9}{16}$	$\frac{13}{32}$	..	**5/3**

Each Eccentric is bored the exact size to suit the shaft. A boss is put upon each Eccentric, with a set screw to fix it.

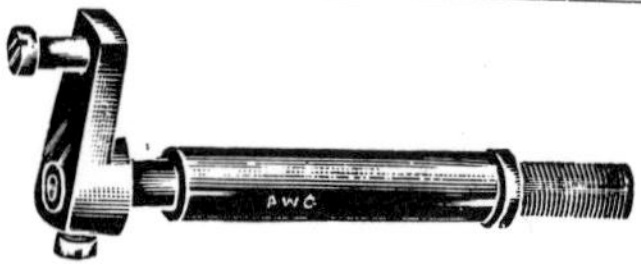

Crank Shafts.

With Gunmetal Half-cranks and Steel Pins.

No.		in.		No.		in.	
1.	Diam. of Shaft	$\frac{1}{4}$	.. **2/2**	6.	Diam. of Shaft	$\frac{21}{64}$	.. **4/10**
2.	,, ,,	$\frac{1}{4}$	.. **2/11**	7.	,, ,,	$\frac{7}{16}$	.. **6/3**
3.	,, ,,	$\frac{5}{16}$	.. **3/5**	8.	,, ,,	$\frac{7}{16}$	.. **7/3**
4.	,, ,,	$\frac{21}{64}$	.. **3/11**	9.	,, ,,	$\frac{1}{2}$	.. **9/3**
5.	,, ,,	$\frac{21}{64}$	.. **4/2**	10.	,, ,,	$\frac{9}{16}$	.. **12/3**

NOTE.—Collars are not wanted with these Half-crank shafts.

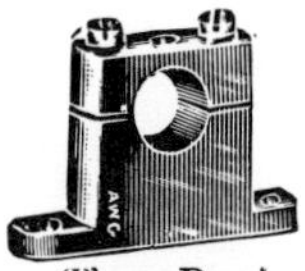

Bearings to suit Shafts.

No.	..	1	2	3	4	5
Per pair	..	**2/4**	**2/5**	**2/9**	**3/3**	**3/6**
No.	..	6	7	8	9	10
Per pair	..	**4/3**	**5/-**	**5/9**	**6/6**	**8/-**

These Bearings are bored out exactly to suit the shafts, so that in a pair two different size holes are used, but in the Bearings for whole throw cranks the holes are the same size in each case, so kindly state which is required when ordering.

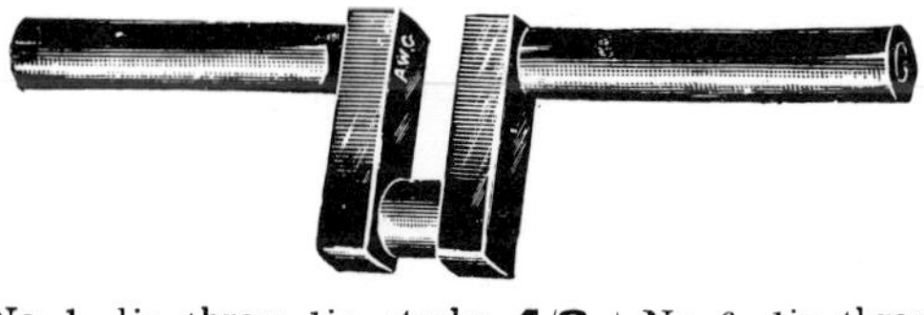

Best Forged and Turned

Whole-Crank Shafts.

No. 1. $\frac{1}{2}$in. throw, 1in. stroke,	**4/3**	No. 6. 1in. throw, 2in. stroke,	**7/-**
,, 2. $\frac{1}{2}$,, 1 ,,	**4/3**	,, 7. $1\frac{1}{4}$,, $2\frac{1}{2}$,,	**8/-**
,, 3. $\frac{5}{8}$,, $1\frac{1}{4}$,,	**5/-**	,, 8. $1\frac{1}{2}$,, 3 ,,	**9/-**
,, 4. $\frac{3}{4}$,, $1\frac{1}{2}$,,	**5/3**	,, 9. $1\frac{3}{4}$,, $3\frac{1}{2}$,,	**11 9**
,, 5. $\frac{7}{8}$,, $1\frac{3}{4}$,,	**6/-**	,, 10. 2 ,, 4 ,,	**16/-**

Loose Collars and Set Screws.

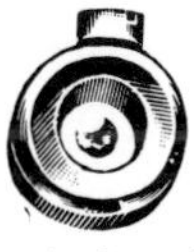

No. 1. $\frac{1}{4}$in. bore,	**6**d. pair	No. 6. $\frac{21}{64}$in. bore,	**10**d. pair
,, 2. $\frac{1}{4}$,,	**7**d. ,,	,, 7. $\frac{7}{16}$,,	**1/3** ,,
,, 3. $\frac{9}{16}$,,	**9**d. ,,	,, 8. $\frac{7}{16}$,,	**1/3** ,,
,, 4. $\frac{21}{64}$,,	**11**d. ,,	,, 9. $\frac{1}{2}$,,	**1/9** ,,
,, 5. $\frac{21}{64}$,,	**11**d. ,,	,, 10. $\frac{9}{16}$,,	**2/3** ,,

NOTE.—Only one pair is required, and both used for one bearing.

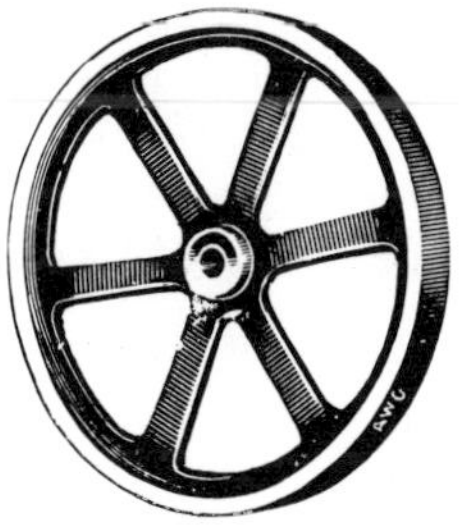

Flywheels.

These wheels are turned and polished on rim and bosses, and bored to suit crank shafts

No.	0	1	2	3	4	5	6	7	8
In. Dia.	$2\frac{1}{4}$	3	$3\frac{1}{2}$	$4\frac{1}{4}$	$5\frac{1}{2}$	6	$6\frac{1}{2}$	$7\frac{1}{2}$	$8\frac{1}{2}$
	1/5	**1/10**	**2/4**	**3/3**	**4/3**	**5/3**	**6/6**	**8/6**	**10/6**

Waste Pipes and Elbows.

	2	3	4	5	6	7	8	9	10
6d.	**6**d.	**8**d.	**8**d.	**8**d.	**10**d.	**1/6**	**2/-**	**2/4**	**2/8**

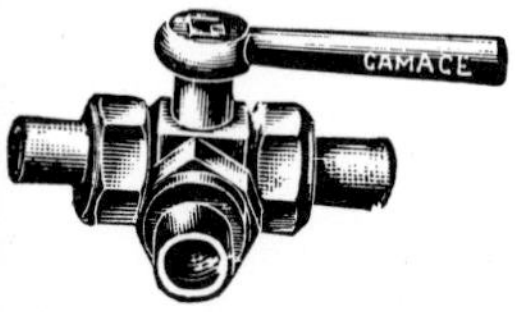

Three-Way Cocks.

With loose handle Handle, and 3 Ground Unions.

No. 1	For $\frac{1}{8}$ in. pipe	**2/9**
,, 2	,, $\frac{5}{32}$ in. ,, ...	**3/3**
,, 3	,, $\frac{3}{16}$ in. ,, ...	**4/-**
,, 4	,, $\frac{1}{4}$ in. ,, ...	**4/10**
,, 5	,, $\frac{5}{16}$ in. ,, ...	**6/6**
,, 6	,, $\frac{3}{8}$ in.	**8/3**

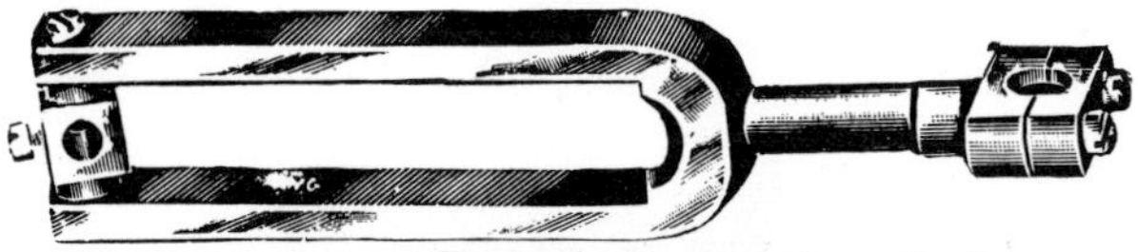

Forked Connecting Rods.

No. 1.	With solid head	**2/9**
,, 2.	,, ,, ...	**2/10**
,, 3	,, ,, ...	**3/3**
,, 4.	With loose head	**4/3**
,, 5.	,, ,, ...	**5/-**
,, 6	,, ,, ...	**5/9**
,, 7.	,, ,, ...	**6/6**
,, 8.	,, ,, ...	**8/-**
,, 9.	,, ,, ...	**9/6**
,, 10.	,, ,, ...	**12/-**

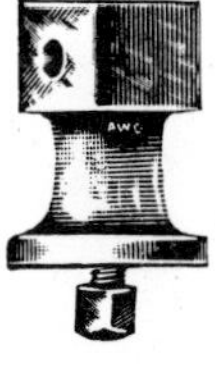

Guide Posts.

To guide piston rods when fork rods are used.

No. 1	2	3	4	5	
7d.	**8**d.	**9**d.	**10**d.	**1/4**	each.
No. 6	7	8	9	10	
1/7	**2/-**	**2/4**	**3/3**	**4/3**	each

Each post is fitted with screw or bolt, according to size, to fit on to bed plate.

Postage extra on all Fittings.

Water Motors and Lighting Plants.

THE "EDNA" Water Motor.

A High-class Water Motor, fitted with brass wheel, gun metal bearings, steel shaft and jointless case, WILL WORK FROM ANY HOUSE TAP. Supply pipe screwed to $\frac{3}{8}$ in. Diam. of pulley 1 in. Approximate speed per minute under load 2·900. Approximate power at 90 lb pressure $\frac{1}{12}$ h.p.

Will drive Dynamo giving 6 volts 2 amperes sufficient for charging a 4-volt accumulator.

PRICE .. .. .. **8/9** Carriage 6d.

No. 2 Ditto, suitable for driving our No. 1. "DEFIANCE" Dynamo Diameter of pulley 1½ in. Supply pipe screwed to $\frac{3}{8}$ in. Approximate speed per minute 2,500. Approximate power at 90lb. pressure $\frac{1}{16}$ h.p. Price **17/6** Carriage 1/-

"Hector" Water Motor.
Similar to Illustration.

The Motor is fitted in a cast iron case, with removable flanged cover. Can be used for driving all descriptions of machinery. They are silent and clean, compact, instantly fixed; absolutely reliable. WILL WORK FROM ORDINARY DOMESTIC WATER SUPPLY or any water under pressure. Two-speed grooved pulley. H.P. $\frac{1}{16}$. Revolutions per minute, 2,500.

PRICE .. .. **20/-** Stop Valve extra, if required, **5/-**

Diam. of Inlet Pipe ½ in. The above power is taken with 80 lbs. pressure.

PETROL-DRIVEN Racing Boat Engine

Fitted with Pulley for Belt-drive Transmission.
1¾ in. Bore × 1¾ in. Stroke.

Cast Iron Cylinder, with steel water jacket, and water connection sockets brazed in.

Aluminium Crankcase, with the timing gear enclosed in a removable case at the side.

The Flywheel is fitted to a taper on Crankshaft with a key and outside nut.

The Connecting Rod is made with a split big end.

All the Bearings have oil holes and grooves to ensure efficient lubrication.

Total height, 4½ in. Over-all length, 10 in. Maximum width. 6 in. Weight complete, 7½ lbs.

PRICE of finished Engine .. .. .. **£7 12 6.** Castings and Material, with Drawings .. **29/6**

Gamage complete Lighting and Generating Plant.

$\frac{3}{4}$ in. Bore. 2½in. Stroke. Water-cooled **PETROL ENGINE.**

General Specification.

Engine fitted with three piston rings, phosphor-bronze bearings throughout, forged steel crank shafts, aluminium crank cases. **Dynamo,** 15 volts 4 amperes or 10 volts 6 amperes. **Fields,** enclosed type, ironclad, one single jointless casting in best grey iron. **Armature,** slotted-drum type, built of best annealed charcoal iron aminations and fitted with efficient oil throws, wound D.C.C. wire.

Commutator, hard-drawn copper segments, insulated throughout with mica.

Bearings, self oiling, ring type, radial bearing seats fitted with oil collecting hoods.

Brush Gear, improved type with carbon brushes, requiring no adjustment until worn out.

Fixed Position of Commutation at all loads.

Bedplate is of cast iron.

ENGINE, with carburettor, water-cooling tank, mounted on bedplate, with dynamo and belt, as illustration. **£10 10 0**

Ignition Coil .. .. **10/6** extra

Petrol Tank .. .. **7/6** ,,

These Plants can also be supplied in parts:—

ENGINE only .. .. price **£5 10 0**	DYNAMO .. .. price **£2 0 0**	BELT .. .. .. price **£0 2 6**
BEDPLATE .. .. ,, **1 1 0**	CARBURETTOR .. ,, **0 15 6**	WATER TANK .. ,, **0 2 6**

Petrol Motor Boat and Aeroplane Engines, Castings, &c.

"STENTOR" Motors have won First Prize in every Race entered.

1st prize. Model Yacht Racing Association Regatta, Clapham, July 6th, 1911

1st prize. Model Yacht Racing Association, London Branch Regatta, V.P., Oct. 15th, 1912

1st prize. Model Yacht Racing Association Regatta, V.P., Oct. 15th, 1912

1st prize. Class B "Model Engineer" Speed Boat Competition, 1912

1st prize. Class C "Model Engineer" Speed Boat Competition, 1912

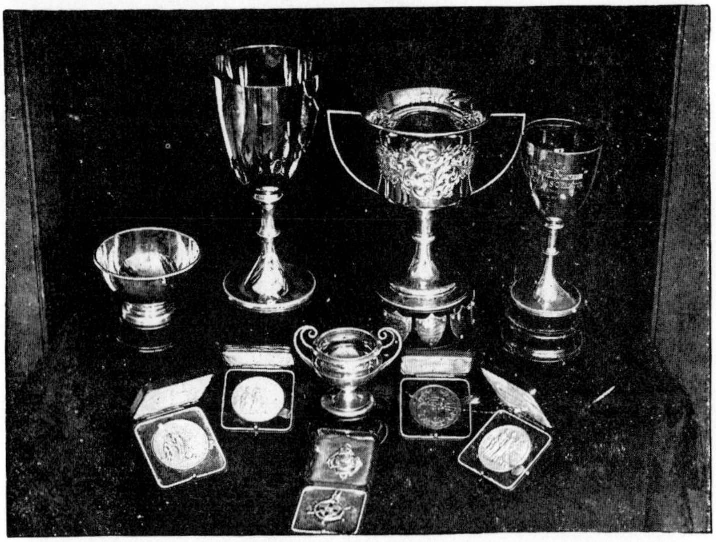

Some Silver Prizes won by "Stentor" Engines.

Bronze Medal. Class D "Model Engineer" Speed Boat Competition, 1912

1st prize. V.M.S.C. Regatta, Oct. 15th, 1910

1st prize. Coronation Regatta, V.P., June 26, 1911

1st prize. "Model Engineer," Speed Boat Competition, 1911

1st prize. V.M.S.C. Regatta, Good Friday, 1912

1st prize. V.M.S.C. Regatta, Whit Monday, 1912

1st prize. Model Yacht Racing Association Regatta, Clapham, 1911

"Stentor" Engines and Castings

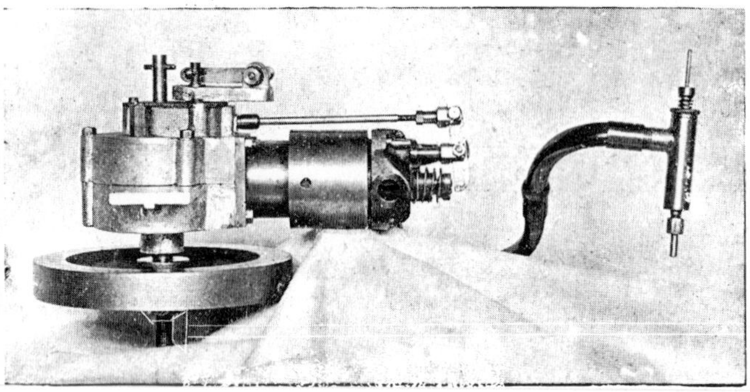

Illustration of $1\frac{1}{8}$ by $1\frac{1}{8}$ in. "Stentor" Engine for 2 ft. Boats.

Transmission is by bevel wheel on engine shaft and bevel wheel on propellor shaft.

$1\frac{1}{8}$ in. bore, $1\frac{1}{8}$ in. stroke, weight $3\frac{1}{2}$ lbs., including carburettor, 11 in. long by 5 in. wide, **£6 0 0** Castings and all materials ... **2 ε $\frac{1}{2}$** Speed up to 4,500 r.p.m.

$1\frac{3}{8}$ in. bore, $1\frac{3}{8}$ in. stroke, weight $5\frac{1}{2}$ lbs., including carburettor, 11 in long by $6\frac{1}{2}$ in. wide, **£6 10 0** Castings and all materials ... **30/-** Speed up to 4,000 r.p.m.

$1\frac{5}{8}$ in. bore, $1\frac{5}{8}$ in. stroke, weight 7 lbs., including carburettor, $13\frac{1}{2}$ long by 8 in. wide, **£7 0 0** Castings and all materials ... **35/-** Speed up to 3,000 r.p,m.

$1\frac{3}{8}$ in. bore, $1\frac{3}{8}$ in. stroke, weight $6\frac{1}{2}$ lbs. Twin for Aeroplanes, b,h.-p. .. **£10 10 0** Castings and all materials ... **£2 2 0** Speed up to 2,500 r.p.m., 6 lb. thrust.

Racing Boats Equipped Ready for the Water.

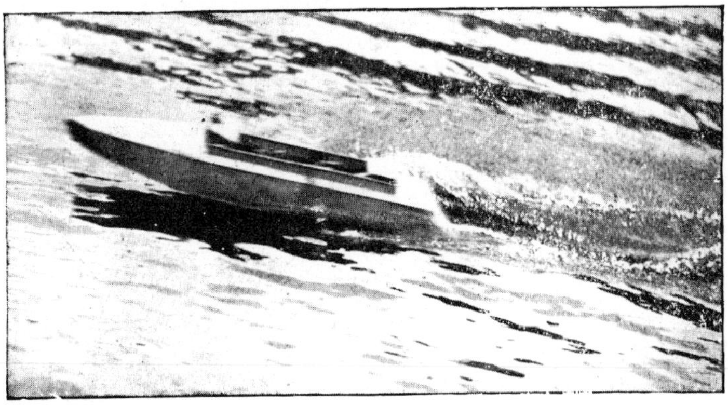

Illustration of "Stentor Minor" travelling at 12 miles per hour.

2-ft. Hydroplane as "Stentorette," complete, ready for running.. **£12 5 0**
Weight complete $5\frac{1}{2}$ lbs.

1-metre Hydroplane as "Stentor Minor," complete, ready for running **12 15**
Weight complete $11\frac{3}{4}$ lbs.

$1\frac{1}{2}$-metre Hydroplane as "Stentor Major," complete, ready for running **14 0 0**
Weight complete 15 lbs.

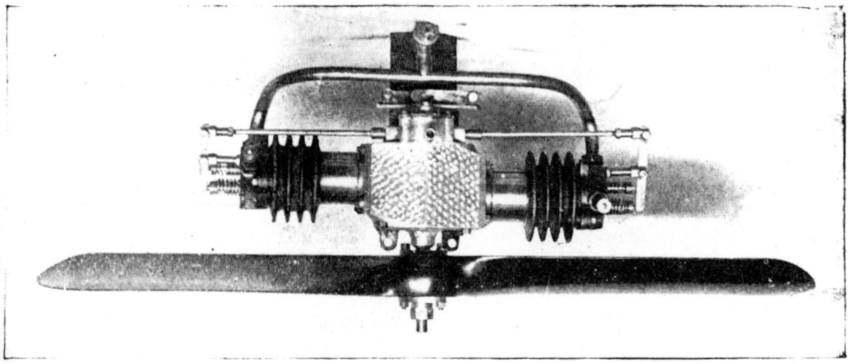

Illustration of $1\frac{3}{8}$ by $1\frac{3}{8}$ in. Twin Aero Engine.

Sets of Castings include—

Aluminium—1 crank case (2 halves).

Cast Iron—1 flywheel, 2 pistons, 2 cylinder heads, piston ring piece, 2 cylinders.

Phosphor Bronze—2 connecting rods, 2 bearing bushes, gear box cover, contact breaker.

Materials comprise everything required to finish engine, including pair of finished gears.

MOTOR BOAT ACCESSORIES:—

Lightweight Tremble Coils	**10/6**	Post 3d.
,, ,, Twin..	**21/-**	,, 4d.
,, Accumulators (4 amp.)	**5/6**	,, 4d.
Spray Carburettors (all sizes)	**7/6**	,, 3d,
Special Sparking Plugs	**2/6**	,, 2d.

Propellors—

2 in.	**2/6**	,, 2d.
3 in.	**3/9**	,, 2d.
4 in.	**4/9**	,, 2d.

Bevel Gears—

For $1\frac{1}{8}$ in. engine, gun-metal	per pair	**4/-**	Post 2d
,, $1\frac{1}{8}$ in. ,, steel (case hardened)..	,,	**12/6**	,. 2d.
,, $1\frac{3}{8}$ in. ,, gun-metal	,,	**4/6**	,, 2d.
,, $1\frac{3}{8}$ in. ,, steel (case hardened)..	,,	**12/6**	,, 2d.
,, $1\frac{5}{8}$ in. ,, gun-metal	,,	**5/-**	,, 2d.
,, $1\frac{5}{8}$ in. ,, steel (case hardened)..	,,	**12/6**	,, 2d.

We strongly recommend Case Hardened Steel.

Lightweight Pumps (centrifugal) for engines up to $1\frac{3}{8}$ in.	**4/6**	Post 2d.
,, ,, ,, ,, ,, $1\frac{5}{8}$ in.	**6/6**	,, 2d.

½-h.p.

Petrol Engine.

Price complete

£6 10 0

CYLINDER.—Water cooled, bore 2¼ in., stroke 3 in., accurately bored and ground. Piston fitted with two or three rings. The water jacket is of ample proportion, thus ensuring efficient cooling under extreme conditions. The crank shaft is of best quality steel, having square webbs, machined all over. Connecting rod of the marine type, fitted with adjustable bronze bearings to big end.

CARBURETTOR,—Latest type spray, fitted with gas and air control.

LUBRICATION.—Sight feed lubricator, fitted on cylinder; bearings fitted with oil cups.

IGNITION.—High tension electric.

ACCESSORIES include water vessel, exhaust box, petrol tank, and sparking plug.

HEAVY TYPE

Gas and

Petrol

Engines.

The above illustration represents our new type of engine, which has been designed for those who require something more massive and elaborate in detail than is at present on the market.

Cylinders are fitted with loose liners, which can easily be replaced when worn, thus prolonging the life of the engine indefinitely.

Pistons have ample wearing surface, being in length more than twice their diameter, and are provided with three accurately fitting rings.

Valves are mechanically operated by cam and roller action.

Governor is of the latest rotary ball type, driven by bevel gearing from the side shaft. The governor controls automatically the amount of fuel consumed in strict proportion to the load.

Ignition.—High tension electric by coil, accumulator and variable commutator.

No. 1 Size.—⅓ H.P., 2 in. bore, 3½ in. stroke. Flywheel, 10 by 1½ in. Speed, 750 R.P.M. Price for gas or petrol engine .. **£10 10 0**

No. 2 Size.—½ H.P., 2½ in. bore, 4 in. stroke. Flywheel, 12 by 2 in. Speed, 650 R.P.M. Price for gas or petrol **11 15 0**

No. 3 Size.—¾ H.P., 3 in. bore, 4½ in. stroke. Flywheel, 14 by 2½ in. Speed, 550 R.P.M. Price for gas or petrol **13 10 0**

No. 4 Size.—1 H.P., 3½ in. bore, 5 in. stroke. Flywheel, 16 by 2¼ in. Speed, 500 R.P.M. Price for gas or petrol **16 10 0**

The H.P. Ratings stated above are taken on gas. When running on petrol 25 per cent. more power will be developed.

The prices quoted include everything necessary for running, and in comparing our prices with those of other makers this must be taken into consideration.

Accessories include water vessel, exhaust box (gas bag or carburettor and petrol tank), sparking plug, coil, accumulator, and a complete set of pipes and wires for a compact arrangement.

All engines carriage forward outside London carrier radius.

Polarity Indicator.

Can be carried in the Vest Pocket, size 3¼ by ¾ in.

Will instantly indicate the negative and positive when connected in circuit. The nickel plated shell encloses and protects the glass tube from injury while being carried in the pocket or tool bag.

For use with battery .. **6/6**   Post 2d.

Dynamos for Charging and Lighting.

"Defiance" Dynamos.

We assert with every confidence that these dynamos are better value than can be obtained elsewhere. So sure are we of this, that we suggest prospective purchasers compare them with any other make, and if not satisfied we will refund cash on receipt of dynamo.

No. Ty. 1.   Output 10 volts, 3 amperes (30 watts); speed 2,800 revs. per min. ; fitted with spring brushes and oilcups, and properly built up commutator.   Price **14/6**.   Carriage forward.

No. Ty. 2.   Output 10 volts, 3 ampères (30 watts), or 5 volts, 6 ampères (30 watts), with spring brush gear, gun-metal rocking bar and ring oiler bearings. A thoroughly well-made machine that can be run for hours without over heating.   Price **22/6**   Post free

DYNAMO and MOTOR PARTS for Education and Home Construction.

Undertype.

Manchester.

Overtype.

Simplex.

Multipolar.

Ironclad.

Complete sets of parts to make up any one of the above dynamos

This collection of models forms a perfect portable training institution, combining reliable technical instruction with workshop experience. A course of model construction on systematic lines, with these sets of parts, will do more to advance the student in real practical work than will a term of instruction at a technical institute.

It is a well recognised fact that actual personal acquaintance with any apparatus itself is far preferable to and more instructive than the most careful perusal of many a learned treatise on the subject. A few inexpensive tools, such as a file or two, and a few small drills and taps, are all that is necessary, and these are to be found in and amateur's workshop however modest its equipment. No lathe is required.

Not only do these sets include all the parts necessary to build the complete working model down to the smallest detail, but full and concise printed instructions are enclosed, together with carefully prepared scale working drawings, an explanation of the action of the apparatus, and a technical description of its various parts and their functions.

Each set is absolutely complete, and packed in a neat cardboard box accompanied by instructions and working drawings as above. The price for any of these sets is the same viz. : **6/6** each, post free.

The "GAMAGE" Dynamos.
Practical Machines at Low Prices.

The No. 1, will light eighteen 10-c.p. Lamps.

Ty. 1.   32 volts, 6 amps., 2,300 R.P.M. or wound to order .. **£3 15 0**
Ty. 2.   20 volts, 6 amps. or 15 volts, 8 amps. **2 15 0**
Ty. 3.   15 volts, 4 amps. or 10 volts, 6 amps. **2 0 0**
   Carriage forward.

Castings with finished Commutator & Carbon Brushes to Build 120 watt Machine **39/-**
Do.   do.   60   do.   **30/-**

Specification.

Fields—Enclosed type, ironclad, one single jointless casting in best grey iron.

Armature—Slotted drum type, built of best annealed charcoal iron laminations, and fitted with efficient oil throws.   All sizes wound D.C.C. wire.

Commutator—Hard drawn copper segments, insulated throughout with mica.

Bearings—Self-oiling ring type, radial bearing seats, fitted with oil-collecting hoods.

Brush Gear—Improved type, with carbon brushes requiring no adjustment until worn out. Fixed position of commutation at all loads.

Aero Engine
Model A.
Extraordinary value.

Power developed by our Aero Engine under reliable and carefully carried out tests.

1 h.p. Two-Cycle
Air-cooled Petrol Engine.

Horse-power under load, ordinary brake test, lifting 18 lbs. :—

At 2,000 R.P.M. ·458 B.H.P.
   3,000 „   ·80 „
   4,000 „   ·916 „

All Engines are fitted with three piston rings, phosphor-bronze bearings throughout, drop forged steel crankshafts, aluminium crankcases, and specially designed aluminium propellor. 1⅜ in. bore, 2 in. stroke.

Weight with propellor 6¼ lbs.   All parts are made to gauge and standardized, so that spare parts can be supplied.

PRICE—Complete with Spray Carburettor, polished brass Aero pattern Petrol Tank and Aluminium Propellor, **84/-**

Model "**B**" is the same design as Model "**A**" and is complete with Spray Carburettor, and is fitted with a fly-wheel instead of a propellor, and has no Petrol Tank. Weight 16 lbs.   Price **£3 15 0**

DYNAMOS and MOTORS.

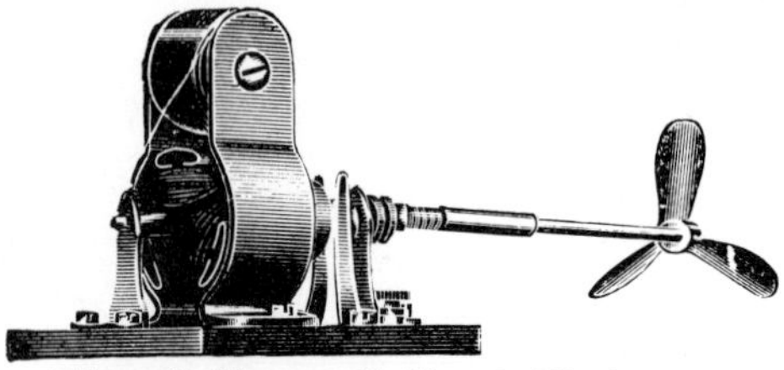

The "ilixum" Boat Motor.
The cheapest motor produced for marine work.
2/9 Postage 3d.
Propeller, with shaft and coupling, **1/-** extra.

Enclosed Magneto Dynamo.
Alternating current with permanent laminated magnet.

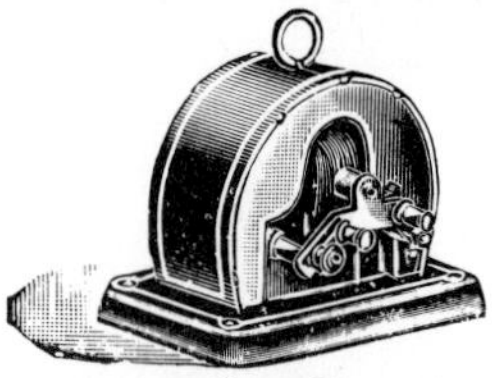

Fitted with 2 pole armature, adjustable slide brush, pole clamps, pulley, on metal base, can be driven by small steam engine.
$2\frac{1}{2}$ volts, 0·3 amp., size $3\frac{3}{8}$ by $2\frac{1}{8}$ by 2 in.
Price **5/6** Postage 4d.

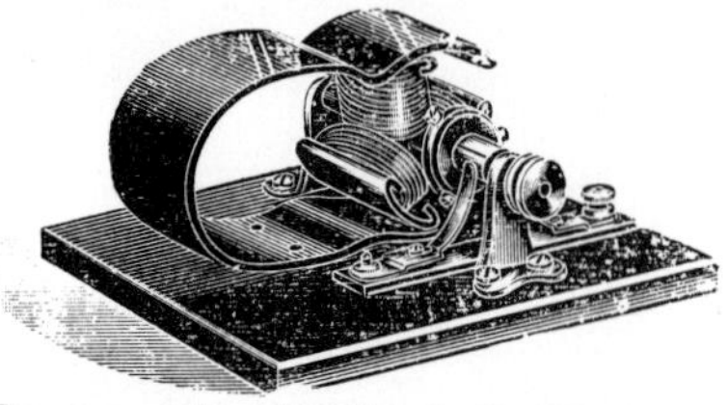

Gamage's "Flash" Motor.
Can be reversed by changing wires of Battery.
The most effective little motor on the market.
Very powerful for its size. Price **2/-** Post 3d.

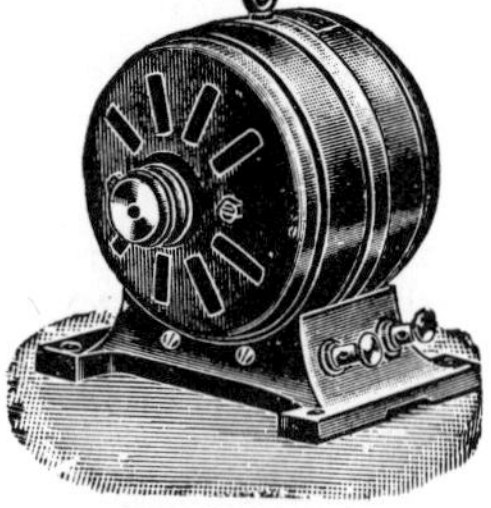

Magneto Dynamo,
(Direct current.)
Double T armature, adjustable slide brush, permanent armature, round metal casing of solid construction.

Black colour. Can be worked by motors and steam engines.

Revolutions per minute.	Volt.	Ampere.	Size inch.	Price
4000	$2\frac{1}{2}$	0.5	$3\frac{1}{2}$x$3\frac{1}{4}$x$3\frac{1}{2}$	**8/6**
3500	$2\frac{1}{2}$	0.8	$4\frac{1}{2}$x$3\frac{3}{4}$x5	**12/6**

Postage 4d.

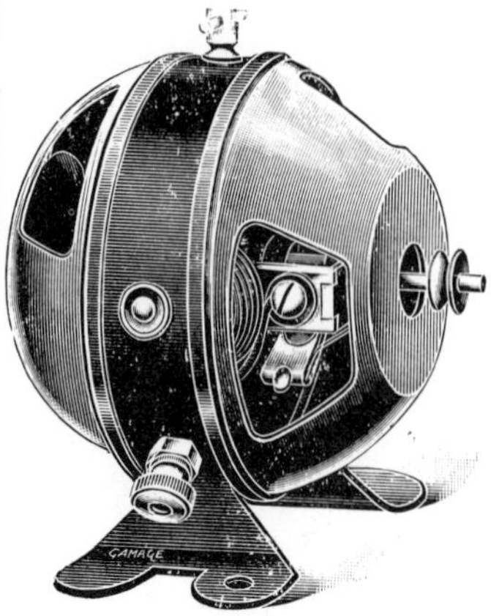

The "Milo" Motor.
This is an exceedingly well made motor with laminated tripolar armature and gauze spring brushes. High Speed is obtained from a 4 volt cell but the motor runs well from two volts.
Fine Value.
Price .. **5/6**
Post 3d.

Gamage'e "Victory" Motor.
This is another of GAMAGE'S surprises this season. This motor has special features which have never been present in any other motor of its size yet produced.

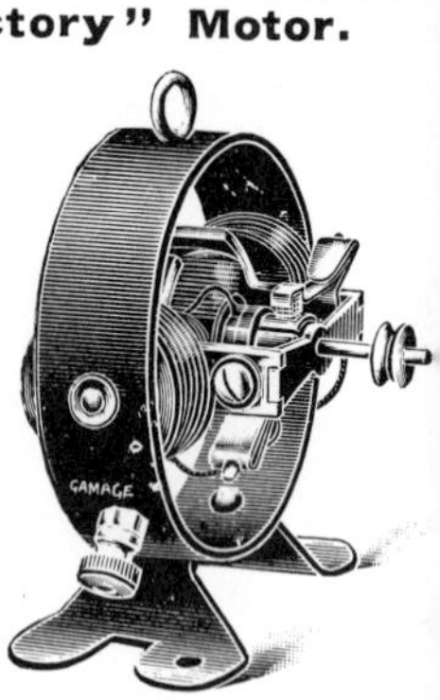

NOTE.—3-pole armature built up of 12 laminations and compressed copper gauge spring brushes.

Runs splendidly on two ordinary dry cells and will take up to 4 volts without undue sparking or heating.
Height $3\frac{1}{4}$, length $2\frac{1}{2}$, width $2\frac{1}{4}$
Gamage's value **4/3** Post 3d

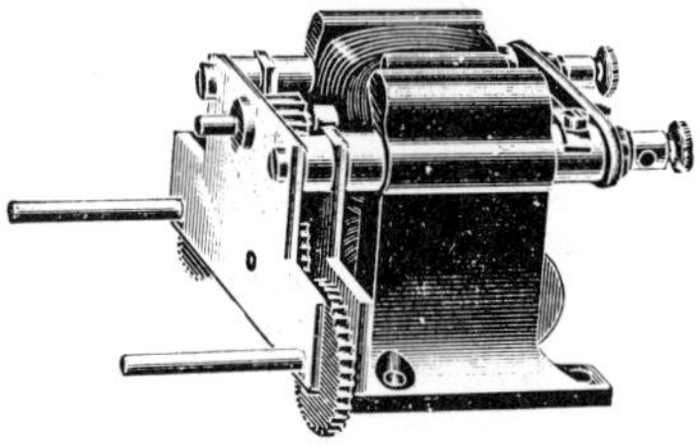

Gamage's "Duplex" Boat and Traction Motor.
4-8 volts. (Patent.)
The gearing is so arranged that the shafts both run in opposite directions, enabling a right and left hand propellor to be used. This motor takes only one ampere at 4 volts, will take up to 16 volts for short runs, and gives greater power than any other motor taking same current. Weight $1\frac{1}{4}$ lbs.
Silk covered windings, with laminated 3-pole armature, self-starting. Price **11/6**
Post 5d.

2 in. 3-blade polished gunmetal propellers and steel shafts, **4/6** pair extra. Post 3d.

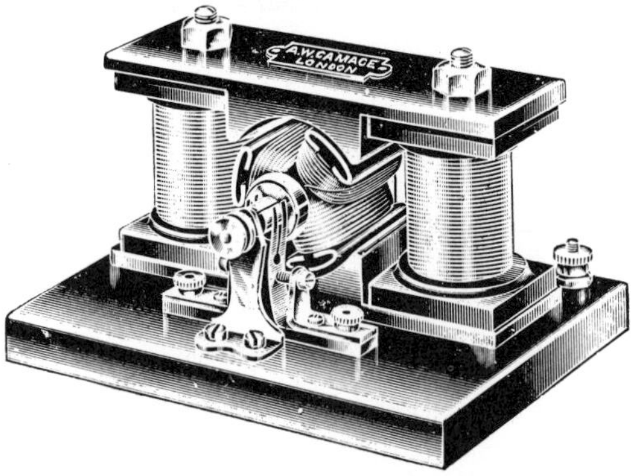

Gamage's "Goliath" Motor.
Unapproachable value. Very solidly built, triple T armature, enamelled iron base and finish. Length $4\frac{1}{2}$ in.. width $3\frac{3}{4}$ in., height $2\frac{3}{4}$ in. Price **4/6** Post 4d.

Dynamo with Street Lamp and Switch.
MOUNTED ON WOODEN BASE.

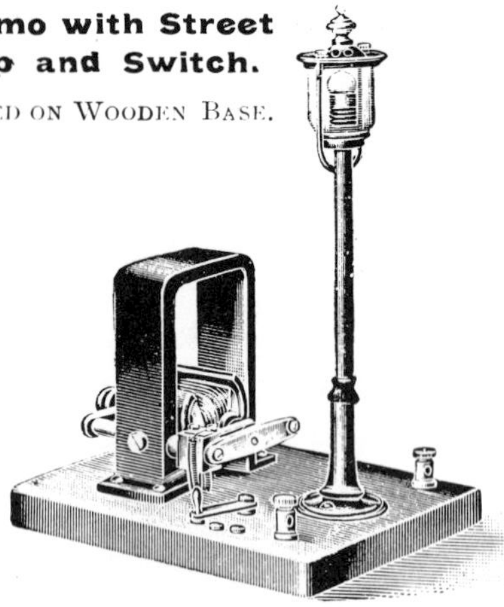

Dynamo with permanent magnet requiring little powe[r] for running. Current produced can be used either t[o] light the street lamp or for other purposes from terminal[s] provided, with switch for lamp and terminals (electri[c] light bulb 3.5 volt). Price **10/6** Post 4d.

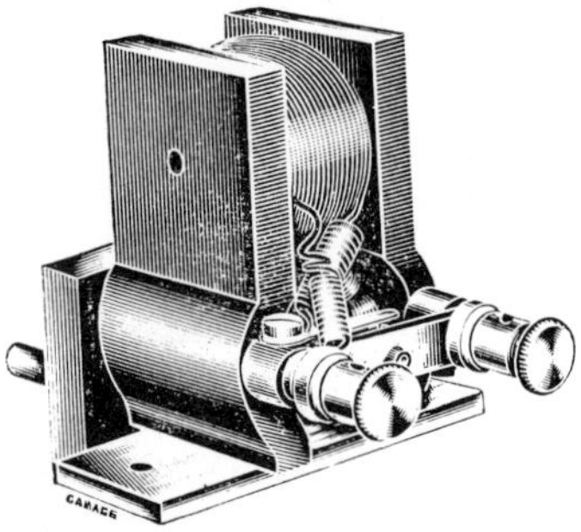

Gamage's "Simplex" (PATENT) **Boat and Traction Motor.**
Fitted with gearing, enclosed in gear case forming an oil bath, which greatly increases power, and allows motor to run at great speed under load. Takes only $\frac{1}{2}$-ampere at 4 volts and will take up to 12 volts for short runs. Silk covered windings, with laminated turned tripolar armature. Self-starting.
Weight 9-ozs. Price **6/6** Post 3d.
With 2 in. 3-blade polished gun-metal propellor and shaft, **2/3** extra. Post 2d.

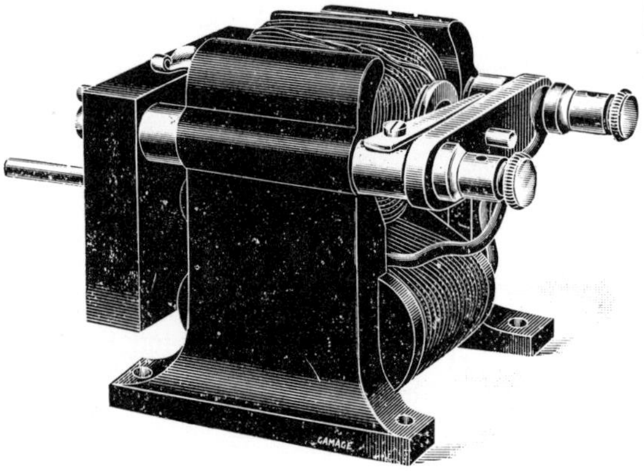

Gamage's "Simplex" Boat & Traction Motor.
(Patent).
Enclosed in a Metal Case forming an Oil Bath.
Fitted with gearing which greatly increases power and prevents motor pulling up when taking a load. Has wonderful power, and takes only one ampere at 4 volt current and will take up to 16 volts for short runs.
Weight 1 lb. 2 oz. Price **10/9** Post 4d.

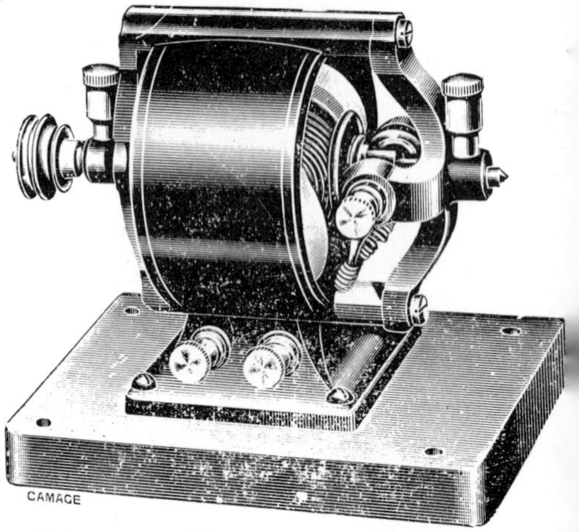

Electric Motor to run from 4-8 volts.
Adjustable spring brushes, tripolar armature, lon[g] bearings, fitted with screw down grease cups. Ver[y] hig[h] speed. Size 5 by $3\frac{1}{4}$ by $4\frac{3}{4}$ in. Price **10/6** Post 4[d].

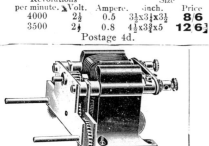

ACCUMULATORS, BATTERIES AND STORAGE CELLS.

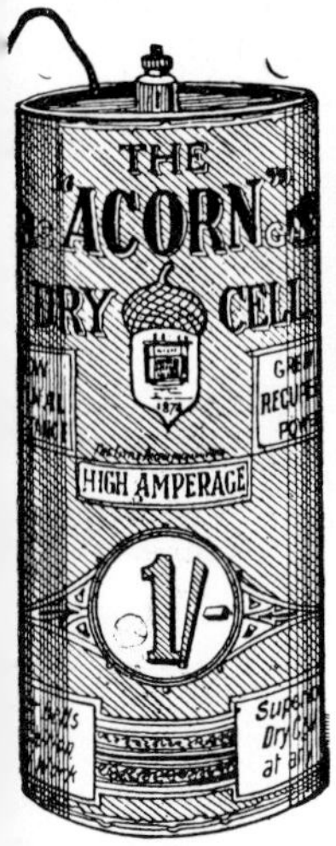

Gamage's "Acorn"
Dry Cell.
London-made. Price **1/-** Very best value obtainable. Equal to many cells in the market at higher prices.
NOTE.—Low internal resistance, high amperage, great recuperative power
Post 3d

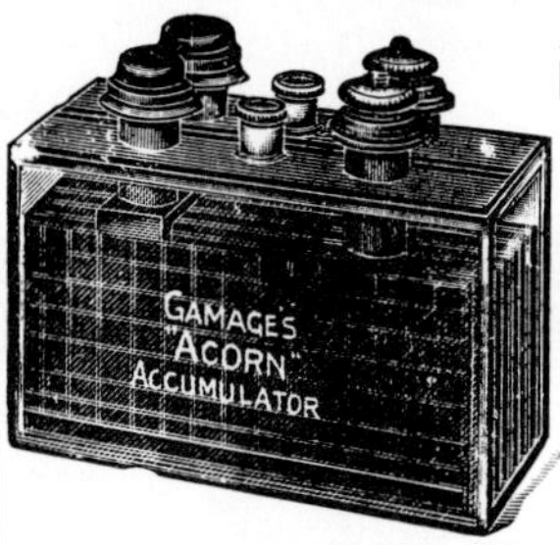

4 volts, 10 amperes, 4 by 2 by 2¾ in.
Price **8/11** Post 6d.

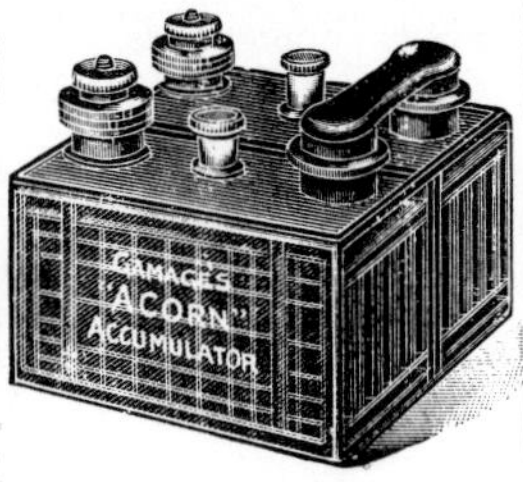

Boat Accumulator.
4 volts, 8 amps., 3⅛ by 3½ by 2 in
Price **7/11** Post 5d.

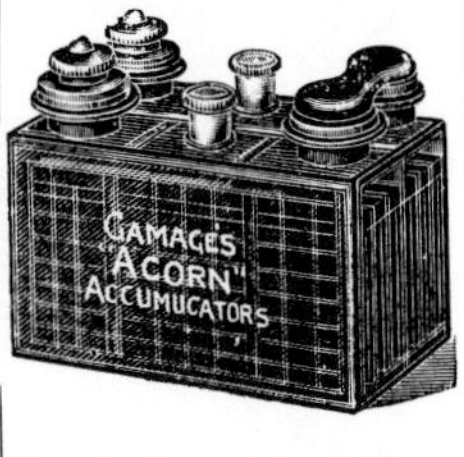

Boat Accumulator
4 volts, 4 amps., 3⅛ by 1¼ by 2 in. Price **5/6** Post 4d.

Complete Bottle Bichromate Batteries.

BEST QUALITY.
½-pint size, 2 carbons & 1 zinc, **1/5** 1-pint, **2/2**
2-pint, **2/9** 4-pint, **4/3**
Ditto, without bottles—
½-pt., **1/1** 1-pt., **1/5**
2-pt., **1/9** 4-pt., **2/9**

ZINCS only—
½-pint, **2**d. 1-pint, **3**d.
2-pint, **4**d. 4-pint, **6**d.

CHROMIC SALT—
Charge, ½-pint, **3**d.
1-pint, **6**d. 2-pint, **1/-**
Carriage extra.

Bottles.	With Brass. Ring.	Coppered Carbons.
½-pint	**1/-**	**2**d.
1 ,,	**1/3**	**3**d.
2 ,,	**1/6**	**4**d.
4 ,,	**2/6**	**9**d.

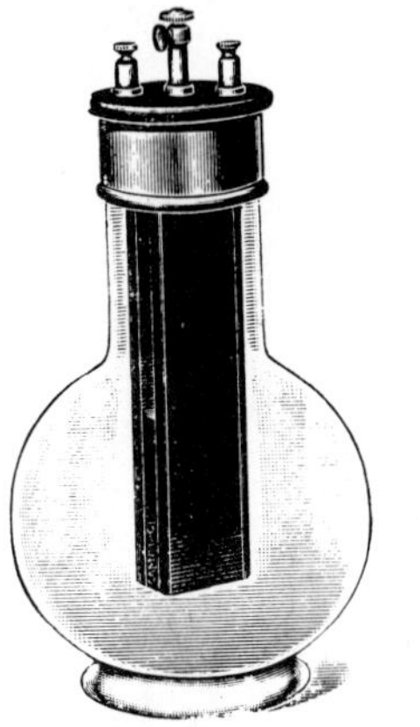

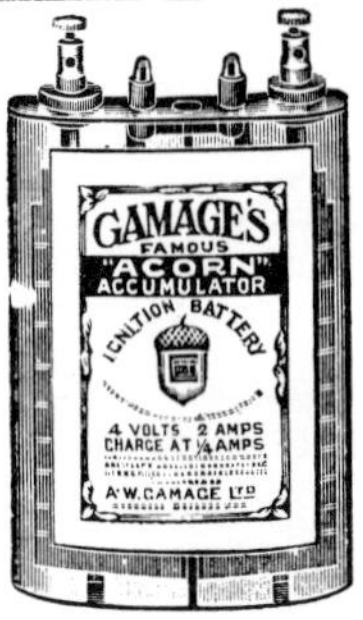

This **Accumulator** represents the last word in cheapness and reliability. English made throughout, stout celluloid case and rubber vent plugs.
4 by 3 by ⅞in. **2/6** Post 2d.

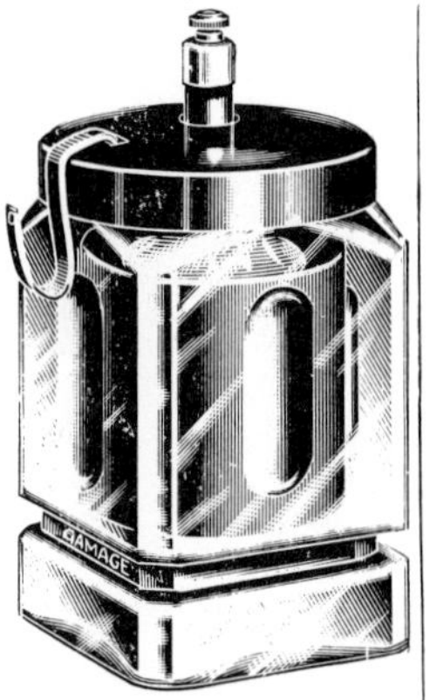

Gamage's Improved Holborn Sac Batteries.
No. 1. 3 by 3 by 7 in. high, Capacity 1 pint ... **1/6**
No. 2. 4 by 4 by 8½ in. high, Capacity 2 pint ... **2/-**
No. 3. 5 by 5 by 12 in. high, Capacity 6 pint ... **3/6**

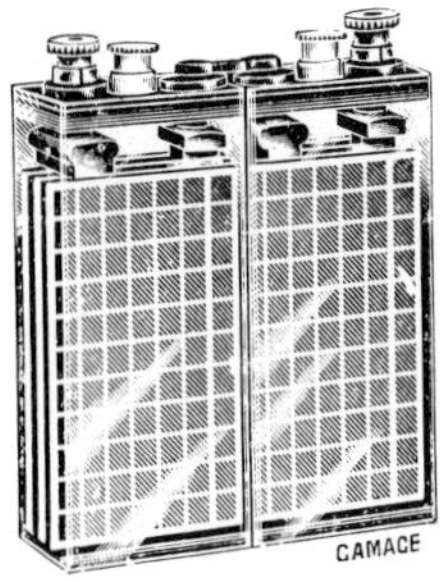

Accumulators.
English made.
Case is all celluloid.
No wax filling.
Weight 14 oz.
4 volts, 3 amperes.
height 4⅝ in., width 3½ by ⅞ in.
Price **3/6** Post 3d.
Do. do. 4 volts, amperes,
Price ... **5/6** Post 4d.

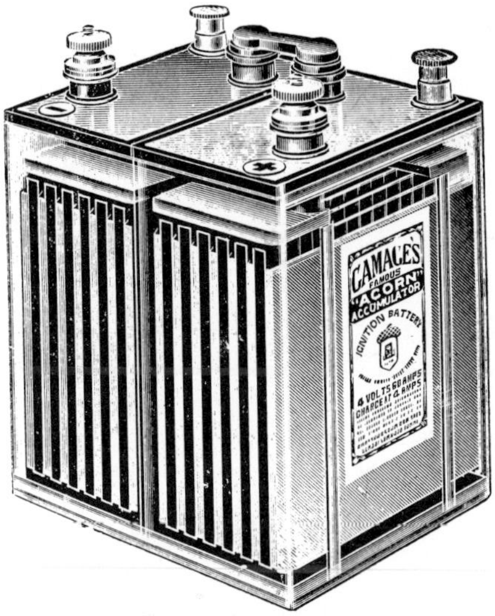

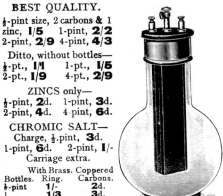

Gamage's Acorn Accumulator.
4 volts, 20 amperes, 5½ by 4⅛ by 2½ in., 6 plates ... **10/-**
4 volts, 40 amperes, 5½ by 4½ by 3⅝ in., 10 plates ... **14/-**
4 volts, 60 amperes, 5½ by 5 by 4½ in., 14 plates ... **19/6**
Carriage forward.

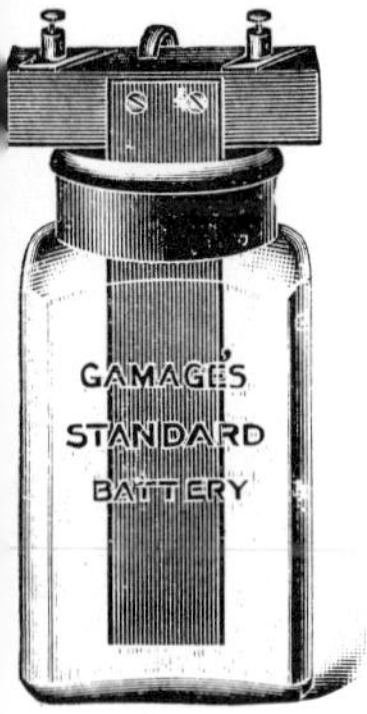

Gamage's "Standard" Bichromate Battery.
10½d. Postage 3d.

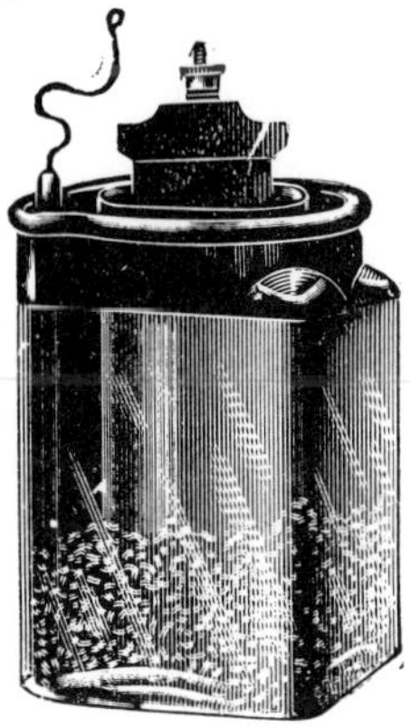

Gamage's "AJAX"
Leclanche Batteries.
Fitted with Bamber's Non-incrusting Zincs.
UNEQUALLED VALUE!
2-pt. size, complete with ¼-lb. salammoniac.
Price **10½**d. **9/9** doz. carr. ex.
Extra Porous Pots **5½**d. **5/-** doz.
Bamber's Zinc Rods **2½**d. **2/-** doz.
Salammoniac, **5**d. lb., **42/-** cwt.
Carriage forward.
Glass Jars, **3**d. each. **2/8** doz.

You can 'Phone YOUR ORDERS by ringing 2700 Holborn.

GAMAGE'S STORAGE CELLS.

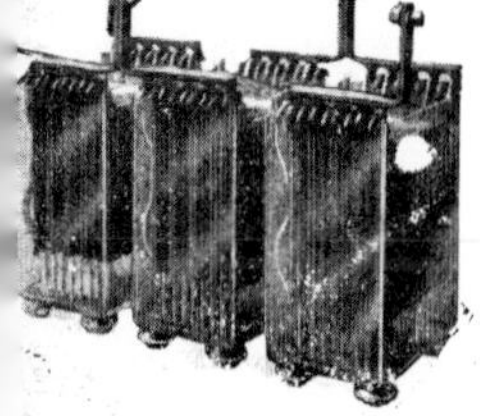

TYPE.	Number of 10 c.p. 10 watt lamps for 5 hours	Capacity in Amp. hours at 10 hr. rate	Discharge rate in ampers. 5 hours	Discharge rate in ampers. 10 hours	Charge rate in amperes Normal.	Charge rate in amperes Maximum	Over all height of Cell	TRAYS. Dimensions in inches	TRAYS. Number of Cells on one tray.	Two-tier Stands, for 14 Cells. PRICE	Two-tier Stands, for 14 Cells. Length ft. in.	Price of Battery Single Cell	Price of Battery of 14 Cells.
Q.H. 3	3	8	1 4	·8	1·1	1·4	9¼ in.	5 by 10½	5	...	2 0	**8/3**	**£5 15 6**
,, 5	7	16	3	1·8	2·2	2·8	9¼ ,,	5 ,, 22¾		...	2 9	**9/9**	**6 9 0**
,, 7	11	24	4·5	2·7	3·3	4·2	9¼ ,,	5 ,, 17		...	3 6	**11/3**	**7 17 6**
,, 9	15	32	6	3·6	4·4	5·6	9¼ ,,	5 ,, 15½		**27/9**	4 3	**13/6**	**9 2 3**
,, 11	19	46	7·6	4·5	5·5	7·0	9¼ ,,	5 ,, 19	3	**31/6**	5 0	**15/-**	**10 7 0**
R.H. 5	25	60	10	6	8	12	16 ,,	9 ,, 14	3	**39/3**	4 0	**18/-**	**12 12 0**
,, 7	37	90	15	9	13	19	16 ,,	9 ,, 18½	3	**31/6**	5 0	**22/6**	**15 13 6**
,, 9	50	120	20	12	17	25	16 ,.	9 ,, 6¾	3	**39/3**	5 6	**27/-**	**18 11 6**

☛ THESE PRICES include Cells complete with glass boxes, dilute acid, glass covers, non-corrosive connectors, glass insulators with oil and india-rubber discs to go between insulators and trays or glass cell.

Note.—For the smaller sizes, the prices are not given for stands, as the trays containing the cells can be arranged on shelving. But prices for stands will be supplied when desired.

DELIVERY IS FREE to any Railway Station in the United Kingdom, including return of empties. If the cases are not returned within 21 days of delivery then the extra cost of cases will be charged in FULL.

PACKAGES charged as under, but credited in full if returned in sound condition to our works within 14 days from date of delivery of the goods.

	Packing Cases.	Carboys or Jars.		Packing Cases.	Carboys or Jars.
4 Q.H. 3 Cells ..	**9/-**	**2/-**	14 Q.H. 11 Cells ..	**16/6**	**4/-**
4 Q.H. 5 ,, ..	**9/-**	**2/-**	14 R.H. 5 ,, ..	**12/-**	**8/-**
4 Q.H. 7 ,, ..	**9/6**	**4/-**	14 R.H. 7 ,, ..	**18/6**	**12/-**
4 Q.H. 9 ,, ..	**13/-**	**4/-**	14 R.H. 9 ,, ..	**22/-**	**16/-**

IF TRAYS ARE NOT REQUIRED, the following prices can be deducted:—

1 Tray to take 5 Q.H. 3 Cells,	**7**d.	1 Tray to take 3 Q.H. 11 Cells,	**8**d.
1 ,, ,, 4 Q.H. 5 ,,	**8**d.	1 ,, ,, 3 R.H. 5 ,,	**10**d.
1 ,, ,, 4 Q.H. 7 ,,	**8**d.	1 ,, ,, 3 R.H. 7 ,,	**11**d.
1 ,, ,, 3 Q.H. 9 ,,	**7**d.	1 ,, ,, 3 R.H. 9 ,,	**1/1**

No. 1.

No. 2.

Electrical Novelties

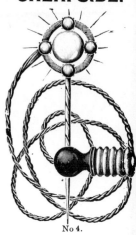

No 4.

No. 6.   Dog Scarf Pin.

Electric Eye.
Very effective for amateur theatricals, etc.
Price, without battery. **6**d.
Postage 1d.
Battery and Case, **5**d. extra.
Postage 2d.

Electric Roses with Maidenhair Fern for Buttonholes.
Finest qual. **1/-** Post 1d each.

Battery and Case **5**d. extra. Post 2d.

Electric Nose.
Made of waxed canvas, semi-transparent.
10d. each.   Post 2d.
Battery and Case.
5d. extra.   Post 2d.
Ears do. **1/11** Post 2d.

No. 5.

Policeman.

Nigger.

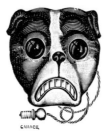

Bull Dog.

The "Glad-eye" Electrical Novelty
Illuminated Grotesque Buttonholes. These grotesque masks have transparent coloured eyes with an electric bulb fitted at the back to which is attached a flexible cord, connected to a battery carried in the pocket. Rare fun for parties, carnivals, etc.   Price complete with Battery and case, **1/11**
Post 3d.

Skull.

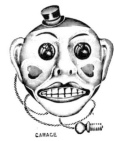

Clown.

"Glad-eye" Electrical Novelty
Illuminated grotesque buttonholes. Light can be flashed on and off by means of switch on battery, producing winking effect. Complete with battery and case, **1/11**
Post 3

Rectangular Tattooing Machine, as illus., best finish. Price **18/9** Post 3d.
Rectangular Tattooing Machine, with 2 terminals, japanned finish.
Price **13/9**   Postage 3d.

Tattooing Colours, in bottles. 2 in. by 9/16 in.
Green, red, brown, blue or yellow, **1/6** bottle.
Indian Ink Liquid in bottles, 1 by 2½ in., **1/6** bottle.
Post and packing, 2d. per bottle.

Tattooing Machine, with 4 coils, as illustration, best finish. Price **52/6** Post free.

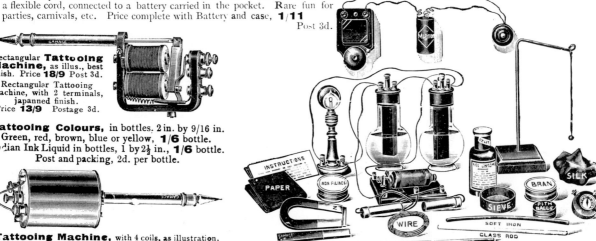

The Gamage Electrical Experiment Outfit.

Comprising two half-pint bichromate batteries, bottle of chromic salt for charging, plated metal bell mounted on japanned iron base with push, battery and 10 yds. wire, highly finished induction or shocking coil, electroscope mounted on polished teak base, galvanometer, silk, wire, paper, horseshoe and bar magnets and keeper, iron filings, brass sieve, bran, pith balls, soft iron rod, steel and glass rods. Complete with instructions for performing experiments in electric lighting, magnetism and frictional electricity.

Price   **15/9**
Post   9d.

Miniature Brass Switch.

With holding down Tugs.

Size as illustration.

Price **3½**d. Postage 1d.

Miniature Batten Holders. As illustration.

Suit any Standard Miniature Screw Lamp.
Price **2**d. each. **1/9** doz.
Exceptional Value.
Metal Filament Screw Lamps, as illustration, 2½ volt.
Price **5**d. each. **4/11** doz.
Post free.

The Gamage No. 2 Bracket Light Set.

With Lamp.
Superior set with heavy brass brackets and back plate mounted on dovetailed teak block with nickel-plated switch.

Only to be obtained from us, far better than any similar article on the market ... **3/6**
Post 4d. Separate shades, **6**d. each.

English-made Electric Table Standard

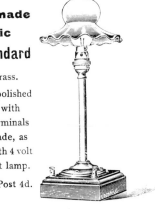

Of heavy brass.
Mounted on polished teak base, with burnished terminals and opal shade, as illustrated, with 4 volt metal filament lamp.

Price **3/3** Post 4d.

Gamages Holborn Light Outfit.
Price
11/6
Carriage forward.

mprising :—3 two pint improved Holborn (re-chargeable) Sac teries (see page 47) and Salammoniac, Brass bracket (6 in. ection), mounted on Teak, dovetailed block 6 in. by 3 in. with ch, 6 in. opal shade, 4 volt Metal Filament Lamp and 30 ft. of wire. Price **11/6**
Do., with 3 one pint batteries and 15 ft. of wire
Price **8/9** Carriage forward.

Terminals.
1 3
(1) **1**d. each, **9**d. doz. (3) **1**d. each, **8**d. doz.
Postage 1d. extra on singles, in doz. lots, 2d.

Gamage s Giant
(2in. dia.)
S.B.C. Lamps
with supported
metal filaments
4 volt, 4 amp., 16C.P. **2/3**
8 „ 4 „ „ **2/3**

Gamage's Special Supported Metal Filament S.B.C. Lamps,
⅜ in. Diameter. English Make.
2 volt, 1 C.P. 4 volt, 4 C.P. 6 volt, 6 C.P.
10d. each. **9/-** doz.

Nickel-plated Reflectors.
1¾ in. diam, **1½**d. 2¼ in., **2**d. 3¼ in. **2½**d.
4in., **3**d. Post 1d.

Gamage No. 1 Electric Bracket.

This is quite a different quality to other similar foreign made articles on the market. The bracket is English-made, of heavy brass ¼ in. diam., highly finished, and the back plate extra heavy and securely fastened. Complete, as illustration. With 4 volt metal filament lamp, **2/3**
Postage 3d.

Ceiling Pendant Light Set, as illust.
Comprising porcelain ceiling rosettes, silk flexible wire and opal shade.
Price with 4 volt metal filament lamp, **2/4½** Post 4d.

Teak-wood Block.
(as illustration.)
Dovetailed and polished 6½ in. by 3½ in.
Price **4**d. Post 2d.
Do. square, 3½ by 3½ in.
2½d. Post 2d

Extra Heavy Solid Brass English-made Bracket.

6 in. projection. Price **9**d. Postage 2½d.
Ditto, with holder and shade carrier, as illustration.
Price **1/1½** Postage 2½d.

Brass Bracket, ⅜in. thread with back plate.
To take ordinary S.B.C. holder, **4½**d. Post 1½d.

Miniature **Key Switch.**
As illustration.
Brass or nickelled cap,
Diam. 1⅛ in. **4**d. Post 1d.

Lamp Stands.

With Reflector and 4 volt metal filament Lamp, (as illustration)
Price .. **1/10** each.
Postage 2d.

Polished Wooden Switch as illus., 2d.
Postage 1d.

Miniature **Batten Holders** with shade carrier, as illus., to take S.B.C. Lamps, **6**d. Post 1d

"Ilixum" Lighting Set.
Special Value.

Consisting of 3 of our noted 1 pint improved Holborn Sack Batteries (with Salammoniac for charging), switch polished teak block, brass bracket lamp-holder with shade carrier, opal shade, with 4 volt 4 candle power Metal Filament Lamp.

20 ft. of Wire.
Price .. **7/6**
Carriage forward.

Brass Electric Bracket.

Wonderful Value.
Mounted on polished teak base, with nickel plated reflector and lamp holder.
Price, without lamp **1/3**
Postage 3d.
Metal Filameht Lamp, 4-volt, 4c.p. **10**d.ea. **9/-** doz.

The 'GLOBE' Lighting Outfit.

Consisting of brass bracket with miniature screw lamp, and reflector mounted on wooden base with terminals and switch also two "Holborn" Sac Replenishable Cells and wire.
Price ... **3/11** Postage 6d

Small Brass Lamp Holders for capped lamps complete with shade carrier and cord grip as illus. **4½**d. Post 1d.

D

Apparatus for Wireless Telegraphy.

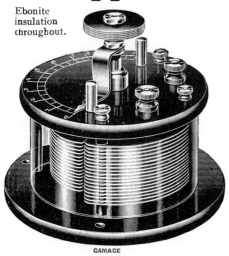

Ebonite insulation throughout.

Receiving Condenser. LONDON MADE. Hardened zinc Vanes, interleaved with ebonite sheet, making such close contact that they keep in any desired place regardless of the position of the instrument. Plates of polished vulcanite, lacquered brass fittings. Capacity ·0043 M.F. **55**/- ·0036 M.F. **60**/-

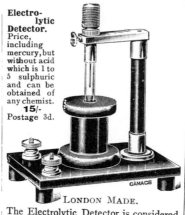

Electrolytic Detector. Price, including mercury, but without acid which is 1 to 5 sulphuric and can be obtained of any chemist. **15**/- Postage 3d.

LONDON MADE.

The Electrolytic Detector is considered by many to be the best of all detectors, and it certainly has the advantage of not being put out of adjustment when transmitting. A battery is essential with this instrument and a Potentiometer should always be used which prevents humming in the 'phones, and also protects the Woolaston wire. **Ebonite Container Case and Base,** metal parts highly finished, lacquered brass.

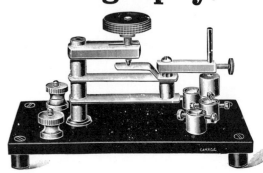

LONDON MADE.

Crystal Detector. This Detector has proved well designed and sensitive instrument. It has 4 cups fitted with crystals, the upper one when remove discloses a gold point which is for use with Silicon. 5½ by 3 by ⅝ in **Ebonite Base,** brass parts burnished and gold lacquered. **15**

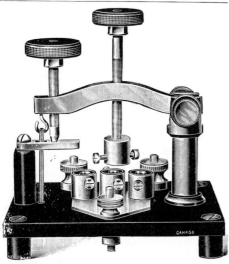

Crystal Detector. LONDON MADE. (Registered design). Without question this is the best Crystal Detector on the market, and quite original in design. It has 4 cups each fitted with a different crystal. The top cup when removed discloses a gold point which is used in conjunction with Silicon. **Base and knobs of best vulcanite,** metal parts burnished and lacquered. Micrometer adjustment. Exceedingly sensitive. **Price 18/6** Post 3d.

Crystal Detector. LONDON MADE. Silicon and Gold Point. This although a small instrument 3½ by 3 by ⅝ in., is an efficient piece of apparatus and suitable for small stations. Polished mahogany base, burnished and lacquered brass work, ebonite knob. **5**/- Post 3d.

Rotary Receiving condenser with Ebonite Top and Bottom Plates

Capacity ·0005 M.F.

Price **20**/-

Variable Condensers. LONDON MADE.
Ebonite insulation throughout with exception of base. Brasswork burnished and lacquered.
Air or Oil Dielectric. Fitted with Ebonite Screw Cap for filling vessel. Glass vessel Rotary type, with moving vanes, perfec insulation and high efficiency. Capacity ·002 m.f., with 9 fixe and 8 moving vanes, **42**/- Height 5in., length 6in., width 5¼in

Capacity ·004 m.f., with 16 fixed and 15 moving vanes Height 6¾ in. Length 6¼ in. Width 6¼ in. Price **50**/-

Do., With Brass Vanes and Massive Ebonite construction Throughout. Faraday House Calibration. Price **84**/-
Capacity stated is obtained when castor oil is used as delectri

Tuning Coils and Transmitting Helices.

Experimenters should remember that they must not transmit on plain aerial. Therefore a Helix is essential:

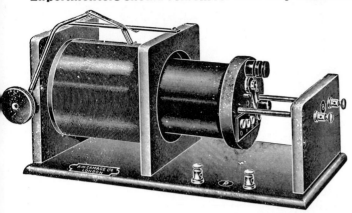

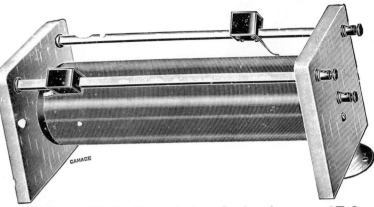

Loose Coupled Tuning Inductance.

A loosed coupled Receiving Inductance or Transformer is without question the most sensitive and selective of all types of Tuners, and will invariably be found in all well equipped stations. It is estimated to give 10 per cent. better results than the ordinary "Tight" type. The Secondary of our Transformer is tapped off in eight sections, which allows the best balancing of the primary and secondary circuits.

The sliding contact permits of the primary being selected at every turn.

If a variable condenser be used in shunt or series with the inductance atmospherics can be cut out and strength of signals increased. Price **45/-**

Since illustration was made the instrument has been very much improved and inductance increased.

Single Slide Receiving Inductance, 17/6

Double Slide Receiving Inductance.

A double contact inductance is used where closer tuning is required than can be obtained with a single slide instrument, and will be found to be very selective. Polished mahogany woodwork. Brass parts gold lacquered. Wound with enamelled copper wire on a prepared solid mandril, and not on a cardboard cylinder as is often the case. Price **21/-** With a double or treble slide inductance a variable or fixed condenser increases the efficiency.

Treble Slide Receiving Inductance.

Greater inductance .. **30/-**

Variable Tubular Condenser.

With ebonite dielectric.

A Tubular Condenser is a useful instrument for close tuning and long distance work. We recommend the connection of the Condenser across the detector, but it may be connected in several ways.

Has a variable capacity from nothing to ·00065 microfarad. Cylinders polished and gold ends lacquered; of polished vulcanite; base, polished mahogany. A first class instrument.

Price **21/-**

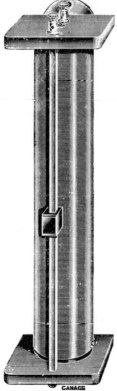

Loose or Inductively Coupled Transmitting Helix.

This Helix is one of the very latest productions of the "Loose" Type. The Drum is constructed of vulcanized fibre and has 44½ ft. of ⅜ in. Copper ribbon. The Rod upon which the slider moves is vulcanized fibre as is also the corresponding tie rod on the other side. The woodwork is polished mahogany.

Price **£4 10 0**

Loading Inductance.

enabling Stations with long wave Lengths to be picked up.

Length over all 17⅝ in. Containing 300 ft. enamelled wire, wound on a solid mandril. Polished mahogany ends with lacquered brass fittings. Price **17/6** Post extra.

Transmitting Helix.

A Helix is of equal importance in the Sending Circuit, as is a Tuning Inductance in the Receiving Circuit, and is essential to comply with Post Office regulations.

No. 1. Extra large Rotary instrument, containing 35 ft. ⅜ in. copper ribbon, with 2 sliders, wound on a Fibre Drum. Any part of Helix can be selected.

Base 14 by 11¼ in. thick, total height 13 in. .. **52/6**

D ..

Spark Coils, Keys, Condensers and Interrupters.

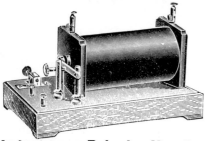

Induct on or Ruhmkorff Coils.

For X-Ray Wireless Telegraphy, Ignition and Experimental Work.

Size No. A.	or Spark.	Without Commu-tator.	With Commu-tator.	Post
0	$\frac{1}{8}$	3/3	—	4d.
1	$\frac{3}{16}$	3/6	4/9	6d.
2	$\frac{4}{4}$	4/3	5/6	6d.
3	$\frac{9}{16}$	6/3	7/6	6d.
4	$\frac{3}{8}$	6/6	8/9	6d.
4B	$\frac{1}{2}$	9 6	11/6	6d.
5	$\frac{5}{8}$	14 6	16/-	7d.
6B	1	22/6	29/-	8d.
8	$1\frac{1}{2}$	33/-	34/6	Free
11	3	89/-	95/-	,,
13	5	—	150/-	,,
15	8	250/-	247/-	,,

Tapping Key.

Well finished and accurate working.
Mounted on polished wooden base.
Length of the Tapping Key, $3\frac{1}{2}$ inches.
Price **2 4** Postage 2d.

Leyden Jars.

For Transmitting Condensers.

Capacity.

·0001 M.F.	..	1/6
·00034 ,,	..	2/6
·00065 ,,	..	3/6
·00082 ,,	..	4/6

Postage 2d. extra on 1 and 2.
3d. on 3 and 4.

Tapping Key. G.P.O. Pattern.

Fitted with Ebonite Protector and knob for Wireless Work. As illustration, highly finished, burnished and lacquered metal parts, mounted on mahogany base silver contacts.
Size $5\frac{3}{8}$ in. by $2\frac{7}{8}$ in.

Price .. **5/6** Post 4d.

Ditto, best finish, mounted on ebonite base.
Price .. **8 6** Post 4d.

Wireless Tapping Key WITH Oil Break.

A highly finished and efficient instrument. Suitable for stations up to 2 Kilowatt. Price .. **25/-**

High-speed Ignition Coils

Fitted with Platinoid Contacts.

Suitable for Motor Cycle Ignition, "X" Ray and experimental work. Make good Wireless Transmitting Coils for short distances.
No. 1. Single Trembler Coil, weight 13 ozs. Size over all, without lid, $1\frac{3}{4}$ in. by 2 5/16ths by $3\frac{1}{4}$ in. Takes about 2 amperes and give 5-16ths spark. Price **10/-** Postage 4d.
No. 2. Turn Trembler Coil same specification as above, and approximately double the size. Price **20/-**
Postage 5d.

Electrolytic Interruptor.

A first class Instrument of proved efficiency. Heavy glass vessel, ebonite cover, brass mountings, accurate adjusting gear. Size over all $13\frac{1}{2}$ by $7\frac{3}{4}$ by $6\frac{1}{2}$ in.

Price **55/-**

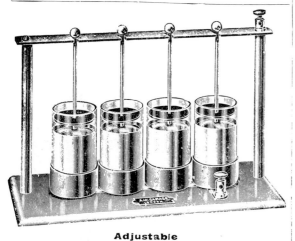

Adjustable Leyden Jar Transmitting Condenser.

As illustration.

Polished Mahogany base, Ebonite standards, burnished and lacquered rack, with four jars, capacity of each jar 0001 M.F.
Price **17/6**

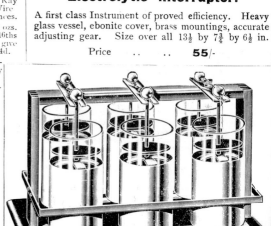

Adjustable Leyden Jar Transmitting Condenser.

With six jars each of ·00034 M.F Capacity. Mahogany and Brass finish. Price **21/-**

SPARK COILS, GAPS, HELICES.

High Efficiency Spark Gap

(Micrometer adjustment).

LONDON MADE.

This Spark Gap is suitable for stations from the smallest up to ¼ K.W. capacity. The base and standards are of polished vulcanite, and of high insulating properties. The vulcanite handles on the brass rods permit the length of the gap to be varied while sending. Spark terminals are of zinc, and fitted with radiation fins. Price **8/6** Post 3d. Larger and more massive gap for stations up to 2 K.W. **32/6**

Zinc Spark Gap Type "A."

LONDON MADE.

For coils up to 2-inch spark

Base of polished mahogany, standards lacquered brass, spark lugs of zinc. Fitted with vulcanite handles, so that the length of the gap can be varied while sending.

Price .. **2/6** Post 2d.

Vertical Spark Gap.

LONDON MADE. Ebonite base, standards and knob zinc spark lugs, brass terminals and adjusting screw. Price .. **5/6** Post 3d.

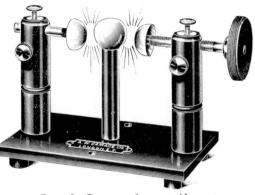

Spark Gap. LONDON MADE.

For Coils up to ½ K.W.

Ebonite Base and Ebonite Pillars, Micrometer, Adjustment, Zinc Spark Lugs. Price **18/6**

Fitted with radiation fins and two adjustable Micrometer rods and handles since illustration made.

Rotary Spark Gear. ¼ K.W.—1 K.W. LONDON MADE.

This Instrument produces a pure musical note, and is a great advantage where power is limited. The Bearing is extra long and is fitted with a lubricator. Suitable for direct belt or gear drive. Base of Marble, and all insulated parts of best Ebonite.

Price **75/-**

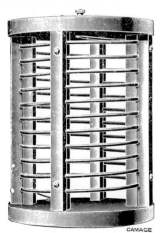

Transmitting Helix. LONDON MADE.

Complete with two clips.

Polished mahogany woodwork, with aluminium helix

8 in. by 10½ high. **17/6** Carriage 6d.

Do. 5 in. by 9 high. **12/6** „ 4d.

Helix Clips, **10**d. each.

Enclosed Spark Gap.

Mounted on Heavy Porcelain Insulator.

Price .. **15/-** Carriage 9d.

Spark Coils for Wireless Telegraphy.

ENGLISH MADE.

Our Coils are section wound on Ebonite Tube and specially constructed for Wireless work, the greatest care being taken in the winding and insulation. The Interruptors are of a patented design, fitted with platinum contacts, giving a high musical note essential for the best results.

½ in.	1 in.	2 in.	3 in.	4 in.	6 in.
18/6	31/-	60/-	£4 3	£5 5	£9 5

N.B.—All Coils are fitted with Primary Condensers and Commutators.

Portable Wireless Stations.

Portable Wireless Transmitting and Receiving Station.

Specification.—TRANSMITTING RANGE, 5-10 MILES.

Receiving Range up to 300 miles.

TRANSMITTING.—Wireless Coil high tension Condenser, with Terminals mounted on ebonite, Spark Gap mounted on ebonite, helix with two Clips, Sending Key with ebonite Protector.

RECEIVING.—Double Slide Tuning Inductance, Crystal Detector, Blocking Condenser, and 1,000 Ohms Wireless Head Gear.

The Apparatus is finished throughout in first-class style, all woodwork polished Mahogany. Brasswork burnished and lacquered.

Price **£12 10 0**

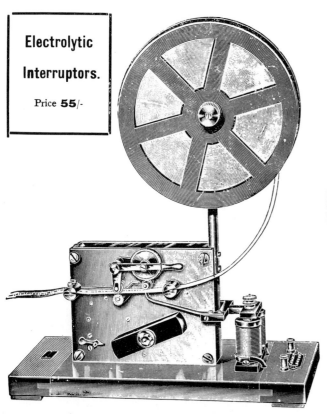

Electrolytic Interruptors.

Price **55/-**

Morse Writing Apparatus.

Well finished and accurately constructed (similar to that used by Post Office), with regulated clockwork stop key and glass cover.

Complete with ink wheel, paper drum, etc.

Mounted on wooden base.

Suitable for use with Wireless or Ordinary Field Telegraphs.

Price **42/-**

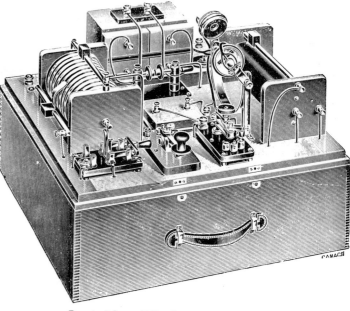

Portable Wireless Station.

Specification.—TRANSMITTING RANGE, 8-12 MILES.

TRANSMITTING.—Special Wireless Coil, with high speed Interrupter and two high tension Condensers, spark gap mounted on ebonite and fitted with radiators, sending helix of copper ribbon wound on vulcanized fibre cylinder, and fitted with two sliding Selectors, change-over switch (from Transmitting to Receiving) mounted on ebonite, and fitted with lightning conductor device to enable aerial connections to be earthed. Sending key with ebonite protector.

RANGE, 300 MILES.

RECEIVING—Two Slide Variable Inductance wound on prepared solid core and fitted with two slide selectors, Crystal Detector mounted on ebonite base and fitted with four crystals and gold point selector, cups arranged to enable crystal combination, Blocking Condenser, pair of double pole high resistance (2,000 ohms) Wireless Phones.

Both the Transmitting and Receiving apparatus is mounted on a polished mahogany base, and has a dovetailed polished mahogany cover with leather handle. Size over all, 22¼ by 19¾ b8¼ in.

Price **£18 10 0**

Transmitting and Receiving Outfits.

We do not make any exaggerated statements regarding the range of our Wireless Outfits.
They will and have given better results.

TRANSMITTING SET.

(Range 1—2 miles).

No. 1. This Set comprises 1 in. Spark Coil (our special wireless pattern with switch), Leyden Jar Condenser, Sending Helix (mahogany woodwork with aluminium Helix), Zinc Spark Gap, 4 volt 20 ampere Accumulator, Wireless Key with ebonite protector.

A well insulated 4-wire Aerial 30—50 ft. above ground should be used, and wire for same is included.   Price **£4 4 0**

TRANSMITTING SET.

(Range 3—5 miles.)

No. 2 Set consists of a Special 1 in. high speed Wireless Coil, Sending Helix, Two-glass Leyden Jar Condensers, High efficiency Spark Gap mounted on Ebonite, 8 volt 20 ampere Accumulator, Wireless Tapping Key, and Double Pole Double Throw Switch mounted on Porcelain, with sufficient insulators and wire for constructing Aerial.

Aerial Masts should, if possible, be 40—60 ft. above the ground to obtain best results. Price **£5 5 0**

TRANSMITTING SET.

(Range 5—10 miles.)

No. 3. This will undoubtedly be a very popular Outfit and one which we can recommend with every confidence.   The apparatus, which is of really good sound construction throughout is as follows :   2 in. Box pattern Wireless Coil with Switch, Sending Helix, Adjustable Leyden Jar, Condenser with 4 Capacities, Zinc Spark Gap mounted on Ebonite, Wireless Key, 8 volt 40 ampere Accumulator, Double Pole Double Throw Switch mounted on Porcelain, Insulators and Wire for Aerial. Price **£7 10 0**

TRANSMITTING SET.

(Range 15—20 miles.)

No. 4. A really nice installation for anyone wishing to fit up a permanent Station.   The instruments comprise our Special 4 in. Box pattern Wireless Coil, Large Sending Helix, Adjustable Condenser, Special Spark Gap, Wireless Key, 8 volt 40 ampere Accumulator, Double Pole Double Throw Porcelain Switch, Insulators and Wire for Aerial.   Price **£12 0 0**
Aerial Mast should be 50—60 ft. above ground.

RECEIVING OUTFIT.

(Range 60—100 miles.)

No. 1. With this Set a 4 wire Aerial 35—50 ft. above the ground is necessary to get good results.

The installation consists of the following instruments : Single Slide Tuning Coil, Crystal Detector with Gold Point Selector, 1,000 ohm Single Head Phone with headband, 250 ft. of Aluminium Aerial Wire, and 6 No. 2 insulators.

This Set is tuneable and capable of receiving signals from a greater distance than stated above if correctly installed with a good Aerial. For diagram of connections see illustration in this List.   Price **£2 5 0**

RECEIVING OUTFIT.

(Range 100—200 miles.)

No. 2. In this Set there is a Double Slide Tuning Inductance which aids materially to cut out unwanted signals and Static interference.

The instruments comprising this Outfit are a Double Slide Tuning Inductance (as supplied by us to the G.P.O.), Crystal Detector with Four Crystals and Gold Point Selector, 2,000 ohm Single Telephone with head band and cushion.   Fixed Condenser with Three Capacities, 250 ft. Aluminium Aerial Wire, Six No. 2 Insulators, Testing Buzzer and Key. Price **£3 15 0**
A 4 Wire Aerial 40—50 ft. above the ground should be used to get good results.

RECEIVING OUTFIT.

Range 500 miles.

No. 3. For those requiring a good experimental Station, we recommend the following apparatus :   Triple Slide Tuning Inductance, Electrolytic Detector, Potentiometer, 2,000 ohms Double Head Gear Commercial Phones, Dry Cell, Rotary Variable Condenser, Fixed Condenser with Three Separate Capacities 250 ft. Aluminium Aerial Wire, and Insulators. Price   ..   **£7 0 0**
The Aerial Masts should be 50—60 ft. above the ground to get good results.

RECEIVING OUTFIT.

No. 4. This Outfit when properly installed, and if located in a favourable position has an exceedingly long range, and is most sensitive and selective, the Oscillation Transformer enables the operator to cut out all undesirable stations with great facility and eliminate static interference.

The Outfit comprises the undermentioned instruments, all of which are of the best make and finish : Oscillation Transformer, Two Variable Condensers, Crystal Detector, Electrolytic Detector, Potentiometer, Fixed Condenser, Two Batteries, Two Switches, 4,000 ohms Double Head Phone, 110 yards 3/19 Phosphor Bronze Aerial Wire and Insulators.   Price **£12 12 0**

NOTE.—All Outfits comprise the instruments mentioned only, and are not connected in any way, but a diagram is supplied if required, showing how instruments are coupled.

Prices for Bamboo Masts and Accessories will be found on another page.

WIRELESS TELEGRAPH (No. Ty. 10250.)

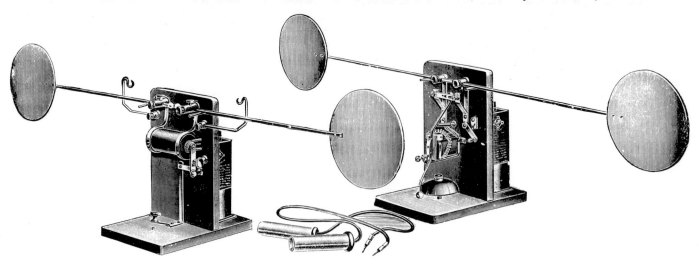

Complete Apparatus for Wireless Telegraphy.

Consisting of—

Sender with Tapping Key, Spark Coil, and Condensers.

Receiver with Coherer, Electric Bell with Decoherer.

Both Sender and Receiver fitted with Antennae and Aluminium discs, and with dependable batteries. Working capacity up to about 10 yards distance.

The Sender is provided with a pair of handles thus converting it into an Induction or Electrifying Apparatus when required, and with a pair of brass hooks to take Vacuum tubes.

Price .. .. **16/6** Postage 10d.

Wireless Distance Switch.

This apparatus is connected with both the receiver of a wireless telegraphy station and with any other objective such as electromotor, incandescent lamp, electric bell, etc. This apparatus can be worked or disconnected through the electric waves from the sender by means of the receiver of the wireless station; also suitable for setting electric railways to work.

Original and instructive, fitted for 5 connections, on polished wooden base 5⅛ in. long 4¾ in. wide. Price **7/6** each. Postage 4d.

Complete Apparatus for Wireless Telegraphy.

No. Ty. 14757/1.

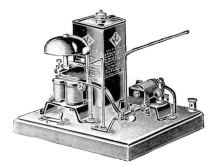

Sender. No. Ty. 13757. Receiver.

Complete Apparatus for Wireless Telegraphy.

Consisting of **Sender** with Tapping Key, Ruhmkorff-Spark-Coil, Condenser, Durable Dry Battery, Air Wire and **Receiver** with Coherer, **Relay,** Electric Bell, Disconnector, Air Wire and Dry Battery and clamps, to be connected with a Morse Writing Apparatus.

Everything finely finished, mounted on polished wooden bases and packed in strong box, working excellent over a distance of 20 yards, furnished with an explicit and interesting description of Wireless Telegraphy.

Price .. .. **25/-** each.

Wireless Telegraph Set

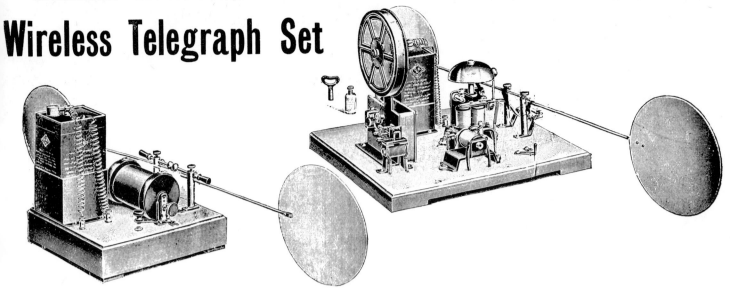

Complete Apparatus for Wireless Telegraphy with Morse Writer.

Consisting of—

Sender with Tapping Key, Spark Coil and Condensers.
Receiver with Coherer, Relay, Electric Bell, Decoherer.
Morse Writing Apparatus with powerful Clockwork and Stop Key.
Both Sender and Receiver are fitted with Antennae and Aluminium Discs (to increase the radius of action) and durable batteries.
The Apparatus will work up to 20 yards.
Explicit and interesting description and history of Wireless Telegraphy in general supplied with each Apparatus.

Price .. .. **39/6** Carriage 1/-

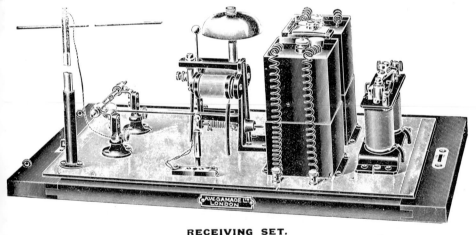

RECEIVING SET.

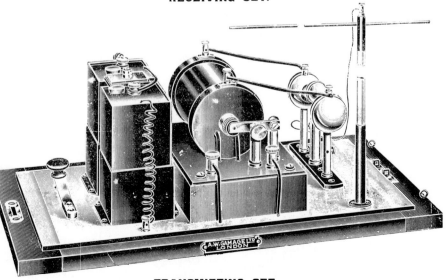

TRANSMITTING SET.

No. Ty. 10201.

Complete Apparatus for Wireless Telegraphy, consisting of Transmitting and Receiving Station.

(IMPROVED MODEL.)

Transmitting Set consists of Tapping **Key**, Spark Coil, Condenser, Aerial and Dry Batteries.

Receiving Station comprises improved Coherer, and Relay Bell, Air Wires with two 8 ft. mast, **Dry Batteries** and Terminal for connecting a Morse Writing Apparatus.

High class finish, strongly constructed and will transmit about 75 yards, mounted on polished wooden base, enclosed in polished cases with lock and key, and furnished with explicit and interesting information.

Complete **90/-**

Special Aerial Outfit for Long Distances.

No. Ty. 10206.

For use with Wireless Telegraph Apparatus, 10201, consisting of two poles about 16 ft. high, with iron ground post, telescopic rods, stays with iron fastening pegs and air wires. By means of these special poles the Wireless Telegraph Apparatus No. 10201 has the capacity of transmitting telegraphic signs about 500 feet, and of giving bell signals 670 feet.

Per Set **42/-**

A set consists of Two Masts, one each for Sender and Receiver.

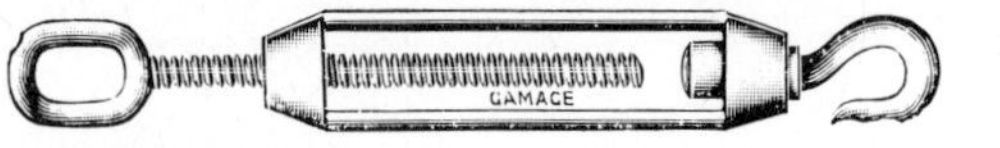

Galvanized Malleable Iron Tightening Screws.

Approx. size of body only	2¾in.	3⅛in.	4¼in.	5⅛in.	6⅛in.	8in.
Prices	**1/6**	**1/6**	**2/3**	**2/9**	**3/6**	**4/6**

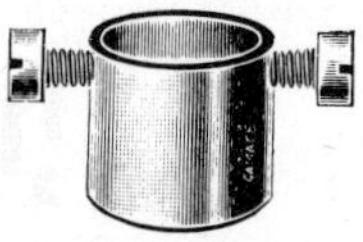

Crystal Cups. Turned brass, burnished and lacquered. Price **6**d. Post 1d.

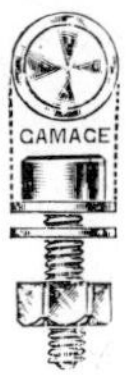

Brass Studs. With nuts and washers. Size as illustration. **2/9** doz.

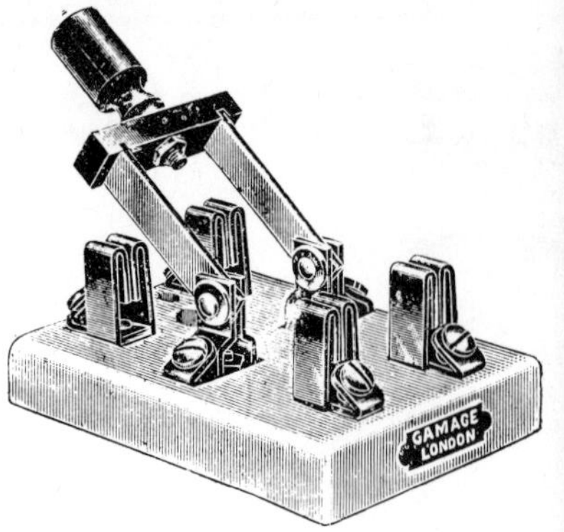

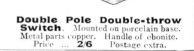

Double Pole Double-throw Switch. Mounted on porcelain base. Metal parts copper. Handle of ebonite. Price ... **2/6** Postage extra.

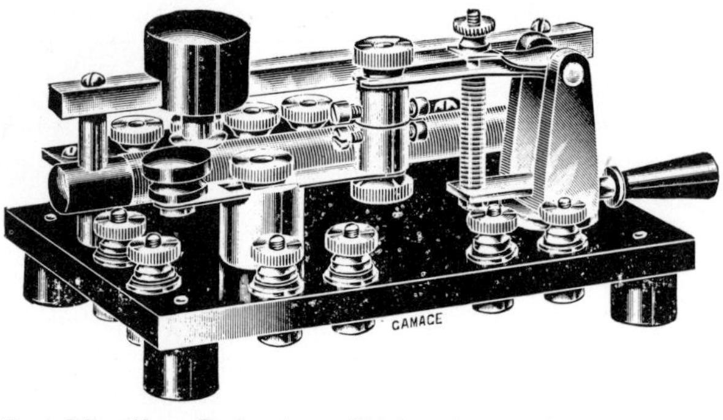

Combination Detector. This is our latest production in Detectors and is a highly sensitive and beautifully finished piece of apparatus. Insulated parts are of polished ebonite, and all metal burnished and lacquered brass. Fitted with Potentiometer and spare interchangeable crystal cups. Price ... **45/-** Post free.

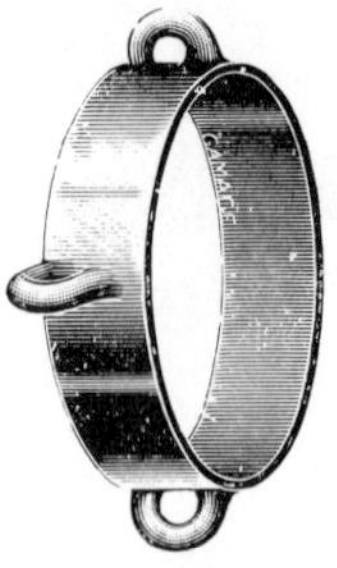

Mast Hoops. Galvanized malleable iron with 1, 2 or 3 eyes.

1½ in.	1¾ in.	2 in.
9d.	**10**d.	**1/-**
2¼ in	2½ in.	3 in.
1/3	**1/6**	**1/9**

3½ in.	4 in.	4½ in.	5 in.
2/-	**3/-**	**3/6**	**3/9**

Inside diameter.

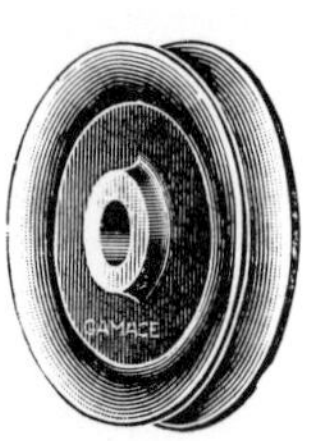

alvanized Malleable Iron **Sheaves,** for masts. ⅞ by ⅜ in. **2**d. 1 by ⅜ in. **2**d. 1½ by ½ in. **3**d. 1¾ by ½ in. **3**d. 2 by ⅝ in. **4** 2½ by ⅝ in. **5**d. 2¾ by ¾ in. **6**d. 3½ by ⅞ in. **10½**d. Postage extra.

Mast Cleats. Galvanized Malleable Iron.

3 in.	3½ in.	4 in.	4½ in.	5 in.	6 in.	7 in.	8 in.	Postag
4d.	**5**d.	**6**d.	**7**d.	**8**d.	**9**d.	**1/3**	**1/6**	3d.

GAMAGE'S PRACTICE BUZZER.

WITH THIS INSTRUMENT one can soon learn the **Morse Code,** and practice the Transmission and Reception of WIRELESS SIGNALS without any further apparatus; the strength and pitch of signals can also be altered in a moment by means of thumbscrews at the side and ends of cabinet.

Price - 21/-

WITHOUT PHONES.

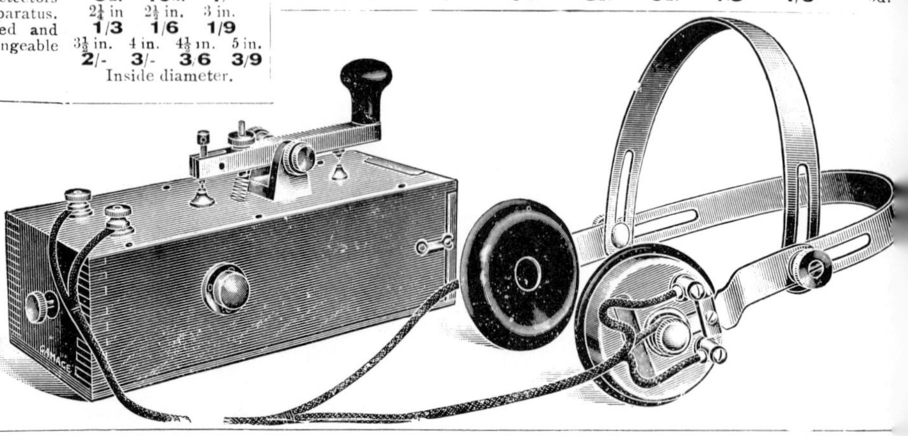

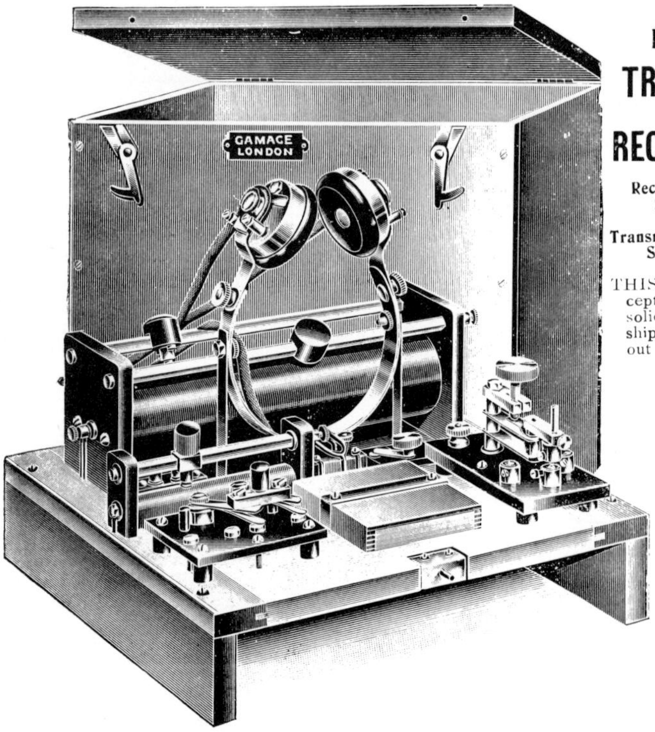

Portable

TRANSMITTING AND RECEIVING SETS

Receiving Set **£9 9s.**

Transmitting Set **£15 15s.**

THIS OUTFIT is of exceptional strength and solidity, and the workmanship and materials throughout are of the very BEST

These sets were originally designed by us for transport on mule-back in a tropical country where they would be subjected to very rough usage. Having proved so efficient we decided to continue their manufacture for Home use.

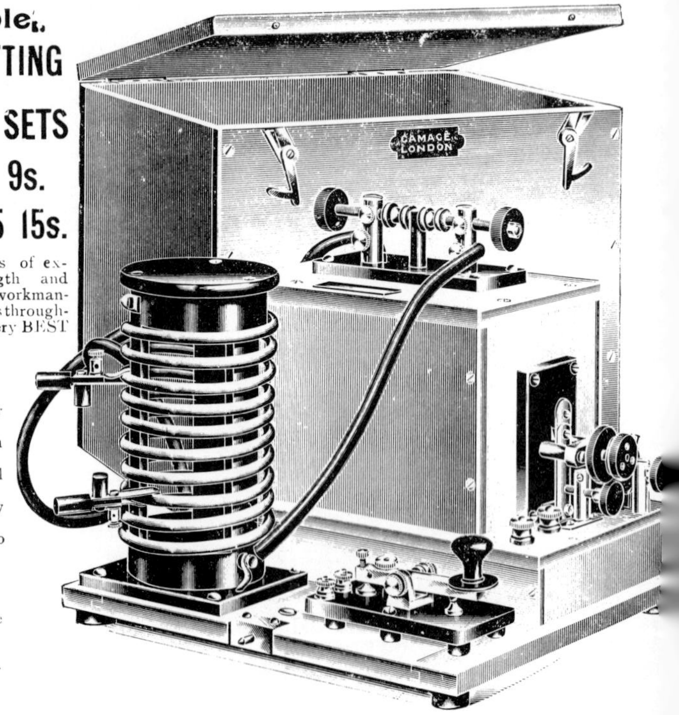

SPECIFICATION

Receiving—Two-slide inductance with ebonite mountings
Crystal Detectors mounted on ebonite with four combinations,
Potentiometer with ebonite slider, knob and ends
Ebonite Switch for cutting out Potentiometer and Local Battery
Change-over Switch for Sending to Receiving
Blocking Condenser and 2,000 Ohms Double Headgear

Sending—High-speed Wireless Coil with Patent Interruptor
Series Spark Gap mounted on ebonite
Oscillation Transformer of Copper Tube, mounted on ebonite
Sending Key mounted on ebonite
Bases and Cabinets of teak

Sounders, Coherers, Relays, etc.

Potentiometer. LONDON MADE

The Potentiometer is used to regulate the voltage and current supplied to detectors, and is necessary for long distance work with most types. Total resistance about 200 ohms. A special form of contact prevents wearing away of resistance rod but always maintains perfect connection. Vulcanite slider rod. Finish, lacquered brass and polished mahogany. **7/6** Post 3d.

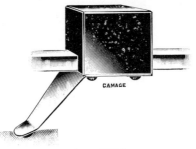

Ebonite Sliders,

LONDON MADE.

With Contact Spring fitted, for Tuning Coils.

Price .. .. .. **2/-** each.

Blocking Condensers.

With Ebonite Insulation.

LONDON MADE.

Total Capacity ·001, ·002, ·003 or ·034 M.F.

Price .. **3/-** each. Post 3d.

Standard Pony Relay.

Mounted on polished mahogany base with metal subbase, will work with perfect accuracy. Recommended when main line sounders fail to give satisfaction. Takes very little current.

0 Ohms. for Lines up to 10 miles, **15/-** Post 5d

5 ,, ,, 30 to 50 ,, **17/6** ,, 6d.

Learner's Outfit.

Comprising Sounder and Key, working from one cell. Improved pattern with Switch.

Price .. .. .. **9/-** Post 5d.

Superior instrument, G.P.O. pattern Sounder and Key mounted together on Mahogany Base with Battery Terminals.

Price .. .. **10/6** Post 5d.

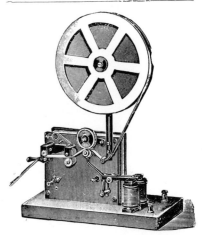

Morse Writing Machine.

With strongly constructed mechanism, enclosed in brass case, lever to stop paper, ink wheel and aluminium paper reel, mounted on polished wooden base.

Total height, 10 in. **17/6** Post 4d.

Smaller and more cheaply constructed Morse Writing Machine, similar design,

Price **7/6** Postage 4d.

Wireless Coherer.

This instrument is exact size as illustration, it has received signals up to 3 miles. The Coherer system of Wireless Telegraphy leaves a big field open to the experimenter as with the Detector Crystal system, it is not possible to call up a station by bell signals as with the Coherer apparatus, the operator being compelled to have the 'phones on continuously.

Price .. **3/-** Post 4d.

Filings for Coherers **4**d.

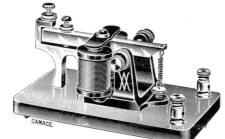

TELEGRAPH SOUNDER.

LONDON MADE.

This sounder is designed specially for Amateur and Private Line work, but can be used in any telegraph circuit. The lever and anvil are of hardened brass and give a clear, sharp sound when operated. It is a well constructed and finished instrument and will give satisfactory service.

Sounder, 5 ohms .. price **5/-** Postage 4d

Sounder, 20 ohms .. ,, **6/-** ,, 4d.

Wireless Coherer.

With bell as used on our 10201 Wireless Set polished base. 9½ in. long, 6½ in. wide.

Price .. .. **10/6** Postage 4d.

TELEGRAPH SOUNDER. G.P.O. Pattern.

LONDON MADE.

Unequalled for quick action, loudness and clear tone.

One cell will operate this instrument, producing a sound louder and clearer than most instruments with two cells.

The clear and distinct sound of this instrument makes it very popular with expert telegraphers.

Sounder, 5 ohms, brass lever, each, **12/6**

,, 20 ohms, ,, ,, ,, **13/6**

Postage 4d.

👉 Leading-in Tubes.

Glazed Vitrified Stoneware, ¾ by 18 in., **1/-** each
Do.   Flanged,   do.   **1/3** ,,
Carriage forward.

Bends charged as 3 feet of straight pipe.

Reel Insulators. Brown Glazed Vitrified
Stoneware. Diam. 1¼ in., **1/-**; 1¾ in. **2/-**;
2 in., **3/-** doz. Carriage forward.

"Leading-in" Insulator.	"Leading-in" Insulator.
With brass core and lock-nut.	With centre bored to take cable.
Price .. **10/6**	Price .. **5/-**
Postage extra.	Postage extra.

Aerial Insulators.

These Insulators have deep corrugations which reduce surface leakage; used at commercial wireless stations heavy galvanized iron rings moulded into ends.

No. 1 will stand a discharge of 20,000 volts, and a mechanical strain of 700 lb.

No. 2 will stand a discharge of 30,000 volts, and a mechanical strain of 1,500 lb.

No. 3 will stand a discharge of 65,000 volts, and a mechanical strain of 1,500 lb.

No. 1—3 in. long by 2 in. diam.	**1/9**	Post 3d.
No. 2—5 in. long by 1½ in. ,,	**2/6**	,, 4d.
No. 3—10½ in. ,, 1½ in. ,,	**3/-**	,, 5d.

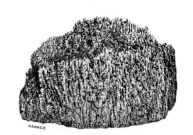

CRYSTALS (Selected).

Fused Silicon	**9**d.	Per specimen
Bornite	**6**d.	,,
Copper Pyrites	**7**d.	,,
Carborundum	**4**d.	,,
Galena	**2**d.	,,
Iron Pyrites	**3**d.	,,
Erubescite	**6**d.	,,
Molybdenite	**6**d.	,,
Pure Zincite	**1**/-	,,
Fusible Alloy (Wood's Metal), for fixing crystals into Detectors	**6**d.	per piece.
Tellurium	**2 6**	,,

GOOD Crystals are rare but we supply them.

Fixed Receiving Condenser.

This fixed condenser is arranged in 3 sections each of ·020 M.F. which are not connected in any way within the case. The leads of each section are brought out to a pair of binding posts mounted on the cover of the case. Five separate capacities are therefore available, which is an advantage where close tuning is required. The case is of mahogany, and the binding posts are lacquered brass. A fixed condenser may be used in the place of a variable condenser, but does not permit of such accurate adjustment.   Price .. **7/6**

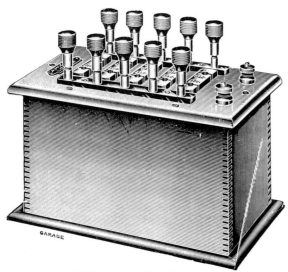

Primary Condenser.

For transmitting up to 4 ins. spark and for receiving; ten capacities, 5 of ·037 m f. and 5 of ·070 m.f. High insulation, first-class finish and efficiency. Price .. **35/-** Post free.

This Condenser must be connected across make and break when used as a Coil Condenser

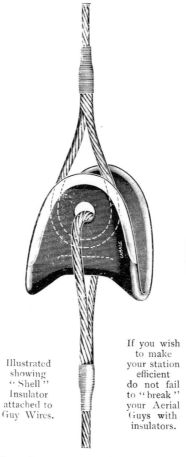

Illustrated showing "Shell" Insulator attached to Guy Wires.

If you wish to make your station efficient do not fail to "break" your Aerial Guys with insulators.

Our Aerial Shell Insulators are particularly suitable for "breaking" the Guy wires of Antennae masts having great strength, and if broken will not allow wire to part.

Aerial Shell Insulators.

This an extremely good Insulator, which, owing to its design, reduces the effects of dampness to a minimum.

	No. 1	2	3
Weight	3½ ozs.	8½ ozs.	30 ozs.
Length	2 in.	3¼ in.	5¾ in.
Breakdown { Dry ..	21,000	38,000	48,000
Volts. } Wet ..	10,000	20,000	28,000
Mechanical Strain, lbs.	2,650	4,000	10,000
Price, dozen	**4/-**	**6/6**	**23/-**

Carriage forward.

Wireless Telephones and Signalling Apparatus.

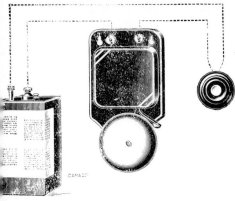

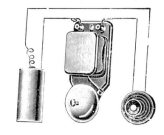

Gamage's Holborn Bell Set.

really soundly constructed and practical article.
th large size nickelled Bell, mounted on japanned
n base, well insulated wire, push and export battery
o action takes place until water is placed in cell).
A splendid example of Gamage value for money.
Price **3/6**   Postage 4d.

Wireless Loud Speaking Receiver.

Large Double-pole Receiver, fitted in Polished Hardwood
Case, with terminals, and including sound director screwed
into top of Receiver Case.

It this instrument be used in conjunction with a suitable
Relay, wireless signals can be distinctly heard without the
use of a Head 'Phone at a distance of 10 to 20 feet.

Price **£2 5 0**

The Little Giant Bell Set.

Wonderful value as illustration.
Consisting of strongly made Bell, with
nickelled gong, push, battery, and
10 yards of wire.

Price **1/10½**   Postage 3d.

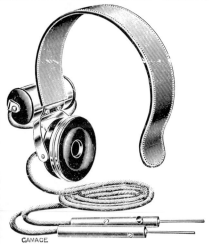

Wireless Telephone Headgear.

Commercial
Pattern, Ball
and Socket
Joints,
minimum
weight,
wound with
50 gauge
copper wire.

Resistances
warranted.

SINGLE
RECEIVER,
with head
band and
cushion.

High Note Buzzer

(size as illustration).

Nickelled Cases, first-
class finish.

Specially constructed for
practicing reception of
Wireless Signals.

Price   ..   **2/9**

Postage 1½d.

This is a combination of a sensitive telephone re-
ver and battery, mounted on a head band.   In use
s placed on the head, and the cord tips touched
the contacts of the circuits to be tested.   The re-
ing "click" or absence of "click" in the re-
ver indicates the presence or absence of complete
ctrical circuit.   Especially handy in a wireless
tion where many tests of this charater are necessary.
eful to test aerial and ground connections, winds
s of spark coils, transformers tuning coils, helices,
eivers, &c.   Indicates short circuits in condensers
d insulation punctures in coil or transformer wind-
gs.   Price   ..   **16/6**   Post 4d

Total resistance 1000 ohms.   .. **16/6**
  ,,   2000   ,,   .. **18/6**
DOUBLE RECEIVER, with adjustable head band.
Total resistance 2000 ohms   .. **29/-**
  ,,   4000   ,,   .. **34/-**
  ,,   8000   ,,   .. **50/-**
Genuine Sullivan 'Phones in stock 2000 to 8000
ohms Double Head Band, **57/6**

BROWN'S Wireless Telephone Relay

In hinged Brass
Case.   Iridium
and Carbon Con-
tacts, resistance
4·400 ohms, or as
required.   When
used in conjunc-
tion with a loud-
speaking receiver,
Wireless Signals
can be heard at a
distance of 10 to
20 ft.

Price—

£12 5 0

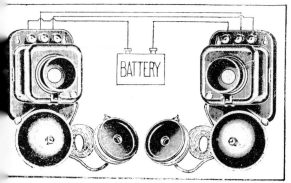

House Telephone Set.

s set is thoroughly well made and is fitted with two sensitive
ceivers and Transmiters enabling every word spoken to be heard
inctly.   Price complete ready for use. with 70 yds. 22 D.C.C.
wire and 2 Batteries, **17/6**   Postage 9d.

Pneumatic Ear Pads.

To fit above receivers, ensures
maximum comfort, **1/6** each.

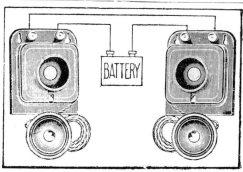

The "Express" Telephone Set.

For use in conjunction with any house bell circuit.
Price without battery or wire, **9/11**
Postage 5d.

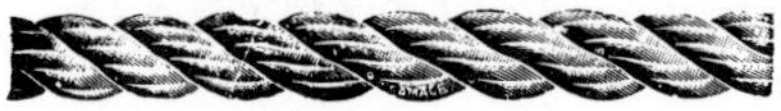

Italian Hemp Line for Aerial Masts. First grade.

Send for sample before ordering elsewhere.

400 lbs. breaking strain, per 100 feet, **3/-** } Post
800 lbs. ,, ,, ,, 100 ,, **4/-** } 3d.

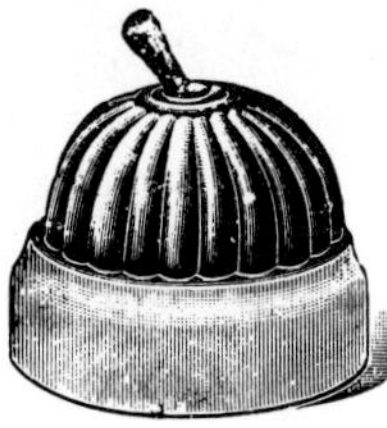

Miniature Tumbler Switch.

On porcelain base with brass cover, 2 in. diameter. Price .. **8**d.

Postage 1½d.

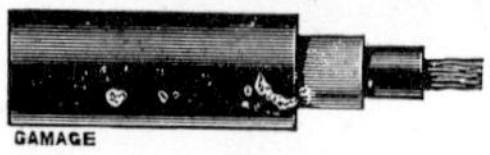

Rubber Insulated Cable for "Leading in."

Diam. 5 m/m, braided, **4**/- doz. yards. Post extr
10 m/m **12**/- doz. yards. do.

A Word about Wires.

A. W. GAMAGE, Ltd. draw attention to the fact that their plain and enamelled Phosphor Bronze Aerial Wires are Admiralt Specification, and further that the enamel has high insulating properties not found in other makes.

The Silcon Bronze Braid is the latest thing in Aerial Wires and has been specially prepared for the purpose. It is relatively light and most easy to handle.

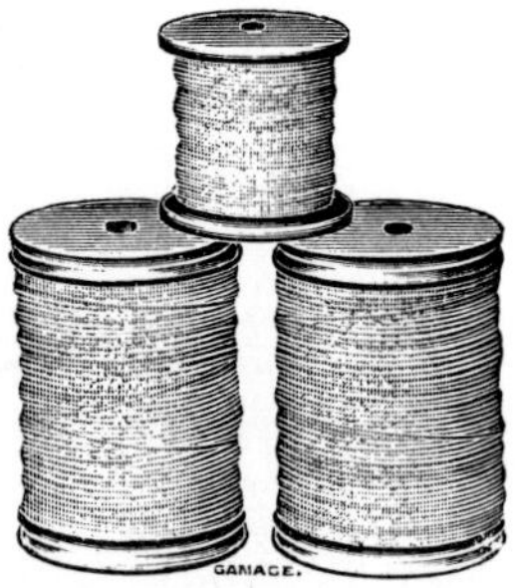

48. **S.W.G. Enamelled Wire** for winding Receivers.

In Bobbins of 1,000 Ohms, **1/3** Post 1d.

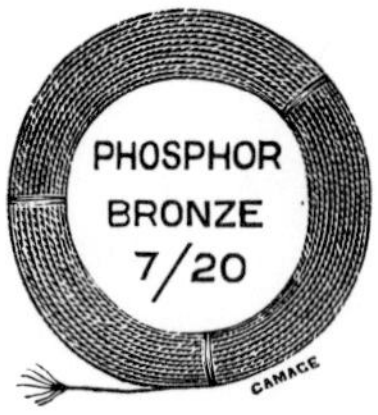

110 yard coils.
Enamelled, **30/-**
Plain .. **25/-**
Carriage forward.

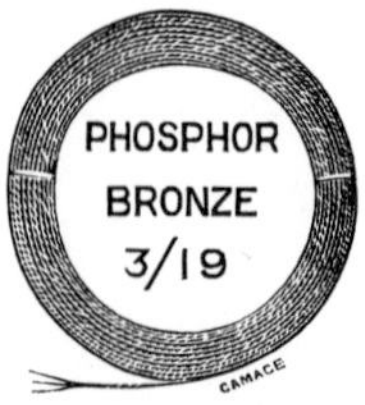

110 yard coils.
Enamelled, **15/-**
Plain .. **12/6**
Carriage forward.

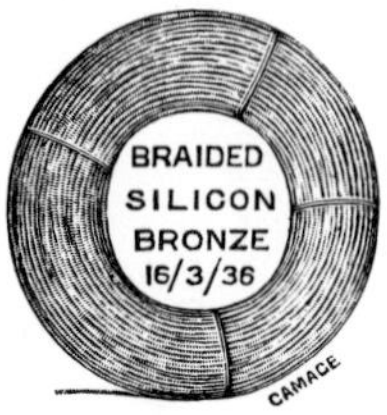

100 yard coils.
16/3/36 plain, **17/6**
16/3/32 do. **27/6**
Carriage forward.

7/22. Plain High Conductivity Hard drawn Copper Wire in 100 yd. coils, **7/6** each.

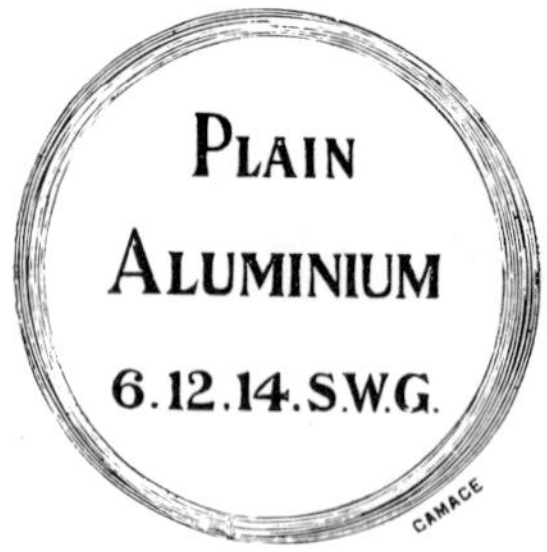

Aluminium Wire.

2/- per lb. Postage extra.

14	16	18	S.W.G.
	270	480	appro feet per lb.

Enamelled Copper Wires.
ADMIRALTY SPECIFICATION.

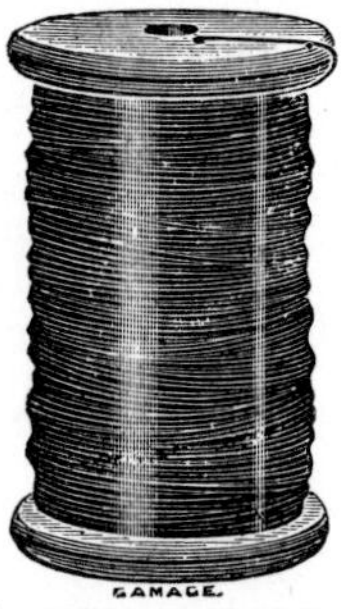

Sizes.	Price.	Yds. per lb. Bare Wire Approrox.
14 ...	**2/-** ...	18
16 ...	**2/-** ...	25
18 ...	**2/-** ...	49
20 ...	**2/3** ...	85
22 ...	**2/3** ...	143
24 ...	**2/3** ...	230
26 ...	**2/6** ...	340
28 ...	**2/9** ...	500
30 ...	**3/-** ...	720
32 ...	**3/6** ...	950
34 ...	**4/-** ...	1300
36 ...	**4/6** ...	1900
38 ...	**7/6** ...	3086
40 ...	**9/6** ...	5200

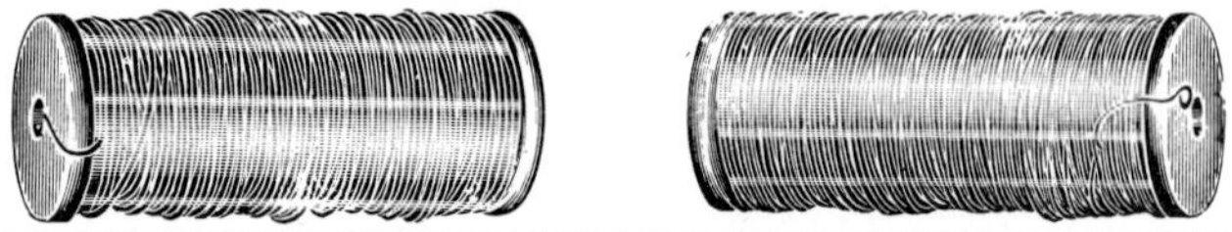

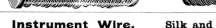

Instrument Wire. Silk and Cotton Covered,
Drawn to Standard Gauge and of Highest Conductivity Copper.

Standard Wire Gauge.	Approx. yards per lb. Bare Wire.	Double Cotton Covered.		Single Silk.	
		Per lb.	Per 4-oz. Reel.	Per lb.	Per 4-oz. Reel
12 ..	10 ..	0 1 2	..	..	0 0 5
14 ..	18 ..	0 1 3	..	..	0 0 5½
16 ..	25 ..	0 1 3	..	..	0 0 5½
18 ..	49 ..	0 1 4	0 0 4	0 1 9	0 0 5½
20 ..	85 ..	0 1 4	0 0 4	0 2 0	0 0 6
22 ..	143 ..	0 1 5	0 0 4½	0 2 0	0 0 6
24 ..	230 ..	0 1 9	0 0 5½	0 2 3	0 0 6
26 ..	340 ..	0 2 0	0 0 6	0 2 6	0 0 7½
28 ..	500 ..	0 2 3	0 0 7	0 3 0	0 0 9½
30 ..	720 ..	0 3 0	0 0 10	0 3 6	per oz. 3½
32 ..	950 ..	0 3 5	per oz. 3	0 4 0	0 0 4
34 ..	1300 ..	0 4 0	0 0 3½	0 4 6	0 0 4½
36 ..	1900 ..	0 5 0	0 0 4	0 4 9	0 0 5
38 ..	3086 ..	0 7 5	0 0 6	0 7 0	0 0 7
40 ..	5200 ..	0 10 0	0 0 9	0 8 0	0 0 8

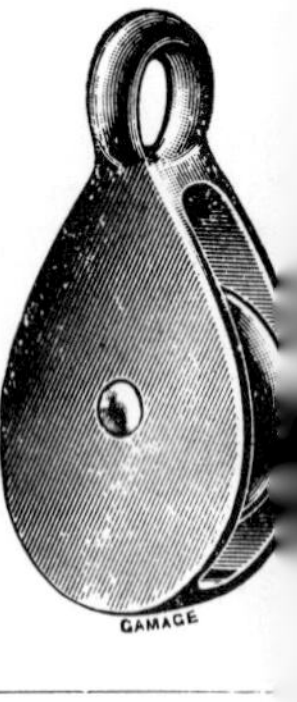

Galvanized Malleable Iron Pulley Blocks

for attaching to masts for raising and lowering aerial

1¼ in...	**6**d.
1¾ ,, ..	**7**d.
2 ,, ..	**9**d.
2¼ ,, ..	**1/-**
2½ ,, ..	**1/3**
3 ,, ..	**1/9**

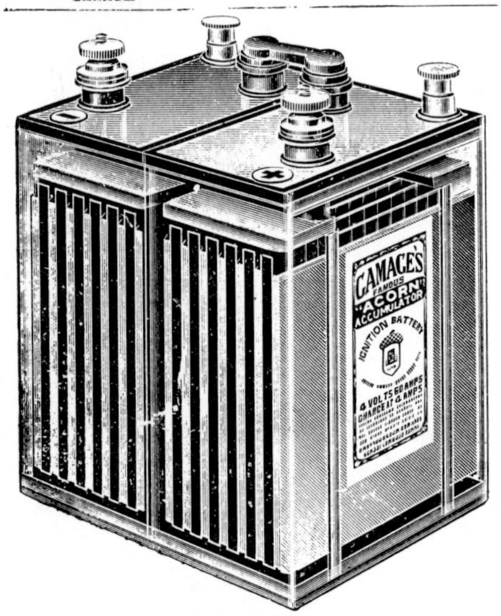

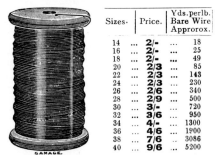

GAMAGE'S "ACORN" Accumulators

4 volts, 20 amperes, 5½ by 4⅛ by 2⅛ in., 6 plates.
Price .. **10/6** Carriage forward.

4 volts, 40 amperes, 5½ by 4⅛ by 3⅝ in., 10 plates.
Price .. **14/6** Carriage forward.

4 volts, 60 amperes, 5½ by 5 by 4⅛ in., 14 plates.
Price .. **20/-** Carriage forward.

Bamboo Aerial Masts, for Wireless.

Length.	Diameter at Butt.	Diameter at Top.	Weight.	Price.
18 ft. ..	1½ in.	About 1 in.	About 4 lbs.	**2/6** each.
18 ,, ..	2 ,,	,, 1½ ,,	,, 7 ,,	**5/-** ,,
24 ,, ..	2½ ,,	,, 1¾ ,,	,, 16 ,,	**9/-** ,,
24 ,, ..	3 ,,	,, 2⅜ ,,	,, 18 ,,	**14/-** ,,
24 ,, ..	3½ ,,	,, 2½ ,,	,, 20 ,,	**20/-** ,,
24 ,, ..	4 ,,	,, 3¼ ,,	,, 26 ,,	**38/-** ,,
35 ,, ..	4½ ,,	,, 3 ,,	,, 41 ,,	**62/-** ,,
35 ,, ..	5 ,,	,, 3¼ ,,	,, 44 ,,	**73/-** ,,
35 ,, ..	6 ,,	,, 3½ ,,	,, 50 ,,	**90/-** ,,
40 ,, ..	7 ,,	,, 3¾ ,,	,, 72 ,,	**130/-** ,,

All Poles Carriage forward direct from Works

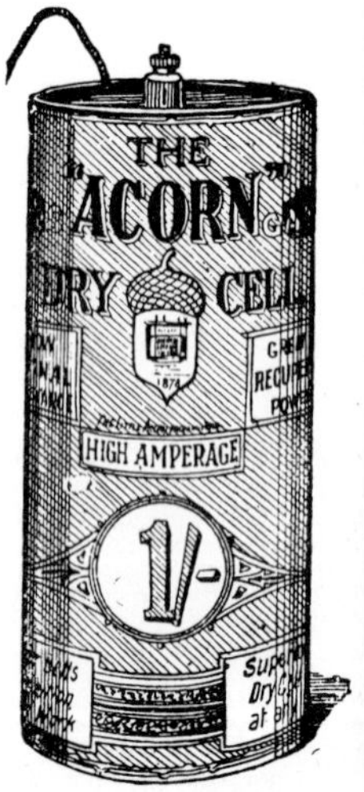

Gamage's "Acorn" Dry Cell.

London Made. Price **1/-** The very best value obtainable. Equal to many Cells in the market at higher prices NOTE.—Low internal resistance, high amperage, great recuperative power. Post 3d

EBONITE TUBES.

¼ in. outside,	⅛ in. inside,	per foot ..	3d.
⅜ in. ,,	⅛ in. ,,	,, ..	3½d
½ in. ,,	¼ in. ,,	,, ..	7d
⅝ in. ,,	⅜ in. ,,	,, ..	9d.
¾ in. ,,	½ in. ,,	,, ..	1/5
⅞ in. ,,	⅝ in. ,,	,, ..	1/-
1 in. ,,	¾ in. ,,	,, ..	1/6

Carriage on above tubes extra.
In stock ebonite rod and sheet, all size .

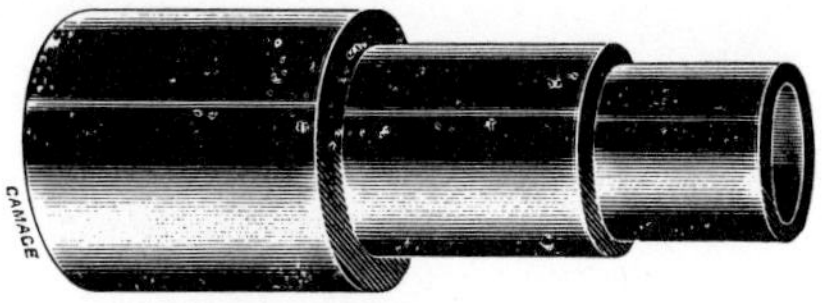

Condenser Foil in Sheets, 12 by 12 in. **1/3** per lb. Post 4d.

Paraffin Wax, Special, 130°, for Sealing Condensers .. **5**d. lb. Post 4d.

Wire Cores, 22 gauge, soft iron wire, in straight 18 in. lengths, **6**d. lb. Post 4d.

EBONITE TUBES.

1⅛ in. outside,	⅞ in. inside,	per foot ..	1/6
1¼ in. ,,	1 in. ,,	,, ..	2/-
1⅜ in. ,,	1⅛ in. ,,	,, ..	2/-
1½ in. ,,	1¼ in. ,,	,, ..	2/-
1⅝ in ,,	1⅜ in. ,,	,, ..	2/-
1¾ in. ,,	1½ in. ,,	,, ..	3/-
1⅞ in. ,,	1⅝ in. ,,	,, ..	3/6
2 in. ,,	1¾ in. ,,	,, ..	4/-

Carriage on above tubes extra.

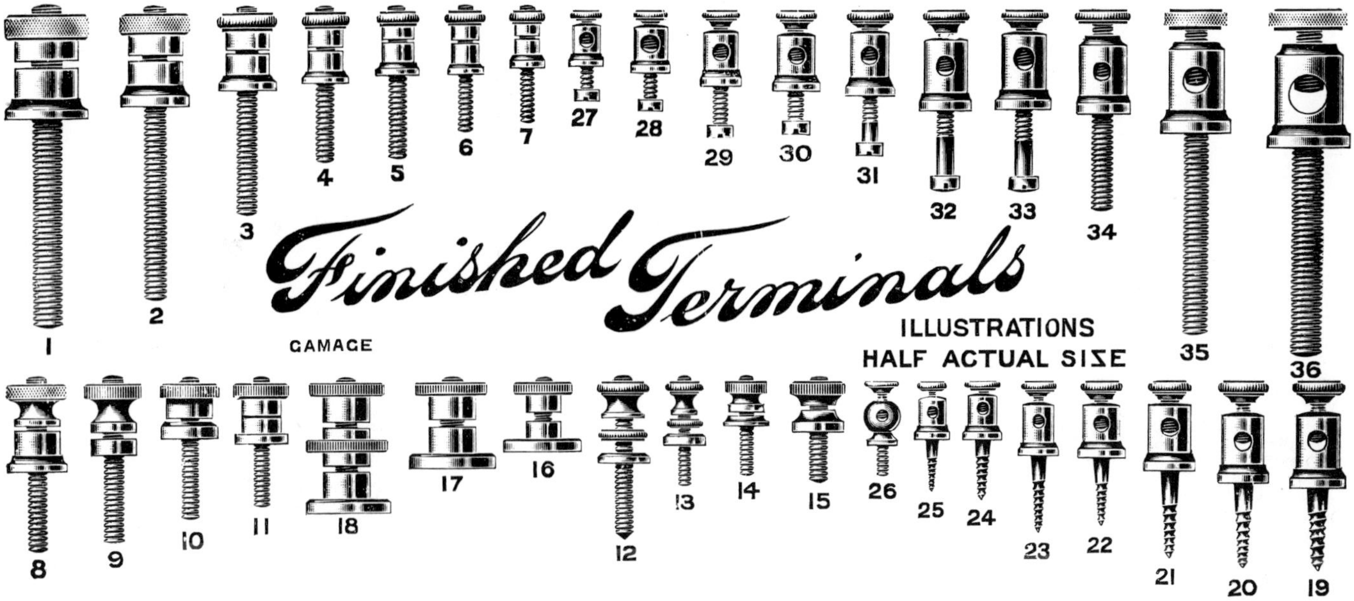

Finished Terminals

ILLUSTRATIONS HALF ACTUAL SIZE

Highly Finished and Lacquered Terminals. London Made.

Fitted with Back Nuts and Washers.

A. W. GAMAGE wish to draw special attention to the fact that the above Terminals are of the very best finish, and every Nut of the same size is interchangeable. ☞ Special quotations given for large quantities and to the Trade.

. 1 ..	**13/-**	doz.	No. 7 ..	**2/-**	doz.	No. 12 ..	**6/-**	doz.	No. 17 ..	**8/-**	doz.	No. 22 ..	**3/6**	doz.	No. 27 ..	**2/9**	doz.	No. 32 ..	**4/9**	doz.
2 ..	**12/6**	,,	,, 8 ..	**5/-**	,,	,, 13 ..	**6/6**	,,	,, 18 ..	**12/-**	,,	,, 23 ..	**3/3**	,,	,, 28 ..	**3/-**	,,	,, 33 ..	**5/-**	,,
3 ..	**5/-**	,,	,, 9 ..	**4/-**	,,	,, 14 ..	**2/6**	,,	,, 19 ..	**5/-**	,,	,, 24 ..	**2/9**	,,	,, 29 ..	**3/6**	,,	,, 34 ..	**5/9**	,,
4 ..	**3/6**	,,	,, 10 ..	**4/-**	,,	,, 15 ..	**3/6**	,,	,, 20 ..	**4/9**	,,	,, 25 ..	**2/6**	,,	,, 30 ..	**3 9**	,,	,, 35 ..	**8/6**	,,
5 ..	**2/10**	,,	,, 11 ..	**3/6**	,,	,, 16 ..	**6/6**	,,	,, 21 ..	**4/-**	,,	,, 26 ..	**2/6**	,,	,, 31 ..	**4/6**	,,	,, 36 ..	**13/-**	,,
6 ..	**2/6**	,,																		

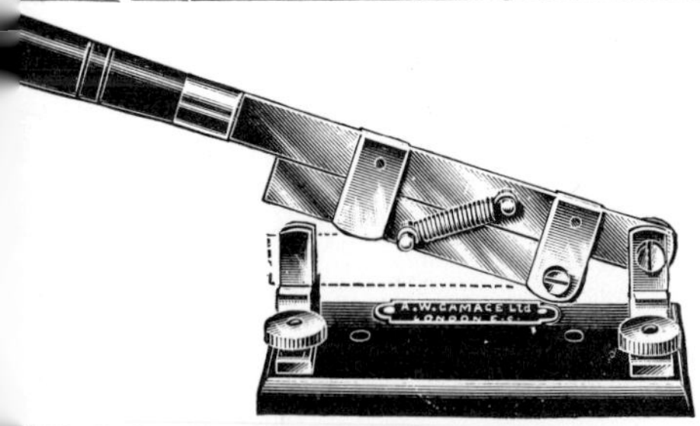

Quick Break Knife Switch.
As illustration. London Made.
Mounted on ebonite base, price, **7/6** Post 3d.

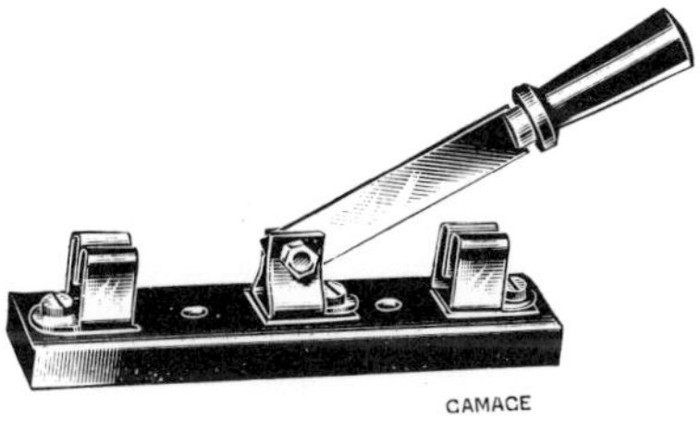

Single Pole Double-throw Switch, mounted on ebonite base. London Made.
Price .. **5 6** Postage 3d.

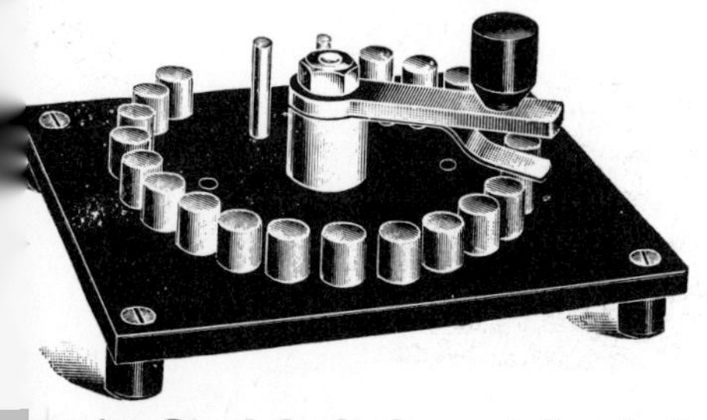

Twenty-Stud Switch, mounted on ebonite base, as illustration. High-class instrument finish. London Made. Price .. **17/6** Post 4d.

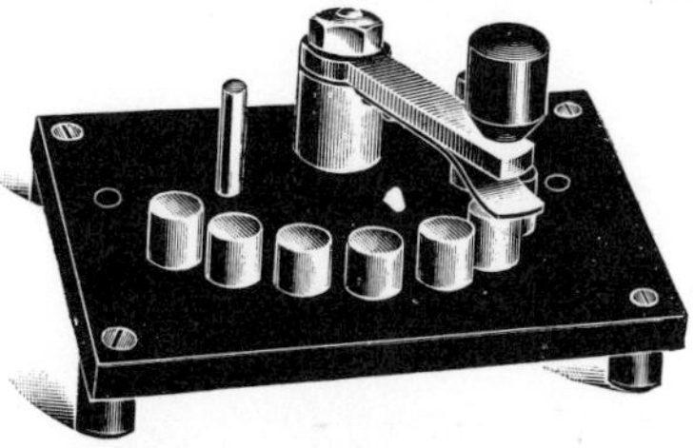

Six-Stud Switch, mounted on ebonite base, as illustration. First-class instrument finish.
London Made.
Price .. **12/6** Postage 4d.

Antennæ or Aerial Switch.

London Made.

Double Pole, Double Switch.
Mounted on ebonite .. **7/6**

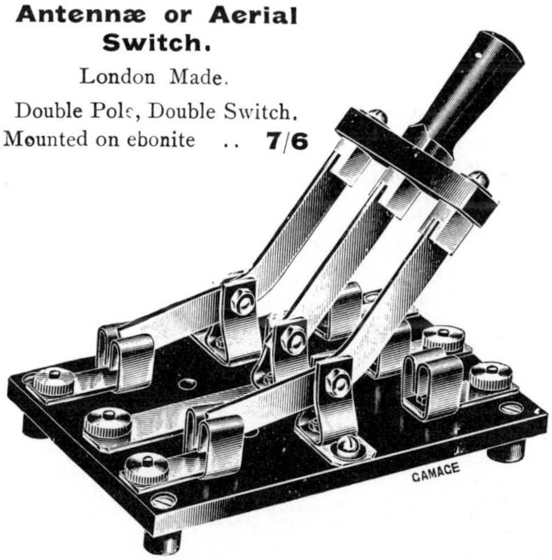

For disconnecting the transmitting apparatus while receiving. The switch has two high tension and three low tension clips, and is so arranged that either a straight away or loop aerial may be used, and several low-tension circuits made or broken.
Mounted on ebonite base. Best workmanship and finish. Suitable for stations from the smallest up to 2 K.W. capacity. No. 1 .. **17/6** No. 2 .. **25/-** Post 4d.

Automatic Morse Code Dictating Machines.

The "Dictamorse" is an Automatic Instrument which sends perfect Morse Signals either in connection with a Buzzer or Sounder and a Battery. It consists of a Clockwork Motor which rotates one or more discs, each being cut in such a manner that it operates a circuit breaker. When used in conjunction with our High Note Buzzer and a Battery, **perfectly Wireless Signals are produced.**

The "Dictamorse" will send at any speed from **10** to **100** words per minute, and, in the case of the Nos. **2** and **3** Instruments, you can change the message in the fraction of a second, even while the Machine is running. The same message may be sent continuously or a fifth part repeatedly.

This Machine sends a Message of 50 Words.

Size 11 by 6 by 5 inches. Weight 5 lbs. Will work with any sounder and operate a Buzzer imitating Wireless.

Price, with set of 5 Records, 63/-

Sounders to suit any "Dictamorse" machine 5/6		12/6
Buzzers .. .. each		2/9
Batteries .. .. ,,		1/-
Extra Set of 5 Record Dials		3/6

The "Dictamorse" No. 2.

The "Dictamorse," No. I,

IS ESSENTIALLY FOR THOSE WHO WISH TO LEARN THE MORSE CODE. :: :: ::

IT CAN BE WORKED BY HAND OR BY THE CLOCKWORK MOTOR, GIVING A VERY WIDE RANGE OF SPEEDS.

Two Discs only are supplied.
Extra Record Dials **6**d. each.

Price - 35/-

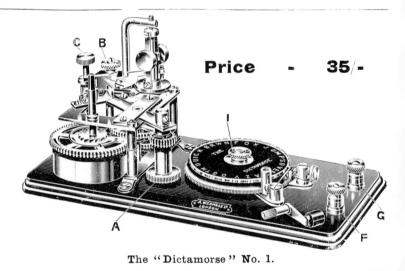

The "Dictamorse" No. 1.

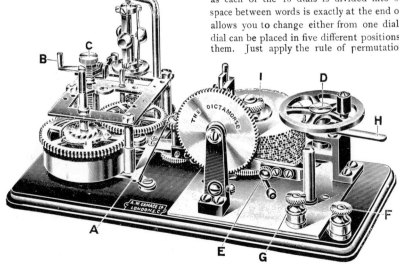

The "Dictamorse," No. 3.

The "Dictamorse," No. 3, has a full Set of 15 dials, equivalent to 75 dials, as each of the 15 dials is divided into 5 equal parts. The message is cut into the metal disc and the space between words is exactly at the end of each section. There are five movable message changers which allows you to change either from one dial to another, or from one word to another, automatically. Each dial can be placed in five different positions on the spindle, the changes are made quicker than you can write them. Just apply the rule of permutation to the "Dictamorse" and you will agree that you can send

Millions of Messages.

The message can be easy or difficult, or you may send what is on each dial continuously and both see and hear. The dials send a straight message of 150 words containing all punctuations, numerals and characters.

Size 11 by 6 by 5 inches. Weight 6 lbs.

Price - - £4 17 6

EXTRA SETS OF 15 RECORD DIALS, **12**/- per Set.

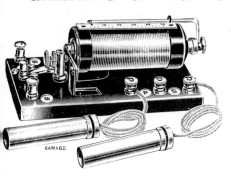

Medical Coil.

Mounted on japanned wrought Iron base, with three terminals for primary and secondary current, regulating scale, etc. All metal parts well nickelled.

A thoroughly reliable and practical article.

Price .. **4/3** Postage 3d.

"Acorn" Dry Battery for use with above, **1/-** Postage 3d.

Improved Magneto Electric Machine.

For stimulating and strengthening the nerves and muscles.

No. 1. With 6 in. magnet and polished wooden box, **9/.** Post 6d.

No. 2. With 7 in. magnet and polished wooden box with lock and key, **12/9** Post 6d.

No. 3. With two 7½ in. magnets, cog-wheel gearing mahogany box with lock and key, **25/-** Post 9d

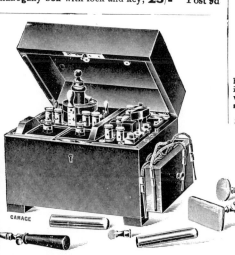

High-class Medical Coil

(Dr. Taub's System).

Fitted with all the latest improvements for regulating, varying and increasing the current. Mounted in polished mahogany case, with lock and key.

Complete with electrodes and dry cells, ready for use. A thoroughly reliable and efficient coil for medical use. Size, 7½ in. by 5½ in. by 5½ in.

Price **59/6** Post free.

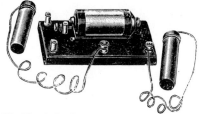

Medical Coil. Mounted on japanned wrought iron base; metal parts nickelled; strong action. Complete with handles, cords and tube regulator. Wonderful Value .. **2/-** Post 3d.

Magneto Machine.

For Rheumatism, Neuralgia, Neuritis, Headache and Stiff Joints. Complete ready for use, as illustration. Price **2/6** Post 3d.

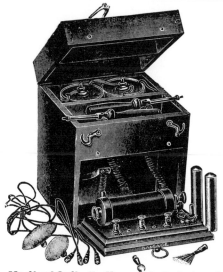

Medical Coil.—For Home and the Profession. A handsome and powerful Coil, fitted with 2 dry batteries in solid walnut polished case. A 2-way switch is supplied which enables the operator to use one or two batteries as required. In addition the slide tube also regulates the current. A full set of electrodes are supplied. Size 7 in. by 6¾ in. by 6¼ in. **22/6** complete. Post 6d.

SPECIAL VALUE. **Handsome Medical Coil,** (as illustration) with primary and secondary currents, electrodes and batteries Complete in polished mahogany cabinet, **17/6** Post 6d.

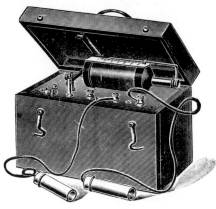

Very Fine Medical Coil.

As illustration. With primary and secondary currents, switch and regulating scale for increasing and decreasing current. In polished mahogany case.

Complete with battery, **10/9** Post 5d.

HIGH-CLASS ENGLISH MADE **Medical Coil.**

Enclosed in polished and screwed Walnut Case with dry cell. This is an exceedingly well made coil and splendid value. It has platinum contact and draw tube for regulating current, also switch.

Price, **21/-** Post free.

Exceptionally Handsome Self-starting Medical Coil.

Fitted with rotary dial regulator (under glass), polished walnut case, 6½ by 6½ in., with carrying strap, primary and secondary currents, button and brush, electrodes and drawer for same, 2 powerful dry cells. Current is automatically cut off when case is closed.

Price .. **21/9** Post 6d.

E

STATHAM'S CHEMICAL CABINETS.

Statham's Boxes of Chemical Magic.

Have been prepared to meet the demand for inexpensive instructive and amusing experiments, free from danger. Each box contains chemical re-agents apparatus, and full instructions for performing a series of experiments, expressly arranged for beginners, and as they can be sent by post to all parts of the globe with perfect safety, they cannot fail to afford a world-wide source of instruction and amusement.

No. 628. Box containing 16 chemicals or
No. 629. 35 chemicals.

628. No. 1. Price 10½d. Postage 2d. List price 1/-
For performing 50 experiments. Weight under 4 ounces. Sent to any part of the world for 10½d. and cost of postage for 4 ounces.
629. No. 2. Price 2/3 Postage 3d. List price 2/6
Sufficient material for performing 100 experiments. Weight under 8 ounces. Sent to any part of the world for 2/3 and cost of postage for 8 ounces.

Statham's Youths' Chemical Cabinets.

Weight from 3 to 4 lb., packed.
No. 1 & 2. Size of case, closed,
6 by 5 by 5 in.
Ditto, open,
12 by 4 by 5 in.

No. 3. Size of case, closed, 6¼ by 5 by 6 in. Ditto. open, 13 by 5 by 6¼ in.
Contain 60 chemical tests and apparatus, without strong acids or other dangerous articles they are safe in the hands of youth, and are admirably adapted as presents, prizes, &c., and for fostering a taste for chemistry in the youthful mind.

831. No. 1. In fancy case, with book of experiments.
Price with book, 7/-   Postage 6d.   List price 7/6
632. No. 2. Pine case, unpolished, with book of experiments.
Price with book, 9/6   Postage 6d.   List price 10/-
683. No. 3. Polished pine case, with lock, with book of experiments.
Price with book, 11/9   Postage 7d   List price 12/6

The Boy's Own Laboratory.

Price with book, 17/- List price 18/- Parcel post, 9d. ex.
634. Size, closed, 11½ by 8 by 3½ in. Weight about 5 lb.

Containing 54 chemical preparations and 30 pieces of useful apparatus, arranged for performing an endless series of instructive and amusing experiments in chemical magic. Stained and polished pine case with tray, lock, etc.

APPARATUS, &c.

Glass spiri lamp	Bohemian flask
Mortar and pestle	Pipette
Triangular crucible	3 glass tubes
	2 glass stirrers
Conical test glass	Litmus paper
	Turmeric paper
Ribed glass funnel	Slip of copper
	Slip of zinc
Packet of filters	Tin foil
Tripod stand	2 glass slips for testing
2 test tubes	Iron rod for ditto
Test tube holder	Copper rod for ditto
Test tube cleaner	Bibulous paper
Tin capsule	
Porcelain evaporating basin	

Students' Chemical Cabinets.

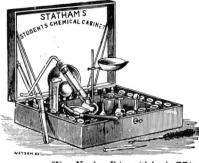

635. No. 1. Price with book, 25/- List price 26/-
Size, closed, 14 by 11 by 4 in. Packing case for country, 9d. Weight about 8 lb., packed.
Fitted up with 36 boxes and 12 bottles filled with chemicals and a large assortment of apparatus of a practically useful size, in all 81 articles carefully arranged, with green varnished labels, in a polished stained pine cabinet with lock, &c.

APPARATUS.

Mortar and pestel	Ribbed glass funnel
Spirit lamp	Packet of filter for ditto
Wick for ditto	
Evaporating basin	2 glass stirring rods
test tubes, assorted	Oxygen tub retort
Test tube cleaner	Watch glass
Test tube holder	Tinned sand bath
Bohemian flask	
Bulb boiling tube	Tinned capsule
2 glass tubes	Cylindrical tes glass
Sheet Litmus paper	Dutch metal
Sheet turmeric paper	Pipette
	Retort stand
Sheet bibulous paper	Hydrogen, &c. gas bottle, fitte

NOTICE.—In this edition it has been found necessary to leave out the "Lists of Chemicals" heretofore given in previous catalogues, the "List or Apparatus" being still retained. Every cabinet and laboratory is supplied with a careful selection of the most generally used re-agents, &c., in accordance with the number of bottles and boxes contained in each set, preference being given to those chemicals necessary for performing the experiments given in Stathams' "First and Second Steps in Chemistry."

Students' Chemical Cabinets.

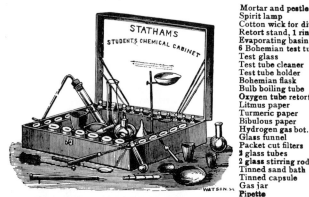

636. No. 2. Price with book, 35/- List price 37/6
Size, closed, 14 by 11 by 4 in. Packing case for country, 9d. Weight about 9 lb., packed.

A handsome polished stained cabinet, fitted with 12 stoppered bottles, and 48 turned wood boxes, filled with 52 chemical tests, &c., and about 30 pieces of apparatus and materials, in all 100 articles. French-polished mahogany cabinet, 3/6 extra.

APPARATUS

Mortar and pestle
Spirit lamp
Cotton wick for ditto
Retort stand, 1 ring
Evaporating basin
6 Bohemian test tubes
Test glass
Test tube cleaner
Test tube holder
Bohemian flask
Bulb boiling tube
Oxygen tube retort
Litmus paper
Turmeric paper
Bibulous paper
Hydrogen gas bot., fitted
Glass funnel
Packet cut filters
3 glass tubes
2 glass stirring rods
Tinned sand bath
Tinned capsule
Gas jar
Pipette
Watch glass
Watch glass holder
Dr. Black's blow pipe
Dutch metal

Students' Chemical Cabinets.

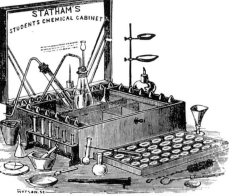

637. No. 3. Price with book, 47/6 List price 50/-
Size, closed, 15½ by 10½ by 5½ in.
Packing case for country, 9d.
Weight of cabinet 12 lb., packed.

Contains 61 chemical preparations and re-agents, in larger bottles an boxes than Nos. 1 and 2, in corked and stoppered bottles and turned wood boxes, and a large assortment of useful apparatus, in a handsome French-polished stained pine case, with tray for boxes and partitions for apparatus, in all about 100 articles.

APPARATUS.

Porcelain mortar & pestle
Spirit lamp
Cotton wick for ditto
Retort stand, 2 rings
Porcelain evaporating basi
1 porcelain crucible
6 Bohemian test tubes
Test tube stand
Test tube holder
Test tube cleaner
Watch glass
Watch glass holder
Red Litmus, Turner
Blue Litmus papers
2 glass rods
3 glass tubes
Bibulous paper
Dutch metal
Tinned sand bath
Tinned capsule
Gas bottle, fitted
Jet for ditto
Clark's test glass
Upright gas jar
Watch glass holder
Iron spoon
Bohemian flask
Bulb tube
Oxygen tube retort
Dr. Black's blow pipe
Glass funnel, 2, 2½ in.
Packet filters, 2½, 3½ in.
Pipette
Deflagrating spoon
Glass boiling flask

PHARMACY ACTS—POISONS.—NOTICE.—Chemicals listed as contained in Statham's Chemical Cabinets, which come within the meaning of the Pharmacy Acts are withdrawn. The boxes or bottles intended to contain them are sent EMPTY.

N.B.—It is necessary to sign purchaser's name (with a witness) in a chemist's poisons book to obtain them.—W. E. STATHAM & SON.

STATHAM'S STUDENTS' CHEMICAL CABINET.

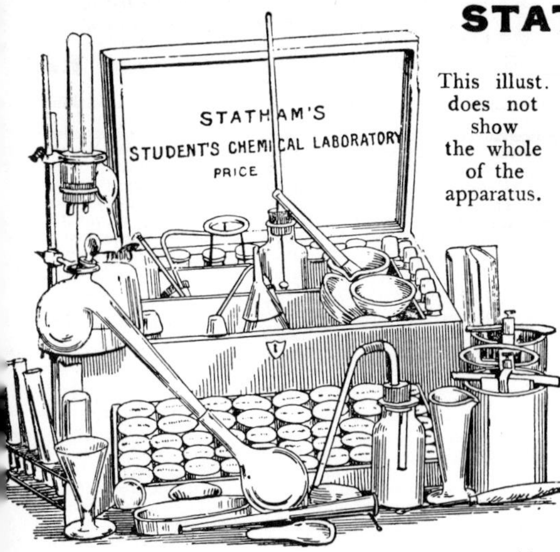

This illust. does not show the whole of the apparatus.

638. No. **4.** Price with book **£4 4 0** Size, closed, 18 by 11 by 6 in. Packing Case, for country, **9**d. Carriage free. Weight, packed, about 18 lbs.

Will be found a good useful working chest. It contains 66 chemical preparations in larger quantities and re-agents in turned wood boxes, and larger size stoppered and plain bottles, with green varnished labels, and is fitted with a very large assortment of apparatus of superior size, comprising the articles necessary for manipulation with the gases, in all about 120 articles; the whole carefully arranged in bottle racks, tray, and appropriate partitions, in a very superio French-polished stained pine cabinet, with lock. French-polished mahogany cabinet, with brass name-plate, lock, etc., **7/6** extra.

List of Apparatus.

Graduatedmeasuregasjar
Porcelain crucible, with cover
Pipette
4 Glass stirring rods
Blue litmus paper
Red litmus paper
Turmeric paper
Glass retort, stoppered
Glass receiver
Battery plates, 3 each
Carbon and zinc
Brass tongs
Gas flask, fitted with funnel and bent tubes
Mounted jet for ditto
Gas receiver, bell
Deflagrating spoon
2 mounted tubes to fit above flask, for use as a wash bottle
2 Bohemian flasks
Bulb boiling tube
Oxygen tube retort and 1 boiling flask
Brass clamps
Spirit lamp
Cotton wick for ditto
Porcelain mortar and pestle
Retort stand, 3 rings
Iron spoon
12 Bohemian test tubes
Test tube stand
Test tube holder
Test tube cleaner
Apparatus to electrolyse water and collect two gases separately
Watch glass
Watch glass holder
3-in. rubber tubing
Dr. Black's blow pipe
Dr. Clark's test glass
Glass funnel, 2 in.
Glass funnel, 2½ in.
Packet cut filters, 2¾ in.
Packet cut filters, 3¾ in.
Porcelain evaporating basin

This Set contains the 3-cell battery minus the outside cells (for which jam pots will answer), also the apparatus for decomposing water by electric current.

Statham's Students' Chemical Cabinet.

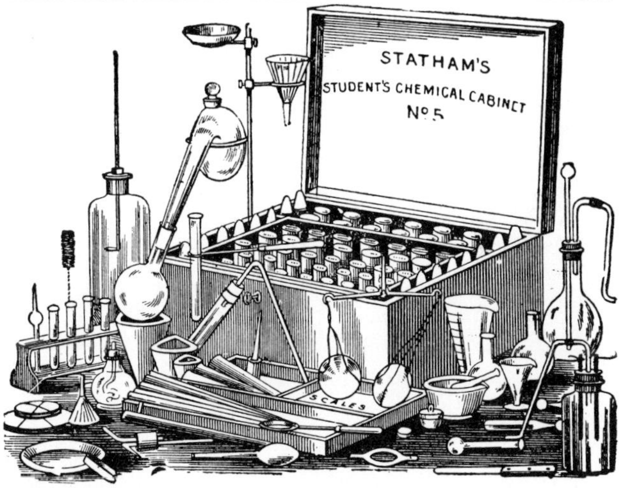

No. **5.** Price **£5 5 0** with book. Size, closed, 18 by 12½ by 7½ in.
Packing Case for country, **9**d. Weight, packed, about, 25 lbs. Carriage free.

This is the latest of the original Students' Cabinets, and besides being larger than No. 4, contains an extra tray for tube apparatus, additional large size bottles of chemicals, and larger apparatus, rendering it more useful. There are over 70 chemical re-agents, etc., in large size stoppered and plain bottles, fitted in racks and turned wood boxes, in tray, and about 77 pieces of apparatus, etc., in all about 150 articles, including those for experimenting with the gases; the whole carefully arranged in a handsome polished stained pine cabinet, having tumbler lock and brass name-plate.

NOTE.—Weight packed does not include the OUTSIDE packing case. **This applies to all Cabinets when weight is given.**

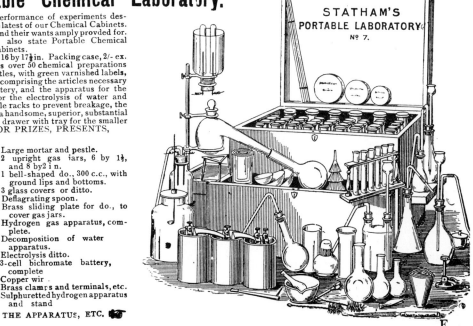

List of Apparatus.

pirit lamp
otton wick for ditto
etort stand, 3 rings
on spoon
test tubes
est tube stand
est tube holder
est tube cleaner
'atch glass
'atch glass holder
raduated measure
ark's ditto
erlin Porcelain crucible and cover
n. rubber tubing
Porcelain capsule
Porcelain evaporating basin, 2¾ in.
Ditto, 3¼ in.
Bulb pipette
2 glass rods, 6 in.
Ditto, 3 in.
6 glass tubes, 8 in.
Book blue litmus paper
Stoppered retort, bell
Receiver for ditto
Flask, fitted with funnel and bent tube for making gases
Porcelain filter support
Glass jet, mounted for do.
Gas jar, bell
Deflagrating ladle
Bohemian flask
Bohemian flasks, 2 & 4 oz.
Bulb boiling tube
Brass tongs
Tinned iron sand bath
Book red litmus paper
Book turmeric paper
Dutch metal
Glass funnel, 2 in.
Ditto 2½ in.
Packet filters, 2¾ in.
Upright gas jar
Packet filters, 3¾ in.
Tinned capsule
Oxygen tube retort
Porcelain mortar & pestle
Dr. Black's blow-pipe
Set of wash bottle tubes
3 hard glass beakers
2 carbon and 2 zinc plates for battery
2 brass clamps
2 brass terminals for ditto

This Set contains the 3-cell battery minus the outside cells (for which jam pots will answer), also the apparatus for decomposign water by electric current.

Statham's Students' Portable Chemical Laboratory.

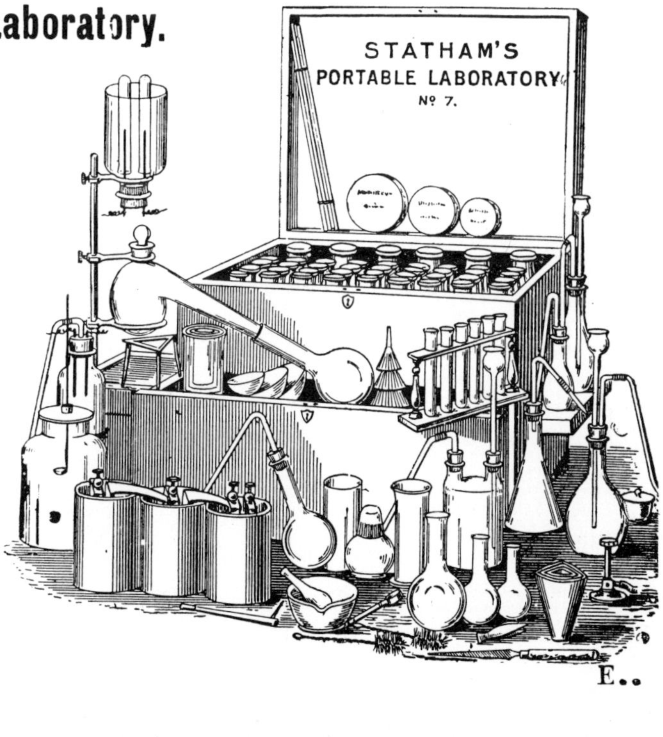

is Cabinet has been prepared with special reference to the performance of experiments described in Statham's "Second Steps in Chemistry," and is also the latest of our Chemical Cabinets. ose, however, who purchase them with more exalted aim, will find their wants amply provded for.
OTE.—Please quote the number and price when ordering; also state Portable Chemical Laboratory, as we have other Students' Chemical Cabinets.

00. No. 7. **170/-** with book. Carriage free. Size of case, 23 by 16 by 17½ in. Packing case, 2/- ex. . L900 will be found a good useful working chest. It contains over 50 chemical preparations d re agents, in large size stoppered and plain white glass bottles, with green varnished labels, d is fitted with a large assortment of apparatus of superior size, comprising the articles necessary manipulation of the gases, including a 3-cell bichromate battery, and the apparatus for the composition of water by an electric current; also apparatus for the electrolysis of water and llection of 2 gases. The bottles are securely packed in double racks to prevent breakage, the paratus in partitioned spaces; the whole carefully arranged in a handsome, superior, substantial e cabinet, stained mahogany and polished, with bottle racks, drawer with tray for the smaller paratus, etc., handles, stop hinges, 2 locks. SUITABLE FOR PRIZES, PRESENTS, mbining Instruction with Amusement. APPARATUS.

cket circular filter papers, , 3¾, and 4½ in.
lass funnels, 2, 2½, 3 in.
lass flasks, 2, 4, 8, and 2 oz.
ass tubing, assorted.
lass stirring rods.
rks, assorted.
iangle file, in handle.
nsen's lamp.
ass receiver.
hemian stoppered glass etort.
ge retort stand, 3 rings, in. rod and tube holder.
of cork borers.
celain Evaporating asins, 2½ and 3½ in.
iam.
st tube brushes
Glass spirit lamp.
Rubber tubing, 3/16 diam.
Nest of 3 Bohemian glass beakers.
Florence flask, 300 c.c.
3 doz. test tubes, 4 by ½, 5 by ⅝, and 6 by ¾
Japanned pneumatic trough with side and beehive shelves.
6-hole teak test tube stand or folding japanned tin ditto.
Pair nickelled orceps.
Test tube holder (brass).
1 rose burner for Bunsen's lamp.
Oxygen flasks, cork and tube.
Wash bottle, complete.
Large mortar and pestle.
2 upright gas iars, 6 by 1½, and 8 by2 in.
1 bell-shaped do., 300 c.c., with ground lips and bottoms.
3 glass covers or ditto.
Deflagrating spoon.
Brass sliding plate for do., to cover gas jars.
Hydrogen gas apparatus, complete.
Decomposition of water apparatus.
Electrolysis ditto.
3-cell bichromate battery, complete
Copper wir .
Brass clamps and terminals, etc.
Sulphuretted hydrogen apparatus and stand

OPEN—SHOWING PART OF THE APPARATUS, ETC. ☛

E..

CHEMICAL CABINETS.

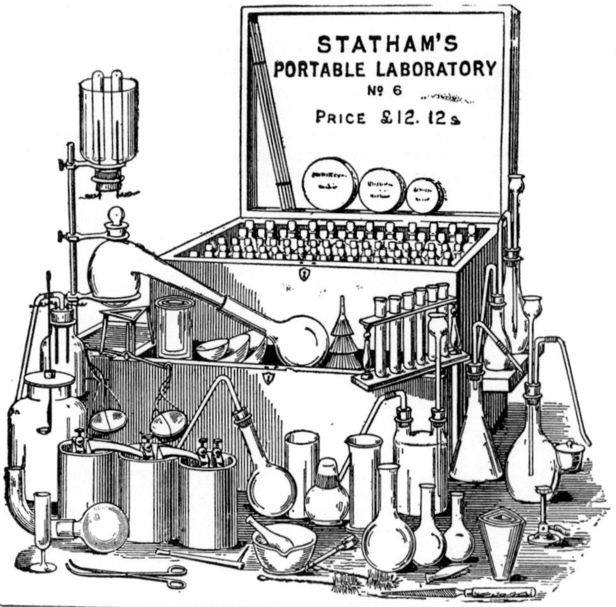

Statham's Student's Cabinet. No. 6. £12 12 0

Size of case, 23 by 16 by 17½ in.   Packing case for country, 1/-

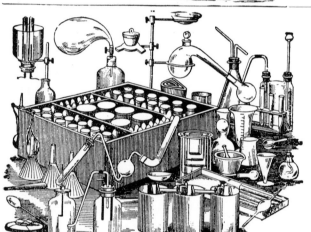

This cabinet is prepared with special reference to the performance of the various operations of qualitative analysis. It contains the necessary re-agents and apparatus for testing in the "humid" way, as also blow-pipe apparatus, fluxes, and tests for the discrimination of minerals, ores, etc. The fluid re-agents are of testing strength and chemically pure and in large size stoppered bottles, as also are those used in blow-pipe analyses, or necessary to be kept in the "dry" state, and are securely packed in double racks to prevent breakage. The apparatus and instruments are of large size, and comprise all that is necessary, and the whole are carefully arranged in a handsome polished stained pine cabinet, having drawer and tray, brass name plate, handles, lock, etc. This cabinet contains about 80 bottles of tests, 136 pieces of apparatus, tubes, etc., in all 216 articles. Polished mahogany case, £1 1 0 extra.

Retort stand, 3 rings	Spirit lamp, with brass screw wick holder	Lead paper	Phillip's precipitating glass
Tube holder for ditto	Cotton wick for ditto	Brazil wood paper	2 cylindrical test glasses
2 wire triangles	5 bohemian beakers	Book starch paper	2 Dr. Clark's ditto
3 evaporating basins	Stoppered retort, 8 oz.	2 iron spoons	Steel spatula
2 porcelain crucibles	Clark's retort	Rat-tail file in handle	Glass Measure, 2 oz.
Steel crucible tongs	Receiver for ditto	Triangular file do.	3 boiling tubes
6 bohemian flasks	Dr. Black's blow-pipe	3 watch glasses	2 chloride calcium tubes
Sulph. Hydrogen Aps. on stand	Blow-pipe lamp	Holder for ditto	Combustion tube
Wash bottle	Lamp Tongs	Ribbed glass funnels— 2, 2½, 3 in.	Wills' nitrogen bulbs
Oxygen retort	2 carbon plates	100 cut filters— 2¾, 3½, 4½ in	2 tinned iron capsules
24 test tubes, assorted	2 zinc plates	Filter support	Gas bottle, fitted with tubes, etc.
Test tube stand	2 brass terminals	6 glass stirring rods	Deflagrating spoon
Test tube holder	2 brass clamps for battery	12 glass tubes, 12 in.	Bunsen gas burner
2 test tube cleaners	6 hard glass tubes	Porcelain mortar and pestle	Brass rose for ditto
Scales, with set of weights in box	Blue litmus paper	Iron sand bath	1 3000 bell gas receiver
6 arsenic tubes	Red litmus paper		Nest 3 clay crucibles
Bulb pipette	Turmeric paper		

This set contains the 3-cell battery, the apparatus for decomposing water by electric current. Apparatus to electrolyse water and collect two gases separately.

Statham's Economic Laboratory

Or Lecturers' and Students' Chemical Vade-Mecum.

No. 1.   Price £7 7 0   Carriage free.   Packing Case for country, 1/- extra.

Being an adaptation of Statham's hydro-pneumatic apparatus to the purposes of a portable chemical laboratory, by the addition of a japanned tin case with trays and partitions containing chemicals and apparatus, including a bichromate battery for the decomposition of water by an electric current, and apparatus for the electrolysis of water and collection of two gases and book, also apparatus for decomposing water, ditto for electrolysis of water and collecting two gases separately.

This illus. represents the TOP PART only of the No. 1 Laboratory open, showing the arrangement of the chemicals, and also some of the apparatus, which is of larger size than that in the Students' Cabinets. There are 74 re-agents and chemical preparations, in stoppered and plain bottles, and turned wood boxes, labelled with white varnished labels, and 90 pieces of large size apparatus, etc., gas jars, and other necessaries for manipulation in the gases, in all about 160 articles.

The LOWER PART of the case is convertible at pleasure into a large pneumatic trough, a hydraulic blow-pipe (useful for bending and blowing glass, making tube apparatus, etc.), and a gasometer for storing gases; it serves also for packing away the general apparatus when not in use, or for travelling.

This Set contains one 3-cell battery minus the OUTSIDE cells (for which ordinary jam pots will answer.)

List of Apparatus.

2-pint gas jar, fitted with brass cap for collecting gases	Bladder, mounted with female screw	Scales and weights in oak box	Cotton wick, for spirit lamp	Bohemian flask, 1 oz.	Brass stop-cock
1-pint deflagrating jar	12 test tubes, assorted	Ribbed glass funnel, 2 in.	6 glass tubes, 8 in.	Ditto 2 oz.	Brass elbow piece
½-pint ditto	Test tube stand	Ditto ditto 2½ in.	3 glass stirring rods	Ditto 4 oz.	Brass blow-pipe
Deflagrating spoon	Ditto holder	Ditto ditto 3 in.	Wash bottle	Iron spoon	Flexible tube, with mouthpiece and brass screw, for hydraulic blow-pipe
Hard glass retort	Ditto cleaner	Packet filters, 2½ in.	Dr. Black's Blow-pipe	Tinned sand bath	Sliding shelf and funnels, for use with pneumatic trough
Receiver, for ditto	Dr. Clark's test glass	Ditto 3½ in.	Blue litmus paper	2 tinned capsules	
Oxygen tube retort	Cylindrical ditto	Mortar and Pestle	Red ditto	Bulb pipette	
Flask filled with acid	Phillip's precipitating test glass	2 porcelain evaporating basins	Lead paper	3 Bohemian beakers, or hot solutions	Apparatus complete to decompose water by electric current
Funnel and bent tube, for making gases	Graduated measure	Porcelain crucible & cover	Turmeric paper	Clark's tube retort	Apparatus to electrolyse water and collect the two gases separately
Mounted glass jet	Retort stand, 3 rings	3 Hessian ditto	Carbon and zinc plates	Ditto receiver	
	2 watch glasses	Spirit lamp, with screw wick holder	Brass clamps and terminals for battery	Lamp for hydraulic blow-pipe	
	Watch glass holder		Tin foil	Cotton wick for ditto	
			Bulb boiling tube	Lamp tongs	

Statham's Economic Laboratory. 652. No. 2, £12 12 0

Is considerably larger than No. 1, and contains the requisites for the performance of complete courses of lectures or experiments, or for the various operations of qualitative analysis and chemical research, includes a battery, also apparatus to decompose water by an electric current and to electrolyse water, and the apparatus necessary for the collection of two gases. The lower part of the case is arranged, as in No. 1, for use as a pneumatic trough, a hydraulic blow-pipe and a gasometer; and the upper compartment contains over 100 re-agents, etc., which are in large size stoppered and plain bottles. There is also a very extensive assortment of large size apparatus, including gas jars and other necessaries for experimenting with the gases. Size, closed, 19 by 12½ by 17 in. Packing case for country, 1/6

APPARATUS.

4-pint gas jar, fitted with brass cap, for collecting gases.	Bohemian flasks— 1, 2, 3, 4, 6, 8 oz.	2 test tube cleaners	Sand bath	Turmeric	Steel spatula
2-pint deflagrating jar	Retort stand, 3 rings	Brass clip holder	5 bohemian beakers	Brazil Wood	Lamp for hydraulic blow-pipe
1-pint ditto	Tube holder for ditto	3 arsenic tubes	Ribbed glass funnels— 2, 2½, 3 in.	Starch	Cotton for ditto
½-pint ditto	Spirit lamp, with screw wick holder	2 bulb boiling tubes	Pack. cut filters, 2¾, 3½, 4½ in.	Lead	Tongs for ditto
Deflagrating spoon	Cotton wick for ditto	Mortar and pestle	2 wire triangles	Triangular file in handle	Elbow piece
Bladder, mounted with brass female screw	Blow-pipe lamp	Glass mortar and pestle	Washing bottle	Rat-tail rasp ditto	Brass blow-pipe
Stop-cock for ditto	Dr. Black's blow-pipe	4 porcelain evaporating basins	Bulb pipette	6 glass stirring rods	Flexible tube, with mouthpiece and brass screw
2 flasks, fitted with acid funnel and bent tubes, for making gases	Piece platinum foil	2 porcelain crucibles and covers	Bohemian retort, stoppered	12 glass tubes	Sliding shelf for pneumatic trough
Jet mounted for ditto	2 platinum wires	4 hessian ditto	Bohemian retort receiver	Phillip's precipitating glass	Apparatus complete to decompose water by electric current
Oxygen flask retort	6 hard glass tubes	Crucible tongs	Clark's tube retort	2 cylindrical test glasses	Apparatus to electrolyse water and collect the two gases separately
	Test tube stand, 8 holes, with pegs	Iron spoon	Clark's receiver	2 Clark's ditto	
	24 test tubes	3 watch glasses	Box of test papers	Glass measure, graduated	
		Watch glass holder	Blue litmus	Porcelain Filter support	
			Red litmus	Pair 7 in. scales, with grain and drahm weights, in oak box	

The completeness and portability of the "Economic Laboratories" render them peculiarly available to lecturers in general for class instruction in schools, mechanics' and scientific institutions, and all interested in chemical pursuits; and from their being made of japanned iron plate instead of wood, they are especially suited for exportation to hot countries, as the cases are not liable to warp or split in tropical climates. They are recommended as being the best adapted of all Statham's Chests for pursuing a general course of chemical research. We have received many testimonials to their usefulness, and have sold a large number of them.

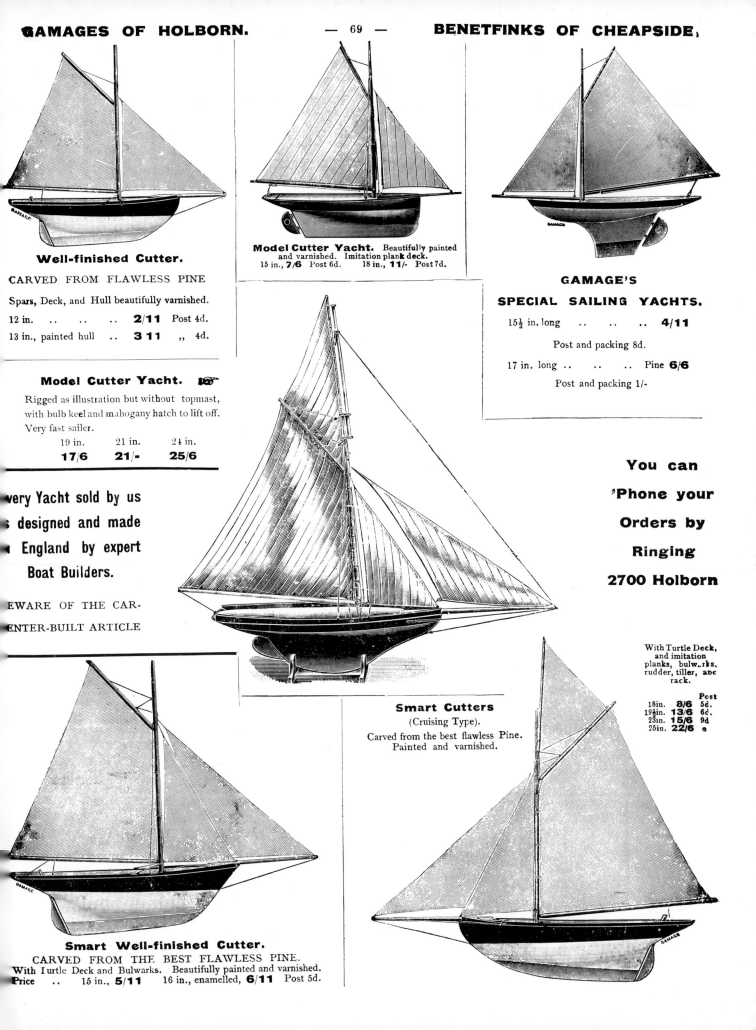

Well-finished Cutter.

CARVED FROM FLAWLESS PINE

Spars, Deck, and Hull beautifully varnished.

12 in.	**2/11**	Post 4d.
13 in., painted hull ..	**3 11**	,, 4d.

Model Cutter Yacht.

Rigged as illustration but without topmast, with bulb keel and mahogany hatch to lift off. Very fast sailer.

19 in.	21 in.	24 in.
17/6	**21/-**	**25/6**

very Yacht sold by us

s designed and made

England by expert

Boat Builders.

EWARE OF THE CAR-
ENTER-BUILT ARTICLE

Model Cutter Yacht. Beautifully painted and varnished. Imitation plank deck.
15 in., **7/6** Post 6d. 18 in., **11/-** Post 7d.

GAMAGE'S
SPECIAL SAILING YACHTS.

15½ in. long	**4/11**
Post and packing 8d.	
17 in. long	Pine **6/6**
Post and packing 1/-	

You can
'Phone your
Orders by
Ringing
2700 Holborn

With Turtle Deck, and imitation planks, bulwarks, rudder, tiller, and rack.

		Post
18in.	**8/6**	5d.
19½in.	**13/6**	6d.
23in.	**15/6**	9d.
25in.	**22/6**	c

Smart Cutters
(Cruising Type).
Carved from the best flawless Pine.
Painted and varnished.

Smart Well-finished Cutter.
CARVED FROM THE BEST FLAWLESS PINE.
With Turtle Deck and Bulwarks. Beautifully painted and varnished.
Price .. 15 in., **5/11** 16 in., enamelled, **6/11** Post 5d.

Class Racing Yachts for Clubs.

8 metre Built Models.

41 in.—42 in. long overall, with automatic steering gear, first-class fittings and union silk sails.

Price - £4 4 0

To Order.

47 in.—48 in. overall.

Price - £5 5 0

To Order.

10 Rater Built Models.

58 in.—60 in. overall.

W.L. 40 in.

With two suits of sails, shifting mast step and latest automatic steering gear.

First-Class Models.

Price - £9 9 0

(Built by Experts)

12 metre Built Models.

With shifting mast step and automatic steering gear.

Price - £14 0 0

To Order.

We are in a position to supply the VERY FINEST RACING CRAFT it is possible to produce.

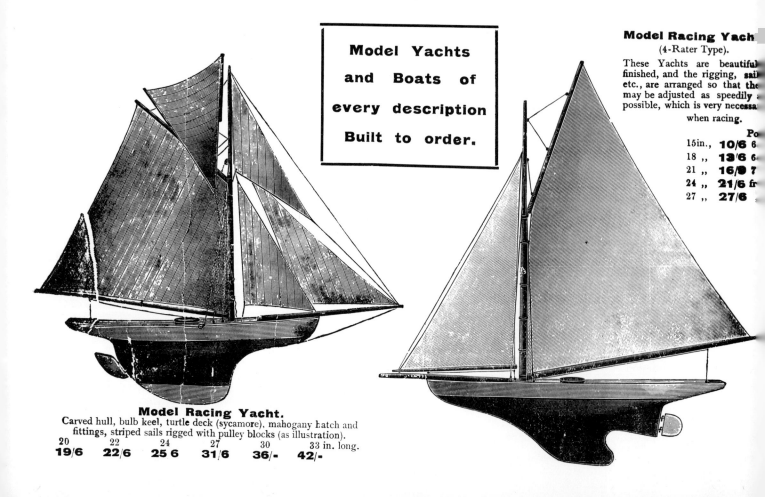

Model Yachts and Boats of every description Built to order.

Model Racing Yacht.

Carved hull, bulb keel, turtle deck (sycamore), mahogany hatch and fittings, striped sails rigged with pulley blocks (as illustration).

20	22	24	27	30	33 in. long.
19/6	22/6	25 6	31/6	36/-	42/-

Model Racing Yacht
(4-Rater Type).

These Yachts are beautiful finished, and the rigging, sail etc., are arranged so that the may be adjusted as speedily possible, which is very necessa when racing.

	Po
15in.,	**10/6** 6
18 ,,	**13/6** 6
21 ,,	**16/9** 7
24 ,,	**21/6** fr
27 ,,	**27/6**

Model Yachts.

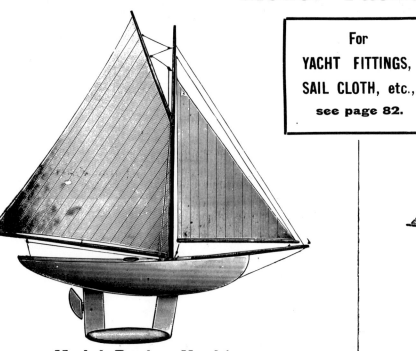

For
YACHT FITTINGS,
SAIL CLOTH, etc.,
see page 82.

Model Racing Yacht.

(Canoe Type).

These are most graceful and speedy boats, specially designed for racing, the general style and finish throughout being of the best.

CARVED FROM THE BEST FLAWLESS LIGHT PINE, and enamel finished.

The lead keel is torpedo shaped and the rudder self-adjusting.

20 in.	22 in.	24 in.	27 in.	30 in.	33 in.
22/6	25/-	27/6	35/-	39/6	57/6

Half-built Racing Yacht.

CARVED FROM BEST FLAWLESS PINE,

mahogany upper streak and stem turtle deck, mahogany hatch, bulb keel, mahogany fittings, striped sailcloth, rigged with pulley blocks and beautifully enamelled (as illustration)

20	24	27	30	33	36 in. long
22/6	29/6	37/6	45/-	50/-	59/6

39	42	45	48 in. long.
72/-	82/-	93/-	105/-

Fast Racing Cutter (Clyde Type).

in. (3 sails), **10/6**	Post 6d.	23 in. (4 sails), **20/-**	Post 9d.
,, (4 ,,), **12/-**	,, 6d.	25 ,, (4 ,,), **25/-**	,, free.
,, (4 ,,), **15/6**	,, 8d.		

CARVED FROM LIGHT FLAWLESS PINE.

beautifully finished throughout, with enamelled hull, turtle and deck with imitation planks.

Scale Model Self-righting Life Boat.

With air-tight boxes and relieving valves. Impossible to sink and bound to right itself when capsized. Beautifully enamelled and finished in correct colours. Complete with oars. As illustration.

| 18 in. long | .. | .. | **32/6** | 26 in. long | .. | .. | **47/6** | } Post free. |
| 22 in. ,, | .. | .. | **39/6** | 30 in. ,, | .. | .. | **55/-** | |

Working Drawings for Yacht Building.

SCALE MODEL WORKING DRAWINGS of the undermentioned Yachts have been specially designed for A. W. GAMAGE, Ltd., by Mr. C. F. BRIERLEY. Marine Architect.

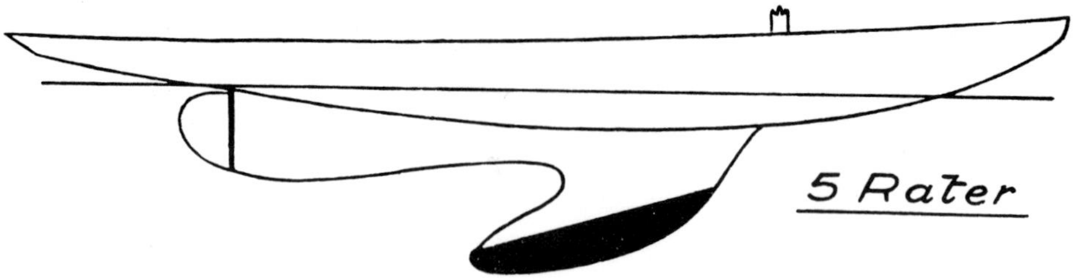

Full size Scale Drawing for 5 Rater Yacht (L. & S.A. Rule) with Sail Plans. Scale ¼ in.=1 in.
Price .. .. **4/-** Postage 1½d.

Material for cutting out above to drawings, including wood for deck and spars, also lead keel and rudder for same .. .. Price .. **32/6** Post 9d.

Ditto, for Built Boats.	Cedar ¼ in.	Price	**9**d.	per square foot.
,, ,,	Mahogany ¼ in.	.. ..	**9**d.	,, ,,
,, ,,	,, ⅜ in.	,, ...	**1/-**	,, ,,
,, ,,	,, ½ in.	.. ..	**1/6**	,, ,,
White Holly for Decks,	⅛ in.	Price	**1/-**	,, ,,
,, ,,	3/16 in.	,, ...	**1/9**	,, ,,
Chesnut ,,	⅛ in.	,, ...	**1/-**	,, ,,
,, ,,	3/16 in.	,, ...	**1/3**	,, ,,
Ash or American Elm for Frames,	⅛ by ¼ in.	Price	**1/6**	per 25 ft.
,, ,, ,,	3/16 by 5/16 in.	,, ...	**2/3**	,,

Post extra.

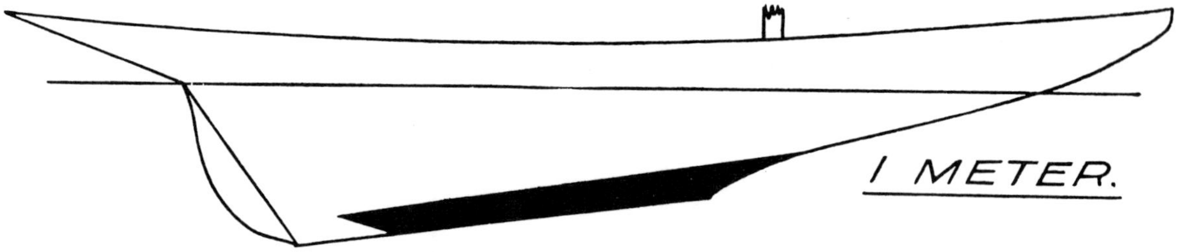

Working Drawings for 1 Meter Yacht (International Rule) with Sail Plans. Scale ⅛ in.=1 in. Sheer and half-breadth Plans half size. Body Plans full size. Price .. **5/-** Postage 1½d.

Material for cutting out above, including wood for deck, and spars, also lead keel and rudder **70/-**

For Material for Built Boats see prices for 5 Rater above.

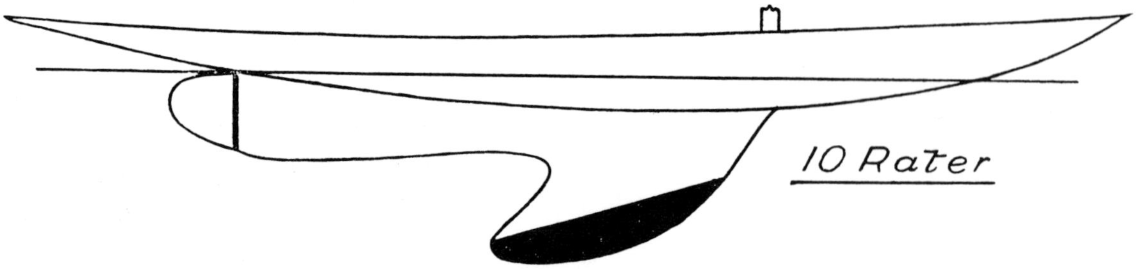

Working Drawing for 10 Rater Yacht (L. & S.A. Rules) with Sail Plans. Scale ⅛ in.=1 in.
Price .. .. .. **5/-** Postage 1½d. Sheer and half-breadth Plans half size. Body Plan full size.

Materials for cutting out same, including wood for deck, spars, and lead keel and rudder for same .. **63/-**

For Material for Built Boats see prices for 5 Rater Yacht.

Working Drawings for Model Motor Boats.

SCALE MODEL DRAWINGS of the undermentioned Motor Boats have been specially designed for A. W. GAMAGE, Ltd., by Mr. C. F. BRIERLEY, Marine Architect.

1 METER.

Full size Working Drawings for 1 Meter Sharpie Type Speed Launch.   Price   .. **2/6** each.   Post 1½d.

Complete Set of Materials, less rudder and fittings, to build above with screws and stocks to build boats on.

Price   ..   ..   .. **18/6**   Post 8d.

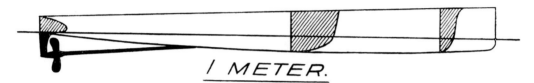

1 METER.

Full size Working Drawings for 1 Meter Speed Launch.   Price   ..   ..   .. **2/6**   Post 1½d.

Complete Set of Materials, less rudder and fittings, to build above with screws and stocks to build boat on.

Price   ..   .. **18/6**   Post 8d.

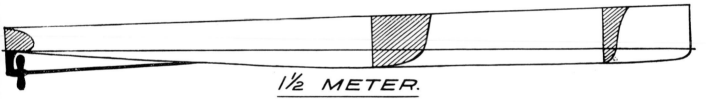

1½ METER.

Drawings for 1½ Meter Speed Launch. Sheer and half breadth Plans half size. Body Plans full size.

Price   .. **3/6**   Post 1½d.

Complete Set of Materials, less rudder and fittings for constructing same with screws and stocks to build boat on.

Price   ..   .. **32/6** Post 9d.

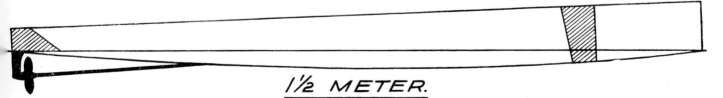

1½ METER.

Scale Model Drawings for 1½ Meter Sharpie Type Speed Launch.   Sheer and half breadth Plans half size.   Body Plans full size.

Price ..   .. **3,6**   Post 1½d.

Complete Set of Materials, less rudder and fittings, for constructing same with screws and stocks to build boat on.

Price ..   ..   .. **32/6**   Post 9d.

High-Class Motor Boats, Launches, etc.

All Boats on this page (with the exception of Ocean Liner and Cargo Steamer) are finished and only require Engines or Motors Fitted.

MOTOR BOATS,

LINERS,

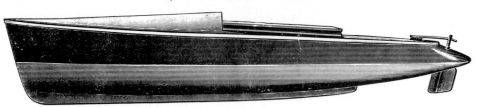

CARGO

STEAMERS.

Napier-Type Motor Boat. (without machinery). Carved from best flawless pine, with mahogany top sides, turtle deck, hatch to lift off and brass rudder. Best enamel and polish finish,

	23	27	30	33	36	42 in.
Prices	**23,6**	**29/6**	**34/6**	**39/6**	**42/-**	**48/-**

For
ELECTRIC MOTORS,
See page 46.

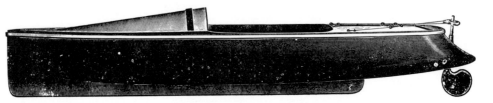

For
ACCUMULATORS
See page 47.

Motor Boat (without machinery). Carved from best flawless yellow pine, long hatch, mahogany fittings, turtle deck (sycamore), beautifully enamelled. **As illustration.**

	24 in.	27 in.	30 in.	33 in.	36 in.
Prices	**19,6**	**22/6**	**27/6**	**35/-**	**39/6**

These Motor Boats and Launches can be fitted with electric or clockwork motors or steam engines, as required, at extra cost according to size and quality.

For
PROPELLORS,
See page 81

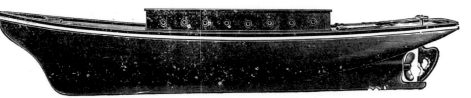

For MARINE
ENGINES and
BOILERS,
See pages 33-34.

Hutton Type Motor Boat. (Without Machinery). Carved from best flawless pine, with turtle deck, mahogany lift-off hatch and brass rudder. Best enamel finish.

	24 in.	27 in.	30 in.	33 in.	36 in	39 in.	42 in.	44 in.	48 in.
Prices ..	**21/-**	**25/6**	**29/6**	**35/-**	**39/6**	**45/-**	**49/6**	**55/-**	**59/6**

For
PETROL BOAT ENGINES,
See page 43.

For
BOAT
FITTINGS,
See page 72.

Steam or Electric Launch (without machinery). Carved from best flawless yellow pine, sycamore deck, with long hatch to take machinery, mahogany fittings, beautifully enamelled. As illustration.

Prices	24 in., **15/6**	27 in., **18/6**	30 in., **24/6**	33 in. **32/6**

Finished and Enamelled Hull of Ocean Liner to Scale, 36 in. long, 4½ in. beam, 3½ in. depth.
Price **32/6**

Ditto   ditto   Cargo Steamer, 36 in. long, 5 in. beam, 3¾ in. depth.
Price **35/-**

MOTOR BOATS and TORPEDO BOATS,

Torpedo Hulls, with Deck.

These Boats are built and designed by experienced boat builders. They are exceedingly cleanly finished both inside and out and are lighter for their respective sizes than any other similar boats now on the market.

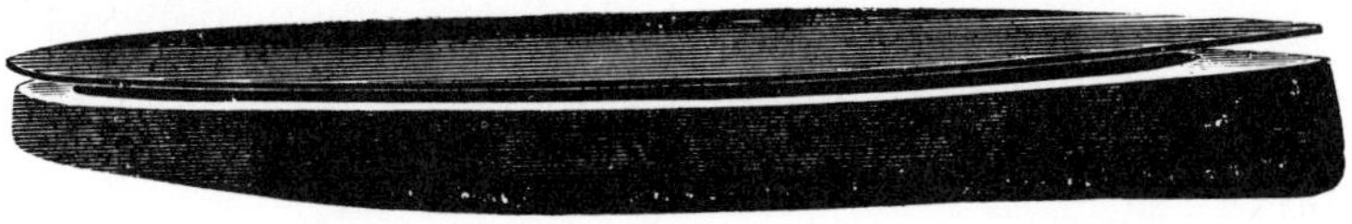

AA—Length 24 in., beam 3¾ in., depth 2⅜ in., **9/6** This size is fitted with Conning Tower and Hatch. Painted 2 coats.

		Length	beam	depth	Price	
	A	2 ft. 6 in.	4½ in.	2½ in.	**9/6**	Carriage extra.
	B	2 ,, 6 ,,	4½ ,,	3 ,,	**10/6**	,, ,,
Metre size,	C	3 ,, 3⅜ ,,	4¾ ,,	3¾ ,,	**18/6**	,, ,,
	D	3 ,, 3⅜ ,,	4¾ ,,	4 ,,	**20/-**	,, paid.
	E	4 ,, 6 ,,	6½ ,,	4½ ,,	**33/6**	,, ,,
	F	5 ,, 6 ,,	8 ,,	6½ ,,	**49/6**	,, ,,

Metre Feather-weight Torpedo Hulls,

With prepared **canvas timbers, deck** and hatch fitted.

Weight about 1 lb.

beam 4¾ in., depth 3¼ **in.**

Price **27/-**

SPECIAL VALUE.

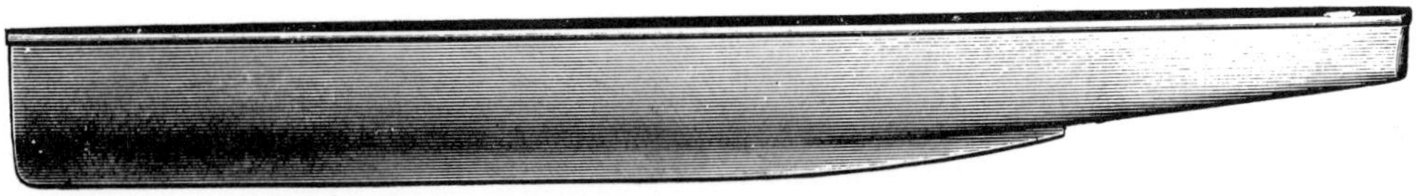

We build Hulls **of** All Sizes and Types To Order.

The "Challenge" Motor Boat Hulls.

Unpainted. 24 in long by 3 in. beam .. **5/6** 30 in. long .. **9/6** 39 in. long .. **17/6**

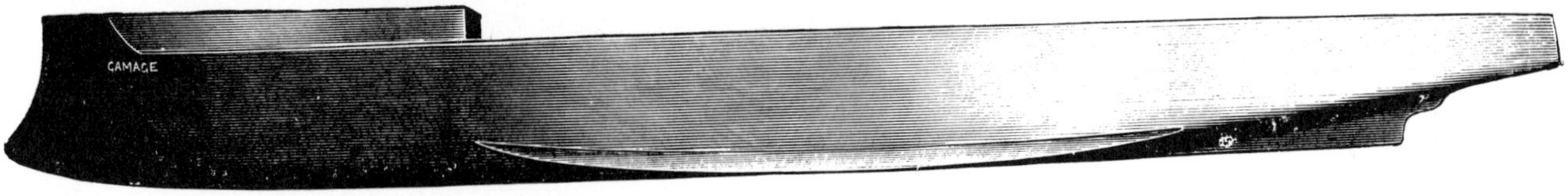

Dreadnought Battleship Hulls. Carved from best quality light pine, ready for Painting.
42 in. long, 7½ in. beam .. .. .. Price **33/6**

Dreadnought Cruiser Hulls. Carved from best quality light pine, ready for Painting.
42 in. long, 6¾ in. beam .. .. .. Price **29/6**

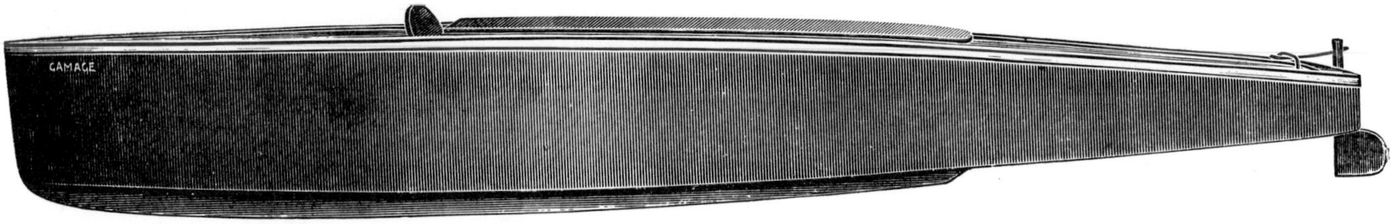

The "Challenge" Motor Boat. Finished and enamelled ready for fitting Motor. 30 in. long .. **17/6** 42 in. long .. **25/-**
These boats are made by a new system which greatly reduces the labour and expense. Every one is well finished and enamelled. They are, undoubtedly the most remarkable value.

Metre Torpedo Boat Destroyers,

High-class scale model of a British Torpedo Boat Destroyer. Fitted with conning tower, turtle deck, steering platform, 2 anchors, quick firing guns, 4 ventilators, 3 funnels, mast, adjusting rudder.

Fitted with our twin screw motor and 2 "Acorn" accumulators. Size, 1 metre (39 in.). Supplied painted black or grey.

Price, ready for use **£4 19 6**

These Destroyers can also be supplied fitted with a powerful clockwork spring in place of electric motor, to run 5 minutes in the water Price .. **72/-**

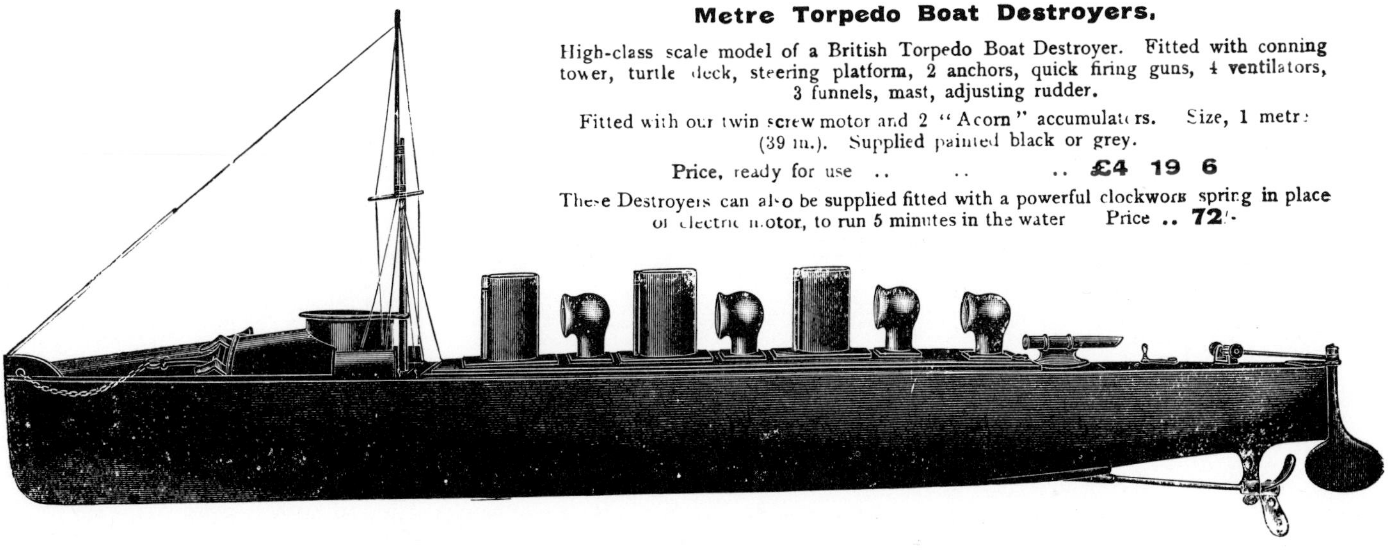

BRITISH ARMOURED CRUISERS.

Modern Type, with 4 Funnels, and complete set of large and small guns.   Best make and finish.

Accurate Details in every respect, bridge, lifeboats, etc., good outlines.

155/441.	New Armoured Cruiser, driven by clockwork, 17 in. long					..	..			..	..	..	**10/9**
,, /442	,,	,,	,,	,,	21¼ in. long with 2 lifeboats	..	..		..		..	**16/6**
,, /444	,,	,,	,,	,,	29½ in. ,, 2 ,,	..	..		..	..	..	**22/6**
,, /445	,,	,,	,,	,,	33¼ in. ,, 4 ,,	..	..		..	..	..	**45/-**
,, /446	,,	,,	,,	,,	37¼ in. ,, 4 ,,	..	..		..	..	..	**55/-**

Fine Model Liner "OLYMPIC" Type.

STRONGLY MADE AND BEAUTIFULLY ENAMELLED.

Fitted with finest clockwork mechanism.   A portion of deck can be removed at a moment's notice for oiling or inspecting works.

No. 0   16½ in. long, without lifeboats .. **11/6** Post 7d.   No. 2.   25¼ in. long, with 4 lifeboats .. **25/6** Carriage free.

No. 1.   ,,   ,,   ,,   .. **15/-**   ,, 9d.   No. 3.   32¼ in. long, with 6 lifeboats .. **45/-**   ,,

No. 4.   30½ in. long with 10 lifeboats .. **65/-** Carriage free.

Clockwork & Steam Torpedo Boats & Destroyers.

Exact models, superfine grey or all black japanning.

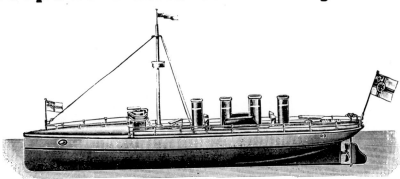

No. 1. CLOCKWORK TORPEDO BOAT, 12¼ in. long, 2 funnels, 3 cannons, 2 torpedo tubes, **4.9** Post 4d.

No. 2. CLOCKWORK DESTROYER. 17 in. long, 4 funnels, 4 cannons, 2 torpedo tubes, **7.6** 6d.

No. 3. CLOCKWORK DESTROYER, 22⅝ in. long, 4 funnels, 4 cannons, 3 torpedo tubes, **9/11** 8d.

With superior **Clockwork movement**, 23½ in. long with torpedo tube and lifeboats .. .. .. **15/6** 9d.

Driven by steam, 23½ in. long with torpedo tube and lifeboats .. .. **16/6** 9d.

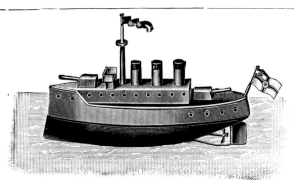

New Range of Gun Boats with best Clockwork Movements.

Gun Boat, finely japanned, with 2 funnels, 2 guns, 7¼ in. long, **1/-** Post 3d.

,, ,, ,, ,, 3 ,, 2 ,, 8¾ ,, ,, **2/-** ,, 3d.

,, ,, ,, ,, 3 ,, 2 ,, 10½ ,, ,, **3 -** ,, 4d.

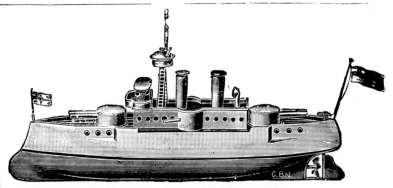

Model Dreadnought, with strong reliable Clockwork Movements, finely japanned. Price **5/11** Postage 4d.

Dreadnought, with strong reliable Clockwork Movements, finely japanned, correct naval grey, 11¾ in. long Price ... ... **3/11** Postage 4d.

Automatically Firing Gun Boats.

After winding up the clockwork, put boat on the water. It will go straight ahead for some distance, then, as if intending to attack an enemy, it will suddenly fire a shot. After this, the boats (size 1 and 2), will sail on in a circle, whilst boat size 3 will turn round and steer back to its original starting place.

Finely finished and beautifully japanned, with best quality clockwork and with automatic steering gear.

No. 1. With 1 gun, 12 in. long .. **5/9** Post 5d.

,, 2. ,, 1 ,, 15¾ ,, .. **8/11** ,, 7d.

,, 3. ,, 2 guns, firing 2 shots at intervals, 19¼ in. lon , **13/9** ,, 9d.

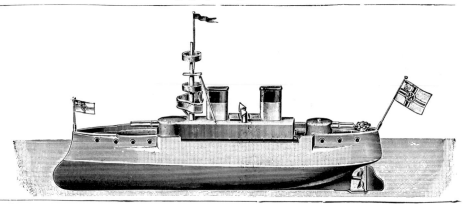

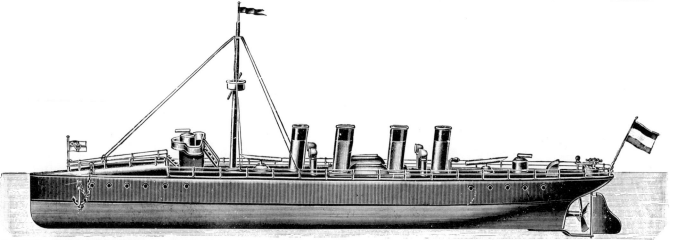

LARGE DESTROYER. Finely japanned, typical, narrow shape, with very strong superior Clockwork, torpedo tubes, Lifeboats and 2 anchors, 39½ in long, **39/6** each. Post free. | Ditto ditto ditto 27½ in long .. .. **23/6** each Post free

Ditto ditto steam propelled .. **39/6** | Ditto ditto ditto steam propelled .. **22/6** ,, ,,

Model Submarines, Motor Boats, etc.

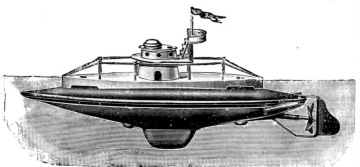

Latest Type Clockwork Submarine Boat.

First-class Models in shape and construction.
Will dive and rise to the surface quite automatically.
Most fascinating and instructive Toy.
Length 12 in. **7/11** Post 5d.   Length 17 in. **15/6** Post 8d.

Clockwork Submarine Boat

FINE MODEL.   STRONGLY MADE & WELL FINISHED.

6½ in., **10½d.**   9 in., **1/6**

Postage 3d.   3d.

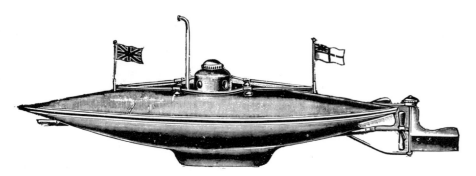

Model Submarine Boats.

**Alternately diving and rising to the sur-
face**, imitating in a surprising manner, the
movements of their large prototype. Finely
japanned, with strong clockwork, working ex-
cellently. Packed in boxes.

10½ in. long, with strong clockwork.
Price **2/3**   Postage 4d.

13¾ in. long, large size, finely made and richly
fitted up.   Price **4/11**   Post 5d.

Steam Motor Racing Boat   Driven by Steam.
Finely japanned, with brass boiler and oscillating brass cylinder.
Hull, 18 in. long.

Price .. .. **8/6**   Post 6d.

Do.   do.   22 in. long .. .. .. **14/6**   Post 9d.

Clockwork Racing Motor Boats

8½ in. long, with rudder .. .. **2/3**   Post 4d.

With two figures   10¼ in. long .. .. **3/6**   ,, 4d.

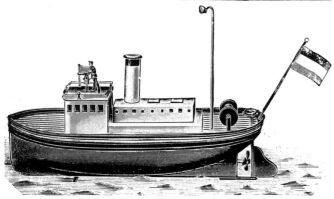

Fire Boat with Pump and Nozzle.

Superior finish, with reliable clockwork mechanism which works propeller
and pump simultaneously.

7½ in. long .. .. **3/6**   Post 4d.
With observation bridge, 7½ in. long, **4/11**   ,, 4d.
Do.   11¾ ,,   **7/6**   ,, 6d.

Clockwork Ocean Liners

Smart well
finished
Boats, with
good
quality
Clock-
work.
Beautifully
enamelled.

With 2 Funnels.	Length 7½ in. ..	..	..	**1/6**	Post 4d.
,, 4 ,,	,, 10¼ in. ..	..	..	**3/9**	,, 5d.
,, 4 ,,	,, 12½ in. ..	..	..	**5/11**	,, 6d.

Boats, Seaplanes, etc.

Clockwork Paddle Steamer.

As illustration.

Strong clockwork movement.

Finely japanned.   7½ in. long.

Price **2/3**   Post 3d.

Clockwork Seaplane.

Special strong clockwork.

4½ in. high, 9¾ in. long, 11½ in. wide.

Price **2/11**   Postage 4d.

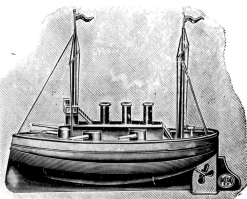

Clockwork Gun-boat.

9½ inch long.   2 masts and revolving guns.

Price **2/11**   Postage 4d.

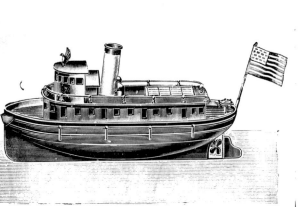

Tug-boat.

Realistic model of a Tug-boat, complete with all fittings.

Superior clockwork movement, strictly reliable.

12 in. long.   4 in. wide.

Price **5/11**   Postage 4d.

Yacht.   Peasure boat of accurate construction.   2 decks, 2 masts, saloon, awning, chimney, strong clockwork, screw propeller.   Hand-made, hand-painted in pretty colours.
Length 16 in.   Height 10½ in.   Breadth 3¼ in   Ptice **17/6**

With screw propeller and regulated clockwork.   Actual shape.   Very effective.
Double deck with saloon, 2 masts with ropes, 4 lifeboats, ventilators, windable anchor.
Length 24½ in.   Breadth 4⅜ in.   Height 16 in.   Price **38/6**

THE "BARRY" SCULLER.   This Toy is a realistic production in minature of a Sculler in his Racing Boat   The motive power is India Rubber, which can be replaced when worn or broken in a few minutes, and at a cost of about twopence.   Quite apart from the indestructable nature of this Toy the feature is the **realistic and graceful action** characteristic of a good Sculler.

Length over all 15½ in.   Price ..   .. **8/9**   Postage 4d.

WATER TOYS AND SWIMMING NOVELTIES.

Miniature Dread-nought.

Realistic Miniature Model of the latest Type Battleship, made of wood, correct colours. Perfectly proportioned, will swim in a basin of water. 5¼ in. long, 1 in. broad .. **10½d.** Post 2d.

Miniature Ocean Liner.

As illustration.

Realistic Miniature Model of a large Atlantic Ocean Liner, correct colours. Perfectly proportioned, made of wood, will swim in a basin of water. 8¾ in. long, 1 in. broad. Price .. .. **1/6** Post 2d.

Divers. As illustration. Finely Japanned. They dive into water and rise to surface again by air blown into rubber tubes. 5⅞ in. high. Price .. **10½d.** Post 2d.

Mechanical Swimming Duck. Propelled by elastic. As illustration.

Price .. **10½d.** Post 3d.

Swimming Frog.

As illustration.

Made of Rubber and propelled by means of a Ball and Rubber Tube.

Price .. .. **10½d.**

Post 2d.

Mechanical Swimming Swan. Propelled by elastic. As illustration.

Price .. **1/-** Post 2d.

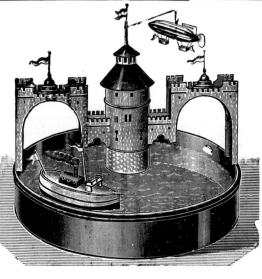

Clockwork Swimming Lady (as illustration). This is one of the most realistic Swimming Toys imaginable, it represents a girl in silk costume swimming the breast stroke, and propelled solely by the action of the legs and arms. Does not easily get out of order.

Price .. .. .. **6/11** Post 3d.

Island Towers with Magnetic Animals. The Tower and Basin are made of stout enamelled metal. The water is moved by mechanism enclosed in base of tower. Very realistic effect. As illustration.

Price .. .. **10/6** Post 6d.

Similar to illustration. Price .. **2/11** Post 3d.

Larger.. .. .. ,, .. **4/11** ,, 4d.

Mechanical Duck.

To run on the ground. Propelled by momentum of flywheel. Cannot get out of order. Splendid value .. .. **6d.** Post 3d.

'NOVELTY!

Clockwork Pond.

As illustration.

The mechanism is so arranged that the water is continually on the move, the boat travelling round and round for two hours without stopping.

No. 1 .. **3/11**

Post 5d.

Clockwork Swimming Frog.
As illustration.
Price .. .. .. **2/11** Post 3d.

Full-size Working Drawings for Yacht Building.

Full-size Working Drawings enabling Amateurs to build their own Craft. Prepared specially for GAMAGES by a Model Yacht expert. Attention should be drawn to the fact that nothing of this description has ever before been placed on the market. Unlike the ordinary designs published, ours are FULL SIZE, ON PAPER **90** BY **20** in. WITH TEMPLATES OF ALL PARTS. Designs published in books or magazines are always on a small scale, and as full-size Working Drawings and Templates are a necessity, these have to be made from the designs. This to the average man is more difficult than building a boat, and costs money, as a drawing board and instruments are required, hence the majority build their boats by guesswork, and they are seldom a success and cannot compete against those who can afford to pay for a properly-designed craft. There are about 100 Model Yacht Clubs in England with from 40 to 100 members each, making a total of quite 6,000, chiefly composed of clerks, better-class working men, etc., who cannot afford to pay for high-class designs, or buy a boat for £15 to £20, and we feel quite sure they will appreciate our offer.

The Drawings are of a 12-metre Yacht, MM. Rating.   If we find that there is sufficient demand we shall from time to

PRICE, each .. .. **10/6** Post 3d.   time place other Drawings on the market.

Hawkins' Patent Propellers.

A. W. Gamage, Ltd., have acquired the sole selling rights of this propeller, and any person infringing will be proceeded against.

$1\frac{1}{4}$ in. 3-blade .. .. .. **3/6** Post 2d.
$1\frac{1}{2}$,, ,, ... **3/9** ,, 2d.
2 ,, ,, ... **4/-** ,, 2d.

1 in. 2-blade **1/9** $1\frac{3}{4}$ in. 2-blade **3/-** ⎫
$1\frac{1}{4}$,, ,, **2/-** 2 ,, ,, **3/6** ⎬ Post 2d.
$1\frac{1}{2}$,, ,, **2/9** 3 ,, ,, **5/-** ⎭

Bevelled Gear Wheels.

Hard Brass.

No. 1. $\frac{1}{2}$ in. diam. .. **4d.** pair.
,, 2. $\frac{5}{8}$ in. diam. .. **8d.** ,,

Brass Pinions. With centre hole & 10 teeth.

No. 59/3. $\frac{1}{8}$ in. long, $\frac{1}{4}$ in. diam. .. **6d.** doz.
,, 59/4. $\frac{3}{16}$ in. ,, $\frac{1}{4}$ in. ,, .. **7d.** ,,
,, 59/4A. $\frac{3}{16}$ in. ,, $\frac{1}{4}$ in. ,, with joining piece **8d.** ,,
,, 59/6L. $\frac{1}{4}$ in. ,, $\frac{1}{4}$ in. diam. .. **9d.** ,,
,, 52/6. $\frac{1}{4}$ in. ,, $\frac{5}{16}$ in. ,, .. **1/-** ,,

Brass Cog Wheels.

With centre hole.

STRONG MAKE.

No. 58/28.	30	40	45	50	60
Width	40	40	48	66	60	68 teeth
Diam.	1	$1\frac{1}{8}$	$1\frac{9}{16}$	$1\frac{13}{16}$	2	$2\frac{3}{8}$ in.
Price	3d.	4d.	5d.	7d.	8d.	1/- each.
,,	1/-	1/5	1/6	2/5	2/8	3/11 doz.

Postage extra.

Steel Pinions. With holes.

No. 59/10. 12 teeth, $\frac{1}{4}$ in. long, $\frac{5}{16}$ in. diam. .. **3/-** doz.
No. 59/11. 14 teeth, $\frac{1}{4}$ in. long, $\frac{7}{16}$ in. diam. .. **5/-** ,,
Post extra.

High-class Gun-metal and Phosphor Bronze Propellers For Model Racing Craft.

No. 1.   Phosphor Bronze.
3 in., **3/9** $3\frac{1}{4}$ in., **4/-** $3\frac{1}{2}$ in., **4/3**
$3\frac{3}{4}$ in., **4/6**   4 in., **4/9** $4\frac{1}{4}$ in., **5/-**
No. 2. Gun-metal, complete with Steel Shaft and Spring Coupling, right or left hand.
2 in., **2/3** $2\frac{1}{2}$ in., **2/6**   3 in., **3/6**
Postage extra.

TORPEDO BOAT FITTINGS

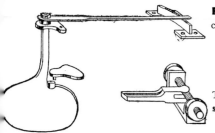

Rudder & Fittings,

complete, and finished ready for fixing to boat.

3 ft. 3 in. .. **3/-**
4 ft. 6 in. .. **6/-**
5 ft. 6 in. .. **7/6**

The two larger sizes have screw adjusting Rudders, and the smaller a plain rack.

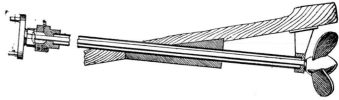

Complete finished **Stern Tube** and **Propeller Shaft Gear**
In Brass and Gun-metal (as illustration), without Propellors.
Made specially for use in conjunction with our other Torpedo Boat Fittings
For 3 ft. 3 in.. **3/9**   For 4 ft. 6 in., **6/6**   For 5 ft. 6 in., **10/6**

Torpedo Tubes. Fitted as Switches. Complete, ready for use. For 3 ft. 3 in. Boat.. .. **3/-**

For 4 ft. 6 in. Boat .. .. **4/-**   For 5 ft. 6 in. Boat **5/-**

Conning Tower with Turtle Deck, Stanchions, Gun Chains and Anchor

Funnel with Steam Pipe. Anchor. **TORPEDO DESTROYER DECK FITTINGS.** Ventilator. Quick Firing Gun.

These fittings are a great advance on the old type made of aluminium, inasmuch as they are nearly half the weight, and vastly stronger, being constructed of **pressed steel** with steel stanchions (not brass), and are lacquered with two coats of dead black. Anyone having experience in boat building knows that the least weight that there is above the deck line the more stable the craft, and it is only by using pressed steel that the weight can be kept down. Aluminium cannot be cast thin enough. Made in three sizes. Suit Boats of undermentioned sizes.

	3 ft. 3 in. (1 metre)	4 ft. 6 in.	5 ft. 6 in.
Complete **Conning Tower Turtle Deck**, Stanchions, Chains and Anchors (as illustration), ready to fit to boat ..	10/-	17/6	25/- set.
Funnels, complete, ready for fitting	—	2/6	3/6 each.
Ventilators, complete, ready for fitting	9d. & 1/-	3/-	4/- each.

N.B.—All above fittings are complete and ready to use and are sent post free. **Anchors** (finished) .. .. .. 1/3 .. 2/ .. 3/- each.

F

Model Ship and Boat Fittings.

No.		Price. s. d.
1H.	Belaying Pins, Racks, Brass or Wood ..per pair 1/- &	1 6
2B.	Best Rigging Cord, various sizes .. per hank 2d., 4d. &	0 6
3H.	Catheads .. .. per pair 9d., 1/- &	1 6
4B.	Steering Wheels, various sizes.. each 1/-, 1/6, 2/-, 2/6 &	3 6
4H.	Do. do. on stand .. .. .. each 2/6 &	2 9
5H.	Plain Deadeyes, sizes, ¼, ⁵⁄₁₆, ⅜ and ½ in. .. per doz.	0 6
6H.	Masthead Trucks do. do. 1d. each or ,,	0 10
7B.	Wood Binnacle, with Compass.. .. .. each	0 6
7H.	Binnacle Compasses, brass .. .. .. each 1/- &	1 3
8H.	Windlasses .. .. 1/6 &	2 0
9W.	Bronzed Anchors.. .. each 2d., 3d., 4d., 6d. &	0 8
9A.	Miniature Brass Anchors .. .. each 2d., 3d., 4d. &	0 6
11H.	Stropt Deadeyes, sizes, ¼, ⁵⁄₁₆, ⅜ and ½ in. per doz.	1 0
12H.	Do. Bullseyes do. .. .. .. ,,	1 0
13B.	Brass Tiller Racks, 2 in. to 3½ in. each 6d. 3¾ & 4 in.	0 8
14B.	Do. Tillers, 2 in to 3½ in. .. .. .. each	0 6
15B.	Masthead, Port and Starboard Lights .. .. ,,	0 6
16H.	Cleats (Brass) .. .. per doz.	0 6
16H.	Do. (Wood) .. .. ,,	0 10
17H	Brass Ships' Bells .. .. .. each 9d. &	1 0
18	Do. Eyebolts with Screw .. .. ,,	0 2
18A.	Do. do. extra large .. .. .. ,,	0 3
19H.	Masthead Caps with Crosstrees.. .. each 1/- &	1 6
23H.	Plain Single and Double Blocks, sizes ³⁄₁₆, ¼, ⁵⁄₁₆, ⅜, ⁷⁄₁₆ and ½ in. per doz.	0 7
24H.	Do., double with brass sheaves, sizes, ⁵⁄₁₆, ⅜, ⁷⁄₁₆ and ½ in. ,,	3 6
25H.	Plain Single, do., do., sizes, do., do. .. ,,	3 0
27H.	Stropt Blocks, single or double, with hooks .. ,,	0 10
28.	Stropt Sheaved Blocks (single).. .. .. per doz.	3 0
30.	Do. do. (double) .. .. ,,	4 0
32H.	Wood Buckets .. .. each	0 6
33H.	Fire do. .. .. ,,	0 6
34H.	Brass Davits, with Blocks and Falls .. per pair 9d. &	1 0
35H.	Do. Ringbolts .. .. per doz.	0 4
36H.	Do. Bowsies .. .. ,,	1 3
37H.	Brass Shroudhooks .. .. ,,	0 3
38G.	Do. Eyebolts .. .. ,,	0 1½
39H.	Plain Bullseyes, sizes, ¼, ⁵⁄₁₆, ⅜ and ½ in. .. ,,	0 6
40.	Brass Sheaves for Running Gear .. .. ,,	1 0
40H.	Bollards (Wood), each 9d. Brass .. .. each	1 0
41B.	Brass Cringles .. .. per doz.	0 9
42H.	Do. Rings for Stays .. .. .. ,,	0 3
43H.	Do. do. Masts do. .. .. .. ,,	0 3

See our Stock of Model Boats and Yachts.

Signal Flags. Commercial Code Set of 19 Flags.

Per Set .. .. 1 in., 4/6 ; 2½ in., 6/9

POSTAGE EXTRA ON ALL SHIP FITTINGS.

Any part of a Boat made to order on receipt of designs and full instructions; also to scale.

Boats and Yachts Made to Customer's own Specification.

No.		Price. s. d.
44H.	Brass Ventilators .. .. each 1/3 &	1 9
45H.	Bowsies, Wood .. .. per doz.	0 8
45H.	Wooden Ventilators, each ¾ to 1¼ in., each, 6d. 1¾ to 2¼ in.	0 8
46T.	BEST SILK FLAGS, Union Jacks, Ensigns, &c.	
	1½ in., 3d. 3 in., 4½d. 3½ in., 8½d. 6 in., each	1 0
47H.	Stropt Sister or Fiddle Blocks, sizes ½ to 1 in. per doz.	1 3
48H.	Wood Skylights with glass tops .. .. each 1/- &	1 6
49H.	Life Buoys .. .. ,, 6d. &	0 9
50H.	Wood Hatchways .. .. .. each 1/- 1/3 &	1 6
51H.	Masthead Caps, brass bound, various sizes ,, 4d. &	0 6
53B.	Companions, with open doors .. .. ,, 1/6 2/- &	2 6
54W.	Brass Mounted Cannon, Government proved	
	each, 2½ in., 1/9 3 in., 2/6 4 in.	4 0
55.	Miniature Ship's Boats, common .. each 1d. &	0 2
55.	Do. do. best .. .. .. ,, 2/- &	2 6
56W.	GUN METAL CANON, Government proved. Model of	
	81-ton Gun .. each, 9d. 1/- 1/6 2/6 3/6 &	4 6
57B.	Brass Chain, Cable Link .. .. .. per yard	0 6
58B	Do. Plain .. .. ,,	0 3
59H	Wood Capstans .. .. each 6d.	0 9
59H	Brass do. .. .. each	1 0
60B.	Small Silk Burgees, 3 in. .. .. .. ,,	0 5

No.		Price s. d.
	Burgees, with name as follow :—	
	SYLPH COLUMBIA FIREFLY	
	PRINCE ALERT ROSE	
	SEA-GULL SUNBEAM ROB ROY	
	SHAMROCK PEARLE WASP	
	SPRITE MERMAID	
	Price .. 3 in., each 6d., per doz.	5 0
61.	Dressed Sailors .. .. each 6d. &	0 9
	Officers .. .. ,,	0 9
62B.	Spider Hoops, Brass .. .. .. 1/3 &	1 6
63H.	Ship's Gratings .. each 1/6, 1/9, 2/-, 2/3, 2/6 &	2 9
65H.	Do. Ladders (Wood), 9 step.. ..each 6d., 9d., 1/- &	1 6
68	Do. Propellers, see Engine Fittings.	
71H.	Carved Figure Heads .. .. .. each 1/- &	1 6
72.	Silver Plated Stanchions, 2 and 3 holes .. .. doz.	1 6
74.	Sailcloth (best striped) per yard	0 10½
75B.	Boom Holder and Spider Hoop .. .. each	2 6
76B.	Mast Sockets .. .. ,,	0 7
77H.	Racks for Sidelights .. .. pair	1 2
78H.	Water Casks .. .. each	0 6
79H.	Port and Starboard Signals (Wood) .. .. ,,	0 6
80H.	Ship's Telegraph (Brass) .. .. .. ,,	1 0
81H.	Brass Hawses .. .. ,,	0 8
82H.	Gammon Irons for Bowsprit .. .. each 8d. 10d. &	1 0

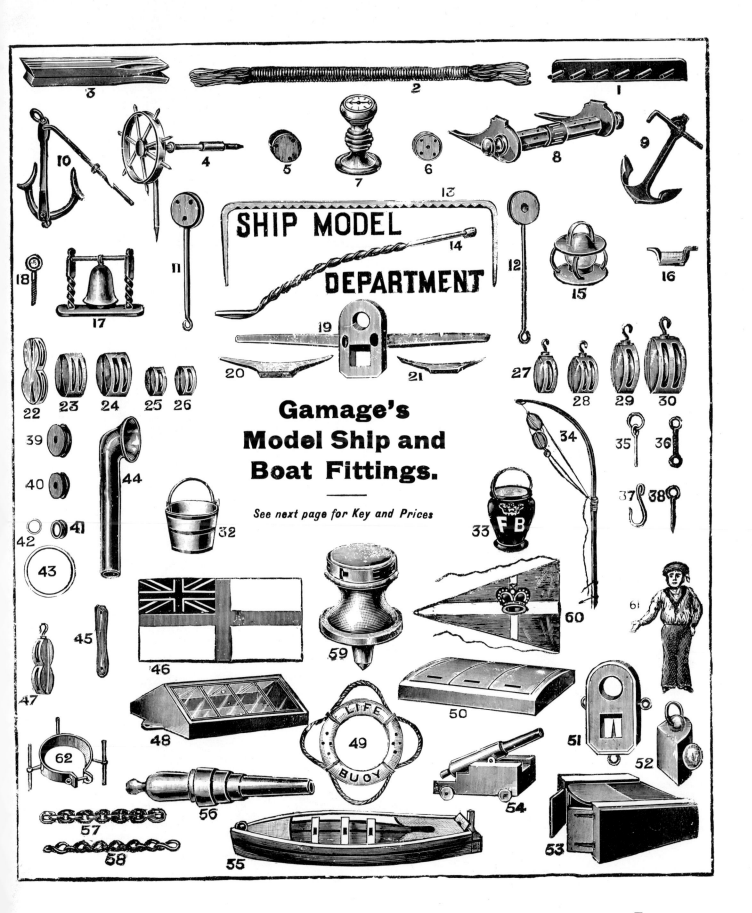

SHIP MODEL DEPARTMENT

Gamage's
Model Ship and
Boat Fittings.

See next page for Key and Prices

AEROPLANES.

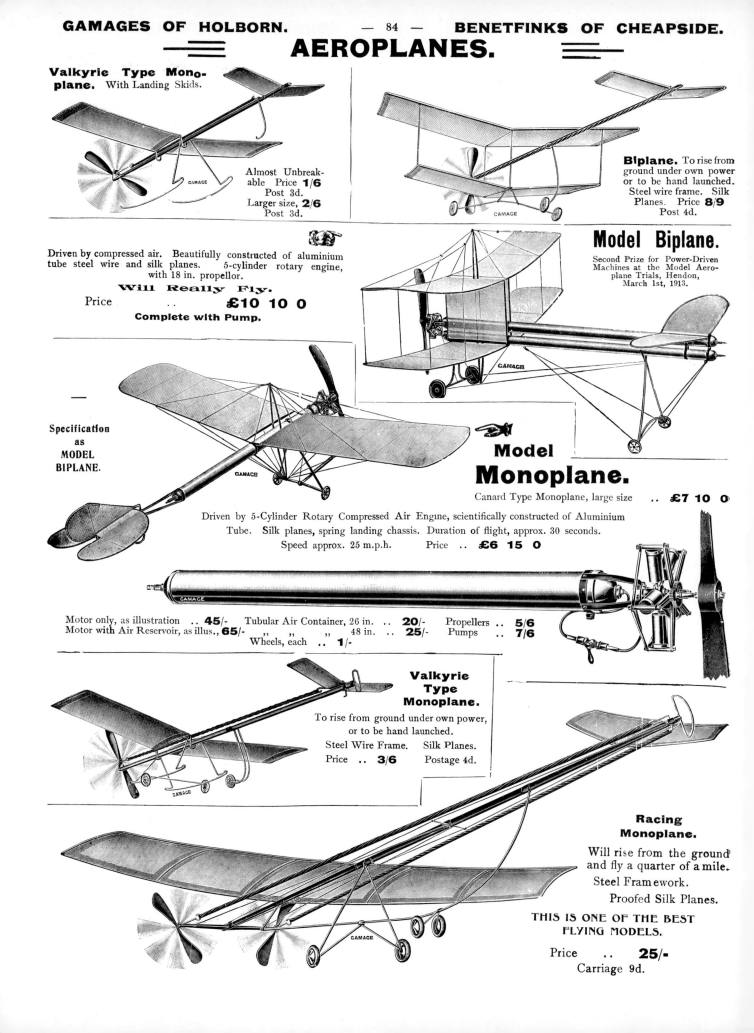

Valkyrie Type Monoplane. With Landing Skids.

Almost Unbreakable Price **1/6**
Post 3d.
Larger size, **2/6**
Post 3d.

Driven by compressed air. Beautifully constructed of aluminium tube steel wire and silk planes. 5-cylinder rotary engine, with 18 in. propellor.

Will Really Fly.

Price .. **£10 10 0**

Complete with Pump.

Biplane. To rise from ground under own power or to be hand launched. Steel wire frame. Silk Planes. Price **8/9** Post 4d.

Model Biplane.

Second Prize for Power-Driven Machines at the Model Aeroplane Trials, Hendon, March 1st, 1913.

Specification as MODEL BIPLANE.

Model Monoplane.

Canard Type Monoplane, large size .. **£7 10 0**

Driven by 5-Cylinder Rotary Compressed Air Engine, scientifically constructed of Aluminium Tube. Silk planes, spring landing chassis. Duration of flight, approx. 30 seconds. Speed approx. 25 m.p.h. Price .. **£6 15 0**

Motor only, as illustration .. **45/-** Tubular Air Container, 26 in. .. **20/-** Propellers .. **5/6**
Motor with Air Reservoir, as illus., **65/-** ,, ,, ,, 48 in. .. **25/-** Pumps .. **7/6**
Wheels, each .. **1/-**

Valkyrie Type Monoplane.

To rise from ground under own power, or to be hand launched.
Steel Wire Frame. Silk Planes.
Price .. **3/6** Postage 4d.

Racing Monoplane.

Will rise from the ground and fly a quarter of a mile.
Steel Framework.
Proofed Silk Planes.

THIS IS ONE OF THE BEST FLYING MODELS.

Price .. **25/-**
Carriage 9d.

Model Aeroplanes and Hydroplanes.

"Aeroplane Al-Ma."

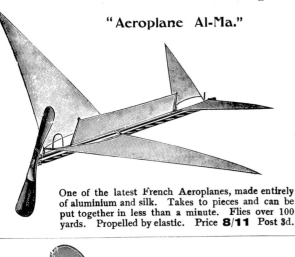

One of the latest French Aeroplanes, made entirely of aluminium and silk. Takes to pieces and can be put together in less than a minute. Flies over 100 yards. Propelled by elastic. Price 8/11 Post 3d.

Leblanc Monoplane.

Copy of LEBLANC'S BLERIOT. Winner of the French Eastern Circuit Race. Aluminium frame and Pegamoid wings. Rises from the ground by its own power. If launched by hand flies 150 to 200 yds. Price .. .. **12/9** Post 6d.

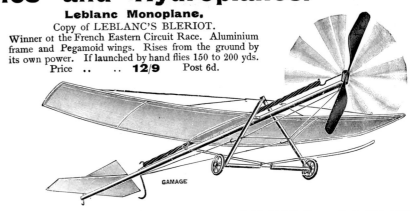

Bristol No 1. Monoplane.

Rises from ground and flies about 180 ft. Strongly made of ash with cambered silk covered planes. Carved Tractor Screw.

No. 1. .. .. Price **6/6** Post 4d.
No. 2. Ditto, larger, ,, **10/6** ,, 5d.

Complete set of materials, with full size drawings, to build No. 2 Machine, **5/-** Post 4d.

Fine Model Racing Monoplane.

Rises off ground and flies about 200 yards. Can be steered and banks like real machine. Strongly made of ash with cambered silk planes. Price .. **12/6** Post 6d.
Complete set of parts, with full size drawings, to build this machine, **8/9** Post 4d.

The Famous Bragg-Smith Biplane.

Patent No. 27812-08. Winner of **27** HIGHEST AWARDS in Model competitions open to the world, including **3** GOLD MEDALS for Stability, Altitude, Distance, Duration, Design, Construction, and general all-round Excellence.

Parcels containing complete sets of materials, including blue print working drawing half full size, full instructions and finished propeller, bearing bracket, and elevator support, which considerably simplifies the making of the models.

No. 1. Bragg-Smith Monoplane, **4/6** Post 4d.
,, 2. ,, Biplane **6/-** ,, 4d.
,, 3. ,, ,, **8/6** ,, 4d.
,, 4. ,, ,, to rise off ground,
Price **9/6** Post 6d.

Antoinette Hydro Aeroplane.

Price .. **17/6** Post 4d.

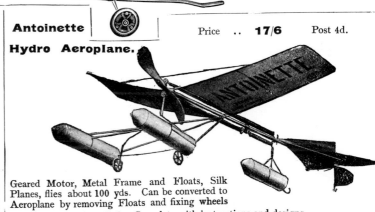

Geared Motor, Metal Frame and Floats, Silk Planes, flies about 100 yds. Can be converted to Aeroplane by removing Floats and fixing wheels supplied. Complete with instructions and designs. A splendid flier, will rise from water or ground under its own power.

TYPE **B.**	Dimensions. 18 by 20.	Will fly 75 yards	..	..	price	**12/6**
,, **C.**	,, 21 by 22.	,, 100 ,,	..	..	,,	**21/-**
TYPE **D.**	Dimensions, 27 by 29.	Will fly 200 yards	..	..	,,	**42/6**
,, **E.**	,, 38 by 38.	,, 300 ,,	..	..	,,	**73/6**

Special Bragg-Smith Hydro-biplane, fitted with floats and rises from the water, dimensions 21 by 22 .. .. price **42/-**
Special Biplanes, to rise from ground (fitted with wheels) same dimensions, **37/6**
Bragg-Smith Monoplanes. No. 1. Dimens. 21 by 22. With 1 propeller, **8/6** No. 2. Long distance, 21 by 22. With 2 propellers, **12/6**

Splendid Flyer. Beautifully made. Will not Upset in the wind.

Fine Model Hydroplane.

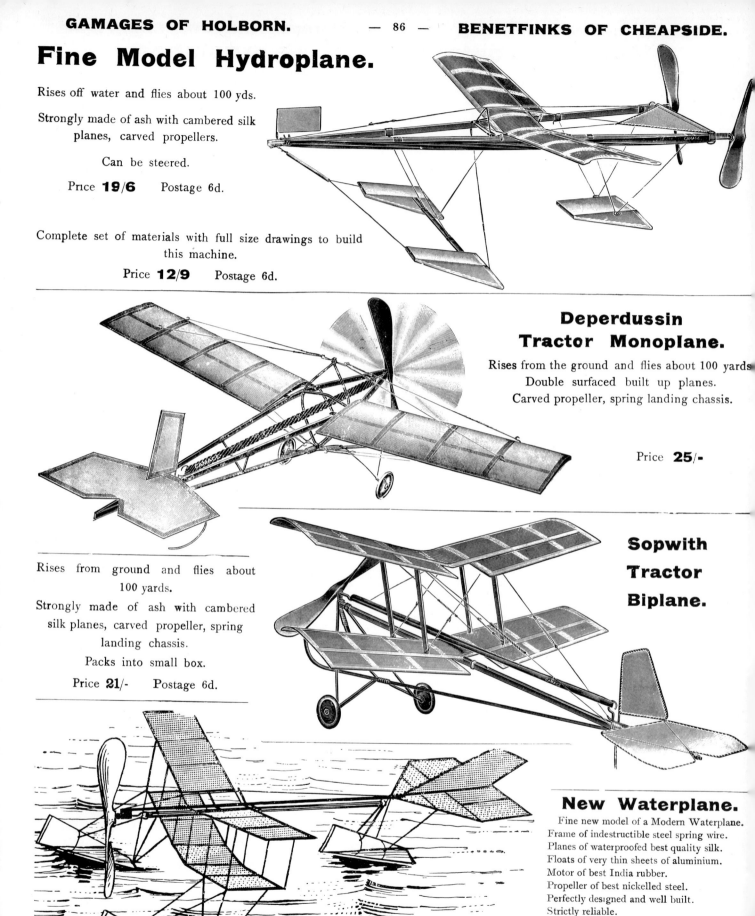

Rises off water and flies about 100 yds.

Strongly made of ash with cambered silk planes, carved propellers.

Can be steered.

Price **19/6** Postage 6d.

Complete set of materials with full size drawings to build this machine.

Price **12/9** Postage 6d.

Deperdussin Tractor Monoplane.

Rises from the ground and flies about 100 yards
Double surfaced built up planes.
Carved propeller, spring landing chassis.

Price **25/-**

Rises from ground and flies about 100 yards.

Strongly made of ash with cambered silk planes, carved propeller, spring landing chassis.

Packs into small box.

Price **21/-** Postage 6d.

Sopwith Tractor Biplane.

New Waterplane.

Fine new model of a Modern Waterplane.
Frame of indestructible steel spring wire.
Planes of waterproofed best quality silk.
Floats of very thin sheets of aluminium.
Motor of best India rubber.
Propeller of best nickelled steel.
Perfectly designed and well built.
Strictly reliable.
Will fly from the surface of the water or will also fly from the hand.
Explicit and detailed instructions with each.
24 in. long, 17 in. across.

Price **10/9** Postage 6d.

Model Aeroplane Accessories.

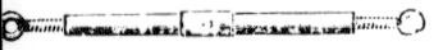

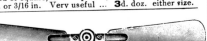

Brass Wire Strainers.

With Steel Screws, for Model Aeroplanes.
Breaking strain, 200 lbs.
Size as illustration.
Price **2**d each **1/6** dozen.

Full size.

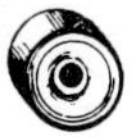

Ball Thrusts.

Smallest in the world, weighing 110 to the oz. Contains 7 Hoffmann's Balls running in grooved pen steel races with German silver dust-proof cases. Price **4½**d. each.

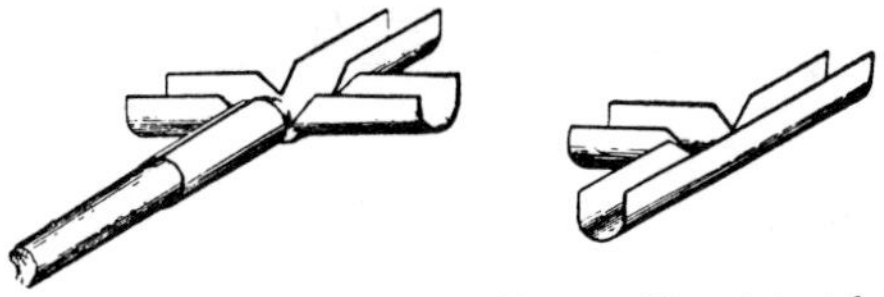

Full size **Strut Connections** (Brass) to take round or square, + or T pieces, two sizes each, to take ⅛ in. or 3/16 in. Very useful ... **3**d. doz. either size.

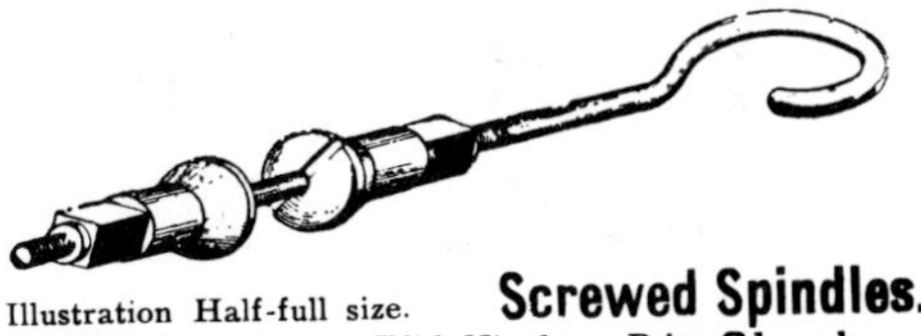

Illustration Half-full size.

Screwed Spindles.

(16th in. gauge). With Nipples. Price **2**d. each.

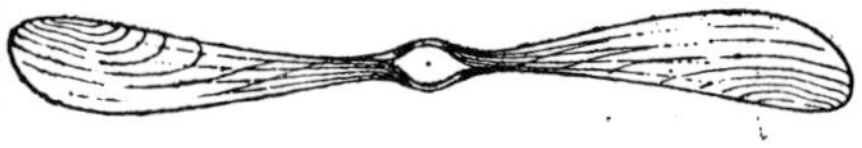

Centrale Propellers.

Right or Left Hand.

	8 in.	10in.	12in.	14in.	16in.	18in.	20in.
Price	**1/6**	**1/6**	**1/9**	**3/6**	**4/-**	**6/-**	**8/-**
Post	2d.	2d.	2d.	3d.	3d.	4d.	4d.

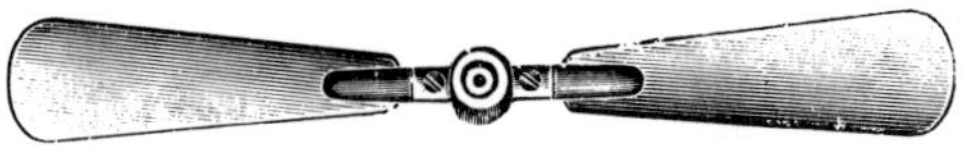

Variable Pitch Propeller.

With aluminium hub and adjusting screws.
12 in. Price **2/-** Postage 2d.

Chauviere Propellers.
6½ in., **1/-**, 8 in. **1/3**, 10 in. **1/6**, 12 in, **1/9.** Post. 2d.

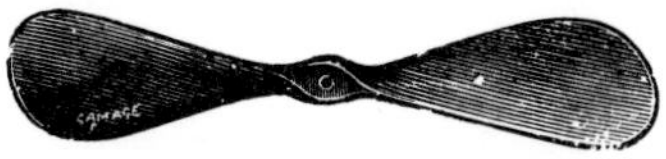

"Venna" Propellers.

High-class, extra light, high efficiency Propellers, as illustration. Perfect Miniatures.

4¾ in.	5½ in.	6½ in.	7 in.	8 in.	8¾ in.	9½ in
9d.	**1/-**	**1/3**	**1/9**	**2/3**	**2/9**	**3/-**
10 in.	16 in.	18 in.	20 in.	22 in.	24 in.	
3/6	**6/6**	**7/6**	**8/6**	**10/6**	**12/6**	

Forks for Miniature Bicycle Wheels.

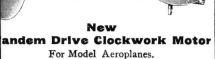

Three Sizes.
5d. each.
Postage 1d.

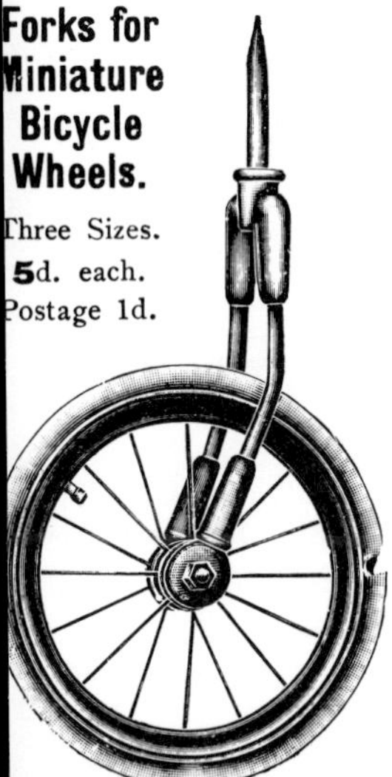

Spoked Rubber-tyred Wheels.

For Model AEROPLANES

Diam.	Each.
¾ in.,	**5**d.
1¼ ,,	**6**d.
¾ ,,	**7**d.
2¾ ,,	**9**d.
3½ ,,	**1/1**
4¼ ,,	**1/7**
6 ,,	**2/6**

Post extra.

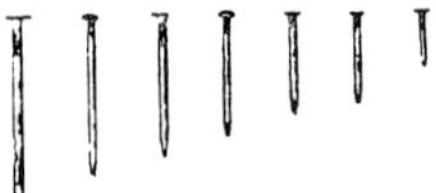

Full size
Model-making Nails.

Smallest Steel Pins. 3/16 in. long.
Packet of about ⅛ oz., **7**d. Postage 1d.
Steel and Copper assorted, packet of about 1½ oz. **9**d.
Post. 1d.

Para Rubber Strip.

For Aeroplane Motors.

⅛ in. wide approx. **1**d. per yard
12 Yards **9**d. Post 1d. 50 Yards **3/-** Post 1½d.

3/16 in. wide approx.

Yards		Post
12	**10**d.	1d.
50	**3/3**	1½d.

¼ in. wide approx.

Yards		Post
12	**1/3**	1d.
50	**5/-**	1½d.

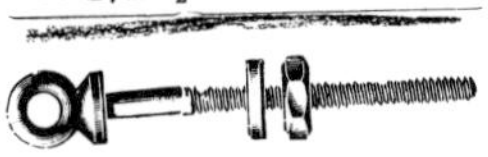

Steel Eyebolt.

With Nut and Washer for Model Aeroplanes.
Size as illus. **2**d. ea. **1/9** doz.

Stamped Aluminium Wheels,

With Brass Axle Bushes and Rubber Tyres.
Very strong and light.

1¼ in. **3**d. 1¾ in. **5**d. 2¾ in dia. **6**d. ea.
3½ in. **8**d. 4¼ in. dia **9**d. ea.

Postage 1d.

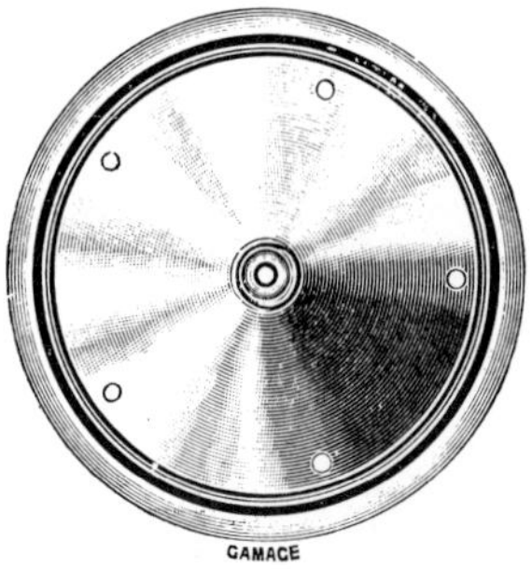

Gold Beaters' Skin Balloons.

Coloured sections for experimental work.

SPHERICAL.

12	14	16	18	20	22	24	30	36	42	48 in.
1/4	**1/10**	**2/6**	**3/-**	**3/9**	**4/11**	**6/6**	**12/-**	**17/6**	**25/-**	**35/-**

ELONGATED.

4ft. 6in. by 2ft.	5ft. by 2ft.	8ft. by 2ft.	8ft. by 3ft.
17/6	**21/-**	**25/-**	**32/6**

12ft. by 2ft., **55/-** 12ft. by 3ft., **85/-**

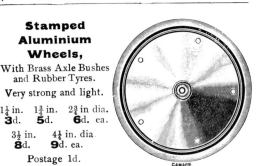

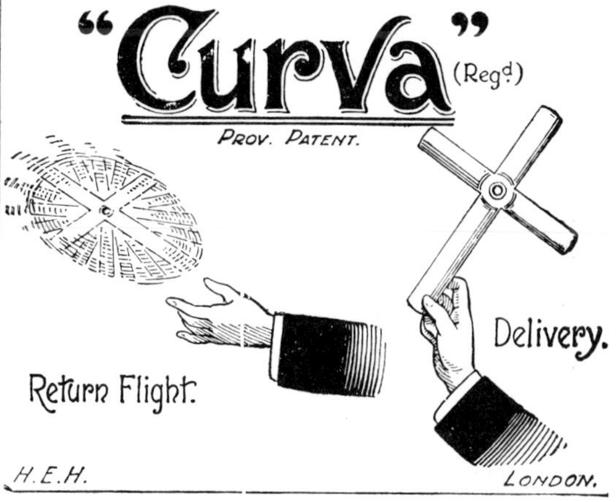
"Curva" (Regd.)
PROV. PATENT.
Return Flight.
Delivery.
H.E.H.
LONDON.

Patented in England, Patents applied for in all Countries.

10½d.
Post 2d.

CURVA is nothing short of a wooden mystery apparently it is simple enough, having the appearance of a cross with the vertical bar a little longer than the h rizontal; there is however, far more in it than its simple form indicates; it has taken many months of experimental work perfecting these mysterious pieces of wood to make them easy fliers.

If a right-handed curve is thrown at a mark on the ground twenty yards ahead it will turn on its side, make a c rcle to the left and return to the thrower's hand.

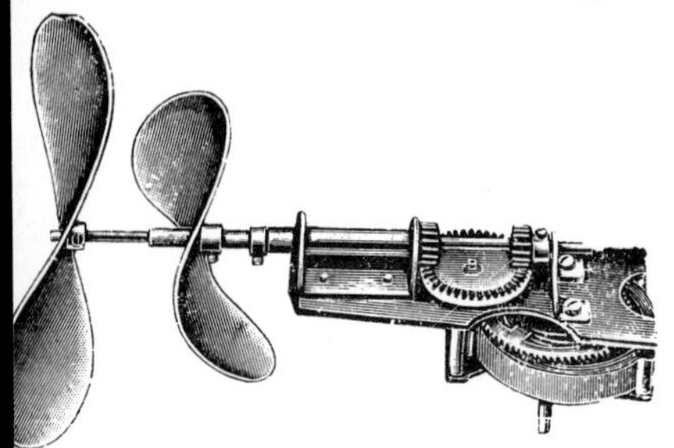

New andem Drive Clockwork Motor

For Model Aeroplanes.

his Motor is fitted with special gearing to drive e propellers in opposite directions, making it the best Clockwork Motor on the market.
Weight 8¼ oz. Price .. **5/6** Post 4d.

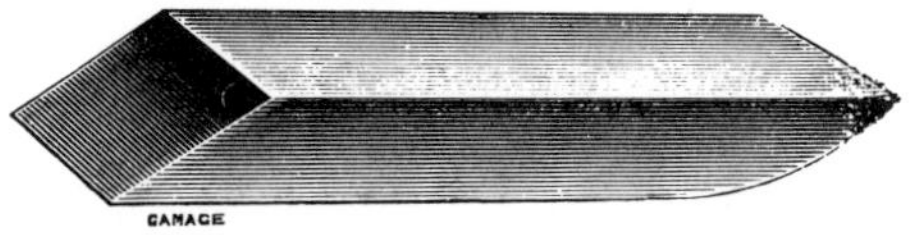

Floats for Model Hydro-Aeroplanes.

Best construction, perfectly watertight.
3/- set of 3. Postage 3d.

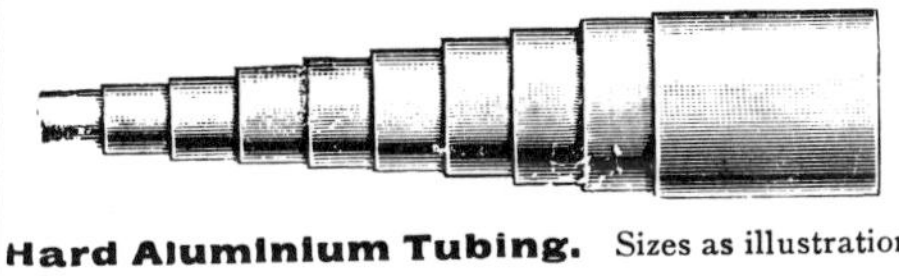

Hard Aluminium Tubing. Sizes as illustration.

	No. 1	2	3	4	5	6	7	8	9	10
Per foot ..	2d	2d	2½d	2½d	3d	3d	3½d	4d	4½d	5d

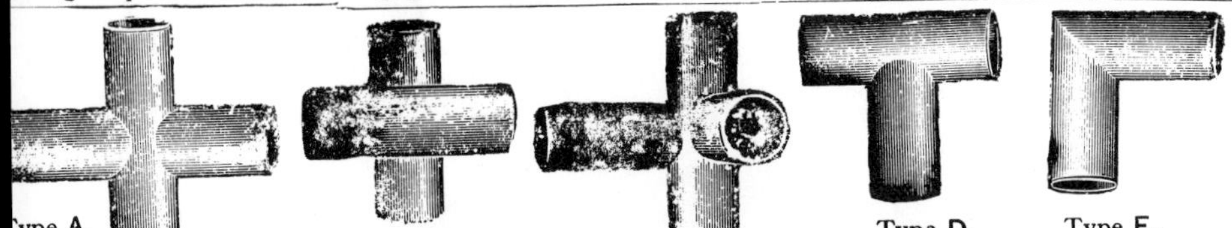

ype A. Type B. Type C. Type D. Type E.

BRAZED HARDENED ALUMINIUM JOINTS.

hese Joints are made in sizes to suit the Hard Aluminium Tubing illustrated above

Size. ..	No. 1.	No. 2.	No. 3.	No. 4.	No. 5.	No. 6.	No. 7.	No. 8.	No. 9	No. 10
ype A	**5**d.	**5**d.	**5**d.	**6**d.	**6**d.	**6**d.	7d.	**7**d.	**7**d.	**8**d.
ype B	**5**d.	**5**d.	**5**d.	**6**d.	**6**d.	**6**d.	7d.	**7**d.	**7**d.	**8**d.
ype C	**8**d.	**8**d.	**8**d.	**10**d.	**10**d.	**10**d.	1/-	**1/-**	**1/-**	**1/-**
ype D	**4**d.	**4**d.	**4**d.	**5**d.	**5**d.	**5**d.	3d.	**6**d.	**6**d.	**6**d.
ype E	**3½**d.	**3½**d.	**3½**d.	4½d.	**4½**d.	**4½**d.	3d.	**6**d.	**6**d.	**6**d.

Clockwork Motors.

With key.

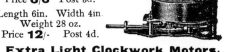

Length over all 5 in. Width 3in. Weight 12 oz.
Price **6/6** Post 3d.

Length 6in. Width 4in. Weight 28 oz.
Price **12/-** Post 4d.

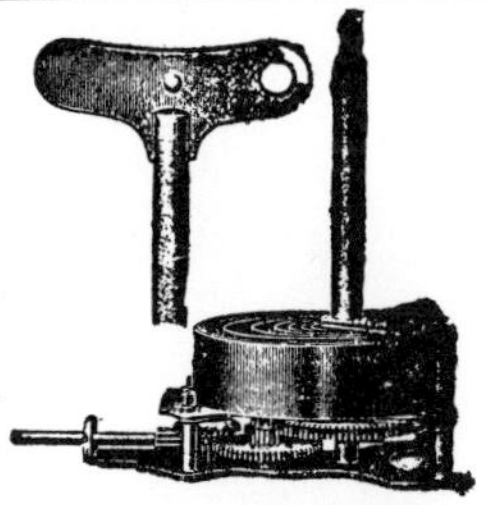

Extra Light Clockwork Motors.

For Small Machines.

No. 1.	Weight 2 oz.	.. ..	**1/6**	Post 1½d.
No. 2.	,, 3 oz.	.. ..	**2/-**	,, 1½d.
No. 3.	,, 5 oz.	.. ..	**2/6**	,, 2d.

MODEL Aeroplane Parts

No. 18. Complete set of materials and parts with drawings to construct Bleriot Monoplane, wi h finished propellor and fuselage. Price **8/11** Post extra

No. 22a. Complete set of materials and parts with fin shed propellor, to construct Monoplane 18 by 19 in., **4/6** Post extra

No. 20a. Complete set of materials and parts, with finished propellor, to construct Etrich-Rumpler Monoplane (main plane, tail and rudder finished), **6/6** Post extra

No. 22. Complete set of materials and parts, including finished propellor, to construct Etrich-Rumpler Monoplane, 18 by 19 in. and Pause Monoplane, 18 by 19 in., Price .. **11/6** Post extra

No. 21. Complete set of parts to construct a large Etrich-Rumpler and Pause Monoplane, with extra parts to construct other models. Price .. **18/6** Post extra

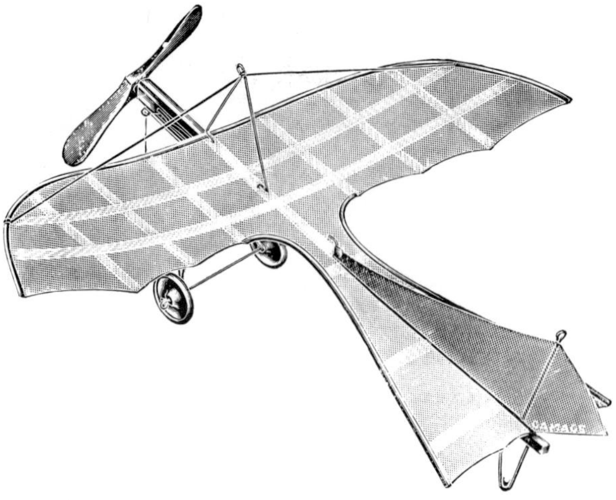

ILLUSTRATION OF ETRICH-REMPLER MONOPLANE.

FOR Home Construction

No. A. Complete set of finished parts, with finished propellor, with drawings, to construct a Monoplane which will fly for 60 seconds Price .. **2/6** Post 3d

No. Z. Ditto do. Monoplane to fly for quarter of a mile. Price **4/6** Post 4d

No. X. Complete set of materials and parts with full-size drawings, to construct Deperdussin Monoplane. **5/-** Post 4d

No. XI. Ditto do. to construct Waterplane Monoplane. Price **12/9** Post 4d

No. XII. Ditto do. to construct Monoplane. Price .. **4/-** Post 4d

No. XIII. Ditto do. to construct Bleriot Canard Monoplane. Price **8/9** Post 6d

Wood, Fabric, Wire, Rubber, Etc., for Model Aeroplane Construction.

American Poplar, Cut to sizes in lengths, 2 ft., 3 ft., 3 ft. 6 in. Small Section, $\frac{1}{8}$ in. by 3/16 in.; 3/16 in. by 3/16 in.; 3/16 in by $\frac{1}{4}$ in.; $\frac{1}{4}$ in. by $\frac{1}{4}$ in. Fine Sawn. 48 feet **1/-**
Larger Sections, 3/16 in. by $\frac{3}{8}$ in.; $\frac{1}{4}$ in. by $\frac{3}{8}$ in. Fine Sawn 36 feet **1/-**
Larger Sections, $\frac{3}{8}$ in. square. Fine Sawn. 24 feet **1/-**

Cane, about 3/16 in. diameter .. .. .. per ft. **1**d.

WOOD.

Spruce, 1/30 in. scaled in sheets 3 ft. 6 in. by 6 in .. **2**d. per sheet.

Birch Propeller Planks, 12 in. by 2 in. **10**d. doz. Post 1½d.

Bentwood Propellers, 6 in., **10**d. pair; 8 in., **1/-**; 10 in., **1/3** pair .. .. Post 2d.

Propellers (Carved). With hook and shaft. Specially large pitch for elastic motors. 6 in. **1/-**; 8 in. **1/3** 9 in. **1/6**; 10 in. **1/9**; 12 in. **2/-**

			planed.	Planed both sides.
American Poplar, extremely light and easy to work 1/16 in. thick in boards, 9 in. wide	..	per ft. run	**3½**d.	**4**d.
,, ,, ,, 6 ,,	..	,,	**1½**d.	**3**d.

Model Flying Machines: Their Design and Construction. By W. G. ASTON. Price **1/-** Postage 2d.

The Aero Manual. A manual of mechanically propelled human flight covering the history of the work of early investigators and of the pioneer work of the last century. Recent successes and the reasons therefore are dealt with, together with full constructive details concerning airships, aeroplanes, gliders, etc. Revised edition. Price **1/6** Post 2d.

Flying; The Why and the Wherefore: Flying and some of its mysteries. By V. E. JOHNSON, M.A. Deals with the construction of Model Airships and Aeroplanes. Price **1/6** Post 2d.

The Aeroplane Portfolio.

Containing Nine Sheets of Scale Drawings of the following celebrated Aeroplanes, Farman, Cody, Bleriot, Antoinette and Rep with a description of each machine. Price .. **1/-** Postage 2d.

Bragg-Smith Special Waterproof Varnish for Model Aeroplanes, Propellers, Floats, etc., and all Woodwork. Dries a Splendid Finish. Price .. **9**d. Post 1½d.

Gamage Model Aero Fabric.

A. W. GAMAGE, LTD., have purchased a huge parcel of Fabric which they are proofing themselves. It makes an exceedingly fine Fabric with a surface like glass. Does not stretch or lose its shape. Extraordinary strength. Try it

APPROXIMATE SIZES:

11 in. by 38 in. **8**d. a piece. Post 1d. 15 in. by 38 in. **10**d. Post 1d. 16 in. by 28 in. **6**d. Post 1d.

Proofed Silk Aeroplane Fabric. Green or Yellow. 36 in. by 36 in. **3/-** Post 1d. 12 in. by 36 in. **1/1** Post 1d.

Gamage's Rubber Lubricant .. .. **6**d. Tube.

Para Rubber Strip for Motors.

$\frac{1}{8}$ in. wide.	12 yards	.. **9**d.	Post 1d.	50 yards	.. **3/-**	Post 1½d
$\frac{3}{16}$,,	12 ,,	.. **10**d.	Post 1d.	50 ,,	.. **3/3**	,, 1½d
$\frac{1}{4}$,,	12 ,,	.. **1/3**	,, 1½d.	50 ,,	.. **5/-**	,, 1½d

SPECIAL.—Ball-Thrust Mounted Spindle and Bearing, beautifully made in hard brass, self-centring bearing, spindle screwed, and nippled to take any propeller, bearing can be lashed to any stick .. .. each **8**d. Post 1d

Steel Colletts .. .. .. **2**d. per dozen.

Bolt with Nuts. Short round-headed Brass Bolts, with hexagon brass nuts .. .. each post **1½**d

Propellor-bearing, drilled ready for use .. each **3**d. post **1**d

Small Bolts with Nuts, Brass and Steel, about 1/16 in. diam. .. .. pair **2½**d

Small Bobbins of Plated Music Wire.

For Model Aeroplane construction, 30 Gauge. Price .. **5**d. each. Post 1d.

Piano Wire, 18 and 20 Gauge Price **1/6** per ½-lb. coil. ¼ coil **6**d. These wires are all plated.

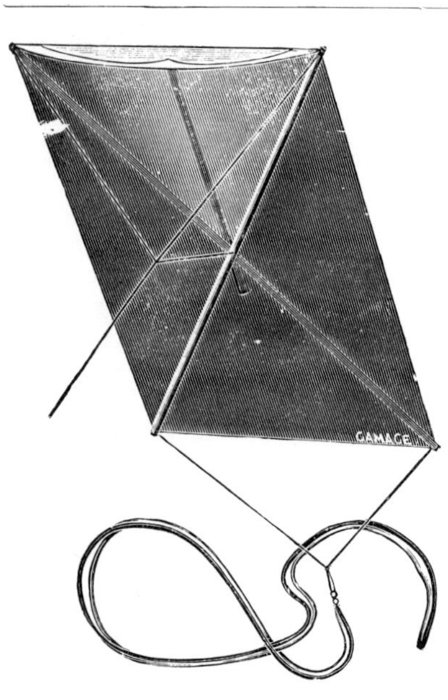

"Music in the Air."

THE WONDERFUL

"Orpheusplane,"

OR

MUSICAL KITE!

Made on an entirely new principle, with whip tail feet long.

This Kite can be manœuvred while flying, and will rise and descend by the manipulation of the cord.

Price .. 2/6

Postage 2d.

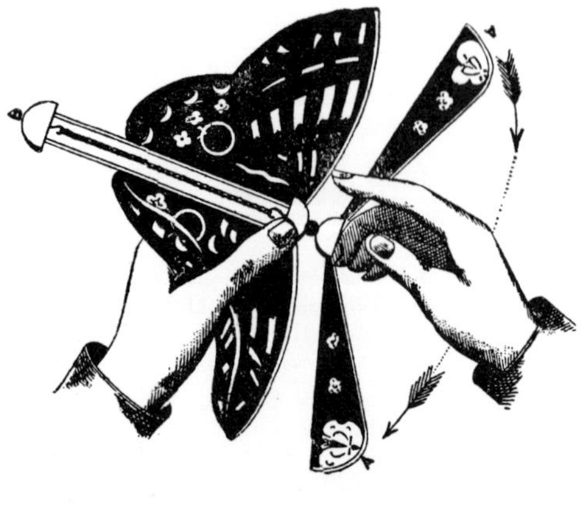

Flying Bats.

SPLENDID FOR INDOOR OR OUTDOOR AMUSEMENT.

Price **6**d. Post 2d.

Ditto, SILK .. **1/-** Post 2d.

KITES.

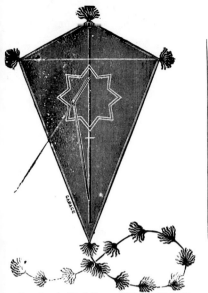

Hawk Kite.

Made of Linen to imitate a Hawk, 8 ft. across wings. Very useful to sportsmen for keeping down Partridges, &c. .. **5/6**
Ditto in Silk .. **15/-** Packing and post 4d.

Since we introduced this Kite some years ago we have sold thousands, and they have given every satisfaction.

Parrot Kite. Most life-like. Flies very steadily. Made of Linen, and coloured to imitate a parrot. 6 ft. across wings. Folds up to 29 in.

Price .. .. **3/6** Post 4d.

The Quadroplane Kite.

In the Altitude Display given by the Council of the Kite and Model Aeroplane Association October, 1910, one of our No. Ty. 9 Quadroplane Kites attained the highest altitude, carrying out 2¼ miles of 22 gauge wire. Winner of the First Prize, Kite Flying Association Meeting, Wimbledon Common, 1910. Awarded highest marks for stability, Kite and Aeroplane Association Competition for Baden-Powell Shield, June 22nd, 1910.

No.	Area of Fabric.		Price.	Carriage
Ty. 1.	7 square ft., similar to illustration		**3/6**	3d
Ty. 2.	9 ,, ...		**4/6**	3d
Ty. 3.	13 ,, ...		**5/11**	4d.
Ty. 4.	15 ,, ...as illustration		**7/6**	6d.
Ty. 5.	21 ,, ...		**10/6**	Forward.

Pocket Folding Kite. (Patent).

Since we first introduced this Kite many years ago, thousands have been sold, and it is still in great demand. Owing to its simplicity of construction, it can be produced quite cheaply. A very suitable Kite for young beginners. Strongly made of linen. with bamboo stays.

No. Ty. 1.	Height 45 in. ..	**1/4½**	Post 3d,
,, 2.	,, 4 ft. 9 in.	**2/4½**	,, 4d.
,, 3.	,, 6 ft.	**4/9**	,, 6d.

Kite Parachutes.

Containing 4 Parachutes and releaser.

5d. a box. Post 1d.

Kite Cords.

No	Breaking Strain.	Length per lb.	Price per Roll of 300 yds.	Carriage.
1	105 lbs.	150 yds.	5/-	5d
2	160 ,,	100 ,,	**7 6**	6d.
3	264 ,,	75 ,,	**10/-**	7d.
4	460 ,,	37 ,,	**20/-**	11d.
5	800 ,,	21 ,,	**42/-**	1/-

N.B.—All above Cords are in one continuous length without joins.

KITE TWINES.

These Twines are made of precisely the same yarns as the cords, but spun in a different manner, and are intended for smaller Kites, having an exceptional length per lb. in relation to their strength.

No.	Breaking Strain.	Length per lb.	Price per lb.	Price per ½-lb.	Price per ¼-lb.
1	45 lbs.	540 yds.	**1/6**	9d.	4½d.
2	69 ,,	324 ,,	**1 6**	9d.	4½d.
3	120 ,,	216 ,,	**1/6**	9d.	4½d.

Postage ¼-lb. 1½d., ½-lb. 2½d. 1-lb. 4d.

The Gamage "Compactum" Folding Kite Windlass.

The most comfortable Winder possible.

No. Ty. 1. Height to seat, 13 in., height to top of windlass, 26 in. ... **5/6**
,, 2. Height of seat, 20 in., height to top of windlass, 37 in. ... **15/-** Carriage forward.

The "Scout" Kite.

This is a very popular Kite, and owing to its relative lightness, is in great demand as a pilot to assist in raising the larger aeroplanes in light breezes. Sizes No. 5 and upwards are fitted with an adjustable bridle special feature. By this arrangement they will adjust themselves while in the air to suit the wind thus obviating the necessity of altering the bridle.

No.	1	2	3	4
Height	24	30	33	38 ins.
Price	1/-	**1/6**	**2/6**	**3/6** each. Car. forward.

Carriage 3d.

No.	5	6	7
Height	42	48	54 ins.
Price	**4/6**	**5/-**	**6/6** each.

Carriage forward.

No.	8	9	10
Height	60	66	72 inch.
Price	**10/6**	**14/6**	**19/6** each.

Carriage forward.

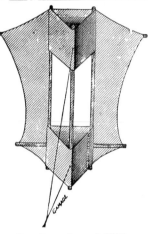

Gamage Professional Kite.

This Kite is well-known for its remarkable lifting power and steadiness in flight. Folds up into a small space.

No. Ty. 1. 7 square feet.. **3/6** Post 4d.
,, 2. .. .. **6/6** ,, 5d.

You can 'Phone your Orders by ringing 2,700 Holborn.

Miniature Kite Man Lifting.

Ty. 1. Kite Basket, **6**d. Post 2d.
Ty. 2. Kite Basket, **9**d. Post 2½d.
Ty. 3. Kite Basket, **1/4½** Post 3d.

The Gamage Kite Winder.

Compact and easy to carry.

Supersedes the old style.

Cord can be wound up quickly.

Made of hardwood.

Ty. 1 .. **8**d. Post 3d.
,, 2 .. **1/-** ,, 3d.
,, 3 .. **1/6** .. 4d.

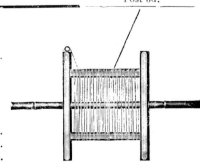

Superior Motor Cars and Lorries.

Clockwork Motor Bus in fine polychrome japanning, with strong clockwork. 12¾ in. long. 6¼ in. wide, with driver.
Price .. **2/11** Post 3d.

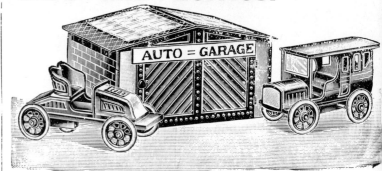

Extraordinary Value, A complete Motor Garage with doors to ope and 2 clockwork Motor Cars, exactly as illustration **1/-** Post 3d.

Limousine Motor Car. Strong clockwork movement, will run forward and backwards, also stop by lever in cab, can run straight or circular Length 12 in. Height 4½ in. Wide 5¾ in. Price **13 6** Post 6d.

New Model Broughams. Torpedo bodies, strong clockwork move ment, rubber tyres, doors to open, fitted with brake, Bevel Glass Windows front axle adjustable to straight or circular run.
No. 3. 16 in. long, 6½ in. wide .. price, **25/-**
" 4. 18⅓ " 7 " .. " **35/-**

New Model Open Touring Car. Torpedo bodies, superior quality best hand-painted, strong, powerful clockwork movement, nicely regulated, rubber tyres. correct pattern seat, with brake, front axe adjustable for straight or circular run. No. 1, 12¾ in. long, 5¾ in. wide ... **11/9** Post 6d.
No. 2. 15¾ in. long, 6⅛ wide **21/-**

New Model Broughams. Torpedo bodies, superior quality strong clockwork movement with brake and rubber tyres, doors to ope Bevel Glass windows, front axle adjustable for straight or circular run No. 1. 10½ in. long, 4½ in. wide, price **8/11** Post 4d.
" 2. 13 " 5¼ " " **14 6** " 5d.

Motor Lorry with Tip-Up Body. Can be tip-- as illustration. Superior quality and finish, strong clockwork movement, rubber tyres, front axle adjustable to --llow either straight or circular run. 11¾ in. long, 3½ in. wide .. **5/11** Post 4d.

Motor Lorry. Loaded with sacks, and covered with tarpauli Very realistic. Strong clockwork movement.
8¼ in. long, 3½ in. wide .. .. price **2/11** Post 3d.

Clockwork Motor Cars, 'Busses, etc.

Double Torpedo Phaeton Motor Car with powerful clockwork spring, fitted brake. Can be made to run backwards and forwards, also straight or circular by means of lever in car.   Finely enamelled.

No. 1. 14½ in. long, 5 in. high, 5 in. wide **22/6**
2. 17½ ,,   5¾ ,,   6¼ ,, ... **32/6**

Motor Cyclist.
One of the best novelties of the season. Propelled by momentum of heavy fly wheels. Does not get of order.
Price **1/10½**   Postage 3d.

Motor Car (open touring car).
Up-to-date body.   Superior finish. Reliable clockwork mechanism. In two colours, red or blue.   Streamline body.
10480/0. 7½ in. long, 2¼ in. wide. **6**d. Post 2d.

Clockwork Motor Car.
Lithographed in green. Fitted with imitation tyres, and roof to take off.
Price **10½**d.   Postage 3d.

Clockwork Motor Bus as illustration.
Price **10½**d.   Postage 3d.

Clockwork Motor Car as illustration. Painted green, and roof to take off, and imitation tyres.
Price **1/10½**   Postage 3d.
Ditto, larger, fitted with imitation lamps, **2/11** Post 4d.

Momentum Motor Car.
No springs to get out of order.   Propelled by momentum of fly wheel. Will run up an incline and travel further than most clockwork cars.
Price **1/11**   Postage 3d.

New Model Open Touring Car.   Torpedo body.
Superior quality, best hand-painted, strong clockwork movement, nicely regulated rubber tyres, correct pattern seat with brake, front axle adjusted for straight or circle run. 9¼ in. long, 3⅞ in. wide. Price **5/11** Postage 4d.

Open Touring Car as illustration.   Up-to-date body.
Superior finish.   Reliable clockwork mechanism. Painted red or blue.   Stream line body.

1. 9 in. long, 4 in. wide .. .. .. **10½**d. Post 3d.
2. 10½ ,,   4¼ ,,   with brake .. .. **24½** ,, 3d.
3. 12¼ ,,   4⅔ ,,   ,, windscreen, 2 lamps, **3/6** ,, 4d.

New 4-seater Momentum Motor Car.
No spring to get out of order.   Driven by heavy fly-wheel, which enables them to run up an incline or down a decline at regular speed. Price **2/11** Post 4d.

Superior Clockwork Fire Engines, etc.

Clockwork Motor Fire Engine
(as illustration, with imitation rubber tyre and hose. Price .. **10½d.** Post 3d.

Clockwork Fire Escape (as illustration),
with removable Ladders and Hose Pipe.
Price **3 11** Post 5d.

Clockwork Fire Engine.
With Rubber Wheels. Price **2/11** Post 4

Latest Type Motor Fire Engine. Superior finish. Superior clockwork movement, fitted with change over gear, which will either run car or work the pump with water reservoir, complete pump gear, hose, bell, rubber tyres, front axle adjustable for straight or circular runs, fitted with brake, bell rings when running. 12 in. long. 4½ in. wide. 6½ in. high. **16/6** Post 6d.

Fine Model Clockwork Fire Engine. Hand-painted fitted with brass boiler and head light, india rubber tyres. Fitted with Automatic Pump, as illustration. Price .. **11/6** Post 6d.

Clockwork Steam Roller (as illustration. Runs forward and backwards. Price .. **10½d.** Post 3d.

Fine Model Clockwork Carpet Locomotive.
Price .. .. .. **3/11** Post 4d.
Ditto, smaller and without cylinder. Price .. **10½d.** Post 3d.
Larger .. .. **1/10½d.** Post 4d.
Ditto, with tender. Price .. .. **2/6** Post 4d.

Fine Model Fire Escape.
Ladder 34 in. high. Price .. **5 11** Post 4d.

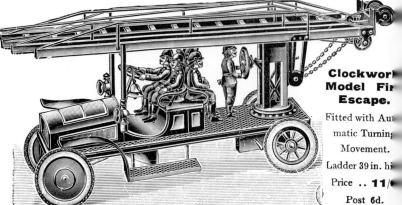

Clockwork Model Fire Escape.
Fitted with Automatic Turning Movement.
Ladder 39 in. hi
Price .. **11/**
Post 6d.

MECHANICAL TOYS.

Oxford and Cambridge Eights. Clockwork Rowing Boat (as illustration) to run on table, &c., coloured in Oxford or Cambridge Blue
Very realistic   Price ...   ... **10½d.**   Post 3d.

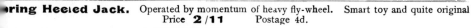

Spring Heeled Jack. Operated by momentum of heavy fly-wheel.   Smart toy and quite original
Price **2/11**   Postage 4d.

Mechanical Billiard Table
(as illustration). Fresh ball rises
automatically as player plays first ball.
Price ...   **1/10½**   Post 3d.

The Jibbing Donkey.
Laughable clever mechanical
Toy.

Price .. **1/-**
Post 3d.

Mechanical Skittle Alley.

As illustration,
Fresh ball rises
automatically
and rolls into
player's hand.

Price .. **2/11**

Post 3d.

MOUNTAIN RAILWAY

(as illustration).

No clockwork to get out of order.   Price .. **2/11**   Post 5d.

CLOCKWORK LOOPING THE LOOP

(as illustration).

Length   Price ..   .. **1/10½**   Post 4d.

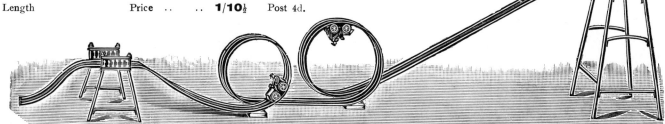

MECHANICAL NOVELTIES.

The Two-horse Race consists of a stand supporting two jockeys on horses, who, when the race is started, race round and round, passing and repassing one another in such a manner that it is positively impossible to tell which will win until the race is over. With this game children can be kept amused for hours. It is strongly made and not likely to get out of order. Price **10½**d. Larger size, with 4 horses, **2/3** Postage 3d.

Children's Ice Cream Freezer
Real working model. Makes Ice Crea of all flavours in a few minutes by turni handle. Strongly made with brass c wheels, enamelled blue and gold. Each in box with directions.
No. 1. Size 5 by 5½ in. **10½**d. Post 3
Ditto Larger .. **3/11** ,, 4

Clockwork Tiger. Most life-like in its movement. When wound up it crouches and then jumps forward. Price .. **32/6** Post 6d.
Ditto LION. Price .. **32/6** ,, 6d.

Folleron Train

The ideal toy for lit children

The carriages are arranged that they follo in an exact line of the e gine when running alon therefore giving a m realistic and charmi effect This toy absolutely unbreakab

No. 1. Loco. and Tend with 3 carriages, fitt Clockwork .. **2/**
Post 3d.

The Equestrienne.

This is an exceedingly clever toy and one which will not readily get out of order. It is operated by winding with string in a similar way to a Gyroscope Top. The momentum of a heavy wheel is the motive power.
As the horse runs round the ring the lady rider jumps the obstacles in a most realistic manner, each time alighting on the back of the horse. Price **10½**d. Post 3d.

Gamage's Popular Racing Cyclist.   Price .. **2/9** Postage 3d.

Without question this is the most clever Mechanical Toy that has been produced for many years. The mechanism differs from that of the ordinary clockwork toy, inasmuch as it is almost impossible to overwind it. An extraordinary feature of the Cycle is that, although the front wheel has entirely free play and the Cycle is in no way held up, it starts off with a characteristic "Wobble," gradually gaining speed and steadiness which it maintains in a circle of about 6 to 8 feet, covering altogether at one winding about 80 to 90 yards.

MECHANICAL TOYS.

Clockwork Clowns.

Clockwork Boy and Cart.

Mechanical Mouse.

NO SPRING TO GET OUT OF ORDER

Propelled by means of heavy flywheel.
Price .. **3**d. Post 2d.

You can 'Phone your Orders by ringing up
— 2700 HOLBORN. —

Clockwork Motor Cycle and Side Car.

Forms figure 8 while running.
Price **10½**d. Post 3d.

...s illustration. One performs while the
...her drives along. Price **1**/- post 3d.

As illustration. Runs about in zigzag
fashion. Price **10½**d. Post 3d.

Clockwork Beetle.

...ith natural movement. Raises its wings and puts
out feelers while walking. Price **10½**d Post 3d.

Clockwork Rat.

Clockwork Goose.

With moveable head. Natural movement with
Voice. Price **10½**d. Post 3d.

As Illustration.

...y a most ingenious arrangement of mechanism
...e Rat will always turn on reaching the edge of
...e table, or on whatever it may be placed, regardless of shape. Almost human.
Price **6**d. Post 2d.

Clockwork Tricky Lobster.

This clever Toy will always turn on reaching
edge of table and go off in another direction.
Will not fall off. Price **10½**d. Post 3d.

The Children's **Picturedrome.**
Complete with 3 sets of Pictures.
Price **10½**d. Post 3d.

Clockwork Horse and Clown.

Very realistic.
Price **10½**d.
Post 3d.

Clockwork Duck and Hen.

Fighting for Frog while running. Price **10½**d. Post 3d.

LATEST

NOVELTY.

Clockwork Clown with Donkey.

...Clown has moveable head and arms.
Price **10½**d. Post 3d.

Mechanical Railway Porter.

An exceedingly clever Toy, with most
lifelike movement. The man bends
his knees and walks by mechanism contained in his body. Price **1/3** post 3d.

Ragtime Joe.

This is the most clever dancing Toy
invented, the movement being very
natural. While dancing the Nigger
turns round in orthodox fashion.
Price **1/3** Post 3d.

When the Box is opened the bird
springs up, flaps its wings, and sings.
Exceedingly clever.
Price **1**/- Post 3d.

"VORTEX"

British Patent

No. 24253.

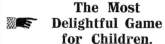

VORTEX NURSERY RHYMES.

THREE little Vortex men are we,
    Out for a rollicking, romping spree,
    Jumping about with a one-two-three!
                    —Three little Vortex men.

One of us is a policeman bold,
Seeing we all do what we're told,
Trying to catch—though he can't hold
                    —Two little Vortex men.

One of us is a merry clown,
Like old Grimaldi of great renown,
Springing about—for he won't lie down
                    —(Nor will) Three little Vortex men.

One of us is a merry Swiss,
Straight from the country of Edelweiss,
Oh, such a jolly fellow this   —Dear little Vortex man!

THREE LITTLE VORTEX MEN are we,
Happy as Vortex men should be!
WHY DON'T YOU BUY US AND THEN YOU'LL SEE
                    —THREE LITTLE VORTEX MEN.

Patent No. 24253. This is a screamingly funny toy and game. It never fails to attract and amuse. When the handle is turned the figures make the most extraordinary movements, providing roars of laughter.

See the Comic Policeman in his efforts to arrest and he can't do it !

Children love it because it is a most amusing toy, new and different from anything they have ever seen before.

Parents buy it because its merits are obvious.

Unbreakable !   Indestructible !   No Springs to get out of order !

The Vortex Wheel has sold by the thousand in all parts of the world !   **Send for one to-day !**

THE VORTEX PATENT TOY COMPANY.

Can be obtained from Gamages .. Price complete, with full instructions, **2/-** Postage 4d.

 # No more dull days in the Nursery

The "Tessted" 'WALKABOUT' Animals.

SOFT PLUSH ANIMALS
that really "Walkabout."

[T]he Mechanical Movement is on entirely [n]ovel lines and patented in all Countries.

[T]he most life-like and natural Toy Animal ever introduced to the public.

[E]LEPHANT,   TERRIER,
[W]HITE CAT,   CÆSAR,
[B]LACK CAT,   LION,
[PO]LAR BEAR,   TEDDY BEAR,
[P]OMMERANIAN DOG, POODLE.

WE CAN ALL WALKABOUT NOW!

Special Demonstration in our Toy Department.

Simply wind them up and they "walk about" in life-like manner. Elephants with slow and stately tread, Lions fast and furious, Cæsar trots along, while Pussie's gentle tread is natural to a degree.

PRICES:

Small.	Large.
3/6	**5/-**
each.	

Each animal is fitted with guaranteed **best quality** mechanism, practically unbreakable—made to last for years. The key is attached to each animal, so that it cannot get lost.

Trippel=Trappel Toys.

By a clever arrangement, without any Clockwork or complicated mechanism, the natural movement of the animals is exactly imitated.

No. **1. Clockwork Clowns,** assorted costumes, felt dressed.   Price .. **10½**d.   Post 2d.

No. **2. Walking Terriers,** with Trippel-Trappel movement. With White Long Hair. Mohair Plush.   Price .. **1/10½**.   Post 3d.

No. **3.   Lamb,** with Trippel-Trappel movement. White Mohair Plush. With Bells and Silk Ribbons.   Price .. **2/6**   Post 4d.

No. **4. Clockwork Jumping Monkey,** with life-like face. Brown Mohair. Price .. **2/6**   Post 3d.

No. **5. Clockwork Jumping Frog,** made of Felt in natural colours. With voice in hat.   Price .. **2/11**   Post 3d

No. 1.

No. 2.

No. 3.

No. 4.

No. 5.

G

Balancing Jockey
The rider runs round an oblong track, maintaining his balance on a very narrow ledge. Price **9**d. Post 2d.

Choral Top.
6d. **10½**d. **1/6**
Large size **2/-** Post d

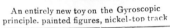

Disc Tops.
A set of three Disc Tops enamelled brilliant colours can be spun at enormous pace by use of the striker supplied, **10½**d. Post 3d

Ring of Roses.
Price **9**d. Post 3d.

An entirely new toy on the Gyroscopic principle. painted figures, nickel-top track

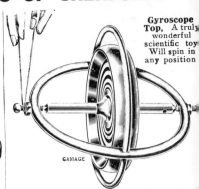

Gyroscope Top, A truly wonderful scientific toy Will spin in any position

With stand, **6**d. **10½**d. **1/4½ 2/6** Post 3d. & 4
Extra large, **3/6 5/11 7/6** Post 5d. & 6

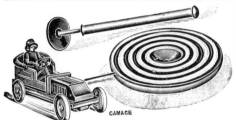

The Mad Motorist. This is a really smart toy and one not likely to get broken owing to its substantial construction. Worked by plunging Striker in centre of Disc. Price ... ... **2/3** Post 3d.

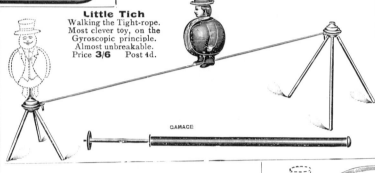

Little Tich
Walking the Tight-rope. Most clever toy, on the Gyroscopic principle. Almost unbreakable. Price **3/6** Post 4d.

Little Tich Top.
On spiral wire.
As illustration.
Price **5/6** Post 4d.

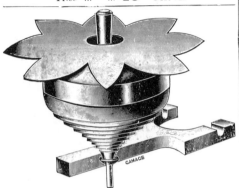

Fifteen-Minute Top. The longest spinning top in the world. Complete with fancy discs, for producing Kaleidoscopic effects Price ... **1 6** Post 3d.

New Tireless Spinning Top.
Spins with a twist of finger and thumb. Runs ten minutes. Price ... **6**d. Post 2d.

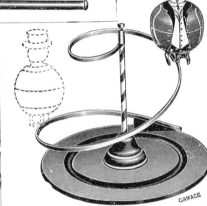

The Concord Top.
Set spinning by a driving stick. Plays two tunes and changes independently during motion of top. The tone is exceedingly sweet and musical. Mechanical parts are of best possible quality and manufacture, enclosed in an embossed nickel-plated body. **4/11** Post 4d.

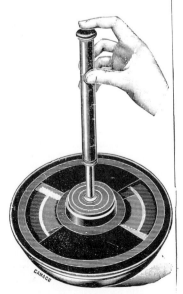

New Changing Disc or Chameleon Top. Price **1/6** Post 3d.
tto, smaller, ,, **10½**d. ,, 2d

The Gyro Happy Dancer.
Unique Mechanical Marvel. Worked upon an entirely new principle. No spring. No clockwork to get out of order **1/-** Post 3d.

Horse Training. A good lasting toy. Worked by means of a plunger and circular disc, **2/3** Post 3d.

Balancing Clown. Disc Top. 2/3 Post 3d.

Choral Top, with spring starter Price **1/6** Post 3d.
Larger size ,, **2/11** ,, 3d.

Gyroscopic and Hopping Tops.

ON THE TRACK.

"GYRO" MONO-RAIL TOP.

Gives double the performance of any other Top, and is capable of high climbing and various performances on the Mono-Rail. The only Top that will travel uphill. Will also travel 100 yards on string with one spin or round a Tumbler, etc. The most fascinating Toy ever invented.

In attractive box with 5 ft. Mono-Rail Track.

Price .. .. **10½**d. ;Postage 3d.

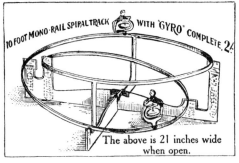

A GYROSCOPE WONDER. BRITISH INVENTION.

AERIAL SPIRAL MONO-RAILWAY.

Showing the travelling, climbing and balancing power of the "Gyro" as it climbs and descends round and round the spiral track.

Top complete with 10 ft. Mono-Rail and Stand, **1/9** Post 3d.

Also the **Giant Aerial Spiral** with 35 ft. Mono-Rail.

Price **5/-**

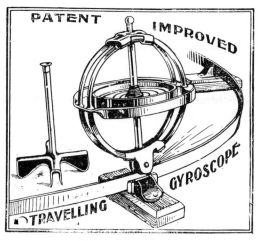

GYRO-DE-LUXE.

For scientific-minded Youths and Adults.

Capable of every revolution of the Gyroscope, in addition to the Patent Travelling Attachment. Boxed with 6 rails and sleepers, and also pillar.

Price .. .. **1/10½**d. Postage 4d.

Extra rails can be had, 8 for **10½**d. Postage 3d.

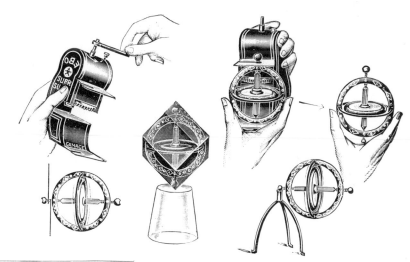

Novelty.

GYRO TOP. TO SPIN WITHOUT STRING.

Wind up Spinner with Crank key, place top in position and release. Perfectly simple to use.

Price **10½**d. Postage 3d.

Novelty.

THE HOPPING TOP.

This is a well made Toy and can be spun by quite young children. To operate place spinner on spindle of Top turn several times to the right, then release by pressing knob.

Price .. .. **6**d. Postage 1½d.

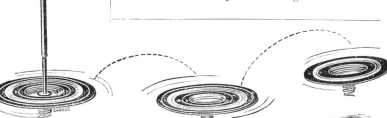

DISC HOPPING TOPS. The latest Novelty.

Can be made to spin at a tremendous speed by the use only of the spinning stick and jump about like cats on hot bricks.

No. 1. Complete set .. .. **10½**d. Postage 2d.
Containing 3 Tops and striker.

No. 2. Containing 2 large Tops and striker. **2/11** Postage 3d.

G..

ARMIES OF LEAD!

Gamages have made a special feature of Toy Soldiers since the institution of their famous Toy Galleries twenty years ago. The endless Battalions which have passed through their famous Store has prompted the Press to describe it as the "Aldershot of the Toy Soldier World," and Gamage as a "British Napoleon!"

All the Soldiers illustrated on the opposite and succeeding pages (with the exception of those having the letter "B" after the number) are the exact size of the large illustrations on page 101. The "B" series are about two-thirds the size of the standard make.

Price .. **4½d.**   Postage 3d. up to 3 Boxes.

1B 1st Life Guards
6B 2nd Dragoons (Scots Greys)
10B 11th Hussars   11B Japanese Cavalry
12B 16th Lancers (active service
13B 17th Lancers   14 Russian Cavalry
15B Mounted Infanty   16B Coldstream Guards
17B Lancashire Fusiliers 18B Grenadier Guards
19B Dublin Fusiliers   20B Manchester Regiment
21B Northumberland Fusiliers
22B Blue Jackets (H.M. Navy)
23B Cameron Highlanders (active service)
24B White Jackets (H.M. Navy)
25B Japanese Infantry   26B Russian Infantry

Boxes contain 4 Horse Soldiers or 7 Infantry.

Price .. **10½**   Post 3d.

1   1st Life Guards   2   Royal Horse Guards
3   5th Dragoon Guards
7   The 7th Royal Fusiliers
8   4th Hussars (Queen's Own)
9   Rifle Brigade
11 Black Watch Highlanders
12 11th Hussars
13 3rd Hussars (King's Own)
15 Argyle and Sutherland Highlanders
16 The Buffs (East Kent Regiment)
17 Somerset Light Infantry
18 Worcester Regiment
19 West India Regiment
23 5th Lancers (Royal Irish)
24 9th Lancers (Queen's Royal)
25 Soldiers to shoot   26 Boer Infantry
30 Drums and Buglers of the Line
31 1st Royal Dragoons
32 2nd Dragoons (Royal Scots Greys)
33 16th Lancers (Queen's)
34 Grenadier Guards
35 Royal Marine Artillery   36 Royal Sussex
38 South African Mounted Infantry
43 2nd Life Guards
44 2nd Dragoon Guards (Queen's Bays)
46 10th Bengal Lancers
47 1st Royal Bengal Cavalry
69 Pipers of Scots Guards   71 Turkish Cavalry
74 Royal Welsh Fusiliers   75 Scots Guards
76 Middlesex Regiment (5th Foot)
77 Gordon Highlanders and Pipers
78 Blue Jackets (Royal Navy)
80 White Jackets (Royal Navy)
81 17th Lancers (Active Service Order)
82 Colours and Pioneers (Scots Guards)
94 The 21st Empress of India's Own Lancers
    (Foreign Service Order)
96 York and Lancaster Regiment
97 Royal Marine Light Infantry
98 King's Royal Rifle Corps
99 The 13th Hussars
100 21st Empress of India's Own Lancers (Review
    Order)
106 6th Dragoon Guards   107 Irish Guards
108 Inniskilling Dragoons (Active Service Order)
109 Dublin Fusiliers
110 Devonshire Regiment
111 Grenadier Guards   112 Seaforth Highlanders

114 Cameron Highlanders (Active Service)
118 Gordon Highlanders (Active Service)
119 Gloucester Regiment
120 The Coldstream Guards
122 Black Watch Highlanders
123 Bihanir Camel Corps   127 7th Dragoons
124 The Irish Guards   133 Russian Infantry
128 12th Lancers   138 Cuirassiers
134 Japanese Infantry   140 Dragoons
139 Chasseurs á cheval   142 Zouaves
141 Infanterie de Ligne   147 Zulus
150 North American Indians (Unmounted)
152 North American Indians (Mounted)
153 Prussian Hussars   154 Prussian Infantry
156 Irish Regiment Standing, Kneeling and Lying
157 Gordon Highlanders Standing, Kneeling and
    Lying
155 Railway Station, Staff, Porters, etc.
160 Territorial Infantry   161 Boy Scouts
163 Boy Scout Signallers   164 Bedouin Arabs
165 Italian Cavalry   166 Italian Infantry
167 Turkish Infantry

Types of the British Army.

Price .. **1/10½**   Post 3d.

No. 41. Containing 2nd Dragoons (Royal Scots Greys). Grenadier Guards.
No. 40. Containing 1st Dragoons (Royal). Somersetshire Light Infantry (13th).
No. 42. Containing 1st Life Guards. Royal Sussex Regiment (35th).
No. 62. 1st Bengal Lancers (10 pieces)
No. 59. 2nd Dragoons (Royal Scots Greys).
No. 50. 1st Life Guards and 4th Queen's Own Hussars.
No. 27. Brass Band of the Line.
No. 52. Containing 2nd Life Guards. 5th Lancers (Royal Irish).

Price .. **2/-**   Post 4d.

No. 125. The Royal Horse Artillery (Review Order)
No. 126. The Royal Horse Artillery (Active Service Order).

Price .. **2/4½**   Post 4d.

No. 55. Containing 2nd Dragoons (Royal Scots Greys), 3rd Hussars (King's Own), and 16th Lancers (Queen's).
No. 54. Containing 1st Life Guards, 2nd Dragoon Guards (Queen's Bays), and 9th Lancers (Queen's Royal).
No. 53. Containing Royal Horse Guards, 4th Hussars, and Grenadier Guards.
No. 61. Our Indian Army, 3rd Madras Light Cavalry (15 mounted).
No. 60. 1st Bombay Lancers.

Price .. **3/3**   Post 4d.

No. 22. Containing Royal Horse Guards, 5th Lancers, The Black Watch (Royal Highlanders 42nd), Worcester Regiment (29th).
No. 102. Containing the Grenadiers, Coldstreams Scots and Irish Guards.
No. 21. 1st Life Guards, 11th Hussars, West India Regiment, The Buffs (East Kent Regiment, 3rd).
No. 37. Full Band of the Coldstream Guards.

No. 101. Full Band of the 1st Life Guards. Modelled and painted in the very best style.

Price .. **4/9**   Post 4d.

No. 129. Containing the 12th Lancers, 2nd Dragoons (Scots Greys), 1st Dragoon Guards, 11th Hussars and 2nd Life Guards, totalling 70 pieces of cavalry. Size of case 2 ft. 1 in. by 1 ft. 5 in. by 3 ins., with one inside tray.

Price .. **13/6**   Post 9d.

No. 130. Containing a splendid collection of the Scots Guards, marching, running, standing-at ease, standing, lying, and kneeling firing, together with Pipers, Drum and Bugle Band Colours and Pioneers, mounted and unmounted officers. Size of case 2 ft. 1 in. by 1 ft. 5 in. by 3 ins., with one inside tray, totalling 118 pieces of infantry.

Price .. **12/9**   Post 9d.

No. 131. Containing: The Royal Horse Artillery, Mountain Battery, Camel Corps, Scots Greys, 11th Hussars, 5th Dragoon Guards, 17th Lancers, 2nd Life Guards, Horse Guards, full Band of the Coldstream Guards, the Scots Guards, lying, kneeling, and standing firing, the Gordon Highlanders with Pipers, the Worcestershire Regiment, Bluejackets and Whitejackets with 4·7 naval guns and General Officer, totalling 275 pieces of cavalry and infantry. Size of case 3 ft. 9 ins. by 1 ft. 11 ins. by 6 ins., with two inside trays.

Price .. **70/-**   Carriage free.

No. 132. Containing: The Royal Horse Artillery, 2nd Dragoons (Scots Greys), 11th Hussars, 12th Lancers, 2nd Life Guards, Horse Guards, 7th Dragoon Guards, full Band of the Line, the Seaforth Highlanders with Pipers, Welsh Fusiliers with Goat, the Coldstream Guards, standing, lying and kneeling firing, the East Kent Regiment, Mountain Battery, 4.7 Naval Gun, and a General Officer, totalling 167 pieces of infantry and cavalry. Size of case 2 ft. 10 ins. by 1 ft. 7 ins. by 6 ins., with two inside trays.

Price complete .. **47/6**   Carriage free.

No. 73. Containing the following regiments—Royal Horse Artillery, 2nd Life Guards, 12th Lancers, Royal Welsh Fusiliers, Scots Greys, Band of the Line, the Gordon Highlanders, and a General Officer. Size of case, 2 ft. 2 in. by 1 ft. 3 ins.

Price complete .. **21/9**   Carriage free.

SOLDIERS.

Prospective Customers should note that all GAMAGE'S "SOLDIERS" are the Best Make obtainable, being hand painted and correct in colours and all details.
AVOID CHEAP IMITATIONS!

No. 1. 1st Life Guards, containing 5 soldiers.
Price .. **10½d.**   Post 3d.

80. White Jackets **10½d.** Post 3d.
81. Blue Jackets **10½d.**   ,,

No. 150.   North American Indians, unmounted.
Price .. .. .. **10½d.**
Post 3d.

Complete Mountain Artillery with quick firing guns to take on and off ammunition included in each box. A perfect and well working model.
Price ... ... **2/3**   Post 4d.

No. 144.   Royal Field Artillery.   Price .. **4/9**   Post 4d.

No. 90.   Containing the Coldstream Guards, in three positions (firing)
Price .. .. .. **2/4½**   Post 4d.

No. 137.   Royal Army Medical Corps, as illust., with Nursing Sisters Wounded, Stretchers, Tent, &c.   Price .. **3/3**   Post 3d.

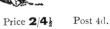

No. 89.   Cameron Highlanders, in three positions   Price **2/4½**   Post 4d.

No. 48.   Egyptian Camel Corps with detachable men.
Price .. .. **1/10½**   Post 3d.

No. 145.   Royal Army Medical Corps. Red Cross Waggon.
Price .. .. **2/4½**   Post 4d.

No. 39.   Royal Horse Artillery.   Price .. .. **4/11**   Post 4d.

No. 29.   Types of the British Army, consisting of complete Mule Battery, 1st Life Guards, 3rd Hussars, 9th Lancers, 2nd Queen's Royal West Surrey Regiment.   Price .. **5/11** per box. Post 6d.

No. 112. Seaforth Highlanders.
Price .. **10½d.**   Post 3d.

Hospital Tents, with Guy Ropes.

Price .. .. **1/-** and **1/6** Post 2d.

ARMY SERVICE SUPPLY COLUMN

COMPLETE WITH SUPPLIES AND ESCORT

MANUFACTURED IN LONDON

Army Service Supply Column,

with Supplies and Escort, **8/9** Post 6d.

No. Ty. 162. **Boy Scouts Encampment**

A combination set of Boy Scouts, consisting of tree, gate, hurdles and movable-arm figures, by manipulating which many varieties of camp enclosure can be formed. The boys can climb into eight different positions in the tree, swing on the gate, mount the hurdles and assume many other positions that the ingenuity of the possessor may suggest, **2/3** Post 3d.

No. Ty. 161.

Boy Scouts

Price .. **10½d.**

War Game as illustration, complete with Book of Instructions.

Price .. **3/6** Post 5d.

Ditto, Larger .. **5/6** ,, 6d.

Army Bell Tent.

Size 1 .. **2d.** Size 3 .. **4d**

,, 2 .. **3d** ,, 4 .. **6d.**

Postage on quantities of 1 to 3, 1d.

3 to 6, 2d. 6 to 12, 2d.

Orders for 1 dozen or more, post free.

No. Ty. 128. **12th Lancers.**

Price .. **10½d.** Post 3d.

Soldiers.

Tents.

As illustration.

4d. **6**d. **9**d. **1/-**

Post 1d. 1d. 2d. 2d.

Boy Scouts, with Scoutmaster and Truck

No. 1, **10½d.**

Post 3d.

No. 2, **1/9**

Post 4d.

No. 3, **2/6**

Post 4d.

No. Ty. 146. **Army Service Corps Transport Waggon.** Price .. **1/10½** Post 4d.

No. Ty. 72. **Landing Party of British Sailors.**

With breech-loading field gun, complete with ammunition.

Price **2/3** Post 3d.

No. Ty. 100. **21st Empress of India's Own Lancers** Price ... **10½d.** Post 3d.

No. Ty. 93. This Presentation Case consists of a **complete Company of Cold-stream Guards,** with Officers, Full Band Colours and Pioneers, with a **Squadron of Royal Horse Guards,** with Trumpeters, etc. Packed in well-made wooden framed box with tray to lift out. Size of box, 2 ft. by 1 ft. by 1 in. Price complete, **10/9** Post 8d.

SOLDIERS, FORTS, etc.

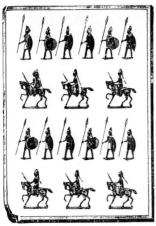

AMERICAN INDIAN WARRIORS
(as illustration).
Price .. **4/11** Post 4d.

KING GEORGE IN INDIA (as illustration).
Price .. **2/11** Post 3d.

ROMAN SOLDIERS (as illustration).
Price .. **4/6** Post 4d.

REALISTIC TOY FORT.

Price	..	**1/6**	**2/11**	**4/11**
Post	..	4d	5d.	6d.

KING GEORGE ON HORSE BACK
(as illustration). Price **2/11** Post. 3d.

REALISTIC TOY FORTS (as illustration).

Price	..	**7/11**	**10/9**	**15/6**	**25/-**
		Post 6d.	8d.	10d.	free.

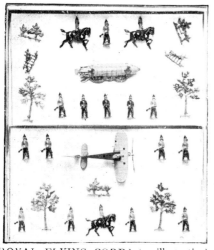

ROYAL FLYING CORPS (as illustration).

Price	..	**10½d.**	**1/9**	**4/6**
Post	..	3d.	4d.	6d.

ROMAN SOLDIERS

(as illustration).

Price .. **17/6**

Post free.

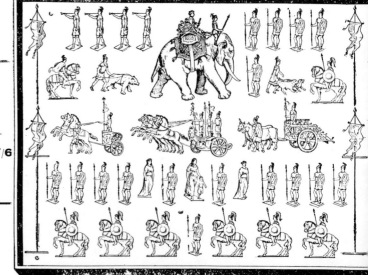

Harmless Pistols and Cannons.

Toy Cap Guns, 1/4½ 1/10½   Post 4d.   **2/6**
Post 6d.   Bayonet and Belt, **3/6**   Post 5d.

Toy Cap Pop Guns, 10½d. 1/4½
Post 4d.   Post 4d.

Metal Field Gun.

Strongly made.   Enamelled only.

To fire peas or small leaden bullets.

Price .. **6**d.   Post 2d.

GUN. Field piece with spring stretching. Nicely burnished gun of metal, breech and mouth of nickelled brass, metal carriage, iron wheels, japanned by hand. Adjustable range finder, with trigger. To fire with peas, rubber balls, &c.

Size 6¾ by 3 by 3¼ in

Price **1/6**

Post 2d.

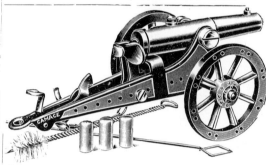

The Gun of the Royal Horse Artillery (Patented).

Price **10½**d.   Postage 2d.

Field-Howitzer to Fire Amorces and Rubber-Shells.

(HARMLESS.)

Solid construction with detachable breech and striking-pin. Barrel with two chambers for double charge of amorces. Burnished barrel of solid brass with adjustments. Metal carriage finely enamelled. Length 6 in. Calibre ½ in. Length of barrel 3 in. Complete with 4 rubber-shells, wire and sponge.

Price .. **5/11**   Postage 5d.

Harmless Modern Coast Cannon.

For double charge to fire amorces and rubber-shells Armoured carriage with ingenious mechanism for revolving to any direction. Massive barrel of burnished brass, with striking pin and 2 chambers for double charging with amorces and adjustable for sighting. Carriage mounted with crane, enamelled iron plate, brass mounted. Accessories—1 box of amorces and rubber-shells. Length 7 in. Height 6½ in. Length of barrel 3½ in. Calibre ⅜ in. **Price 9/6** Post 4d. Ty. 2. For double charge with amorces and rubber-shells. Amoured carriage with ingenious mechanism for revolving to any direction. Massive barrel of burnished brass, with striking pin and two chambers for double charging with amorces, adjustable for sighting. Carriage mounted with crane, enamelled iron-plate, brass mounted. Length 10 in. Height 8½ in. Length of the barrel, 5 in. Caliber, ½ in. With 4 rubber-shells and 1 box of amorces. Price **16/6** Postage 6d.

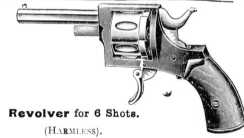

Cannon, FIELD PIECE (HARMLESS). Breech loader with powder, caps and RUBBER SHELLS. Shells to be pressed into the muzzle. Solid construction—Gun metal barrel, steel blue burnished, cast iron wheels, metal carriage, grey colour. New handy loading and firing mechanism, detachable breech bolt with bayonet closure, fixed chamber, trigger with spiral spring.
Length of barrel 2½ in., total length 5½ in.
Caliber 7/32 in.   Price .. **2/6**   Post 3d.
Length of barrel 3½ in., total length 7½ in.
Caliber 9/32 in.   Price .. **3/11**   Post 4d.

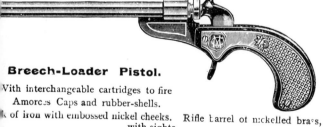

Breech-Loader Pistol.

With interchangeable cartridges to fire Amorces Caps and rubber-shells.

Of iron with embossed nickel cheeks. Rifle barrel of nickelled brass, with sights.

Accessories—Sponge, 1 box of amorces caps, 10 rubber-shells.
Length 10 in.   Calibre 5/16 in.   Price .. **3/11**   Post 4d.
Extra rubber shells, **6**d. per doz. Post 4d.

Toy Sentry Box.

Size 2 by 2 by 3½ in.

Price **6**½d.   Post 2d.

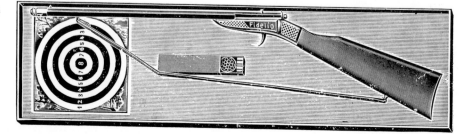

Revolver for 6 Shots.

(HARMLESS).

Ammunition : Amorces and rubber-shells. Original design, automatic revolving, detachable breech part, holding both the amorces caps and shells. Wooden stock, iron frame, nickelled and rifled barrel of massive brass.   Length 6½ in.   Calibre 7/16 in.
Size of card-board box, 8 by 3¾ by 1¼ in.
Accessories : 20 rubber-shells, 1 box of amorces 1 sponge, and 1 wire.   Price **8/11**   Post 5d.

Harmless Muzzle-Loader Rifle with Cartridges.

With automatic cocking mechanism.
Beech wood stock, burnished steel plate barrel.
On fine cardboard with target.
Caliber ¼ in.
Complete with 10 rubber shells.

Price ..   ..   ..   **5/11**   Post 6d.

Cowboy and Indian Outfits.

Indian Necklet.
With imitation teeth ornaments.
Price 10½d.   1/6
Post 2d.   2d.

Indian Spear, with Feather Decorations,
Price .. .. 2/3   Carriage 6d.

Medicine Man's Drum.
Price 4/11   Post 6d.
Tom-tom, as illustration.
Price 8/11   Post 9d.

Indian Knife, with imitation crocodile sheath and belt.
2/3
Post 4d.

Imitation tiger skin
Quiver
(without Arrows).
1/6   Post 3d.

Indian Pipe, with Feathers.
1/3
Post 3d.

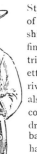

Style 402. **Cowboy Outfit.** Made of khaki drill. This outfit consists of a shirt made open coat style, with pocket and finished with pearl buttons. Trousers trimmed down each side with wide leatherette strip decorated with metal shells and rivets. This outfit also contains a large cowboy hat of khaki drill with leatherette band, red bandanna handkerchief, white rope lariat and pistol pocket, belt and pistol

Price 5/11

Post 4d.

Style 3155. **Cowboy Outfit** consists of a shirt made of a fine grade of khaki twill in open coat style, genuine leather pocket on shirt trimmed with metal shell and rivet; genuine leather fringes in sleeves and band round cuffs. Trousers have fancy imitation fur fronts trimmed in 'chaps' style, with leather pieces round crotch, and leather belt finished with rivets; wide side pieces of genuine leath r finished with metal shells and rivets, back of trousers of fine grade khaki twill. This outfit also includes a large felt cowboy hat, a large red bandanna hankerchief, white rope lariat, a fine genuine leather pistol pocket and belt, fringed throughout, and pistol.

Price .. 19/6   Post 8d.

Imitation tiger skin
Shields,
3/11   Post 9d.

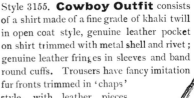

Imitation tiger skin
Shields,
1/10½
Post 6d.
Larger
2/6
Post 6d.

Indian Tomahawk
1/-   Post 3d.

Indian Club,
10½d.   Post 3d.

Cowboy Outfit. Made of khaki drill, and consists of a shirt made in open coat style, with leather pocket, trimmed with metal shell and rivet and finished with pearl buttons; leather fringes on sleeves and leather band on cuff. Trousers have large triangular-shaped pieces of leather down each side, finished with metal shells and rivets; pockets are leather trimmed with metal shell and rivet. The outfit also contains a large cowboy hat trimmed with leatherette band and rivets; large bandanna handkerchief, white rope lariat, pistol pocket, belt,, and pistol.

Price .. .. 8/11   Post 6d.

Cowboy Outfit. Made of a fine grade of khaki twill. This outfit consists of a shirt made in open coat style, leather pocket on shirt, trimmed with metal shell and rivet, leather fringes on sleeves and band round cuffs. Trousers have wide side pieces of leather trimmed with metal shells and rivets, as are also the two leather pockets. Leather belt and leather pieces round crotch are decorated with rivets. This outfit also includes a large cowboy hat of khaki twill with wide leather band finished with rivets; a large red bandanna handkerchief, white rope lariat and leather pistol pocket, and belt and pistol.

Price .. .. 13/6   Postage 6d.

GENUINE IMPORTED
American Indian Warrior Suits.

GENUINE IMPORTED
American Indian Wigwams.

Style 1010. Indian Chief Outfit made of khaki drill, and consists of a coat with coloured front, trimmed with coloured fringes and yellow edging throughout; trousers same trimming. Bonnet of similar material, in cap style, trimmed tapes and fringes, and coloured feathers, **3/11** Post 4d.

Cheaper qualities, **3/11 4/11 5/11** Post 4d.

Style S O 2. Outfit consists of coat made of khaki drill with blue facings piped yellow braid and trimmed red fringe; trousers of khaki with khaki felt trimmings and red fringe. Bonnet of Sioux style with 26 coloured feathers. Exceedingly well made - **22/6** Ditto, with less trimmings and feathers, **17/6**

Style 1375. Indian Chief Outfit. Fine grade of khaki, consists of coat with genuine leather inserts on front, fully beaded; trimmed throughout with woven non-curling fringes; trousers have coloured genuine leather inserts on each side, fully beaded, trimmed with woven non-curling fringes. Bonnet has a full crown of coloured felt, wide front band of genuine coloured leather, fully beaded, and 24 large tipped (two colour) feathers, taped at bottom with coloured cloth, **16/6** Post 6d.

Style 3035. Outfit consists of coat made of red drill, with non-curling felt fringe, green felt piping on coat and trousers with leather fringe. Bonnet made in Sioux style with leather front and felt band, containing 29 coloured feathers, with bells and red and khaki ribbons. **13/6**

Style 1142. Indian Chief Outfit, in khaki drill, consists of a coat with coloured front, trimmed throughout with double colour non-curling felt fringes and yellow edging; trousers similarly trimmed. Bonnet made in Sioux style, khaki front trimmed with coloured fringes and tapes, and with 20 coloured feathers. Price ... **5/11** Post 6d.

Style 1091. Indian Chief Outfit in khaki drill, consists of a coat with double colour felt non-curling fringes, 2 pockets similarly trimmed; trousers same trimming down sides. Bonnet of similar material trimmed coloured fringes and tapes, and with 12 coloured feathers. Price ... **4/11** Post 4d.

Style 3041. Coat made of khaki drill with green felt stripes and yellow fringe, red collar. Skirt khaki drill piped with green and red felt with yellow fringe. Bonnet of red felt and 9 coloured feathers. Price **10/6** Post 6d.

Style 3033. Outfit made of khaki and consists of coat with red and yellow and green non-curling felt fringe with Sioux style bonnet with leather front and 30 coloured feathers. Price **10/6**

Style 1163. Indian Chief Outfit, in khaki drill, consists of a coat elaborately trimmed with wide coloured felt bands, fully decorated double colour non-curling felt fringes; trousers with similar trimming; bonnet with full crown of coloured felt, wide felt front band trimmed with beads, and 20 coloured feathers taped at bottom with coloured cloth. Price **8/11** Post 6d.

Indian Wigwams.

No.		Height.			Price.
1	Unbleached Sheeting,	5 ft.,	3 poles		6/11
13	Khaki Drill ..	.. 5 ,,	3 ,,		8/11
2	White Drill ..	.. 6 ,,	3 ,,		8/11
3	White Drill ..	.. 6 ,,	5 ,,		15/-
4	White Duck..	.. 6 ,,	5 ,,		18/6
5	Waterproof Khaki ..	6 ,,	5 ,,		25/-
6	Waterproof Khaki ..	8 ,,	5 ,,		37/6
8	Khaki Drill ..	.. 6 ,,	5 ,,		18/6
9	Khaki Drill ..	.. 5 ,,	5 ,,		15/-
10	Waterproof Khaki ..	5 ,,	5 ,,		18/6

Style 1182. Indian Chief Outfit, made of khaki drill, consists of a coat with coloured cloth inserts on front, trimmed with beads and finished with felt non-curling fringes and yellow tapes. Trousers have felt non-curling fringes and yellow tapes. Bonnet in Sioux style, khaki front trimmed with coloured fringes and tapes, and 20 coloured feathers. **7/11** Post 6d.

Style 3031. This Outfit is made of khaki drill with red front and green-and-yellow trimming and fringe; trousers green felt stripe and red non-curling fringe. Bonnet made Sioux style with leather front and 24 coloured feathers. Price ... **10/6**

Harmless Shooting Outfits with Vacuum Arrows.

HARMLESS RIFLE as illustration.

Complete with Rifle, 1 Arrow, and Enamelled Target.

Price .. **3/11**

Post 6d.

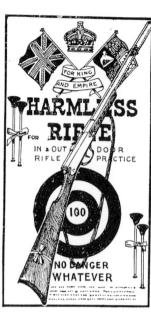

No. 113.   RIFLE 29 in., with Japanned Fittings and Strap, adjustable Sight, 4 Arrows, and Target, 12 by 27 in.

Price .. **5/11**

Post 6d.

NEW HARMLESS PISTOL SET.

British Made.

No. 6. Heavy Browning Repeater pattern Pistol, three rubber-tipped arrows, strong leather belt with bolster. Target 18 by 13 in. Each in box .. **4/6**

Post 4d.

"CATAWAULING."
SCREAMINGLY FUNNY.

Cats painted in life-like colours in fighting attitude on garden wall. Arranged to stand on table. When hit they give a shriek of pain and disappear behind the wall. Each mounted on card in box.   No. 325. As illustration, Rifle 19 in., 2 Arrows, wall 2 in. long with 2 Cats and Target, **2/11**   Post 3d.
No. 326.   Larger size.   Rifle 27 in., 3 Arrows, wall 15 in. long, with 3 Cats and Target   ..   ..   **5/11**   Post 6d.

HARMLESS RIFLE SET, As illustration.

Complete with Rifle and Arrow, with enamelled Target,

2/11   Post 4d.

HARMLESS RIFLE SE
Complete with Superior Rifle, Arrow and enamelle
Target ...   **7/6**   Post 8
Do , with cheaper Rifle,
fires caps ...   **5/6**   Post 6

HARMLESS RIFLE SETS.

Complete with Rifle, Rubber-tipped Arrows and Targets.

Price ..   **10½d.**   Post 3d.

Do.   do.   PISTOL SETS ..   **10½d.**

Post 3d.

HUNTING THE ROARING LION.

When shot in the centre the Lion roars with pain, and a baby Lion appears from behind the target. Made of stout wood and arranged to stand firmly on table. Rifle 27 in., 2 arrows, &c. Target mounted on card.   Each in box   ..   ..   ..   **5/6**   Post 5d.

TIGER HUNTING.   When shot the Tiger rolls over and gives a death gasp.   The voice is automatic and does not require re-setting. Mounted on card in box.   No. 340. Rifle 23 in, 2 Arrows, Tiger painted on wood.   Each set in box, 24 by 11 in. ..   **3/11**   Post 6d.

No. 112.   HEAVY RIFLE
with Strap, 2 Arrows and
Target 10 by 36 in. ..   **5/**
Post 6d.

Toy Uniforms.

LANCER'S UNIFORM, as illustration ... **2/11** Post 4d,
Ditto, superior ... **5/11** Post 5d.

POLICEMAN'S OUTFIT, as illustration ... **3/11** Post 4d.

INDIAN WARRIOR'S OUTIT, as illustration. Price **5/11**

SMART INDIAN WARRIOR'S OUTFIT, similar to illustration. but without shield ... **3/11**

COWBOY SETS. Quite new **3/11**
4/11 As illus., **10/6** Post 3d. 4d. 6d

FIREMAN'S UNIFORM, as illustration,
Price **3/11**
Post. 4d.

SCOUTS' OUTFIT Special Quality. As illus,
4/6 4/11 6/11 8/11 Post 4d,, 5d., 6d.

HIGHLANDER'S UNIFORM (as illustration) ... **15/-** Post 6d.

Cowboy Outfit.
10½d. 1/10½
Post 3d. and 4d.

YOUNG TERRITORIAL OFFICER'S OUTFITS.
1/10¼ 2/6 As illustration, **3/6** Post 3d. and 4d.

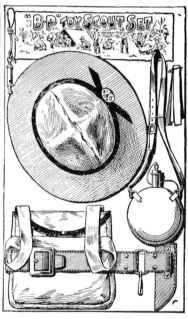

BOY SCOUT OUTFITS ... **1/10½** Post 3d,
As illustration, **2 4 3 3 3 11 5/ 11 8/11** Post 3d., 4d., 5d. and 6d.

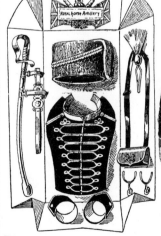

Best quality London Made INFANTRY UNIFORM, as illustration, **12/6** Containing spiked helmet painted red, red coat, with white facings, dark blue knickers, with red line, buff belt and dagger. Carriage free.

Best quality, London Made DRAGOON UNIFORM as illustration, **13/6** Containing green hat, red tunic with green facings, dark blue trousers with wide yellow stripe spurs, sword sheath and whip. Carriage free.

ROYAL HORSE ARTILLERY UNIFORM, as illustration.
2/11 5/11 7/11 Post 4d. 5d. 6d.

Best quality London Made DRAGOON GUARDS' UNIFORM as illustration. **15/6** Helmet painted aluminium with coat of arms and plumes, red tunic with red facings, knickers royal blue with wide yellow line, leggings, sword, sheath and gun. Carriage free.

Best quality London Made LANCER UNIFORM as illustration **15/6** With red hat with royal blue band, red tunic with red facings, blue cuffs with yellow edgings, royal blue trousers with double yellow stripe field glasses, sword, sheath, spurs and whip. Carriage free.

Harmless Guns, Pistols, Swords, Bows and Arrows.

Metal Breast Plates.

Highly nickelled.

4/6   6/11
Post 6d.   8d.

Complete Armour Set,

37/6 Carriage 1/-

The Gatling-Pop-Gun.

By turning handle at side, a sound is given off like the firing of a Gatling Gun.

Price **10½d.**   Post 3d.

Lancer's Helmet.
1/-
Post 3d.

Dragoon Guard's Helmet.
9d.
Post 3d.

LIfe Guard's Helmet.
1/-
Post 3d.

Life Guard's Helmet

as illustrated.

Strongly made and highly nickelled.

Price .. **6/11**
Post 6d.

Miniature Warships.

Beautifully modelled and correctly painted.

Price **10½d.**   **1/6**   **1/10½**
Postage 3d.   3d.   4d.

Miniature Fleet of Warships.

Correct class models of the latest types.

First class finish.

Just the set to "Play Sea Fights."

Price in strong box, **5/11**

Postage 6d.

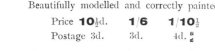

Toy Swords.

Price	Post
1/-	4d.
1/6	4d.
1/10½d.	4d.
2/6	4d.
3/11	4d.
5/6	4d.
7/11	6d.

Court Swords.
5/6
Postage 4d.

Naval Swords.
Price **5/6**   Post 6d.

Military Camp.
Price **18/9**   Postage 10d.

No. 1. **Lancewood Bow,** 3 ft. 9 in. enamelled Targe 24 in. by 9 in., two Arrows, 20 in. long, **2/6** Carriage 4d

No. 2. **Lancewood Bow,** three Arrows, Target 18 in by 14 in. .. .. **3/-** Carriage 5d

No. 3. **Lancewood Bow,** 5 ft., six Arrows, Targe 27 in. by 14 in. .. .. .. **4/11** Carriage 6d

IDEAL PISTOL.

D.R. PATENT
D.R.G.M.

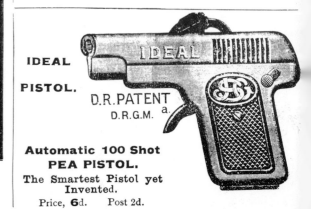

Automatic 100 Shot PEA PISTOL.
The Smartest Pistol yet Invented.
Price, **6d.**   Post 2d.

Drums. Bagpipes. Pianos.

Metal Head Drum.

as illustration **6½**d. Post 3d.
Ditto, 10 in **1/-** Post 4d.

Drums with Metal Rims, vellum heads and tightening screws, 9½ in.
1/- Post 4d.

Ditto 12 in. **2/6** Post 4d.

Side Drum.

as illustration with vellum heads.
Price **2/11** Post.

Organ Chimes.

When the Toy is twirled round it gives off sounds similar to that of an organ. Price **6d.** Post 2d.

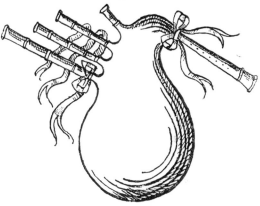

Bagpipes.

Best Rubber Bags and turned painted pipes and Drones
No. 1 Pipe without Drone Price **6d.** Post 1d.
No. 2 ,, with two Drones **10½d.** ,, 1½d.
No. 3 ,, ,, three ,, as illus. **2/-** ,, 2d.
No. 4 ,, ,, three ,, extra large as illustration
3/6 Post 3d.

Strongly made Nickel Drum.

Tightening Screws
Vellum Heads.

As illustration,
10¼ in. diam.

2/6 Post 5d.

Model Pianos with Metal Notes.

Superior finish.

8 Notes..	**4/11**	Post 6d.
10 ,, ..	**5/11**	,, 7d.
12 ,, ..	**7/6**	,, 9d.

Drum Major's Baton.

With metal head, 34 in. long .. **10½**d. Post 3d.
Ditto, with brass head, 34 in. long .. **1/9** ,, 3d.

Novelty Drum

Mechanical part inside drum. Drum fitted with handle, which, when turned, produces sounds equal to an expert Drummer.

Metal Rims, Brass Body.
8 in. Head .. **2/6** Post 4d.

Drums with Wooden Rims solid brass body, vellum heads, belt hook and knee rest, 10½in.
Price .. **4/11** Post 6d.
Do., do., 11 in. .. .. **5/11** Post 6d.
Do., do., 10½ in., extra strong **7/11** ,, 8d.
Do., do., 11¼ in. ,, ,, **8/11** ,, 9d.
,, ,, 13 in. .. ,, **11/9** ,, 10d.

Bass Drum.

as illustration with Vellum heads
3/11 Post 5d.

Smart Toy Piano.

WIRE STRUNG. CAN BE TUNED.

No.					
1.	With 8 Notes	..	**8/11**	Post and packing,	7d.
2.	,, 10 Notes	..	**10/9**	,, ,,	8d.
3.	,, 14 Notes	..	**13/6**	,, ,,	8d.
4.	,, 16 Notes	..	**15/6**	,, ,,	9d.
5.	,, 18 Notes	..	**18/9**	,, ,,	1/-
6.	,, 20 Notes	..	**23/9**	,, ,,	1/-

New Model Piano with Metal Notes,

With 6 Notes	..	..	..	**1/9**	Post 4d.
,, 8 ,,	..	..	..	**2/3**	,, 5d.
,, 10 ,,	..	..	..	**2/11**	,, 6d.
,, 12 ,,	..	..	..	**3/11**	,, 6d.

FINE MODEL
Overstrung
Baby Grand
Piano,
with Playable Sharps on Raised Keys.

Style D. As illustration.
Height 8½ in. Length 20½ in.
Width 15½ in.
Height, with lid up, 18 in.
25 notes .. **35/-**

Style B. Without sharps.
Height 7½ in. Length 20½ in.
Width 12½ in.
Height, with lid up, 14 in.
15 notes .. **21/-**

TOY MUSICAL INSTRUMENTS.

Real Horn Horns.
Price .. **1/10½** Postage 3d.

Sword Pop Gun.
Price .. .. **6**d. Postage 2d.

Guitar.
With 4 strings,
Price .. **6½**d.
Post 2d.

Ditto, larger.
With 8 strings, as
Illustration.
Price .. **1/-**
Post 3d.

Autoharp.
with 12 strings.
Price .. **1/-**
Post 3d.

Accordeons.
With 6 Notes.
Price .. **1/-** Post 3d.
Smaller size. Price .. **6**d. Post 2d.

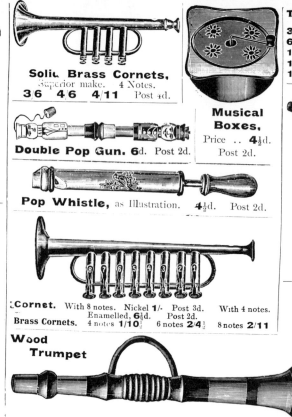

Soli. Brass Cornets,
Superior make. 4 Notes.
3 6 4 6 4/11 Post 4d.

Double Pop Gun. 6d. Post 2d.

Pop Whistle, as Illustration. **4½**d. Post 2d.

Cornet. With 8 notes. Nickel **1/-** Post 3d. With 4 notes.
Brass Cornets. Enamelled, **6½**d. Post 2d.
4 notes **1/10½** 6 notes **2/4½** 8 notes **2/11**

Wood Trumpet

As illustration. **4½**d. Post 2d. **6**d. Post 3d.

Painted Trombone .. **1/-** Post 3d.
Ditto Brass **2/-** ,, 3d.
Ditto (larger) ,, .. **2/11** ,, 3d.

Tubephones, superior quality, price **10½**d., **1/6**,
2/4½, 3/6, 4/6, 5/11. 10/6 Postage extra.

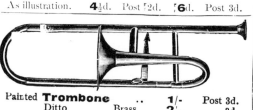

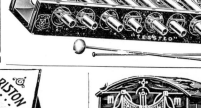

Ariston Musical Box. As illustration. With 18 notes
and Moveable Pictures. Price .. **1/-** Post 3d.

MUSICAL VARIETY SHOW.
As illustration With Six Notes and changeable pictures.
Price .. .. **6**d. Post 2d.

Metal Trumpets.
3d. ... Post 2d.
6d. ... ,,
1/- ... Post 3d.
1/4½ ... ,,
1/10½ ,,

Musical Boxes,
Price .. **4½**d.
Post 2d.

Police Rattles
As illustration.
Price **2**d. Post 2d.
,, **4**d. ,, 2d.

Musical Bottle.
Price .. **4½**d.
Postage 2d.

Mandoline
As illustration.
Price .. **6**d.
Post 2d.

Concertinas.
Price, **6**d. and **1/-**
Post 2d. and 3d.
Extra large,
Price **2/-** Post 4d.

PAINTED WOODEN HORN.
Price **4½**d.
Postage 2d.

Zithers.
With 8 Strings.
Price .. **6½**d.
Postage 3d.

Clown Pop Gun.
6d. Post 2d.

Drum Mouth Organ. As illustration. Price **1/-**
Postage 3d.

Bell Chimes, Reins, Conductors' Sets, Violin, etc.

Bell Chimes with Beater.

With Bells	6	8	10	12	16
Price	10½d.	1/4½	1/10½	2/11	4/11
Post	3d.	4d.	4d.	4d.	5d.

Push Wheel Chimes.

Price **10½d.**   Postage 3d.

Donkey Chimes.

Price	10½d.	1/4½	2/4½	3/11
Post	3d.	3d.	4d.	4d

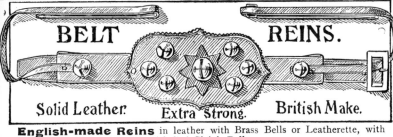

BELT REINS.

Solid Leather.   Extra Strong.   British Make.

English-made Reins in leather with Brass Bells or Leatherette, with nickelled Sleigh Bells.

	6d.	10½d.	1/4½	1/10½	2/4½	2/11	3/6	4/6	5/11
Post 3d.		3d.	4d.	4d.	4d.	5d.	4d.	5d.	5d.

PETS REINS

Horse Chimes.
Price **6/11**   Post 6d.

Duck Chimes,
similar to illustration.
Price **10½d**   **1/4½**   **2/4½**
Post   3d.   3d.   4d.

Cow Chimes.
Price **2/4½**   Post 4d.

Dog Chimes.
Price **3/6**   Post 3d.

Conductor's Sets as illustration.
Price **10½d.**   Postage 3d.
Superior quality. **1/10½ 3/6**   Post 3d. & 4d.

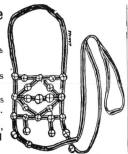

English-made Toy Reins.

With 3 Sleigh Bells
6d.   Post 2d.
With 5 Sleigh Bells
10½d.   Post 3d.
With 7 Sleigh Bells
1/10½d.   Post 3d.
Superior qualities,
2/4½ 3/6 3/11
Post 4d.

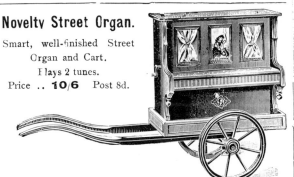

Novelty Street Organ.

Smart, well-finished Street
Organ and Cart.
Plays 2 tunes.
Price .. **10/6**   Post 8d.

Knitted Woollen Reins

with Bells
as illustration.

Price .. **2/-**
Post 3d.

Conductor's Sets as illustration.
10½d. each.   Post 3d.
Superior quality, **1/10½   3/6**
Postage 3d.   3d.

Organ with Music, drawn by Horse.

Wonderful value.
Price **6**d.
Larger size,
1/-
Post 2d.

Miniature Violin and Bow in Case
as illustration.

Price **1/-**
Splendid Value.
Post 3d.

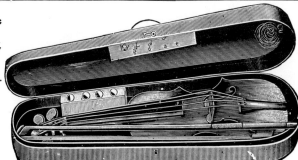

H

Skipping Ropes, Skittles, Garden Games, etc.

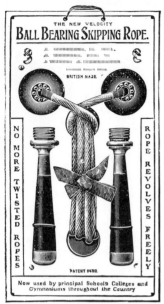

THE NEW VELOCITY
BALL BEARING SKIPPING ROPE.

BRITISH MADE

NO MORE TWISTED ROPES

ROPE REVOLVES FREELY

PATENT 8482.

Now used by principal Schools Colleges and Gymnasiums throughout the Country

12 ft. Ball-Bearing Skipping Ropes. 2/6 Post 3d.

Do. cardboard handles, **2/11** ,, 3d.
Do. cork or leather
covered handles, **3/6** ,, 3d.

Suitable for Schools & Gymnasiums

Skipping Ropes. Best qual. plaited rope with boxwood handles. Price **6½d.** & **10½d.** Post 3d. & 4d.

Skyscrapers. The name of this Toy gives an idea of what it really is. Can be sent right out of sight. Price **1/3** Postage 3d.

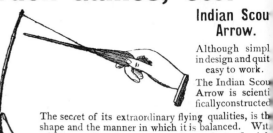

Indian Scout Arrow.

Although simple in design and quite easy to work.

The Indian Scout Arrow is scientifically constructed

The secret of its extraordinary flying qualities, is the shape and the manner in which it is balanced. With a little practice, the arrow can be made to fly right out of sight, always ascending and descending point foremost. Great accuracy of aim is soon acquired.

The Scout Arrow is in daily use among the savage tribes for killing birds and ground game.

Price of complete set, consisting of Sling Stick and 3 Arrows, packed in box with instructions. **1/-** Post 3d.

Kaleidoscope.
ENGLISH MAKE.

Strongly made Kaleidoscope, producing everchanging coloured designs.

7½ in., **6**d.		13 in., **1/4½**
11 in., **10½**d.		14 in., **2/4½**

Post 3d.

A. Contains 2 vellum battledores, 2 shuttlecocks, 2 strong celluloid balls, and skipping rope, in box complete. **1/10½** Post 3d.

B. Contains 2 vellum battledores, 2 shuttlecocks, 2 strong celluloid balls, and 1 boxwood handle skipping rope, in box complete. Price **2/6** Post 4d.

C. Contains 2 vellum battledores, 2 shuttlecocks, 2 strong celluloid balls, and 2 boxwood handle skipping rope, in box complete. Price **3/6**

D. Contains 2 vellum battledores of very best quality, 2 celluloid balls, 2 superior shuttlecocks, 1 boxwood handle skipping rope. Price **4/6**

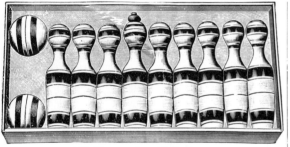

Well-made Skittles.
Nicely enamelled in colours. Price **2/4½** Carriage 6d.

Complete Sets of Painted Wood

Skittles

Price	Post
4d.	2d.
6d.	2d.
1/2	3d.
1/6	3d.
2/-	4d.
2/6	5d.

GAMAGE'S GARDEN & NURSERY GAMES.

Shuttlecocks.
18 feather ... **2½**d. each.
20 ,, larger, **3½**d. ,,
24 ,, ,, **5**d. ,,
Postage 1d.

Novelty Skittles
Turned hard wood enamelled in colours. Packed in box complete. Special value **3/6** post 6d

Nigger Skittles.
The latest novelty made from hard wood and enamelled in colours. Packed in box complete. Special value **3/6** post 6d

Money Boxes, Banks, Balls, etc.

Assorted Rubber
Novelty Balls.
Figures appear on pressing the ball.
Price **4½**d. Post 1d.

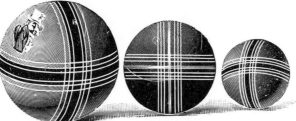

Rubber Coloured Balls. 2¾ in. **6**d. 3½ in. **9**d.
4 in. **1/-** 5 in. **1/6** 5½ in. **2/-** 6 in. **2/6** 7 in. **3/6** 7½ in. **4/6**

Taxi Cab Bank.
Save your pennies by Taxi Bank. The clock registers deposits up to 20/-. and shows at any time the correct amount saved.
For Pennies only.

Price ... ... **10½**d. Postage 2d.

N.B.—When the Register shows 20/-, run Taxi to the nearest Post Office and deposit the sovereign.

Automatic Spring Money Safe.

Pull out drawer, place coin in slot and release.
Money cannot be taken out except by opening bottom with key.
Price .. **1/-** Post 2d.

Novelty Pipes. Most interesting Corn Cob Pipe with rubber figure, which can be made to pop in and out .. **3**d. Post 1d.

Novelty Donkey Camera.
Squeeze the ball and take your friend's photo Price .. **5½**d.
Post 1d.

Nodding or Pendulum Toys,
Cleverly carved and hand painted in colours.
Price .. **6**d.
Post 1½d.

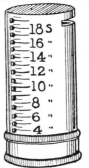

To hold **40 Sixpences,** with indicator showing exact number of sixpences in bank. Opens when 40 are saved.
Price **4½**d. Post 1d.

Play Store Register.
Actual size. Height 4 in., width 4 in. length 3½ in, weight ⅞ lb.
Made of cold rolled steel. Perfect in every respect. Registers every coin put in and shows amount of purchase. Imitation coin furnished with each Register. Price .. .. **2/6** Post 3d.

Fairy Parlour Balls

	2¾	4	5	6	7	8 in.
Price ...	**6**d.	**1/-**	**1/9**	**2/3**	**2/11**	**3/11**
Postage ...	1d.	1d.	1½d.	2d.	2d.	2d.

Exceedingly light and strong, will not break the windows.

BANK is 4½ in. long, in. high, 3 in. wide, weight ⅞ lb. Made from heavy cold rolled steel, securely riveted, forming a closed deposit vault in which mechanism is securely placed away from meddlesome fingers, money can be taken out when 100 deposits have been made when figures will read (000), at which point coins are shaken out through slot in back of the bank, holding upside down, pressing and holding lever down.

Bank is finished in black japan enamel. Beautifully ornamented and everlasting. When coin is inserted in slot in front of bank marked deposit press lever down, which rings bell, and deposit is registered and amount shown on indicator, be sure and register each coin before depositing another, use only 1 coin at a time. If you need the money before bank contains 100 deposits, use an axe.
Price **2/6** Postage 3d.

Novelty Money Boxes
with lock and key, turned hardwood, nicely enamelled in bright colours. Splendid value.
Price **1/-** each.
Post 2d.

The Mysterious Magic Box.

This consists of a box covered with glass and sealed inside, with figures, balls, etc., on rubbing the glass with a special pad which is supplied the figures dance and jump in a most extraordinary way.

Price **10½**d. and **1/6**
Postage 2d. and 3d.

H ..

MIRTH MAKERS.

The Wonderful Air Torpedo

Makes a report like a Gun. No Smoke.

No Explosive. No Danger.

Simply place a piece of paper inside lid, fasten down, then strike any object with the round end (which is flexible and cannot cause any damage). Try hitting your friend on the shoulder unawares! The greatest Boy's Toy invented for years. A ripper for Carnivals. Price **10½**d. Post 3d.

Singing Tie Pin

This novelty will cause great wonderment if fitted in the tie and worked by the small ball which is concealed in the waistcoat pocket. When singing, the bird moves its beak in a most realistic manner. Price ... **1**/- Postage 1d.

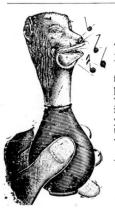

Where is that Dog?

The "Yapper" Dog Barker will produce endless fun for the person possessing one, with a "Yapper" in your pocket, you are a person to be reckoned with at parties, carnivals, etc.

Price .. **6**d.
Postage 2d.

Ditto, larger, **10½**d. Post 2d.

ONE DOZEN RUBBER Blow-out "Dying" Novelties.

Eight different kinds — Horse, Bear, Swan, Donkey, Elephant, Cockerel, Humpty-Dumpty & Monkey .. **1**/-   Post 1½d

The "Dying" Baby.

Extra stout rubber.
Composition head.
Price **5½**d.   Post 1d.

Harry Lauder.

Amusing "dying" toy.
Price **5½**d. Post 2d.

The Whistling Nigger.

Exceedingly clever. By pressing the ball, the Nigger-Hustler puts out his tongue, whistles and rolls his eyes.
Price **1**/-   Post 2d.

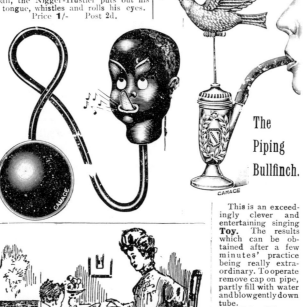

Plate Lifters.

UP-TO-DATE SPIRITUALISM.
DISHES AND PLATES WILL DANCE!

Plate Lifters are made of thin rubber tubing with small rubber ball at one end, which is inflated by squeezing the ball fixed at the other end of tube. When placed under the plates of your guests at supper (under cloth, so that the tube is out of sight), endless fun is caused as the plate is made to jump up and down at will.

Price **3**d. each. Extra long, **4½**d. Postage 1½d.
New Winged Plated Lifter, lifts two articles at once .. **5½**d.   Postage 1½d.

The Piping Bullfinch.

This is an exceedingly clever and entertaining singing **Toy**. The results which can be obtained after a few minutes' practice being really extraordinary. To operate remove cap on pipe, partly fill with water and blow gently down tube.
Price **8**d.
Postage 2d.

The Vocophone.

An Evening's Entertainment in your Waistcoat Pocket.

Try this simple MUSICAL NOVELTY. It will strengthen your Voice, and develop true sounds.

You can imitate all Brass Instruments, rendering good Solos.

The effect of harmonizing is good. It is a companion to the Cyclist and Scout. The Vocophone will do anything you wish it to do, as regards intensifying vocal sounds. By removing the cap and speaking through the tube, it will increase the sound given forth, and will answer the purpose of a **Pocket Megaphone.**
Price, with instructions, **6**d. Post 1d.

Surprise Water Camera.   As illustration.

AN AMUSING NOVELTY.   Price .. **1**/-   Post 3d.
Cheaper quality, without View-finder, **6**d. Post 2d.

Kindergarten Toys.

Tiny Town Telegraph Office.

As illustration.

Price **10½**d. Post 3d. **2/4½** Post 4d.

Dolly's School contains a large blackboard on wooden stand, chalk, sponge, bell, pencil, pen, penholder and pen case, pencil sharpener, ruler, 6 tiny slates with sponges, 1 drawing board, numeral frame, pictures for object-lesson, the A B C for spelling lesson, and a pair of eye-glasses for the little teacher.

It is packed in a solid box with beautiful coloured label.

Price .. **2/6** **3/11**
Post .. 3d. 4d.

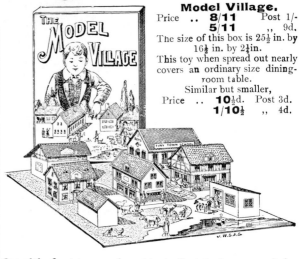

Model Village.

Price .. **8/11** Post 1/-
5/11 ,, 9d.

The size of this box is 25½ in. by 16½ in. by 2⅛ in.
This toy when spread out nearly covers an ordinary size dining-room table.
Similar but smaller,
Price .. **10½**d. Post 3d.
1/10½ ,, 4d.

One of the finest toys ever brought out. Contains large ground plan lithographed in bright colours, on which the children have to build up the village. For this purpose there are provided cottages, a church, railway station, farmhouse, a boathouse, a blacksmith's shop, an inn, windmill, etc. They are all made collapsible and consist of various parts, which the children have to put together. They are all made of strong cardboard and are printed in artistic colours. There is a further tin train, consisting of locomotive, tender and passenger car, a cab, a motor car and a donkey cart, all made of tin, and a set of wooden carved animals which are painted life-like. There are also a signal-box and signals. Keeps children quiet for hours. Packed in a large and solid box. with bright label, which depicts the village, when built up, as seen above.

WITH ALL PARTS NECESSARY FOR A GOOD GAME OF TRAINS

BOX 12 × 20 IN.

Let's Play Trains.

Great fun for the boys. Contains best quality cap, green and red flags, tickets, etc., labels, clippers, alarm signal, lantern, and whistle, in box with coloured label and full instructions. Price **2/6** Post 3d.

Drawing Stencils.

As illustration.
10½d. Post 3d. **6**d. Post 2d.

A Nice Toy for young children.

Price.	Post.
10½d.	.. 3d.
1/10½	.. 4d.

The Skittles are decorated with pictures of Fairy Tales, like Red Riding Hood, Cinderella, etc., and are made of strong cardboard on wooden stands.

Bead Pleasures.

Price **10½**d. **1/10½** **2/11** Postage 3d. 3d. 4d.

Clean Cuts. A fascinating pastime for children. Price **10½**d. Postage 2d.

Paper Cutting and Pasting.

As illustration.
Price .. .. **2/6** Post 3d.

Character Dolls.

Smaller **10½**d. Post 3d. As illus. **2/6** Post 4d.

Quick-Change Motorists.

A really interesting Toy for children, consisting of a Motor Car with two figures, and two complete sets of clothes which can be taken off and on at will.

Price **1/-**
Postage 3d.

Educational Constructional Toys.

The Joiboy Card Building.

The Cards interlock into each other.

Price .. .. .. **1/10½** Post 3d.

The Young Crane Builder.

Contains wood blocks, pulleys, wheels, etc., in mahogany, for constructing a model working Crane. When erected can be wheeled about and made to hoist any weight. The revolving platform and brake make this toy specially interesting and instructive.

No. 1, size 10 by 10 in. **2/6** Post 4d.
No. 2 (in wood box), size 15½ by 14 in.
Price .. **4/6** Post 6d.

Spelling Board.

This is an exceedingly clever arrangement, enabling any word to be made and brought into the centre of board. Will keep children amused and teach at the same time.

Price .. .. **3/9** Postage 5d.

Drawing Slates.

Strongly made with stout glass and assorted pictures.

6d. **10½** **1/6** **1/10½**

Post 2d., 3d. and 4d.

Constructional Houses.

As illustration.

Complete box of building materials, making 5 charming houses of latest design.

Nicely painted. With full plan for building.

Size of box, 10 in. by 7 in.

Price .. .. **5/11** Post 6d.

The Young Signal Builder.

Complete set as illustration, in wood.
Price .. **10½d.** Post 3d.

"JEAN-JEAN."

It consists of cardboard forms such as walls, windows, outer and inner doors, gables, roofs, floors, staircases, balconies, etc. It is formed into one solid body by metal clasps fixed from within.

JEAN-JEAN enables a child to build houses complete with all details and inner walls, and each article is accompanied by three pictures which serve as models for object lessons. Its fitting together is so simple a method that a description is unnecessary.

The variety of houses to be built is numberless, and in order to permit as wide a margin as possible to a child's impression and intelligence, we supply:—

Model I. containing 160 single parts with 24 patterns and designs, **3 11**
Model II. containing 220 single parts with 24 patterns and designs, **5 11**
Model III. contains 320 single parts with 40 patterns and designs, **7/11**
Postage 4d., 5d., 6d.

JEAN-JEAN is the finest building toy of any kind which by its simple construction forms a solid structure, and even in a semi-finished condition can be moved or turned upside down without tumbling to pieces.

KINDERGARTEN TOYS.

The Liliputian Writing Companion.

Price	**10½**d.	**3/6**
Post	2d.	3d.

CHINA BALL MOSAIC.
A most interesting pastime for young children, who can make up pretty designs with the differently coloured balls. Price **6**d. Post 2d.

Basket Work and Stick Building.

Price.		Post.
6d.	..	2d.
10½d	..	3d.
1/9	..	3d.

Is a very useful and instructive toy for children. By means of the cut-out pieces, the wooden sticks, paper strips, etc., etc., the chi'dren can make all sorts of different objects, as houses, baskets, etc.

Character Dolls.

Price	..	..	**10½**d.
	Post 2d.		

Wood Mosaic.
By means of the 108 highly varnished and differently colored wooden pieces of various shapes, children can make up hundreds of different designs. Provides hours of amusements for children.
Price **6**d. **10½**d. **1/10½** Post 2d. 3d. 3d.

DOLLY'S WARDROBE.
The favourite of our girls consists of a wardrobe made of thick cardboard and decorated in modern style. The Wardrobe contains 2 cardboard dolls, 8 hats and bonnets, 8 dresses (latest fashions, also umbrella, muff, boa, school bag, tennis racket, etc. The dresses are fastened in the wardrobe on metal hooks, and the hats, etc., are kept in the drawer. Each wardrobe is packed in leatherette box with gold lettering. The dolls as well as the dresses, etc., are printed in full colours on stout cardboard and are nicely embossed.
Undoubtedly one of the best presents for our Girls.
Smaller, **6**d. Post 2d. As illustration. **2/6** Post 3d.

The Mosaic Designer.
ingenious arrangement of cups and coloured balls for forming various designs.

rice	..	..	..	**10½**d.	**1/9**	**2/6**
ost	..	..	..	3d.	3d.	4d.

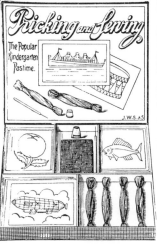

Pricking and Sewing.
As illustration.

Price	..	..	**10½**d.
	Post 3d.		

WEAVING AND PAPER PLAITING

The pretty designs into which our little ones have to work the paper strips will not fail to arouse their interest.

Price	..	..	**6**d.	**10½**d.	**1/4½**	**1/10½**
Post	..	..	2d.	3d.	3d.	3d.

KINDERGARTEN TOYS.

Fairy Photos. An entirely new idea. Each box contains a packet of 12 sensitized cards which merely require washing in soda water to develop into 12 beautiful photographs. These represent the well-known fairy tale of "Little Red Riding Hood," &c. Can be put into an album, specially designed for them. All the necessary parts complete in neat box. 8 by 5 in. Price **10½**d. Post 3d.

Mosaic Painting.
Price .. **6**d. Postage 2d.

Colour Stencils.

Price .. .. **1/4½** Postage 3d.
Larger size .. **2/11** ,, 4d.

Kitty's Painting Box.

Price **1/3**

Post 3d.

MARVELLOUS VALUE.
Japanned Metal Paint Box with paint as illustration.
Good soluble colours. Price **6½**d. Post 2d.

Dolly Dimple.
The favourite pastime of our girls. Each box contains dainty dresses and hats to match with the doll; each one is printed on stout cardboard in bright colours.
Price **6**d.
Post 2d.

The Little Ones' Games.
Instructive and amusing pastime for children.
Price **10½**d. Postage 3d.

Drawing and Painting.
Of all the many occupations for boys and girls, this game is to be particularly recommended.
Price **6**d. and **10½**d. Postage 2d. and 3d.

The Artists of Nursery Land.
The best and most useful Kindergarten and Nursery Pastime. Contains the finest quality of paints and crayons with designs for drawing, and coloured sketches as guide for colouring.
Packed in fine box, with artistic label. Price **2/6** Post 4d.

Transfer Pictures.

A delightful pastime for children of all ages.

The pictures are of the highest class obtainable (the same as used by manufacturers for decorating enamelled ware, etc.), and may be transferred to any object of wood, cardboard, tin, china, terra cotta, etc.

Packed in neat boxes.

Price **6**d. **10½**d. **2 3**
Post 2d. 3d. 3d.

Flower Making at Home.
Complete Outfit for Flower Making.

Price	10½d.	1/4½	1/10½	2/4½	3/6	4/11	5/11
Post	2d.	3d.	3d.	3d.	4d.	4d.	5d.

Price	6/11	9/6	Post	6d.	8d.

Toy Village, as illustration.
Complete with Cottages, Flowers, Trees, etc.

Price	..	..	10½d.	1/10½	3/6
Postage	..	..	2d.	3d.	4d.

Models for Embroidery
Containing 12 perforated coloured designed cards for embroidery according to Froebels principles
Price **2/11**   Post 3d.

Threadwork Pictures.
Containing coloured pencils, coloured thread, needles, model, and designed perforated cards for colouring, cutting out and erecting.

Price .. **2/-**   Post 3d.

Artistic Pea and Bean Work.
Containing 6 different coloured lots of Peas and Beans rubber stalk tubing, elastic fasteners and wire also, model making an amusing occupation for girls.

Price .. **2/-**   Post 4d.

Little Canvas Embroiderer
Containing 16 canvas sheets, model with skeins of thread, needles and designs.
2/6 smaller **6d. 1/0** Post 2d. 3d.

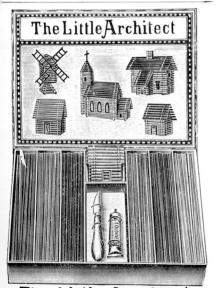

The Little Architect.
Containing cardboard stands, steel knife, tube of liquid glue, 4 different lots of coloured sticks, with diagrams showing how to build houses, churches, etc

Price .. **2/11**   Post 3d.

Mosaic Cubes
Beautifully enamelled in colours.

Price **1/-**   Post 3d.

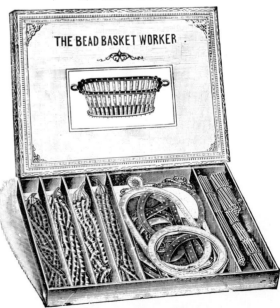

Bread Basket Worker
Containing sticks, 3 coloured strings of Beads, and cardboard material for Basket making.   Price **1/0, 3/6, 4,6.**   Post 2d. 4d. 4d.

KINDERGARTEN TOYS.

Art Needlework.

Price .. **6**d. **10½**d. **2/11** Post 2d. 3d. & **3**d.

Fancy Needlework.

Price **6**d. **10½**d. **1/10½**
Postage .. .. 2d. 3d. 3d.
Larger, Price **3/11** Post 4d.

Bead Weaving Loom.

A favorite Kindergarten Pastime for our Girls, who can make by means of the beads and the wooden weaving loom a lot of useful little things, like book-marks, fobs, etc. Complete, in strong box, with bright label and full instructions.
Price .. **10½**d. Post 3d.
Larger, price **2/11** and **3/11** Post 3d. and 4d.

Scandinavian Tapestry.

An Instructive Kindergarten Toy. Designs stencilled on gauze must be filled in with wool of the same color as the colored sketches given with each box. A beautiful tapestry effect is thus produced.

No. 15, size of box .. .. 17 ins. by 11 ins.
Price .. **3/11** Post .. 4d.

Thoroughly well-made wooden **Blackboard and Easel,** as illustration.
Really substantial in all details.

No. 00	0	1	2	3
3/11	**4/11**	**6/11**	**7/11**	**13/6**
Carr. 6d.	8d.	9d.	1/-	1/-

An entirely new idea in Mosaic Spindles, containing wool of various colours, are laid into a frame side by side and thus form most realistic designs of Carpets, Landscapes, Houses, etc. Each box is supplied with a Carpet or Landscape already fitted in frame as well as a book of coloured designs.

			Price	Post
No. 1 Box, size 10 by 7½ ins. with 500 spindles			**3/6**	4d.
,, 2 ,, 14 by 9½ ,, 1000 ,,			**5/11**	5d.

Animated Pets.

Beautifully coloured animals, birds, etc. So jointed that they may be placed in the most life-like positions.
Price **6**d. Postage 2d.

Sewing and Embroidery

Gives great pleasure to our Little Girls who, with their busy hands are always ready to make useful little Articles.
Price **6**d. **10½**d.
Post 2d. 3d.

The Little Folks Railway Play Box.

The latest Novelty! A fine present for our boys, who are always interested in Railway playthings. Put up in a very pretty box containing a tiny booking office (as seen above), a "right away" flag and a "danger flag," a bell, a good supply of tickets, ticket punch, luggage labels, whistle, a conductor mask, etc., etc. Undoubtedly the best present for the boys.
Price **3/6** Post 6d. Ditto. smaller **2/4½** Post 4d.

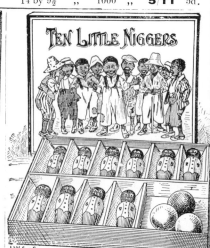

A game of ten pins. Very nicely got up in solid box with full colored label, contains 10 wooden figures of Nigger Boys, which are painted in life-like colours and are numbered differently, also 3 polished wooden balls Price **3/6** Post 4d.

KINDERGARTEN TOYS.

Quite a Novel Comb.na..on.

The Ideal Toy for Boys Contains: A Model of "Tiny Town" Station, to be
built up on a coloured base, Tin Train, Coal Cart, Hansom, &c.
Packed in box complete with Station.

Price **6**d.   Post 2d.   **10½**d.   Post 3d.   **2 6**   Post 4d.

Pets Bookstall. Containing little books, little newspapers
specially prepared for young people, full of fun. British manufacture

Price **10½**d. Postage 3d.   Smaller size, **6** l. Postage 2d.

Tiny Town G.P.O.

Improved Edition.   Complete with dainty Note
Paper, Envelopes, tiny Picture Postcards, Stamps, Stamp
Pad, Cheque Books, &c.
With Miniature Post Office.   Price **6**d.   Post 2d.
  ,,   and Postman Mask **10½**d.   ,,   3d.
  ,,   ,,   **2/4½**   ,,   4d.
Edition de luxe, with Miniature Post Office, Postman
Mask, Inkstand, Penholder, &c.   Price **3/6**   Post 4d

Tiny Town Bank.

By means of this outfit the children
can play at bank, for this purpose
being provided with a bank counter
with two windows, behind which
the Cashier stands, cheques, £5 toy
notes, toy money, deposit forms and
account books, in which the amounts
paid out or in have to be entered.

Price **10½**d.   Postage 3d.

Noahs Ark.

This set contains a fine large collapsible Noah's Ark,
which has to be set up. It also contains a set of **24** animals
printed in life-like colours on stout cardboard, and mounted
on wooden bases.   The whole set is arranged in a nice box
with wooden partitions, and with a beautiful label on
the outside.

Price ..	..	..	**10½**d.	**3/6**
Postage	..	..	2d.	3d.

Bobbies and Thieves.

A Splendid Present for a Boy.   Price **10½**d.   Postage 3d.

PETS SAND TOY

Pets Sand Toys.   The box exactly as this model can be made from this box.
Real sand, real figures, real spade, real pail, real sea-weed, real shells. Just borrow
mother's tea tray, the right thing to play on.   British manufacture.

Price **10½**d.   Post 3d.   Do. large **1/10½**   Post 4d.

Kindergarten Toys, etc.

The Word Builder.

Most interesting way of Teaching Children to Read.

Price **6**d. Post 2d. **10½**d. Post 3d.
,, **1/9** ,, 3d. **2/11** ,, 4d.

Funny Faces.

Makes over 2,000 Funny Heads.

Price .. .. **6**d. each.
Postage 2d.
Larger size **10½**d.
Postage 3d.

——

British Manufacture.

Counting Frames

10½d.
1/4½
1/10½
2/4½
Post 3d., 4d. & 6d.

Pet's Boarding School Box.

Note Paper and Envelopes in assorted size and fancy design. Calendar for every in the year. Blotting Pad, Pens and sealing wax.

Just the Thing for a Girl.

British Manufacture. **10½**d. Post 3d. Larger, **1/10½** Post 4d.

Rubber Bubble Blowers.

Containing 2 wooden pipes and 4 rubber balloons, assorted colours.

Price .. **10½**d.

Post 3d.

Washing Set.	Containing, Tubs, Pails, Washing Board, etc.				
Price ..	**6**d.	**10½**d.	**1/10½**	**2/11**	**3/11**
Post ..	3d.	3d.	4d.	4d.	5d.

The Little Picture Makers.

The latest Kindergarten Pastime in connection with Transfer Pictures.

There are 12 sheets, with pictures of farms, meadows, seaside, railway station, &c., and the children have to complete these pictures by means of the Transfer Pictures provided for that purpose, according to the outlined design sheets which come with each set. A very interesting Kindergarten outfit, complete with two mixing trays, bottles of gum and varnish, and sponge and brush. In strong box, with highly artistic labels, **2/11** Post 3d. Ditto smaller, **10½**d. Post 3d.

Pet's Transfers and Scraps.

Price **10**d.
Postage 2d.

Larger,
Price **1/10½**
Postage 3d.

Pet's Pastry Maker.

Containing all the fittings for Pastry Making and instructions how to ma few simple tarts.
British Manufacture.

Price ..	**6**d.	Post 3d.	**10½**d.	Post 4d.
Larger ..	**2/-**	Post 4d.	**3/11**	Post 5d.

ZILLOGRAPH or SHADOW THEATRE.
Price ... **6**d. and **10½**d. Post 2d. and 3d.

SHADOW PICTURES, containing shadow sheet & various figures for fitting on to finger tips, forming an amusing Punch and Judy Show ... **2/-** Post 3d.

British Made.
CLOCK MAKING MADE EASY.
Every part is numbered and can easily be fitted together by a boy of 8. Guaranteed to keep good time. Complete and clear instructions given. All parts for making a complete 30-hour clock, with wood case, brass wheels, escapement and and metal back.
Price .. **5/6** Post 6d.

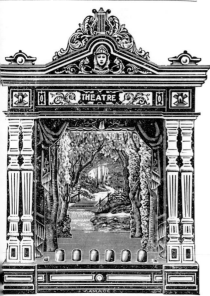

THEATRE, WITH FOOTLIGHTS.
The best Miniature Toy Theatre in the market. Strongly made and fitted with properly working curtain, English pattern, footlights to burn oil, beautifully lithographed characters, mounted on cardboard and cut ready for use. These Theatres have complete set of characters, etc., as per book.

No.	2a	3a	5a	6a
	7/11	13/9	18/6	37/6

Postage 6d. under 20/- in value.

THE INDIAN'S CAMP. A marvellously clever idea. Contains 22 Jointed Figures of Indians, Cowboys, Cowgirls, Horses, &c., all being painted in bright colours on heavy cardboard and securely riveted at the joints. Also contains a large stained wooden board, with grooves, size 24 by 12 by 2 in.. on which

NEW PUNCH AND JUDY SHOW.
No toy has ever yet captivated the heart of a child of any age quite as much as a Punch and Judy Show. These Punch and Judy Shows are strongly made and nicely ornamented. Supplied complete with life-like figures. The figures for the 2 largest sizes are specially made of solid wood, beautifully painted and of large size. Made in the following sizes:
No. 1. 25½ by 12 in. with 6 figures: **5/6** Carriage 6d.
No. 2. 28 by 14 in. ditto, **7/11** Carriage 8d.
No. 3. 38 by 18 in. ditto, **10/6** Carriage 10d.
No. 4. 43½ by 20¾ in. ditto, **14/6** Carriage 1/-
No. 5 49¼ by 23 in, ditto, **20/-** Carriage 1/3
No. 6. 65 by 29½ in. with 6 wooden figures, **35/-** Carriage 1/6

PET PLAYS. Box containing Theatre, Stage Front, Scenery and the Figures. Price .. **6**d. Post 2d.

TINY TOWN ZOO, as illustration, complete set in cardboard figures, animals, houses, &c.
Price .. .. **7/11** Carriage 10d.

These figures can be made to stand up in hundreds of different positions. There is also a Folding Tent and Blockhouse with it. The game is most artistically got up in a large showy box ... **4/11** Post 6d.

No. 7, 78 by 34½ in, with 6 wooden figures ... ... **45/-** Carriage 2/-
The comicalities of the game brings forth refreshing laughter and real enjoyment to both young and old.

ILLUSTRATIONS ARE FROM PHOTOGRAPHS OF ACTUAL MODELS MADE IN PERMODELLE.

What IT is— and something about IT !		IT is SO clean! Does not stick to the fingers!

PERMODELLE

Registered Trade Mark,   Patent 4949 of 1912.

MADE IN ENGLAND.

A NEW MODELLING WAX.

No laborious working required !		There is NO grease in IT.

PERMODELLE is hard but becomes plastic when held in the hand for a few seconds. NO LABORIOUS WORKING REQUIRED. When plastic it will keep so whilst it is being modelled, and when finished it sets hard in a few minutes and becomes a real model one can keep. It does not alter in any other way. It can be softened and modelled, and softened and re-modelled as many times as desired. Years after, an old model can be softened and re-modelled. PRACTICALLY IT LASTS FOR EVER AND NEVER ALTERS. It never uses away because it does not stick to everything it touches and does not waste. It is more easy to model than Clay and is the

The "Plastic at will" Feature.

CHEAPEST & BEST

MODELLING MATERIAL OBTAINABLE.

PERMODELLE has many advantages over other Modelling Materials. IT IS SO CLEAN, IT DOES NOT STAIN OR MARK THE HANDS.

It will not stain the most delicate dress and even if a soft piece be stamped into the carpet it will pick up without leaving a trace behind. THERE IS NO GREASE IN IT. Once realise that it is perfectly clean and you will never use anything else for modelling. All modelling is done entirely with the fingers. Even the most fragile flower can be made more easily with the fingers with PERMODELLE than with a tool.

WONDERFUL PICTURES can be made with PERMODELLE. Real-looking FLOWERS, FRUITS, VEGETABLES, FIGURES, ANIMALS, MAPS, ETC. Rough Wood covered with it. You can do anything with PERMODELLE that you can do with any other Modelling Material and a great deal more.

PERMODELLE has no smell, is non-poisonous and does not stain.

Practically it lasts for ever and never alters.

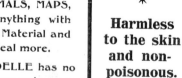

Permodelle the NEW— It is SO clean —Modelling Wax.

✳

Hard in its normal state.

✳

Made in 20 bright colours

✳

Harmless to the skin and non-poisonous.

Supplied in **1**d. SAMPLE PACKETS, containing 4 Sticks, also in BOXES, containing good Assortment of Material—

	6d.	**1**/-	**2 6**	each.
	Post 2d.	3d.	4d.	

Also in BOXES, containing Material and Models—Each. Post

	1/- Post 3d.	**2 6** Post 4d.	**5**/-	5d.
Pottery Moulding Outfit, with Tools..	..	..	**3**/-	4d.
Alphabet Moulding Outfit, with Brass Mould		..	**3**/-	4d.
Animal Moulding Outfit, with 3 Brass Moulds		..	**3/6**	4d.
,, ,, ,, ,, 6 ,, ,,			**5**/-	5d.
The LITTLE GEM LATHE & MATERIAL, &c.			**5**/-	5d.

Bricks, Dissected Puzzles, Picture Cubes.

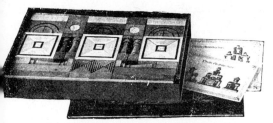

Fine Wood Building Blocks.

6 1/10½ 2/6 2/11 3/6 3/11 4/11 5/6 6/11 7/6 9/6 17/6
Post 4d. 4d. 5d. 5d. 6d. 6d. 7d. 9d. 10d. 1/- 1/- 1/3

A want supplied.

arge plain Square and Oblong Hardwood Bricks, cannot
et broken and are easy to build **2/11 3/11 4/11 7/11**
Post 6d. 6d. 7d. 1/-

itto, with Pyramid Cubes. **5/11 7/11 10/6 13/6**
Post 9d. 10d. 1/- 1/3

Embossed Wooden Cubes.

Almost everlasting.

4d. Post 2d. **1/-** Post 3d.
2/6 Post 5d. **3/6** Post 6d.

Pyramid Nested Cubes

No. 1 8 pieces 6½d.
„ 2. 10 „ **1/-**
Postage 3d.
„ 3 12 large pcs. 1/11
„ 5 13 „ „ **2/11**
Postage 4d.

Slate Slates.

10½d.
Postage 4d.

Drawing Slates,

6½d. 10½d.
Post 3d., 4d.

1/6 1/10½d.
4d. 5d.

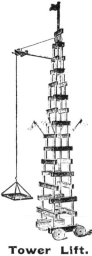

Tower Lift.

Wooden Blocks and
Rods, to build a Work-
ing Tower Lift, nearly
6 feet high 4 · each
BRITISH MAKE.

"Playmates." The Little Folks Picture Blocks.

Solid wooden Blocks with beautifully coloured pictures.
Packed in strong box. Price **2/11** Postage 5d.

Picture or A.B.C. Cubes.

Best quality Cubes, to form amusing and interesting Pictures.
Packed in box complete.

No. 0 6½d. 1 **1/-** 2 **1/4½** 3 **1/6½** 4 **2/-**
Postage 3d. 4d. 4d. 5d. 6d.
No. 5 **2/6** 6 **2/11** 7 **4/11** 8 **6/6**
Postage 6d. 7d. 7d. 8d.

Novelty Cubes. With voice 2/4½ B, with 4 voices, 3/6
Larger size, **4/6 6/11** Cubes with music 1/6 2/11 4/6

Burlington Building Blocks

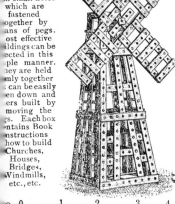

re made of
rdwood slabs
h small holes
which are
fastened
ogether by
ans of pegs.
ost effective
ildings can be
ected in this
ple manner.
ey are held
ly together
can be easily
en down and
ers built by
moving the
s. Each box
ntains Book
nstructions
how to build
Churches,
Houses,
Bridges,
Windmills,
etc., etc.

o. 0 1 2 3 4
0½d. **1/3** **2/-** **3/6** **4/6**
st 3d. 3d. 4d. 4d. 6d.

"Tudor" Stone Building Bricks

e surface of the bricks being modelled to imitate the
pearance of the rough hewn stone, magnificent modern
ildings as well as faithful reproductions of the beautiful
chitecture of Mediæval Times can be erected. Each
contains a coloured book of instructions of about 29
es, with ground plans, showing how to build Castles,
urches, Houses, Towers, etc.

1. Box contains 86 stones **4/11** No. 2. 160 stones **7/6**
3. „ 200 „ **10/6** „ 4. 270 „ **13/6**

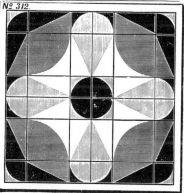

Mosaic Cubes.

Very fine finish in Coloured Enamel,
making numerous designs. 10 in. squ.
Price 6d 10½d. 1/10½d. 2/11
3/11 5/11
Post 2d. 3d. 3d. 4d. 5d. 6d.

GEOGRAPHICAL DISSECTED PUZZLES.

England and Wales, Europe the World,
Scotland, Ireland.

No. 1, containing 100 pieces, **1/6** Post 4d.
No. 2, containing 160 pieces, **2/9** Post 5d.
No. 3, containing 260 pieces, **3/11** Post 6d.

A Selection of Dissected Puzzles.

An almost endless variety of subjects
Post 6d. 2d, 10½d. 3d. 1/10½d. 3d. 2/4½d. 4d. 2/11 5d. 3/11 5d

Constructional Toys.

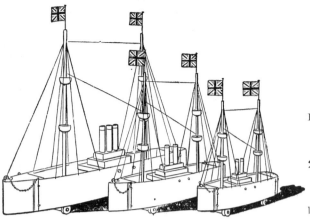

Model Steamers.

Exceptionally well made.

Packed in box with Hull assembled.

Mast and Riggings separate.

Easy to put together or take apart.

Travel on Wheels.

No. 1. 12 in. long, **2/11** ea. Post 4d.

No. 2. 17½ in. long, **4/11** Post 5d.

No. 3. 2 ft. 4 in. long, **6/11** Post 6d.

Battleship Building Bricks. Beautifully carved i hardwood and enamelled in colours for building different model battle ships. Made to float. Box to hold 3 boats, **8/6** Post 6d. Ditt 4 boats, **12/6** Post 8d. Ditto 6 boats, **18/6** Post 10d.

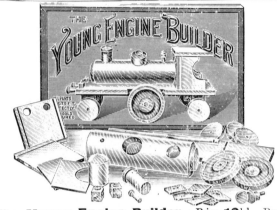

The Young Engine Builder. Price **10½**d. Post 3 **1/10½** Post 3d. **2/11½** Post 4d. **3/11** Post 4d. **4/11** Post 5d. **7/11** Post 6d.

"KLIPTIKO."

"Kliptiko" is simple enough to joyfully interest a young child, while its possibilities are expansive enough to preven that interest from flagging as the child grows up.

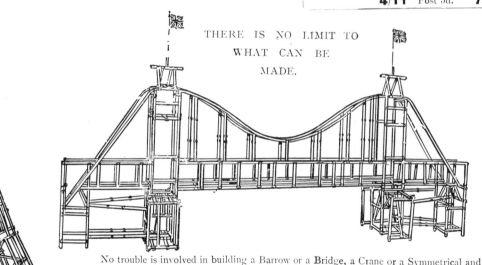

THERE IS NO LIMIT TO WHAT CAN BE MADE.

No trouble is involved in building a Barrow or a Bridge, a Crane or a Symmetrical and graceful Tower. There are no irritating small parts to get into the wrong place, or in the reverse position to that which that they should be. All Constructions are quite rigid and steady, and working models may be operated without slackness or fear of collapse. The Standard Units are the same in each set, making all pieces interchangeable, and allowing one set to be added to another of a lesser or a greater price. No. 1 **10½**d. Post 3d. No. 2 **2/4½** Post 4d. No. 3 **4/11** Post 5d. No. 4 **9/11** Post 6d.

The Young Motor Maker.

Complete set of parts in wood to make a Motor Van.

10½d. **1/10½** **2/6**
Post 4d. 5d.

Fire Escape.

A complete set of materials and instructions for building above.

Price **2/6** Post 3d.

Wooden Constructional Toys.

HOW TO BUILD "DREADNOUGHTS" THAT FLOAT.   (Patent applied for No. 12653/13.)

A VALUABLE IMPROVEMENT ON OUR WELL-KNOWN DREADNOUGHT SHIPBUILDING BLOCKS.

All ships are fitted with a special keel which enables them to **float upright in water.**

These Shipbuilding Blocks are undoubtedly amongst the finest Toys on the Market. Each Box contains Wood Blocks, Guns, Flags, &c., with instructions for building Warships, type: H.M.S. "Dreadnought," H.M.S. "Lord Nelson," H.M.S. "King Edward VII," etc., as well as Cruisers, type: H.M.S. "Invincible," etc., Torpedo Boats, Forts, etc. This Toy is not only very entertaining, but most instructive.

	No. 1	1½	2	3
	1/10½	**2/11**	**6/6**	**10/6**
Postage ..	4d.	5d.	8d.	10d.

INTERLOCKING BUILDING BRICKS.

Fort.
Built with Gamage's Interlocking Bricks.

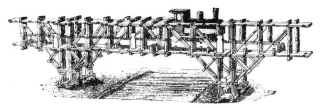

Bridge.
Built with Gamage's Interlocking Bricks.

House.
Built with Gamage's Interlocking Bricks.

The Gamage Interlocking Building Bricks, without question, are far and away the best bricks ever invented for children. Their chief feature is, of course, the notches or slots into which the bricks interlock, so that when a model has been constructed, whether it be a House, Fort, or Windmill, it can be carried about and played with as if it were nailed or glued together. Even apart from the interlocking arrangement the shapes and sizes have been so arranged that the number of different models which can be made from a single box, is quite extraordinary. The Bricks are of Best Beech Hardwood, machined and planed to gauge, so that any brick (no matter what size) will interlock with another and will not come apart until required.

An illustrated Booklet is supplied with each Box. showing how to construct
Model Bridges, Churches, Windmills, Houses, Forts, Monuments, &c., &c.

No. 1. **10½d.** Post 3d.	No. 1½. **1/9** Post 4d.	No. 2. **2/4½** Post 5d.	No. 2½. **3/11** Post 9d.

A DELIGHTFUL & FASCINATING TOY

Consisting of wood Blocks, wheels, axles, pulleys, rods, pins and tongues with tools and manual of illustrated instructions for constructing Cranes, Motor Cars, Engines, and all sorts of Models that work.

Open Motor Car.

All Models can be taken to pieces and used over and over again.

All Models when made are Strong and Rigid Toys for Practical use.

Pin-Tung   Or Model Making Made Easy.

The Tower Bridge. A correct Model.

Trip Hammer.

2/6	Box makes	11	Models.	Post	4d.
3/6	,,	23	,,	,,	5d.
5/6	,,	28	,,	,,	6d.
8/6	,,	40	,,	,,	8d.
12/6	,,	46	,,	,,	10d.
17/6	,,	50	,,	,,	1/-
21/-	,,	53	,,	,,	1/-

I

WHITE HARDWOOD MODELS. Can be taken apart and re-assembled.

Horizontal Engine, with Motar Mill.
With the above models there is no danger. Children will derive great amusement from turning the engines and watching the revolutions of the wheels and the movements of the piston rods. Can also be used to drive other small models. Sand is supplied for grinding in the pan .. **4/11** Post 6d.

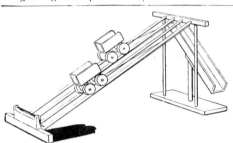

Double Colliery Tip, as illustration.
One waggon descends while other ascends and automatically empty themselves. With shoot to collect contents of waggons .. **3/6** Post 3d.

Cannon.
A good strong serviceable Toy, strong and well finished. Length of barrel 10 in. Complete with 12 balls .. **3/6** Post 4d.

Potter's Wheel.
Many varieties of shaped Vases and Plain and Fancy Pieces that are made in Pottery, can be produced with this Toy. Complete in box, with Clay, Tools and Booklet of full instructions, **3/6** Post 4d. Made in England.

Horizontal Engine. Working Model.
Very useful for driving other small models, toys, &c., by connecting up to the pulleys by small belts. Driven by turning handle. Realistic movements.
Price .. **2/4½** Post 3d.

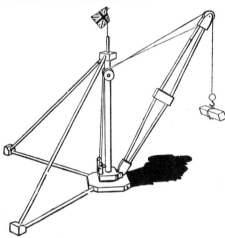

Derrick.
When taken apart packs compact in box. Arm 18 in. long.
Price .. .. .. **2/4½** Post 3d.

Model Stationary Crane.
Perfect in every detail.

Arm detaches and all packs into small compass.

Length of arm 16 inches.

Good Design.

Strongly Made.

Complete with Clamp in Box.

Price .. **4/11**

Post 6d.

Steam Crane on Wheels.

In addition to hoisting, this can be used to drive any small models by connecting up, with belts, to pulleys on shafting.
Handle is turned to drive engine.
Price .. .. **3/11** Post 4d.

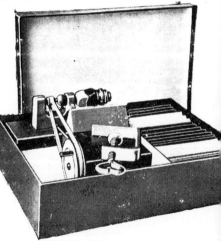

The "Wheelboy."
Combining Fun with Physical Culture.
No Playground or Gymnasium complete without. Carefully constructed so as to prevent injury to the knuckles.
Developes the muscles of the arms, shoulders and back.
With rubber tyre .. .. **1/9** Post 4d.
Without rubber tyre .. **10½d.** ,,

The Little Gem Lathe, for Turning Permodelle.
Permodelle is a most delightful material from which to turn small articles. This lathe is a perfect mode Cannot get out of order. Quite easy and simple work. Outfit includes Lathe and Belt, Cramp Rest, Tools, &c., supply of Permodelle.
Price in box, with full instructions, **4/11** Post 6d.

Jolly Joe.

comical dancing figure. The youngest
ild can make this amusing figure dance
endless variety of steps. Danced to
music is great fun. A very strong toy.
Price .. **10½d.**
tto, made of muslin, **10½d.** Post 1½d.

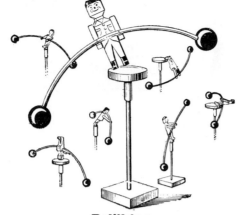

Rollikins.

Rollikins is a well made toy. He has movable arms,
and the centre of gravity is altered by altering the
position of his arms. He will balance anywhere, on his
head or toes. He always appears to be just going to
tumble off the Stand, but just manages to keep on.

Price .. .. **10½d.** Post 3d.

The French Knitting Machine

Girls will appreciate this Machine the most, but
boys will find a great interest in knitting Scarves,
Neckties, Mats, and various other useful articles.
Quite easy to use.
With a little skill, Socks and Stockings may be
knitted, and Mittens are simplicity itself.
Complete in box. Used with any wool.
1/10½ each. Post 3d. Made in England.

A Strong Pair of Sturdy Boxers

which fight until one knocks out his opponent.
Price .. .. **10½d.** Post 3d.

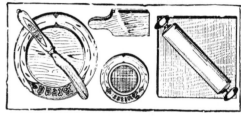

The Little Dairy Set.

A very useful set consisting of Paste Board, Rolling-pin,
Bread Board, Bread Knife, Butter Dish, and Butter
Workers. Price .. **2/3½** Post 3d.

Butter Workers & Board
And Butter Dish.

means of the model pair of Scotch
nds, girls will be able to learn how to
make Butter Pats and Rolls, etc.
he set complete in box, as illustrated.
Price .. **10½d.** Post 3d.

Bread Board and Knife.

A nicely carved Bread Board, 6½ in. diameter,
and Bread Knife, complete in box.
Price .. **10½d.** Post 3d.

e Celebrated "Mr. Jollyboy."

he most
musing of
Dancers.
e King of
Dancers.
e Jolliest of
Jollyboys.

Patent
o. 7725.
Made in
England.

Toy with
normous
ssibilities.

re is no end
e Variety
steps to be
ormed by
Jollyboy.'

0½ each,
ost 4d.

uperior quality, specially finished, **2/10½**
Post 4d.

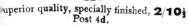

Model Scaffolding.

A Novel Set of Scaffold Poles, Tubs and Planks, including
Pulley Block for hoisting materials.

In conjunction with a few books, or toy bricks, the scaffolding
can be erected in any form desired, affording much amusement.

1/- Post 3d. **2/-** Post 4d.

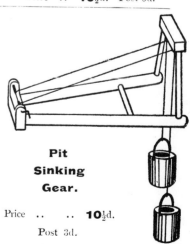

Pit
Sinking
Gear.

Price .. .. **10½d.**

Post 3d.

With 2 buckets, each of which automatically
descends as the other ascends on working the
winch.

I...

ANIMALS, STABLES, etc.

Jumping Rabbit.
Operated by squeezing ball.
Most realistic. Does not
get out of order.
Price **5½**d. Post 2d.
Larger size, **10½**d. Post 3d

Jumping Dog.
Worked by a rubber ball.
Will not get out of
order.
Price **5½**d. Post 2d.
Larger, **10½**d. Post 3d.

Large Felt
Covered
Horses
to ride upon.

Price	Post
8/11	4d.
10/9	5d.
13/9	6d.
15/6	7d.

**Mascot
Black Cat.**
With label on marked
"For Luck." 3½in. high
Price **5½**d. Post 2d.
British Manufacture.

**Smallest
Teddy Bear**
ever made in
plush. 3 in. high
5½d. Post 2d
British
Manufacture.

"TUBBY" and "FIFI"
The Famous Nursery Pets.

"TUBBY" with Coat as illustration.
Price **10½**d. **1/10½** **2/11**

"Fi Fi."
The Cat of the
Season.
This is one of
the novelties in
soft plush toys,
and one which
has already be-
come a great
favourite.
Beautifully made
of silky plush.
(Grey Plush).

Price	Post
10½d.	3d.
1/4½	3d.
2/3	3d.
3/6	4d.
4/6	4d.

Can also be
supplied in
standing position
jointed.

Also supplied in
red or blue plush
Most attractive.

"Fi Fi."

"TUBBY."
"Tubby" is a fine specimen of a mischievous puppy, and
together with his "pal" "Fi Fi" make a fine pair.
A really fascinating toy, splendidly made of soft plush with
"expression" eyes.

Prices	**10½**d.	**1/4½**	**2/3**	**3/6**	**4/6**
Post	3d.	3d.	3d.	4d.	4d.

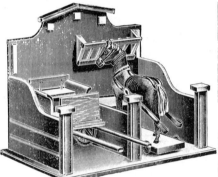

Special value. Strongly made **Stable.**
As illustration. Price **1/11** Post 4d.
Similar style, smaller, **1/-** " 3d.

Sweet Stalls. 5/11
Butchers' Shops.

Price	**1/10½**	**2/11**	**3/11**	**4/11**	**5/11**
Post	4d.	4d.	5d.	6d.	6d.

Grocers' Shops.

Price	**2/6**	**3/6**	**4/6**	**5/11**	**7/11**	**11/9**	**16/6**	**23/6**	**35/-**
Post	5d.	6d.	7d.	8d.	9d.	10d.	1/-	free.	free.

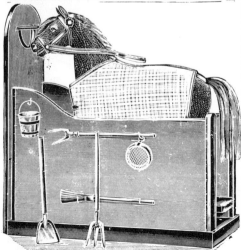

Real Skin Covered Horse and Stall.
Complete with clothing and stable utensils as illustration.
Special value. Price **5/11** Post 6d.

Stables. Similar to Illustration. **1/10½** **-/11**

Price	**3/6**	**4/11**	**6/11**	**8/11**	**10/9**	**15/6**	**19/6**
Post	5d.	6d.	7d.	8d.	8d.	9d.	free.

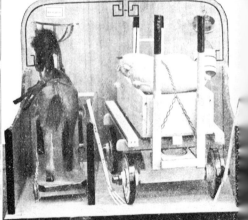

STABLES.

Price	**10/9**	**15/9**	**29/6**
Post	8d.	9d.	free

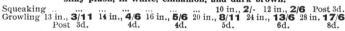

STEIFF HIGH-CLASS TOY AND RIDING ANIMALS IN FELT AND PLUSH

In offering STEIFF TOYS again we wish to inform our customers of the high satisfaction these goods have always given to their purchasers, and of the marvellous success they have achieved all the world over. The secret of this will be found in their character as Toys, which they are in the full sense of the word, combining durability and lifelike models which are unsurpassed.

Irish Terrier on wheels.
Light brown fine plush. Realistic model.

14 in.	17 in.	20 in.
7/11	**11/6**	**15/-**
Post 6d.	9d.	1/-

Lion on wheels.
Light brown fine plush, long silky mane.

9 in.	11 in.	14 in.	17 in.	20 in.	24 in.
4/6	**6/6**	**11/9**	**18/6**	**30/-**	**39/6**
Post 4d.	6d.	9d.	1/-	Free.	Free.

Fine model of a Circus Horse, white silky plush skin, steering apparatus, saddle with stirrups
36 in. **£5 5 0**

Lamb. Curly white lambskin.

9 in.	11½ in.	14 in.	17 in.	20 in.	24 in.
2/6	**4/6**	**7/11**	**10/9**	**18/9**	**27/6**
Post 3d.	4d.	6d.	9d.	1/-	Free.

Fox Terrier on wheels.
White felt skin.

7 in.	11 in.	14 in.	17 in.	20 in.
1/6	**3/6**	**5/11**	**6/11**	**10/6**
Post 3d.	5d.	6d.	7d.	9d.

In fine plush.
17 in. ... **10/6** Post 9d.

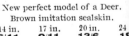

New perfect model of a Deer.
Brown imitation sealskin.

14 in.	17 in.	20 in.	24
6/11	**9/11**	**13/6**	**18**
Post 6d.	7d.	9d.	

Polar Bear on wheels.
White silky plush skin.

9 in.	14 in.	24 in.
4/11	**13/6**	**27/6**
Post 6d.	9d.	Free.

Fine Brown Plush Bear on wheels. A Special Favorite.

7 in.	9 in.	11½ in.	14 in.	17 in.	20 in.	24 in.
3/6	**5/11**	**7/11**	**13/6**	**18/9**	**26/6**	**39/6**
Post 4d.	5d.	6d.	9d.	1/-	Free.	Free.

Brown Bear on wheels.
Imitation sealskin.

7 in.	...	**2/6**	...	Post 3d
9 in.	...	**4/6**	...	" 4d
11½ in.	...	**5/11**	...	" 5d
14 in.	...	**8/11**	...	" 8d
17 in.	...	**13/6**	...	" 10d
20 in.	...	**18/6**	...	" 1/
24 in.	...	**27/6**	...	" Free
32 in.	...	**45/-**	...	" Fr

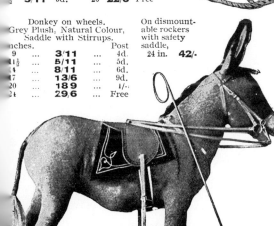

STEIFF Popular Grotesque & Character Dolls

Individual features, Unbreakable, Jointed, Comical, Soft stuffed.

Mrs. Captain.
14¾ in., **3/3** Post 4d.

Captain.
14 in. **3/3** Post 4d.

Golliwog, fully jointed,
attractively dressed.

Inches.		Post
11½	**2/6**	3d.
14	**3/6**	4d.
17	**4/6**	5d.
20	**7/6**	6d.

ALFONS   GASTON.
The Two Polite Frenchmen.
11½ in. **2/3** Post 4d.   20 in. **2 6** Post 4d.

Thin Postman.
20 in. **2/11** Post 4d.

Comic Policeman.
17 in. fat **2/11** Post 4d.
20 ,, thin **2/6** ,, 4d.

Soldier, red jacket, blue
trousers, Fat, 17 in. **3/6**
Thin, 20 in. **3/6** Post 4d.

Hunter Hubertus.
Red jersey, grey trousers, grey hat, garters.

11½ in.	14 in.	17 in.	20 in.	24 in.
4/11	**5/11**	**7/11**	**12/6**	**14/6**
Post 4d.	5d.	6d.	8d.	10d.

Esquimaux Doll.
Fine Brown Plush Dress.
11½ in. **2/6** Post 4d.

Dutch Girl,
Helen.

Inches.		Post
11½	**4/11**	4d.
14	**5/11**	5d.
17	**9/6**	6d.
20	**12/6**	8d.
24	**15/-**	1/-

Dutch Boy,
Harry.

Inches.		Post
11½	**4/6**	4d.
14	**7/11**	5d.
17	**12/6**	6d.
20	**14/6**	9d.

STEIFF'S

Stuffed Character Dolls, the
best in the world, will stand
without support, their clothes
take off, are fully jointed, do
not break, have individual
fascinating features, and
their hair will not come out.

Boy in
delaine suit

In		Post
11½	**4/11**	4d.
14	**5/11**	5d.
17	**7/11**	6d.
20	**12 6**	8d.
24	**15/**	9d.

Girl in
delaine
dress.

In.		Post
11½	**4/11**	4d.
14	**5/11**	5d.
17	**9/6**	6d.
20	**15 -**	9d.
24	**18/-**	1/-

Highlander.
Uniform true to life.

17 in.	20 in.	2
5/6	**6/6**	7
Post 4d.	5d.	

Monkey on Speedaway.
"Record Peter."
Most unique movements,
in red felt dress.
8 in. **2/11** 10 in. **4/6**
Post 4d.   4d.

In Brown Plush.

8 in.	10 in.	12 in.
3/6	**4/6**	**6/6**
Post 4d.	5d.	5d.

Duck waddling & quacking
6 in. **2/3** 7 in. **3/6** 9 in. **4/6**
Post 4d.   5d.   6d.

Life-like Moving Monkey
7 in. **2/3**   9 in. **2/11**
Post 3d.   4d.

Natural Running Rabbit, Brown Felt
5 in. **1/4½** 6 in. **2/3** 9 in. **3/6**
Post 3d.   4d.   5d.
Grey Plush, 7 in. **3 6**   Post 5d.
Fine Plush, Spotted, 7 in. **4/3** ,, 6d.
                        9 in. **5/6** ,, 6d.

STEIFF Natural Running Animals and those on
Speedaway are new and most amusing for children
—There is no clockwork to get out of order, the
movements are realistic and comical. See them
**racing each other on the Racing Track
in our Xmas Bazaar. Father Xmas has
never before provided more joy.**

Red Riding Hood.

11½ in.	**4/11**	Post
14 ,,	**6/6**	,,
17 ,,	**9/6**	,,
20 ,,	**15/-**	,,

Noah's Arks, Farmyards, etc.

Sheep with Shepherd and Dog, most realistic models; correctly painted. Practically unbreakable. Price **2 6** Post 3d.

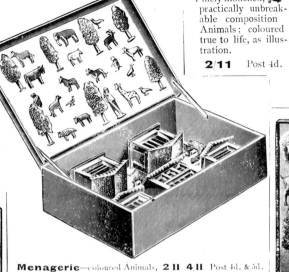

Finely modelled, practically unbreakable composition Animals; coloured true to life, as illustration. **2/11** Post 4d.

Superior quality Farmyard Animals—fine models, beautifully coloured and almost unbreakable. Complete box, as illustration. **3/6** Post 7d.

Menagerie—coloured Animals, **2 11 4 11** Post 4d. & 5d.

Farmyard, with nicely painted Animals, etc. **1 6** Post 3d. **2 -** Post 4d. **3/6** Post 5d. **5/11** Post 6d.

Poultry Farms, 4/11 Post extra.

Fine models of Farmyard Animals, as illustration, beautifully painted and practically unbreakable.
Price .. **5 11** Post 5d.

Farmyard Pets, well-modelled Animals in practically unbreakable composition, as illus. **2/-** Post 3d.
Three Animals, **1/-** Post 3d.

Plain whitewood Animals in boxes. Postage 3d. and 4d.
On wheels, **1/- 1/6 2/11** Without wheels, **1/- 1/4 2/4½**
Whitewood Animals, as illus., best quality, very finely carved Price **3/11** and **4/11** Post 4d. and 5d.

Boat-shaped Arks, as illust.
in. long, with 32 whitewood animals, **1/-**
in. ,, ,, 50 ,, ,, **1/6**
in. ,, ,, 60 ,, ,, **2/11**
in. ,, ,, 90 ,, ,, **4/6**
Postage 2d., 3d., 3d., 4d.

Ark, as illustration, with rustic roof, containing—
64 varnished Animals, 14½ in. long, **1/11** Post 2d.
104 ,, ,, 17 in. ,, **3/3** ,, 5d.
112 ,, ,, 19 in. ,, **4/11** ,, 3d.

Noah's Ark, White Animals.
11½ in., 96 Anmls **2/11**
16 in., 96 Anmls. **3/11**
152 Anmls. **5/11**

Boat-shaped Ark, as illustration, complete with whitewood Animals.
19½ in. 50 animals, **7/11** Post 4d. 24 in. 50 animals, **12/9** Post 6d.
27 in. 50 animals, **15/6** Post 8d.

Noah's Arks, complete with twelve Animals, 5½ in. long, **6d.** Post 3d.

New Model Ark, with polished Animals.
17 in., 100, **4/11**
18½ in., 152, **8/11**
Post 6d., 8d.

New Stable Ark, as illustration, opens out as shown. Fitted with 36 animals, 8 attendants and furniture complete. 20½ in., **8/6** Post 4d. 26 in., **12/6** Post 6d. 31 in., **22/6** Post free. No. 1227. Noah's Ark, containing 28 skin and felt covered animals ... **23/6** Carriage free.

DOLLS MANSIONS.

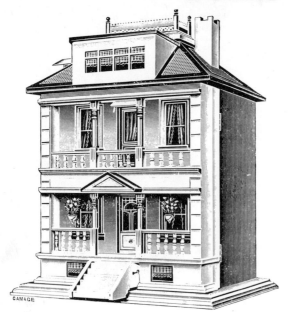

Handsome Dolls House.   As illustration.

With 4 rooms, windows fitted with curtains, balcony on first floor
Beautifully enamelled and finished, imitation tile roof and brick walls.

30 in. High.   25 in. Wide.   20 in. Deep.

Price **42/-**

Handsome Villa.   As illustration.

With 4 rooms and staircase, imitation electric door bell to ring, all windows
fitted with curtains, doors to open, imitation tile roof and brick walls

Beautifully finished.   31½ in. High.   30½ in. Wide.   20 in. Deep.

Price   ..   **59/6**

Doll House.   As illustration.

Beautifully enamelled and finished

With 5 rooms and staircase, all doors to open, fitted with imitation electric door
bell to ring. All windows fitted with curtains, imitation tile roof

38 in. High   35 Wide.   26 in. Deep.

Price   ..   **97/6**

Superior Model Dolls House.

With 5 rooms, windows fitted with curtains, 1 window at rear of house
imitation tile roof and brick walls.

Strongly   made   and   well   finished.

36 in. High   29 in. Wide.   19 in. Deep.

Price   ..   **49/6**

Carriage extra on all Dolls' Houses outside London Carrier Radius.

Dolls' Houses.

Stylish and strongly made

Doll's House,

With 2 rooms. Height 18 in.

Price .. .. 5/11 Carriage 8d.

Smart Doll's Villa,

With two rooms. Over all dimensions, 15½ in. high, 9 in. wide, 7 in. deep.

Price **2/11**

Carriage 6d.

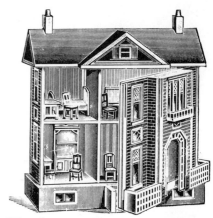

Handsome Doll's Mansion,

With four rooms, each fitted with furniture. Total height 18 in., width 18½ in., depth 8 in.

Price .. .. **11/9** Carriage 1/-

The New Screen Doll's House. (Improved.)

It stands about 4 ft. high, and can be folded up flat. The centre fold has a Door with Lock and Key and Letter Slit. The Door is quite large enough for a child to walk through. The Side Leaves are provided with Windows (to open). The idea is to stretch the Screen across the corner of a Room and Children can then "Play at Houses" in quite a realistic way. Tea Parties could be held inside, etc. The outside is finished in White and Red Brick, inside nicely Papered, Glass in Windows, etc.

No. 1. About 4 ft. high .. .. Price **37/6** each. Carriage and packing, 2/-

" 2. " 5 ft. " .. .. " **50/-** " do. 2/6

Strongly made Doll's Villa,

With two rooms furnished. 18 in. high, 14½ in. wide, 7 in. deep. Price .. **7/11** Carriage 10d.

Doll's Villa, as illustration. With four rooms, windows fitted with curtains. All doors to open.

27 in. high, 18½ in. wide, 12¼ in. deep.

Price **21/-**

The front of this large House opens in centre. Four rooms with fireplaces fitted.

The special novelty is the clock in the tower. This goes for 24 hours without re-winding.

30 in. high, 28 in. wide, 18 in. deep.

Price .. **30/-**

Doll's House, as illustration. Complete with furniture. 22½ in. high, 17 in. wide, 12½ in. deep. With two rooms, windows, fitted with curtains, all doors to open, nicely finished.

Price .. **17/6**

Dolls' Carriages.

The "Eclipse" Doll's Carriage.
Wood Body (measures at top, 18½ in. by 9 in.). Concealed Foot-well, ⅝ in. Rubber-tyred Wheels (12 in. and 8 in. diam.), Narrow Metal Hubs, Reversible Brass-jointed Hood.
Stock Colours . Dark Blue, Dark Green and Motor Striped. Price **9/11**

The "Gamage" Doll's Cariage.
Wood Body (measures at top, 20 in. by 9¾ in.) with Reversible Brass-jointed Hood and China Handle 12 in. and 8 in. by ⅝ in. Rubber-tyred Wheels.
Stock Colours : Dark Blue, Dark Green. **12/9**

Smart Wooden Body (measures at top, 22½ in. by 10¾ in.), Plain Cee Springs, Reversible Brass-jointed Hood fitted with Thumbscrews and Stops, ⅝ in. Rubber-tyred Wheels (12 in. and 8 in. diam.), Waist Straps.
Stock Colours: Dark Blue, Dark Green. **27/**

The "Ascot" Doll's Carriage.
Large Size Wooden Body (measures at top, 22½ in. by 10¾ in.), ⅝ in. Rubber-tyred Wheels (12 in. and 8 in. diam.), Brass-jointed Reversible Hood, fitted with Thumbscrews and Stops, China Handle, Strap Cee Springs, Waist Straps.
Stock Colours: Dark Green, Dark Blue **19/11**

The "Mayfair" Doll's Carriage.
Large Size Wood Body with Motor Stripes (measures at top, 22½ in. by 10¾ in.), ⅝ in. Rubber-tyred Wheels (12 in. and 8 in. diam.), Reversible Hood fitted with Thumbscrews, Stops, and Brass Joints, China Handle, Waist Straps.
Stock Colour : Dark Green with Motor Stripes in Black. **22/6**

The "Victoria" Doll's Carrjage
Special Large Wooden Body (27½ in. by 12½ in. at top, Plain Cee Springs, ⅝ in. Rubber-tyred Wheels (14 in. and 10 in. diam.), Reversible Brass-jointed Hood, fitted with Thumbscrews and Stops, Extended Wood Cross Hand'e.
Stock Colours: Dark Green, Dark Blue **25/9**

The "Empress" Doll's Carriage
Large Size Wooden Body, with Moulded Sides. ⅝ in. Rubber-tyred Wheels (14 in. and 2⁰ in. diam.). Strap Cee Springs, Steadying Straps, Apron, Cot Seat, Loose Cushions, Extended China Handle, Brass-jointed Hood. Best Finish throughout.
Stock Colours: Dark Green, Dark Blue. **30/-**

The "Royal" Doll's Carriage.
Large Size Body, with Swelled Sides. ⅝ in. Rubber-tyred Wheels (14 in. and 10 in. diam.). Strap Cee Springs, Steadying Straps, Long (over-end) Apron, Centre Seat, Loose Cushions, Extended China Handle, Brass-jointed Hood. Best Finish throughout.
Stock Colours : Dark Green, Dark Blue. **32/6**

The "Albermarle" Doll's Carriage
Large Sized Body (measures at top. 24¾ in. by 12 in.), beautifully Coach Painted and Upholstered, Convex Sides, with Raised Moulding of smart design, Reversible Hood with Brass Joints, Complete with Loose Cushions, Well Cover, and Overend Apron, Strap Cee Springs of easy riding pattern, 14 in. and 10 in. Rubber-tyred Wheels. Best Finish throughout.
Stock Colours : Dark Blue, Dark Green' **35**

arriage Extra on all Dolls Carriages outside London Carrier Radius.   Crate. 6d. extra, not returnab

The "Promenade" Doll's Carriage.

Carriage extra on all Doll's Carriages outside London Carrier Radius. Crate 6d. extra, not returnable.

Wicker Umbrella or Sunshade Holders for Toy Prams, **1/6** each. Post 3d.

Rugs for ditto, **10½**d. & **2/6** Postage 3d.

All Dolls Carriages (except the "WONDER" & "GAMAGE") are supplied without extra charges in the following colours: Peacock Green, Sage Green, Dark Tan, Light Tan, Bronze, Claret, Dark Blue, and Dark Green.

Extra **9**d. per carriage:—Pale Blue, Coffee, Gobelin Green, Mignonette Green.

Extra **3/6** per carriage (best Enamel finish): White, Ivory, Biscuit and Pale Pearl Grey. Dolls' Sunshades, **1/- 2- 2/6 3/-** extra.

Special Large Size Wooden Body (27½ in. by 12½ in. at top), Cane Beaded Panels, Strap Cee Springs, ⅜ in. Rubber-tyred Wheels (14 in. and 10 in. diam.), Reversible Brass-jointed Hood fitted with thumbscrews and stops, Loose Well Cover, Extended Wood Cross Handle. Stock colours : Dark Green, Dark Blue. Price **32/6**

The "Mall" Doll's Carriage.

Extra Large "Twin" Carriage.

Strap Cee Springs, ½ in. Rubber-tyred Wheels, 16 in. and 12 in. diam. Reversible Hoods as in illus. Apron, Well Cover, Loose Cushions. Absolutely Best Finish throughout.

Umbrella Basket, **1/6** extra Stock colour — Dark Green, **47/6**

The "Durbar" Doll's Carriage.

ecial Large Size Body (27½ in. by 12½ in. at top), Concave acks, Cane Beaded Panels, beautifully coach painted, Strap ee Springs, Reversible Hood is fitted complete with brass ints, Loose Cushions, Well Cover and Overend Apron, n. Rubber-tyred Wheels, 16 in. and 12 in. diameter. Stock colours: Dark Blue, Dark Green. **42/-**

The "Cinderella" Doll's Carriage.

American Reed Body, ⅜ in. Rubber-tyred Wheels (12 in. & 5 in. diam. Strong Springs. A useful simple Toy. **8/11**

Tne "Cupid" Doll's Carriage.

Special Large Size Wooden Body (27½ in. by 12½ in. at top), Strap Cee Springs, ⅜ in. Rubber-tyred Wheels, 14 in. and 10 in. diam.), Reversible Brass-jointed Hood fitted with thumbscrews and stops. Extended Wood Cross Handle.

Stock colours : Dark Green, Dark Blue. Price **28/9**

The "Phyllis" Doll's Mail Cart.

Convertible Body in American Reed with roll side.

Leg-rest can be lowered.

⅜ in. Rubber-tyred Wheels (14 in. and 5 in. diameter), Strap Cee Springs, Brass-jointed Hood, Upholstered in Leather Cloth.

Stock colours : Reed work left natural, other parts Dark Blue or Peacock Green. **21/-**

The "Belgravia" Doll's Carriage

Large-sized Body with convex sides and raised mouldings, measures at top 23¼ in. by 11¼ in., reversible Hood with brass joints, Strap Cee Springs, China Handle. and 14 in. & 10 in. Rubber-tyred ⅜ in. Wheels. Stock colour : Dark Green with vertical striping as illustration. **31/9**

Sewing Machines, Tea Sets, etc.

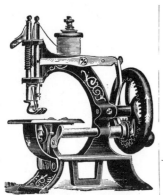

No 10 **New Model Sewing Machine** as illus. Does real work. **4/11** Post 4d.

No. 1. **Smart Working Sewing Machine.** A Real Worker. **1/9** Post 4d.

Needles for No. 1 & 2 Machines, **6**d. packet. of 1 doz. 10, 12 & 15, **10½**d. packet.

No. 15. Substantial Extra Heavy **Sewing Machine.** Larger Ssize. A first-class worker. A splendid Girl's Present. Price .. **11/6** Post 9d.

No. 2. **New Type Sewing Machine** as illustration. Works exceedingly well. Price **3/6** Post 4d.

No. 12. Fine Heavy **Sewing Machine** as illustration Does really good work. Price **8/6** Post 8d.

Enamelled Wooden **Washstands** with china utensils.

No. 1. Ivory china with gold lines, 8in. wide, 11½ in. high, **5/11** Post 6d.

No. 2. Do. do. 11½in. high, 9in. wide, **6/11** Post 7d.

No. 3. Assorted china ivory and gold lines, blue rimmed, etc. **8/11** Post 8d.

Doll's Washing Set as illustration. Beautifully enamelled in colours, **6/11** Post 6d. Larger, **12/6** Post 10d.

China Dinner Set as illustration. White with decorations, also other designs. Price **2/-** Post 5d.

China Tea Sets. Assorted patterns and shapes. **6½**d. Post 3d.

China Tea Set as illustration. 9 pieces white with blue band floral decorations also many other designs, **1/6** Post 4d.

Blue Enamelled Tea Set as illustration.

Price **3/6** Post 6d.

Splendid Value.

China Tea Set with assorted floral decorations.

Price **3/6** Post 6d.

Do. do. larger, **4/6** Post 8d.

TOY TEA AND DINNER SERVICES, TOILET SETS, &c.

Enamelled Tea Set.

As illustration.

With 2 cups and saucers, Blue enamel **10½d**
Post 3d.

Ditto, with 4 cups and saucers **1/9** Post 3d.
Ditto, with 6 cups and saucers **2/3** ,, 3d.

Enamel Dinner Set.

As illustration.

Price **2/4½** Post 4d. Ditto larger **3/6** Post 5d.
Ditto **6/11** Post 6d.

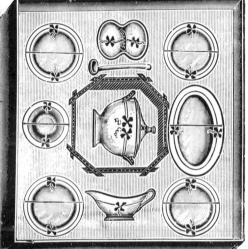

Enamel Dinner Set, as illustration, with 4 lea clover decoration with gold lines. Price **3/6** Post 5d.
More elaborate designs. Price **5/11** Post 6d.
Price **9/11** Post 7d. Price **21/-** Post free.

Aluminium Tea Sets.

Beautifully finished, as illustration

1/- Post 3d.

Cup, Saucer and Plate.

Stamped enamelled White, with plastical paintings and gold decorations, Dutch scenes.

Plate 8 in., Cup 3 in., Saucer 5 in. diam.

2/6 Post 3d.

Aluminium Dinner Set with knives forks and spoons, as illustration. very fine value **1/4½** Post 3d.

Enamel Tea Sets, with assorted Highgrade decorations, with 4 cups.
Price 6/6 Post 6d.
Ditto with 6 cups. **Price 8/11** Post 7d.

Enamelled Cup, Saucer and Plate stamped White with plastical Paintings and Gold Decorations.

Dutch Scenes.

Plate 8 in. Cup 3 in. Saucer 5in. dia.

2/6 Post 3d.

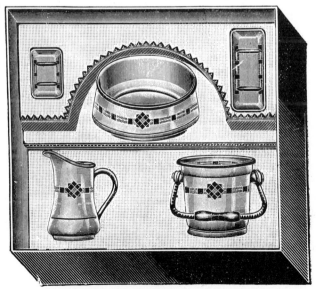

Artistic Enamelled Toilet Sets

2/6	**3/6**	**3/11**	**5/11**	**6/11**
Post 4d.	5d.	5d.	6d.	6d.

The illustration represents the **3/6** set. The Higher prices have more elaborate designs and are larger.

DOLLS' FURNITURE, STOVES, PASTRY SETS, etc.

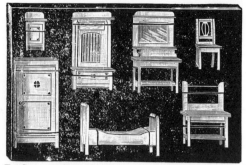

Bedroom Furniture, as illustration. Price .. **2/11**

Similar, **1/6** Post 3d. **4/11** Post 4d.

Well-made **Cooking Stove,** as illus.
3/11 Post 5d. Do. larger **5/11** Post 6d.

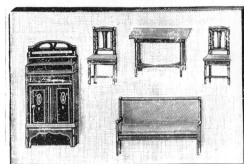

Drawing and Dining Room Furniture
1/6 Post 3d. **2/11** Post 4d. **4/11** Post 6d.

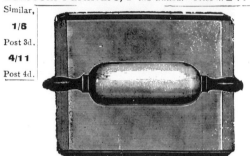

Wooden Rolling Pin and Paste Board.
12 in. long. Price ... ... **1/-** Post 3d.

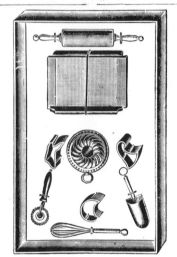
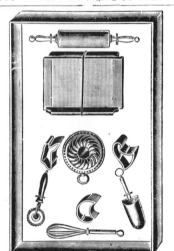

Kitchen Sets, on Cards. Strong and
instructive toys ... **2/3** Post 3d.
Ditto ... **2** ... **5/11** Post 4d.

Toy Garden Set, as illustration ... **4/11** Post 4d.

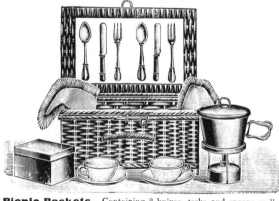

Picnic Baskets. Containing 2 knives. forks and spoons, well
finished and nickelled. nicely carded, travelling stove with spirit lamp
(fitting inside the pan), biscuit box, 2 enamelled cups and saucers, 2
serviettes, packed in brown wicker basket with handle, 10 in. long,
6¼ in. wide, 4 in. high. Price ... ... **6/6** Post 5d.

Chest of Drawers. Strongly made of wood.
Painted in white enamel, 14 in. high, 17½ in. wide.
4/6 Post 4d. **6/11** Post 6d. **10/9** Post 10d

Oak Wardrobe, 9/11 Post 6d. **15/-** Post 1

Handsome Toy Cooking Stove.

As illustrated, with spirit
lamp .. **8/11** Post 6d
Do. larger **11/9** ,, 7d
Do. larger **15/-** ,, 3d.

Strongly made Cooking Stove. Complete
with lamp, as illustration ... **1/11** Post 4d.
Ditto larger ... **2/11** Post 5d.

Children's Smart
Cooking Stov
Complete with lam
Price .. **6/11**
Post 5d.

TRUNKS AND TROUSSEAU.

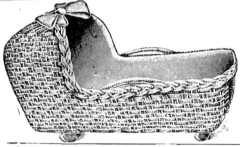

The Rock-a-bye Cot, 24 in.
by 14 in. by 19 in. high, as
illustration, Price **8/6**
Carriage forward.
Complete with mattress and bolster.

Doll's Swinging Bassinette.

Size	1	2	
Length	16½	20½	in.
Width	9½	11	,,
Height	7	8	,,
Price	**3/11**	**4/6**	
	Post 6d.		
Size	3	4	
Length	24	27½	in.
Width	14	16	,,
Height	9	10	,,
Price	**5/9**	**6/11**	
Postage	6d.	8d.	

The Dolly Cot. Size 24 in.
by 13 in. by 17 in. high , as
illus. .. **7/6** Carr. forward
The Daydreams Bedstead, 24 in by 13 in. by
17in., without side rails .. **6 6** Carriage forward.
Both above complete with mattress and bolster.

Specialite.— Woven Wicker Cradles.

Lined. Wooden Rockers.
Very strong.

Size—			
12 in., to take 9 in. doll,	**1/6**
17 in. ,, 12 in. ,,	**2/-**
21 in. ,, 16 in. ,,	**2/9**
25 in. ,, 21 in. ,,	**3,6**

Compacta Cot and Basket

SPECIALITE—Plaited Straw Cradles.
Lined Pink. Wooden Rockers. Very Strong.
Price **1/4½** **1/11** **2 9**
14 in. long **3/11**
17 ,, ,, ... **4/11**
20 ,, ,, ... **5/11**
Postage 6d.

"Compacta" Cots. Trimmed. Enamelled Frames, with Mattress.
PACKED IN A BOX

"Compacta Cots" trimmed and Furnished.
Cot frames trimmed and furnished with Mattress, Pillow, pair of Blankets, pair of Sheets
Sateen frilled quilt and Lace Coverlet.

		*Folding 21 in.	*Folding 28 in.	*Folding 31 in.	*Folding 36 in.	*Folding 24 in.	Folding 21 in.	Folding 28 in.	Folding 31 in.	Folding 36 in.
DC 7	Trimmed Art Muslin and Lace	**7/6**	**10/6**	**11/9**	**16/9**	**8/11**	**10/6**	—	**21/-**	**23/9**
DC 8	Trimmed White Muslin, or Cream, Sky or Pink Sateen, Lace and Ribbon	—	**11/9**	**15/9**	**19/6**	**10/6**	**14/9**	—	**23/9**	**25/9**
DC 9	White Fancy Striped Muslin, or Cream, Sky or Pink Sateen, Mercerised Lawn & Ribbon	—	**13/9**	**17/6**	**21/-**	**11/9**	—	**20/-**		
DC 10	White open work Muslin, or Cream, Sky or Pink Sateen, Fringe and Ribbon	—	**15 9**	—	—	—	—	—		
DC 11	White open work Muslin, or Cream, Sky or Pink Sateen, Lace Insertion and Ribbon ..	—	**16,9**	—	—	—	—	—		
DC 12	White and Cream Mercerised and Fancy Muslin, Ribbon and Ball Fringe	—	**21/-**	—	—	—	—	**26/9**		
DC 13	White Muslin over Sateen, or embossed Sateen trimmed Lace, Insertion and Ribbon ..	—	**22 6**	—	—	—	—	**28/6**	—	—

*The Cot folding 21 in. will take dolls up to 15 in. ; folding 28 in. will take dolls up to 21 in.
,, ,, 31 in. ,, ,, 24 in. ; ,, 36 in. ,, ,, 28 in.

Compacta Baskets to match.

Carriage on Cots, 6d. and 9d.
Carriage on Baskets, 4d. and 6d.

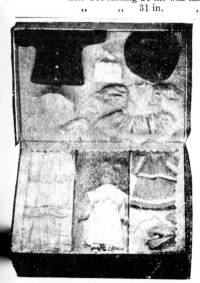

Fitted Doll's Trunks.
Best quality.
No. 36. Doll's Trunk, about 10 in. long, containing best
quality dressed Doll.
Complete with satin dresses, etc., **8/11** Postage 6d.
No. 37. Trunk, 10½ in. long, containing best quality
dressed Doll, long hair, moving eyes, extra dresses, night
dress, complete set of underclothing, 2 hats, handkerchief
and scent. Price **10,9** Postage 6d.
No. 40. Do., 11½ in. Price .. **13 6** Postage 6d.
No. 39. Do., 12½ in. Price .. **15,9** ,, 6d.
No. 4. Do., 11½ in. Containing 1 Boy and Girl Doll
with movable eyes and joints, both dressed in sailor
clothes, with complete change for each, hand glass, etc.
Price .. **18/6** Postage 6d.
Empty Trunks .. **4/6 5/3 5/11 7/6 8 9 10/6**
Post 3d. 4d. 4d. 5d. 5d. 6d.

Special Value. Dolls' Trunks with Doll and		
Trousseau	**1/-**	Post 2d.
Ditto ditto larger	**2/-**	Post 3d.

DOLL'S TRUNK. OPEN.

Dolls' Trousseau.
26 **36** **4/6**
Post 3d. 4d. 5d.

Dolls' Fitted Baskets.
4 6 **6 6** **8/9** **14/9**
Post 4d. 5d. 5d. 6d.

Dolls and Dolls' House Novelties.

Pet's Dresser.

Fine model of a kitchen dresser, complete as illustration. Just the thing for a Doll's House.

No. 1 .. **6**d.   No. 2 .. **10½**d.
Postage 2d.   3d.

'Our Baby"

An unbreakable baby doll of fine quality as illustration or with long clothes

2/11   5/6

Post 3d. & 4d.

Pet's Kitchen Set.

A most attractive little outfit, as illustration. Will keep children amused for hours.

Price .. **1/10½**   Postage 3d.

The "Fairy" Doll

A smartly dressed doll with well made clothes

Unbreakable head.

Price **4/6**

Postage 4d.

The Famous "Campbell Kids"

These dolls still maintain their popularity, due to a great extent to the fact that they are quite unbreakable.

Price .. **4/11**   Postage 4d.

Japanese Dolls

These are genuine imported Japanese Dolls of fine quality.

			Price	P
No. 6	5 ins.	..	6½d.	1½
,, 1	10 ins.	..	7½d.	2
,, 2	12½ ins.	..	1/-	3
,, 3	14 ins.	..	1/9	4

EXTERIOR OF THE "WENDY" PLAY HOUSE

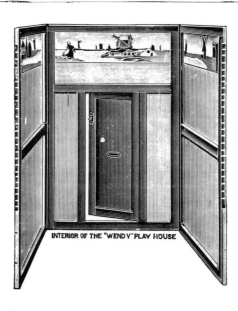

INTERIOR OF THE "WENDY" PLAY HOUSE

The "Wendy" Play House.

The latest "Screen" or Folding Play House, strongly made, light and portable. Hand painted on strong canvas.

Folds flat when not in use.

Handsomely decorated both inside and o

Price **35/-**
Carriage extra outside London Carrier Radius.

THE "WENDY" PLAY HOUSE FOLDED

Finest Quality Jointed, Character Baby Dolls

No. 1.	Height, sitting,	14 in.	Price	8/11	Post 4d.
,, 2.	,,	16½ in.	,,	11/9	,, 6d.
,, 3.	,,	20 in.	,,	13/9	,, 7d.
,, 4.	,,	22½ in.	,,	21/-	,, free
,, 5.	,,	25 in.	,,	25/-	,, free

Cheaper quality, with hair. No. 1. 9¼ in., 1/11 Post 3d.
No. 2. 12 in., 2/11 Post 4d. No. 3. 14½ in., 3/11 ,, 4d.

Undressed Baby Doll.
Wonderful Value.
eight, sitting, 8¼ in., 1/6 Post 5d.

SPECIAL VALUE.
Hair-stuffed Doll.
Blue body, with moving eyes.
11½ in. Price 6d. Post 2d.
16 in. ,, 1/- ,, 3d.

Best quality Kid-body Dolls

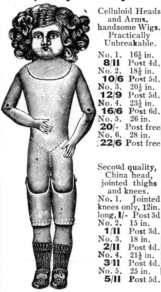

Celluloid Heads and Arms,
handsome Wigs.
Practically Unbreakable.

No. 1.	16½ in.
	8/11 Post 4d.
No. 2.	18½ in.
	10/6 Post 5d.
No. 3.	20½ in.
	12/9 Post 5d.
No. 4.	23½ in.
	16/6 Post 6d.
No. 5.	26 in.
	20/- Post free
No. 6.	28 in.
	22/6 Post free

Second quality,
China head,
jointed thighs
and knees.

No. 1.	Jointed knees only, 12in. long, 1/- Post 3d
No. 2.	15 in.
	1/11 Post 3d.
No. 3.	18 in.
	2/11 Post 4d.
No. 4.	21½ in.
	3/11 Post 4d.
No. 5.	25 in.
	5/11 Post 5d.

Water Babies.
Loofah.
No. 1 ... 5½d.
,, 2 ... 10½d.
Post 2d.

Unbreakable Dolls.
Close-grained wood.
Jointed limbs, curly wigs.

No. 1.	11 in.
	3/11 Post 3d.
No. 2.	12½ in.
	5/6 Post 3d.
No. 3.	14 in.
	6/6 Post 4d.
No. 4.	16 in.
	7/11 Post 5d.

Cheaper quality

No. 1.	10 in.
	1/- Post 3d.
No. 2.	11 in.
	1/11 Post 3d.
No. 3.	14 in.
	2/11 Post 4d.

WATER BABY.CB
RD. N5 570749

GAMAGE'S FAMOUS "Salome" Dolls.

These are the very finest Dolls manufactured, the modelling of the limbs and body being exceptionally good. The heads, of character type, are made of first grade biscuit china. Ball and socket jointed throughout. Fine long sewn curly wigs.

No.				Post
1.	15½ in. long,	6/11	4d.
2.	18 ,, ,,	9/11	5d.
3.	22 ,, ,,	11/9	5d.
4.	24 ,, ,,	13/9	6d.
5.	26 ,, ,,	15/9	7d.
6.	28 ,, ,,	19/11	8d.
7.	30 ,, ,,	23/9	free
8.	32 ,, ,,	27/9	free

Baby Pierrot.
The latest Doll for Baby.
Soft and light, with
Musical Rattle inside.
Price 1/10½ Post 3d.

THE "Dorothy" Doll.
Wonderful Value. Jointed limbs, Sleeping Eyes, long real Hair. Length 10½ in.
Price 1/- Postage 3d.

THE "Marvel."
JOINTED DOLL.
11 in. long.
Price 6d. Post 3d.

No. 1.

No. 2.

No. 3.

No. 4.

Gamage's Famous "Phyllis" Dolls.

THESE DOLLS are most astonishing value and will be found *great bargains* to those requiring a good medium quality Doll. All sizes have jointed limbs throughout, sleeping eyes and sewn wigs. Nos. 2, 3 & 4 also have eyelashes.
No. 1, 14½in., 1/- Post 3d. No. 2, 17½in., 1/11 Post 4d. No. 3, 21in., 2/11 Post 4d. No. 4, 25in., 3/11 Post 5d.

DRESSED DOLLS.

A. W. Gamage, Ltd., draw special attention to the fact that they have recently removed their Doll section to a larger Department and have now in Stock and on show the largest and most varied collection of dressed and undressed dolls ever seen in an English Store. A visit will please you and save you money!

Long Clothes Baby Doll.
Good medium quality at exceptionally low prices. **2/4½ 2/11 3/11 5/11**
Post 3d. 3d. 4d. 4d.

Baby Dolls in Short Clothes.
Our range of these is a particularly large one, containing a really wonderful variety of designs in the best taste.
11/6 15/9 18/9
Post 5d. 6d. 6d.
26/9 29/6 39/6 52/6

Red Riding Hood Dolls
7/11 17/6 17/6 22/6
3d. 6d. 7d. Free.

Short Clothes Baby Dolls.
Good Quality and Value
2/11 3/11 4/11
Post 3d. 4d. 4d.

Baby Dolls in Long Clothes.
We have a really magnificent assortment of the very finest quality Baby dolls exquisitely dressed.
6/11 7/11 10/6 15/6 18/9
4d. 4d. 5d. 6d. 1/6
23/9 27/9 29/6 30/- 32/6

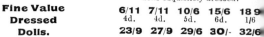

Cheap Quality Dressed Dolls

12 ins long with moving eyes **1/-**
Postage 3d.

8 ins long with fixed eyes **6½d.**
Postage 2d.

The "Kiddieland" Doll
With the Baby stare. Expression can be altered in a moment by turning the eyes.
1/10½ 2/6
Post 3d. 3d.

Fine Value Dressed Dolls.

We are offering during our Xmas Bazaar an exceptionally fine collection of dolls dressed in a variety of smart costumes, with moving eyes, superior jointed Length.
12 ins. **1/10½**
14½ ins. **2/11**
16 ins. **3/11**
18½ ins. **6/11**
Post 4d. 5d. 5d. 6d.

The Kiddieland Muff Doll
The expression can be instantly changed by turning the eyes.

One of the most attractive dolls introduced as illustration
2/11 3/11
Post 3d. 3d.

SOFT BODY.
Wool dressed dolls with celluloid heads. Almost unbreakable.
Price **1/10½** Postage 3d.

Rag Dolls.
New models with life-like faces **2/8**
Postage 3d.

London Dressed Dolls
In up-to-date Costumes.
Large selection **8/11** Post 6d.

Smart London Dressed Dolls
In a variety of styles **6/11**
Postage 5d.

Dressed Dolls
Finest Quality
Handsomely dressed in the latest London and Parisian styles
10/6 12/6 13/6
Post 5d. 6d. 6d.
15/6 16/6 18/6 30/-
7d. 7d. 8d. Free
32/6 37/6 45/- 63/-

Walking and Talking Dolls. Fairy Dolls.

Little Sailor Boys.

Very pretty, natural, life-like faces, best jointed Doll, dressed in dainty well-made suits and caps, with inscription.

15 in. high
Price **7/9** .. Post 4d.

18 in. high.
Price **10/9** .. Post 5d.

Dainty Wax Fairy Dolls.

FOR 'XMAS TREES.

1/-	.. Post	3d.
1/11	.. ,,	3d.
2/6	.. ,,	4d.
3/6	.. ,,	4d.
3/11	.. ,,	4d.
4/11	.. ,,	4d.
5/11	.. ,,	5d.

Sambo's Baby Brother.

Natural life-like faces with two teeth, very pretty face, curly locks. To sit or lie down. New original joints. 12in. high, **3 11** Post 4d.

Spoon Set.

As illustration **10½d.** Post 2d.

D lls **Dolls**
that that
Really Really
Walk Walk
and and
Talk. Talk.

Knife and Fork Set,

As illustration.
Price .. **1/-** Post 2d.

Knife, Fork, and Serviette Set.

As illustration
Price **1/6**
Post 2d.

Fitted Knife, Fork and Spoon Baskets.

6d. and **1**/-each. Post 1d. and 2d.

No clockwork or complicated mechanism to get out of order. Place the heels of the Doll alternately on the ground and push the Doll forward, when it will go through the actual movements of a child walking. Very ingenious and can be worked by anyone.

Undressed Doll, best quality wig, sleeping eyes and lashes, 10 in. high .. .. **2/3** Post 3d.

Dressed Doll, assorted pattern dresses, 14 in. high, **2/6** Post 4d.

Scotch Boys and Girls, with sleeping eyes and lashes, will sit down, and moves head and hands whilst walking, 14 in. high .. **5/6** Post 5d.

Sailor Boys and Girls, ditto ditto **5/6** Post 5d.

Dressed Doll, dainty dress and bonnet, sleeping eyes with lashes, talks—Papa and Mama whilst walking, 19½ in. high. **12/6** Post 6d.

Dressed Doll, dainty silk dress, says Papa and Mama whilst walking, 22 in. high .. **16/9** Post 9d.

Paris Dressed Dolls, walking and talking, very pretty face, flirting eyes, real hair wig can be combed, moving head and hands to throw kisses whilst walking, fully jointed, stand or sit down, clothes take off, 22 in. high. **27/6** Post free.

Sambo's Little Sister.

New, very pretty, lifelike face, with sleeping eyes.

BEST QUALITY,
BLACK SILKY WIG.

Dressed in coloured loose dress and gold bead necklace.

14½ in. high .. **4/6**
Post 4d.

17 in. high .. **5/11**
Post 5d.

Laughing Black Sambo.

Very pretty, natural, life-like face, best joints, short hair, dressed in coloured loose suit and gold bead necklace.

14 in. high
Price **5/6**

Postage 4d.

Jumeau Dolls.

Absolutely THE BEST Jointed Doll made, body and limbs being entirely of wood are perfectly unbreakable; with skirt, shoes and socks, eyelashes, and real hair wig that can be combed.

A perfect Model Doll.

Talking, Papa & Mama.

Will stand ALONE.

Height.		Post
18 in.	**15/9**	8d.
19½ ,,	**19/6**	10d.
21 ,,	**23/6**	1/-
23 ,,	**25/-**	1/-
27 ,,	**35/-**	free
28½ ,,	**42/-**	free

K

Children's Toy Motor Cars

To Pedal.

For Children 3 to 6 years old.

Order Style A. This pedal driven motor car is finished in Dark Green with fine lines only. Specification includes 12 in. rubber-tyred wheels, wings and steps, speedometer and motor clock .. .. Price **25/9**

For Children 4 to 8 years old.

Order Style B. The exclusive model shown above is up to date in all respects. It has the fashionable round-fronted radiator and is fitted with motor headlight, horn, machine cut chain wheels. Finished in Dark Green or Dark Blue with fine lines.
Price **35/-**

For Children 4 to 8 years old.

Order Style C. Style C. is complete with mud-guards and step-boards, round-fronted radiator, motor lamp and horn, speedometer and motor clock. Machine cut chain wheels, cycle type chain, knuckle-jointed steering gear, stove enamelled ironwork. Adjustable upholstered seat, finished Dark Green or Dark Blue .. Price **42/-**

For Children 4 to 8 years old.

Order Style D. A handsome model with realistic artillery type wheels fitted with solid rubber wired-on tyres. Very nicely finished in Bright Red or Dark Green. Adjustable upholstered seat, speedometer, motor clock, motor lamp and horn, new round-fronted radiator .. .. Price **52/-**

For Children 6 to 10 years old.

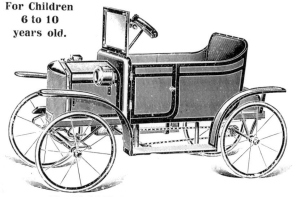

Order Style E. The Model E. Motor is a reproduction of the torpedo shape touring body now so popular on large cars. It includes the new round-fronted radiator, side door, wind screen two motor lamps, horn, adjustable seat, extra wide mud-guards and steps, speedometer and clock, and upholstered back. Finished in Motor Fawn or Dark Green .. .. .. Price **59/6**

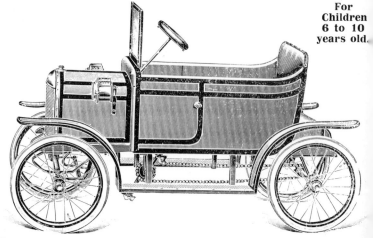

For Children 6 to 10 years old.

Order Style F. This car is a marvel of value, being fitted with good pneumatic tyres, tangent-spoke wheels, wind-screen, motor clock, speedometer, two motor lamps, horn, and round-fronted radiator included. Upholstered adjustable seat, finished in Fawn or Dark Green .. Price **97/-**

Carriage extra on all above Cars outside our London Carrier radius.

Hundreds in Stock.

Children's Toy Motor Cars

Value and Quality.

To Pedal.

For Children 6 to 10 years old.

For Children 6 to 10 years old.

Order Style G. A luxurious car, finished specially throughout. Ball-bearing pedals, wheels, and bottom bracket. Fitted wind-screen, adjustable seat, two plated lamps and twisted horn, ⅞ in. wired-on tyres. tangent spokes, ball-bearing wheels. Beautifully upholstered and painted dark green, dark blue, suede, grey. Speedometer, brake, motor clock and free wheel included. **£6 15 6**

Order Style H. THE LAST WORD IN CHILDREN'S AUTOMOBILES It is mounted on tangent spoke wheels with pneumatic tyres, and includes all fittings shown as well as a pump for tyres. Finished in suede grey, French grey, dark green, or dark blue. Price .. **£7 10 0**

For Children to 12 years old.

For Children 6 to 12 years old.

Order Style I. This commercial motor is modelled on the **B** type 'bus chassis, and has a tipping body operated in a very simple manner. Band brake, speedometer, clock, etc., included. Finished in bright red, black, and grey decoration. Price .. **£2 7 6**

Order Style K. A superior town carriage, nicely upholstered and finished coach style, Cape hood, wind-screen, two plated lamps, horn, tangent spoke wheels, ⅞ tyres wired on, speedometer and clock; ball-bearing pedals and bottom bracket, adjustable seat. Finished dark green or carmine with striped panels. Price **£4 19 6**

Order No. 25.

Tandem Toy Automobile.

The flush-sided body is a really good model of the latest practice. Curvated panels with ½-round beading. Specially well painted, lined and varnished and upholstered in sanitary leather. The chassis is fitted with ball bearings throughout, and is cycle made. Front axle will be appreciated by motorists. Fittings include speedometer, motor clock, two plated lamps and horn, wind-screen, adjustable seat, side doors, band brake, starting handle, finished any colour,

THE LAST WORD IN TOY AUTOS.

Ball-bearing pedals.

Pneumatic tyred wheels. Price **£11 9 6**

Carriage extra on all above motors outside our London Carrier radius

K..

"Handsmobiles" and Hand Propelled Cycle Cars.

The Safety "Scooter."

This is a perfectly safe Toy but at the same time, on from which plenty of excitement, and healthy exercise can be obtained. One foot is placed on the platform while the other is used to strike out skating fashion, and when sufficient speed is attained the operator can put both feet on the platform or sit on the seat.
Price as illust., **10/6**

Without seat and pillar, **7/11**

Cycle Car No. 1.

This is the simplest type of hand propelled Cycle Car with rubber tyred wheels working on the crank principle.

It runs easily and can be used by quite young children without the slightest danger.

Very strongly built.

Price **17/6**

Cycle Car No. 2.

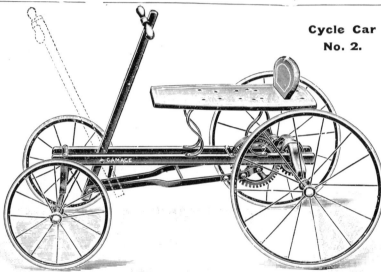

This is a very popular Car operating with steel cranks and cogwheels. Very strongly built with adjustable seat mounted on steel springs, and best quality rubber-tyred wheels. For children of all ages. Price **25/-**

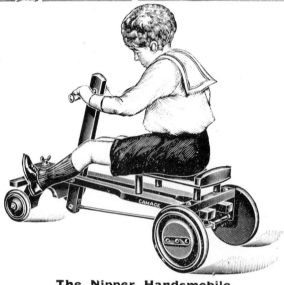

The Nipper Handsmobile.

This is a grand little hand propelled Car working on the crank system. Strong and perfectly safe. Splendid value. Price **8/9**

Cycle Car No. 3.

This is the finest Car produced, and is propelled by means of cogwheels operating a cycle chain.

It has a free wheel attachment and can be propelled backwards and forwards.

The seat is padded and mounted on steel springs.

Motor type Bonnet rubber-tyred wheels and mudguards.

Price .. **42/-**

Carriage extra on all goods on this page outside London Carrier Radius.

Old Style Rocking Horses.

—

Saddle Panniers and Straps.

No. 2, **11/6** extra.

No. 3, **13/9** extra.

No.	Height of Saddle.	Length of Rocker.	Price.
0	2 ft. 2 in.	4 ft. 4 in.	14 6
1	2 ft. 6 in.	5 ft. 0 in.	19 6
2	2 ft. 11 in.	6 ft. 3 in.	27/-
3	3 ft. 3 in.	6 ft. 6 in.	37/6

With two End Seats.

No.	Height to Saddle.	Length of Rocker.	Price.
2	2 ft. 11 in.	6 ft. 3 in.	38/9
3	3 ft. 3 in.	6 ft. 6 in.	49/9

Gamage's GEE SWING

The latest Novelty for the Nursery and Gymnasium, very strongly made and finished in best style with adjustable hemp ropes. One size only suitable for children up to 10 years of age.   Price **42/-**

THE SCOTS' GREYS ROCKING HORSE.

Real Detachable Cavalry Harness, with Shoe Cases, Valise, Holsters, Martingale, Saddle Cloth, Military Bridle, etc.

Plated Metal-work on Stand.

Special Finish Horse and Stand. Harness as above.

No.	Height to Saddle.	Length to Stand.	Price.
2	2 ft. 7½ in.	3 ft. 8 in.	55/-
3	3 ft. 0½ in.	4 ft. 4 in.	75/-
4	3 ft. 4½ in.	4 ft. 9½ in.	95/-

Special Clothing for these Horses in Royal Blue and Red with Braided edges, etc.

No. 2, 3/6 each ; No. 3, 4/6 each ; No. 4, 5/6 each,

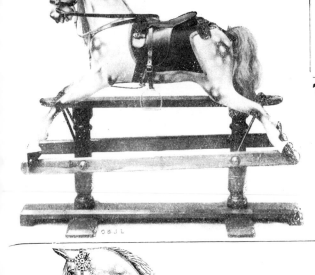

mproved Hobby Horse.

With two end Chair Seats for Children.

Very strongly made in best quality only.
Ty. 2. **46/6**
Ty. 3. **65/6**

A good horse for families, schools, nurseries, etc.

When fixed to the floor, three children can rock it as hard as they like with perfect safety.

Carriage and Packing extra on all above goods outside London Carrier Radius.

Gamage's Celebrated Hobby Horses.

Very strongly made and finished in best style.
Quite safe and practically unbreakable. Painted in various colours.

No.	About height to saddle.	Length of St and.	Price.
Ty. 1	2 ft. 3½ in.	3 ft. 0½ in.	19/6
Ty. 2	2 ft. 7½ in.	3 ft. 8 in.	28/-
Ty. 3	3 ft. 0 in.	4 in. 4 in.	41/-
Ty. 4	3 ft. 4½ in.	4 ft. 9½ in.	49/-

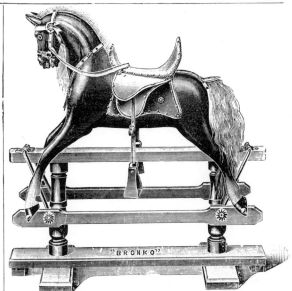

Gamage's "Bronk" Safety Hobby Horse.

Registered No. Ty. 467,670. This horse is specially constructed our own designs. Fitted with cowboy saddle and stirrups, which not only give it an elegant appearance, but render it a much safer horse for a child than the old style. Made in four sizes.

	No. B	No. C	No. D	No. E
	34/6	**42/6**	**63/-**	**75/-**
Hei. to saddle,	27½ in.	31½ in.	36½ in.	40½ in.
Len. of stand,	36½ in.	44 in.	52 in.	57½ in.

Tricycle Horses, Push Horses, Cavalry Horses.

The 'Startler' Tricycle Horse.

THE "STARTLER" No 1905 G.R.J.L.

Unique. Great Novelty.

Iron tyred wheels	**10/9**
Rubber tyred do.	**12/9**

Tricycle Horses. Best London Make.

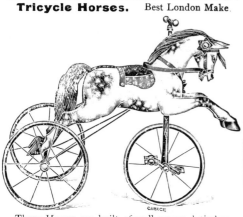

These Horses are built of well-seasoned timber soundly constructed and well finished, with trappings complete
Iron frame and supports, rubber tyres, handsomely painted, framework lined. **All with glass eye and padded saddles.**

To suit age.	No.	Height of Wheels.	Rubber Wheel
4 to 6	00	12 in.	**17/6**
4 to 6	0	14 in.	**19/6**
6 to 8	1	15 in.	**22/6**
8 to 10	2	18 in.	**27/6**

British Cavalry Horses.
(Large).

These Horses are far superior to the usual Carved Horse. The proportions are exceptionally good.

The Harness is magnificently made of splendid material, it is all detachable and is made on the Cavalry Model, with all fittings as shown. Sandow Wheels and Handles are fitted. Will be the pride of any boy or girl lucky enough to receive one.

Height to top of Head.	As Illustrated.	With Push Handles.
1B 19 in.	**14/6** each.	**16/6** each.
2B 22¼ in.	**21/-** ,,	**22/6** ,,
3B 24 in.	**24/6** ,,	**25/6** ,,
4B 25½ in.	**29/6** ,,	**29/6** ,,
5B 27½ in.	**33/9** ,,	**35/-** ,,

Stool Horses. English made.

No. 1, **2/11** No. 2, **3/11** No. 3, **4/11**

Best Quality strongly made Beech **Push Horses.**

No.	5	6	7
	9d.	**1-**	**1/6**

No.	8	9	10	11	12	13
	2/-	**2/6**	**2/11**	**3/11**	**4/11**	**5/11**

Carriage Extra on all above Toys outside London Carrier Radius.

Best Quality Carved Pole Horses.

No.	Height.	Length of Base.	Wooden wheels.	Iron wheels.
Ty. 1	19	18 in.	**3/6**	**3/11**
Ty. 2	21	20 in.	**4/11**	**5/6**
Ty. 3	25	23 in.	**6/11**	**7/11**
Ty. 4	28	26 in.	**8/6**	**8/11**
Ty. 5	30	28 in.	**12/9**	

No. Ty. 5, with spider rubber wheels **17/6**

Best Quality Carved Push Horses.

No.		Height to Handle.	Wood wheels.	Iron wheels.	Rub whe
No.	Ty. 1	21 in.	**4/6**	**4/11**	—
,,	Ty. 2	23 ,,	**5/6**	**6/6**	—
,,	Ty. 3	25 ,,	**7/6**	**7/11**	11
,,	Ty. 4	29 ,,	—	**10/9**	13
,,	Ty. 5	33 ,,	**13/6**	**13/9**	18
,,	Ty. 6		**19/9**	**21/6**	23

No. Ty. 5, with spider rubber wheels, height to handles 33 in.. **18/9**

Horses and Carts, Milk Carts, Garden Rollers, etc.

Timber Van (Loaded).

well-made article, fitted with strong Cart Horse and loaded
with Cut Timber.
Price : 32 in. long over all   .. **10/9**

Pickford's Lorry. Very strong Cart Horse and
Lorry, loaded with Six Cases, the lids of which slid
off. Nicely painted. Mounted on Gilt Iron Wheels.
Total length 25 ins. Price   **6/11**   Rubber Tyres, **8/6**

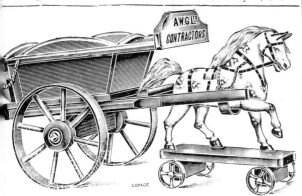

Horse and Carts with Wooden Wheels,

No	Total Length.	Height.	Price.
Ty. 0	25	12 in.	**6/6**
Ty. 1	26	13	**7/11**
Ty. 2	28	15	**9/9**
Ty. 3	31	18	**12 9**

Dairy Cart.

No. 1. It is very strong. Good churn with brass tap.
Two brass-mounted delivery cans. Nicely painted and gold lined.
Price   ..   **8/9** each.
Rubber Spider Wheels, **1/7** extra.

The V.V. Bread Cart & Horse.

This is a finely finished Toy
modelled on the **van** which
is so familiar nowadays.
Neat wicker Basket included.
Length over all, 28½ in.

Price complete, **7/9**

Railway Van and Pair Horses

This is a good model of a heavy Railway Delivery Wagon An
adjustable Tail-board is fitted, and a strong pair of Horses mounted
on Gilt Iron Wheels. It is supplied with and without Sacks.

No.	Long.	High.	Wide.	With Sacks.
1	28 in.	15 in.	11 in.	**9/9**
2	30½ in.	16½ in.	12 in.	**12/6**

Horse and Carts with Rubber-Tyred Wheels.

No.	Total Length.	Height.	Wheels.	Price.
3	31	18	10 in.	**15/-**
4	20½	19½	12 in.	**18/9**
5	22	21	14	**23/9**
6	25	21¾	15½	**28/9**
7	27½	24	16	**37/6**

Garden Roller.

No.	Height.	Price
1	26 in.	**3/9**
2	29 ,,	**4/11**
3	35 ,,	**6/9**

Dairy Cart.

Superior make throughout, large Horse and
Churn, Delivery Cans, etc., as illustration.
Varnish Finish, **14/-**   Painted Finish, **16 6**

Milk Floats, Gipsy Vans, Bakers' Barrows, Tally-ho Horses, &c.

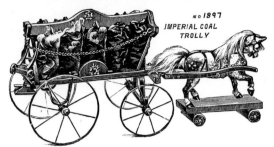

Coal Trolley.

Strong Elm Varnished; loaded with sacks of Black Wood Blocks on four strong Spider Wheels.

No. 1 .. **13/9**   No. 2 .. **19/6**

The Galloping Scooter.

(Prov. Patent No. 23416.)

A Great Novelty.
The Rider propels the toy by means of pedals and chain, and the horses gallop as the toy moves along. Lamp and Horn provided. Suitable for children 6-10 years.

Price .. **52/6**

Push handles fitted behind when required Extra .. **3/6**

Shooting Cart and Horse.

Length 48 in.

A very large toy. We strongly recommend this Toy as a Good Selling Line. It exceptional good value. Must be seen to be appreciated.

Style A has fixed back to Cart **25/**

Style C — Ordinary finish on large Rubber-tyred Wheels, Cart nicely varnished light oak shade, with adjustable tailboard and Sandow wheels on horse **31/**

Style E — Extra Finish, Woodwork nicely painted in various fancy colours (Pale Blue, White, &c.) and Gold Lined, Brass Rails, Whip-Socket, Rubber Spider Wheels on Horse. A Splendid Toy **49/**

This Model is mounted on Strong Rubber Wheels, and is finely painted, lined and varnished. Front lets down on Chains and top lifts up.   Price .. **13**

Large G.P.O. Barrow.

Similar in size and finish to the Baker's Barrow **13/9**

Milk Float.

Realistic Toy, nicely painted in bright colours and lined out in gold; with Churn, Cans, and Dipper; mounted on Rubber-tyred Wheels, China Handles.

No. 1 **11/9**   No. 2 Larger Size **19/6**

ADAMS' TALLY-HO HORSES.

This Toy is supplied with a pair of horses only as illustrated, or with four horses. This splendid novelty was invented by a well-known jockey. It has an advantage over many toys in that it teaches the young idea how to drive, and this is one of the greatest ambitions of all juveniles.

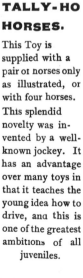

The attention to detail and careful handling of the reins is as necessary when driving this pair of horses as when driving their living prototypes; in fact, there can be no better method for the small boy or girl to learn how to handle the reins properly. The horses are splendidly finished in dapple grey or chesnut, and are nicely harnessed in calf leather. Rubber-tyred wheels are fitted, and a strong strap is placed ready for attaching the propeller-crossbar to the child's waist.

Price per pair (two horses), size as illustrated, no whip, **25/-**

Price per team (four horses), no whip, **50/-**

Carriage and Packing extra on all above Toys outside London Carrier Radius.

Playgrounds, Baby Walkers, Hobby Horses, etc.

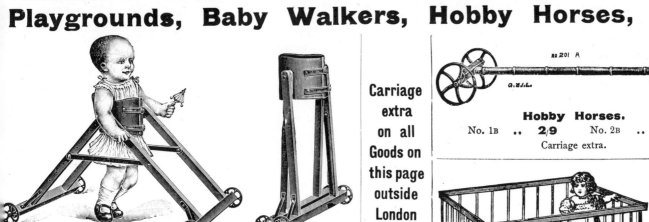

Carriage extra on all Goods on this page outside London Radius.

Hobby Horses.

No. 1B .. **2/9**   No. 2B .. **3/6**

Carriage extra.

Children's Folding Play Ground.

Size 4 ft. by 3 ft. by 22½ in. high.

The Gamage Baby Walker and Supporter is undoubtedly the most sensible and practical Baby Walker yet invented. The child is partially supported, preventing undue weight on the legs and when in the Walker is perfectly safe. Can be adjusted to suit children of various heights. Price **5/6**

The "Children's Hour." No more tears No more danger. Folds Flat. Teaches Babies to Walk and helps them to play. Keeps them safe. Makes them quiet   Price .. **12/6** Larger size, 5 ft. by 4 ft. by 26 in. **18/6**

Baby's Pair-Horse Galloping Gig.

Full Size.

Height of handle, about 3 feet, ordinary finish wicker seat, 2 horses, painted grey, **39/6**

The "Old Time" Hobby Horse.

This production is sure to be favoured with the little riders' approval. The illustration shows size and method of driving. It is very light (3 lb.) and strong and folds up when not in use (no loose parts). 33 ins. long overall. Price **6/6** each.

Royal Gig Horses.

Best finish. Wicker seat, spider wheels.
No. 2 .. Price **21/-**
Superior quality. Size 3. Price **25/-**

The "Wobbling Goblin."

Pattern No. 9703.

This highly amusing and novel toy will be one of the novelties of 1913 Season. By an arrangement of springs, the little rider imparts a natural trotting motion to the horse. It is upholstered in velvet and handsomely trimmed. Wide polished hardwood rests are provided to steady the little rider, and polished Sandow wheels are fitted. Price **9/6**

The Giant Dairy Cart

This excellent large model appeals to the imagination of the child as "big enough to ride in." The churns and cans and dippers are all real A beautiful horse with sandow wheels and pull handle is fitted Ball-bearing castors on the step make the cart safe from tipping, and the wheels are rubber-tyred. Measures 70in. overall. **55/-**

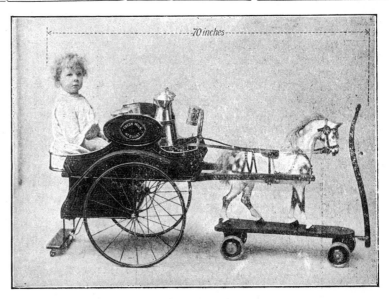

Wood Engines, Trams, etc.

Double Deck Electric Tram.
Hardwood, nicely varnished, 19 in. Price, **4/11**

The Rapid Motor Bus as illustrated.
Is a very strong and attractive toy.
Solid construction and splendid finish.
More lettering than on illustrations.
Length 23 inches
Price on cast iron gilt Wheels .. **6/11**

Strong wooden Tram with iron wheels. Price **10**

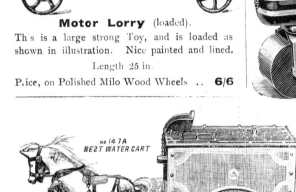

Motor Lorry (loaded).
This is a large strong Toy, and is loaded as
shown in illustration. Nice painted and lined.
Length 25 in.
Price, on Polished Milo Wood Wheels .. **6/6**

Motor Mail Van.
A good Model of the real article. Round top;
back doors open. Well painted and lined.
Length 24 in.
Price, on Polished Milo Wood Wheels, **5/11**

Steam Roller.
Strong Toy, painted bright red, solid wood
rollers, imitation brake, brass fittings. Price **6/6**

Water Cart and Horse.
These are proper work-
ing Models. Tin Lined.
Brass Valves and Brass
Sprays. Rubber
Wheels. Splendidly
painted and finished Cart
Horse.

As illustrated,
21/- each.

Organ Cart,
No. 1.
A new cheap Organ and Cart, one Tune.
A splendid line, similar to illustration, but with
One Tune Organ.
9/11

The Nipper Lawn Mower.
Registered.

This captivating Little Toy is
a certain seller.

The Knives revolve in exactly
the same way as a big Mower,
and it is quite easy to push. A
polished Handle is fitted, and
the Metal work is finished in
Blue, Green, Red and Black
Enamel; the Knives in Aluminium Paint. The whole is neatly
cardboard boxed. It is not
intended to cut much grass, but
it snips off some, so may be
truly said to cut grass.

Price with detached Grass Box,
each **6/3**
Without Grass Box, each **4/11**

Horse Rocking Chair.
As Illustration.
Built of Polished Hardwood .. **13/6**

Gamage's Famous American Daisy Waggon.

Substantially built of hardwood, well varnished. Size of body 30 by 14 in., wheels 12 in. and 18 in. with heavy ¾ in. welded tyres, shaved spokes and hub caps. **17/6** Carriage forward.

These waggons have locked corner bodies, steel [ax]les and boxes, iron and tongued draw, with improved pressed steel rocker plates.

Gamage's Famous Express Waggons.

Soundly constructed of good strong hardwood, well varnished These waggons have frame bottoms with hardwood sills and body braces, locked corners, square steel axles with turned bearings, morticed hubs, shaved spokes, heavy welded tyres and hub caps. as illustration, and with seat. **27/6** Carriage forward.

With locked corner bodies, steel axles and boxes, iron tongue draw, and improved steel rocker plates. Body 26 by 13 in. of sound hardwood well varnished. Wheels 10 in. and 15 in., with rivetted tyres, **8/6** Carr. forwd. Similar to illustration, but without splashboard, No. 38, Larger, **13/6**

Hand Carts with Racks

These are specially roomy, light and strong; has folding prop under front, which is easily adjusted with a touch of the foot. Square axles with turned bearings. Wheels have shaved spokes, welded tyres, and steel hub boxes. Bodies set on steel springs. Cut shows top rack on, which can be easily detached when not required. Varnished on the wood. Size 24 by 16 in. body, 18 in. wheels ... **17/6** Carriage extra

G. & J.L. No. 161.

Painted Wood Barrow

Best quality only.

No. 1 .. **1/6**
No. 2 .. **2/-**
No. 3 .. **2/11**

Birch Barrow.

Beautifully finished and well varnished.

No. 1 **4/6** No. 4, **9/11**
" 2 **5/11** " 5, **15/6**
" 3 **7/11**

Playcart.

A handsome, easy riding Playcart. The shafts can be used for pushing or drawing.
Price **21/-** Carr. extra.

DIMENSIONS.—Length of body, 24 in.; width of body, 13 in.; width of seat, 12 in.; depth of seat, 10 in.; height of seat from floor, 5 in.; height of seat back, 8 in.. The wheels are 14 in. in diam., rubber-tyred, nutless, with brass hub caps.

The Elm Sandow Express

The Strongest Pole Cart made. Registered design.

[Siz]e O, **5/11** Size A, Size of Body, 23 by 15 in., upholstered seat, **8/6**

[Al]l goods on this page CARRIAGE PAID within [o]ur London Carrier radius; outside, extra.

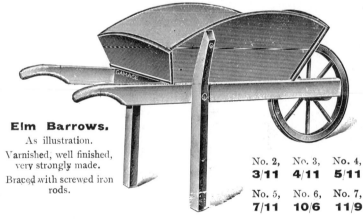

Elm Barrows.

As illustration.
Varnished, well finished, very strongly made.
Braced with screwed iron rods.

No. 2,	No. 3,	No. 4,
3/11	**4/11**	**5/11**
No. 5,	No. 6,	No. 7,
7/11	**10/6**	**11/9**

Price .. **13/9**
Carriage extra.

[Th]is cart is modelled on much [the] same lines as the Playcart, [bu]t is not fitted with convertible handle.

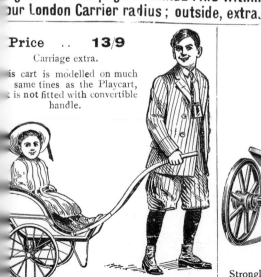

[The] axles are set in a wooden bolster and bolted [thro]ugh the body. It has both front and back safety stops, as shown in the illustration.

Strongly made Hardwood **Waggons** As illustration. Large enough for two big children.
Price **20/-** Carriage extra.
Ditto, similar to illustration. Upper length 26 in., width 17½ in., diam. of wheels 12 by 16 in., **16/6**

Gamages' New Pole Carts.

Strongly made of American Birch and varnished.

1. 16¾ by 9 in. ... **3/11**	3. 30 by 11¾ in. ... **6/11**
2. 18¾ by 11 in. ... **5/11**	4. 22½ by 13½ in. ... **7/11**

With ¾ in. iron wheels.

Switchbacks See-saws, etc.

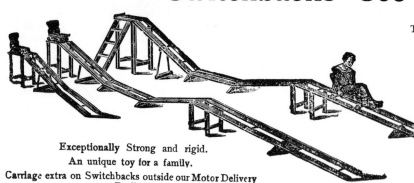

Switchbacks.

Ty. 1.   12 ft. 2 in. long, by 8 in. wide, 11½ in. high, with Car fitte with boxwood wheels; length of car, 22 in. by 8 in. wide.. **15/-**

,,   2.   15 ft. long by 10 in. wide, 17¼ in. high, Car 22 in. long b 10 in. wide **19**

,,   3.   30 ft. long by 10 in. wide, 21 in. high, Car fitted with adjustab foot rest, Car 31 in. long by 11 in. wide **31/**

,,   4.   50 ft. long by 11 in. wide by 30 in. high, Car as No. 3, lengt of Car 31 in. by 11 in. wide.   This is a very firm Switch back, and is fitted at end with steps..   ..   ..   **57/**

Exceptionally Strong and rigid.

An unique toy for a family.

Carriage extra on Switchbacks outside our Motor Delivery Radius.

Combination See-Saw and Roundabout

Very strongly made (as illustration).

New Model with Improved Seats, Bar to take apart.

No. 1.   Size 6 ft. bar, **18/9**   No. 2.   Size 8 ft. bar, **23/6**

Larger ..   ..   **37/6**   Carriage extra.

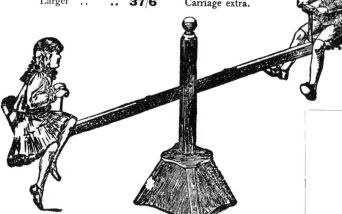

See-Saws.

Made from Birch.   Are very strong, and can be set to four differen heights.   A good toy for children.   Price **8/1**

Size 8 ft. long, 13 in. wide.   Height—Lowest 23 in.   Highest 28 i

Toy Motor Cars, with wooden Samson Wheels, as fitted on engines, **2/11   3/11   5/11   6/11**

Extra large Wooden Engines.

with four rubber-tyred wheels.

No. 1, **15/9**

No. 2, **27/6**

Wood Engines, with Samson metal brushed wheels and steel axles, painted red picked out green and yellow.

Price, No 0, **1/11**   No. 1, **2/11**   No. 2, **4/6**

Trucks, to match,   **1/3**   **1/9**   **2/3**

Solid wood, painted bright red and green, picked out yellow, solid brass bands, with patent *Hercules roller-bearing wheels,* *steel axles,* noiseless and easy running.   Perfect models.

Nos. 1,   2   3
4/6   5/11   7/11

Nos. 4   5
10/9   14/6

No. 1 has steel axles only, no roller-bearing.

Trucks, to match, **2/11   4/11   5/6** **6/11**

THE JOIBOY TRAINS are very strongly built, and made so that they can twist about in any direction without upsetting. A single truck of the smallest train will bear a 20 stone man.

No. 1.	Goods Train (length 7 ft. as illustrated)			35/-
,, 2.	,, ,,	,,	4 ,,	17/-
,, 3.	,, ,,	,,	3 ,,	8/6
,, 4.	,, ,,	,,	2½ ,,	5/6

LARGE ENGINES. Splendid out door Toys.
No. 1. With 10 in. back wheels and strong foot brakes. Total length 3½ ft. ... **35/-**
No. 2. With 7 in. back wheels, length 3 ft. ... **22/6**
No. 3. (As illustrated), length 2¼ ft. ... **15/-**

MOTOR TIP WAGGONS.
Small (length 1 ft. 8 in.) ... **5/6**
Large ,, 2 ft. 6 in. ... **12/6**

"BUMPO." The horse that moves along when the saddle is bumped up and down. Height of saddle 22 in. Steered by turning the head.
17/6

— THE —

JOIBOY
TOYS

ARE BUILT TO STAND KNOCKING ABOUT.

They are made of the best and strongest material, and are beautifully finished.
Steel axles and malleable iron wheels.

ROCKING BOATS that move along when rocked, and can be steered in any direction. Will carry 2 or 3 children. A splendid exerciser.
No. 1. Length 4 ft. ... **32/6**
No. 2. ,, 3½ ft. ... **21/-**

CRANES. Strong enough to lift ½ cwt. 10 feet. Ball bearing Turn Table, Clamp to fix it to table.
20/-

HAY WAGGONS.
No. 2. as illustrated 2½ ft. long.
17/6

Excellent Garden Toys with strong malleable iron wheels, best steel axles, and long handle.
Very safe for children

Strength in the **TOY** *... is* **JOY** *to the* **BOY**
— **ALL** BRITISH MADE

NEW OAK CONVERTIBLE EXPRESS CARRIAGES.
Very light yet very strong. Wooden wheels with polished brass caps. The seats can either be used in dogcart fashion or swung over to make an open waggon. Length 3 ft. **22/6** each.

CHRISTMAS CRACKERS, 1913-1914.

GAMAGE'S

Crackers

are packed in

strong Boxes

labelled with

attractive

labels.

Specially

designed by

LAWSON WOOD.

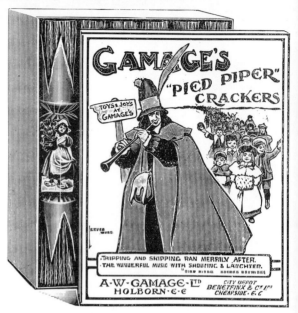

SERIES A. 5½d. box. 5/3 doz.

Postage—1 box 2d., 2 boxes 3d., 12 boxes 5d.

No. 4000. Here We Are Again.
Crackers in bright colours, decorated with amusing reliefs and containing hats and caps.

No. 4005. Jewel.
Pretty crackers in blue and cerise, containing jewellery.

No. 4008. Eastern Beauties.
Crackers in bright coloured Japanese paper, decorated with suitable reliefs. Containing Japanese toys.

No. 4009. Skating.
An assortment of musical toys is found in these pretty crackers of white holly printed paper.

No. 4012. Happy Moments.
Dainty floral paper crackers, containing an assortment of amusing toys and pretty jewels.

No. 4015. Wonderland.
An assortment of novelties is found in these dainty pink crackers.

SERIES C. 10½d. box. 10/- doz

Postage—1 box 2d., 2 boxes 3d., 12 boxes 5d.

No. 4064. Children's Fireworks.
A good variety of harmless fireworks is found in these crackers.

No. 4067. Hippodrome.
Musical cigar, whistle, trumpet, birdcall, &c., are contained in these crackers.

No. 4063. She Won't be Happy Till She Gets One.
These showy crackers contain amusing toys.

No. 4069. The Surprise.
These crackers, of scarlet and white crepe, contain toys, jewels, hats and caps.

No. 4070. The Geisha.
Crackers composed of Japanese crepe in bright colours, containing Jap Toys.

No. 4071. The Millstream.
Very pretty crackers containing amusing head-dresses.

SERIES E. 1/9 box 20/- doz

Postage —1 box 2d., 2 boxes 3d., 12 boxes 5d.

No. 4101. Woodland.
Model birds and animals are found in these attractive crackers of floral crepe.

No. 4102. Amateur Orchestral.
These choice crackers contain trumpet, musical cigar, whistle, birdcall, squeaker, &c.

No. 4104. Wedding Bells.
Dainty jewellery is found in these very bright crackers.

No. 4107. Sporting.
These crackers are designed with centres of white crepe and bands of gelatine over embossed gold on ends and tissue. They contain toys.

No. 4109. Bric-a-Brac.
Choice crackers in cerise gelatine over gold, decorated with floral reliefs. Miniature presents are found inside.

No. 4114. Venice.
These crackers of embossed gold with fringes of green tissue make a very attractive box. The contents are Venetian and other pretty jewellery

SERIES D. 1/3 box. 14/- doz.

Postage—1 box 2d., 2 boxes 3d. 12 boxes, 5d.

No. 4082.

The Jester.

These crackers in embossed gold have dainty reliefs in the centre of each, and contain amusing head-dresses.

No. 4084.

Cornfield.

These crackers are designed in orange gelatine and embossed gold, and contain amusing toys.

No. 4086.

Any Luck.

Dainty trinkets will be found in these pale green crepe crackers.

Series D.—Continued.

No. 4087.

Poppyland.

Choice crackers with embossed gold centres and fine fringes of scarlet tissue. They contain a good assortment of amusing toys.

No. 4090.

Army & Navy.

Crackers decorated with reliefs of soldiers and sailors. Containing toys

No. 4091.

Moonlight.

These crackers are designed in silver and blue foil, creating a moonlight effect. Containing various toys, jewels and costumes.

GAMAGES CRACKERS—*continued*.

SERIES G.   2/6 box.   28/- doz.

Postage—1 box 2d., 2 boxes 3d., 12 boxes 5d.

No. 4130.   Seaside.
These attractive crackers are designed in silver, with fringes of green and white. The contents are amusing toys.

No. 4132.   All round the World.
These fine crackers in scarlet gelatine. Contain a good assortment of amusing costumes.

No. 4133.   The face that counted.
These crackers in green gelatine. Contain pretty jewellery.

No. 4134.   Fancy Dress.
Very bright crackers with centres of embossed gold, containing costumes.

No. 4138.   Firework Crackers.
Showy crackers containing electric wire, fire balloon, shotting picture in addition to amusing hats and caps.

No. 4139.   Winter Sports.
Toys, puzzles and games are contained in these snow-white crepe crackers.

SERIES L.   5/- box.

Postage—1 box 2d., 2 boxes 3d., 12 boxes free.

No. 4170.   At the Meet.
Bright and showy crackers in scarlet with broad stamped bands of embossed silver on the ends and sporting reliefs.
Containing toys and jewellery.

No. 4171.   Sunset.
Toys, jewels and costumes are found in these large gelatine crackers which are relieved with fine bands of embossed gold.

No. 4172.   The Young Troubadour.
Very artistic crackers in two shades of yellow gelatine, containing an assortment of musical toys.

No. 4173.   Touring.
The centres of these crackers are of blue silk line decorated with floral and other reliefs, fine bands of gold lace ornament the ends. Motor accessories are found inside.

Series L.—*Continued*.

No. 4174.   Lily of the Valley.
Handsome shoulder box covered with lily of the valley paper, containing pale green gelatine crackers, in which will be found costumes.

No. 4175.   Venice.
Venitian and other pretty jewellery is found in these showy crackers of scarlet gelatine, with little seascapes in the centre and gold cord ties.

SERIES J.   3/6 Box.   40/- doz.

Postage—1 box 2d., 2 boxes 3d., 12 boxes free.

No. 4150.   Springtime.
These attractive crackers have centres of rose pink gelatine, containing toys, jewels, and costumes.

No. 4151.   The Christmas Greeting.
A seasonable box of crackers in scarlet gelatine. Containing musical toys.

No. 4152.   The Smart Set.
Up-to-date crackers designed in orange and green. Containing an assortment of pretty jewellery.

No. 4153.   Under Venetian Skies.
These crackers are designed in a pretty combination of blue and silver.
Containing venetian and other jewellery.

No. 4154.   Sporting Life.
Amusing toys form the contents of these bright crackers in scarlet gelatine.

No. 4155.   The Sunny South.
A most attractive box.
The crackers are made of orange gelatine. Costumes are found inside.

SERIES M.   6/- box.

Postage—1 box 2d., 2 boxes 3d., 12 boxes free.

No. 4180.   The Little Princess.
These exceedingly handsome crackers have centres of embossed gold and fine fringes of purple and white gelatine, containing good costumes.

No. 4181.   Autumn.
Dainty floral and other reliefs decorate these choice crackers in shades of orange gelatine.
An assortment of toys, jewels, and costumes is found inside.

Series M.—*Continued*.

No. 4182.   Poinsettia.
Elegant box covered in Poinsettia fancy paper, containing fine crackers in scarlet gelatine. Jewels and knick-knacks are found inside.

No. 4183.   Fairy Tale.
Fine photograveur in Sepia forms the box top. Amusing toys are found in the crackers which are composed of red silk gelatine and ornamented with silver lace, etc.

No. 4184.   Fancy Dress.
Charming crackers designed in rose pink gelatine over embossed gold, and tied with delicate green fancy ribbon. Containing costumes.

No. 4185.   Go Ahead.
Motor accessories are found in these charming green gelatine crackers with handsome bands and fine fringes.

SERIES K.   4/6 Box.

Postage—1 box 2d., 2 boxes 3d., 12 boxes free.

No. 4160.   The Little Minstrel.
A charming coloured photograveur forms the box top. The crackers are designed in scarlet silk gelatine, relieved with bands of burnished gold. Containing musical toys.

No. 4161.   O'er Hill and Dale.
Little sporting pictures under transparent gelatine form the centres of these attractive red crackers. Suitable toys inside.

No. 4162.   Loch Lomond.
Fine amber gelatine crackers with broad bends of specially embossed gold.
A coloured print of Loch Lomond forms the box top, and the crackers contain Trinkets.

No. 4163.   Miniatures.
Fine medallions of ladies' heads ornament these choice crackers in purple gelatine.
They are packed in a fine box and contain toys, jewels and costumes.

No. 4164.   Westward Ho!
These quite novel crackers are made in embossed silver with fringes of Cambridge blue gelatine and tissue, and ribbon ties of the same colour. Costumes form the contents.

No. 4165.   Umbrella Courtship.
Amusing costumes are contained in these bright emerald green gelatine crackers with floral reliefs and dainty ribbon ties.

---

a Quality Crackers containing Jewels, Miniature Presents, etc.   Price 9/6 and 12/6 Box.   Post free

Decoration Crackers and Novelty Cracker Boxes.

The Rose Bush.

No. K. 831.

6 in Box.

Dainty Crackers, decorated with graceful bows and artificial roses, green rose leaves and grasses.

They contain Jewellery and Toy Novelties, and can be had either in pink, crimson, or gold.

2/11

Post 3d.

Holly Bush.

No. J. 677.

6 in Box.

Effective Crackers trimmed with graceful bows and sprays of light green holly leaves and red berries.

They can be had in white or crimson.

Each Cracker contains two articles, a Head-dress and Jewel or Toy Novelty.

2/6

Post 3d.

Carnation.

No. K. 802.

6 in Box.

Crackers of white crêpe decorated with sprays of red carnations with shaded red leaves, silver tinted, and red grasses.

They contain Jewellery and Bric-à-Brac.

2/11

Post 3d.

Sweet Violets.

No. K. 806.

6 in Box.

Charming Crackers in pale green, profusely decorated with silken violets, shimmering green leaves and grasses.

Each Cracker contains two articles, viz., a Head-dress and a Novelty.

3/6

Post 3d.

Orchid.

No. K. 804.

6 in Box.

Made up in very prettily designed pink floral crêpe.

Decorated with beautiful pink silken orchids and shaded leaves, and containing jewellery and head-dresses, etc.

No. 805 is the same as above, but in mauve floral crêpe with mauve silken orchids.

3/6

Post 3d.

Dreadnought.

No. S. 347.

A magnificent model box of modern Battleship, containing 12 brilliant crackers. The contents include miniature sailor figures, models of battleships, life-boats, anchors, cannon, revolvers, syrens, etc.

Price **2/2**   Post 3d.

Fire Brigade.

No. S 352.

A most excellent model of the latest Motor Fire Engines, in colours, containing 12 brilliant crackers with miniature models of Motor Fire Engines. Fire Serpents, Fire Balloons, Fountains of Perfume. Miniature Pails, Masks, etc.

Price **2/6**   Post 3d.

Sweet Peas

No. J. 630.

12 in Box.

Crackers of finest crêpe in rich soft colouring, ornamented with beautiful sprays of sweet peas and grasses.

They can be had in pink, crimson, gold, or heliotrope.

Each Cracker contains two articles—a Head-dress and a Toy Novelty.

3/6

Post 3d.

Apple Blossom,

No. K. 703.

12 in Box.

Made up in soft delicate shades of the finest pink crêpe and ornamented with sprays of finely-coloured apple blossom, together with foliage of darker shade, making a perfect harmony of contrasts. They contain Toys, Jewels, and Bric-à-Brac.

3/6   Post 3d.

No. S. 350.

This very novel box of 12 attractive Crackers contains Musical and Lucky Charm Novelties, Musical Toys, etc.

Price .. **1/6**

Post 3d.

Mistletoe,

No. K. 701.

2 in Box.

Bright crimson Crackers, decorated with sprays of Mistletoe Leaves and Berries, together with Grasses.

They contain a variety of Novelty Head-dresses and Jewels.

Price **2/11**

Post 3d.

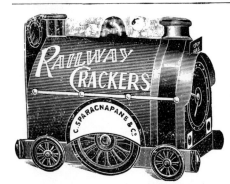

No. S351. **Railway.** Splendid model of the latest type of Railway Engine, filled with 12 bright red crackers, they contain miniature models of Railway trains including engine, tender and carriage (all detachable), Railway bells, whistles, kaleidoscopes, hats, caps, etc. **2/-** Post 3d.

No. S. 349. This Box, called "Calendar Cottage," has the almanack printed on it, each month representing a window, and contains 12 exceedingly pretty crackers. They contain Bric-a-Brac Novelties, including coloured Figures, pretty Vases, Jugs, etc., Gilt Ornamental Thimbles, dainty Muff Chains, Hand Mirrors, etc. .. **2/-** Post 3d.

No. S 348. **Electric.** Interesting model of Electric Car filled with 12 crackers. They contain Electric Car Charms, Electric Lights, Necklets, Brooches, Bracelets, Chains, etc. .. **2/-** Post 3d.

No. 4007. Bryant & May.

dozen bright Crackers containing HATS and CAPS acked in an exact fac-simile of a packet of Bryant & May's Matches. A capital urprise for Children. Price **5½d.** per Box. Post 2d.

No. 4106. Nigger Minstrel.

A most attractive label of a Minstrel on the box top. Crackers are designed in white Crepe with fringes of black and white tissue, and fine bands of scarlet gelatine. Containing Toys & Costumes. **1/6** per Box. Post 2d.

No 4100. Double Dutch.

Bands of red and blue Foil. and splendidly-printed little pictures, in keeping with the label, decorate these pretty Crepe crackers. Containing HEAD-DRESSES. **1/6** per Box. Post 2d.

---

ke your child's happiness complete by adding **1** of Gamage's Santa Clause Stockings to your Presents.

GAMAGE'S LUCKY STOCKING *for a* Good Boy

PRICES OF Gamage's Stockings For Boys.

ch one packed with Best Toys, etc.

WITH OR WITHOUT CONFECTIONERY.

5½d.	Postage & packing,		3d.
10½d.	,,	,,	3d.
1/4½	,,	,,	4d.
1/10½	,,	,,	4d.
2/4½	,,	,,	5d.
4/11	,,	,,	6d.

Pretty Basket of Bon-Bons.

1/- each.   Postage 2d.

GAMAGE'S LUCKY STOCKING *for a* Good Girl

PRICES OF Gamage's Stockings For Girls.

Each one packed with Best Toys, etc.

WITH OR WITHOUT CONFECTIONERY.

5½d.	Postage & packing,		3d.
10½d.	,,	,,	3d.
1/4½	,,	,,	4d.
1/10½	,,	,,	4d.
2/4½	,,	,,	5d.
4/11	,,	,,	6d.

Pretty Basket of Bon-Bons.

1/- each.   Postage 2d.

Gamage's MONSTER Crackers.

Any Size Made to Order.

MONSTER CRACKERS can be supplied any length and price, the quality of the contents depending on the quantity.

Hundreds of others to choose from.

SUITABLE FOR use or School Parties.

GE CRACKERS, assorted oice designs in Fancy epe, Gelatine, etc.

H containing VARIED les TOYS, COSTUMES and JEWELLERY.

Length		Price	Post and Packing		Contents
th 15in.	,,	Price **5½d.**	2d.	Contents: —12 Toys, etc.
17 ,,	,,	**10½d.**	3d.	,, 12 ,,
18 ,,	,,	**1 3**	3d.	, 12 ,,
20 ,,	,,	**1 9**	3d.	,, 12 ,,
21 ,,	,,	**2/6**	4d.	,, 12 ,,
25 ,,	,,	**3/6**	4d.	,, 18 ,,

Length 28 in.	Price **4/11**	Post and Packing 5d.	Contents: —24 Toys, etc.
,, 32 ,,	**6/6**	6d.	,, 36 ,,
,, 36 ,,	**9/11**	6d.	,, 50 ,,
,, 48 ,,	**13/6**	Free.	,, 60 ,,
,, 54 ,,	**16/6**	Free.	,, 80 ,,

Also made to take Customers' own selection of contents.

L

BEADS! BEADS!! BEADS!!!

A. W. GAMAGE draw attention to the fact that they are making a very special feature of Beads at their Xmas Bazaar. The selection, which is very varied, comprises the cheapest and also the very best art varieties, the stock amounting to **many Tons.**

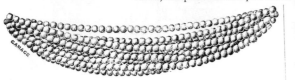

Best Quality Transparent **Beads** in Bunches of **200**.
Price .. **6**d. Post 1d.

Transparent Imitation Brilliant Cut-glass **Bead**
Bunch of **500** .. **9**d. Post 1½d. Superior qual
in Bunches of **200** .. **4½**d. Post 1d.

Beads in Bunches of **500**. As illustration.
One colour to each bunch. **6**d. a bunch. Post 3d.
6 for **2/6** Post 8d. Supplied in the following colours :—
SEMI-TRANSPARENT : Emerald Green, Old Gold, White, Sky Blue, Claret.
OPAQUE : White, Royal Blue, Pea Green, Cloudy White, Light Turquoise Blue, Light Canary.
Beads, 500 in a bunch, as illustration. One Colour to each bunch. Opaque amber, **1/-** bunch.
Vermillion, **2/-** bunch. Post 3d.

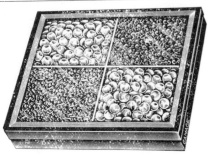

Special Value Large Box of Assorted Beads.
As illustration. In glass top box.
Price .. **1/-** Post 4d.

A limited number only. Assortment of either large or small **Beads,** or both, in strong wooden box, as illustration. Size, 6½in. by 4in. by 1¼in. Price **1/-** Post 4d.

Wonderful Value. Japanned metal Lock-up Cash
Fitted with tray and filled with an assortment of Beads
illustration, but without handles on inner tray.
Size 6 by 3¼ by 2¼ in. Price **1/4½** Post 4

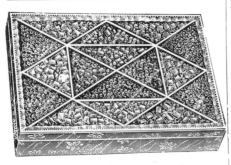

Assorted Beads in artistic glass top boxes.
10½d. Post 2d. **1/4½** 4d. **1/10½** 5d.

A variety of Doll's
Comb, Bag, Scent and Toilet Sets.

Price.	Post.
6d.	.. 1d.
1/-	.. 2d.
1/6	.. 2d.
1/10½	.. 3d.
2/4½	.. 3d.

Pets Cafe.
Box containing tea things, table and table cloth.
British manufacture.
10½d.
Post 3d

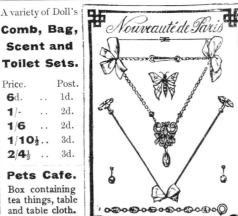

Nouveauté de Paris

Polished Wooden Boxes containing an assortmen
Beads. As illustration. **1/-** Post 4d.

Pet's Candy Stores.

Price.	Post.
10½d.	.. 3d.
1/10½	.. 4d.
2/11	.. 5d.
4/11	.. 6d.

A FINE PRESENT FOR A GIRL.
Polished Cabinet. Size 9 by 6 by 3 in., with lock and key.
Filled with an assortment of Large, Medium, Small and Tubular Beads. Price .. **2/11** Post 7d.

Doll's **Chatelaine** Sets.
1/- **1/6** **3/6**
Post 2d. 2d. 3d.

Strongly made **Scales,** as illustration.
10½d. Post 3d. **1/4½** Post 3d. **1/10½** Post

Ornaments, Garlands, etc., for Christmas Trees.

per Bells, as illus., assorted red, gold,
green and pink. **1**d., **2**d., **3**d., **4**d.
and **6**d. each. Postage 1d. & 2d.

**A Large Assort-
ment
of
Garlands
from 1d.
to 10½d.
each.**

Garland, as illus., 3½ yds. long, green, with 17 assorted coloured fans, **6**d.

Silver Leaf Garland, as illus., very effective, 2½ yds. long, **4**d. Post 2d.
Holly, similar to illustration, price **4**d. Post 2d.

**Coloured
Confetti
for
Wedding
Parties,
Carnivals,
etc.,
28-lb. bag
5/6**
Carr. forwd.

Garland. 👉
As illustration.
quare with Roses
aced on each side,
124 roses in all.
Four yards long.
ice 1(½d. Post 3d.

Acorn Leaf Garland, as illus.,
4½ yds. long, with 28 roses placed at
either side. **10½**d. Post 3d.

Green Garland, as illustration, 👉
4½ yds. long with 18 large Roses.
Price **6**d. Post 2d.

Hanging Decoration
of imitation paper
Flowers.

Price .. **5½**d.

Post 2d.

**Boxes of Assorted Toys for Xmas
resents, Bran Tubs, etc. Splendid
lue ! Price .. 1/- each.**
Post 3d.

**ANCY ORNAMENTS FOR
OP OF CHRISTMAS TREES.**
., **4½**d., **6**d., **9**d. and **1/-** each. Post 2d.

**GAMAGE'S
TOY GALLERIES
1 doz TOYS AND GAMES
Price 1/-
HOLBORN. LONDON E.C.**

TINSEL STRINGS,
1d., **2**d., **3**d., **4½**d. **6**d. & **7½**d. Post 1d.

FATHER CHRISTMAS.
Suitable for Christmas Tree, Table or
other Decorations.
7½d., **1/10½** & **2/6** Post 3d., 4d. & 5d.

**GLASS BELLS FOR
'XMAS TREES.**
6d. and **1/-** box of 12. Postage 3d.

**Gamage's Celebrated
Candles for Xmas Trees.**
½-lb. Boxes **3**d. Postage 3d.

Fancy Glass Ornaments for Christmas Tree Decorations.

XMAS TREE ORNAMENTS.
n Fancy Glass in a great variety of Designs.
6d. and **1/-** box of 12. Postage 3d.
CICLES for Christmas Trees, **4½**d. dozen.
Postage 1½d.
ANCY GLASS BALLS in variety of
Colours in string of 10 Balls,
Price **6**d., **1/-** and **1/3** doz. strings. Post 3d.

Gamage's Dainty Wax Fairy Dolls
For 'Xmas Trees, etc.
Prices **1/- 1/4 2/6 3/6 4/11 5/11 6/11**
Post 3d., 4d. and 5d.

**FANCY
GLASS ORNAMENTS.**
For Christmas Trees. Assorted Shapes.
Beautifully Coloured **6**d. and **1/-** box
of one dozen. Postage 3d.

Candle Clips for Xmas Trees.
5½d. and **10½**d. dozen. Post 2d. and 3d.

L..

A Feature to be Remembered

Pascall's Countess Chocolates.
½-lb. boxes, **1/-** and **2/6**
Postage 2½d. Postage 3d.

RIGHT IN GAMAGE'S BAZAAR THIS CHRISTMAS
.. WILL BE A STALL FOR THE SALE OF ..

PASCALL'S Novelties in

CHOCOLATES & CONFECTIONERY

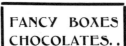

Pascall's White Heather Chocolates.
½-lb. and 1-lb. boxes ... **1/-** and **2/6**
Postage 2½d. & 3d.

FANCY BOXES CHOCOLATES..

6d. 1/- 1/6 2/6
5/- 7/6 10/- 15/-
20/-

Large Assortment of Sweets in Boxes, Bottles & Tins.

Pascall's Bitter Sweet Chocolates.
½-lb., 1-lb. & 2-lb. boxes, **1/- 2/6 4/11**

PASCALLS' CONFECTIONERY

The Purest Bottled Sweets.

6d. and 1/- each

Barley Sugar,
Mixed Fruits,
Golden Maltex,
Glace Pralines,
Silver Mints,
Butter Almonds,
Butter Walnuts,
etc., etc.

Student's Paint Box.
A Chocolate Novelty ... **6d.** and **1/-**
Postage 2d. & 3d.

Pascall's Chocolate Xmas Tree Novelties.
"Just the Thing" ... **1/-**
Postage 3d.

Pascall's Original Parlour ... **6d. 11d. 1/5 26 5/-**
Butchers' Shops, 1/-   Shops at all prices to suit all purses.

Assorted 1lb. & 2lb. Boxes of Pure Confectionery containing Fondant Marzipans Gum Jellies, etc.
11d. & 1/10½

Pascall's Smokers' Companion.
Naval Cadets, Boy Scouts, etc. ... **6d.** and **1/-**
Postage 2d. & 3d.

Novelties containing Chocolates Suitable for Christmas Trees, &c.

Bedsteads, Swings, Figures, etc.   ...   **1/-** doz. Post 3d.
Wooden Punts, Bedsteads, Cigar and Cigarette Boxes, Wind-bells,
etc. **3**d. each, **2 9** doz. Packing and Post, 4d. doz.
Tricycle Carriers, Cradles, etc., etc.   ...   **6**d. each, **5 6** doz.
Packing and Post, 8d. each.
Hawkers' Trays, Railway Refreshment Trollys, Shooting Galleries,
Cradles, Imitation Cigar and Cigarette Boxes containing chocolate
cigars and cigarettes, Lacquer Boxes, etc., **1/-** each, **11/6** doz.
3d. each.   Packing and Post, 1/- doz.

Carriage and Packing extra outside our Motor Delivery radius.

Fancy Boxes, Wallets, etc., containing superior Chocolates,
6d. **1/- 16 26 5/- 76 10 - 15 - 21/-** Post extra.

GAMAGE'S MAGICAL DEPARTMENT.

The One Great House for Everything Magical.

Department Manager ... ... **Mr. WILL GOLDSTON.**

THE completeness of our stock can only be realised to the full by means of an actual visit and a tour of inspection. If any client has not yet seen this great Magical Department, let him now hasten to do so. It is, in truth, a great Magical Department. There is not a rival to it in this or any other country. It could equip at an hour's notice a hundred conjurors and illusionists with full apparatus for all their effects. And even then there would be enough left in its store rooms to provide material for hundreds more. Its customers come from all parts of the world. On its books are the names of the leading magicians— British, American and Continental. They have made practical tests of its capabilities, and have found that it can supply them promptly with anything they want executed in the best possible style. Gamage's Magical Department is well equipped from every point of view. It has brains and ideas behind it. The mechanics who work for it have special knowledge as to all the intricacies of magical apparatus. Its salesmen are experienced conjurers able to explain the mode of operation of every trick they handle. Nothing is too big for it and nothing too small. It can supply everything ranging from the most elaborate illusion to the simplest pocket trick. And it is always first in the field with novelties. A customer might visit it a dozen times in a month, and on every occasion find something new among its stock. In this respect, as in others, Gamage's Magical Department is an easy winner.

No. E. 236. The Japanese Rings.

large rings with which many extraordinary manœuvres can be performed.

he rings are proved to be solid and are handed round for examination but at the command the performer they become linked together in chains of two, three or more, and yet continually keep becoming connected and disconnected. Finally when the rings appear to be in inextricable confusion, they suddenly disentangle and fall on the floor.

Price, complete with full instructions, **2/6** Post 3d.
Larger size **5/-** Post td.
Brass, full size, **12/6** Post 9d.
Extra heavy **20/6**

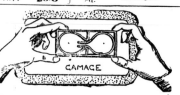

No. E. 246. "It Puzzles Me."

This wonderful puzzle is highly recommended. Ask your friend who knows all "to have a try."
Price **6d.** Postage 3d.

No. E. 263 The Welsh Rabbit Saucepan.

a large saucepan are placed the various ingredients for Welsh rabbit. A handkerchief is placed in a borrowed ignited, and the saucepan is held over the flames to the ingredients. Upon opening the lid of the saucepan out jumps a live rabbit, and the hat and handkerchief are restored uninjured to their respective owners. very effective. Best make. Handle made to take on off, for convenience when travelling.
Price, with full instructions, **4/6** Postage 6d.

No E. 268. The Dove Pan Illusion.

A very interesting and telling illusion.

The performer borrows two rings and drops them into the pan, then he breaks in eggs and other ingredients to suit taste. He now mixes the whole lot together, finally setting fire to it a d putting the lid on. After a few seconds he removes the lid, and out fly two dives with the borrowed rings tied around their necks with ribbon.
Price, complete with full instructions, **4/6** Postage 6d.

No. E. 280. The Vanishing Canary and Cage.

You show a pretty cage, 6 in. square containing a live canary, and then cover it with a large handkerchief which you take into the middle of the spectators, and throwing the handkerchief in the air the bird and cage vanish.
Price, complete with full instructions, **6/6** Post 6d.

The Magician Monthly.

Specimen Copy, **5d.**
Post free.

No. E. 310. The "Yelit" Squeeker.

Specially made to produce unearthly noises in Punch and Judy Shows, or for imitating various animals, &c.
Price .. **9**d.
Post 1d.

No. 388. The Collapsible Walking Stick.

The performer walks forward with an ordinary looking walking stick in his hand. He is seen to press both ends and the walking stick gradually decreases in size until it can be easily placed in the vest pocket. Very handsome stick, complete with case.
Price **6/9** Postage 1d.

No. E. 410. The (Un) Musical Watch Winder.

Most useful to a conjuror for winding a borrowed watch. The unearthly din resembles a meatjack and is guaranteed to create great laughter Price- complete with full instructions, **6**d. Postage 2d.

The Changing Cords.

A little puzzle that can be presented as a conjuring trick.
A very pretty and puzzling effect.
Price **9d.** Postage 2d.

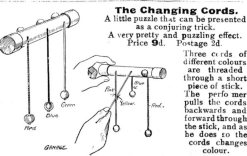

Three cords of different colours are threaded through a short piece of stick. The performer pulls the cords backwards and forward through the stick, and as he does so the cords changes colour.

The Magic Mint

This wonderful piece of apparatus changes discs of metal into real money. Can be performed anywhere without fear of detection.
9d. Post 1d.

Theatrical and Conjuring Goods listed in this Catalogue cannot be sent on Approval or Exchanged.

CATALOGUE OF TRICKS AND JOKES POST FREE ON APPLICATION.

COMPLETE SET OF CONJURING TRICKS.

No. E. 198.

Set of Conjuring Tricks.

No. E. 1. Containing several good tricks **2/3** Post 3d.

No. E. 2. Containing many good tricks **3/3** Post 4d.

No. E. 199. **Gamage's Boys' Box of Conjuring Tricks.**

With instructions .. **1/-** Post 2d.

The GAMAGE Special Boxes of Conjuring Tricks.

No. E. 200

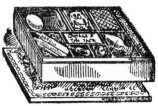

Box A contains 10 really good tricks as follows : The String Trick, The Egg Ball Illusion, The Bottle Imp, The Magic Book, The Card Book, The Magic Handkerchief, The Candle Case, The Marvellous Ball Box, The Cap and Halfpence, &c.

Extraordinarily Cheap. English Made.

Thorough good workmanship. The youngsters' delight, complete with instructions for performing every trick .. .. **4/3** Post 4d.

Box B contains 12 good effective tricks, viz.: The Figure-it-out Trick, The Penetrative Coin, The Penny in the Bottle, The Enchanted Corks, The Magic Candle Case; The Magic Handkerchief, The Wizard's Changing Cards, The Ball Box, The Magic Book, The Card under Glass Trick, The Changing Card, The Enchanted Rose Trick and a Book of Modern Tricks. With full and lucid instructions to enable anyone with a little practice to perform all the foregoing marvellous illusions. Price ... **5 6** Post 4d.

No. E 423.

The Cabinet of Latest Conjuring Tricks.

This Cabinet contains a complete set of well made conjuring tricks. With a little practice, the performer should be able to give a full hour's entertainment in the drawing room.

Contents—Chinese Linking Rings, polished steel ; plated set of Tambourine Rings, 100 Spring Flowers, assorted set of 6 Trick Cards, 6 coloured Hat Coils, 6 strong Tambourine Coils, Conjuror's Wand, New Changing Cards, Magic Brass Snuff Box, Magic Brass Fire Bowl, Book of Up-to-date Tricks, useful card box of Enchanted Flowers and Ribbon, wonderful Glass Casket, Mysterous Rising Cards. Handkerchief Illusion. Price complete with full instructions, **42/-** Car. free.

All Cabinets and Boxes of Tricks

described on this page (with the exception of Nos. 198 and 199) are of **British Manufacture and Materials,** and are the most complete sets that have ever been offered to the public at the prices quoted. Every person interested in the facinating art of Legerdemain should send for one of these cabinets at once. The wonderful value will greatly surprise them, and the effect of the tricks will astonish and mystify their friends. So if you will be a social lion, invest in a cabinet of conjuring tricks, and be the envy of all your friends.

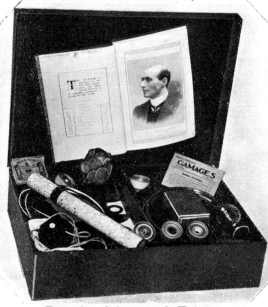

Box C. Advanced Tricks.

Containing a number of first-class Illusions, strongly made and very effective to work. The box contains a valuable Manual on Conjuring, viz.: **"Tricks and Illusions."** Besides this book which explains a host of other tricks, there is The Chinese Ring Trick as performed by the great Oriental Magicians, The Drawer Box, The Demon Envelope, The Figure-it-out Trick, several Coin Tricks, large size Ball Box, Obedient Ball and Enchanted Rose. The whole comprising the most complete set of tricks sold at this price .. **10/6** Post 6d.

Box D. The Gamage Guinea Cabinet.

Complete set of Tricks for a Drawing Room Entertainment. Contains all the latest tricks, viz.: An Up-to-date Treatise on Magic, a splendid Wand, The Enchanted Rose and Ribbon, Ball and String Trick, Bran Box, The 3-change Flower (large size) Ball and Glass Casket, The Tambourine Illusion and Set of Hat Coils, Magic Plate for Coins, The Handkerchief Case, The Egg Ball Illusion, The Cap and Halfpence, The Enchanted Padlock, The Cigar Case Novelty, The Fakir's Bands of Paper, The Walking Pip Card .. **21/.** Post 10d.

We might mention that the value of this cabinet greatly exceeds the price charged. We are enabled to do this owing to the enormous quantity that we sell. This speaks for itself.

British Work and Good Material.

Catalogue of Tricks and Puzzles post free on application

Cabinets of Conjuring Tricks.

This Cabinet .. **12/6** Post 9d.

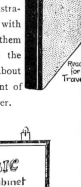

For the convenience of Amateur Conjurors we are putting up Cabinets of Conjuring Tricks in the form of Attache Cases. As will be seen from the illustration these cases are fitted with handles, the things in them pack nearly flat, and so the tricks can be carried about with the minimum amount of discomfort to the performer.

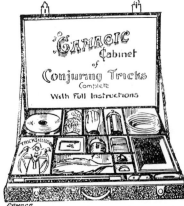

This Cabinet .. **25/.** Carriage 1/-

The Cases are in two sizes.

The smaller one, containing sufficient apparatus for one hour's entertainment, is

12/6 Post 9d.

The larger one, containing sufficient tricks for an interesting performance lasting an hour-and-a-half, is to be had for

25/- Carriage 1/-

Either Cabinet make a very handsome present.

Sissa.

A very entertaining puzzle.

Price **5½**d.
Postage 1d.

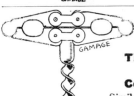

No. E. 542.

The Unique Surprise Corkscrew.

Similar to 544, but very superior quality and different in shape.

Price, complete with full instructions, **1/-**

Postage 1d.

E. 544. The Surprise Corkscrew.

AN IDEAL JOKE.

Great amusement may be caused with one of these corkscrews, which folds up so that it will go into the waistcoat pocket.

The idea is to ask someone to draw out a cork with the corkscrew, but much to his annoyance and perplexity he finds he cannot make the cork budge, although he cannot tell why. At last you say you cannot wait longer but must draw the cork yourself, which you do with the greatest ease.

Price, complete with full instructions, **6**d. Post 1d.

No. E. 545.

The Ebony Ball.

The puzzle in this most beautiful apparatus is to gain possession of the concealed coin.

We are at a loss to describe the workmanship, but assure our numerous customers that no expense is spared in producing this neat article.

Price **1/9**   Postage 2d.

Match Puzzle.

Collection of surprising puzzles can be made after following directions.

Price **3**d.
Postage 1d.

MORE TRICKS and PUZZLES
without
Mechanical Apparatus
By WILL GOLDSTON.

128 Pages. Board Covers (handsome 3-colour design) and about 100 illustrations.

Price **1/-** net, Post 3d.

This Book is highly recommended to all persons interested in Magic.

66 Pocket Tricks with Humorous Patter. The only book of its kind.

The Spade and the Bullet.

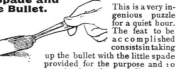

This is a very ingenious puzzle for a quiet hour. The feat to be accomplished consists in taking up the bullet with the little spade provided for the purpose and so carrying it to the cup. The puzzle can be done, but it is a feat of skill which will not be accomplished without some practice.

Price .. .. **4**d.   Postage 1d.

No. E. 86. The New Card Change.

Invented by WILL GOLDSTON.

A card held in performer's hand is seen to change four times. Entirely new method.

Price **6**d.   Postage 1d.

No. E. 552.

The Gamage Puzzle.

A very perplexing Boxwood puzzle. Just as you think you have done it, you find you have not.

Price, complete with full instructions .. **9**d.

Postage 2d.

No. E. 555.

Egyptian Match Box.

A box without an opening of any kind. Beautifully made in brass with a real halfpenny pivoted on top. Anyone can turn box over and over, and turn halfpenny on top round for hours without being able to get at the matches which they can hear inside, yet you can get them out yourself with ease.

Price, complete with full directions, **1/6** Post 2d.

No. E. 556.

Diplomacy Puzzle.

You have to get a coin out of the lid; although it is under a piece of glass and can be seen, you cannot get it unless you know how.

Price, complete with full illustrated instructions, **9**d. Postage 2d.

No. E. 557. Boxes of Puzzles.

Price, complete with full illustrated instructions,

6d. **2/6 5/- 10/6 21/- 42/-**

Postage 2d., **3**d. and 6d.

No. E. 558. The Persian.

This is a box which will contain rings, &c. A rod runs through the centre of it and each part will move separately, yet the whole are bound together in the securest manner.

Price, complete with full instructions. **9**d.

Postage 1d.

No. E. 559

Screw Box.

The lid of box turns freely, but will not come off; the puzzle is to get it off.

Price, complete with full illustrated instructions, **6½**d.

Postage 1d.

No. E. 560.

Cannon and Ball Puzzle.

A wooden cannon with a glass ball inside it. The ball can be got out by those in the secret.

Price, complete with full illustrated instructions, **1/-** Postage 2d.

No. E. 561.

Dumbell Puzzle.

A wooden dumbell with a ring on it; the puzzle is to get the ring off.

Price, complete with full illustrated instructions, **1/-** Postage 2d.

No. E. 562.

The Tower Puzzle.

A box in the shape of a tower without an opening, will contain money, but the puzzle is to get it out.

Highly recommended.

Send for one; you will be delighted.

Price, complete with full instructions, **6½**d.

Postage 1d.

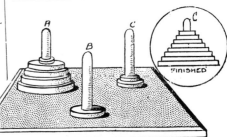

The "Bramah" Puzzle.

The original of this interesting and ingenious puzzle is said to date back to the legendary history of the creation. This puzzle has 8 discs, and **can be solved in four minutes, 15 seconds.** If there were 64 discs, it would take 5,849,424,173 centuries to accomplish.

5½d. Post 1d.

Catalogue of Tricks and Puzzles post free on application.

A Card of Puzzle.

The "PATIENCE" Card Puzzle.

Very interesting and not so easy as it looks.

Price **5½**d. Postage 1d.

No. E. 532.

Puzzle Money Box.

A coin is put in the box and heard to rattle, all at once rattle ceases and coin has gone. Audience cannot detect how, though done under their eyes. Neither can they find any secret opening. Price, complete with full directions, **1/-**

Superior make, in brass, **2/-**

Postage 2d.

The Kalcograph.

(Patented).

A Marvellous Mathematical Mystery.
Price **5½**d. Postage 1d.

No. E. 534.

Dissecting Puzzle.

Price .. **10½**d.

Postage 2d.

Box of Wire Puzzles.

No. E. 531.
10½d. Post 2d

Puzzles with instructions.

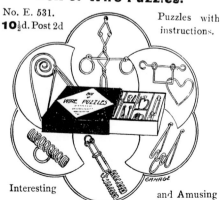

Interesting

and Amusing

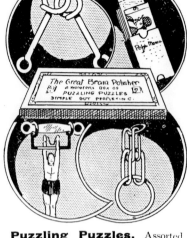

Puzzling Puzzles. Assorted.

A wonderful box containing four to six interesting puzzles.

Price **6**d. Postage 2d.

No. E. 524.

Wonderful Puzzle Key

(Steel).

You show a door key and borrow someone's ring. Ask the company to put the ring on the key, but they will find it impossible, yet you can do so with ease. Price complete with full instructions **1/-** each. Post 1d.

No. E. 529.

Cube Barrels and Balls.

These Puzzles are beautifully made of different coloured woods. They take to pieces and the puzzle is either to take apart or put them together.

In various shapes as shown, Cube, Ball, Egg shape and Barrel.

Price, complete with full instructions **2/-** ea Postage 2d.

By far the handsomest puzzle made.

No. E. 535. The Ring Box Puzzle.

A pretty boxwood box contains a ring yet same cannot be extracted by any person not knowing the secret. Highly recommended.

Price, complete with full instructions, **6½**d. Postage 1d.

The Holborn Box of Wonderful Puzzles.

Positively the Greatest Value offered for the money.

Five Novel and Instructive Puzzles with Instructions. **6d.**

Postage 2d.

No. E. 536. The Zulu Box Puzzle.

Handsomely made of Boxwood.

Unless in the secret box cannot be opened.

Instead of opening the box, try as they might, the lid absolutely refuses to come off.

Yet it will turn.

Price, complete with full instructions, **6½**d. Postage 1d.

See Saw.

Secure the three steel balls into position.

Price **6**d. Postage 2d.

The Bowling Green.

To get the quicksilver into the holes—the highest score wins.

Price **6**d. Postage 1d.

No. E. 538.

The Great Jubilee Puzzle.

A very neat looking boxwood puzzle. You may place a sovereign inside, and may safely promise it to any person who can get it out. A very smart puzzle, and nicely and neatly made.

Very amusing for parties, social gatherings, etc.

Price, complete with full instructions, **6½**d. Postage 1d.

The Balls in the Hole Puzzle.

Interesting and Entertaining.

Price .. **4**d.

Postage 1d.

No. E. 564. The Invisible Gift.

A piece of money is concealed somewhere in the box. If anyone can discover it within a certain time, you tell them they can have it, but they never succeed. Price, complete with full instructions, **6½**d. Postage 1d.

No. E. 565. Lighthouse Puzzle.

The lantern of which turns round. There is a ring round the body of lighthouse, which is very difficult to get off unless in the secret.

Price, complete with full instructions .. **6**d. Postage 1d.

No. E. 565A. The Barrel and Ball.

To get a marble out of the barrel.

Price, complete with full illustrated instructions, **6½**d. Postage 1d.

The Electric Pencil.

This pencil can write any colour.

The catch of the season.

Price .. **3**d. Postage 1d.

The Ring Box Puzzle.

A pretty boxwood box contains a ring, yet same cannot be extracted by any person not knowing the secret. Highly recommended. Price, complete with full instructions, **6½**d. Postage 1d.

The Seven Ring Puzzle.

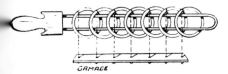

You are clever if you can do it without being shown. Superior make, **5½**d. Post 2d.

The Green Star Puzzle.

Ingenious, Entertaining, and New.

Price **5½**d. Post 1d.

The Great Four Ace Puzzle.

Looks good and easy. You must have this.

Price **5½**d. Post 1d.

The See-Saw Puzzle.

Price .. **5½**d. Postage 2d.

The puzzle is to get the three balls into the holes.

No. E. 141. The Finger through the Hat.

You borrow a hat from a gentleman in the audience, when you immediately push your finger through the crown; you appear to be sorry for doing such a silly thing, but the owner feels annoyed, and the audience are highly amused at the joke; yet the conjuror returns the hat in a perfect condition.

Price, complete with full instructions, **6**d. Postage 1d.

No. E. 141E. The Whistling Nigger.

The head can either be fastened to the coat lapel or waistcoat.

The wearer can at any moment he pleases make the head whistle, move its eyes, and shoot out its tongue. Great Effect.

Price **1/-** Postage 2d

Two Eyes and a Mouth.

A good puzzle for anyone. In the Nigger's Head are 3 bullets, two to represent the eyes and one for the mouth. The puzzle is to pick them out with the fingers. It looks easy enough, but—

Price .. **9**d. Postage 2d.

Table Tricks. This Cabinet comprises a number of tricks and novelties. Great funs for the guests. Price **10½**d. Postage 3d.

The Dancing Skeleton.

Mysterious and novel.

Reduced price **5½**d.

Postage 1d.

The "Hello" Puzzle

Craze has struck the Country.

Can you ring off?

The newest brain teaser. You simply can't drop it until you have removed the steel ring from the celluloid disc. Easy when you know how, but—!!

5½d. Post 1d.

The Corkscrew Puzzle.

Not so easy as it looks.

Price .. **2**d. Post 1d.

Catalogue of Puzzles and Tricks post free on application.

The Improved "HOLBORN" Box of Puzzles.

This Box contains five selected puzzles, all strongly made and well finished.

Price .. **6**d.

Generally sold elsewhere at 2/-

Complete with illustrated instructions.

Ball and Maze Puzzle.

Splendid Pastime.

2d.

Post 1d.

"A FAIR COP."

Purse and Snake Joke.

Great fun can be obtained from this purse.

Price **1**/-   Postage 2d.

The "Octo" Star Puzzle.

The object being to place seven counters on seven of the eight points.   Price **5½**d.   Post 1d.

The Young Conjuror.

VOLUME II.
OF
The Young Conjuror.

A wonderful collection of secrets will be found. They are explained in such a way, that the youngest magician can understand them. The book is thoroughly well illustrated and, at the price, there is no better book on the art of magic.
Fully illustrated.
Paper covers ... **6**d.
Cloth bound ... **1**/-
Postage 2d.

SIXTY GOOD AND EFFECTIVE TRICKS, WITH AND WITHOUT APPARATUS, FULLY EXPLAINED AND ILLUSTRATED

VOL. 2   By Will Goldston   **6**D. NET.

A. W. GAMAGE, LTD.

CARRY THE LARGEST STOCK OF JOKES AND PUZZLES. IN THE WORLD.

Ha! Ha!   Oh! Oh.

Novel Views.
This novel spy glass arrangement will keep a company amused for hours.   Price **8½**d.   Post 1d.

JOKES and TRICKS
CANNOT
BE EXCHANGED.

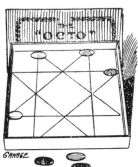

GAMAGE

Gamage's Knife.
Cannot be opened unless you are in the secret.
Price .. .. **6**d.   Post 1d.

START ALL FROM HERE

COWS IN THE PASTURE

Cows in the Pasture.
Novel and Clever.
5½d.
Post 1d.

Tri-Trix Puzzle.
This neatly made puzzle is highly recommended to persons who are fond of a pastime requiring skill.
Price .. **5½**d.   Post 1d.

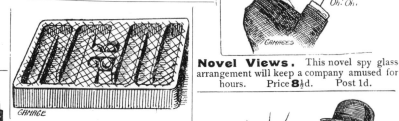

The Funny Patent Lighter.
Creates more laughter than can be imagined. Just out.   Price **1**/-   Postage 1d.

The Snuff Box Puzzle.

The most useful box made.   Great fun when handing the box round to your friends

Price **1**/-   Postage 1d.

DONT MOVE I CAN REACH

The Ever Growing Cigar Holder.
Very useful for parties to create fun.
Get one of these holders and be the envy of your friends.
Price **1/6**   Postage 1d.

The Electric Flash Joke.
Ask your friend to watch the bull's-eye for coloured flash. Instead of light he receives a steady stream of water in the eye, Great joke for any time.

Price .. **6½**d.

Post 1d.

Catalogue of Jokes and Tricks post free on application.

Oh! Oh!!

A Coon Baby, many feet in length, is shot out of a case without the least warning. The Latest Design.

Price, **1/-** Post 2d   Smaller size, **9**d. Post 1d.

'MAGICIAN SECRETS.'

Edited by WILL GOLDSTON.

This booklet contains a good number of Tricks suitable for the beginner and advanced amateur conjuror.

Price .. **3**d.

Post 2d.

Oh, Mother!

Ask your Mother to sew a button on, at the same time hand her the reel of cotton, and wait for developments. Price **9**d. Post 3d.

The Go-Bang Cigarette Box.

When this pretty Cigarette Box is opened, a loud report is heard. Great joke for parties, etc.

Price .. .. **6**d. Post 1d.

No. E. 430.
Beetles in the Beer.

Most remarkable imitation. The joker quietly drops one of these beetles into his beer and then objects to drink it until an offer is made to exchange the liquor. However, on second thoughts, after removing the beetle, he drinks the beer. The company feel ill at the sickly sight.

Great joke to those in the secret.

Per packet of 3 for **5**d. Postage 1d.

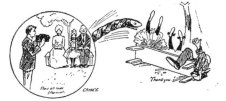

The Latest Snake Camera.

Just as you are about to snap your friends, a huge snake jumps out of the Camera.

YOU MUST HAVE ONE!

Small sizes	..	..	..	..	**1/-** and **1/6**
Medium size	..	..	..		**1/11½**
Full size	..	..	..		**2/6**

Post 3d. and 4d.

The Seback-roscope.

With the aid of this instrument the possessor can see behind him. You will find lots of fun in owning a Sebackroscope Made of hard rubber and finished in an excellent manner.

6d. Post 1d.

No need to wish for eyes in the back of your head, as with this article you can observe all that occurs in that direction without even turning the head. How often you are anxious to see faces in back of you or to observe who is following without attracting attention by turning around. This instrument does this for you.

The Joke of the Season!

A monster pencil 25 inches long is produced from the waiscoat pocket. Handsomely made.

Price .. **1/-** Post 3d.

Well worth 2/6

The Ladies' Cigarette Box.

This dainty box has a small ball fitted in the cover.

When your lady friend presses the ball to obtain a cigarette, she receives a spray of water on the nose.

Price .. .. **1/-** Post 1d.

Well I Never!

Offer your friend the Smoker a Cigar from your Case, when he attempts to take one the fun commences. The Cigar when lifted has a habit of returning to the Case **rather quickly.**

Price .. **8½**d. Postage 1d.

The Mysterious Mutoscope.

A little innocent-looking mutoscope is on the table. If your friend does not pick it up and begin to turn the handle you can suggest to him that the mutoscope contains some of the latest pictures. He will then become curious and will probably gaze into the machine and turn the handle. Immediately he does so he receives the surprise of his life, for a large snake suddenly springs out of the mutoscope and shoots out its fangs at your inquisitive friend.

Price **1/9**

Post 2d.

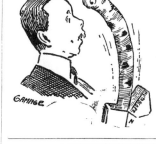

"A FAIR COP"

A Snake Purse.

Attempts to snatch this purse from its fair owner will get a bad shock to his system, for the moment he touches the purse a large snake will spring out at him and cause him to wish he had never attempted to rob the lady.

Price, **1/-** Postage 2d.

What Next!

A capital joke for smoking rooms, &c. The smoker goes up to the match stand, takes a match and lights it. As he does so all the matches fly upwards from the stand.

Play this on to your friends at Christmas.

Price .. **1/6** Price 3d.

Have one of my New Cigarettes?

When your friend is about to take a Cigarette, you release a catch and the concealed flap drops upon his finger, giving him a shock which creates laughter.   Price .. **6**d.   Postage 1d.

Seven Novel Jokes FOR **1/6** Post 3d.

Other Boxes can be supplied :
2/6   3/9   5/6   10/6 and **21/-**
Postage 3d., 4d. and 6d.

Crystal Gazing.

Anyone who may be possessed of latest "mediumistic" powers may possibly be able to bring them into use by looking at the Crystal Ball, in other words by "Crystal Gazing." Faces and scenes, both past and in the future may be seen by highly strung persons with keen imaginative powers.   The accompanying illustrations is a picture of a "scene" actually "discovered" in the Crystal by a lady.   The scene is that of a wedding, and 21 days after seeing it the lady was actually married although at the time she took up the Crystal she had no thoughts of matrimony.   A copy of "Looking into the Future," an interesting booklet, compiled and edited by Will Goldston, which explains Crystal Gazing. Spiritualism, Palmistry, &c., &c , is given away with every Crystal Ball we supply.

Large size **4/9**   Second size **3/3**
Third ,, **2/9**   Small ,, **2/-**
Postage 4d. and 3d.

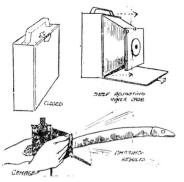

The Camera Fiend.

Everyone has heard of the camera fiend—the man who takes snap-shots of people at inconvenient moments. Tell someone that you have captured the camera fiend and have got him inside the camera. Then touch the button and the fiend—in the form of a snake—will jump. Your friend will also jump, and if he is bigger than you—why, then, perhaps you had better jump too!

Price ..   .. **2/6**   Post 4d.

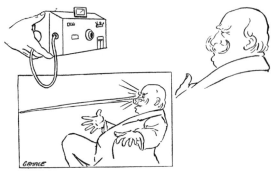

The Snap Shooter.

The boy who handles this joke must be careful in the selection of his victims! Bachelor uncles of proved good tempers will probably appreciate the little attention, but the puzzle worker will be advised to give "crusty old uncles" a wide berth. You merely offer to take a snap-shot of your victim, and the apparatus you handle seems exactly like a small camera. However, when you have your sitter full face towards you the poor man suddenly discovers that the camera is not quite so innocent as it looks. He receives a little stream of scent or water in his face.

The "camera" can be loaded again and again.

Price ..   .. **1/-**   Post 3d.
Second quality ..   **9**d.   Post 2d.

Pointless Jokes.
Four Peculiar Pencils.

"A pencil? Certainly." You hand one to a friend who drops it. The pencil is so much heavier than an ordinary pencil that when a man attempts to take hold of it he does not put out sufficient strength to grasp it. The second pencil has a "point" made of indiarubber; this looks so much like lead that your victim is sure to try and write with it—until he gives it up in disgust. Number three pencil collapses directly you press on it, and after folding in half returns to its normal state, and the point of the last pencil disappears inside the pencil when you try to use it.

Price **2**d. each. ..   ..   Post 1d.

Who Upset the Mustard ?

A joke for the breakfast table on a Sunday morning—or any other morning. The mustard pot is obviously upset, and the mustard is on the table. Cries of indignation from the lady of the house ! "Who upset the mustard ?" The mustard is quickly cleared up, and no harm is done to the cloth.

The joke can be repeated any number of times.

Price ..   .. **6**d.   Postage 3d.

Shocking Cigarettes.

An innocent little box of cigarettes. When your unsuspecting friend attempts to open the box and help himself he discovers that the cigarettes are truly shocking.

Price ..   .. **6**d.   Post 1d.

A Pencil ?   Certainly.

A man wants to borrow a pencil.   You ha[ve] him this one and then watch him. He strugg[les] to get the point protector off the pencil a[nd] finally puts it in his mouth in his effort to [get] at the pencil. Finally he has to give it up [as] the pencil will always remain with its p[oint] covered.   Price **3**d.   Postage 1d.

Catalogue of Jokes and Tricks Post Free on Application.

Novelties and Jokes.—*continued.*

Have a Cigarette?

A novel kind of Cigarette Case. You hand it to a friend and ask him to help himself. He opens the lid and receives a tiny stream of water in his face. The Case can be loaded again and again.

Price .. **1/-**
Postage 2d.

Jumping Cigar.

When your friend goes to take a cigar, it is shot into his mouth.

Harmless and Funny.

Price .. **8½d.**
Postage 2d.

Sampling The Scent.

Tell your friend that you have obtained a sample of a new and rare perfume, and ask him to be good enough to take out the cork for you. If he is one of those men who "hate being laughed at" the subsequent joke will be well "up against him," because, however careful he may be to draw the cork of the bottle nicely, he will certainly spill the scent. He will not be able to help this, because the moment the cork is removed the scent drips through the bottle. Price **3**d. Postage 1d.
Superior quality .. .. **6**d.

The Opera Case Joke.

On opening the case a monster snake jumps.
Price **1/9**   Postage 3d.

"Oh! Oh!" she cried

Snake jumps out of Jewel Box. Creates screams of laughter.

Price.. **1/-**
Post 2d.

Not for Teetotallers!

A nice joke to play on a man who is "fond of a glass of Good Beer." One of these Beetles placed in his glass of beer can be guaranteed to give him quite a sudden shock when he discovers it there.

The "Beetles" are made of indiarubber.

Price .. .. **3 for 5d.** Post 1d.

The Distorting Mirror.

Price **3**d. and **6**d.   Postage 1d.

The Burning Cigarette.

Hold the Cigarette between your fingers and go close up to your friend.—See him edge away from you so that his fingers shall not be scorched with the end of your cigarette. Put the cigarette on your hostess's piano, and listen to her scream of surprise at your carelessness! You can do many other things with this cigarette without doing any damage, because the lighted end is not really alight. The resemblance to the real thing is so good, however, that it takes in everybody.

An excellent fun-producer at any Party.

Price **1**d. each, **7** for **6**d. Post 1d.

A Smash Somewhere!

A few pieces of metal dropped on to the floor—or the pavement outside the house—make a tremendous crash! People who hear it will come running up, wondering what motor 'bus has run into the window, or how many cups and saucers the housemaid has broken this time! While they are all looking for the cause of the row, you quietly pick up the plates and drop them again in another place. Continue in the same way until you are found out and then disappear quickly.

Price .. **5½d.**   Postage 2d.

The Kaliscope Joke.

You hand the Kaliscope to your friend requesting him to look through the glass and see the Ballet dancer.

When he remarks there is nothing to be seen, then ask him to press the spring at the side, which he does, and receives a shock.

8½d. Post 1d.

Squinting Eyeglasses.

Make everyone laugh. Mechanical movements.
Price **4½d.**   Postage 1d.

OH MY POOR FEET!
6D A PAIR
A TOE-TALLY NEW JOKE

Just Out!

THE NOVELTY OF THE SEASON.

A Pair of Monster Feet.

Nicely coloured.
Price .. **6**d.
Post 1d.

Superior quality, strongly made, **2/6** Post 4d.

A Present for Sister.

A neat little Case containing a **Mirror** (?) is presented to a lady in the company. Upon the Mirror (?) being removed it flies out of her hand, giving her a start. YOU MUST HAVE ONE OF THESE.

Price .. .. **6**d. Postage 1d.

A Catalogue of Jokes and Tricks Post Free on Application.

No. E. 386.

Great Novelty.

By turning a knob at the side of holder the victim receives a spray of water in the face, although he expected to see a pretty picture.

The Kinematograph is handsomely made in metal, mickel plated.

Price **6½**d. Post 1d.

The Gamage Box of Wonderful Puzzles.

Positively the Greatest Value offered for the money. Fine novel and instructive Puzzles with instructions
Price .. **6**d. Worth 2/- Postage 2d.

The Electric Flash Joke.

Ask your friend to watch the bull's-eye for coloured flash. Instead of light he receives a steady stream of water in the eye. Great joke for any time.

Price **6½**d Postage 1d.

The Scissors Joke.

This pair of Scissors and Cigar Cutter cannot be opened. Get one if you are fond of joking.
Plain, **4½**d. Superior plated, **1**/- Postage 1d.

The Sympathetic Ink.

If you wish your letter kept secret, use this ink. The writing is invisible until heated.
Price **6**d. Postage 1d.

The Giant's Penknife

The joke of the season.

You must have this.

Price .. **1/6**

Post 1d.

The Beer Jug Joke.

The contents of the Jug make a speedy exit in the wrong direction. Price **2/9** Postage 4d.

The Hinged Pencil.

Nothing like it for laughter. Price **2**d. Post 1d.

The Stocking Purse.

The owner of one of these Stocking Purses creates great laughter every time he pays.

Price .. **1/6**

Post 1d.

The Baby Crier.

That machine imitates the crying of a baby to the very life MA-MA. Price **1 9** Post 3d.

The Nailed Pencil.

The fun is to watch your guest attempt to lift the Pencil. It cannot be done.

Price .. **3**d.

Post 1d.

The Musical Chair.

This ingenious device will be the means of making your party a high success.
Price **3**d. Improved Method, **6**d. Post 1d.

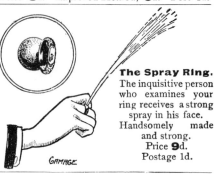

The Spray Ring.

The inquisitive person who examines your ring receives a strong spray in his face. Handsomely made and strong.
Price **9**d.
Postage 1d.

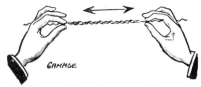

The Endless Wire. A Puzzle and Trick combined
Price .. **3**d. Postage 1d.

The Bank Note Maker.

This machine will turn sheets of plain paper into bank notes. **2/-**
Postage 3d.

One for the Scotchman.

An ideal trick to play on that Scotch friend of yours, or anyone who is fond of a "drop of good Scotch." You present him with a little glass flask containing some of his favourite liquor; you talk eloquently about it—its age, blend, origin and so on. You apologise for the absence of a glass and suggest that "Its not worth while putting a little drop like that into a glass; drink it as it is—out of the bottle," And your friend tries to drink it. He tries, and tries, and tries. Finally he sees the joke! (Even a Scotchman will see this joke.)
Not a drop of licquor will come from the flask.
Price ... **1/-** Post 3d.

Catalogue of Jokes and Tricks post free on application.

The Explosive Mat.

Everytime a glass is placed on this mat and removed a loud explosion occurs.

The most effective way of using this joke is to put the mat on the table, place a glass on it, and wait until some inquisitive friend comes along.

Price **3**d.   Postage 2d.

Not Real Jam.

An excellent imitation of a jar of jam. A great deal of fun can be got out of this simple article. For instance smuggle it into the drawing-room and quietly slip it on to the top of the piano, then watch your hostess's face when she goes to the piano and rings indignantly for the servant to "take that away".

Price **6**d.   Postage 3d.

The Magic Mirror.

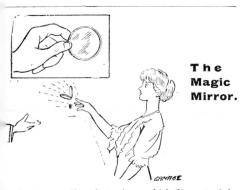

This is a small pocket mirror which flies out of the hand in a very startling manner.

The "operator" merely hands it to someone and the mirror does the rest.

Price **6**d.   Postage 1d.

The Surprise Mat chox.

The box should be handed to a man who wants a light. He opens it carelessly and then drops it suddenly, for the box seems to come to pieces in his hands. The owner can quickly put it right again in readiness for the next victim.

A capital joke.

Postage **1**/-   Postage 1d.

"That" Match Box.

The clever young man who "knows all about puzzles" will take some little time to discover this one, for the innocent looking box of matches does not open.

A good joke to play on a man who never carries matches and is always ready to borrow yours.

Price **3**d.   Postage 1d.

Touch the Button.

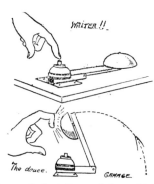

You touch the bell to call the maid, but the bell does not ring in the approved fashion. It does something else. The moment the finger is placed on the button the gong of the bell flies up and hits the back of the hand.

No harm is done. A good joke to leave on the table meal times.

Price **9**d.   Postage 2d.

No. E. 65.

The "Devo" Torn Card.

Regd. No 52421. This latest addition to an already large collection of clever card fakes is far and away the neatest and most finished piece of card mechanism which we have ever had the pleasure of seeing. It will be seen by the illustration that unlike all other cards of this nature—no flap or spring is employed. It will be obvious that unlike most cards which are used for this capital experiment, the card may be seen to be actually minus the torn piece, and may not only be freely shown back and front in this condition which is quite impossible in any other case, but it may be actually thrown down upon the table, &c., face up or down, and yet may be restored completely and shown back and front immediately afterwards. We can confidently recommend this card as a really capital and practical accessory. Price, complete with full instructions, **9**d.   Postage 1d.

A Funny Match Box.

The illustrations show what happens when anybody opens this match box. The box is thoroughly well made and the mechanism does not get out of order.

Price **9**d.   Postage 1d.

The Mysterious Fountain Pen.

This is a good imitation of a fountain pen and the joke lies in the fact that the cap of the pen cannot be removed. Therefore if the pen is handed to a man who is in a hurry to write a note, one can imagine what the result will be. The man may struggle with it as he pleases but no amount of strength will enable him to take cap from the pen.   Price **1**/-   Postage 1d.

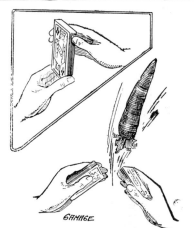

The Vegetarian's Pack of Cards.

Suggest a game of cards and produce this pack. Ask your friend if he is a vegetarian. No sooner are the words out of your mouth when a large Carrot springs quickly from the case. **1/6** Post 3d

A Curious Cigarette Lighter.

This little box has the appearance of being an ordinary "lighter" but when the knob is pressed, the smoker hears a mild explosion and his cigarette remains unlighted.

Price .. **1**/-

Postage 1d.

A Quaint Telescope.

The telescope is supposed to contain a number of pictures which move when the outside case of the telescope is turned round. Having announced what the pictures are, you will have no difficulty in finding some one who would like to see them. He puts the telescope to his eyes and unknown to himself, has a black eye before he has finished with the telescope. Price **9**d. Postage 3d.

Catalogue of Jokes and Tricks post free on application.

The Jumping Bean.

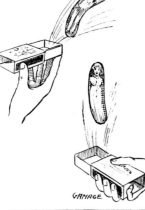

A member of the company is requested to open a box, when to their astonishment a spring bean jumps out of the box.

Price **3**d.

Postage 1d.

The Comic Cigar Case.

Just when your friend is about to take a cigar a dummy jumps up, as illustrated.

Price **8½**d.   Postage 2d.

The Shooting Cigar Case.
A novelty much sought after. **8½**d. Post 2d.

What's That?

Why, an imitation of those cigar lighters you see everywhere. When requested for a match just hand the person the box and watch developments.

Price **1/-**

Postage 2d.

What the Deuce Pencil.

One of the latest jokes invented. **2**d. Post 1d.

The Straw of Terror.

A really good harmless joke.

Price **3**d.

Post 1d.

The Endless Cotton.

Mrs. Caudle discovers a piece of cotton on her husband's coat, tries to take it off—the result, as she pulls away, to her astonishment, there is no end. Funnier than a Pantomime!

Price ..   .. **6**d. Post 1d.

The Tongue of Simon.

A mysterious head is seen on the wearer's waistcoat with projecting tongue. At command the tongue grows large, then small, and makes many other astounding movements.

Price **3**d.   Post 1d.

The Magic Lighter.

This is a capital joke to play on the man who has developed the unfortunate habit of being without matches—the man who is always asking other men if they can "oblige him with a light."

You hand such a man this magic lighter. He presses the botton and a small explosion occurs!

Perfectly harmless
Price .. **1/-**
Postage 1d.

The Weather Flower.

This flower has the power to tell the kind of weather.

A very Mysterious Novelty,

Price **3**d.

Post 1d.

A Matchless Joke.

A Match Stand, as illustrated, is seen on the smoker's table. Immediately a match is struck on the box, the whole of the contents are shot out of the box.

A Startling Novelty.

Price .. **1/6**

Post 3d.

The Catch Pencil.

Although you can write with the Pencil, your friends will fail unless they are in the secret.

A good joke that can be done anywhere ! **2**d. Post 1d.

The Nile Fortune Telling Cards.

This splendid Game should be in every home, and will be found a welcome game during winter months.   Can be played by two or more persons. Cards and full instructions. Price **1/9** Post 2d.

STANLEY COLLINS' Sympathetic Ace Trick
(FULLY PROTECTED).

A most puzzling and weird effect in which the four Aces taken from the pack of cards and placed on four corners of a handkerchief or serviette, mysteriously pass one by one under a piece of paper put on one corner.

Startling! Simple! Original!

Concise and valuable Instructions written by the Inventor, together with all accessories. Price **9**d. Postage 1d.

The "Convivial" Cards.
Introduced by STANLEY COLLINS
(Fully Protected).

No "Man about Town" can afford to be without this little Pocket Trick, as it enables the possessor to have refreshment at some one else's expense each time the trick is shown. ROARS OF LAUGHTER.

Invaluable to Professionals and Amateurs.

Price, complete with instructions. **6**d.   Postage 1d.

STANLEY COLLINS' "Eclipse" Card Transit.
(Fully Protected).

Having selected the four Aces and the four Tens from his pack, the performer very deliberately places the Aces in a borrowed silk hat, and the "Tens" in a borrowed "bowler." At the word of command the respective sets changes places, the Tens being found in the silk hat, whilst the Aces are taken from the "bowler."

Backs of Cards shown !   No Sleight-of-hand required.

Price complete with instructions. **6**d. Postage 1d.

Catalogue of Jokes and Tricks post free on application.

The Musical Pincushion.

A Joke for the Girls.

Get one of these pincushions and leave it on your friend's dressing table. She will be surprised to hear weird noises every time she takes a pin from the cushion. The joke can be repeated any number of times, and there is nothing to get out of order.

Price **6**d.   Postage 1d.

A Purse of Money.

A sub-title for this joke might be "The Waiter's Surprise." The moment anyone attempts to open the purse, a shower of money falls from it and the inquisitive finder of the purse is "given away."

Price **9**d.   Postage 1d.

The Jumping Cigarettes

You must have this!

An innocent looking box of cigarettes is handed to you. You open the box if you do not know the joke and are surprised when all the cigarettes jump out of the box.   Price **6**d. Postage 1d.

Beautiful Scent.

Improved make.

A small bottle of exquisite perfume. You dilate on its charm and then ask some one to smell it. The moment the cork is removed, all the scent runs out of the bottle. The joke can be repeated any number of times. Price **6**d. Inferior quality Price **3**d. Postage 1d.

Not much of a Glass.

Price .. **3**d.

Postage 1d.

This is what a lady will think of the dainty little mirror which you hand to her. She will try and take it from the case and will be puzzled to find that there is any difficulty in doing this. As a matter of fact the feat is impossible because it is really not much of a glass. It cannot be taken from the case.

The Cigar-cutter Joke.

This pair of scissors has the appearance of the genuine article. The fact it cannot be opened—therein lies the joke.

Get one and fool your friends.
Price **4½**d. Superior finish, **1/-** Post 1d.

The "Shmendrick" Head.

This is somewhat similar to "the Sensitive Fish," but instead of the fortunes of the holder being foretold by a wish they are indicated by the eyes of the monster which roll about in a weird and very mystifying fashion.

Price **9**d.   Post 3d

Jokes and Catches.

For the convenience of customers at a distance we are now putting up

Boxes of the Latest Jokes and Catches.

Each box contains sufficient material
To Amuse a Large Party of People.
Full instructions are given.

No Christmas Party is complete without some of these Jokes. They are the "very thing" to bring out when the fun is flagging and the youngsters are wondering "what next to do" START A FEW JOKES & CATCHES ON THEIR ROUNDS and soon the fun will be fast and furious again.

Prices   **1/-   1/9   2/6   3/6   6/6**
Postage 3d. and 4d.

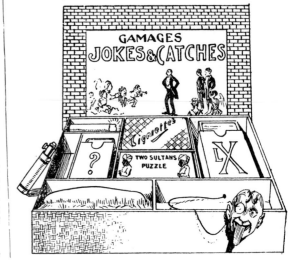

"A Night in Paris."

The unsuspecting person, seeing this book on the table, will wait an opportunity of reading it. You give him the chance he is eagerly waiting for by leaving the room.

On opening the cover of the book a loud report is heard.

"Laugh! why I thought I should have died."

Price **1/6**
Postage 2d.

Catalogue of Jokes and Tricks post free on application.

M

WILL GOLDSTON'S PUBLICATIONS on MAGIC AND INDOOR PASTIMES

THE NAME OF WILL GOLDSTON is one to conjure with in conjuring matters. And in other matters as well. He has written and compiled many books on many subjects, and all of them deal adequately with the respective subjects. Some particulars of the latest are given below. ¶ What do you require? Are you a beginner in Magic anxious to master the first principles quickly? If so, *The Young Conjurer* is just the book for you. Buy a copy and study carefully. You will be astonished with the progress you make in the art, and your audiences will be equally astonished with the manifestations of that art you present to them. Perhaps you have passed the elementary stage; perhaps you are working on a fairly big scale and merely need new material for that work. You will find that material in *More Tricks and Puzzles, Tricks and Illusions*, and *Stage Illusions*. All these books realize their titles. The first is a miscellany suitable for the drawing-room performer; the second forms a sort of silver bridge between the impromptu platform and the regular stage; the third deals with bold effects which will appeal to the biggest variety theatre audiences. ¶ Some Magicians combine juggling with their magic. More might well do so. You, for instance. Why not buy *Juggling Secrets*, and use some of the effects described in it to give variety to your customary show? Juggling is simple enough—when you know how—and *Juggling Secrets* tells you how in the simplest possible manner. If you want further variety, it is to your hand in *Sand, Smoke and Rag Pictures*. A good act this; yet one little practised now-a-days. Every detail of it is described in the book. Why not add it to your repertoire? You may not be able to produce pictures in oil or water colours for the Royal Academy, but you can, with the help of this book, produce them in sand, smoke or rags, for the public at large. ¶ Perhaps you are not a Magician in the technical sense of the word; perhaps you are simply an ordinary member of society, wishing to do your duty to society. Will Goldston has something for you. His *Indoor Pastimes* describes the newest and most laughable of parlour games. Study it, and you will be an acquisition to every party you visit this winter. Whenever the jollity flags you will be prepared to revive it. The vote of thanks at the end of the evening will be yours.

SMOKE AND RAG PICTURES.—How to make them in an entertaining manner. The only Book on the subject in existence. Edited by Will Goldston. Fully illustrated. The Editor has pleasure in announcing that he has obtained from Mr. David Devant the only explanation ever given by Mr. Devant of the way to make Paper Pictures. If the book contained nothing else it would be well worth many times its price.
1/- Post 2d.

THE YOUNG CONJUROR. By Will Goldston. Big and Small Mechanical and Sleight-of-hand Tricks for the Amateur. 104 pages, about 150 illustrations, handsomely bound in cloth. Vol. II. Vol. I. out of print. **1/-** each. Post 3d.

TRICKS AND ILLUSIONS. 3rd Edition. By Will Goldston. 136 pages. Nearly 300 illustrations. The latest and best Tricks and Illusions explained. Board Covers, **2/6** Cloth, **3/6** Post 3d. and 4d.

LOOKING INTO THE FUTURE. Compiled by WILL GOLDSTON. Whatever may be the reader's views regarding such matters as Fortune telling Crystal Gazing, Palmistry, etc., he will certainly find plenty of food for thought in this volume. The chapters dealing with these subjects contain an abundance of most interesting material. **6d.** Post 1d

JUGGLING SECRETS. Compiled and Edited by Will Goldston. THE ONLY book of its kind Published. 96 Pages. About 50 illustrations. **1/-** Post 2d.

MORE TRICKS AND PUZZLES. Without mechanical apparatus. By Will Goldston. 60 Tricks, 12 Puzzles, 72 Total. Nearly 200 illustrations. Positively the greatest Book on this fascinating Art published. Patter with each Trick. **1/-** Post 3d.

EASY TRICKS FOR TRICKSTERS. **4**d. Post 1d.

Catalogue of Conjuring Books and Tricks, Post Free on application.

INDOOR PASTIMES —Compiled and edited by Will Goldston. "THE" book of the season. No party should be attempted until someone who is coming to it has bought this book and mastered some of its contents. Fully illustrated. **1/-** Post 2d.

STAGE ILLUSIONS. — Compiled and edited by Will Goldston. This book contains complete explanations of some of the best illusions now being performed on the stage. By the student of magic, amateur and professional, it will be found to be an excellent Manual of the Art; in fact no conjurer can afford to be without it. The text is simple and the illustrations are so elaborate that the learner can understand all the lessons this excellent book has to teach.

Magical Secrets.
EDITED BY WILL GOLDSTON.

This booklet contains a good number of Tricks suitable for the beginner and advanced amateur conjuror. Price **3**d. Postage 2d.

JUST PUBLISHED

1/- **Juggling Secrets.** **1/-**

Compiled and Edited by Will Goldston. 96 pages. About 100 illustrations. Post 2d.

After Dinner Sleights.

A collection of Interesting Pocket Tricks.

Handsomely Illustrated.

Price **9**d. Post 2d.

The Secrets of Stage Hypnotism, &c., &c.

By **KARLYN** (J.F.Burrows)

Just Published.

Full explanations of all the secrets employed by stage hypnotists, stage electricity "workers," and "bloodless surgeons" are explained in this book. The author is a genuine hypnotist, but at the same time he is fully conversant with the methods adopted by those who only pretend to have the hypnotist's powers. This is the first time that the secrets have ever been divulged in book form, and the book will therefore be interesting both to the lay reader and to the man who is interested in every branch of magic.

Price .. **1/-** net. Postage 2d.

Tricks for Everyone.

Clever Conjuring with Common Objects.

BY **DAVID DEVANT.**

(Of Maskeline and Devant, St. George's Hall, London)

Illustrated with over **150** Photographs showing the complete working of the experiments.

A volume by one of our leading magicians, suitable to the capacity of amateurs, but by no means to be despised by the professional conjuror.

The contents include:—Tricks at the Writing Table—Tricks in the Smoking Room—Tricks at the Work Table—Tricks at the Dinner Table—Tricks in the Garden—Card Tricks—Thought Reading Tricks, etc. Stiff Wrapper, **1**/- post free.

Just Published.

Simple Conjuring Tricks.

By **WILL GOLDSTON**

PROFUSELY ILLUSTRATED.

Part I.—Tricks without Apparatus.
Part II.—Tricks with Apparatus.

This New Book contains a number of simple but effective Conjuring Tricks that anybody can perform. Price **1**/- Postage 2d.

Will Goldston's
Exclusive Magical Secrets

A book essential to all who wish to Excel in Magic—An Epoch Making Book—A book that will repay its cost many times over.

Exclusive Magical Secrets is to the student who specialises in magic what the Encyclopedia Brittanica is to the student concerned with the general field of knowledge. It deals with all the departments of magic, and gives the fullest and most up-to-date particulars about them. The magician who wants information on any point connected with his work has only to refer to Exclusive Magical Secrets and he will find it there. But the number of magicians who will be able to refer to it is a strictly limited one. Only 1,000 copies of the book have been printed. They are being issued on subscription terms, and every subscriber has to sign an undertaking to keep his copy for his own exclusive use.

There are many other books on magic, but none of them can compare with Exclusive Magical Secrets. It is the first real attempt to collect within one cover the best and biggest of modern tricks and illusions; the first real attempt to explain the methods employed by the most successful of the present day magicians specialising in the different branches of the art; the first real attempt to supply a complete and accurate guide to twentieth century magic;

The first real attempt to give the ordinary magician at a normal cost the means of improving the quality, and extending the scope of his work.

How has the attempt succeeded? The answer to this is supplied by the letters which have been received from the first subscribers. Two of them are printed below.

HARRY HOUDINI writes:—"I have just finished reading Exclusive Magical Secrets, and must say that at the price you charge it is an absolute gift. The first white man entering that mysterious country L'Hassa did not find so many exclusive secrets as will the fortunate possessor of your great book. It is, according to my mind a volume of such importance that it will live for ages after you and all the original subscribers have shuffled off this mortal coil. I offer my heartiest congratulations to you and also to the thousand "Knights of Mystery" who are the happy owners of copies of Exclusive Magical Secrets."

PROFESSOR HOFFMANN writes:—I must write to congratulate you upon a genuine success. You have produced a fine book; a regular storehouse of magical ideas. Indeed, it would be difficult to name any other volume displaying such varied results of inventive genius in the magical direction. I trust that the book may prove as successful commercially as it certainly is magically."

Many more such letters have been received from magicians in all parts of the world. The first subscribers have indeed, without exception united in praising the book. They agree that it fulfils every claim made on its behalf by Will Goldston—every inducement held out by him to subscribers.

The majority of the 1,000 copies have already been subscribed for. Early application for the remainder is recommended. A fully illustrated prospectus of the book can be obtained from

Gamages Magical Department.

Attached to it is the form of undertaking as to secrecy, which all subscribers are required to sign. This should be posted, together with the amount of the subscription, to A. W. Gamage, Ltd., Holborn, London, E.C., the Sole Agents, for the distribution of Exclusive Magical Secrets.

Every copy of the book is numbered and embossed in gold with the name of the subscriber.

Catalogue of Books and Tricks Post Free on application.

M

MISCELLANEOUS ASSORTMENT OF MASKS AND NOSES

GAMAGE'S GAUZE MASKS. These Masks are beautifully cool, as, being made of Gauze, they allow perfect ventilation. They can also be folded without danger of breaking them as you would an ordinary cardboard mask. **Postage on any of these Masks, 3d. each.**

577. Old Lady, very pleasant face, painted front of bonnet, real hair, with curls at side. **10½d.**

No. 574. With real hair and frill. **6d.**

979

No. 979. Very funny **Skeleton Mask.** Woolly hair and beard. Very effective and comfortable to wear. Price 1/- Post 3d.

415

No. 415.

The Magician's or Wizard's Hat and Make-up.

Very effective Make-up, strongly reminiscent of the old time sorcerer. The hat is conical and of a peculiar pattern. The face is that of the proverbial "Wise Man," and the hair is long at the back and finishes the mask off beautifully.

Price 1/- Postage 3d.

No. 249.

Red Riding Hood.

Very dainty mask and make-up of the principal character in this popular and pretty fairy tale.

The child-like expression of the mask causes much wonderment. Light and comfortable to wear.

Price **2/6**

Postage 3d.

1093

The "Express" Driver's Mask.

Very strong Gauze, half-mask, with paper hat. There is a gold band round hat with the word "Express" printed. Very bushy hair and whiskers, black.

Price 1/9 Post 3d.

No. 263/8.

Oily Mike.

This mask is highly recommended for character.

Price .. **1/6½**

Postage 3d.

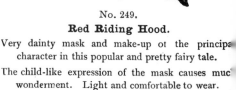

1086

No. 1086.

Tramp's Hat and Make-up.

Very strong and effective part-mask and make-up.

The hat has a tuft of hair protruding through the side, and looks very natural.

Pirce .. **1/4½**

Postage 3d.

No. 6000.

The Ogre's Mask.

Very peculiar and fierce expression.

Large tombstone teeth.

Price 10½d. Post 3d.

969

No. 969.

Skeleton Mask.

With long hair, moustache and big teeth.

Price .. **10½d.**

Postage 2d.

The Continental Jockey.

Half Mask, wax gauze, with striped jockey's cap and long black whiskers. Very good make-up.

Price **1/9**

Postage 3d.

No. B 76BB.

Father-in-Law.

A perfect scream. Only a limited number in stock.

Price .. **1/4½**

Postage 3d.

No. 619.

Tramp Make-up.

This is a very fine wax mask, with real hair, beard and moustache, all of which has the matted, unkempt appearance of a tramp.

Price .. **1/6**

Postage 3d.

109S

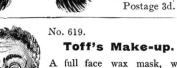

No. 619.

Toff's Make-up.

A full face wax mask, with spectacles, fancy stand-up collar, long nose, real hair and eyebrows. The face has a jolly, funny appearance, which is sure to cause plenty of fun.

Price **1/6** Postage 3d.

No. 750.

The Patch Eye Mask

Very comical Mask of Tramp, with bandage over one eye. Very large nose. Most comical effect.

Price **1/6**

Postage 3d.

No. B 44A.

Half Mask.

Very funny, cool and easy fitting.

Price 10½d.

Postage 3d.

Theatrical Catalogue post free on application.

Wigs and Whiskers.

No. 510.
Barrister Wig (grey).
Price .. **4/-**
Post 3d.

Wigs Made to Order.

No. 509.
Judge's Wig (white).
Price **3/6**
Postage 3d.

—

No. 30.
English design, superior make.
Price **5/-**
Postage 3d.

No. 504.
Fancy Clown.
Four colours in each.
Price **2/6**
Postage **3d.**

No. 508.
Without tuft,
Price **1/9**
Postage 3d.

No. 1a.
Scratch Straight Hair Wig
Suitable for beggar or tramp
Price **2/6** Post 3d

No. 494. Nigger Wigs.
1/- each. **10/6** doz.
No. 495. Corner Man, with tuft,
1/6 each. **16/-** doz.
496. Nigger Wig, with moving tuft, **3/6** each.
497. Bald Nigger Wig, black, white or grey,
2/9 each.

No. 498. Astrachan Nigger Wig, **5/6 ea.** Post 3d.

Nigger Wig with Moving Tuft.
Price **3/6**
Post 3d.

GAMAGE

WHITE COURT WIGS.

All these wigs are made on a wire frame, so that they will instantly adapt and fit any size head.

Enormous Variety of Wigs in Stock.

No. 16. Lady's
Price **2/9**

No. 17. Gent's
Price **3/-**

No. 506.
White Statuary Wig,
Price .. **2/6**
Postage 3d.

Wigs on Stockinette foundation.
Beautifully cool and light.

No. 488.
Plain Scalp, Flesh, White or Black.
Price .. **6d.**
Postage 3d.

No. 491.
Old Man, bald.
Price **6d.** Postage 3d.

No. 489.
Chinese .. .. Price **9**d.
Postage 3d.

Superior qualities,
3/6 7/6 10/6 and **21/-**

—

No. 492.
Old Gent's Bald Front, with parting.
Price **1/6**
Postage 3d.

No. 490.
Clown, **9**d.
Postage 3d.

—

No. 111A.
Just out.
New Pattern Wig.
Nicely finished.
Price **3/9**
Postage 3d.

GAMAGE

JUST PUBLISHED.

Secrets of Scene Painting and Stage Effects.

Secrets of Scene Painting and Stage Effects
by Van Dyke Browne

Profusely illustrated with Black and White Drawings.
Also several Colored Plates.

Price .. **2/6** Net.
Postage 3d.

Theatrical Catalogue post free on application.

German Moustache.

Real Hair, **1/4½**

Manufactured Hair, **4½d.** and **10½d.**

Postage 1d.

Military Moustache.

Real Hair, **1/4½**

Manufactured Hair, **4½d.** and **10½d.**

Postage 1d.

American Cup Beard.

On Gauze.

Real Hair, **3/6**

Manufactured Hair, **1/-**

Postage 3d.

Frenchman's Moustache.

Real Hair, **1/4½**

Manufactured Hair, **4½d.** and **10½d.**

Postage 1d.

The Butler Mutton Chops

Real Hair on Gauze, **3/6**
Manufactured Hair on Wire Frame, **9d.**
Postage 3d.

Tramp Beard.

On Wire Frame.

Real Hair on Gauze, **6/6**

Manufactured Hair, **1/9**

Postage 3d.

The Footman Side Whiskers.

Real Hair on Gauze, **4/3**

Manufactured Hair on Wire Frames, **1/-**

Postage 3d.

Dude Moustache.

Real Hair, **1/4½**

Manufactured Hair, **4½d.** and **10½d.**

Postage 1d.

Middle Age Beard.

On Gauze,

Real Hair, **5/6**

The Dundreary Whiskers.

On Wire Frame.

Real Hair on Gauze, **5 6**

Manufactured Hair, **9d.** and **1/4½**

Postage 3d.

Manufactured Hair, **1/-** and **1/4½**

Postage 3d.

Handsome Moustache.

Real Hair, **1/4½**

Manufactured Hair, **4½d.** and **10½d.**

Postage 1d.

We Stock every kind of Moustaches and Beards.

Theatrical Catalogue post free on application.

Gamage's Grease Paints

With the help of Grease Paints the art of making up has been greatly simplified and made more effective, as they give a much clearer and more life-like appearance to the skin than any other form of make up can possibly do. The lights and shades for making up character parts being more easily graduated.

An additional advantage is, that on account of their greasy nature, they are not easily affected by perspiration. This should recommend their use especially for any arduous character. We have had large quantities of grease paints especially manufactured for us and are thus enabled to supply our numerous customers with the finest grease paint procurable at less than half the usual price. These grease paints are made from the very best materials and guaranteed absolutely pure. They are very soft and easy to use, and require no heating or hard rubbing, at the same time they obtain a good body.

Gamage's Grease Paints are extensively used by the theatrical profession who recommend them very highly.

Grease Paint about actual size. Our Grease Paints are packed in the following colors :—

No. 1. The lightest flesh color made, mostly used by ladies of delicate complexion, also for lightening the complexion when found too dark.

No. 1½. Slightly darker, the favourite colour with ladies, very useful for chambermaid parts.

No. 2. The lightest flesh color used by gentlemen and is also used by ladies.

No. 2½. The most popular colors for all youthful make-ups.

No. 3. The most popular color with gentlemen.

No. 3½. Slightly darker, suitable for men 30-35.

No. 4. Very dark, suitable for countryman, soldier, sailor, etc.

No. 5. A light yellow, for very sallow old man.

No. 5½. For Chinaman, improved if used with No. 7.

No. 6. A yellow flesh tint for old man, darker than No. 5.

No. 7. Brown shade, copper color.

No. 8. Japanese.　　No. 11. Othello.
No. 9. Red Indian.　　No. 12. Negro black.
No. 10. Opera, "Aida."　　No. 13. Mulatto.
No. 14. Moor, North African
No. 15. Indian.
No. 16. Bohemian (gipsy).
No. 17. Deep yellow.
No. 18. Yellow.
No. 19. Carmen, Spain.
No. 20. White, for statuary and clowns faces and heightening the effect of flesh tints.

Light, dark and middle blue, for unshaven chins, or making up old men.

Grey, light and dark, for hollows in old age, also useful for death scenes.

Carmine, vermilion, carmine 1 and 2 for clown's faces, the lips, cheek and burlesque characters. Carmines for dark cheeks. Rose for ladies' cheeks.

Gamage's Grease Paint, **3d.** per stick. Post 1d.
2/9 per dozen. Postage 3d.

Liners.
EVERY SHADE SUPPLIED.

The following are in thin sticks and are used for lining purposes only :—

Black for making very strong wrinkles and darkening the eyebrows; also for the eyelids.

Brown, light and dark, more suitable for wrinkling the face when the characters are near the audience.

Lake, the most popular liner, has a very soft appearance when used for wrinkles, and is most effective and useful for blotches, &c.

Blue, light and dark, also medium blue, for the veins, also round the eyes. A line made with this color round the eyelashes and a second line with the black will be most effective.

Carmines, for lining round mouth and face for character parts.

Grey, light and dark, for shading the wrinkles on face, and for the high lights.

Long Liners. 3d. per stick. Postage 1d.

Gamage's Special Short Liners, the same length as a stick of grease paint.
Price 2d. each.　　Postage 1d.

 Actual size. Small Liner.

No. 153.
Specially prepared
Spirit Gum,
for Theatrical purposes.

The best spirit gum, specially manufactured, will adhere strongly in the hottest weather.

Price .. 4½d. bottle.
Postage 1d.
In metal screw stoppered bottle, 10½d. Postage 2d.

No. 154.
Specially made Crepe Hair. For making false moustache, etc., in all colors. 4½d. per yd. Post 1d.

No. 155. **Moustache Fixture.**

For hiding the moustache in powder costume pieces, etc. Also so that you may make up over it. This article may also be used in place of cosmetique.
Price 4½d. Postage 1d.

No. 152. **Gamage's Cocoa Butter.**
Special Manufacture.
An article which is universally used for effectually and quickly removing grease paint, spirit gum, and all make-up and colour from the face. A cooling and health application.
Price 4½d. or 4/- per doz.
Large size 9d. per stick.
8/- per doz. Postage extra.

No. 156. Joining Paste.
For joining the bald fronts of wigs to the forehead
Price **4½d.**　　Postage 1d.

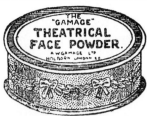

No. 157
GAMAGE'S POWDER.

The very best powder that it is possible to use for the stage or toilet, it is specially made to absorb grease and moisture. After making up with grease paint it is necessary to powder over the face to finish the make up, and thus give the face a very natural appearance. This powder is the best powder to use for this purpose. Gamage's powder is of a higher quality than any other make, and is sold at a very low price.

In addition to being the finest theatrical powder on the market, it cannot be surpassed as an ordinary complexion powder. In three shades, white, cream, and pink.

Price 3d. per box.　Postage 1d.
Highly perfumed, 4½d. per box. Postage 1d.
Large box .. 8½d. " " 2d.

No. 158. **Harefeet.** Specially manufactured

Mounted with handle. Price, 10½d. Post 1d.
Superior quality .. ., 1/3 ,,

No. 159. **Nose Paste.** Price 4½d. Post 1d.

No. 3001. **MAKE-UPS, Gamage's Special Nigger Black.**
Always Ready for Use.
After much careful study and experiment we have succeeded in producing a really good nigger black. This nigger black is packed in tubes, and the great advantage of this is that it is always in a liquid condition and applied more easily than any other preparation. An additional advantage is that it washes off quite easily with a little soap and cold water. We should esteem it a great favour if our numerous customers will give it a trial as we feel certain they will never afterwards use any other.

Price only 4½d. per tube.　Postage 1d.

GAMAGE'S CLEANER.

No. 157. Grease Paint Remover.

Price **4½d.** per box.　Postage 1d.

Fuller's Earth. Burnt Cork, Prepared Whiting, Burnt Umber, Carmine, Blue, Antimony, Mongolian, and all powder make-ups.
. Price 4½d. per box. Postage 1d.

MAKE-UPS.

No. 788.   The Handy Make-up Box.

Strong Metal Make-up Box, with tray to lift in or out for holding paints, has a separate division for liners, space beneath tray will hold powders, towels, and one or two wigs.

Price fitted ..	..	8/6 Postage 8d.
,, fitted with Leichner's Grease Paints,	14 6	
,, empty ..	..	2/11 Postage 6d.

No. 790.   The Gamage
Expanding Make-up Box.

Closed.

Open.

Above box, Japanned, Empty, **5/6**   Filled, **15/6**
Postage 8d.

This box opens up in 3 tiers with support at back, top tier has separate divisions for holding sticks of paint with shallow tray at side for liners.

Second tray will hold folding mirror, haresfoot, etc. Space below will carry wigs, towel, etc. This is the cheapest and most complete make-up box offered to the public and contains every article required for successful making-up; including a neat folding mirror.

No. 791.
The Lady's Make-up Box.

If required for a lady the boxes can be had at same price when Creme Imperatrice, Patches, Curling Tongs, Hair-pins, and other articles are substituted for Joining Paste, Crepe, Hair, Gum, etc.   Price .. **15/6**   Postage 8d.

If Desired   Customers may have Make-up Boxes fitted with goods of their own selection.

No. 787.
Pocket Grease Paint Case.

A flat black enamelled box which may be carried in the pocket, will pack flat in a bag, and contains 12 sticks of grease paint and liners, and has separate divisions for each stick.
Price—Filled, **3/4¼**   Unfilled, **1/4½**   Postage 3d.

No. 100.   Burnt Umber.

This specially prepared powder is absolutely pure, and is highly recommended by us for theatrical purposes, **4½**d.   Postage 1d.

No. 101.
Carmine

A specially prepared highly-coloured powder, used extensively for make-up purposes.
Price .. **4½**d.
Postage 1d.

No. 104.   Prepared Whitning.

This splendid preparation has been specially manufactured for us, and is of very best quality.

Price .. **4½**d.
Postage 1d.

No. 105.   Burnt Cork.

Of high-class manufacture, used largely by nigger minstrels of every class,
4½d. Post 1d.

Ruddy Rouge.

No. 106.

A soft and delicate preparation for the face.
Price **4½**d. box
Post 1d.

No. 102.

Eyebrow Pencils.

In metal case.
Black or Brown.
Price **4½**d.
Postage 1d.

No. 103.

Ema l Noir.

To stop out teeth for old men characters, etc.
Extensively used by actors and comedians of all classes.
Price **1/-**   Postage 1d.

Gamage's Celebrated Liquid White and Pink.

Used by leading Professionals for beautifying the skin.

1/- size bottle	..	**8½**d.
6d. size ,,	..	**4½**d.

Postage 3d. and 4d.

No. 789.   Spirit Gum Bottles.

This screw-stoppered gum bottle, including brush, is an article we can recommend.

No cork is required and the brush is always moist.

The advantage of having one of these bottles is easily realized (with gum), **10½**d. Post 2d.

No. 792.   Folding Mirror.

A compact folding mirror in a neat wooden frame. Can be easily carried in pocket.
Marvellous Value.   Price **1/3**   Postage 2d.

No. 107.   Rouge Pads.

These pads are extensively used by theatrical ladies, and are absolutely the finest value obtainable. Very useful for putting rouge, powders, etc., on the face.

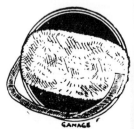

Small	..	**4½**d.
Large	..	**9**d.

Postage 1d.

Theatrical Catalogue post free on application.

Air-Float TALCUM POWDER SPECIALITIES

The "Air-Float" Talcum Face and Toilet Powder Specialities have the highest reputation in the United States of America, and they promise to acquire a similar reputation in this country. The basis of these powders is, as the name suggests, "Talc."

"There is," says the Company manufacturing these "Air-Float Powders," "just one mine in the United States producing Talc fit for use for toilet purposes—that mine is located right here where we are—that mine is ours. From that mine comes the Talc we use—it is pure as freshly fallen snow—free from iron, aluminium, feldspar, or any other foreign ingredients."

"One very important part of the process we alone employ. The Talc is first thoroughly cleansed by a strong stream of filtered water running through nickelled pipes at a tremendous pressure. It is then crushed and reduced to fine pebble form in one mill, finely pulverised in a second, and finished into impalpable powder in a third. After this treatment the fine particles—and only the finest—are allowed to literally float in the air. This is like vapour—the lower grades cannot float so high, and fall to the ground—and as it so floats it is drawn away by air suction pipes to be carefully gathered, delicately perfumed, and packed in distinctly attractive packages. There is nothing like 'Air-Float' in all the world for fineness, purity and excellence, so much so that it can be used with perfect safety even on the skin of the youngest and most delicate infant."

A bold announcement this, but not in our opinion too bold. We have tried the Talcum Powder Specialities, and have found them to be of supreme excellence. They are most suitable for ordinary toilet purposes, and also the best for make-up purposes. Many public entertainers of our acquaintance have suffered from the use of badly prepared face powders.

The ill effects of these cannot be exaggerated. The complexion may be injured, may be made permanently unsightly, may even be ruined. All risk of this is avoided by the use of the "Air-Float" Talcum Powders. They will not impair the most delicate complexion. Indeed their effect is in all cases guaranteed to be advantageous. Particularly to be recommended are the "Air-Float" Talcum Flesh Tint Powders. They will suit everybody who has to make up for stage purposes. The tint is perfect, the powder a delight to use.

STEIN & Co.'s

**World Famous
Theatrical MAKE-UPS.**

Stein's Alpine Mascaro.
ONCE TRIED, ALWAYS USED.
Price **1/6**   Postage 2d.

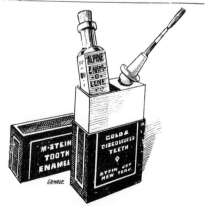

Stein's E-nam-o-lene Tooth Enamel
For whitening gold or discoloured teeth.
Price **1/-**   Postage 2d.

STEIN'S
Moist Rouge.

The most perfect Rouge invented.
Absolutely pure.

Highly recommended

Price . **1/-**
Postage 2d.

Stein's Rouges.
Price **10**d. each.
Postage 1d.

Stein's Lip Stick.
Price **7**d. Post 1d.

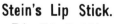

Eye Pencil.
Price **4½**d. Post 1d.

Giant Sticks
OF
Grease Paints.

American Artistes playing in Great Britain will be pleased to learn that we are now carrying complete stock of Stein's Grease Paints Giant Sticks.

Price .. **1/-**
Postage 2d.

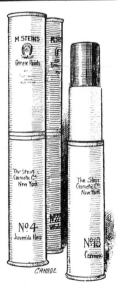

The Regent Skin Cream.

Of all Skin Creams the Regent is the most popular.
Used by thousands of professionals.

The most perfect Skin Cream invented.

Price .. **1/-**
P. stage 2d.

Santa Claus.

This Costume is made up in cheap materials, but has the desired effect.

Complete Outfit, but not including Boots and Bag,
Price **30/-**
35/-
42/-
To **£5 5 0**
Carriage 1/- extra.

Wigs.
2/6 6/6
10/6 21/-

Beards.
3/6 6/6
Postage 4d.

Plate of Assorted Fruit. Price **2/6** Post 9d.

Cheese, with Plate. Price .. **1/-**
Poached Egg on Plate .. .. **1/-** Post 4d.

Short Hair Beard.
Real Hair	.. ..	**10/**
Good Imitation	..	**4/6**
Third quality..	..	**1/**

Postage 3d.

Stockinette Marks.
Very useful to save making-up the face; they can be slipped on in an instant and they also have the advantage of comprising Mask, Wig, Whiskers, etc. in one.

Latest Novelties for the Table.
VERY REALISTIC.
Each Article contains a Surprise
Pastries .. Assorted, 2½d., 3d., 3½d. each. Post 1d.
Fruits .. Pear, Peach, Apple, Orange, **8d.** each. ,, 1d.
Ditto ditto ditto **7/3** doz. .. 4d.
Nuts .. Walnuts **2/9** doz. Chestnuts .. **2/9** doz.
Fish .. Mussels .. .. **2/4** doz. Post 3d.
6 in. French Fish .. .. **1/-** each. ,, 2d.
Cheese on Plate .. **1/6** and **2/-** per plate. Post 4d.

Plate and Half-doz. Mixed Nuts.
Price .. **1/6** Post 6d.

They carry everything but the smell.

Potatoes	.. each	**6d.**
Bananas	,,	**6d.**
Grapes	per bunch	**4d.**
Radishes	,,	**6d.**
Oranges	.. each	**6d.**
Assorted Sweets ..	per plate	**1/-**
Poached Egg on Toast ..	..	**1/-**
Sausage and Mashed		**1/-**
Bacon and Egg	..	**1/-**

Postage 4d.

No. E. 337.
Father Xmas
LONG BEARD, WHITE HAIR AND EYEBROWS.
Price .. **3/3**
Post 3d.

Noses, in three sizes: Large, Medium and Small. Price 2d. & 3d. each. Post

Stockinette Animal Mask
OUR PRICE, **3/6** Postage 3d.

No. E. 750.
Indians,
With War Paint and Feathers.
Price .. **4/3**
Post 3d.

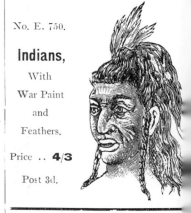

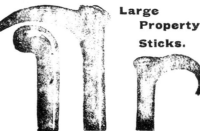

Large Property Sticks.

89. Big Stick, with strap for carrying over shoulder, **1/6**
690. Big Stick with staghorn handle **1/-**
691. With knotty handle **1/-**
692. Slightly hooked knot handle **1/-**
Postage and Packing 4d.

Plate of Mixed Sweets. Price .. **1/-** Post 6d.

THEATRICAL CATALOGUE
POST FREE ON APPLICATION.

Theatrical Goods
CANNOT be sent
ON APPROVAL
OR EXCHANGED.

SCENERY FOR THE DRAWING-ROOM AND STAGE

With a view to obviate the great difficulty experienced by Amateurs (particularly in country houses) in obtaining Scenery, etc., to fix in a Drawing Room, and then only by considerable outlay for hire and great damage caused to walls, we have decided to keep a **Series of Coloured Scenes,** mounted on Canvas, which are ready for immediate use, or they can be had unmounted on thirty sheets of strong paper, and can be joined together or pasted on canvas or wood, according to requirements. Full directions, with diagrams showing exact size of BACK SCENES, BORDERS AND WINGS, can be had FREE on application.

Foliage.

This is a sheet of paper on which foliage is drawn, which can be repeated and cut in any shape that is required. It is kept in two sizes. Per sheet

Small size, 30 in. by 20 in. **8d.**
Large „ 40 in. by 30 in. **1/-**

Street.

This scene can be purchased in any size. It is not kept mounted. It consists of brickwork, coping stone, windows and door. The above represents the back scene only; wings can be made by using a door each side, with brickwork above; the border can be made with blue paper. The brickwork will also be found very useful for making garden walls, so often required in plays.

Brickwork, 40 in. by 30 in. ... per sheet **1/-**
Coping-stone, 40 in. by 30 in. (making 28 ft.) „ **1/-**
Exterior Door, comprising 3 sheets, 7 ft. by 3 ft. ... **3/-**
Exterior Window „ 2 „ 6½ ft. by 2½ ft. **2/6**
Blue Paper, 30 in. by 20 in. ... per sheet **2d.**

Tree Trunk.

This is to be used with the Foliage sheets and placed at the bottom of the scene.

Price and size same as Foliage.

Garden.

Kept in 2 sizes. The size of the back scene of the smaller one is nearly 10ft. long and 6½ft. high, and extends with the wings and border to 15ft. long and 8ft. high. The back scene of the large one is 13 ft. long and 9 ft. high, and extends with the wings and border to 20 ft. long and 11⅓ ft. high. It is not necessary to have the scene the height of the room, as blue paper to represent sky is usually hung at the top. Price, complete:—

Small size with Wings and Border, unmounted ... **20**
Do. do. do. mounted ... **50**
Large size, do. do. unmounted ... **25**
Do. do. do. mounted ... **70/-**
Blue Paper, 20 in. by 30 in. per sheet .. **2d.**

Canvas.

Canvas for scene painting, drop scenes and so forth, very strong (two yds. wide), per yard, **1/9**

All canvas, calico, or other material used for scenery should be sewn in horizontal strips. This prevents tucking when rolled up.

Any Woodwork for these scenes can easily be made by a local carpenter.

Proscenium and Drop Scene.

Proscenium.

A most effective Proscenium can be formed by utilising the paper made for this purpose. Three pieces of wood are merely required, shaped according to the above design and covered with the paper, the Proscenium having the appearance of puffed satin panels in gold frames, with Shakespeare Medallion in the centre.

Puffed Satin Paper, light blue, 20 by 30 in., per sht. **6d.**
Imitation Gold Bordering, making 14 ft. „ **6d.**
Shakespearean Medallion, 18 in. diameter **1/-**

Drop Scene.

The picture shewn above is an illustration of this scene. It comprises four sheets of paper, which are to be pasted in the centre of any sized canvas that may be requisite for the Drop Curtain. Size 6½ by 5 ft. Price ... **7/6**

Wood.

Kept in two sizes, same as the Garden Scene, and at similar prices.

French Window.

Consisting of four sheets of paper, representing a window containing four large ornamental frosted glass panes with coloured glass round.

Size 6½ ft. high by 5 ft.

Price, complete **7/6**

Interior Doors.

These comprise three sheets of paper each, and can be had either for Drawing Room or Cottage purposes. For EXTERIOR DOOR, see under Street Scene.
Size 7 ft. by 3 ft. Price, complete ... **3/-**

Calico.

Calico to mount the above scenes (62 in. wide)
Per yard .. **11½d.**

Transparent Gelatine Papers.

19 in. by 23 in., in the following colours: White, Green, Pink, Blue, Red, Lemon, Orange & Violet, **1/-** per sheet

Interior Window.

This is a parlour window, formed with two sheets of paper and could be made practicable to slide up and down by mounting on two pieces of wood, allowing one to groove into the other at the sides. The introduction of curtains each side would make it very effective.

For EXTERIOR WINDOW, see under Street scene.

Size 3ft. in. by 4 ft. Price, complete ... **2/6**

Cottage.

This is kept in the large size only. In the centre is a door, leading outside. On the left centre is a rustic fireplace, and the right centre is a window. On the wings are painted shelves, etc., to complete the scene. The above is a representation of this scene with one set of wings only (not a box scene), but a box scene can be made by purchasing the extra set of wings

Prices and size same as Drawing Room Scene.

Cottage or Drawing Room Fireplace.

This is made with two sheets of paper. The fire is lighted, but should this not be required, a fire-paper can be hung over it. It will be found most useful in many farces wherein a character has to climb up a chimney and many plays where a fireplace is indispensable By purchasing a door, window, and fireplace, any ordinary room scene could easily be constructed with the addition of some wall paper. Size 3 by 4½ ft. Price, complete, **3/-**

Drawing Room.

Only kept in the large size. The back scene is 13 ft. long and 9 ft. high, and extends with the wings and borders to 20 ft. long and 11⅓ ft. high. In the centre is a French window leading down to the ground. On the left wing is a fireplace with mirror above, and on the right wing is an oil painting. The whole scene is tastefully ornamented and beautifully coloured, forming a most elegant picture. The above is a representation of a box scene, consisting of 38 sheets of paper, the extra sheets being used for the doors each side.

Back Scene, Border and 1 set of Wings, unmounted. **25/-**
Do. do. do. mounted, **70/-**
Back Scene, Border with 2 sets of Wings, as above, to form box scene ... unmounted, **35/-**
Do. do. do mounted, **90/-**

Theatrical Catalogue post free on application.

ENTERTAINMENTS OF·EVERY·DESCRIPTION· PROVIDED

Artistes of every description for every style of Entertainment. **NONE** but First-class Talent whose performances are well known by Mr. WILL GOLDSTON, the Departmental Manager. **THE FEES** quoted will be found **LESS** than any other agency in London. **SPECIAL ENTERTAINMENT LIST POST FREE** on request.

H. HEWSON-BROWN,
The Popular Dicken's Impersonater & Entertainer

STANLEY COLLINS
England's Favourite CONJURER and VENTRILOQUIST.

ACCOUNTS will be forwarded by post day after performance, and cheques should be remitted by return, as Entertainments are provided strictly on the CASH BASIS.

When an Entertainment is ordered, it cannot be cancelled except under the following conditions : If cancelled or postponed two clear days before date of Entertainment, half fees will be charged ; and if postponed and held within one month of original date, three-quarter fee will be charged in addition to half fee already paid.

SPECIAL QUOTATIONS where repetition is desired for BAZAARS, FETES, etc.

CLIENTS are requested to note that Artistes should not under any circumstances leave their cards or accept orders other than through the AGENCY.

Should Clients wish to re-book Artistes they will kindly send order to HOLBORN, where it will receive prompt attention.

THE FEES include all expenses within a radius of 4 miles from Holborn and not more than half mile from local station.

Entertainments outside above radius will be especially quoted for, and inclusive prices given.

PUNCTUALITY is expected and strictly observed by the Artistes, it is respectfully intimated that clients have claim upon the performers time only so long as engagement specifies.

A. W. GAMAGE, LTD., cannot be held responsible for any delay in the arrival of Artistes which may be caused by fogs, trains or any unforseen circumstances.

Should Artistes be unable to return to London same night, reasonable accommodation and conveyance to and from station must be provided, in addition to fee quoted.

It is respectfully requested (unless otherwise arranged) that no payments be made to Artistes.

Entertainment List Post Free on application. ESTIMATES FREE.

All enquireies respecting Entertainments should be addressed to
Department Manager : WILL GOLDSTON, Entertainment Department.
Telephone ; No. 2700 Holborn.   Telegraphic Address ; "Gamage, Holborn" London.

"WILKIE"   The Greatest of all Humanet Artistes.

Billiard Tables and Accessories.

BILLIARD TABLES
Special Half
and
Three-Quarter Size
Tables.

BILLIARD TABLES
suitable for
CLUBS,
MISSIONS,
etc.

.G. 1. 6 ft. Billiard Table, solid mahogany frame on stained and polished hardwood stand, complete with 3 ivory balls, 2 cues, rest, marking board, chalk, spirit level and rules, complete .. .. Price **£7 0 0**

,, 2. A superior mahogany Billiard Table, as above on 4 solid mahogany turned and carved legs, fitted with low, fast, frost-proof cushions, covered with West of England billiard cloth, best thick Bangor slate bed, with the following accessories : 6 cues, rest with brass head, 30 in. solid mahogany marking board, rules, 2 metal chalk cups, billiard iron and shoe and 3 $1\frac{7}{8}$ in. ivory balls. Price **12 18 6**

,, 3. A 7 ft. by 3 ft. 6 in. do. do. do. do. do. Price **15 15 0**

,, 4. An 8 ft. by 4 ft. do. do. do. do. 2 in. ivory balls do. **18 12 6**

,, 4* 8 ft. by 4 ft. mahogany Billiard Table, covered with West of England Cloth, $1\frac{5}{8}$ extra thick slates, 6 9 in. solid mahogany legs. A very massive table, nothing better made, complete with accessories .. .. Price **30 0 0**

,, 5. A 9 ft. by 4 ft. 6 in. on 6 in. legs, 6 cues, set 2 in. balls, 2 short rests, half butt and rest, marking board, 4 chalk cups, and framed rules, complete .. .. .. Price **29 10 0**

,, . A 10 ft. by 5 ft. do. do. $2\frac{1}{8}$ in. balanced ivory balls, cue rack, brush, holland cover, etc. do. **37 0 0**

All TABLES
Delivered and
Fixed
FREE IN
LONDON.

General Repairs
a Speciality.
Experienced
Workmen sent to
all parts.
Estimates Free

perior Full-size Billiard Table in mahogany, specially finished throughout, on 8 solid mahogany fluted legs, bolted slate bed, fitted with extra low, fast, silent, frost-proof cushions, covered with good West of England cloth, and including 1 set balanced $2\frac{1}{16}$ in. ivory balls, 6 cues, cue rack with brass springs, marking board to match table, long and short butt and rests with brass heads, 1 5 ft. rest, iron and shoe, brush, holland cover, flush pocket plates, 6 chalk cups and rules complete. Built expressly for Working Men's Clubs, Institutes, &c. .. Price **£47 0 0**

perior Full-size Billiard Table, in mahogany, specially finished throughout, on 8 solid mahogany fluted legs, with panels, knees, $1\frac{1}{2}$ in. thick Bangor slate bed fitted with our extra low, fast, silent, frost-proof cushions, covered with good West of England billiard cloth, and including the following accessories : 1 set of ivory balls $2\frac{1}{8}$ in. balanced, 12 cues best selected ash, cue rack for 12 cues with brass springs, marking board for billiards, large size to match table, long and short butts, long and short rests with brass heads, 15 ft. rest with brass head, 4 brass rest supports fitted to table, iron and shoe, brush, holland cover, framed rules of billiards, flush pocket plates, stout pocket nets, and 6 brass chalk cups .. .. Price **52 0 0**

ssive Full-size Billiard Table, in mahogany, specially finished throughout, 8 turned and fluted solid mahogany legs, with panels to knees, arved brackets, $1\frac{1}{2}$ in. thick best Bangor slate bed, fitted with our extra low, fast, silent, frost-proof cushions, covered with superfine West f England billiard cloth, and including the following accessories : 1 set of best ivory balls, $2\frac{1}{8}$ in. balanced, 12 cues best selected ash, cue ack for 12 cues with brass springs, handsome mahogany marking board large size to match table, long and short butts, long and short rests ith brass heads, 1 5 ft. rest with brass head, 4 brass rest supports fitted to table, iron and shoe, brush, holland cover, framed rules of billiards, ush pocket plates, stout pocket nets, and 6 brass chalk cups .. .. Price **57 10 0**

perb and very massive Full-size Billiard Table in very fine mahogany, 8 handsome reeded legs, 8 in. diameter with reeded panels on the knees nd carved brackets, frame, extra thick Bangor slate bed covered with fine quality West of England billiard cloth, fitted with our extra low, ast, silent, frost-proof cushions and including the following accessories : 1 set of ivory balls, $2\frac{1}{8}$ in. best balanced, 12 butted cues, cue rack or 12 cues for brass springs, marking board for billiards large size to match table, long and short butts, long and short rests with brass heads, ft. ash rest with brass head, 4 brass rest supports fitted to table, iron and shoe, brush, holland cover, framed rules of billiards, flush pocket lates, best cord bottomless pockets, and 6 automatic chalk cups .. .. Price **63 10 0**

BILLIARD DEPARTMENT.

Our Speciality.

6 by 3 ft. mahogany frame Billiard Table, covered with good quality cloth. Set of Ivory Balls, 2 Cues, Rest, Marker, Chalk, Level, etc. For standing on dining table.

£4 4 0

Miniature Slate Bed Billiard Tables.

For Standing on Dining Table.

Fitted with adjustable Screw Legs for levelling. Rubber Cushions, Ivory Balls, 2 Cues, Marking Board, Chalk, Spirit Level, Rules, etc.

Outside Measure.	Size of Balls.	Price.		Outside Measure.	Size of Balls.	Price.	
4 ft. 4 in. by 2 ft. 4 in.	.. 1½ in. ..	£3 6 6		6 ft. 4 in. by 3 ft. 4 in. ..	1⅝ in. ..	£7 15 0	C quality
5 ,, 4 ,, ,, 2 ,, 10 ,,	.. 1⅝ ,, ..	4 6 6		7 ,, 4 ,, ,, 3 ,, 10 ,, ..	1⅞ ,, ..	7 10 0	A ,,
6 ,, 4 ,, ,, 3 ,, 4 ,,	.. 1¾ ,, ..	4 15 0	A quality	7 ,, 4 ,, ,, 3 ,, 10 ,, ..	1⅞ ,, ..	9 10 0	C ,,
6 ,, 4 ,, ,, 3 ,, 4 ,,	.. 1¾ ,, ..	6 0 0	B ,,				

Carriage extra. 10/- charged for cases which is refunded on their return carriage paid.
Rests supplied with Tables, 6 ft. and upwards.

COMBINED BILLIARD AND DINING TABLES.

THE REVERSIBLE.

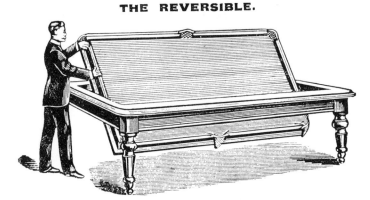

Showing manner of Reversing.

These Tables are of simple construction and of the finest quality material, they are fitted with screw toes, whereby a perfect level can be obtained, covered with superior West of England Cloth. Best rubber cushions, ivory balls, cues, etc.

Billiard Table.	Dining Table.		Price.
6 by 3 ft.	7 by 4 ft.	Stained and Polished ..	£12 12 0
7 ,, 3 ft. 6 in.	8 ,, 4 ft. 6 in.	,, ,,	16 10 0
8 ,, 4 ft.	9 ,, 5 ft.	,, ,,	22 7 6
6 ,, 3 ft.	7 ,, 4 ft.	Mahogany ..	18 10 0
7 ,, 3 ft. 6 in.	8 ,, 4 ft. 6 in.	,,	22 12 6
8 ,, 4 ft.	9 ,, 5 ft.	,,	28 0 0

These Tables to order only, sample on show in Showroom. Carriage extra.

THE "IDEAL" TABLE.

In solid Mahogany, Walnut or Oak.   To order only.

6 by 3 ft.	..	Suitable for a Room 14 by 11 ft. ..	..	£19 0 0
7 ,, 3 ft. 6 in.	,,	,, ,, ,,	15 ,, 11 ft. 6 in.	25 5 0
8 ,, 4 ft.	,,	,, ,, ,,	16 ,, 12 ft. ..	30 0 0
9 ,, 4 ft. 6 in.	,,	,, ,, ,,	17 ,, 12 ft. 6 in. ..	35 0 0

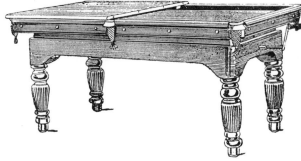

THE "IDEAL."

The distinguishing feature of the "Ideal" is the extreme ease with which the change from billiard to dining table—or *vice versa*—is effected. merely working handle (see illustration above) the adjustment to correct height can be quickly made by one person, and, even in the largest size, no exertion is required. The mechanism employed is of the simplest and not liable to get out of order. Recommended where an inexpensive but reliable and accurate table is required.

SPECIFICATION.—Made in stained hardwood (polished any colour) with slate bed, low and fast rubber cushions, good West of England cloth, improved invisible pocket plates, and stout cord nets, turned legs with adjusting toes. **Metal** raising rollers. Tables with wood raising slides can be supplied to order at cheaper rates. Complete with accessories as follow: 3 ivory or Crystalate balls, 2 ash cues, marking board, rest, spirit level, chalks, Rules, Extra cue tips and waters.

5 by 2 ft. 6 in.,	£12 2 6	6 by 3 ft.,	£13 17 6	7 by 3 ft. 6 in.,	
8 by 4 ft.,	£22 15 0	9 by 4 ft. 6 in.,	£27 17 6		

All prices include delivery in London or packing for country and abroad. Any of the above tables can be polished to match existing furniture, colour pattern should be sent with order. The billiard table can be made with pockets for playing the cannon game.

All Tables Delivered and Fixed Free in London.   **Cases and Carriage Extra.**

BILLIARD TABLE DEPT.—*continued.*

A Quality.

lished Mahogany Folding Bagatelle ›ard, lined green cloth, complete with ›, mace, bridge, nine ivory balls, rules and pegs.

Sizes.	Price.
t. by 15 in., 1 in. balls ..	**31**/-
t. 6 in. by 16 in., 1 in. balls	**35**/-
t. by 18 in., 1⅛ in. balls ..	**40**/-
t. by 21 in., 1¼ in. balls ..	**54/6**

B Quality.

lished Mahogany Folding Bagatelle ›ard, lined with super. green cloth, fitted h india rubber cushions, well finished, nplete with cue, mace, bridge, nine ivory balls, rules and pegs.

Sizes.	Price.
. by 20 in., 1⅛ in. balls	.. **50**/-
. by 22 in., 1⅜ in. balls	.. **66/6**
. by 25 in., 1½ in. balls	.. **86**/-

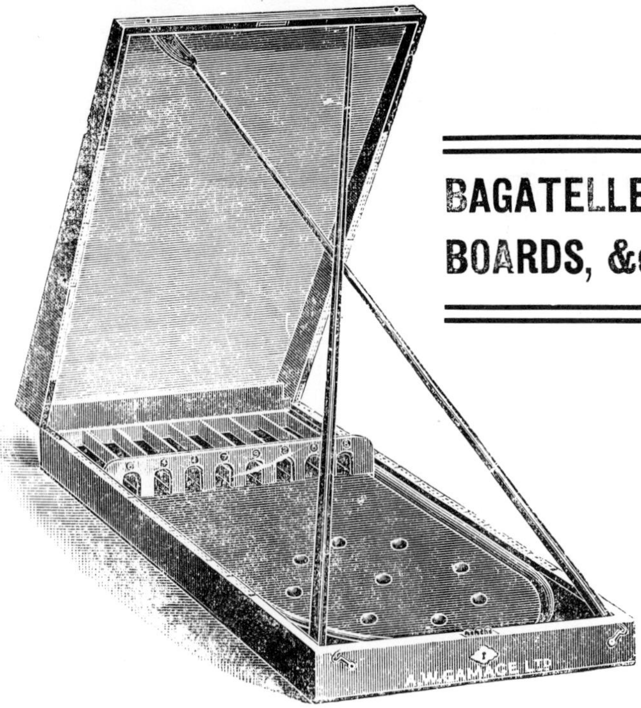

BAGATELLE BOARDS, &c

C Quality.

Best Polished Solid Mahogany Folding Bagatelle Board, lined best green cloth, best india rubber cushions, complete with nine best ivory balls, cue, mace, bridge, pegs and rules.

Sizes.	Price.
6 ft. by 20 in., 1⅛ in. balls ..	**63**/-
7 ft. by 22 in., 1⅜ in. balls ..	**77/6**
8 ft. by 25 in., 1⅝ in. balls ..	**95**/-

Special Quality.

Size 9 ft. by 30 in., 1¾ in. balls.

Price .. **£6 19 6**

Panel Top Boards.

Sizes.	Price.
7 ft. by 24 in., 1½ in. balls ..	**84**/-
8 ft. by 27 in., 1¾ in. balls ..	**126**/-

Carriage and packing extra on all Bagatelle Boards. 7/6 charged for cases, which is refunded on their return carriage paid.

TABLE BILLIARDS.

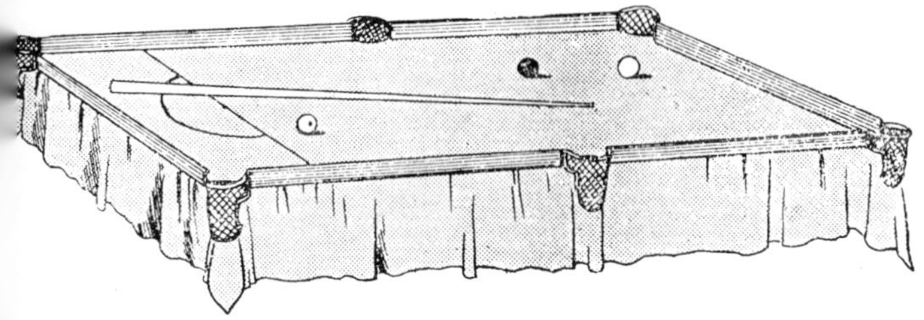

adaptation to an ordinary dining table, the ordinary table cover forming billiard cloth. Can be fitted in a few minutes to any table.

G0. Containing 6 pockets to screw on to table, set of stout linen bands to form cushions, 2 cues, rest, boxwood balls, each .. **10/6**

G1. Complete in box, containing a set of billiard pockets with india-rubber fittings, a set of boxwood billiard balls, 2 polished ash cues 38 in. long, cue rest, a set of stout linen bands with buckles, markers, marking board and French chalk **15/9**
Suit a table not exceeding 8 ft. by 4 ft. 6 in.

G1x. Ditto with composition balls **21**/-
Suit a table not exceeding 12 ft. by 6 ft.

G1a. Ditto, in polished box, extra quality ivorine balls, 4 ft. cues, etc. **33**/-
Suit a table not exceeding 12 ft. by 6 ft.
Carriage extra.

Special Small Size Billiard Tables.

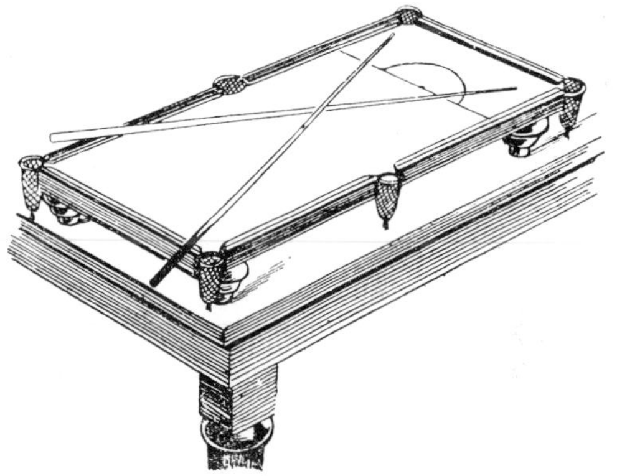

3 ft. 4 in. by 1 ft. 9 in. solid mahogany frame, slate bed, covered with billiard cloth, on short adjusting legs, complete with marking board, 3 ivory balls, 2 cues, indiarubber cushions, spirit level, rules, chalk, &c.

Price .. **50**/- Cases 5/- returnable. Carriage extra.

›EN SLATE BED BAGATELLE BOARDS.

Suitable for Clubs, Missions, etc.

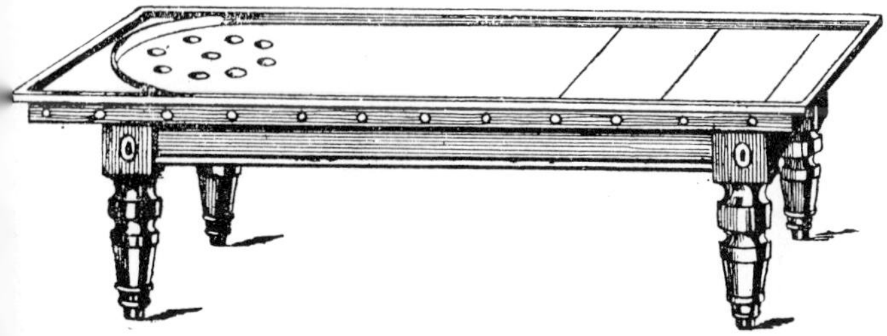

.e Tables are made of thoroughly seasoned wood, best Bangor slates, fitted best rubber cushions and cloths, including 4 cues, 9 balls, marking board, , etc. Complete with Stand as illustrated.

8 ft. by 2 ft. 9 in., 1¾ in. balls ..	..	**£8**	**15**	**0**
9 ft. by 3 ft. 3 in., 1⅞ in. balls ..	..	**10**	**0**	**0**
10 ft. by 3 ft. 4 in., 1⅞ in. balls ..	..	**11**	**2**	**6**

2 Pockets, **12/6** extra Carriage extra.

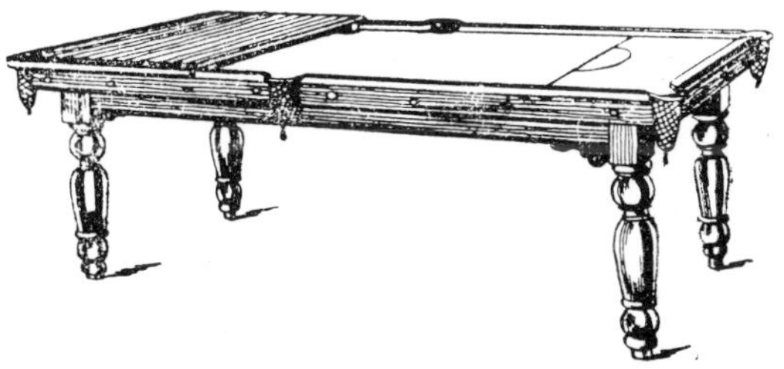

The Holborn Combination Billiard and Dining Table.

Instantaneous Action.

Perfectly rigid when in use, is quite portable, and can be quickly stored away if necessary, no expert knowledge being required to fix it. Made in hardwood, stained and polished any colour, with mahogany cushion rails, slate bed, best frost-proof cushions, West of England cloth. Complete with two cues, ivory balls, rules, spirit level, marking board, &c. To order only. Carriage extra.

6 by 3 ft., **£9 17 6** 7 by 3 ft. 6 in., **£12 17 6** 8 by 4 ft., **£16 12 0**

BILLIARDS, BAGATELLE, POOL AND PYRAMID BALLS.

Pool Balls.

1¾ in. Boxwood Pool Balls with Markers, box complete .. **7/6**
1¾ in. Ivory Pool Balls .. .. **5**/- each **60**/- set
1⅞ in. ,, ,, ... **6**/- ,, **72**/- ,,
2 in. ,, ,, ... **7**/- ,, **84**/- ,,
2 1/16 in. and 2⅛ in. Ivory Pool Balls, from **7/6** to **21**/- per ball

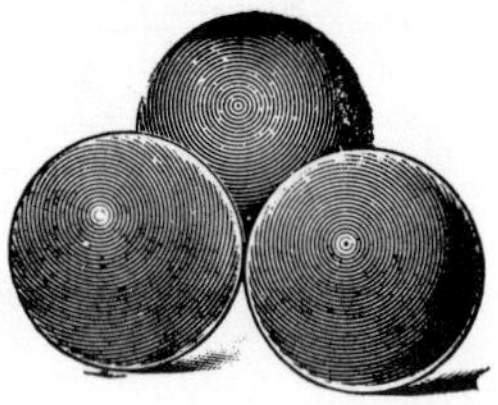

Pyramid Balls.

1¾ in. Boxwood Pyramid Balls **10/6**
1⅞ in. ,, ,, ... **11/6**
Combination Pool and Pyramid Balls .. **11/6** and **12/6**
Snooker Sets, 22 Balls .. **16/6** and **17/6**
Pyramid Triangles, 1¾ and 1⅞ in. **2/6**
,, ,, 2 and 2 1/16 in. **3**/-

Bagatelle Balls.

Per Set	1	1⅛	1¼	1⅜	1½	1⅝	1¾	1⅞ in.
Ivory ..	**14/6**	**16/6**	**18/6**	**22/6**	**27/6**	**30/-**	**35/-**	**45/-**
Crystalate or Bonzoline	**5/3**	**6/9**	**9/6**	**12/6**	**16/6**	**19/6**	**22/6**	**25/6**
Boxwood	**2/6**	**2/6**	**3/-**	**3/9**	**4/3**	**4/9**	**5/9**	—

Boxwood Balls, ⅞ in. **3/3** 1 in. **3/6** the set of 20. Postage extra under 10/-

Billiard Balls.

Per Set	1¾	1⅞	2	2 1/16	2
Best quality Ivory	**18/-**	**21/-**	**24/-**	**55/-**	**6**
Second quality Ivory	**14/6**	**16/6**	**20/-**	**32/6**	
Crystalate, guaranteed	**10/6**	**14/6**	**17/6**	**31/6**	**3**
Bonzoline	**10/6**	**14/6**	**17/6**	**31/6**	**3**
Polished Boxwood	**2/3**	**2/3**	**2/9** set	**1/-** each.	

Match Billiard Balls "Selected Ivory" from .. **21**/- to **30**/- ball.

BILLIARD SUNDRIES.

Per set.

Numbered Boxwood Balls, 1 to 16 per set **2/3**
Pool Skittles for Miniature Tables .. **2/6**
,, full size, with Rules .. **3/9**
Billiard Rules .. .. .. **6d.**
Bagatelle ,, ... **3d.**
Skittle Pool Rules .. .. **6d.**
Pool or Pyramid Rules .. **6d.**
Cue Tips, per box of 50, assorted sizes, **7½d.**
,, ,, 100, ,, **1/3**
,, best quality **1/6**
Cue Tip Wafers, obviating the use of glue or cement .. .. per box **4d.**
Billiard Spots, (Silk) Black or White, per box .. .. .. **4½d.**
Billiard Silk Plaster for repairing Cloth, per yard **1/6**
Chalk, White. Per doz. **1½d.** Per gross **1/3**

The "Premier" Chalk, Very Superior Quality, small size square blocks, blue or green .. **10½**d. per doz. Per gross **9/-**
The Saloon, Round blocks, green only. Per dozen **1/3** Per gross **13/6**
St. Martins, large square blocks, blue only. Per dozen **1/3** Per gross **13/-**
The Professional large square blocks, green only. Per doz. **1/6** Gross **16/6**
Cork Cased Pocket Chalk, large size, green only. Per doz. .. **2/-**
Billiard Pockets, for 6 ft. tables, set of 6 **1/6**
,, full size ,, ,, **3/6**
Cue Cement (Kay's) small **4½**d., large **9**d.
Wire Shade Frames **1/-**
Best ditto, with Gas Bracket **3/-**
Billiard Shades, 1/- each; dozen **11/-**

Billiard Shades, Scolloped ..each
,, ,, with Silk Fringe ,,
Covers, Holland, 6 ft. .. ..
,, ,, 7 ft. .. ..
,, ,, full size **1**

Waterproof Covers—

	6 ft.	7 ft.	8 ft.	Full
Drab Proof or Check	**13/9**	**16/-**	**21/-**	**27**
Drab Cambric ..	**18/9**	**23/6**	**26/6**	**3**
Heavy Sheeting ..	**19/9**	**21/-**	**25/6**	**4**
Drab Cambric, lined red, blue or green	**21/6**	**24/-**	**27/6**	**4**

Carriage Paid.

The "A.W.G." Patent Brass Cue Tip, complete .. ..each
Additional Tips .. .. .. ,,
Handicap Sheets 16 32 48 64 players. **8d. 10d. 1/- 1/3** each.

BILLIARD AND BAGATELLE CUES.

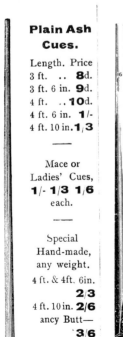

Plain Ash Cues.

Length.	Price
3 ft. ..	**8d.**
3 ft. 6 in.	**9d.**
4 ft. ..	**10d.**
4 ft. 6 in.	**1/-**
4 ft. 10 in.	**1/3**

Mace or Ladies' Cues, **1/- 1/3 1/6** each.

Special Hand-made, any weight. 4 ft. & 4ft. 6in. **2/3**
4 ft. 10 in. **2/6**
ancy Butt— **3/6**

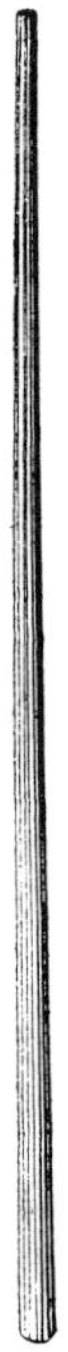

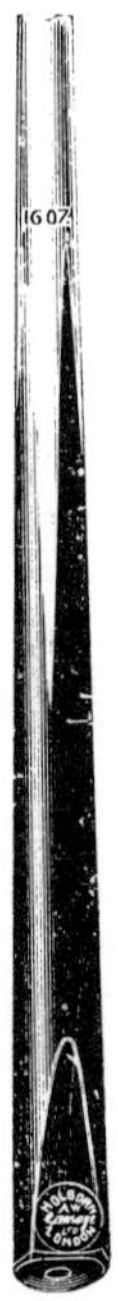

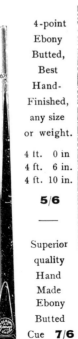

4-point Ebony Butted, Best Hand-Finished, any size or weight.
4 ft. 0 in
4 ft. 6 in.
4 ft. 10 in.
5/6

Superior quality Hand Made Ebony Butted Cue **7/6**

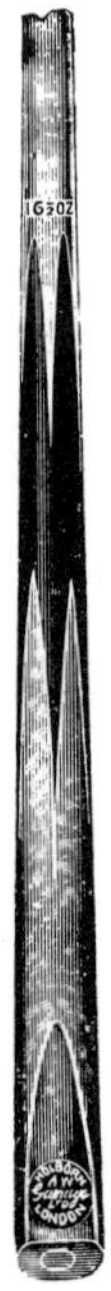

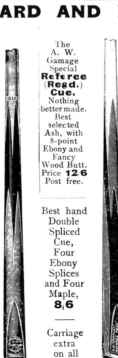

The A. W. Gamage Special **Referee (Regd.) Cue.** Nothing better made. Best selected Ash, with 8-point Ebony and Fancy Wood Butt. Price **12/6** Post free.

Best hand Double Spliced Cue, Four Ebony Splices and Four Maple, **8/6**

Carriage extra on all Cues.

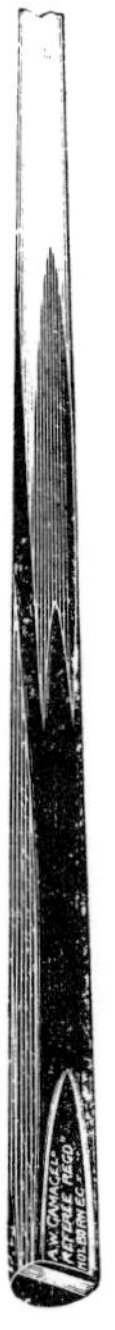

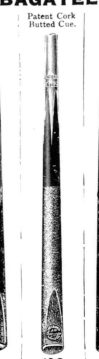

Patent Cork Butted Cue.

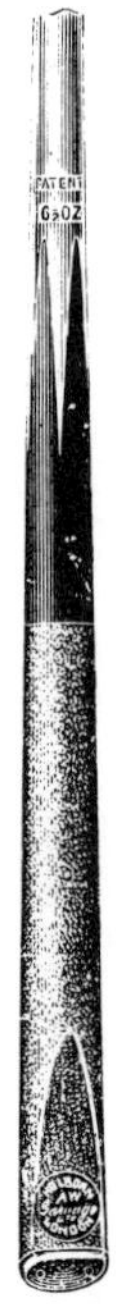

10/6

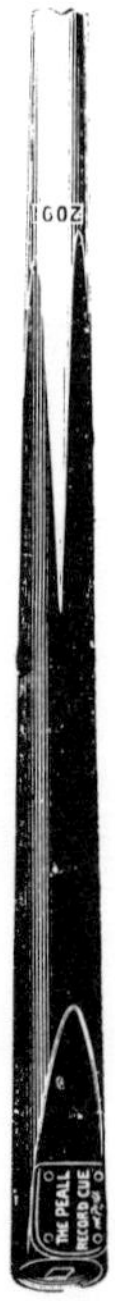

Patent Cork Butted Cue.

Excellent grip. **10/6** Post free.

The Peall Record Cue.

As used in making the Record Break of 3,304 **14/6**

Butts, **10/6** pair

Half Butts, **8/9** pair.

Carriage extra.

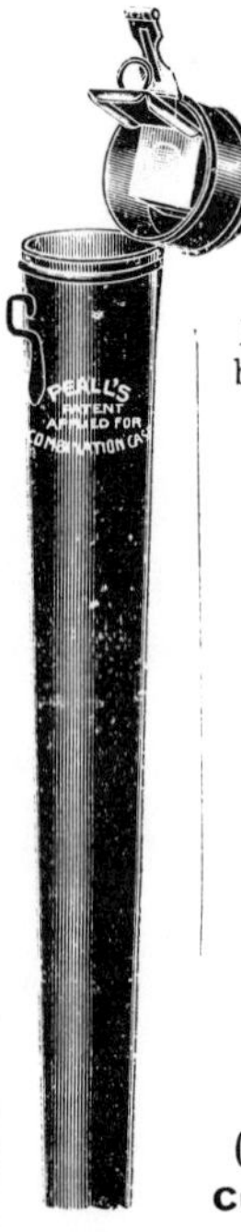

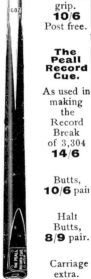

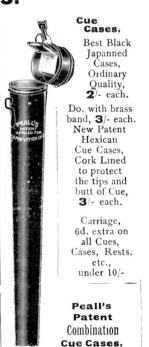

Cue Cases.

Best Black Japanned Cases, Ordinary Quality, **2**/- each.
Do. with brass band, **3**/- each.
New Patent Hexican Cue Cases, Cork Lined to protect the tips and butt of Cue, **3**/- each.

Carriage, 6d. extra on all Cues, Cases, Rests, etc., under 10/-

Peall's Patent Combination Cue Cases.

With receptacle for Chalk. Price
Locks for Cue Cases .. **6d.**
Yale Loocks **2**

Lettering on Cue Cases, 1/- each.

Cue Rests.

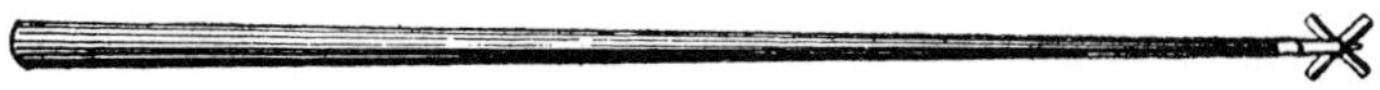

BILLIARD RESTS and SUNDRIES.

Round Brass Rest.
Price .. **1/-**
Full size, Flat or Round **1/9**
Postage, 3d.
Polished Wooden Handles
for Rests **1/-** each.

Brass Butt Rest.
Leather Tips.
2/9 each. Postage 3d.
Polished Wood Butt Handles,
3/3 extra. Carriage extra.

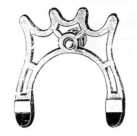

Brass Spider Rest,
Special light make, **1/9** Do., with best
quality Leather Tips, **2/3** each. Post 3d.
Polished Sticks **1/-** extra. Carriage ex.

Flat Brass Cushion Rests
3/- each. Post 3d.
Plated brass **1/3**
Post 2d.

Flat Brass Combination X and Cushion Rest.
Price **2/3** Post

New Patent Billiard Games Regulator

SAVES TIME. SAVES MONEY.

The difficulty of keeping an efficient record of money taken and games played in billiard rooms has very frequently been noticed, but is now satisfactorily overcome by the use of the BILLIARD GAMES REGISTER, which, being placed on the wall at a convenient height, not only shows who has or who has not paid for their game, holds for inspection all moneys taken for ten or more games, but enables players, on entering the room, to record their names on a card register and so secure their priority of play over later comers. It thus serves proprietor and players alike—at the same time preventing disputes. The proprietor can at any time enter the room and ascertain at a glance whether any game played, or in progress, has been paid for. Price **27/6** Carriage paid.

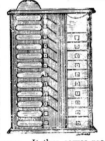

Solid Mahogany Triangles.
For 1½ in. and 1¾ in. Balls,
2/6 each.
For 2 in., 2 1/16 in. and 2⅛ in.
3/- each.
Postage 3d.

Pool Baskets.
Small size, **2/3**
Full ,, **3/6**
Postage 3d

Hard Table Brushes. Best Make and Finish.
Well-made Brush, suitable for small tables, as illustration. Price **1/9** each.
Best Bristle Brushes, black centre, white border, as illustration No. 1, **2/11** No. 2, **3/11** No. 3, **4/11**, No. 4, **6/6** Postage 3d.

LATEST SHAPE PURE BRISTLE Billiard Brush.
Shaped as illust. With end piece which goes well under the cushion.
Price .. .. **5/11** Post 4d.

Gamage's Patent Cue Rest.
With Adjusting Head.
By a simple turn of the handle the head can be adjusted to any angle. Price **5/6** each.

Billiard Table Irons and Shoes.
Small size Iron and Shoe, 7½ by 3⅝ **3/9**
Full size ditto 10¼ by 5 ... ... **6/9**
Carriage extra.

Brass Cue Tip Fasteners.
Small size, **1/-** each.

Do., large size,
1/9 each.
Postage 2d.

Boxwood Cue Tip Fastener.
With File. Price—
1/11 each. Post 2d

The New Handy Chalk Holder.
Easily attached to ceiling. Complete with cords and fittings, **1/-**
As illustration, **1/6** each
Chalk for do., per doz.—
White **4**d. Blue **7½**d.
Postage 3d.

(Watkins' Patent).
The Automatic Delivery Machine.
Supplies a piece of Blue Chalk in Case for **1**d.
Indispensable in every well-conducted Billiard Room, and a boon to every player.
A Source of Profit to the Proprietor.
A Great Convenience to the Customer.
Size 14 by 7 by 5 in. ; in Polished Oak, with Brass Fittings.
21/- each. Chalk, **9/-** gross. Carriage Paid.

Pocket Spirit Level.
Polished brass, 2½ in. long. In boxwood case **10½**d.
Ditto 4 in. long **1/6** Postage 2d.

Patent Cue Tip.
As illustration, **5**d. each.
Postage 1d.
Loose Tips, **2**d. each.

6 in. flat Spirit Level, **8½**d.
Post 2d

6 in. superior ditto, as illustration **1/4½** Post 2d.
8 in. ditto ditto **2/-** ,, 3d.

Seccotine.
Per Tube .. **5**d.
Post 1d.
A splendid cue-tip fastener.

Pocket Chalk Holders
Celluloid .. **3**d. each.
Boxwood or Ebony .. **5**d. each
Plated Steel, **9**d. each.
Post 1d.

Chalk Cups.
Brass Chalk Cups **9**d. each.
Mahogany ditto, **1/3** each.
Post .. 3d.

Watkin's Patent Chalk Holder
Made expressly for DAWON'S Champion Chalk.
Nickel-plated, **6**d.
Suspenders for same, **2**d. each.

The New Crystalate Snooker Marker.

White enamelled face. Black figures. Size 14 by 7 in. Price **7/6** Post free.

Brass Spring Cue Clips.

As illustration.

Price .. **2/9** dozen

Postage 3d

Do. with rubber flanges in place of bone **2/9** doz.

Polished Mahogany Cue Rack.

With brass cue springs. For 4 cues, **5/6**
For 6 cues, **6/3** 12 cues, **11/6** 18 cues, **17/3**
For 24 cues, **22/6** Carriage extra.

26 in. Polished Mahogany Marking Board.

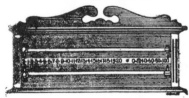

With two brass slides and pointers.
14/6 each.
30 in ditto, 3 brass slides .. **27/6** to order.

Cue Stand.

Polished Mahogany
As illustration.

Circular Stand, revolving
with clips for 12 cues, **35/-**
Ditto 18 ,, **42/6**
Ditto, Non-revolving. for
12 cues, **25/-**
Ditto 18 ,, **32/6**
To order.

Superior well-made Polished Combination Marking Boards

With Roller Markers for Billiards, Pool for 12 players, with Secret
Money Till, Ball Box and Slate in centre.
Price **£6 10 0** Carriage paid.

BILLIARD TABLE REPAIRS executed on the Shortest
Notice. Experienced Men sent to all parts. ESTIMATES FREE.

PATTERNS OF CLOTH SENT ON APPLICATION.

Bes Billiard Chalk.

The Professional
Super Quality, Large Square Blocks
Green only, **1/6** doz., **16/6** gross.

The Cork Cased Pocket Chalk.
Green only, **2/-** dozen.

Billiard Table Surrounds and Settees.

Approximate size room required for Billiard Tables.

6 ft. table requires a room	..	..	14 ft. by 11 ft.
7 ,, ,,	..	..	15 ,, 11 ,, 6 in.
8 ,, ,,	..	..	16 ,, 12 ,,
9 ,, ,,	..	..	17 ,, 13 ,,
12 ft. full size ,,	..	..	21 ft. 6 in. by 15 ,.

Skittle Bagatelle or Doddie'em Board.

An open stained and polished pine board, lined with green cloth, and
including skittles, balls and two cues.

No. G. 1. 6 ft. by 2 ft. 6 in. **46/-**
,, G. 2. 7 ft. by 2 ft. 9 in. **52/-**

Carriage paid.

Marking Boards.

Solid Mahogany Marking Board, Gold Letters and Boxwood Pointers.

No. G. 1. No. G. 2. No. G. 3.
21 by 7 in., **6/9** 26 by 7 in., **8/3** 30 by 11 in., **12/6** Carriage 9d

Special Marking Board.

For Miniature Tables, stained and polished, 16 by 6½ in.
Price .. **3/3** each. Carriage 4d.

Superior Polished Mahogany Pool Marker.

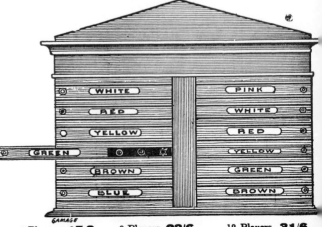

6 Players, **17/9** 9 Players, **23/6** 12 Players, **31/6**
Carriage extra on No. 1.

MINIATURE BILLIARD TABLES, &c.

BILLIARDS IN EVERY HOME
A Perfect Game on the Smallest Table in the World

Patented.

Outside Dimensions of Table: 20 x 11 inches.

Manufactured in Fumed Oak or Mahogany, with Levelling Screws, Rubber Cushions, Crystalate Balls, and a Slate Bed. Supplied Complete in Wooden Box with Marker.

IN FUMED OAK 27/6 WITH ONE CUE

A little practice with the **Patent Spring Cue** enables the same shots to be made on this small table as on a full sized one, and gives full scope to the individual skill of the player.

IN MAHOGANY 32/6 WITH TWO CUES

Carriage paid.

Larger size, do. 38 by 21 in. in Oak or Mahogany complete with 2 cues' set of balls, marker, spirit level, rules, &c.   Price **£3 7 6**

Snooker Sets, **£1 5 0**   Carriage paid.

Miniature Billiards.

The "Tessted" Miniature Billiard Table with plate glass bed, covered with cloth, ensuring absolutely level surface, adjustable feet, rubber cushions, imitation Ivory balls, 2 cues, chalk, etc. The game can be skilfully played on the table. Size 22½ × 14¼ in. Price **15/-** each.

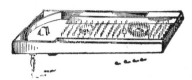

Tivoli Games.
Board lined Green Baize, and played with springs or cue

19½	23½	27½	35	39 in.
3/6	**4/6**	**5/11**	**8/11**	**11/6**

Carriage extra.

German Billiards.
A capital game played on a Board.

The balls are struck by pulling the spring fitted at the side and count according to the recesses or holes they stop in.

No. 1, **10½**d.   2, **1/4½**   3, **1/11**   4, **2/9**

Carriage extra.

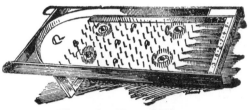

French Bagatelle.
Hardwood, stained Mahogany colour.
Superior make and finish.

2 ft. 10 in. by 12 in., 1 bell		**12/6**
3 ,, 4 ,, by 14 ,, 2 bells		**14/6**
3 ,, 10 ,, by 18 ,, 2 ,, ...		**18/9**
4 ,, 4 ,, by 19 ,, 3 ,, ...		**21/6**
4 ,, 4 ,, by 19 ,, ,, ...		**25/-**
4 ,, 6 ,, by 19 ,, 4 ,, and fitted with Boxwood Sets		**32/6**

Carriage and packing extra.

PEALL'S RECORD BILLIARD TABLE
(A PERFECT MINIATURE):

Solid Oak Frame,

Best Rubber Cushions,

Brass Pocket Plates,

Adjustable Screw Legs,

Special Composition Bed.

Everything in Exact Proportion to a Full-Sized Billiard Table.

No Table genuine without the "Peall Record" plate

(Mr. W. J. Peall, Holder of the World's Record Break, 3304, accompanied many of his finest performances with these Balls).

Price with all Accessories,

30/-

Complete with 2 Cues, Miniature Board, Chalk, Triangle, and a complete set of the finest **Composition Balls** (18 in all) for playing every known game on a Billiard Table, including Pool, Pyramids, Smoker Pool, English Pool, Russian Pool, and Ordinary Billiards

ENGLISH AND AMERICAN PLAYING CARDS.

Columbines and Racers.
Duplex, Round Corners,
Price 7½d. pk   Post 2d.
**New Cambric
or Linen print
Faced Cards.**
9d. pack.   8 9 doz.
Post 4d. doz.

**Viceroys and
Dexter Harrys.**
Printed in Colour.   Thin,
Porcelain Face, in New
designs, with Joker.
Price **8½d.** per pack.
A good wearing card for
club use, in 28 different
patterns.

**Our Special
Playing Cards.**
Round Corners, Gilt Edges,
Highly Enamelled.
Price **8½d.** pack.   Postage 2d.
These Cards are specially
made for A. W. G. Ltd., in
England, and are wonderful
value.

Sultans.
Duplex, Round Corners,
various designs, Porcelain
Face.
Price **I/-** pack.
A very large variety of
patterns and designs always
in stock.

Clan Tartan.
Printed with the Arms and
Tartans of the Macdonald
Stuart, Campbell, Gordon
Graham, Mackenzie, etc.
Clans.   24 Varieties.
1/2 per pack.   Post 2d
24 Different Tartans.

**THE SALON SERIES
of very superlor Playing Cards.**
Special Designs, gilt edges.
FANCY BOXES.
Price   **1/6** pack.   Postage 2d.

Society Playing Cards.
Very superior quality and artistic designs.
Each pack boxed.   Price **1/3** Post 2d.
**National Playing Cards of Eng'and,
Scotland & Ireland**   Price **1/2** pack.   Post 2d

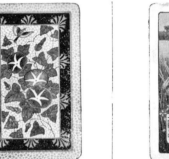

Canadian Souvenir.
2 PATTERNS ONLY.   GILT EDGES
The World's Granary, **1/6**   Post 2
  „   Orchard, **I 6**   „   2

**HANDLE-BAR.
808 Bicycle.**
Bicycle Cards, including the
'Joker.' Porcelain face Bicycle
9½d. pack. **8/6** doz. Post 2d.
Air Cushion Finish, **10½d.** pack,
post 2d.

No. 515 Picket.
FORT. Red and Blue.
The Picket, a special cheap
line. **8½d.** pack   Post 2d
SPECIAL VALUE.

AUTO GIRL
83. Vogue.
**AMERICAN
PLAYING
CARDS.**
8½d. pack.   Post 2d.

Linenette Playing Cards. The surfaces
on both back and front are granulated or linen-grained—
a special feature.   Instead of being smooth as usual they
can be easily dealt and the chance of a mis-deal is very
much lessened.   Price **9d.** pack.   Post 2d.
Society Linette, Gilt Edges, **1/6** Salon do., **1/9** Post 2d.

INITIAL SERIES.
Copyright, 1904, by
the U. S. Playing Card Co.
New Series, any initial in c
of Card in Roman chara
Handsome designs, **1/9** Po
Air Cushion Finish, Gilt F

**De LaRue's Pneumatic
Playing Cards.**
Fancy Designs (Boxed).
1/- 1/4½ 1/9 pack.   Post 2d.

164—STORM CLOUDS.
**Congress Playing
Cards.**
Air Cushion Finish.
Gilt Edges.
Various Pictorial designs.
Price **1/9** Post 2d.

Special Linen Covered
Playing Card Case
AND
Trump Indicator,
4d. each.
Or with pack of cards
complete, **1/-** Post 2d.

165—SOUTH SEAS.
**Congress Playing
Cards.**
Pictorial or Figure designs.
Gilt Edges.
Rough back.
Price **1/9** Post 2d.

**Wedgwood and Pompeii
Designs.** Very effective Colour
Price **1/2** per pack.   Postage 2

Progressive Whist, Bridge, Trump Whist, Klondyke, Court, Golf, Goblin Whist, etc.

Court Whist.

One of the best varieties of Whist introducing the Coronation, Prosperity, Conspiracy, Revolution, Confiscation and Restoration. Being played in series of 4 tricks.

Cards and Pencils complete in box. **10½d.** & **1/4** doz. Cards. Post 2d.

.09. Zoological. 24 well-known Animals carved in wood. An actual Charm.
.10. Thumb Prints. 24 Humorous Characters with descriptive title. Founded on a thumb print.
.11. Noah's Ark. 24 comic designs of its inhabitants. In attractive colours.
.13. Still Life. 24 humorous designs of household objects. Printed in delicate tints.
.14. Sporting. 24 best-known Sports, well illustrated.
.15. Comic Band. 24 Instrumentalists caricatured in amusing style. **1/4¼** doz. Post 1d.

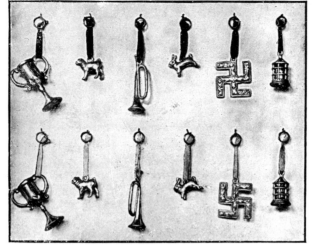

Metal Charm Whist Badges, 10½d. doz. Post 3d.
60 varieties.

Progressive Whist.

Scoring Card, folding, ivory, round corners, title and design, on first page in gold and colours, table inside to score 24 deals, complete with pencil and tassel, boxed in dozens.

9½d. per doz.
9/- per gross.
Post 2d. doz.

A very large variety always in stock at 9½d. dozen cards.

Progressive Bridge.

Scoring Cards, folding Ivory Cards, Round Corners, Title and Design on front page; each complete with Pencil and Silk Tassel, **9½d.** doz. Postage 2d.

Dance and Whist Programmes.
9½d. dozen.

Win and Lose Scoring Cards and Blocks.

Goblin Whist.

The variations introduced are of an attractive yet simple character, so that the game can be played by anyone acquainted with ordinary Whist.

Per doz.
G421 Herald design, printed in red and black **10½d**
G393 Comic design of Goblin palming a coin, printed in one colour **10½d**
Superior Do. Printed on best Cards in Art Colours. Price **1/4½d**. Post 1½d.

Point Bridge.

This new progressive game retains the present method of scoring with an additional score board on a system which enables merit to win, and eliminates wild calling.

With pencils, per doz.
G331. Elf with Cards, stamped coloured relief **1/4**
G332. Elf on Toadstool, stamped coloured relief, **1/4**

.3. As illustration, stamped gold relief **1/4**
.4. "Hearts are Trumps," ,, **1/4**
Postage 2d.

Grand National Whist.

Combines the excitement of a Steeplechase with the attractions of a card table. The variations are easy enough to be understood by an ordinary whist player. The headings of the various sections indicate incidents on the course, such as Handicap, The Start, They're Off, Ditch, A Foul, Fence, Water Jump, and Winning Post.

G410 The Paddock, with king, queen & knave, printed in playing card colours Box of 12 Cards and Pencils ... **1/4**

Horse and Rider Jumping Fence, printed in three colours. Box of 12 Cards and Pencils **1/4**
Post 2d.

Progressive Games.

These Games are arranged for family and social gatherings, and are intended to give the minimum trouble to those who have to entertain large parties, as, beside the games, there are full directions, scoring cards, etc. **1/9** Post 3d.

Afternoon Tea Games.

1/2 per Box of **12**. Post 2d.

The following Games are attractively printed on folding Ivory Card, Round Cornered, complete with Pencil and Tassel; boxed in dozens, with Key :—

No.	Questions	No.	Questions
1701	Troublesome Imps, 28	1720	Magazines and Periodicals .. 30
1702	A Transposition Competition .. 26	1721	The 'Age' of Jones 30
1703	The Problem of our Sons .. 27	1722	Noah's Ark Competition .. 50
1704	What is it .. 30	1888	Old Friends in Disguise .. 24
1705	The Game of Terminals .. 26	1889	Word Pictures . 24
1706	Shooting .. 26	1890	Delineated Authors, 41
1707	Through Constantinople .. 19	1891	By Waters, Mountains and Moors.. 24
1708	Subject and Object 24	1892	Highly Coloured .. 28
1709	The Game of Kings 20	1893	The Magic Hour.. 28
1710	The New Game, or I wish I knew it, 24	1894	Ills that Afflict us, 28
1711	The Sights of London .. 42	1895	Ann's Antics .. 50
		1896	A Nursery Game.. 20
1712	Alphabetical Celebrities .. 26	1897	Reflex Words .. 28
1713	Puzzling Creatures, 38	1898	On the Rails .. 28
1714	Popular Advertisements .. 38	1899	The 'late' Vicar of Great Boring .. 32
1715	The Most Stirring Events of 1911 .. 31	1900	Guess my Name .. 41
		1901	Find our Names .. 43
1716	Animal Life .. 30	1902	Beheaded Words.. 24
1717	Up in Town .. 24	1903	Poetical Titles .. 29
1718	A Love Story .. 24	1904	Fascinating Doubles 42
1719	An Operatic and Dramatic Romance 38	1905	The Balkan War.. 50
		1906	A Bridge Competition 43
		1907	Alphabetical Amusements .. 26

1908 Celebrities, Past and Present, comprising 36 illustrations, with descriptive matter, to the set, attractively printed on Ivory Card, Round Cornered, with Key, **2/-** set.

SCORING CARDS for ditto, attractively printed on Ivory, folding, complete with Pencil and Tassel, **9½d.** doz.

Round Games and Competitions for Evening Parties.

What despair often fills the mind of those who have to cater for the entertainment of a large company. This Compendium of Round Games and Competitions is the Host's *Vade Mecum*. Nothing like them has been published before. Every particular is tabulated, commencing with the invitation to the guests, and all the appliances are provided for a novel and entertaining evening's enjoyment. Armed with this Compendium, no host need fear a dull moment during three to four hours' entertainment.

All necessary appliances for a party of 20, **9d.** Post 3d.
Superior appliances for a party of 36 .. **1/4½** ,, 3d.

Scoring Cards for Trump Whist, Solo Whist, Progressive Hearts, Golf Whist, Sporting Whist, Matrimonial Whist.
9½d. per doz. cards of 24 deals. Post 1½d.

Table Numbers and Trump Indicators.

Table Number Cards, printed in black and red, 1 to 12, **4½d.** 1 to 24, **9d.** 1 to 50, **1/6**
Do. with Trump Indicator and Number, black and red, 1 to 12, **4½d.** 1 to 24, **9d.** 1 to 50, **1/6**
Postage 1½d. and 2d.

request the pleasure of
Company
RSVP

Invitations.

No. G404. **Company.**
No. G405. **At Home.**

Suitable for any Card Game.

Folding Sheets, Notepaper size, with Envelopes to take the Invitation without folding.

10 Invitations, 10 Large Envelopes In box for **10½d.** Post 2d.

Also in Heart, Goblin and Tartan Designs.
Postage on Scoring Cards, 2d. per box.

Invitation Cards and Envelopes.

In boxes containing 12 Cards and 12 Envelopes for all kinds of Progressive Games, per box ... **6d.**
Ditto, containing 12 sheets of Note Paper and 12 Envelopes to match, (post 3d.), per box ... **1/-**

Golfanwhist

is a happy combination of the popular games of Golf and Whist. There are nine holes, each of which is divided into three deals, representing the tee, the course, and the green.

Bunkers, foozles, and other difficulties are encountered and penalised, and good strokes rewarded. The game is equally interesting to those who have never seen a golf course.

With pencils, per doz. **1/4**

WHIST.

G345. Golf Girl, printed in dainty colours, stamped in gold relief. **1/4** doz. Post 2d.
G346. Golf Man. A realistic picture in natural colours stamped in gold relief. **1/4** doz. Postage 2d.

Popular Bridge Sets and Sundries.

The Camden Bridge Set.
Cloth, blocked in gold, containing 2 packs Viceroy Cards, duplex, round corners, thin; 2 scoring Blocks and Book of Rules.

Price .. **3/3** Postage 3d.

Silver Mounted Bridge Set.
Long grain leather case with silver title and catch, 2 packs linette cards, 2 scoring blocks, and book of Rules **8/11**

Ditto. with Silver Title Catch and Four Corners **10/6**

Very Superior Mounted Cases at **14/6** **18/6** **22/6** **27/6** each.

"Double Dummy" Patent Bridge and Whist Board.
Superior to any other device for the game of two-handed Bridge, the best card game for two players ever invented. Four hands are dealt as in ordinary Bridge but the arrangement of the board prevents either player seeing more than his own Dummy Hand. Each complete in a box with Scorer.
6070. Mahogany finish **3/6** Postage 3d.

Draw Bridge Card Holders.
As illustration. Polished Walnut.
8/6 pair. Post 4d.

This invention provides for the first time, games of cards in which two persons can play four-handed games, such as Bridge, Whist, etc. This result is obtained by each player using an Automatic Partner as illustrated. The cards held by the 'Dummies' can be seen by their respective partners, but not by their opponents. It is particularly adapted to Bridge and Whist. Price **8/6** per pair. Post 4d.

The Holborn Bridge Set.
No. 103. Long Grain Leather Case. title printed in gold, containing 2 packs Linette Cards, 2 scoring blocks and book of rules.
Price **5/11**
Superior Leather Cases ditto **7/11** Post 4d.

The "G.B." Bridge Set.
Agate Persian Case, blocked in gold, containing 2 packs Imperial Club Playing Cards, duplex, round corners, thin; 2 Acme Scoring Blocks, and Book of Rules. by Professor Hoffman **10/6**
Russian Leather **14/6**
Crushed Levant, Beaver or Kangaroo .. **18/6**
Post 4d.

Draw Bridge Card Holders or Automatic Partners.
Compact, Model B. grooved Mahogany or Walnut, **4/6** pair. Postage 4d.
Patience Card Size .. .. **3/6** Post 3d.

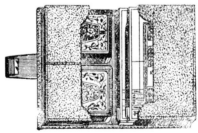

The Compactum.
Seal Grain Leather Case, made expressly for travelling, containing 2 packs superior Linen Grained Playing Cards, 2 scoring blocks and book of rules. .. **5/11**
Pigskin do., **7/6** Post 4d.

The Ideal Pocket Bridge Set.
Cigar Case Bridge Set containing 2 packs Linette Cards, 2 Scoring Blocks, and guide to Bridge. Price **13/6** Post Free

Royal Auction Bridge or Royal Spades.

Cloth blocked in gold containing 2 packs Viceroy Cards 2 Scoring Blocks, and Book of Rules. **2/3** Post 3d.
Imitation Real Grain Case complete with cards and markers. **5/4** Post 4d.
Long Grain Leather Case containing 2 packs of Linette Cards, 2 Scoring Blocks and Book of Rules. **7/11** Post 4d.
Silver Mounted Sets. **13/6** Post 4d.

Scoring Blocks Long Pattern.
The Lilly 3 Column **4½d.** Post 1d.
The Holborn 2 ,, **3½d.** Post 1d.
The Acme 3 ,, **4½d.** Post 1d.
Guide to Auction Bridge **4½d**

"The Pocket Laws of Auction Bridge," as framed by a Joint Committee of the Portland and Bath Clubs, 1908. Price **6d.** net.

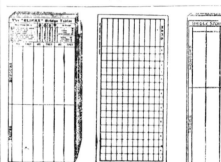

Tear-off Bridge Scoring Blocks.

The Midget Bridge Score Block.
Very convenient where room is limited. These Blocks are only half the width of the ordinary size.
Size 7 in. by 2¾ in. Price **2/-** doz. Post 4d.

Gamage's Special Bridge Scoring Block.
Full size with Pencil, well printed, **3d.** each. Post 4d. doz.
The Acme Bridge Tablets, 7½ by 3½ in., with pencil and table of scores, **4½d.** each.
The Holborn ditto, as illustration, leather loop and pencil, **5d.** each. **4/9** per doz.
The Triple, complete with 60 sheets on front, 15 sheets on back for totals, with pencil.
6d. each. **5/6** per doz. Postage 2d.

The New Addeesi Bridge Table
7¾ by 3⅜, with Scoring Formula to show Nett Difference in score at any stage of the Game.
Price **4/9** doz. **5d.** each.

Rules of Playing Card Games.
Whist, Bridge, Bridge Solo, Poker, Bezique, Progressive Whist, Patience Nos. 1 and 2,
Price .. **4½d.** each. Post 1d
Cases containing set of 14 Books on Card Games bound in morocco
Price **10/6**
Usual Price **21/-**

"KUHN KHAN" THE ROYAL GAME OF BEZIQUE. COON CAN, &c.

G. 6254.—Enamelled Box, 2 packs Highlander Cards Rules, and 2 enamelled Registers.
Price **1/9**   Postage 3d.

G. 6253.—Enamelled Box, 2 packs Imperial Club Cards, Rules, and 2 enamelled Registers.
Price **2/3**   Postage 3d.

G. 6251.—Enamelled Box, blocked in gold "Bezique," 2 packs Imperial Club Cards duplex, round corners, thin, Rules, and 2 Enamelled Registers.   Price **2/11**

The 'Camden Cloth Box

No. G. 9492 Gilt, 2 packs Imperial Club Cards, 2 enamelled Registers, and Book of Rules.
Price **3/6**
Postage 3d.

For Four Players
No. G. 6248. Enamelled Box, four packs Highlander Cards Rules, and four Enamelled Registers.   Price .. **4/-**   Postage 3d.

45. Cloth Box, gilt, 4 packs Imperial Club Cards duplex, round corners, thin, Rules and 4 four enamelled Registers.   Price .. **5/6**   Postage 4d.

The "Royal" Bezique.

Beautiful Paste Grain Leather Case, with Tray containing 4 packs best Cards, 2 Club Bezique Markers, and 2 Scoring Blocks.
Price **1 6**   List price 21/-   Post free

The Camden Patent Card Shuffler.

Place the pack in the Shuffler held in the left hand and press the gripper with the left thumb. Draw out with the thumb and second finger of the right and the cards ungripped, keeping the gripper depressed at the same time.
Price—Patience size, **2/9** Full size, **3/-** Post 3d

Bezique Markers. Emerald Cardboard for Scoring 10 0000 points **3d.** each.
French Morocco do. **8d.** ,,

EVERYBODY'S PLAYING IT.
THE LATEST OF CARD GAMES.

COON CAN. "KAHN KHAN"

COON CAN. "De La Rues"
Complete sets in leather cases, containing two pack of cards, two scoring blocks, and rules as adapted by the Bath Club.
Price .. .. .. **5/9** per set.   Post 4d.
,, Superior do. .. **6/11** ,,   ,,
Scoring blocks **6d.** each.   Book of rules **6d.** each.
Postage 1d.

"KUHN KHAN." The New and Popular Card Game.

The "Windsor" No. G. 1734. Long Grain Leather Case, blocked in Gold, containing two packs "Linette" Cards. Duplex, Round Corners, Thin, two folding Scoring Blocks with Pencils, and Book of Rules by Nemo. **7/11** each.

The "Camden" No. G. 1732. Cloth Case, blocked in Gold, containing two packs "Linette" Cards, Duplex, Round Corners, Thin, two folding Scoring Blocks with Pencils, and Book of Rules by Nemo **3 11** each.
Scoring Blocks, **6d.** each.   Rules, **4½d.**   Post 4d. set.

The "Camden."   No. G. 9494.

Cloth blocked in Gold, containing 2 pack Viceroy Cards, duplex, round corners, thin 2 Scoring Blocks and Book of Rules.
Price .. .. **3/9**   Postage 3d.

Mahogany Playing Card Cabinets
To hold 6 packs **4 3**
,, 12 ,, .. **5 11**
Post 4d.
A very convenient Cabinet for all Card Players.

Eureka polished wood Poker Chip Block

The Eureka Chip Holder is a great acquisition to every poker table, the chips being easy to handle, the blocks revolving round as required. It is made in polished mahogany or ebonised wood with nickel-plated handle and pasteboard cover.
Price **15/6** each.
Postage 5d.
Superior, nickelled .. .. **25/-** & **30/-**

1⅝ in.   **Compo Poker Chips,** 100 in Box
1 6   Postage 3d.

Large size Numbered Poker Chips.
3/6 per 100.   Plain ditto, **2/6** per 100.   Post 3d.

Sole London Agents for
HARRIS'S Genuine American Composition Poker Chips,
Engraved and Embossed Designs.
A Good Stock always on Hand.
3/9   5/-   7/6   8/6   10/- 100,
Price .. .. **4d.** per 100.

Poker Cards.
Goodall's Poker Cards, size 3½ by 2¼ in., duplex, round corners, thin .. .. **9½d.** pack.
De La Rue's ditto .. .. **9½d.** ,,
Linette Poker Cards .. .. **9½d.** ,,
Postage 3d.

Five Hundred.
The Popular American Card Game. Cloth, blocked in Gold, containing 2 packs Imperial Club Cards, duplex, round corners, thin; 2 Scoring Blocks and Book of Rules by Professor Hoffman.
Price .. **3/11** Postage 4d.

The "Balmoral" Cabinet.
Imitation Long Grain, block in gold, containing 2 packs Imperial Club Cards, duplex, round corners, thin; 2 Scoring Blocks and Book of Rules by Professor Hoffman.
Price .. **5 11**   Postage 4d.

The "Pall Mall" Whist Marker

In Light and Dark Woods **2 3** pair.   Post 2d

Whist Markers. Enamelled Cardboard, **3d.** each.
French Morocco do. **8d.** each.
Post 1d. each.

A large selection of superior sets suitable for presents always in stock

PATIENCE SETS AND CARD COUNTERS.

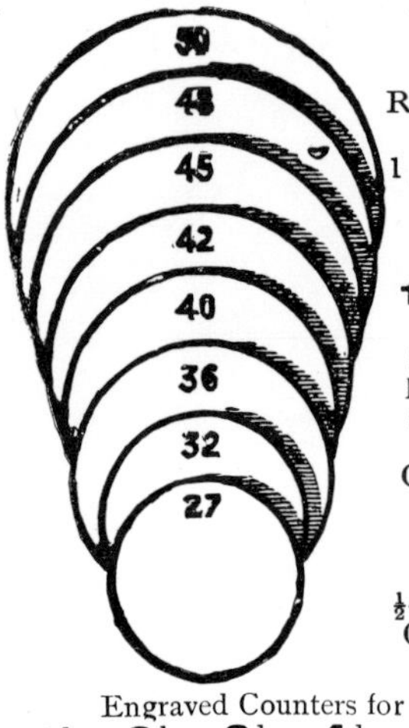

Card Counters.

Round Bone Counters.
1 gross in box, assorted 2 or 4 colours.

27   32   36 line.
10d. **1/3 1/9** gro.

40   45   50 line.
2 6 3 6 4/3 gro.

Postage 3d. gross.

Special Line.

Cowrie Shell Counters, **4½**d. per large box.
Postage 3d.

Coin ditto, gilt.
½-Guineas, **2 3** gro.
Guineas, **2 9** gross.
Postage 3d.

Engraved Counters for Waiters, &c.
1d **2**d. **3**d. **4**d. **5**d. **6**d. **1/-**
1/6 per doz. Postage 2d.

Bone Counters

Wood boxes. 100 Counters in strong wood boxes with divisions.

10½d. **1/6**
2/- per gross.

Solitaire and Solitaire & Tactic Board.

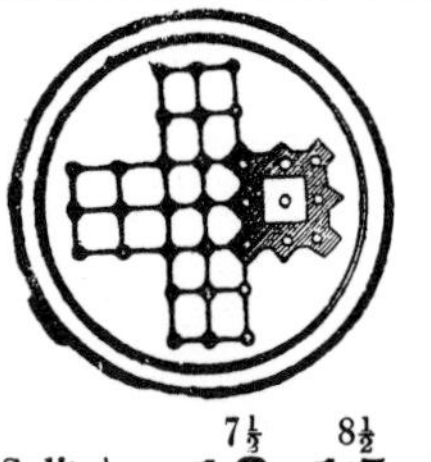

The **1/-** Solitaire Board and Marbles in box, **8½**d.
Solitaire, with box fitted under board. **6½**d. & **1**/-
Polished Mahogany, with glass marbles.

	7½	8½	9½	10½	12 in. Brd.
Solitaire	**1 3**	**1 5**	**1/10**	—	—
Do. with	**1/6**	**1 9**	**2/3**	**3/9**	**4/6**
Tactics	Postage 3d., 4d. and 6d.				

Patience Cards and Sets in Cases.

Cards—Size 2⅝ by 1¾ in., printed backs, duplex, round corners, thin.

8143. Fancy enamelled cardboard box, pull-off lid, containing 2 packs Patience Cards—Linette grained **1/4½**

8788. Paste grain leather, blocked in gold—"Patience," hinge lid, containing two packs Patience Cards—Series A or B, and Book of Rules, as illustration **2 11**

Paste grain leather, with hinged lid and catch, superior cards **3/11**

8788/F. Morocco Patience Sets, blocked in gold, containing two packs Patience Cards and Rules **4/11**

93. Upright leather case, with "Patience" in gilt on lid, containing two packs De la Rue's Patience Cards. **4 9** Post 3d. set.

Ditto, silver mounted, **6/6** Post 6d.

Oblong ditto, crushed morocco case, name stamped in gold, superior cards, **7/6** set. Postage 3d.

Folding Patience Boards.

Folding Leatherette Covered Boards, lined baize,
15 in. square .. **1/9**

Patience Boards, folding, as illustration, with clips. Covered with Maroon Kera morocco lined with smooth green baize.

Ditto, 14½ by 21½ **2 6**

Ditto, 14½ by 22½, baize both sides, edged imitation morocco. Price .. **4/11**

Size, folded, 15⅝ by 11½ in. Open, 15⅝ by 23 in. Price **6/-**

Ditto, superior quality .. **8/11** Post 4d.

Non-folding Patience Board, with box attached for cards, stamped "Patience is a Virtue." Price .. **9/11** Postage 6d.

Patience Playing Cards.

A. Fancy figured backs, round corners, thin indexed .. **8½**d. and **10½**d. pack.

Pneumatic ditto, **1/-** Post 1d.
Linette „ **8½**d. „

Medusa Patience Playing Cards.

As illustration.

1/- pack, or 2 packs in box, **1/11** Post 2d.

The New Tabart Patience Cards

With Large Index. Pip in centre.
2 packs in box **1/11** Postage 2d.

Goodall's 'Elfin' Playing Cards.

Size 1¾ by 1¼ in. Series A, duplex, round corners, thin, **2**d pack. Post 1d.

'Pigmy' Playing Cards.

Size 1¾ by 1¼ in. Enamelled both sides, assorted patterns, with rounded corners, in neat sliding boxes, each containing two packs, **8½**d. Post 2d.

Leather Pocket Playing Card Cases.

Pigskin, purse shape .. .. .. **10½**d.
Black seal with clip **1/3**

Do., containing one pack of full size cards .. **1/4½** and **2/-** Post 2d.

POKER-PATIENCE AND PROGRESSIVE POKER-PATIENCE.

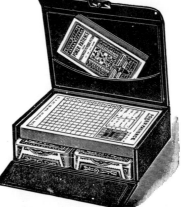

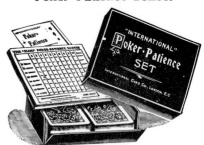

Poker Patience Boxes.

In Cardboard Box, Gold Blocked, contains 4 Packs Midget Cards, Book of Rules and Scoring Block **1/9**

Fancy enamelled Cardboard Box, pull-off lid, containing 2 Packs Patience Cards, Scoring Block and Book of Rules **2/3**

Poker-Patience Scoring Blocks.

The "Gem" Poker-Patience Scoring Block with loop and pencil .. .. .. **4½**d. each.

The "Gem" Poker-Patience Scoring Block without loop and pencil .. **3**d. each.

The "Bijou" Poker-Patience Scoring Block **2**d. each.

The "International" Poker Patience Rules **4½**d. each.

Post 1d. each.

No. G. 1.

Fancy cardboard box, pull-off lid, containing two Packs Patience Cards, Scoring Block and Book of Rules, also Rules for various Patience games.

Price ... **2/3**

Post 3d.

THE NEW POCKET SET POKER-PATIENCE

(As illustration).
Folding Board and Cards complete.
2 6 Postage 3d.
Rules for Poker-Patience, **4½**d. Post 1d.

No. G. 11 Set. In real pigskin, for the pocket contains 2 packs full size Patience Cards, Scoring Block and Book of Rules. **4 9** each.

No. G. 10 Set. In real pigskin, for travelling, contains 4 packs full size Patience Cards, Book of Rules, Scorer and Pencil. **9 6** each. Post 4d.

The Midget.

Long Grain Leather, Hinge Lid, blocked in Gold, containing 4 Packs Miniature Playing Cards, 2 Scoring Blocks and Book of Rules, **2/6** Post 3d

The Miniature.

Long Grain Leather, blocked in Gold, containing 2 Packs Patience Cards, 2 Scoring Blocks and Book of Rules ... **3/3**

The Balmoral.

Long Grain Leather, blocked in Gold, containing 4 Packs Patience Cards, Two Scoring Blocks and Book of Rules ... **5/11**

In Paste Grain Leather, full flap (as illustration), contains 4 Packs "LINETTE" Patience Cards, 100 Score Cards, Book of Rules and Scoring Block **7/6**

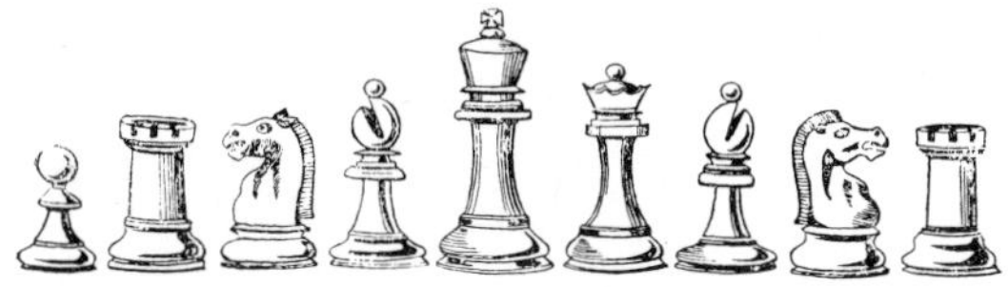

Chessmen, Pocket Chess, Draughts, &c.

The Real Staunton Chessmen

Postage under 20/- 4d.

No.		Our Price	List Price
Gxxx.	Ebony and boxwood, small size, in mahogany box, lined, base of King 1¼ in. diameter. Height 2¾ in.	**10/3**	12/6
G000.	Ebony and boxwood, in polished mahogany box, velvet lined, base of King 1⅜ in. diameter. Height 3 in.	**12/3**	15/-
G00.	Ebony and boxwood, large size, in polished mahogany box, velvet lined, base of King, 1¾ in. diameter. Height 3½ in.	**14/3**	17/6
G0.	Ebony and boxwood, loaded with lead, superior finish in mahogany cases, same size as No. G00	**20/6**	25/-
G1½.	Ebony and boxwood, loaded with lead, small size Club, in mahogany case, base of King, 1⅞ in. diameter, Height 3⅞ in.	**28/9**	35/-
G1.	Ebony and boxwood, loaded with lead, Club size, in strong mahogany case, base of King, 2 in. diameter. Height 4¼ in.	**36/6**	45/-

Gamage's Bone Chessmen.

Packed in strong polished wood box.
Plain size, 1, **9/6**
Green Baize bottoms, in polished wood box.
Size 1, **12/6** Size 2, **14/6**
A handsome present. Postage 4d. under 20/

Special Line Chessmen.

Size 0, **6½**d., boxed complete.
Size 1 **10**d., ,,
Postage 3d. per set.

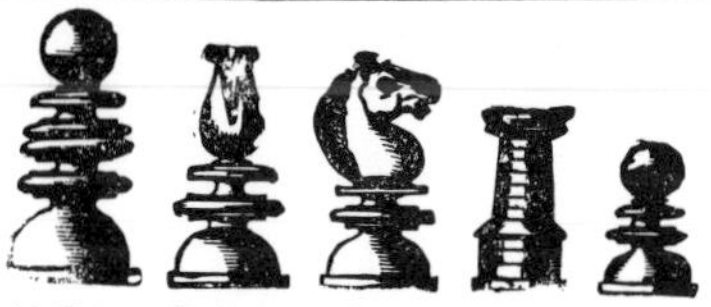

"St. George's" Pattern Chessmen.

Boxwood and ebony stained in rosewood box.

Size	0	1	2	3	4	5	6
	10d.	**1/1½**	**1/8**	**2/-**	**2/6**	**3/3**	**3/11**

Postage 3d. per set.

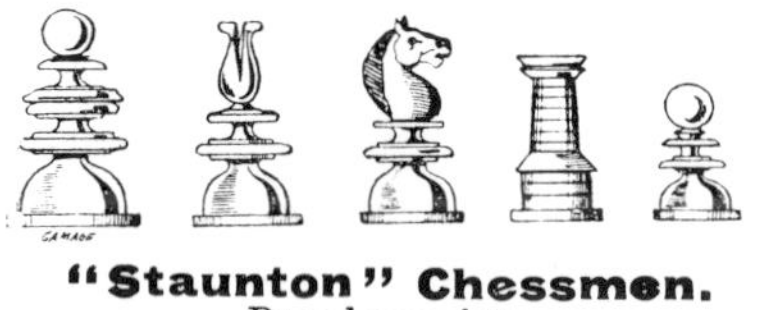

"Staunton" Chessmen.

Boxed complete.

Size	0	1	2	3	4	5	6
Boxwood	**2/1**	**2/4½**	**2/7½**	**3/-**	**3/6**	**3/11**	**4/6**
Do., Draped green baize in polished boxes					**4/6**	**4/11**	**5/6**
Do., Loaded					**6/6**	—	**7/6**

Special No. 7 Large size Loaded Staunton Pattern Chess, for Club use, **10/6** set.

Draught Board and Draughts Combination.

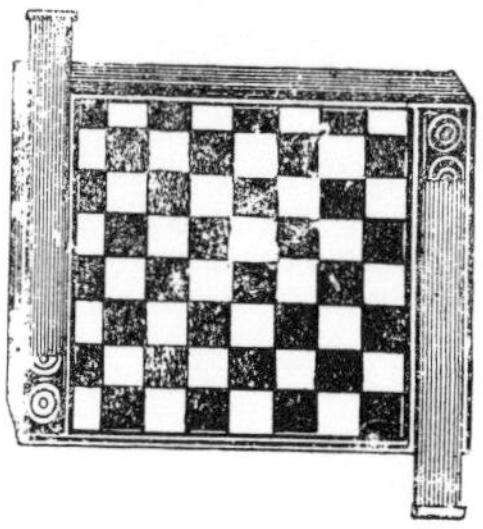

With Draw-out Lids.
Complete, 10 in., **2/-** unpolished.
Walnut wood, 10 in., **2/6** unpolished.
Stained Mahogany, 10 in., **3/11** polished
Postage 4d.

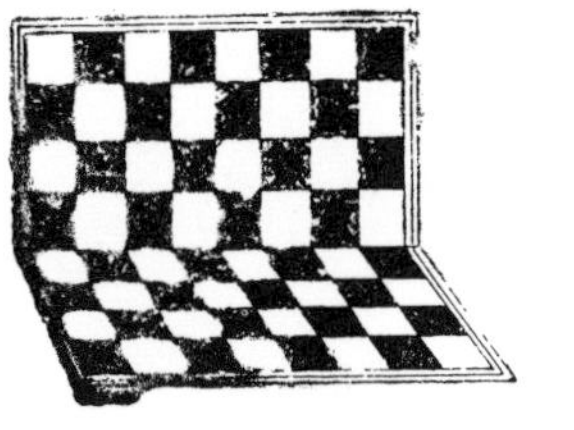

Folding Boards.

Inches	12	14	16	16	18	20
Fancy Boards	—	**5½**d.	**7½**d.	**9**d.	—	—
Half leather	**1/-**	**1/2**	**1/4**	—	—	—
Best leather	—	**2/-**	**2/3**	—	**3/-**	**3/9**
Red and Buff	—	**2/3**	**2/7**	—	**3/6**	**4/6**

Very superior paste grain Leather Chess Boards. Red and buff or green and buff squares. Suitable for presentation.
16 in., **10/6** 18 in., **12/6** Postage 4d.

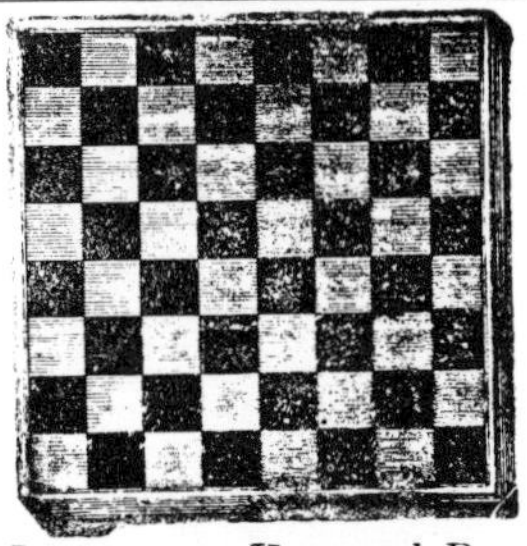

Strong Hard-wood Club Boards.

Walnut and white squares
14 in. .. **3/6**
16 ,, .. **4/3**
18 ,, .. **5/6**

Superior do., Holly and Rosewood Squares, mahogany frame, polished.
14in., **4/6** 16in., **5/11** 18in., **7/6** 20in., **10/6**
Postage 4d. and 6d. each.
Polished Walnut Chess Board, with inlaid edge, polished back.
14 in., **6/6** 16 in., **7/6** 18 in., **8/6**
Postage 4d. and 6d.

Wood Boards.—Special Line.

Wooden Chess Boards, polished board, stained frame. 12¾ in., **1/6** 14½ in., **1/9** 16 in., **2/-**
Polished black edges. 10¾ in., **1/9** 12½ in., **2/3** 14½ in., **2/9** 16 in., **3/3** 17½ in., **3/9**
Postage 3d. Large size 4d.

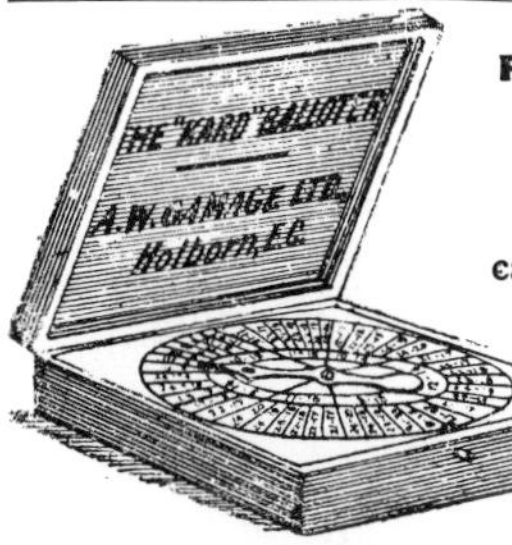

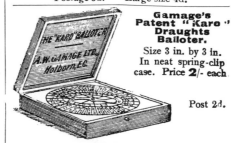

Gamage's Patent "Karo" Draughts Balloter.

Size 3 in. by 3 in.
In neat spring-clip case. Price **2/-** each

Post 2d.

The Holborn Note Book Pocket Chess Board.

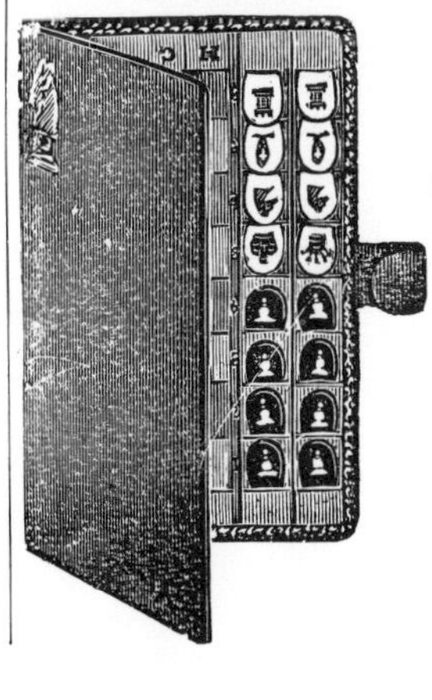

Leather Case.
Lined sheep, fitted wtih Celluloid Men.
Price .. **2/3**
Size 5¼ by 3½ in. closed

Large do., with Pocket for Problems.
Price .. **3/11**
Postage 2d.
Size 6½ by 4¼ in. closed

Superior do., with Envelope Case.
Price .. **6/9** each.
Postage 2d.
Size 5¼ by 3½ in. open.

Mahogany Pocket Chess Boards.

With pegged men for railway or sea use.

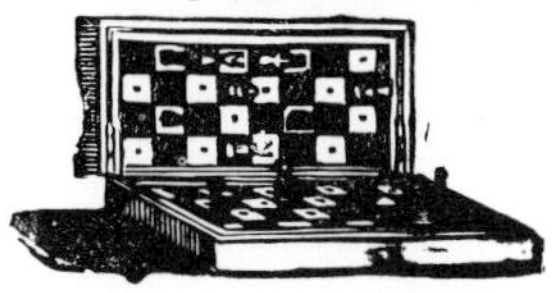

5 in. .. **4/9**
6 in. .. **6/-**
8 in. .. **8/-**
9 in. .. **9/-**
Post 3d. per set.

Special Line Pocket Chess Board (as above) **3/11** Postage 3d.

Travelling Folding Flap Chess Boards.

Polished Mahogany Board Boxes. Pegged Men.
6 in. **8/3**
8 ,, **10/6**
10 ,, **13/9**
12 ,, **17/3**
Postage 4d. under 10/-

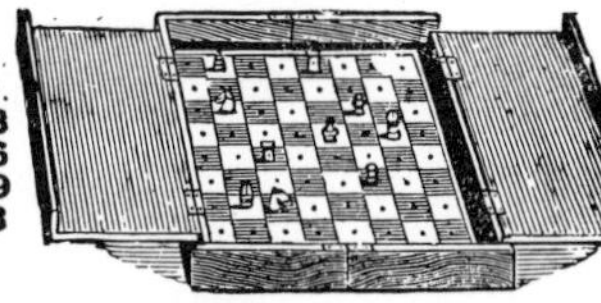

The "Whittington" Mahogany.

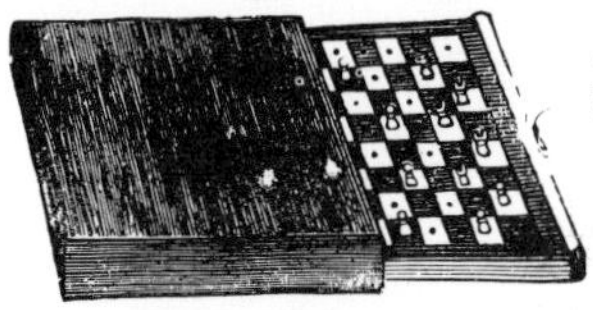

To draw out.
Size 5in. Bone men **7/9** Postage 3d per set.
Do., with Slide Lid, **6/11**
Postage 3d.

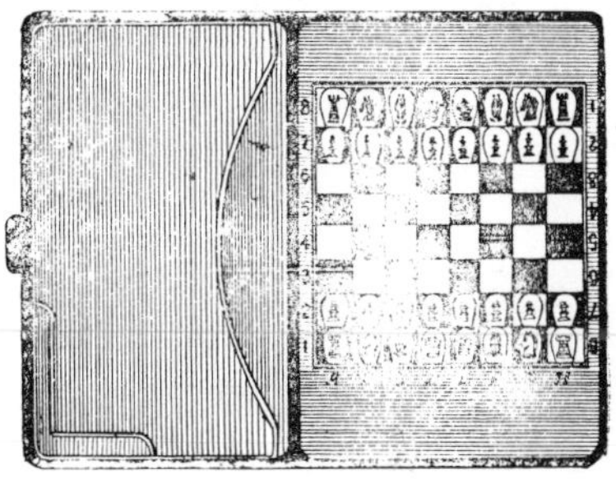

The Dexter Pocket Chess or Draughts Board (in Note Case form).

With pocket for holding chess diagrams, and a corner piece in which to place the particular problem being worked out. The pieces are printed on thin Xylonite, and the slots for their reception are so made that they can be placed or withdrawn with the greatest ease.

In French Morocco lined Sheep **4/3**
Size—Closed 6½ in. by 4½ in.
Superior Leather Case **6/3**
Crocodile, Silver mounted **12/6**
Draughts same price Postage 3d.

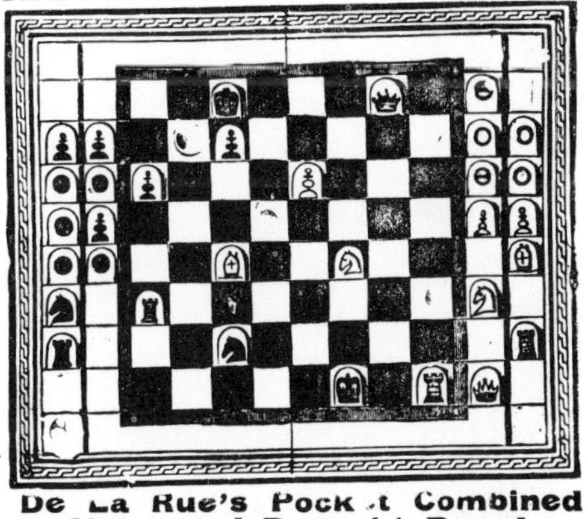

De La Rue's Pocket Combined Chess and Draught Board.

Open In Case. Price **2/-** Postage 2d.

Dominoes, Draughts, Dice, Crib Boards, etc.

Straight Cribbage Boards.

4½d. 6½d. 1/-
1/6 & 1/11
Postage 3d.

Inlaid Ivory .. **1/11 2/6 3/4** and **4/11**
Including pegs.   Postage 3d.
New Large Club size Boards **2/6** and **3/6** each.

Crib Pegs.

1 in. **1**d. set. 1½ in. **2**d. set. Postage 1d.

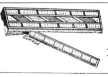

3 handed Lap out Cribbage Boards.

Inlaid Fancy Woods.
Price **1/3 1/9 2/6**
Postage 3d.

Triangle Boards.

Price
10½d. 1/4½ 2/-
Including pegs.
Postage 2d.

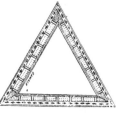

Single Pack Card Boxes and Cribbage Marker.

Price **10½d. 1/4½**
2/- 2/11
Including Pegs.
Postage 3d.

Double Pack Card Boxes and Cribbage Markers

Inlaid Tops. No. 1, **2/-** and **3/-** Postage 4d.
Inlaid Ivory, etc., **4/6** and **6/6** Post 4d.
A large variety of Designs in all Prices.

Celluloid Poker Dice.
2/6 set of 5.
Postage 2d.
Leather Poker Dice Cups.
1/9 each.
Postage 3d.

Dice (6 sizes).
Size 0, 1 & 2, **1½**d. set of 3.
  ,, 3, 4 & 5, **2**d. ,,

What constitutes the Main Advantages of
The British Domino.
MADE IN ONE PIECE OF SOLID EBONITE.
SPOTS CANNOT WEAR OFF.
COLOUR CANNOT CHANGE OR GET YELLOW.
DOES NOT CHIP.
MAKES A **GAME** OF A GAME OF DOMINOES.

Combination Boxes and Scoring Board.

Most useful for Clubs, etc. The lid being made to
reverse. Prices: No. 1, **1/-**   No. 2, **1/6**
No. 3, **2/-** Postage 3d. each.
Price does not include Dominoes.

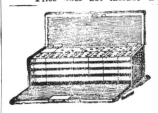

Dominoes
In wood slide lid boxes.
Double sixes.

	No. G.18	G.20	G.2	G24
Good quality ..	**10½**d.	—	—	—
Superior	**1/2½**	**1/4½**	**1/9**	—
Extra thick polished boxes		**2/3**	**2/11**	**3/6**
22 line bevel face polished box	..	..		**3/6**

Double Nines.

Thick, in wood boxes	..	**3/6**	**4/6**	**5/9**

Postage 3d. per box.

Superior quality polished Dominoes, secured with
3 nails (flat), suitable for private use. Will not
scratch table. In very strong polished box, with
fall front. Size 22 line, **5/6** Postage 4d.
Best quality, bevelled edges, polished Dominoes,
in polished mahogany box, slide lid, 20 line, **6/6**
22 line, very superior Dominoes, in polished
mahogany box with fall front, **8/6** Post 4d.

Universal Portable Draughts.

With board, in box complete, **4½**d., **9**d. and
1/4½ each. Postage 3d.

THE BRITISH DOMINO

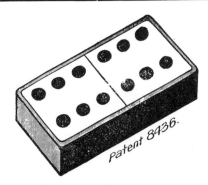

Patent 8436.

No. 1. Plain face as illustration fancy back in
tin box. **2/9** set.
Do. in mahogany fall front box, **4/6** set.
9 by 9 Do. Do. tin box **5/11** set.

Black fancy back, Brass pivot in centre, **3/6**
Do., composition pivot for Club use, **4/3**
Plain back, fancy colours, **3/6**
Post 4d. set.

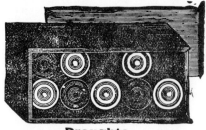

Draughts.

Ebonised & Boxwood, polished in mahogany box.
1-in. **10½**d. 1½-in. **1/1½** 1½-in. **1/4½** Post 3d.
Ebony and Boxwood in polished, mahogany box.
1-in. **1/4½** 1½-in. **1/6** 1½-in. **1/8** 1½-in. **1/11**
Postage 3d.
Hollow Edge Draughts.
Ebony and Boxwood, best quality.
1-in. **2/3** 1½-in. **2/6** 1½-in. **3/-** Postage 3d.

Blundell's Registered Draughts.

New Ebony and Boxwood Interlocking Match
Draughts. Registered Design.
Price **1⅛, 1 3** set. **1¼, 1/6** set. Post 3d.

Gamage's Bone Draughts
Red and White, in polished boxes.
1-in. **5/6** 1¼-in. **8/11** Postage 3d.

Chairman's Hammer
Best Boxwood or Ebonised, **1/3** each. Post 3d.

Crown & Anchor Dice, **6**d. & **9**d. each
Do. Cloths, 18 in. by 18 in. .. **2 6** ,,
Do. Cloths, 27 in. by 18 in., **3 6** Post 3d.

Continental Pattern Solid Leather
Dice Cups.
Specially suitable for Crown and Anchor.
Small **1/-**
Large **1/6**
Post 2d.

Dice Cups
Boxwood, 3⅜ in. **4**d.
  ,, 3¾ in. **6**d.
Leather, 6½d. & **10½**d.
Large Leather Poker
Dice Cups
1/9 each Post 2d.

Duplex Card Dominoes.
In enamelled and printed cardboard pull-off boxes.
Price **5**d. Post 1d.

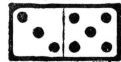

No. 68. In French Morocco Leather Case,
blocked in gold. Price **10**d. Postage 1d.

Leather Backgammon Boards.

Cups and Draughts complete.
Half leather, black and white squares.

12	14	17 in.
2/-	**2/9**	**3/6**

Superior, all leather—
3/3 **4/3** **5/3**

Best quality black leather, extra gilt.
12 in., **5 3** 14 in., **7/-** 17 in., **10/-**
Red and white squares, 6d. extra.

Postage extra under 10/-

Best quality maroon leather.
13 in., **11/6** 15 in., **17/-** 18 in., **23/6**

Flat Folding Backgammon Boards.
Covered black and red cloth.
16 in., **1/9** 18 in., **2 3** Postage 3d.

Winged Compendiums.

Complete
Containing
Backgammon,
Chess, Draughts,
Dominoes,
Race Game,
Cribbag, Whist,
Bezique,
Bell, and Hammer
with illustrated
book of
instructions.

Stained Rosewood, **43/-** Mahogauy, **52/-**
Walnut, **62/-** Mahogany, **66/-** Oak, **71/-**
Mahogany (brass capped and cornered) **82/-**

Combination Set of Parlour Games,

Large set.

Comprises :

Table Croquet
Race Game,
Puff and Dart,
Expert Angler
Tails, Snail,
Ton-ton, Go-
bang. Star
Ringolette,
Tactics,
Skittles, Fox and Geese, Solitaire, Aunt Sally,

Small Set, containing 6 games	..	**7/9**
Middle size ,, 10 ,,	..	**13 9**
Large Set ,, 14 ,,	..	**23/6**

Add for carriage 6d., 9d., and 1/6.

The New Combination of Parlour Games

Containing 7 games, viz., Carpet Croquet,
Parlour Lapelle, Parlour Quoits, Parlour Bowls,
Dolphin Expert Angler and Skittles.

In strong deal box	..	**15/-**
Superior fittings	..	**25/-**

Carriage extra.

Flat Compendiums.

G. XXX. Pine, containing 4 games, viz. :—
Chess, Draughts, Go-Bang and Race Game
with book and instructions. Price .. **2/9**

G. 0. Pine, containing 6 games, viz. :—Chess,
Draughts, Race, Dominoes Go-Bang and
Spellicans. Price **5/-**

G. 1. The School Prize, containing Halma,
Reversi, Trails, Dominoes, Race, Draughts,
Solitaire, Snail, German Tactics, Fox and
Geese. Price **7/6**

G. 2. Pine, superior, containing 10 games,
viz., Go-Bang, Chess, Draughts, Dominoes,
Race Game, Cribbage, Bezique, Whist, Spoil
Five and Pope Joan, with book of instructions.
Price **9/6**

G. 3. Pine (excluding cards and the use of dice),
containing 10 games, viz., Chess, Draughts,
Go-Bang, Race Game, Spellicans, Solitaire,
German Tactics, Fox and Geese, Snail Game
and Trails, with book of instructions .. **10/6**

G. 4. Mahogany Box, containing 11 Games,
viz., Chess, Draughts, Race, Halma, Reversi,
Dominoes, Go-Bang, Whist, Bezique, Spoil
Five and Spellicans. Price .. **13/9**

G. 5. Mahogany, containing 10 games, viz.:—
Backgammon, Chess, Draughts, Cribbage, Be-
zique, Whist, Spoil Five, Dominoes, Race
Game and Pope Joan, with book of instructions.
Price **15/-** Carriage extra.

G. 6. Pine, containing 14 games, viz., Back-
gammon, Chess, Draughts, Dominoes, Race
Game, Bezique, Whist, Cribbage, Spoil Five,
Go-Bang, German Tactics, Solitaire, Fox and
Geese, Snail Game, with book of instructions.
Price .. **18/9** Carriage extra.

G. 7. Mahogany ditto (similar to 6) .. **23/-**

G. 8. Solid Walnut, containing 12 games, viz.,
Chess, Draughts, Backgammon, Dominoes,
Halma, Race, Reversi, Bezique, Whist, Crib-
bage, Spoil Five and Spellicans. Price **30/9**

G. 9. Oak, containing 15 games, viz., Bone
Chess, Draughts and Dominoes, Race Game,
Backgammon, Cribbage, Whist, Bezique, Spoil
Five, Snail Game, Fox and Geese, Bell and
Hammer, Spellicans, Solitaire, German Tactics,
with book of instructions. Price .. **40/-**

G. 10. Pine, containing 17 games, viz., Chess,
Draughts, Backgammon, Cribbage, Whist,
Bezique, Spoil Five, Dominoes, Race Game,
Spellicans, Solitaire, German Tactics, Siege of
Paris, Fox and Geese, Snail Game, Bell and
Hammer, Table Croquet, with book of instruc-
tions. Price **43/6**

Carriage Paid on above over 20/- Carriage Free Inside London Radius.

Useful Boxes of
Standard Games.

Compendium of Standard Games.

1.	Containing 4 games	..	..	..	**9**d.	Post 3d.
2.	,, 4 ,,	..	..	..	**1 9**	,, 4d.
3.	,, 5 ,,	..	..	..	**2 6**	,, 4d.
3A.	,, 5 ,,	..	..	..	**3/3**	,, 4d.
4.	,, Che-s, Draughts, Dominoes, Halma and Race ..			..	**4/11**	,, 6d.
5.	,, With Ludo and Porchese, and without Race	..		..	**7/6**	,, 6d.

The Compendiums are complete with fittings
Rules, Boards, Counters, Dice, and all accessories for the
playing of 50 different games.
Price .. **4/11** Post 4d.

The "Dreadnought."
Complete with all accessories, for playing 46 different games
Price .. **3/3** Post 4d.

The "King"
Compendium of 34 selected games.
Complete with book of instructions. Price **6/3**
Postage 4d.

THE "TORMENTUM"
Series of Jig-saw Picture Puzzles.

A SCANTY MEAL.

PUBLISHED BY
A. W. GAMAGE, Ltd.
HOLBORN.

The Puzzles are beautifully cut and finished by the most up-to-date machinery and skilled work people. The Pictures are all selected from Genuine Works of Art and in many cases Artist-proof Pictures are used.

All Pictures are sent out in neat attractive boxes and sealed.

When ordering, please state whether Landscape, Historical, Sporting, etc., etc., subjects are required.

All Puzzles are checked and re-checked before being sent out.

Famous Cricketers Puzzle

Containing the Photo of 120 celebrated Cricketers.

Key Plate with each Puzzle.

Price **2/6**   Post 4d.

GEMS from the ART GALLERIES.

A very fine selection of Pictures being copies of some of the most valuable pictures in England.

Price **2 6** each about 130 pieces.

See next page for list of Titles.

THE PORT OF LONDON.

The Dickens Period of
Coaching Scenes.
Size 15 by 11 in.
200 piece 4/6 each.   Post 4d.

DRUMMOND'S SPORTING SERES
about 550 pieces.

"GOOD BYE & GOOD LUCK"
"HOMEWARD BOUND"
"The CLOSE of a GOOD DAY"
Price **15/6** each.

These pictures are all signed copies and were originally sold at 21/- per copy.

THE "TORMENTUM" SERIES.

No. 1.	80 piece Set, approx. size 8 by 6 in.	**10½d.**	No. 4.	260 piece Set, approx. size 16 by 14 in.	**5/9**
,, 2.	110 ,, ,, ,, ,, 10 ,, 8 in.	**1/9**	,, 5.	300 ,, ,, ,, ,, 20 ,, 15 in.	**7/6**
,, 3.	160 ,, ,, ,, ,, 13 ,, 9 in.	**3/-**	,, 7.	400 ,, ,, ,, ,, assd.	**9/6**
,, 3x.	200 ,, ,, ,, ,, 15 ,, 11 in.	**4/6**	,, 9.	500 ,, ,, ,, ,, 24 by 17 in.	**12/6**

Postage 3d., 4d. and 6d.   No. 1. **100** Double pieces, i.e., Picture both sides, **2/3**   Postage 3d., 4d. and 6d.

600 piece Set	..	..	**18/6** each.	Post free.
750 ,, ,,	..	..	**21/-** ,,	,,
1000 ,, ,,	..	..	**30/-** ,,	,,

Map Puzzles.

80 pieces	..	**10½d.**	250 pieces	..	**4/6**
125 ,,	..	**1/9**	300 ,,	..	**5/6**
200 ,,	..	**3/-**	Postage 3d. and 4d.		

Puzzles for Progressive Parties.

In Sets of 4, 6 and 8 players.

Price .. **1/10½** **2/9** **3/11**   Postage 4d.

Oak Frame Trays
On which to make up Puzzles.

14 by 11 in.	27 by 14 in.	29 by 20 n.	33 by 29 in.
2/-	**3/9**	**5/3**	**6/9**

Carriage extra.

YE OLD TABARD INN.   DICKENS' SERIES.

List of Subjects for Tormentum Picture Puzzles.

No. 1. About 80 Pieces. Approx. size 8 by 6. An endless variety in colour and black and white.

No. 2. About 110 Pieces.

THREE JOLLY HUNTSMEN. Hunting Subject	THE STORY OF THE RUN. Hunting Subject	THE VOICE OF THE DEEP
CHANGING HORSES ditto	A SEA PICTURE	A GOOD CATCH
THE MEET ditto	HAYMAKING	THE PIONEER
THE START ditto	THE MAN IN POSSESSION. Sporting	THE BEST OF FRIENDS
WOO-WHOOP ditto	IN THE HIGHLANDS	THE KING AND QUEEN IN ROBES OF STATE
THE KILL ditto	THE COLLEEN BAWN ROCK	Etc., etc., etc.

No. 2F. About 130 Pieces. 2/6 "Gems" from the Art Galleries.

INSIDE A STABLE.	G. Morland.	*Exhibited at the National Gallery*		WOODY LANDSCAPE.	Hobberna.	*Exhibited at the National Gallery*	
THE AVENUE.	Hobberna.	do.	do.	SHOEING THE BAY MARE.	Sir E. Landseer.	do.	do.
PATH THOUGH THE WOOD.	Hobberna.	do.	do.	MRS. SIDDONS.	Gainsborough.	do.	do.
THE VILLAGE FESTIVAL.	Sir David Wilkie.	do.	do.	LADY WITH A CHILD.	George Romney.	do.	do.
HIGHLAND MUSIC	Sir E. Landseer.	do.	do.	FLATFORD MILL.	Constable.	do.	do.
KING CHARLES SPANIELS.	Sir E. Landseer.	do.	do.	THE POOL OF LONDON.	Vicat Cole.	do.	*Tate Gallery*
HALTING AT AN INN.	Meissonier.	do.	*Wallace Collection*	NOONDAY REST.	John Linnell.	do.	do.
GIRL WITH DOVES.	Greuze.	do.	do.	A SCANTY MEAL.	Herring.	do.	do.
THE LAUGHING CAVALIER.	Frans Hals.	do.	do.	HAYMAKING.	Glendening.	do.	do.
DIGNITY AND IMPUDENCE.	Sir E. Landseer.	do.	*National Gallery*	MISS CAROLINE FRY.	Lawrence.	do.	do.
SLEEPING BLOODHOUND.	Sir E. Landseer.	do.	do.	THE CORN FIELD.	Constable.	do.	do.
THE HAY WAIN.	Constable.	do.	do.	HIS OWN PORTRAIT.	Rembrandt.	do.	do.
THE VALLEY FARM.	Constable.	do.	do.	THE INFANT SAMUEL			
HIS OWN PORTRAIT.	Rembrandt	do.	do.	KNEELING AT PRAYER.	Reynolds.	do.	do.
INNOCENCE.	Greuze.	do.	*Wallace Collection*	MRS. H. W. LAWZUN.	Sir H. Raeburn.	do.	do.
A CAVALIER.	Meissonier.	do.	do.	THE BLIND FIDDLER.	Sir David Wilkie	do.	do.

No. 3. About 160 Pieces.

A CAVALRY CHARGE	THE FLOWER GARDEN	THIS WAY, PLEASE	A LANDSCAPE
A CRITICAL MOMENT	THE FINISH. Hunting	GLEANERS	WAR
SHEEP GRAZING	THE FERRY	SUNSET	IN THE HAYFIELDS
LAND OF THE MIDNIGHT SUN	COUNTRY LIFE	WATER FROM THE SPRING	Etc., etc.

No. 32. About 200 Pieces.

A DESPERATE ENCOUNTER	A GOOD JOKE	AT THE COVERT. Hunting	FULL CRY. Hunting
THE HUNTSMAN'S STORY	THE COMBAT	RELEASE FROM THE KENNELS.	A LANDSCAPE
CATTLE IN MEADOWS	THE OLD HOMESTEAD	Hunting	A CORNER OF THE MEADOW
THE RECITAL			

Famous Old Coaching Scenes. (Dickens' Period.)

Bath Coach Arrives in Ladd Lane, E.C. Scene in an Old Country Inn Yard. The North Mail Coach. At ye Old Tabard Inn. Liverpool Coach Leaving the City. The Brighton Coach at Marine Parade, 1820. York Coach Passing the Old Queen's Head. Leeds Coach Leaving St. Martin's-le-Grand. Etc., Etc.

No. 4. About 260 Pieces.

RUN TO EARTH. Fox Hunting	A LANDSCAPE	A SEASCAPE	SCENE FROM "CARMEN" (1)
ARAB HORSEMEN	ENQUIRING THE WAY	THE VILLAGE SMITHY	LA REVE. Military picture
WHEN HEARTS ARE YOUNG	A CANTER ON THE SANDS	THE MILL RACE	WAR
BLIND MAN'S BUFF			

No. 5. About 300 Pieces.

A COUNCIL OF WAR	SCENE FROM "CARMEN" (2)	VANITY FAIR	CHARLES I. ON THE WAY TO EXECUTION
A WAYSIDE INN	A LANDSCAPE	A SONG WITHOUT WORDS	MARY QUEEN OF SCOTS
SCENE FROM "CAVALERIA RUSTICANA"	IN GREEN PASTURES	INSIDE THE CASINO AT MONTE CARLO	Etc., etc.
	A FLOWER STUDY		

No. 7. About 400 Pieces.

RIVAL PETS	A LANDSCAPE	THE FAVOURITE	THE LAKE OF THUN
A FINE CATCH	THE BARBER'S DAUGHTER	PETER PAN SERIES	THE MEETING OF DANTE AND BEATRICE Etc., etc.
RETURNING HOME	THE HUNT	THE SPORTSMAN'S SPOIL	

No. 9. About 500 Pieces.

SCENE FROM "RIGOLETTO"	SCENE FROM "CARMEN"	SPORTING DOGS	THE MORNING OF THE DERBY
SCENE FROM "CAVALERIA RUSTICANA"	THE TUG OF WAR	A LANDSCAPE	DEPARTURE OF THE TROOPS
	THE SWING	GRETNA GREEN	Etc., etc.

Drummond Sports. About 550 Pieces.

GOOD-BYE AND GOOD LUCK. HOMEWARD BOUND. THE CLOSE OF A GOOD DAY.

Tormentums can also be had in 600, 750 and 1,000 Pieces. Various Subjects.

No. 2a. About 100 Double Pieces (*i.e.*, Pictures both sides). A most fascinating puzzle. Various Subjects.

Contest Sets	FOR 4 PLAYERS	FOR 8 PLAYERS	FOR 12 PLAYERS

Tormentum Maps, England and Wales, Europe, Scotland, and Ireland. 80 pcs. 125 pcs. 200 pcs. 250 pcs. 300 pcs.

☞ *Customers are advised to give a second Choice when ordering, as owing to the great demand for Tormentums, the first may be out of Stock.*

IT IS IMPOSSIBLE to give a more complete list as new subjects are being continually added. Owing to the excellence of Manufacture, the splendid variety, and quality of the Pictures, **the sale of our "Tormentum" Puzzles is as vigorous as ever.**

The Latest in Card Games.

An amusing Game of Adventure and Travel.
Price .. **9**d. Post 2d.

A Novel Game of Dominoes which will be found most interesting and cause a lot of fun.
Price .. **9**d. Post 3d.

PAK.

A GAME OF CARDS FOR TWO PLAYERS.

A long-felt Want.

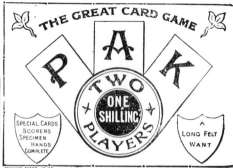

Pak is not a game imported from abroad or a variation of an old game, but the invention of a well-known writer, who, feeling the need of a card game for two persons involving more skill than any of those at present known designed an entirely new one for his own amusement.

A rubber of Pak occupies about half-an-hour.

Price, complete with special cards, scorers, rules and specimen hands, **1/-**

Club Sets (two packs), 2/- Post free.

A New Round Game for several players.
Price .. **9**d. Post 2d.

An entire New Card Game. Beautifully illustrated.
Price .. **9**d. Post 2d.

MANX

The Latest of

CARD GAMES.

Easy to Learn.

"**MANX**" (COPYRIGHT). The new and original Card Game, suitable for any number of players from two to eight, appears alike to the home circle and the skilled card player. The pack consists of 60 cards, the usual 52, 4 Billikens and 4 Manx Cards. The novelty of the game consists of the use of the Manx Card, which when played, brings the running up total to zero. Can be easily learnt in its first principles, yet contains many fine points in play, that appeal to the expert and club player, principally as to when and how to play the Manx Card.

Books of Rules. Blocks for Scoring, and the Set containing 2 packs, 2 blocks and book of rules (suitable for Manx and Manx Bridge), issued at popular prices. Pack of Manx Cards, containing 60, i.e., the ordinary 52 with 4 Billikens and 4 Manx Cards, with short paper rules in puff box, blocked in gold. **2/-** Post Free. Book of Rules, **6**d. Scoring Blocks, **7**d. each. Complete Set in Cases, containing 2 Scoring Blocks, 2 Packs Cards, Rules, &c., **5 11** Post 4d. Ditto, in Antique Rexine, **7/11** Superior Sets. **10/6**, **15/-**, &c.

THE "TESSTED"
PATENT CARD DEALER & SHUFFLER
PRICE **2/6** BRITISH MAKE

Bridge Scorer.

The "**Everthere**" Scorer is neat and effective, and as its name implies can always be relied upon to be in place when the table is set up. It is also cheaper as refill paper rolls can be obtained for **2½**d. each, with 50 per cent more scoring space than the ordinary bridge blocks. The great advantage however of "EVERTHERE" Scorer is that it is not loose on the card table and avoids, as frequently happens, the Bridge Blocks being put on some other piece of furniture, in order to be out of the way.

Price .. .. **3/6** each. Post paid

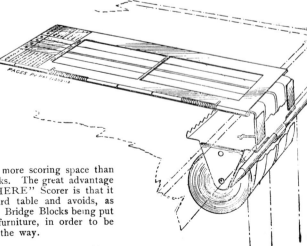

Pictorial Card Games.

ALICE IN WONDERLAND.

10d. each. Post 2d.

"Shilling" Pictorial CARD GAMES.

Painted on fine Cardboard. Enamelled on both sides and printed with Ornamental Design at back. Each pack, with Rules, neatly boxed. The Cards composing the Games are printed in colours from new and original designs of a most taking character, and the Games will be found highly amusing both to young and old.

10d. each. Post 2d.

A Round Game with Cards. Price **9d.** Post 2d.

Price .. **1/4½**
Postage 2d.
The one and only original card game

Snap, original edition .. **9d.** Post 2d.
Happy Families .. .. .. **9d.** Post 2d.
Kingdoms of Europe, 3 series .. **9d.** ,, 2d.
Counties of England, 2 ,, .. **9d.** ,, 2d.

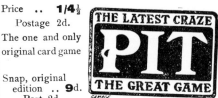

Quit.
A good game for four players.
Price .. **1/4**

Latest Card Games.
Birds,
Music,
Our Fleet,
Flowers,
Derby Day.
Price **9d.**
Post 2d.

American Blue Jay,

Cavalry.
A New Round Card Game for 4, 6 or 8 players. Beautifully illustrated.
Price .. **1/9**

Cavalry.
41 Cards.
Illustrated with the numbers and names of the British Cavalry Regiments.
Price .. **1/9**

UNITED STATES OF AMERICA.

Latest Card Games.
Language of Flowers,
Flags,
Domestic Animals,
Wild Animals,
Authors.
Price .. **9d.**
Postage 2d.

The Edition de Luxe
Happy Family Card Game.
Price .. **4½d. & 9d.** Post 2d.

PETER PAN.

JUMBO AND THE BULL.
THOMAS DE LA RUE & CO. Ltd.

The Old Familiar Game of Snap.
Price **4½d. and 9d.** Postage 2d.

Sherlock Holmes.
An exciting Card Game,
Price .. **1/4**
Post 2d.

Peter Pan.
A Card Game founded on the well-known play, all the principal figures introduced.
If you have seen the play you must have the game.
Published with the authority of J. M. BARRIE.
The Drawings are by CHAS. A. BUCHEL.
Price .. **1/9** Post 2.

Jungle Jinks.
The latest and one of the most Amusing Card Games ever published.
Consisting of 48 Pictorial cards illustrating the adventures and games of Dr. Lion and his School.
Price .. **1/9**
Post free.

The New Card Game "Precedence."
Dedicated (by permission) to the Speaker of the House of Commons (Rt. Hon. James W. Lowther, M.P.)
By Royal Letters Patent. Copyright Gt. Brit. & U.S.A., 1906. Price ... **1/4½** set. Post 2d.
The great feature of the game is that it permits of playing with any number of persons from two to six being able to take part. Although the Rules are easily mastered there is great scope for judgment and skill.

Card Games.

Pit ..	.. .. **1/4½**	Post 2d.
Quit ..	.. .. **1/4½**	,, 2d.
Rook ..	.. .. **1/4½**	

Card Games.

Counties of England ..	**1/2**	Post 2d.
Kingdoms of Europe ..	**9d.**	,, 2d.

Misfitz and other Card Games.

9d. each. Post 2d.

The Misfitz Series consist of 72 beautifully illustrated Cards, making up 24 complete Pictures.

9d. each. Post 2d.

The Misfitz Series consist of 72 beautifully illustrated Cards, making up 24 complete Pictures.

These Series are well known for the Fun and Amusement they cause at Children's Parties, etc.

Star Tidleywinks.

Price .. .. .. **1/9** Post 3d.

A New Top Spinning Game,
which scatters the marbles on the board.
Price **9d., 2/3** and **3/3** Post 3d. & 4d

Nations and Flags.

An amusing and educational game for children. Printed in correct colours. Very artistic.

Price .. **9d.** and **2/3** Post 3d. and 4d

The Game of Goose. A decided novelty in games played with realistic Model Geese. Price **5/11** Post 6d. Smaller size **4½d.** & **9d.** Post 3d.

Fox Hunting.

A Game of Real Fun and Excitement, bringing in all the exciting elements of the chase.

Price	..	..	..	3/3	5/11	7/6
Post	..	..	..	4d.	5d.	6d.

FASCINATING RACE GAMES.

Sandown Race Games.

Pocket size, wood disc, leatherette box ..	**2/6**
Do., with counters and cloth ..	**3/3**
Do., Metal disc, with cards, counters and cloth	**10 6**

Postage 3d.

Do., in mahogany case with glass top, cards and counters	**26/6**
Medium size do., cloth case, with cards and counters	**25/-**
Do., in polished pine case, cards and counters	**37/6**
Large size do., in cloth case	**45/-**
Do., in polished pine case	**60/-**

Postage free.

Cloths extra with medium and large size boards.
Cloths for do., **6/6** and **10/6** each. Post 3d.

ASCOT RACE GAME.

		List price.
G. 1. Polished wood box, 4 horses	**3/3**	4/-
G. 2. ,, ,, ,, 6 ,,	**4/10**	6/-
G. 3. Mahogany case 6 ,,	**7/-**	8/6
G. 4. Superior do., with lock and 6 large horses	**8 6**	10/6
G. 5. Club size do. ..	**12 3**	15/-
G. 6. Do., superior with 8 horses .	**17/3**	21/-
G. 7. Polished oak, nickel fittings, 8 horses ..	**23/6**	30/-

Self-Winding Set.

C. Handsome mahogany case, clockwork motor, 6 horses	**33/6**	42/-

Postage extra under 10/-

Petits Chevaux Race Game.

No. G. 2—1 row 6 horses		**3/3**
No. G. 3—2 rows 8 horses ..		**4/9**
No. G. 4—2 rows 8 horses ..		**7/6**
No. G. 5—2 rows 6 horses, superior ditto		**9/6**

Postage extra under 10/-

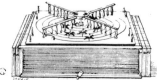

The Family Petits Chevaux Race Game.

In strong ebonized case, green baize top and nickel plated fittings.
Each horse having a separate action.

6	7	8 horses.
70/-	**80/-**	**126/-**

Carriage paid. Crate 1/6 extra.

The Family Petits Chevaux.

Stained ebony case, with 9 horses in 3 rows. Same superior quality as above. Best French make.
Price **63/-** Crate 1/-

A small selection is shown here from a large variety.

MINORU.

The most realistic Race Game ever invented.

Played on an entire new principle.

ONCE PLAYED, ALWAYS PLAYED.

No. G. 0 Complete with Horses, Rules, etc.	..	**4/3**
,, G. 1. ,, ,, ,,	..	**6/3**
,, G. 2. Superior ditto, with Pack of Cards	..	**8/9**
,, G. 3. Full-size Set	..	**12/6**
,, G. 4. Superior ditto, in polished mahogany box	**16/9**

Carriage 4d. and 6d. per set.

MANIFESTO.

The New Race Game by the inventor of "Minoru." Unlike most race games each throw of the dice affects the positions of all the horses on the course, keeping up the interest of each player until the game is actually finished.

No. 0. Popular set for 8 players	..	..	**6/9**
,, 1. 9 6	No. 2.		**13 6**
,, 3 Polished Wood Box		..	**18 6**
,, 4. Mahogany Box	..	..	**25 6**

Postage 5d.

Complete with horse, elegant folding board and dice cups.

| **9**d. | **1/9** | **2/4½** | **3/3** |

Do. with very superior horses on springs giving realistic action.

4 6 and **7 6** set. Post 3d., 4d. and 6d.

Racing Games.

Cardboard, folding, complete with horse, dice and instructions.

| No. G. 0, **4½**d. | 1, **9**d. | 2, **1/4½** |
| 3, **1/10½** | 4, **3/6** |

Superior quality, with extra gilt cloth band.

| No. G. 1, **3/9** | 2, **4/9** | 3, **6/5** |

Postage 3d. & 4d.

Extra large size Club board folding size, 5 ft. by 2 ft. 4 ins.. Complete with 6 large size. Solid metal horses and dice.
15/- Complete.

Metal Race Horses.

| **1**d. | **2**d. | **3**d. | **4½**d. | **6**d. each. |

Post 1d.

Hedges and Ditches

4½d. **6**d. and **9**d. set.
Postage 2d.

PUFF BILLIARDS.

Puff Billiards or Billiard Nicholas.
(Best Quality.)

| FOUR PLAYERS | .. | .. | **35/-** |
| SIX PLAYERS | .. | .. | **50/-** |

Carriage extra.

ACCESSORIES:—
Metal Supports, **8**d. each. Puffs, size 1, **3/6** ea. Sizes 2 and 3d, **4 6** each. Post 3d, Balls—**4**d. set of 3. **6**d. set of 4. **8**½ set of 6. Postage extra.

The Royal Race Game.

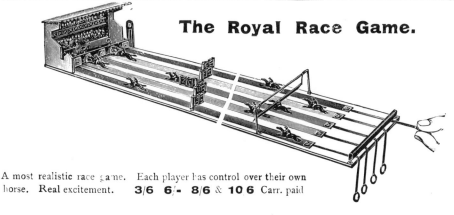

A most realistic race game. Each player has control over their own horse. Real excitement. **3/6 6/- 8/6 & 10 6** Carr. paid

O

Roulette, Watches, Boards and Accessories.

New Watch Roulette.
Nickel-plated. With Spring.
Price .. 5½d.
Post 3d

Superior ditto in Oxydised Steel Case, Spring movement.
Price .. 3/6
Post 3d.

No more Cheating at Dice!

Watch Race Game.
With fly-back movement, horses painted on dial.
Price 3/11
Post 2d.

The Dice Watch
prevents it.
Price
5½d. & 2/3
Postage 2d.

Crown and Anchor, ditto, 2/3
Postage 2d.

Roulette Watch

This Roulette Watch works on the same system and principle as the large Roulette Games with a small spinning ball.

Price .. 2/6
Postage 2d.

Roulette Boards.
Superior quality, best French pattern.

8½	10	12	13½
10/6	13/6	17/6	23/6

Carriage paid over 10/-

Roulette Cloths. painted on green American cloth.
Single, 24 by 18 in., 1/- .. 30 by 22 in. 1/9
Double, 56 by 22 ,, 2/6 .. 72 ,, 26 ,, 4/6
Postage 3d.

Best French Green Melton Cloths with printed figures. 72 by 19½, 8/6 77 by 20, 10 6
93 by 27, 12/6 each.
Single ditto. Small, 3/9 Large, 6/3
Roulette Rules, 3d. Postage 1d.

Roulette Balls, 4d. 6d. and 8d. Postage 1d.
Croupier Rakes, Plain, polished black .. 1/6
Inlaid ivory 2/6
Superior quality French make 3/6 & 5/- Post 4d.

The fairest, cleverest, simplest and most fascinating game of chance ever invented.
Played with pack of cards and Twirlette. **5/6** Post free.

Baccaratte Accessories.
Sabots or Slippers, best French make with ball-bearing block, **45/-**
Cloths, &c., to Order only.

Bone Checks.
1d. 2l. 3d. 4d. 6d. 1/-
18/- per gross.

Roulette Boards.
Polished wood. Fancy coloured disc.
No. G. 1 6½d. No. G. 2 1/- Post 3d
As illust. Ordinary qua'ity, best black finish
7 in. 3/- 8 in., 3 9 9½ in., 5/3
Nickel mountings and zinc bottom—

10½	12	13½	17½	19 in
10/6	15 6	21/-	37/6	45/-

Carriage paid over 10/-

Crown and Anchor Game.
Cloths 18 by 18, 2/6 18 by 27, 3/-
27 by 27, 4/6 Post 3d.
Dice .. .. .. 6d. and 9d. each
Dice Cups .. 1/- and 1/6 each. Post 2d

"Derbygo."
The only realistic mechanical Horse Racing Game existing.
Instructions for use.
The racing cloth is spread on a table at least 6 ft. 6 in. in length, after which the apparatus is placed to the right end of it, the crank handle in front. Open the box and give the crank handle two or three turns to the left, then place the horses in position at the other end of the cloth.
The box may now be closed again.
The racing game is worked by turning the handle to the right
The race is over as soon as the base of the first horse touches the box.
5 Horses with cloth, 25/6 7 do., 32/6 10 do., 45/-
Straight Wood Track. 5 Horses, 42/-
Circular Track as illustrated. 50/- Carriage paid

GAMAGE'S

TABLE TENNIS

Interest in this old famous Game is being revived.

TABLE TENNIS.
No. G. 1. Containing 2 wood bats, 1 pair strong clamps, net and 3 balls in box. 2/3
No. G. 2. Superior bats and fittings, 6 balls 3/3
No. G. 3. With projecting iron clamps and 6 balls .. 4/6
Superior qualities at 6/11 7/6 10/6 and 14/6
Carriage extra under 10/-
Table Tennis Nets. 6d. and 9d. each. Post 2d.
Wood Table Tennis Bats.
Plain Wood, 4½d. and 6d. each. Superior do. 10½d. each.
Cork Faced, single side, 1/3 ,, Cork Faced, on both sides, 1/6 ,,
Rubber Faced, 2/6 each.
Table Tennis Balls. Best quality. 10d. and 1/- per doz.
9 by 5 ft. Table Tops.
Painted and Lined, 25/- each. Trestles for do., 2/9 each.
Carriage extra.

Amusing Table Games.

Scouting or On The War Path.

Complete with Soldiers, Scouts, Cannon, Tent, Aeroplane, Motor Car, &c. A game crammed full of excitement and fun.

Price **3/-** Complete. Post Free.

Great Siege. A Military Game of Attack and Defence, comprising Officers and Men of two opposing Armies, (Infantry & Mounted). Full equipment of Cannon, Sharpshooters, Pompoms, Ammunition, Hospital Tents, Flags, etc., etc., Two Novel and Realistic Forts.

A Game for Young Britons. Price **5/6** Complete.

The Game of Great Raid.

Comprising Officers and Men of two opposing armies (Infantry and Mounted) and full field equipment of Cannons, Ammunition, &c. Complete with a novel and realistic Battle Field, **5/-**

RAZZLE DAZZLE

An Exciting R.C.Co Ltd New Game

An Interesting Game for any Number of Players.

Price **2/11** Post 4d.

JIGGERIES
A · MERRY · ROUND · GAME

A Fine round game any child can play it. All adults will play it.

Price **1/-** Post Free.

THE ALL RED ROUTE

Complete with Railway Cars, Terminus and Distance Guage, an exciting race to the Colonies.

Price **1/-** Post Free.

TWILBEATU.

A New Game of Skill, one man against the Board.

Price **1/-**

Post free.

THE NAUGHTY PIGGIWIGS

Piggiwigs. A real jolcy game, causing roars of laughter. The object is to push the naughty Pigs (marbles) up the slopes into the Pen by means of wire pushers. The unsteadiness of these pushers has a very tantalising and comical effect. The player who first gets his 6 Piggiwigs into the Pen wins the game.

No. 2. For 4 players (as illustration) **1/9** Post 3d.
No. 1. „ 2 „ **10½d.** „

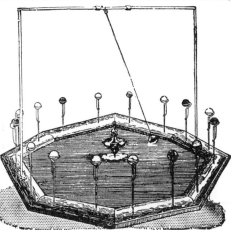

The invention of W. PEALL, Esq., the noted Snooker player. This game is one of the novelties of the season excitement intensifies while the top is spinning.

No. 1. Very portable with balls and standards, fixed on collapsible metal frame. Price .. **5/6** each.
Superior qualities .. .. **10/6** and **15/-** „
Extra Tops, **1/6** each. Coloured Balls, **3d.** „
Carriage paid.

TID-OLF.

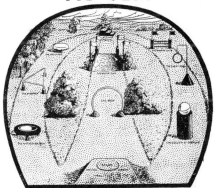

Complete with Clubs for Driving, Lofting, Putting,&c. Discs, and a complete 10 foot Novel Golf Course.
A Unique and Clever Game of Skill for All at All Times.
A Perfect Miniature Nine Hole Golf Course.
A Game for one to any number of Players.
Can be played on any size Dining Table
Price .. **5/6** complete.

O ..

Frogs are made to walk tight ropes, and when proficiency is gained, racing and tandem driving on tight ropes, the whole produce exciting and grotesque movements.

9d   19   33
Postage 3d.

Roly Poly an amusing game for children.
Price **4½**d. & **9**d.   Post 3d.

Hopla.
The favorite game.
No. G. 0. **4½**d. Post 3d.
No. G. 1.
2 hands and cones,
9d. Post 3d
No. G. 2.
4 hands and cones,
1/9 Post 3d.
No. G. 3.
4 hands and cones,
2/11 Post 4d.

No. 4.   Edition de Luxe, with 4 hands and celluloid cones .. **3/11**   Post 4d.
Extra Cones, **1**d. each.

The Maze.

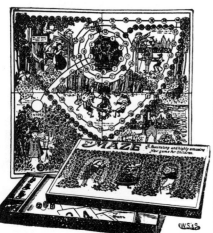

A good Game for several players.

Prices	..	**4½**d.	**9**d.	**3/3**
Post	..	3d.	3d.	5d.

Magnetic Fishponds.

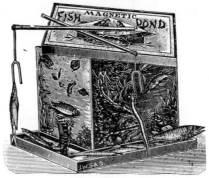

Price 4½d.	**9**d.	**1,9**	**33**	**4/11**
Post 3d.	3d.	3d.	4d.	4d.

A game that will be the children's delight. A real game of Hide-and-Seek between Prince and Princess.

Price **9**d. and **1/9**   Postage 3d.

With Bone Counters, **4½**d. and **6**d. set. With Vegetable Ivory Counters, **6**d., **1/10½**d. Post 3d.

Familiar Objects.—An instructive and amusing game for children's parties of 4 and 6 players.

Price 4½d.	**9**d.	**1/10½**	**3/3**
Post 3d.	3d.	3d.	4d.

Always a favourite game.   Trains of the world.
Price **1/9**   Post 3d.

The Old Original Game with 6 tails to each set.

4½d.   **9**d. and **1/9**

Post **3**d. & 4d.

Comical Dominoes.

Very amusing game for children, causing roars of laughter.

Price **4½**d. & **9**d. per Set.

Postage 3d.

Tiddley Wink ten pins.   Price **9**d.   Postage 3d.

For several Players.   British Manufacture.

This is a Naval Game the board showing the chief Ports in England and Germany. Each player has a battleship, destroyer and torpedo boat and the game is to disable your opponents' fleet or to capture towns belonging to your opponents. The board and pieces are contained in the box.   Price **9**d. and **1/9**   Postage 3d.

This is a Fishing Game of quite original conception. A characteristic of the Tarpon is its leaping out of the water. In this game the fish are made to leap by an original method. The Game being to catch them in the nets provided.   Price **9**d.   **1/9** and **3/6**
Postage 3d. and 4d.

The Season's Novelties in Table Games.

LAYING the Ghost.

decided novelty in games. The object of the player being to make the ghost lay down

Price **9**d. **1/9 3/6**. Post 3d. & 4d.

Just the thing for Parties.

rice **9**d. **1/9 2/6** Post 3d. 4d. 6d.

Across Canada.

Played on the familiar lines cf Ludo, etc., enabling children to gain a good geographical knowledge of the country.

Price **4½**d. **9**d. **1/9**
Post 3d. 3d. 4d.

The New Game of MOTOR TOUR

A New Game. Price **9**d. Post 3d.

New Harbour Puzzle

How to get the ships into safety.

rice .. **4½**d.

Post 2d.

Ski-ing. The New Game.

An Up-to-Date Game, founded on the favourite pastime of Ski-ing.

Prices **9**d. Post 3d. **1/10½** Post 4d. **4/11** Post 5d.

Published by C.W. FAULKNER & Cº London·E·C·

The prettiest and most novel card game of the age"

ASK TO SEE THE NEW GAME "NATIONAL MISFITZ"

Price .. .. .. **9**d. Post. 2d.

A Trip on the Continent.

A Game of never-failing interest, educational and amusing, always interesting. Price **4½**d. **9**d. **1/10½**. **4/9**

Post 3d. 3d. 4d. 5d.

SUITABLE FOR ANY NUMBER OF PLAYERS. **9**d. and **1/10½** Post 2d.

Howitzer Game.

A most interesting game for children, With real Spring Cannons which fire small pellets, and soldiers, by which a continuous bombardment of the opposite player's camp is kept up.

Price **9**d. & **1/9**

Postage 3d. & 4d

The player starts the auction, putting up one of the articles he happens to have, the other members bid as in real auction, the higher bidders being the purchasers. The purchaser then becomes the auctioneer and so on.

THE NEW GAME "AUCTIONEER" OR "GOING! GOING! GONE!" COMPLETE OUTFIT ARTICLES, CASH, HAMMER. NOT A DULL MOMENT. SCOPE FOR FUN, WIT & HUMOUR.

Price **4½**d, **9**d. and **1/9** Post 3d

Cats and Catapults.

Something quite novel, the scoring by being made of the number cats knocked off the roof.

Price **4½**d. & **9**d. Post 3d.

CATS AND CATAPULTS OR ON THE TILES

Rope Quoits

BRITISH MANUFACTURE

Always enjoyable, suitable for parlour or lawn.

Substantial Board and 4 Quoits **1/9**
Do. for in or out door use **2/6**
Strong Board with 5 Pegs and Quoits **3/6**
Polished Board, 5 Screw Pegs and 5 rope Quoits **5/11** Carriage 3d. 4d. & 6d.

NEW AND UP-TO-DATE GAMES.

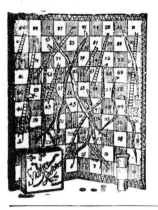

The Original Snakes and Ladder Game.

Price. Post
4½d. .. 3d.
9d. .. 3 l.
1/9 .. 4d

Published by
C. W. FAULKNER & Cº. London. E.C

ASK TO SEE THE NEW GAME "FAIRY TALES"

This attractive Game consists of 56 Cards, divided into five sets of five in halves, each set of five bearing the same title, and one set of six entire cards, and is perhaps the prettiest, most interesting, and amusing of card games. The rules are quite on original ines.

Price .. 9d. Post 3d.

J. W. S. & S.

An interesting game for any number of playe[?]
Price .. 4½d. Postage 3d.

An Aerial Race Game.

The designs are doubly interesting in that they accurately depict a large number of distinct flying machines recently constructed, and the adventures of the experimenters are very droll and amusing. Price 9d. Postage 3d

This is a board game of unusual interest and contains many novel features. The trains call at stations, pick up and put down passengers. Flags have to be exhibited at various signal boxes to prevent collisions.

Price .. 4½d. 9d. 1/9 Post 3d. and 4d.

The Game of
Aerial Contest or Flight.

The up-to-date Aeroplane Game, in which [?] incidents of a flight in an Aeroplane are though[t] out. A very amusing gar e for 2 to 6 player[s]

Price .. 4½d. 9d 1 10½ 3 6
Postage 3d 3d 4 . 4d.

An instructive and amusing Game of Flying
Price .. 4½d. 9d 1/9 and 3/6
Postage 3d. and 4d.

The Game of Cargoes.

A most instructive game for players of all ages.
Price .. .. 2/6 Post 4d.

Tidley Winks,
Complete with Cup, Counters and Rules.
Price .. 4½d. 9d. 1 10½ Postage 3d.
New Series with Vegetable Ivory Counters.
Price .. 6d. and 1 10½ Postage 3d.

Winkle's Wedding.
One of the exceptionally funny serie of Card Games. Roars of laughter.
Price .. .. 9d. Postage 3d.

A never failing source of enjoyment for Chil r[?]
Price .. .. 9d. Post 3d.

LATEST TABLE GAMES.

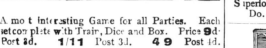

GAMES FOR BOY SCOUTS.

The Game of Boys Scouts.
Invented by an Officer.   Price **9**d.   Post **2**d.

Scouting.

A GRAND GAME FOR BOYS.
Price **4½**d., **9**d. and **1/9**   Post **3**d.

"Bobs" A new Bagatelle Bridge Game.
The rules are few and very simple. but it is a game requiring plenty of skill.

Price **9**d. **1/9 2/6 3/6**   Postage 3d. 4d. & 6d.

A New round Game for Scouts.   Price **9**d.
Postage 2d.

SPECIAL LINE.   4 Players.
Puff Billiards.
Very similar in appearance to the original.
Nicely finished.
Price **20/-** each.   Carriage extra.

King's Scouts.

A BOARD GAME IN PORTABLE FORM
The object of the game is to acquaint Boy Scouts with all the Badges they have to obtain before they are entitled to that of the King's Scout. Besides being a very interesting game, the Board is a very showy one and contains much interesting matter that every Scout should know. This is true in every detail, having been verified by an eminent Scout Master.

Price   **4½**d., **9**d. and **1/9**   Postage 3d. and 4d.

Siege.

A real good Game of Skill for two or four players

Price   **2/6**   Post 3d.

L'Attaque.   The new War Game.
A troupe of 36 officers and men on each side, in beautifully coloured uniforms of various nations manœuvring against each other. Complete in boxes   **2/4½ 2/11 3/9 5/- 9/6** set.
Post 3d.,   4d.,   and   5d.   Post free.

Naval Battle.
A Game of Skill for two players.
Superior finish.
Price   **9/9**   Post free.

Well-known Scout in colours is placed on the table and when the bulls' eye at base of Scout is struck, by means of the pistol provided, the Scout's arms are liberated and they rise waving a flag in each hand.
Price **9**d. and **1/9**   Postage 3d.

The New SCOUT SIGNALLING GAME.
Price .. **9**d.   Postage 3d.

New and Up-to-Date **Scouting Game** of unfailing interest to Boy Scouts.
Price .. **4½**d. and **9**d.   Postage 3d.

Invasion of Europe.
A CAPITAL GAME FOR ALL,
In which the Principal Towns and Ports of Europe are captured by the opposing sides.

Price ..	**4½**d.	**9**d.	**1/9**	**3/6**
Postage ..	2d.	3d.	3d.	4d.

LATEST PARLOUR GAMES.

Realistic **Model Fort,** with Towers, Gateways, Ramparts and Soldiers.

Complete **4½d.**   Post 3d.

With Machine Guns   **..**   **9**d.

Superior quality, **1/9** Post 4d.

Ratat.

The novelty for this season can be fitted on to any table. Simple rules, hours of amusement. A great rival of Ping Pong.

Price **5/- 7/6 10/-**   Carriage paid.

Bubbles.

THE CHILDREN'S DELIGHT.

Price   **..**   **..**   **4½**d., **9**d. and **1/10½**

Post 3d. and 4d.

The Detective Game.

Board game for boys.   With many thrills.

Price   **..**   **9**d.

Post 3d.

Tapette.   A new and novel game of skill for 2 or 4 players.
Price **3/6** and **7/6**   Carriage paid.

Pop-in-Taw.

POP-IN-TAW is a rollicking game of class, which only makes its appearance at intervals of a few years. It is a "Society" game. Pop-in-Taw is full of life, "go" and fun. Played with steel ball which are picked up upon small wooden shovels. The object of each player is to deposit as many of the steel balls as possible into cone-like receptacles which are placed in the middle of the table. Two, three or four at a table. Pop-in-Taw is immensely popular.

Price   **..**   **...**   **...**   **9**d.

Brush Archery.   Latest Novelty.

Indoor pastime, quite harmless.

Price   **..**   **..**   **5/11**   Post 4d.

A most interesting game for children. Played with Animals and Board.

Price   **..**   **9**d.   Post 3d.

A Simple Game for Children.   Plenty of fun and no complicated rules.   Price **9**d.   Post 3d.

A Simple Ball Rolling Game for Children.

Price **9**d.   Post 3d.

A game of great Fun. The antics of the tumbling figures are very funny, and much skill is required to control them. Price **9**d.   Larger sizes **1/9** & **3/11**   Post 3d., 4d., 5d.

An instructive game, imparting knowledge in a pleasant fashion, the players learning much about the countries visited during the game.

Price **9**d.

Post 3d.

The Latest in Table Games.

Laripino,

A Game of Chance played with Marbles.

Price .. .. **4½d.** Pos. 3d.

Who Knows?

The original game of Questions and Answers.

Price .. .. **9**d. Post 3d.

Royal Ludo.

Price .. **9**d. **1/6**

Postage 3d. and 4d.

Superior Ditto, in Box.

Price .. **2/6**

Postage 4d.

Ordinary Ludo.

Price .. **4½**d **9**d. **1/4½** **1/9** Per Set.

Postage 3d. and 4d.

Acrobats.

The Board, which is a representation of an Acrobat or his back holding a barrel on his feet, is set up in the box. By means of a special figure which is actuated by a spring, a small figure of an acrobat is propelled.

Price **9**d. & **1/9**

Postage 3d.

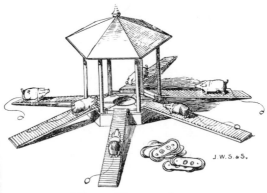

The Piggeries.

Good party game, the pigs being made to race each other to the wall.

For 2 players .. .. **1/10½** Post 3d.
For 4 players .. .. **3/9** ,, 4d.

Edition de Luxe, with painted wood house.

For 3 players, with Model Shaped Pigs .. **5/11**
For 6 players ditto ditto .. **8/6**

Postage 5d.

Correct Cardboard Models. Price .. **9**d. Post 3d.

Always a great source of amusement for Children of all ages

Price **4½**d. **9**d. **1/10½** **3/3**
Postage .. .. 3d. 3d. 4d. 4d.

Price **4½**d. **9**d. **1/9**
Post .. .. 2d. 3d. 3d.

A Voyage through the Clouds.

Describing an adventurous race in balloon over Europe.

Price .. Post
4½d. .. .. .. 2d.
9d. .. .. .. 3d.
1/10½ .. .. .. 3d.
3/3 .. .. .. 4d.

Skilly, or Bobs.

The Bagatelle Bridge Game

Price **9**d. **1/9** **2/6**
Postage .. 3d. 3d. 4d.

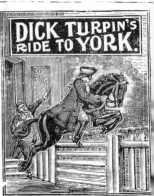

A game brimful of interest, founded on the old historical ride of the famous Dick Turpin from London to York.

Price .. .. .. **9**d.

Postage 6d.

Latest Novelties in Parlour Games.

Busy Bees.

Charming Game for Children.

e board represents a honeycomb, which the Bees work from cell to l until they become surrounded by the various coloured flowers.

| ce | .. | 9d. | 1/9 | 3/6 |
| stage | .. | 3d. | 3d. | 4d. |

Rescue.

A very Exciting Game.

players racing their boats to and the wreck to try and save the greatest number of lives.

| e | .. | 4½d. | 9d. | 1/9 |
| age | .. | 2d. | 3d. | 3d. |

ost facinating game for an evening in which the coloured balls have knocked off the wire stands into the box.

| ce .. | .. | 9d , | 1/9 and | 3 6 |

Post 3d. an 1 4d.

teresting and amusing game of By means of the special shaped rs, the players endeavour to blow arious coloured balls in the division of the box.

| e .. | .. | 9d., | 1/9 and | 3 6 |

Post 3d. and 4d.

Latest London Society Craze.

Dormy Golf Game.

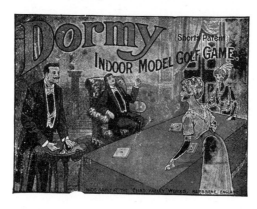

Dormy Golf for the Table is the closest reproduction of the outdoor Game ever invented, as it follows the features of the outdoor Game in every respect.

It is complete with miniature MODEL SPRING GOLF CLUBS (Drivers, Mashies and Putters).

Specially Prepared Balls, Putting Green and Bunkers.

The Balls being specially prepared will not travel more than three to four yards for a hard drive, and an excellent game may be obtained by using two tables, driving from one table to the other.

PRICE .. **14/6** POST FREE.

Oval Cricket.

A capital game for Boys, worked out on scientific principles. Runs, &c., being scored on a unique device. A most enjoyable game for a family.

Price **4½d.** and **9d.**

Post 3d.

Fantails.

The Game comprises a neat cage with four openings, and a number of variously coloured paper birds. Each player is provided with a fan with which to fan the birds of his own colour into the cage, the one who first cages all his birds being the winner. The fun becomes fast and furious when birds caged by one player are fanned out again by another.

The Game is produced in a very attractive form, and makes an excellent item for PROGRESSIVE GAME PARTIES

PRICE **2/6** AND **4/6** POST FREE.

Fantails, the only Game since the advent of Ping-Pong, that has become popular with a rush, its simplicity and its originality being at once its charm.

Blue Birds.

A delightful Game.

Founded on the charming Play and Story by M. Maettincks.

The players pass from scene to scene until Blue Bird is attained.

| Price | .. | .. | 9d. | 1/9 | 3/6 |
| Postage | .. | 3d. | 3d. | 4d. |

Atlantic Records.

A game representing the Sea

And Different Steamship Routes between Europe and America.

Miniature steamships are used, together with obstacles to make the game exciting.

| Price | .. | .. | 4½d. | 9d. | 1/9 |
| Postage | .. | 3d. | 3d. | 4d. |

By SIR FREDERICK FRANKLAND, Bart. A game that will be found to have great interest to the average golfer and should be found in every club room .. **9d.** and **1/9** Postage 3d.

An instructive and amusing game of Flying. **4½d. 9d. 1/9** and **3 6** Post 3d. and 4d.

Played on the familiar lines of Ludo, etc. enabling children to gain a good geographical knowledge of the country.

| Price | .. | .. | 4½d. | 9d. | 1/9 |
| Post | .. | .. | 3d. | 3d. | 4d. |

LATEST GAMES.

Lotto or House.
No. 400.

4½d.   9d.
1/9 and 2 6

New Edition in polished box, superior fittings.

3 6

Post 3d. & 4d.

CUEPING
A NEW & FASCINATING GAME OF SKILL.

ENGLISH MANUFACTURE

A capital game for winter evenings.
Complete with cue, plain and coloured posts, ball and rules in box.   Price 2/-   Postage 4d.

Four Corners.
An Ideal Game for Dull Evenings.
For 2 or 4 players.   Price 9d.   Post 3d.

HOKO   The New Ring Game.
10 heads and rings complete in Box.
Price 9d.   Postage 3d.

Blow Football.
Rare Fun for Evening Parties.

Price 4½d. 9d. 1/9 & 3 3   With bellows 3 11
Post 3d. 3d. 4d. 4d.   4d.

Gamage's Patent Game—
"Wibbly-Wob"
or Parlour Football.

Every Footballer or lover of the Game should have one. It gives as much amusement to the lookers on as to the players.
Endless amusement combined with science.

"Wibbly-Wob." (Registered Name).
No. 0. Special for 2 players 1/-
  ,, 1. For 2 Players 1/6
  ,, 2. For 4 Players 2 6
Postage 3d.
Superior quality, wire goal nets.
Packed in strong box.

No. 3. For 2 Players 5/-
  ,, 4. For 4 Players 6/-
Extras— Strikers 6d. each.   Balls 2d. each.
Postage 3d.

Prices :

9d. 1/9

3/6 & 7/3

Post 3d., 4d. & 6d.

Kick.
Latest and Best of all Football Games, each one complete with metal figures which kick the ball.

Socker.   Price 9d. and 2/3
Larger size with full teams, 3 11   Post 3d. 4d. 5d.

Snipkick.   New Football Game.
Price   ..   9d. and 2/6   Postage 3d. and 4d.

No. 1.   Board and Men or 4 players   ..   9d.
  ,, 2.   Leatherette ditto 1 4½
  ,, 3.   Cloth-covered Board and box to
match 1 9
  ,, 6.   Ditto 3 3
Postage 3d.

The Great Game of Motor Tour
or Motor Ride.
A grand Motoring Game full of exciting incidents.
Price   4½d.   9d.   2/3   4/9
Postage   3d.   3d.   4d.   5d.

One of the Novelties of the season. By a novel arrangement the dogs are made to go along the table and bring back a stick in their mouths.
Price 9d. and 1/9   Post 3d.

Word Making.   The old familiar Game
Price 4½d.   9d   1/3   Postage 3d.
Extra large 2 6   Postage d.

An Interesting Game for Parti
Price   ..   9d.   Post 2d.

Latest Table Games.

A Jolly Game for 4 players.

Complete with beans, pockets and gatherers.

Price .. **9**d.

Post 3d.

Price .. **2/6** and **4/6**

Post 3d.   3d.

A novel and interesting Railway Race Game.

Price **4½**d., **9**d. and **1/9**   Post 3d. and 4d.

Stepping Stones.   (Registered.)

This is an amusing game which the spectators enjoy the most. It is difficult to balance a ball on a platter it is not easy to walk over stepping stones, but when both are attempted at the same time a steady hand as well as ready confidence and determination are needed. The game may be played in the drawing room or nursery or upon the lawn.

Price .. **5/-**   Carr. extra.

NEW STANDARD INDOOR GAME.

"BATTLE"
EXCITING WAR GAME.

Played by 2 or 4 persons, by pieces representing Generals, Cavalry, Guns Infantry and Ammunition, on a battlefield

The Season's Craze. Endless combinations and problems. Supersedes Chess, Draughts and Cards.

2/6

Or **2/10** post free

Military and Social Clubs and Cafes, wishing to be up-to-date, should immediately introduce it. —Vide Daily Press.

A novel and up-to-date game.   For two or four players.

Price .. **9**d.   Post 3d.

Novel game with rolling marbles.   Price **9**d.   Post 3d.

This game consists of an egg box or "roost" in which there are a series of holes or "nests," a number of imitation eggs, and small spoons or "shovels." The game may be arranged for either two or more players, who, in the latter case, take sides. The players endeavour to pick up the eggs with their flat spoons and drop them into their respective nests—a task requiring considerable skill and creating endless amusement.

Price, for 2 or 4 players   ..   ..   **9**d. and **1/9**

Postage 3d. and 4d.

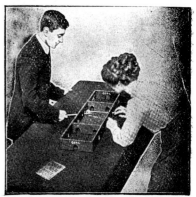

Holo. (Registered). Here is a game at once fast and furious. The players bend their energies and their backs to secure a goal. The excitement from start to finish is intense, as one cannot be certain till the very end that the game is lost or won.   Price ... **3/3**   Post 4d.

An ingenious puzzle .. **4½**d.   Post 2d.

Flip Figure Game with Goblin.

Very strong .. **3/11**   Post 4d.

Square Board ditto for 4 players, with centre cup and 24 counters .. **5/11**   Post 6d.

A simple and amusing Game with Ring and Counters.

Price .. **4½**d. **9**d. **1/9** and **3 6**

Postage 3d. and 4d.

Amusing Games.

The most realistic Fishing Game.
Very different to all other fish-pond games.
The fish when caught are weighed in the scales.
The first totalling 14 lbs. being the winner.

Price .. .. **2/10½** Post 3d.

Bagg It. The New Mirth Maker in two Series for Adults and Children.
Your future can always be found in Bragg It.

Price .. **1/10½** Post 3d.

Cherry Bobs. A simple and most interesting game for all. The one getting the largest number of Bobs on the Tree being the winner. Price .. **1/9** Post 3d.

The Old Game of Tiddley Winks made very interesting with the Model of a Battleship.
The scoring being taken from the different part on which the shots land Price .. **9**d. & **2/-** Post 3d.

Aladdin.

A fascinating children's game, based on the old fairy tale and exquisitely carried out. Each player takes a magic lamp and the lucky one wins his way to fortune and marries the Princess.

Price.		Post.
4½d.	..	3d.
9d.	..	3d.
1/9	..	4d.
3/6	..	5d.

Silent Billiards.

A capital game. Very strong. Nothing to get out of order.

20½ by 20½   For 4 players

Price **25/-**

Carriage 9d.

Advance Australia.

An Instructive Geographical Game on Ludo lines.

Price .. **9**d. Post 3d.

Cape to Zambesi ditto. Price .. **9**d.

Post 3d.

Edition de Luxe Tiddley Winks,
Enamelled cup and vegetable ivory counters ..
Post 3d.

The Game of Travel.
One of the most instructive games ever published.
Always interesting.

Price **6/6**
Post paid.

A New Table Football Game,

With goal posts, ball and set of flippers.

Price .. .. .. **9**d. and **1/9**

Post 3d. and 4d.

POPULAR PARLOUR GAMES.

Shooting the Chute.

A Game of Skill for the Table on quite a novel principle.

Price .. .. **1/-** and **2/6**

Post free.

MADROLO

FOR ANY NUMBER OF PLAYERS.

Game consists of a Board, containing, Holes numbered 1 to 7, and a ball of a very uncontrolable and illusive nature, which runs

HERE, THERE & EVERYWHERE.

Can you control it in its
MAD = ROLL - O.

Price **1/-**

Hands Up. Wild West Shooting Range.

The target is represented by an Indian, Cowboy and Cowgirl, who on being shot immediately put up their hands.

Complete with Shooting Range and perfectly harmless Pistol.

Price, ... **2/9** complete.

TIMI TIPP.

Jolly Nigger Boys race along poles by tapping each pole at one end. For 2, 3, 4 and 6 players.

Prices **2/9 3/9 5/6**

Post free.

The Great Test Match.

A Game combining Skill and Chance.

Complete with 11 men, cricket field, ball, and a scoring board as used at all the great test matches.

Price .. .. **1/-** and **2/6**

Post free.

Tilting Targets.

A Table Shooting Game.

Compact with gun shots and six automatic targets.

Price **1/-**

Post free.

Bauko Billiards.

A never ending source of amusement. Can be played on any size table. For any number of players.

———

Complete with 6 Balls, Bauko Board, and Billiard Cue.

———

Interesting. Exciting. Entertaining. A Game of Skill.

Price **3/-**

Captive Table Tennis.

Easily adjusted to any ordinary dining table, no screws or clamps required.

Price .. **7/6**

Post 4d.

Bobs or Bridge Bagatelle.

An Ideal Parlour Game.

Complete with Bridge, Cue and Balls.

PRICES :—

9d.	..	Post 3d.
1/9	..	,,
2/6	..	Post 4d.
3/6	..	,,

New and Standard Games.

Table Bowls.

An adaptation of the Game of **Lawn Bowls** and can be played on an ordinary table.

Size 1.   Containing 4 pairs Lignum Vitæ Bowls, Jack and Shoot and Rules .. **2/6**
Size 2.   Ditto,   ditto **3/3**
Size 3.   Ditto,   ditto **4/6**
Size 4.   Ditto,   ditto **5/11**
Superior Ebony ditto, small size Bowls .. **7/6**
  „   „   „   2¼ in. „   „   set **10/6**
Postage 4d. and 5d. per set.

Home Cricket.

The most successful effort yet made to introduce the national game into the category of parlour games.

Price .. **5/11**

Postage 4d

Combination Carroms and Crokenhole Boards.

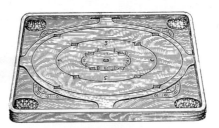

50 games on the one board.   The board is 29 in. square with rounded corners and four pockets, the centre of board being of white maple with a natural colour polish, the Crokenhole side being fitted with an imitation mahogany centre. Sent out complete with all accessories.
Price **18/6**

The C. B. Fry Cricket Game.

The only game in which the runs are recorded and are accurately made

Price .. **1/9**

Post Cd.

Mixed Pickles.

A GAME FOR OLD AND YOUNG.

A great amusement for progressive and social gatherings.

A Real Mirth Maker.

A game founded on the selecting of one's own favourite pickle.
Price .. **2/-**
List price 2/6
Post 3d.

Parlour Cricket.

The ball is aimed at the bat, and the batsman strikes it as in the real game, runs being scored when the ball stops in the numbered holes.

The player keeps in till the ball hits the wicket or he is "caught out."
Special quality ... **9d**
Postage 3d.
"A" quality. with full directions, **1/9**

Size of Field, 18 in. long by 13 in. wide.   Post 4d
Larger size, **3/6** „ **6**

Table Golf.

A fascinating parlour game.

Neatly boxed with cloth.

Obstacles, counters and drivers.

Price .. **3/3**

Post 4d.

The New Game Of
TABLE GOLF

Crazey Traveller.
A good strong parlour game with spring top.
Price **10½d.**   Postage 4d.

The New Indoor Game.   ARBOCU.

A new and diverting game with a spinning top which the players have to work over the board on the branches of the tree.
Price **4½d.** and **9d.**   Post 3d.

THE SENSATION OF THE YEAR.
A game of skill which will amuse your friends whether they be young or old. Strength or agility not necessary.
Playable on any dining-room table from six to nine feet long.
Complete in box with cloth, nickel plated propelling bow on polished oak base, clamp, twelve compressed fibre discs, scoring block and rules.
Price **21/-** each.   Carriage paid.

A new puzzle of perforated cards with Spots.   The puzzle being to arrange the cards so that only certain coloured spots are left in view   Price **4½d.**   Post 1½

Table Croquet and Parlour Games.

No. 1. For 4 players, mallets, balls, &c. **9**d.

2. Ditto Superior **2/-**

3. 4 mallets, balls, 2 starting pins, hoops, rules &c., in box complete **2/11**

4. 4 best quality Boxwood mallets and balls, Patent Self Clipping hoops, complete with Clamp and Webbing, to go round table, in Strong Box.
Price **4/9**. Post 4d.

6. Comprising 8 Boxwood mallets, 8 balls, hoops, 2 starting pins and rules. In box complete **6/3**

6A. Superior Finish, ditto, with Polished Mahogany mallet and ball stand. **11/6** Post 6d.

Postage on 1 & 2 3d.

,, ,, 3 & 4 4d.

The N**l** e Series. **Table Croquet.**

With Patent Self-Clipping Hooks.

1. Comprising 4 mallets, 6 patent spring hoops, 2 posts, and book of rules .. .. **9**d.

2. Ditto, with boxwood mallets **2/-**

3. Ditto, with celluloid-headed mallets and superior quality fittings.. .. .. **3/-**

4. Ditto, with 4 solid celluloid mallets best quality fittings, &c. **3/11**

Post 3d. set.

A most fascinating game for young and old. The game is played by placing sleepers and metals in position on a railway track which is divided into sections for 2, 3 or 4 players. The excitement in the game is in **all players commencing at once** and endeavouring to get their section finished first; all parts to be lifted and placed in position with the wire spoon or lifter.

No piece may be touched with the hands.

Price .. .. **9**d. Post 3d.

Springbock.

An exciting Game of Skill, each player being provided with a mallet, with which he strikes the spring bearers with the object of making the ball fly through the square at the end of the board.

Price .. .. **1/9 3/3** and **5/11**

Carriage extra.

No. 7. Set. Consisting of 4 best quality boxwood mallets, 4 balls, 2 posts. Complete with set of good quality hoops, plated clamps and table webbing. In best finished **polished Oak Box**, fitted with Clasp .. **8/11**

No. 8. Do. do. containing materials for 8 players in Oak Box.
Price **14/6** Post Free.

No. 9. Edition De Luxe comprising 8 extra quality boxwood mallets, eight best balls, 2 coloured posts, complete set of hoops, clamps, bands &c., with polished mahogany stand to take mallets, and balls in best quality polished oak box.
Price **18/6** Carriage Paid.

Three Little Kittens.

A Harmless and amusing ball game for Children.

Price 2 Kittens **1/10½**

,, 3 ,, **3/3**

Post 3d. and 4d.

Ditto, with Tiddley Winks .. **4½1**
and **9**d. Post 3d.

An amusing Ball Game.

Price.. .. **9**d. Post 3d.

Chinaman ditto .. **9**d. Post 3d

Ally Sloper **6**d. & **9**d. Post 3d.

Snappo. A most amusing game of Skill. The clowns caps having to be tossed into the rings attached to a Screen. Price **4/3** Post 6d.

A good party game for young people.

An original Game for two or more players, the Frogs being made to jump down the Swan's mouth Price .. **9**d. Post 3d.

P

Table Croquet and other Games.

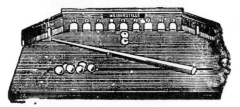

"BILLIARDETTE." The New Table Game

A game of skill for those who cannot afford the space for Billiards. Some of the strokes are similar to those used in billiards, some similar to bagatelle. Simple enough for youngsters—interesting enough for adults. Any number can play. It is played on an ordinary table. The fittings comprise : Cloth ready marked up, 8 balls, cue, billiardette frame, marking board, etc.

Price, complete .. .. **8/6** Carriage extra.

Bagatelle.

Bagatelle board with solid oak cushions covered in green cloth, cue chalk and 9 of the finest Composition Balls. With rules and all accessories for playing the following games : Cannon Game, Sans Egal, Bagatelle and All Cannon Game.

Price .. .. **12/6** complete.

Patent No. 12701.

A Game of Skill.

The balls are shot out of t Projector into the net, Project sliding along rod to enable playe to play for any particular net.

Price **10/6** Carriage Paid.

A magnetic yacht race over two courses with 6 steel yachts 6 docks. The yachts are steered with poles from underneath the board. An exciting game to avoid getting "On the Rocks." **5/-** each.

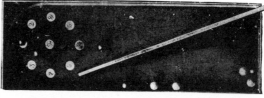

Children's Bagatelle Board.

Complete with Cue and Balls.

Price		**4½d.**
With Wood Frame	**10½d.**	**1/9**
Post	3d.	4d.

Epsom.

An up-to-date race game with the odds scientifically worked out

Price **9**d. & **2/-** Post 3d.

Skittle-Chute

A capital Game for Club use. The ball can be directed on to any direction on the board and great skill is required to knock down all the skittles at one time.

Price .. .. **8/11** Post 6d.

Dominoe Pool.

Consists of 9 best quality dominoes fastened on to a polished walnut stand. Each player throws 2 dice and turns back dominoes of equal value to his throw. He continues until his throw cannot be represented by the dominoes which are not turned back. Any number can play and the player who is left with the lowest score is the winner and takes the pool A handsomely finished article. **10/6** Post free.

An entirely new game, using a patent screen, behind which Artillery and Infantry manœuvre for positions, with railways, bridges, houses, churches on canvas sheet, size
Complete with instructions .. .. .. **12/6** each.

Pop it in.

A Game of Skill.

Large board with captive b on long elastic strings, w clamp to attach to table.

Price complete .. **3/3** &

Post 4d. & 6d.

GAMES FOR CLUBS, INSTITUTES, &c.

Ring or Dart Boards

9d

Throw Darts.
Complete with Strong Board and Darts.
Price **9**d. Postage 3d.
Combination Dart and Ring Board.
Price **9**d. Post 4d.

Ring Boards.

The ever popular game. Price **4½**d. and **9**d.
Postage 3d.

Peg Quoits.

Small size, polished wood, Stand and Peg with superior velvet-covered Rings.
Price .. **1/10½**
Postage 3d.
Large size, ditto,
Price .. **4/11**
Postage 4d.

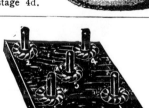

The Rope Quoit Board.

Five-peg Board complete with 4 rope
quoits **3/11**
Superior ditto **5/11**
Ditto **7/6**
Double quoit board suitable for deck
use .. .. .. set **10/6**
Carriage Extra.

Puff and Dart.
Wood Target, Metal Blow Pipe and set of Darts.
No. G. 1 **9**d. G. 2 **1/4½**d. G. 3 **2/3**
With Bell .. 1 **3/-** 2 **4/6**
Postage 3d.

Solid Wood Dart Board

2-in. solid wood Dart Board, with stout wire divisions and numbers, wired on one side, **5/-** each
Reversible, **6/9** Complete with 3 darts.

Large reversible, with 6 darts, **8/11** Carriage ex.
Cane darts with brass ferrule, **4**d. each. Small feather darts, **1**d. each. **10**d. doz. Small loaded darts, **1½**d. each, **1/3** doz. Postage 2d.

"Hook it."
The New Quoit Game for the Wall.

The Board having been hung up, the players throw the rubber quoits at the hooks, and endeavour to gain the highest numbers.

The quoits are noiseless and can be used in a drawing room.

No.				Post
G. 0.	Square Board, with 4 rings ..	**4½**d.	3d.
G. 1.	,, ,, ..	**9**d.	3d.
G. 2.	,, ,, ..	**1/4½**	3d.
	Do. with cardboard ring catcher	**1/6½**	5d.
G. 3.	,, Green baize covered	**1/6**	4d.
G. 4.	,, ,, ..	**2/6**	4d.
G. 5.	Round polished board, with brass hook and 4 rubber rings ..	**2/11**	5d.
G. 6.	Shield shape, stained and polished, brass hook and 6 rubber rings	**4/-**	6d.
G. 7.	Large ditto	**5/-**	6d.

Extra Large size **9/11** Carriage Extra.
Extra Rubber Rings for Boards, **1/3** doz.
Postage 3d.
Folding Table Stand, for Puff and Dart Boards and Ring Boards.
Plain, **1/6** Polished, **2/-** Postage 4d.

Tipply Web.

An amusing game of skill for any number of Players. The balls having to be rolled down the shoot into the Pockets, scoring accordingly.

Price
1/4½ & **2/9**
Post 3d. & 4d.

Ring Boards for Club Use.

Polished Board with 13 Brass Hooks and 4 Rings.
Price .. **2/11**
Postage 4d.

Parlour Quoits.

Good strong Board with Peg and Rubber Rings complete.

14 by 14, **2/3**
18 by 18, **3/6**
Post extra.

Parlour Quoit Boards
Sunk Centre.

Complete with rubber rings, **8/3**
Postage 9d.
Extra rings, **6**d. each.

The body of this board is sunk to prevent the rings jumping off. Carriage extra.

Shove Half-penny Board.

Plain, with brass band,
7/9
Do., with brass lifts, as illustration .. **17/6**
Solid Mahogany, with lifts **25/-**
Carriage extra.

P..

Parlour and Lawn Games.

We carry a large assortment of Parlour Games which cannot be Illustrated.

Three Figure Head Ball Target.
39 in. high.

Price **5/11**　　　Carriage extra.

The New Ring Shuttlecock Game.
Something New.
Very fascinating and harmless Toy for Children.
Price, with 2 sticks and 1 shuttlecock, **2/11**
Postage 4d.

The Popular Game of La Grace.
10½d. **1/9 2/6** and **4/6** per set.
Postage 4d.

New Victoria Ball Game.
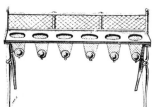

39 in. long, 23½ in. high.
A harmless, interesting game of skill for any number of players.
For either in or out-door use.

Complete with all accessories, **8/6** Carriage extra

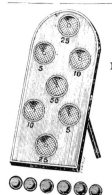

Indian Ball Game.

No. 0	..	**3/6**
,, 1	..	**4/11**
,, 2	..	**6/11**
,, 3	..	**7/11**
,, 4	..	**8/11**
,, 5	..	**10/6**

Complete.
Carriage extra.

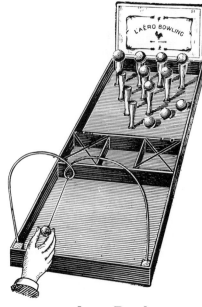

Aero Bowls.
A splendid game for club use played as illustration
Folding up into neat box.

Price **10/6**　　　Post free.

New Cue and Ball Game.

On Stand, as illustration, Brightly Painted and finished.

Price complete .. **9/6**
Carriage extra.

The Three Bell Rolling Ball Game.
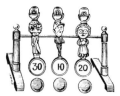

An amusing and scientific game requiring great skill
Very superior finish.

Price .. **7/6**　　　Carriage extra.

Five Figure Ball Target Game.
Very strong.　Suitable for Lawn or Parlour use.

Price **7/6**　　　Carriage extra.

Bull Board.
(SOLID WOOD TOP.)
For Deck or Lawn use.　Complete with 6 Disc
No. G. 1.　33 by 25　..　..　**10/-**
No. G. 2.　Superior ditto ..　..　**14/6**
Carriage paid.

Revolving Hoopla.

Stand with Animals and Rings complet
Good strong game.　Price **11/6**

Frog Race.
Suitable for Garden Parties, Bazaars, etc.
Quite a new fun maker.
With 3 Frogs and rules complete, **1/9** Post 3d.
With 6 Frogs and rules complete, **3/3** Post 3d.

Provisionall Protected

Polished and Painted Hardw
Skittles.
In strong wood box.
8 in., **6/3**　　9½ in., **7/9**　　11 in., **8/1**
Carriage extra.
Cheaper quality, ordinary pattern.
No. 1, **1/5**　　No. 2, **1/8**　　No. 3, **2**
No. 4, **4/-**　　Carriage extra.

HOME GYMNASTIC SETS, etc. for XMAS PRESENTS.

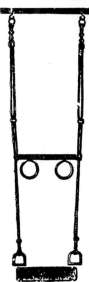

Complete Set,
comprising Trapeze Bar, Leather covered Rings, Swing Board, Stirrup-shaped Irons, Ropes adjustable and interchangeable with two N.-P. Dog hooks. Two Safety Ceiling Hooks.

Price **14/6**
Stronger do. **18/6**

Do. cheaper quality with uncovered Rings, **8/11** Set.

Carriage Extra.

All in Strong Wood Boxes.

Nursery Swing, with Trapeze.

Can be used as a Swing or Trapeze.

Easily adjusted to any doorway.

Price, complete with Swing.

4/11 each.

Carriage extra.

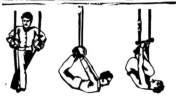

Trapeze Bars and Ropes.
SPECIAL LINE

No. 1—Polished Trapeze Bar with Ropes		**2/6**
,, 2—Stronger do		**4/6**
,, 3—Do., with leather covered hand rings .. .. .. set		**8/6**
,, 4—As No. 3, with adjustable ropes ,,		**11/6**

Carriage 4d., 5d., and 6d. set.

The 'Athleticon,' or Home Gymnasium.
Comprises—Horizontal Bar, Trapeze Bar, with iron core, Hand rings. Can be fixed in a few minutes in any room, and as quickly removed. The ropes can be adjusted to any height. Complete in box, price **24/6**. Sitting Swing, **5/6** extra. Carriage extra.

The Cheapest Horizontal Bar, light portable, fixed in a few minutes, either in or out of doors. The bar is constructed of the very best ash, with a ¾ in iron core.

Price, complete	**£1**	**5**	**0**
Larger and stronger ditto ..	**1**	**12**	**6**

Carriage extra.

Trapeze Bar and Leather Covered Rings.
Interchangeable with N.P. Dog Hooks, adjustable Ropes and Safety Ceiling Hooks.
Price **8/6** and **11/6** Set. Carriage extra.

New Cane Foot Rest Swing.

Very Safe and Light.

No. 1, **4/6**   No. 2, **5/11**   Carriage 4d.
No. 3, Special Finish, complete with Cushion, **8/6**   Carriage 6d.

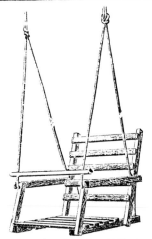

Perfection" Porch Swing.
Made of Hardwood, nicely finished with waterproof varnish. Light and portable, folds flat for storing when not in use. Will support weight of half-grown person. Can be hung in doorway, porch or from tree. Screwhooks and rings supplied. Adjustable to height and pose. Back 13 in. high, seat 13 in. deep, distance between arms 14 in.
Price .. **4/6**   Carriage 6d.

Baby's Network Swings.

Impossible to fall out.

Very strong.

4/11   Post 4d.

Nursery Swing Frame.
Made from Hardwood. Very rigid, can be taken apart and packed into small space.
Weight 21 lbs.   Price **8/11**   Carriage extra.

Nursery Swings.

Children's Safety Swings, as illustrated.

Strongly made and polished black and white.

No 1 ..	..	**3/6**
,, 2 ..	..	**5/11**
,, 3 ..	..	**6/11**
,, 4 ..	..	**10/6**

Carriage 6d.

Footballs and Hockey Sticks for our Boys.

Rugby Balls same price.

The "REFEREE"
(Regd.)

Made from the Celebrated Tufine Chrome Leather. Thoroughly waterproof, does not get heavy. **12/6** Post free.

Tennis Rackets for Presents.

Gamage's Fishtail, with Demon Shaped Handle, **5/6**

The Champion, 6/9

The Referee, 8/11

The Special Club Double Strung Centre, **10/6**

The A.W.G., 14/6

The Gamage, 18/6

Very Best Quality Gut and Selected Frames.

For full range of Racquets write for Sports & Games List

The "A.W.G."
New and Perfect shape. Selected hides cut on a new principle. Thoroughly recommended for hard wear .. **10/6** Post free.

HOCKEY STICKS.

Superior plain Ash, Bound Handles .. **2/6** each.

Flat or Bandy Hockey Sticks, Bound Handles, suitable for Ladies .. **2/-** ..

"The School," Cane Handle, Bound with twine .. .. **2/3** ..

Post 4d.

The "Referee Regd. All-Cane Cricket Bat Handle.

Heads polished to keep out the damp. The BEST Stick on the market. In all weights.
Men's New Bulged Head .. **4/6** each.
52/- dozen.

The "Junior Referee," (Regd.),
with Cane Handle and Bulged Heads. Specially adapted for Schools and Junior Clubs.
3/6 each. **40/-** doz. Post 4d.

BOYS Footballs **BOYS** Footballs

No. 2.	**Universal**	.. .. ..	**2/9**
3.	,,	.. ..	**3/3**
4.	,,	.. ..	**3/9**
5.	,,	.. ..	**4/6**
3.	**School**	.. ..	**4/3**
4.	,,	.. ..	**5/6**
5.	,,	.. ..	**6/-**
No. 3.	**Holborn**	.. ..	**5/-**
4.	,, ..	.. ..	**6/-**
5.	,,	.. ..	**6/11**

The Circus, Chrome Dressed.
No. 4 .. . **9/6** No. 5 .. **10/6**
Post 3d. and 4d. per ball.

HOCKEY STICKS.
The "A.W.G."
Selected Cane and Rubber Spring Handle and Polished Bulged Head. Round or Square Toe.
All weights .. **5/11** each. Post 4d.
68/- dozen.
Ditto, with Cork Handle .. **6/6** Post 4d.
75/- dozen.

"The Champion."
Specially selected Ash, Double Rubber, Spiced Handles, with improved Double Binding.
All Weights. Price .. **7/3** Post 4d.
84/- dozen.

Ditto, specially selected, Leather Bound Handles, New Bulged Head Hockey Stick .. **7/11**
Post 4d. **92/-** dozen.

Webber's Celebrated **AYTENPAN.**
As used in the English Cup Final, **12/6** Post free

Best English Association Badminton Rackets.

No. 1. Thin ash frame, good gut, handles as illus., Bound Shoulders.
4/9 Post 4d.
Superior qualities,
6/6, 7/6 & 9/6 each.

The Sparton (Davis) ...**11/6**
The Lambert Chambers (Slazenger) ..**14/6**
The Hydera (Ayres) ...**11/6**
The A.D.P. (Sheffield) **14/-**
The E.D.B. (Sykes) ...**12/3**
The Special Corona **14/6**
The Extra Special (Prosser) ... **9/6**
Feltham's Climax ... **12/6**
Post free.

Association
Shuttles ... **4/9** doz.
Post 3d.
F. H. Ayres ... **5/9** doz. Post free.

The "GAMAGE."
Best quality Cowhide handsewn and fitted with superior red rubber bladder, **8/11** Post 4d.

Presents for Our Golfing Friends.

Our Speciality.

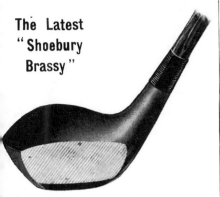

The Latest "Shoebury Brassy"

The Club with the Projecting Rim.

The Club that will keep your ball low and will be of great assistance to the novice or expert.

Price **6/6**.   Post free.

complete range of Boys and Girls Clubs at 2/9 and 3/9 each.

Juvenile Golf Sets.

Containing Driver, Brassie and 3 Irons in Bag.

Complete **10/6** Set.

The "St. Andrew's"

Series of Boys Clubs.

2/9 each.   All patterns

The "Gamage"

Series of Boys Clubs.

Selected models. A perfect Club

Price **3/9**.   All patterns

Post 4d. each

"Potted Golf." By Harry Fulford.

1/- Edition Half-price, **6**d. Post 1d.

The Never Stoop
Golf Bag Stand

Fits any Bag.

Easy to fix, strongly made

Price **3/9**   Post 4d

Colt Bags.

4½ in. ring, in Bedford cord, brown or green twill, canvas pocket, sling, leather bottom and fittings **2/11**
4½ in. ring, heavier canvas and fittings, brown or white only **3/6**
In brown, olive green or drab canvas, waterproof with super quality leather fittings, Gent's **5/9**
Best quality, brown and olive green waterproof canvas, holdfast handle, superior fittings, nothing better in canvas; umbrella loop. Gent's **8/11**
Ditto   Ditto   Ladies' **7/6**
Ladies' or Gent's Cowhide **12/6**
Do   Do   best Calfskin **21/-**
Best white, green or brown bag with hood as illustration **14/6**
Do   Do   fitted Rhino's bottom **17/6**
Best calf leather (a handsome present) .. **27/6**

Post, under 10/-, 4d.

Golf Balls.   Post free.

Challengers, all ptns.	**19/-** doz.	The Referee	..	**14/6** doz
Dunlops	,, **18/6** ,,	Gamage's "Ariel"		**18/6** ,,
V Dunlops	.. **24/6** ,,	Zome Zodiacs all ptns		**24/-** ,,
Patent Colonels	.. **19/-** ,,	Midget Dimples	..	**24/-** ,.
White	,, **24/-** ,,	Glory	,, ..	**24/-** ,,
Arch	,, **24/-** ,,	Recovered Balls	..	**8/9** ,,
The Ilixum	.. **11/6** ,,	Selected Named	..	**12/6** ..

The Boomerang Golf Ball

Always returns to the same spot.

Price .. **2/11**   **4/6**   Post 3d.

Golf Practice Nets

For practising golf in your own Garden.
Best Hemp net, ¾-in. mesh, complete with 2 Poles, Guy Rope, Pegs, etc.

Size 10 ft. by 8 ft. .. .. price **19/6**
,, 10 ft. by 9 ft. .. .. ,, **21/6**
,, 10 ft. by 10 ft. .. .. ,, **23/-**

The "Referee" Regd. Fibre Faced Drivers and Brassies.

With Black Rubber Cloth Grip	..	..		**6/6**
Plain Faced Drivers	..	..	..	**4/3**
Brassies ..	..	..	..	**4/6**
All patterns, Irons	..	..	..	**4/3**

THE "Stet Solus" Golf Bag.

(Patent.)

Exactly meets the requirements of the Golfer who carries his own Clubs.

Saves all stooping.

Prevents damage to heads of Wood Clubs caused by throwing bag on the ground.

Prevents shafts 'going' caused by their getting wet from bag laying on ground.

It has no unsightly or cumbersome external attachment.

Can be made to stand upright without the least exertion.

Gent's Bags
14/9 16/9 23/9
Ladies' Bags
14/3   15/9
Carriage paid.

The Home-Putt

Is invaluable to every Golfer.

A few minutes' home practice at spare moments with Home-Putt gives the average golfer the correct strength and aim as well as the necessary confidence for accurate Putting from varying distances on the Green.

(Regd. design 610,326) costs only **1/6**. Post free

Useful Presents.

Whitely Adjustable 5-Strand Chest Expanders.

Lady's	..	..	**2/9**
Man's..	..	..	**3/9**
Athlete's	..	..	**4/9**
Hercules	..	..	**5/9**

Complete with Chart. Post 4d.

BOXING GLOVES.

American Pattern.

Gold Cape Gloves, padded horse hair, laced palms. **7/6** set. Post 4d.

Superior quality, **10/6** and **12/6** set

Our Famous N.S.C., **14/6** set.

Special do., **16/6** 6 or 8 oz.

Boys' Cape Boxing Gloves .. **6/6** and **8/6** set.

Youths' .. **3/11 5/3 6/9** and **8/3** ,,

Post 4d.

Children's Doorway Trapeze and Horizontal Bar.

Consisting of 2 Brass Brackets and Ash Bar.

Price .. **5/6** Post 4d.

Sandow's Latest Spring Grip Dumb-bells.

Special Spring Grip Gumb-bells for men at a popular price.

Enamelled in black, with 5 nickelled steel springs fitted complete in box, with illustrated charts of instruction, specially drawn up by Sandow. 1 piece of Sylvet supplied with each pair.. Weight 3 lbs. per bell. Our price .. .. **7/6** pair.

Nickel-plated ditto .. **12/6** pair. Ladies .. **10/6**
Youth's .. **10/6**　　　Boy's .. **7/6**　　　Girl's .. **7/6**

Children's .. **5/** pair. Post free.

Sandow's Improved Model Developer.

May be used by Man, Woman or Child.

This apparatus is absolutely unique. It is specially designed by EUGEN SANDOW to enable users to carry out his World Famous System of Physical Culture.

Price **12/6** with full set of Charts.

Child's ditto .. **8/6**

Sandow's Symmetrion.

FOR PROMOTING HEALTH AND BEAUTY IN WOMEN.

Neat and artistic, easily fixed and removed, enables women to defy the ravages of time.

Price **12/6** with full instructions.

The Referee.

Adjustable Portable Striking Bag, with Spiral Springs.

Price .. **32/6**

Carriage paid.

The Whitely Exerciser.

Lady's	..	**2/9**
Man's	..	**3/9**
Athlete's..		**4/9**
Hercules..		**5/9**

Post 4d. each.

Door Hooks for attaching Exercisers to door in place of screw hooks.

Self-adjusting. Nickel-plated .. **1/3** pair. Post 2d.

The Holborn Punch Ball Drum.

Very Strong.

The Iron Work being made of best Angle Iron, is adjustable to three different heights, and suitable for gymnasium or private use.

Platform only .. **30/-** Carriage paid.

Weighing Machine.

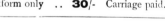
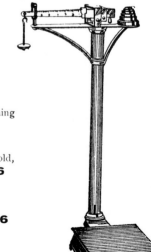

Small size Personal weighing machine .. **22/6** each.

Enamelled Green and Gold, 37 in. high .. **32/6**

5 feet ditto, Enamelled Green.
Price **59/6**

Height Measuring Standards.
Price .. **14/6** each.

Carriage extra.

Roller Skates make Ideal Presents.

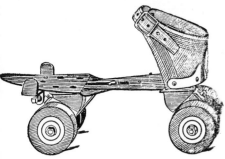

The Celebrated "Union" American Roller Skate.

One Skate for all sizes.
Gents' all Clamp or Ladies ½.Clamp.
No. 12. Plain Bearings, Steel Wheels, bright finish ..   .. **4/9** per pair.
No. 6. Do., Ball Bearings, Steel Wheel, do., **7/3** per pair

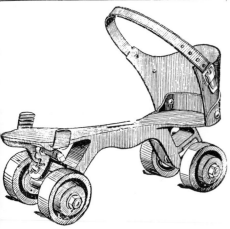

The Birmalium Roller Skate

The frames are cast in one piece from the well-known Birmalium Aluminium Alloy, which is renowned for its strength and lightness.
One price only, Lady's or Gents', **21/-** per pair.
Racing Model same price.

Ladies' Pattern—Sizes 8, 8½, 9, and 9½ in.
Gents' Patterns with narrow strap fitted at back—
Sizes, 10, 10½, 11, 11½ in.
Undoubtedly far and away the lightest and sweetest Running Skates on the Market.

WE ARE THE SOLE AGENTS FOR LONDON AND DISTRICT.
Wholesale and Retail.

The Latest Book on Roller Skates
BY CLARICE HEWETT, **6**d. Post 4d.

Figure and Racing Skates.

The "Elite," with Boxwood Wheels **24/6**
Ditto with Grappite Wheels .. **29/6**
The "Dexter" with Boxwood Wheels. **27/6**
Ditto with Aluminium Wheels **35/-**

When ordering send size or sketch of Sole of Boots.

The World-Famed "Ariel" Skate.

This Skate is English-made throughout, made in the same factory as our World-famed Cycles.
There is noting better..   One quality only.
Ladies or Gents .. **12/6** per pair.
Ditto, with Aluminium Wheels .. **17/6** per pair.
Ladies' ½-Clamp, same price.

The "Referee" Rink Boot.

Cut by expert Craftmen. Designed by an expert Skater. An Ideal Boot for Roller Skating.

In Tan and Black Hide .. **10/6**
In fine quality Tan Willow and Box Calf, **14/6**
Best quality Welted..   ..   .. **16/6**
Made to Special Order .. **2/-** extra.

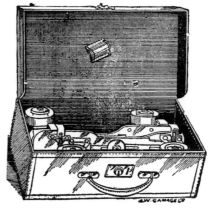

Roller Skate Cases.

Compressed Compo., box shape, as illust.. **3/9**
Ditto to hold Skates and Boots..   .. **4/11**
Best Leather Case, Nickel-plated Lock and Key, Strong Handle, as illustration **8/9**
Ditto, for ½-Clamp Skates **8/11**
Ditto, to take Skates and Boots .. **11/6**
Postage extra.

Gamage's Special Boys' Skates.

With Iron Wheels, very strongly made, easily adjusted, with spanner shown in illustration.
Price ..   .. **1/9½** Post 4d.

Winslow Skates.

No. G. 25 & G. 27. Ladies' or Gent's ½-clamp plain bearing Extension Steel Skates with rubber springs. Ladies' extending from 8 to 10 in. Gentlemen's extending from 10 to 11½ in.
Price **5/6** per pair.   Postage 4d. per pair.
Ditto with Steel Wheels **6/6** per pair.
Postage 5d. per pair.
No. G. 35 & G. 37. Ladies' or Gents' ½-Clamp Extension Steel Skates, with Rubber Springs and Ball-Bearing Wheels. Ladies extending from 8 to 10 in. Gentlemen's extending from 10 to 11½ in.
Price **12/6** per pair.
Ditto with Aluminium Wheels **21/-**

The "Express" Skate.

Aluminium Body very light Circular Rubber Cushion, best Ball-Bearing Aluminium Wheels.
In all sizes. Price **15/3** List price 21/-
Post 5d.

All Skates should be ordered one inch shorter than the Boots worn.

The "Elite" Ball-bearing Roller Skates. (Ladies' or Gent's).

English make, Nickel Plated, highly finished, all clamp for Gentlemen or half-clamp for Ladies, with Boxwood Wheels .. per pair **24/6**
Ditto, with Aluminium Wheels ,, **29/6**
"Dexter" Skates, with Boxwood wheels .. .. .. per pair **27/6**
Ditto, with Aluminium Wheels ,, **35/-**

SHEFFIELD SKATES.—For the Continental Winter Season.

Wilson's New Pattern Monier Williams.

Registered swelled blades, .. **18/6**   Ordinary pattern, .. **17/6**
The G.B. Monier Williams Pattern, **12/6** per pair.   Post **4**d.

Wilson's Celebrated "Mount Charles."

Fitted with Dowler blades, nickel-plated, complete, **20/6** per pair.
Wood's ditto .. .. **18/6** Post **4**d.

The "Houghton" Figure Skate.

High-class English style Figure Skate.   English Standard radius.
Rectangular blades, nickel-plated and polished.   Built in every
detail to particulars supplied by H. J. Houghton, Esq.
22/6 per pair.   Post paid.

The "Solid Champion."

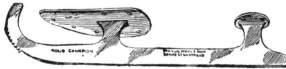

The "Solid Champion" is built for the most advanced Figure Skaters.
Has swelled blades, acute angle skating edges.   Nickel-plated and
polished .. **30/-** per pair.   Post paid.

New Style Adjustable Skates.

No straps or screws required, can be fastened quite easily, **15/6** pair.
The runners of these skates are made from forged Sheffield steel of
the hardest quality.   The whole skate is heavily nickel-plated and
bevelled.

The "Presto" Skates.

Sheffield made, nickel-plated and polished,
8/6 pair.   Post **4**d.

Wilson's Celebrated "Mount Charles" Skates.

Brass or aluminium
fittings, nickel-plated.
Acme pattern iron
complete, **16/-** pair.
Wood's 14/6 pair.
Post **4**d.

Best Sheffield Make.   The "Mount Charles."

Wilson's 16/6

Wood's with
Interchangeable
Dowler Blades,
27/6 pair.
Post paid.

The Special "Prince's" Skate.

Superb quality Sheffield blades, nickel-plated.   Highly finished, with screwdriver, gimlet and
screws complete.   As used at the London Ice Rinks.   Manufactured by J. WILSON, Sheffield.
27/6 pair.   WOOD'S **24/6** pair.   Carriage paid.

The Ladies' Princess.   Will take any size Heel.

One of the smartest
and easiest detachable
skates, made expressly
for ladies' use
Price .. **6/11**
Post **4**d.

Gamages Unique Skates.

Regd. pin.
No. 146,690.

Has a distinctive advantage of having the exact shape of the foot,
being made on the same principle as a boot.   Therefore this pattern
will fit in every instance in the centre of the foot, and the blade will
always have, without any adjusting, the correct position.   Another
great advantage is that the skate will open very wide and will never
be found too narrow for any broad boot form.
Fitted with best welted Rattler blades, nickel-plated **8/6** pair.   Post **6**d.

Toboggans.

4 ft., **10/-**   5 ft., **11/3**   6 ft., **13/9**   7 ft., **17/-**   8 ft., **25/-**
Best Selected, with Steel runners—
5 ft., **15/-**   6 ft., **18/6**   7 ft., **22/6**   8 ft., **30/-** Carriage paid.

The Lightening Guider Sled

has more lateral curve than
any sled on the market.   It
has less friction.   There is
positively no lost motion.
The sled responds quickly to
the touch of the guiding bar.
With these advantages you
obtain better results on the
hill.   The Lightning Guider
Sled is made of the best
grade of white ash wood and
spring steel.   The construction, workmanship and finish,
is perfect.   It is strictly a
high class article.

Every sled guaranteed.

No.	Length, in.	Height, in.	Width, in.	Weight, lbs	Price.
G. 18.	32	6	12	6	**7/11**
G. 21.	36	6¼	13	7¼	**10/6**
G. 22.	40	6½	13	9½	**13/6**
G. 24.	50	8	14	15	**17/6**

Carriage extra under 10/-

The Davos.

GENUINE SWISS SLEIGHS.

	31½ in.	36½ in.	48 in.
Price	**11/6**	**14/6**	**18/6**

Carriage paid.

Hard Wood Coasters.

No. G. 4.   Hardwood body on round steel runners, top painted
and decorated, length of runners, 32 in. **3/11**
No. G. 8.   Ditto   do.   do.   36 in. **5/11**
No. G. 11.   Ditto   do.   do.   48 in. **7/11**
Carriage extra.

Genuine Imported Norwegian and Swiss
SKIS, TOBOGGANS, SLEIGHS, COASTERS, etc.

SKIS.

Norwegian Skis, selected Hickory or Ash with Huitfeldt Binding and Clamps.

88 in.	84 in.	80 in.	76 in.
29/6	**28/-**	**27/-**	**26/-**

Hoyer Ellefsen Binding and Clamp.

31/6	**30/-**	**28/6**	**27/6**

Carriage Paid.

Swiss Skis.

By Dethleffsen & Co., Berne, with Huitfeldt Bindings and Strainers.

80 in.	84 in.	88 in.
26/6	**27/6**	**28/6**

Do. with Ellefsen Binding.

28/6	**30/-**	**31/6**

Carriage paid.

By Staub of Zurich fitted with Huitfeldt Binding and Strainers.

76 in.	80 in.	84 in.
26/6	**27/6**	**28/6**

English-made Skis.

Procured to order.

Ladies' **26/6**   Men's **27/6** and **28/6**

Huitfeldt Binding.

8/6 per pair.   Postage 4d.

Foot Plates, **2**/. per pair.

Ellefsen Binding.

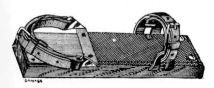

Extra Binding, **8/6** per set.   Postage 4d.

ICE AXES.

Genuine Swiss Make.

Ash handles.

Tourists' Model.

12/6	**17/6**
19/6	**21/-**

each.

Leather Head and Point Cases.

Small size **1/6** set.   Large size **2/3** set.

Portage 3d.

A. W. GAMAGE, Ltd. are agents for STAUB'S Zurich and Dethleffsen GENUINE SWISS & VICTOR THORN'S NORWEGIAN SKIS.

SKI STICKS.

Cane or Bamboo with Cane Rings.

Price **2/6** each.

Carriage paid.

STRAINERS.

For Bindings,

3/- each.

Postage 4d.

Any make of Binding can be procured and fitted to order.

Ice Creepers.

Absolutely the best Ice Creeper in the market. Best hardened steel points This is no doubt the most convenient pattern ever made, largely used and highly approved not only by walkers and tourists, but also by ski-runners and lugers.

Price **1/6** pair.

Alpine Ropes.

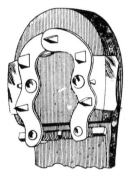

Very best Italian hemp ¾ in. diameter. Breaking strain 47 cwt.

6d. per foot.

Made up in any length or pattern.

Cleaning Outfits.

For Skis, including Scraper and Wax.

   **2/6** each.   Postage 8d.

Wax for Skis.

10½d. per tube.

Hard or soft.

Postage 2d.

Clamps for Skis.

3/6 per set.   Postage 8d.

The Davos.

GENUINE SWISS SLEIGHS.

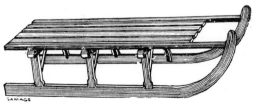

31½ in.	39¼ in.	48 in.
11/6	**14/6**	**18/6**

Carriage extra.

Automatic Penny-in-Slot Machines

These Machines are wonderful money-takers and will earn their cost over and over again.

The Pickwick Three-ball Skill Machine, £4 4 0.

ORIGINAL DESIGN.

PENNY IN SLOT.

THIS MACHINE can only be supplied SECOND-HAND.

The coin is placed in the slot and the three balls are then released into play; one ball is shot at a time, and the object is to catch it in the *sliding cup* after it falls through the nails. If successful, a check value 2d. to be exchanged at counter is obtained.

Automatic Shooting for Goal

Penny and Halfpenny in Slot. £3 10s.

☞ This being a game, and for amusement only, no objection can be raised on the score of gambling.

This Machine is the latest of our Novelties. It is arranged for one player only. On placing the coin in the slot a ball is released, and the operator then has to shoot it up the platform with sufficient force to send it under the *red flag*, when the coin is at once returned. Plenty of play is obtained; and only when the ball is shot under the *blue flag* is it lost. A most attractive machine, in polished cabinet, with plated fittings, Yale lock, etc. We can, without hesitation, recommend it to our customers as a really first-rate money-taker.

Automatic Imperial Electric Machine. PENNY IN SLOT.

For Licensed Houses, Exhibitions, Shops,&c.

☞ It is always a ready-money taker and cannot be objected to on any ground whatever

The Imperial Electric Machine is operated by the insertion of a Penny in the Slot. The handles are then grasped on each side—the right-hand one being moved round to indicate the strength of the current, which is indicated on the dial. The current comes on very mildly at first, there is therefore no shock or danger. The electric treatment is strongly recommended as a cure for rheumatism, nervousness, headache and neuralgia.

No. 1. Nickel-plated all over, **£3 3s.**

No. 2. Bronzed, and handles only nickel-plated. **2 2s.**

Automatic Double-event Machine. Profitable to owner

The Double-Event Machine operated by the insertion of a Penny in the Slot. The balls are then released into play, and the object is shoot each ball so as to drop it in one or other of the bull's eyes marked RED. If successful pull out draw at left-hand side and receive a me check, to be exchanged at counter value. If not successful, try again score. Every ball falling into the divisions marked BLUE is return for another shot, and it is possible get two checks for a penny. In nicely polished cabinet, nickel-plat fittings ivory balls, and **£4 4** gross of checks complete

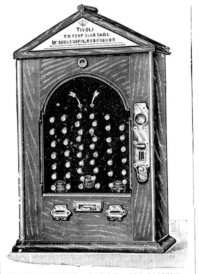

The Running Hare Machine. (LA CHASSE) PENNY IN SLOT. £4 10s.

This Machine is specially designed for Licensed Houses, Shops, etc. It provides amusement and skill combined, and is very profitable to the owner. This is not a game of chance, but REAL test of **skill**, and therefore not liable to be objected to.

The Running Hare (La Chasse) Machine is worked by the insertion of a penny in the slot. The handle at right hand side is then turned round and released, and off goes the hare. The object is to hit the bull's eye marked on it as it goes round. If successful, a check is *automatically delivered* as the Hare squeals. The check must be exchanged for value at the counter. In highly finished cabinet, with polished brass fittings, all latest improvements, and a full supply of special checks complete.

THE TIVOLI CIGAR MACHINE.

Best of all Skilled Machines.

PENNY & HALFPENNY IN SLOT.

The Tivoli Cigar Machine is known all over the country. It can be seen in most Licensed Houses, also in Tobacco and Sweet Shops, etc. The coin is placed in the slot and then shot by means of a trigger, the object being to drop it in the *centre row of Pegs* between the arrows. If successful, this releases the drawer, and a ticket is obtained which has to be exchanged for value at the counter. If the coin goes down either of the *side rows* it is returned for another shot. The Tivoli is a source of profit wherever it is placed; also it ASSISTS the SALE of GOODS. **40/-**

150 Tickets and Top Weight included.

ALL MACHINES SENT CARRIAGE FORWARD. 1/- CHARGED FOR PACKING.

The Success (Crowing Cock) Reserve Ball Machine

For Licensed Houses, Shops, etc. Very Profitable to the Owner

Special Coin Slot to reject lead discs. Magnet to eject steel or

The Success Reserve Ball Machine is worked by placing Penny in the slot, and a ball is then released into play. ALL the top divi are winning ones, and there is only ONE loser. Every successful is indicated at the top, and a check is also obtained for every loser. In highly finished cabinet with nickel-plated fittings, and one gross of special checks complete, **£6**

Note.—This Machine is now made to *deliver all the Balls* i "Reserve" Division each time a check is obtained.

"His Master's Voice" GRAMOPHONES

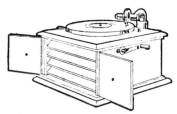

Hornless —Model No. 1
Price £4
Specification

CABINET : Fumed Plain Oak, nickel-plated fittings ; internal horn with wooden grille. Size 6¾ in. high, 14½ in. wide.

MECHANISM : Single-spring spiral-drive motor ; 10 inch turntable, playing 10 in. and 12 in. records ; speed indicator ; "His Master's Voice" tapering tonearm with patent "Gooseneck" ; "Exhibition" soundbox.

Nett Weight, 16¾ lbs. Gross Weight when packed, 34 lbs.

Hornless —Model No. 3
Price £6
Specification

CABINET : Polished Quartered Oak, with solid moulded doors ; nickel-plated cabinet fittings ; full size internal horn with wooden grille. Size—Base 17 in. height 9 in, depth 17 in.

MECHANISM : Small double-spring spiral-drive motor ; 12 inch turntable ; speed indicator ; "His Master's Voice" tapering tonearm, with patent "Goos-neck"; "Exhibition" soundbox.

Nett Weight 26 lbs. Gross Weight when packed, 48 lbs.

Horn—Model No. 5
Specification

CABINET : Polished Mahogany ; nickel-plated fittings ; large coloured metal horn, 24 inch bell Size—Base 14¾ in. ; height, 6½ in.

MECHANISM : Double-spring spiral-drive motor ; 10 inch turntable, to play 10 in. and 12 in. records ; speed indicator ; "His Master's Voice" tapering tonearm with patent "Goose-neck"; "Exhibition" soundbox.

Nett Weight, 28 lbs. Gross Weight, when packed, 76 lbs. **Price £7 10.**

If fitted with Wooden Horn, £8 10.

Also made in Oak at same prices

Table Grand— Model No. 6
£8 8s.
Specification

CABINET : Dull polished Quartered Oak ; nickel-plated fittings ; internal horn with wooden grille ; wooden needle bowl. Size—Base 15¼ in. ; height 12¾ in. ; depth 19 in.

MECHANISM : Small double-spring spiral-drive motor ; 10 inch turntable ; speed indicator ; "His Master's Voice" tapering tonearm with patent "Gooseneck"; "Exhibition" soundbox.

Nett Weight, 31 lbs. ; Gross Weight when packed, 87 lbs.

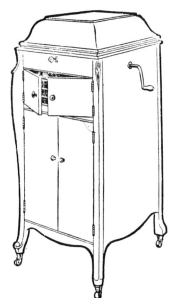

Cabinet Grand— Model No. 12
£25
Specification

CABINET : Highly polished mahogany, brass gilt fittings ; internal horn of special metal which enhances the tone ; wooden grille and needle bowl. Under the horn is a chamber for storing records with record albums for 72 records. Size—Height 43¾ in. ; width 19½ in. ; depth 23¾ in.

MECHANISM : Double-spring spiral-drive motor ; 12 inch turntable ; new automatic brake and speed indicator ; "His Master's Voice" tapering tonearm with patent "Gooseneck"; "Exhibition" soundbox.

Nett Weight, 101½ lbs. Gross Weight when packed, 285 lbs.

Also manufactured in Oak at same price

Horn— Model No. 7
Price £12
Specification

CABINET : Polished Mahogany ; nickel-plated fittings ; horn of cross-banded Mahogany, 22 inch bell. Size, Base 16½ in. ; height 7½ in.

MECHANISM : Triple spring spiral-drive motor ; 12 inch turntable ; speed indicator ; "His Master's Voice" tapering tonearm with patent "Goose-neck"; "Exhibition" soundbox.

Nett Weight, 29½ lbs. Gross Weight when packed, 87 lbs.

Or fitted with coloured Metal Flower Horn, 24 inch bell— **Price £11**

Also made in Oak at same price

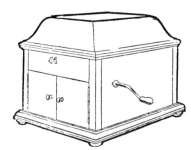

Table Grand—Model No. 8
Specification

CABINET : Dull polished Quartered Oak ; brass gilt cabinet fittings ; internal horn with wooden grille ; needle bowl. Size—Base, 18¼ in. ; height, 14¼ in. ; depth, 22½ in.

MECHANISM : Double-spring, spiral-drive motor ; 12 inch turntable ; speed indicator ; "His Master's Voice" tapering tonearm with patent "Goose-neck"; "Exhibition" soundbox.

Nett Weight, 52½ lbs. Gross weight when packed, 115 lbs. **Price £12 10.**

HOLBORN GRAMOPHONES (1914 Models).

The Holborn Model I.

Cabinet 12 by 12 by 5½in. Oak polished. Turntable, 10 in. green felt. Tone Arm, tapered and nickelled. Motor plays one 10 in. record. Sound Box — "Expression." Horn — Size 17 by 17 in., seamless pattern.

As illustration **18/6**

The Holborn Model II.

Cabinet—Dark Oak, ornamental base, size 12½ by 12½ by 6 in. Turntable—10 in. covered green baize. Tone Arm—Tapered, highly nickel-plated. Motor — Superior, playing one 12 in. record. Sound Box—"Alexophone," fine tone. Horn—18 by 18 in., seamless.

Price **25/6**

The Holborn Model III.

FINEST VALUE ON THE MARKET

Cabinet—English Solid Oak, 13 by 13 by 7 in. with hinged lid to Motor. Turntable—10 in. covered green baize, nickel-plated. Tone Arm — Tapered, nickel-plated, highly polished. Motor—Extra strong worm gear, silent running and perfectly reliable. Speed Indicator. Sound Box—Gamage Famous Model B. Horn, size 19 by 19in. seamless. **32/6**

The Holborn Model VII.

Cabinet—English Solid Oak, 16 by 16 by 7 in., with hinged lid to Motor. Turntable 10 in. green baize covered. Tone Arm—Heavy quality nickel-plated. Tapered, neat design. Motor—Double spring, worm gear, silent running. Sound Box—"Apollo." Horn—Wood Horn, matching cabinet. size 24 by 22 in.

Price **£2 10 0**

The Holborn Cabinet Model X.

FINE VALUE.
An entirely New and Chaste Design.
Cabinet Disc Machine
Made of solid Mahogany, polished in Chippendale style or oak, 42 in. high, 21 in. wide. Drawer for sundries. Powerful Motor, running two 12 in. Records. 12 in. Turntable Speed-dial Indicator. Latest pattern Tone Arm. "Sonoria" Sound Box.
£7 10 0 Carriage paid.

The Holborn Model VIII.

MOST PERFECT OBTAINABLE.

Cabinet—Best English manufactured Oak, finely polished, hinged top to Motor. Motor —New Patent worm gear, silent running. extra strong double spring, accurate speed indicator. 12 in. Turntable. Tone Arm—Finely adjusted with patent swivel, extra heavy and well tapered. Sound Box—The Famous "Crescendo." Horn—Dark Oak polished, new design Bell 22 in., length 26 in.

Price **£3 15 0**

Holborn Hornless Gramophones.

The Holborn Model IV.

CABINET.—15 by 13 by 7 in., highly polished Mahogany with solid hinged door admitting to the wooden sound chamber.

TURN TABLE.—9 inch nickel-plated.

TONE ARM.—Tapered inverted nickel-plated.

MOTOR.—Reliable playing 1 12-inch Records.

SOUND BOX.—Tresor.

This Model is fitted with a **speed indicator.**

Price .. **25/-**

The Holborn Model V.

CABINET.—English Oak Case, 15 by 15 by 7 in., fitted with wooden grill and hinged doors to sound chamber.

TURN TABLE.—10-inch covered Green Baize.

TONE ARM.—Patent extension, tapered, giving a rich tone.

MOTOR.—Powerful worm gear, thoroughly reliable and silent running.

SOUND BOX.—Gamage special rubber insulated.

Price .. **33/-**

The Holborn Model VI.

CABINET.—Handsome polished Oak, 16 by 16 by 12 in., with hinged doors to sound chamber. Large size as illustration. Can be closed down while playing, with lock and key, and handle at side for carrying.

MOTOR.—Strong latest type spring motor playing 2 10-inch Records.

TONE ARM.—Inverted tone arm, nickel-plated.

SOUND BOX.—Model B, latest pattern, improved model with a human tone.. **55/-**

Columbia Graphophones

No. 3. ("Junior Regal")

CABINET.—Mahogany or Oak throughout, piano finish, round corners, size 13½ by 13½ by 7.

MOTOR.—Columbia, powerful double-spring to run about three 10 inch records, silent running.

TONE-ARM.—Columbia tapered arm, with sound-tight universal joint, detachable "Regal" sound box.

HORN.—Wood horn (oak) to match cabinet, bell 21 in., length 23½ in.

No. 3.	Brass Horn	..	£5 10 0
No. 4.	Wood Horn	..	£7 10 0

No. 6. ("Regal")

CABINET.—Oak throughout, piano finish, round corners, size 16½ by 16½ by 8½.

MOTOR.—Columbia, powerful Triple-spring to run fifteen minutes or about six 10 inch records, silent running.

TONE ARM.—Columbia tapered arm, with sound-tight universal joint, detachable "Regal" sound box.

HORN.—Brass or Wood Horn (oak) to match cabinet, bell 21 in., length 23½ in.

No. 6.	Brass Horn	..	£7 10 0
No. 7.	Wood Horn	..	£9 10 0

No. 18. ("Crescent" Hornless).

"The Open Tone that Surprises."

CABINET.—Solid oak, piano finish, round corners, hinged lid, size 16½ by 16½ by 8½.

TONE CHAMBER.—Specially large interior ampli-fying chamber, fitted with new tone shutters, controlled by a button, for regulation of volume.

MOTOR—Genuine Columbia, powerful double-spring to run about three 10-inch records, silent running.

TONE ARM.—Columbia tapered arm, with sound-tight universal joint, nickelled horn-bracket and elbow, detachable "Regal" sound box.

No. 18 Oak, **£5 10 0**   No. 19 Mahogany, **£6 6 0**

No. 22. "Columbia" Grafonola.

No. 22 Oak, or

No. 23 Mahogany

£10.10.

CABINET—Oak (or Mahogany), with Hinged Cover, fitted with release button to faciliate opening and closing. Size 21½ in. deep (back to front), 18 in. wide, 14 in. high.

TONES CHAMBER—Polished Oak (or Mahogany). Fitted with new Tone-Shutters for regulation of volume.

MOTOR—Genuine Columbia, Powerful TRIPLE-Spring, constructed on Metal Motor-Board and Insulated. New Self-Registering Speedometer. Winding-key Escutcheon fitted with "Rubberoid" to prevent creaking.

TONE-ARM—Columbia Tapered Arm, New shape Seamless, with Bayouet-joint. New Detachable "Regal" Sound Box.

TURNTABLE—12 in., with Nickelled Flange.

Four Needlecups for new and used needles fitted to Cabinet.

No. 2. ("Regent")

CABINET.—Solid oak, highly polished, round corners, size 13½ by 13½ by 7.

MOTOR.—Columbia, powerful double-spring to run about three 10 in. records, silent running.

TONE ARM.—Columbia tapered arm, with sound-tight universal joint, detachable "Regal" sound box.

HORN.—New style metal horn, enamelled oak finish to match cabinet, bell 20¾ in., guaranteed not to rattle or spoil reproduction with vibratory noises.

Price .. **£4 4 0**

No. 1. ("Prince")

CABINET.—Solid oak, highly polished, with hinged lid, size 13 by 13 by 7.

MOTOR.—Columbia, single-spring to run about five minutes.

TONE ARM.—Columbia tapered arm, with sound-tight universal joint, detachable "Regal" sound box.

HORN.—New shape metal horn, enamelled oak finish to match cabinet, bell 20¾ in., guarantee not to rattle or spoil reproduction with vibratory noises.

New Speed Regulator Pointer and Indicator D

Price .. **60/-**

DULCEPHONES,

The High-grade Gramophones at a Popular Price.

Model No. 51.

This compact little Model can be strongly recommended for out-door use on account of its portability.

Full grain polished oak cabinet. Hinged doors. Base 13½ in. square. Height 7½ in. New pattern worm gear motor, ratchet and pawl wind.

Price - £2 2s.

Model No. 53.

A hornless model possessing all the advantages of an ordinary Gramophone in a most compact form. The style and finish are of the best, and whilst primarily designed for portability, its tone and appearance make it well suited for indoor use.

Figured oak, fumed finish cabinet, hinged doors, wooden sound chamber. Base 15½ in. square. Height 8 in. Motor will play three 10¾ in. records.

Price - £3.

Model No. 50.

This instrument, lowest in price of all Dulce-phone models, can be thorough'y relied on in every detail. A special feature is the "Swan Neck" Tone Arm, a device which greatly facilitates the operation of changing the needle.

Polished oak cabinet: hinged top. Base 13 in. square. Height 7 in. New pattern worm gear motor, ratchet and pawl wind. **£2 2s.**

Model No. 55.

This is an entirely new hornless model fitted with a hinged dome-shaped lid, and the new "modulator shutters," which allow of the tone being regulated according to the volume required.

Dark polished oak cabinet, hinged dome-shaped lid, tone modulators, wooden sound chamber. Base 18 in. square. Height (over all) 13 in. Powerful single spring, worm gear motor.

Price - £3 15s.

Model No. 62.

A hornless model of exquisite design and construction. The finish and fittings are of the highest possible grade, and we have every confidence in stating that no finer instrument of this type can be obtained, irrespective of price.

Figured oak cabinet. best fumed finish. Hinged dome lid and doors, best nickel plated fittings. Base 22 by 18 in. Height (over all) 14 in. Large double spring motor. Will play four 10¾ in. rcds.

Price - £6 10s.

Figured oak stand for this Model, **£1 17 6**
In solid Mahogany. Price ... **9 9 0**

Model No. 56

An elegantly designed hornless model of superior workmanship and finish, and possessing exceptionally good tonal qualities.

Fumed oak cabinet, hinged top. Base 20½ in. by 16 in. Height 14½ in Motor will play three 10¾ in. records. **Price £4 10s.**

Boudoir Model No. 59

Cabinet types of Gramophones have recently become very popular, and this, our cheapest "Boudoir" Model, is tastefully designed in fumed oak with ebony inlays.

Fumed oak cabinet, height 3 ft. 5 in., top 22 by 17 in. Motor will play three 10¾ in. records.

Price £5 15s. Better qualities up to **£24**

THE COMPLETE REPERTOIRE OF THE WORLD-FAMED

JUMBO RECORDS

IS NOW
1/6

SPECIAL STAR REPERTOIRE.

VESTA TILLEY
GEORGE FORMBY
GERTIE GITANA
BILLY WILLIAMS
ELLA RETFORD
HAPPY FANNY FIELDS
WILKIE BARD
MARK SHERIDAN
VICTORIA MONKS
ALBERT WHELAN
THREE RASCALS

THE complete Jumbo Repertoire, which contains names that top the bills at London's leading Music Halls—stars of such renown as Vesta Tilley, George Formby, Gertie Gitana, etc.—is now reduced to **EIGHTEENPENCE.** The eighteen-penny Jumbos are not a new brand, but the same world-famed Jumbos that have proved so popular in the past at **2 6**

ORIGINAL SONGS BY THE ORIGINAL SINGERS.

SAM MAYO
JACK LORIMER
MORNY CASH
WHIT CUNLIFFE
TOM JONES
ARTHUR AISTON
GEORGE GROSSMITH, Jun.
DAISY JEROME
VIOLET LORAINE
JOCK WHITEFORD
ADAM TOMLINSON

Q

Gramophone Sundries.

The Gamage Index Disc Record Case

With Strap and Catch.
As illustration.
Made of stout wood.
Covered Leatherette.

To hold 25 10-in. Discs, **2/3**
  ,,   50 10-in.   ,,   **2/11**
           12-in. Cases
To hold 25 12-in. Discs, **2/9**
  ,,   50 12-in.   ,,   **3/11**
  ,,   25 10¾-in.   ,,   **2/9**
Very superior quality, cloth
         covered.
To hold 25 10-in. Discs, **2/6**
,   50 10-in.   ,,   **3/9**
          12-in. Cases.
To hold 25 12-in. Discs, **3/6**
  ,,   50 12-in.   ,,   **4/11**

The Gamage Expanding Disc Record Albums.

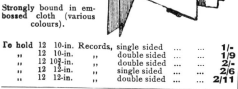

With expanding back and thick manilla pockets.

Strongly bound in embossed cloth (various colours).

To hold 12 10-in. Records, single sided **1/-**
,,   12 10-in.   ,,   double sided **1/9**
,,   12 10¾-in.   ,,   double sided **2/-**
,,   12 12-in.   ,,   single sided **2/6**
,,   12 12-in.   ,,   double sided **2/11**

The 'Holborn' Extra Strong Album

With solid blocked back.

Record pockets of untearable paper.
To hold 12 10-in. Records, single sided .. **2/3**
,,   12 10-in.   ,,   double sided .. **2/6**
,,   12 12-in.   ,,   single sided .. **2/9**
,,   12 12-in.   ,,   double sided .. **3/-**

The "Dreadnought" Disc Albums.

This is an entirely NEW ALBUM being extra strong, made of untearable paper with patent binding, making it impossible for records to slip out. Edges of each page bound with wood, with two clasp fastening.   PRICES :—
To hold 12 12-in., **4/6**   To hold 12 10-in., **3/6**
,,   24 12-in., **8/-**   ,,   24 10-in., **6/-**

For Double sided Records :
To hold 12 10-in., **4/9**   To hold 12 12-in., **5/9**

The "Fibrex" Disc Record Case.

These handsome leather grained cases are made from genuine flax fibre, nicely lined inside and fitted with our expanding compartment system, extra strong leather strap handle and plated spring lock.

To hold 25 10-in. records **3/11**
,,   50 10-in.   ,, ... **4/11**
,,   25 12-in.   ,, ... **4/9**
,,   50 12-in.   ,, ... **5/9**

Collapsible Brass Horns.

In five pieces, screwing on to one another. Most compact Horn on the market, giving a loud, clear, living tone. Price .. **12/6** each.

Gramophone Records.

" Grand Concert," 10 in., **3/6**   " Monarch," 12 in., **5/6**
" Red Label," 10 in., **6/-**   12 in., **9/-**   " Melba " ... **12/6**
" Violet Label," 12 in., **6/6**   10 in., **4/6**   " Patti " ... **12/6**
Special " Caruso," 12 in., **12/6**   " Tetrazzini," **12/6**
Double Sided, 10 in. **3/6**   Ditto, 12 in. **5/6**

Post free.

The New "Odeon" Double-sided Disc Records.

10¾ in., reduced to **2 6**   12 in.   ... **5/-**   Post free.

Pathe Records—Double-sided.

8½ in., reduced to **1/-**   Standard **2/-**   11 in. **3/-**
PLAYED WITH SAPPHIRE POINT.   Post free.

Zonophone Double-Sided Records.

10-in., **2/6**   12-in., **4/-**   Grand Opera (double sided), **3/6**
Post free.

Edison-Bell Double Sided.

10¼ in., reduced to **1/9**   10½ in., velvet face, **2/3**

Marathon Records.

10 in. **2/6**   12 in. **4/-**   The Record that is twice as long.

The "Gamage" Disc Records (Double Sided).

ALL BRITISH.—These Records are specially made for us by one of the largest Record Manufacturers. They are recorded by experts with a new patent process, and the quality and tone are exceedingly fine. 10 in. diam. (Double sided), **1/6**

Send for New and Up-to-Date Catalogue, Post Free.

Needle Boxes.

4½d. each

Tone-Arms.

No. 1. Tone-arm, including elbow, screws and nuts, and nickel-plated bracket, richly ornamented.

Price **4/6**

Superior and extra strong

10/6

GRAMOPHONE ACCESSORIES

Brakes .. .. **1/3** and **1/9**
Governor Springs ..   **1d.**   Keys ..   **1/-** to **2/6**
Horns, Metal, 20 by 19 in. **4/6**
  ,,   ,,   23 ,, 22 in. **6/-**
  ,,   ,,   26 ,, 23½ in. **8/-**
  ,,   Polished Mahogany or Oak, 24 by 22 in.   **15/-**
Motors, single spring, complete with turntable
    and all fittings **7/6**
  ,,   Do., extra strong and superior .. **10/9**
  ,,   Do., double spring **16/6**
  ,,   Do., 12 in. Turntable, extra strong **21/-**
        Sound Boxes, **1/6 2/6 3/6**
Speed Regulators **3/-**   Springs **1/9**
Tone Arm and Bracket for hornless machines..   **4/6**
   Ditto, superior, heavy make **10/6**

SPECIAL ATTENTION GIVEN TO REPAIRS, which are executed in our own workshops.

Trumpet Baskets.

Best quality basket, lined green baize for Gramophone Flower Horn, All sizes, **16/6**

Special Baskets Made to Order

Gamage Sound Boxes.

To suit all Gramophones.

Model B. This Sound Box is constructed entirely different from any on the market at the present time. The parts are not stamped out, but pressed; it is fitted with an india-rubber ring which makes the connection with the tone-arm sound-tight. Every care has been taken to get the absolutely best and most perfect results. **5/-**

The "Exception" Sound Box

It is always advisable to have an extra Sound Box. This Sound Box is made to fit " His Master's Voice " and similar Machines.
Very fine tone.   Price .. **6/-**

Gamage's English-made best quality Steel Needles.

200 BEST ENGLISH. **NEEDLES** FOR **DISC MACHINES** A.W. GAMAGE LTD HOLBORN LONDON E.C.

Box of 200 **6d.**
Per 1000 **2/-**
Post free

Loud, medium or soft tone.

For use with Gramophones and other Disc Records. There are none so superior. no matter what price you pay.

The "Vitesse" Record Holder

By means of this Cabinet the problem is solved of storing an unlimited number of records, so that any one record can be found without disturbing any of its neighbours.

By this system any disc may be found immediately by simply referring to the index supplied therewith.

A pivotted receptacle is pulled forward allowing easy removal of record required, and a slight push is sufficient to send it back into its place.

Cabinets in solid Oak or Mahogany

To hold 100 Oak **4** gns.   Mahogany **4½** gns.
Ditto   140   ,,   **5** ,,   ,   **6** ,,
Ditto   300 sup. Queen Anne style **15** ,,

Gramophone Pedestals.

Imitation Rosewood, nicely made and polished, fitted with divisions, and shelf for Records, drawer for sundries, lock and key.
Height 3 ft.   Top 14 in. square.   Price **25/-**

Phonographs—Genuine Edison.

The Edison "Gem" honograph

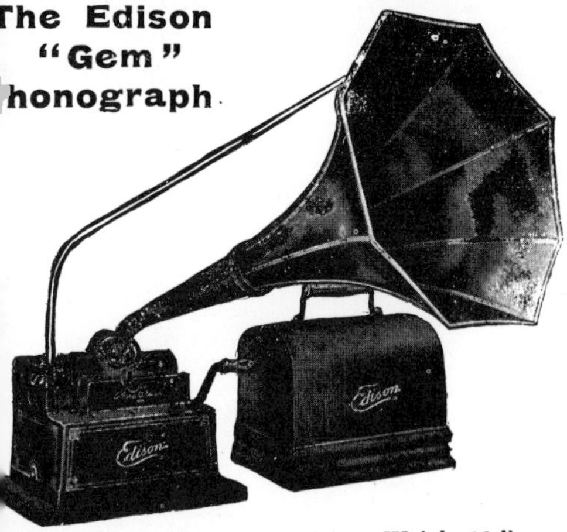

Height 8¾ in. Base 9⅜ by 6⅝ in. Weight 13 lbs.
EQUIPMENT—Model C Reproducer, Flower Horn with ane, Winding Key, carrying Cover, camel's hair Brush.
Price **£2 6 0**

Edison Gem. Combination Type.

ame size as ordinary Gem with K Reproducer, playing ther the Standard or Amberol Records. New Improved orn. Made in two sections, maroon coloured with gilt corations; polygonal shaped; 19 in. long; bell 11 in. de. Supported by nickel-plated crane, with improved Motor. Price **£3 0 0**

The "Puck" Phonograph.

This Machine outdistances anything on the market at e price, it being a superior machine in every way. tted with good reproducing diaphragm, trumpet, gulator, and levelling screw.

'ill take any Standard size cylinder cord. Wonderfully effective.

ew **Model.** Price **3/9** Post 4d.

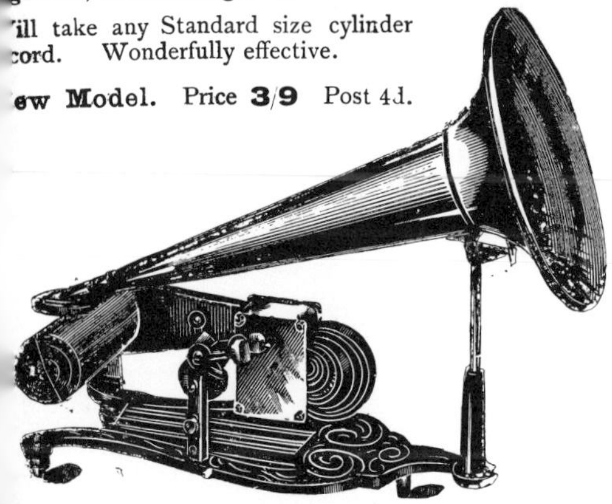

Edison Fireside Phonograph. £4 4 0

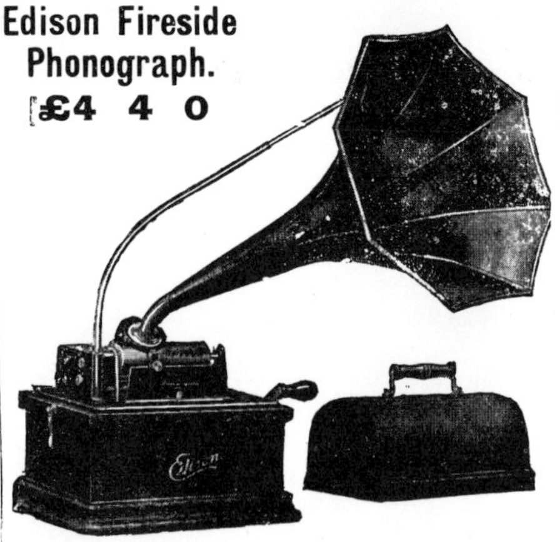

Cabinet—Antique oak, new style design, with cover to match, both highly polished.
Horn—Fireside type sectional horn, maroon japanned with gilt decorations; 19 in. long. Supported by nickel-plated crane.
Mandrel—Nickel-plated and polished. Will play all Edison Records.
Motor—Newly designed, single spring; runs noiselessly. Can be wound while running. Improved start and stop regulating device.
Reproducer—New style combination Model K.
Size of Machine—Height 11 in., base 9¼ by 11¾ in. Weight, net 18 lbs.; gross, 42 lbs. Packed in one case. Horn packed with machine

The "Fairy" Phonograph.

This is an entirely new machine, and gives a really good reproduction. All parts are finished in best style, and highly nickelled, except horn, which is finely enamelled. Will play any standard size cylinder record. Complete with highly polished cabinet and cover. 8/9 Carriage 9d.

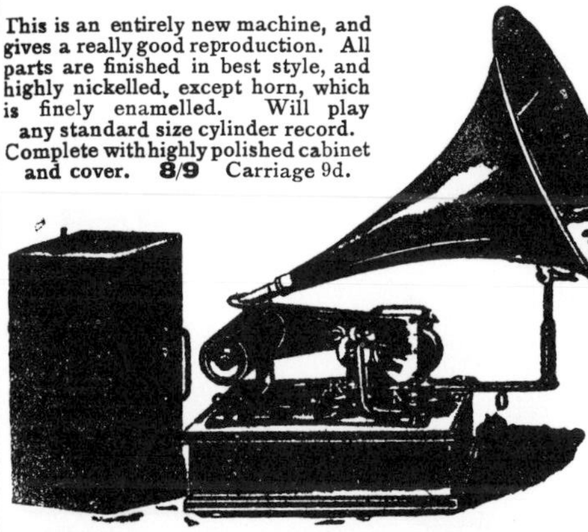

EDISON Standard Phonograph £5 15 0

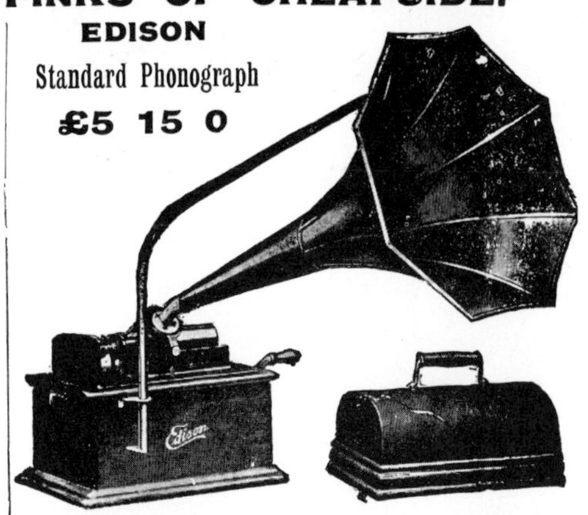

Cabinet—Antique oak with cover to match, both highly polished.
Finish—Black enamel with gilt decorations.
Horn—Same as Fireside Model. Supported by nickel-plated swinging crane.
Mandrel—Nickel-plated and polished; firmly supported to ensure steady and uniform reproduction, will play Edison Amberol, Standard and Grand Opera Records.
Motor—Powerful single spring with improved motor suspension insuring perfect regulation and noiseless operation.
Reproducers—Model C for Standard Records and Model H for Amberol Records.

Size of Machine—
Height 11¼ in., base 13½ by 9½ in. Weight, net 21½ lbs. gross 43 lbs. Packed in one case.
Horn weight 9 lbs.

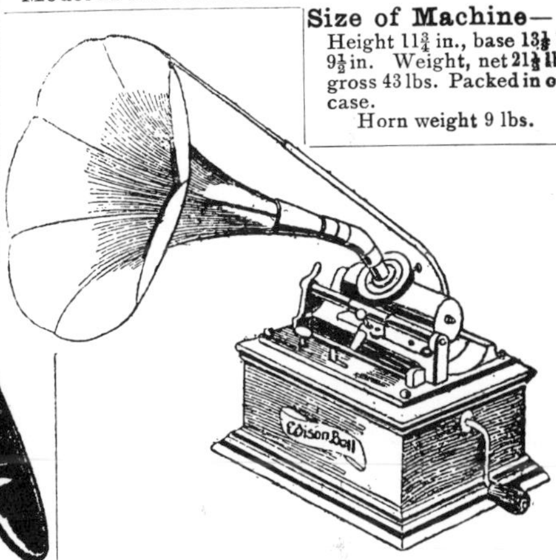

Edison Bell Phonograph. "THE GEM."

Fitted with Modern Fantail Reproducer, with carrying Crane and Large Horn.

Price .. **37/6**

PHONOGRAPH ACCESSORIES.

Cases to hold Cylinder Records.

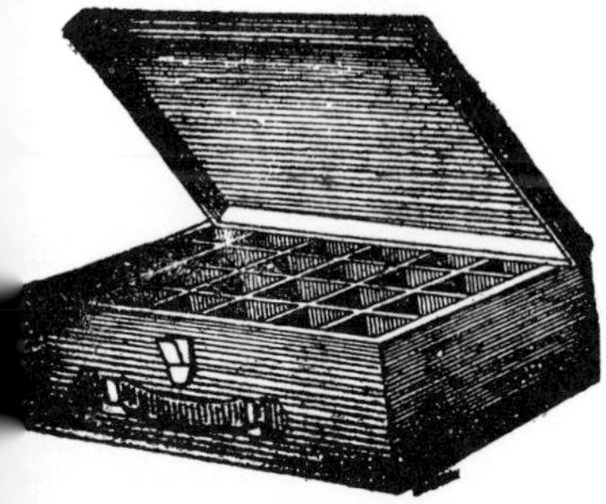

Card-board Case, covered leatherette, fitted with partitions, and lined flannelette.

Special value.

o hold 2 doz., **1/3** Post 4d. 3 doz., **1/9** Post 4d.
uperior quality, Wooden Frame and Leather Handle.
With Catch, see illustration.
o hold 3 doz., **2/6** Post 6d. 4 doz., **3/3** Post 7d.

ECORDS.		
	Clarion	**9**d. each
	Edison Amberol	**1/6** ,,
	Do. Blue Amberol	**2/-** ,,

Catalogue of Records on Application.

SUNDRIES.

Diaphragm Glass, Edison's	**2**d.
Governor Spring and spindle for Puck .. each,	**9**d.
Glass Points for Reproducing .. .. dozen,	**3**d.
Gamage Phono Oil .. .. .. per bottle,	**2**d.
,, Oiler	**1**d.
Horns for Phonographs, Best Brass,	
24 in. long, 11½ in. bell, **4/-** 42 in. long, 16½ in. bell,	**13/9**
30 in. ,, 15 in. ,, **6/6** 56 in. ,, 20½ in. ,,	**23/-**
Keys for Puck or Fairy .. .. .. each,	**2**d.
Motors for ditto .. .. .. ,,	**1/3**
Reproducers, Polyglot .. .. .. ,,	**2/6**
Musica, best quality	**3/-**
Puck, small size ... **3**d. Puck, large size ...	**9**d.
,, superior ... **6**d. ,, Grand Opera ...	**1/-**
Rubber Connections	**3**d.
Ditto, Best Flexible (metal ends)	**6**d.
Sapphire Points for Reproducing .. each,	**6**d.
,, ,, ,, Recording .. .. ,,	**1/-**
Spiders for Puck or Fairy .. .. .. ,,	**1**d.
Springs	
Edison, "Home," **2/9** "Standard," **1/9** Gem,"	**9**d.
,, "Fireside" ... **2/-** Combination ...	**1/3**
Puck Type Machines	**3**d.

Genuine Edison Reproducers.

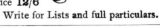

Model G **9/-**
,, H **9/-**
,, K **21/-**
,, R **21/-**
Diamond Reproducer **32/-**

Edison Recorder, Price **12/6**

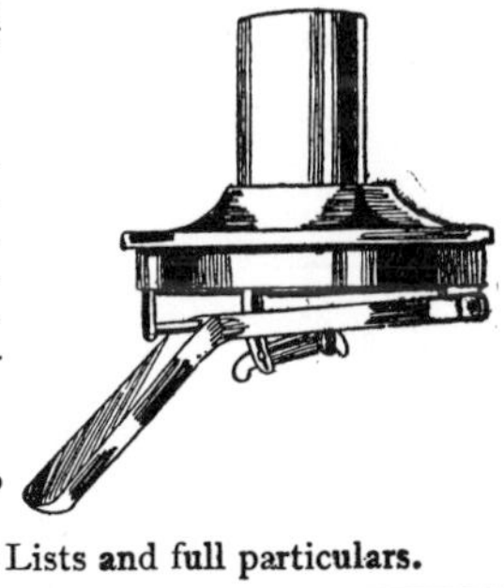

Write for Lists and full particulars.

Attachments for Playing Amberol Records.

For Gem Phonograph	**9/6**
For Standard Phonograph	**21/-**
For Home and Triumph Phonographs	**31/-**

An Amberol or Four-minute Reproducer is also included in each of these Attachments.

We fit to your Machine free of charge.

VIOLINS.

W. 31. The Hoff Model. Remarkable value. A good beginner's instrument, as illus. **5/11** Full or ¾ size.

W. 32. Violin, correct shape, purfled ebony fittings, brown varnish, in ½, ¾, and full sizes, **8/6**

W. 33. Strad Model, fine gold amber full varnish, good ebony fittings, finely marked wood, in ¾ and full sizes. Price .. **10/6**

W. 34. Dulcis and Fortis Model, amber varnish, well fitted and good finish, in ½, ¾ and full sizes .. **12/6**

W. 35. Strad Model, rich, reddish full-spirit varnish, one-piece back, ebony fittings; splendid instrument, well proportioned .. **15/-**

W. 36. Amati Model, very hollow borders, light brown shaded varnish in imitation, ebony fittings .. **17/6**

W. 37. Strad Mdl., dark amber full varnish, finely marked back in 1 piece, rosewood pegs, scroll and edges black lined after French style, fine tone .. **20/-**

W. 38. Stradivarius Mdl., medium amber full varnish, finely mrkd. back, with well matched table front, finest ebony fittings, artiste taste **27/6**

W. 39. Copy, Italian Masters, very fine wood and varnish ebony fittings, rosewood pegs, **32/6** Do., Ladies' size, **30/-**

Faithful Reproductions of the Old Masters—
Hand-made English.

A.	Fine copy Amati	**30/-**
B.	Seigfrieds, copy of Strad. Splendid tone	**45/-**
C.	Buthod, copy of very old Strad. Excellent tone	**50/-**
D.	Sarasate Artiste, splendid varnish. Very fine instrument	**65/-**
E.	Strad. Most perfect, even to the tone	**8** gns.
F.	Guarnarius. Hand - made, best oil varnish, finely marked, powerful tone ...	**10** ,,
G.	Amati. Hand-made, very old wood, splendidly marked and shaded, excellent tone	**15** ,,

Tenor Violins or Violas.

Well made and proportioned Instruments. Red shaded varnish, good tone.

Tenor Violin, copy Michael Angelo Garini, ebony fittings throughout **15/-**

Tenor Violin, copy Italian Masters, ebony fittings, fine old wood, reliable instrument. rich tone, **29/6**

Tenor Violin, copy Barnabethi, thoroughly well seasoned, old wood; a concert instrument, **38/-**

Viola Bows, 2/6 4/6 5/6

Violin Cases.

Leatherette Cases.

A.C. Black leatherette covered Violin Case, green cloth lined, small nickel button fasteners, inside lock, flat leather handle. ... ... Price **7/6** Post 6d.

A.E. Black leatherette covered Violin Case, superior finish, blue swansdown lining, spring clasps, inside lock, strong round leather handle ... price **9/6** Post 6d.

A.F. Black or brown leatherette covered Violin Case, swansdown Quaker-grey lining, nickel double slide, outside lock, with latest improved spring fasteners, heavy N.P. protecting guard at end, round leather handle ... ... price **12/6** Post 6d

A.G. Black or brown leatherette covered Violin Case, superior finish, cord edging, improved patent spring fasteners, nickel double slide, out side lock, heavy N.P. protecting guard at end, round leather handle ... ... price **15/6** Post 6d.

Canvas Violin Case Covers.

Best make Shaped or Straight. Bound with leather **10/6**
Cheaper Quality **8/6**

Cheap Wood Cases.

A. Wooden Violin Case, half lined, hook fasteners, brass handle, price **3/11** Post 6d.

A.A. Wooden Violin Case, superior finish, full lined, brass button fasteners, lock and key, heavy brass handle. ... ... price **4/11** Post 6d.

A.B. Wooden Violin Case, best varnish, full cloth lined, brass spring clasps, superior lock and key, as illustration ... ... price **5/11** Post 6d.

Shaped Wood Cases.

A.G. Violin Case, black varnish, bandeau round lid, hook fastenings, round lock, felt lining, flat leather handle; made in ½, ¾ and full sizes .. **5/9**

Black Polished Cases

A.A.E. Violin Case, fine black varnish, American spring fittings, round lock, marino plush lining, leather bag handle, embossed bottom and top, **11/9**

A.M. Ditto, ditto, but varnished brilliant black, and silk plush lining à la Parisienne .. .. price **19/-**

A.B. Violin Case, fine dull polished varnish, new style, spring fasteners on plates, rich silk plush lining, padded leather bag handle .. price **37/-**

Imitation Walnut Cases.

1A. Imitation Walnut, merino lining, round lock, patent clip fasteners, nickel fittings, leather bag handle .. .. .. price **11/6**

2A. Ditto, ditto, as 1A, with superior lock, French plush lining, leather bag handle .. .. price **15/6**

3A. Similar to 2A, with silk plush lining .. .. .. ,, **21/-**

4A. Imitation Walnut, new shape, bottom and top shaped alike, fancy carved bandeau round lid, strong outside lock, nickel clip fasteners, round leather bag handle, French plush lining .. .. price **18/-**

5A. Similar to 4A, with silk plush lining, Parisienne .. .. ,, **24/-**

Leather Cases.

American Violin Cases, brown, large grain crocodile leather, very rounded, new style fittings, silk plush lining, padded, leather handle, new bow holders, very best finish .. .. price **55/-**

Violin Strings.

The great trouble encountered by musicians using stringed instruments is undoutedly the difficulty experienced in obtaining reliable strings at a reasonable price. We beg to inform all musicians, that having fully appreciated this difficulty we have made very special efforts to obtain absolutely the best possible strings, and to list them at an exceptionally low price, in the hope that the quality and value will draw attention to our musical instruments, which will be found of equal value and excellence.

"E" Violin Gut Strings, 4 lengths.

No. W. 2.	Good quality	...	3d. each.
" 8.	very good quality clear white	...	4d. "
" 11.	Russian gut, good quality	...	4d. "
" 10.	Russian gut, very superior white smooth...		5d. "
" 7.	Very best selected smooth	...	6d. "
" 6.	" " " rough	...	8d. "
" 1.	" " " white	...	8d. "

"A" Violin Strings, 2 lengths.

No. W. 28. **3d.** each. No. W. 29. **4d.** each.
" 31. Russian gut, good quality **5d.** "
" 30. " " best selected white **8d.** "

"D" Violin Strings, 2 lengths.

No. W. 38. ... **3d.** each. No. W. 39. ... **4d.** each.
" 41. Fine selected **6d.** "
" 40. Very finest selected white **8d.** "

"G" Violin Strings

No. W. 60. Silver plated, on best selected gut **4d.** each.
" 52. Sterling silver, very fine ... **1/-** "
" 50. Ditto, finest quality ... **1/3** "

Gamage's Special **Acribelle Violin Strings**
Two full lengths ... ... **4d.** each.
Three " ... ... **6d.** "

Sundries for the Violin.

Violin Resin.

In Card Box **1d.**
Larger size in card-board box ... **2d.**
In book form, resin fitted in wood **3d.**
Dustproof, square size ... **4d.**
Gamage's "Sampo" fitted on chamois leather ... **6d.**

No. 43.
Ebonite (double screw) Pan-shape

Chin Rest,

Price **1/-** Post **2d.**
No. 45. Ebony

Chin Rest.

Improved shape pan.
Price **1/6** Post **2d.**

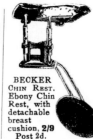

BECKER CHIN REST. Ebony Chin Rest, with detachable breast cushion, **2/9** Post **2d.**

Stabil Chin Rest

Improved Model.
As illustration, **3/3**

Violin Tailpiece.

All Sizes in Stock.

Ebony...	**3d.**
Better finish with gut ...	**5d.**
Finest Ebony	**6d.**
do. Best finish	**9d.**

Violin Bridges. Any size, all fitted

Plain wood, kidney ...	**2d.**
Buthod model...	**4d.**
Grandini "	**6d.**

Violin Tuners.

1 note, E A D or G **3d.** each
4 tubes. 4 notes, ditto **9d.** "
6 " 6 " " **10d.** "
2 " 4 " " **6d.** "
Chromatic (full compass) **2/3**

Tuning Forks ... **9d. & 1/-**

Mutes.

Solid Ebony.
each. **2d.**

Mutes.

German Silver.
3d. each.
Better quality,
4d. each.

Violin Pegs, 4/4 and ¾ size.

Black, wood polished ... **2d.** each
Rosewood or Ebony. Paris pattern, **3d.** "
Ditto, Fluted ... **6d.** "

Violin End Pins, 2d. each.

Finger-boards, Ebony, 9d.; superior quality, 1/-

Bow Hair, 4d.; best quality, 6d.

String Gauges, 1/-

Sound-Post Setters, 6d.

String Pliers ... ... **10d.**

VIOLIN BOWS.

No. W. 1. Violin Bow, dark colour, ebony nut, cloth lapping... ... **1/3**
" W. 2. Violin Bow, light coloured Brazilette stick, half silver mounted, German silver screw, ebony nut, German silver lapping **1/6**
" W. 3. Violin Bow, dark polished Brazilette stick, full German silver mounted, ebony mounted, German silver screw, silver wire lapping, finished with black leather rings **2/6**
" W. 4. Violin Bow, Tourte Model, imitation Fernambucco wood, full German silver mounted, octagon stick, fine silver wire lapping **3/6**
" W. 5. Violin Bow, Tourte Model, finest imitation Fernambucco wood, octagon stick, ebony full mounted nut, superior lapping, bound with brown leather rings, splendid balance **4/6**
" W. 6. Tourte Model, Dark Fernambucco octagon stick, imitation old finish, German silver full mounted, ebony nut, silver wire lapping with leather rings ... **6/-**
" W. 7. Violin Bow, Bausch Model, dark polished, finest Fernambucco round stick, German silver full mounted, fine ebony nut, silver wire lapping, bound with leather ring **7/6**
" W. 8. Violin Bow, Dodd's Model, light Fernambucco stick, with fine ebony nut, pearl slide, silver wire lapping, finished with leather rings **9/6**
" W. 9. Violin Bow, Bausch Model, light round Fernambucco stick, real silver full mounted ebony nut, with metal lined slide, silver wire lapping, bound with two leather rings **12/6**
" W. 10. Violin Bow, Tourte Model, light octagon Fernambucco stick bound with silver wire lappings, finished with two leather rings, real silver full mounted, ebony nut, solid silver screw ... **15/-**
" W. 11. Violin Bow, Tubb Model, fine selected round Fernambuco stick full silver mounted, leather and silver lapped, silver bow screw, best finish **21/-**

Postage 3d.

CONDUCTORS' BATONS.

No. W. 3. Selected wood, white enamelled ... ... **6d.**
" 4. " ebonized ... ... **6d.**
" 5. Finest selected ebony **1/-**

Sterling Silver Mounts.

No. W. 12. Ebony, 3 plain 1in. silver mounts **4/6**
" 14. " 3 engraved 1in. " **7/6**
" 15. " 3 engraved 1½in. " **9/6**
" 16A. " 3 fancy, chased 1½in. silver mounts... **12/6**
" 17A. " 3 " " 2½in. " **15/-**
" 19A. " 3 engraved, handsome design, octagonal 3in. silver mounts **17/6**
" 21 " 3 fluted, pear-shape handsome design, 3½in. silver mounts ... **22/6**
" 30 " 3 engraved handsome, extra heavy silver mounts ... **30/-**
" 32. Ivory, 3 do. do. **52/6**

Cases for above Batons.

A. Cloth covered, velvet lined, two clasps ... **4/6**
B. Leather covered, velvet and silk lined **5/9**

POCKET BATONS. Sterling Silver Mounts.

No. W. 17B. Ebony, jointed, 3 silver mounts, 2⅛in. chased pear design, in lined case **15/6**
" 19B. Ebony, patent folding joint, 3 silver mounts 3in. beautifully engraved, in velvet lined case **22/6**
" 28. Ivory, jointed, 3 beautifully chased silver mounts, in velvet lined case **45/-**

Metronomes

Best quality.

Mahogany with fixed key **7/6**
Walnut do. .. **7/9**
Mahogany, with bell, fixed key .. **11/6**
Walnut do. .. **11/9**
Rosewood, fixed key .. **10/6**
Ditto, with bell .. **14/6**

Postage 6d.

Piano Insulators.

Amber, Crystal and Green.

In three patterns. Per set of 4 **1/3**
Oriental, blue and white, set of 4 **1/8**
" extra strong, amber " **1/10½**

Carriage extra.

Telescopic Folding Music Stands,

Adjustable to any height. Extremely compact when folded

No.
W. 1A. Bronzed metal, loose desk . **2/-**
W. 1B. Superior do., extra heavy **2/6**
W. 2. Bronzed metal, connected desk .. . **2/9**
W. 3. Nickel plated, loose desk **3/6**
W. 4. Copper " " **3/9**
W. 5. Nickel " very strong, patent quick adjustment **5/9**
W. 6. Nickel plated, extra strong, well made, sup. qual. **10/6**
W. 7 Full size stand, nickel plated, will fold up small and go in box 14 by 1⅜ by 1½ in. for pocket **13/6**
W. 8. Nickel Stand for fixing on end of piano, useful when playing violin, when not in use it is easily detached **5/11**
W. 9. Bronze do. .. **2/6**
W. 10. Table Stand .. **2/11**

Music Rolls and Cases.

W. 1. American cloth, waterproof roll .. **1/-**
W. 2 Stout leather roll with strap and handle **2/9**
W. 3. Pigskin grain leather, roll, with strap & handle **3/3**
W. 4. Cloth, duplex, to take music, flat or folded **2/6**
W. 5. Flat leather music case with bar .. **5/11**
W. 6. Do. Pigskin grain, green or brown **7/6**
W. 7. Do. do. do. superior **9/6**

Music Cases.

Keep your music clean and tidy.
Made of stout wood. body leatherette covered, front of drawers covered in cloth, **5/11**

VIOLONCELLOS.

A. Brown varnished, purfled, well marked, labelled Antonius Sladinarius **26/6**

B. Well seasoned Maple wood. rich crown varnish, good purfling, white edging, entire ebony fittings, telescopic end pin. Most extraordinary value because of its ebony fittings **35/-**

C. Old seasoned Swiss Pine, French varnished, finely marked back, broad purfling, fine Maple neck, entire Ebony fittings, telescopic end pin, well finished throughout **£2 5 0**

D. Old seasoned Swiss Pine, spirit varnish in gold amber, slightly shaded and finely marked, highly finished scroll, Maple neck, entire best Ebony fittings and telescopic end pin. A fine tone instrument **£3 15 0**

E. Selected old wood, fine amber spirit varnish, well marked, best finish throughout, finest ebony fittings, telescopic end pin. Rich tone **£5 12 6**

Violoncello Sundries.

Bridges	..	..	..	**6d.**
Ditto, with kidney, well cut ..		..	..	**9d.**
Very rich wood Bridges, well cut		..	..	**1/6**
Resin, in case	..	..	..	**6d.**
End Pins, Ebony	..	..	..	**9d.**
Ditto, with metal Sliding Rod..		..	..	**2/3**

Violoncello Strings. First quality. A 6d. D 8d. G 9d. C 10d. Finest selected. A 8d. D 10d. G 1/- C. 1/2

Violoncello Bows.

1A. Round Brazil wood stick, with wire lapping, ebony nut with pearl eye, German silver screw **2/9**

1B. Round Brazil wood stick, superior and full mounted **3/6**

1C. Best imitation Fernambucco round stick, silver wire lapping with leather rings, full German silver mounted ebony nut... ... ... **4/6**

1D. Octagon Fernambucco stick, silver wire lapping leather rings, full German silver mounted, ebony nut, superior finish **9/6**

1E. Do. do., specially selected stick ... **10/6**

Brown Waterproof Cases.

Canvas Bag, with pockets for bow, leather straps and handle ..		..	..	**10/6**
Ditto, do., superior quality, bound leather ..	..	..	..	**13/6**
Extra strong canvas, superior bound..		..	..	**17/6**

Violoncello Cases.

Black varnish, hook clasps	..	..	..	**24/-**
Ditto, with spring clasps	..	..	..	**25/6**
Best quality, raised edges, fine flannel lining	..	..	**50/-**

GUITARS.

W. 1. With Machine Head, varnished belly. Price ... ... **10/6** Carriage 9d.

W. 2. Maple, yellow, purfled machine head. Price ... ... **17/6** Carriage 9d.

W. 3. Maple, German silver frets, varnished belly, rosette machine head. Price **22/6** Carriage 9d.

W. 4. Maple, fine wood, brown, pearl rosette, machine head, with large screw cogs. Price **29/6** Carriage 9d.

W. 5. Rosewood, German silver frets, pearl rosette, machine head and screw cogs. Special value. Price **37/6**

Guitar Cases and Bags.

Guitar Case, American cloth, stitched with lock	...	**6/3**
Ditto ditto superior quality	... ...	**9/-**
Ditto brown basil leather, lined scarlet, nickel double-action lock	... ...	**24/-**
Guitar Bag, green felt	... ...	**2/6**
Ditto Brown waterproof check	... ...	**7/3**

The "B.D." Guitar Strings. New Process.

W. 88.	E firsts, silver-plated steel	...	...	**2/-** doz.
,, 92.	B seconds	,,	,,	**2/-** ,,
,, 94.	G thirds, wound on silver-plated steel			**2/8** ,,
,, 96.	D fourths	,,	,,	**3d.** each
,, 98.	D fourths, wound on silk	,,		**4½d.** ,,
,, 102.	A fifths, wound on silver-plated steel...			**3½d.** ,,
,, 104.	A ,, ,, silk		...	**5d.** ,,
,, 106.	E sixths, ,, silver-plated steel ...			**3½d.** ,,
,, 108.	E ,, ,, silk	...	...	**6d.** ,,
	Set of six steel strings		...	**1/6** set.

MANDOLINES.

W. 1. G.B. Genuine Italian Mandoline. In polished rosewood, tulip-wood profile, rosewood escutcheon, and machine head, good tone. Special value. Price **8/9** Post 6d.

W. 2. T.B. Genuine Italian Mandoline. Of selected rosewood, with tulip-wood profile, pearl rosette, tortoise-shell escutcheon, pearl borders round belly and open machine head Price ... **12/9** Post 6d.

Y.T. Genuine Italian Mandoline. Of best selected, finely marked rosewood, pear rosette, tortoiseshell escutcheon, inlaid with pearl, borders, with enclosed nickel-plated machine head. A fine instrument. Price ... **21/-** Post free.

W. 7. Fine Quality Italian Mandoline. Neapolitan model, labelled "Phébé," best selected rosewood, with 13 ribs, pearl inlaid escutcheon, pearl rosette, pearl borders and machine head. Price ... **27/6** Post free.

W. 8. Very Handsom Italian Mandoline. Latest Neapolitan model label Carlo Martello, with 25 ribs, pe inlaid escutcheon, pearl rosette, tended finger board and enclos machine head **33/9** Post fr

W. 9. Very Fine Italia Artist Mandoline. Labelled "Phébé" of finest qual rosewood, 17 hollowed ribs, cellul escutcheon, with pearl inlaying, pe rosette, pearl imitation tortoisesh border round belly, with cover machine head. Fine tone, **45/**

W. 10. De Meglio Mand line. Rosewood, 17 ebony purf ribs outside, rosewood cap and r tulipwood, bevelled border, large cutcheon extending over sound ho pressure bar and sound hole ... **47**

W. 11. High-class Italia Mandoline. Of finely marked rosewood, with hollowed ribs, finger board edg with pearl, ebony and pearl edgi round belly, best quality cover machine head with pearl pegs. artist's instrument. Price ... **6** Post free.

Aluminium Mandolines.

Aluminium Mandolines are not influenced by any change of temperature and are therefore specially fit for tropical climates. They are v light and have a sonorous, powerful tone of great beauty.

No. W 34. With Round Aluminium Body. Neapolitan Model, cord pattern, wooden edges, sound hole and butte escutcheon, richly pearl inlaid with machine head and sleeve gua as illustration **27**

No. W 03. With Flat Aluminium Body. Flat Back Model, machine head, wooden edges, ornamented so hole, with sleeve guard. Fine tone **13**

Mandoline Cases.

Mandoline Case, American cloth, stitched, with lock	...	...	...		**2**
,, ,, ,, stronger, round leather handle...					**3**
,, ,, ,, nickel lock and two clasps					**4**
,, ,, ,, best grained cloth, superior nickel fittings					**7**
,, ,, ,, stamped leather, imitation crocodile, super. fittings					**11**
,, ,, ,, brown cowhide, nickel fittings					**16**

Mandoline Plectras.

Real Tortoiseshell	...		... per doz.
,, ,, larger	...	...	,,
,, ,, extra large	...	...	,,
3-point triangular	...		,,
Ivory, ordinary shape	...	...	,,
Cherry-wood	...		,,

MANDOLINE STRINGS.

The "B.D." Mandoline Strings. New Process.

W. 12.	E firsts, silver-plated steel	...	...	... per doz.	**2/-**
,, 14.	A seconds		...	...	,,	**2/-**
,, 16.	D thirds, wound on silver-plated steel	...	...	,,	**2/8**
,, 18.	G forths		...	...	,,	**3/-**
	Set of Six Strings in neat box		...	,,	**1/8**

The "B.B." Mandoline Strings.

W. 2.	E firsts, silver-plated steel	...	... per doz.	,,
,, 4.	A seconds		...	,,
,, 6.	D thirds, wound on silver-plated steel	...	...	,,
,, 8.	G fourths		...	,,
	Set of Eight Strings in neat box		... per set	,,

Mandoline Bridges. Well cut ... **4d.** Ebony ... **6d.**
Sleeve Guard. Celluloid ... **2d.** Imitation Tortoiseshell ... **3**

TEMLETT BANJOS.

WE desire to draw special attention to the undermentioned BANJOS and to recommend them with every confidence to our customers. TEMLETT BANJOS have a reputation of over 40 years, and are admitted to be the finest instruments on the market. Hitherto, it has been impossible to obtain Banjos except at high prices. We are now offering these instruments at prices less than the inferior machine-made Banjos.

ZITHER BANJOS

A. Walnut neck and hoop, nickel-plated tension ring, eight brackets raised frets, machine head, pearl position marks, ebony finger board. Price .. .. **16/6** List price 27/6

Veneered Rosewood or walnut hoop, nickel silver tension ring, brass machine head, 12 brackets, solid cast straining. Gamage's price .. .. **26/9** List price, 39/-

Superior veneered rosewood or walnut hoop, nickel silver tension rings, pearl inlaid edge of hoop and finger board, nickel silver machine head, solid cast straining beyel, 12 tightening bolts and 12 supporting brackets, superior vellum head, solid German silver frets. Gamage's price ... ... **30/-** List price, 45/-

Extra stout hoop veneered with rosewood, finger board and edge of hoop handsomely inlaid with pearl, fancy cut tension hoop, 13 tightening bolts and 13 supporting brackets, engraved nickelplated machine head, new pressure bar tail-piece, ebony and sycamore finger board. Gamage's price ... ... **41/6** List price, 70/-

2 Solid rosewood neck, four panels of ebony and sycamore on finger board, beautifully moulded rosewood back, finger board and edge of hoop handsomely inlaid with pearl raised frets, first class machine head. First-class Instrument. Gamage's price ... ... **84/-** List price, 126/-

GENUINE WINDSOR BANJOS.
No. W. 65. Zither Banjo.

eal Italian walnut, shaped back, purfled edges, solid cast brass tension hoop and strong rim, 8½ ins. diameter, ebony finger board inlaid with pearls, open machine of good quality, walnut neck, good strong selected vellum, 12 hexagonal-head tension bolts to tighten with a key, and 12 brackets. Price **25/6** List price 30/-

Banjo Strings. Black Diamond.

First, silver plated steel, **2/-** doz.   C Fourths, wound on silver-plated steel, **2/-** doz.
Seconds ,, ,, **2/-** ,,   C ,, ,, silk **3/6** ,,
Thirds ,, ,, **2/-** ,,   G Fifths, or Octaves, silver-plated steel **2/-** ,,

Gut Banjo Strings.

also 5th. Very finest quality gut **3d.** ea.   4th. Silver-plated wound on gut **3d.** ea.
ditto ditto ... **4d.** ,,   4th. Ditto, wound on silk ... **3d.** ,,
ditto ditto **6d.** ,,

Banjo Vellums. Allow 3 to 4 inches for fitting.

n. .. 10½d.   13 in. ... **1/-**   14 in. ... **1/3**   15 in. ... **1/6**   16 in. ... **2/6**

Banjo Bridges.

itewood not fitted ... ... price **1d.**
ony, fitted ... ... ,, **2d.**
'ever-slip'' Pattern—Whitewood or ebony, not fitted ... ... ,, **2d.**
uine ''Never-slip,'' fitted ... ... ,, **4d.**

The Weaver Patent Non-slip Pegs.

r Banjo (or Guitar) .. **6/-** per set of Five,   Or **1/3** single peg.

ORDINARY BANJOS.

Ordinary Banjo, veneered handle, vellum head, brass band and screws, 5 strings. Price **4/9** Postage 6d.

Ordinary Banjo, veneered handle, vellum head, brass band, six brackets, five strings. Larger size Price ... ... **6/6** Postage 9d.
Ditto, ditto, better quality, eight brackets, best vellum ... Price **8/6**
Ordinary Banjo, 11-in. nickel-plated double spun hoop, elm lined, 16 plated brackets, walnut neck, pearl inlaid, veneered face, celluloid pegs, raised frets. Price **18/6** Post 9d.
Ditto, with nickel-plated rim, 12 nickel-plated brackets ... ,, **14/9** ,, 9d.

High-class Concert Banjos.

Grand tone of considerable carrying power, walnut neck, Ebony finger board, rim spun over maple, heavily nickel-plated. 20 brackets sunk into bezel. Price ... ... **27/6** List price 42/-

AWG. Notched flushed nickel-silver hoop, 24 supporting brackets, fine vellum, patent non-slipping pegs, ebony in laid finger board (perfectly fretted) walnut arm. **42/6**
This Banjo is made exclusively for us, and is the finest value possible to obtain.

Temlett's Celebrated ''Ajax'' Banjo.

Nickel-silver hoop, Canadian walnut neck, notched flush rim and finest vellum, with two panels of ebony and sycamore on finger board, raised frets, non-slipping pegs 24 brackets Gamage's price ... ... ,, **57/6** List price 84/-
Ditto ditto, extra stout, ebony finger board, raised frets, spliced neck (absolutely unwarpable), non-slipping pegs and tailpiece. Gamage's price... **75/-** List price 110/-

''Reliance'' Banjo Cases.

American cloth, scarlet lined, leather handle and hinge, nickelled double lock ... **6/3**
With better quality fittings, **7/6**
Superior American cloth, scarlet lined, fitted with 3 pockets, best quality lock, **12/6**
Cowhide, chocolate colour, fitted, **31/3**

The ''Gamage'' Banjo Cases.
This is exceptionally good value and is strongly and neatly stitched, in good American cloth, with solid leather handle and hinge. Price **5/11** Postage 6d.

When ordering, state wether for ordinary or Zither Banjo and diameter of hoop.
No. W. 1. Imperial Cloth, lined, with nickel lock, leather hinge and round leather handle, **7/6** Post 6d.
No W. 4. Basil leather, with nickel double-action lock, swansdown lined, round leather handle, **17/3** Post 4d.
No. W. 5. Best Cowhide Black or Brown, lined scarlet swansdown, full-shaped lip, double-action lock, **27/6** Post 8d.

he Gamage Violin Outfit.   Special Value.

Comprising Full or ¾-Size HOPF MODEL VIOLIN.
th light Brazilwood Bow. Mounted with German Silver fittings, Ebony Frog. ther-of-Pearl Eye, and inlaid with Mother-of-Pearl. One extra set of Strings, in and Tutor. Complete in light wooden case, painted black and polished. Lined inside. **Price complete .. 12/6**   Carriage 9d.

Student's Violin Outfit.

Comprising Full-size Strad Model Violin, Bow, Case, Resin, extra set of strings, tutor, etc.

Price .. **21/-**
Carriage 9d.

Mandoline Outfit.

A Good Opportunity for Beginners.
Outfit contains first-class Mandoline, with Case, Tutor, and Set of Strings.
Price .. **12/6**   Postage 6d.

Japanese Fiddles, etc.

The Fiddlephone.

In spite of the novel construction of the Fiddlephone, the tone is really melodious, and is quite twice as loud as that of any ordinary Japanese Fiddle. The Fiddlephone is played in a similar manner to the Japanese fiddle, the fingering is the same also. The lower part of the instrument is gripped between the knees, the cross piece preventing slipping. The string should be tuned to A, but may be varied to suit the taste of the player. To obtain the full tone, the bow should cross the string at right angles, close to the bridge, the motion coming from the fore arm, the wrist being loose. Anyone possessing an ear for music can rapidly master this instrument, obtaining really beautiful effects especially when accompanied by the Piano or Organ.

I. Small model, stained walnut wood, fretted. fitted with flower trumpet (as illustration) .. **4/11** Post 6d.
II. Medium model, length 2ft. 9in., hand stained wood, mother-of-pearl fretted fitting with aluminium trumpet.
    Price **6/9**   Post 8d.
III. Large model, suitable for stage work, fine tone, fitted with non-slipping peg, large reproducer, ebony finger-board and extra large solid aluminium trumpet .. **15/6**
      Post 9d.
Bows, for same, extra.
(See Bows.)

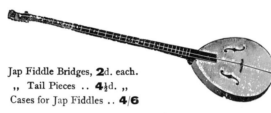

Japanese Fiddles.

White wood, nicely varnished, dotted finger-board for position. Price **5/-**
Ditto, with reproducer and flower trumpet, giving better volume Price **8/6**
Walnut, with reproducer and aluminium trumpet, fitted with non-slipping peg .. **10/6**
Square Style Fiddlephone, best quality, white wood, varnished back, plain white wood belly. Ivory infrets pearl dotted finger board **4/6**
Ditto, with reproducer and flower horn, giving better tone and volume. Price **8/-**
    Cigar Box pattern   **3/6**

Jap Fiddle Bridges, **2**d. each.
 ,, Tail Pieces .. **4½**d. ,,
Cases for Jap Fiddles .. **4/6**

Gamage Violo Fiddle.

Splendid tone.

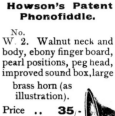

No. W. 1.
Violin shape body, walnut neck, ebony finger board and tail-piece, non-slipping peg .. **10/6**

No. W. 2.
Ditto, ditto, superior finish, and highly polished varnish.
    Price .. **15/-**

Howson's Patent Phonofiddle.

No.
W. 2. Walnut neck and body, ebony finger board, pearl positions, peg head, improved sound box, large brass horn (as illustration).

Price .. **35,-**

No.
W. 4. GRAND CONCERT, with all improvements, and as used by Chirgwin (to order only).
£2 15 6

OCARINAS.

No.	With Tuning Slide.	
W. 1.	Superior Quality, pocket size	**3/-**
W. 2.	Ditto, large size	**3/6**
W. 3.	Ditto, extra large ..	**4/9**
	Post 4d.	

OCARINA (Mezetti's make)   Post 3d.

No. W. 2. Small **9**d. W. 3. Medium **1/-**
  ,, 4. Large **1/6** ,, 5. Ex. large **1/9**

Mandoline Harp.

In white or black enamel, as illustrated. Chromatic scale. Each harp complete with tuning key, plectrum, and packed in strong cardboard case.
CAN BE LEARNT IN ONE HOUR.
    Price .. **12/6**

Auto Harps. Each Instrumnt in cardboard box with Tuning Key, Plectrum and Tutor.
No. W. 1. Imitation rosewood with 3 bars and 20 strings, producing the following three chords—C major, F major and G 7th .. **3/9** Post 6d.
  W. 2. Ditto, with 6 bars and 25 strings, producing chords—G major, C major, D 7th, E minor, A minor and B minor.. .. .. .. **6/6** Post 9d.
  ,,   6¾. Ebonised case, nobly ornamented with gilt mountings, etc. 6 bars, 25 strings, producing 6 chords, with outside tuning string **9/9** Post 9d.
  ,,   8. Ditto, with 9 bars, 32 strings, producing 9 chords—D, G and B major, B, A and E minor, A, G and D 7th .. .. .. **11/9** Post 9d.
  ,,   8½. Ditto FULLY CHROMATIC, with 6 changing bars, producing 72 chords, with outside tuning **21/6** Carriage free.
Muller's Erato Ebonised and inlaid with Marqueterie, perfect chromatic scale, 37 strings, producing 36 chords, gives minor, major and chords of 7th upon every degree of scale **£2 10 0**

MUSIC for 3 6, or 9 bar Auto Harps :—Instruction Book, **9**d. English Popular Songs (Vol. I. & II.) each **1/6**. Hymns and Sacred Songs, **1/2**.

BONES.

Rosewood or Ebony
6 in. **10½**d.
Ditto, 7 in. **1/2**

CASTANETS.

Whitewood	...	**8**d.
Boxwood	...	**10**d.
Ebony	...	**1/6**

Nigger Tambourines.

Plain Varnish Hoop, Vellum Head.
8 in., 3 pairs gingles, 1**0**d. each ; **9/-** doz.
No. W. 75. 9 in., 3 pairs gingles, **1/-** each ; **10/6** doz.
  76. 10 in., 3 pairs gingles, **1/2** each ; **12/6** doz.
Plain Hoops, Painted Red and Blue.
No. W. 80. 9 in., 3 pairs gingles, **1/-** each **10/6** doz.
  ,, 81. 10 in., 3 pairs gingles, **1/2** each ; **12/6** doz.
Best Oak Scolloped Hoop.
No. W. 84. 9 in., 3 pairs gingles, **1/8** each ; **15/-** doz.
  ,, 85. 10 in., 3 pairs gingles, **1/9** each ; **18/6** doz.
Best Oak, Painted Red & Blue Plain Hoops
No. W. 88. 10 in., 6 pairs gingles, **2/-** each ; **21/6** doz.
  ,, 89. 11 in., 6 pairs gingles, **2/6** each ; **28/6** doz.
  ,, 90. 12 in., 9 pairs gingles, **3/3** each ; **30/-** doz.
  ,, 91. 12in., 12 pairs gingles, **3/9** each ; **42/-** doz.
Nickel-plated Hoops.
No. W. 100. 9 in., 6 pairs gingles, **5/6** each ; **60/-** doz.
  ,, 101. 10 in., 6 pairs gingles, **5/-** each ; **54/-** doz.
Professional Tambourines, with Brass Brackets, Screws and Bands.
No. W. 58. 10 in., 6 pairs gingles, **3/3** each ; **36/-** doz.
  ,, 59. 11 in., 6 pairs gingles, **3/6** each ; **39/-** doz.
  ,, 60. 12 in., 6 pairs gingles **4/-** each ; **44/-** doz.

Dulcimers.

No.		
W. 3.	3 Octaves, stained polished walnut, black sound board 3 strings to each note	**16/3**
W. 4½.	3 Octaves, in polished oak (larger size), 4 strings to each note (best London make)	**25/-**
W. 6.	3 Octaves, do., best polished mahogany inlaid with rosewood	**41/3**

Xylophones.

No.	notes		rows			
W. 1.	18 notes	Swiss Pine	2 rows	...	...	**9/-**
,, 2.	26 ,,		3 ,,	...	...	**12/6**
,, 3.	36 ,,		4 ,,	...	...	**17/3**
,, 4.	26 ,,	Walnut	3 ,,	...	...	**18/6**
,, 5.	36 ,,		4 ,,	...	...	**24/-**

Regulation Artillery Field Bugles.

Suitable for Territorials, Boys' Brigades, Scouts, etc. Astounding Value.

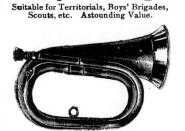

Copper Bugles.

Bb. Heavy Pattern, weight 20½ oz.
Rifle or Artillery Field Bugle, Regulation pattern and size, Copper, with German Silver Lipped Mouthpiece ... ... **11/3** Post 6d.
Ditto, light pattern, 14½ oz. ... **9/9** ,, 5d.
Ditto, in brass ... ... **8/3** ,, 5d.
Regulation pattern. Smaller size. Bb. **7/-** each. Postage 4d.

The Leader.

Silver Plated Bugles. Bb. Heavy pattern.
Regulation pattern and size.
German Silver-lipped mouthpiece. Price **21/-**

Post Horns.

Best Heavy Make.

1 and 2.   4 and 5.
No. 1. Two Turns, brass **2/9**
,, 2. ,, ,, copper ... **3/6**
,, 4. Three ,, brass ... **4/-**
,, 5. ,, ,, copper ... **4/9**
Postage 4d.

Bugle Mouth Pieces.

Nickel Plated. **1/3**   Silver Plated, **1/8**
Brass, **9d.**   Brass, German Silver Lipped, **1/-**
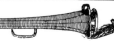 Bb Crook, Copper, **1/6**

Eb Cavalry Trumpets.

Current British Army Pattern.

Regulation Eb Cavalry Trumpet, Brass with genuine German Silver Mouthpiece With Slide and Brass Chain. **17/6**
Eb Cavalry Trumpet, brass Regulation Model and chain attached (As illustration). Price ... **10/6**

Best English Flageolets.

G	Brass	...	**3½d.**	Nickel plated	**5½d.**
F	,,	...	**4d.**	,,	**6d.**
E flat	,,	...	**5d.**	,,	**7d.**
D	,,	...	**6d.**	,,	**8d.**
C	,,	...	**7d.**	,,	**9d.**
B flat	,,	...	**8d.**	,,	**1/-**

Cocus Bark Flageolets. 1 Brass Key, Bb, **4/6**   D or Eb. **3/-** each.

Bugle Cords.

Regulation Pattern, in Green, Scarlet, Tri-colour. Khaki, or White, **1/6**   Cheap quality, **1/3**   Dress Cords. **3/6**

Lipped Mail Horns.   Best Quality, Heavy Make.

Straight, 30 in., G.S. rim and mouthpiece. Brass,	**4/9**	each.	Copper,	**5/6**	each.	Postage 5d.
,, 36 in.	,,	,,	,,	**5/3**	,,	,,	**6/3**	,,	,, 5d.
,, 40 in.	,,	,,	,,	**5/9**	,,	,,	**6/11**	,,	,, 6d.
,, 44 in.	,,	,,	,,	**6/6**	,,	,,	**7/3**	,,	,, 6d.
,, 48 in.	,,	,,	,,	**6/9**	,,	,,	**7/11**	,,	,, 7d.

Mail Horn Baskets.

Baskets for the 30, 36 and 40 in. **2/-** Postage 4d.
,, ,, 44 and 48 in. ... **2/6** ,, 4d.

Hunting and Post Horns.

Straight Model.

				Best quality
Brass, 10 in.	...	...	...	**1/3**
Copper, 10 in.	...	...	...	**1/6**
Brass, 12 in.	...	...	...	**1/6**
Copper, 12 in.	...	...	...	**1/9**
Brass, 14 in.	...	...	...	**2/-**
Copper, 14 in.	...	...	...	**2/3**
Circular Horn	...	...	...	**2/6**
Horn, 2 Notes	...	...	...	**3/6**
,, 4 ,,	...	...	...	**6/6**
Carriage extra.				

Clarionets.

Cocus or Ebony, 13 German Silver Keys, special cheap lines	**35/-**
,, 13 ,, ,, 2 rings, cork joints, copy of Albert model ...	**44/9**
,, 14 ,, ,, new pattern keys to facilitate the C sharp cadence ...	**57/6**
Clarionet, Cocus or Ebony, 13 German Silver Keys and Tips, 2 rings, double filleted keys, German Silver lining to joints and cork bindings, superior quality	**75/-**
Ditto, with patent C sharp key	**88/-**

Lyre Music Desk.

Flute Desk, with strap for arm, tin buckle.

Price **1/3**

Do., brass buckle, **1/6**

Postage 3d.

Band Flutes. Bb. Best London Make. Best Quality.

E flat" Cocus 1 Brass Key **1/3**	Do., 4 G.S. Pillar Keys, slide head **5/9**
,, 1 G.S. Key and Tips **2/3**	Do., 6 ,, Keys, slide head .. **6/6**
,, 1 Pillar Key and tips ... **2/6**	Do., 6 ,, do. Pillar Keys **7/3**
,, 1 Cross Key and Tips (slide head) **3/6**	Do., 6 ,, do., slide head,
,, 4 ,, Keys, plain head **4/9**	best finish, Pillar Keys ... **12/-**

Clarionet Cases.

Good Quality Stitched Duck,	**3/11**	Post 4d.
Best ,, ,, ,,	**4/11**	,, 4d.
Solid Leather	**10/6**	,, 4d.

D Concert Flutes.

Cocus Wood, 1 G. S. Key, plain head	... **6/-**
,, 2 ,, slide head ...	**8/6**
,, 4 ,, ,, ...	**12/9**
,, 6 ,, ,, ...	**13/6**
,, 6 ,, ,, ...	**15/-**
,, 8 ,, ,, ...	**18/6**
,, 9 ,, with pillar keys	**21/-**

F Flutes.

Cocus Wood, 1 G. S. key and tips ...	**2/6**
,, 4 ,, slide head ...	**6/6**
,, 6 ,, ,, ...	**8/-**

Piccolos (English), D, Eb or F. Best Quality

Cocus 1 Brass Key, plain, 2 joints ... **1/-**	Cocus, 6 G.S. Keys, slide head ... **6/9**
,, do. 3 brass tips and ferrules **1/6**	,, Do., with Pillar Keys... **7/6**
,, 1 German Silver key plain head **2/-**	Army Model Pattern.
,, 4 do. Pillar Keys, plain head **4/9**	,, 6 G. S. Pillar Keys slide head **15/-**
,, 4 do. do. slide head **5/9**	,, Do., bushed holes, lip plate **18/-**

Flute Cases.

Best quality, **4/6**   Good quality, **3/6**

Piccolo Cases.

Best quality, **3/6**   Good quality, **2/6**

Reeds.

Musette	**9d.**
Clarionet, cheap	**2d.**
,, superior	**3d.**
,, best tested	**6d.**

Panpipes.

Full Compass best make metal.
Medium size **2/3**   Large size **3/6**

Musettes.   London Made.

No.	Cocus Wood.				Post
1.	Plain, with Reed...	**2/11**	4d.
2.	Large Bell, with Reed	**4/3**	4d.
3.	With Reed, small Bell and 1 G. S. Key on pillars	**3/9**	4d.
4.	,, ,, large ,, ,, ,,	**4/9**	4d.
5.	German Silver tipped, with Reed, large Bell and 1 German Silver Key on pillars	**5/9**	4d.
6.	Ditto, with 4 German Silver Keys on pillars ...	**7/9**	4d.
7.	Ditto, with 5 ,, ,, ,, ,,	**8/3**	4d.
8.	Ditto, with 6 ,, ,, ,, ,,	**9/6**	4d.

DRUMS.—Specially made for Boy Scouts and Boys' Brigades.

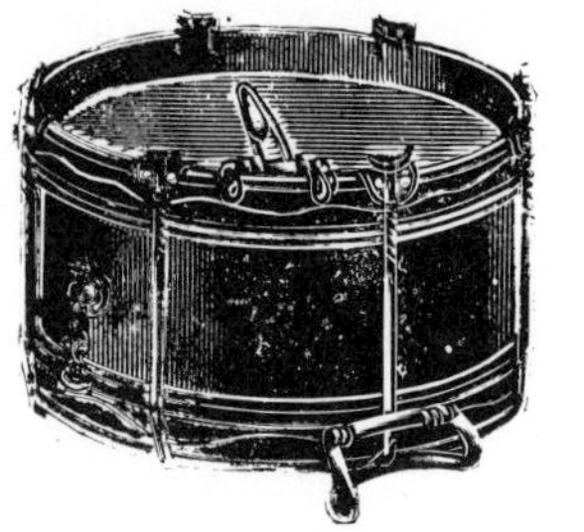

SIDE DRUMS.

BEST ENGLISH MAKE.

REGULATION PATTERN.

Best Workmanship throughout, and all fitted with knee supports.

First Quality.

		Stout seamed brass shells. plain nuts.	Stout brazed brass shells, washered nuts.
12-in.	5 tuning rods	**18/6**	**25/-**
14-in.	6 ,,	**24/-**	**29/3**
15-in.	6 ,,	**25/6**	**32/6**

Second Quality.

		Seamed brass shells.
12-in.	5 tuning rods ..	**15/6**
14-in.	5 ,, ..	**21/-**
15-in.	6 ,, ..	**24/-**

Cheap Quality.

		Brass shells.
12-in.	5 tuning rods ..	**13/9**
14-in.	5 ,, ..	**17/6**
15-in,	6 ,, ..	**19/6**

Carriage extra.

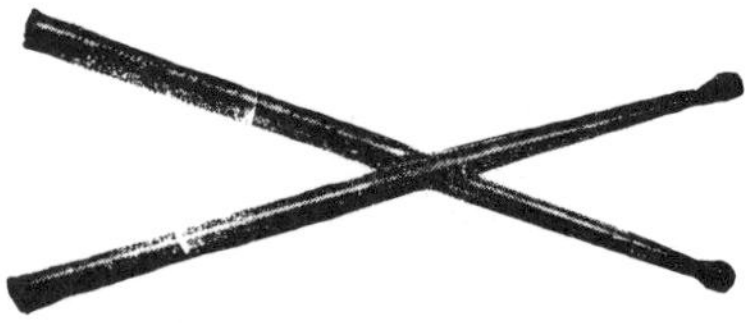

Side Drum Sticks.

W. 1.	Hardwood, good quality ..	**1/-**	pair.
W. 2.	Cocus, best quality	**1/6**	,,
W. 3.	Ebony ,, ..	**2/3**	,,
W. 4	Rosewood ,, ..	**2/9**	,,

Postage extra.

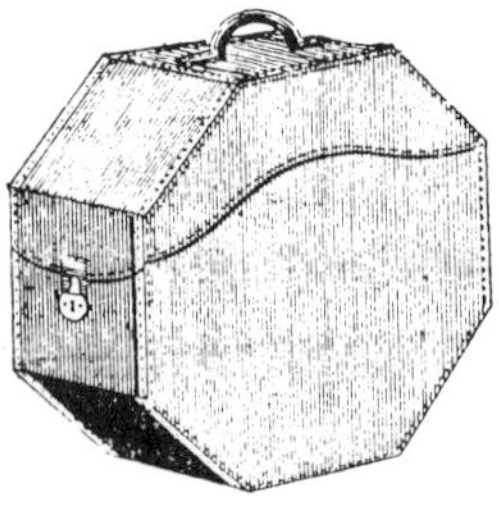

Side Drum Case.

American cloth, lined grey swansdown, leather bound, strong leather handle, nickel double-action lock.

Price .. .. .. 12/- Postage 7d.

Ditto, superior quality Tan Canvas.

Price .. .. .. 15/6 Postage 9d.

Brass Cymbals.

	6	10	12	13	15 inches
1st quality	— **6/6**	**11/-**	**13/-**	**16/6**	pair
2nd ,,	**2/3**	**5/6**	**7/6**	**9/6**	**14/-** ,,

Triangles with beaters.

3	6	8	10	12 inches.
10d.	**1/8**	**2/3**	**2/9**	**3/3**

Excelsior Model Side Drums.

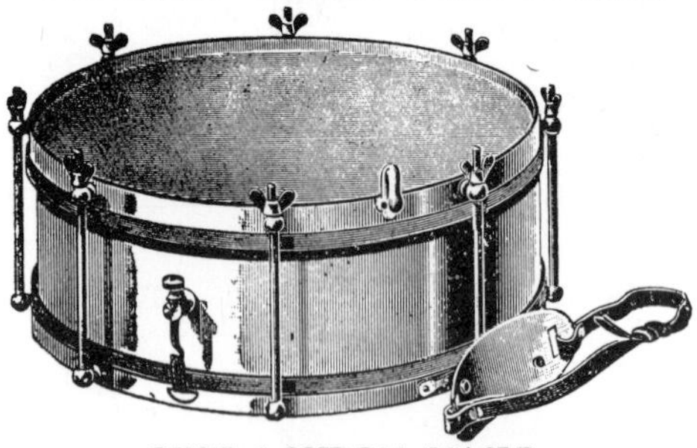

BEST LONDON MAKE.
Stout Brazed Brass Shells and Hoops,
Brass Tuning Rods, Knee Rests.
14-in., 8 tuning rods, **42/-** 15-in., 8 tuning rods, **44/6**

BASS DRUMS. ARMY MODEL.

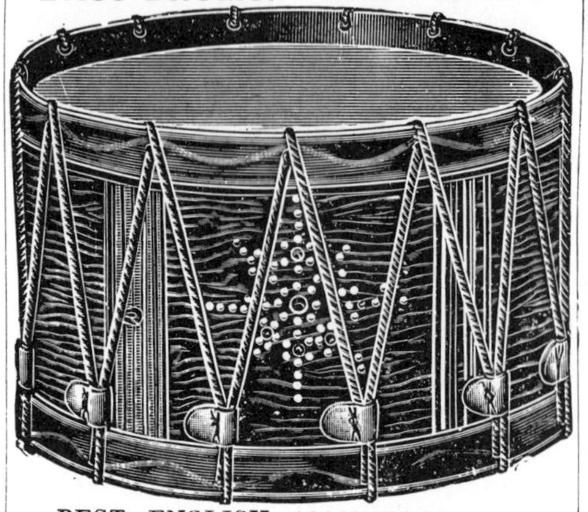

BEST ENGLISH MANUFACTURE.

Second Quality.	First Quality.
Painted ornamental lines. Well finished.	Red and Blue Hoops. Polished ash shells, painted aprons. Best finish.
28 in. **49/9** 30 in. **57/-** 32 in. **62/-**	28 in. **58/6** 30 in. **63/-** 32 in. **68/6**

Carriage extra on all Bass Drums.
Third Quality.
Painted Red and Blue Aprons, ornamental lines,
Varnished ash shell. Price **44/6** each.
Bass Drums Painted with crest and title from **7/6** extra.

DRUM SUNDRIES.

Bass Drum Aprons, black or brown leather	**21/6**
Ditto, medium quality **15/6** ordinary qual.	**10/6**
Ditto, in white buff	**38/6**
Bass Drum Covers, best quality teak ..	**10/6**
Side Drum Covers, all sizes	**3/9**
Side Drum Thigh Pieces or Aprons—	
Sheep Skin, small, **2/6**; medium	**3/9**
full size, **5/9** White Buff ..	**13/-**
Drum Cord for Guards' Model, 13 yards (pure white)	**4/6**
Dress Drum Cord	**1/9**
Bronze Side Drum Stands	**7/9**
Bass Drum Stands	**18/-**
Belt Hook to fix on Hoop	**1/-**
Knee Rest Leather, covered and painted ..	**1/6**
Do. all brass leather covered	**2/6**
Wing Nuts, Steel Bushed .. .. each	**9d.**
Do. large plain .. .. ,,	**4½d.**
Heavy Drum Rod and plain nut .. ,,	**9d.**
Snare Hook and Nut. Iron and Lever Brass Nut .. .. each	**4½d.**
Snare Gut .. .. .. per length	**10½d.**
Heavy Claw Bracket .. .. .. each	**4½d.**
,, Single ,, ... ,,	**3d.**
Flesh Hoops, any size .. .. ,,	**6d.**
Buff Braces for Guard's Model .. ,,	**6d.**
Guard's Drum Belt Hook .. .. ,,	**9d.**
Painted Drum Hoops .. .. per pair	**8/-**

Postage extra.

SIDE DRUMS.

BEST LONDON MANUFACTURE
GUARDS' MODEL.

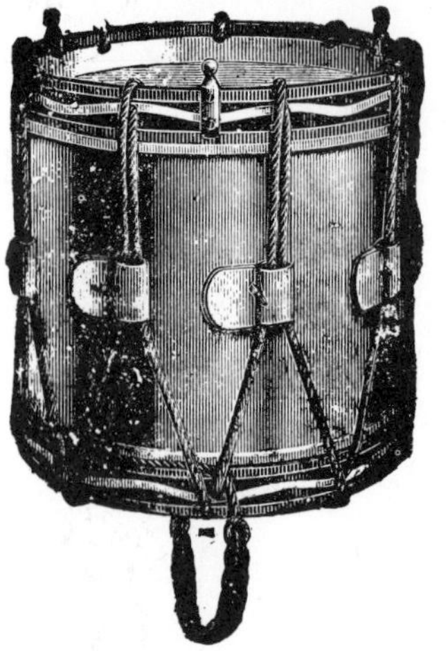

Extra deep and stout seamless brass shells, cord, braces, and carriage hook.
Best Quality.
15 in. by 14½ in. **44/6** 14 in. by 14½ in. **42/6**
Carriage free.

The Scout Tenor Drum.

Ash shells, best vellums, white ropes, &c.
16 in. by 16½ in... .. .. .. **30/-**

Side Drum Vellums.

Best French.

14 in.	15 in.	16 in.	17 in.	18 in.	19 in.
1/3	**1/6**	**2/-**	**2/9**	**3/3**	**3/9**

Bass Drum Sticks.

W. 1.	Cork, leather covered brass cap	**2/9**	pair.
W. 2.	Lamb's Wool, medium size ..	**6/-**	,,
W. 3.	Lamb's ,, large ,,	**6/9**	,,
W. 4.	White Felt, 3 pieces	**6/6**	,,
W. 5.	,, solid head ..	**9/6**	,,

Postage extra.

Bass Drum Belts.

In. wide.		Each.	Post.
1½	Black Leather	**4/6**	3d.
1½	Brown Leather	**4/9**	3d.
1½	Black Brass Fittings ..	**6/9**	4d

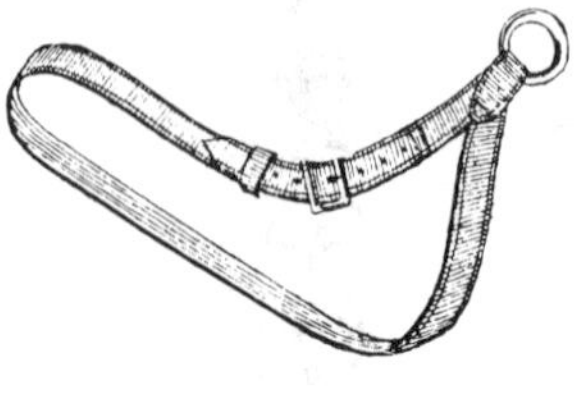

Side Drum Belts.

WIDTH.		
1 in.	Black or Brown leather	**1/9**
1¼ in.	Do. Do.	**2/1**
1½ in.	Do., Brass ring only	**3/-**
1½ in.	Do., Brass fittings	**3/3**

Postage 3d.

BAND INSTRUMENTS.

Cornets.

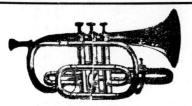

SPECIAL VALUE.

W. 200.   Bb and A shank, detached bell, single water key, 3 light-action German silver valves, with German silver mouthpiece.

Complete with music desk   ..   **27/6**

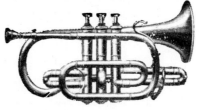

FINE VALUE.   W. 20.   Bb and A shanks. Single water key.   All fittings.   Price, **21/6**

Bb Baritone Saxhorns.

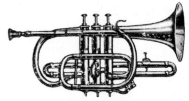

EXTRA QUALITY.

Courtois Model.   Bb and A shank,   Full bore detached bell with stays, double water key, 3 light-action German silver piston valves, German silver mouthpiece.

Complete with polished music desk   ..   **35/6**

Eb Tenor Saxhorns.

Eb Tenor Saxhorns.   First quality.

Light action, German silver Valves, German silver mouthpiece.

Complete with music desk   ..   **35/-**

Euphoniums.

Bb Euphonium.   With 3 valves.

Light action, German silver piston valves, water key, German silver mouthpiece, music desk.

As illustration.   Price   ..   **47/6**

Bb Tenor Slide Trombones.

Silver plated mouthpiece, water key and music desk.
Price   ..   **21/-**
Superior improved model **27/6**

Bb Baritone Saxhorns.   Bb, first quality, 1 water key, light action, German silver piston valves, German silver mouthpiece.
Complete with music desk   ..   **39/6**
Electro quality ditto, with quick change for high or low pitch **45/-**

Eb Bombardons or Contra Basses

Eb Bombardons.   Extra Quality.
Light action, extra German silver pistons, water key, German silver mouthpiece.   Complete with music desk.

As illustration.   Price **60/-**

Fluegel Horns.

(Contraltos).

W. 225.   **Bb Fluegel Horn.**   With light action, German silver piston valves, with water key and German silver mouthpiece.   Complete with music desk **32/6**

W. 226.   Ditto ditto fitted with tuning slide or high or low pitch.   Price **35/-**

Bb Bombardons.

Bb Bombardons.
Three valves, light action, extra German silver pistons, water key, German silver mouthpiece.
Complete with music desk   ..   **84/-**

Cornet Cases.

3rd quality   ..   **3/6**   2nd quality   ..   **4/6**
Best quality   **10/6**

ACCORDIONS.

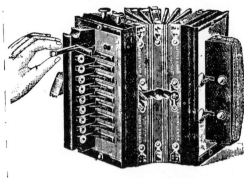

"Gamage" Accordions.

Black moulded case, single bellows, nickel key pallets, 1 set of reeds, 2 stops, 10 keys.
Price .. .. .. **3/-** Post 6d.

Same as above, but with double bellows.
Price .. .. .. **3/9** Post 6d.

Black moulded case, blue tops, open action, nickel keys, double bellows, 6 folds, 10 keys, 2 stops, 2 sets of reeds .. **4/3** Post 6d.

Black mouldings, nickel pallets, double bellows, nickel corners to folds, imitation crocodile skin covered bellows, 2 stops, 2 sets of reeds, 10 keys (as illustration) .. .. **5/-** Post 6d.

Black mouldings, nickel pallets, 8-fold treble bellows, with nickel corners to each fold, fancy sides, 2 wood stops, 2 sets of reeds, 10 bone keys .. .. **6/3** Post 6d.

The "Empress" Brand, 8-fold treble bellows, with nickel corners to each, fancy coloured cloth sides, open key action, moulded case, 3 stops, 3 sets of extra broad reeds, 10 keys.
Price .. .. **11/6** Post 6d.

The "Empress" Brand, new Improved Model, walnut finish, 11-fold bellows, with nickel corners to each, fancy coloured cloth sides, open key action, moulded case, 3 stops, 3 sets of extra broad reeds, 10 keys.
Price .. .. .. **12/9** Post 6d.

"Imperial" Accordions.

"The Prince of Wales," extra small size, 10 keys, 2 stops, 2 sets of extra broad reeds, polished case, light panels **8/6**

'Little Lord Fauntleroy," black polished mouldings, nickel border to panel, nickel pallets, new action keys, 2 sets of reeds, 2 stops (as illus.) .. **10/6**

Ten keys, black polished case, white moulding, patented simplex key action, fine nickel baguettes, double bellows, each fold entirely fitted with steel wire riveted nickel rims, 2 sets of reeds .. **11/-**

Ten keys, the smallest size with 3 sets of reeds, very loud music, by means of the stops the tones can be changed five times.. .. .. .. **14/-**

"Virtuose Grandini," stained rosewood tops, nickel edges, 10 keys, 3 stops and bass stop, 3 sets of steel reeds and 2 sets in bass, 20th Century patent key action **21/-**

Chromatic Accordion.

"Gamage" Chromatic, the "Empress" Brand, black moulded case, 11-fold treble bellows, with nickel corners to each, variegated coloured sides, 2 stops, 2 sets of reeds, 19 keys, 4 bass chords, **15/9**

Imperial Chromatic Accordions.

19 keys, 2 stops, the smallest Imperial with 2 rows of key with open key action, 2 sets of broad reeds, bla polished case **21/-**

19 keys, 2 stops, ebonized moulding, open nickel valve silver stamped bellow frame, 8-fold double bellow leather straps, 2 sets of broad reeds .. **25/-**

19 keys, 2 stops, 4 bass chords, Vox humana, oak ca nickel pallets, double bellows, leather straps, bro reeds **31/6**

Italian Accordions.

No. W. 345. Size 10 by 5½ in. Imitation rosewood w nickel corners, 12-fold bellows with nickel corners each fold, fretwork tops, 10 pearl keys, 4 pearl b keys, cloth lined straps, 2 sets of reeds **9/9**

No. W. 346. 11 by 6 in. Imitation rosewood with nic corners, 14-fold bellows with nickel corners to e fold, fretwork tops, 19 pearl keys, 8 pearl bass ke cloth straps, 4 sets of reeds .. **16/9**

No. W. 347. 12 by 6 in. Imitation rosewood with nic corners, 14-fold bellows with nickel corners to each fo fretwork tops inlaid, 21 pearl keys, 8 pearl bass ke cloth lined leather straps, 4 sets of reeds .. **22/6**

No. W. 289. Sovereign Professional. 11 by 6 in. Ro wood tops, ebonized frame with nickel corners, 14-f bellows with nickel corners to each fold, fretwork t 21 pearl keys, 8 pearl bass keys, cloth-lined lea straps, 4 sets of steel bronzed reeds .. **27/9**

CONCERTINAS.

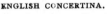
ENGLISH CONCERTINA.

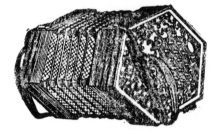
ANGLO-GERMAN CONCERTINA.

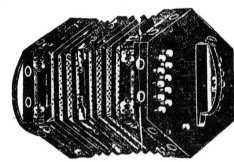

Lachenal's English Patent Concertinas.

Keys, Double Action, Screwed Notes, and Warranted. Compass, 3⅜ Octaves from G below to second C above stave.

MAHOGANY—In Deal, paper covered box	35/9
ROSEWOOD—Superior tone and finish, mahogany box	44/9
ROSEWOOD—Extra superior tone and finish, five-fold bellows, mahogany box	53/6
ROSEWOOD—Best finish five-fold morocco bellows, moulded edges, keyholes, bushed with cloth, to prevent rattling, rosewood box	72/-
ROSEWOOD—Extra best finish, five-fold morocco bellows, German Silver keys, rosewood box ...	95/-
ROSEWOOD—Newly improved, ornamented throughout, silver-tip keys, fine and pure tone, rosewood box ...	99/-
ROSEWOOD—Same finish as No. W 4. with tempered steel reeds, rosewood box	112/-

Lachenal's Anglo-German Concertinas.

All with separately fitted Screwed Notes.

MAHO-GANY	20 keys.	26 keys.	28 keys.	30 keys	MAHO-GANY	20 keys.	26 keys.	28 keys.	30 keys.
	19/6	26/9	27/6	29/6		23/9	32/6	35/-	38/9
	With Yellow Metal Reeds.					With Steel Reeds.			

Special Quotations given for any of Lachenal's Concertinas not Listed

German Concertinas.

			Post
20 keys, imitation rosewood, hexagon ..		**2/9**	6d.
20 Ditto do. G.S. bound trumpet holes		**3/9**	6d.
20 keys, rosewood, hollowed, double G.S. bound trumpet holes		**5/9**	6d.
20 bone keys, rosewood, 6 folds, double bellows, bellows clasps, trumpet holes		**6/3**	7d.
20 bone keys, Anglo-German, rosewood ..		**8/3**	7d.
20 bone keys, Anglo-German, rosewood, steel reeds, 6 folds		**12/-**	7d.
20 keys, Anglo-German, rosewood, 8 folds, broad reeds, in wood case		**14/9**	7d.

MUSICAL BOXES.

Self-acting Musical Boxes.

Plays 2 tunes, in polished wood box, 4¾ by 3¼ by 2⅜ in ... **3/9** Post 3d.

With glass cover to works, winds at side. Plays 3 tunes ... **4 9** Post 3d.

Plays 4 tunes, in polished wood box, 4¾ by 3¼ by 2¼ in., with glass cover to works, winds at bottom. **5/6** Post 3d.

Highly polished Walnut 4¾ by 3¼ in.

Extra long superior music.

Playing 2 tunes	..	..	..	**6/6**
Do. 3 ,,	..	..	..	**8/-**
Do. 4 ,,	..	..	..	**9/6**

Hand Organs.

In wooden case, 4 by 2 by 1⅜ in. To play 1 tune, As illustration. **1/6** Post 3d.

Do., 4 by 3¼ by 2¼ in. To play 2 tunes ... **2/6** Post 3d.

Do., 4½ by 3¼ by 3 in. To play 4 tunes ... **3 6** Post 4d.

In Round Nickelled Cases.

To play 1 tune	..	..	**1/2**
Do. 2 tunes	..	..	**2/-**

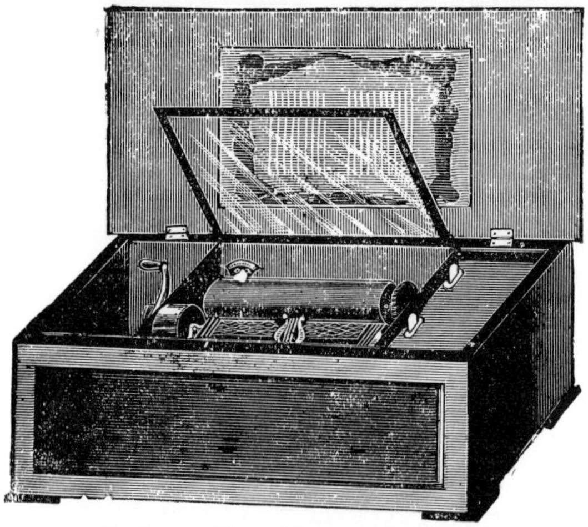

Musical Piano.

Light oak. To turn by hand. Size of piano 9 by 4 by 9½ in. Price, including 6 metal tunes .. **12/6** **A very fine Present.**

Automatic Musical Boxes

In highly finished imitation rosewood cabinets.

No.		
W. 1.	Has 3½ in. barrel, plays 8 tunes, 14 by 7½ by 5 in.	**23/6**
W. 2.	Has 6 in. ,, 10 ,, stop, start, change, repeat levers, size 17½ by 8½ by 5½ in. ..	**35/-**
W. 3.	Ditto, with Bells	**38/6**
W. 4.	Has 7 in. barrel, plays 12 tunes, 4 bells, stop, start, change and repeat levers, size 20 by 11 by 9 in.	**45/-**
W. 5.	Has 7½ in. barrel, plays 20 tunes, start, change and repeat lever, with optional mute, size 22 by 12 by 7¼ in...	**59/6**

Polyphons.

These boxes are automatic and have a strong well-made motor and cabinet. Complete Catalogue on application, New Tunes always to be obtained. When ordering, mention the diameter of your tunes or send us one as a sample.

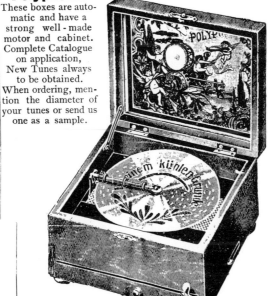

Polyphon No. 28|S. 30 notes, rosewood case, 7⅝ by 7½ by 4¾ in. Price, including 6 tunes, **25/6** Diameter of tunes 6½ in., price per dozen.. **4/-**

Polyphon No. 41. 41 notes, polished walnut case, size 10½ by 9⅞ by 6⅝ in. Price, including 6 tunes .. .. **38/6** Diameter of tunes 8¼ in., price per doz. .. **6/-** Timbro-variante (Zither arrangement) extra **2/-**

Polyphon No. 46. 46 notes, highly polished walnut case, size 12 in. by 10¾ by 7½ in. Price, including 6 tunes .. .. **57/6** Diameter of tunes 9⅝ in. Price per dozen .. .. .. **11/-** Timbro-variante (Zither arrangement) extra **3/6**

EDELWEISS
With Changeable Tunes

Hand Organs in polished wood case, 6 by 4⅛ by 3 in., and three interchangeable tunes .. **7/11** Do., 8¼ by 6 by 5⅓ in , with carrying sling and three interchangeable tunes .. **10/6** Post 4d. Extra tunes 4d. each. Do., 11 in. by 9½ in. by 6⅜ in., with 6 tunes Long Tunes, Superior Music and Motor, **22/6** Extra tunes 8d. each. **Automatic** with changeable tunes, as illustration, in polished mahogany wood case, strong clockwork motor. Complete with 6 tunes ... **12/6** Post 6d. Extra tunes 4d. each.

CHRISTMAS PRESENTS.

Musical Tobacco Jar

(Plays when lifted).

Height 7 in.

With 2 tunes.

Price .. **9/6**

as illustration.

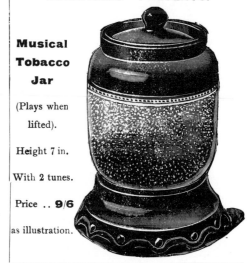

Musical Cigarette Box

(Plays when opened). Carved wood, size 8 by 3¼ by 3½ in., with 2 tunes Price **9/6**

Mouth Organs.

Hohner Echo,

Double-sided Tremolo, in 2 Keys, 40 double holes, 80 Reeds, Brass Plates, as illustration.
In Fancy Box .. **2/6** Post 3d.

Small Single-sided Echo.

Vampers, **6**d. Post 2d. Tremolo, **6**d. Post 2d

King George Harp.

Tremolo, 16 double holes, 32 Reeds, solid Brass Plates, nickel covers.
Price .. .. **1/-** Post 2d.
Ditto do., with 20 double holes, 40 Reeds,
Price .. .. **1/6** Post 2d.

The "Scout."

14 double-sided holes 28 reeds .. **6**d.
16 ,, superior) **9**d.

The Ironclad Harp.

Vamper, 10 holes, 20 Reeds, solid Brass Plates. Solid metal division between each reed. Nickel corners. Price **1/1** Post 2d.
Ditto do. with 14 holes, 24 Reeds. **1/6** Post 2d.

The Fortissima Harmonico

Wonderful Novelty.
Phonograph tone, 32 Reeds. 3 in. Brass Bell.
Price **2/11** Post 4d.

M Hohner Harmonette.

Vamper, 10 single holes, 20 Reeds, **1/3** each.

Ragtime Band.

17 double holes, 34 Reeds, fine tone, improved model .. .. **1/3** Post 2d.

Musical Clown.

20 double holes, 40 Reeds, Brassed Plates, 2 Bells, nickel covers, in fancy hinged box .. **1/6** Post 2d.

M Hohner Chromatic Harmonica

10 single holes, 40 Reeds, Brass Plates, Strong N steel covers, in Fancy hinged Box, **4/-** Post 4d

Up-to-Date Harp, double-sided (as illustration), 20 double holes each side, 80 Reeds. concert tuning, richest tone, in silk-lined case.
3/6 Post 3d.

Up-to-Date, single-sided, 20 holes, 40 Re Brass Plates, full concert octave size, in neat s lined leatherette case, **1/10½**

Mandola Harmonica,

40 reeds, 6½ in. long. Pleasing crescendo effe easily obtainable. Printed instructions and se of tunes, **1/6**
Larger .. **1/9** Post 2d.

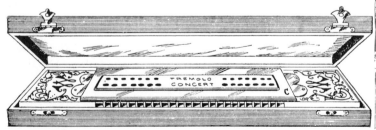

The Opal Grand Concert Harmonica,

96 Reeds, 2 Keys, 10 in. long **3/11** Post 4d.

Up-to-Date Goliath Harp. Single-sided, 24 double holes, 48 Reeds, solid Brass Plate, fine tone. **1/10½** Post 3d.

The Elegie. Grand Concert Harmonica, 128 Reeds, 4 Keys,

Double-sided, 64 double holes. **4/11** Post 4d.

The Trumpet Call. Single-sided, 28 double holes, 56 Ree solid Brass Plate, fine tone and finish. **2/6** Post 3d.

PIANOS AND PLAYER PIANOS.

COTTAGE PIANO.

15 guineas.

Ideal instruments for the Drawing Room, at the right price. Made of selected well-seasoned material, and by a firm with over 50 years' experience. Iron Frame, Full Compass, Full Trichord, Swiss Pine Sounding Board, Gilt Panel and Sconces, Check Action. These Pianos have an ideal touch and a brilliant tone, combined with durability.

Cottage Piano.—Iron Frame, Full Trichord, 7 Octaves, Check Action, Moulded Door, Lined Panel with either Shell or Flower Centre, Gilt Sconces, Walnut Case. Height 3 ft. 10 in., width 4 ft. 6 in.
Price .. .. .. **15 guineas.**

The Boudoir Model.—Iron Frame, Full Trichord, 7 Octaves, Check Action, Bushed Keys, Moulded Top Door and Lock Board, Square Columns Pearl and Marqueterie Panel, Brass Pedals, Gilt Sconces, Walnut Case. Height 4 ft. 2 in., width 4 ft. 7 in. Price .. **16 guineas.**

Overstrung Model.—Iron Frame, Full Trichord, 7 Octaves, Overstrung, French Type Check Action, Bushed Keys, Moulded 3 Compartment, Top Door and Lock Board, Pearl and Marqueterie Centre, Square Columns, Gilt Sconces, Brass Pedals, Walnut Case .. **20 guineas.**

You can easily give a good deal more money and get an inferior instrument.

The "IDEAL" PLAYER PIANO.

45 guineas.

The Most Perfect and Up-to-Date Player Piano.

Well made of best seasoned wood with fine finish. Has a singing tone and splendid touch. The Player answers readily to the levers, both the finest crescendo to dim, being easily obtained either in treble or bass. Only very light pedalling required. A child can play it. Best workmanship throughout.

Specialities.—Standard Compass, 65 Notes. Perfect Repetition. New Six-fold Motor. Noiseless Tracker. Transposing Device, 5 Keys. Divided Key-board. Accentuation Stops. Forte and Tempo Stops.

Height 4 ft. 5 in., width 4 ft 10½ in., depth 2 ft. 1½ in.

DAMP IS THE GREATEST ENEMY OF YOUR PIANO. Get the "Ajax" Damp Preventer, small size 2/- Large 2/6

ORGANS AND HARMONIUMS.

The "Baby" Portable Organ.

Best English Manufacture.

DESCRIPTION.
Style A.—Solid Oak Case, 1 row of 8 ft. Reeds, 4 Octaves C to C, Knee swell. Weight about 42 lbs. Closes up to form an oblong box 2ft. 5in. 12in. by 17in.
£4 15 0
Style 1.—1 row of 8ft. Reeds, 4 Octaves, Compass C to C, with Knee swell, no Stops, weight about 40 lbs. **£5 5 0**
Style 2.—2 rows of Reeds, 4 Octaves, Compass C to C, Bass 2 Octaves, Treble 2 Octaves. 4 Stops, viz., Diapson 8 ft., Principal 4 ft., Melodia 8 ft., Flute 4 ft. With Knee swell. Weight about 48 lbs.
£6 7 6

These Organs are made with Full-size Keys. The Reeds are most carefully voiced, and possess a powerful, strong, rich, sympathetic tone. Strongly made for hard wear. Suitable for Parlour or Mission Hall.

Imperial Linenized Music Rolls.

For use with all makes of Piano Players.

From **9**d. each. Write for Catalogue of Tunes.

These Rolls are Standard size, with 65 Notes, and will suit all Standard Piano Players.

You can 'Phone your Orders by ringing 2,700 Holborn.

The ANGELUS Organ.

Height 61 in. length 41 in., depth 18 in.

DESCRIPTION OF CASE.
Case in Walnut Veneer, highly polished; large Bellows; Removable Panel over pedals, giving access to Webbings; large bevelled Mirror; fitted with Actions 1, or 3.
DESCRIPTION OF ACTIONS.
Class 3x, with Action 1: One Row of 8-ft. Reeds; 61 Notes; No Stops; Forte Knee Swell. **£7 2 6**
Class 3x, with Action 3: One row of 8-ft. Reeds; 61 Notes; Five Stops; Diapason, Dulciana, Melodia, Echo, Vox Humana. Forte Knee Swell. **£7 17 6**

Join our Lending Library for Music Rolls.

Send for full particulars

24 Rolls per Month.		12 Rolls per Month.	
Period.	Subscription.	Period.	Subscription.
One Year ..	**73/6**	One Year ..	**52/6**
Six Months ..	**47/6**	Six Months ..	**34/-**
Three Months ..	**31/6**	Three Months..	**21/6**
One Month ..	**11/6**	One Month ..	**8/6**

Carriage free both ways on One Consignment each Month, within our Vans' district.

SHEET MUSIC DEPARTMENT.

A Large Selection of New and Popular Songs, Vocal Duets, Pianoforte Solos, Pianoforte Duets, Dance Music, Comic Operas, &c., in addition to those mentioned in Catalogue, kept in stock. Music not in stock will be procured to order at the usual discount. Customers are particularly requested when ordering Songs, to state the **Key or Voice** they require; also, if possible, give name of Composer and Publisher. List of Popular Songs and Piano Solos on application. **Music procured to order or sent through the Post, cannot be exchanged or allowed for if returned.**
SPECIAL LOW TERMS to Teachers and Schools, will be sent on receipt of professional card or letter heading.

TUTORS.

Accordian—
Howard (with Tunes) 4½d.
Auto Harp Tutor—
Turner 1/2 Harvey 4½d.
Banjo—
Ellis Banjo School.. 1/11
Wickins 4½d. Hawkes 1/2
B♭ Baritone—
Hawkes 1/2
Bugle—
Dallas .. .. 9d.
Clarionet—
Kappey's 10d. Hawkes 1/2
Coach Horn—
Dalla's complete .. 9d.
Concertina—
Wickins .. .. 4½d.
Metzler English .. 1/6

Cornet—
Wickins .. .. 4½d.
Hawkes 1/2
Stanton Jones .. 10d.
Double Bass—
Hawkes 1/2
Drum—
Hawkes 1/6
Dallas .. .. 9d.
Dulcimer—
Podecta .. .. 6d.
Euphonium. B♭.
Hawkes 1/2
Flute—
Pratten 9d. Wickins 4½d.
Guitar—
Dallas 1/0
Hawkes 1/6

Harmonium—
Clark Scotson .. 1/8
Read .. .. 9d.
Jap. Fiddle—
Howson 2/6 Turner 1/0
Mandoline—
Wickins 4½d. Turner 1/2
Melodeon—
Tutor with Tunes .. 4½d.
Musette—
Turner .. .. 9d.
Oboe—
Metzler 1/6
Organ—
Stainer 1/8
Pianoforte—
Beringer's Tutor .. 1/11
Bonheur 1/8

Curwen — Grade I., Step IV. .. 1/6
,, I., II., III. each 1/2
Pianoforte—
Czerny .. .. 9d.
Engel, in 4 Books .. 1/3
Gurlitt 1/8 Hamilton 1/4
Hemy 1/8 Ezra Read 9d.
Scott's 1/0
Smallwood 1/8
Smith's Vamping Tutor 9d.
Vincents New Century 1/6
Waldstein Giant Note (4 parts) each 9d.
Piccolo—
Hawkes 1/1½ Hardwick 9d.
Trombone. B♭ slide—
Hawkes 1/2

Trumpet—
Hawkes 1/2
Viola—
Hawkes 1/2
Violin—
Wickins Rapid .. 4½d.
Leyland 1/8
Farmer 1/8 Tours 1/8
Violoncello—
Dallas 9d. Hawkes 1/6
Piatti (3 parts) each 1/8
Vocal—
Behnke—Mezzo, Soprano each 1/6
Contralto, Tenor ,, 1/6
Baritone, Bass ,, 1/6
Randegger 3/4
Marchesi 3/10 Nava 1/11

PIANO.

Beringer, Daily Technical Studies 2/8
Bertini, 25 Easy Studies, Op. 100 .. 9d.
,, Studies, Op. 29, Op. 32 .. each 9d.
Burgmullar, Studies .. .. 9d.
Cramer, ,, (4 Books) .. each 9d.
Czerny, 101 Studies .. .. 9d.
Etude de la Velocity .. .. 9d.
Fingerfertigkeit 2/1
24 Five-finger Exercises .. .. 4½d.
Heller, Studies, Books 1 to 8 .. each 10d.
Herz, Scales and Exercises .. .. .. 10d.
Kalkbrenner, Scales .. .. .. 6d.
Klitz, Scale and Arpeggio Manual, complete 9d.
Köhler, 6 Books .. .. .. each 9d.
Macfarren, Scales 2/0
Plaidy, Technical Studies 1/8
Schmidt, Five-finger Exercises .. .. 4½d.
Wiecks, Studies 1/3

STUDIES.

VOCAL.

Behnke, Voice Training Exercises—
Soprano, Tenor, Mezzo or Bass each 1/6
Concone, 50 Exercises for Medium of Voice 9d.
25 ,, ,, ,, 9d.
40 Contralto .. .. .. 11d.
40 Baritone or Bass .. .. 11d.
Nava, 25 Solfeggi .. .. .. 10d.
Panseron, Vocalises .. .. .. 10d.
Tosti, 50 Solfeggi, Books I. II. .. each 1/11

VIOLIN.

Hermann, Studies, 1st position .. .. 10d.
Kayser, Studies, Books I. II. III. each 10d.
Krutzer, 42 Studies .. .. .. 10d.
Laubach, Scales and Arpeggios 1/8
Mazas, Studies, 3 Books .. .. each 10d.

VIOLONCELLO.

Bast, Scale Manual .. .. 10d.
Grutzmacher, Daily Exercises 1/1
Squire, Easy Exercises .. .. .. 10d.

THEORY BOOKS.

Catechism (Read) .. .. 6d.
Composition (Stainer) 1/8
Counterpoint (Bridge) 1/8
,, (Prout) 4/2
Harmony (Stainer) 1/8
,, (Prout) 4/2
Instrumentation (Prout) 1/8 Musical Terms 9d.
Rudiments of Music (Cummings) .. 10d.
Elements of Music (Davenport) .. 10d.
Rudiments of Music (Holmes) .. .. 9d.
Musical Form (Prout) 4/2
Fugue (Prout) 4/2

COMIC OPERAS.

	Vocal Score.	Piano Score.	Piano Selection.
Arcadians	6/0	3/6	1/6
Autumn Manœuvres	5/0	3/0	1/4
Baron Trenk	5/0	3/0	1/4
Bohemians, The	4/6	2/3	1/6
Chocolate Soldier	7/6	4/0	1/6
Count Luxemberg	6/0	3/6	1/6
Dancing Mistress	6/0	3/6	1/6
Gipsy Love	6/0	3/6	1/6
Girl in the Taxi	5/0	2/8	1/4
Girl on the Film	6/0	3/6	1/6
Gondoliers (Sullivan)	5/0	3/0	1/6
H.M.S. Pinafore	3/10	2/3	1/4
Merrie England (German)	5/0	3/0	1/6
Mikado (Sullivan)	5/0	3/0	1/6
Oh, Delphine	6/0	3/6	1/6
Our Miss Gibbs	5/0	3/0	1/6
Patience (Sullivan)	5/0	3/0	1/6
Pirates of Penzance	5/0	3/0	1/6
Princess Caprice	6/0	3/6	1/6
Quaker Girl	6/0	3/6	1/6
Yeoman of the Guard	5/0	3/0	1/6

STANDARD OPERAS (Vocal Scores).

Barbiere (1) .. 2/11
Bohemian Girl (Balfe) 2/11
Carmen (English) 4/6
Cavalleria Rusticana 5/8
Das Rheingold 7/6
Die Miestersinger .. 7/6
Die Walküre (Wagner) 7/6
Don Giovanni (Mozart) .. 2/11
Faust (Gounod) .. 3/6
Fliegend Hollander 2/11
Freischutz (Weber) 2/11
Götterdammerung 7/6
Guillaume Tell (Rossini) .. 4/2
Huguenots, Meyerbeer 4/2
Lohengrin (Wagner) 2/8
Lucia di Lammermoor 2/11
Lucrezia Borgia .. 2/11
Madama Butterfly (Puccini) .. 6/0
Maritana (Wallace) 2/11
Martha (Flotow) .. 2/11
Massaniello .. 2/11
Norma (Bellini) .. 2/11
Nozze di Figaro .. 2/11
Pagliacci, Leoncavallo 5/8
Parsifal (Wagner) 7/6
Rigoletto .. 2/11
Romeo and Juliet 3/6
Siegfried (Wagner) 7/6
Sonnambula (Bellini) 2/11
Tannhauser (Wagner) 2/8
Tosca (Puccini) .. 6/0
Traviata (Verdi) .. 2/11
Tristan and Isolde 2/8
Trovatore (Verdi) 2/11

ORATORIOS, CANTATAS, &c. (Vocal Scores)

	Paper.	Boards.	Cloth.
Acis and Galatea (Handel)	10d.	1/3	2/1
As the Hart Pants (Mend'sohn)	9d.	—	—
Athalie (Mendelssohn)	9d.	1/6	2/3
Creation (Haydn)	1/0	1/11	2/3
Crucifixion (Stainer)	1/3	1/8	—
Dream of Gerontius (Elgar)	3/0	—	—
Elijah (Mendelssohn)	1/0	1/11	3/0
Golden Legend (Sullivan)	2/8	3/0	3/10
Hear my Prayer (Mendelssohn)	9d.	—	—
Holy City (Gaul)	1/11	—	—
Hymn of Praise (Mendelssohn)	9d.	1/1½	1/11
Israel in Egypt (Handel)	1/0	1/11	3/0
Judas Maccabæus (Handel)	1/0	1/6	2/6
Kingdom, The (Elgar)	4/2	—	—
Last Judgment (Spohr)	10d.	1/3	2/1
Mass in B minor (Bach)	1/11	—	—
Messiah (Handel)	1/0	1/11	3/0
Passion Music (Bach) St. John	1/8	—	—
Passion Music ,, St. Matthew	1/8	2/1	—
Redemption (Gounod)	2/1	2/6	4/2
Samson (Handel)	1/6	1/11	3/0
Stabat Mater (Rossini)	9d.	1/1½	1/11
Stabat Mater (Dvorak)	1/11	—	—
St. Paul (Mendelssohn)	1/0	1/11	3/0
Twelfth Mass (Mozart)	9d.	1/1½	1/11
Woman of Samaria (Sir S. Bennett)	10d.	1/3	2/6

POPULAR ORATORIOS

CHEAP 10½d. EDITIONS

EACH.

Handel's Messiah
Haydn's Creation
Rossini's Stabat Mater
Handel's Judas Maccabæus
Handel's Samson
Mendelssohn's Hymn of Praise
Mendelssohn's Elijah
Handel's Israel in Egypt
Mozart's 12th Mass

Augener Edition.

Beethoven—Sonatas (Buonamici) 2 vols. each 2/9
Brahms—Sonatas I. II. III. .. .. ,, 1/3
Chopin—Valses, Ballades (complete) .. ,, 10d.
,, Polonaises, Nocturnes ,, .. ,, 1/3
,, Mazurkas ,, .. ,, 1/8
Coleridge Taylor—African Suite 1/8
Farjeon—Night Music 1/6
Gurlitt—Op. 101, Album leaves for the young 1/8
,, Op. 107, Buds and Blossoms .. 1/8
Heller—Sleepless Nights 1/3
Jensen—Songs and Dances .. .. 10d.
Liszt—Rhapsodies .. .. .. each 9d.
Moszkowski—Valse Brilliante .. .. ,, 1/3
Nineteenth Century, 8 vols. .. .. each 1/8
Scharwenka—Polish Dance 1/3
Schumann—Novelletten .. .. .. 10d.
,, Carnival Jest .. .. 10d.
Spanish Dances and Romances 2/1

Complete Catalogue on application.

Peters Edition.

Bach—48 Preludes and Fugues, 2 vols. each 1/10
,, Inventions 2 & 3 .. .. .. 1/1
Beethoven—Sonatas (complete) 4/2
Grieg—Op. 12, Lyric Pieces, Book I. .. 1/5
,, ,, 43, ,, ,, III. 1/10
,, ,, 46, Peer Gynt, Suite I. .. 1/5
Haydn—Sonatas, 4 vols. .. .. each 1/5
Moszkowski—Spanish Dances 2/9
Mozart—18 Sonatas 2/4
Schubert—Impromptu and Moment Musicales 11d.
Sinding—Rustle of Spring .. .. 11d.

Complete Catalogue on application.

B. F. Wood Edition.

Bertini—Studies, Op. 29 .. .. .. 9d.
Chopin—Impromptus .. .. .. 9d.
Gade—Aquarellen, Op. 19 .. .. 9d.
Liszt—Consolations .. .. .. 9d.
Mendelssohn—Songs without words .. 1/6
,, Six Christmas Pieces .. 9d.
Plaidy—Studies 1/6

Complete Catalogue on application.

Handsome Cloth Bound Volumes Suitable for Christmas Presents.

PIANO ALBUMS.

Beethoven—Sonatas, 2 vols.	ea.	4/2
,, complete 1 vol.	..	5/8
,, 10 selected		
(gilt edges)		3/9
Brahms—Best selected works	..	5/5
Chopin—Album, most popular pieces	..	2/11
Do. larger, collection with portrait	..	4/2
Waltzes, complete	..	2/8
Mazurkas ,,	..	3/5
Polonaises ,,	..	2/11
Nocturnes ,,	..	2/11
Classical Companion—Album of pieces by the best composers	.. ..	1/11
Clementi Album of famous pieces	..	3/5
Christmas Album (music suitable for Xmas)		3/6

PIANO ALBUMS.

German—20 pieces with portrait	..	4/2
Grieg—Album of popular pieces	..	2/8
36 pieces with portrait	..	4/2
Liszt—20 do. do.	..	4/2
Mendelssohn—Songs witnout words	..	3/5
Do. (edited by Taylor)		4/7
Modern Masters.—Collection of all the best pieces by the best composers	..	5/5
Our Piano Album, fine selection of good pieces (moderately easy)		3/0
Portfolio—40 selected pieces by the best composers	.. .. ..	1/11
Rubinstein Album, 20 pieces with portrait		4/2
Score of Romantique Fragments		4/2
Tschaikowsky Album of popular pieces		2/11
,, ,, 20 pieces with portrait		4/2
Weber Album of popular pieces	..	4/2

SONG ALBUMS.

British Nursery Rhymes	..	2/6
Imperial Edition—Baritone, Bass, Contralto, Soprano, Tenor, Mezzo Sop. Handsome, limp leather binding, ea.		4/0
Our Old Nursery Rhymes	..	4/11
Scottish Student Song Book		3/11
Tiny Tunes for Tiny Folk (Boards)		1/11

VARIOUS.

Music Song and Dance, piano solos, duets, songs, violin and piano complete	..	3/9
Morceaux Choises.—Selected pieces for violin and piano	..	2/11
Cello and piano	..	2/3
Schubert Album of popular pieces for violin and piano	..	4/6
The Life of Famous Musical Composers, with their portraits. Handsomely bound with gilt edges, complete	..	2/11

PIANOFORTE SOLOS.

Aletter—Rendez Vous	1/6	Gillet—Loin du Bal	1/4	Rubenstein—Melody in F	0/8
Ascher—Alice	1/4	Godard, B.—Au Matin	1/4	Romance E♭	0/8
Baderewski—Maiden's Prayer	0/6	Berceuse de Jocelyn	1/6	Saint-Saens—Le Cygne	1/4
Beethoven—Adieu to the Piano	0/6	Deuxieme Mazurka	1/4	Scharwenka—Polish Dance	1/0
Idyll in G.	1/4	Fourth Mazurka	1/6	Schutt—A la bien aimée	1/6
Moonlight Sonata	0/8	5th Valse Chromatique	1/8	Carnival Mignon	2/8
Pathetique ,,	0/10	Gounod—Funeral March of a Marionette	1/6	Etude Mignon	1/6
Sonata Op. 49 No. 2	0/8	Handel—Harmonius Blacksmith	0/8	Pour tous les ages	1/6
Sonatas complete :		Largo	0/8	Valse Bluette	1/6
Augener ed'n.	4/2	Haydn—Gipsy Rondo	0/8	Valse Lente	1/6
Peters ,,	4/2	Heller—Tarantelle A flat	0/8	Schytte—Berceuse	1/0
Cloth	6/0	Hill—March in G	1/0	Schumann—Arabesque	0/6
Bennett—Barcarole	0/8	Hogwill—Weymouth Chimes	1/0	Merry Peasant	0/4
Three Musical Sketches	1/0	Jensen—The Mill	1/0	Schlummerlied	0/8
Blake—Grand March	0/8	Jungman—Heimweh (Home)	1/6	Novelette F	0/8
Waves of the Ocean	0/8	Ketterer—Caprice Hongroise	0/6	Scott, Cyril—Allegretto Gracioso	1/6
Blon—Sizilleta	1/6	Lack—Cabaletta	1/4	Colombine	1/6
Boccherini—Celebrated Minuet	0/6	Pendant la Valse	1/4	Sibelius—Romance	1/4
Bohm—Lyrische Suite	2/3	Valse Arabesque	2/0	Deux Miniatures	2/3
Spinnlied	1/4	Lange—Blumenlied	0/6	Smith, Sydney—Le Jet d'eau	0/8
Borowski—La Coquette	1/6	Edelweiss	0/6	Maypole Dance	1/4
Minuet	1/6	Lasson—Crescendo	0/6	Tarantelle	0/8
Valsette	1/6	Leybach—2nd Nocturne	0/8	Sousa—King Cotton March	1/4
Melodie	1/4	Litolff—Spinnlied	0/8	El Capitan	1/4
Braga—Serenata	1/4	Lincke—Glow Worm	1/6	Liberty Bell	1/0
Brahms—Drei Intermezzi, Op. 117	2/8	Magnus—Barcarolle from Tales of Hofman	1/6	Stars and Stripes	1/4
Hungarian Dances (21)	2/6	Mascagni—Intermezzo from Cavalleria Rusticana	1/6	Washington Post	0/8
Chaminade—Air de Ballet	1/6	MacDowell—Fireside Tales	3/0	Spindler—Husarenritt	1/6
Arabesque	1/6	Woodland Sketches	3/0	Taylor Coleridge — Four Characteristic Dances	1/11
Automne	1/6	Sea Pieces	3/0	Thomas—Gavotte from Mignon	1/0
Danse Creole	1/6	Mattei—Grand Valse	1/8	Thomé—Andante Religioso	1/8
Dance Pastorale	1/6	Mendelssohn—Andante and Rondo	0/8	Illusion	1/4
Fileuse	1/6	Capriccioso	0/8	L'Extase	1/6
La Lisonjera	1/8	Fragment	0/8	Simple Aveu	1/4
Les Sylvains	1/6	Six Christmas Pieces	0/8	Sous les Feuilleé	1/4
Pas des Amphores	1/6	Wedding March	0/8	Tschaikowsky—Chanson Triste	0/8
Pas des Echarpes	1/6	Songs without Words (Leider ohne worte)		Chant sans Paroles	0/8
Pierette	1/6	Cheap Ed'n	1/6	Barcarolle	0/8
Ritournelle	1/6	Superior ,,	2/3	Valse des Fleurs	1/0
Serenade	1/6	Michaelis—Turkish Patrol	1/6	Wachs—Capricante	1/6
Costa—March of the Israelites	1/0	Moszkowski—Polish Dances	1/6	Wagner, O.—Under the Double Eagle March	1/4
Cowen—Four English Dances	1/11	Pres du Berceau	1/6	Wagner, R.—March Tannhauser	0/8
Debussy—Children's Corner	3/9	Serenata	1/6	Weber—Invitation to the Waltz	0/8
Deux Arabesque	2/3	Spanish Dances, Op. 12	2/9	Il moto continuo	0/8
Delibes—Pizzicato Sylvia	1/4	Mozart—Sonatas	2/1	Rondo Brilliante E♭	0/8
Coppelia Valse	2/0	Nevin—Rosary	1/6	Last Waltz	0/8
Durand—Chacone, Op. 62	1/4	Narcissus	1/0	Wely—Les Cloches du Monasters	0/8
1st Valse	1/4	Paderewski—Melodie	1/0	Whitney—Mosquitoes Parade	1/6
Dussek—Consolation	0/8	Minuet	1/6	Wilson—Chapel in the Mountains	0/8
Matinee	0/8	Pauer—Cascade	1/6	Moonlight on the Hudson	0/8
Dvorak—Humoresque	1/6	Pierne—Serenade	1/6	Shepherd Boy	0/8
Eilenberg—March of the Mountain Gnomes	1/6	Rachmaninoff—Prelude	0/8	Wayside Chapel	0/8
Elgar—Pomp and Circumstance	1/6	Raff—Cavatina	0/6	Wollenhaupt—Grand March Militaire	1/0
Salut d'Amour	1/6	La Fileuse	1/4	La Gazelle	0/8
Finck—In the Shadows	1/6	Polka de la reine	0/10	Wyman—Silvery Waves	1/0
Fucik—Entry of the Gladiators	1/6	Rigaudon	1/4	Yardier—La Paloma	1/4
Ganne—March Lorraine	1/6	Tarantelle	0/9		
La Czarine	1/6				
Ganz—Qui Vive Galop	1/4				
German—Three Dances (Henry VIII.)	1/6				
Three Dances (Nell Gwyn)	2/0				

R

Albums of Songs.

	EACH
Brahms, J., 20 selected Songs (low and high),	3/-
,, Second Collection of 20 selected Songs (low and high)	3/-
Clutsam, Songs from Turkish Hills (low, medium or high voice)	3/-
Coningsby Clarke, First Sheaf of Little Songs (low and high)	3/-
,, Second Sheaf of Little Songs (low and high)	3/-
,, Perfect Tune (high and low) ..	3/-
Elgar, Sea Pictures	3/4
,, Seven Songs (low and high) ..	2/3
Finden, Five Little Japanese Songs (low and high)	3/-
,, Four Indian Love Lyrics (low and high)	3/-
,, Dream of Egypt (low and high) ..	3/4
,, Golden Hours (low and high) ..	2/8
,, Lover in Damascus (high and low) ..	4/-
,, On Jhelum River do.	4/-
,, Stars of the Dessert do.	3/-
Gatty's Six Plantation Songs, four books ..	1/8
Gaudeamus Book of Songs.. ..	3/10
Greig's 20 selected Songs ..	2/3
Guy D Hardelot, Eight Songs ..	2/6
Handel's Twelve Songs, arranged by A. Randegger for Contralto or Soprano	1/8
Imperial Edition, Baritone Songs ..	2/1
,, Bass Songs ..	2/1
,, Contralto Songs	2/1
,, Soprano Songs ..	2/1
,, Tenor Songs	2/1
,, Mezzo-soprano Songs ..	2/1
Johnson (Noel), Eight Songs ..	2/6
"Just So" Song Book (German, E.) ..	4/6
Korbay, Hungarian Melodies ..	3/4
Lehmann, Four Cautionary Tales and a Moral	3/6
,, Daisy Chain	4/2
,, Nonsense Song, from Alice in Wonderland	3/6
,, More Daises	4/2
,, Bird Songs (Mezzo and Soprano) ..	2/11
,, In a Persian Garden ..	3/10
,, Five Little Love Songs (med. and high)	3/-
,, Songs of the Flapper (high and low)..	3/-
Lohr, Songs of the Norseland (low and high)	4/-
,, Songs in Exile (low and high)	3/6
,, Romany Songs ,, ,,	3/-
,, Songs of Roumania do.	2/-
Martin, Four Songs of the Fair (low and high)	2/6
McGeoch, Kiddies	9d.
,, Five Miniature Songs (low and high)	9d.
,, Flowers from a Cottage Garden (low and high)	2/3
,, Seven Popular Songs (with portrait) ..	2/1
Needham, Album of Hush Songs	4/2
Nevin, Album of 24 Songs ..	3/4
Peel (Graham), Country Lover ..	3/-
Oliver Herbert, Songs of Old London ..	2/1
,, The Passing Show.. ..	2/4
,, Songs of Merrie England ..	2/6
Quilter, Three Shakespeare Songs.. ..	2/1
Raymond, Wayside Songs do. ..	1/8
Ronald, Cycle of Life (low and high) ..	2/3
,, Four Songs of the Hill (low and high)..	2/3
,, Summertime (medium and high) ..	2/3
Scottish Students' Song Book ..	2/6
,, ,, ,, ,, cloth ..	3/5
Stanford, Songs of the Sea ..	2/1
Taylor Col., Five Fairy Ballads ..	4/-
Weckerlin, Bergerettes	3/10
,, Pastourelles	3/10
Wishaw's Russian Songs. Two books ..	2/1

Albums of Comic Songs.

Price **1/-** each. Postage extra.

The Monster Budget of Comic Songs. Revised "up-to-date." Best Songs with patter.

The Humorous Vocal Entertainer. Revised edition. The best book of really good, modern, popular humorous songs. Suitable for the home.

Forty Famous Funny Songs ..	1/-
Francis & Day's Album of Coon Songs ..	9d.

Albums of Songs for Children
AND
Nursery Rhyme Books.

Animals at Play (Illustrated) ..	1/6
Bedtime Lullabies	1/3
British Nursery Rhymes (Moffat) ..	2/6
Dittyland Songs for Children ..	9d.
French Nursery Rhymes ..	1/8
Gatty Songs, Vol. I., II., III. .. each	2/1
Kiddies' Songs (McGeoch) ..	9d.
Motto Action Songs ..	9d.
Mr. Coggs and other Songs (Lehmann) ..	3/-
Our Old Nursery Rhymes. (Bound in Cloth)..	5/-
Pillowland (Bingham) ..	9d.
Rounds (for Singing and Dancing) ..	1/8
Rub-a-dub-dub	9d.
Sing-Song (100 Nursery Rhymes) ..	1/6
Songland (Songs for Children) ..	9d.
Tiny Tunes for Tiny Tots (Illustrated) ..	1/11
Twelve Childen's Songs	1/6

Gamage's Special, 1/-

Postage extra.

The Young Folks' Song and Rhyme Book Suitable for grown up Girls and Boys, as well as the Children. 70 Songs and 90 illustrations.

Popular Song Albums.

	EACH
"Follies" Albums. Nos. 1, 2 and 3. Each containing six of the "Follies" well-known Songs	9d.
Portrait Series (containing eight Songs in each) Guy d'Hardelot, Liza Lehman, Ed. German, Noel Johnson, Del Riego, Tosti, Lambert, each	2/6
Vagabond Albums. Nos. 1 and 2. Containing eight songs as sung in the Vagabond entertainment	1/-
Irish Song Book. Containing 40 of the best Irish Songs	1/-
Favourite Song Albums—	
No. I. Containing 6 of Madame Melba's favourite Songs	1/-
No. II. Containing 6 of Madame Tetrazzini's Operatic Songs ..	1/-
No. III. Containing 8 of Mr. Ben Davis' well-known Tenor Songs ..	1/-
No. IV. Containing 11 of Clara Butt's well-known songs, for Contralto voice ..	1/-

Gamage's Special. 1/- each.

Postage extra.

The Monster Folio of Sacred Songs. Revised edition. Well-known Hymns and Songs for Sundays.

The Monster Mezzo-Soprano Folio. Containing 62 very fine Soprano (Mezzo) Songs.

The Monster Contralto Folio. Containing 58 up-to-date Songs.

The Monster Tenor Folio. Containing 58 very fine Tenor Songs.

The Monster Soprano Folio. Containing 56 refined Songs.

The Monster Folio of Bass Songs. Containing 68 Songs.

This Year's Song Albums.

Francis & Day's. Feldman's. Planet's. All contain LATEST POPULAR SONGS. GAMAGE'S PRICE .. 9d. each; post free 10½d. Write for Contents.

Large Selection of Popular Songs always in Stock .. .. 4½d. each. Write for Lists (post free).

Vocal Duets.

Awake (Pellissier)	..	..	1/6
Beauty's Eyes (Tosti)	F	..	1/6
Come, Sing to Me	D, F	..	1/6
Down the Vale	F, G	..	1/6
Excelsior	C, D	..	1/4
Friendship	F, G	..	1/6
Go, Pretty Rose	F, G	..	1/6
Joy (St. Quintin)	E♭	..	1/6
Keys of Heaven	G, B♭	..	1/4
Larboard Watch	G	..	1/4

Comic, Humorous and Coo[n] Songs.

	EAC[H]
Archibald (Braham)	1[/]
Billy Brown (Fragson)	1[/]
Bovine Barcarolle ..	1[/]
Cow Jumped over the Moon (Tom Clare) ..	1[/]
Don't Play in the Shadows ..	1[/]
Dinah's Wedding (Gatty) 1/- De Old Banjo	1[/]
De Lecture .. 1/- De Sun is A-sinking	1[/]
Ding Dong Ding (Gatty) ..	1[/]
Insurance Agent (Will Edwards) ..	1[/]
Married v. Single, 1/6 My Word	1[/]
Mr. & Mrs. Bee (Duet) 1/6 Modern Courtship	1[/]
My Jobs .. 1/6 My Bungalow in Bond Street	9[d.]
My Beastly Eyeglass	1[/]
Posers (Vagabonds)	1[/]
Three Feminine Questions	1[/]
Village Pump (Naish)	1[/]
When Richard I. sat on the Throne ..	1[/]

Monologues.

A Fallen Star (Chevalier)	1[/]
A False Alarm (Jackson) ..	1[/]
Devil-may-care (B. Williams) ..	1[/]
Green Eye of the Yellow God ..	1[/]
How I Drove the Special (Graham)..	1[/]
How we Saved the Barge (B. Williams) ..	1[/]
Street Watchman's Story..	1[/]
The 11.69 Express	1[/]
The Man with the Single Hair ..	1[/]
Wot ver do 'e luv oi (Chevalier) ..	1[/]

(Complete Catalogue free on application).

Recitations, etc.

Coming a Cropper (Duologne) ..	6[d.]
Extra Turns by Cue ..	1[/]
Funny Recitals by French ..	1[/]
Fun Encyclopædia (Foster) ..	1[/]
Glimpses of Life. A series of Humorous Oration[s] By Charles Pond. Price 6d. each.	
I.—The Fully-licensed Man. II.—Greefenstee[]	
III.—On Strike. IV.—Who'll have a Blood Orang[e]	
V.—My Brother George	
VI.—"'Evings! Dorg 'Ospital"!	
VII.—The Last Cigarette and the Last 'Arf-pint.	
Kiss me quick (Rae Brown) ..	6[d.]
Laughing Gas or Gags that get grins ..	1[/]
Patter Stories and Cross Talk ..	6[d.]
Seven for Sixpence (popular parodies) ..	6[d.]
Six for Sixpence (side splitters) ..	6[d.]
Six Humorous Recitations. By L. Pond ..	6[d.]
Ditto ditto ,, Will Terry ..	6[d.]
Six Nonsense Songs ,, ,,	6[d.]
Ten Character Sketches from Charles Dickens (Bransby Williams)	1[/]

Scout Songs, Marches and Call[s]

Baden Powell Scout March (Cleve).. ..	1[/]
Do. do. (Vocal part) ..	2[/]
Be Prepared (Leo) ..	1[/]
Book of Bugle Calls and Marches ..	6[d.]
Do. do. larger and including Trumpet Calls	1[/]
Boys be prepared (Rubens) ..	1[/]
Boys of the Empire	4[/]
Keep Whistling (Leo) ..	1[/]
When the camp fires brightly burn	1[/]

Life's Dream is O'er	..	1[/]
Night Hymn at Sea	C, E♭	1[/]
Night of Stars (Barcarolle) D.F.	..	1[/]
Oh ! That we Two were Maying	F	1[/]
Sailor Sighs (Balfe)	..	1[/]
Snowdrops (Lehmann)	E, G	1[/]
Still as the Night (Bohm)	C	1[/]
Sous les Etoiles	C, E♭	1[/]
Tenor and Baritone	G, A	1[/]
Venetian Song (Tosti)	D♭, F	1[/]

NEW AND POPULAR SONGS.

Title.	Composer.	Key.	Compass.	
April Song	Newton	F, G, A	C to F	1/6
At Santa Barbara	Russell	G, A♭, B♭,	D to D	1/6
April Morn	Batten	B♭, C, D	B♭ to G	1/6
Abide with Me	Liddle	C, D♭, E	G to E	1/6
Absent	Metcalf	E♭, F, G, A♭	B♭ to C	1/6
Angus MacDonald	Roeckel	C, D	B to E	1/6
An Old Garden	Temple	G, A♭, B♭	B to E	1/6
Anchored	Watson	C, D	B to E	1/6
Admiral's Broom	Bevan	D, E, F	A to D	1/6
All Through the Night	Somerset	C, E♭, F	C to D	1/6
Always	Bowers	A, C, E♭	B to C	1/6
Angels Guard Thee	Godard	B♭, C, D♭, E♭	B♭ to D	1/4
Arrow and the song	Balfe	A, C	C to D	1/4
Asleep in the Deep	Petrie	D, F	D to B	1/4
Ave Maria	Mascagni	C, E♭, F	A to E	1/6
Bowl of Roses	Clark	B♭, D, E	B♭ to D	1/6
Brown Eyes	Riego	B♭, C, D	C to E	1/6
Because	d'Hardelot	A♭, B♭, C	C to E♭	1/6
Beloved, It is Morn	Aylward	C, D, F	C to C	1/6
Beauty's Eyes	Tosti	C, E♭, F	A to C	1/6
Bedouin Love Song	Pinsuti	B, D, C minor	F to D sharp	1/6
Believe Me, if all those endearing young Charms	Landon Ronald	E♭, F, G, A♭	B♭ to E♭	1/6
Beyond	St. Quinten	C, D, E♭, F	A to D	1/4
Bird of Love Divine	Haydon-Wood	F,G,A♭,	C to F	1/6
Blow, Blow, Thou Winter Wind	Sarjeant	B♭, C, D	F sharp to D	1/6
Buglar, The	Pinsuti	D, F, G	A to D	1/6
Coolan Dhu	Leoni	D, E, F minor	C to E	1/6
Corisande	Sanderson	D, E, F	A to D	1/6
Corporals Ditty	Squire	E♭, F, G	A♭ to C	1/6
Catch Me	Margaret Cooper	D	D to F	1/6
Chorus, Gentlemen	Löhr	F, A♭	C to C	1/6
Chip of the Old Block	Squire	B♭, C	B♭ to D	1/6
Captain's Yarn	Hubert Bath	B♭, C, D	B to D	1/4
Children's Home	Cowen	B, C, D, E♭, F	B to D	1/6
Come, Sing to Me	Thompson	D, E♭, F, G	C to D	1/6
Come back to Erin	Claribel	C	B to E	6d.
Constancy	Hill	A♭, B♭, C	C to E♭	1/4
Crossing the Bar	Willeby	E, F, G, A minor	B to D	1/6
Drum Major	Newton	F, G	C to D	1/6
Dawn, The	d'Hardelot	D♭, E♭, F, G		1/6
Dear Eyes	McGeoch	B♭, C, D	B♭ to E♭	1/4
Dear Little Soul	Travers	B♭, C, D	C to D♭	1/4
Dear Little Star	Dorothy Foster	E♭, F, G	C to E	1/6
Devotion	Hill	D, E♭, F	A to D	1/4
Devout Lover	Maud V. White	E♭, F	E to F	1/6
Down in the Forest	Landon Ronald	B♭, C, D, E♭	B♭ to E♭	1/6
Drake goes West	Sanderson	C, D	G to D	1/6
Dreams	Chaminade	G, A minor	C to E♭	1/6
Drinking Song	Thomas	E♭, F	A♭ to E♭	1/4
Dumbledum Day	Löhr	C, E♭	B to C	1/6
Emblem, An	Thompson	B♭, C, D, E♭	B♭ to C	1/6
Enchantress	Hatton	A, B♭	A to E	1/4
Folk Song	Clutsam	G, A, A♭	C to D	1/6
Farewell	Liddle	G, A♭, B♭, C	D to D	1/6
Four Jolly Sailorman	German	C, D	G to E	1/6
Fairy's Lullaby	Needham	E♭, F, G, A♭	B♭ to E♭	1/6
Flight of Ages	Bevan	G, A♭, B♭	B to D	1/6
Franklin's Maid	Cowen	E, G minor	D to E	1/6
Grey Eyes	Phillips	B♭, C, D	B to E♭	1/6
Good Company	Adams	E♭, F, G, A	B♭ to E♭	1/6
Glorious Devon	German	C, D, F	B to E♭	1/6
Go to Sea	Trotére	F, G, A♭, C	A to C	1/6
Garden of Love	d'Hardelot	B♭, D♭, E♭	C to E♭	1/6
Good-bye	Tosti	A♭, G, F, E♭	E♭ to A	1/6
Good-night	Cowen	E, G	D to E	1/6
Green Isle of Erin	Roeckel	D, E♭, F, G	B to D	1/4
Happy Song	Reigo	D, E♭, F	D to F	1/6
Hallo, Tu-Tu	Scott-Gatty	G	D to E	1/6
Husheen	Needham	B♭, C, D	B♭ to D	1/6
Holy City	Adams	A♭, B♭, C, D	C to E♭	1/6
In Sympathy	Leoni	C, D, E	C to E	1/6
I Hid My Love	d'Hardelot	B♭, D♭, E♭	A to E♭	1/6
I Know a Lovely Garden	d'Hardelot	E♭, F, G	D to E♭	1/6
If Love were All	Foster	D, E♭, F	B to E	1/6
I'll Sing Thee Songs of Araby	Clay	E♭, F, G, A♭		1/6
Irish Folk Song	Foote	E, F, G	B to E	1/6
I Bring My Roses	Carse	D, C	C to F	1/6
If I Built a World for You	Lehman	C, E♭, F	C to C	1/6
If Thou wert Blind	Noel Johnson	D, F, G, A, B mr.	A to B	1/6
I Hear You Calling	Marshall	G, A♭, B♭, C	D to E	1/6
I Know of Two Bright Eyes	Clutsam	E♭, F, G, A♭	C to C	1/6
In Fair Arcadia	Foster	E♭, G	B to E	1/6
In the Heather, my Lads	Löhr	A, B, C minor	A to C sharp	1/6
Invitation	Barry	B♭, C, D♭, E♭	B♭ to D	1/6
Jest Her Way	Aitken	B♭, C, D	C to D	1/6
Jack Briton	Squire	C, D	B to D	1/6
Joy	St. Quinten	D, E♭, F, G	B to D	1/6
Kashmiri Song	Woodforde-Finden	B♭, C, D	B♭ to D	1/6
Kathleen Mavourneen	Crouch	E♭	B to F	6d.
Killarney	Balfe	F	C to F	6d.
King's Minstrel	Pinsuti	G, A	G to D	1/6
Kiss, A	McGeoch	E♭, F, G	A to E	1/6
Kisses	Trotére	G, B♭, C	D to D	1/6
Love in a Cottage	Bath	G, B♭, C	B to D	1/6
Lowland Sea	Coates			1/6
Love is Meant to Make us Glad	German	D♭, E♭, F	A♭ to E♭	1/6
Little Irish Girl	Löhr	B♭, C, D	B♭ to D	1/6
Lighterman Tom	Squire	E♭, F	B♭ to E♭	1/6
Land of Hope and Glory	Elgar	B♭, C, D	B♭ to E♭	1/6
Land of Violets	Cowen	D, E	E to F	1/6
Lead Kindly Light	Pinsuti	A, B♭, C, D, E	A to C sharp	1/4
Life is but a Song	Petrie	E♭, F	E to D	1/4
Life's Lullaby	Lane	F, G, A♭, B♭	C to D	1/6
Life's Maytime	Newton	F, G, A♭	C to F	1/6
Little Irish Girl	Löhr	B♭, C, D	B♭ to D	1/6
Long Live the King	Andrews	G		6d.
Lost Chord	Sullivan	E♭ F, G, A♭, A	C to D	1/6
Love, Could I only Tell Thee	Capel	C, D, F	A to D	1/6
Lute Player	Allitsen	B, C, D minor	F to D	1/6
My Old Shako	Trotére	B♭, C, E♭	B♭ to D	1/6
Magic Month of May	Newton	C, D, E	C to F	1/6

Title.	Composer.	Key.	Compass.	
Macushla	MacMurrough	F, A♭, B♭	C to E♭	1/6
Mandalay	Willeby			1/6
May Mourning	Denza	D, E♭, F, G	C to D	1/6
Mother o' Mine	Tours	B♭, D	C to D	1/6
Mairie My Girl	Aitken	C, D, E	C to E	1/6
Mifanwy	Foster	E♭, F, G	C to D	1/6
Melisande in the Woods	Goetz	B♭, C, D minor	B♭ to D♭	1/6
My Dreams	Tosti	B♭, C, D♭, E♭	D, E♭	1/6
Master and Man	Clark	C, E♭	C to E	1/6
My Ain Folk	Lemon	D♭, E♭, F, G	A♭ to D♭	1/6
My Dear Soul	Sanderson	A♭, B♭, C	A♭ to E♭	1/6
Magic of your Voice	Hardy	C, D, F	B to D	1/4
Maying	Smith	F, G, A♭	C to E♭	1/4
Message, The	Blumenthal	C, D, E♭	A to E	1/6
Micky's Advice	Löhr	B♭, C, D,	G to C	1/6
Mighty Deep	Jude	F, G	F to F	1/4
Mighty Like a Rose	Nevin	F, G, A	C to D	1/6
Moira of My Heart	Thomson	F, G, B	A to D	1/6
Mother MaChree	Olcott & Ball	D, F	D to F	1/6
Mountain Lovers	Squire	B♭, C, E♭, F	B♭ to D	1/6
Mountains o' Mourne	Collisson	G	D to D	1/6
Muleteer of Malaga	Trotére	C, D, G	G to C	1/6
My Love's Grey Eyes	McGeoch	E♭, F, G	B♭ to D	1/6
My Ships	Barratt	C, D	B♭ to F	1/6
My Sweetheart when a Boy	Morgan	C, D, E♭	D to F	1/4
Nita Gitana	Newton	A, C	B to E	1/6
Nightingales of Lincoln's Inn	Oliver			1/6
Nirvana	Adams	B♭, C, D, E♭	C to E♭	1/6
Night has One Thousand Eyes	Lambert	F, A♭	C to C	1/6
O, my Garden full of Roses	Clark	B♭, D, E	C to D	1/6
Oh, oh! Hear the Wild Winds Blow	Mattei	D, E♭, F	A to D	1/6
Oh, Promise Me	De Koven	F, G, A♭, B♭	C to D	1/6
Old Admiral Benbow	Somervell	F, G, B♭	C to D	1/4
O Lovely Night	Ronald	B♭, D♭	B to D	1/4
Onaway, Awake	Cowen	C, D, E	C to F	1/6
Once	Hervey	C, E♭, F, G	C to C	1/-
Our Land of Dreams	Thompson	E♭, F, G	B♭ to E♭	1/6
Out on the Deep	Löhr	G, A, B♭	G to D	1/6
Prince Charming	Lehman	B♭, D♭	C to G	1/6
Perfect Day	Jacobs Bond	C, D♭, F	C to B	1/4
Peace and Rest	Batten	A♭, B♭, C, D♭	B♭ to E♭	1/6
Parted	Tosti	B, A♭, F♭,	D to E	1/6
Pipes of Pan	Elgar	G, A, B	B♭ to D	1/6
Plumstones	Cooper			1/6
Powder Monkey	Watson	F, G	C to D	1/6
Rosamond	Foster	F, G, A♭	C to F	1/6
Rose in the Bud	Foster	B♭, C, D♭, E♭	G to D	1/6
Reuben Ranzo	Coates	C, D, E♭	C to D	1/6
Remembrance	Noel Johnson	A♭, F	E to G	1/6
Richard of Taunton Deane	Gould	E♭, F, G	B♭ to C	1/4
Rock Me to Sleep	Greene	E♭, F, G, A	B♭ to D	1/6
Rosary	Nevin	B♭, C, D♭, E♭, F	C to D	1/6
River of Years	Marzials			1/6
Slave Song	Riego	D, E, F G minor	C to D	1/6
She is Far from the Land	Lambert	G, A♭, C	C to E♭	1/6
Song of Thanksgiving	Allitsen	C, E♭, F, G	A to C	1/6
Stone Cracker John	Coates	D, E♭	A to D	1/6
Swallows	Cowen	F, G, A	C to F	1/6
Sailor's Dance	Molloy	D, E♭, F	A to D	1/6
Serjeant of the Line	Squire	F, G, A	A to C	1/6
Sailor's Grave	Sullivan	C, D, E♭, F	B to D	1/6
Sergeant of Horse	Dix	B♭, C	B to E♭	1/4
Shadows	Finck	B♭, C, D	A to D	1/6
Silver Ring	Chaminade	D♭, E♭, F	A to E♭	1/6
Sincerity	Clarke	D, E♭, F, G	A to D	1/6
Song of Thanksgiving	Allitsen	C, E♭, F, G	A to C sharp	1/6
Softly Awakes My Heart	S. Saens	B, C, D♭, E	G to E	1/8
Solveig Song	Grieg	F, G, A	C to F	1/6
Somewhere a Voice is Calling	Tate	D, E♭, F, G	B to D	1/5
Spring	Tosti	F, A♭, B♭, C	C to D	1/6
Stormfiend	Roeckel	C, D, E♭	G to D	1/4
Summer Night	Goring Thomas	C, D♭, D	A to F	1/6
Sweet and Twenty	Eric Coates	C, E♭,	C to F	1/6
Sweetest Flower that Blows	Hawley	D♭, E♭, F	B♭ to D	1/6
Sympathy	Marshall	D, E♭, F, G	B to E	1/6
Tommy, Lad	Margetson	D, E♭	B to E	1/6
Take a Pair of Sparkling Eyes	Sullivan			1/6
Thoughts have Wings	Lehman	D♭, E♭, F	C to E♭	1/6
Three Little Songs	M. V. White	Low, med., high	A to E	1/6
Two Songs	Noel Johnson	Low, med, high	C to D	1/6
Two Little Irish Songs	Löhr	Low, med., high	C to D	1/6
Three for Jack	Squire	F, G	B♭ to D	1/6
There's a Land	Allitsen	D, E♭, F, G	A to D	1/6
Trumpeter	Dix	F, G, A, C	A to C	1/6
Thora	Adams	D, E♭, F, G	A to D	1/6
Thousand Fathoms Deep	Petrie	C, D	G to C	1/4
Time's Roses	Barry	E♭, F, G	A to E	1/6
Toilers	Piccolomini	B♭, C, D, E♭	D to F	1/6
Tommy, Lad	Margetson	C, D, E♭	A to D	1/6
True till Death	Gatty	F, G, A, C	A to C	1/4
Two Eyes of Grey	McGeoch	B♭, C, D	B to D	1/6
Two Little Irish Songs	Löhr	Low, med., high	C to D	1/6
Two Songs	M. V. White	Low, med., high	A to E	1/6
Until	Sanderson	D♭, E♭, F	B♭ to E♭	1/6
Valley of Laughter	Sanderson	E♭, F, G	C to F	1/6
When Shadows Gather	Marshall	B♭, C, D, E	B♭ to E♭	1/6
Where My Caravan has Rested	Löhr	F, A♭,	D to F	1/6
Where Corals Lie	Elgar	D, F minor	A to D	1/6
When I Survey the Wondrous Cross	Hope	C, D♭, E♭	C to E	1/4
When the Ebb-tide Flows	Gordon	E♭, F, G	G to C	1/4
Where the River Shannon Flows	Russell	E♭	E to F	1/6
Who	Tosti	E, E♭, D♭, C	B to E	1/6
Widdicombe Fair	Old Devonshire	G	D, D	6d.
Willow Song	Col. Taylor	B♭	B, G	1/6
Within Your Heart	Trotére	D, E♭, F, G	A, D	1/6
Yeoman of England	German	C, D	C to D	1/6
Yeomans Wedding Song	Poniatowski	G, A, B♭	C to D	1/6
Young Tom o' Devon	Russell	A♭, B♭	A♭ to E♭	1/6
Yeoman, The	Dix	G, B♭	C to D	1/6
You, Just You	Thompson	B♭, C	D to E♭	1/6
Your Eyes Have Told Me So	Hardy	F, G, A	C, D	1/4

Compass of lowest key is given.

New and Popular Dance Music.

Ragtimes, Two Steps, &c.

Amblin Ambros..	..	(two-step)	1/6
Burglar Bill	..	do.	1/6
Bustlin Billy	..	do.	1/4
Bogey Walk	..(one or two-step) ..		1/6
Crab Crawl	..	(one-step)	1/6
Down in Jungle Town	..	(two-step)	1/4
Fluffy Ruffles	..	do.	1/4
Gaby Glide	..	do.	4½d.
Gaily through the Woods..	do.	..	1/6
Gin and Bitters ..	..	do.	1/6
Gnats ..	..	do.	1/6
Hitchy Koo	..	do.	4½d.
How do You do, Miss Ragtime	do.	..	4½d.
Hullo, Ragtime ..	..	do.	1/6
Interruptions	..	do.	1/6
I want to be in Dixie	..	do.	4½d.
Little Peter	..	do.	1/4
Lobster's Promenade	..	do.	1/6
Oh you beautiful Doll	..	(Ragtime)	4½d.
On the Mississipi ..	..	do.	4½d.
Paddling Puddles	..	(two-step)	1/6
Policeman's Holiday	..	do.	1/6
Rag-a-Muffin ..	..	do.	1/4
Red Pepper	..	(Ragtime)	1 6
Ring o' Roses ..	..	(two-step)	1/6
Teddy Bear's Pic-nic	..	do.	1/6
Temptation Rag	..	do.	1/6
There's a Girl in Havana ..	do.	..	4½d.
Toboggan	..	do.	1/6
Top Dog	..	do.	1/6
Tortoise Patrol ..	..	do.	1/4
Très Moutarde	..(one or two-step)..		1/6
Waiting for Robert E. Lee	..	do.	4½d.
'Way Down Colon Town ..	(two-step)	..	1/6
Wedding Glide ..	..	do.	1/6
Whistler and his Dog	..	do.	1/6
Wiggle Woggle	..	do.	1/6
Yankee Grit ..	..	do.	1/6
Ye Gods and Little Fishes	do.	..	1/4

Waltzes.

Always Gay	..	(Joyce)	1/6
Amoureuse	..	(Berger)	1/6
Blue Danube	..	(Strauss)	1/4
Cassandra	..	(Lemon)	1/6
Chant d'Hier	..	(Hughes)	1 6
Charming	..	(Joyce)	1/6
Columbine	..	(Gardener)	1/6
Corisande	..	(Breville	1 6
Dancing Mistress	..	..	1/6
Coquetterie	..	(Wood)	1/6
D'Avril	..	(Godin)	1 6
Daybreak	..	(Brunet)	1,6
Décembre	..	(Godin)	1/6
Donan Wellen	..	..	8d.
Dreaming	..	(Joyce)	1/6
Dream Kisses	..	(Rolfe)	1/6
Druid's Prayer	..	(Davson)	1/6
Enchantress	..	(Gastelle)	1/6
Eternal Waltz	..	(Fall)	1/6
Eva Waltz	..	do.	1/6
Gipsy Love	..	do.	1/6
Girl in the Taxi ..	..		1/6
Girl on the Film	..	..	1/6
Golden Land of Fairy Tales	..		1/6
Gold and Silver ..	..	(Lehar)	1/6
Juillet	..	(Godin)	1/6
Kiss of Spring ..	..		1/4
Klytemnestra	..	(Lotter)	1/6
La Tristesse	..	(Deacon)	1/6
Le Desir d'Amour	..	(Bréville)	1/6
Look Down Dear Eyes	..		1/6
Luna Waltz	..	(Lincke)	1/6
Luxe d'Amour	..	..	1/6
Luxemberg Waltz	..	..	1/6
Ma Blonde Aimée	..	..	1/6
Malmaison	..	..	1/6

Waltzes—(continued).

Marsinah	..	(Carton)	1
Melisande	..	(Lambert)	1
Midsummer Eve..	..		1
Nights of Gladness	..		1
Monte Christo	..	(Kotlar)	1
Nightbirds	..	(Kaps)	1/
Norvégienne	..	(Van Dyck)	1/
Oh, Oh, Delphine	..		1
Passing of Salome	..	(Joyce)	1
Pink Lady	..	(Caryll)	1/
Princess Caprice	..		1/
Remembrance	..	(Joyce)	1/
Saints and Sinners	..		1/
Sanctuary	..	(Baldock)	1/
Sheila..	..	(Nemo)	1/
Siziletta	..	(Blon)	1/
Sobre las olas	..	(Roses)	1/
Songe d'Automne	..	(Joyce)	1/
Sumurun	..	..	1/
Sunshine Girl	..		1/
Sweet Memories	..	(Joyce)	1/
Sylvana	..	(Martel)	1/
Thousand Kisses	..	(Joyce)	1/
Under my Darling's Window	(Lincke)		1/
Unrequitted Love	..	do.	1/
Valse Mai	..	(Godin)	1/
Valse Novembre	..		1/
Valse Septembre	..		1/
Venus on Earth ..	..		1/
Vera Dear	..		1/
Vision of Salome	..		1/
Wedding Dance..	..		1/
When the Birds began to Sing	..		1/
Whirl of the Whirl	..	..	1/
Yeux Turquoises	..		1/
Your Eyes have told me so	..		1

THIS YEAR'S DANCE ALBUM.

Francis & Day's. Feldman's. Planet's. Just Published. GAMAGE'S PRICE, 9d. each; post free, 10½d. Write for Contents.
Contains all the Latest Popular Dances.

Gamage's Special ☞ **The Monster Budget of Dance Music,** **One Shilling.** Pos
Revised "up-to-date," containing Waltzes, Ragtimes, Two-steps, etc. ext

---

Ragtime Albums.

FRANCIS & DAY. FELDMAN. **Contain all Latest and Popular Ragtimes.** Post free,
Gamage Price, 9d. each. 10½d.

Popular Pianoforte Albums.

The Eclipse Pianoforte Album, containing 52 selections. Fine value 1/-
Bound in cloth cover, printed on better paper, 2/6
Sousa's March Folio, containing 12 of Sousa's best Marches 1/6
GAMAGE'S SPECIAL .. 1/- post extra: The Monster Pianoforte Folio. Standard and Popular Pieces. Very fine, for advanced pupils.
March Album. 20 Up-to-date and Popular Marches 1/-
Melodious Memories. A Selection introducing 74 of the most popular airs of the last fifty years 2/-
Liszt Album of 20 Pieces 2/1
Score of Romantique Fragments .. 2/1
Greig Album of 50 most popular pieces 2/1
German Album of 12 most popular pieces 2/1

Easy Pianoforte Albums for Children.

The Ideal Music Book, published in 6 different books, each containing 12 easy pieces for piano .. 4½d.
My Child's Music Book, published in 6 different books, each containing 12 easy pieces for piano .. 4½d.
Merry Little Tunes for Children, including all the original melodies to the nursery rhymes .. 9d.
Cole's Music of the Bells, in two volumes, containing 12 easy pieces for wrist bell playing .. 9d.
Wicken's March Album, containing sixteen fine Marches .. .. 9d.
Wicken's Simple Tunes for Little Players, containing 32 easy and short pieces .. .. 9d.

Manuscript Music Paper.

Size 12 by 9½ in. Good quality. Upright.
2 staves for Instrument ⎫
4 3's for Vocal   ⎬ Double Sheets,
6 2's for Piano..   ⎭ **6d. per doz.**

VIOLIN and PIANO.

Barcarolle. Tales of Hoffman	..	..	1/6
Bolero	..	Whitaker	1/4
Broken Melody ..	..	..	1/6
Cavalleria Rusticana. Selection ..			1/6
Cavatina	..	(Raff)	1/-
Humoreske	..	(Dvorak)	1/6
Intermezzo, Cavalleria Rusticana	..		1/6
In the Shadows ..	..	..	1/6
Kol Nidrei	..	(Bruch)	2/-
Largo..	..	(Handel)	1/-
Le Cygne	..	(St. Saëns)	1/8
L'Extase	..	(Thomé)	1/6
Madrigale	..	(Simonetti)	1/-
Martha. Selection	..	..	1/-
Melody. F	..	(Rubinstein)	1/-
Serenade	..	(Drdla)	1/6
Simple Aveu	..	(Thomé)	1/4
Sous la Feuillee ..	..	..	1/4
Spring Song	..	(Mendelssohn)..	1/-
Tarantella	..	(Poole)	1/4
Two Hungarian Dances	..	(Brahms)	1/6
Valse. Septembre	..	..	1/6
William Tell. Selection	..	..	1/-
Zigeunerweisen ..	..	(Sarasate)	2/3
Zapateado	..	do.	3/4

MANDOLINE and PIANO.

Alice, where art thou 6d.		Poet and Peasant,	
Carmena (Distin) 1/4		Overture	1/4
Faust. Selection .. 6d.		Rosy Dawn, Polka..	6d.
Killarney .. .. 6d.		Simple Aveu (Thome)	1/4
Album of 8 Marches, Mandoline and Piano .. 10d.			

MANUSCRIPT BOOKS.

Paper Covers, 6 staves. Oblong 12 pages..			1d.
,, ,, 12 ,, Upright 8 ,,			1d.
Leatherette Covers, 6 staves. Oblong 24 pages			3d.
,, ,, 6 ,, ,, 48 ,,			4½d.
,, ,, 12 ,, Upright 20 ,,			4½d.
,, ,, 12 ,, ,, 36 ,,			6d.

Instrumental Albums.

Recordi Flute and Piano Albums. Published in t
volumes, each containing 12 Classical Pieces, w
separate part edition for Flute, 147 pages, 2/- ea
Recordi Instrumental Albums, for Violin, Clarion
Mandoline and Cornet, each containing 6 pre
Pieces, with Pianoforte-part edition for instrum
for duets .. .. .. 9d. each
Squire's Violoncello Albums. Nos. 1, 2 and 3. Ea
containing Popular Pieces.. .. .. 1/6
Wicken's Easy Violin Books, containing 7 Piec
Several different editions .. 9d. each
Gamage Folio. Collection of all the Popular Pie
for Violin and Piano .. .. ..
Pleyel. Op. 8. 6 easy Duets. Violin & Piano
Beethoven. Collection of easy Pieces for 'Cello
and Piano .. ..
Mendelssohn. Songs without words. 'Cello
and Piano .. ..
Popular Melodies. By Popp. Flute and Piano
Operatic do. do. do.
Hermann. 50 favorite Melodies. 'Cello & Piano
Squire. Five easy Pieces. do.
Scottish Songs. .. Violin and Piano
March Album. 14 popular Pieces. do. 1
Hermann Album. Modern Pieces. do.

Physical Drill Books for Schools

With Music by Beatrice Wickens. These
are strongly bound and very clearly printed..
Musical Drill Book. Published by Williams.
For Public and High Schools .. ..

Band Cards.

Stout Cardboard, 7¼ by 5⅜ in. Nine Staves, mach
ruled .. .. .. 9d. doz
Thin Cardboard, lined-lined, 7¼ by 5⅜ in.
Ten Staves, machine ruled .. .. 1/- e

Pictures in Your Own Home this Christmas.

For particulars see page 262.

THE "GAMAGE" KINOSCOPE.

A Simple self-contained Cinematograph for Home use.

The brilliancy of the picture given by the Kinoscope is considerably greater than that given by any existing machine of the same style whether fitted with accumulator or self generating plant. The reason lies in the optical system.

In our optical system the condensers and the lens are specially adapted one to the other so that the greatest possible light passing properties are obtained.

The focus of the lens is 2¼ inches, and it is not possible to use a lens of longer focus. At the same time the lamps are specially constructed for the purpose and give the greatest possible light that is obtainable by this system.

Lastly the silver screen is a specially prepared one that is almost totally reflecting, and seeing for private work that the angle of view need not be so wide as in ordinary theatres, we have been able to produce a screen that gives best possible results with a minimum light.

The machine is well and solidly built, and the wearing properties should be beyond reproach. It is quiet in working and there is no difficulty in delivering a lecture or description of the film in an ordinary voice. The size of the picture 2 ft. 8 ins. by 3 ft. 6 ins. is comparatively large, quite big enough for ordinary class rooms so that the Kinoscope should find its way into a good many schools, its cost of maintainance being low, and the results in every way being equal to those obtained in the Picture Theatres. The machine is light, easy of transport and simple to manipulate, there is no delicate mechanism to go wrong, and no adjustments required. It is sent out ready for immediate use.

Further advantages of this apparatus over others are :—

No. 1. The apparatus can be used for ordinary films so that any film that is used for theatrical use can be run through this machine, and now in most Towns there is a film hiring depot where standard size films are stocked.

No. 2. The film spools hold 200 yards of film, the other machines so far only take 100.

No. 3. The apparatus contains its own re-winder so that the films can be immediately re-wound without a further piece of apparatus.

No. 4. The apparatus runs extremely easily, it is no more difficult to turn than an ordinary sewing machine.

No. 5. The light continues to shine whether the machine is running or at rest. This enables the operator to handle his films more easily, at the same time there is not sufficient heat generated to cause the slightest danger of fire.

The precision of the apparatus is extraordinary, and the work is the highest quality.

This Kinoscope is supplied in three different models:

Kinoscope Model "A" is for use where an electrical current available. The machine is supplied complete with contact plug for attachment to an ordinary lamp in the room, and consists of a special resistance lamp and long length of connecting cable. This ends in an ordinary plug, the current being turned on, and the plug pushed into the proper position in the Kinoscope makes up the circuit, and illuminates the projector.

When ordering it is necessary to state the voltage of current available.

The price of this model complete consisting of the machine with cover, to solid and one dividing spool, five 8 volt lamps, 1 resistance lamp, fittings a attachments with cable, silver projecting screen 32 ins. by 42 ins. with erecting frame **£15 0**

Kinoscope Model "B" is for use where there is no electric current available but where there is a possibility of recharging accumulators which course occurs in every place where there is a motor garage. The outfit is slightly more expensive, but the running of an accumulator is cheaper than running with dry batteries. The accumulator supplied has about 13 hours burning output whether it is used for one continuous projection or in a number of short periods. The cost of recharging accumulators is extremely small being only a few pence. As the accumulator is specially prepared for our machine it is undesirable to use it for working anything else, such as children's toys, toy railways, or other purposes.

The price of this outfit complete with the machine, two solid and dividing spool, five six volt lamps, accumulator as described **£17 0** with connecting cable, silver screen as above with erecting stand

Kinoscope Model "C" is for use where electric current is obtainable, and where there is no chance of recharging accumulators. It consists of the apparatus as described with a dry battery. On connecting the dry battery with the machine the six volt incandescent lamp is illuminated. The battery will last for five hours at least under continual work, but it is recommended to run not more than an hour at a time and then it will last very considerably longer as it recuperates.

The price of this outfit consisting of the machine with cover, two solid and dividing spool, five six volt lamps, dry battery with connections, silver screen as above with erecting stand complete **£15 0**

Price List of Extras and Replacements.

Folding Table to hold the machine for all models **£2 2 0**	Extra accumulator for model "B" .. **2 7 6**	22 volt resistance lamps each **3**
Extra dry batteries each for model "C" .. **7 6**	Replacement lamps six or eight volts per box of 4 **6 0**	Extra spools (solid) each **2 3**
	110 volt resistance lamps each **2 0**	,, ,, (dividing) **3**

Working Parts of Kinoscope.

A Focussing Lens. **C** Film Gate Clip. **E** Film Gate. **G** Lower Film Clamp. **I** Film Receiving Wheel. **L** Plug for attaching Lumina

B Film Centeirng Adjustment. **D** Lamp Holder. **F** Top Film Clamp. **H** Driving Handle. **K** Film Holder and Re-winding Wheel.

CINEMATOGRAPHS FOR WINTER EVENINGS.

The "SILENT" Home and Educational Cinematograph

NEW MODEL. WITH STANDARD LAMP HOUSE.

An absolutely perfect, safe and cheap projector, designed especially for use in the Home, the School, or the small Hall for use with Standard Size Films.

This Cinematograph is a thoroughly practical instrument for showing both living pictures and lantern slides.

With this projector a perfect moving picture exhibition can be given by anyone — previous knowledge & experience being quite unnecessary

Any size picture can be obtained according to the power of the illuminant used and the distance available from the screen. The picture on the screen is as steady as a lantern slide and as flickerless. The machine is so perfectly made and works so smoothly that it is practically silent when running,

Prices: complete as illustration **£10 19 6**

Adjustable iron legs for fitting to baseboard, making a strong serviceable stand that can be adjusted for height or tilted in any direction, **£1 9 6** Extra spools, 8 in. 2/6
Spool boxes for 8 in. spools, per pair **£1 9 6** Extra Spools, 2 in. 2/6

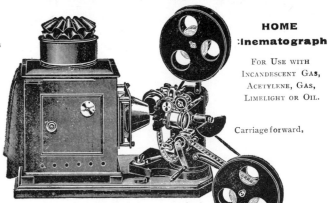

Prices:
With two Lenses and strong Wooden Case, **£5 13 6**

Mechanism only without Lenses, **£2 7 6**

Ditto. with Cinematograph Lens. **£2 17 0**

HOME Cinematograph

FOR USE WITH INCANDESCENT GAS, ACETYLENE, GAS, LIMELIGHT OR OIL.

Carriage forward.

A first-rate living picture machine for side shows, home use, schools, bazaars, &c. This is an excellent cinematograph and will project a steady, clear picture, with the standard size films. It is provided with feed and take-up sprockets. The re winding gear is perfectly efficient and works on the steel band system, the same as the No. 1 Machine. It takes the standard Edison gauge films, but is, of course, much smaller in all its parts, with the exception of the sprockets, gate and hanging mechanism.
Cheap continuous films are made for this Machine either in real photographic subjects or in lithographic.

The No. 3 Holborn Cinematograph.

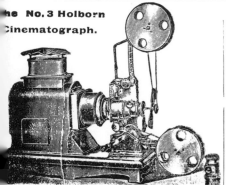

Suitable for displays on larger scale than No. 2, being fitted with full-size 4-in. condenser, and large size objectives, and an extra lens being provided for ordinary lantern projection. It is an exceptionally strong instrument, and is almost noiseless in action. It can be used with limelight, electric, acetylene, incandescent gas, or oil, according to customers requirements. No illuminants being included at price quoted.

Price with extra lantern lens, £6 6 0

NOTE—This machine takes full-size lantern slides.
Carriage forward.

Holborn Cinematograph Nos. Nos. 71 & 61.

No. 71. Entirely new model. Beautifully finished, and absolutely rigid. Arranged to take longer lengths of film than is usual in cheap machines, fitted with powerful oil lamp. Price, complete with 1 dozen lantern slides, 6 colored cinematograph films, and 1 photographic film, **70/-**

"Superior Cinematograph

Packed in strong Wood box.

Complete

50/-

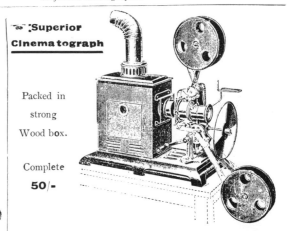

Lantern body of sheet iron mounted on cast iron base, takes all films with standard "Edison Perforation," also suitable as magic lantern for the projection of glass slides 2¾ in. wide, or ood-framed slides, 2¼ in. wide. Dogaction mechanism, top sprocket, almost noiseless film movement, lower and upper film spool fitted for re-winding. Oblong coloured films, 3 superior photo-process films, 12 glass slides, lantern body sheet iron dull black finish, base, cast iron. Superior quality set of lenses, brass objective with rack and pinion, focussing movement, double condenser (2⅜ in.) and 12 in. duplex oil lamp.

Miniature Combination Cinematograph and Magic Lantern. No. 783/1.

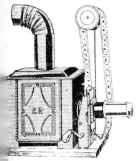

Strongly made metal body, fitted with lens, condenser and paraffin lamp. Complete with 3 films producing living pictures and 6 slides, 1¾ in.

Price complete, .. **4/6**

Postage 6d. extra.

Miniature Combination Cinematograph and Lantern.

No. 785. Strongly made iron body, mounted on metal base, fitted with lens, condenser, and paraffin lamp. 3 coloured films are supplied for producing the living pictures. Provision is made for using ordinary lantern slides, 1¾ in. wide, 6 are supplied with lantern.

Price complete in box with instructions

7/11.

Postage 9d.

Miniature Combination Cinematograph and Magic Lantern.

No. 786. Strongly made, iron body, mounted on metal base, fitted with lens, condenser, and paraffin lamp. 3 long coloured films are supplied for producing the living pictures. Provision is made for using ordinary magic lantern slides, 1¾ in. wide. Price, complete in box with full instructions, including 6 slides, **12/6**

Postage 9d.

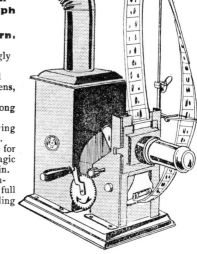

Get a Copy of our Cinematograph Book 6d. Post free.

Toy and Post-card Lanterns.

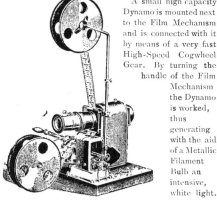

Our Boys' Lantern.

No. 1400/1 3 slides, 1¹³⁄₁₆ in. .. **10½d.** Post 2d.
,, 1400/2 6 ,, 1³⁄₁₆ in. .. **1/3** ,, 3d.
,, 1400/4 12 ,, 1⅜ in. .. **2/6** ,, 4d.

THE DYNAMOGRAPH.

A Cinematograph with a Dynamo attached, automatically generating its own light.

No. P. 2000. THE STANDARD LANTERN SET.
Well-finished Magic Lantern.
Fitted with Petroleum Lamp, Reflector, brass Sliding Tubes to

lens, with twelve colored slides, assorted subjects, complete in strong box.

Postage extra.

No. 2000. Size Slides, 1⅜ in. wide .. **4/6**
,, 2002. ,, 1½ in. ,, .. **6/6**
,, 2003. ,, 2 in. ,, .. **8/11**
,, 2004. ,, 2⅜ in. ,, .. **9/11**

Postage 4d., 5d., 6d., 6d.

A small high capacity Dynamo is mounted next to the Film Mechanism and is connected with it by means of a very fast High-Speed Cogwheel Gear. By turning the handle of the Film Mechanism the Dynamo is worked, thus generating with the aid of a Metallic Filament Bulb an intensive white light.

For focussing and other purposes a small auxiliary battery is fitted into the base of the apparatus and this battery can be used whenever the handle of the mechanism is not being turned.

Suitable for all Films with "Standard Edison Perforation." The Apparatus can also be transformed into a Magic Lantern in which case the Dynamo also provides the necessary light.

222/300 "Dynamograph." with fine objective with cog wheel for focussing, 6 coloured films, 12 glass slides, 2 in. wide, metal filament electric lamp, 4 Volt, 0,3—0,4 ampère each... ... ... **29/6**

222/303 Same Apparatus, but larger, with strong mechanism superior workmanship, fine objective and large film spool 6 Photobing Films, 1 original photographic film, 1 series (3 slides of Photobing slides, 2⅔ in. wide fitted for wooden framed slides of 2 in. width), metal filament electric lamp, 5 Volts 0,3—0,4 ampere and with 2 large film spools, lower and upper spool for automatically winding up the film ... ... each **57/6**

Combination Cinematograph and Magic Lantern.

Superior make, most substantial and fitted with a best quality lamp, also six long coloured films for producing the living pictures, and adapted for using ordinary magic lantern slides 2 in. wide.

Nos. 799/1 & 791.

Complete in box with full instructions, including 1 dozen long coloured slides, **32/6**
Do. smaller size **25/-**
Carriage forward.

No. P. 105.

Mirroscope Projector.

Fitted for electricity, gas or acetylene, **21/-** Carr. paid.

Construction: Made of steel throughout, two parts being die pressed, curled or seamed together, no solder or screws used in this machine. Finished Oxidize copper. Interior: white enamel.

Lenses: Gun metal tube with stationary diaphragm and two plano convex lenses of good quality.

Reflectors: Two concave reflectors, nickel plated, instantly detachable for polishing

Card Holder : Concave card holder with air cooling device, or holding postcards, photographs, etc., either vertically or horizontally.
Specify voltage required.

No. P. 103. Mirroscope Projector.

Fitted for electricity, gas or acetylene, **31/6** Carr. paid.

Construction: Highly finished steel throughout, all parts are die pressed, curled or seamed together, no solder or screws used in this machine.
Finish : Oxidized coppered.
Interior : White enamel.
Lenses : Two plano convex lenses of fine quality, fitted in gun metal plated tube with stationary diaphragm. Lenses can be readily cleaned and polished.
Reflectors : Two genuine parobolic brass reflectors, heavily nickel plated, instantly detachable.
Specify voltage required.

Construction: Highly finished steel throughout, all parts being die pressed, curled or seamed together, no solder or screws used in this machine.
Finish : Oxidized coppered.
Interior : White enamel.
Lenses : Two plano convex lenses of fine quality, both lenses may be taken out readily for cleaning and polishing. Reflectors : Two concave brass parobolic, heavily nickel plated, instantly detachable for polishing.
Card Holder : Double dropping. This carrier permits insertion of the card while a card or other subject is in instrument being reflected on the screen, thus making the rapid changing of subjects extremely simple.
Specify voltage required.

Toy Magic Lantern.

The "Gloria."

The body is handsomely constructed of Russian iron, with a specially constructed kerosene burner, producing a very powerful light. The optical lenses, both in the condenser and front objectives, are specially prepared. Each lantern is fitted with twelve long slides, one chromotrope, one slipping slide in wooden frame, and one comic slipping slide.

No. P. 4005. Complete in strong fancy wood case with 12 slides. Price **19,9** each. Post 1

N P. 209. **Mirroscope Projector**
Fitted for electricity, gas or acetylene.

This instrument is designed especially to meet a tremendous demand for a thoroughly practical low priced Mirroscope which will project a subject clearly and well defined. All customers who have inspected this model frankly admit that they do not see how the machine can be offered at such a ridiculous price.

Construction Made of steel throughout, the parts being die pressed, curled or seamed together no solder or screws are used. Lenses : One 3½ diameter double convex lense of fine quality, fitted in metal tube with stationary diaphragm. Lenses can be readily cleaned and polished. Reflectors Two nickel tin reflectors of good quality. Card Holder : Concave card holder with cooling device is included.

Specify voltage required. **15/-** Carr. paid.

Full Catalogue of Cinematographs sent Post 6d.

No. P. 101. **Mirroscope Projector.**
Fitted for electricity, gas or acetylene ... **42/-** Carriage paid.

MAGIC LANTERNS.

LANTERNS AT EXCEPTIONALLY LOW PRICES

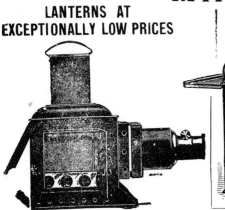

THE Gamage Special

Large Objective 2⅜ in. dia. and Condenser, 4½ in.

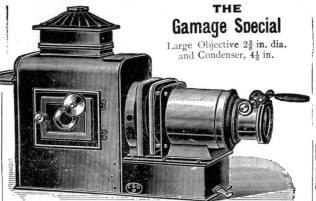

Optimus Magic Lantern.

31/-

No. 1001. Japanned tin body, with dome shape top and side door. Fitted with 4-in. Plano-convex Condenser, and Double Combination Achromatic Front Lenses, in Brass Mount, with Rack and Pinion Adjustment, a 3-wick Petroleum Lamp (with wicks 2-in. wide), and Jointed Russian Iron Chimney **17/10**
Lightning Carriers .. .. ..**10**d. each

No. 1002. Japanned tin body with dome shape top and side door. Fitted with 4-in. Plano-convex Condenser, and Double Combination Achromatic Front Lenses, in Brass Mount, with Rack and Pinion Adjustment and Flasher, a four Wick Petroleum Lamp (with wick 2-in. wide), and Jointed Russian Iron Chimney.
Complete in Carrying Case **22/3**
Lightning Carriers.. .. .. **10**d. each

32/6

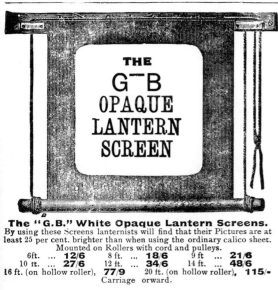

No. 1004. Russian Iron Lantern with Sliding Brass Front, adapted for burning Incandescent Gas, with 4-in. Plano-convex Condensers, Double Combination Achromatic Front Lenses, mounted in Brass, with Rack and Pinion Adjustment and Flasher, fitted with Incandescent Burner and Mantle, Chimney, Gas Jet, Reflectors and Jet Tray.
Complete in Metal Box **32/6**

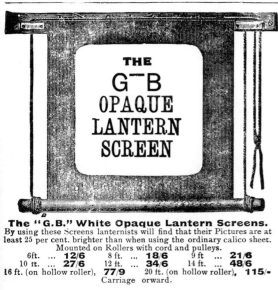

THE G⁻B OPAQUE LANTERN SCREEN

The "G.B." White Opaque Lantern Screens.
By using these Screens lanternists will find that their Pictures are at least 25 per cent. brighter than when using the ordinary calico sheet. Mounted on Rollers with cord and pulleys.

6ft. ... **12/6**	8 ft. ... **18/6**	9 ft. ... **21/6**
10 ft. ... **27/6**	12 ft. ... **34/6**	14 ft. ... **48/6**
16 ft. (on hollow roller), **77/9**	20 ft. (on hollow roller), **115/-**

Carriage orward.

Body—Heavy Russian Iron, Solid Brass Front.
Condenser—4½ in. Plano-convex.
Objective—2⅜ in. double achromatic, with flap shutter and tinter shot, cowl top and tray for limelight.
Russian Iron Case, with handle **69/6**
Extra for—Blow-through jet, **13/6** Mixed **13/6**
Stock's lamp, **19/9** 4-wick lamp, best qua. **10/6**
Acetylene lamp **42/-**
Telescopic front and jacket lens, allgwing lenses of various foci to be used, **32/6** extra.

94/6

Polished Mahogany Lantern.

⸢The outside body is of superior and well-seasoned mahogany, having a panelled door on either side into which sight holes are recessed. The interior lining is of strong metal ; between it and the mahogany body is a space for air to circulate freely and so keep the outside cool and convenient to the touch. The Stage Plate and Telescopic Tubes are of highly finished brass, as is also the O.G. Flange for connecting a specially selected Petzval Portrait Combination Front Lense (Achromatic) which gives brilliant and crisp definition. It has Rack and Pinion Focussing Adjustment. The Condenser, which is a picked one and free from flaws, is composed of two Plano-convex Lenses of 4 in. diameter. The 3-wick Refulgent Lamp, best make, is specially selected. Wicks are 2 in. wide and burn paraffin oil. Chimney is of Russian Iron, securely jointed without solder.

Complete in outside box, which is arranged to be used as a support for the Lantern during an exhibition or lecture.

Price **94/6**

Fig. 1. Superior Japanned metal body, fitted with Achromatic Lens, 3-wick Lamp, 4-in. Condenser, etc.
Complete in wood box **31/-**

36/-

Optimus College Magic Lantern.

Fig. 2. Superior Japanned metal body, with Open Stage, fitted with Achromatic Lens, 3-wick Lamp, 4-in. Condenser, etc.
Complete in Wood Box **36/-**

Superior quality Russian Iron Lantern, with 4-inch Plano-convex Condensers, Double Combination Achromatic Front Lenses, Double Pinion Focussing Adjustment, Sliding Brass Tubes, fitted with best quality 3-wick Petroleum Lamp, wick 2-in. wide. Complete in Wood Box with nstruction for use **48/-**

75/-

Optimus Educational Magic Lantern

STRONGLY RECOMMENDED.

The body is made of substantial Russian Ion. The Stage Plate and Sliding Tube are of well-finished Brass. The Lens is a first-class Portrait Combination, giving really excellent definition.
The Lamp is a 3-wick Refulgent.

Complete in outside box for carrying .. **75/-**
Telescopic Tubes **40/-** xtra

Daylight Enlargers and Accessories.

The Express Adjustable Enlarger.

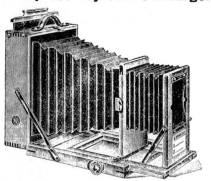

The enlarger is marked so that various degrees of enlargement can be obtained. It is very compact, folding into a small space for storing, yet most rigid when erected for use; has a single achromatic lens, exposing shutter, and loose dark slide. Made of bird's-eye marble.

No. 35/1. ¼-plate to ½-plate or 1/1 plate .. **25/-**
,, 35/2. ¼-plate to 1/1 plate or 12 by 10 .. **35/-**
,, 35/3. Post-Card to 1/1 plate or 12 by 10 **35/-**
,, 35/4. ½-plate to 12 by 10 or 10 by 12 .. **47/6**
,, 35/5. 9 by 12 to 18 by 24 ,, 24 by 30cm. **40/-**

Carriage paid.

The "Klimax" Acetylene Generator.

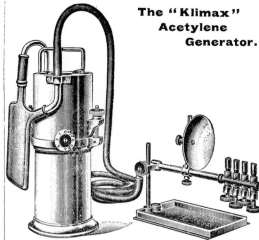

Acetylene is a form of illuminant favoured by those who cannot use gas or electric light. It gives a pure white light, which lends itself particularly well to enlarging purpos s. Exposures are reasonably short. The Klimax Generator is simple to use and is from smell.

Price—Generator, 4-burner Jet and india-rubber tubing **42/-**

The "Pilot" Enlarger.

The simplest form of enlar er made.

The negative is placed in the small end, th bromide paper in the large ; there is no focussin or any other adjustment to make.

Made of wood, covered in leatherette, wi sinple achromatic lens, and exposure shutte Loose wood detachable dark slide.

No.	To enlarge from	
20/1.	¼-plate to ½-plate, & 3½ by 2½ to 6½ by 4¾ ..	**10**/
	Extra dark slides, 8½ by 6½ ..	**4**/
20/2.	¼-plate to 12 by 10, & 3½ by 2½ to 8½ by 6½ ..	**16**/
	Extra dark slides, 12 by 10 ..	**7**/
20 3.	Post-card to 12 by 8 ..	**16**/
	Extra dark slides, 11 by 12 ..	**7**/

Electric Projecting Lamp, "Nernst."

Extra Resistances ... **2/6**
Extra Filaments ... **4/-**

This well-known type of Lamp is constructed on the lines that have been proved to be the most serviceable, *i.e.* with the filaments covered by means of a cap when the lamp is not being used.

The filaments are extremely fragile and consequently require the utmost care when out of use. The advantage of the Nernst Lamp over others is that the resistances are wired in such a manner that one, two or three filaments can be used as desired. It is substantially made in nickel-plated brass, and the whole Outfit comprises the following :—Lamp Holder, Resistance, Filament, Plug for conuection, Cast-iron Tray with Standard, Lighting Torch and three yards of Flexible Wire. Price—With 1 Resistance and 1 Filament, **32/6** With 2 Resistances and 2 Filaments, **39/-** With 3 Resistances and 3 Filaments, **45/-**

Incandescent Gas Outfit.

For burning the Incandescent Gas in ordinary Lanterns, which with the aid of Reflector, as shown in above illustration, gives a beautifully clear light, without the bother, smell or smoke experienced with oil lamps. Outfit consists of Tray, Arm for holding Burner, Incandescent Gas Burner, Adjustable Reflector, short Chimney and Mantle.

Price, complete .. **6/9** Post 4d.

The "Meta" High-Pressure Spirit Lamp.

The best form of illum'nent where the gas electric light is not ava lable. The Meta lan gives an intense white light from methylate spirit, is extremely simple to manipulate an perfectly safe.

No. 0. Circular reservoir, holds 8 ozs. spirit **9/1**
,, 1. As illustrated, superior quality .. **14**/
,, 2. Very powerful **23/1**

Stocks Patent Oil Lamp

130 Candle power.

The most powerful oil lamp mad

Gamage's price **18/9**

Postage 6d.

Best 3-wick Lamp

(2in. wide).

For full-sized Lanterns.

Russian Iron Body and Chimney.

Price **4/2**

4-wick ditto.

Price **5/3** Post 4d.

"Holborn" Arc Lamp.

This lamp has been specially made to take the ordinary house current and small pencil carbons, will carry up to 7 amperes, and gives a very fine light. The Outfit is complete with Lamp, Resistance. 2 yards of flexible wire, plug connection, and solid cast trap with brass standard.

Model No. 1.

Carriage paid.

Complete with 100 volt Resistance, **28 6** 250, **39 10** Lamp only, without Flex Tray, **13 6** Extra Resistance, 100 volt, **12**/- 2 0, **24**/- Carbons, per 100, **4** Model No. 2. Fitted with Mechanical Adjustments. Simila to the No. 1 patte but fitted with mechanical raising and lowering gear and lateral adjustments. Co plete, 150 volt resistance, **34**/- 250, **45**/- Lamp only without Flex or Tray, **20**

CINEMATOGRAPH FILMS.

New Non-Flam Photographic Films for Cinematographs. 50 ft. Lengths.

A splendid series of films, each 50 ft. long, selected to give excellent results with the Cinematographs illustrated in this Catalogue.

No. P.
1. Polar bears fighting.
2. Rough sea, Hastings.
3. Feeding pelicans.
4. Snowballing in Switzerland.
5. Our sailor boys.
7. River Thames & Tower Bridge.
8. Salt industry in south of France.
9. Boating on the Thames.
11. Ladies jumping on horseback.
13. An elephant ride.
14. Canadian express train.
15. Sports at Cairo.
16. Tigers.
17. Lions.
18. Giraffes.
19. Fire engines.
20. King leaving Buckingham Palace
21. Marble Arch.
22. Piccadilly Circus.
23. Fishing trip in Canada.
24. Waterloo Bridge and Somerset House.
26. Houses of Parliament.
27. Westminster Bridge.
28. Trafalgar Square.
29. Scottish sword dance.
30. An Irish jig.
31. A scarf dance.
32. An Indian ballet.

No. P.
34. Miss Brown's tea party.
35. His wedding morn.
36. The lunatic's conversation.
37. The strong arm of the law.
38. Road making in Canada.
39. When donkeys meet.
41. Black and white artists.
42. Let's be boys again : Father's ghost.
43. Let's be boys again : A fishing expedition.
44. Polly & the paperhanger
45. An Indian street.
46. Lachine Rapids, Montreal.
47. Trip down St. Lawrence River, Canada,
48. Funeral of King Edward VII.
49. Soldiers riding past.
50. Royal carriages in procession.
51. Canadian scenery.
52. Canoe race & boys diving
53. Buffaloes in the Rockie mountains.
54. Railway ride in France.
55. Lake scenery in Canada.
56. Building a railway in Canada.
57. Harvesting in Canada.

Price **19/10** per film, including title slide. Postage 3d.

List of Films—Cinematograph, Lithographic Coloured.

Fine Long Coloured Films, each about 43½ in. long with Edison Perforation.

No. P. **Series No. I.**
1. The rehearsal.
2. The magic head.
3. The merry clowns.
4. Approaching train.
5. Dancer.
6. Children with cats.

Series No. IV.
1. Clown tricks.
2. Carriage drive.
3. Marionette.
4. Spanish dancer.
5. Winter games.
6. Monkey at breakfast.

Series No. VII.
1. Boxer. [bird cage.
2. Lady conjuror with
3. Baker and professor.
4. Gymnastics on the
5. The stupid dog. [horse
6. Horse racing on the ski-rink.

Series No. X.
1. Leaving the ski-course
2. Teasing at the fountain.
3. Tobogganing.
4. The clumsy waiter.
5. Balloon race.
6. Cycling.

No. P. **Series No. II.**
1. Battleship.
2. Jumping artists.
3. Boys at the spring.
4. Acrobats. [pot.
5. Magician with flower-
6. Child with cat.

Series No. V.
1. Somersault.
2. Performing dogs.
3. The industrious cooper
4. Pierette.
5. Card players.
6. Magician with rabbit.

Series No. VIII.
1. Ski-race.
2. Hare chasing.
3. Fencing lesson.
4. A bet for an apple.
5. Comical street cleaner.
6. Loading stones.

Series No. XI.
1. Leaving the ski-course
2. Man balancing top hat.
3. Clown.
4. The inattentive pupil.
5. The vain cook.
6. Boys on see-saw.

No. P. **Series No. III.**
1. Skater.
2. Magic performance.
3. Tramway.
4. Hard work. [stress.
5. Shortsighted seam-
6. Living wheel-barrow.

Series No. VI.
1. Magician with egg.
2. Playing ball on the ice
3. Throwing bricks.
4. Serpentine dance.
5. Boys bathing.
6. Somersaults.

Series No. IX.
1. Training.
2. Ski-runner.
3. Professional pianist.
4. Circus.
5. Steerable airship in the air.
6. Motor race.

Series No. XII.
1. Winter sport.
2. Pantomime.
3. Fencer on horse-back.
4. The disturbed tea-party.
5. Girl playing diabolo.
6. Kettle-drummer.

P. **Series No. XIII.**
The airship fleet leaving the port.
Bleriot's trial flight.
Zeppelin's flight.
Parceval III and Zeppelin III.
Flying week at Rheims.
Zeppelin flying over imperial train.

No. P. **Series No. XIV.**
1. Discovery of the North Pole.
2. Hunting polar bears.
3. Returning from the North Pole.
4. Cake-walk.
5. Quick artist.
6. Box on the ears.

10d. each. 4/3 per Box of 6 as Series listed. Post 3d.

COLOURED LITHOGRAPHIC SLIDES.

The Holborn Series of 3¼ by 3¼ full-size Lantern Slides. The most complete Series of Lithographic Slides yet published.

1/7½ Per Set of 1 doz. With Reading.

From "Jack the Giant Killer" Set. For Full-size Lanterns. Size 3¼ by 3¼ in.

RELIGIOUS SETS.

No. P. of Set.
17 David, Life of 180 Joseph, Life of
41 Life of Christ, series 1 100 Do., series 2
170 Life of Moses 50 Miracles of Christ
164 Miracles and Life of Christ, Nicodemus, the Last Supper, Martha and Mary, etc.
165 New Testament pictures, further Miracles and the Apostles
166 New Testament pictures, parables, Zachariah in the Temple, etc.
167 Old Testament pictures, Joseph, Ruth, Nebuchadnezzar, Darius, Cyrus, etc.

Postage on single set of Slides, 5d. extra.

RELIGIOUS SETS.

No. P. of Set.
168 Old Testament pictures, Samuel Naaman, Elijah, Elisha, Daniel, etc.
169 Old Testament pictures, Adam and Eve, Noah & the Flood, Tower of Babel, &c.
57 Palestine, series 1 120 ditto, series 2
61 Pictures from the New Testament
62 Pictures from the Old Testament
64 Pilgrim's Progress, series 1 130 ditto, series
69 Prodigal Son, The 84 Stations of the Cross

1/7½ Per Set of 1 doz. With Reading.

TEMPERANCE SETS.

6 Calculating Cobbler, The 9 Cash Thre
39 How Cissie saved her Father
31 Slaves of drink, The 106 Two drunkar
NOTE.—A special long Reading, forming a book itself, entitled "The Calculating Cobbler," can had for 1d. extra.

NURSERY AND FAIRY TALES.

No. P.
201 Aesops' Fables
107 Alladin, series 1 102 Do., series 2
108 Ali Baba, or the Forty Thieves
1 Babes in the wood, The
2 Beauty and the beast
4 Bluebeard 7 Caliph stork, The
14 Cinderella
18 Dick Whittington
22 Dwarf Long Nose
24 Elephant's revenge, The
26 Gulliver's travels, series 1
101 ,, ,, ,, 2
32 House that Jack built
33 Jack and the beanstalk
34 Jack the giant killer
46 John Gilpin 43 Little Muck
83 Marquis Carrabas and his cab
47 Mother Hubbard
59 Phantom ship
68 Precocious piggies, The
70 Punch and Judy
71 Puss in boots
72 Pussy's road to ruin
73 Red Riding Hood
75 Reynard the fox, series 1
109 ,, ,, ,, 2
76 Robinson Crusoe, series 1
110 Do., series 2 111 Do., series 3
78 Santa Claus
80 Sinbad the sailor, series 1
103 ,, ,, ,, 2
83 St. George and the dragon
85 Swiss Family Robinson
87 The three bears
88 The tiger and the tub
89 Tom Thumb and his seven brothers

COMIC SETS.

21 Don Quixote 23 Educated cats
25 Fine Art Gallery
27 Handy Andy
35 Jackdaw of Rheims
36 Jackie Marlingspike
51 Mischievous Tommy

No. P.
60 Pickwick, Scenes from
66 Pompey's joys and sorrows
67 Poor "Jerimi"
90 Utopia (the world governed by law 1,000 years hence)
93 Naughty Normau, the boy who would not be photographed
94 Belle Bilton and her bicycle
95 The Artist and the musician
105 Rain while you wait
171 Baker and the tarred fence
172 Rival billposters
173 A lively snowball
174 Doctor's boy and the whitewasher
175 The crocodile, elephant and the monkeys
176 The sailor and the donkey
209 The Magic Lamp and the Genii

TRAVELS, INTERESTING and EDUCATIONAL SETS

No. P. 111 Africa, Life in
113 American Views, series 1, American cities, etc.
152 American Views, series 2, opium dens, mammoth caves, etc.
153 American Views, series 3, Indian encampments, etc.
154 American Views, series 4, Negro scenes, etc.
182 Arctic circle 115 Arctic regions
116 Arctic expedition
8 Canadian Life
10 Celebrated castles, palaces, etc., series 1
155 Celebrated castles, palaces, etc., series 2
11 Celebrated places of the World
145 Centinental views
200 Churches, Monuments and Places of Interest in Paris
19 Discovery of America by Columbus
No. P. 114 Effect slides, day and night scenes, series 1, Houses of Parliament, Niagra Falls, etc.

No. P.
157 Effect slides, day and night scenes, series 2, The Tower of London, Cologne Cathedral, etc.
158 Effect slides, day and night scenes, series 3, Venice, Eddystone lighthouse, etc.
104 Emigrants' voyage, The
63 Ireland, Views of
40 Land of the pigtail
42 Life on board an ocean palace
44 London views (modern), series 1
121 ,, ,, ,, ,, 2
45 ,, ,, (old London)
52 Natural history, animals, series 1
99 ,, ,, ,, ,, 2
159 ,, ,, birds ,, 1
160 ,, ,, ,, ,, 2
161 ,, ,, Reptiles ,, 1
162 ,, ,, ,, ,, 2
117 Natural phenomena, series 1
118 Do., series 2 128 Do., series 3
54 Nile, On the banks of the
56 Overland route to India, series 1
98 ,, ,, ,, ,, 2
86 Switzerland, series 1
163 ,, ,, 2
205 Tour Round the World, series 1
206 ,, ,, ,, ,, 2
207 ,, ,, ,, ,, 3
208 ,, ,, ,, ,, 4
177 Bonny Scotland

MISCELLANEOUS SUBJECTS.

204 The Dragon of Rhodes
146 Life and death of Queen Victoria
147 Life of King Edward, series 1
148 ,, ,, ,, 2
48 Mottoes, Good-night, Welcome, Merry Xmas, God save the King, Interval, Happy New Year, Silence, etc., series 1
184 Mottoes, different illustrations of above, series 2

MILITARY SUBJECTS.

No. P.
12 Charge of the Light Brigade, a Life in the Army
129 Heroes of the Victoria Cross
37 Jessie's Dream, or the Relief Lucknow 53 Nellie's pray
202 The Story of the Bell, series 1
203 ,, ,, ,, 2

DEEDS OF HEROISM, SENTIMENTAL, etc.

119 Adventures with wild beasts
3 Binger on the Rhine
5 Bob the fireman
13 Christmas Carol, A (Dickens)
16 Curfew must not ring to-night
29 Dogs and monks of St. Bernard
28 Heroes of the lifeboat
181 How Jane Conquest rang the be
96 Jack's treasure, a London waif
135 Loved unto death, series 1
136 ,, ,, ,, 2
55 On the brink. Tale of Monte Ca
58 Paul and Virginia
133 Peter the fisherman, series 1
134 ,, ,, ,, 2
65 Pilot's story
97 Poor Tom : A boy's temptatio
74 Reuben Davidger, or captured pirates 77 Romeo and Ju
79 Settler's life among the Indians
82 Soudan, Life in the
91 Village Blacksmith, The
92 Western pioneers and life amon Indians

NOTE.—A special Service of Song B with words and music can be had "Peter the fisherman" and "Lo unto death." Price 4d. each.

Projection Postcards.

Owners of picture postcard projectors have long experienced the want for sets coloured postcards which illustrate tales familiar to the young. The Primus Jun Lecturer Postcards fill this want ; they are made up in sets of eight, each of which form complete story, and are supplied with either reading or wording on cards so that no difficu need be experienced in explaining the pictures.

The cards are lithographed in light colours and show up well on the screen :

Set No.		Set No.	
1	Sweep and Whitewasher	11	British Army, Chap. I.
2	Foolish Bird	12	British Army, Chap. II.
3	Elephant's Revenge	13	British Navy, Chap. I.
4	Tiger and Tub	14	British Navy, Chap. II.
5	Ten Little Nigger Boys	15	Lifeboatmen
6	Robinson Crusoe	16	Firemen
7	Aladdin	17	British Express Trains
8	Peter Pan, Chap. I.	18	Doré Bible, Chap. I.
9	Peter Pan, Chap. II.	19	Doré Bible, Chap. II.
10	Peter Pan, Chap. III.	20	Doré Bible, Chap. III.

Price per ser of 8 .. .. **11½d.** (A)

With printed Reading complete in carton.

Full Size Lantern Slides.
New Series of Lithographic Lantern Slides.

These Slides are vastly superior in quality to the ordinary Lithographic Slides, and being made up in smaller sets they are bound to be more useful for Children's Amusement. Size 3¼ in. square. These sets are arranged in two series: SERIES **A** have the matter printed in bold letters on the slides, thus dispensing with reading; SERIES **B** are complete with Readings in each box.

NEW SERIES. JUST OUT. 3¼ by 3¼ in. 2/6 per set of 8 slides.

Life of King Edward. 2/- Set.
No. P. 791. Chapter I. Early Life.
,, P. 792. ,, II. A Popular Prince.
,, P. 793. ,, III. Edward the Peacemaker.
,, P. 794. ,, IV. The King is Dead : Long Live the King.

Peter Pan. 2/6 Set.
An abridged edition of Mr. J. M. Barrie's delightful story "Peter Pan," and is published by permission. The slides are produced from photographs by Messrs. Ellis and Walery.
No. P. 773. Chapter I. Nursery to Never Never Land.
,, P. 774. ,, II. Never Never Land.
,, P. 775. ,, III. Peter and Pirates.

Dore Bible. 2/- Set.
No. P. 785. Chapter I. Bible Heroes.
,, P. 786. ,, II. The Life of Jesus.
,, P. 787. ,, III. Christ the Teacher.

Boy Scouts. 2/6 Set.
Three Chapters—In Camp with Baden-Powell. Campaigning. Scouts, Law and Chivalry.

British Battleships. 2/6 Set.
Three Chapters—No. P. 799. The Dreadnoughts.
No. P. 780. The Cruiser Life Aboard.
,, P. 781. Destroyers and Submarines.

The Conquest of the Air. 2/6 Set.
No. P. 795. Chapter I. Balloons
,, P. 796. ,, II. Air Ships.
,, P. 797. ,, III. Aeroplanes.

Uncle Tom's Cabin. 2/- Set.
No. P. 801. Chapter I. Mr. Shelby sells Uncle Tom.
,, P. 802. ,, II. Eva and Uncle Tom.
,, P. 803. ,, III. Legree's Plantation.

Alice in Wonderland.
This is an abridged story from the world-famous "Alice's Adventures in Wonderland," and is published by permission of Messrs. Macmillan & Co., Ltd. The slides produced from Sir John Tenniel's original drawings.
No. P. 776. Chapter I. Down the Rabbit Hole.
,, P. 777. ,, II. Mad Tea Party.
,, P. 778. ,, III. Who Stole Tarts.

Series D. 3¼ by 3¼. **Water Babies.**
The best thing ever done in inexpensive Slides. A delightful fairy story from the beautiful story of Chas. Kingsley, re-produced from the drawings of Warwick Goble, by permission of Messrs. Macmillan and Co., Ltd.
P. 1. Tom and his Master meet the Irishwoman
P. 2. Tom runs away from the Nurse
P. 3. Tom sees a clear stream
P. 4. Tom turned into a Water Baby
P. 5. The Fairy Queen protects Tom from the angry Trout
P. 6. Tom sees a Gorgeous Dragon-Fly
P. 7. Tom watches the Moonlight on the River
P. 8. Past the Great Town
P. 9. Tom sees the Sea Anemones
P. 10. A Lobster for a Playfellow
P. 11. The Fairies Fixing Wings on Elsie
P. 12. Tom finds another Water Baby
P. 13. The Fairy Isle of St. Brandans
P. 14. Tom frightens the Crabs
P. 15. Mrs. Be-done by-as-you-did tells Tom to behave himself
P. 16. Tom and the Good Fairy
P. 17. Tom finds where the Sea Bull's Eyes are kept
P. 18. Tom asks the way of the last of the Gair Fowl
P. 19. The Fairies carry the Shipwrecked Baby to their home
P. 20. The Ice Fairies on Shiny Wall. 21. Tom sees Mother Carey
P. 22. The Great Sea Serpent lying dead
P. 23. In the Legs of a Great Bogey
P. 24. Grimes stuck fast in the Chimney
Price **10/6** per set of 24 Slides, in handsome carrying case. Carriage 1/- extra.

Series "A."

No.		No.	
P. 500	Sweep the Whitewasher	P. 509	The Elephant's revenge
P. 501	Willie's Revenge	P. 510	Mr. and Mrs. Brown and the Mouse
P. 502	Never ride a strange Horse	P. 511	Puss in Boots
P. 503	Nursery Rhymes	P. 512	Jack and the Beanstalk
P. 504	How Jing-Jing bagged his Quarry	P. 513	Old Mother Hubbard
P. 505	Gag-Jag the Rejecter	P. 514	The Tiger and the Tub
P. 506	Where there's a will there's way	P. 515	Ten Little Nigger Boys
		P. 516	A Frog he would a-Wooing
P. 507	The foolish Bird and the artful Hedgehog	P. 517	Hey ! diddle, diddle [go
P. 508	Jack the Giant Killer	P. 518	There was an Old Woman
		P. 519	Sing a Song of Sixpence

Size 3¼ by 3¼ in. Price **2/-** per Set of 8 Slides.

Series "B."

P. 601	A Country Courtship	P. 743	Our Colonies, India
P. 602	The death and burial of Cock Robin.	P. 744	,, ,, South Africa
		P. 732/33	Gulliver's Travels (2 chaps.)
P. 603	Red Riding Hood	P. 745/50	Animals (6 chaps.)
P. 606	Living Statuary	P. 751/53	Birds (3 chaps.)
P. 607	Caudle's Curtain Lectures	P. 754/56	Reptiles (3 chaps.)
P. 608	Comical Cats and Dogs	P. 760/62	Sea Animals (3 chaps.)
P. 609	Every-day Street Sounds	P. 757/59	Butterflies and Moths (3 chaps.)
P. 610	John Gilpin		
P. 611	Robinson Crusoe	P. 765	Cinderella
P. 712/13	The British Army (2 chaps.)	P. 763	The House that Jack
P. 714/15	The British Navy (2 chaps.)	P. 764	The Three Bears [Built
P. 716	Our Lifeboatmen	P. 766/8	Children's Life of Jesus (3 chaps.)
P. 717	Our Firemen		
P. 722	Brave Deeds	P. 769/70	Æsop's Fables (2 chaps.)
P. 723	Birds and their Nests	P. 771	Sindbad the Sailor
P. 724	Wild Animals & how hunted	P. 772	Aladdin
P. 725/6	Views of London (2 chaps.)	P. 613	Robin Hood
P. 729/31	Japan and its People (3 chaps.)	P. 614	The Babes in the Wood
		P. 615	Ali Baba & the 40 Thieves
P. 740	Our Colonies, Canada	P. 616	Pied Piper of Hamelin
P. 741	,, ,, New Zealand	P. 798	Famous British Locos.
P. 742	,, ,, Australia	P. 799	British Express Trains
		P. 788/90	Pilgrims Progress

Size 3¼ by 3¼ in. Price **2/-** per set of 8 slides.

Famous Pictures of the World.

A **Series of choice subjects**, illustrating the old masters, collected from the Galleries of Europe. The work of reproduction has been carried out in a most lavish manner to faithfully portray the originals.

Per Set of 8 Slides 3¼ by 3¼ in., with Printed Reading, price **4/-**
Postage 4d.

The complete set of 80 Slides is supplied in handsome polished mahogany transit case, lined inside with felt, and hinged in centre for convenience when exhibiting, the slides being transferred from one side to the other. With snap fastenings and carrying handle.
Price **40/-** complete. Carriage 1/- extra.

A reading for the complete set of 80 Slides is also published.
Price .. **6**d. Postage 1d.

No. P. 800.
Illustrated History of the Union Jack.

P. 1. Title Slide showing the complete "Union Jack"
P. 2. Flag of St. George for England of the Royal Navy
P. 3. Flag of St. Andrew for Scotland
P. 4. Flag of St. George and St. Andrew combined
P. 5. Flag of St. Patrick of Ireland
P. 6. Flag of St. George, St. Andrew and St. Patrick combined
Per set of 6 slides .. **1/9**

Postage on Single sets of slides, 4d.

MECHANICAL LANTERN SLIDES.

Lightning Lantern Slide Carrier.
Mahogany, **11**d.   Mahogany, with Raising Lever, **1/2** each.
Postage 2d.

Slipping Slides.
With metal frames, for Magic Lanterns, per box of 1 doz. Comic subjects.
1¾ & 1⅝   1⅞   2   2⅜   2¾ in.
2/6   3/-   4/-   5/6   7/-   Post 4d. doz

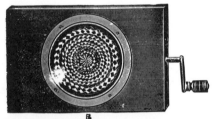

Rackwork Slides.
Chromotrope, double rack frame, producing a remarkable combination of coloured effects, by revolving process, hand-painted photographic, **8/-** each.   Post **3d.** each.

Movable Skipping Slides.
Hand-painted, **3/-**   Post 3d. each.

Chromotrope Set.
Consisting of 6 pairs coloured discs, producing a variety of different effects; also Rackwork Carrier Frame. The discs can easily be removed at will. Price, complete in wood box for full-sized lanterns, **17/6**   Post 9d.

We have an exceptionally large and varied selection of Lantern Slides, Topical Up-to-date Subjects, Humorous, Pathetic, Scientific, &c., to suit every class of audience.
For 'XMAS ENTERTAINMENTS the Magic Lantern is unrivalled, and we have all the popular Slides Illustrating Fairy Tales with readings, Comic Tales with readings, and technical slides.

Fig. 5.   Movable Lever Slides.
In Wood Frames.   Comic Subjects.
1¾   2   2¼   3⅞   3½ in. wide.
7d.   **9**d.   **1/-**   **1/2**   **1/4** each.   Post 4d. doz.

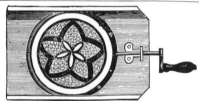

Fig 7.   Mechanical Lantern Slides,
Chromotrope.   Post 3d. each.
2 in., **10½**d.   2¾ in., **1/1**   4 in., **1/9** each.
A variety of other effects.

Changing Comic Slipping Slides.
With mahogany frames.   Suitable for full-size Lanterns, **6/-** doz.   Post 1/- doz.

Fig. 8.   Lithographic Chromotrope Rackwork Slides.
For full-sized Lanterns, **1/9** each.   Post 4d. each.

Double Rackwork Chromotropes
Assorted designs.   Coloured Lithographic.
2/- each.   Post 1/- doz.

Lantern Slide Carriers.
Carrier, giving dissolving effect, as illustration .. **9/10**   Postage 4d.

Fig. 9.   Mechanical Rackwork Lantern Slides.   (Fire Scene).
2   2¼   2¾   3⅛   3½ in.
1/4   1/6   1/9   1/11   2/2 ea.   Post 2d. ea.
A variety of other effects.

Rackwork Slides (best quality).
Hand-painted, photographic, double movement. "Man Swallowing Rats," etc., **8/-** each.   Post **3d.** each.

Movable Slides.
Hand-painted Comic subjects.   Very amusing.
1/4 each.   Post 3d. each.

Mechanical Rackwork Set.
Consisting of 6 hand-painted Lantern Slide (full-size), 6 pairs of Coloured discs, and Rackwork Carrier Frame. The slides are inserted at the top of carrier, and 2 of the discs, 1 on either side, are used in conjunction with each, which revolve around the fixed slide, producing a beautiful and life-like effect. The discs can easily be removed at will. Price, complete in wood box, **25/-** for full-sized Lanterns.   Postage 9d.

"KODAKS" as Christmas Presents.

The Folding Pocket Kodaks.

All Kodak Goods

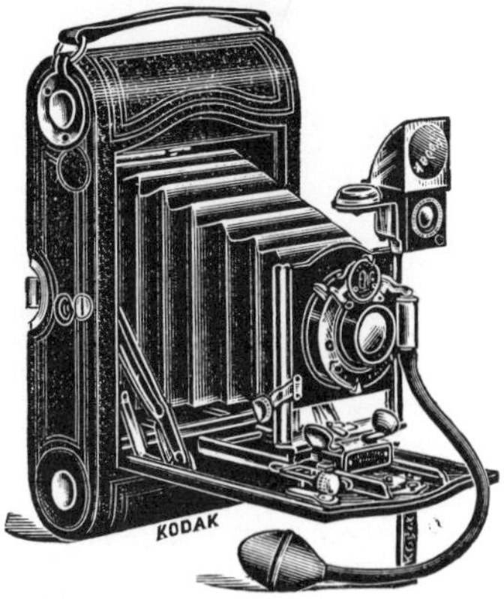

sent Post Free.

The Folding Pocket Kodaks range in size from the No. P. 1, which akes a picture 3¼ by 2¼ ins., to the No. P. 4a, which takes a picture 6½ by ¼ ins. These Kodaks are of the best workmanship throughout. They re fitted with good quality lenses and shutters and all movemennts ecessary to first-class picture-making. They have no complicated adjust-nents aud the working of any of the Folding Pocket Kodaks can be nastered in half-an-hour.

Io, P. 1 takes pictures 3¼ by 2¼ ins. **42/-**	No P. 1a takes pictures 4¼ by 2½ ins. **50/-**	No. P. 3 takes pictures 4¼ by 3¼ ins. **72/6**
Io. P. 3a takes pictures 5½ by 3¼ ins. **90/-**	No. P. 4 takes pictures 5 by 4 ins. **90/-**	No. P. 4a takes pictures 6½ by 4¼ ins. **147/-**

Vith Kodak Auto Shutter } No. P. 3, **85/-**; No. P. 4, **102/6**; No. P. 4a, **102/6**

All Folding Pocket Kodaks can be fitted with special anastigmat lenses. Prices on application.

Nos. P. 1 and P. 2 "Brownie" Outfits.

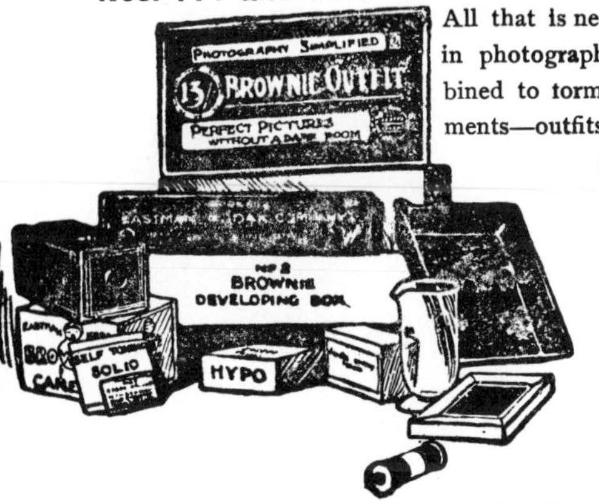

All that is necessary for a start in photography has been combined to torm complete equipments—outfits that, requiring no dark room, can be taken up by anybody without the slightest experience, and with the confidence that he will be able to produce pictures of a high degree of excellence.

The 13/6 Brownie Outfit.

ncludes No. P. 1 Brownie for 2¼ by 2¼ pictures, film for 6 pictures, the ew Brownie Daylight Developing Box and all necessary paper, chemicals nd accessories.

No. P. 2 Brownie Outfit.

ncludes the No 2Brownie, for 3¼ by 2¼ pictures, and details as above. Price **18/6**

he Nos. P. 1, P. 2, P. 2a and P. 3 'Brownie' Kodaks.

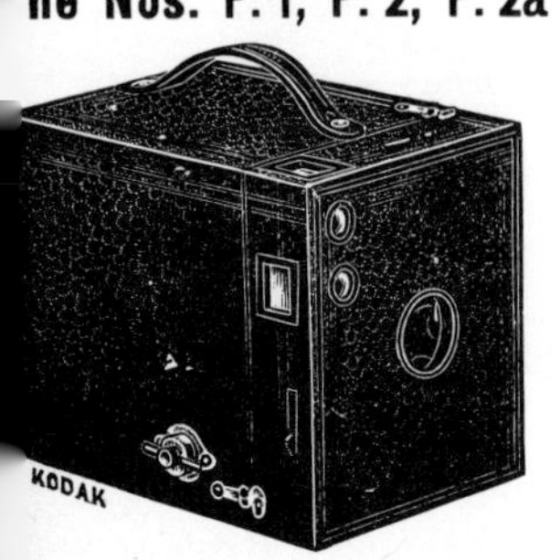

The No. P. 1 Brownie gives six 2¼ by 2¼ pictures, and the No. P. 2 Brownie six 3¼ by 2¼ pictures without reloading. The No. P. 2a Brownie gives 4¼ by 2½ pictures, and takes spools for either six or twelve exposures. The No. P. 3 Brownie gives pictures 4¼ by 3¼, and takes spools for either six or twelve exposures. The No. P. 2, No. P. 2a, and No. P. 3 models have each a pair of finders, showing exactly the extent of view embraced by the film.

For the No. P. 1 Brownie, we supply a self-attaching finder at a small extra ost of 1/-

No. P. 1 .. **5/-** No. P. 2 .. **10/-** No. P. 2a .. **12/6** No. P. 3 .. **17/6**

The Vest Pocket Kodak, for Roll Films only.

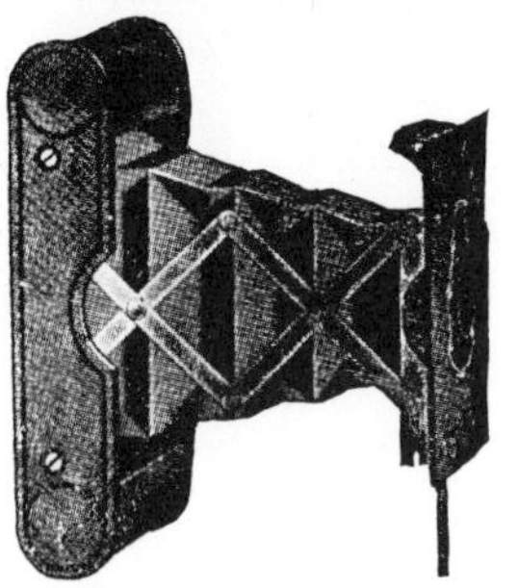

The smallest Kodak made, so flat and smooth as to go easily into the waistcoat pocket, yet giving a thoroughly good sharp picture (4½ by 1⅝ in.), and one that can be enlarged to postcard size with the help of the Vest Pocket Kodak Enlarger, or to a still greater size by the usual methods. No focussing is required; the camera is practically always ready for action, one second being sufficient for the pulling out of the front.

The Shutter is the Kodak ball-bearing, and the lens a meniscus achromatic of exceptional quality. The body of camera is made of metal, with black enamel finish, and the bellows are of black leather.

All difficulties of estimating exposure are removed by the Autotime Scale which is fitted to the front of the Kodak.

The Vest Pocket Kodak is not only for those who have never taken a picture before, but is also for past masters in photography

Takes a picture 2½ by 1⅝ in. Capacity, 8 exposures without re-loading. Size of Kodak, 4¾ by 2½ by 1 in. Weight, 8½ oz. Fitted with meniscus achromatic lens, 3 in. focus, Kodak ball bearing shutter, giving exposures of 1/25th and 1/30th sec., as well as time and bulb. Automatic scale, Iris diaphragm and brilliant reversible finder.

	£	s.	d.
Price of Vest Pocket Kodak, in Black Leather Case	**£1**	**10**	**0**
Ditto, in Velvet Calf Case	**1**	**12**	**6**
Ditto, in Finest Crushed Morocco Case	**1**	**16**	**0**
N.C. Film Cartridge, 8 Exposures	0	0	10
Vest Pocket Kodak Film Tank	0	10	0
Tank Developing Powders, per packet of 6	0	0	6
Vest Pocket Kodak Enlarger...	0	7	6
Portrait Attachment	0	1	6

The "Ensignette" Pocket Camera.

REDUCED IN PRICE AND GREATLY IMPFOVED.

The "Ensignette" is now made in 2 sizes—The No. P. 1 "Ensignette" (**21/-**) which measures when closed 3⅞ by 1⅞ in and is only ⅜ in. in thickness and yet gives negatives 2¼ by 1½ in. in diameter.

The No. P. 2 "Ensignette" (**31/6**), measurng when closed 5 by 2¾ in. by ⅞ in. in thickness and giving pictures 3 in. by 2 in.i

With the **21/-** and **31/6** "Ensignettes" there is no focussing to bother about. Everything is sharp, bright and clear, from objects 6 feet away right to the horizon. Unless snapshot exposures are made in dark and deeply shaded places, every picture taken with the "Ensignette" will be a successful one. There need be no failures, and if one is quite a beginner at photography good crisp pictures will be obtained even from the very first spool.

The Watch Pocket Carbine.

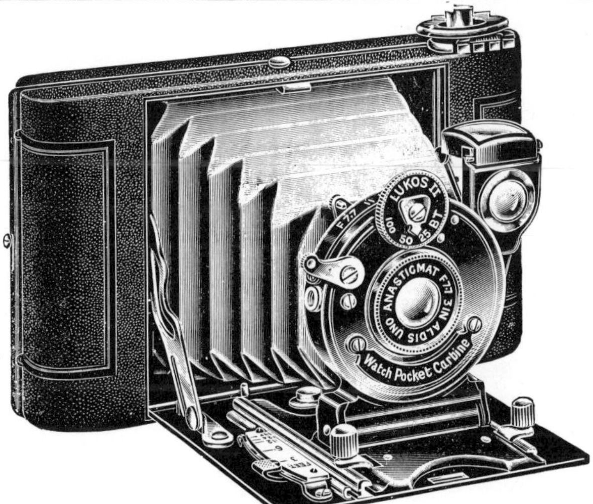

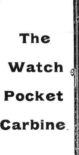

The Perfect Miniature Camera. Takes pictures on roll films 2¼ by 2¼ the universal size. A perfectly designed miniature roll film Camera with every essential adjustment and movement. The Camera is made entirely of metal, has a folding baseboard, Lukos speeded shutter, focussing movement and Aldis Uno Anastigmat lens f7·7. There is a large brilliant finder. Every part is constructed in a solid and rigid manner. It takes the standard 2¼ by 2¼ films so that any make can be used, and supplies obtained everywhere.

	Model I. With Lukos Shutter	Model II. With Compound Shutter
Aldis Uno Anastigmat f/7.7	**£2 5 0**	**£3 7 6**
Beck Mutar f/4·9	—	**4 17 6**
Zeiss "Triotar" f/6·3	4 10 0	**5 12 6**
Cooke f/5·6..	—	**6 15 0**
Ross Homocentric f/6·8		**7 5 0**
Dallmeyer "Carfac" f/6·3		**7 0 0**
Zeiss "Tessar" f/6·3		**7 10 0**
Goerz Dagor f/6·8		**8 15 0**

Accessories.

Leather wrist case with shoulder extension **3/-**
Enlarger for enlarging up to ½ plate.. .. .. **7/6**

Full Catalogue of Cameras post free. All Cameras on this page sent post free.

BINOCULAR and THEATRE GLASSES. Ideal Christmas Presents.

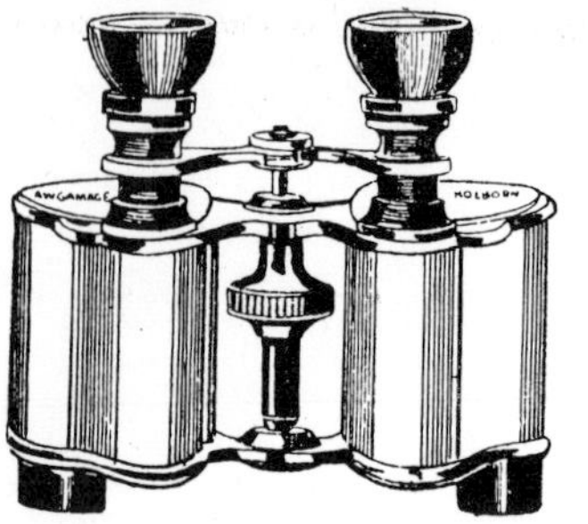

The Gamage Prism Binocular.

A first-rate Binocular at half usual price, giving a magnification of 8 times, with brilliant definition and exceptionally large field; has simultaneous focussing and convenient eye distance adjustments, and focussing eyepiece. The mechanical construction is perfect and finish elegant.

Price including Leather Case and Sling

8 magnifications **67/-**
12 ,, ... **80/-**

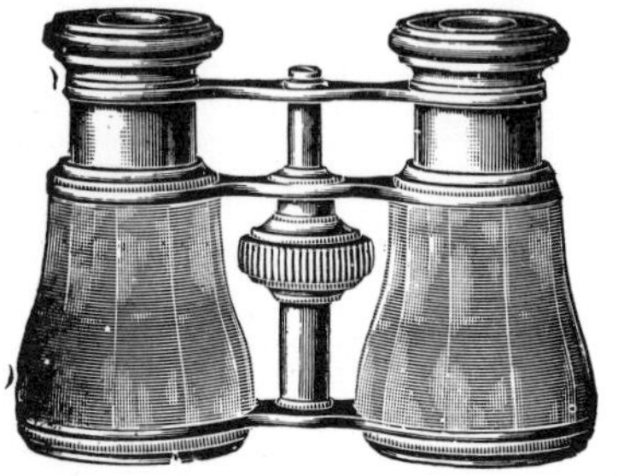

Fancy Pearl and Aluminium Opera Glass.

Diameter of object Glass..	$1\frac{1}{8}$	$1\frac{3}{8}$ in.
	27/6	**31/6**
Best qlty. 12 lens, as illus.	**67/6**	**72/6**

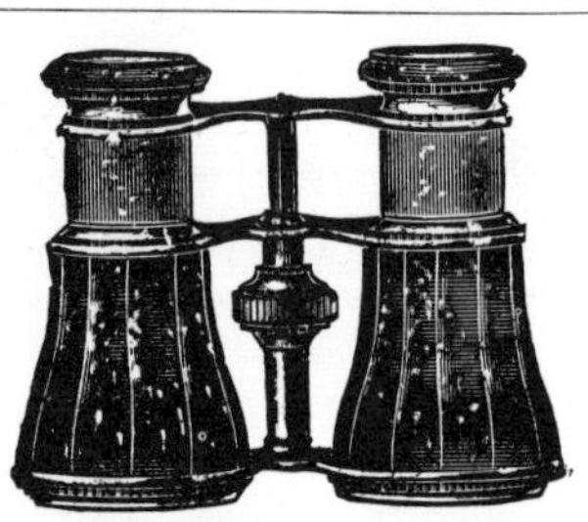

Pearl Opera Glasses.

Suitable for Presents. Splendid Value. In case, complete.

Small size, **10/6** Medium size, **13/6**
Large size, **14/6** Do., 12 lens, **35/-**

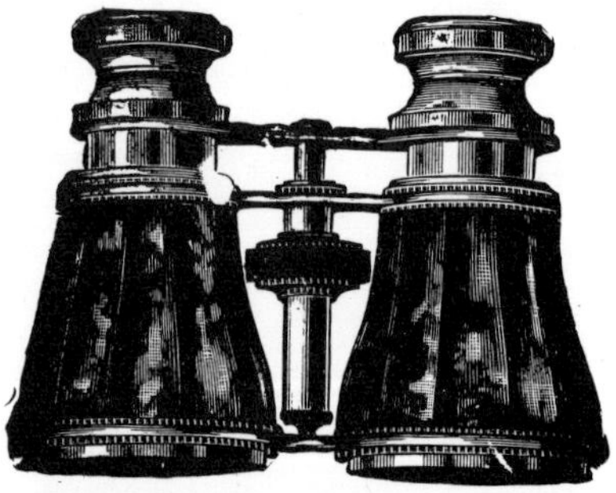

Fancy Pearl and Aluminium Opera. Very best make and finish.

Diam. of object glass ...	$1\frac{1}{8}$ in.	$1\frac{3}{8}$ in.	$1\frac{1}{2}$ in.
Price	**67/6**	**72/6**	**82/6**

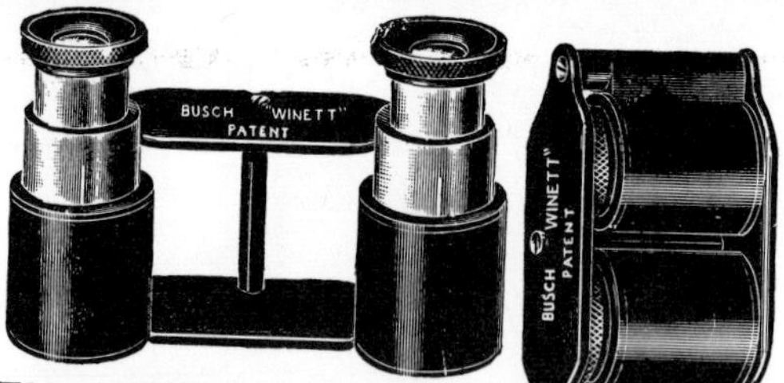

The "Winnet" Pocket Binocular.

Open Ready for Use.

Is the most wonderful little instrument ever put before the public. It embodies in the smallest possible form, features that are usually found only in binoculars both expensive and bulky. It folds up like a small pocket magnifying glass, and can be carried with less inconvenience than a purse. The magnifying power equals that of many binoculars of the old type, and the definition and other optical qualities are of the very best. An ingenious arrangement permits the adjustment of the occulars to any pupillary distance. For normal vision the glass can be opened out ready focussed for instant use, and an adjustment is provided by means of which any difference in the power of the two eyes can be allowed for. Never before has an aid to vision been offered to the public in a form so novel and compact as to warrant its universal use. As a constant companion on land, sea and racecourse, in the football, hunting and battle field, as well as the theatres it will be found invaluable.

Price, in Snap Leather Case **25/-**

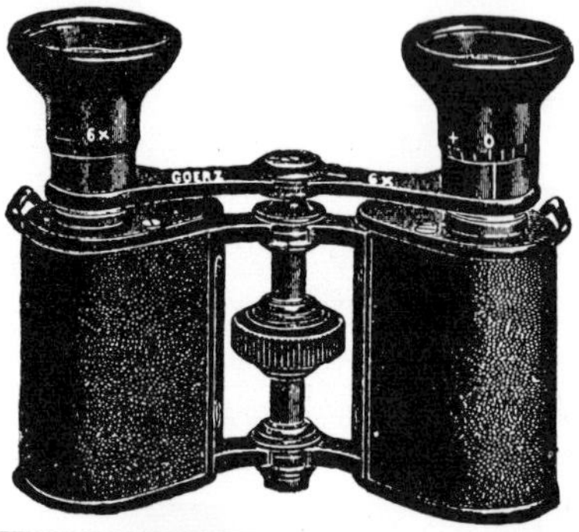

Goerz "Pagor."

A New Prism Binocular.

Very light and portable.

6 magnification, **£6 10**

8 ditto. **£7 0 0**

10 ditto, **£8 0 0**

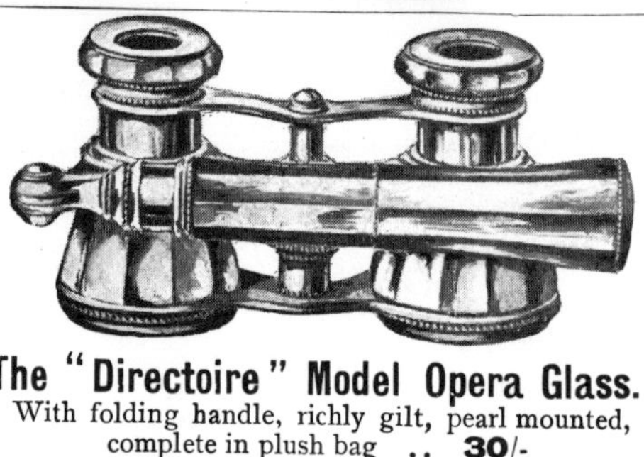

The "Directoire" Model Opera Glass.

With folding handle, richly gilt, pearl mounted, complete in plush bag .. **30/-**
Ditto, aluminium and pearl **37/-**
Ditto, tortoiseshell **40/-**

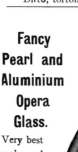

Fancy Pearl and Aluminium Opera Glass.

Very best make and finish. High magnification. Complete in leather vanity bag .. **47/6**

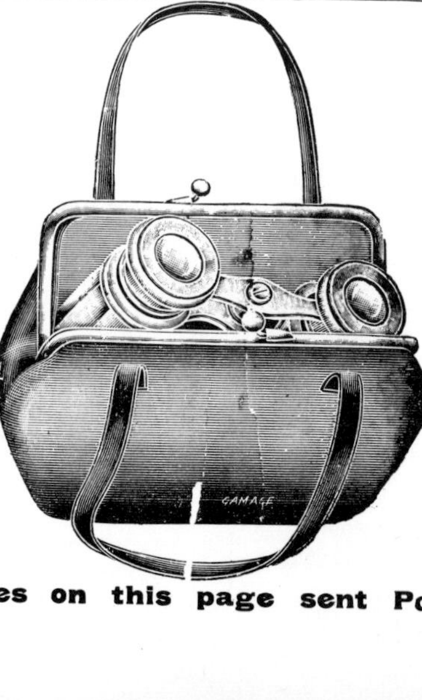

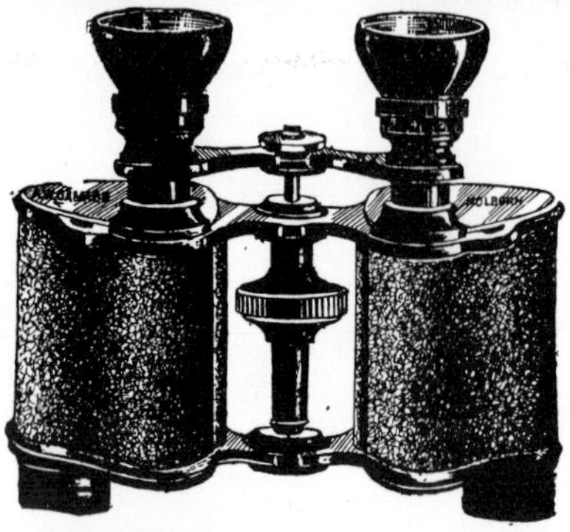

The GAMAGE Stereoscopic Binocular.

X 8. A new pattern Prism Binocular, giving perfe steeroscopic vision and greater illumination than o 1911 Model. Magnifying X 8 times, has the separa eye focussing, and adjustable wheel focussing Ea glass is carefully tested before being sent out from o works. Complete in Leather Cas .. **£3 18**

Theatre Glasses.

X 3 times **63/-**

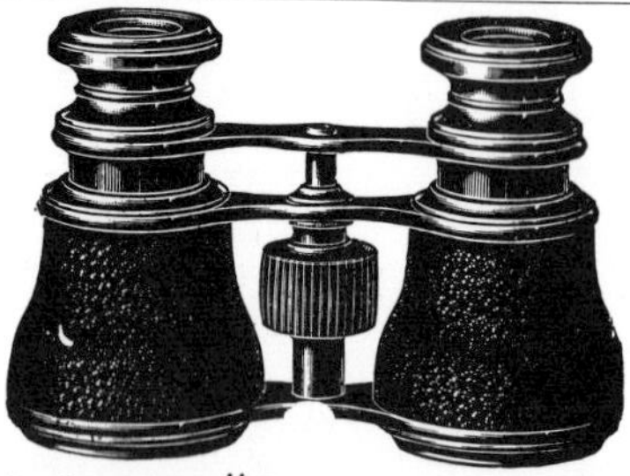

Voigtlander "Tannhauser" Opera.

Aluminium mounts, morocco covered.
Magnifying 3 diameters. Price .. **£2 10 0**

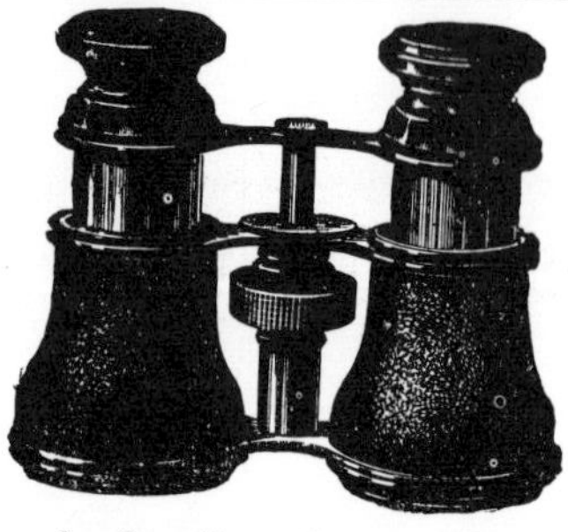

Good Quality Opera Glass.

Japanned brass, morocco covered.

Diameter of object glass—			
$1\frac{1}{8}$	$1\frac{1}{8}$	$1\frac{1}{8}$	$1\frac{1}{8}$ in
6/9	**7/6**	**9/-**	**10/-**
Superior quality Lenses—			
12/6	**14/-**	**15/6**	**18/6**

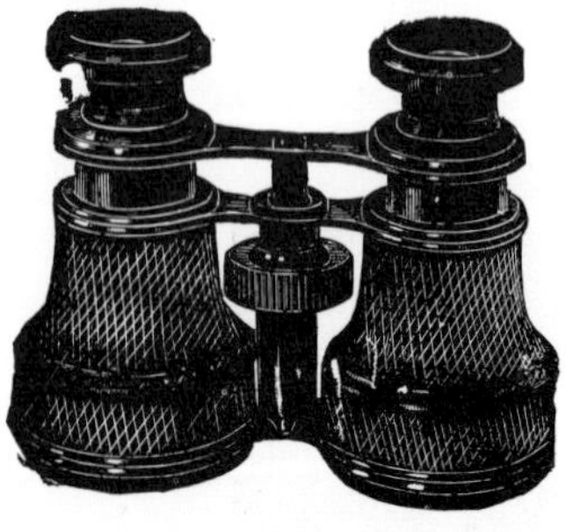

Special Line.

Medium size Field or Opera Glass, Russia co in Sling Case **12/6**
Worth 21/-

All Glasses on this page sent Post Free.

Aneroid Gift Barometers.

A remarkable example of Value.

No. 56. Carved Oak Barometer and Thermometer combined.

Guaranteed for two years.

Height 33½ in. Width 10½ in.

17/6

No. 156. Carved Oak Aneroid Barometer and Thermometer combined.

Height 34 in. Width 11 in.

£1 5 0

No. 24. Height 36½ in. Width 13 in. Carved Oak Aneroid Barometer & Thermometer. **47/6**

Solid Mahogany Inlaid Design with Silvered Dials. Best London movement. **58/6**

No. 52. Height 37 in. Width 13½ in. Mahogany Inlaid Aneroid Barometer and Thermometer. Very effective design. Sheraton style. **£2 18 6**

The Miniature Pocket Tourist Set.

Fig. P. 17.

Aneroid Barometer and Transparent Compass in Snap Pigskin Case.

Oxydised	.. ..	**£3 10 0**
H.M. Silver ..	..	**£5 0 0**
Gold	from	**£8 10 0**

No. 49. Carved Polished Oak Aneroid Barometer. China dial. Diameter, 9½ in., **18/-** 11¼ in., **21/-**

No. 51.

Carved Polished Oak Aneroid Barometer.

Diam.
6½ in. **10/6**
7½ in. **12/6**
9¼ in. **15/-**
11 in. **17/6**

A choice assortment of other patterns on show.

Fancy Wood Aneroid Inlaid Design Assorted Patterns.

English-made Walnut Inlaid Aneroid. Very special value. 6½ in., porcelain dial. .. in. over all, **32/6** Plain Oak, **25/-**

With open front porcelain dial. 8½ in. over all, **15/6** 9½ in., **16/3** Post 9d.

New Pattern Aneroid. Mounted on fancy coloured polished wood framed.

3½ in. diam. over all, **4/6** each ⎫ Postage
,, ,, ,, **6/6** ,, ⎭ 6d. extra.

Rustic Weather Houses.

As illustrated **3/11**

Cheaper Models, **2/3** & **1/4½**

Postage 4d.

Carriage extra outside L. P. D. Co.'s Radius.

Stereoscopes and Monoscopes for Presents.

Graphoscope and Stereoscope combined.

4 in. lens, **14/-**   5 in., **23/6**
6 in. ,, **32/6**   Postage 9d

Monocle Graphoscopes.
Various Woods.

4 in. diam., **10/-**   5 in., **20/-**
Postage 9d.

Best wood, with folding handle,
1/2 each.
Ditto, with velvet bound hood
2/5 each

The "Perfectoscope."

Handsomely made throughout in aluminium, with polished sliding view holder, large size prisms in metal mounts with shaped plush covered edge to hood.

Price **4/11**. Postage 4d.
Stands for hand stereoscopes,
6d. each. Post 2d.

Stereoscopic Slides.
In great variety.

"Universal" Series, opaque, all countries, from photos. **4/6** doz
The "S.P." Series. Large variety English Views and Comics **3/6**
English Views on P.O.P. paper, best quality, well selected **6/-**
Views of almost any subject can be supplied at **6/-** per doz.
Postage 2d. doz.

Hand Stereoscopes.
(American model).

Revolving Stereoscope
To hold 50 views.
Price **45/-**   Carriage extra.

Folding Stereoscope
Handy for pocket.

Price .. **3/6**

Postage 2d.

Box-Form Stereoscopes.

Box-form mahogany, with glass reflector	**3/-**
Polished walnut, with glass reflector, superior	**5/-**
Polished walnut, with ebonised eye-pieces	**7/6**
Polished walnut, with opera adjustment well-finished ..	**11/6**
Superior quality walnut Stereoscope, with shaped body and large ebonised mounted eye-pieces	**18/-**
Walnut Stereoscope, with large lenses, fitted with opera adjustment and side rack movement	**20/-**
Superior walnut Stereoscope, extra large Prisms, shaped body, rack focussing, and adjustment for width of eyes	

Postage 6d.

Brass Pocket Microscopes having a magnification of 50 times complete in handsome polished wood box, with 3 mounted objects, 2 Slides and 1 Carity Slide and full instructions.

To clear at

2/9 each.

Postage 2d.

Special Selection of 'Xmas Telescopes and Microscopes.

No. 296.	Tubular Microscope, in polished case, 1 power **4/11**	Post 4d.
,, 297.	Ditto, 3 power ..	,, 4d. **7/6**
,, 299.	Column do., 2 power .. **11/6**	,, 6d.
,, 280.	Ditto, with rack .. **16/6**	,, free.

Microscopic Slides for the above :—
Assorted objects .. .. **2/-** per dozen.
Better quality for large Microscopes,
3 in. by 1 in., **4/6 6/6** and **11/6**
Unmounted Objects .. .. **11**d. per box of 12.
Micrometer Slide .. .. .. **2/6** Post 4d.

BOOK ON MICROSCOPE.
Common Objects of the Microscope **1/-** Post 2d.

Cabinets for Microscopic Slides, polished pine.

To hold	24	36	48	72	144
	1/10½	**2/1½**	**2/10**	**3/-**	**5/9**

Postage 6d.

"Optimus" School Microscope.

Highly finished bronzed foot, sliding coarse adjustment, fine adjustment by milled head, ¼ in., ½ in. and 1 in. dividing objective, one eyepiece and condenser, in upright mahogany case with drawer for objects.

Price **£2 15 3**   Postage 9d.

Powerful Students' Microscopes.

With 3 powers, rack adjustment, without condenser. Price **21/-**

With condenser, better quality. Price **32/6**

Each Microscope packed in polished mahogany case with forceps and 1 slide.

Postage 6d.

The "MONOSCOPE"

POST CARD

For viewing
Picture Postcards and Photographs.

A Novelty both pleasing and entertaining.

Consists of a concave mirror, 5 in. diameter, set in a wood frame covered with leatherette, the mirror being held in a place by a polished aluminium ring

A base board is attached to the frame with self-locking device, at the extreme end of this base is a spring holder in which to place the postcard or photograph to be viewed.

In use, the Monoscope is held so that the light falls directly on the picture, and by looking over the edge of picture into the mirror and at such a distance from it that the picture just fills the mirror, a very pleasing effect is produced.

The picture is not only magnified but a stereoscopic effect is produced.

As a means of utilising collections of postcards and photographs for table entertainment it is altogether unique.

Price **2/9** each.   Postage free.

Telescopes.
Pocket size, 3 draw tubes, leather covered body.

1	1¼	1½ in. diam.	Postage
5/6	**6/6**	**11/6**	3d.

The Scholar's Microscope.
8 in. Rack and Pinion Focussing and Tilting Movement, **16/6**
9 in. ditto, **19/6** Post 9d.

This Year's Books for Boys and Girls

A NEW STORY FOR GIRLS.

GLADYS AND JACK. A Story of Australian Life.   By J. M. WHITFELD.   Coloured Illustrations by N. TENISON. Crown 8vo, Cloth **5/-**

Edited by Mrs. HERBERT STRANG.

THE BLUE BOOK FOR GIRLS. A splendid Gift Book containing a large store of miscellaneous reading matter for girls : Stories, Articles, Poems, etc., by well-known writers. Twelve plates in colour and many other illustrations. Cloth, gilt, bevelled boards, gilt top, **5/-** ; Cloth, **3/6** ; Picture Boards, **2/6**

New Editions of Famous Books for Girls.

THE STORY BOOK GIRLS. By CHRISTINA G. WHYTE.   With coloured illustrations by J. DURDEN.   Cloth, olivine edges, **3/6**

TOM, WHO WAS RACHEL? An Australian Story for Girls.   By J. M. WHITFELD.   Cloth, olivine edges, **3/6**

STORIES FOR CHILDREN.

THE UNLUCKY FAMILY. By Mrs. HENRY DE LA PASTURE.   New edition, with coloured plates by C. E. BROCK. Crown 8vo, cloth, **3/6**

THE MYSTERIOUS SHIN SHIRA. By G. E. FARROW.   Illustrated in colour and black-and-white. Picture boards **1/6**

THE HAPPY FAMILIES. By VOILET BRADBY.   A story based upon the well-known Parlour Game.   ,,   ,,   **1/6**

SONGS FOR LITTLE CHILDREN. A Book of Children's Poems with new musical settings by T. W. STEPHENSON, and many illustrations.   Cloth, **3/6** ; Picture Boards, **2 6**

The Children's Holiday Series.

Edited by Mrs. HERBERT STRANG.

Each book contains a selection of reading matter for children in prose and verse, and many illustrations in colour and black-and-white.   Picture boards, **1/6** each.

THE PANSY BOOK.   THE PRIMROSE BOOK.   THE ROSE BOOK.   THE VIOLET BOOK.

NEW PICTURE BOOKS AND TOY BOOKS.

CECIL ALDIN'S Annual Books.

FARM BABIES. Containing 24 full-page colour pictures by CECIL ALDIN, and amusing letterpress by MAY BYRON. New Edition,   Cloth, **3/6**   Picture boards, **2 6**

THE NIGHT BEFORE CHRISTMAS   ..   ..   ..   Illustrated throughout in two colours, by J. C. CHASE. Cloth, **2 6**   Picture boards, **1/6**

MY OWN NURSERY RHYME BOOK. With many illustrations in colour and black-and-white by HELEN JACOBS. Cloth, **2** -   Picture boards, cloth back, **1/** -

BABIES OF OTHER LANDS.
LITTLE PEOPLE OF OTHER LANDS } Illustrated in colour by ROSA PETHERICK,   Picture boards, **1/-** each,

MY PRETTY NURSERY RHYMES.   **MY FAVOURITE NURSERY RHYMES.** Picture boards, **6**d. each.

HENRY FROWDE and HODDER & STOUGHTON

S...

GIFT BOOKS that are appreciated.

Books for Boys.

Herbert Strang's New Book.
Sultan Jim : Empire Builder.
The Air Patrol. A Story of the North-West Frontier.
The Air Scout.
Heroes of the Air.
With the Airmen.
Pub. at 6/- each.
Our Price **4 6**
Postage 4d.

The Romance of the World Series.
By Herbert Strang.
The Romance of Canada.
The Romance of Australia.
The Romance of India.
60 pp. Illustrated with 16 plates in colour and 4 maps. Demy 8vo, cloth, gilt top. Pub. at 6/-
Our price **4/6**
Postage 4d.

Books for Boys.

The Race Round the World.
By Captain GILSON.
An account of the Contest for the £100,000 Prize offered by the Combined Newspaper League. Coloured illustrations by Cyrus Cuneo, and a Map of the Route of "The Swallow."
Published at 3/6   Our price **2/7½**
Postage 4d.

The Henty and Kingston Series.

By G. A. HENTY—
Out on the Pampas
The Young Franctireurs
Friends though Divided
By W. H. G. KINGSTON—
The Three Midshipmen
The Three Lieutenants
The Three Commanders
The Three Admirals
The Missing Ship
Roger Willoughby
From Powder Monkey to Admiral
Hendricks the Hunter
By HERBERT STRANG—
The Adventures of Dick Trevanion
One of Clive's Heroes
Rob the Ranger
Humphrey Bold
Setlers and Scouts
By Capt. GILSON—
The Spy
By DESMOND COKE—
The School Across the Road
By G. SURREY—
'Mid Clash of Swords
By A. C. CURTIS—
The Good Sword Belgarde
By LILIAN QUILLER-COUCH—
The Romance of Every Day
By H. G. ADAMS—
David Livingstone : Centenary Edition
By H. C. ADAMS—
In the Fifteen
Charlie Lucken
By JULES VERNE—
A Journey to the Centre of the Earth
By H. COLLINGWOOD—
A Pirate of the Caribbees
By G. MANVILLE-FENN
Cutlass and Cudgel
By T. BAINES REED—
The Willoughby Captains
By GORDON STABLES—
Just Like Jack
From Pole to Pole
On Special Service
Frank Hardinge
By Dr. MACAULAY—
Stirring Stories
Thrilling Tales
By W. O. STODDARD—
Montezumas
Our price **2/7½**
Postage 4d.

Hurricane Hurry. Published at 5/-
Our price **3/9**   Postage 4d.

The Herbert Strang Series.

Samba : A Story of the Congo. Illustrated in colour
With Drake on the Spanish Main. Illustrated in colour
Barclay of the Guides. A Story of the Indian Mutiny. Illustrated in colour, with Maps
Published at 5/-   Our price **3/9**   Post 4d.

The Adventures of Phyllis, By Bessie Marchant
Three Girls on a Yacht, By E.E. Cowper.
Sister-in-Chief. By Dorothy A Beckett Terreil.
Peggy, D.O. By Helen H. Watson.
Peggy, S.G. By Helen H. Watson.
Penelope Intrudes. By Katharine Newlin.
Etheldreda the Ready. By Mrs. G. De Horne Vaizey.
The Mysterious Twins. By Brenda Girvin
Published at 3/6   Our price **2/7½**   Post 4d.

Books for Girls.

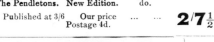

The Unlucky Family
The Girl Scout, by Brenda Girvin.
The Girl Crusoes, by Mrs. H. Strang
A Sage of Sixteen, by L. B. Walford.
The Ogilvies' Adventures
Sylvia's Victory
Audrey's'Awak'ning
The Conquest of Claudia
Dauntless Patty
The above 5 books by E. L Haverford
Phœbe : Her Profession
Sidney : Her Summer on the St. Lawrence
Teddy : Her Daughter
Teddy : Her Book
Nathalie's Sister
Nathalie's Chum
Janet : Her Winter in Quebec
The above 7 books by Anna Chapin Ray

Peggy Pendleton's Plan E. M. Jameson
The Pendletons. New Edition.   do.
Published at 3/6   Our price **2/7½**
Postage 4d.

JUST LIKE JACK

HERBERT STRANG'S ANNUAL

Herbert Strang's Annual.
(Sixth year of issue.)
Cloth, Olivine edges **5/-**
Picture boards, cloth back **3/6**

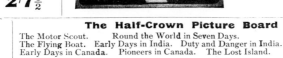

The Half-Crown Picture Board Series.

The Motor Scout.   Round the World in Seven Days.
The Flying Boat.   Early Days in India.   Duty and Danger in India.
Early Days in Canada.   Pioneers in Canada.   The Lost Island.

By various authors. 2/6 each.
For the Admiral
Comrades
The Three Lieutenants
The Three Midshipmen
From Powder Monkey to Admiral
The Three Commanders
The Three Admirals
Audrey's Awakening
The Conquest of Claudia
Peggy Pendleton's Plan
Our price **1/10½**   Post 3d.

The above Series contain both new books and new editions of old favourites. Strongly & artistically bound. Illustrated in Colours.

By HERBERT STRANG. Post 4d.
The Purple Book for Boys
The Blue Book for Boys
The Red Book for Boys
The Green Book for Boys.
Crown 4to, cloth, bevelled bds. gilt top, 5/- ; cloth, 3/6. Picture bds., cloth back. 2/6
Our price **3/9   2/7½   1/10½**

King of the Air : or, To Morocco on an Aeroplane.
Illustrated in colour by W. E. Webster. Cloth, 2/6
Our price ... **1/10½**
Postage 3d.

Nelson's Very Popular Annual.
Always Delights.
Published at 2/6
Our price **1/10½**
Postage 4d.

Gift Books for Boys and Girls.

Published at 5/- Our Cash Price **3/9**
Postage 4d.

Published at 6/- Our Cash Price **4/6**
Postage 4d.

Published at 6/- Our Cash Price **4/6** Postage 4d.

Select Books for Girls.

New Book by CAPTAIN F. S. BRERETON.

The Great Airship: A tale of Stirring Adventure. Fully Illustrated.

Captain F. S. Brereton's

ory of the Dominion: A Tale of Canadian Immigration
dian and Scout
hn Bargreave's Gold
oughriders of the Pampas
oldier of Japan, A
nder the Chinese Dragon
ith Roberts to Candahar

Fleet-Surgeon Jeans'

ord of H.M.S. " Vigilant "
r. Midshipman Glover, R.N.

New book by CAPTAIN BRERETON.

With Wellington in Spain: A Story of the Peninsula. Illustrated by W. Rainey, R.I. In coloured wrapper.

Captain F. S. Brereton's

Foes of the Red Cockade
Great Aeroplane, The
Hero of Panama, The. Hero of Sedan, A
How Canada was Won
Kidnapped by Moors: A Story of Morocco
Roger the Bold. With Dyaks of Borneo
With Wolseley to Kumasi

Fleet-Surgeon Jeans'

John Graham, Sub-Lieutenant, R.N.: A Tale of the Atlantic Fleet
On Foreign Service

Harry Collingwood's

Middy in Command
With Airship and Submarine

Alexander Macdonald's

Lost Explorers, The. Pearl Seeker's, The
Through Heart of Tibet
White Trail, The

Sir Harry H. Johnston

The " Real Adventures " of those Pioneers who have helped to lay the Foundations of the British Empire. Edited by Sir Harry H. Johnston, G.C.M.G., K.C.B. Demy 8vo, cloth extra. With 8 full-page coloured and many other illustrations.

Old School Friends: A Tale of Modern Life. By Rosa Mulholland
The Daughter of the Manor. By Katharine Tynan. Illustrated by John Campbell
Twin Sisters. A Story by Rosa Mulholland
Saturday's Children. By Winifred James
Girl Comrades. By Ethel F. Heddle
Strangers in the Land. By Ethel F. Heddle
Fair Noreen. By Rosa Mulholland
Cousin Sara. By Rosa Mulholland
O'Shaughnessy Girls. By Rosa Mulholland
Our Sister Maisie. By Rosa Mulholland

Grand Books for Boys.

Published at 3/6 Our Cash Price **2/7½** Postage 4d.

New Book
By HARRY COLLINGWOOD.
Turned Adrift: An Adventurous Voyage

G. A. Henty's

At the Point of the Bayonet
A Knight of the White Cross
Tiger of Mysore
At Agincourt: A Story of the White Hoods of Paris
Both Sides the Border
By England's Aid
By Pike and Dyke
By Right of Conquest
Captain Bayley's Heir
Cat of Bubastes. Facing Death
Chapter of Adventures
Condemned as a Nihilist
Dragon and Raven. Jacobite Exile
Final Reckoning. For the Temple
In Freedom's Cause
In Greek Waters. One of the 28th
True to the Old Flag: The American War of Independence
Under Drake's Flag
Under Wellington's Command
With Clive in India
With Cochrane the Dauntless
With Frederick the Great
With Moore at Corunna
Young Carthaginian
Young Colonists

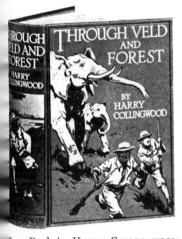

New Book by HARRY COLLINGWOOD.

hrough Veld and Forest: An African Story. Illustrated by Archibald Webb.

Harry Collingwood's

Middy of the King
Middy of the Slave Squadron
uise of the " Thetis "
wo Gallant Sons of Devon: A Tale of the Days of Queen Bess.

G. A. Henty's

Aboukir and Acre. By Sheer Pluck
eld Fast for England
the Heart of the Rockies
Surrender. St. George for England
rough Russian Snows
Herat and Cabul
easure of the Incas

Herbert Strang's

own of Moukden. Kobo
m Burnaby
est of the Black Opals. A. Macdonald
e Invisible Hand. A. Macdonald

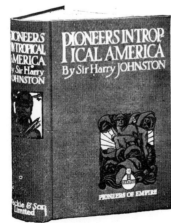

Pioneers in Tropical America. By Sir Harry H. Johnston. Illustrated in colour by Charles H. Sheldon.
Pioneers in South Africa. By Sir Harry H. Johnston. Illustrated in colour by Wal Paget.
Pioneers in India. Pioneers in Canada
Pioneers in Australasia
Pioneers in West Africa

Through Three Compaigns: A Story of Chitral and Ashanti
Lion of St. Mark
Lion of the North
Maori and Settler
March on London
On the Irrawaddy
Orange and Green
Through the Fray
Through the Sikh War

Captain Brereton's

Under the Spangled Banner
With the Dyaks of Borneo
Foes of the Red Cockade: A Story of the French Revolution
In the King's Service: A Tale of Cromwell
Tom Stapleton, the Boy Scout
Knight of St. John: A Tale of the Siege of Malta
In the Grip of the Mullah: A Tale of Somaliland
Gallant Grenadier. Dragon of Pekin
With Rifle and Bayonet
One of the Fighting Scouts
With Shield and Assegai

Harry Collingwood's

Adventures of Dick Maitland
Overdue. Harry Escombe
A Strange Cruise
Log of the " Flying Fish "

G. Manville Fenn's

Devon Boys. Dick o' the Fens
In the King's Name. Quicksilver
Captured Cruiser. C. J. Cutcliffe Hyne
Hidden Nugget. A. Macdonald

JUST OUT.
When East Meets West: A Story of the Yellow Peril. By Percy J. Westerman

Christmas Gift Books for Boys and Girls.

Good Girls' Story Books.

Published at 3/6

Our Cash Price **2/7½**

Postage 4d.

The Youngest Girl in the Fifth. By Angela Brazil.
The Loyalty of Esther Hope: A Story of Vancouver. By Bessie Marchant.
A Girl of Galway. By Katharine Tynan.
Betty's First Term — Lilian F. Wevile
Betty's Next Term — ,,
Courageous Girl, A — Bessie Marchant
Daughter of the Ranges — ,,
Ferry House Girls — ,,
Girl's Loyalty — F. Armstrong
New Girl at St. Chad's — Angela Brazil
No Ordinary Girl — B. Marchant
Original Girl, An — E. F. Heddle
A Princess of Servia — Bessie Marchant

2/6 Books.

Cash **1/10½**
Postage 3d.

For Girls.

The Leader of the Lower School.

ANGELA BRAZIL.

Cousins in Camp. Theodora Wilson Wilson
The Adventurous Seven: Their Hazardous Undertaking. Bessie Marchant
The King's Knight. G. I. Whitham

For Boys.

Published at 2/6

Our Price **1/10**

Postage 3d.

Boys of the Priory School.

F. COOMBE.

Brave Sidney Somers — F. M. Holmes
Captured at Tripoli — P. F. Westerman

The Pilots of Pomona — R. Leighton
Carbineer and Scout — E. H. Burrage
Dr. Joliffe's Boys — Louis Hough
Hallowe'en Ahoy ! — Hugh St Leger
Champion of the Faith — J. M. Callwell
Wulfric the Weapon Thane — C. Whistler
Sou'wester and Sword — H. St. Leger
The Thirsty Sword — R. Leighton

Triumphs OF Enterprise Series.

Profusely illustrated.

Wonders of Transport.

Conquests of Engineering.

Wood and What We Make of It.

By CYRIL HALL.

Published at 3/6   Our Cash Price **2/7½**   Post 4d.

Published at 3/6

Our Cash Price **2/7½**

Postage 5d.

Blackie's Standard Library.

Children of the New Forest — Marryat
The Coral Island — R. M. Ballantyne
The Cruise of the Midge — Michael Scott
Faith Gartney's Girlhood — Whitney
Feats on the Fiord — H. Martineau
Good Wives — Louisa M. Alcott
The Gorilla Hunters — R. M. Ballantyne
Hans Brinker — Mary M. Dodge
The Heroes — Charles Kingsley
The Lamplighter — Miss Cummins
The Last of the Mohicans — J. F. Cooper
Little Women — Louisa M. Alcott
Martin Rattler — R. M. Ballantyne
Masterman Ready — Captain Marryat
The Pathfinder — J. Fenimore Cooper
Peter the Whaler — W. H. G. Kingston
Poor Jack — Captain Marryat
The Rifle Rangers — Mayne Reid
Robinson Crusoe — Daniel Defoe

Gamage's price, 9d.

Published at 1/-

Post 3d.

Andersen's Favourite Fairy Tales
Andersen's Popular Fairy Tales
Grimm's Fairy Tales
Deerslayer — J. Fenimore Cooper
Dog Crusoes — R. M. Ballantyne
Southey's Life of Nelson

The Settlers in Canada — Captain Marryat
Swiss Family Robinson — M. Wiss
Tales from Shakespeare — Charles Lamb
Tom Brown's Schooldays — T. Hughes
Tom Cringle's Log — Michael Scott
Uncle Tom's Cabin — H. B. Stowe
Ungava — R. M. Ballantyne
The Vicar of Wakefield — O. Goldsmith
What Katy did — Susan Coolidge
What Katy did at School — Susan Coolidge
The World of Ice — R. M. Ballantyne

The Youth' Library

Entirely N
Binding.

Splendid p
sentation
Books.

Gamage'
price .. 1/

Published

Post 3d.

From Log Cabin to White House — W. M. Thay
Robinson Crusoe — Daniel Def
The Pilgrim's Progress — John Buny
Grimm's Fairy Stories — Grimm's Fairy Ta
The Swiss Family Robinson. — Æsop's Fabl
Andersen's Popular Tales. — Andersen's Stori
Boys' Own Sea Stories
Scottish Chiefs — Jane Port
Ivanhoe — Sir Walter Sco
Prisoners of the Sea — F. M. Kingsl
Westward Ho ! — Charles Kingsl
Arabian Nights' Entertainments
Two Years Ago — Charles Kings
The Last of the Barons — Bulwer Lytt
Harold — ,,
The Heroes — Charles Kings
Willis, the Pilot. Sequel to " Swiss Family Robinson "
The Coral Island — R. M. Ballanty
Martin Rattler. Ungava. — ,,
The Young Fur Traders — ,,
Peter the Whaler — W. H. G. Kingst
Sent to the Rescue — E. H. Coo
The World of Ice — R. M. Ballanty
Old Jack — W. H. G. Kingst
The Dog Crusoe — R. M. Ballanty
Tom Brown's Schooldays — T. Hug
A Wonder Book — Nathaniel Hawthor
Tanglewood Tales — ,,
The Last of the Mohicans — J. Fenimore Coo
The Gorilla Hunters — R. M. Ballanty
The Red Eric — ,,
The Water Babies — Charles Kings
The Lighthouse — R. M. Ballanty
Hereward the Wake — Charles Kings
The Three Midshipmen — W. H. G. Kingst
Andy — Lucill Lov
Fighting the Flames — R. M. Ballanty
True Blue — W. H. G. Kingst
Eric, or Little by Little — F. W. Far
St. Winifred's, or the World of School — ,,
Julian Home : A Tale of College Life
Deep Down — R. M. Ballanty
Granny's Wonderful Chair — Frances Brow

Jules Verne's Works.

Crown 8vo, cloth gilt, with Frontispiece.
Gamage's price 9d.   Published at 1/-   Post 3d.

20,000 Leagues under the Sea.
From the Earth to the Moon.
The English at the North Pole
The Ice Desert.   Round the World in 80 Da
Interior of the Earth.   Five Weeks in a Ballo
The Mysterious Document
On the Track.   Among the Cannibals

Books That Are Greatly Appreciated.

THE CECIL ALDIN EDITION OF BLACK BEAUTY.

Black Beauty: The Autobiography of a Horse. By Anna Sewell.
With 18 charming plates in colour specially painted by Cecil Aldin.
Size of work 9 by 7, 292 pages. Handsome cloth gilt binding. Intaglio end papers by Cecil Aldin. Second edition, **7/6**

Limited edition, hand-made paper,
£1 1 0 Post 4d.

The most sumptuous edition of "Black Beauty" ever printed. It combines charming illustrations, delightfully printed. Probably no living artist could illustrate "Black Beauty" so sympathetically as Cecil Aldin.

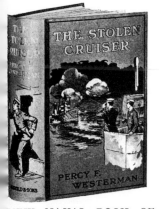

NEW NAVAL BOOK OF ADVENTURES, 3/6

Our price .. **2/7½** Post 4d.

SPLENDID GIRL'S STORY.

Just published, 2/6
Our price .. **1/11½** Post 4d.

TWO-AND-SIXPENNY GIFT BOOKS.

Crown 8vo, cloth gilt. Illustrated.

By Ethel Turner.

Price **2/6**

Our price .. .. **1/10½** Post 4d.

1	Seven Little Australians	10	Mother's Little girls
2	The Family at Misrule	11	The White Roof-Tree
3	The Little Larrikin	12	In the Mist of the Mountains
4	Miss Bobbie		
5	The Camp at Wandinong	13	The Stolen Voyage
6	Three Little Maids	14	Fugitives from Fortune
7	Story of a Baby	15	The Raft in the Bush
8	Little Mother Meg	16	An Ogre Up-to-Date
9	Betty and Co.	17	That Girl

JARROLDS' CELEBRATED BOOKS ON DOGS.

Dogs: Their Selection, Breeding and Keeping. By F. T. Barton, M.R.C.V.S. Size 7⅜ by 5⅛. Frontispiece in colours, 256 pp. with about 40 photographs illustrating the various breeds and types of dogs included. Cloth boards, **3/6**

This work is a companion volume to "Dog and All About Them." It is in no sense competitive, but is supplementary to it. No dog breeder or keeper should be without this most valuable new volume on the Dog.

The contents include chapters on the following:—Choice of a dog. Purchasing dogs. Dogs for children. Dogs for sport. Water dogs. Dogs for foreign climes. Temperament of dogs. Choosing puppies. Various breeds and types of dogs, with their qualities and characteristics discussed at length in a lengthy series of chapters. Keeping and management of dogs. Dog breeding. Breeding for points. Preparing for shows. Impairment of the senses in dogs. Fashion in dogs. Hiring dogs, Best food for dogs. Dog bites. Refractory dogs, &c. &c. Post 4d.

HORSES AND PRACTICAL HORSE KEEPING.

By Frank Townend Barton, M.R.C.V.S.
Second Edition. Demy 8vo (9 by 5½).
10/6 net. Post 4d.

The Horse Keeper's vade mecum.
A complete practical guide to Horses.
Practically all varieties of Horses dealt with.
100 illustrations including 56 art plates.
650 pp. of text. Handsome binding.

Horse and Hound.—"The result of the co-operation of author and publisher to produce a reliable and practical book on the Horse, which shall stand out from among the mass of horse literature at present in existence; and there will be small doubt among its readers that that object has been worthily achieved. Though bulky in form, it is extremely light and comfortable to handle, is well printed, capitally illustrated, and wholly recommendable."

EVERYONE'S LIBRARY.

1/- Our price .. .. **9d.**
Post 3d.

A re-issue of standard works in a cheap form. These books contain between 320 to 500 pages, printed in the best style with illustrations on art papers and tastefully bound in cloth board.

The Young Fur Trader. By R. M. Ballantyne.
Tales from Shakespeare. By Charles and Mary Lamb.
Daisy. By Elizabeth Wetherell.
Daisy in the Field. By the same author.
Julian Home. By F. W. Farrar.
Roland Yorke. By Mrs. Henry Wood.
Lorna Doone. By R. D. Blackmore.
The Little Duke. By Charlotte M. Yonge.
The Book of Golden Deeds. By the same author.
Eric; or, Little by Little.
By F. W. Farrar.
St. Winifred's.
By the same author.
From Log Cabin to White House.
By M. M. Thayer.
The Gorilla Hunters.
By R. M. Ballantyne.
The Children of the New Forest.
By Captain Marryatt.
The Heroes. By Chas. Kingsley.
Alice in Wonderland.
By Lewis Carroll.
What Katy Did.
By Susan Coolidge.
Peter the Whaler.
By W. H. G. Kingston.
The Lamplighter.
By Miss Cummins.
Stepping Heavenward.
By E. Prentiss.
Melbourne House.
By Susan Warner.

John Halifax, Gentleman.
By Mrs. Craik.
Little Women and Good Wives.
By Louisa M. Alcott.
Coral Islands.
By R. M. Ballantyne.
Hans Andersen's Fairy Tales.
Grimm's Fairy Tales.
By the Brothers Grimm.
Swiss Family Robinson.
Westward Ho!
By Charles Kingsley.
The Water-Babies.
By the same author.
Tom Brown's Schooldays.
By an old Boy.
The Wide, Wide World.
By Susan Warner.
Life and Adventures of Robinson Crusoe. By Daniel Defoe.
Uncle Tom's Cabin.
By H. B. Stowe.
Mark Desborough's Vow.

NEW BOOK OF ADVENTURES FOR BOYS, 2/6

Our price .. **1/10½** Post 4d.

THE BIRDS' SCOUT BOOK,
2/6 net. Post 4d.

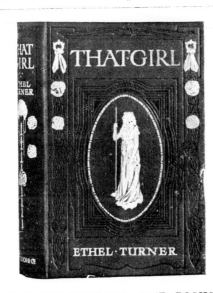

NEW BOOKS FROM PARTRIDGE'S LIST

Christmas Gift Books for Boys and Girls.

5/-

Paper, **1/6**   Cloth, **2/-**

6/-

1/6

Boys' and Girls' Tales.

Always a Favourite.

Paper Boards, **3/6**   Cloth, **5/-**

2/-

1/6

Paper, **1/6**   Cloth, **2/-**

3/6

NEW BOOKS FROM PARTRIDGE'S LIST

Ask for **CAPT. BRERETON'S** great school story

PERCY WESTERMAN'S Latest Book.

THE KING OF RANLEIGH.

A masterpiece of glorious Fun and Adventure.

THE RIVAL SUBMARINES.

A vivid story of Under Sea Mystery.

6/-

6/-

Always a Favourite.

The Infant's Magazine.
Picture Boards, **1/6**
Cloth Boards, **2/-** Ditto, extra, **2/6**

Picture Boards, **3/6**   Cloth Boards, **5/-**

The Children's Friend.
Paper Boards, **1/6**
Cloth Boards, **2/-** Ditto, extra, **2/6**

2/6
By Dorothea Moore.

5/-
By Dorothea Moore.

THE GIRL WHO LOST THINGS.

ROSEMARY, THE REBEL!

ASK TO SEE

Partridge's Publications.

Full range of Partridge's Works.
See this very interesting Collection.

S. W. Partridge & Co., Ltd., London, E.C.

Gamage's Price, 3d. in the 1/- discount.

Postages : 4d. on **3/6, 5/-** and **6/-**; 3d. on **2/-** and **1/6** Books.

New and Interesting Books for Boys and Girls.

The Girls' Budget

(2nd year).

Edited by
JEAN
MINTOSH

List price
3/6

Cash price
2/7½

Post 4d.

This volume contains a collection of stories suitable for girls from 14 to 20. The writers include Annie Swan, Mr. L. B. Walford, Alice Chesterton, Ethel M. Wilmot-Buxton, Gladys Davidson, Geraldine Mockler, and May Wynne, and the stories are for the most part of a modern character. The book is beautifully produced in every respect and illustrated with reproductions from 16 water colour drawings by first-class artists.

Wild Animals ot Yesterday and To-day.

Net price **6/-**

Postage 4d.

Beyond the Dragon Temple

ROBERT
HUDSON.

List price
3/6

Our price
2/7½

Post 4d.

A rattling adventure story for boys in their "teens" dealing with a remarkable quest which has a highly successful issue. With six coloured plates.

Cousin Betty.

Edited by
GERALDINE
MOCKLER.

A story for older girls of the type of "Little Women," showing how difficulties disappear in the face of pluck and determination. With six coloured plates

List price 3/6   Our price **2/7½**   Postage 4d.

The Rival Submarines. By PERCY F. WESTERMAN.
Author of "A Lad of Grit," etc.   Uniform with above.
List price 6/-   Our price **4/6**   Postage 4d.

The appearance in British waters of a mysterious submarine owned & commanded by Captain Restronguet, causes considerable misgivings in Naval circles. The unknown craft performs a number of harmless evolutions, demonstrating the powerful means of offence and defence at his command. Simultaneously a series of outrages, stated to be the work of Captain Restronguet, take place in Continental ports. Captain Restronguet disowns the authorship of these acts, and declares them to be the work of a renegade German, owning a rival submarine, the *Vorwartz.*

The British Admiralty issues orders for Captain Restronguet's submarine, the *Aphrodite,* to be captured. Elaborate precautions are taken in order to do so. Captain Restronguet easily escapes, taking with him Arnold Hythe, a young Sub-lieutenant, whom he makes prisoner in a submarine encounter.

The *Aphrodite* starts in pursuit of the *Vorwartz,* Captain Restronguet deeming it his duty to rid the seas of the modern buccaneer, von Harburg. Then follows most startling adventures in quick succession.

Sub lieutenant Hythe figures prominently, and the story concludes by relating how the young naval officer dramatically seizes the *Aphrodite,* which becomes a powerful unit of the British Navy.

The Fight at Summerdale

JOHN
GUNN.

List price
3/6

Our price
2/7½

Post 4d.

This battle forms the centre of a historical romance of the sixteenth century. The scene is laid chiefly among the Orkney Islands. The book is full of incident and adventure, and is specially rich in "local colour" as regards these islands.

With Axe and Rifle.

List price
2/6

Our price
1/6½

Postage 3d.

Kingston Series.   Coloured Plates.

With Axe and Rifle	Saved from the Sea
Snow-shoes and Canoes	The South Sea
In the Eastern Seas	Whaler
In the Wilds of Africa	Twice Lost
In the Wilds of Florida	Voyage round the
My First Voyage to	World
Southern Seas	The Wanderers
Old Jack	The Young Llanero
On the Banks of the	Dick Cheveley
Amazon	Two Supercargoes

Ballantyne Series.   Coloured Plates.

Freaks on the Fells	Gorilla Hunters
Erling the Bold	Hudson Bay
Deep Down	Martin Rattler
The Wild Man of the	Ungava
West	The World of Ice
The Coral Island	The Young Fur
Dog Crusoe	Traders

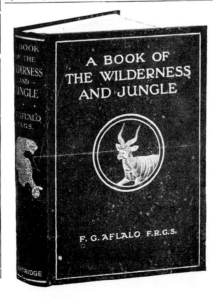

A Book ot the Wilderness and Jungle.

Net price
6/-

Post 4d.

Things to Make

ARCHIBALD
WILLIAMS.

List price
3/6

Our price
2/7½

Post

This is just the book for the active youth who has got beyond the period when he asks "How is it done?" and now wishes to do it himself. Mr. William's new volume will show him how to make an engine, a box kite, an aeroplane, and dozens of other fascinating things; further, the instructions are of such a workmanlike character that when made the things will really go. The book is very fully illustrated with useful diagrams drawn exactly to scale.

Also How it is made, 3/6   How it works,
How to Fly, 3/6   Our price **2/7½**   Post 4

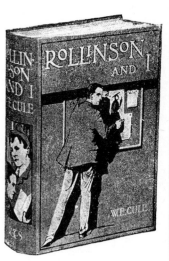
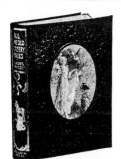

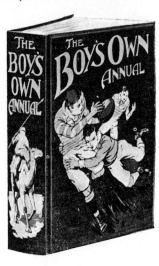
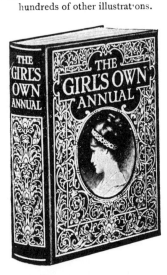

Splendid Gift Books for Boys and Girls.

Published Price 3/6

Our Price **2/7½** Post 4d.

By Evelyn Everett Green.

A Disputed Heritage, with illustrations and coloured frontispiece by Saville Lumley.

Gabriel Garth, Chartist, illustrated by J. Aylin Symington.

Hilary Quest 8 illustrations by Watson Charlton.

The Book of the Fire Brigade, by A. L. Haydon. Coloured frontispiece and numerous photographs.

The Earl's Signature, by Albert Lee. Coloured Frontispiece and 4 illustrations.

The King's Ring, by Z. Topelius. Coloured frontispiece and 4 illustrations.

Sunshine and Moonshine, by Grace Carlton. Coloured frontispiece and 4 illustrations.

The Kidnapped Regiment, by Robert Leighton. Coloured frontispiece and 4 illustrations.

The Boys of Huntingley: a School Story, by K. M Eady. Illustrated.

A Rank Outsider: a School Story, by Kent Carr. 8 illustrations by Hutton Mitchell.

Famous British Admirals, by Albert Lee. Numerous illustrations and portraits.

England's Sea Story, by Albert Lee. Illustrations and portraits.

The World's Exploration Story, by Albert Lee. Numerous illustrations and portraits.

By Evelyn Everett-Green.

Madam of Clyst Peveril

Illustrated by Watson Charlter.

Miss Lorimer of Chard

Illustrated by Collron Pearse.

The Squire's Heir

Illustrated by E. Woolmer.

Published at 3/6

Our price .. **2 7½**

Postage 4d.

Published at 1/-

Our Price **9d.**

Postage 3d.

—

THE OLDEST OF NURSERY FAVOURITES.

Published at 2/6

Our Price .. **1/10½**

Postage 3d.

Miss Greyshott's Girls, by E. Everett Green.

Stepsister Stella, by E. Everett Green.

The Gold Seekers.

A Lad of London Town, by E. Everett Green.

Five Years on a Training Ship, by J. Dunn Bush, F R.C.S , with coloured frontispiece and 3 illustrations by Saville Lumley.

he Kid and the Captain. Adventures on an Indian Island, by Jack Heron. Coloured frontispiece and 3 illustrations, by Bertram Gilbert.

Northumbrian Rebel, by Percy T. Lee.

ens. A Story of School Girl Life in Australia, by Louise Mack.

Wilful Girl, by Helen Griffith.

TORY BOOKS at 1/6

Our price, **1/1½**

Post 3d.

arge size volumes. Illustrated.

ys of the Red House nd Sandys.

By Evelyn Everett Green and Lucretia Mayberry.

e Browning Boys and nd Long Morley.

By Pansy and E. Larter.

mphill Minor and enshawe of Greyotes.

By Kent Carr and I. Suart Robson.

Sisters of Silver Sands and Miss Irving's Bible.

By Evelyn Everett Green and Sarah Doudne;.

rtin Rattler. By R. M. Ballantyne.

field's Blazer. By W. E. Cule.

Young England.

An Illustrated Magazine for Boys all over the world.

Three Serial Stories.

Up-to-date Articles, &c.

Cloth.

Published at 5/- Price **3/9**

Postage 6d.

The Red Nursery Series.

Alice in Wonderland.

Nursery Rhymes.

Tales told at the Zoo.

Very funny stories in Rhyme.

Dick the Gipsy.

The Magic Uncle.

That Lucky Visit.

Robins Chrissie and the Corporal.

Published at 1/- Our price **9**d.

Postage 3d.

Books by FRANK UNDELL.

The "Heroines" Library

Heroines of History and Travel.

Heroines of Mercy & Daily Life.

Heroines of Cross and Faith.

"Adventure" Series.

Stories of the Lifeboat and Fire Brigade.

Stories of the Victoria Cross and Humane Society.

Stories of Alpine and Balloon Adventure.

Stories of Sea and Travel Adventure.

Pub. at 2/- Our price **1/6**

Postage 3d.

Andersen's Fairy Tales. By H. S. Andersen.

Basket of Flowers, The.

Boy Who Sailed with Blake. By W. H. G. Kinsgton.

Captives, The. By Emma Leslie.

Charley Laurel. By W. H. G. Kingston.

Clever Daughter, A. By Mrs. Henry Clarke.

Coral Island. By R. M. Ballantyne.

Danesbury House. By Mrs. Henry Wood.

Dog Crusoe. By R. M. Ballantyne.

Driven into the Ranks. By Rev. Rabson Vennell.

Good Wives. By Louisa M. Alcott.

Gorilla Hunters, The. By R. M. Ballantyne.

High School Girl, A. By Mrs. Henry Clarke.

Little Women. By Louisa M. Alcott.

Martin Battler. By R. M. Ballantyne.

Masterman Ready. By Captain Marryat.

Medland Boys, The. By A. L. Haydon.

Ministering Children. By Maria Charlesworth.

Mischievous Moncton. By Evelyn Everett-Green.

Miss Merivale's Mistake. By Mrs. Henry Clarke.

Monksbury College. By Sarah Doudney.

Peter Biddulph. By W. H. G. Kingston.

Pilgrim's Progress, The. By John Bunyan.

Ralph Roxburgh's Revengs. By Evelyn Everett-Green.

Uncle Tom's Cabin. By Harriet Beecher Stowe.

The "Premier" Shilling Library.

Large handsome Volumes of extra size, well illustrated and strongly bound in Cloth.

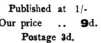

Published at 1/-

Our price .. **9d.**

Postage 3d.

CASSELL'S GIFT BOOKS

CHUMS. Yearly Volume.
This Volume is literally packed from cover to cover with all that a British boy loves—high-class stories of adventure and fun. Nearly 1,000 pages, profusely illustrated. Cloth gilt, **8/-**

BRITISH BOYS' ANNUAL.
Fourth Year of Issue. Profusely illustrated by Gordon Browne, H. M. Brock, Albert Morrow, etc., in colour and black-and-white. With seven magnificent Colour Plates. Cloth gilt, **5/-**

BRITISH GIRLS' ANNUAL.
Fourth Year of Issue. Contains articles and short stories by Dorothy à Beckett Terrell, Olaf Baker, Dorothea Moore, E. E. Cowper, Angelia Brazil, Ralph Simmonds, etc. With seven Colour Pictures, and many in black-and-white. Cloth gilt, **5/-**

CASSELL'S ANNUAL

FOR BOYS AND GIRLS.

Picture Boards, **3/6**

Cassell's Annual is still the children's favourite.

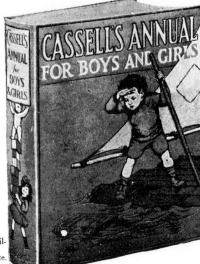

FIFTH YEAR OF ISSUE.

Cloth Gilt, **5,-**

Containing about 200 colour pictures by John Hassall, Lucie Attwell, Rose Petherick, Harry B. Neilson, etc.

And Stories by the best of writers for children.

ALL ABOUT ENGINEERING
By Gordon D. Knox.
"All About Engineering" tells, in a graphic way, how the great mechanical engineering wonders of the world have been accomplished. With two colour and numerous illustrations from photographs. Cloth gilt, **6/-**

THE AIR-KING'S TREASURE.
By Claude Grahame-White and Harry Harper.
Many of the graphic incidents which happen to the great air machine are based on the authors' actual experiences. They are facts—not the products of imagination. With four colour illustrations by Dudley Tennant. Cloth gilt, **3/6**

LITTLE FOLKS. Christmas Volume.
Contains a large number of stories, recitations, articles, and pictures that will appeal to children of all ages and tastes.
Picture Boards, **3/6** Cloth gilt, **5/-**

TINY TOTS.
A Picture-Book Annual for the very Little Ones. With beautiful colour Frontispiece and large number of pictures in colour and black-and-white. Picture Boards, **1/6** Cloth, **2/-**

BO-PEEP.
A Picture-Book Annual for Little Folk. With over 30 Pictures beautifully printed in colour, and many in black-and-white.
Picture Boards **2/6** Cloth, **3/6**

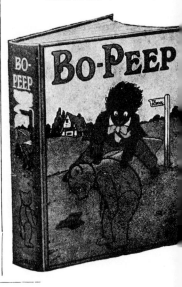

CASSELL & CO., LTD., LA BELLE SAUVAGE, LONDON, E.C.

Sold by A. W. GAMAGE, Ltd., at 3d. in the 1/- discount. Postage ext

---

REMARKABLE OFFER.

The "MARVEL" Lever Embossing Press.

PRICE :—

3/11

Complete with any Address up to 24 letters.

Postage extra 6d.

Extra letters over 24 are charged at the rate of

1/6

Per dozen.

Die must not exceed 2¼ by ¾ in.

POINTS WORTH KNOWING.

1. English Manufacture throughout, NOT foreign. 2. Solid Copper Counterpart, NOT soft composition.
3. Half-inch Steel Die, NOT thin soft Steel Die. 4. Selection of Types, NOT tied to one style.
5. Malleable Iron Handle, NOT Cast Iron.

A PERFECT PRESS THAT WILL LAST FOR YEARS.

Grand Selection of Gift Books.

The "All About" Series.

Books for Boys

AT **3/6**
OUR PRICE **2/7½**
Postage 4d.

The Air King's Treasure.
By CLAUDE GRAHAME-WHITE and HARRY HARPER.

All About Engineering. GORDON D. KNOX. Price **4/6**

"All About Engineering" tells in a graphic way how the great mechanical engineering wonders of the world have been accomplished. It is written by an author who not only knows his subject thoroughly, but has also a wide experience of presenting scientific and technical subjects in a popular and readable form. The volume ends with a most valuable chapter, entitled "The Making of an Engineer."
With 2 Colour Plates and numerous Illustrations from Photographs. Cloth gilt, coloured edges.

All About Ships. LIEUT. TAPRELL DORLING, R.N. Price **4/6**

With Colour Illustrations showing the "Flags and Funnels of the principal Shipping Companies," "Lights and the Rule of the Road," and "Flags of the Chief Maritime Nations," and numerous Black-and-White Illustrations. Cloth gilt, Olivine edges.

All About Airships. RALPH SIMMONDS. Price **4/6**

With Colour Frontispiece by Charles Dixon, R.I., and numerous Illustrations from Photographs.

All About Railways. F. S. HARTNELL. Price **4/6**

With Colour Frontispiece and 48 pages of Illustrations.

The above are published at **6/-** each. Our price **4/6** Postage 4d.

Published at **3/6**
OUR PRICE **2/7½**
Postage 4d.

The Cragsmen.
By W. BOURNE COOKE. With 4 full-page Colour Plates by H. M. Brock.

As a story of thrilling adventure, vivid realism, and literary quality and power 'The Cragsmen' stands shoulder to shoulder with R. L. Stevenson's 'Treasure Island.' It is safe to prophesy that this will become a standard adventure book for boys. Cloth gilt.

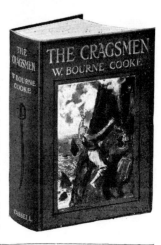

Books for Boys

AT **3/6**
OUR PRICE **2/7½**
Postage 4d.

Adventure Books. By EDWARD S. ELLIS.

Every one of Mr. Edward S. Ellis's stories is full of wholesome fun and adventure, such as every healthy boy revels in, and each is told with all the skill for narrative that has made and maintains Mr. Ellis's fame in many countries.

"Ellis" Books at **2/6** OUR PRICE **1/10½** Postage 4d.

Each contains about 4 full-page Illustrations. Cloth gilt.

The Mountain Star
The Forest Messengers
A Hunt on Snowshoes
Shod with Silence
The Phantom of the River
In the Days of the Pioneers
The Hunters of the Ozark
The Camp in the Mountains.
The Last War Trail
The Lost Trail
Camp Fire and Wigwam
Footprints in the Forest
Iron Heart   River and Jungle
Fire, Snow and Water
Red Jacket
In Red Indian Trails
The Last Struggle
Deerfoot in the Forest
Deerfoot on the Prairies
Deerfoot in the Mountains

Boy's Book of Battles. ERIC WOOD. With 4 Colour and 12 Black-and-White Illustrations. Cloth gilt, coloured cover.

Boy's Book of Adventure. ERIC WOOD. With 4 Colour and 12 Black-and-White Illustrations.

Sons of the Sea. Capt. FRANK H. SHAW. With 4 Colour Illustrations by E. S. Hodgson. Cloth gilt.

Champion of the School. Capt. FRANK H. SHAW. With 4 Colour Plates by Ernest Prater.

For School and Country. RALPH SIMMONDS. With 4 Colour Plates by Harold Earnshaw. Cloth gilt.

The School Mystery. RALPH SIMMONDS. With 4 Colour Plates by Tom Day.

Follow My Leader. TALBOT BAINES REED. With 4 Colour Plates by W. H. C. Groome. Cloth gilt.

Yo-ho! for the Spanish Main. S. WALKEY. With 4 Colour Illustrations by Archie Webb. Cloth gilt.

The Three Homes. DEAN FARRAR. With Colour Frontispiece by Geo. Soper, and 4 Black-and-White Illustrations.

"Ellis" Books at **2/-** each. OUR PRICE **1/6**
About 4 full-page Illustrations. Cloth gilt. Post 4d.

The Path in the Ravine   Blazing Arrow
The Young Ranchers   Chieftain and Scout
Ned in the Woods   Klondike Nuggets
Ned on the River   Pontiac, Chief of the Ottawas
Ned in the Block House   Lost in the Wilds
The Rubber Hunters

"Ellis" Books at **1/-** each. OUR PRICE **9d.**
About 4 full-page Illustrations. Cloth gilt. Post 3d.

Lost in the Rockies   Red Feather
The Lost River   Wolf Ear the Indian
Captured by Indians   River and Forest
The Daughter of the Chieftain

T

A GRAND SERIES OF BOOKS FOR BOYS AND GIRLS.

The Chesterton Girl Graduates. By L. T. Meade. With 6 illustrations in colour by Harold C. Earnshaw.
5/- Our price ... **3/9** Post 4d.

Moll Meredyth, Madcap. By May Baldwin. With 6 illustrations in colour by W. H. C. Groome. 3/6 Our price **2/7½** Post 4d.

The Girls of King's Royal. By L. T. Meade. With 8 illustrations in colour by Gordon Browne. 6/- Our price ... **4/6** Post 4d.

The Girls of Abinger Close. By L. T. Meade. With 6 illustrations in colour by Percy Tarrant 3/6 Our price ... **2/7½** Post 4d.

The Hero of the Mutiny. By Escott Lynn. With 6 illustrations in colour by W. Rainey 5/- Our price ... **3/9** Post 4d.

A Boy Scout in the Balkans. By J. Finnemore. With 6 illustrations in colours by by W. H. C. Groome. 5/- Our price **3/9** Post 4d.

Jo Maxwell, School Girl. By Lizzie C. Reid. With 4 illustrations by Percy Tarrant. 2/6 Our price **1/10½** Post 4d.

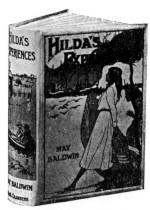

Hilda's Experiences. By May Baldwin. With 6 illustrations in colour by W. Rainey. 5/- Our price ... **3 9** Post 4d.

Holly House and Ridge's Row: A Tale of London Old and New. By May Baldwin. Illus. in colour. Dainty Pen-and-Ink Sketches M. Wheelhouse. 3/6 Our price **2/7½** Post 4d.

Troublesome Topsy and her Friends. By May Baldwin. With 6 illustrations in colour by Mabel L. Attwell. 3/6 Our price ... **2/7½** Post 4d.

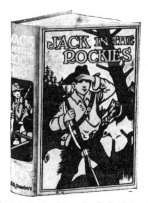

Jack in the Rockies. B. G. B. Grinnell. Cheap Edition. With 8 illustrations by E. W. Deming. 2/- Our price ... **1/6** Post 4d.

Jack the Young Ranchman. By G. B. Grinnell. Cheap Edition. With 8 illustrations by E. W. Deming. 2/- Our price ... **1/6** Post 4d.

Little Tin Soldiers. By Graham Mar. With 6 illustrations by Mabel L. Attwell. 1/6 Our price **1/1½** Post 4d.

April Fool Twins. By E. Timlow. Cheap Edition. With 5 illustrations by H. R. Richards. 1/6 Our price **1/1½** Post 4d.

Our Agreeable Friends. By F. G. Aflalo. Admirably illustrated in colour and Black & White by Miss N. Parker. 3/6 Our price **2/7½** Post 4d.

Rosaly's New School. By Elsie Oxenham With 4 illustrations in colour by T. J. Overnell. 3/6 Our price ... **2/7½** Post 4d

T..

Gift Books for Boys and Girls.

Half-crown Gift Books for Girls.

A New Series of Books, specially selected for girls, charmingly bound. With Colour Frontispiece and 3 Half tone Illustrations in each.

Sisters Three. By Mrs. G. de Horne Vaizey
Tom and Some Other Girls. By Mrs. G. de Horne Vizey
Mrs. Pederson's Niece. By Isabel Suart Robson

Uniform with this Series Little Mother Bunch. By Mrs. Molesworth Containing about 288 pages with full-page illusts., cloth gilt.

A. W. Gamage's price **1/10½**
Post 4d.

Showing format of the Volumes.

The Prize Library.

Entirely New Editions, well printed on good paper. Each volume illustrated by well-known artists, and attractively bound.

Published at 2/- Gamage's price **1/6**
Postage 4d.

1	Little Women	L. M. Alcott
2	Good Wives	"
3	The Lamplighter	Miss Cummins
4	Uncle Tom's Cabin	H. B. Stowe
5	The Wide, Wide World	Wetherell
6	Queechy	"
7	The Prince of the House of David	{ Rev. J. H.
8	The Throne of David	Ingraham
9	Melbourne House	E. Wetherell
10	From Jest to Earnest	E. P. Roe
12	A Knight of the 19th Century	"
13	What Katy Did at Home and at School	Susan Coolidge
14	The Old Helmet	E. Wetherell
15	Daisy	"
17	Barriers Burned Away	E. P. Roe
18	Ben-Hur	Lew Wallace
19	Beulah	A. J. Evans Wilson
20	Infelice	"
21	St. Elmo	"
22	At the Mercy of Tiberius	"
24	John Halifax, Gentleman	Mrs. Craik
25	The Pillar of Fire	Rev. G. H. Ingraham
30	Opening a Chestnut Burr	E. P. Roe
31	Macaria	A. J. Evans Wilson
34	Prisoners of the Sea	F. M. Kingsley
37	The Mill on the Floss	George Eliot
38	Monica	E. Everett Green
39	A Face Illumined	E. P. Roe
40	Vashti	A. J. Evans Wilson
44	Daisy in the Field	E. Wetherell
47	Adam Bede	George Eliot
48	Danesbury House	Mrs. Henry Wood
49	Inez	A. J. Evans Wilson
50	Helen's Babies	John Habberton
51	Agatha's Husband	Mrs. Craik
52	The Head of the Family	"
53	The Days of Bruce	Grace Aguilar

Mrs. Henry Wood

54	East Lynne
55	The Channings
56	Mrs. Halliburton's Troubles
57	Lord Oakburn's Daughters
58	Mildred Arkell
59	Verner's Pride
60	The Shadow of Ashlydyat
61	St. Martin's Eve
62	Trevlyn Hold

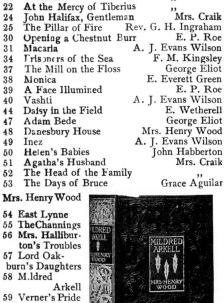

THE FAMOUS 52 STORY SERIES OF BOOKS FOR BOYS AND GIRLS.

Published, 5/-
Gamage's price .. **3/9**
Post 4d.

The Fifty-two Library.

Edited by Alfred H. Miles. In large crown 8vo, 400—500 pp., cloth, bevelled boards richly gilt, gilt edges, well illustrated. 5/- each. The "Fifty-two series" forms an excellent library of fiction for young people. The stories are by the best writers for boys and girls including—

G. A. Henty	Gordon Stables, M.D., R.N.
W. Clark Russell	Ascott Hope
G. Manville Fenn	F. C. Selous
W. H. G. Kingston	Robert Chambers
R. M. Ballantyne	R. E. Francillon
Captain Mayne Reid	David Ker
Rosa Mulholland	Mrs. G. Linnæus Banks
Alice Cockran	Sarah Doudney

And many other well-known writers.

Fifty-two Stories for Boys
Fifty-two Stories for Girls
Fifty-two More Stories for Boys
Fifty-two More Stories for Girls
Fifty-two Further Stories for Boys
Fifty-two Further Stories for Girls
Fifty-two Other Stories for Boys
Fifty-two Other Stories for Girls
Fifty-two Stories for Boyhood and Youth
Fifty-two Stories for Girlhood and Youth
Fifty-two Stories for Children
Fifty-two Stories of Boy Life
Fifty-two Stories of Girl Life
Fifty-two Stories of Life and Adventure for Boys
Fifty-two Stories of Life and Adventure for Girls
Fifty-two Stories of Indian Mutiny and the Men who saved India. By A. H. Miles & A. J. Pattle
Fifty-two Stories of Pluck and Peril for Boys
Fifty-two Stories of Pluck, Peril, and Romance for Girls Fifty-two Fairy Tales
Fifty-two Stories of the British Navy
Fifty-two Stories of Duty and Daring for Boys
Fifty-two Stories of Duty and Daring for Girls
Fifty-two Stories of the British Army
Fifty-two Holiday Stories for Boys
Fifty-two Holiday Stories for Girls
Fifty-two Sunday Stories for Boys and Girls
Fifty-two Stories of Heroism in Life and Action for Boys [for Girls
Fifty-two Stories of Heroism in Life and Action
Fifty-two Stories of the Wide, Wide World
Fifty-two Stirring Stories for Boys
Fifty-two Stirring Stories for Girls
Fifty-two Stories of the British Empire
Fifty-two Stories of Courage and Endeavour for Boys [Girls]
Fifty-two Stories of Courage and Endeavour for
Fifty-two Stories of Greater Britain.
Fifty-two Stories of the Brave and True for Boys
Fifty-two Stories of the Brave and True for Girls
Fifty-two Stories for the Little Ones
Fifty-two Stories of School Life and After for Boys
Fifty-two Stories of School Life and After for Girls
Fifty-two Stories of Animal Life and Adventure
Fifty-two Stories of Grit and Character for Boys
Fifty-two Stories of Grit and Character for Girls
Fifty-two Stories of Wild Life East and West
Fifty-two Stories of Head, Heart, and Hand for Boys [Girls
Fifty-two Stories of Head, Heart, and Hand for
Fifty-two Thrilling Stories of Life at Home and
Fifty-two New Stories for Boys [Abroad
Fifty-two New stories for Girls
Fifty-two Pioneer Stories all round the Compass
Fifty-two Excelsior Stories for Boys
Fifty-two Excelsior Stories for Girls

The Captain Library.

Each volume illustrated by well-known artists and attractively bound.

Published at 2/- Gamage's price **1/6**
Postage 3d.

1	Westward Ho!	Charles Kingsley
2	From Log Cabin to White House	W. Thayer
3	Robinson Crusoe	Daniel Defoe
4	The Pilgrim's Progress	John Bunyan
5	Grimm's Fairy Stories	
6	Grimm's Fairy Tales	
7	Swiss Family Robinson	
8	Andersen's Fairy Stories	
9	Andersen's Fairy Tales	
12	The Scottish Chiefs	Jane Porter
13	Ivanhoe	Sir Walter Scott
15	Two Years Ago	Charles Kingsley
16	The Last of the Barons	Bulwer Lytton
17	Harold	Di
18	Arabian Night's Entertainments	
26	20,000 Leagues under the Sea	Jules Verne
27	The Wonderful Travels	Di
28	Among the Cannibals	Di
29	The Moon Voyage	Di
30	The Adventures of Captain Hatteras	Di
31	Willis the Pilot. Sequel to "Swiss Family Robinson"	
32	The Coral Island	R. M. Ballantyne
33	Martin Rattler	Di
34	Ungava	Di
35	The Young Fur-Traders	Di
36	Peter the Whaler	W. H. G. Kingston
38	The World of Ice	R. M. Ballantyne
39	Old Jack	W. H. G. Kingston
40	The Dog Crusoe	R. M. Ballantyne
41	Tom Brown's School Days	Thomas Hughes
44	The Gorilla Hunters	R. M. Ballantyne
45	The Red Eric	Di
47	The Lighthouse	Di
48	Hereward the Wake	Charles Kingsley
49	The Three Midshipmen	W. H. G. Kingston
52	Fighting the Flames R. M. Ballantyne	
53	True Blue W. H. G. Kingston	
54	Eric, or Little by Little F. W. Farrar	
55	St. Winifred's; or The World of School F. W. Farrar	
56	Julian Home. A tale of College Life F. W. Farrar	
57	Deep Down R. M. Ballantyne	

Books for Young Women.

A Country Corner By Amy Le Feuvre
With colour frontispiece by T. Dugdale, R.O. and 8 illustrations by Steven Spurrier 352 pages, cloth gilt.
Other volumes this Series.
Wild Heather. Mrs. L. T. Meade
With colour frontispiece and 3 full page illustrations by Elizabeth Earnshaw
Betty of the Rectory Mrs. L. T. Meade
With colour frontispiece and 4 full page illustrations by Charles H. Martel.

Flaming June By Mrs. G. de Horne Vaizey
With colour frontispiece and 3 full page illustrations by A. Gilbert.
Price A. W. Gamage's price ... **2/7½** Post 4d.

Every Volume full of sustained Interest.

A. W. Gamage's Annual Volumes,
GIFTS FOR BOYS AND GIRLS.

The New Wonder Book.
Better than ever.

Picture boards, 3/6   Our price **2/7½**

Cloth gilt, 5/-   Our price **3/9**   Post 4d.

Chums.
Published at 8/-   Our price **6/-**   Post 6d.

ALSO

Boy's Own Annual.
Published at 8/-   Our price **6/-**   Post 6d.

AND

The Girl's Own Annual.
Published at 8/-   Our price **6/-**   Post 4d.

Rosebud Annual.
icture boards, 3/-   Cloth, 4/-

Our price **2/3**   **3/**   Post 5d.

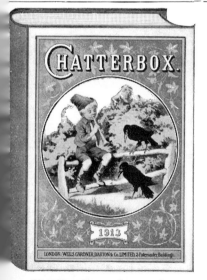

Chatterbox Annual.
Picture boards, 3/-   Cloth, 5/-

Our price **2/3** and **3/9**   Post 5d.

Sunday Volume.   Same price.

Fifth Year. Better than ever.
Full good things, 3/-
Our price **2/3** Post 4d.

The new Book for Girls.
8 full-page colored illustrations
and numerous black and white
do., 230 pages of the most interesting reading matter for girls.
Published at 5/-
A. W. Gamage's price, **3/9**
Postage 6d.

ALSO

The Empire Annual for Girls.
Edited by A. R. Buckland, M.A
Containing 38 complete stories
and articles by favourite writers.
With 8 colored plates and 16 in
black and white.
Demy 8vo, 384 pp.
Gamage's price, **2/7½**
Published at 3/6 Post 4d,

Published at 1/6
Our price .. **1/1½**
Post 4d.

A New Volume that appeals to
Boys fond of adventure Stories.
Second year of publication.
Greatly enlarged.
Gamage's price ... **3/9**
Published at 5/- Postage 6d.

ALSO

The Empire Annual for Boys.
Edited by A. R. Buckland, M.A.
Containing 46 complete stories
and articles by popular authors.
With 8 colored plates and 16 in
black and white.
Demy 8vo., 384 pp.
Published at 3/6 Postage 4d.
Our price **2/7½**

Published at 3/6   Cloth 5/-
Our price **2/7½** and **3/9**   Post 5d.

ALSO

Partridge's Children Annual.
Published at 3/6 and 5/-
Our price **2/7½** and **3/9**   Post 5d.

Blackie's Children's Annual.
Published at 3/6 and 5/-
Our price **2/7½** and **3/9**   Post 5d.

The Children's Empire Picture Album.
Published at 3/6
Our price **2/7½**   Post 5d.

Nister's Annual.
Published at 3/6 and 5/-
Our price **2/7½** and **3/9**   Post 5d.

Tuck's Annual.
Published at 3/6
Our price **2/7½**   Post 4d.

Picture Boards, **2/6**

Cloth Bevil Gilt Edges, **3/6**

Postage 4d.

A Manual of Scoutcraft. Edited by
Morley Adams. 416 pages. Over 200
Illustrations. Price **2/7½** Published
at 3/6 Postage 4d.

Quite new, bright and sparkling.

Full of Fun. Published at 2/6

Our price **1/10½**   Post 4d.

CHARMING CHILDREN'S GIFT BOOKS.

The Changing A.B.C.

A novel mechanical Book for children, changing pictures of common objects for each letter, printed in full colours. Verses by L. L. Weedon.

Published at 1/6   Our price **1/1½**   Post 3d.

Moving Pictures.

A new mechanical book of four full-paged moving pictures.

Verses by L. L. Weedon.

Pub. at 1/-

Our price **9**d.

Post 3d.

Of great educational value and Universal Interest.

Half-hours with Natural History.

Written in an intensely interesting and attractive style by Mr. Alfred Miles, Mrs. Yeatman Woolf, and the Editor, Mr. Edric Vredenburg, and lavishly illustrated with excellent lifelike drawings, in colour and black and white, by well-known artists. Bound in an elegant cover, with inset colour picture, and effective lettering in the margin. 16 coloured plates. 192 pp. letterpress. Crown 4to Illuminated boards, bevelled. Cloth, gilt, gilt top.

Animals, Wild and Domestic.

By Alfred Miles and Edric Vredenburg.

Delightful description of life in the Animal World, illustrated with numerous spirited drawings in colour and black and white by M. Scrivener, N. Drummond, and others. Bound in decorative cloth cover with inset colour pictures. 8 colour plates.

48 pp. letterpres.   Crown 4to.

Pub. at 5/-   Our price **3**/- nett. Post 4d.

A Splendid Gift for Boys and Girls.

Children's Stories from the Arabian Nights.

Illustrated by H. G. Theaker Edited by Edric Vredenburg. An admirable collection of the most popular tales carefully compiled so as to form an entirely delightful and charming volume.

The writer, Mrs. Yeatman Woolf, in re-telling the stories has followed, with brilliant success, the fascinating style of the early translations.

The book is beautifully illustrated with 12 full-page pictures gorgeous in their Eastern colours, and innumerable black and white drawings. Printed on rough art paper. 144 pp. letterpress, crown 8vo. Pictorial boards, cloth back, 3/6 net.   Our price **2/7½** Cloth, bevelled, gilt edges, 5/-   ,,   **3/9**   Post 5d.

FULL OF DELIGHT AND CHARM.

Curly Heads and Long Legs.

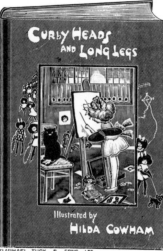

Illustrated by Hilda Cowham with stories by Edric Vredenburg and others. Hilda Cowham's inimitable children in the delightful situations she depicts for the fascination of all beholders, with verses by Norman Gale and charming stories by Edric Vredenburg and others.

A vast number of black & white drawings and 12 full-page coloured pictures. 144 pp. crown 4to.

Pictorial boards, cloth back, 3/6 net. Our price **2/7½** Cloth, bevelled, gilt edges, 5/-   ,,   **3/9**   Post 5d.

Birds, Reptiles and Insects.

By Edric Vredenburg and Rose Yeatman Woolf.

The every-day life of these interesting creatures, told in fascinating language, and profusely illustrated in colour and black and white by E. Drummond, C. F. Newall, R. J. Wealthy, and others.

Bound in decorative cloth cover, with inset colour picture.

8 Colour Plates.

48 pp.   Letterpress   Crown vo.

Price **3**/- net.

Postage 4d. extra.

A most beautiful edition of these exquisite Stories.

Hans Andersen's Fairy Tales.

Illustrated by Mabel Lucie Attwell.
Edited by Edric Vredenburg.

Dainty grace and quaint charm pervade this exquisite edition of the beloved fairy tales. The illustrator has entered into the spirit of the stories, and the result is an exceedingly beautiful book which will be warmly welcomed and dearly cherished. 12 full-page coloured pictures and numerous black and white drawings.

Printed on rough art paper.   144 pp., crown 4to. Pictorial boards, cloth back, 3/6 net.   Our price **2/7½** Cloth, bevelled, gilt edges, 5/-   ,,   **3/9**   Post 5d

THE EVER-WELCOME

FATHER TUCK'S ANNUAL.

With an Additional Thirty-two Coloured Pictures.

A Store house of good things such as girls & boys love, and the grown-up thoroughly appreciate. Stories in prose and in verse, songs, etc.

Over 200 pictures coloured and black and white.

Father Tuck's Annual in flourishing condition.

Printed on rough art paper.   208 pp., crown 4to. Pictorial boards, cloth back, 3/6   Our price **2/7½** Cloth, bevelled, gilt edges, 5/-   ,,   **3/9**   Post 5d

Books for the Little Ones.

ub. at 3/6 & 2/6 Our price **2/7½** & **1/10½** Post 3d.

Two New Books by Frank Adams.

Little Jack Sprat.

Quaint Old Rhymes.

Sam the Sportsman.

Old Mother Goose.

Simple Simon

Tom the Piper's Son.

Jack and Bill.

The Frog who Would A-wooing go.

Pub. at 2/-

Our price **1/6**

Post 4d.

Mr. Frank Adams has exuberant spirits and a true
re for the old nursery rhymes. His interpretations
full of life and go, and a perpetual source of delight.
Large 4to, Art boards. Each book contains 12 full-
ge superb coloured illustrations.

This Way to Jolly Town.

Just What I Wanted.

Rocking Chair Tales.

New Volumes The Surprise Packet.

Draw up Your Chairs.

Just Before Bedtime.

Our price **1/6**

Post 4d.

Children will be delighted with the new volumes or
s series for they are brighter and more attractive
n ever. Each volume contains about 60 colour
tures and is full of charming stories and amusing
se, carefully selected to please little folks.

Each containing about 50 colour pictures and other
ck and White illustrations. Picture boards. **1/6** ea.

Our price **3/6** Postage 4d.

Our price **3/6** Postage 4d.

The Story of Angelina Wacks by
Mrs. CLAYTON PALMER.
Author of "Only Pretendin'," &c.
Illustrated in colours from drawings by Sybil Barham.

Angelina Wacks is a beautiful doll belonging to a little
girl named Ursula.   She was very happy for a long time,
lived in a lovely nursery, went out to parties, and made
lots of doll friends.   One day she met with an accident,
and was taken to the Dolls' Hospital, where they made
her a new head, and when she got old, Ursula gave her to
a poor little child in the Children's Hospital, who loved
her dearly, and she lived happily ever after.

Published at 2/6   Our price **1/10½** Post 4d.

Also by the same Authoress Only Pretendin', 2/6
Our price **1/10½** Postage 4d.

Published at 2/6 and 1/6
Our price **1/10½** and **1/1½** Post 4d.

"Tales and Talks" Series.

200 pages fully illustrated in colour by leading
artists.   Picture boards.

Blackie's Popular Nursery Rhymes. 200 pages
of coloured pictures by John Hassall, R.I.

Blackie's Popular Fairy Tales. Illustrations
by John Hassall.

Tales and Talks in Nature's Garden.
Illustrations by Gordon Browne.

Tales and Talks about Children. Illustrations
by Charles Robinson.

Tales and Talks about Animals.

Tales and Talks from History. Illustrations
by T. Heath Robinson.

Mr. Jumbo at Home. Illust. by Harry B. Neilson

Happy Days by Road and River.

Stories from Grimm. Illust. by Helen Stratton

Pub. at 2/6   Our price **1/10½** Postage 4d.

Each vol.
contains
a large
number or
pictures in
colour and
black-and-
white.
Picture
boards.

My Book
of Engines
Trains and
Ships.
My Book
of Ships.

1/- each.
Our's **9d.**
Post 3d.

Juvenile Gift Books.

Stift covers, picture boards, untearable leaves. Size 13 by 9½. 28 pages. Coloured throughout. Twenty-four full-page coloured pictures. Published at 3/6

Our price, 2/7½ Postage 4d.

Our price, 2/7½ Postage 4d.

Mother Goose.

Edited by EDRIC VREDENBURG

Re-arranged with charming illustrations in colour and black and white, specially designed by Mabel Lucie Attwell.

Consisting of 144 pages of letterpress and pictures in black and white, with 12 full-page illustrations printed in colour. Printed on rough Art Paper. Crown 4to. Pictorial boards, cloth back, 3/6

OUR PRICE, **2/7½**

Cloth, bevelled, gilt edges, 5/- OUR PRICE, **3/9** Post 4d.

"OUR PRIZE PICTURE BOOK." Size 13 by 9½. Paper, 34 pp. Coloured throughout. Pub. at 5/-

"ALL ABOUT ANIMALS. Pub. at 3/6.

Our price, 3/9 Postage 4d.

Our price, 2/7½ Postage 4d.

An exceptionally attractive Edition of **"Alice in Wonderland."** By LEWIS CARROLL.

Most characteristically and charmingly illustrated by Mabel Lucie Attwell. Third edition. Twelve coloured pictures and innumerable black and white drawings. Printed on rought Art paper, making an exceedingly beautiful Gift Book. 148 pp. Crown 4to. Pictorial boards, cloth back, 3/6 OUR PRICE, **2/7½**

Cloth, bevelled, gilt edges, 5/- OUR PRICE, **3/9** Post 4d.

Size 13¾ by 10. 24 coloured pictures and numerous other illustrations. 72 pages. Picture boards.

"PICTURE STORIES FROM THE BIBLE." Published at 5/-

Our price, 3/9 Postage 4d.

Post-card Painting Books.

24 Post-cards in Colour and 24 Post-cards in Outline.

Each Post-card is perforated all around so that it can be detached and sent through the post when painted.

No. 2761. "ANIMALS AND BIRDS" Post-card Painting Book Price 1/-

No. 2754. "SOMETHING TO LAUGH AT" Postcard Painting Book." 1/-

No. 2756. "FLAGS OF THE BRITISH ARMY" Post-card Painting Book. 1/-

No. 2757. ' FATHER TUCK'S POST-CARD " Painting Book. Price 1/-

Our price .. 9d. each. Postage ?d.

The old Fairy Stories ever in demand.

Re-told by EDRIC VREDENBURG and others. Two vols.

"Old Fairy Tales."

Selection of the popular old-time FairyStories delightfully illustrated with eight full-page colour pictures and a large number of drawings in black and white, by M. and A. L. Bowley, E. J. Andrews and others. Printed on rough Art Paper, bound in attractive cover. 112 pp. letterpress. Crown 4to. Pictorial boards, cloth back. Price 2/6. Our price **1/10½**

Favourite Fairy Stories

A splendid collection of the old tales, with charming illustraitons, eight full-page colour and numerous

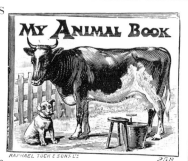

"FRIENDS AND FAVOUR-ITES." Price 2/6.

"MY ANIMAL BOOK." Price 2/6.

"HAPPY HEARTS PICTURE BOOK." 2/6

Our price .. .. 1/10½ each. Postage 4d.

black and white pictures by well-known Artists. Printed on rough Art Paper, with a fascinating cover by Agnes Savage. 112 pages letterpress. Pictorial boards, cloth back, Price 2/6 OUR PRICE, **1/10½** Post 4

Delightful New Books for the Children.

FINE ART GIFT BOOKS,

The Book of the Sagas. By Alice S. Hoffman, illustrated with full-page coloured illustrations and pen-and-ink sketches, by Gordon Brown, R.I. A charming gift book. Price 7/6

Heroes and Heroines of English History. In this beautiful book Mrs. Hoffman brings back to us the romantic days of English chivalry and stirring warfare. The chief heroes and heroines of whom the children have read in their history books become real and living personalities.

The book is beautifully illustrated by Gordon Browne, R.I., and contains six full-page coloured illustrations and twelve full-page black and white drawings, besides numerous vignettes. Bound in cloth elegant, gilt edges. Price 7/6

The Arabian Nights. This is undoubtedly one of the finest editions published of these ever-popular stories. It is edited and has an introduction by W. H. D. Rouse, M.A., Litt.D, etc. The beautiful illustrations in colour and black and white are by Walter Paget. Handsomely bound in cloth elegant, with gilt edges. Price 7/6

The Pilgrim's Progress. A very beautiful edition of this world-renowned work, with an introduction by the Right Rev. Handley C. G. Moule, D.D., Bishop of Durham. The illustrations in colour and black and white are by Walter Paget. Price 7/6

Child Characters from Dickens. Letterpress by L. L. Weedon. Coloured and black and white drawings by Arthur A. Dixon. Price 7/6

Tales from Shakespeare. By Charles and Mary Lamb. Six full-page coloured plates and 70 half-tone illustrations by Walter Paget. Price 7/6

Gulliver's Travels. Dean Swift's wonderful book of adventures is here presented in a most delightful form. It has been specially adapted for children and is most charmingly illustrated by A. E. Jackson. Bound in cloth elegant, gilt edges. Price 7/6

Hauff's Fairy Tales. A first-rate book of fairy tales, translated from the German of Wilhelm Hauff by L. L. Weedon. None of the interest has been lost in the translating, and the masterly drawings by Arthur A. Dixon make the stories very realistic. Bound in cloth elegant, gilt edges. Price 7/6

The Water Babies. By Charles Kingsley. A beautiful edition of this popular work, illustrated by A. A. Dixon. Bound in cloth elegant, gilt edges. Price 7/6

Laboulaye's Fairy Tales. A very beautiful edition of fairy tales from the French of Edouard Laboulaye. These tales are as clever and entertaining as any that have ever been written. This particular edition is charmingly illustrated by Arthur A. Dixon. Bound in cloth elegant, gilt edges. Price 7/6

A. W. Gamage price 5/9

Postage 4d.

Wonderland Series.

A charming series of volumes in colour for younger children, combining delightful painting with humour, adventure and anecdote, such as cannot fail to win the favour of every healthy child.

Price **1/-** net.

Paper Boards.

Post 3d.

Each book contains 12 plates in colour beautifully painted by some of the cleverest "children's artists, with 48 pages of delightfully written letterpress, dainty end papers in colour, title pages in colour, with plate in colour pasted on the cover. There are also a number of humorous line blocks running through the text. Size of each volume 6¾ by 5¼, 76 pages.

1. **The Flying House**: or, what happened to Sunny Babe and Baby Son.
2. **Sea Foam,** the Amazing Adventures of a Doll.
3. **Tiny Wee Wun,** the Little Fairy of the Forest.
   Other titles will be announced.

Companion volume, also **1/-** net. **Baby Bunting & Co.,** by IRENE PAYNE. Size 5½ by 3¾ in., with 20 plates in colour, 91 pages inclusive.

My Picture Scrap Book.

A large scrap book for young children. Coloured picture boards with cloth backs.

Price 3/6

Our price **2/7½**

Post 4d.

Stories for All Times.

A monster book of stories for young children, with 288 pages and 12 full page coloured plates, a large quantity of pen and ink sketches picture boards with cloth backs.

The publisher wishes to draw special attention to this book as being of quite extraordinary value.

Price 3/6 .. Our price .. **1/10½** Post 4d.

Our New Story Book. A monster volume of full page coloured pictures, numerous pen and ink sketches, verses for children by well known authors. Price 3/6 Our price .. **2/7½** Post 4d.

Merchant Ships and what they bring us. A book for boys and girls by Sheila E. Braine. The 8 full-page coloured pictures and numerous pen and ink sketches are by Chas. J. De Lacy. An exceptionally strong colour book. Price 2/6 Our price .. **1/10½** Post 4d.

The Little Home Decorators Scrap Book. No. 1—Nursery Rhymes. No. 2—Nursery Tales. The above are two new books of large coloured pictures, illustrating the well-known nursery rhymes and tales. Each page is perforated, and the figures are intended for cutting out and pasting around the nursery wall. Price 1/- Our price **9d.** Post 3d.

Dean's Patent Rag Books

Stands alone, representing the highest obtainable standard of excellence in the production of Picture Books for Little Children

Only the most simple subjects suitable for young children are dealt with, such as A.B.C.'s, Animal Books, Train Books, Nursery Rhymes, Fairy Tales, etc. In many cases the designs are from originals by the foremost artists of the day, including John Hassall, Cecil Aldin, Stanley Berkeley, and David Brett, whose aptitude in illustrating books which form the delight of the Nursery is indisputable.

Dean's 6d. Patent Rag Books

Containing 12 pages of Designs in full colours on strong cotton cloth. Size 4⅝ by 6¼ in. Ditto Long size. Size 4½ by 9¼ in. Containing 6 pages of Designs in full colours on strong cotton paper.

No. 12. Pets (a book of pet domestic animals
„ 13. What is it? (An object book)
„ 91. Home Pets (a domestic animal book)
„ 92. Jumbo (a bold animal book)
„ 95. 1, 2, 3, 4 (an easy counting book)
„ 96. The Lucky Tub (a book of pretty toys)
„ 108. The Puffer (a train book)
„ 109. Jingles (old nursery rhymes)
„ 112. Quaint A.B.C. Zoo
„ 113. Playthings A.B.C.
„ 127. Baby Bunting (nursery rhyme book)
„ 128. Dolly Dimple's A.B.C. (a little folk's alphabet)
„ 142. All Sorts of Things (an object book)
„ 143. Kittycats (a book of pretty pussies)
„ 83. Iron Horses (a train book)
„ 84. The Doll's House (a pretty story for girls)
„ 85. Jumble A.B.C. (an alphabet book)
„ 86. Small Tot's A.B.C. (an alphabet for "tinies")
„ 129. The Farm (a book of tame animals)
„ 130. Forest Friends
„ 131. A.B.C. (a nursery alphabet
„ 132. Toy Town (a book of play things)
GAMAGES price 4½d. Post 1d.

Dean's New "Roly Poly" Rag Books, Nursery Friezes and Dados

A Novelty which is creating its own demand.
A 'Roly Poly' Rag Book is a Roll neatly tied with ribbon, opening out in panoramic fashion, and displaying along its entire length a continuous picture in full and fast colours.
In the 6d. Series, the Roll is 5½in. wide, 4in in circumference, opening out to 4ft. in length. 6d. Roly Poly Rag Books N. 137. A.B.C. N. 138. The Farm 139. Wild Animals. „ 140. Fairy Wood
GAMAGES price 4½d. Post 1d.
In the 1/- Series, the Roll is 6in. wide, 5½in. in circumference, opening out to 6ft. in length. 1/- Roly Poly Rag Books No. N. 135. Trains.
No. N. 136. Mother Goose's Visto
GAMAGES price 9d. Post 3d.

Dean's 1/6 Patent Rag Books

The daintiest of dainty Rag Books, containing 32 pages of designs in full colours, on strong cotton cloth. Size 4½ by 5½ in
Indestructible, Washable. Entirely British manufacture
No. 133. An Odd A.B.C. (a very amusing alphabet)
No. 134. Toddles (the adventures of a very cute little boy) **Gamages price 1/2 Post 3d**

Dean's 1/- Patent Rag Books

Containing 12 pages of designs in full colours, on strong cotton cloth.
No.   Size 6 by 8¾ in.
2. What is this? What is that? (an object book)
48 One, Two, Three (a Kindergarten counting book).
65. Tick, Tick (a book by which a child easily learn to tell the time)
89 Wee Chick's Alphabet (an animal alphabet)
90. What's that? (an object book)
106. Noah's A.B.C. (Quaint animals from the Ark)
110. Neddy and other friends.
111. On Wheels and Wings (A book of trains and airships)
114. Baby's Diary (a day's delightful doings)
125. The Express (an up-to-date train book)
126. Sugar Candy A.B.C. (a book of sweetmeats)
144. Pussycats A.B.C. (a book of quaint cats)
145. Mother Goose Rhymes (Tales for the bairns)

Dean's 1/- Patent Rag Books

(Long size) Containing 6 pages of designs in full colours on strong cotton cloth. Size 6½ by 13 in.
No. 75. An Animal Rag Book (a book of favourite animals)
„ 76. Baby's Rag Book (an object book)
„ 104. A.B.C. (an alphabet of well-known things)
„ 105. The Garden (a book of familiar objects a child would see in a garden)
GAMAGES price .. 9d. Post 3d.

Dean's 2/6 Patent Rag Books

Containing 16 pages of designs in full colours on strong cotton cloth. Size 9 by 8 in.
No. 56. Gee Gee Book. (Designed by Stanley Berkeley.)
„ 69. The Jungle. (A Bold Animal Book.)
„ 78. Sunbonnet Babies. (Designed by Gladys Hall.)
„ 100. A Bow-Wow Book. (Designed by Stanley Berkeley.)
„ 101. Pussikins. (A book of dear little kittens.) Designed by M. Morris.
„ 124. Lullaby Rhymes. (Designed by H. G. C. Marsh.)
„ 148. The House that Jack Built. (Designed by R. J. Williams.)
Awarded Two Gold Medals, Brussels Exhibition 1910.
GAMAGES price 1/10½ Post 3d.

Dean's 2/- Patent Rag Books

Containing 14 pages Charming Illustrations in Full Colours on Strong Cotton Cloth. Size 7 by 8 ins.
No. 61. Trains. (Showing Railroads throughout the world).
„ 62. Animals and their Little Ones.
„ 81. The Animal's Circus. (A book of Comical Animals)
„ 82. Ten Little Niggers. (With Music).
„ 102. The Menagerie. (Bold Animals from the Zoo).
„ 107. My Boat Book. (The Seaside Rag Book).
„ 123. Knockabout Land. (Happy Doings in Toy Land).
„ 146. Tiny Mites' A.B.C. (An Animal Alphabet).
„ 147. Bo-Peep's Rhyme Book.
GAMAGES price, 1/6 Post 3d.

Dean's 6/- Patent Rag Books

Containing 24 pages of Coloured Illustrations on Strong Cotton Cloth. Size 9¼ by 11¼ ins.
Cecil Aldin's Rag Book. No. 70. The Animal's School Treat. (Verses by Clifton Bingham.)
The John Hassall Rag Book. No. 141. Mother Goose Nursery Rhymes.
GAMAGES price 4/6 Post 4d.

Dean's 36 Patent Rag Books

Size 8 by 11¾ ins. Containing pages of Artistically Produced Design and Clear Text Matter on Strong Cotton Cloth. Amusing and Instructiv

No.
57. Just Off (designed by Vernon Barre
79. Noah's Zoo. (designed by All Wright)
80. Baby's A.B.C. (designed David Brett)
97. Pets at Home. (designed C. Pearse
103. Pretty Tails. (designed M. Morris
149. A Funny A.B.C Book. (designed by G. H. Dodd)
150. The Railway Rag Book. (designed by E. Travis)

GAMAGES price, 2/7½ Post 3d.

Painting Books and Children's Gift Books.

Dean's Canvassed Painting Books.

The great novelty of this series is that the canvassed paper is specially prepared for the purpose of giving all pictures painted thereon the appearance of having been coloured on actual canvas. The coloured originals are brilliant but simple, the books being not too difficult, but not too easy.

6d. Canvassed Painting Books.

Size 10¼ by 7¾ in.

Gamage's price 4½d. Post 3d.

Published at 6d.

1 The Greenhouse Painting Book
12 Spring Flowers do
13 Forest Foliage do.
14 Leaves of Trees to Paint
15 Dessert Painting Book
16 Fruit do.
17 Country Views to Paint
18 Rural Painting Book

NEW TITLES,
19 Butterflies Painting Book
20 Birds' Feathers and Eggs Painting Book
21 Water Plants Painting Book
22 Wayside Flowers Painting Book

1/- Canvassed Painting Books

Size 10¼ by 7¾ in.

The great novelty of this series is that the canvassed paper is specially prepared for the purpose of giving all pictures painted thereon the appearance of having been coloured on actual canvas

Gamage's price 9d. Post 3d.

Published at 1/-

Landscape and Floral Painting Book
4 Leaves and Flowers to Paint
5 Beautiful Flowers Painting Book
6 Woodland trees Painting Book
7 The Orchard Painting Book
8 Countryside Painting Book

NEW TITLES,
Butterflies and Feathers Painting Book
Wild Flowers Painting Book

Sixpenny Patchpuz Series.

Size, 8¾ by 12½ in. PATCHPUZ constitutes an entirely new idea for making most artistic and attractive pictures without paints or crayons The pictures are formed by cutting out and fixing to an outline sketch a number of coloured pieces provided on gummed sheets, fitting the whole together after the style of a Dissecting Puzzle.

Our Cash Price.
6d. Books, 4½d.
1/- ,, 9d.
Post 3d.

NEW TITLES,
Dean's Patchpuz Book, Nos. 7, 8, 9 and 10.
Also in Series :
Dean's Patchpuz Book, Nos. 3, 4, 5 and 6.

Shilling Patchpuz Series.

Dean's Patchpuz Book, Nos. 7, 8, 9 & 10.

Pictured by GLADYS HALL.

Shilling Kiddieland Series.

Stiff Covers. 16 Pages. 15 by 8 in. Coloured pictures and attractive verses in bold type. Big value.
1. Peggy. Gladys Hall.
2. Teddie. Eugénie Richards.
3. Puggydog. Gladys Hall.
4. Kittycat. Eugénie Richards,
Our price 9d. Post 3d.

Little Mother's Dolly Book. A model book of dolls for cutting out and dressing, by Sheila Young. Printed in full colours.

Olden Day Dollies. Similar to above, but the dolls will be dressed in costumes of the olden times.

The A B C Model Maker
The Circus Model Book
The Doll's House Model Book
Going Shopping
My Menagerie Model Book
The Model Book of Games
,, Book of Horses
,, Motor Car Model Book
,, Book of Trains
The Animals' Model Book
Dainty Dollies and their Dresses
The Farmyard Model Book
The Little Model Maker
The Model Puzzle Book
,, Book of Ships
,, Book of the Zoo
,, Peep Show
,, Book of Soldiers

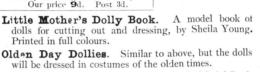

WE TWO & OTHERS ! !

2/6 Grand Prize Series.

10¼ by 10¼ in. Containing 96 pages of Pictures and Stories in full Colours and Tints, and bound cloth gilt bevelled boards with picture cover.

We Two and Others.

All about Animals.

Our price 1/10½

The CHIEF SCOUT SIR ROBERT BADEN-POWELL

W. FRANCIS AITKEN

The Boys' Hero

Life of Baden Powell attractively told.

Published at 1/-

Our price ... 9d.

Postage 3d.

3/6 Cloth Bound Series.

Size, 12 by 10 in.

Handsomely bound cloth gilt bevelled boards and picture covers.

Mounted on Cotton Cloth.

Containing 28 pages of Art Lithographed pictures, and in full Colours and Tints.

NEW TITLES.
Toddles   A Present for You

Also in Series :
Babykins Book
The Delightful Book
Musical Mites Book
Tingle Town   For Rainy Days
Lots of Fun

Paper. Containing 56 pages of Art Lithographic Pictures and in full Colours and Tints.

NEW TITLES.
My Picture Book
Peggy and Teddy.   (15 by 8 in.)
Kittycat & Puggydog. ,,   ,,

Also in Series :
The Overseas Book
Nursery Rhymes and Tales
An Animal and Train Book
The Real Life Picture Book
(Size 10¼ by 7¾ in.)

MY PICTURE BOOK

Model Books Children's At 1/-

THE LITTLE ANIMAL MODEL MAKER

The Model Book of Dolls
The Sunday Model Book
The Young Rider's Model Book

Only for Very Good Children.

A book of simple Stories and Verses, charmingly illustrated, and suitable for the very little ones. Usual price 2/6. A. W. Gamage's price 1/10½ Postage 4d.

CALENDARS, WRITING TABLETS, Etc.

Vest Pocket Calendars.

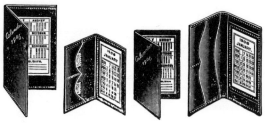

No. 611.   No. 612.   No. 613.   No. 614.

No. 611 Printed on Silk, in red and black and bound in fine leather ... ... 5d.

No. 612 Stamp Case and Monthly Midget Calender, in assorted leathers ... ... 5d.

No. 613 Calendar (printed on Silk), and Gentleman's Card Case, in fine leather ... ...10d.

No. 614 Gentleman's Card Case and Monthly Midget Calendars, assorted leathers ... ...10d.

Miniature Calendars.

No. 620.   No. 625.

Postal Regulations, Holidays, Moon Phases, and clear Calendar—one month to a page.

No. 620 Fast Bound Leather... 5d.

No. 621 Fast Bound Leather, loop and pencil ... 10d.

No. 625 Renewable Long Grain Leather, with pockets 4½d.

No. 626 Do. Russia, with pockets ... ...10d.

Bijou Calendars.

No. 630.   No. 632.

Daintily printed in red and black, with daily events, etc., and full postal information.

No. 630 Limp Leather, with stamp pockets ... 5d.

No. 631 Limp Leather, mounted on Greeting Card 5d.

No. 632 Tuck Case, Velvet Calf, with pocket ... 10d.

Happy Months Calendar.

A Purse Calendar in booklet form, with quotations suitable to each month, illustrated and printed on art paper, bound in Dainty Parchment and Orient Leather Covers ... ... 5d.

And in various elegant styles of Leather ... ... } at 10d.

Solid Brass Pedestal Date Stand.

(Protected.)

Elegant and Novel,

Exact size as shown .. **1/-**
Midget size **1/4**
Carte ,, ... **3/-**
Cabinet ,, ... **4/4**

The "Zenobia" Purse Calendar.

Price ... ... **5d.**

A dainty little Calendar, printed in red and black, with full postal information, charmingly bound in Parchment; Covers illuminated and ornamented in artistic styles. The feature of this Calendar is the "Zenobia" Scent Sachet with which it is interleaved. An attractive and pleasing novelty.

Hasty Notes Writing Tablet.

Padded Leather, complete with pencil.

Renewable inside.

Renewable Calendar.

Price **2/11**

Postage 4d.

Block Calendars.

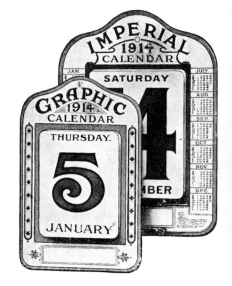

Block Calendars, with bold imposing figures, lithographed in colours. Very striking and handsome.

These Calendars include the dates for Sundays.

Fitted with Patented Holder.

The Graphic, size of actual block without mount, 5½ by 4½ .. .. each 10½d.

The Imperial, size of actual block without mount, 6¾ by 5 ... ... each 1/6

YOU CAN 'PHONE

YOUR ORDERS

BY RINGING

2700 HOLBORN.

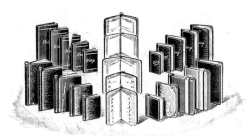

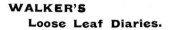

WALKER'S Loose Leaf Diaries.

Complete List on application.

Walker's Diaries, 1914.

STYLE OF COVER.	No. 1. SIZE OF LEAF, 3 in. by 2 in.		No. 2. SIZE OF LEAF, 4 in. by 2½ in.		No. 3. SIZE OF LEAF, 5 in. by 3⅛ in.		No. 4. SIZE OF LEAF, 5¾ in. by 3½ in,		No. 7. SIZE OF LEAF, 5¾ in. by 2¾ in.	
A WEEK at an opening.										
Cloth	51	6d.	52	6d.	53	9d.	54	1/-	57	9d.
Roan, Gilt edges	101	9d.	102	1/-	103	1/3	104	1/6	107	1/3
Velvet Calf	131	1/6	132	2/-	133	2/3	134	2/6	137	2/3
Roan, with Back Loop & Pencil	61	1/-	62	1/3	63	1/6	64	1/9	67	1/6
Renewable Binding. FULLY EQUIPPED WITH POCKETS.										
Long Grain	151	1/6	152	2/-	153	2/6	154	3/-	157	2/6
Morocco	181	3/-	182	3/6	183	4/6	184	5/-	187	4/6
Pigskin	301	3/-	302	4/-	303	5/-	304	6/-	307	5/6
TWO DAYS to a page.										
Cloth	511	9d.	512	1/-	513	1/3	514	1/6	517	1/3
Roan	111	1/3	112	1/6	113	1/9	114	2/3	117	2/-
Pigskin	811	1/6	812	2/3	813	3/-	814	3/6	817	3/-
Roan, with Back Loop & Pencil	611	1/6	612	1/9	613	2/-	614	2/3	617	2/-
ONE DAY to a page.										
Cloth	501	9d.	502	1/-	503	1/3	504	1/6	507	1/3
Roan	601	1/3	602	1/6	603	2/-	604	2/6	607	2/-
Pigskin	801	2/-	802	2/6	803	3/-	804	3/6	807	3/-
Velvet Calf	1001	1/9	1002	2/3	1003	3/-	1004	3/6	1007	3/-
A WEEK to a page (Graphic).										
Roan	011	9d.	012	1/-	013	1/3	014	1/6	017	1/3
Pigskin	021	1/3	022	1/6	023	2/-	024/1	2/3	027	2/-
Velvet Calf	091	1/6	092	2/-	093	2/3	094	2/6	097	2/3
Roan, with Back Loop & Pencil	061	9d.	062	1/-	063	1/3	064	1/6	067	1/3
Renewable Binding. FULLY EQUIPPED WITH POCKETS.										
Roan	110	1/9	120	2/3	130	2/9	140	3/6	170	3/-
Pigskin	310	2/9	320	3/6	330	4/6	340	5/6	370	4/6
Velvet Calf	810	4/-	820	5/-	830	6/3	840	8/-	870	6/9

The Pearl.

Size of Leaf, 2 in. by 1¾ in.

No. 30. Paste Grain .. **6½d.**

,, 30sc. Paste Grain, with silver corners **1/-**

,, 32. Velvet Calf .. **1/-**

,, 35. Crushed Morocco **1/-**

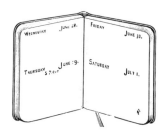

The Diamond.

Size of Leaf, 2¾ in. by 2 in.

No. 40. Paste Grain .. .. **9**d.

,, 40. Paste Grain, with silver corners .. **1/-**

,, 42. Velvet Calf **1/3**

,, 45. Crushed Morocco .. **1/3**

Paste Grain, with back loop and pencil **1/-**

Year-by-year Books,

CAN BE STARTED ANY DAY IN ANY YEAR.

Price .. **3/4 4/2 5/4**

Postage 3d.

Silver Bar Mounted Diaries.

A NEW IDEA.

VARIOUS BINDINGS.

Gordon Browne's Novelty Calendars for 1914.

Wot's 'e done?

A Hunting Engagement.

Golfer.

Winter Sport.

Harmony.

Obstruction.

Fashion.

"The quintessence of quaint-
ness"

Hand Carved and Hand Coloured
Wooden Figures by

GORDON BROWNE, R.I.

Each in box packed securely for
post.

Price .. **1/4** Post 3d.

All New Designs for 1914.

Towser.

In the Park.

Canvas Panel Calendars in Oak Frames.

Hand-coloured Designs by

John Hassall and Cecil Aldin.

Eight varieties. Price .. .. **1/4** each.

Walker's Memo Calendar.

Both dates and spaces for Memos. and Engagements for every day.
Renewable Blocks issued yearly .. **1/-**
Bronzed Metal, very strong and handsome .. .. **2/6** Post
Also in various Leather Styles for Presents .. **3/3 4/9** 4d.

Solid Brass Rim Calenda

Midget, upright or oblong .. 8
Carte 10
Cabinet 1/
Postage 3d.

J.W.

"Year By Year"
A condensed comparative record of
5 years. Can be commenced on
any day in any year.
An Ideal Gift.
Made in Two Sizes.
Roan .. .. **3/4** and **4/2**
Pigskin or Velvet
Calf .. .. **4/2** ,, **5/4**
Postage 3d.

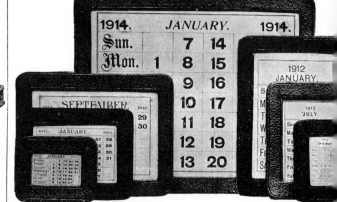

Boudoir Calendar Cases. New series of Regal Grained Le
Two Colours, Upright or Oblong.
Midget size **5**d. Carte, **10**d. Cabinet, **1/4** Mammoth, Oblong only
Postage 3d. Largest 5d.

Charles Letts's School-boy's Pocket Diary and Note Book.

(Compiled by MARC CEPPI, Whitgift School.)

Containing much useful information and many Tables helpful for his work & games.

A similar Diary is published for girls at same prices, under the title **The School-girls' Pocket Diary.**

Also a Diary specially arranged for those engaged in the Scholastic Profession, **The School Teacher's Pocket Diary.**

This Diary, which was only recently introduced, becomes more and more popular, so much so that, though it was reprinted no less than four times, it went right out of print, and many who wished to obtain a copy were unable to do so. A Diary or a Note Book is necessary to all Schoolboys. Even the youngest pupil requires some little book in which to note down the work set for Home preparation and the thousand and one things that he is expected to remember.

The SCHOOL-BOY'S DIARY is intended to take the place of the nondescript note books to be found in all schoolboys' pockets. It is of real use to the owner, for, in addition to the Diary proper, it contains :—Latin, French and German Irregular Verbs, Historical Events proper for every day of the year. Valuable Mathematical Tables and Constants. Science Notes and Constants. Numerous pages in which a boy can keep a record of books lent and borrowed, pocket money, letters written and received, marks, results of school matches (cricket, football and hockey) and of school sports. Also Cricket and Football Championship Tables, etc.

With very few exceptions, the Mathematical and Scientific Constants are those which the student cannot be expected to remember, so that the Diary may be admitted in the Classroom or the Laboratory without fear of "cribbing."

ART LINEN, with back loop pencil .. **1/-**   LEATHER, with pocket and back loop pencil .. **2/-**
MOROCCO, card and stamp pockets and back loop pencil **3/-**

Charles Letts's Boy Scout's Note Book and Diary.

With a mass of USEFUL information . to Boy Scouts

Bound in Khaki Cloth **6**d. copy, or in Leather **1/-** per copy.

Size 4⅛ by 2¾ in.

Issued under the direction of
Lt.-Gen. Sir Robt. BADEN-POWELL, KCB.

This book is the Official Handbook of Boy Scouts, and contains a mass of information which makes it invaluable to every scout. It is very suitable for adoption as the Hand-book of Scout Patrols ; special terms will be quoted by the Publishers when ordered in quantity.

Charles Letts's "R.H.S." Gardener's Pocket Diary & Note Book

With a mass of useful information invaluable to Gardeners—amateur and professional.
Edited by Rev. W. WILKS.

Bound in Art Leather Cloth PLUVIUSIN BRAND **1/-**
Bound in Leather, with pocket and back loop pencil **2/-**

Printed and Published for
The Royal Horticultural Society by **Charles Letts & Co** *Diarists and Manufacturers,* LONDON.

The above Diary is a book which will appeal to all garden lovers; it gives weekly suggestions and reminders of work to be done—pages for the record of seed sowings and results—pages useful to growers—and many pages of useful suggestions and recipes. It is of handy size, suitable for the pocket, measuring 4⅝ in. by 3⅛ in.

Charles Letts's Poultry Keeper's Diary & Note Book

This Diary issued to enable systematic methods in the keeping of Poultry to be rendered simple and easy, and thus reduce the costs and increase the profits where Poultry are kept for profit.

Edited by C. E. J. WALKEY,
Member of Committee of Utility Poultry Club, Instructor in Poultry to Somerset County Council, etc.

It contains Monthly Notes on Poultry Keeping, Instructions for preparing Birds for Show, Treatment of all Ailments and Diseases, Standards of various Breeds, Dates, etc., of Shows, Prices of Eggs, Particulars of different Clubs, etc. Many pages of Tables, etc., which make it

INVALUABLE TO ALL WHO KEEP POULTRY FOR PROFIT or PLEASURE

Published jointly with THE POULTRY PRESS, LTD.

Bound in Art Leather Cloth, with Pencil,

ONE SHILLING.

A Large Variety of CHARLES LETTS'S DIARIES and Note Books may be seen at A. W. GAMAGE, Ltd. .. STATIONERY DEPARTMENT ..

Christmas Cards and Calendar Values.

The Bird Calendars.

No. 16. Bird is composed of real Feathers. Various Birds

Price .. **1/9½** each. Post free 2/-

No. 1026. No. 1029.

A series of four British sports (aviation, tennis, cricket, golf), figures artistically moulded in metal.

Size 13¼ by 6. Price **1/3½** each. Postage 2d.

New ART Calendars.

PRICE **10½**d.

Postage 3d.

Real feathers.

WONDERFUL VALUE!

GAMAGE'S
BOX OF TWELVE
Christmas Leaflet Greeting Cards
With Envelopes. ALL DIFFERENT.
PRICE **1/0½** POST FREE.

Containing nine beautifully executed Black and White Leaflet Christmas and New Year Cards (assorted designs), complete with envelopes.

Price .. .. **1/0½** Post free.

Special Values in Calendars & Christmas Cards.

THE
GIFT FOR FATHER.

The Fox.
Novelty Metal Calendar, with Calendar in Gilt Frame (renewable).

Price .. .. **3/6** Post 4d.

Novelty Miniature Fox.
Metal Calendar. Price .. **9½d.**
Post 3d.

The Eagle
Paper Weight and Brush Penwiper.

Penholders and pencils extra.

6½ in. high.

A very useful Present.

Price .. **3/6**

Post 4d.

The Boy Scout
Calendar. Metal.

Price .. **6½d.**

Post 3d.

THE GEM
Box of 6 Leaflet and Corded Children's Christmas Cards. beautifully coloured. Per box .. **6½d.** Post free.

THE GEM
Box of Christmas Cards. 6 Beautiful subjects. Black and White studies. Ribboned and Leaflets. Per box .. **6½d.** 6 Cards. Post free.

DOES YOUR MOTHER KNOW YOUR'E OUT ?
Novelty Metal Calendar.

Companion Calendar. Does your Father Know you are out? Same price.

Price **9½d.**

Post 2d.

Novel Metal Calendar.

Price **6½d.**

Post 3d.

No. 81.
The Comic Calendar.
12 Designs. Various Characters.
Price **1/-** Post free.

No. 28. The beautiful
Panel Calendar.
Assorted Designs. High Art Coloured. A complete picture when Calendar is detached.
Price **3/6** Post free.

No. 20.
The Portrait Panel
Various Heads Calendar.
Very decorative.
Latest Novelty.
Price .. **2/3** Post free.

U

ORDER EARLY TO PREVENT DISAPPOINTMENT, MANY GOOD DESIGNS ARE SOLD OUT QUICKLY.

Private Greeting-Cards.
BOOKS SENT ON APPLICATION.
Unrivalled Selection from all the Leading Publishers.

1s. CALENDARS.

The Novelty of the Season

THE
Lifebuoy Calendar

(Perpetual

TO ALT\
DATE,\
PULL T\
ANCHOR

That's a

VERY\
SIMPLE

Lasts with ordinary care scores of ye

Price   ..   **1/6**   Postage 4d

Ernest Nisters & Co.'s

Fine Art Block Calendars.

Longfellow\
Shakespearian Year\
Tennyson\
Christian Year\
The Dickens\
Longfellow\
Ruskin

Published at 1/-\
Gamage's price   **9**d.\
Postage 3d.

Any Calendar sold out will be substituted unless otherwise ordered.

THE PRESENT FOR EVERY GOOD BOY OR GIRL.

DRAWING AND PAINTING MADE EASY.
"PICTURES, AND HOW TO MAKE THEM."

A beautifully pictured Box containing eighteen perfect models Animals, Birds, etc., to guide the young artist in drawing. T Colour and Twelve outline pictures are also given as examples, Six Sheets of Drawing Paper and a pencil.   Price **1/6**   Post 4d

Entertaining and Educational.

Come unto me\
Gems of Thoughts\
Published at 6d.

Days with Shakespeare\
Gamage's price **4½**d.

Through the Year\
Daily Light\
Post 2d.

6d. CALENDARS

A delightful Pastime and a great aid in learning how to draw and paint.\
Pictures, and How to make Them.   Series I.   "Country Life."\
Full instructions in each Box.   Size 13¼ by 10¼\
Pictures, and How to make Them.   Series II.   "Forest and Jungle.

DOLLIES ON THEIR TRAVELS,
with their Trunk, Suit Case, Bags, Dresses and Hats.

In attractive Coloured Picture Envelope,\
Price 6d.

This pleasing novelty consists of Four Dolls with their Luggage affixed to effective background which stands firmly, the Trunk, Suit Case and Bag containing Twelve articles of clothing—Frocks, Coats and Hats, by a simple arrangement made to take off and put on, and forming a large variety of attire.

Cut out in stiff card. Size 9¾ in. by 6in. closed,\
21 in. by 6 in. extended.

Our price, **5**d.   Postage 2d.

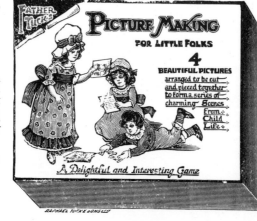

FATHER TUCK'S PICTURE MAKING FOR LITTLE FOLK

Price **1/-** per Box of Four Pictures.\
Postage 4d.

The box contains Four sheets of Coloured Obj and Four Pictures in Outline. The colou objects are to be cut out and affixed to t respective positions shown on the outline she when a beautiful picture will be formed. Gun upon the back of the coloured sheet, and a br is given in each box, so that only a little wate necessary for making the pictures. A short desc tive story is on the back of each outline sheet

Series I.   "The Punch and Judy Show," "Go to School," The Three Friend "The Little Flower Seller."

Series II.   "Blind Man's Buff," "In Fa Dress," "Off to Town," "The Swin

Fancy Boxes of Christmas Stationery.

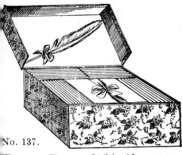

No. 137.

Fancy Box of Stationery.

Contains 50 sheets linen note fashionable size and 50 envelopes, Quill pen, artistically faded and fancy box, only **1/6½**. Post 4d.

No. 136.   Very Handsome

Cabinet of Stationery.

With pull-out drawer and tied with ribbons. Most artistic and seasonable box.

Only .. **2/3½**   Postage 4d.

No. 133.   **A Splendid Gift.**

Large cabinet of stationery, leatherette red covered with picture in lid.
A most desirable present.

Only .. **2/3½**   Postage 5d.

The Fleet.

A most greatly appreciated gift by Boys and Girls.
The Complete Correspondence Outfit.

A magnificent case, containing a liberal supply of good stationery, as illustrated. The case is water-proof with spring lock and key and leather handle, a very useful Attache Case when empty.

Size, 12½ by 8½ by 3¼.   **5/6** each, post free.

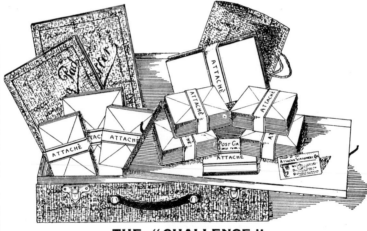

THE "CHALLENGE."

A wonderful case for **3/11**.   Postage 4d.

Good Linen-faced Stationery, tray in case and contents as illustrated.
The cheapest and most useful case ever sold.   Size, 15½ by 9 by 3⅜.

Grand Value!!

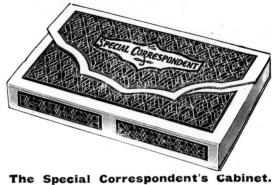

The Special Correspondent's Cabinet.

Contains 50 sheets of linen faced note paper, pad, and 50 envelopes to match.   Duchess shape.

Only **10½d**. Postage 3d.   **10/3** doz. Carriage extra.

No. 139

Fancy Box of Stationery.

60 sheets and 60 envelopes, tied with fancy ribbons only **10½d**.

Postage 3d.

Novelty!
Travelling Pad Companion.

Contains linen faced pad and envelopes to match.
Art colours.
Fitted with quill as sketch.

Only .. **10½d**.

Postage 3d.

The New Art Linen Companion.

Writing pad with pocket containing Envelopes to match.
Heliotrope, White, Blue, and Green.
Quite an acceptable gift.

Price **10½d.** each.   Postage 3d.   **10/3** dozen.

No. 212.   **Linen Cabinet.**

Cream or White.
100 Sheets, 100 Envelopes to match.
10½d. Post 4d.

No. 213.

New Parchment Cabinet.

100 Sheets and 100 Envelopes to match.
10½d. Post 4d.

U..

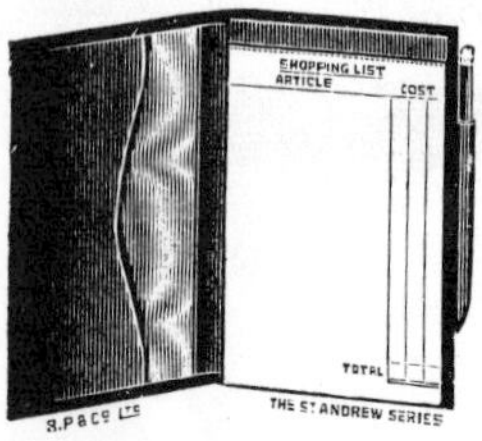

Shopping Lists.

Polished straight grain Roan with Ladies' Card Pocket .. **1/11**
Crushed leather do. **3/3**
Pigskin do. **3/11**
Russia do. **4/6**
Seal do. **4/11**
Crushed Morocco do **6/6**

Post 2d.

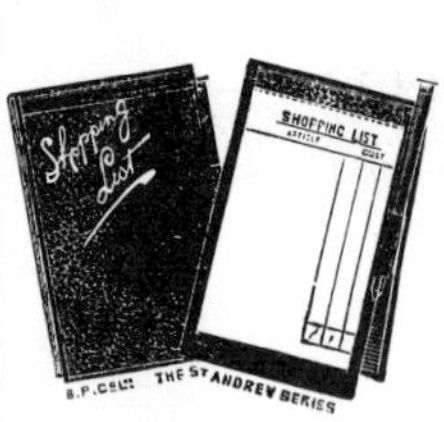

Shopping Lists.

French Morocco **9½d.**
Refills .. **3d.**
Crushed leather **1/3½**
Refills .. **5d.**

Ruled for articles purchased and cost

Small size to fit Lady's Purse. Post 2d.

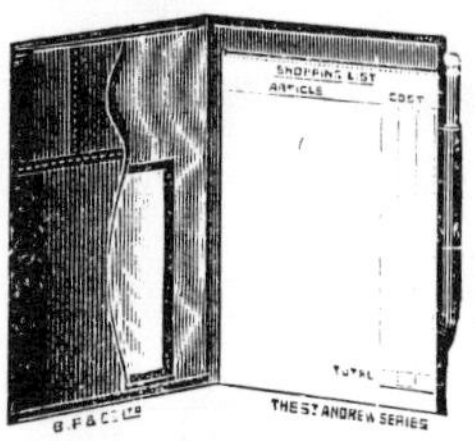

Shopping Lists.

Lined satin with mirro stamp pocket and gold top pencil.

		Refil
Polished Roan	**2/6**	6½
Crushed leather	**3/6**	7½
Pigskin ..	**4/6**	8½
Russia ..	**5/6**	9½
Seal ..	**6/6**	10

Post 2d.

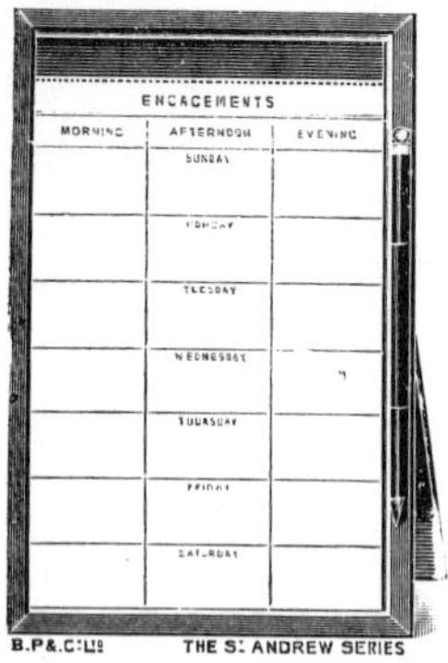

Engagement Tablet.

For Morning and Afternoon Engagements. 52 leaves. One week at view. Perforated at top. Undated so that tablets may be commenced at any time.

Fancy art vellum cloth .. **1/6**
Polished long grain Roan .. **2/6**
Do. with limp flap .. **3/6**

Post 4d.

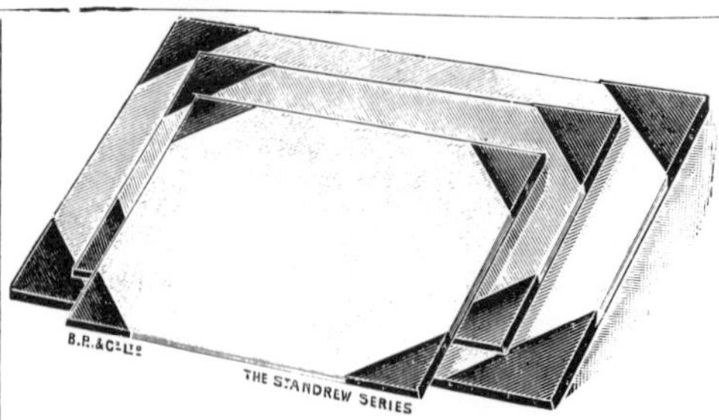

Blotting Pads.

French Morocco Leather Corners
11⅜ by 8⅝ **5½d.** 13⅜ by 8⅝ **7½d.** 17¾ by 11 **10½d.**

Russia Leather Corners
11⅜ by 8⅝ **1/3** 13⅜ by 8⅝ **1/11** 17¾ by 11 **2/6**

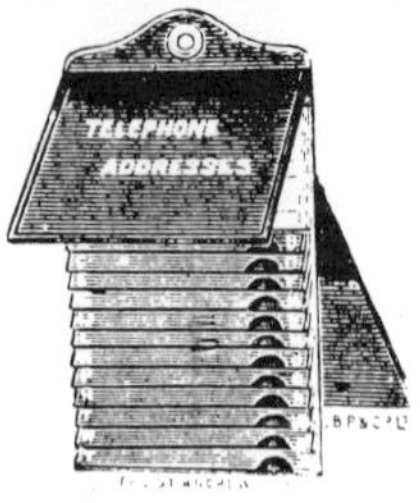

Telephone Address Stand

Alphabetically arranged Lettered in gold.
Polished staight grain Roan, with strut **2/6**
Postage 3d.

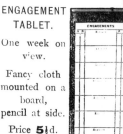

ENGAGEMENT TABLET.

One week on view.

Fancy cloth mounted on a board, pencil at side.

Price **5½d.**

Postage 2d.

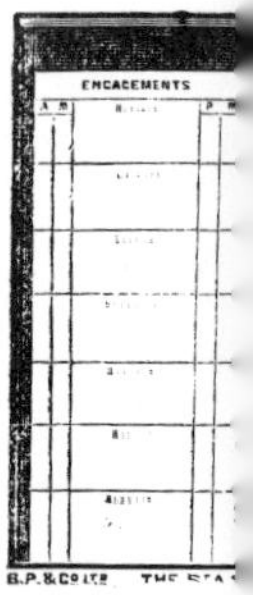

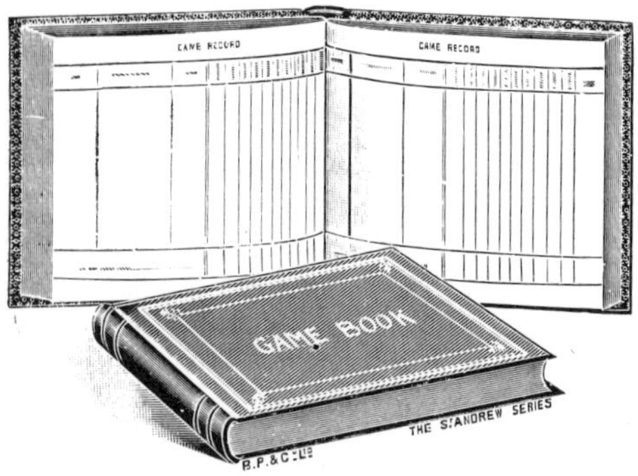

Game Books.

40 leaves, whole limp cloth, marble edge, lettered gold **2/11**
40 leaxes, ½ bound French Morocco, marble paper sides lettered **3/11**
40 leaves, whole bound stiff Roan, marble edges lettered **7/11**
80 leaves, whole limp polished Roan, gilt edges lettered **11/6**
120 leaves, whole bound diced Persian, gilt edges lettered **23/6**
120 leaves, whole bound hard grained Morocco, gilt edges, lettered **24/6**
120 leaves, whole bound Russia, gilt edges, lettered **32/6**
120 leaves, whole bound Pigskin, gilt edges, lettered **35/9**

Postage 5d.

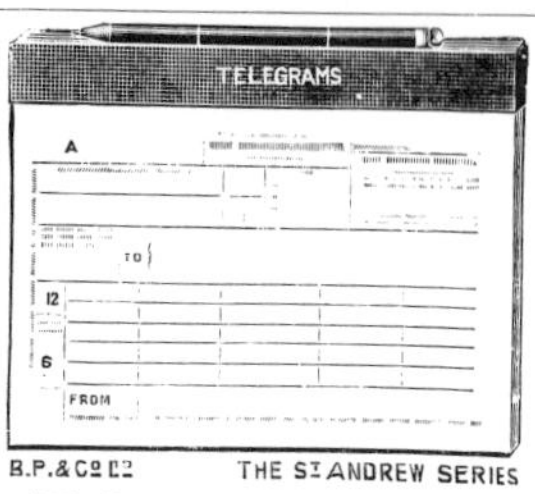

Telegram Block.

Refillable.

Art Linen tops, perforated, with pencil .. **1/3**
Polished Roan do. **1/9**

Post 3d.

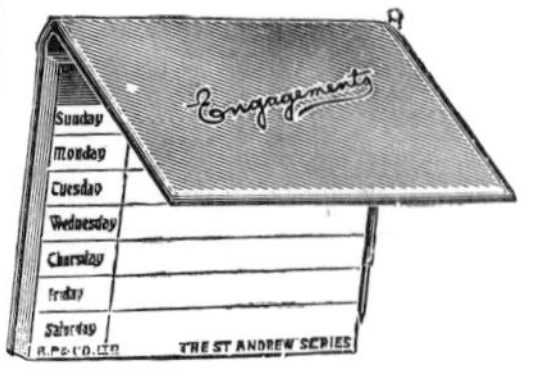

Daily Engagement Block.

Size of leaves 5¾ by 4¾ ins. oblong.

Fancy art vellum cloth, with pencil **1/1½**
Polished straight grain Roan ditto **2/3½**

Postage 3d.

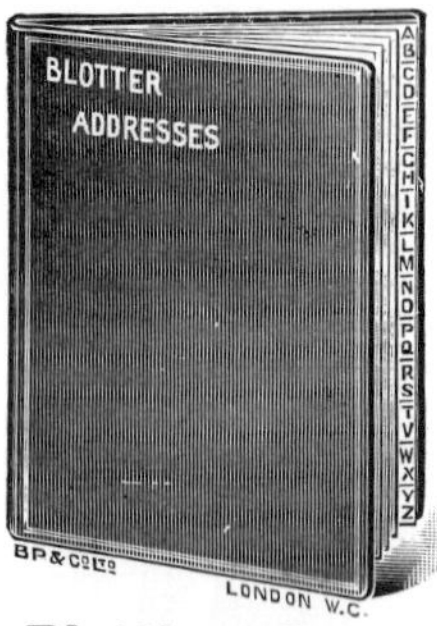

Blotting Case.

With address book, in fancy art vellum cloth, size 12 by 10 ins. .. **1/4**
Padded straight grain Roan .. **2/1**

Pos 3d.

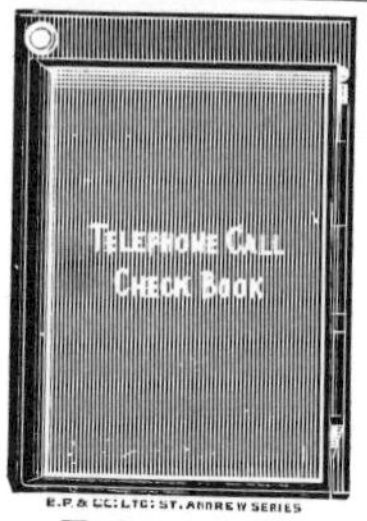

The Telephone Call Check Book

A complete record of the number of times a Subscriber uses the telephone
In patent leather, lett'd ... **10½d.**
In fancy art vellum, lett'd ... **1/9½**
Postage 2d.

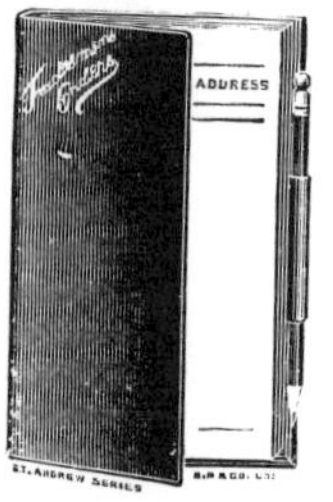

Tradesmen's Orders

In polished Roan, limp flap lined satin gold top pencil. Block stamped die in color, mauve, green, scarlet or dark red. Price **1/9½**
Refills 9½d Post 2d.

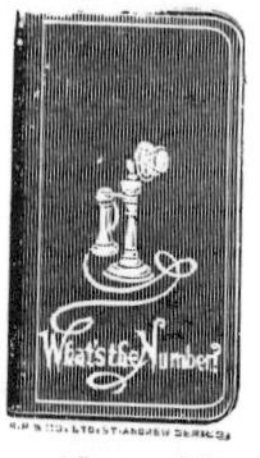

What's the Number.

Concise register of Telephone addresses for vest pocket or purse.
In polished Roan .. **9½d.**
In Calf, Seal or Crushed Mor. **1/3**
Postage 2d.

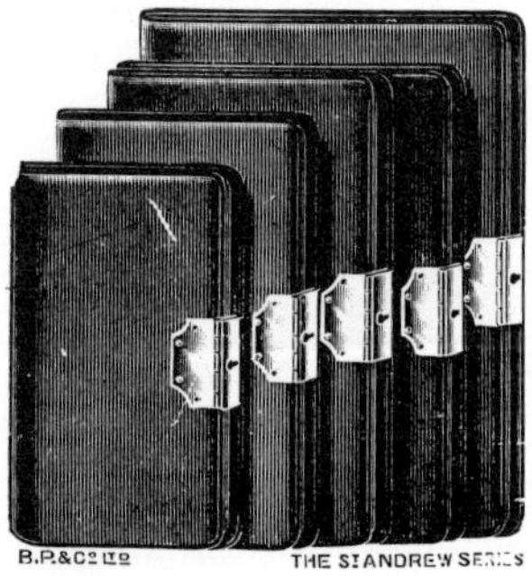

Private Manuscript and Cash Account Book

Best polished long grained Roan, round corners, Towgoods cream laid paper, gilt edges, nickel lock and 2 keys

F'lscap 8vo leaves	6 by 4	**4/6**
Post 8vo leaves	7 by 4½	**4/11**
L-post 8vo ,,	8 by 5	**5/11**
F'lscap 4to ,,	8 by 6	**7/6**
Post 4to ,,	8½ by 7	**8/6**

Post 5d

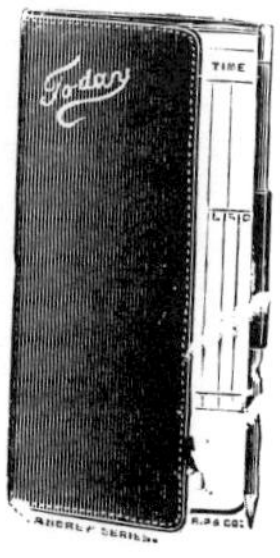

To-day.

A combined engagement tablet, shopping list and note book.

Limp cases, satin lined flaps, oval nickel top pencils, loose refills, gilt edges, lettered in gold

		Refills
Limp Roan	**2/6**	6½
Velvet Persian	**3/6**	7½
Crushed Morocco	**5/6**	8½
Real Seal	**6/6**	9½

Postage 2d.

Visitors Books

Oblong Series.

Ruled on cream wove paper, bound with bevelled boards, gilt edges and gilt linen roll, lettered.

Polished straight grain ruled and printed **10/6**
Hard grained Mor. **12/6**
Russia ... **15/6**
Pigskin ... **20/-**
Post, Small 4d. Large 6d

Upright Series.

Limp French Morocco ruled and printed, marble edges **4/-**
Padded polished Roan gilt edges **5/-**
Padded Morocco do **9/6**
Padded Russia **9/6**
Stiff Pigskin **12/6**
Post, Small 4d. Large 6d

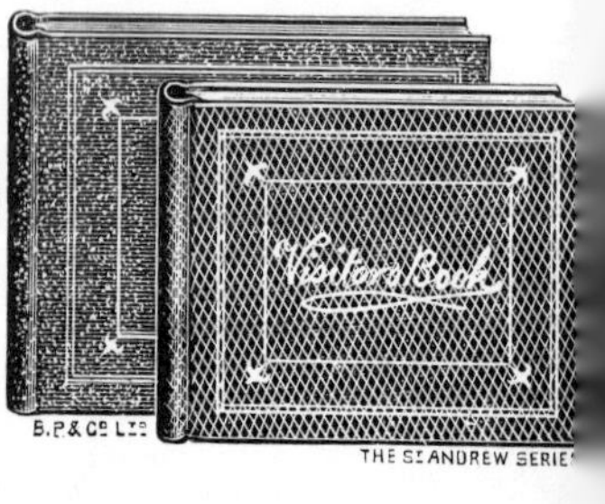

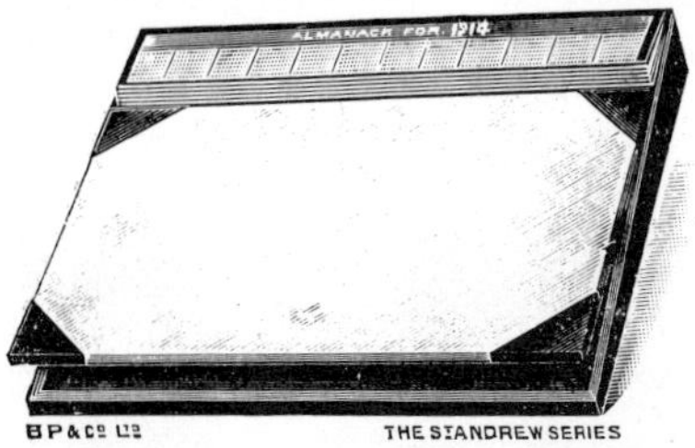

Calendar Blotting Pad and Desk Slope with diary, one week at view.
Price **1/11** Post 4d.

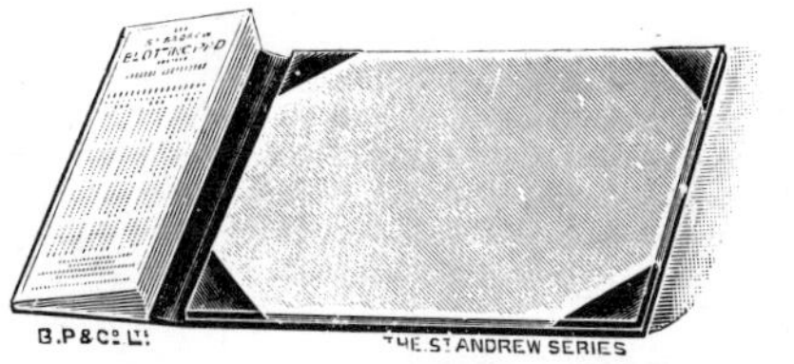

Blotting Pad with Diary.
Interleaved Blotting. Giving postal and other useful information with pencil.
Price **2/-** Post 4d

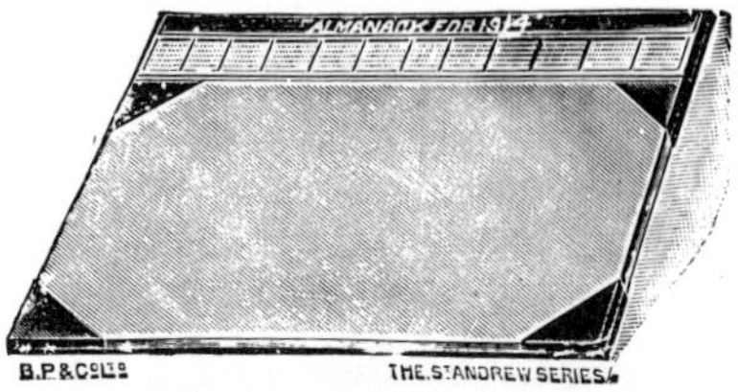

Calendar Blotting Pad.
Printed 1 week to an opening perforated at top with printed almanack on outside.
Price **1/-** Post 4d.

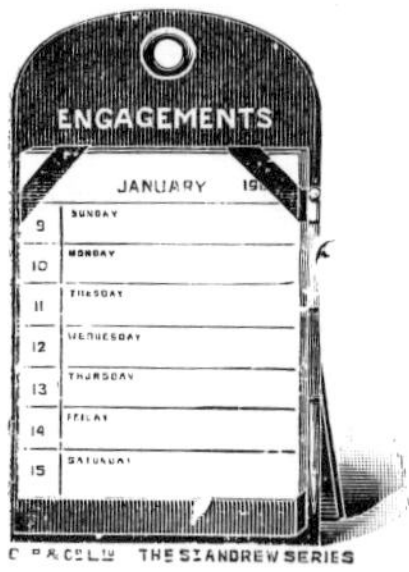

A Concise WeeklyMemo Diary Stand for 1914.

Fancy cloth with strout and pencil.

Price **10½**d.

Polished Roan ditto.

Price **1/4½**

Post 3d.

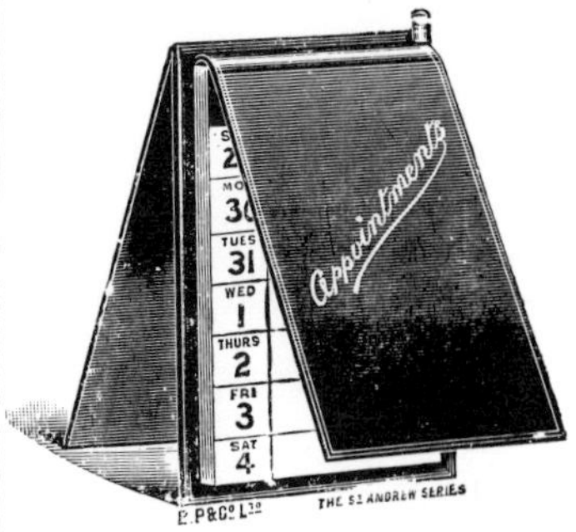

Upright 'Appointment' Stand.

Printed in black and red for 1914.

Art Vellum Cloth, **1/4**

Polished Roan, **2/9**

Post 3d.

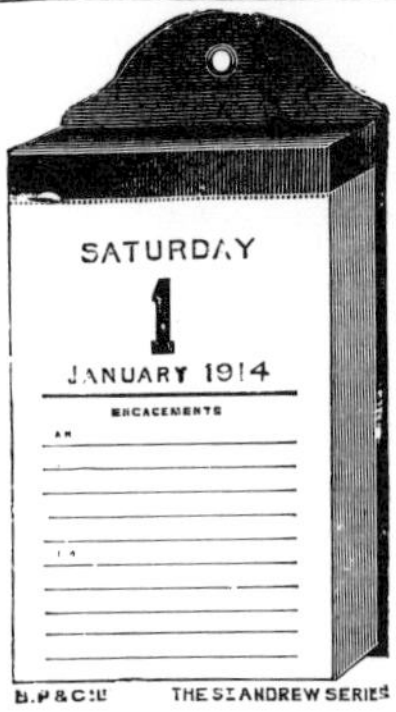

The "St. Andrew" Dated Note and Engagement Block for 1914.

Printed in bold type black and red.

To hang up.

Price **1/4** Post 4d

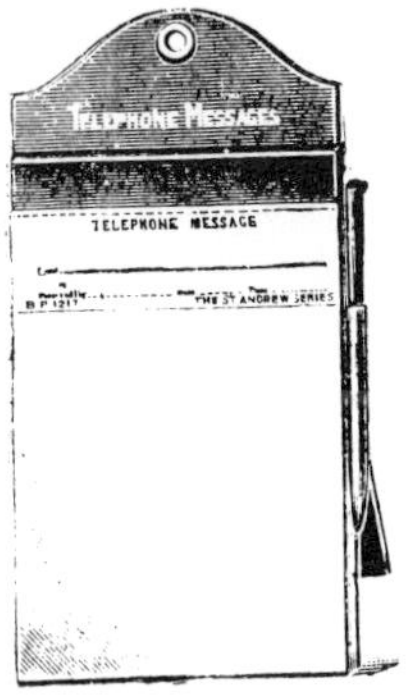

Telephone Message Block.
Fancy Art Vellum Cloth, **10½**d.
Loose Refills, **6½**d.
Polished Roan ... **1/9½**
Loose Refills, **9½**d. Post 3d.

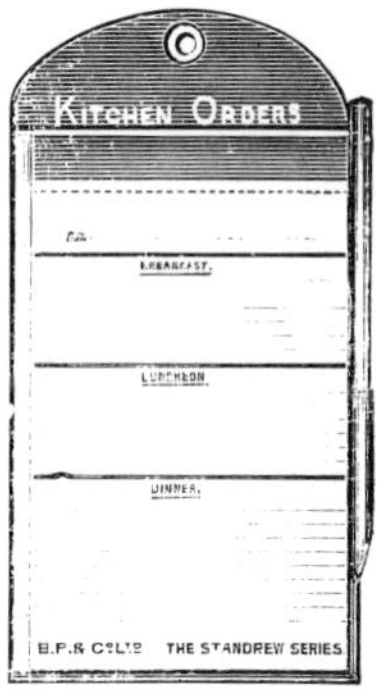

Kitchen Order Block.
Fancy Art Vellum Cloth **10½**d.
Loose Refills, **6½**d.
Polished Roan ... **1/9½**
Loose Refills, **9½**d. Post 3d.

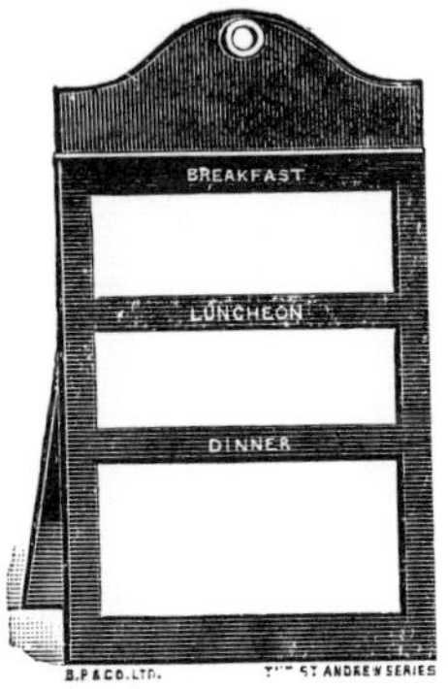

Kitchen Order Slates.
Porcelain mounted in polished roan, stand.
Refillable, **2/3½** Post 4d.

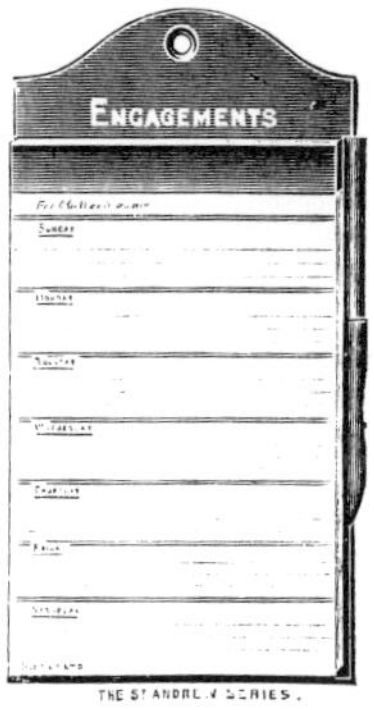

Engagement Block.
1 week at view. Fancy Art Vellum Cloth, **10½**d. Loose refills, **6½**d.
Polished Roan ... **1/9½**
Loose Refills, **9½**d. Post 3d.

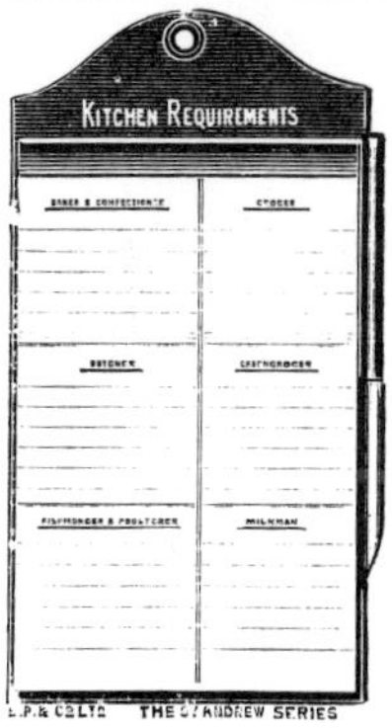

Instructions to Kitchen Block.
Fancy Art Vellum Cloth, **10½**d.
Loose Refills, **6½**d.
Polished Roan ... ...
Loose Refills **9½**d. Post 3d

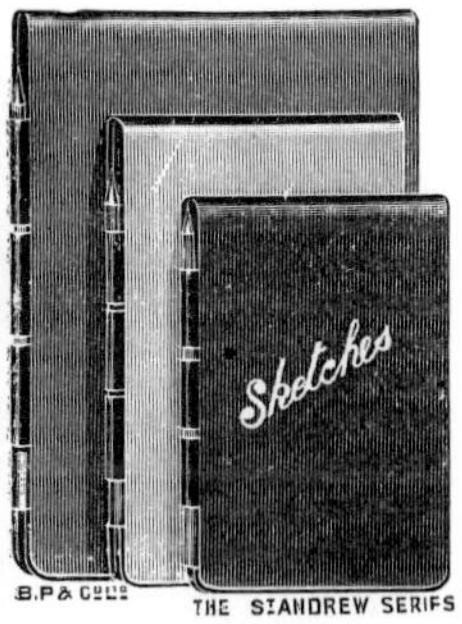

Sketch Books.

Cartridge leaves.

Fancy Art Colour Vellum Cloth.

Pencils at side.

Price

6½d. **7½**d. **10½**d.

Post 3d.

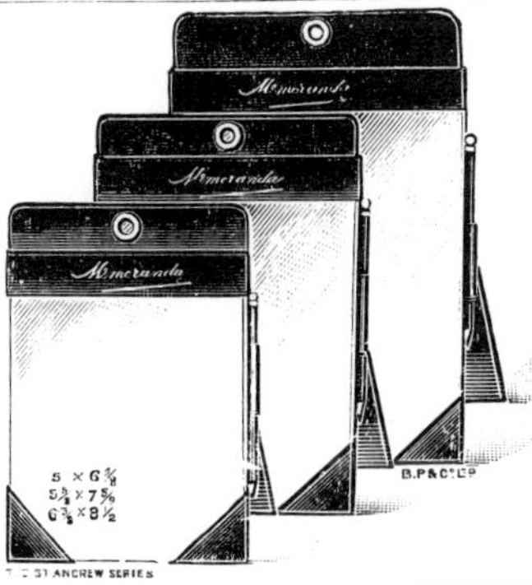

Memoranda Slates.

Art Vellum Cloth.

Lettered white.

5 by 6⅜ .. **10½**d.
5⅝ by 7¾ .. **1/1½**
6⅞ by 8½ .. **1/4½**

Straight grain leather.

Lettered gold.

5 by 6⅜ .. **1/3½**
5⅝ by 7⅜ .. **1/6½**
6⅞ by 8½ .. **1/11½**

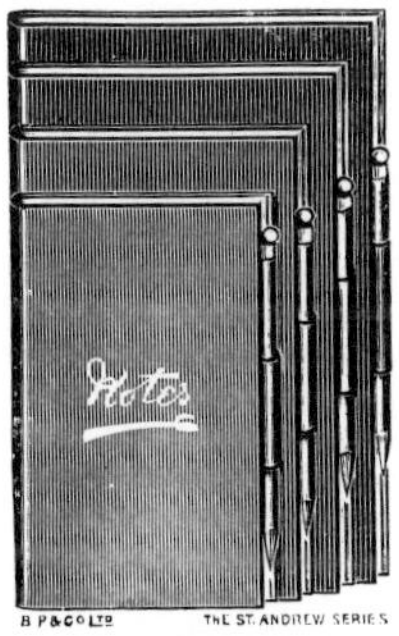

Notes Blocks

Fancy Art Vellum Cloth.

Lettered in gold.

Pencil at side.

Loose Refills.

		Refills.
5¾ by 3¾ ..	**6**d.	**3**d.
5½ by 4¼ ..	**9**d.	**3½**d.
7¼ by 4⅞	**11**d.	**5**d.
8 by 5¼	**1/1½**	**6**d.

Post 2d.

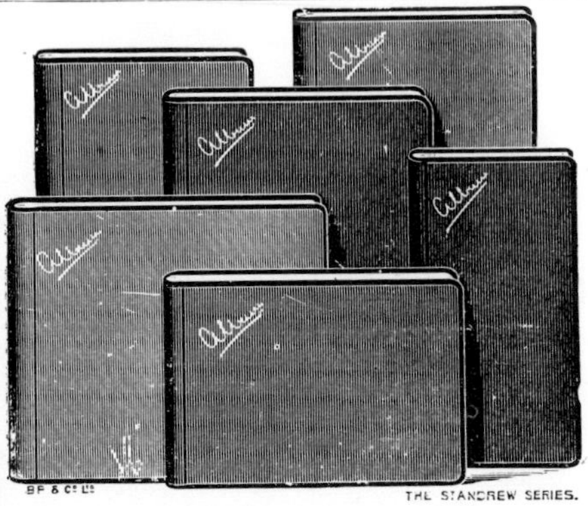

Padded Writing Albums.

In polished Roan.

Tinted leaves, interleaved drawing paper.

Round corners, gilt edges and fancy linings.

Oblong or upright.

Large 8vo,	8 by 5	..	**2/11**
Foolscap 4to,	6¾ by 7¼	..	**3/11**
Post 4to	9 by 7	..	**4/11**

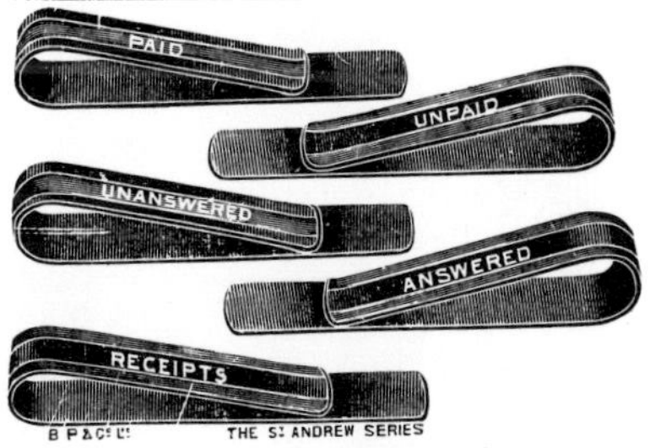

Sheffield Steel Spring Clips.

In 1 color leather .. **10½**d. In 2 colors leather .. **1/0½**
In 1 ,, lettered, **1/3½** In 2 ,, lettered, **1/4½**
Any regimental colors can be supplied to customers requirements. Postage 1d.

Very Useful Christmas Gifts.

Addresses

Roan, with pencil. Size 6 by 4 in. **2 6 3/11**
,,   ,,   ,, 6½ ,, 4½ ,, **2 11 4/6**
,,   ,,   ,, 7¼ ,, 5 ,, **3 6 5/6**
Crushed Morocco with pencil do. **4/6 5/6**
do.   do.   do. **5/11 6/11**
do.   do.   do. **6/11 8/11**
Postage 3d. and 4d.

(With Silver Price Corners)

No. N. 9297.   Telegram Case.
Silver Corners and Silver Word Telegrams.
French Morocco. **10/6** Postage 4d.

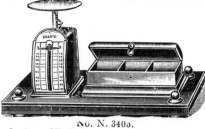

No. N. 3400.
Letter Weigher and Stamp Box.
Size of the base 6 by 3½ in. Nickel.
White Crystal base **10/9** Postage 5d.

No. N. 3260.   Letter Openers.
White Crystal with Nickel Fittings.
Length 8½ in.   Price **1/11½**   Postage 4d.

No. N. 3305.   Crystal Seal.
White Crystal. Length 3¾ in. Nickel fittings.
Price .. **1/11½**   Postage 3d.

No. N. 693.
Paper Weight.
Nickel fittings.
Crystal Base.
Size 3½ by 2¾ in.
Price **2/3**
Postage 3d.

Leather Autograph Books.
With Gilt Tooling Gilt Edges.
Prices **2/6, 3/6, 4/6** and **5/6**   Postage 4d.

New Writing Pad.

100 Sheets Linen Bond .. **5½d.**   Post 3d.
5/3 dozen.   Carriage extra.

Writing Pad.

100 Sheets Linen Bond, Ruled .. **5½d.**   Post 3d.
5/3 dozen.   Carriage extra.

No. N. 3375.   Nickel Sealing Set.
Complete Seal, Wax and Lamp.   Crystal Base.
Size of Tray, 6¼ by 4¾ in.   **10/9**   Postage 4d.

No N 9825.   Telegram Case.
Straight Grain Roan.   Price **2/6**   Post 3d.

No. N. 2200.
Menu or Note Porcelain Slate.
In Nickel Frames.
Size 5¾ by 3¼ in.
Price .. **1/4½**
Postage 4d.

No. N. 3331.
Penwiper and Stamp Box.
With Stamp.   Size 4½ by 3½ in.
Height 3¼ in.   Nickel.   **6/6**   Post 4d.

No. N. 2356.
Gumpot.
White Pearled Glass.
Nickel fittings.
Price **2/6**
Postage 3d.

No. N. 3390.
Letter Weigher.
Size of the base 2¾ by 3½
Nickel.   White Crystal Base.
Price **5/1**
Postage 4d.

No. N. 817.
String Holder
With cutter on top.
5 in. long.
Nickel on crystal glass base.
With string.
Price .. .. **4/11**   Postage 3d.

Useful Christmas Gifts.

Guide Covers.

In Polished L.G. Roan.
With Binder for holding Books
securely.

or Bradshaw	..	B. 9221
A.B.C.	..	B. 9229
Post Office Guide	..	B. 9225
Army List	..	B. 9233
Navy List	..	B. 9237

Price .. **4/6**   Post 4d.

Address Books.

Limp Covers. Gilt Edges,
Double Thickness.
Size.
5⅞ by 4½, French Morocco.
B. 9109 .. **2/9**
6½ by 5, French Morocco.
B. 9410 .. **3/3**
7¼ by 5½, French Morocco.
B. 9411 .. **3/6**
Post 2d.

Address Books.

Very limp and thin.   Bank paper.
Gilt Edges.

No.	Size	Roan.	Pig-skins	Post
B. 9385 ..	3¼ by 2¼ in.	**9½d.**	**1/-**	2d.
B. 9386 ..	3½ ,, 2¾ in.	**1/0½**	**1/3½**	,,
B. 9387 ..	4 ,, 2⅝ in.	**1/3½**	**1/6½**	,,
B. 9388 ..	4½ ,, 3⅛ in.	**1/6½**	**1/11½**	,,

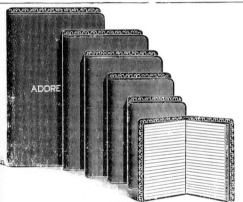

Address Books.

Padded Velvet Calf Covers.
Gilt Edges. Lettered in Go'd.

Size.	No.	Price.	
3½ by 2¼	B. 4845	**1/11½**	each.
4 by 2½	B. 4846	**2/3**	,,
4½ by 3	B. 4847	**2/9**	,,
5½ by 3⅝	B. 4848	**3 3**	,,
6½ by 3⅞	B. 4849	**3/11**	,,
7½ by 4¾	B. 4850	**5/3**	,.

Post 2d.

Telephone No. Register.

With Tab
and Eyelets
to Hang
Gilt Edges.
With
Alphabetical
Index.
Size 8½ by 5.
French
Morocco.

B. 1713/ABC.
2/9
Post 4d.

A Greatly Appreciated Gift.

Dictionary Set. Padded Spring-hinged Top.
SIZE OF BOOKS 4 by 2⅝ in.
French Morocco   No. B. 14216.
Price .. .. .. **31/6**   Post 6d.

Kelly's Code Perpetual Calendar. Patented.

A Calendar that Lasts for Ever.

The Utility of this Calendar to Students,
Journalists, Professional and Business
men is apparent.
No time is lost in referring to Old Diaries, etc.
The Calendar will give *any* date for *any* year.
A Permanent and Useful Present.
vered Leather, **24/**, **26/-** and **35** .
Postage 6d.
r convenience, the Code on the Calendar is set for
years, but a Code Card for a Century 1851-1950 A.D.
is obtainable. No. N. K5010. Price, **6d.** nett.

A Greatly Appreciated Gift.

For the Lady's Boudoir.

Set of Three Dictionaries.

SIZE OF BOOKS 4 by 2⅝ in.
English, English-French, English-German.
French Morocco,   No. 14225.
Price .. .. **16/6** each.
Postage 4d.

Engagement Calendars, Memos., Albums., etc.

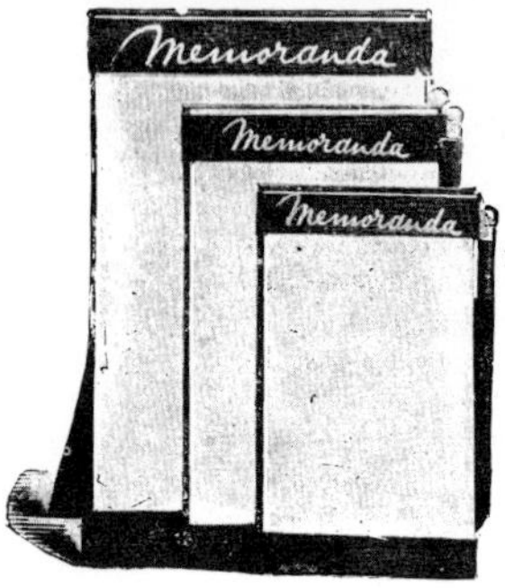
Memoranda
Memoranda
Memoranda

Opal Slates for Memoranda Engagements.

In Ripplegrain cloth frame, lettered in white, with pencil.

MEMORANDA

Size.	No.	Each
4 by $2\frac{1}{2}$	R 952	**$5\frac{1}{2}$**d.
6 by 3	R 953	**8**d.
6 by 4	R 954	**11**d.

ENGAGEMENTS.

Size.	No.	Each.
4 by $2\frac{1}{2}$	R 583	**$5\frac{1}{2}$**d.
5 by 3	R 584	**8**d.
6 by 4	R 585	**11**d.

Post 3d.

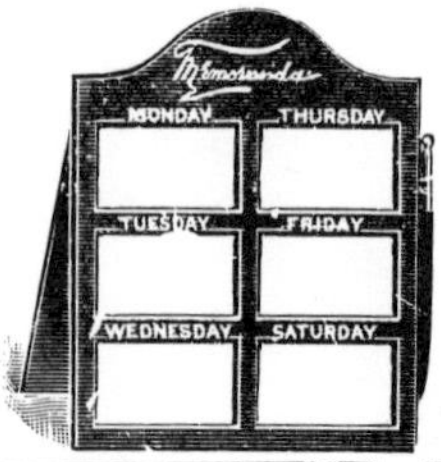
Memoranda
MONDAY
THURSDAY
TUESDAY
FRIDAY
WEDNESDAY
SATURDAY

Opal Engagement Slate.

Leatherette.

Size.	No.	Each.
8 by 7	H 35	**$1/7\frac{1}{2}$**

Spanish Roan.

Size.	No.	Each.
8 by 7	H 36	**2/3**

Post 3d.

Autograph Albums.

THE "THACKERY" ALBUM.

Full bound Art Cloth, padded, with line border and lettering in white, tinted paper leaves for writing on, interleaved with cartridge paper for sketches, gilt edges, upright.

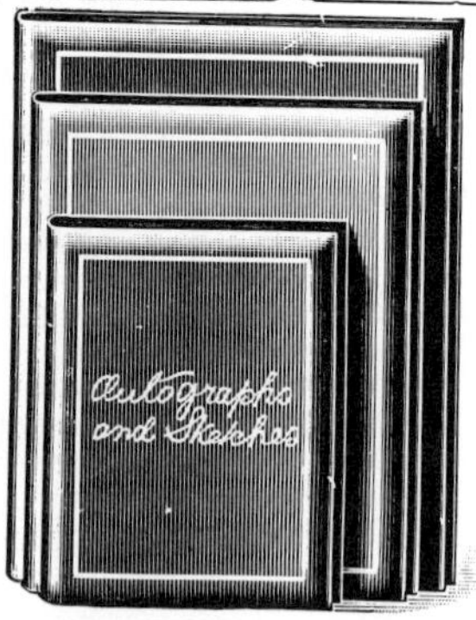
Autographs and Sketches

Size.	No.	Each.
$5\frac{7}{8}$ by $4\frac{1}{2}$	M 642	**$1/7\frac{1}{2}$**
$7\frac{7}{8}$ by $6\frac{1}{4}$	M 643	**$2/3\frac{1}{2}$**
$8\frac{3}{4}$ by 7	M 644	**2/8**

Post 3d.

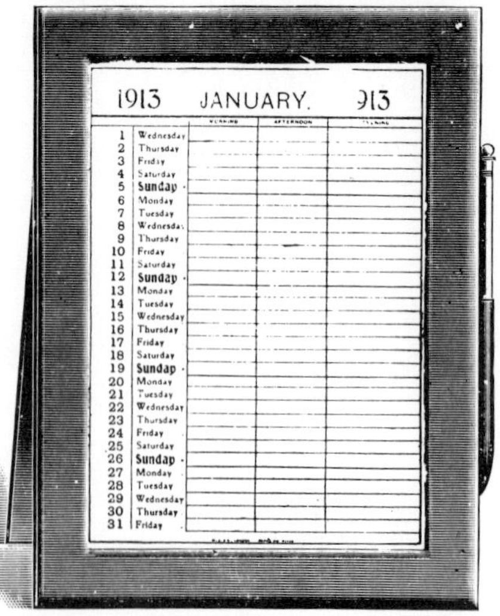
1913 JANUARY 913
1 Wednesday
2 Thursday
3 Friday
4 Saturday
5 Sunday
6 Monday
7 Tuesday
8 Wednesday
9 Thursday
10 Friday
11 Saturday
12 Sunday
13 Monday
14 Tuesday
15 Wednesday
16 Thursday
17 Friday
18 Saturday
19 Sunday
20 Monday
21 Tuesday
22 Wednesday
23 Thursday
24 Friday
25 Saturday
26 Sunday
27 Monday
28 Tuesday
29 Wednesday
30 Thursday
31 Friday

The "Carlton" Engagement Calendar.

14 Cards $9\frac{3}{4}$ by 7, ruled and printed to show morning, afternoon and evening engagements for a month at a glance. In frame, with strut at back to stand and ring to hang.

Ripplegrain Cloth, with cloth back. No. R 1719... **$23/\frac{1}{2}$** each.
Spanish Roan, with nickel pencil No. R 1109 ... **4/11** ,,
Crushed Morocco, with nickel pencil. No. 1146 ... **9/6** ,,
Refills . **8**d. per set. Post **4**d.

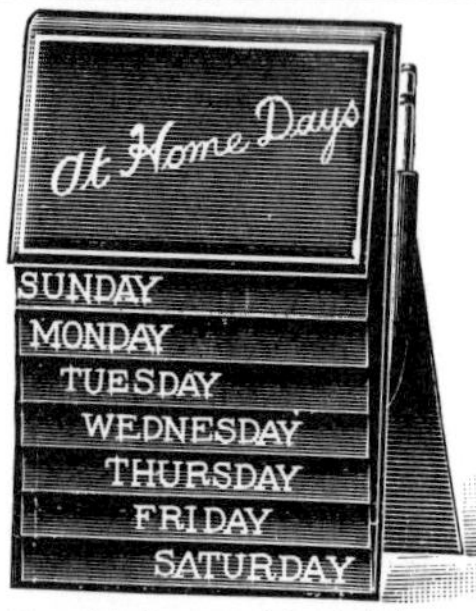
At Home Days
SUNDAY
MONDAY
TUESDAY
WEDNESDAY
THURSDAY
FRIDAY
SATURDAY

Address and "At Home" Stands.

Leatherette, cloth back lettered in white, wooden pencil.

Addresses—

Size.	No.	Each.
6 by $4\frac{1}{4}$	R 1457	**$1/11\frac{1}{2}$**

Do. do. "At Home" Days—
6 by $4\frac{1}{4}$ R 1456 **11**d.

Spanish Roan, with nickel pencil.
Addresses—
6 by $4\frac{1}{4}$ R 923 **3/11**

Spanish Roan, with nickel pencil "At Home" Days—
Size 6 by $4\frac{1}{4}$ No. R 924 **2/11** each.
Do. with silver corners. Addresses—
Size 6 by $4\frac{1}{4}$ No. R 1096 **4/11** each.
Do. do. do. "At Home" Days—
Size 6 by $4\frac{1}{4}$ No. R 1097 **4/2** each.
Post 3d.

The Best Boy's School Present.

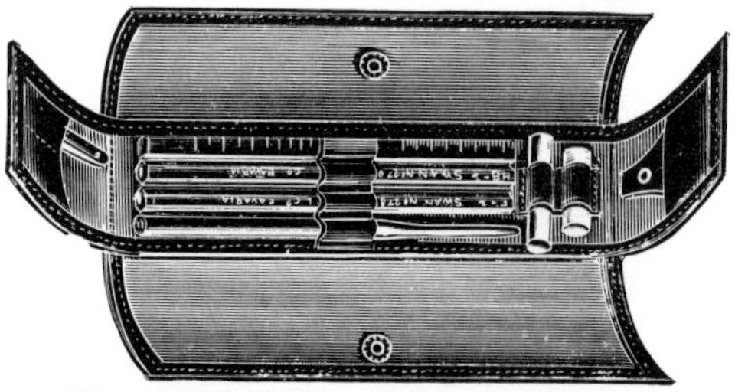

Every Boy and Girl uses the Fold-up Pen and Pencil Set.

The Best Girl's School Present.

Exact as sketch, **2/9** Other designs fold up, **$6\frac{1}{2}$**d., **$10\frac{1}{2}$**d., **$1/0\frac{1}{2}$**, **$1/4\frac{1}{2}$**, **$1/6\frac{1}{2}$**, **$1/9\frac{1}{2}$**, **$1/11\frac{1}{2}$**, **$2/3\frac{1}{2}$**, **2/6** The Largest Selection to be seen anywhere and at cut prices. Postage 3d.

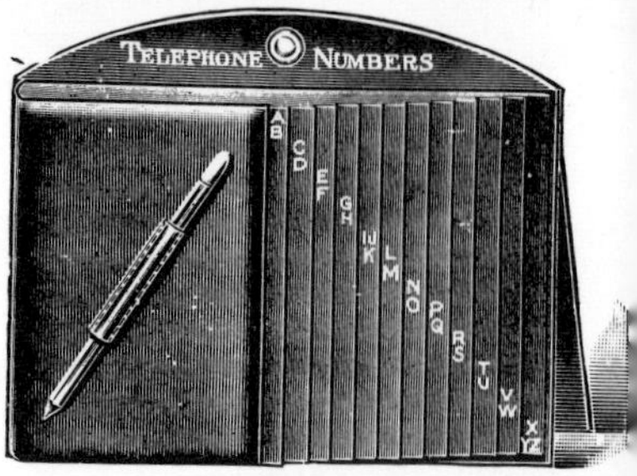
TELEPHONE NUMBERS

The Telephone Directories.

Size $9\frac{1}{4}$ by $7\frac{1}{2}$ in. Spanish Roan, with 12 leav tipped Spanish Roan, lettered in gold, with g tipped pencil. To stand or hang.

No. R 2036 .. .. **5/9** each.
Crushed Morocco, with gilt pencil.
No. R 2181 .. **14/3** each. Post 3

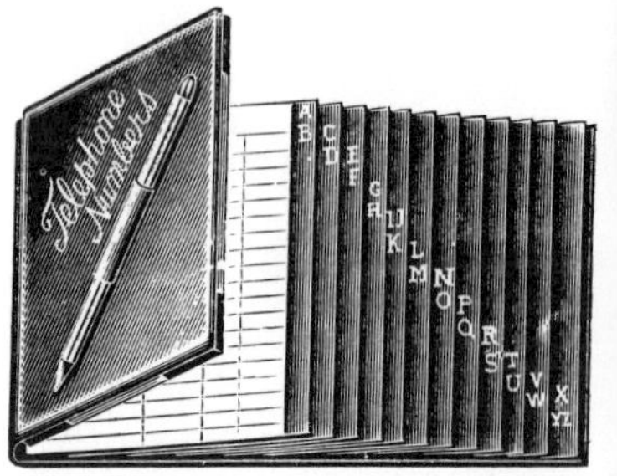
Telephone Numbers

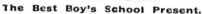

Regd. No. 618661. Spanish Roan, white card lea tipped Spanish Roan and lettered in gold. A bloc 50 leaves for messages under flap. No. R 2221 each. Refill blocks 2d. each. Post 3d.

The "Tudor" Post Card Album.

3 on a page.

Half-bound in Seal-grain leather with Art cloth sides, gold finish and lettering, leaves of very strong dark green Manilla paper. To take 3 oblong or 2 upright cards on a page.

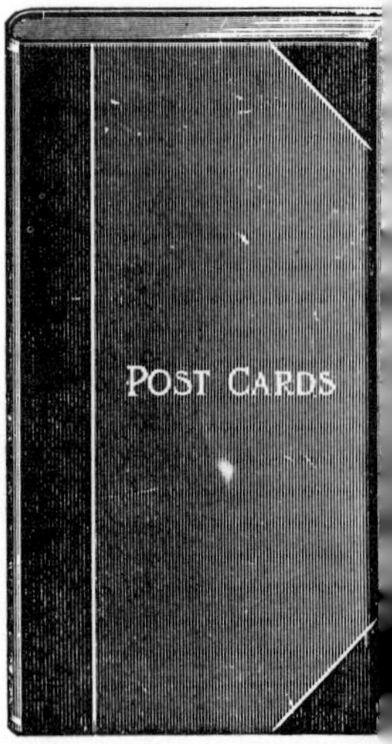
POST CARDS

Holding	Size of Book.	No.
300	$15\frac{3}{4}$ by 8	S 1523
400	$15\frac{3}{4}$ by 8	S 1524
500	$15\frac{3}{4}$ by 8	S 1525

Post 6d.

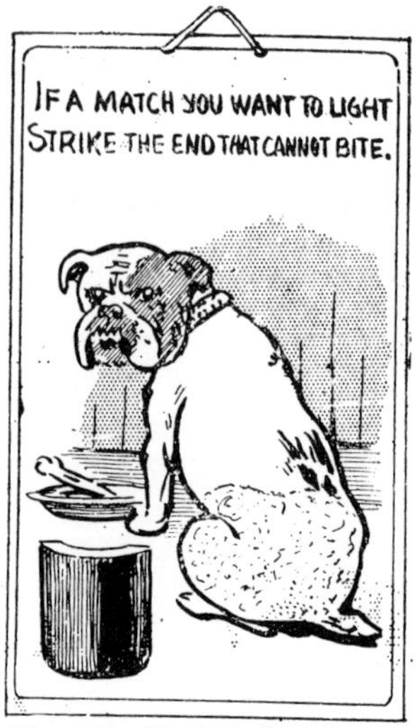
IF A MATCH YOU WANT TO LIGHT
STRIKE THE END THAT CANNOT BITE.

Novelty Match-holder.
To hang. Small shelf for matches. Strikes on the dog.
Regular price 6d.
Our price **$3\frac{1}{2}$**d. Postage 2d.

Initial Seals for Stationery Wax.

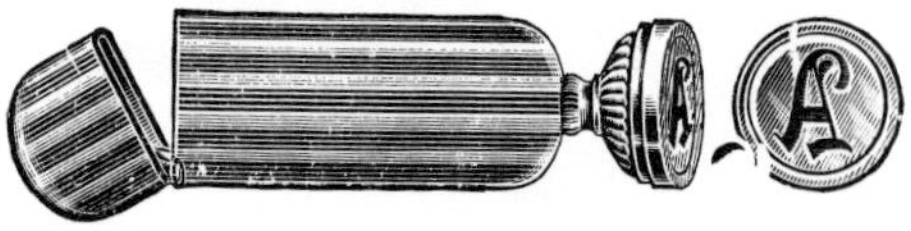

New Handle. Brass Match Box with Seal.
Price complete **$1/4\frac{1}{2}$** Useful Novelty.

These Seals are made of best brass, beautifully chased.

Various designs. The handles are made so that any initial can be screwed in.

Price complete with any initial, **$1/4\frac{1}{2}$**

Postage 1d.

SPECIAL VALUE! Box of assorted shades of Fancy Sealing Wax.
Containing six pieces. Price .. .. **9**d. Post 2d.

The New Patent Reform Refill Pocket Books and Pocket Cases.

THE BEST PRESENT FOR A GENTLEMAN.

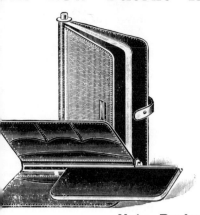

A Series of Pocket Books, Wallets and Small Cases

IN VARIOUS FINE LEATHERS.

Fitted with the New Patent Reform Refill.

The most compact system yet devised.

Easily adjusted, flat opening, and very thin.

Note Books.

Size of leaf	4 by 2 in.	4½ by 2½ in.	5 by 3 in.	6 by 3½ in.
...an	1/6	1/9	2/3	2/6
...rocco	2/6	3/-	4/-	5/-
...skin	2/6	3/-	4/-	5/-
...ssia	4/6	5/-	6/-	7/-
...vet Calf	6/-	7/-	8/-	10/-

Postage 3d.

Pocket Wallets with Silk Lined Refills.

Size of leaf	3½ by 2 in.	4½ by 4½ in.	5 by 3 in.	6 by 4 in.
Roan	1/9	2/-	2/6	3/6
Morocco	2/9	3/6	4/3	6/6
Pigskin	2/9	3/5	4/6	6/6
Velvet Calf	5/-	6/-	8/-	11/-

Postage 4d.

San Remo Writing Case.

Fully equipped with Pockets, Pen, Pencils, Blotter, &c., and containing a renewable Tablet of San Remo Notelettes, complete.

Price	..	..	3/9
Better quality	..	..	4/9

Post 3d.

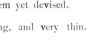

"Remember" Tablet.

Best quality, with renewable refill and good pencil. Two sizes.

Nos. 131 and 132 .. **2/6** and **3/6** each.

Post 3d.

New Notelette Case.

Fully equipped with Pockets, &c., &c., and with Patent Strap Fastener.

Each Case contains a folding Tablet of "Notelettes" (Notepaper and Envelopes combined) with Blotter, &c., as shewn.

In Padded French Morocco, Note size	..	1/11
,, ,, ,, Viceroy ,,	..	2/4½
Crushed Morocco, Note size..	..	..	2/8
,, ,, Viceroy size	..	..	3/4

Post 3d.

Refill Tablets of "Notelettes," either size, **6**d. each. Post 2d.

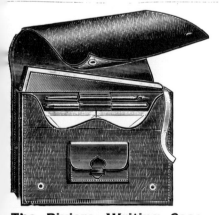

The Riviera Writing Case.

...ontaining a Quarto Tablet of the fashionable "Society Bond" Notepaper with Envelopes to match.

...lly equipped with Pen, Pencil, Stamp Pockets, &c., perfectly limp and flat.

...his forms the most compact case ever devised, and especially suitable for use in travel.

...ench Morocco, fitted complete	..	10/6
...lid Pigskin	..	15/-
...id Morocco	..	15/-

Post 4d.

The Stationery Kit Wallet.

A simple Leather Envelope with two Gusset Pockets.

Fitted with a supply of Notepaper and Envelopes, and equipped with Pen and Pencil, &c.

This has been devised for a new travelling companion, and is very limp and compact for packing in one's bag.

Solid Basil	..	..	..	5/-
French Morocco	..	..	5/6
Solid Pigskin..	..	..	7/6

Post 4d.

Elegant Library Blotting Pad.

With Engagement Tablet and Folding Leather Flap.

Very Handsome Gift.

Two sizes.

Price .. .. 4/6 6/- Post 5d.

GAMAGE'S, ☞ THE RENOWNED FOUNTAIN PEN HOUSE

MOST ACCEPTABLE GIFTS FOR ALL.

The "Waverley" Fountain Pen.

10/6

Ordinary Barrel.

Fitted with 14-carat solid gold nib and gold feed .. **10/6** Post free.
Also fitted with gold bands for Presentation, from **12/6**
This pen has been designed to meet the demand for a Fountain Pen with a turned-up point. It is a replica of the "Waverley" nib; for smooth and easy writing is unsurpassed.

The "Pelican" Non-leakable Pen (Sold elsewhere at 10/6).

This pen is fitted with 14-carat solid gold nib with twin gold feed. Has patent shut-off valve by which the flow of ink can be adjusted to a nicety, and can be carried in any position in the pocket. Fine. Medium. Broad and Stub Points. **8/6** Post 2d.

Gamage's Taxi Stylo.

The handsomest little pen made. Will fit into the vest pocket or wrist bag, takes up very little room. Fitted with spring needle, in polished vulcanite case, red or black. Price ... **10½d** Post 1d, Ditto, chased barrel, superior needle. **1/6**

The "Gamage" Fountain Pen.

The best value pen yet offered. It is of the finest quality throughout; fitted with extra heavy solid 14-ct. gold nib with Waterman-pattern feed, in chased vulcanite barrel. Fine, Medium, Broad & Oblique Points. **7/6** Post free.

The Gamage "Fleet" Self-filling Fountain Pen.
"The Record Value."

Fitted with 14-ct gold-plated nib. The biggest value ever offered.
Price .. .. **1/-** Post 1d

Gamage's Marvellous Self-filling Pen.

4½d.

The most wonderful Self-filling Pen made. Takes any nib. Easy to fill. No dirty fingers or ink-fillers. Price **4½d** Postage 1d.

The New "Onostyle" Self-filling Stylo Pen.

A perfect Self-filling Stylo, Pen made on exactly the same principle as the "Onoto" Pen. Has large ink reservoir and perfect ink trap, allowing the pen to be carried in any position in the pocket without fear of leakage.
Length Open, 5 in. closed, 4 in. Price **5/-**

Gamage's Red or Green Pocket Stylo Pen. A perfect pocket Stylo, in best red or green vulcanite case. Has best quality spring needle and platinum point. Every pen guaranteed. A wonderful value pen. Price **2/6**

The Guildhall Self-Filling Pen.

The Guildhall Self-filling Pen, 14-ct. Nib, Iridium points. Quickly fills. Worth **10/6**. Our Price **5/6**

The "Phonetic" Stylo.

1/6

The cheapest spring-point Stylo made. Thoroughly reliable. Polished vulcanite case. Complete in box, etc. Price .. **1/6** Post free.

The "Gamage" Improved Safety Pen, With Screw Cap.

Ladder feed, to ensure correct flow of ink, fitted with 14-ct. finest qual. gold nib, iridium pointed. Fine, Medium, Broad and Oblique Nibs, **5**

The "Crown" Pen.

The finest and largest pen ever offered at anything approaching the price. The is equal in size and appearance to the 'Waterman' at 17/6; has specially large s 14-ct. gold nib, iridium pointed, large duct feeder. handsome chased barrel. Suppl in Fine, Medium Broad, and Stub oblique Points. Gamage's price **4/11**

The "Gamage" Patent Self-filling Pen. IMPROVED PATTERN

The finest and easiest Self-filling Pen made. Has larger ink capacity than any other pen. Simple to use. No part to get out of order. Fills itself in a second from any ink supply. So simple a child can use it. Fitted with a Gamage special quality 14-ct iridium pointed nib, chased barrel. Price **3/6**
Supplied in Fine, Medium, Broad and Oblique Nibs.

Gamage's New Safety and Non-Leakable Pen.

Specially made for carrying in the waistcoat pocket. Fitted with Gamage special 14-ct gold nib, iridium pointed. Handsome chase barrel. Size, closed, 4½ in.; open 5½ in. Price .. **3/.**
Supplied in Fine. Medium, Broad and Oblique Nibs.

The Olympic, Extra Large Barrel.

The Olympic.
Large Barrel, carries increased Ink Supply, 14-ct. Gold Nib, Iridium pointed.
Worth **10/6** Our Price **6/9**

The Speedy, Gold Nib and Feed.

The Speedy and Reliable Fountain Pen, 14-ct. Gold Nib and Feed. Rapid Writer.
Worth **10/6** Our Price **5/11**

The "Rex" Pen.

A really marvellous value pen. Has specially selected solid 14-ct. iridium pointed twin feed, in handsome chased vulcanite case. Price .. **2/6**

The "A.W.G." Pen THE PEN WITH A REPUTATION.

Our special value pen. Equal to most pens at 10/6 Has beautiful solid 14-ct. gold twin feed, chased vulcanite barrel. Fine, Medium and Broad Points, ... **2**

Gamage's New Phono or Desk Pen.

This pen has been specially made for those requiring a pen for shorthand or desk u Is fitted with a solid 14-ct. gold nib with special gold ink regulating top feed a vulcanite under feed. Long tapered barrel in chased vulcanite. Price **3/6**

The "School" Pen.

1/11

Our New Pattern School Pen. The best value pen ever offered. Has extra lar solid 14-ct. gold nib, iridium pointed. Beautifully chased barrel and twin feed.
Fine, Medium and Broad Points. Price ... . **1/11** Post 2d.
Equal to most pens at double the price.

POST CARD ALBUMS.

No. 164.

To hold—

200 Cards	..	**1/6**
300 ,,	..	**2/-**
400 ,,	..	**2/6**

Post 4d.

Assorted Designs.

No. 150.

Presentation Album.

Handsomely Bound.

Half Panne Calf

Morris paper sides

To hold —

200	..	**4/6**
300	..	**5/6**
400	..	**6/-**
500	..	**7/6**

Postage 4d.

No. 142.

Artistic Cloth Binding.

To hold—

200 Cards	..	**1/6**
300 ,,	..	**2/-**
400 ,,	..	**2/6**

Post 4d.

Very smart Design.

No. 900.

Best Quality Leaves.

To hold—

200 Cards	..	**2 6**
300 ,,	..	**3/-**
400 ,,	..	**3/6**
500 ,,	..	**4/-**

Post 6d.

Assorted Designs.

SCRAP ALBUMS.

Bound in Assorted Linen Grain Cloths.

Blocked as illustration, with letterings on back and side in gold.

	No. 1.					No. 2.
20 Leaves (= 40 pages)	..	..	..	..	..	.. **1/0½**
45 Leaves (= 90 pages)	..	..	..	..	..	.. **1/6½**
70 Leaves (= 140 pages)	..	..	..	..	..	.. **1/11½** Post 4d.

No. 252.

Handsome Presentation Album.

Bound in best quality Panne Calf, padded. Design on Cover.

To hold—

200 Cards	..	**12/-**
300 ,,	..	**13/-**
400 ,,	..	**14/-**
500 ,,	..	**15/-**

Post free.

Best Quality Art Cloth Binding, various art shades. Strong Manilla leaves, thread sewn   To hold 4 upright or 3 oblong cards on one page

No. 1. To hold 500 cards **5 3**

Postage, 6d.

The Sylvia Post Card Album

Post Card Album, handsomely bound in Panne Calf a very effective binding. Makes an Ideal Art gift. Leaves are of best quality and all thread sewn.
To hold 200 cards **11/6** 300 **12/-** 400 **13/-** 500 **13/9**

Postage 4d.

No. 30.

Strong, half-bound brilliant Morocco.

To hold 150 Cards.

Price **1/11**

Postage 3d.

Album.

To hold 100 Cards One on a page Bound art cloth Best paper leaves Thread sewn

Price .. **10½d.**

Postage 3d.

May also be had in Spanish Roan .. **3/3**

Bound in Art Cloth with white lettering and decoration Very strong and thick green Manilla paper leaves A thoroughly serviceable

and durable book for large collections.
No. 932. Holding 500, **5/6**   No. 933. 700, **7/3**

Postage 6d.

Cheap Packets of Foreign Stamps.

POSTAGE STAMP ALBUMS.

The following Albums are carefully compiled and are UP-TO-DATE.

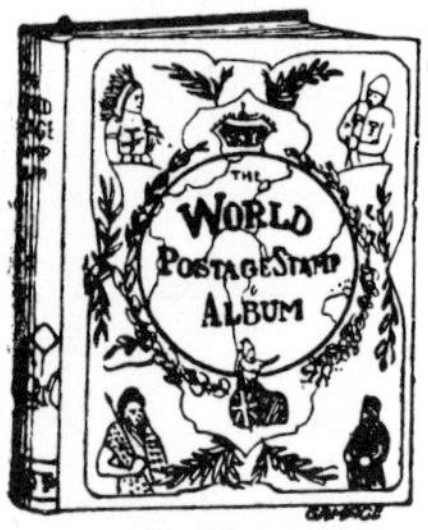

The World, No. 3 Album.

The **Victoria** Stamp Album, strongly bound in fancy board, 80 pages, including illustrations, with space for 1,500 varieties, **6**d. Post 2d.

The **Rowland Hill** Album, 152 pages, illustrated, bound in cloth, with space for about 3,500 varieties, **11**d. Postage 3d.

The **World** Album, crown quarto, 144 pages, with illustrations of rare and obsolete stamps; space for more than 4,000 varieties.

No.			Post.
N. 1.	Cloth bds., coloured design on cover.	**1/4½**	3d.
N. 2.	Cloth boards, extra gilt lettered.	**1/10½**	3d.
N. 3.	Enlarged edition. Cloth, extra gilt,	**2 4½**	4d.

The **Queen** Album contains 272 pages, well guarded and handsomely bound in cloth, gilt lettering, space for 7,500 varieties, coloured map of the British Empire, with useful hints on collecting. Price **3/3** Postage 4d.

The **Empire** Album contains 288 pages, printed on extra thick paper, full pages coloured maps, with spaces for 8,500 varieties.

No.
N.1. In neat cloth, extra sprinkled edges, **4/9** Post 4d.
N.2. Strongly half-bound, leather back, gilt edge, Price **7/3** Postage 4d.
N.3. Art canvas binding, interleaved plain leaves, **7,3**

ENLARGED EDITION.

No. N. 1.	Handsomely bound in extra Cloth, bevelled boards, sprinkled edges, gilt back and side	**9/11**
No. N. 2.	Ditto ditto Interleaved ..	**11 9**
No. N. 3.	Half bound, Leather back and corners, bevelled boards, red edges	**14/9**
No. N. 4.	Ditto ditto Interleaved ..	**16/6**
No. N. 5.	Whole bound Morocco gilt, bevelled boards, gilt edges	**18/9**
No. N. 6.	Ditto ditto Interleaved ..	**23 6**

No. N. 1. **The Lincoln Stamp Album.** With spaces for 3,650 Stamps. 6th Edition. Strongly bound cloth, **10½**d. Post 3d.

The Lincoln Album Strongly bound cloth. Spaces for 7,200 stamps. Price **2/6** Post 3d.

Ditto, as above, but containing 16 coloured maps, complete Stamp Catalogue, showing value of stamps. Price **4 6** Postage 4d.

Cigarette Card Albums.

For holding Picture Cigarette Cards.

Each leaf is cut ready for placing the cards under; dark green leaves, best linen covers.

To hold	250	50	700	1000 cards.
Price	**6½**d	**1/-**	**1 11**	**2/11** each.
		Postage 3d.		Postage 4d.

Cigarette Card Albums

To Slip under. Each leaf on separate guard.

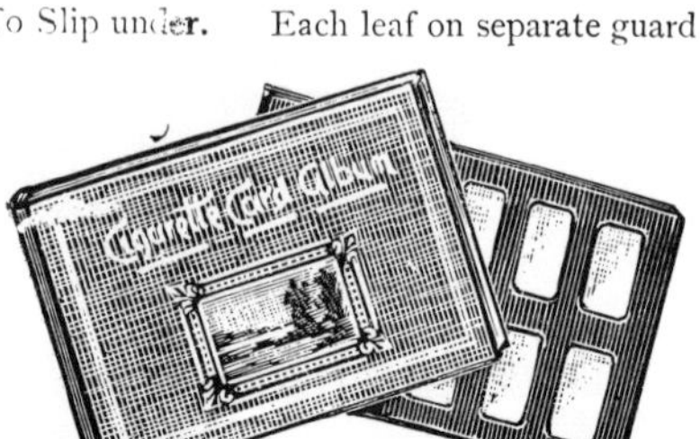

Strongly bound in art canvas.

160	300	500 cards.	
10½d.	**1/3**	**1/9**	Post. 4d.

THE "NEW ISSUE" PACKET.

Contains 13 used and unused but only NEW ISSUES that have come out recently. Everyone wishing to keep his collection up-to-date, should purchase this packet. It includes 2 Bosnia 1912, Emperor's head unused, Australia (Map), Cayman Islands ¼d., King George V., British East Africa and Uganda, French Oceania 1913, Leeward Islands, Russia 1913, 3 Chinese Republic surcharged, Macedonia 1913, Mauritania pictorial 1913, Russia head issue.

9½d. post free. Foreign postage, 2½d. extra.

Why not buy this with the Pictorial Packet, as the two packets contain NO duplicates?

THE "MAP" PACKET.

Packet (A). Contains 10 different Stamps each of which has a map on it as part of the design. A most interesting packet, it includes Newfoundland (map of the Island), Canada, Xmas Stamp (map of the World), a fine set of Nicaragua (maps), new issue, Panama (map of the Isthmus), and a fine set of Reunion, used and unused. Many of the above stamps sell at 1½d. or 2d. each.

Prlce of Packet, **5½**d. Foreign postage 2½d. extra.

THE "SHIP" PACKET.

Packet (A). Contains 12 stamps, set of British Guiana (ship in full sail), Bermuda (ship in dock), Malta (harbour with ships), Cuba 5c. (U.S.A. dreadnought), Portugal (Vasco de Gama's ship), Venezuela (ship) provisional unused, 2 U.S.A. war tax (ironclad) also 1902 issue (Columbus in sight of land), Costa Rica (view of harbour of San Jose with ships).

Pr·ce **6½**d. Foreign postage 2½d. extra.

"BALKAN WAR" PACKET.

Packet A. Contains 20 stamps, all different, set of 6 Turkey with new issue, 2 Greece, 2 Servia (King Peter), also obsolete issue, 4 Bulgaria (Ferdinand), Austria Jubilee (high value), and a set of 5 Roumania obsolete.

Post free, **4½**d. Foreign postage 2½d. extra.

THE "ZOOLOGICAL" PACKET.

Contains 30 stamps, all different, many beautifully engraved and each having the picture of some bird or animal. 1 British North Borneo (peacock), 2 Sudan (camel), Malay (tiger), 2 Mexico (eagles), 3 West Australia (swans), a fine set of 4 China (dragons), Nyassaland (camels), New Caledonia (bird), 2 British North Borneo, postage due (stag and monkey), a fine Negri Semblain (tiger) obsolete, Middle Congo (leopard), and a set of 10 Hungary (pigeon).

Post free, **1/1** Foreign postage, 2½d extra.

THE "PICTORIAL" PACKET

Contains 20 Pictorial Stamps, including Federat Malayasia (1c tiger), Costa Rica, 2 Jamaica, 2 N Zealand, Borneo (native), West Australia (Swa 30 h Hungary (bird), British Guiana (ship), Eg (Pyramids, Trinidad (Britannia), 3 U.S.A. (ironclad Orange River Colony (antelopes), 2 China (dragon U.S.A., Columbus and Cuba (Palm Tree).

Price **6½**d. post free. Foreign postage 2½d. ext

Why not buy this with the "New Issue" as they contain NO duplicates.

THE "MAP" PACKET.

Packet (B). 20 Stamps, in all a really uni packet contains all the stamps mentioned above packet A, and in addition, 2 Nicaragua, Maps (offici 2 more Canada (maps) showing varieties of col Reunion 10c. (map) used, Australia (map), 1913, a fine set of the Miranda issue of Venezuela, the M shewing the disputed boundary between Venezu and British Guiana. This packet contains specim of almost all the principal map designed stamps of world up-to-date.

Satisfaction Guaranteed or money returned.

Post free, **1/-** Foreign postage 2½d. extra.

THE "SHIP" PACKET.

Packet (B). Contains 12 different stamps, Bri North Borneo 8c. (native boat), usually sold at 2 British Guiana (ship in full sail), including coloured stamp, German, China (ship). Bermuda (1 century ship in full sail), 2 Venezuela (Revolution steamer "Bankigh"), these stamps alone are ca logued at 1/-. British Solom n Islands, Protecto unused (native war canoe), 3 U.S.A., War T (ironclad), and Grenada, 1906 (wooden battleshi the Columbus period).

Price **1/1** post free. Foreign postage 2½d. ext

"BALKAN WAR" PACKET.

Packet (B). Contains 25 stamps, all different, set of 6 Turkey including surcharged, Austria Jubi 3 Servia, including the famous Coronation (de mask) stamp, 4 Bulgaria, pictorials, etc. C (unpaid) unused. Greece, 3 Roumania (latest iss Montenegro 18-8, 2 Bosnia Pictorials (views of and Valley of Viba), British Levant, issued for us British Post Office at Constantinople.

Price **1/-** post free. Foreign postage 2½d extr

THE "UNUSED" PACKET.

Contains 20 Stamps, all different, and all unu New Caledonia (bird), 2 Argentine (head ½ and current issue), Guinée, St. Pierre and Mic (pictorial), Ivory Coast (head), Spanish Moro Bulgaria (obsolete), a fine set of 3 Cuba, Nicara Martinique (head of native), Spain, 1879, Gu (postage due), Madagascar (bi-coloured), Pict Gaudeloupe, 2 Prussia and Porto Rico.

Price **6½**d. post free. Foreign postage 2½d. ex

Special Variety Packets.

These contain a really excellent selection of Foreign Stamps. EVERY STAMP DIFFERENT. Many new and obsolete issues.

200 .. price **1/-**	300 .. price **2/6**
250 .. ,, **1/6**	500 .. ,, **6/-**

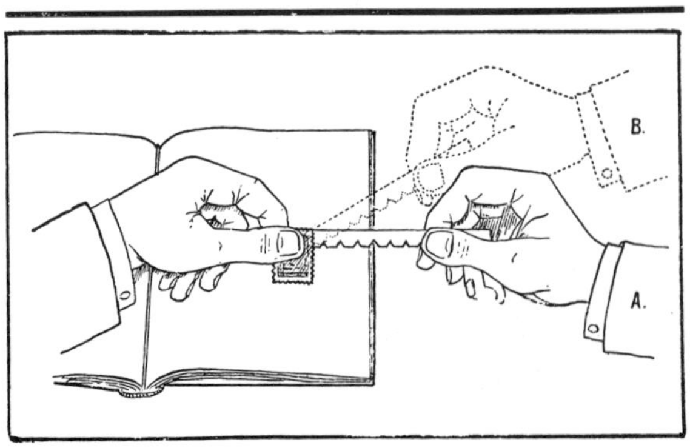

The New "STRIP" MOUN

Patented.

WATKIN'S PATENT.

These mounts are the *only patented* st mounts on the market, and admit of st being neatly hinged *three times as qu* as by any other method and are far away simpler and better than the fashioned *single* mounts.

SATISFACTION GUARANTEE

DIRECTIONS.

Fold the strips gummed side outw moisten the end mount with the lips, it where the stamp is required, ther the stamp on it, pressing firmly with th of left hand (fig. A). Now move hand upwards with a **steady** te movement (fig. B). Do **not** give a su jerk; the mount will break off quite c leaving stamp firmly fixed.

500 .. **3**d. 1000 .. **6**

Writing Sets and Pencil Boxes for 'Xmas Presents.

The Academy Set of Pencils, etc.

A very dainty and useful Gift. In neatly finished pale blue box. Art Shaded Pencils, etc.

Price .. **1/11**   Postage 3d.

No. 5014. **Crayon Set.**

Fourteen Crayons (assorted colours) and an economy holder with nickel Tip. Book of 12 designs for colouring, and a packet of 48 pieces of drawing paper.

Price **6½d.**   Postage 2d.

Superior Rubber Type Outfit.

Outfit neatly boxed in polished wood containing extra quality deep Solid Rubber Type, special pattern.

Letter, pair Tweezers and Self Inking Pad. No. 9 Fount contains 1 fount each capitals, small letters, numerals, display signs. 4-line Holder. Price **5/6** Post 3d.

No. 44 Fount contains 2 founts type as above, but smaller quantity, 1 3-line Holder. Price **4/9** Post 3d.

No. 45 Fount contains large fount type—capital and small letters—smaller size type as above founts, 4-line Holder, and Self Inking Pad Price **3/9** Post 3d.

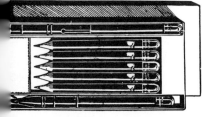

No. 895. Containing one Art Penholder with Nickel Tip, Combination Pen and Pencil, five extra Pencils, and piece of Rubber.

Price **5½d.**   Postage 1d.

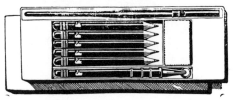

No. 1 X 32. Contains one Art Pocket Pencil with nickel Tip, five Refill Leads (assorted colours), one Art Coloured Penholder, and piece of Artist's Rubber. Price **5½d.** Post 1d.

The Man of War Set of Pencils.

Containing 4 Pencils, 2 with nickel sheaths, 2 Rubbers and metal box for same.   Splendid value.

Price **4½d.**   Postage 1d.

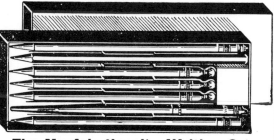

The Mayfair Novelty Writing Set.

Containing an assortment of Art Coloured Pencils, four with Inserted Jewels and three with Pearls.

WONDERFUL VALUE.   Price **6½d.**   Postage 1d.

Novelty Pencil Box.

A beautifully made flat box. polished Enamel outside in 3 dainty tints : Pink, Green and Mauve. Fitted with Pencils, Pens, etc.. **1/11** Post 2d.

Box of 12 **Coloured Crayons** in Cedarwood. Full size.   Price .. **5½d.**   Post 2d.

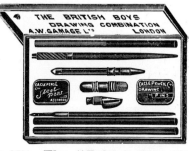

No. 2554. **The "British Boys'" Drawing Combination.**

Containing 1 Mapping Pen, 1 hexagon Drawing Pencil, 1 Copying Ink Pencil, 1 red and blue Crayon in cedar, 1 Japanned Penholder, 1 pocket Pencil and point Protector, 1 box of Drawing Pins, 1 box of assorted steel Pens, 1 Eagle Pencil Sharpener, 1 Rubber Eraser in nickel case. **9½d.**   Post 2d.

Printing Outfits.

Each set contains a full font of Rubber Type, self-inking pad, 3-line holder and pair of tweezers. The Cheapest Outfit Made.

Gamage's price ... **9d.** Postage 2d.

Ditto, Larger Type, more complete. Price ... **1/=**   Post 2d.

Ditto., as above, smaller size ... **6d.**   Post 1d

Larger Sizes **1/6** Post 3d.   **2/3** Post 4d. **2/11** Post 4d.   **3/6** Post 4d.   **3/11** Post 4d.

"VERONIQUE" Pencil Set, in finest art colours, polished. Six H.B. pocket pencils, containing : one H.B. Hexagonal drawing pencil, one H.B. pocket pencil with gilt protector, one H.B. tablet ink and pencil eraser, one gilt flat pocket pencil, two flat pocket pencil refills, one high class penholder, one nickel box of pen nibs. **10½d.**   Post 2d.

The Boudoir Writing Set.

Containing four Art Coloured Pencils, 2 Pocket Pencils with gilt protectors, two Art Coloured Penholders with nibs.   Price **6½d.**   Postage 1d.

TYPEWRITERS, etc., for CHRISTMAS PRESENTS.

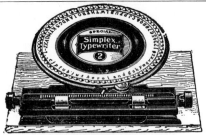

The Improved Simplex Typewriter.

No. 1. This is a very complete Machine, having key for each letter roller fed, automatic inking and spacing, sight writing. Will take a small letter head, and can be easily and rapidly operated. Has 36 characters and stops. With full instructions. Price **4/6** Postage 4d.

The Simplex. No. 2.

GREATLY ENLARGED AND IMPROVED.
Similar to No. 1, but has two sets of alphabets, capital and small, numerals and punctuation stops. Fitted on wood base, price **8/6** Postage 6d.

Dear Sir;
See! This
is the best
present I ev-
er got.

The Simplex Typewriter. No. 3.

Similar in style to No. 2, has 2 sets Alphabets, Numerals, etc. Will take paper up to Foolscap size. Will print very clearly and has perfect alignment. Price **12/6** Postage 4d

A Scientific Marvel. The Varystyle.

An improved and large Designograph, executive thousands of artistic designs made of best quality throughout. Size of design, dial 6 in.
Gamage's price **4/6** Post 4d.
Also supplied in superior wooden case with 8½ in. dia superior fittings. Gamage's price **11/3** Post 6d.

A USEFUL 'XMAS PRESENT.
The "Bijou" Typewriter.
NEW MODEL.

Weighs only 12 lbs.. Complete in case. Perfect visible writing, universal keyboard, every modern improvement, single or two-colour ribbons can be used. Specially suitable for Travellers, Ministers, Secretaries, &c. Price, complete in solid leather case .. **£12 0 0** net.

The Home Model Blickensderfer Typewriter. Price **£5 17 6** net
Interchangeable Type Wheel.
Perfect Sight Writing.

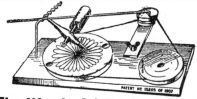

The Wonderful Designograph.

For reproducing Geometrical Designs.
A marvellous mechanical instrument, which draws geometrical designs in endless variety. Thousands of designs can be made from this little machine.
Gamage's price **10½d.** List price 1/- Post 3d.
Do., larger size, superior make.
Price **2/-** List price 2/6 Post 3d.

The Oliver, Rebuilt, No. 3.
Complete with metal cover.

£10 10 net. No. 4 Oliver **£13 10** net

The Latest Model.

PARTICULARS OF THE NO. 6 SIMPLEX TYPEWRITER. This machine has many new features of practical va never attempted before in any other typewriter at price. It will write on paper of any width, envelo cardboard or tablet, in book form, or any package. carriage moves over the surface space by space, and l by line, and may readily be moved back to re details, or add omissions. The paper is held flat on bed, and the machine and every part of the work is plain sight at all times. The ruling and register scales, both vertical and horizontal, are useful in mak out tallies, accentuating phrases, words, or figures, may also be used for many forms of tally work, and forming squares and oblongs; also for making desig

Price **21/-**

The Remington, Rebuilt.

No. 7. Price .. **£10 10 0** net.
Two-Colour Ribbon Attachment **8/6** extra.

Metal Case .. .. .. **12/6** extra.

The "Plex" Duplicator.

No Stencils. No Gelatine. 100 perfect copies can taken from 1 original. Prints in a variety of col simultaneously. The cheapest and most effective co made. After using wipe off with a damp spo Machine is then ready for use again. Apparatus comp

Octavo 9 by 6, **9/6** Foolscap size, **15/-**
Double size, **30/-** Post free.

Plex Ink, **1/-** per bot.
Black, Violet, Green, Brown, Red, Blue, Yello
Postage 1d.

Illustrated Booklet forwarded on applicat:

Useful and Instructive Gifts.

S. & S. Young Artist's Outfit.

Patent No. 22382.

A HANDSOME
CHRISTMAS
GIFT
FOR EITHER
BOY OR GIRL.

This charming Outfit comprises everything required by the young artist for drawing with pencil and crayon, or painting with water colours.

A Constant Delight.

Gives new pleasure each time it is taken up.

CONTENTS OF OUTFIT:

(1) A PATENT DRAWING SLAB which is suitable either for pencil or brush work, and as the drawings will clean off, it affords the pupil unlimited practice without waste of paper. Progress is therefore much more rapid.

(2) A PAINTING BOOK, entitled, "The Young Artist's Guide." This contains a series of copies in black and white, and in colours, representing the different kinds of drawing and painting. The copies are graded and full instructions are given, to suit pupils of different ages and ability.

(3) DRAWING UTENSILS, including a box of colours, crayons, pencil, brush, rubber, pins, etc.

These are all packed in a handsome cabinet.

PRICES.

No. 1. The Complete Outfit with Painting Book .. **4/11** net.
No. 2. The Outfit with Loose Copies .. .. .. **26** net.
S. & S. Painting Book. By R. E. Green, Art Master **1/6** net.

The copies include object drawing (single and in groups), nature drawing, and landscape painting.

Massive Inkstand.

A HANDSOME GIFT.

Two Bottle on Glass Base, and Perpetual Calendar.

A favourite and appreciated Gift. Price **21/-**
Carriage 9d. extra.

Penwiper.

And Pen Rest. Nickel.
With holder for a Fountain Pen. Diameter 3¾ in. Height 3¾ in.

Price .. **3/6** Post 3d.

Letter Rack.

Price **4/11** Post 4d.

"KO-MIO"

Komio Pencil.

THE PENCIL OF THE MOMENT. THE FAVOURITE PENCIL.

Propelling, Reserve Leads, and Point Sharpener. Black, Copying, Red, Blue.

10½d. each. **10/3** per dozen. Refills, **4½d.** per box.

The New Globe.

Showing the Panama Canal Route and various steamship direct services and the shortening of the sea passage by this wonderful engineering triumph.
Published at 2/6
Our price **2/3** Post 4d.

String Holder.

4¼ in. long. Nickel on crystal glass base, with string.
Price **4/11** Postage 3d.

The Little Draughtsmen's Set.

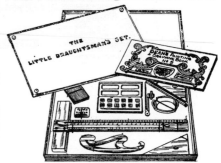

Complete Outfit. Drawing Board, T-square, Set Square, French Curved Drawing Pins, Compass, Pencil, Rubber, Crayons, Box of Colours and Mixing Palette, Ruler, Painting Book.

Complete .. **3/6** Carriage 6d. extra.

Most Useful

Date Stand.

Price

6/11

Post 4d.

All Nickel

Penwiper.

Price .. **3/11**

Post 4d.

Novelty in Sealing Sets.
The Georgian.

The Set comprises Spirit Lamp, Wax Crucible, Initial Seal, box of matches, and about 30 Sealing Balls, in handsome Presentation Case.
Price **5/-** As illustration.
Ditto in smaller case. Price **2/-**
Refills can be had at **6**d. per box of about 30 assorted colors. Post 3d.

Very Useful

Date Stand.

2/11

Post 4d.

Inkstands and Cabinets.

Very Handsome Oak Inlaid Cabinet and Inkstand.

Size 13¾ in. by 10½ in.

Price .. .. **25/-** Post free.

Oak Inlaid Stationery Cabinet and Inkstand combined.

Size 12 in. by 9 in.

Price .. .. .. **21/-** Post free.

Stationery Cabinet and Inkstand combined.

Beautifully made of polished oak throughout.
Fitted with 2 best quality glass bottles, best quality nickel silver mounts.

No. 4D. Price **22/6**
Post free.

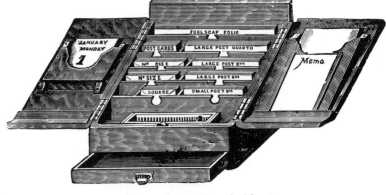

Strongly-made Cabinet.

Polished either light or dark oak, with pocket for loose papers.
Porcelain slate. Drawer for sundries. Perpetual date case and loose glass pen tray.

No. N. 822. Folio size **23/6**
Post free.

Balances.

No. 33.
Weighs up to 4 lbs.

Price .. **26/6** each. Post free.

Very Strong Balance for Book or Parcel Post.

8 16 33 oz.
No. 27 .. **10/3 14/- 21/-** each. Post free.
Extra Strong Solid Brass Balance on Moulded Edge Stand.

No. 11.
4 8 16 32 oz.
Price .. **4/9 7/3 10/9 17/6** each.
Cheaper, **2/11 3/11 4/11 12/9** Post free.

Children's Water Colour Boxes
REEVES' CELEBRATED STUDENTS OUTFITS.

Elementary Boxes.

No. N.21. Contains 12 moist water colours and 2 brushes, **10½d.** List price 1/- Post 3d.

No. N. 21A. Contains 12 moist water colours in pans, 2 tubes and 3 brushes .. **1/4** List price, 1/6 Postage 2d.

No. N.21B. Contains 16 moist water colours in pans, 2 tubes and 3 brushes.. **1/9** List price 2/- Postage 3d.

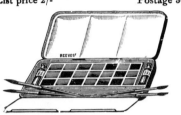

No. N. 23. Contains 21 moist water colours in pans, 2 tubes and 3 brushes.. **2/2** List price 2/6 Postage 3d.

Reeves' Students' Water Colours in Tubes.

No. N. 40. Contains 6 tubes and 1 brush, in japanned tin case, **1/6** List price, 1/8

No. N. 41A. Contains 9 ditto, ditto .. **2/2** List price 2/6

No. N. 42A. Contains 15 ditto and 4 ditto **4/4½** List price 5/-

No. N. 42B. Contains 12 tubes, 3 brushes, china palette and water cup, **5/3** List price 6/-

No. N. 41A.

No. N. 27.
Contains 10 China Pans and 1 Tube of Moist Water Colours, China Palette and Brushes.
Price **2/7** List price 3/-
Postage 4d.

Superior Japanned Half-Pan Boxes Best Students' Colours.

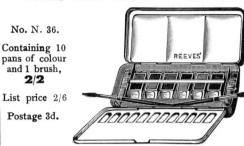

No. N. 36.

Containing 10 pans of colour and 1 brush, **2/2**

List price 2/6

Postage 3d.

No. N. 35. Contains 12 pans and 2 tubes of colour, 2 brushes, **3/-** List price 3/6 Postage 3d.

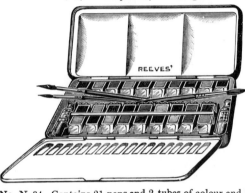

No. N. 34. Contains 21 pans and 2 tubes of colour and 3 brushes, **4/4½** List price 5/- Postage 4d.

No. N. 33. Contains 28 pans and 2 tubes of colour and 3 brushes, **6/6** List price 7/6 Post 4d.

No. N. 42B.

Children's Water Colours,
in polished mahogany boxes.

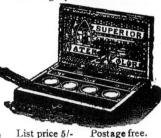

No. N.16, with hinged lid, contains 10 large cakes, saucers and brushes .. **2/2** List price 2/6 Postage 4d.

No. N.7, ditto, contains 12 ditto, ditto, **3/-** Post 4d. List price 3/6

No. N. 9 contains 18 ditto, etc. **4/4½** List price 5/- Postage free.

Polished Mahogany Colour Boxes.
Containing Students' Pan Colours.
Thoroughly reliable well-made boxes, much appreciated as 'Xmas Presents and School Prizes.

No. N. 29.

Polished Mahogany Box, with lock, containing 20 Pans and Tube of Moist Water Colors, China Tile and Brushes. Price **6/6** List price 7/6 Postage free.

No. N. 28. Contains 16 China Pans and Tube of Moist Water Colours, China Slab and Brushes. **4/4½** List price 5/- Postage 6d.

No. N. 30. Polished Mahogany Box, with lock, containing 27 Pans and Tube of Moist Water Colours, China Tile, Indiarubber and Brushes. Price **9/4** List price 10/6 Postage 8d.

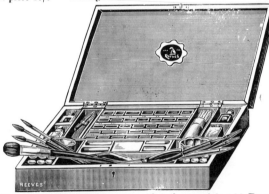

No. N. 31. Polished Mahogany Box, with lock, containing 36 Pans of Moist Water Colors, Bottle of Chinese White, China Tile, Indiarubber, Water Glass, Drawing Pins, Pencil and Brushes. **13/-** List price 15/- Postage 9d.

No. N 32. Polished Mahogany Box, with lock and key, containing 36 China Pans of Moist Colors, Bottles of Chinese White, Indian Ink, Gold and Silver Ink, China divided Palette, 2 Water Glasses, Pencils, Rubber, Drawing Pins, Pencil Compass, box of Pastel Crayons, Port Crayon, Camel Hair Brushes and Sky Brush Price **18/4** List price 21/- Postage 9d.

Reeves Pen Painting Materials.

Set A. In strong Cardboard Box, complete	**5/-** net.
„ B. In Japanned Tin Box	7/6 „
„ C.	10/6 „
„ D.	15/- „
Reeves' Pen Painter's Work Board	8d. „

MATERIALS TO REFILL THE BOXES.
Reeves' Improved Pen Painting Colours, all at **3d.** net.
Alizarin Crimson, Black, Burnt Sienna, Carmine Tint, Chrome Yellow, Pale, Mid., Deep, Cinnabar Green, Crimson Lake, Mauve, New Blue, Permanent Blue, Prussian Blue, Raw Sienna, Rose Madder, Sap Green, Scarlet Lake, Vandyke Brown, Vermilion, Mid Tint, White No. 1 Stiff, No. 2 Extra Stiff. White, Nos. 1 and 2, in half-pound tubes, 8d. net.

Reeves' Pen Painting Powder ...	...	per bottle, **5d.** net, per ½-lb. **1/3** net.
„ Medium ...	...	„ **5d.** „	½-pt. **2/6** „
Japan Pens	...	...	„ per dozen **3d.** „

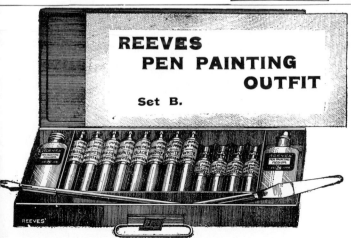

REEVES PEN PAINTING OUTFIT Set B.

V

USEFUL CHRISTMAS PRESENTS.

Reeves & Sons' New Walnut Wood Boxes for Oil Painting.

Reeves' New Walnut Wood Boxes for Oil Painting.

Polished Boxes. Leather Handles.
Mahogany Palettes.

No. N. 350s.

Empty with palette **6/-**
Fitted with 12 tubes of Students' oil colours, bottles of linseed oil and turpentine, dipper, 6 hog hair brushes, palette knife and palette **10/-**

No. N. 350. Same box fitted with Artist's Colours **12/-**

No. N. 351s.

Empty with palette **8/6**
Fitted with 1 double and 19 single tubes of Students' oil colours, large bottles of linseed oil and turpentine, 7 hog hair brushes, covered dipper, palette knife, rag and palette **15/-**

No. N. 351. SKETCHING BOX.

Empty with palette **8/6**
Fitted with 1 double and 19 single tubes of Artists' oil colours, large bottle of linseed oil and turpentine, 6 hog hair and 1 fitch brush, covered dipper, palette knife, rag and palette **20/-**

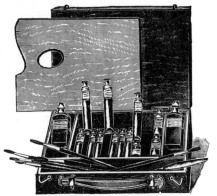

No. N. 350. (10 by 7¾ in.)

STUDENTS' OIL BOXES.
Japanned Tin.

Reeves' Student's Oil Colours.

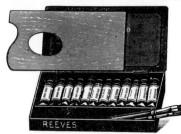

No. N. 301. Size 7 by 3¼ in., contains 12 tubes of Art Students' oil colours, palette and 2 hog brushes.
Price **3/-** List price 3/6 Postage free.
Empty box, **1/4** Palette 6d.

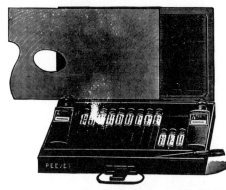

No. N. 302. Size 9½ by 5¼ in., as No. N. 301, 12 tubes and bottle of oil and turps.
The palette slides in a groove over the colours.
Price **4/4½** List price 5/- Postage free.
Empty box, **2/-** Palette, **6d.**

No. 303. Size 9⅓ by 6¾ in., contains 16 tubes of Art Students' oil colours, 2 hog brushs, palette, dipper, bottles of oil and turpentine. The palette slides in a groove over the colours.
Price **6/6** List price 7/6
Empty box, **3/6** Palette, **8d.**

No. 304. Size 10½ by 7½ in., contains 18 single and 1 double tube of Art Students' oil colours, hog brushes, palette, dipper, knife, bottles of oil and turpentine. The palette slides in a groove over the colours.
Price **9/2** List price 10/6
Empty box, **4 3** Palette, **10d.**

No. N. 305. Size 12½ by 8½ in., contains 18 tubes of Art Students' oil colours, 9 artists' brushes, palette, dipper, knife, 2 bottles of oil and 1 of turpentine, etc.
Price **13/-** List price 15/-
Empty box, **6/-** Palette, **1/-**

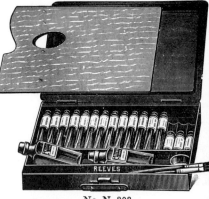

No. N. 303.

Japanned Boxes for Oil Painting

Fitted with ARTISTS' Oil Colours.
Finest Quality Japanned Tin. Extra Finish.

No. N. 315. Fitted with Artists' colours and brushes. Price **15/-** List price 20/-
Same contents as No. N. 305, but fitted with artists' colours.

No. 328. Studio Box.

Containing palette, 12 hog hair, 3 fitch hair and 8 sable brushes, badger hair softener, varnish brush, japanned bottles of turpentine, linseed, poppy and drying oils, mastic and copal varnishes, 3 steel and an ivory palette knife, scraper, double dipper, 3 prepared academy boards, 15 by 11, mahl stick, 4 double and 38 single tubes of artists' oil colors.

No. 328. (16½ by 11½ in.)
Complete .. **£3 19 0** List Price, £5

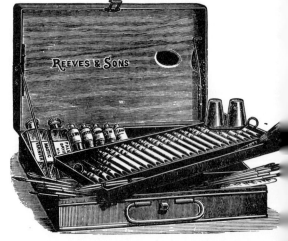

No. N 325. Contains palette, 10 hog hair and 3 fitch brushes, badger hair softener, japanned bottles of turpentine, linseed oil, drying oil and mastic varnish, palette knife, double dipper, 6 double and 21 single tubes of Artists' oil colours

Price **30/-** List price 42/-

Box, with empty japanned bottles, **13/6**
Palette, **1/-**

Japanned Tin Boxes "Landseer" Students' Moist Water Colours

No. 1 Box. Size 4⅝ in. by 2¾ in.,
1 in. deep. Containing—
10 China Pans of "Landseer" Students' Moist Water Colour.
1 Brush.
Price **1/9**

No. 2 Box. Size 6⅞ in. by 3 in.
1 in. deep. Containing—
14 China Pans of "Landseer" Students' Moist Water Colour.
1 Tube of Chinese White.
2 Brushes.
Price **2/6**

No. 3 Box. Size 6⅞ in. by 3⅞ in.
1 in. deep. Containing—
China Pans of "Landseer" Students' Moist Water Colour.
Tube of Chinese White.
3 Brushes.
Price **3/6**

No. 4 Box. Containing 30 Pans, Tube of Chinese White and 3 Brushes. Price .. **5/-**

No. 9 Box. Containing 12 Pans, Tube of Chinese White and 3 Brushes. Price .. **2/-**

No. 10 Box. Size 7⅞ by 2⅜ in. ⅞ in. deep.
Containing—
8 Pans of "Landseer" Students' Moist Water Colour, and 2 Brushes.
Price .. **1/6**

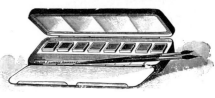

No. 11 Box. Containing 6 Tubes and Brush. Price **1/4**
No. 12 Box. Containing 9 Tubes and 2 Brushes .. **2/-**
No. 13 Box. 7 by 3⅞ in. 1 in. deep. Containing 12 Tubes of "Landseer" Students' Moist Water Colour, and 3 Brushes. Price **3/4**
No. 14 Box. Containing 15 Tubes and 3 Brushes .. **4/-**

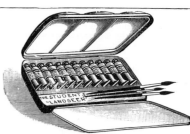

No. 15 Box. Containing 8 Half-tubes and Brush .. **1/3**
No. 16 Box. 6¼ by 2⅞ in. ⅞ in. deep. Containing 12 Half-tubes of "Landseer" Students' Water Colour, and 1 Brush. Price .. **1/8**
No. 17 Box. Containing 6 Half-tubes and 2 Brushes, **2/-**

"Gainsborough" Japanned Tin Juvenile Boxes.

No. 0. 9 Pans and Brush,   **No. 1.** 12 Pans and 2 Brushes,

Polished Mahogany Boxes of "Landseer" Colours.

No. 21 Box. Containing 16 Pans, Tube of Chinese White, Centre Slant, and 3 Brushes. Price .. **3/6**

No. 22 Box. 20 Pans, Tube of Chinese White, Centre Slant, Water Glass, and 3 Brushes. Price **5/3**

No. 23 Box. Size 10⅛ by 7⅝ in. 2 in. deep. Containing 27 Pans, Tube of Chinese White, Centre Slant, large Water Glass, piece India-rubber, 2 Brushes. Price .. **7/6**

No. 24 Box. 36 Pans, Tube of Chinese White, and good assortment of materials. Price .. **11/3**

No. 25 Box. 35 Pans, and a larger and more varied assortment of materials than in No. 24 Box. Price **15/9**

No. 2 Box. Containing 12 Metal Pans and 2 Tubes of "Landseer" Students' Water Colour and 3 Brushes. Price **1 3**
No. 3 Box. Containing 16 Pans, 2 Tubes and 3 Brushes. Price **1/6**

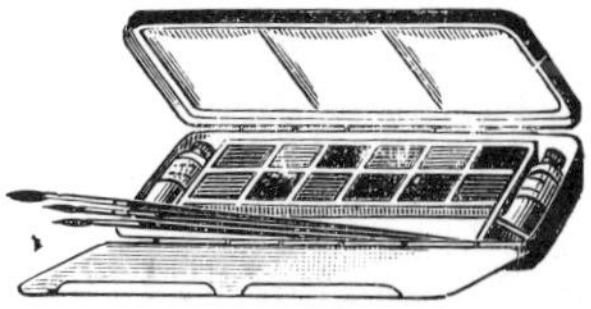

No 4 Box. Containing 21 Metal Pans and 2 Tubes of "Landseer" Students' Water Colour and three Brushes. Price **2/-**

Winsor & Newton's Pen-Painting Colours and Materials.

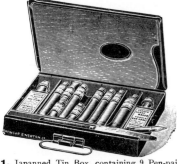

No. 1, Japanned Tin Box, containing 9 Pen-painting Oil Colours in tubes, Bottle of Special Medium, Bottle of Special Powder, Mahogany Pallette or Opal Tile, Pallette Knife, Pen-holder and Pens. Price **7/6**

No. 2, Japanned Tin Box, measuring 10½ in. by 7⅞ in., containing 17 Pen-painting Oil Colours in Tubes, Bottles of Special Medium and Powder, Pallette, Pallette Knife, 2 Pen-holders with Pens, 12 loose Pens, Traced Designs, Traced and Partly-painted D'oyley, and 6 pieces of Silk Gauze. Price ... **15/-**

No. 3, Polished Walnut Box, 13 by 9 in., containing colours and other fittings as above. Price **17/6**

Winsor & Newton's Stencilling Outfit.
Fitted with Artists' Oil Colours and Stencilling Materials

Containing 9 Colours, Bottle of Medium, 3 Brushes, Opal Tile, Cutting Knife and Stencil. Price **5/-**

WINSOR & NEWTON'S

Polished Mahogany Box of Artists' Moist Water Colours in Half-tubes, specially selected for Transparent Painting. Containing 16 Artists' Colours, a large Tube of Chinese White Bottle of Francis-Lewis Transparent Painting Medium, 8 Tinting Saucers and 3 Red Sable Hair Brushes, **16/-** The Box empty, **3/6**

A SMALLER Box, containing Half-tubes instead of Large, **11/6**

V..

Mathematical Instrument Sets for Xmas Presents.

Pocket Sets.

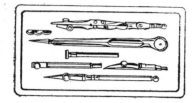

The Technical School Set in Electrum

No. N. 1.   Leather Snap Case.

5 in. elec. bow-pencil compass with double knee-joints, pen points and lengthening bar, divider ruling pen, case of leads, steel-jointed throughout.

Price .. **7/6**   Postage free.

The Technical School Set. No. N. 2.

Leather Pocket Case   Containing 5 in. Compass, with double knee-joints, pen and pencil points, spring bow pen and pencil (nut and bolt adjustment), ruling pen and case of leads.

Price .. **8/3**   Postage free.

Gamage's Universal Case.

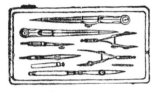

The finest value case ever offered.

As sold elsewhere at 15/6

5 in. Electrum Compass with round points, pen and pencil points, 4½ in. divider, spring bow pen and pencil (nut and bolt adjustment), ruling pen and case of leads.

Price .. **10/6**   Postage free.

The Improved Technical Set.

German Silver Instruments.

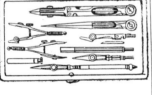

Containing 5½ in. needle pointed, steel jointed compass, double knee joints, nut and bolt adjustment, pen and pencil points, divider, lengthening bar, 2 spring bows, ruling pen, lift up nib, box of leads and key, in morocco leather case, silk lined.

Price .. **13/9**   Postage free.

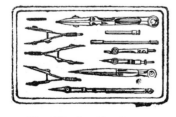

The Student's Case.

N. 2.   5½ in. steel-jointed needle-pointed compass, double knee joints, pen and pencil points, lengthening bar, ruling pen, 3 spring bows and divider.

Price .. **18/6**   Postage free.

School Sets.

No. 1.   No. 3.   No. 4.

No. 1. contains compass, pen and pencil points, slip rule and compass key, in stained wood box   ...   **1/-**

No. 2. contains 4½ in. compass, pen and pencil points, lengthening bar, pencil holder, slip rule, compass key and brass protractor **1/4**

No. 3. contains ditto with ruling pen added **1/9**

No. 3½. contains do. with divider added in polished rosewood box **2/6**

No. 4. contains 6 in. compass, pen and pencil points, lengthening bar, divider, as illustration, in polished rosewood box   **3/3**

No. 5. contains ditto ditto but with bow compass, set of three points, instead of pencil holder, in polished rosewood box   **4/6**

No. 6. **Pocket Case** containing 5½ in. compass, pen and pencil points, bar, divider, compass, set of three movable points, ruling pen, slip rule and half circle protractor   **4/-**   Post. 3d.

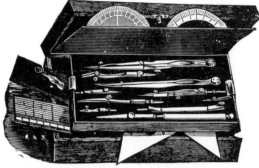

No. 7. Polished Rosewood Box.

With lock, containing 5-in. needle pointed compass, pen and pencil points, bar, divider, bow compass, set of 3 points ruling pen, half-circle protractor, parallel rule, scale and rule

Price   ...   **6/-**   Postage 3d.

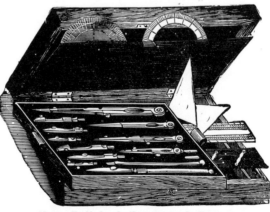

No. 8. Polished Rosewood Box.

with lock, containing 6-in. compass, pen and pencil points, bar, 4-in. compass, with pen and pencil points, bow compass, set of 3 points, divider, ruling pen, two protractors, parallel rule, scale and angles.

Price   ...   **8/-**   Postage 4d.

No. 9. Polished Rosewood Box.

With lock, containing 6 in. compass, with pen and pencil, points and bar, divider, 4 in. compass, with pen and pencil points, patent pencil point holders, box of leads, ivory hand-ruling pen, long spring bow with ivory handle, parallel rule, scale and angles.

Price   **9/11**   Postage 4d.

Presentation Sets.

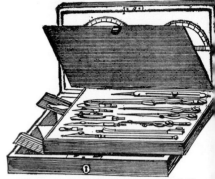

No. N. 10. Polished Rosewood Box.

With lock containing 6 in. needle pointed compass, pen and pencil points, bar, 4 in. compass, pen and pencil points, bow compass, set of 3 points, divider, proportional compass, ruling pen, 2 protractors, rule, scale and angles.

Price .. **12/6**   Postage free.

No. 11. Handsome Rosewood Box

Inlaid with brass, containing 6 in. needle pointed compass, pen and pencil points, bar, 4 in. needle pointed compass, pen and pencil points, divider, proportional compass, 2 spring bows, 2 ivory ruling pens, 2 protractors, parallel, scale and angles

Price   **19/6**   Postage free·

English Pattern Elechum Instruments.

The Gamage Set.

Nut and Bolt Needle-pointed Instruments

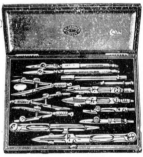

Special morocco pocket case, silk lined with lift-up inside of lid, containing: 5½ in. electrum steel jointed compass with two knee joints, pen and pencil legs, lengthening bar, hollow bow pen and pencil, set of 3 spring bows, hair-spring divider, 2 ruling pens and compass key.

Price .. **30/-**   Postage free.

The "Holborn" Set.

Special neat leather snap case, silk lined, with lift-up flap inside lid.

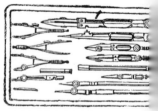

Contains 6-in. sector-jointed compass, german silver with nut and bolt needle points, 2 knee joints, deep hollow, lengthening bar, hinged pen and pencil points, hair-spring divider, and 2 ruling pens, 3 improved spring bows with needle points and nut and bolt adjustment, case of leads and key

Price .. **40/-**

The above set also supplied in real Russia leather case   Price **50/-**   Postage free.

The London Set.

Best English Drawing Instruments.

Morocco pocket case, silk-lined, electrum name-plate centre of lid, containing the following superior german silver instruments: Compass with double knee-joints, needle points, pen and pencil points, lengthening bar, hair-spring divider, 3 needle-pointed spring bows, in pencil needle-pointed double knee-jointed bows, jointed ivory pen, steel ditto.   Price .. **50/-**   Post fr.

Prayer and Hymn Books for Presents.

Morocco Grained Leather, with or without cross.
Colours: Black, Green & Maroon, Ruby type .. **2/-**
Also in Velvet, Persian Calf, and various colours, **2/11 3/6 4/6**
Large print edition 24mo on Oxford India paper. A nice light book, Morocco grained leather .. **7/6**
Velvet Calf **12/-**

Ivorine, with Hall-marked Silver Cross or I.H.S. on side.
4/-
Also in superior finish, the covers lined with silk.
6/-

Velvet Persian Calf, Yapp binding.
Pearl type, on India paper.
A small Pocket Edition with good print **3/6**
Ruby type .. **2/3**
Superior quality—
4/-

The New Satchel Carrying Case.

Containing Prayer and Hymn Book.
Made in Velvet Persian Calf, all the fashionable colours.. .. .. .. **10/6**
Real Seal Leather **17/6**
Also in a cheaper quality of Velvet Calf with long silk cord handle **8/-**
Each of these has a pocket for offertory.

Church Services

In various types and bindings, **1/-** to **40/-**

Prayer Book with Hymns.

Two volumes, in leather case, with Hall-marked Silver Front.
Thumb edition, **6/6**   48mo edition, **5/9**
48mo edition, superior make   .. **7/-**
Also with Cherub design, stout silver front **10/6**

EXACT SIZE).   J.
"Thumb" Prayer Book **3/6**
  ,,   Hymn Book **4/3**
  ,,   Prayer and Hymns, in 1 Volume **5/6**
In a superior Leather Binding, with stout Silver London-made front, as above, and other designs.
Also in a cheaper quality—
Prayer Book, **2/6**   Hymn Book, **3/3**
Prayer Book with Hymns in 1 Volume, **4/6**
Larger type editions   ditto   **10/6**

Prayer and Hymn Books.

Ruby Edition.   Leather Bindings.

4½ by 3 in. French Morocco, Paste Grain and other bindings **1/-**
Ditto, Limp and Padded, round corners, superior finish **1/6**
Persian Calf, straight grain and other leathers, limp and padded **2/-**
Ditto, in superior styles **2/6**
Rutland Morocco, padded Persian, &c., plain and fancy bindings .. **3/-** **3/6**
German Calf, Turkey Morocco, real Russia, limp and padded, various styles of finish .. **4/6 5/6 6/6 7/6**
In White Bindings, for Weddings, Confirmations, etc. **1/4 1/9 2/6 3/- 3/6 to 7/6**

Imitation of Christ, and all the Popular Devotional Books kept in stock or obtained to order immediately.

Large print, 32mo.
French Morocco, rounded covers **3/-**
Superior Leather—
  4/- 5/- 6/6 etc.

Larger type, 24mo.
French Morocco .. **4/-**
Superior Leather—
  5/- 6/- 7/6 etc.

2 Vols. in Case, 48mo.
Leather, with cord or leather handle .. **2/6**
As illustration .. **3/-**
Upright or Oblong Cases in various superior leathers—
3/6 4/- 4/6 5/- 6/- 6/6 7/6 9/- etc.
Also in larger types.

Gamage 1/- Prayer and Hymn Book.

With handle.
Marvellous value.
Bound in levantine straight grain and imitation calf, round corners, gilt edges.
(Post 2d.

Velvet Persian Calf,
Price **5/-**
In Mauve, Green, Mole, Grey, Brown, etc.

Gamage's New Illustrated Prayer and Hymns

With Old Master Coloured Plates.
A beautiful Gift.
Leather binding.
1/6 2/- 2/6

Hymns A. & M., Hymnal Companion, and other Hymnbooks, kept in stock or supplied to order.

THE POETS in Dainty Binding, &c., for PRESENTS.

The New Oxford Pocket Poets.

Good clear type on thin opaque paper.

Each volume has a portrait.

Size 6 by 4 in.

Arnold (Matthew)
Æschylus
Aristophanes
Browning, E. B.
Browning's (Robert) Poems, 1833-1842
Browning's (Robert) Poems, 1842-1864
Burns
Chaucer's Canterbury Tales
Coleridge
Dryden's Virgil
English Songs
Goethe's Faust and Crosland
Marlowe's Dr. Faustus
Goldsmith's Poems

Herbert (George)
Herrick
Homer's Iliad, Pope
  ,,   Odyssey ,,
Hood (Thomas)
Ingoldsby Legends
Keats
Longfellow's Evangeline, etc.
Longfellow's Hiawatha, etc.
Macaulay's Lays of Ancient Rome, etc.
Palgrave's Golden Treasury
Sheridan's Plays
Sophocles
Tennyson

Cloth, gilt edges .. .. .. **1/-** net.
Lambskin, gilt lines, gilt edges **2/3** ,,
Velvet, Persian calf, padded, Author's mono. on side colour under gold edges as illustration .. .. **3/6** ,,

Postage 2d. extra.

Tennyson.—Complete Works.

Straight grain roan, round corners, gilt finishings, gilt edges .. 12/6 **9/6**
Straight grain roan, padded, round corners, extra gilt finishings, red under gold edges 15/- **11/3**
Rutland morocco, padded, best style ditto 17/6 **13/2**
Real morocco, padded, best finish ditto 21/- **15/9**
Also in vellum, tree calf, polished levant and other presentation bindings. Postage 4d.

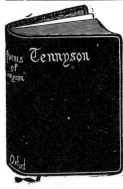

The Oxford Illustrated Tennyson.

With two coloured pictures after G. F. Watts and 91 illustrations in Black and White by Millais, Rossetti, Maclise and others.

Large Type.

Size 7¾ by   in.

Straight grain, limp, gilt line, round corners, gilt edges **7/6**
Rutland, padded, gilt line, round corners, red under gilt edges, gilt roll .. **10/-**
Tree calf, gilt edges **12/6**

The Oxford Illustrated Shakespeare.

Complete in volume with Glossary and 32 pictures taken from the Boydell Gallery.
Size 7¾ by 6½ inches in large print.
Straight grain leather, round corners, gilt finishings .. .. .. **6/-** net.
Tree calf, marbled edges .. .. **10/-** ,,

The Oxford Editions of Standard Authors.

" Delightful Editions all of them and wonderful for money."— *Daily Graphic.*

Crown 8vo.

Good print, each with a portrait or other illustrations.

POETRY.

Arnold (Matthew), 1849-1867
Book of Light Verse
Bridges (Robert)
Browning (E. B.)
Browning (Robert), 1833-1864
Browning. The Ring and the Book
Burns
Byron
Campbell
Chaucer
Coleridge
Cowper
Dante:
  Cary's Translation. 109 illustrations
Dryden
Goldsmith. 21 illustrations
Gordon (Adam Lindsay)
Herbert
Hood
Ingoldsby Legends. 25 illustrations
Keats
Longfellow

Lowell
Milton
Moore
Pageant of English Poetry
Palgrave's Golden Treasury. With Additional Poems
Poe (Edgar Allan)
Scott
Shakespeare. Complete
Shakespeare's Comedies. Large type edition
Shakespeare's Histories and Poems. Large type edition
Shakespeare's Tragedies. Large type edition
Shelley
Southey
Spenser
Tennyson, 1829-1868
Thomson
Whittier
Wordsworth

PROSE.

Boswell's Life of Johnson. 2 vols.
Bunyan's Pilgrim's Progress. 24 illustrations.
Goldsmith's Plays and the Vicar of Wakefield. 16 illustrations.
Grimms' Popular Stories. 22 illustrations.
Kingsley's Hereward the Wake. 14 illustrations
Kingsley's Westward Ho! 12 illustrations.
Lamb's Tales from Shakespeare. 16 illustrations.
Lamb's Works. 2 vols.
Pageant of English Prose.
Robinson Crusoe. (Defoe). 55 illustrations.
Sheridan's Plays. 15 illustrations.
Southey's Life of Nelson. 24 illustrations.
Tom Brown's School Days. (Hughes). 14 illus.

Cloth boards, gilt back .. .. 2/- **1/6** net.
Leather, round corners, gilt edges 3/6 **2/8** ,,
Paste grain leather (as illustration) gilt design on side, colour under gold edges .. .. .. 4/- **3/-** ,,
Padded leather, round corners, extra gilt finishings, colour under gold edges .. .. 5/- **3/9** ,,
Quarter vellum, gilt back, cloth sides, gilt top edges .. .. 5/6 **4/2** ,,
Italian morocco, padded, round corners, colour under gold edges 6/6 **4/11** ,,
Rutland morocco, ditto .. .. 7/6 **5/8** ,,
Velvet calf, padded, ditto,
  a very pretty present 10/- **7/6** ,,
Morocco boards, full gilt side and back .. .. 10/- **7/6** ,,

Postage 4d. extra.

The Oxford Edition of the Poets.

" Now by far the best in the market." *Sphere.*

" Remarkable for cheapness and excellence." *Manchester Guardian.*

Large crown 8vo, on superior paper, each with photogravure portrait.

Arnold, M.
Browning, E. B.
Browning, Robt.
Bing and the Book
Burns
Bridges, Robt.
Byron
Campbell
Chaucer
Coleridge
Cowper

Crabbe
Dante
Dryden
Goldsmith
Hood
Ingoldsby
Keats
Longfellow
Lowell
Milton
Moore

Pageant of Eng. Poe
Poe
Scott
Shakespeare
Shelley
Southey
Spencer
Tennyson
Thomson
Whittier
Wordsworth

Straight grain roan, round borners, gilt finishings and edges .. .. .. 6/6 **4/1** net
Ditto, padded, round edges, extra gilt finishings, red under gold edges .. 8/- **6/-**
Half vellum, gold blocked back, marbled sides, gilt top edges 9/- **6/9**
Tree calf, gilt back, extra gold finishings, gilt edges 12/- **9/-**
Three-quarter Levant polished morocco, gilt tooled back, art linen sides .. 16/- **12/**
Printed on Oxford thin India paper, velvet Persian calf, supple yapp, red under gold edges, 9/- **6/**

Postage 4d. extra.

The complete works of Shakespeare, 12 handy vols. in case 32mo, each vol. 4½ by 2¾ in., size of case 9½ by 4   **3½** net
Cloth, in cloth or oak case .. .. .. **12/6** net
Paste grain, in oak case .. .. .. **20/-** ,,
Straight grain, in oak case .. .. **27/6** ,,
Quarter vellum, hand tooled back, in oak case, **38/-** ,,
The complete works of Shakespeare, 9 pocket volumes Lambskin, extra gilt, gilt edges, **20/-** net.
The complete works of Shakespeare, in 3 vols. Large print Size 7¾ by 5¼ in. Cloth boards, **4/6** Leather, round corners, gilt edge, **8/-** Half calf, gilt back, cloth side. **12/**

BIRTHDAY BOOKS.   32mo Edition.

Burns
Dickens, Charles
Emerson
Great Thoughts
Hermans, Mrs
Keats
Keepsake
Links of Memory
Little Folks

A Guide, a comforter
Abide in Me
Album Scripture Text Book
Bible Gems
Bible Words
Birthday Greeting
  ,, Motto Book
  ,, Scripture Text Book
Browning, Robert E. B.

Longfellow
Lowell
Merry Thoughts
Moore
Scott
Shakespeare
Shelley
Tennyson
What Saith the Master
Whit and Honour
Whittier & Wilcox
Wordsworth

Cloth, padded sides, round corners, gilt edges, **1/-** net
Leather, square corners, gilt edges, as illust., **1/-** ,,
Leather, round corners, gilt lines, as illust., **1/6** ,,
Italian morocco, padded, round corners .. **2/-** ,,
Velvet, Persian calf, yapp, as illustration .. **2/-** ,,
Ivorine, padded, round corners .. .. **2/6** ,,

Oxford Reference Bibles.

THE NEW CLARENDON—PEARL 32mo, ¾ in. by 3¼ in. A clear print in a small book.

ench morocco, gilt edges, round corners 1/6
„ yapp 2/6
perior ditto, leather lined, red-gilt edges, round corners 3/6
Printed on Oxford thin India paper.
ench morocco, yapp, cloth lined, red-gilt edges, round corners 4/6
rsian morocco, yapp, leather lined, red-gilt edges, round corners 6/6

RUBY 24mo., 5⅝ by 4 in.

ench morocco, yapp, gilt edges, round corners 2/6
perior ditto, yapp, leather lined, red-gilt edges, round corners 4/6
Printed on Oxford thin India paper.
orocco grained leather, yapp, cloth lined, red-gilt edges 5/6
sian morocco, yapp, leather lined, silk sewn, red-gilt edges 7/6
dras ditto ditto .. 10/6

EMERALD 16mo, 7 by 4⅝ in.

ench morocco, gilt edges 2/6
„ round corners .. 3/-
„ yapp, round corners.. 3/9
perior ditto, yapp, leather lined, red-gilt edges round corners 5/6
Printed on Oxford thin India paper.
l grained leather, yapp, cloth lined, red-gilt edges, round corneers .. 6/-
sian morocco, yapp, leather lined, silk sewn, red-gilt edges, round corners 9/6
key ditto ditto .. 13/6

CLARENDON BREVIER 16mo, 7¼ by 4⅝ in.
A bold black print, easy to read, in almost a pocket volume.

nch morocco, round corners, red-gilt edges 4/6
nch morocco, yapp, red-gilt edges .. 5/6
perior ditto, yapp. leather lined, red-gilt edges, round corners 8/-
sian ditto, yapp, leather lined, silk sewn, red-gilt edges, round corners 10/6
Printed on Oxford thin India paper.
A very light and beautiful Bible.
sian morocco yapp, leather lined, silk sewn 12/-
ant ditto ditto .. 18/6

Cheap School Bibles.

In clear print.

rl 24mo, cloth, red edges ... ... 9d.
y 32mo, cloth, gilt edges 1/-
ch morocco, round corners, red gilt edges ... 1/6
pareil 16mo, cloth, red edges 1/2
„ „ paste grain leather, red edges ... 1/9
ion 12mo, cloth, red edges 1/6
rl 32mo, references, cloth, red edges 1/-
rald 16mo „ „ 1 9

The Holy Bible. Revised Version.

Pearl 16mo.

h, red edges 8d. Paste grain limp, gilt edges 1/9
nch morocco yapp 2/6

Nonpareil 16mo.

h, red edges 1/-
nch morocco, round corners, gilt edges . 2 3
„ yapp, red gilt edges .. 3/6

Brevier 16mo., with references.

h boards 6/-
nch morocco, round corners, red gilt edges 7/6
ian morocco yapp, leather lined .. 13 6
„ „ Oxford India paper.. 16/-
ant morocco „ „ .. 25/-

The Oxford Bible for Teachers.

Complete illustrated edition, with concordance, &c.
Ruby 24mo. 5⅝ by 4 in.

French morocco, yapp, round corners 4/6
„ „ superior yapp, leather lined 6/-
Printed on Oxford thin Indian paper.
Seal grained leather, yapp, leather lined, red gilt edges 8/-
Persian morocco yapp, leather lined, red gilt edges 10/-

Emerald 16mo. 7 by 4⅝ in.

French morocco limp, round corners, red gilt edges.. .. .. 5/6
French morocco, yapp, round corners, red gilt edges.. .. .. 6/9
Printed on Oxford thin India paper.
Seal grained leather, yapp, leather lined, round corners 10/-
Persian morocco, yapp, leather lined, silk sewn 12/-
Levant morocco, yapp 19/-

Long Primer 8vo. 8 by 5½ in.

Persian morocco, yapp, leather lined, round corners, red gilt edges 16/6
Levant morocco, yapp, leather lined, round corners, red gilt edges 25/-

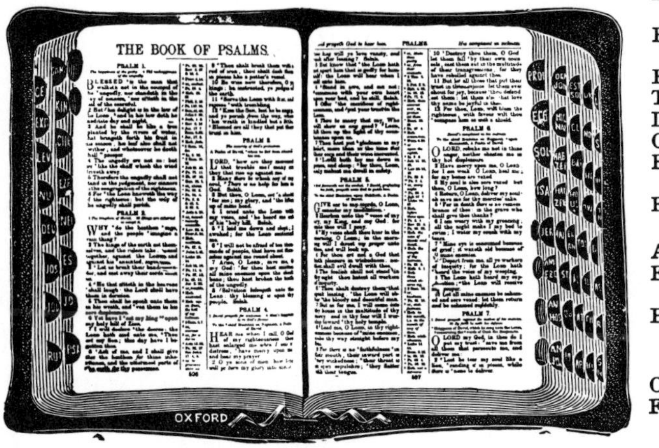
THE BOOK OF PSALMS
OXFORD

The Oxford Thumb Index Bibles.

For convenience of reference, the titles of the various Books are printed in gold on spaces cut in the Bibles' edges Any part desired may thus be instantly turned to.

Pocket Bibles. Diamond 32mo.

Morocco grained cloth, round corners, red gilt edges.. .. .. 1/9
French morocco, yapp 2/6
Paste grain, yapp, cloth lined 3 6

Pocket Bible. Diamond 32mo. Printed on Oxford thin India paper.

French morocco, yapp, cloth lined 4/6

Text Bible. Ruby 32mo.

Morocco grained leather, round corners, red gilt edges 2/3

Referrence Bible. Pearl 32mo.

French morocco, yapp, red gilt edges.. .. 3/3
Printed on Oxford thin India paper.
French morocco, yapp, cloth lined 4/-
Persian morocco, leather lined.. .. .. 6/-

Reference Bible. Ruby 24mo.

French morocco, yapp 3/9
„ „ cloth lined 4/6
Printed on Oxford thin India Paper.
French morocco, yapp, leather lined 6/6
Persian „ „ „ „ 8/6

Reference Bible. Emerald 16mo.

French morocco, yapp, cloth lined 5/6
Printed on Oxford thin India paper.
French morocco, yapp 6/9
Persian morocco, yapp, leather lined 10 6

Postage 3d. extra.
Any other Bible in this catalogue may be had with this most useful Thumb-Index, specially cut 1/3 additional cost.

New Testaments.

A great variety at 6d., 8d., 10d., 1/-, etc.
Authorised and Revised Versions.

Small Bibles for the Pocket.

BRILLIANT 48mo, 2⅝ by 2⅛ in.

French morocco yapp, red-gilt edges, 3/6
Persian morocco yapp, leather lined, 5/6

BRILLIANT 48mo, with References.

French morocco, limp, round corners .. 4/-
French morocco, yapp, cloth lined, round corners, red-gilt edges 5/6
Persian morocco, yapp, leather lined, round corners, red-gilt edges 7/-
Levant morocco, yapp, leather lined, round corners, red-gilt edges 10/6

DIAMOND 32mo, 4¾ by 2¼ in.

Cloth, round corners, red-gilt edges .. 1/-
French morocco, yapp, gilt edges .. 1/6
„ „ superior yapp, red-gilt edges 2/6
Printed on Oxford thin India paper.
French morocco, round corners, red-gilt edges 2/6
French morocco, yapp, cloth lined, round corners, red-gilt edges .. 3/6
Persian morocco, yapp, leather lined .. 5/-
Turkey morocco, „ „ „ .. 7/6

DIAMOND 24mo, with References, 5 by 3½ in.

Cloth, round corners, gilt edges .. 1/-
French morocco, round corners, red-gilt edges 1/6
Fench morocco, yapp, „ „ „ 2/-

CLARENDON PEARL 32mo, 5¼ by 5⅜ in.
A very readable type on Oxford thin India paper.

French morocco, yapp, round corners, red gilt edges 3/-
Persian morocco, yapp, leather lined, red gilt edges 5/6

PEARL 24mo, 5½ by 3½ in.

Cloth, round corners, gilt edges .. 1/-
French morocco, yapp, round corners, red gilt edges 1/9

The Palestine Pictorial Bible.

The Authorised Version. Emerald 16mo with references and 116 engravings and coloured pictures from drawings made in Bible lands.
The most beautifully illustrated Bible published.

Cloth boards, gilt edges 4/-
„ padded, full gilt sides and back gilt edges 5/-
French morocco, yapp round corners .. 6/6
Straight grain roan boards, full gilt side and back red gilt edges 7/6
Printed on Oxford thin India paper.
French morocco, yapp silk lined 10/6
Persian morocco, yapp leather lined .. 12/6
Also in Cheaper editions for school use.

PEARL TYPE, 24mo, with 32 engravings.

Cloth .. 1/- French Morocco .. 1/6

RUBY TYPE. 32mo, with 32 coloured pictures.

Morocco grained cloth, red edges 2/-
Italian yapp 3/-

PEARL TYPE, with References, 32 engravings.

Cloth, gilt edges 1/9
With 32 coloured pictures, leather binding 2/6

Cheap Large-print Bibles.

Cloth, red edges 1/6
French morocco, round corners, gilt edges 2/11
French morocco yapp, round corners, red gilt edges 3/11

CLARENDON BREVIER 16mo. 6¼ by 4½ in.
A good bold black type.

French morocco, round corners, red gilt edges 3/9
French morocco yapp, round corners, red gilt edges 4/6

LONG PRIMER 16mo. 7½ by 5 in.

Cloth, round corners, red edges .. 2/9
French morocco, round corners, gilt edges. 4/6

SMALL PICA 8vo. 9½ by 6 in.

Cloth, round corners, red gilt edges .. 4/-
French morocco, round corners, red gilt edges 5/9

All Bibles are Net. Postage 2d. and 3d. each extra.

The "Little Joiner" Polished Tool Chests and Juvenile Tool Sets on Card.

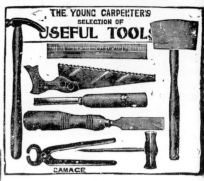

No. 2. Tool Set.

Price, on Card complete 10½d

Postage 3d.

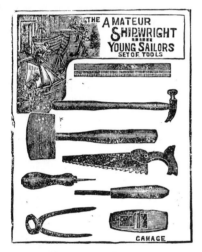

No. 1. Tool Set.

Price, complete on Card .. .. **6½d.**

THE TRIUMPH OF VALUE.

Postage 3d.

Tool Chests.

No. 0. SPECIAL. Contains **mallet**, hand-saw, hammer, pincers, bradawl, turnscrew.

Price .. .. **1/-** Postage 3d.

No. 0 10 P. contains hand-saw, gimlet, turn-screw, hammer, mallet, bradawl, rule, chisel.

Price .. .. **1 6** Postage 3d.

No. A contains hand-saw, mallet, hammer, gimlet, bradawl, chisel, gouge, turnscrew.

Price .. .. **2/-** Postage 4d.

No. 1 A contains brass-back saw, hammer, gimlet, chisel, gouge, mallet, rule, pincers, turnscrew.

Price .. .. **2/6** Postage 4d.

No. C contains hand-saw, mallet, hammer, large gimlet, small gimlet, large bradawl, small bradawl, steel chisel, steel turnscrew, steel tack-lifter, rule, gouge.

Price .. .. **3/6** Postage 4d.

No. C S contains hand-saw, mallet, large gimlet, small gimlet, large bradawl, small bradawl, steel chisel, spokeshave, steel turnscrew, steel tack-lifter, rule, gouge.

Price .. .. **4/3** Postage 5d.

No. D contains hand-saw, mallet, hammer, large gimlet, small gimlet, pliers, large bradawl, small bradawl, steel chisel, steel turnscrew, steel tack-lifter, gouge, rule, smooth plane.

Price .. .. **5/-** Postage 6d.

No. S D contains spokeshave, large gimlet, small gimlet, hand-saw, steel chisel, steel gouge, steel turnscrew, steel tack-lifter, large bradawl, small bradawl, rule, pliers, square iron plane, mallet, hammer.

Price .. .. **6/-** Postage 6d.

Soldering Set.

Contains—

Soldering Iron,
File,
Solder,
Lamp,
Brush, etc.
Superior Quality.

Price .. **6/3**

Postage 3d.

No. 4. Tool Set.

Price, complete on Card **1/9**

Postage 3d.

No. 3. Tool Set.

Complete on Card.

Price .. .. .. **1/3** Postage 3d.

No. 5. Tool Set.

Price, complete on Card **2/3**

Postage 3d.

GAMAGE'S TOOL CHESTS—Sheffield Make.

THE "TECHNICAL" SETS.

Strong Deal Chests, fitted with Useful Tools, splendid value.

D 1. Contains Plane, Hammer, Turnscrew, Chisel, Bradawl, Boxwood Rule, Gimlet, File, Handsaw, Tacklifter, and Pincers. Price **7/6** Carriage 6d.

D 3. Contains Saw, Chisel, Punch, Bradawl, Plane, Hammer, File, Pincers, Turnscrew, Gimlet, Boxwood Rule, Gouge, Gluepot and Brush, Spokeshave and Beech Marking Gauge. Price **10/6** Carriage 6d.

D 5. Containing Morticed Mallet, Boxwood Rule, ½ in. Chisel, Gluepot and Brush, Pincers, ½ in. Chisel, Marking Gauge, Walnut Spirit Level, Gouge, Hammer, Shell Gimlet, Spokeshave, mahogany Square, Twist Gimlet, 2 Bradawls, Plane, Turnscrew and Handsaw. Price **18/9** Carriage paid.

D 6. 4½ in. Mortice Mallet, Hatchet, 1¾ in. Smoothing Plane, Rivetting Hammer, 6 in. Tower Pincers, Gluepot and Brush, Patent Marking Gauge, 1 in. handled Chisel, ½ in. handled Chisel, ¼ in. handled Chisel, ¼ in. handled Gouge, ft. (4-fold) Boxwood Rule, small London pattern Turnscrew, 6 in. London pattern Turnscrew, 4½ in. Mahogany Square, 2 Bradawls, Twist Gimlet, Shell Gimlet, iron handle, Spokeshave, handled File, 8 in. Mahogany Spirit Level, Joiner's Brace Centrebits, Swiss Bit, Nail Punch, 12 in. Handsaw.

Price .. .. **25/-** Carriage free.

GENTLEMEN'S OAK TOOL CHESTS.

Sheffield Make. Best Quality. Carriage Paid.

No. 20.

16 in. by 8½ in. by 5 in.

20/- each. Contains—

Handsaw	Two Bradawls
Claw Hammer	Two Gimlets
Mallet	Compasses
Chisel	Brad Punch
Gouge	Pincers
Oil Stone, in case	Square
	Pliers
Spokeshave	Saw File
Saw Wrench	Arch Joint Rule
Marking Awl	Furniture, &c.
Turnscrew	

No. 21.

17 in. by 9¾ in. by 6 in.

30/- each. Contains—

Handsaw	Marking Gauge
Mallet	Saw File
Claw Hammer	Smoothing
File	Plane
Rasp	Oil Stone, in case
Chisel	
Gouge	Marking Awl
Keyhole Saw	Two Gimlets
Turnscrew	Two Bradawls.
Spokeshave	Brad Punch
Claw Wrench	Pliers
Plated Bevel	Hand Pad, with 8 Tools
Square	Pincers
Compasses	Furniture, &c.
Arch Joint Rule	

No. 22.

19 in. by 11½ in. by 8 in.

39/- each. Contains—

Handsaw	Three Chisels
Hatchet	Two Gouges
Hammer	Two Files
Mallet	One Rasp
Rule	Oil Stone, in case
Pincers	
Marking Awl	Pliers
Punch	Compasses
Two Turnscrews	Lock Saw
Spokeshave	Plane
Square	Wing Pad and Tools
Claw Wrench	
Three Gimlets	Furniture, &c.
Three Bradawls	

No. 23.

19¼ in. by 11 in. by 8¼ in., with Drawer.

45/- each. Contains—

Best Hand Saw	Three Firmer Chisels	Plated Square
Best Hatchet	Two Gouges	Claw Wrench
London Turnscrew	Saw File	Flat Nose Pliers
Joiner's Mallet	Flat File	Pair of Compasses
Best Rule	Cabinet Rasp	Lock Saw
Tower Pincers	Oil Stone, in case	Smoothing Plane
Three Shell Gimlets	Marking Awl	Marking Gauge
Three Round Bradawls	Brad Punch	Glue Pot
	London Hammer	Keyhole Saw
	Spokeshave	Furniture, &c.

No. 24.

21 in. by 12 in. by 8¼ in., with Drawer.

50/- each. Contains—

Handsaw	Square	Brad Punch
Hatchet	Brick Chisel	Pliers
Hammer	Keyhole Saw	Compasses
Rule	Four Gimlets	Smoothing Plane
Mallet	Four Bradawls	
Pincers	Two Gouges	Gluepot and Brush
Marking Awl	Four Chisels	Furniture, &c.
Two Turnscrews	Three Files	
Spokeshave	Oil Stone, in case	

No. 25.

23 in. by 13½ in. by 9 in., with Drawer

75/- each. Contains—

Two Saws	Jack Plane	Two Turnscrews
Axe, Rule	Marking Gauge	One Spokeshave
Two Hammers	Glue Pot and Brush	Square
Mallet	Acorn Pad and Tools	Claw Wrench
Pincers		Pliers
Six Gimlets	Two Files	Compasses
Six Bradawls	Two Rasps	Drawing Knife
Six Chisels	Oil Stone, in case	Cutting Punch
Four Gouges	Marking Awl	Scraper, mounted
Keyhole Saw	Two Punches	Bevel
Smooth Plane		Furniture, &c.

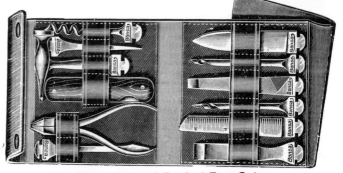

No. 4899. "Bonsa Pocket Tool Set. Consists of 10 Best Warranted Quality Tools, polished bright finish and handles. With Coco. Scales. In Brown Leather Case. As illustrated **8/9** Post 3d.

The "Sabina" Pocket Tool Set

Contains 11 Tools, including Tube Wrench with Wire Cutter, and Pliers Metal Handle. All instruments polished, Nickel-plated finish, and fitted in Leather Case.

Price ... ... **10/6** Post 4d.

Special Set for Electricians, &c.

Tool Pads

Containing 12 Tools.

Price **1/6**

Post 3d.

The Special Tool Pad

Price **2/9**

Post 4d.

The "Bonsa" Pocket Tool Set.

No. 5652. Contains 12 Best Quality Tools, including Pliers, all polished bright finish, and Handle, with Coco. Scales. In Fold-up Leather Case. **12/3** Post 4d.

Specially adapted for Cyclists, Sportsmen, etc.

No. 5979. **The "Sabina."** Contains 10 Best Warranted Tools, polished bright finish, and Holder. With Coco. wood Scales. In Fold-up Leather Case. **7/3** Post 3d.

Gamage's Tool Racks and Cabinets.—Sheffield Tools.

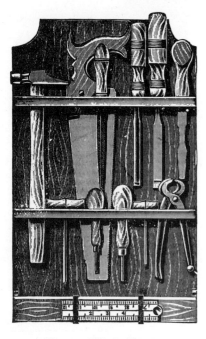

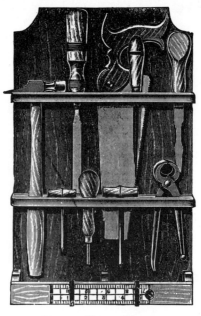

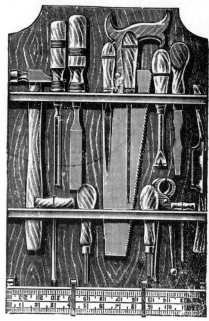

No. 61. Tool Rack.

Polished pine, contains hammer, chisel, saw, file, screwdriver, pincers, 2 gimlets, bradawl and rule. **7/6**   Postage 4d.

No. 60. Tool Rack.

Polished pine, guaranteed quality tools, contains hammer, saw, file, gouge, chisel, screwdriver, 2 bradawls, 2 gimlets and rule. **5/11**   Postage 6d.

No. 62. Tool Rack.

Polished pine, guaranteed quality tools, contains hammer, gouge, chisel, saw, tacklifter, screwdriver, spokeshave, pincers, 2 gimlets, 2 bradawls, file and 2-foot rule. **10/6**   Postage 6d.

All Tools guaranteed best quality.

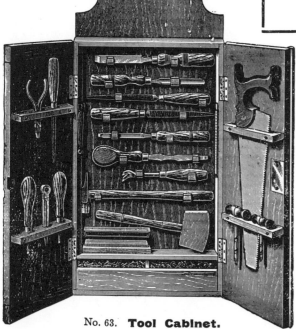

Write for our Complete List of Tools Lamps, Stoves and Electrical Fittings.

No. 63. Tool Cabinet.
Guaranteed Quality Tools.

Pine .. .. **29/6** | Oak **39/6**

Cabinet, with brass clips inside, 20 in. by 13 in. by 4½ in. deep, contains tools as follows:—Hand saw, 2 gimlets, pliers, pincers, compasses, 2 files, 1 rasp, 2 bradawls, claw wrench, mallet, hammer, 2 chisels, gouge, turnscrew, cased hone, rule.

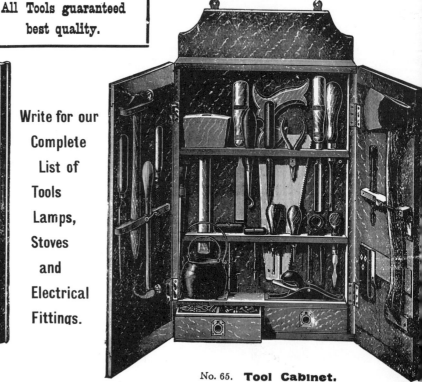

No. 65. Tool Cabinet.
Guaranteed Quality Tools.

Pine .. .. **39/6** | Oak **47/6**

Cabinet, 21 in. by 14 in. by 5½ in. deep, contains tools as follows Handsaw, 2 hammers, 1 hatchet, 2 turnscrews, 3 files, chisel, gouge, mallet, plane, pincers, 2 bradawls, 2 gimlets, glue pot and brush, pliers, claw wrench, square, whetstone, rule, compasses, nails and screws.

No. 67. Oak Cabinet, 26 in. high by 16 in. wide by 7½ in. deep, fitted with tools as follows:—2 saws, 2 hammers, 2 turnscrews, plated square, 3 files, 1 rasp, spokeshave, saw pad, brace and 6 bits, 2 chisels, 2 gouges, pincers, mallet, hatchet, plane, glue pot and brush, cutting pliers, compasses, 3 gimlets, 3 bradawls, marking awl, hand vice, brad punch, spirit level, coach wrench, cabinet scraper, box rule, oilstone, cold chisel, nails and screws.

Price **£3 19 0**

STRIP WOODWORK.

:: A NEW AND INTERESTING HOBBY. ::

THE great possibilities of Strip Woodwork are so apparent that it will at once appeal to every class of Amateur Worker, and whether it is the Woodworker or Cabinet Maker, the Mechanic, the Model Maker or the Engineer; it will be seen that it adapts itself to the needs of all.

Hobbies No. Ir. 1 Strip Woodworkers' Outfit.

THIS complete Outfit is attractively made up in a strong handsome Box with hinged lid. The Tools are held in place by Hobbies Patent Permanent Steel Clips, in order that each tool may be replaced when not in use.

Model Garden Arch

The No. Ir. 1 Outfit contains :—
Hobbies Special Cutting Board (with length gauge).
Tenon Saw.
Hammer.   Square.
Awl.   Nails.
25 ft. Strips and Hobbies 32 page Handbook of Instructions and a selection of full sized Working Drawings.

Price - - 5/-
Post Free - 5/7

To enable the worker to build up complete Working Models a range of wheels, Pulleys, Axles, etc., can be obtained, which can be adapted to any desired Model for all kinds of gearing, etc.

With the aid of these it is possible to construct mechanical parts of Models such as Swing Bridges, Cranes, Lifts, etc.

Model Barrows and Trucks.

Satin Walnut Strips.

Planed on all sides and beautifully finished.

				Price	Post
$\frac{1}{8}$ in	by $\frac{1}{4}$ in.	by 2 ft.	per 100 ft. run	2/3	3d
$\frac{1}{8}$,,	by $\frac{3}{8}$,,	by 2 ,,	,,	2/6	3d
$\frac{1}{4}$,,	by $\frac{1}{2}$,,	by 2 ,,	,,	2/9	4d
$\frac{1}{4}$,,	by $\frac{1}{4}$,,	by 2 ,,	,,	2/9	4d
$\frac{1}{4}$,,	by $\frac{3}{4}$,,	by 2 ,,	,,	3/-	6d
$\frac{3}{4}$,,	by $\frac{3}{8}$,,	by 2 ,,	,,	3/3	6d.
$\frac{1}{2}$,,	by 1 ,,	by 2 ,,	,,	3/9	8d
$\frac{1}{2}$,,	by $\frac{1}{2}$,,	by 2 ,,	,,	3/9	6d.

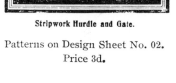

Stripwork Hurdle and Gate.

Patterns on Design Sheet No. 02.
Price 3d.

Hobbies No. Ir. 3 Strip Woodworkers' Outfit.

THE Outfit here illustrated is similar to No. Ir. 1 Outfit, but contains a larger selection of Tools. It is supplied in a strong handsome Box, and the Tools are neatly arranged, being held in place by Hobbies Patent Spring Steel Tool Clips, thus making a permanent receptacle for the Tools.

The No. Ir. 3. Outfit contains :—
Hobbies Special Cutting Board, (with Length Gauge).
Tenon Saw.   Hammer.
Angle Square.
Steel Rule.   Metal Plane.
Sandpaper Block.
Hex. Head Drill Awl.
Nails (two boxes).
50 ft. Strips. 32 page Handbook of Instructions and a selection of full sized Working Drawings.

Price - 7/6
Post Free - 8/2

A Fully Illustrated Booklet showing complete list of Tools and Requisites for this New and Interesting hobby can be obtained on application.

Fretwork Tools, Machines and Materials. Of British Manufacture throughout.
Carded Outfits with Steel Clips for Holding Tools.

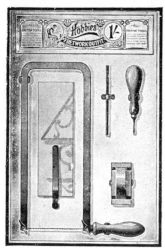

Contains 12-in. Frame, Sandpapering Block, Bradawl, Half Dozen Saw-blades, and Design.

Price **1/-** Postage 4d.

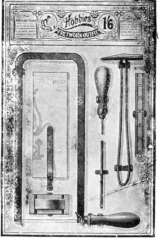

Contains 12 in. Frame, Hammer, steel Rule, Sandpapering Block, Half Dozen Saw-blades, Bradawl and Design. Price **1/6** Postage 4d.

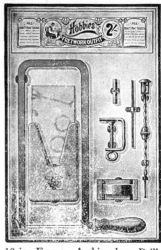

Contains 12-in. Frame, Archimedean Drill, with Bit and Nickelled Drill Box, Steel Cutting Table, Iron Cramp, Half dozen Saw-blades, Sandpapering Block and Design.
Price **2/-** Postage 4d.

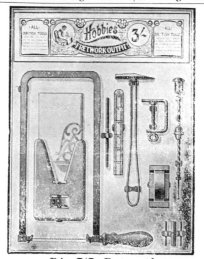

Price **2/6** Postage 4d.
Contains a superior 12-in. Hobbies Hand Fretsaw Frame, Archimedean Drill with 3 Bits, Nickelled Drill Box, Steel Cutting Table, Iron Cramp, Fretwork Hammer, Sandpapering Block, One Dozen Saw-Blades, and Design.

Price **3/-** Postage 5d.
Contains a superior 12-in. Spring Fretsaw Frame, Archimedean Drill with 3 Bits, Nickelled Drill Box, Steel Cutting Table, Iron Cramp, Fretwork Hammer, 6 in. Steel Rule, Sandpapering Block, One Dozen Saw-blades, and Design.

Price **3/6** Postage 5d.
Contains a superior 12-in. Spring Fretsaw Frame, One Dozen Hobbies Saw-blades, Archimedean Drill with 3 Bits, Nickelled Drill Box, Steel Cutting Table, Iron Cramp, Fretwork Hammer, Fretwork Plane, Sandpapering Block, 6-in. Steel Rule, and Design.

Price **4/-** Postage 5d.
Contains superior 12-in. Spring Fretsaw Frame, Two Dozen Hobbies Saw-blades in Nickel-plated Saw Case, Archimedean Drill with 3 Bits, Nickelled Drill Box, Steel Cutting Table, Iron Cramp, Fretwork Plane, Fretwork Hammer, 6-in. Steel Rule, Sandpapering Block, and Design.

Price **5/-** Postage 6d.
Contains Special Screw-handled Fretsaw Frame with Shaped Top Clamp, Steel Cutting Table, Iron Cramp, Archimedean Drill with 3 Bits, Nickelled Drill Box, Fretwork Plane, Two Dozen Hobbies Saw-blades, in Nickelled Saw Case, 6-in. Steel Rule, Fretwork Hammer, Sandpapering Block, and Design.

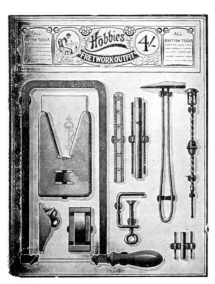

Hobbies 6/- Fretwork Outfit.

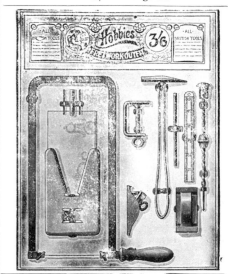

Price
6/-
Postage 4d.

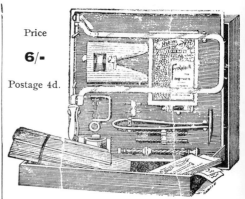

6/- OUTFIT contains :—14 in Patent Lever Hand Fretsaw Frame, Archimedean Drill with 2 Bits, Pressed Steel Cutting Table with Iron Cramp, Fretwork Saw Blades, 2 dozen, Liquid Glue in Collapsible Tube, Fretwork Hammer, Sandpapering Block, Illustrated Handbook, Parcel of "Gem" Designs, with sufficient Fretwork for making six articles.

Larger Size Boxed Outfits.
Price .. **8/6** post 7d.   **11/6** Post 8d.

Fretwork Machines. Of British Manufacture Throughout.

Young Briton, 13/6

The Young Briton is a new model this season and is a cheap and reliable Fretsaw. The frame of the Machine is made entirely of iron finished in cycle enamel. The Balance-Wheel Pulley and Table are the same as used on our "Briton" Machine. The Saw Clamps are our Patent Spring Open pattern. A Wrench, one dozen Saws and Design are sent with each machine.

No. 1. **A1 Treadle Fretsaw. 21/-**
No. 2. **With Nickle-Plated Table and Emery Wheel** **23/6**

Considering its low price of one guinea, the Hobbies A1 Fretsaw is acknowledged to be unsurpassed. The Machine is fitted with the Hobbies Patent Lever Clamps. These will securely grip the finest Saw Blades, and they are so made that the Lever cannot fly back and loosen the tension of the Saw.

The end of Balance-Wheel Spindle is arranged to hold a Drill, and there is also an improved Dust Blower.

A Drill Bit, Oil Can, Screwdriver, Spanner, one dozen Saws, and two Designs are sent with each Machine.

No. 1. **Briton Fretsaw** .. **14/6**
No. 2. **Ditto, with Nickel Plated Tilting Table and Emery Wheel 17/-**

The "BRITON" Machine is one of the cheapest reliable Treadle Fretsaws on the market. The arms will take 18 in. work, and the height to the Table is 32 in. The Machine is fitted with Hobbies Patent Lever Steel Clamps with new patent screws and shackles. There is also an improved Dust Blower, and the end of the Balance-Wheel Spindle is pierced for holding a Drill. A Drill Bit, Wrench, Oil Can, Saws, and two Designs are sent out with each Machine.

The "Companion" Lathe and Fretsaw.

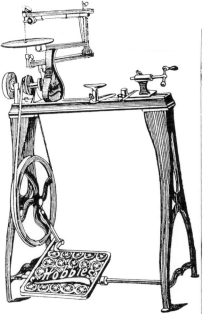

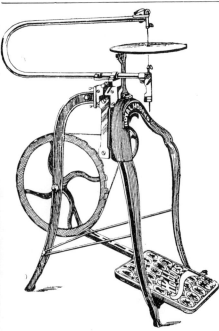

Royal Hobbies Fretsaw.

No. 1   As illustrated, with Dulled Nickelled Table and
     Japanned Saw Frame **32/-**
     Ditto, with Plated Table **34/-**
No. 2,   With all Bright Parts Plated, including
     Table and Saw Frame **37/-**

TREADLE CIRCULAR SAW.

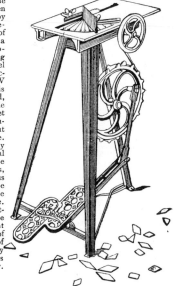

This neat little Treadle Circular Saw has been specially designed by us at the urgent request of a number of customers. It takes a 4-in. Saw and is provided with a Sliding Table moving parallel with the Saw on accurately machined V Slides. This Table is machine graduated, and has an adjustable fence which can be set to any angle, thus enabling wood to be cut to any desired angle. This tool is splendidly suited for geometrical inlaying, as by its use any number of Squares, Triangles, Rhombus or Rhomboids, may be cut identical in size and accurate in shape. Most delightful patterns can thus be formed from different coloured varieties of wood. Examples of Geometrical Inlay work cut with Hobbies Treadle Circular Saw. Price ... **22/6** Carriage forward.

This "Companion" Machine forms a useful Amateur's Lathe and Fretsaw. The large Driving Wheel has two groves of varying depths to give a change of speed. The Lathe head is provided with a 2-in. Face Plate, a Spur Centre, and a Screw Centre for turning Cups It has also a solid Emery Wheel and a Drill Spindle. The Tail Stock has a Screw Feed Centre. The Lathe is provided with two Rests. three Turning Tools, Wrench and Screwdriver, and for the Fretsawing Attachment, Designs, Saws, Drill Points. &c. Swing of Lathe, 5 in. Length of Bed 24 in. Distance between Centres, 14 in. A Circular Saw Attachment with Nickel-plated and polished Table can be fitted to the **"Companion"** Lathe. The Fretsawing Attachment is secured to the Lathe Bed by one bolt, and can be put on and taken off at leisure. It is fitted with 19-in. arms, with Trusses to prevent bending, Dust Blower. nickel-plated Tilting Table, and Hobbies Patent Lever Saw Clamps.

Lathe and Fretsaw. 35/-   **Lathe and Tools, 27/6**   **Fretsaw Attachment. 8/6**   **Circular Saw Attachment, 5/6**

All Machines are carefully tested before being despatched, packed in crates in complete working order, and ready for immediate use. Direct from Works. Machines are sent by Rai at the Railway Company's risk. The purchaser pays carriage on delivery.

ELECTRIC NOVELTIES.

New Electric Ceiling Watch Stand.

Illustration of case open, in use as an ordinary watch stand.

Illustration of case closed ready to reflect dial of watch on to the ceiling.

In the new Ceiling Stand, which takes any watch (except Hunters), the bulb is entirely hidden and is merely used for projecting a huge image of the dial on to the ceiling the moment the button is pressed. The image which is thrown on to the ceiling being so large and clear, and no glare reaching the eyes of the user, it is possible even for persons of weak sight to immediately see the time without any effort.

The cord and push are detachable, and can be placed inside the case, which can then be packed into a trunk, when travelling, without risk of injury.

LONDON MADE THROUGHOUT.

No. 1162. **18/6** each.

Complete as illustrated, but without watch. Covered in real leather—dark green, or royal red, and brown. Refill batteries, 1/3 Spare bulbs, 2/6

Portable Electric Bell Sets.

No. 155. **8/6** each.
Refills, 1/6 each.
Height 2¾ in.
Nickel plated bell on stained and polished wood box, complete with 12 yards silk flex and push.

No. 886. **10/6** each.
Refills, 1/6 each.
Height 5½ in.
Nickel plated bell on highly polished mahogany box, complete with 12 yards silk-covered flex and push. Exceptionally good value at the price.

No. 447. **12/6** each.
Refills, 1/6 each. Height 5¾ in.
Circular bell on highly polished mahogany box, complete with 12 yards silk flex and push.

The "Ever-Ready" Electric Cigar and Pipe Lighters,

As supplied for the use of H.M. THE KING.
No. 296 .. **15/-** complete.
Refill Batteries, 1/6 each.

Heavily plated fittings on polished mahogany box Height over all, 6½ in.
Size of battery box, 5⅛ by 4¼ by 2¼ in.

This Cigar and Pipe Lighter is a thoroughly practical and useful article, and can be highly recommended for everyday use. With the exception of the battery, which will give unlimited service for six to nine months, the only part of the lighter which requires attention is the reservoir, which has to be filled as required.

Saves the danger and expense of matches, and is invaluable on the card table, desk, or in the smoking room.

New Ceiling Clock.
Indispensable for Invalids, etc.

On pressing the button at the end of the flexible cord, there is cast upon the ceiling such a huge reflection of the Dial that anyone, even with the weakest sight, can see the time during the night. If desired to use this model either during the day or as an ordinary illuminated dial clock during the night, the projecting attachment can be instantaneously removed, as shown.

No. 890. Price complete, **27/6**
Refill Batteries, 1/6 Spare Bulbs, 2/6
30-hour movement.

Electric Ceiling Clock.
Model De Luxe.

The particular feature in this model is that it can be used either as a ceiling clock at night or as an ordinary clock in the day time without any alteration whatsoever.

The special advantages which this method of displaying the time at night has over the older method of illuminating the dial by means of a small incandescent electric bulb are :—

1st.—The huge size of the reflection cast on the ceiling, making it easily legible, even for people with weak sight.
2nd.—The total absence of any glare, which, in the ordinary type of clock, makes it difficult to distinguish anything at all for the first few moments.

No. 897. Green crushed morocco, or Violette de Parme crushed morocco. Price **63/-**
Spare Refils, 2/6 Spare Bulbs, 2/6
Fitted with reliable 8-day movement.

The New "Ever-Ready" Combined Pocket Lamp and Writing Pad.

No. 1660
Showing Lamp ready for use as a Pocket Lamp.

No. 1660
Showing Writing Pad open with light and reflector fixed ready for use.

Body covered real leather in red, green or brown. Fittings heavily nickel-plated.

When in use as a note book the reflector, which is hinged, is brought over the lens (as shown above).

Fitted with BEREC SUPERIOR Dry Battery and Metallic-Thamen Bulb.

No. 1660. Price **5/6** complete.

Extra 3-cell Batteries, BEREC SUPERIOR, (No. 1289 B.S.) 9d.

The Gamage Long Life, 6d. Spare Bulbs, 9d.
Size, 4¾ by 2½ by 1 in. Weight, 9½ oz.

Gun Model Ceiling Clock.

Showing clock in horizontal position for use in the day time.

Showing clock tilted for nightly use.

No. 1098. Finished in polished brass, gilt finish.
Price complete **30/-**
Refill Batteries 1/6 Spare Bulbs, 2/6
Ditto. Leather Covered Base.

In these models a beautiful effect is obtained by covering the base with real leather and fitting flexible silk-covered cords to match.

The New "Ever-Ready" Combination Bedroom Clock.

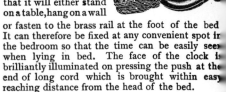

No. 881.
17/6 complete.
Spare Batteries, 1/3
Spare Bulbs, 2/6
Beautifully finished.
Heavily nickel-plated all over.

This cleverly designed Clock is so constructed that it will either stand on a table, hang on a wall or fasten to the brass rail at the foot of the bed. It can therefore be fixed at any convenient spot in the bedroom so that the time can be easily seen when lying in bed. The face of the clock is brilliantly illuminated on pressing the push at the end of long cord which is brought within easy reaching distance from the head of the bed.

No. 40.
3½ volt .. **14/6**
Refills, 1/6 Bulbs, 2/6

Furnished complete with cord and push, as illustrated (not including the watch). Fine nickel plate on fancy wood box.

This is one of the most popular models we make. The watch hangs behind a powerful magnifying glass which can be adjusted to any suitable angle showing the watch face brilliantly illuminated and greatly magnified.

THE NEW PATENT "EVER-READY" UNIVERSAL LAMP.

WITH ADJUSTABLE TOP.

No. 1680. In use as a Pocket Lamp.

No. 1680. In use as an Inspection Lamp.

(Patent applied for 13175.)

Fitted with a BEREC SUPERIOR Dry Battery and a Metallic Filament Bulb.

No. 1680. Price **5/6** complete.

Extra 2-cell Refill Batteries—BEREC SUPERIOR (No. 1289 B.S.), 9d. The Gamage Long Life, 6d. Spare Bulbs, 9d. each. Size 3½ by 2½ 1 in. Weight 9

Covered in real leather in red, green or brown.

Fittings heavily nickel-plated.

ELECTRIC POCKET HAND LAMPS, etc.

Electric Pocket Lamp.

BEST ENGLISH MAKE.

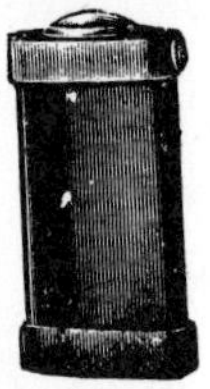

No. 730.
Size 3¾ by 1⅛ by 1 in.

Price complete **4/6**

Refills, 1/- Spare Bulbs, 2/-
Fitted with 2½ volt dry battery.
Leather covered.
Fitted with metallic filament bulb

This Pocket Lamp is very small and neat but gives an exceedingly powerful light.

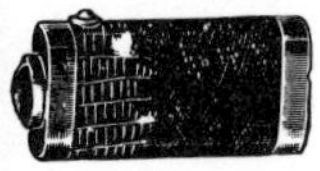

The Smallest **Electric Pocket Lamp** made, gives great light, covered in real lizard skin.
Nickel plated top and bottom caps.

Price **4/6** complete.

Extra Batteries, 9d. each. Extra Bulbs, 2/- each.

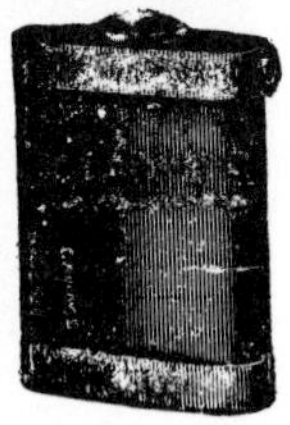

No. 121.
Price complete .. **4/-** each.
Refill Batteries, 1/- each,
Spare Bulbs, 9d. each.
Fitted with 3½ volt, dry battery.
BEST ENGLISH MAKE.
Covered red and black.
Size 3¾ by 2¾ by 1. in

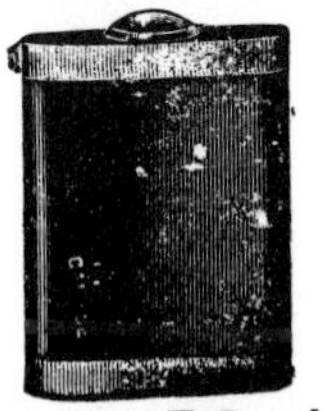

No. 295. Large size.
Size 4½ by 3½ by 1⅛ in.
Fitted with 3½ volt dry battery.
Leather covered body, heavy nickel-plated fittings.
Special "Ever-Ready" Metallic Filament Bulb, giving an exceedingly powerful light.

Price complete .. .. .. **7/6** each.
Spare Refills, 1/3 each. Spare Bulbs, 2/6 each.
It will give fully 4 to 5 hours of light when used intermittently.

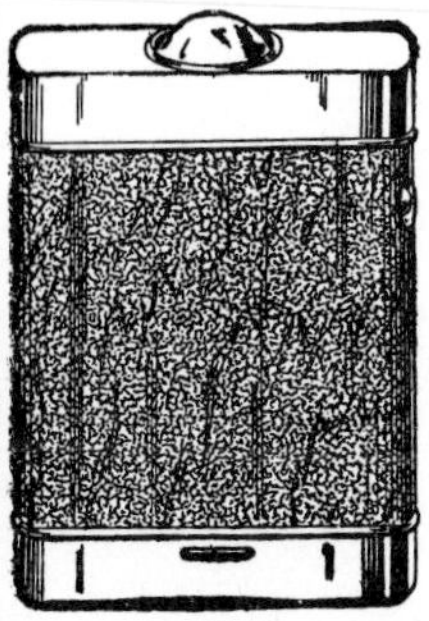

Electric Pocket Lamp

Best Quality.
Fitted with good quality battery and bulb. Price **2/6.**
2nd. Quality .. **1/3**
Do., cheaper quality case, but with good battery and bulb,
Price **10½**d.

Metallic Filament Lamp

Price **6**d. each.

Carbon Ditto Price .. **4**d.

Extra Batteries.

"The Gamage Long-Life Battery"

Price **6**d. each. Postage 2d.

The "Ever-Ready" Electric Hand Lantern.

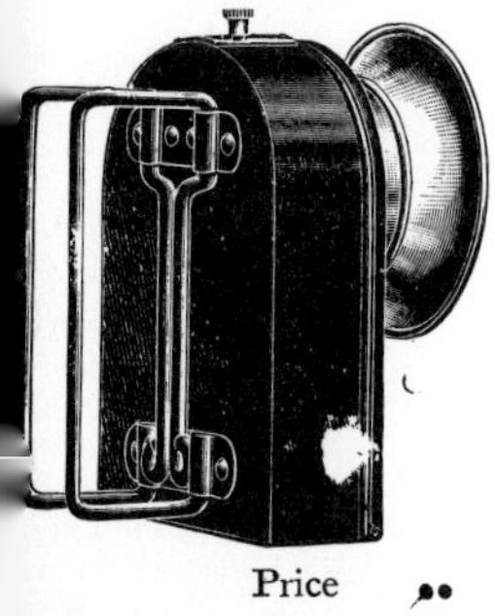

No. 999.

Can be adjusted to throw a concentrated beam of light a good distance ahead or a wide angle ray for a short distance. Well finished in black enamel.

Fitted with best Battery and Bulb.

Price .. **7/6**

Extra Batteries, **1/-** Extra Bulbs, **9**d.

Electric Hand Lamp.

Light and portable.

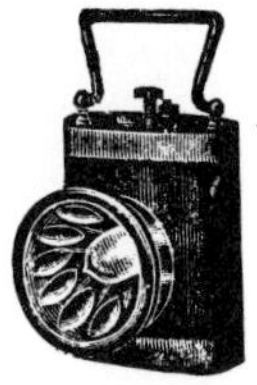

Heavily nickel-plated all over. Body covered real leather in dark green, brown and royal red. Fitted with dry battery and metallic filament bulb, giving very powerful light.
Height over all 5½ in.

No. 878. With white enamelled Reflector .. Complete **10/6**

No. 878a. With Prismatic Reflector .. **12/6**
Spare Batteries, 9d. Spare Bulbs, 2/6

Electric Hand or House Lamp.

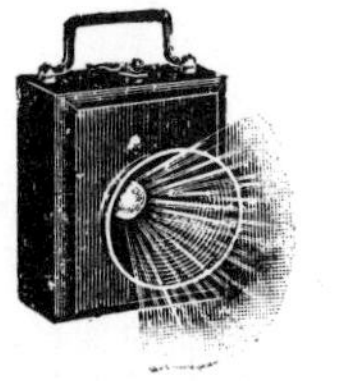

No. 12.
3½ volt, with Parabolic Reflector and dry battery **14/6**

No. 14.
5½ volt, with Parabolic Reflector and dry battery **21/-**
Finished in heavy nickel-plate on finely polished wood box.

Extra battery, 3½ volt for No. 12 .. .. **1/6**
" 5½ " for No. 14 .. .. **2/6**

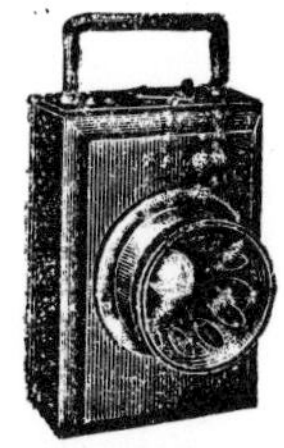

No. **"61 Spec."** 3½ volt, with New Prismatic Reflector, and dry battery. Price **19/-**

No. **"62 Spec."** 5½ volt, with New Prismatic Reflector. Price **25/6**

Finished in heavy nickel-plate on finely polished wood box.
Extra battery, 3½ volt for No. 61 **1/6**
Do. 5½ volt for No. 62 **2/6**

This Prismatic Reflector greatly increases the light.
Extra Metallic Filament Bulbs for same .. **2/6**

No. 500. SPECIAL LINE. Electric Hand Lamp, heaper quality.

Price .. **5/11** Postage 3d.

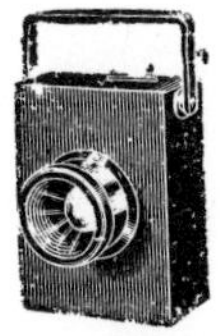

Polished mahogany case, measuring 5 by 3½ by 2½ in.
Nickel-plated fittings.
Fitted with latest type of accumulator with screw terminals.
Fitted with 2-volt metallic filament bulb giving a powerful light.
Burns 8 to 10 hours on a charge.

No. 1073. **16/6** complete, as illustrated.
Spare Accumulators, 7/6 Spare Bulbs, 1/-
Can be had with bull's-eye lens, same price.

Heavily nickel-plated fittings on well polished best quality hardwood box.

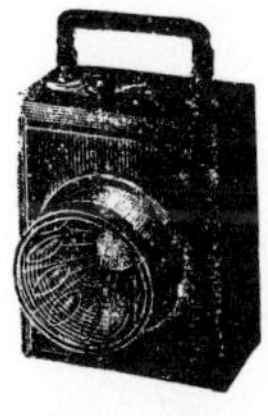

Illustrates 869.

A very great improvement has been effected in these lamps by doing away with troublesome contact screws and so arranging the wiring system that the accumulators make contact automatically upon inserting them into the case, and to obtain light it is only necessary to use the switch.

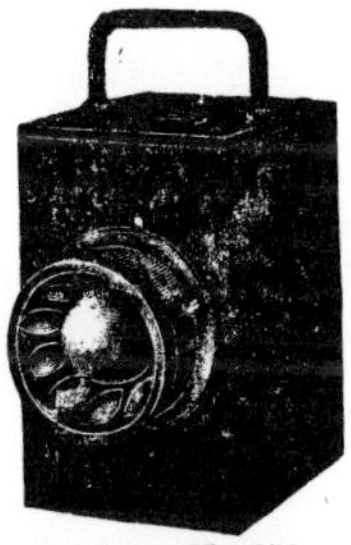

Illustrates No. 876.

No.	Voltage.	C.P.	Hours of light.	Size of Case. Inches.	Price
869.	2	1½	15 to 20	3¾ by 2¾ by 5½	**25/-**
Spare Accumulators, 12/6				Spare Bulbs, 2/-	
876.	4	3	15 to 20	3¾ by 4 by 5⅝	**42/-**
Spare Accumulators, 21/-				Spare Bulbs, 2/-	
876a.	4	6	8 to 10	3¾ by 4 by 5⅝	**42/-**
Spare Accumulators, 21/-				Spare Bulbs, 2/6	

"Ever-Ready" Electric Torch

With New Metallic Filament Bulb giving double the light and twice the number of burning hours.

No. 31. Baby Torch, 2½ volt, 6 by 1⅛ in. **12/6**
Refills, 1/3 Bulbs, 2/6
No. 1. 3½ volt, 1⅛ by 9 in. **12/6**
Refills, 1/6 Bulbs, 2/6
No. 2. 3½ volt, 1⅛ by 11 in. .. . **16/6**
Refills, 1/6 Bulbs, 2/6
No. 3. 5½ volt, 1⅛ by 14 in. **21/-**
Refills, 2/6 Bulbs, 2/6

Torches Nos. 1, 2 and 3 are covered real leather and greatly improved quality and finish.

De Luxe Pattern.

Beautifully polished, indestructible weather-proof casing, improved pattern.

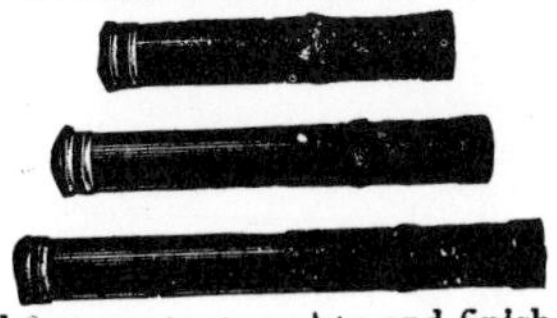

Nickel-plated fittings, best quality and finish
No. 4. 3½ volt, 1⅛ by 9 in. **14/6**
Refills, 1/6 Bulbs, 2/6
No. 5. 3½ volt, 1⅛ by 11 in. **18/6**
Refills, 1/6 Bulbs, 2/6
No. 6. 5½ volt, 1⅛ by 14 in. **24/-**
Refills, 2 6 Bulbs, 2/6

The New "Ever-Ready" Torch.

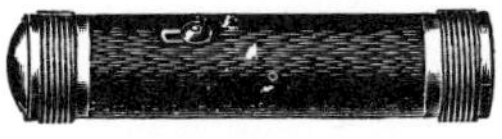

Fitted with metallic filament bulb & permanent switch, size 7½ by 1⅝ in. Nickel plated or covered in black leather.
Price **6/6** complete.

Extra Battery, 1/- Extra Bulb, 10½d.
Do., larger size, 9½ by 1⅝ in. Price **7/6** complete.
Extra Battery, 1/6 Extra bulb, 10½d.

The "Ever-Ready" Electric Hand Lamps.

With unspillable Accumulators.

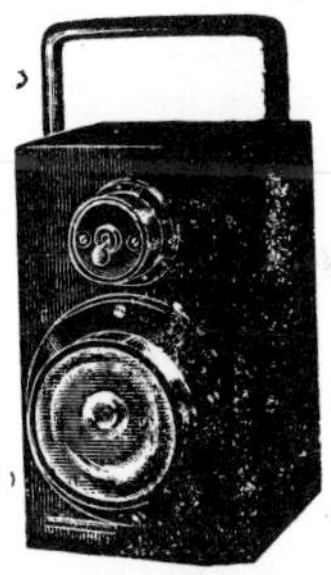

Size of Wooden Case. 3¾ by 4 by 6½.

No. 868.
Fitted with 4-volt unspillable accumulator and powerful metallic filament bulb, giving 3 c.p. for 15 to 20 hours on a charge
Price, complete, **35/-**
Spare Accumulators, 21/-
Spare Bulbs .. 2/-

No. 868a.
Price, complete, **35/-**
Same as above, but fitted with a bulb giving 6 c.p for 8 to 10 hours on charge.

Well-made polished teak case with nickel-plated fittings. Spare bulbs, 2/6

The New E.R. Electric Hand Lamp.

These lamps are fitted with Morse key, useful for Marine, Military, or other signa ling. Also ordinary switch for continuou light. Gives a powerful light. Cases made in polished teak with brass bound corner to stand rough usage Fitted with best dry battery and bulb.

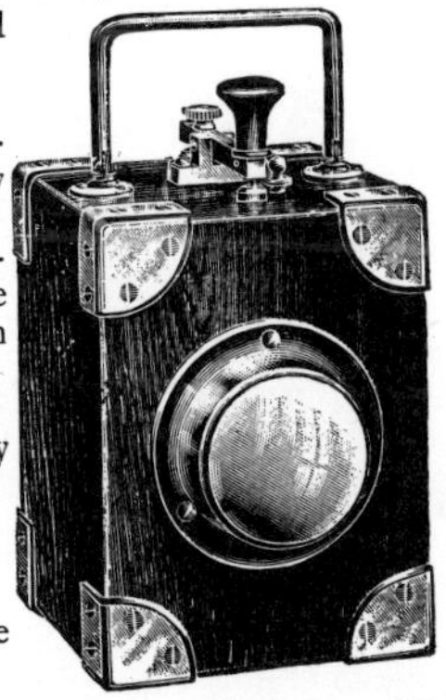

No. 1675.
Price .. **47/6**
Complete with 2 spare bulbs.

No. 1674. Ditto, without Morse key .. **42/-**
No. 1688. Smaller size ditto, fitted with Morse key. Complete with 2 spare bulbs. Price **42/-**
Ditto, without Morse key .. **36/6**

ELECTRIC NOVELTIES

No. 1692. Iris.   1693. Carnation.   1694. Chrysanthemum.   1695. Poppy.

The New "Ever-Ready" Floral Table Decorations

With Electric Light (self-contained). Fitted with Berec Superior extra long life Dry Batteries and Metallic Filament Bulbs. Beautifully made, extremely artistic.

No. 1692.	Height over all about 21 in.	..	..	..	Complete	**6/6**
,, 1693.	,, ,, ,,	20 ,,	with pink or red flower		,,	**7/6**
,, 1694.	,, ,, ,,	22 ,,	,, bronze or pink flower		,,	**7/6**
,, 1695.	,, ,, ,,	18 ,,	,,	..	..	**8 6**

Base finished black. Size 3 in. diam. by 4¼ in. high.

2-cell Berec Superior Refills (No. 800 B.S.) **1/-** each. Spare Bulbs **9**d. each.
Each Berec Superior Battery gives approximately 15 hours light.

The Floral Decorations illustrated above offer an inexpensive but at the same time extremely artistic and novel means of decoration. They consist of beautifully made artificial flowers with an electric light bulb hidden in the centre of the flower itself. The current for the bulb is obtained from a high battery contained in the base, on the top of which is fitted a switch to control the light. They make ideal table decorations, and the base being small, enables the flowers to be grouped in a jardiniere, or several with the bases suitably draped and tastefully arranged on a banqueting table present a very charming and striking appearance. As they are quite independent of the ordinary house current there are no unsightly wires to be disposed of, and this greatly facilitates their artistic arrangement.

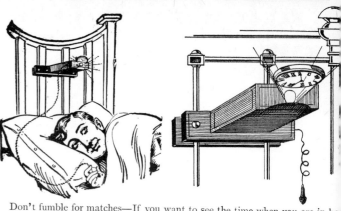

Don't fumble for matches—If you want to see the time when you are in be

The "Time-o'-Night" (Regd. No. 561851)

does away with all that trouble and the risk of knocking the watch— possibly a few other trinkets—over. All you have to do is to press a swi hanging ready to your hands, and the dial of your watch is illuminated b neat electric lamp. No trouble at all. This invention is simplicity itself. electric battery contained in a neat leatherette case, which can be fitted on almost any bedstead, with a spring attachment at top for holding the watch nickel-plated disc reflects the light on the watch and shields the eyes from glare. Ample length of wire with a pear-shaped switch is provided.

5/6 Post free. Complete with watch, **8/6** Extra batteries, 6d., bulbs,

The New "Ever-Ready" Holophane Hand Lam

Fitted with a Dry Battery and a Metallic Filament B
No. 1672. **10/6** each complete.
3-cell Refill Batteries—Berec Superior (Nos. 12 B.S.
15 B.S.) **2/-** Ordinary Type (Nos. 12 or 15), **1/**
Spare Bulbs, **9**d.
Polished Mahogany Case, size 4¾ by 3¾ by 2 in. Nicl plated fittings. Weight 24 oz. In this Hand Lam will be noticed we have introduced the familar holoph glass which is so extensively used in connection with forms of illuminants. As is well known, by the use this glass the light is evenly distributed without waste. the possibility of any glare is eliminated. It has b specially designed for household use and is altogethe very handsome and useful lamp.

New "Ever-Ready" Multiflector Hand Lamp

Fitted with a Dry Battery and a Metallic Filament Bulb.

No. 1686 .. .. **10/6** each complete.

3-cell Refill Batteries—Berec Superior (Nos. 12 B.S. or 15 B.S.) **2/-**

Ordinary Type (Nos. 12 or 15), **1/6**

Spare Bulbs, **9**d.

Polished Mahogany Case, size 4¾ by 3¾ by 2 in. Nickel-plated fittings. Weight, 24 oz.

This is another model of Hand Lamp fitted with our new Multiflector which intensifies the light to a remarkable extent. The lamp itself is of a particularly neat appearance and will be found most useful, especially for domestic purposes.

Electric portable Candle
Matt Gilt Finish.
With Fluted Candle Tube.
8/6 complete.
Extra Bulbs **1/6** Battery **9**d.

The great advantage of this little stove will be found in the fact that it can be used at any time of the day or night by pressing a push or setting the clock

Prices of Apparatus—

Polished Case and Enamelled Fittings Complete with Clock **23/-**

Polished Case with Copper and Plated Fittings. Complete with Clock .. **34/-**

The Latest Automatic Gas Stove.

A wonderful invention! People who rise early in the morning need a cup of t coffee or cocoa before starting for business, yet they frequently have to start with anything warm because of the difficulty of getting boiling water. The use of Automatic Stove enables a cup of anything hot to be obtained within a few minu This small stove can be attached in any room by a flexible pipe. Put the tea in teapot and place it on the stand; set the alarm clock five minutes before the h you wish to rise. In five minutes the water has boiled, the tea has been made, gas turned off, and an electric bell continues ringing until you remove the ves from the stove.

Gentlemen's Umbrellas. Endless Selection.

U. P 16.

Genuine Partridge Cane Handles, 2 Hall-marked Gold Mounts, Twill Silk Covers, Fox's Paragon Frames.

35/- 45/-

U. P 76.

Partridge, Pimento or Cherry crook. Chased Silver Mounts, Bordered Silk Cover, Fox's Frames.

12/6

U. P 79.

Beautiful Horn Crook, Octagon Silver Mounts Hall-marked, Bordered Silk Cover, Fox's Frame.

18/6
21/- 25/-

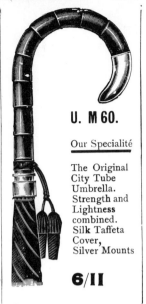

U. M 60.

Our Specialité

The Original City Tube Umbrella. Strength and Lightness combined. Silk Taffeta Cover, Silver Mounts

6/11

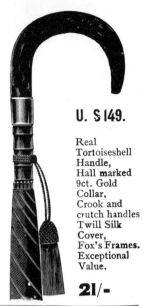

U. S 149.

Real Tortoiseshell Handle, Hall marked 9ct. Gold Collar, Crook and crutch handles Twill Silk Cover, Fox's Frames. Exceptional Value.

21/-

U. M 60.

Real horn, crook handle, Hall-marked Silver collar, strong silk Taffeta cover.

4/11
6/11

U. P 911.

The NewPrince

Our Specialité

Smallest rolling. Strong and neat.

Pure Silk, Fox's Frames, A pleasure to carry.

15/-

U. M 21.

Genuine Horn Crooks, Silver Collars, Bordered Silk, Fox's Frames.

15/6
21/- 25/-

With Solid Gold Collars.

42/-

The 'Everneat'

Smallest Rolling.

Fox's Frame, Silver Mounts, Bordered Silk.

10/6

The 'Tipcup' Umbrella, Silver Mounts.

Design as above,

4/-

U P 56.

Cape Horn Crook, Silver Collar and Tip Cap, Fox's Frames, Bordered Silk Covers.

15/-
18/6
21/-

U. A 96.
Our New Stickbrella

An umbrella in a walking stick .. **5/11**
Finest make. Full size Umbrella ..**10/6**
Two Articles in One **14/6**
With 2 Silver Mounts, **18/6**

The Storm.

Natural Sticks All Shapes. Bordered Covers, Fox's Paragon Frames.

Double ribs.

Verystrong but neat rolling.

10/6

U. H 56.

The NEW Straight Handle, Solid Silver Mount, Strong Taffeta Covers, Lock Rib Frame.

7/11

U. H 60.

The "Excel"

Marvellous Value.

Twill Taffeta Covers, Fox's Paragon Frame, Solid Silver Mount.

6/9

U. P 10.

Partridge Cane Umbrella. Hall-marked 9ct. Gold Mount, Bordered Silk Cover, Fox's Frame.

21/- 25/-

Carriage Paid on all Umbrellas over 10/-

W

No. U. 1103

The New Witchwood Solid Stick.

Smart in appearance.
Stout and strong.
Solid Silver Mount.

6/11

No. U. 1630.

Genuine Kalma Palma Stick. Dark brown colour. Hall-marked 9ct. Gold Mount.

A Stout Stick **15/6**
Also shape as above.

In Real Solid Ebony **Bent Stick,** the strongest and nicest looking stick made to-day. Fine and Strong. Will not break.

Solid Silver Nose Mount **7/11**

As illustration.

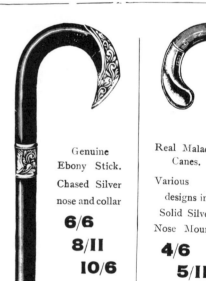

No. U. 1104.

The New Witchwood Stick.

Very strong, dark in colour.

Stout Hall-marked Silver Mount.

7/6

U. 1079

Real Brazilian Vine Stick.

Solid Silver Mounts.

Plain or chased

4/6

U. 1128

Ebony or Partridge Cane with large engraved silver handle.

15/-

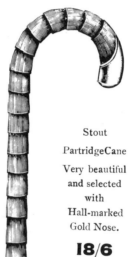

Stout Partridge Cane

Very beautiful and selected with Hall-marked Gold Nose.

18/6

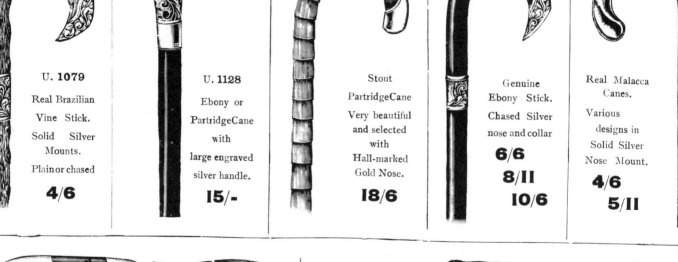

Genuine Ebony Stick.

Chased Silver nose and collar

6/6
8/11
10/6

Real Malacca Canes.

Various designs in Solid Silver Nose Mount.

4/6
5/11

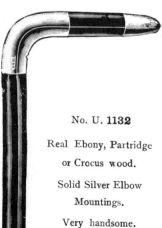

No. U. 1132

Real Ebony, Partridge or Crocus wood.

Solid Silver Elbow Mountings.

Very handsome.

7/11 10/6

No. U. 1073

Horn handle on Ebony, Partridge and Malacca. Silver Mounts.

7/11 10/6

With handle or Real Ivory or real Tortoiseshell. Gold-plate or Silver Mounts.

**25/- 30/-
40/-**

The new Malacca Canes with numerous designs in Silver Caps.

**4/11 5/11
6/11 7/11**

With superior Silver Caps,

8/11

In Ebony or Malacca with large 9ct. gold cap.

30/-

No. U. 1126

Beautiful Ash Plant.

Natural heads.

Stout Sticks.

Silver Mounted.

2/6 3/6

No. U. 112

The new Grey Crocu

Solid Silve nose and coll

Very handsor

4/11

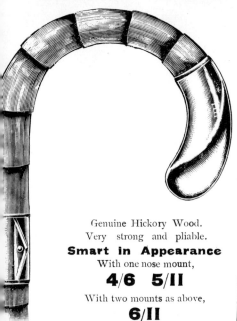

Genuine Hickory Wood.
Very strong and pliable.
Smart in Appearance
With one nose mount,
4/6 5/11
With two mounts as above,
6/11

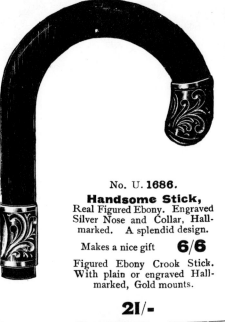

No. U. **1686.**
Handsome Stick,
Real Figured Ebony. Engraved
Silver Nose and Collar, Hall-
marked. A splendid design.

Makes a nice gift **6/6**

Figured Ebony Crook Stick.
With plain or engraved Hall-
marked, Gold mounts.

21/-

No. U. **4111.**
Cape Horn Crook.

Engraved Solid Silver Mounts,
Extra Stout on Ebony Wood,
Malacca or Partridge Cane.

12/6

Real Tortoiseshell crook handle.
Partridge cane or ebony.
28/6
**Genuine Snakewood
Sticks,** Natural Markings.
Large Cape Horn Crook Handles.
Plain Silver Collar Mounts **25/6**

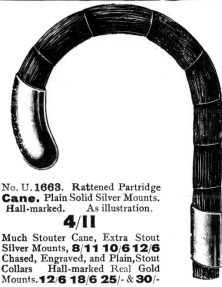

No. U. **1663.** Rattened Partridge
Cane. Plain Solid Silver Mounts.
Hall-marked.   As illustration.
4/11
Much Stouter Cane, Extra Stout
Silver Mounts, **8/11 10/6 12/6**
Chased, Engraved, and Plain, Stout
Collars Hall-marked Real Gold
Mounts. **12/6 18/6 25/- & 30/-**

No. U. **1693.**
Real Partridge Cane.
A Marvel of Value.
Long Hall-marked Silver Mount.
Chased or Engraved.
3/11

No. U. **2211.**
Real Buffalo Horn.
Crook on Ebony.
Exclusive Style **10/6**

With Real Hall-marked Gold
Collar on Solid Ebony.
30/-

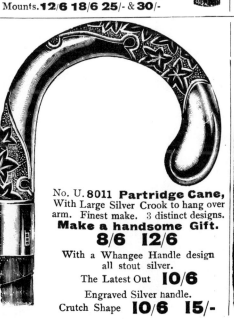

No. U. **8011 Partridge Cane,**
With Large Silver Crook to hang over
arm. Finest make. 3 distinct designs.
Make a handsome Gift.
8/6 12/6
With a Whangee Handle design
all stout silver.
The Latest Out **10/6**
Engraved Silver handle.
Crutch Shape **10/6 15/-**

No. U. **432.**
Handsome Cane.
Crook Handle.
Engraved Silver Mounts, Nose
and Collar.
Imitation Snakewood Stick.
4/11

W..

A Lady's Umbrella is always an acceptable gift.

U. 30 B.

Ladies' Real Gold Mounts.

Hall-marked.

Various Designs in Gold Mounts.

Bordered Silk Cover.

Fox's Frame.

16/6

U. 20 H.

The New Straight Handles.

Finest quality Gold-plate on Partridge Cane.

Bordered Twill Silk and Fox's Frame on Stick or Tube,

10/6
16/6
21/-

U. 20 I.

Plain Partridge Crook, unmounted Handles.

Bordered Twill Silk and Fox's Paragon Frame.

7/11
8/11
10/6
12/6
15/-

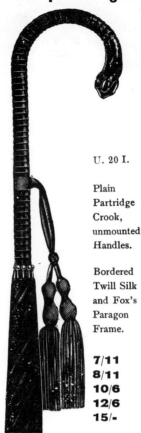

U. 20 E.

Handsome Pattern.

Real Partridge Cane, with Solid Silver Nose Mounts, Various Designs. Bordered Silk and Fox's Paragon Frame Stick or Tube.

10/6
12/6

Wear guaranteed

The Sunbre[...] for sun [...] rain.

Beauti[...] silk cov[...] in Gree[...] or Nav[...] Blue.

Gold Plated Frames and Ferrule[...]

Carved Sticks with B[...] Head Handle[...]

12/6

U. 114 W.

Special Value.

Full size Ladies' Umbrella.

Stout Taffeta Cover on Stick or Tube Frame.

With Solid Nickel Mounting as illus.

4/11

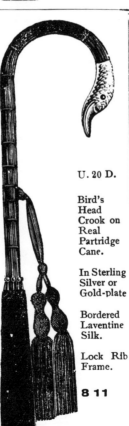

U. 20 B.

Horn Handle on Partridge Cane, Plain Silver Mounts, Hall Marked, Real Taffeta Cover, Lock Rib Frame,

4/11
5/11
6/11
7/11

With Silk Cover and Fox's Frame,

10/6
12/6

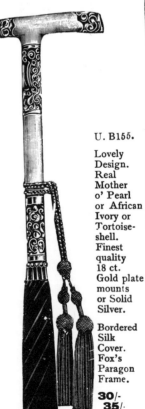

U. 20 D.

Bird's Head Crook on Real Partridge Cane.

In Sterling Silver or Gold-plate

Bordered Laventine Silk.

Lock Rib Frame.

8/11

U. B155.

Lovely Design. Real Mother o' Pearl or African Ivory or Tortoise-shell. Finest quality 18 ct. Gold plate mounts or Solid Silver.

Bordered Silk Cover. Fox's Paragon Frame.

30/-
35/-
40/-
45/-

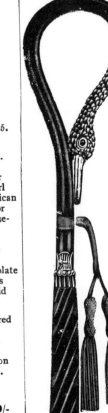

U. B3[...]

Charm[...] Desig[...]

Finest Gold [...] on Ho[...]

Border[...] Twill S[...]

Fox's Frame[...]

25/-

Ladies' Presentation Umbrellas and Sticks made at a few hours' notice

Ladies' Umbrellas and Tassels.

WONDERFUL VALUE.

HORN, GUN METAL, SOLID SILVER
OR
PARTRIDGE CANE HANDLES.
Very Handsome Bordered Silk, Fluted Frames.
Full size covers .. **6/11**

THE LATEST STYLE.

EXTRA LONG HANDLES.

Beautiful Colourings in Exclusive
Designs in
GUN METAL, HORN, THE
NEW BRIARLITE.

Price **8/11**

Fox's Paragon Frames. Bordered
Silk Covers

NEW STYLES IN LADIES' UMBRELLAS.

MOUNTED SOLID SILVER OR GOLD
PLATE.

Handsome Designs in
SILVER, BUFFALO HORN, PARTRIDGE
CANE, &c., &c.

Fox's Paragon Frames. Bordered Silk Cover .. **10/6**

U. C 201.

Lady's all Silver Crook Handle. Fox frame and twill silk cover,

10/6

Best Gun Metal, Mother o' Pearl and Cape Horn Sticks.

21/- 25/- 30/- each.

Cheaper Silver Crooks at

5/11 6/11 7/11 ea.

Similar Design.

U. C 252.

Real Partridge Stick, beautiful design in Silver or Gold Plate Heads best make only.

Fox frame, Laventine silk cover,

12 6

Special Selected Hard Wearing Cover.

The New Black Silk Bangle Tassels.

Worn with
the
New
Straight
Handle
Umbrellas,
6½d.
each.

U. C 303.

Pretty Design.

Finest Gold Plate. or Sterling Silver.

Best Silk.

Guaranteed Fox's frame.

15/- 21/-

U. 20 A.

Partridge Crook Ladies' Umbrellas. Hall Marked Silver, Bordered Laventine Silk Cover, Lock Rib Frame.

7/11 8/11 10/6 12/6

Tube or Stick.

Exclusive Designs in Ivory and Tortoiseshell always in Stock.

Carriage paid on all Umbrellas over **10/-**

Little Boys' & Girls' Umbrellas. Satisfying Gifts.

"JUST LIKE MAMMA'S."

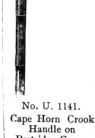

No. U. 1	U. 2	U. 3	U. 4	U. 5	U. 6	U. 7	U. 8	U. 9	U. 10
2/6	3/11	3/6	3/6	4/11	2/6	3/11	4/11	5/6	4/11

Better qualities at **6/11 8/11 10/6** any handles.

Assorted handles in crook and crutches, Rabbits, Cats, Dogs, Monkeys, and Birds' heads in endless variety. Silver and Gold Plate Mounts. **Extra strong Frames and Covers.**

Please give age of child when ordering.

Boys' Walking Sticks. Pretty Gifts.

No. U. 1142.
Boy's Dog's Head Walking Stick. Hall-marked silver collar. **1/-**

No. U. 1140.
Real Tonkin Canes. Engraved silver collar mount. **1/-**

No. U. 1139.
Real Congo Wood. Hall-marked silver mount. **1/9**

No. U. 1145.
Real Partridge Canes. Hall-marked silver nose mount. **1/11**

U. 100. Fancy Dog's Head & sterling silver collar. Head is well carved and mechanical when button is pressed mouth opens & closes. **3/3**

No. U. 1143.
Palm and Partridge Canes. Engraved silver crutch handle. **3/6**

No. U. 1141.
Cape Horn Crook Handle on Partridge Canes. Fancy silver collar. **2/6**

Please state age of Boy when ordering.

Shepherd's Crook Sticks.

About 5 ft. high, in white.

For Plays, Weddings, &c.

1/3 and **1/9** each.

The Idolite Walking Stick.

Real Malacca or Partridge Cane.

Leather covered handles, solid silver mounts beautifully finished. A brilliant light is instantly given from electric lamp concealed.

Strong and lasting. **30/-**

Buy your Golfing Friend A Golf Umbrella.

Root or crook handle.

Double wind proof storm frame.

5/11 and **7/9**

The New Electric Walking Stick.

Neat and smart in appearance. A crook Malacca Cane. nicely mounted with collar. A single movement with the thumb and finger and you get a full brilliant light. Light is completely hidden when not on. Strong, safe and reliable.

Our price **8/-**   Elsewhere 10/6

Ladies' & Gentlemen's Seat Sticks for Presents.

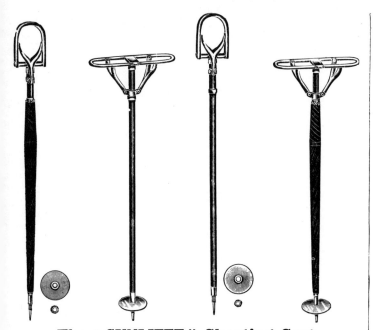

The "CUNLIFFE" Shooting Seat.

As an Umbrella or Walking Stick.   The Latest in Sports Seats.

Gents' Walking Stick	..	..	..	..	**24/-**
Ladies' ,, ,,	..	..	..	..	**21/-**
Gents' Umbrella and Seat combined		..	..	**36/6**
Ladies' ,, ,, ,,		..	..	**33/6**

With Leather Covered Handle, 3/6 extra.

The "REFEREE" Sportsman's Seat Stick

Made entirely of Aluminium.

The neatest and lightest seat stick made. Very comfortable and can be used exactly as a Walking Stick.

Beautifully made, of the Finest Workmanship **16/6**

The "MILLS" (Patent) Seat Stick.

PRICE

15/-

As carried.   As a Seat.

This Stool is made with a wood slide. For people not requiring varied heights of seat.

The seat part is made exactly the same as the seats of the Telescopic Stools.

Wonderfully Light and Smart in Appearance.

The "MILLS" (Patent) Aluminium Telescopic Sportsman's Stools.

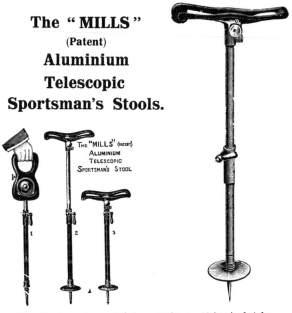

This Seat can be varied from 20 in. to 32 in. in height.

The Seat is perfectly comfortable and impervious to damp. Made almost entirely of Aluminium, will not rust, warp or crack.

Strong and Reliable, of First-class Workmanship.

Black Bronzed	..	..	..	**25/-**
Polished Bright	..	..	..	**21/-**

Distance Piece to fix when using on hard ground extra.

The "GAMAGE" Seat Stick.

Bamboo finish, Plaited Cane Seat. Nickel plated Mounts.

Seat folds up, and can be carried neatly as a Stick.

Price **10/6**

A huge variety of Seat Sticks from 3/6 always in stock.

Hunting Crops and Riding Whips for Presents.

HUNTING CROPS.

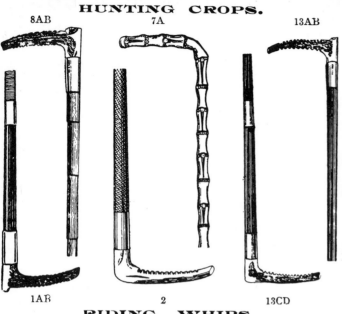

8AB   7A   13AB

1AB   2   13CD

RIDING WHIPS.

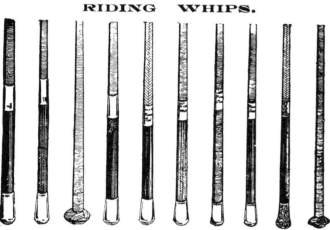

26B   27A   25AB   27B   29A   29B   28   27C   26ABC   24

No. U.

1a (As illus.) **Gent's Crop**, Stag horn, leather handle, solid white metal mount, colour guaranteed, all gut and bone, buff keeper **16/6**
1b Do. do., with extra stout silver collar, plain or chased, h.-m. **21/-**
1c Finest quality **Gent's Crop**, leather handle, all gut and bone, extra stout silver mounts **30/-**
1d Do. do., mounted with chased or plain h.-m. 9-ct. gold mounts **55/-**
Rhinoceros Hide Twigs, **7/6** each.
Birch Rods, **3/11** each.   Whip Cord Scourges, **5/6** each.

No. U.

2 (As illus.) **Gent's Crop**, all gut and bone, very strong wear, thoroughly guaranteed. Finest quality hall marked plain silver collar .. **18/**
3a **Gent's Crop**, Stag hook and Malacca cane, very handsome chased silver mount, hall marked, 2 in. deep, leather keeper .. **12/**
3b Do. do., with 2 in. chased solid white metal mount **9/**
4a **Gent's Crop**, very effective, braided to end, with brass lock smashing hammer, extra strong **8/**
4b Do. do., with nickel hammer **9/**
7a (As illus.) **Gent's Crop**, best quality hard bark Whangee cane .. **6/**
7b Plain ash cross hook crop. Very strong **3/1**
8a (As illus.) **Gent's Crop**, Rattan cane and Stag hook, 1½ in. white metal collar, very strong **7/**
8b Do. do., with hall marked, very stout, sterling silver collar, buff keeper **10/**
11 **Gent's Crop**, Malacca cane, with brass hammer head **6/**
12 **Ladies'** ,, Malacca cane, fancy solid nickel hammer head .. **5/**
13a (As illus.) **Ladies' Crop**, Malacca cane, Stag horn and h.-m. silver. **4/**
13b Do. do., with solid silver, hall marked **6/**
13c Do. do., with leather handle, electro plate mounts and stag hook. A very pretty crop. Exceptional value **4/1**
13d Do. do., with 2 beautifully chased or plain hall-marked silver mounts.. **10/**
13e Finest quality **Ladies' Crop**, stag horn and leather handle, gut and bone body, silver mounts **21/**
13f Beautiful Crop; picked stag horn handle, 9-ct. gold mounts, hall-marked **35/**
Riding Switches for Hot Climates **4/1**

Leather Thongs for Crops.   Best Quality only.   Stock Whips with

Rounding-up Thongs ... **10/6 15/-**   **21/-** each. **To Order only.**

1¼ yard White Melton Plait,	**1/6**	1¼ yd. White Beauford Plait,	**1/10**
1¼ ,, Brown ,, ,,	**2/-**	1¼ ,, Brown ,, ,,	**2/6**
1¾ ,, White Melton Plait,	**1/11**	1¾ ,, White Beauford Plait,	**2/4**
1¾ ,, Brown ,, ,,	**2/11**	1¾ ,, Brown ,, ,,	**3/3**

Ladies' Riding Whips.   Exceptional Value.

No. U.
14a Steel lined, celluloid horse leg handle, nickel mounts **6/**
14b Ditto, ditto, all gut and bone; a very pretty whip **9/**
15a Steel lined, leather handle, nickel mounts **2/**
17a Thread and cane whip, very strong, nickel mounts **1/**
20a Handle, steel lined, chased nickel mounts **2/1**
Ladies' Silver-mounted Whips, **8/6 10/6** and **15/-** each.

Gent's Riding Whips.

No. U.
24 (As illus.) Thread and Cane Rough Rider's Whip, button top .. **1/**
25a (As illus.) Gut and bone, Turk's head handle; a very strong whip .. **12/**
25b (As illus.) Ditto, ditto, high-grade Racing Whip, finest quality obtainable, all gut and whalebone; a very beautiful whip .. **18/**
26a (As illus.) Leather handle, steel lined, chased metal mounts .. **3/**
26b (As illus.) Ditto, ditto, handle, sterling silver mounted, gut and bone. **10/**
26c (As illus.) Ditto, ditto, very best quality, silver or gold plate mounts **18/**

Infantry and Cavalry Whips.

No. U.
27a (As illus.) Steel lined whip, leather handle; a strong and reliable whip, best nickel mounts **1/**
27b (As illus.) Ditto, ditto, best quality gut and bone **2/**
27c (As illus.) Ditto, Ditto, plain or chased sterling silver mounts .. **15/**
28 (As illus.) All thread but steel lined, good wearing whip, electro mounts, leather handle **1/**
29a (As illus.) Raw-hide Whip, plaited, handle, steel lined **3/**
29b (As illus.) Real pigskin handle, electro-plated mounts, gut & steel lined **3/**

Stock Whips.

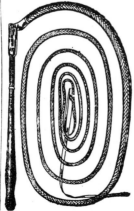

Loaded Hardwood, unmounted.

12 ft. rawhide thongs **15/-**

With natural malacca handle .. **18/6**

Steel lined and gut handle or rawhide **21/-**

All above have 12 ft. thongs.

Special quotation for 15 or 20 ft. thongs.

Various other qualities in Stock Whips are supplied at

25/- 35/- 45/- each.

BICYCLE JOYS

FOR GIRLS AND BOYS.

Give him—or her—a **REAL BICYCLE** for Christmas. A Gamage Juvenile is as soundly constructed as an adult's cycle and will wear as long. Don't buy a toy, get the real thing.

One can find few presents coming nearer to the ideal than Juvenile Cycles. One of the finest, if not THE finest exercise a boy or girl can possibly get to-day is Cycling. Health and Happiness go together on a Cycle, if of the right sort. We were the first to introduce these perfect little machines for Juveniles, and every season finds our sales trebled. "Gamage Juvenile" Cycles are pre-eminent for quality, strength, lightness, easy running and as examples of "VALUE FOR MONEY."

SIZES—No. 1.   22 in. wheels, length of reach adjustable from 24 in. to 28 in.   16 in. frame.
,, 2.   24   ,,   ,,   ,,   26 ,, 30 ,,   18 ,,   ,,
,, 3.   26   ,,   ,,   ,,   28 ,, 32 ,,   20 ,,   ,,

"Gamage" Model.

GENUINE DUNLOP Tyres, plated rims, enamelled centres and edges, divided rubber pedals, plated spring saddle, smaller and finer hubs, etc.
Superior finish throughout and lined in best gold leaf.

Boy's or Girl's same price, £5 5 0
Carriage paid.

SPECIFICATION. The "Gamage."

FRAME.—Best weldless steel tubing.
BEARINGS and HUBS turned from solid "Teutonic" unbreakable bar steel, dust-proof and oil retaining, Hoffmann's balls. True and hard bearings are the secret of easy running.
SPOKES.—Tangent, high tension.
CHAIN.—⅜ in. pitch, roller.
CRANKS.—Square, tapered, bevelled edges, of toughened steel.
GEAR CASE, on Girl's only.—Dover chain cover.
FORKS.—Double-butted stem.

BRAKES.—Back and front rim brakes, worked on the new roller lever principle
MUDGUARDS.—Light steel, enamelled
FREE WHEEL.—Perry's frictionless, ball-bearing with centres and edges enamelled.
RIMS.—Plated with centres and edges enamelled.
FINISH.—Best black enamel and all parts highly plated on copper, lined best gold leaf.
EQUIPMENT.—Saddle, tool bag, pump, tools and oil can.

"Favourite" Model.

A perfect model in miniature of a High Grade Roadster.
Light in weight, suitably geared, easy running, British-made throughout, thoroughly reliable.
As fully guaranteed as the highest priced machine in our Catalogue.

Boy's or Girl's same price, £3 19 9
Carriage forward.

SPECIFICATION. The "Favourite."

FRAME.—Best weldless cold-drawn steel tubing.
BEARINGS and HUBS.—Turned from solid "Teutonic" unbreakable bar steel, dust-proof and oil retaining, Hoffmann's balls. True and hard bearings are the secret of easy running.
SPOKES.—Tangent, high tension, rust-less.
CHAIN. - ⅜ in. pitch, roller.
CRANKS.—Square, tapered, bevelled edges, of toughened steel.
TYRES.—The Holborn Pneumatic.

METAL CHAIN GUARD.—On Girl's only.
BRAKES.—Back and front rim brakes, worked on the new roller lever principle
MUDGUARDS.—Light steel, enamelled
FREE WHEEL.—Perry's frictionless, ball-bearing with centres and edges enamelled.
RIMS.--Plated.
FINISH.—Best black enamel and all parts highly plated on copper.
EQUIPMENT.—Saddle, tool bag, pump, tools and oil can.

Crates 1/- each for Country.   Delivered Free by our own Vans in London Radius.

You cannot please a child better than by giving him one o
GAMAGE'S TRICYCLES.

THE "HOLBORN" TRICYCLE.

Tubular Frame, Plated Handle Bar, Leather Saddle, Brazed Joints, Adjustable Seat, Rubber-tyred Wheels.

Wheels—18 by 12 in.	..	..	..	..	..	..	**33/9**
,, 20 ,, 16 in.	..	..	..	..	..	..	**37/9**
,, 23 ,, 16 in.	..	..	..	..	..	..	**40/9**
,, 25 ,, 16 in.	..	..	..	..	..	..	**43/9**

Complete with Spanner.

THE "A.W.G." CHILDREN'S TRICYCLE.

Frame ⅞ Weldless Steel Tube, Malleable Iron Fittings, Turned and Bored to gauge, Rubber-tyred Wheels, good Adjustable Saddle, Black Enamelled.

Smallest size ..	..	**20/9**	Elsewhere ..	27/6
Wheels—Front 20 in., back 17½ in.	**25/9**	,, ..	30/6
,, ,, 23 ,, ,, 20 ,,	**29/9**	,, ..	35/6
,, ,, 26 ,, ,, 23 ,,	**33/6**	,, ..	47/6

SPECIFICATION.

Frame—Built throughout of Weldless Steel Tubes, and Tubular Front Fork with Box Crown, carefully built up and brazed exactly as our adult cycles
Ball Bearings throughout
Wheels—Built up with Tubular Rims, high tension Tangent Spokes, and fitted with ⅝ in. best grey Rubber Tyres wired on.
Live Axle.
Chain—⅜ in. pitch Roller.
Brake—Pull up, with clip brazed on handle bar.
Gear Case—Metal covering both chain wheels and chain on one side, very nicely finished, and adjusts with chain.
Finish—Four coats finest Black Enamel and beautifully lined, all bright parts plated as illust.

SINGLE TUBE MODEL.

SUITABLE FOR CHILDREN FROM 3½ TO 10 YEARS.

No. 1 Size—Wheels: Front 18 in., back 20 in.	..	..	**55/9**
,, ,, ,, ,, 20 ,, ,, 22 ,,	..	..	**57/9**
,, ,, ,, ,, 22 ,, ,, 24 ,,	..	..	**60/9**

May be fitted with Pneumatic Tyres and Plated Rims for **20/-** extra.

DOUBLE TUBE MODEL.

SUITABLE FOR CHILDREN FROM 3½ TO 10 YEARS.

No. 1 Size—Wheels: Front 18 in., back 20 in.	..	..	5
,, 2 ,, ,, ,, 20 ,, ,, 22 ,,	..	..	6
,, 3 ,, ,, ,, 22 ,, ,, 24 ,,	..	..	6

May be fitted with Pneumatic Tyres and Plated Rims for **20/-** ex

The Machine is fitted with Ball Bearings throughout, has a Roller Chain instead of the old fashioned block, high tension Spokes, and, if desired, Pneumatic Tyres. There can be nothing made to run more easily.

It is built like a Modern Bicycle with Steel Tubes and has a powerful Brake, also Gear Case.

THE "GAMAGE" JUVENILE TRICYCLES.

SPECIFICATION.

Frames—16 in., 18 in. and 20 in.
Wheels—24 in.
Gear—53 in.
Chain—½ in. Pitch Roller.
Inflator—Celluloid with Spring Clips.
Axle—Live Axle, enclosed type, Fived Wheel.
Handle Bar—As illustrated.
Saddle—Juvenile 4-Wire.
Brake—Front Rim Rolling Lever.
Chain Cover—Girls only.
Tyres—Cambridge, 1¾ in.
Finish—Black enamel, lined red.

MODEL as Specified above.

Juvenile Boy's No. 40 .. **£6 15 0**

CARRIAGE EXTRA.

MODEL as Specified above,

Juvenile Girl's No. 41 .. **£6 15**

Suitable Presents for Cyclists in Presentation Boxes.

Electric Cycle Lamp.

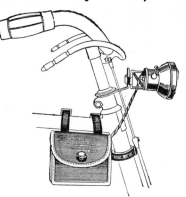

The "Holborn" Set.

ickel-plated. 2¼ in. cut-glass lens and rabolic reflector, canvas case, 3-cell case battery, flexible cord, and bulb.

urns 12 hours continuous, or 16 to 18 hours intermittent.

Price complete .. **7/6**

Refills, **1/-** each.   Bulbs, **1/-** each.
Postage 4d.

The "Special" Set.

urns 80 hours continuous,
100 hours intermittent.

volt dry battery in leather case, complete with wire and 3-amp. lamp.

Price complete .. **21/-**
Separate battery **4/6**   Post free.

The "Luxray" Electric Rear Lamp
(Provisional Patent).

Fits on Cycle Back fork in a few moments in similar manner to other rear lights.

Gives an actual red warning illumination which can be seen at a considerable distance. Price **3/9**

Complete with instructions.

Spare Refills can be kept 12 months without exhaustion.   Price **9**d. each.

The "Gamage" Gas Lamp.

Equipped with condensing lens, very highly polished reflector, and all the latest improvements In fancy box. **6/9** Post free

"Ever-ready" Electric Cycle Lamp.

A very handy lamp.

Eminently suitable for doctors, who may have to ride off at a moments' notice.

Lasts 6 to 15 hours.

Weight 17ozs.

Height 4 ins.

Prices :   **6/6   7/6   8/6** and **9/6**
With Handle and Metal Reflector, **10/6** & **11/6**
In fancy box.   Refill 9d. & 1/-   Postage 3d.

The Nulite Paraffin Lamp.

Made of brass, heavily nickel-plated.

We Guarantee this Lamp.

The "NULITE" burns Paraffin,
The Lamp that won't blow out.
The NOTROUBLE Lamp.
Brilliant White and Steady Light.

The "Nulite" is British made throughout, it is built of solid brass rivetted, and well sprung, heavily plated and beautifully finished. It is fitted with the "Barton" Porcelain Paraffin Burner (Patent) Paraffin. In fancy box.   Price **6/6**

THE "VOLTALITE" MAGNETO ELECTRIC CYCLE LAMP.

"No Battery—No Accumulator—No Recharging"

The **Voltalite** is easily fitted to the front fork of the cycle, by means of a single clip. It is mounted on a supporting stirrup, and by the movement of a small lever the rubber pulley on Voltalite engages or disengages at will on the rim of the cycle wheel, thus turning on or off the light. At 3 miles an hour (small walking speed) the light is produced, and no matter how high the speed of cycle, no injury is caused to the **Voltalite** or its bulb.

The **Voltalite** cannot be exhausted of electricity; it contains no acid, no liquid, no accumulator, no battery, and does not require recharging. In appearance it is neat and compact, being inclosed in a polished aluminium dust-proof case. It can be taken off the machine with the same ease as an oil lamp. It will last for years

Every **Voltalite** is sent out complete, with full instructions, in strong box. It can be readily fitted to the standard cycle in a few minutes. **Prices**—No. 1, with Reflector attached to Voltalite **18/6**
No. 2, with Reflector for head of machine connected to Voltalite by flexible conducting cord **25/-**
The Motor Cycle **Voltalite**, price complete with 2 spare Bulbs and Cord, **£2 16 0**

atent Cycling Muffs or Hand Shields

Speciality for Winter Riding. **For Cyclists** nd Motor Cyclists. Cycling in coldweather pleasure. Indispensable for motor cyclists. asily fixed to handle-bars and allows for the free operation of brake and bell.

Ioleskin lined with fur, Ladies' .. **15/6**
strachan, best   ,,   .. **15/6**
aracal, Ladies' **7/6**
strachan ,, ... **5/6**
eather, lined fur, Gents' **18/6**
est Macintosh, lined tamo, Gent's .. **10/6**
Iacintosh, lined wool   ,,   .. **5/9**

The "Voltalite" Cycle Lamp and Electric Rear Light combined.

Gives a brilliant light in front and a red light behind. Can be attached to any cycle in a few moments with the utmost ease. The rear light is a beautifully-finished lantern of special design and is fitted with ruby glass, metal filament bulb and reflector. It is arranged that the light is generated by the "Voltalite" for rear as well as the head lamp at the same time. The rear light is fitted to the back fork of cycle by means of a screw and a clip and connected up to the "Voltalite" by means of the wire which is provided. The bulb in "Voltalite" Lantern is changed for the one provided with the rear light.

No. V 6. The "Voltalite" Cycle Lamp, complete with head and rear lamps, ready for attachment to cycle, **22/6**

No. V 5. Electric Rear Lamp and attachment, with bulb for Voltalite, and connecting cord, **5/-**

The New Torpedo Lamp.

This Lamp is entirely made of brass.

Stylish shape, burns splendidly, easily cleaned and polished.

Nickel-plated.

Price **6/6**

Post 3d.

Really Useful Presents for Cyclists.

"La Fauvette" Syrens. NEW TYPE.

Very strong, highly finished, aluminium and brass, nickel-plated. Small, **6/8** Large, **10/-** Post 4d.

The New Syren Horn.

Suitable for Cycles, Motor Cycles or Cars. Very powerful and effective. Made in two sizes.
Small size .. **10/6** Large size .. **17/6** Post 4d.

The "OSOEZI" Saddle.

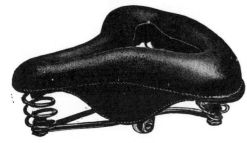

Anatomically correct.
The ideal saddle for ladies or gentlemen.
An ideal 'Xmas present. Price **21/-** Post free.
Illustration shows Gent's pattern.

The Mignon Horn. The very latest production.
Neat and smart, being only 7¾ in. long, yet most powerful
Best finish. The smartest horn ever produced.
A NICE PRESENT. Price **3/6** Postage 3d.

The Metropolitan Police Whistle.

SOLID SILVER, Hall-Marked **12/6**

The Veeder Trip Cyclometer.

List price 8/6
Price .. **6/11**
Post free.

Lucas Medallion Revolving Dome Bell.

No. Cy. 32. With 2⅝ in.
revolving domes. Plated
or Ebony black .. **4/6**
Post free.

The Elite Aluminium Rear Carrier

Rigid and reliable. Combines lightness with strength.
Price, including straps **6/6**
Maker's price - 7/6 Postage 3d.
The Favourite Aluminium Carrier .. **4/6**

The Universal Map Measurer.

In Miles, Versts, and Kilometres.

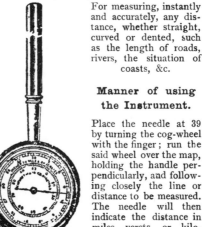

For measuring, instantly and accurately, any distance, whether straight, curved or dented, such as the length of roads, rivers, the situation of coasts, &c.

Manner of using the Instrument.

Place the needle at 39 by turning the cog-wheel with the finger; run the said wheel over the map, holding the handle perpendicularly, and following closely the line or distance to be measured. The needle will then indicate the distance in miles, versts, or kilometres according to the map measured and the dial circle used.
Price **3/9** Post 2d.
Map Measurer (In case) **6/11**

Goodlad's Speed Indicators for Cycles.

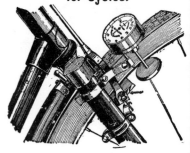

No. 1. Up to 28 miles per hour, fork fitting
Price .. **12/6**
No. 2. For Motor Cycles, up to 42 miles per h
Price .. **15/6**

The Gamage Handle Bar Basket

Made of fine split cane, biscuit colour,
Smart and best finish with straps for bar
Wire Spring Lid. Really a high-class articl
11 by 5 by 6 in. Price **4/9** Post 3d.

Acme Siren Horn

Useful for amateur theatricals for producir
weird sounds—imitating the wind. A mc
efficient road clearer. Highly nickelled, **3**
Smaller size Without horn, **1/10½** Post

Tourist Map Cases, with Clea Celluloid Windows.

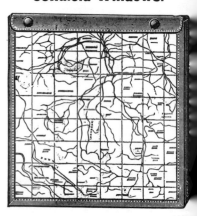

To take two folds of Ordnance Survey a
Bartholomew's Maps.
Pigskin, best quality, ruled up in 1 in. squar
6/6 each. Second quality, **3/6**

The Military Map Case.

Specially made EXTRA STRONG.
Thoroughly waterproof, with adjustable str
for hanging over shoulder. Price **18/**

The "Gamage" Light Weight Motor Cycle.

Are you a Cyclist? **Are you thinking of a Motor Cycle?** The Gamage Lightweight is the one you should buy. Because—
It is light to handle. Has no complicated mechanism. Is quiet when running. Is as simple to control as a push bike. No vibration.
No strain on nerves or injury to health when riding a GAMAGE MOTOR CYCLE. Cost of running very low.

An Astonishing Example of Quality and Low Price.

TESTIMONY FROM HILLY WALES!

Llanfair Hall, Carnarvon,
N. Wales, 3-8-13.
The Motor Cycle is going splendidly.—A. E. SMITH.

17, Church Street, Rhymney, Monmouth,
S. Wales, 11th July, 1913.

The "Gamage" motorcycle is exactly the machine I want, and I am able to say after trial that it runs smoothly, climbs all the hills, is easy to start, and simple to control.—
W. CLARK.

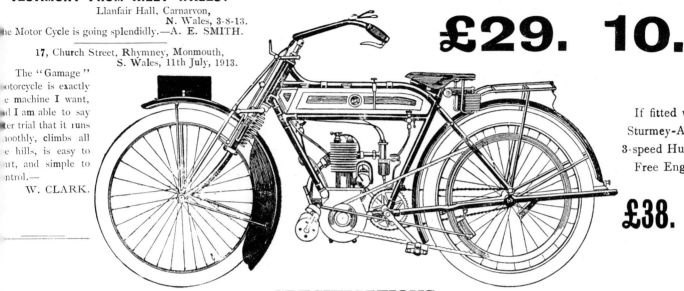

£29. 10.

If fitted with
Sturmey-Archer
3-speed Hub and
Free Engine,

£38. 10.

SPECIFICATIONS.

ENGINE—2¾-h.p. single cylinder, adjustable tappets, ball-bearing main shaft, adjustable pulley, 70 by 76 bore and stroke.
FORKS—The famous Druid spring.
TYRES—Hutchinson 26 by 2 in. beaded edge, rubber studded.
SADDLE—Lycett's La Grande, No. 110.
CARBURETTER—Brown & Barlow, with handle-bar control and variable jet.

IGNITION—Bosch magneto (Z.E.I. ball-bearing) enclosed waterproof type requiring no cover. Gear driven.
TANK—Petrol capacity, one gallon sufficient for about 125 miles, fitted with large filler caps, glass top to petrol cap, drain tap. Oil capacity one quart, internal oil pump.

The Cowey Motor Cycle Speed Indicator.

Can be fitted to any machine, either spring or solid forks. Will fit on either right or left hand side. Will register up to 60 miles per hour guaranteed. Price, with Odometer, **£4 4 0**
When ordering, please give the following particulars : Name of machine, h.p. of machine, front wheel, whether spring or solid forks. If spring forks, name of make.

The New "Veeder" Motor Cycle Cyclometer.

Specially constructed.
Stronger mechanism.
Larger and stronger Star Wheel.
Price .. **11/9**
Post free.
Elsewhere 12/6

Gamage 800 ft. Beam Motor Cycle Lamp Set.

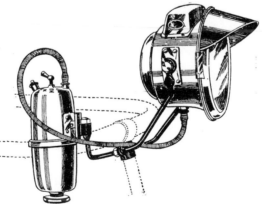

Finest quality material, fitted with Mangin Lens Mirror.
Price complete .. **35/6**

The "Powerful" Motor Cycle Horn.

Thoroughly well made of heavy gauge Brass and N.P. Fitted with dust gauze and strong clip.
Price .. **14/9** Carriage paid
This is the Best Value ever offered in Motor Cycle Horns.

Stewart's Cycle-Car Speed Indicator.

Price **£3** complete.

Stewart's Motor Cycle Speed Indicator.

50/- complete.

When ordering please state make of machine to fit, and also size of wheels.

Write for our Full Motor List,
SENT POST FREE
anywhere.

Acceptable Presents for your Motoring Friends.

Hot Water Foot Warmers.

Highest quality, covered best Brussels carpet.
Tinned steel, brass ends.

12 in.	13½ in.	16 in.	18 in.	22½ in.	24 in.	27 in.
12/6	**12/9**	**14/-**	**14/9**	**16/9**	**17/6**	**19/3**

All copper. Copper ends.

| **16/9** | **17/6** | **18/-** | **20/-** | **22 6** | **25/6** | **26/-** |

Motor Foot Muff.

No. M.18.

In black imitation Astrachan with thick white
wool interior.

Price **15/6**
Smaller size for children .. **14/6**
Post free.

Lucas' Motor-Cycle Handle-Bar Mirror.

Nº16.

3¼ in. diam. glass. Length of arm, 5¾ in.
Price **7/6** Carriage paid.

"Gamage" Slip-on Step Mat.

Quickly detachable for cleaning.
Best quality Mats **8/6**

The New Gamage Quick Detachable Step Mat
(PATENT).

Simply fixed by 2 thumb screws.
Fits more neatly on the running board, and is quicker
to fix or detach than any other pattern. Price **8 6**
Or with border and extra quality, **10/6**

Gamage's "Everlasting" Foot Warmer.

"Boil it like an egg."

No charcoal. No hot water. No handling.

FOR THE MOTOR CAR. FOR THE CARRIAGE.

Leakages and fumes are impossible, the nickel
case being hermetically soldered. Will retain
the heat six times longer than the old-style
foot-warmer. Is everlasting and only requires
"boiling" for a few minutes, just as one would
boil an egg; it then remains hot for a number
of hours, which varies according to the size
selected.

	M. 4.	M. 3.	M. 2.	M. 1.	M. 0
	For the Motor.	For the Carriage.	For the Bed.	For the Pram.	For the Muff.
Size in inches..	16 by 6	10½ by 4½	8 by 4½	6 by 3¼	4½ by 1¾
Boil for	40 min.	30 min.	20 min.	15 min.	10 min.
Remains hot for	15 hrs.	12 hrs.	9 hrs.	6 hrs.	3 hrs.
Price each, inclusive of cloth cover	**35/-**	**19/9**	**17/6**	**12/6**	**7/6**

Latest Pattern Foot Muff.

All Leather outside, trimmed with leather fringe.
Buff, Green or Blue Leather. Lined Fur.
25/6

The New "Gamage" Motor Tool Kit.

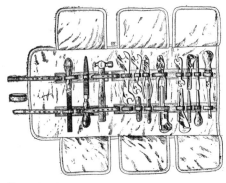

Exceptional Value. All Tools carefully selected.
39/9

Motor Foot Muff.

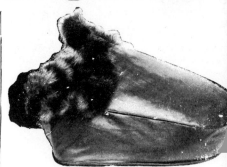

M. 22. In best strong leather-cloth, with fur lining
and edging. Price **4/6** Postage 6d.
Wonderfully good value.

M. 22a. Grey Goat outside, warm fur lining.
Price **7/6** Postage 6d.

FOOT MUFFS, covered cord cloth, lined Fleece
10/6

FOOT MUFFS, covered imitation Mole, lined
Fleece, large size, very warm and comfortable.
21/-

FOOT MUFFS, covered imitation Chinchilla,
lined Fleece **12/6**

Motor Cycle Mirrors
from **5/6**

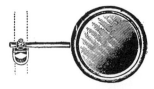

Special Lines in Mirrors.

6 in. Round Brass	..	..	Price	**7/6**
6 ,, ,, Nickel	..	..	,,	**9/-**
7 ,, by 5 in. Oblong Brass	..		,,	**10/6**
7 ,, by 5 ,, ,, Nickel	..		,,	**12/6**
8 ,, by 6 ,, ,, Brass	..		,,	**12/6**
8 ,, by 6 ,, ,, Nickel	..		,,	**15/-**

Flower Vases.

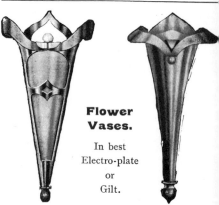

In best
Electro-plate
or
Gilt.

	Electro-plate.	Gilt.
No. M. 102. All Metal ..	**10/6**	**12/6**
,, M. 104. Openwork ..	**10/6**	**12/6**

N.B.—Either pattern can be
obtained with Glass only
at bottom **8/6** **10/6**

London made.

GAMAGES OF HOLBORN.
LADIES' MOTOR COATS.

BENETFINKS OF CHEAPSIDE.
Leather Lined, Fur Lined and Camel Fleece Lined.

THE
'DIAMLER'

THIS SMART COAT

is, in appearance, exactly as any other Motor Coat, but it has this advantage, the detachable leather lining can be taken out bodily, sleeves included, and worn under an ordinary overcoat.

Made in specially selected light fleecy cloths and chrome leather lining.

PRICE :—

No. L. T. 1—
£5 5 0

No. L. T. 2—
6 6 0

No L. T. 3—
7 7 0

The Ladies'
'MOTURA'
Coat.

Perfect cut and finish.

Cut full and comfortable.

The leather lining is attached by a very convenient form of fastening. It is easily detached when the weather turns suddenly mild, and the Coat without the lining is considered warm enough. It is easily inserted again when driving in the evening chills, &c.

Made in fleece, frieze and blanket cloth.

No. L. T. 1—
£3 10 0

No. L. T. 2..**4 4 0**

No. L. T. 3..**5 5 0**

No. L. T. 4..**6 6 0**

PATTERNS AND SELF-MEASUREMENT FORM POST FREE.

The "MOTURA" Coat. Fitted with the 'TRIPCOL' Collar.
A Comfortable, Cosy, and Convenient Coat, with Detachable Leather Collar.

Takes 40 seconds to Insert Lining.

Fig. T. 1.
The Leather Lining ready to attach.

Fig. T. 2.
The Coat Complete with Leather Lining fixed inside the coat.

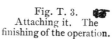

MADE IN REAL IRISH FRIEZE.

A BOON TO EVERY MOTORIST.

Fig. T. 3.
Attaching it. The finishing of the operation.

Perfect cut and finish. Very full and comfortable. The leather lining is attached by a convenient form of fastening. It is easily "stripped" off when the weather suddenly turns mild and the Coat without the lining is thought to give sufficient warmth. Easily inserted again when driving in the evening chill, &c. ces, complete, as illustration :—

No. T. 1. Lined Chrome Dressed Leather	**£3 5 0**	
No. T. 2. Better quality	**4 4 0**	
No. T. 3. Tan Cape Leather, best quality Irish Frieze..	**5 5 0**	

Special in Grey Frieze, Detachable Leather Lining .. **£2 10 0**
This Coat can also be made in better qualities at—
£6 6 0   £7 10 0   8 8 0

FUR RUGS FOR THE CAR.

We have a Large and Varied Selection of MOTOR RUGS on view in our Showrooms. The following which we list are typical of the good value we offer in durable and warm Fur Rugs. Consistent with quality the prices will be found considerably below those of other houses.

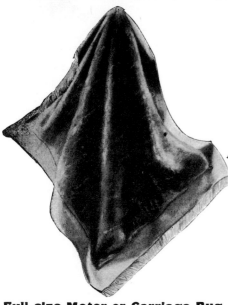

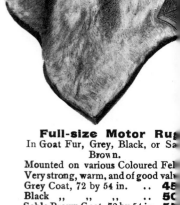

Full-size Motor or Carriage Rug

In Silver Grey Cheverette Fur or Silver Grey Wombat Fur.

Mounted on assorted Coloured Fringed Wool Shawls.

Warm, light, and comfortable.

An Ideal Rug for Ladies' use.

Silver Grey Cheverette	**£3 15 0**	
Silver Grey Wombat ..	**4 4 0**	

Full-size Fur Motor or Carriage Rug

In selected Wolf Skin.

Mounted on good quality strong Felt, in Blue, Green or Brown, or can be mounted upon any desired shade in two days.

Five Skins (as illustration) 72 by 54 in.	**75/-**
Seven Skins, extra large, for three persons, 84 by 54 in.	**110/**

Full-size Motor Rug

In Goat Fur, Grey, Black, or Sable Brown.

Mounted on various Coloured Felt. Very strong, warm, and of good value.

Grey Coat, 72 by 54 in. ..	45
Black ,, ,,	50
Sable Brown Goat, 72 by 54 in.,	55

Also made in extra large size for three persons.

Grey Coat, 84 by 54 in. ..	55
Black ,, ,, ,,	60
Sable Brown Goat, 84 by 54 in.	65

Full-size Motor or Carriage Rug.

In Australian Wallaby Fur.

Made from carefully selected Skins. Mounted on various Coloured Cloths.

Very warm and durable.

10 Skins ..	**£4 15 0**	
12 Skins ..	**£5 10 0**	
14 Skins ..	**£6 5 0**	

Full-size Motor or Carriage Rug.

In specially selected Civet Cat or Brown Jap Badger Fur.

A very handsome, warm and durable Rug.

Mounted on various Coloured Cloths, 72 by 54 in...	**£5 10 0**
Also made in extra large size for three persons, 86 by 54 in. ..	**6 10 0**

Full-size Fur Motor or Carriage Rug

In Hamster Fur. Very strong, warm, and light. Mounted on various coloured fringed shawls.

Price ..	**£5 10 0**

BOYS' & YOUTHS' CLOTHING to Order or for Immediate Wear.
COMPLETE SCHOOL OUTFITS A SPECIALITY.
PERFECT FIT & SATISFACTION GUARANTEED.

"Boys' Reliable Clothing.

We are now stocking in all sizes several numbers of Reliable Standard Tweeds and Serges. These we can strongly recommend for School and General wear. The advantage to our customers who purchase these Standard goods is that they can always be repeated, or odd Knickers and Trousers matched.

Bespoke Department—
In this Department a Staff of Experienced Cutters are kept, thus assuring Perfection of Fit and Style in all Garments Made to Measure.

School Outfits—
In this Department we are making a Speciality of School and College Outfits, and all Orders entrusted to us by parents and guardians will receive immediate and careful attention.

Garments for Immediate Wear—
In this Department we have a Large Stock of every variety of Clothing suitable for Young Gentlemen's Wear.

The Eton Suit.

Is most useful for Dress or School Wear and is made in Vicunas, Twills and Cheviots. The Trousers are made of our Special Untearable West of England Hair Line Cloths.

Eton Jackets and Vests.
15/6   18/6   23/-   25/-

These prices are for Size 6, age 11.

Rise 1/- each size.

Hair Line Trousers.
5/6   7/5   10/-   11/-

T. 2345.

This is a useful style for Best and School wear, and is suitable for Youths from 10 years of age and upwards. They are made in Tweeds, Homespuns, Worsteds and Serges. Very Strong and Durable.

Rugby Suits.
14/6 18/6 22/6 26/6

These prices are for Size 5, age 10.
Rise 1/- each size.

BOYS' and YOUTHS'
Marlborough Suits.

Jackets and Waistcoats in Vicunas and Serges.
17/6   21/6   26/6

Hair Line Trousers—
5/11   7/11   10/6

Stripe Worsted Trousers—
7/6   8/6   10/6

Perfect Fit Guaranteed.
These prices are for size 7.

T. 4564.

T. 4368.

THE
Holborn Suit.

This style of Suit is usually worn by Youths from 12 years of age and upwards, and is made in Tweeds, Homespuns, Worsteds and Serges.

Very Strong and Durable.

18/6 21/6 23/6
25/6 28/6 32/6

These prices are for Size 8, age 10.

Rise 1/- each size.

T. 5612.

THE
Kensington Suit.

Suitable for Boys from 8 to 12 years, made in specially strong Tweeds and Homespuns.

12/6 15/6 18/6 21/6

These prices are for Size 3, age 8.
Rise 1/- each size.

Norfolk Suit.

The Norfolk Suit is now made without a waist-coat, but a detachable imitation Vest is provided fastening close to the neck, giving protection to the chest. They are made in Tweeds, Serge and Homespuns, and are useful for General or School wear, and also for Cycling Very Strong and Durable.

13/6 17/6 21/6
25/6

These prices are for Size 4 age 9. Rise 1/- each size.

T. 5000.

T. 315

X

"BE PREPARED" to Give your Scout Friends a 'XMAS PRESENT.

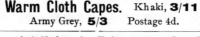

Khaki Flannel Shirts.

2 military pockets and shoulder straps. Boys' sizes up to 14½ in. collar, **3/9** Men's sizes, 15 to 17 in. collar, **4/6**.

Flannel Mixture Khaki Shirts.

Official pattern. Boys' sizes up to 14½ in. collar, **3/4½**. Men's sizes, 15 to 17½ in. collar, **3/10½** Also in navy or green.

Strong Khaki Serge Shirts.

With 2 breast pockets & shoulder straps. Boys' sizes up to 14½ in. collar, **2/-** Larger sizes, **2/3**

Scoutmaster's Shirt.

Khaki Flannel mixture. Official pattern. With detachable collar, **4 11** Postage on each, 3d.

Navy or Green to order in few days

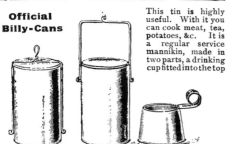

New Mess Tin.

With Tray, fitted with handle for plate or frying pan, with cup and condiment box.

1/9 Post 4d.

Official Billy-Cans

This tin is highly useful. With it you can cook meat, tea, potatoes, &c. It is a regular service mannikin, made in two parts, a drinking cup fitted into the top

It can be easily carried in a haversack, and it is most all-round useful item of a Scout's equipment. **7½**d. Postage 3d.

SCOUTS' AXES.

Gamage's Boy Scout Axe, steel head, ash handle.
Price **1/-** Postage 4d.
Better quality, blade of forged steel.
Price **2/6**
Axe Cases, **9**d. and **10½**d.
Postage 4d.

Scout Steel Axes.
Price **1/6**
Axe Cases, **9**d. and **10½**d.
Postage 4d.

Warm Cloth Capes. Khaki, 3/11

Army Grey, **5/3** Postage 4d.

Special Value in Telescopes for Boy Scouts.

Complete in Leather Case, with loop for fixing to Belt. Price **6/11** Postage 3d.

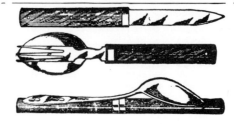

CLOSED.

The "Holborn" Camp Combination.
Knife, Fork and Spoon a necessity to all Scouts and Campers out. Price **1/9** Postage extra.

Superior Knives. Black Handle.

Fitted with screw-driver, corkscrew, marlinespike, tin-opener, large and small blade.
Price .. **2/6**

Superior quality, chequered handle.
Price .. **2/9**
Postage 2d.

Scouts' Knives.

Official pattern.
Stout Bone-handle Knife, with special tool for splicing ropes. Essential for camp life.
Price **10½**d.
Do., with lanyard, **1/-**
Superior quality ditto, chequered handle .. **1/6**
Also first quality nickel-plated,
Price **1/6** With lanyard, **1/7½**
Postage 1d.

Scout's Knife Combination.

Knife, fork and spoon, best nickel silver and cast steel.
Price .. **2/6**
Postage 3d.
The knife, fork and spoon can be used separately.
Superior quality,
4/11
Postage 3d.

Scouts' Jerseys.

"B.P." Official Pattern.

Strong khaki worsted, very warm & comfortable
Boys sizes, 26 to 34 in. chest. Price **3/-** 36 to 40 in., **3/9** Post 4d.
State chest measurement when ordering.
Can also be made in plain navy or green.

Knickers.

No. 2. Official Pattern.

With side hooks for supporting belt.
Superior quality. Strong serge, navy blue or khaki.
Price **2/-** Post 3d.
State waist measurement.

Scouts' Bottle.

Tin, with screw top and web sling, **6½**d. With leather slings, **1/-**
Do., japanned, with web sling, **10½**d. With leather slings, **1/4½**. Postage 3d.
Leather Slings for bottles **7½**d. each. Postage 1½d. Web Slings, **2½**d. each. Postage 1d.

Steel Water Bottle.

Khaki felt covered.
Price **2/6**
Larger size, **4/3**
Postage 4d.

Tan leather, with dull black metal fittings, with two rings and swivels. Price **1**
Ditto, with ring and swivel, **10½**d.
Postage 2d.

Gamage's Scoutmasters' Whist[le]

Best quality, nickel-plated.
Price **1/-** With lanyard, **1/2** Postage 1
African Pattern, **1/-** and **1/6**

Boy Scout's Whistle.

Large size, **7½**d. With lanyard, **9**d.
Smaller size, **5½**d. With lanyard, **7½**
Postage 1½d.

Gamage's Hand Book of Scout Crafts. A useful Book for Scouts ... ... 10½d. Postage 2d.

Dress Shoes and Slippers. Enormous Variety.

Slippers for the Fireside, the Bedroom and the Bath, at fully **25** *o/o less than elsewhere.*

Grecian Slippers.

4/11

n red, tan, marone, morocco, and best black glace kid.

/11   5/11   6/6   8/6   Carriage 4d. extra.

Morocco Albert Slippers.

3/11

3/11   4/11   5/6   6/6

Postage 4d. extra.

Every pair guaranteed **A1 Value**

Patent Dress Shoes in great variety.

4/11

Postage 4d. extra.

Splendid Value.

her qualities .. **6/11   8/9   10/6   12/6**

Fancy-worked Slippers.

3/6

Postage 3d.

Special Value.   Better qualities—
4/11   5/6   6/6

ustomers' own material made up.

and-sewn, **7/6** and **8/6** Carriage 4d. extra.

Colonial Outfits a Speciality.

DRESS SHOES.

The **A.W.G.** Court Shoe.

4/6

Carriage 4d. extra.

Calf patent fronts.   Marvellcus value.

Fully 25 o/o less than elsewhere.
All sizes and fittings.   Every pair perfect.

Glace Court Shoes.
8/6

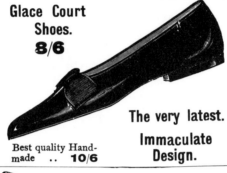

The very latest.
Immaculate Design.

Best quality Hand-made .. **10/6**

The Ideal.
7/9

C.H. patent throughout.   Postage 4d. extra.
Other qualities,
3/11   4/6   5/6   6/11   8/6   10/6   12/6

Boys' and Youths' Dress Shoes.
GREAT VARIETY.

REAL TURKISH SLIPPERS.
Red Leather.   Wool Lined.   SPLENDID VALUE.

Ladies' and Gent's, **2/6** Children's, **1/11** Post 3d.

School Outfits a Speciality.
Estimates by return of post.

DUTCH SABOTS for Fancy Dress.
All sizes .. **2/6**   Carriage 4d. extra.

Bath and Bedroom Slippers.

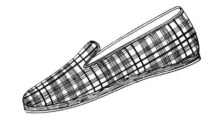

	2/6	3/9
Ladies' ditto	2/6	3/6
Slipper Boots, fine quality..	3/11	4/9

Carriage 3d. extra.

The A.W.G. Grecian Slipper.

3/11   Postage 4d. extra.

Made in Tan and Marone Colour Leathers.

Unprecedented Value.

The Quadrille.

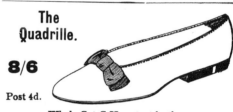

8/6

Post 4d.

Whole Cut C.H. patent leather.

Other qualities .. **10/6   12/6   14/6**

The A.W.G. Albert Slipper.

(As illustration.) **4/11**

Made also in
Black Glace Kid
at **5/11**

Post 4d.

Fine quality Levant Leather Upper.   Warm fleecy lined and stout Leather sole for winter wear. Hard wearing and exceedingly comfortable.

Boys' & Youths' School Slippers
—A Speciality.

Made in Stout Levant Leather, wear guaranteed,
3/11 and **4/6**

Motor Footwear a Speciality.

X

ACCEPTABLE 'XMAS GIFTS.

Ladies' Satin Quilted Slippers.

1/11½

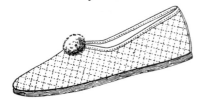

In various colours, viz. :—

Cinamon, Royal Blue, Saxe Blue, Scarlet, Black and Helio.

Splendid Value.

Gent's Slippers.

Made in Tan and Marone Leather.

6/11

Light and Pliant
Yet exceedingly durable.
Perfect fitting.

The "Gamage" Patent Dress Shoes.

FOR BOYS.

(As illustration).

Sizes 2 to 5.

3/11

Made also in C.H. Calt, Patent throughout, at **5/11**

A Large Selection of Slippers always in Stock.

Ladies' Slipper Boots Quilted

2/11½

Marvellous Value.

Fur Bound, exceedingly warm and comfortable.

In various colours, viz. :—
Saxe Blue, Scarlet, Cinamon, and Black.

Special Value.

Ladies' and Gent's.

3/6

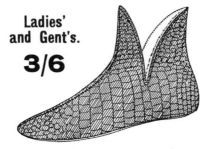

Made in Red Crocodile Leather, and Fleecy lined, exceedingly comfortable. 30 per cent. cheaper than elsewhere.

SCHOOL SLIPPERS IN GREAT VARIETY.

The "Gusset" Slipper, made with **Elastic Slides,** in strong Levant Leather Double Soles.

Boys' sizes 11 to 1	.. ..	**3/11**
Youths' sizes 2 to 5	.. ..	**4/6**
Men's sizes 6 to 11	.. ..	**5/11**

Made also in **Patent Seal Leather.**

Boys' sizes 11 to 1	.. ..	**4/6**
Youths' sizes 2 to 5	.. ..	**4/11**
Men's sizes 6 to 11	.. ..	**5/11**

The A.W.G. "Cosy" Slipper for Ladies.

(As illustration.) **1/11½**

Elsewhere **2/11**

Fine quality Felt Uppers, **padded Leather Soles,** comfort and style combined. An Ideal Slipper.
Colours—Saxe, Cherry, Helio. and Black.

Ladies' Velvet Slippers.

1/11½

Wonderful Value.
Exceedingly Durable.

Variety of colours.

Cinamon, Ruby, Saxe Blue, Emerald and Black.

Gent's Plaid Slipper Boots.

3/11

Best quality .. **4/9**

Ladies' sizes same prices.

This is one of the most comfortable Slipper Boots on the market.

Light in weight, yet durable in wear.

The "Gamage" Patent Court Shoes.

FOR BOYS.

(As Illustration). Sizes 2 to 5,

3/11

Made also in Best C.H. Patent Calf at **5/11**

The A.W.G. "Cosy" Slipper for Gentlemen. (As illustration.)

1/11½ Elsewhere **2/11**

Best Felt Uppers, **padded leather soles,** exceedingly warm and comfortable, and very durable.
Colours—Brown, Navy and Cherry.

HANDSOME PRESENTS
FOR ALL
SPORTSMEN

SPORTING GUNS. BRITISH BUILT. Special Ejector Gun.
Anson & Deeley Hammerless Ejector Gun.

12, ·16 and ·20 Bore, B.S.A. Steel Barrels, boss bite, treble grip, joint finish, beautifully engraved, left choke, nitro proved. Standard stock measuremen ts. Essentially a high-grade, well-finished gun. Sold in the West End at £25. Our price **£14 10 0**
Initials on Silver butt plate engraved free.

The "Holborn."
British made Hammerless Double Barrel Nitro Proved Gun.
Absolutely the best value in Guns ever offered
In 12 and 16 bore.

PRICE **£5 10 0**
Sent on Approval.

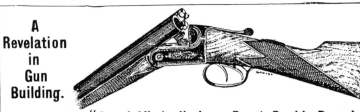

A Revelation in Gun Building.

Harrington & Richardson's and Ivor Johnson Single Ejector 12 & 16 Bore Gun

London proved 12 bore. This takes down in the same way as an ordinary double-barrel gun. Length of barrel 30 in, Standard stock measurement. The Premier value in Single Barrel Ejector Guns. **21/-** Carriage paid.

Gamage's "Special" Ladies' or Boys' Double-Barrel Hammerless Guns. (Carriage paid.

Steel barrels, nitro proved, with cross bolt and border engraving, in 20, 28 & ·410 bore. British made by British labour. Can only be procured from us. **£8 8 0**

The "Triumph" Double-Barrel Hammer Gun.

Of British Manufacture—Of Dependable Quality. Its Perfect Balance and Shooting Qualities are unequalled, and it is the strongest and Most Reliable Gun at the price on the market.

A Gun with a Reputation for Simplicity and Exclusive Features.

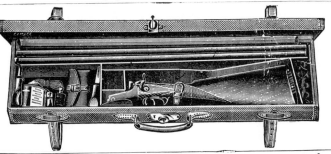

It has the following Specification :

Steel Barrels made by the B.S.A. Co., Ltd., Birmingham ; Nitro proved, Right Barrel Cylinder, Left Barrel Full Choke ; Spring Strikers, Snap Fore-end ; specially selected Walnut Stock, Horn Heel-plate, and a Double Bolt.

Complete Brown or Green Waterproof Canvas Case and all accessories.

£4 4 0 Complete. Carriage paid.

The "Bayard" Auto-Cocking & Ejecting Semi-Automatic Rifle.

Price .. **19/6** Post 6d.

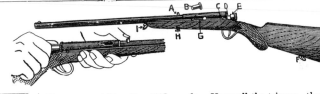

Collector's Gun.

·410 bore, steel barrel, side lever, very best finish **35/-** British made.

The strongest Shooting Rifle made. You pull the trigger, the Bayard does the rest. Made for ·22 short or long rim fire ordinary Smokeless Cartridges. A— Shows adjustable rear sight. B—Shows empty shell flying out. C—Shows safety latch. D—Screw Cap which retains breech block. E—Breech block. F—Sling swivels. G—Breech block catch. H—Take-down screw. Weight 4 lbs. Short Smokeless Cartridges, **1/2** per 100. Long ditto, **1/4** 100.

DESCRIPTION—In firing the cartridges the recoil automatically opens breech block, cocks rifle, ejects empty shell, and leaves it ready for a new cartridge. Merely press breech block G, and pull trigger, then drop in new cartridge.

·410 bore, Folding barrel, superior finish .. **31/6**

Smokeless Cartridges, to suit .. **5/3** per 100.

Walking Stick and Collector's Gun.

The New "B.S.A." Miniature Rifle.

R. 2 Model. With bolt action, ·22 calibre, weight 6 lbs., length of barrel 24in. back sight adjustable up to 200 yards elevation .. **30/-** Carriage paid.

R. 3 Model. Superior finish, with chequered stock, as illustration .. **50/-**
Waterproof Canvas Covers, **1/9 2/11**

London proved. 410 bore, highly tested, superior horn handle, concealed trigger. Length, 35 in. Weight, 1 lb. 6 ozs.
Just the gun for Rabbits, Rooks, &c. Price **35/-** Carriage Paid
Cartridge to fit—Ball **5/9** Shot **4/6 5/3** per 100.

For full list of all makes of Guns and Rifles send Postcard.

B.S.A. Air Rifles.

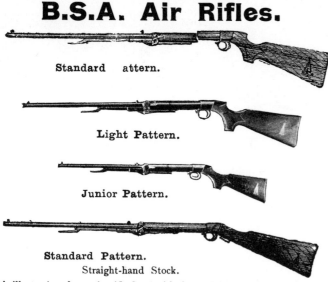

Standard attern.

Light Pattern.

Junior Pattern.

Standard Pattern.
Straight-hand Stock.

This illustration shows the rifle fitted with the straight-hand stock. The other rifles shown above are fitted with stocks with pistol grips.

Military Pattern Air Rifle.

Specifications.

PATTERNS ..	Standard.		Light.	Junior.
Bore	·177 in. or	·22 in.	·177 in. only	·177 in. only
Weight of Rifle ..	7¼ lbs.	7¼ lbs.	6¼ lbs.	5½ lbs.
Length over all } (14¼ in. stock) }	43¾ in.	45¾ in.	39½ in.	34¾ in.
Length of Stock { from trigger to { centre of butt {	14¼ in. (standard) 13¾ or 13¼ in.	14¼ in. (standard) 13¾ or 13¼ in.	13½ in. (standard) 13¾ or 14¼ in.	11¼ in. (standard) One length only supplied
Length of Barrel ..	19¼ in.	19¼ in.	17 in.	15¼ in.
Effective Range ..	50 yards	50 yards	30 yards	20 yards

The various Patterns and their Prices.

Each of the various patterns dealt with opposite has its particular function The Standard Model is the most popular and the pistol-grip stock is generally preferred to the stock with a straight-hand. The Light Models are designed for Ladies and others who are not quite robust enough to handle the 7¼-lb. ordinary pattern, whilst for Boys & Girls there is no better rifle made than the Junior Model

The following are the various Models & their Prices

Standard Pattern	Pistol-hand stock, **50/-**	Straight do. **45**/-
Light or Ladies' Pattern	ditto ditto **50**/-	ditto **45**/-
Junior or Boys' Pattern ..	ditto ditto **45**/-	ditto **40**

The long Military Pattern (complete with push pattern wind-gauge, back sight slide) .. **80**/- The short Military Pattern .. **120**

Prices of "Adder" Pellets.

·177 in. (No. 1) **1/3** box of 1,000. ·22 in. (No. 2) **1/5** box of 500. Post 4d. A.W.G." No. 1 Slug .. .. **1**/- box of 1000. ,,

For full Specifications of

ALL B.S.A. Air Rifles, Sights and Accessories.

Send for " The Book of the B.S.A. Air Rifles." Post free.

For full range of ALL GRADES of Air Guns, Rifles and Accessories, send for Departmental "R" List.

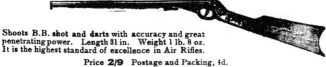

Length of barrel, 16 in. Length over all, 36 in. Weight 4½ lbs.
Boys' Millita, Plain barrel, **14/6** Waterproof Canvas Case, to suit, **1/9** The best Slug is the "Holborn," **7d**. 1,000
HEAVIER MODELS **19/6 23/9 35/- 37/6**

The "King" or "Daisy" Single Shot Air Rifle.
Made of polished steel, handsomely nickelled Genuine walnut stock, splendid sights

Shoots B.B. shot and darts with accuracy and great penetrating power. Length 31 in. Weight 1 lb. 8 oz. It is the highest standard of excellence in Air Rifles.
Price **2/9** Postage and Packing, 4d.

The "King" or "Daisy"
Repeating Air Rifle. Made of polished steel, walnut stock, peep sights. Shoots 350 times without reloading. Shoots B.B. or Air Gun Shot. Length 34 in. Weight 2 lbs. All parts interchangeable ... **3/9** Post 4d The King 350 Shot is a hammerless Air Rifle that loads automatically. The magazine holds 350 Air Rifle Shots, and each shot is swaged to size as it enters the barrel, thus giving it great force and accuracy.

The "King" or "Daisy"
Lever Action Air Rifle. (500 and 1,000 Shot).
A hammerless magazine Repeater with lever action. Loads automatically and shoots with accuracy and great penetration. The frame and barrel are of one piece of nickelled steel—no joints between barrel and frame to work loose. Walnut stock and splendid sights. All parts interchangeable. 500 Shot, **6/6** 1,000 Shot, **7/6** Post 6d.

No. R.1 Holborn Hollow Back Slugs .. **7**d. 1,000
Postage 4d.
No. R.1 A.W.G. Slugs, HANDLED, for Match Shooting **1**/- 1,000
Postage 4d.
Darts .. .. **4½**d. doz. Post 1d.

Gem
Air Guns.

The "Gem" Air-Gun

No. 1 Bore. Top lever, with Slugs, Darts and Dart Extractor (as Illustration Complete with Slugs, Targets, Darts and Dart Extractor .. **11**/-
Waterproof Canvas Cover **1/9**

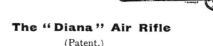

The "Diana" Air Rifle
(Patent.)

The latest creation in Air Gun Manufacture. The "Diana" Air Rifle is not a toy, but an exact model of a real rifle. Very powerful and absolutely accurate. No. 1 Bore, with Slugs, Darts and Targets, price **7/6** Post 6d.

The "Holborn" **Slug, 7**d. per 1,000.
The "A.W.G." Match **Slug, 1**/- per 1,000. Post 4d.
B.B. Shot, **4½**d. box. Post 3d
Bango Bullets, **6**d. box. Post 2d.
Shot Cartridges, **5½**d. box. Post 2d.

THE HOLBORN
Air Pistol.

No License required to purchase this Pistol.
Nickel-plated body and barrel, adjustable elevation and lateral movement, backsight, adjustable trigger, walnut stock. Barrel 9½ in. long. 21 in. over all. Weight 2 lbs. 6 oz. Beautifully balanced. Each one packed in cardboard box with Slugs, Darts and Targets.

Price .. **7/6** Post 6d.

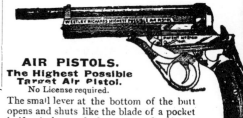

AIR PISTOLS.
The Highest Possible Target Air Pistol.
No License required.

The small lever at the bottom of the butt opens and shuts like the blade of a pocket knife; it has a dual purpose: first it enables the shooter to get more leverage when cocking pistol, and, second, it helps to steady the aim.

The length of the barrel is 9¾ in., and the length of the pistol over all is 12 in., and weighs 2¾ lbs. The pistol is easily manipulated and loaded, with less operations and less effort than ordinary air pistol. It is beautifully balanced, beautifully made and of handsome appearance. It handles well; it shoots well; it has no recoil. It is not a toy, but a weapon of precision recreation by men and women, the use of which, while affording unlimited pleasure, affords tests of skill not hitherto obtainable. The Patent "Highest Possible" Air Pistol, black finish, as illustrated, packed in cardboard box ... ...
Stiff Pegamoid Box with straps and handle, no implements, BRITISH MADE.

The best SLUGS to use in the above pistol are "A.W.G." Price .. **1**/- per 1,000. Post 4d

The "Champion" Water Pistol.

Revolver pattern. Fires 12-15 sprays of water with one loading. Total length 7½ ins. The best and most powerful water pistol on the Market.

The Latest and Best.   Price **1/-** each.

British Made.

U.S.A. Repeating Pistol.

No. R. 2. .. **1/6** Post 2d.

'Wizard' Repeating Liquid Pistol

No. R. 3. Patented. **1/6** Post 2d.

SOMETHING NEW.   BOOMERANGS.

Which behave in an unaccountable way.

These Boomerangs were devised by Mr. M. Holroyd Smith, M.I.M.E., etc., when engaged in studying problems of Flight. They can with a little practice be made to execute curious and extraordinary evolutions in the air. Throwing them is an interesting pastime and an intellectual study. No Scientific explanation has yet been found to account for their behaviour. They differ from the Australian Boomerang in shape, and in the fact that they can be easily thrown. They should be held between the thumb and finger of the right hand, flat side down, and then with a long swing of the arm and a twisting action of the wrist, thrown preferably into the wind when they will travel forward, skimming the ground for thirty, forty or more yards, according to the force exerted, then rise upwards making a graceful curve and return towards the thrower. By varying the angle in which they are held, and the angle above the horizontal at which they are thrown, they can be made to travel in different paths, returning sometimes to the feet of the thrower, sometimes landing far behind him, sometimes making a wide curve to the left, descending, skimming the ground, then rising again and making a graceful curve to the right before landing a hundred yards or more away from the starting point.

THE BLUE BIRDS are the easiest for a beginner to throw.

THE FLAMINGOES travel further before rising.

THE BLACK BATS (which must be held by the wide end) make the more complex and prolonged flight.

2/6 each.   A very welcome present for your boy.

A Very Useful Present for a Territorial.

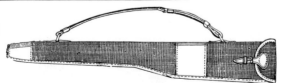

Waterproof Covers for Lee-Metford Rifles.

Cheap Waterproof Cover, strong double texture bound leather, leather nose cap .. **3/11**
Ditto, with Sling, **4/11** each. Brown Canvas with sling, leather at action and nose **7/6**
Postage 6d.

Superior quality, Box nose cap, leather covered action and leather covered flap **9/6** Post 4d.

In ordering, state whether for Service or Sporting Model. Give total length required.

The "Demon" Water Pistol.

BOY'S SIZE.

6d. each.

Latest Novelty—Popular Fireworks.

This very popular form of Indoor Amusement is composed of Miniature Fireworks, manufactured so as to render them absolutely suitable for indoor use.

The following Novelties are included in the **10½**d. and **2/3** box:

The Floating Beacon,	Lightning Paper,
The Striped Cobra,	Will o' the Wisp.
Scintilettes,	Bengal Lights,
Artificial Lighting,	War Pictures,
War Signals, War Balloons,	Growing Ferns,
Electric Sparklers.	

Special Cheap Selection .. .. .. **6**d. per box
One Shilling size .. ..**10½**d. „
Two-and-Sixpenny size .. .. ..**2/3** „

Full directions with each.

Polar Balloons.

First open out the paper and stand it on a plate, then light the two top corners; after burning a short time it ascends and drops several beautiful stars. Quite harmless and a great novelty.

6d. for 20. Post 1d.

The 'Holborn" Brand of Electric Sparklers

Smokeless and without smell. For indoor or outdoor use.

To be placed on metal tray,

3d. box of 12.

The "Stanley" Cartridge Bag.

A perfect Cartridge Bag thoroughly waterproofed. The gussets are made from solid leather cowhide and all the fittings the best possible make.

The new shape of this bag ensures the Cartridges being kept perfectly dry.

To hold	30	50	75	100
Brown Duck	**6/-**	**6/6**	**7/3**	**8/-**
Pigskin ..**12/6**		**13/6**	**15/6**	**19/6**
Cowhide ..**10/-**		**10/6**	**13/6**	**16/6**

Post 4d.

For Handsome Presents
For the Naturalist, Shooter, or Fisherman,
SEND FOR DEPARTMENTAL LIST.

HANDSOME PRESENTS FOR TROUT FISHERMEN.

No. R. 50a.

The "G.B. CHALLENGE" Superior Quality British Built Split Cane Fly Rod.

Two tops, double brazed lock joints, cork grip, Universal winch fittings, rubber button, hollow landing handle.

9 ft., 9½ ft., 10 ft., 10½ ft., 11 ft., 12 ft.	..	**32/6**
If with Steel centre	..	**45/-**

The 'W.S.A.' Light-weight Split Cane Trout Rod

Three joints, two tops in landing handle, suction ferrules, solid cork grip. Special design. Weight from 6 oz.

9 ft., 9½ ft. and 10 ft. only **42/-**

To the Special Design of W. S. Amor, Esq.

NOTED FOR THEIR PERFECT BALANCE.

No. R. 30a.

British-built Split Cane Trout Spinning Rod.

With suction joints, and in every other respect the same quality throughout as our No. R. 50a "Challenge" Rod, with two tops, one making an 11 ft. and the other a 10 ft. ideal spinning rod. Price **35/-**

No. R. 30b. Ditto, ditto, but with steel centre .. **47/6**

The Test Reel.

An Aluminium Reel of the Finest Workmanship.

With an especially large drum for quick winding.

	3 in.	3½ in.	4 in.	4½ in.
Price ..	**17,-**	**20/-**	**23/-**	**25/6** each.

No. R. 16.

The Ariel Dry Fly Box.
ALUMINIUM.

SPECIAL NOTE.—This box has each lid fitted with a spring and catch, so that when the catch is released the lid springs open, and by pressing down is immediately closed.

Transparent lids

12 compartments	..	..	**8/6**
16	,,	.. ..	**10/6**

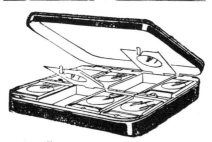

The "Gamage" Dry Fly Box.

Each partition has a separate lid.

The best possible way of keeping dry flies.

6 partitions ..	..	..	**8.6**
8	,,	..	**10/-**
10	,,	..	**13/6**

No. R. 368T.

Handy Cast and Trout Fly Box.

Cast Box has a safety rim.

Holds 75 Flies, small 7's and 10's.

Price .. **9/6** each.

No. R. 1646½.

Cow Hide Trout Fly Book.

Two leather gussetted pockets, all well stitched strap and buckle; eight pages for Trout flies two felt leaves, and the usual parchmen dividing leaves.

5½ in. ..	**3/9**	6 in. ..	**4/6**

No. R 2002.

Pigskin Trout Fly Book.

Strap and buckle; two leather gussett pockets, all well sewn; contains ten pages f Trout flies, four envelope cast pockets wi flaps, two felt leaves, and parchment dividi leaves.

5 in.	5½ in.	6 in.
5/6	**6/-**	**6/9**

The "Shaw" Fly Fisher's Knife.

Contains the eight necessary tools of the Fisherman, viz.: Disgorger, Lancet, Scisso File, Nippers, Screwdriver, Stiletto and Bla All parts highly magnetized, so that which ever tool is being used it will serve to pick any required fly.

Nickel-plated ..	**10/6**	Ivory ..	**15/-**
Silver ..	.. **21/-**	Post paid.	

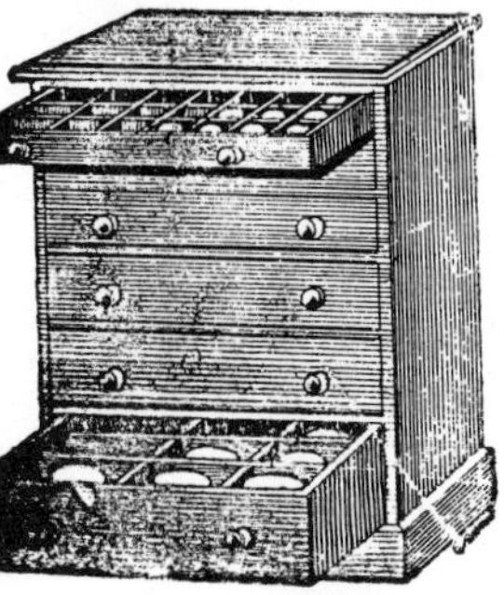

Returnable Crates for all Cabinets, 1/-

In Mahogany to order, same price as for Oak.

Birds' Egg Cabinets

Drawers.	Width.	Height.	Depth.	Polished Stained Basswood. Price.	Old English Oak.
4	12	13	9	**11 3**	**15/-**
6	15	18	9½	**15/-**	**21/-**
8	19	25	11	**27/6**	**35/-**
10	22	35	14	**50/6**	**67/6**

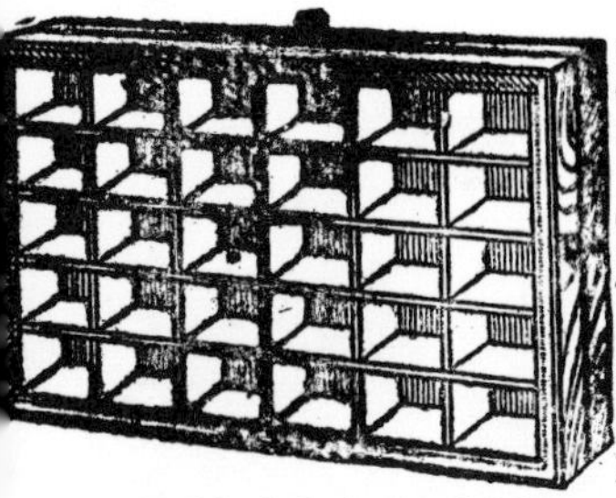

Egg Cases.

With Partitions, Glass Framed Top. Suitable for Exhibition purposes.

Polished Imitation Mahogany.

10x8	13x9	14x10	16x10	16x12	18x14	18x18 in.
2/6	**3/6**	**4/-**	**4/6**	**5/6**	**6 6**	**8/6**
Old English Oak.						
3/6	**5/-**	**5/6**	**6/-**	**7/-**	**8/-**	**11/-**

Post and Packing, 6d.

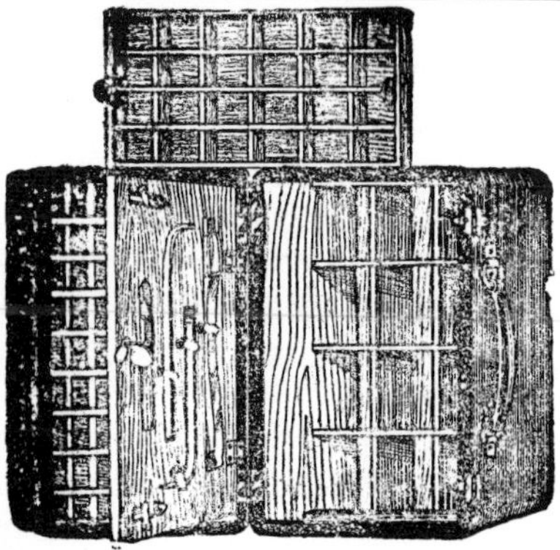

The **"St. Neots"** Handy Egg Case for Collectors. With 3 Trays for storing eggs, and Divisions containing 3 drills, 2 blowpipes, and 1 Egg lifter. Beautifully finished in black with patent catches on top, strong leather handles for carrying .. **12/6** In Old English Oak, self colour .. **15/-** Post 6d.

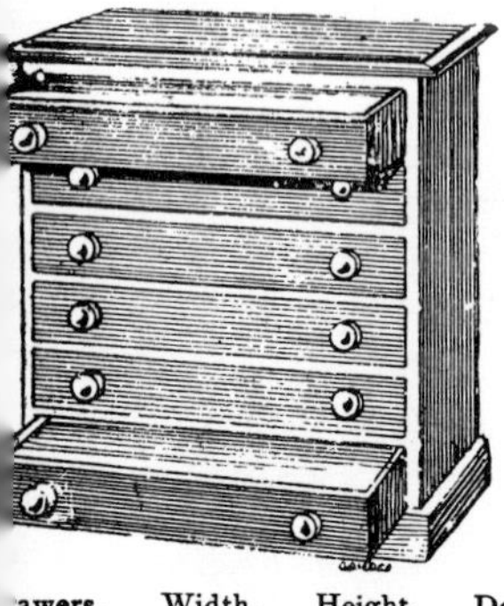

Cabinets for Insects.

Corked and papered.

Same style as illust., only with different compartments in drawers to take Insects or Butterflies.

Carriage forward.

Drawers.	Width.	Height.	Depth.	Price.
4	13 in.	12 in.	8 in.	**12 3**
6	15 ,,	16½ ,,	9 ,,	**16/6**
8	18 ,,	22 ,,	11 ,,	**30/6**
10	19½ ,,	27½ ,,	12 ,,	**39/-**

Old English Oak, **15/-** **21/-** **42/-** **65/-**

Crates (returnable) charged 1/-

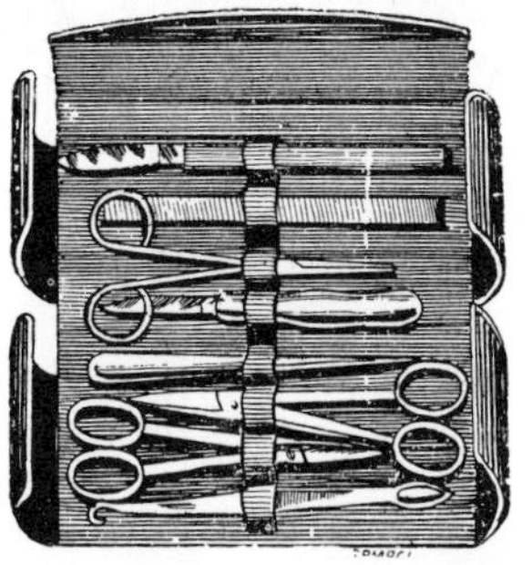

Taxidermist's Companion.

A pocket case in leather, containing 9 useful tools for skinning, viz., 2 pairs scissors, different sizes, 2 scalpels, different sizes, 1 pair tow pliers, 1 small file, 1 brain scoop & hook, 1 pricker. Price **9/-**

Ditto, Superior finish. **10/6** Post paid.

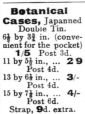

Botanical Cases, Japanned Double Tin. 6½ by 3¾ in. (convenient for the pocket) **1/5** Post 3d.

11 by 5½ in., ... **2 9** Post 4d.

13 by 6½ in., ... **3/-** Post 4d.

15 by 7½ in., ... **4/-** Post 6d.

Strap, **9**d. extra.

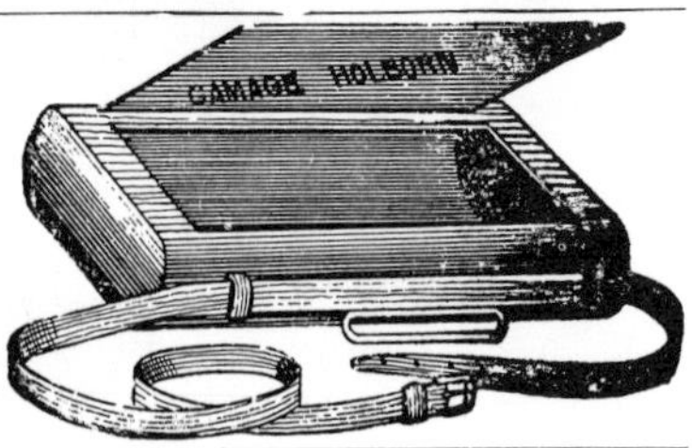

Coin and Microscopic Object Cabinets.

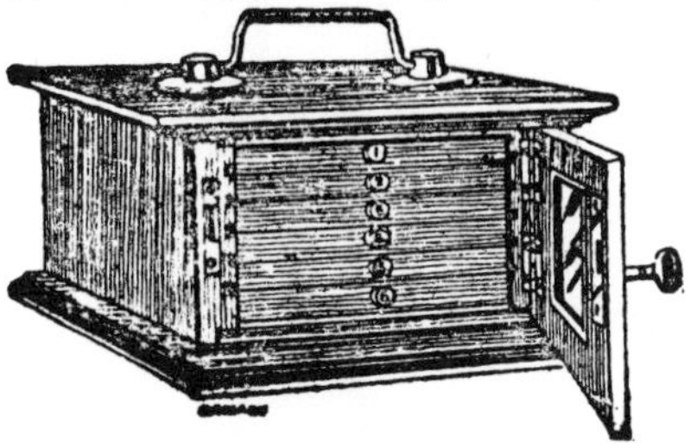

Larger sizes (prices in proportion) to order only. With glass panel door, lock and key, drawers lined velvet.

Drawers.	Height.	Width.	Depth.	Stained and polished.	Old English Oak.
6	5 in.	7½ in.	9 in.	**13/6**	**17/-**
8	7 ,,	7½ ,,	9 ,,	**15/-**	**20/-**
10*	6½ ,,	7½ ,,	9 ,,	**20/-**	**24/6**
12*	7½ ,,	8½ ,,	9 ,,	**26/6**	**32/6**
15*	9 ,,	10 ,,	9 ,,	**37/6**	**47/6**
20*	11½ ,,	11 ,,	9 ,,	**51/6**	**62/6**

*To run on grooves.

Packing Cases, 1/- each extra, returnable.

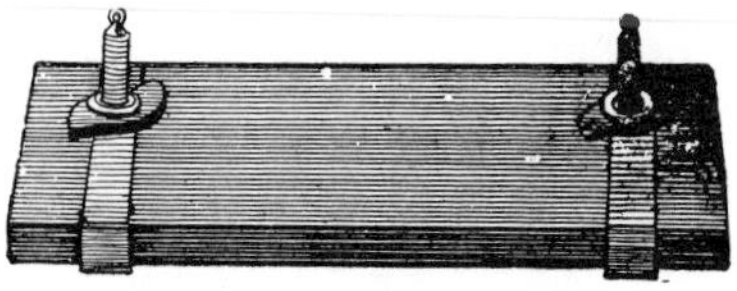

Hardwood Botanical Press.

Size, 16 by 10 in. between screws, ... **4/6**
Larger size, 20 by 12 in. ... ... **6/6** } Post 8d.

For Large Assortment Book Form Botanical Presses See "R" List.

Setting Houses.

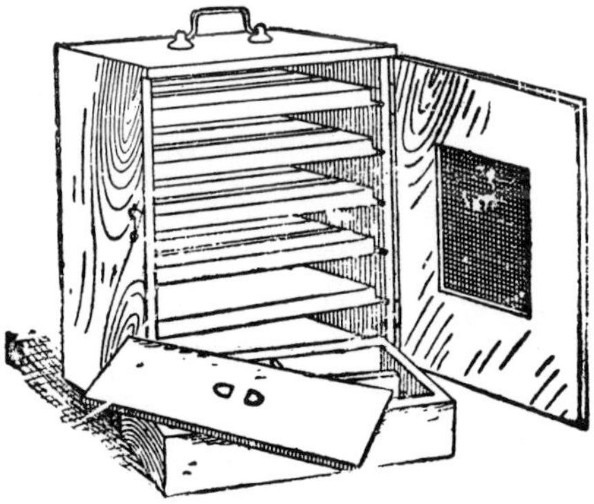

Plain deal drying houses, with 10 corked setting boards (various sizes), drawer for pins, perforated zinc door, brass handle at top, 12 by 9 by 5, **9/-** Post 8d.

Entomologist's Companion, containing every requisite for collecting and preserving, best articles, **66/6**

Insect Cabinet of best quality.

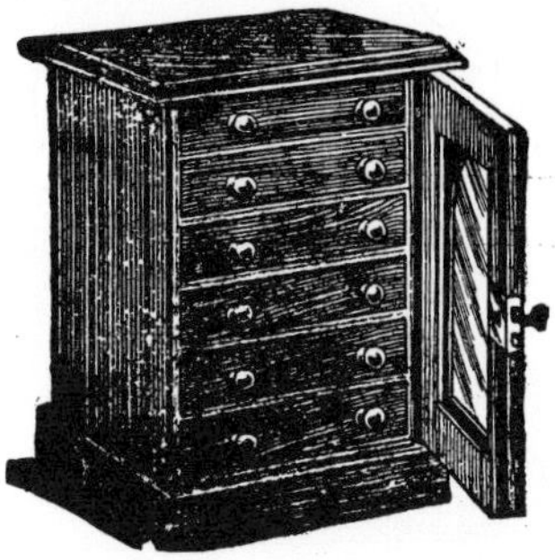

Always in Stock.

Corked, Glazed and Papered.

Drawers.	Height.	Width.	Depth	Polished Deal, Mahogany Glass Panel Door or Rolled Pillars	Polished Mahogany, Glass Panel Door or Rolled Pillars.
4	12in.	13 in.	9in.	**17/6**	**26/6**
6	16½in.	15in.	10in.	**22/-**	**31/6**
8	22in.	18in.	12in.	**37/6**	**54/-**
10	27½in.	19½in.	13in.	**48/-**	**67/6**

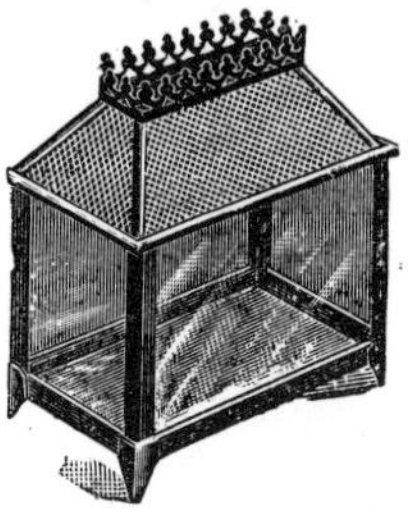

London Made.

Best Make and Finish.

10 in. long by 6 in. wide by 6½ in. high, **3/6**

12 by 7 by 7½ in. .. **6/-**

13 by 8 by 9 in. .. **8/6**

14 by 10 by 10 in. **10/-**

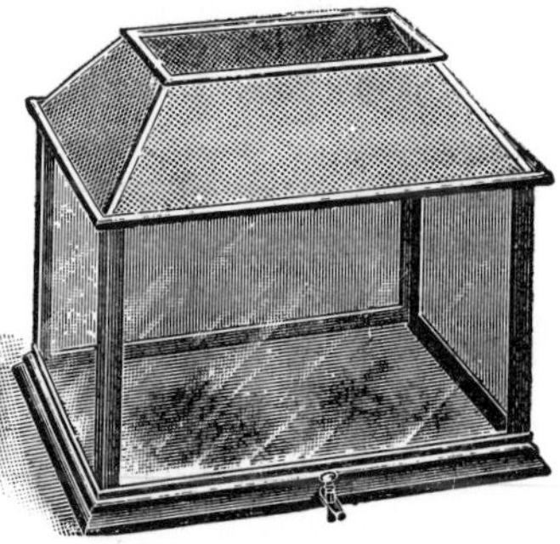

18 in.	.. 8 in.	.. 9 in., with Tap	..	**20/-**
18 ,,	.. 12 ,,	.. 12 ,, ,,	..	**25/-**
24 ,,	.. 12 ,,	.. 12 ,, ,,	..	**35/-**

Packing crate 1/- Returnable.

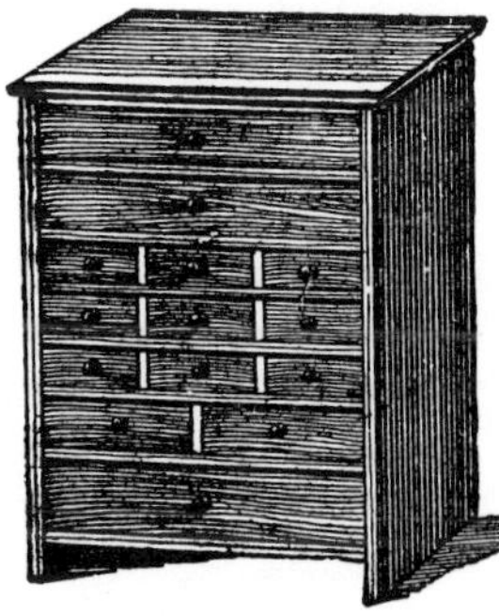

Chest of Drawers for Tools, Shells, Coins, etc.

Other sizes obtained to order.

No. R. 1. Chest of 10 drawers, yellow deal, brass knobs. Dimension: Height 10½ in., width 12⅝ in., depth 10⅝ in. **6/-**

No. R. 2. With 12 drawers. Dimensions: Height 13¼ in., width 11¾ in., depth 9 in. **9/-**

No. R. 3. Width 14 drawers. Dimensions: Height 15¼ in., width 11¾ in., depth 9 in. **10/-**

No. R. 4. Width 16 drawers. Dimensions: Height 17½ in., width 11¾ in., depth 9 in. **12/-**

Carriage forward.

TABLE FOUNTAINS.

A WONDERFUL PEEP INTO NATURE.

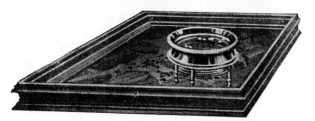

The Lubbock Formicarium,

Or the Nest of Amber-coloured Ants.

A marvellous living object lesson, which leaves a lasting impression on the minds of all observers. As a medium for teaching the wonders and changes of insect life, this Liliputian City stands unsurpassed.

Price of the Nest, with Queen, ...	**10/6**
In Polished Frame	**2/6** extra.
Tripod Magnifier	**1/9** extra.
Extra powerful Reading Glass, ...	**3/9**

Carriage and packing, 1/- extra outside London delivery radius.

Book on "Ants, Bees and Wasps," by Lord Avebury, price .. **5/-**
Postage 3d.

Special Double Exhibition Nest with 2 Queens. Price **42/-**

Silver-plated. All Metal.

Playing $\frac{1}{2}$ hour.

No. R. 1/850.

Price **30/-**

Silver-plated. All Metal.

Playing $\frac{1}{2}$-hour.

No. R. 2/850.

Price **42/-**

Automatic Patent Self-contained Fountains.

For use in Halls, Reception Rooms and Conservatories, and at Dinner and Supper Parties.

FOR WATER OR PERFUME.

Elegant Table Decoration,
Air Purifiers for Private Houses, Hotels, Sanotoriums and Hospitals.
Always ready for Use.
No Noise whilst in action.
No Working Expenses.
Independent of Waterpipes or Motor Power.

The Fountain, as illustration, is 17½ in. high, the base is 11 in. in diameter, and with one winding will play for one hour, and by means of a simple winding movement the fountain is again re-charged. One of the chief points is that the liquid is used for an indefinite period and there is no messing operation to perform. The finish is of a dull silver and is untarnishable, splash spots are removed with a sponge which leaves no trace whatever.

Fresh cut and artificial flowers can be used to advantage (shown in illustration) and when a flower holder is placed in position on top tray a unique effect is produced.

Price of actual Fountain, as illustration—

67/6

Plated Flower Sprayers for top
3/6 each.
Ditto, for base .. **5/6** each.
Plated Splash Dishes for use with top Flower Sprayer,
2/6 each.

Patent Self-contained and absolutely reliable, with no trouble whatever to operate. They are the rage of the Continent, and being so simple and not easily put out of order they are by far the most substantial novelties at present made. Many sizes are made but only one is stocked by us, it being the one adopted and recommended for general utility purposes.

Silver-plated Metal Tray. Cut Glass.

Playing 40 to 45 minutes.

No. R. 5/850. Price **60/-**

Hand Bags and Fitted Cases.

The "Fife" Square Hand Bag from 8/6

No. K. 6.

The "Fife."

Nut brown Hide, with slides and shoes, good lock.

12 in.	..	**8 6**
14 in.	..	**9/6**
16 in.	..	**10/6**
18 in.	..	**12 6**

No. K. 3. Nut brown cowhide, leather covered frame, nickel fittings.

12 in.	... **6/11**
14 in.	... **8/6**
16 in.	... **9/6**

No. K. 4. Brown hide, better quality, linen lined.

12 in.	... **8/6**
14 in.	... **10/6**
16 in.	... **12/6**

No. K. 4A. Ditto, lined leather.

2 in. .. **10/9**   14 in. .. **12/6**   16 in. .. **14/6**

Kit Bags

from

14/6

No. K 16. A most useful bag, made of brown cowhide, lined drill, good lock and clips.

4 in. **14/6**   16 in. **16/6**   18 in. **18/6**   20 in. **21/6**

No. K 17. Better quality hide, finish and fittings.

4 in. **16/6**   16 in. **18/9**   18 in. **21/-**   20 in. **23/6**

No. K 19. Superior quality hide and finish, hand-sewn, brass lock and clips, best drill lining.

16 in. **32/-**   18 in. **36/-**   20 in. **40/-**

Carriage free on Kit Bags 20/- and upwards.
Initials free on Bags 20/- and upwards.

Travelling Kit Bag.

No. K 21. Brown cowhide, lined drill, double handles and end straps.

20 in., **28/9**   22 in.. **32/-**   24 in., **35/-**
26 in., **37/6**

No. K 22. Superior quality London cowhide, as illustrated. Best London frame, brass S. N. lock, end clips and end straps, drill lined, hand-sewn throughout.   20 in. .. **55/-**   22 in. .. **62/-**
24 in. .. **67/6**   26 in. .. **72/6**

Gladstone Bags.

No. K 2. This is a well-known Bag. Made of brown cowhide, 2 straps all round, good lock, slides and shoes.

18 in., **18/-**   20 in., **20/-**   22 in., **22/-**   24 in., **24/-**   26 in., **26/-**

No. K 4. Better quality hide, 2 good locks and superior finish

20 in., **29/-**   22 in., **32/-**   24 in., **35/-**   26 in., **39/-**

Hide Suit Cases, from 25/-

No. K 4. A real smart Case. Made of brown case hide. Two good brass locks, drop back lid, and well finished.

20 in., **25/-**   22 in., **27/6**   24 in., **30/-**   26 in., **32/6**

No. K 6. Superior brown hide, London made, as above,

20 in., **32/6**   22 in., **36/6**   24 in., **42/6**   26 in., **45/6**

No. K 8. Best quality case hide, hand-sewn throughout; 2 good brass locks. Real good value.

20 in., **39/-**   22 in., **43/-**   24 in., **47/-**   26 in., **51/-**

Carriage paid. Initials free on all hide Suit Cases.

The Week-end Hide Case.

Turned edge, nickel exposed frame, expanding top. Very light and strong, lined leather cloth.

14	15	16	17	18	19	20	21	22 in.
23/-	**25/**	**26/6**	**28/6**	**30/-**	**32/6**	**34/-**	**35/-**	**37/6**

Leather Cushions from 7/6

To have a soft springy cushion, just where you want it, is what this cushion affords.

Splendid Value in Square Cushions.

Colours—Blue, Grey, Fawn, Brown, Green, etc.

Size 16 by 13 .. **7/6**

,, 20 by 20, without pocket .. **13/6**

Postage 6d.

No. K 053. **The "Louise" Fitted Case for Ladies.**

Morocco leather or Nut hide. 14 by 11½ by 7 Lined silk with 4 chased silver mounted bottles, silver hair brush and clothes brush, instrument board and folding mirror,

Price .. **85/-**

K 054. **Ladies' Dressing Case**

18 in., polished morocco case, lined watered silk, with 2 locks, fitted with 6 silver-mounted bottles, 2 full-size silver hair brushes, hat and cloth, shoelift, button-hook, blotter, mirror, instrument board, comb, etc. Price **£10**

Ladies' Fitted Blouse Case.

K 052. Size, 16 by 12½ by 5½ in. Green polished Morocco, lined water silk. Fitted with silver hair brush, hat and cloth brush, hand mirror, and 5 silver-mounted chased-top bottles, instrument board fitted with scissors, etc. Splendid value. **£5 17 6**

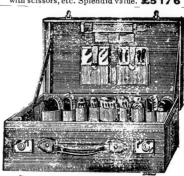

Gentleman's Fitted Suit Case £5 15

K 055. The "HATTON." Solid hide, 21 by 15 by 7½ in., lined leather throughout. Fitted with 5 silver-mounted bottles, 2 ebony hair brushes, cloth and hat mirror, strop, razors, etc.

Hide Attache Cases, from 7/6

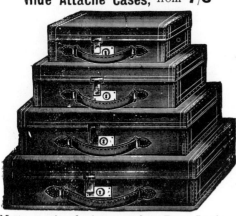

Most convenient for documents &c. Brown Leather, lined Leatherette.

No. K. 1.

10 x 7 x 2¾ 12 x 8 x 3 14 x 9 x 3½ 16 x 10 x 3½ 18 x 11¼ x 4 in.
7/6   9/6   12/6   15/6   16/9

No. K. 2. Better quality Case Hide. lined Leather.
12 in., **13/9** 14 in., **17/6** 16 in., **21/6** 18 in., **25/6**

No. K 3.

12 in., **17/6** 14 in., **20/-** 16 in., **22/6** 18 in., **27/6**

Flaxite Fibre Attache Cases.

10 by 7 by 3 12 by 8 by 3½ 14 by 9 by 4 16 by 10 by 4½ 18 by 11 by 5
3/6   3/11   4/6   4/6   6/11

Leather handle, nickel locks, leather hinge, light and waterproof. 16 in. and 18 in. have two locks.

Brown Fibre Suit Case.

No. K. 31½. 8 Fibre corners, steel frame, leather handle, 2 nickel locks, lined green twill. Exceptionally light and quite strong.

Size 16 by 13 by 5				**9/6**
,, 18 ,, 13½ ,, 5½				**10/9**
,, 20 ,, 14 ,, 6				**12/-**
,, 22 ,, 14½ ,, 6½				**13/6**
,, 24 ,, 15 ,, 7				**14/6**
,, 26 ,, 15½ ,, 8				**15/6**

Send for our Complete List of Bags and Trunks.
The FINEST SELECTION in LONDON

Gamage's "Underbed" Wardrobe Trunk.

USEFUL XMAS PRESENT

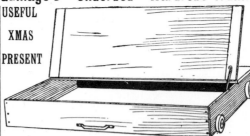

Made on a strong American hard-wood foundation, stained light oak, handles each end and front, four wooden wheels to enable one to pull the trunk out easily from under the bed. Size 47 by 23 by 9½ in. Price **23/9** Carriage forward.

No K. 52.

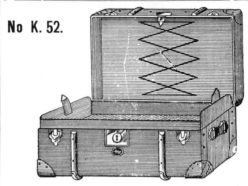

"Flaxite" Fibre Foundation, covered Green Canvas, on steel frame, hard wood battens all round, eight leather capped corners, lever lock, clips, lined holland with tray. (36 in. has four battens and two locks.)

27 in.	30 in.	33 in.	36 in.	39 in.
45/-	**49/6**	**55/-**	**59/6**	**65/-**

The "Universal" Ladies' Hat Case.

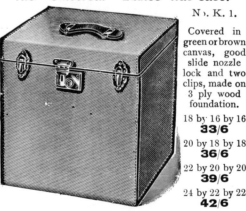

No. K. 1.
Covered in green or brown canvas, good slide nozzle lock and two clips, made on 3 ply wood foundation.

18 by 16 by 16 **33/6**

20 by 18 by 18 **36/6**

22 by 20 by 20 **39/6**

24 by 22 by 22 **42/6**

The Gamage Cane Compartment Case.

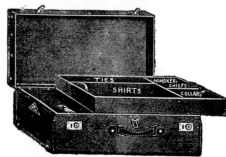

TIES SHIRTS HANDKER-CHIEFS COLLARS

Best quality cane and fittings, useful divided tray, two locks and handle.

26 in., **58/6** 28 in., **62/6** 30 in., **65/-**

Vacuum Flasks.

Gamage's 'Record' Flask.

Pint size, aluminium top and cup, black body.

Price	..	..	**1/11½**
Refills	..	..	**1/6**
Quart size	..	..	**8/6**
Refills	..	..	**5/-**

No. 2. SPLENDID VALUE
Pint size, all nickel covered, good brown cowhide.

GAMAGE'S price .. **6/1**
Actually worth 21/-
Refills **4/-**

The "Henley" Wicker-covered Vacuum Flask.

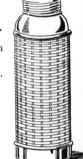

Made on a strong foundation with polished cup and shoulders.

An Ideal Flask for the picnic basket.

Pint size	..	**3/6**
Refills	..	**2/-**
Extra Corks,	**1**d. each.	

Gamage's Thermos Flasks.

Pint size	..	..	**6/6 13/6 21/-**
Quart ,,	..	..	**10/6 31/6**

Flask Cases.

Pint size .. **6/6**

To make the above present more complete, BUY CASE to put the Flask in.

Made of good Cowhide, well finished.

Quart size .. **8/6**

Postage on Cases, 4d. extra if purchased separate.

No. K. 1030c.

Solid Hide Case, lined fawn velvet, with sling strap all round; best finish throughout, including aluminium Sandwich Box.

For Pint size, **13/6**

PINT FLASK, from **1/11½** extra.

Carriage and packing on all Flasks per rail, 9d.

Ladies' Wrist Bags.

Gamages Best Quality School Satchels.

Boys' or Girls' School Bags.

13 in. long.
With outside pockets.
Tweeds, **1/3 1/9**
Tan Waterproof **2 9**
Brown Leather **4/6**
Brown Hide **6/6**
Without pocket.
Tan Canvas **2/6**
Brown Hide **5/6**
Post 3d.

Useful Collar Bags

Will hold from 1 to 1½ doz. collars. Also suitable for ties, handkerchiefs, cuffs, or Lady's Work Bag The most useful article yet introduced.
In Persian Leather—
2/11 3/6 4/6
brown Levant Roans **5/6** In Pigskin, **7/6**
Velvet or Willow Calf **10/-** Post 3d.

6/6

o. **K 22066.** Best morocco, trapeze shape bag, rivetted nickel frame, outside pocket.
8 in. **6/6** 8¾ in. **7/6** 9½ in. **8/6**

6/6

o. **K. 22065.** New flapover envelope bag morocco leather, pocket inside.
8 in. **6/6** 8¾ in. **7/6** 9½ in. **8/6**

8/6

No. K. 21319. New design Mote Cord Handle Bag, gilt frame, with centre division.
6¼ in., **8/6** 7¼ in., **9/6**

6/6

No. K. 21755. The popular shape. Morocco leather, fitted purse, mirror and bottle.
8 in., **6/6** 8¾ in., **7/6** 9½ in., **9/6**

9/6

No. K. 21927. Smart Antelope Leather long shape Bag. Good gilt frame, fitted and leather lining.
8 in., **9/6** 8¾ in., **10/6** 9½ in., **11/6**

Send for our complete Bag and Trunk List.

MUSIC CASES.

Music Cases.

Assorted patterns, **1/11 2/11 3/3 3 6**
4/9 4/11 6/6 6/11 8/6
Music Folios, Flat—
8d. 1/- 1/6 1/10½ 2/10½ 4/6

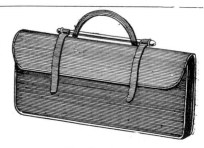

Music Case.

With patent bar handle.
Good solid brown Hide; to take song music.
Price **7/6** Postage 3d.

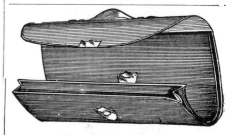

The Duplex Case.

To take song or score music, in brown Hide **5/11**
In Best Grain Cowhide, with 2 locks .. **9/6**
In Finest Smooth Case Hide **11/6**
In Morocco .. **7/6 10/6 12/6 16/6**
Postage 3d.

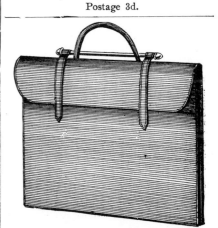

Best Quality Music Cases.

With Patent bar handle. Brown Leather, **5/11**
Grain Bag Hide, **9/6** Smooth Case Hide, **11/6**
Postage 3d.

Useful Xmas and New Year Gifts.

No. F. S 3283 T.

Inexpensive Clock.

Reliable Timekeeper. Gilt Curb
Mount. 3⅜ in. diameter.

Price **3/11**

No. F. 9949.
Splendid Value

Eight-day Timepiece.
Thoroughly reliable.
Nickel finished case 2 in. dial.
Price .. **5/-**

No. F. 3286 T. Superior finish.

Heavy Brass Curb Clock.
Thirty-hour movement.
Good Timekeeper. 4 in. diameter.
Price .. **6 6**

No. F. 600.

**Travelling or Carriage
Clock.**

French movement. Good timekeeper.
Complete in strong Leatherette case.
Price .. **15/6**

Superior quality. Lever movement.
Price .. **21/-**

No. F. 6/4108 T.

A Dainty Clock,

Polished gilt finish. Tortoise-shell coloured
front. Thirty-hour movement.
Good timekeeper. 5 in. high.
Price .. **10/9**

No. F. 300.

**The
"Ever
Ready"
Chronos
Clock.**

These Clocks are wound up, set and regulated the same
as any ordinary Timepiece, and can be relied upon to
keep time accurately. Highly polished Nickel-plate or
Gilt finish. Height about 4¾ in. Price **25/-**

Other styles .. **30/-** and **35/-**

No. F. 6/4164.

Pretty Eight-day Clock.

Polished gilt finish. Onyx colour front. Good
Timekeeper. 5 in. high. Price **14/6**

No. F. 1149. Travelling Clock,
Oval glasses, Superior movement, Leather Case.
Price .. **32/6**

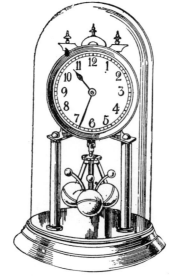

**The Clock that goes for 400 days
with one winding.**
Polished brass base and mounts.
Flat Pendulum, 3½ in. bold dial.
Height complete with glass shade, 11 in. **18/6**
Ball Pendulum as illustration, **21/-**

No. F. 1150. Travelling Clock.
New style. French movement. Polished gilt.
Complete in Leather Case. Price **21/9**
Lever movement, **27/6**

CHRISTMAS AND NEW YEAR PRESENTS.

If in doubt. Give a Clock. They are always acceptable.

EXCEPTIONAL VALUE.
30-Hour Timepiece.
k Colour Case with fancy border.
5¼ in. high.
Price ... **3/6**
LSO IN OTHER SHAPES.

The Finest Value Clock on the Market.
Eight-Day
French movement.
Timed and examined.
3½ in. Enamelled Dial.
English-made Case.
Mahogany or Oak.
Inlaid neat design.
Height 8¼ in. in 3 shapes.
Price **15/9**

No. F. 600.
Travelling Clock.
French Movement.
Leatherette Case.
Price **15/6**

Lever Movement,
Price **21/-**

Leather Case,
2/- extra.

No. F. B 9552/4.
A Reliable Clock at a Low price.
30-Hour movement.
Neat Oak Colour Case with Fancy Border.
8 in. high. Price **7/11**
ALSO IN OTHER SHAPES.

No. F. 66135.
Bold Marble Clock.
ronze Figures, Columns and Mounts.
Gilt Decoration.
Eight-day Lever Movement.
Striking hours and half-hours on rich toned cathedral gong.
Height 16½ in Width 16½ in.
Price **37/6**

LUMINOUS DIAL Repeater Alarm Clock.
Time can be seen quite plainly in the dark. Splendid quality movement. 4½ in. dial Nickel finish Case.
Price .. **6/3**
Without Luminous Dial. Price **5/6**

No. F. 43. SPLENDID VALUE.
arble Clock. Six Bronze Columns.
t Relief. Accurate 8-day Movement.
rikes Hours and Half-hours on Cathedral
ng. Height 13¼ in. Width 16¼ in.
Price **28/9**

F. 33. Style and quality as above,
ut fitted with four Bronze Columns.
ight 12 in. Width 13 in. .. **26/9**
r without visible escapement .. **25/-**

Travelling Clock with Radium Figures and Hands.
Can be seen in the dark. Size 4¼ by 4¼ in.
30-hour reliable movement.
Straight grain leather case. Price **37/6**
Eight-Day movement. Price **52/6**
Crushed Morocco Case. 36-hour movement. Price **42/-**
Eight-Day movement. Price **57/6**

No. F. 731.
Reliable EIGHT DAY CLOCK.
Strikes on rich toned Gong.
Mahogany Inlaid Case. Height 12 in., width 6⅝ in.
Price **38/9**

"Enigma" Watch.
The most reliable inexpensive watch in the market.
Neat in appearance.
Oxydised Steel or Nickel Case.   Price **5/-**

"Excalibar" Lever.
Neat in appearance.   Non-magnetic.
Perfectly regulated.
Oxydised Steel or Nickel Case.   Price **7/6**

Gamage's "Holborn" Lever Watch.
Hundreds sold and giving entire satisfaction.
Smart appearance.   Perfectly regulated.
Oxydised Steel, **10/-**   Sterling Silver, **18/6**

Gamage's English Lever Watch
A triumph of British Wormanship.
Non-magnetic movement.   Accurately adjusted.
Oxydised steel case, **22/6**   Sterling silver, **27/6**
Rolled Gold (10-year case) **35/-**
9-ct. solid gold **£5 0 0**

Radium Dial.   Visible in the dark.
Lever movement.   Timed to perfection.
Nickel Case, **14/6**   Oxydised Steel, **15/6**

The "Uno" 8-day Pocket Watch
15 jewel. Lever movement. Breguet Hairspring.
Timed and adjusted.   Sterling Silver, **47/6**
10-year Gold Filled Case, **50/-**   20-year, **65/-**
9-ct. Gold Dome Case, **£6 6**   18-ct. **£13 13**

Sportsman's Chronograph Watch.
Absolutely reliable.   Highest grade movement.
Oxydised steel or nickel case, **39/6**
Sterling silver, **49/6**   18-ct. gold, **£12 15**

The "Levee" Dress Watch.
As worn at Court functions.
Lever movement.   Timed and examined.
Sterling silver **£2 0 0**
9-ct. gold, **£5 0 0**   18-ct. gold, **£7 10 0**
A similar style of watch in oxydized steel, **9/6**

Gent's Gold Watch.
High-grade lever movement. Timed & examined.
9-ct. gold, **67/6** 15-ct. **£5 5** 18-ct. **£6 15**
Well-built cases for serviceable wear.

A Large Selection of Ladies' and Gent's Watches in Stock.   **We can give you satisfaction.**

Reliable Watches for Xmas and New Year's Gifts.
GUARANTEED TIMEKEEPERS.

Inexpensive Wrist Watches, for every-day use.

SOUND CONSTRUCTION.   GOOD TIME-KEEPERS.   STRONG LEATHER STRAPS IN A VARIETY OF COLOURS.
Neat in appearance

Black Oxydized Steel	..	..	..	..	..	..	5/-	6/-	7/6	10/6	12/6	18/6	21/-
Sterling Silver cases	..	..	..	..	..	..	8/9	10/6	12/6	15/6	17/6	25/-	32/6
9-ct. Gold Cases..	..	..	..	..	..	..		25/-	30/-	38/6	42/-	49/6	66/3

NEW PATTERN.
Expanding Bracelet Watch

Reliable Time-keeper.

9-ct. gold	..	..	**£3 0 0**
Lever movement	..		3 15 0

WEST END PATTERN.
Gold Bracelet Watch.

Lever movement.

9-ct. gold	..	..	**£3 17 6**
15-ct. gold Watch ⎫ 9-ct. Bracelet ⎭			**4 10 0**
18-ct. gold Watch ⎫ 9-ct. Bracelet ⎭			**5 5 0**

THE SMART STYLE.
Gold Bracelet Watch.

Lever movement.

Accurate time-keepers.

9-ct. gold .. **£4 19 6**

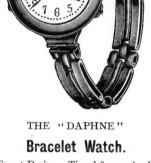

THE "DAPHNE"
Bracelet Watch.

Smart Design.   Timed & examined.
Lever movement.

9-ct. gold	..	..	**£4 4 0**
18-ct. gold Watch ⎫ 9-ct. Bracelet ⎭			**5 15 0**

Wrist Watch.

Leather straps.   High-grade movement.

Sterling silver	..	..	**17,6**
Lever Movement	..	..	**25/-**

The New Tonneau-shaped Wrist Watch.

VERY SMART.   GOOD QUALITY MOVEMENT.
Various Coloured Leather Straps.

Sterling Silver	..	..	**£0 15 0**
Sterling Silver, best lever	..		**1 12 6**
9-ct. gold ..	..	..	**3 10 0**
18-ct. gold ..	..	..	**5 12 6**

Fashionable Wrist Watch.

Reliable Time-keepers.   Leather straps.

9-ct. gold	..	..	**25/-**
Superior quality	..	..	**30/-**
Lever movement	..	**38/6** & **49/6**
18-ct. gold lever movement	**70/-** & **95/-**

Y

Jewellery Department.

No. F. 127. 9 ct. Gold Necklet.
Amethyst and Pearl Pendant.
Price **52/6**

No. F. 7. 9 ct. Gold. Very fine Amethyst Necklace. Filigree Setting.
Price **63/-**

No. F. 761.
9 ct. Gold Necklet.
Amethyst and Pearl Pendant
Price **63/-**

9-ct. Gold Neck Chains for Pendants. Various patterns, 5/6, 7/6, 10/6, 12/6, 15/6, 20/-

No. F. 3328.

Gold Pendant.

Choice Design.

Set Garnet and

Pearl.

Price .. **21/-**

No. F 122.
9 ct. Gold Bangle.
Price ... **23/6**

No. F. 3374.

Handsome Gold
Pendant. Set Amethyst,
Peridots and Pearls.

Price .. **45/-**

No. F. 121a. 9 ct. Gold
Bangle. Engraved,
29/6 Plain, **28/6**

No. F. 3347.

Gold Pendant.

Set Peridots and
Pearls.

Price .. **35/6**

No. F. 227.
9 ct. Gold Bangle.
Price ... **19/6**

No. F. 3369

Gold Pendant

Set Amethyst,

Peridots and

Pearls.

Price .. **19/6**

No. F. 151.
Girls' Bracelet.
9 ct. Gold. Price .. **12/9**

No. F. 156.
Child's Bracelet.
9 ct. Gold. Price .. **7/9**

9 ct. Gold **Bracelets.**
Open Curbe, 21/- 24/6 27/6 30/- 45/-
Close Curbs, 30/- 35/- 39 6 50/-

15 ct. Gold .. .. .. from **50/-**
18 ct. Gold .. .. .. ,, **63/-**

No. F. 146. VERY FINE VALUE. 9 ct. Gold **Bracelet.** Price **21/-**

No. F. 121. NEW PATTERN. 9 ct. Gold **Bracelet.** Price **32/6**

No. F. 142P HEAVY MAKE. 9 ct Gold **Bracelet.** Price **55/-**

A choice selection of Fancy Pattern Bracelets .. .. **from 23/6 each.**

JEWELLERY DEPT. BROOCHES AND RINGS.
We illustrate a few Specimens of our Immense Stock.

No. F. 82
9-ct. Gold "Merry Thought" Brooch. **4/3**

No. F. 1360½.
9 ct. Gold Brooch. Smart design.
Price **4,6**

No. F. 22.
9-ct. Gold "Merry Thought" and Shamrock Brooch.
Price **3/6**

No. F. 39.
9-ct. Gold "Horseshoe" and Fancy Brooch.
Price **4/6**

No. F. 27.
9-ct. Gold "Shamrock" Brooch.
Price **5/-**

No. F. 423.
9-ct. Gold and Amethyst Brooch.
Price **5/6**

No. F. 152.
9-ct. Gold Brooch.
"Faith, Hope and Charity."
Price .. **7/6**

No. F. 171.
9-ct. Gold Brooch.
Price **8/3**

No. F. 1471.
-ct. Gold and Amethyst Brooch **8/6**

No. F. 583.
9-ct. Gold and Amethyst Brooch.
Price .. **10/6**

No. F. 129.
9-ct. Gold Brooch,
Peridot and Pearl, or Turquoise and Pearl.
Price .. **10/6**

No. F. 16480.
9-ct. Gold and Cape Rubies.
Price .. **11/6**

No. F. 193.
9-ct. Brooch.
Turquoise and Pearl.
Price **17/6**

No. F. 106w.
9-ct. Gold Brooch.
Amethyst and Pearl .. **15/6**

No. F. 351.
9-ct. Gold Garnet and Pearl Brooch. **14 9**

No. F. 110A.
9-ct. Gold Brooch.
Peridot and Pearl or Amethyst and Pearl.
Price **21/-**

No. F. 648.
9-ct. Gold and Garnet Brooch. Price **17/6**

No. F. 66.
18-ct. Gold
Coloured Stones and Diamonds.
15/6

No. F. C577.
18-ct. Gold.
Diamonds.
23/6

No. F. 123w.
9-ct. Gold Motor Veil or Lace Pin.
Aquamarine and Pearls or Amethyst and Pearls.
Price **23/6**

No. F. C579.
28-ct. Gold.
Pearl and Coloured Stones.
32/6

No. F. 196.
18-ct. Gold.
Three Brilliants and two Roses.
Price .. **39/6**

No. F. 199.
18-ct. Gold.
Single Stone .. **70/-**
Larger Stone, **95/-** and upwards.

No. F. 170.
18-ct. Gold.
Three Brilliants, **47/6**
Larger size stones,
63/- 75/- 90/- 105/-

No. F. 188.
18-ct. Gold Marquise.
Fine Brilliants, **£7 7 0**

No. F. 145.
18-ct. Gold.
Five Brilliants.
Set Platinum.
Price .. **84/-**

No. F. 121.
18-ct. Gold.
Five Brilliants .. **95/-**
Larger size stones,
£5 5 0 to **£25**

No. F. 116.
18-ct. Gold.
Three Brilliants and two Roses .. **47/6**
Larger stones, **63/- & 75/-**

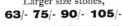

No. F. 158.
18-ct. Gold.
Three Brilliants.
Set Platinum.
Price .. **90/-**

No. F. 177.
18-ct. Gold.
Eleven Brilliants.
Price .. **£20**

No. F. 181.
18-ct. Gold.
Five Brilliants.
Set Platinum.
Price .. **£8 10 0**

No. F. 125.
18-ct. Gold.
Twelve Brilliants.
Set Platinum.
Price .. **£9 10 0**

RING SIZE CARD SENT ON REQUEST.

Y

"Platinon" Set French Paste Jewellery. Effective. Untarnishabl

Inexpensive, Smart Designs. The advantage of the New "Platinon" Metal enables the Paste to be set so that they have every appearance of

Fine Platinum Diamond Work.

No. F. 713088. **NEW DESIGN.**
"Platinon" and Parisian Diamond Brooch
Price **7/6**

No. F. 713530.
"Platinon" and Parisian Diamond Broo
Price **3/9**

No. F. 19752.
"Platinon" and Parisian Diamonds.
Smart Drop Pendant Brooch.
Price .. **8/6**

No. F. 713523. "Platinon" and Parisian Diamonds.
MOTOR VEIL BROOCH.
Price **6/6**

No. F. 10444 "Platinon" and Parisian Diamonds.
MOTOR VEIL BROOCH.
Price **5/6**

No. F. 7133584 **VELVET NECK BAND.**
With "Platinon" and Parisian Diamond Mounts.
Price **15/-**

No. F. 10772.
"Platinon" and Parisian Diamond
NECKLET.
Price **8/6**

No. F. 713357. **VELVET NECK BAND.**
With "Platinon" and Parisian Diamond Mounts.
Price **12/6**

No. F. 712310.
"Platinon" and Parisian Diamond Bangle.
Price **11/6**

"Platinon" and Parisian Diamond Ear-rings.
Very Fashionable.

No F. 65936.	No. F. 6063.	No. F. 5296.
5/6	**9/6**	**8/6**
Per pair.	Per pair.	Per pair.

No. F. 13229.
"Platinon" and Parisian Diamond Bangle.
Price **12/6**

No. F. 713089.
SMART BROOCH.
"Platinon" and Parisian Diamonds.
Price **6/9**

No. F. 713091.
DAINTY BROOCH.
"Platinon" and Parisian Diamonds.
Price **6/9**

No. F. 78821.
"Platinon" and Parisian
Diamond Brooch, **5/6**

No. F. 713520.
Motor Veil Brooch.
"Platinon" and Parisian
Diamonds .. **5/9**

SILVER DEPARTMENT. Toilet Requisites.

No. F. 1140½. Silver-mounted **Hair Brush**.
Price **8/3**
Hand Mirror to match **12/6**
Cloth Brush ,, ... **5/3**
Hat ,, ,, ... **4/11**
Comb ,, ... **2/-**

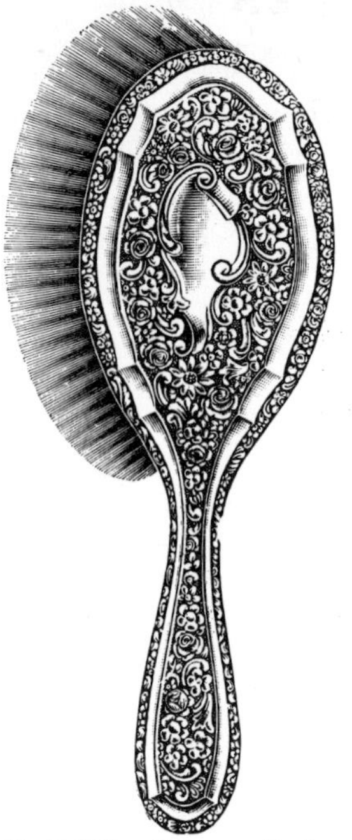

No. F. 1416. Quite new Design.
Silver-mounted **Hair Brush**.
Price ... **7/11**
Hand Mirror to match, **14/9**
Cloth Brush ... **6/5**
Hat ,, ... **6/3**
Com , **2/6**

No. F. 1266. Silver-mounted **Hair Brush.**
Length ⅛ in. Price **10/6**
Hand Mirror to match **14/6**
Cloth Brush ,, **6/6**
Hat ,, ,, **6/3**
Comb **3/6**

No. F. 1544. Smart Design.
Silver-mounted **Hand Brush.**
Price ... **14/6**
Mirror to match, **24/6**
Hat or Cloth Brush, **7/9** Comb **4/6**

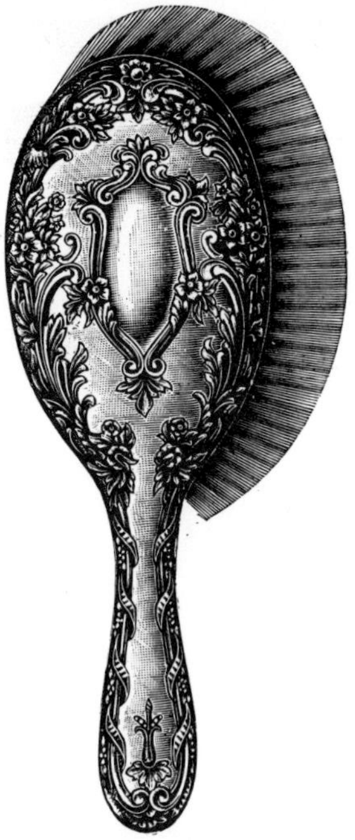

No. F. 1334. Silver-mounted **Hair Brush.** Price **13/6**
Hand Mirror to match **23/6**
Cloth Brush ,, ... **7/3**
Hat ,, ,, ... **6/9**
Comb ,, ... **3/9**

No. F. 707

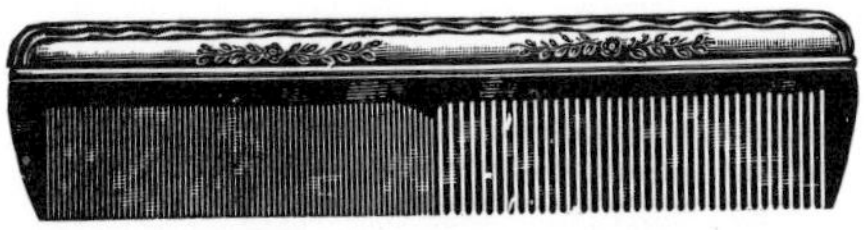

REGISTERED DESIGN

Silver-mounted Toilet Set. English Hall-marked.

Hair Brush, $9\frac{3}{4}$ by 3-1/16 in. **17/9**
Mirror, $10\frac{1}{2}$ by $7\frac{7}{8}$ in. **32/9**
Hat or Cloth Brush, 7 by $1\frac{3}{4}$ in. **10/6**
Comb, $7\frac{3}{4}$ by 2 in. **7/3**
Puff Jar, Hobnail Glass, 3 by $2\frac{3}{4}$ in. **14/6**
Hair Tidy, Hobnail Glass, 3 by $2\frac{3}{4}$ in. **14/3**
Button Hook, Length, $9\frac{3}{4}$ in. **5/9**
Shoe Lift, Length, $9\frac{7}{8}$ in. **6/3**
Curling Tongs, to match, **12/6**
ove Stretchers, to match, **14/9**

Useful Articles for Xmas and New Year Gifts.
SILVER GOODS. ENGLISH MANUFACTURE.

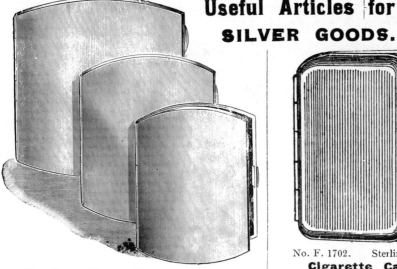

Sterling Silver Cigarette Case.
Single row. Very neat flat case.
No. F. 1889. Size 3⅜ by 2½ in. Price **21/-**
„ F. 1890. „ 3⅝ „ 3¼ in. „ **25/-**
„ F. 1891. „ 3¾ „ 3½ in. „ **30/-**

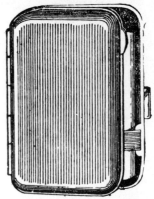

No. F. 1702. Sterling Silver
Cigarette Case.
Size 3⅜ by 2½ in. Price **13/6**
Or richly engraved with plain tablet
for initials. Price **15/6**

Sterling Silver Cigarette Case.
Single row. Suitable for evening dress.
No. F. 830½. Size 3¼ by 2¼ in. Price **15**
„ F. 830. „ 3¼ „ 2½ in. „ **17**
F. 829. „ 3¼ „ 3¼ in. „ **21**

⅔ SIZE
No. F. 9485.
Sterling Silver Tobacco Box, 13/9

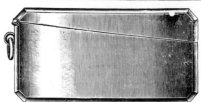

Gent's Sterling Silver Card Case.
Improved shape. No sharp corners.
No. F. 1043. Plain. Price **11/6**
„ F. 1043. Engraved. „ **12/9**

⅔ SIZE
No. F. 10092½. Sterling Silver Tobacco Box.
Richly Engraved Design, **17/9**

No. F. 10909. ⅔rds size.
Smoker's Lamp. Sterling Silver. Price **7/6**

No. F. 3605.
Silver Mounted Cigar Cutter.
Plain, **5/11** Engraved, **6/6**
Solid Gold Mounted.
Plain, **18/9** Engraved, **20/-**

No. F. D5. **Sovereign Purse.**
Sterling Silver, Plain **12/6** Engraved, **13/6**
9 ct. Gold, Plain **75/-** Engine Turned, **77/**
Engraved .. **80/-**

No. F. 2755 Sterling Silver **Toothpick.**
Plain, **10½**d. Engraved, **1/3**
9 ct. Gold „ **5/3** „ **5/9**
15 ct. „ **10/6** „ **11/6**

No. F. 2360.
Silver Cigarette Box, lined cedar wood.
To hold about 25 50 75 100
21/- 28/6 42/ 50/-

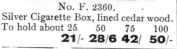

No. F. 2733. Sterling Silver **Toothpick**
Plain, **1/-** Engraved, **1/4½**
Gold—Plain, **6/6** Engraved, **7/6**
Post free.

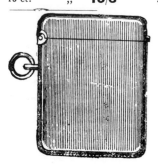

No. F. 215.
Actual Size.
Sterling Silver
Match Box.
Hall Marked,
5/6
Other sizes—
**3/6 4/6
6/6 7/6**
Engraved
5/6 to 10/6

No. F. 3705.
The Most Perfect **Cigar Piercer** on the Market.
Sterling Silver .. **5/11**
9 ct. Gold, **22/9** 15 ct. Gold, **42/-** 18 ct. Gold, **57/6**

Silver
Sovereign
Purse.

Plain, as
illustration
4/6
Also at
5/6 & 6/6

Engraved
Sovereign
Purses,
5/6, 6/6
and **7/6**

Silver Department.

No. F. 255.
Sterling Silver-mounted **Inkstand**
Length of Base, 5¾ in.   Price **17/6**

No. F. 298/59.
Sterling Silver Bags
As illustration.
Prices : **16/9 21/- 25/- 27 6 35/- 42/ 47/6 55/- and 63/-**
according to size.

Sterling Silver Eau-de-Cologne Stands.
No. F. 3206.
Height 2⅝ in. .. **7/9**
No. F. 3207.
Height 3 in. .. **10/-**
No. F. 3208.
Height 3⅜ in. .. **13 6**

No. F. 1831.
Silver Mounted Clock.
Price **19/6**

No. F. 9445.
Embroidery Scissors.
Sterling Silver Handles, Polished Steel Blades.
Price .. **5/9**

No. F. 10438.
Silver Mounted **Shell Pin Tray.**
Price .. **3/9**
Or No. 11214½.
As above, mounted with Miniature Silver Kangaroo.
Price .. **4/9**

No. 9366.
Cutting Out Scissors.
To Match.
Price **7/6**

FULL SIZE
No. F. 101.
Silver Vanity Case.   Price .. **4/9**

No. 8924.
Silver Mounted **Folding Glove Hook**
Price **1/4½**

No. F. 15291.
Cut Crystal Glass **Smelling Salts Bottle.**
Sterling Silver Mounts.   Price **4/9**

Crown Lavender Salts.
Sterling Silver Stand.
No. F. 3205.   Price .. **6/9**
No. F. 3204.   ,, .. **10/6**

No. F. 15289.
Smelling Salts.
Cut Crystal Glass.
Sterling Silver Mount.
Price **3/11**

No. F. 15297.
Perfume Spray.
Crystal Hob Nail Glass.
Sterling Silver Mounts.
Size 4½ in. by 2½ in.
Price .. **4/9**

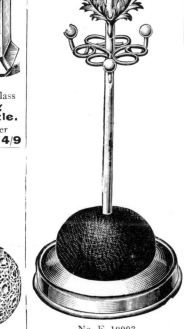

No. F. 10093.
Silver Mounted Hat Pin and Ring Stand.
Price .. **7/9**

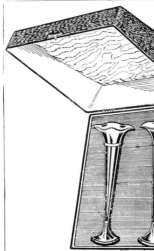

Two Sterling Silver Vases.
Height 7½ in.   Complete in Case .. **2/-**

2/3 SIZE.
No. 11556.
Silver Mounted Hat Pin and Ring Stand.
Real Enamel Top.
Price .. **4/9**

No. F. 10327½.
Sterling Silver Mounted Belt Buckle.
Price **5/6**

Silver and Gold Pencils and Fruit Knives.

No. F. 2555. The New Patented Pointer Pencil.
With space for Reserve Leads.

Pointer at end. Business size.

Sterling Silver, **8/-**   Solid Gold, **42/-**

No. F. 2565. As above, without reserve.
Gent's size.

Sterling Silver ..	**5/-**	Solid Gold .. **24/-**
Do., with Shackle	**5/9**	Do., with Shackle **30/-**

No. F. 2575. As above, Lady's Size, without reserve.

Sterling Silver ..	**3/9**	Solid Gold .. **18/-**
Do., with Shackle	**4/6**	Do., with Shackle **24/-**

No. F. 1205.

Sterling Silver **Flat Pencil,**	Plain	..	**1/-**
,, ,, ,, ,,	Engraved	..	**1/4½**
Solid Gold ,, ,,	Plain	..	**9/9**
,, ,, , ,,	Engraved	..	**10/6**

No. F. 1123.

Sterling Silver **Flat Cedar,**	Plain	..	**1/4½**
,, ,, ,, ,,	Engraved	..	**1/11½**
Solid Gold ,, ,.	Plain	..	**13/9**
,, ,, ,, ,,	Engraved	..	**14/9**

No. F. 1111.

Sterling Silver **Fluted Cedar** ..	..	**2/4½**
Solid Gold ,,	..	**19/6**

No. F. 623.

Sterling Silver **Pencil,**	Plain	..	**2/4½**
,, ,, ,,	Engraved	..	**2/8½**
Solid Gold ,,	Plain	..	**8/3**
,, ,, ,,	Engraved	..	**9/3**

No. F. 1705. Sterling Silver Round **Cedar Pencil.**

	2¼	2½	2¾	3 in.
Plain	**2/6**	**2/10½**	**3/2**	**3/6**
Engraved ..	**3/3**	**3/6**	**3/10**	**4/3**
Solid Gold, Plain ..	**16/6**	**18/6**	**20/-**	**22/6**
,, ,, Engraved	**17/9**	**20/-**	**22/6**	**24/6**

Post free.

No. F. 1315. Sterling Silver Hexagon **Slide Cedar Pencil**

	2½	3	3½ in.
Plain ..	**3/6**	**3/11**	**4/3**
Engraved ..	**4/3**	**5/-**	**5/9**

No. F. 3885. **Registered Nib Ejecting Pen Holder.**

Sterling Silver.

Plain, 6 in. ..	**3/9**
Chased, ,, ..	**4/6**
Plain, 7 in. ..	**5/-**
Chased, ,, ..	**5/9**

⅔ RDS. OF ACTUAL SIZE.

Solid Gold.

Plain, 6 in. ..	**25/-**
,, 7 in. ..	**28/6**

No. F. 167. Pocket Fruit Knife.
Sterling Silver Blade, Pearl Handle.
Price **1/6**   Larger size **2/-**

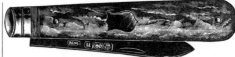

No. F. 104. Pocket Fruit Knife.
Sterling Silver Blade, Pearl Handle.
Price .. **2 6**

No. F. 141. Pocket Fruit Knife.
Sterling Silver Blade, Pearl Handle.   Price **3/-**
Also in other styles, better quality.   Price **3/6 4/6**

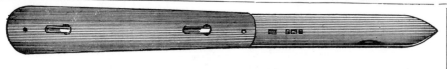

No. F 1012   Combination Fruit Knife and Fork.
Sterling Silver Blade and Fork, Pearl Handle. Very neat and compact. Price **6/-**

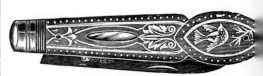

No. F. 225.   Pocket Fruit Knife.
Sterling Silver Blade, Carved Pearl Handle.
Price .. **5/6**

Fancy Combs, etc. Choice Designs.

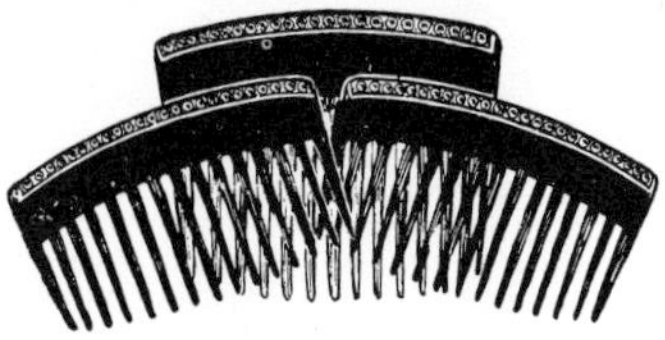

›. F. 23. Shell colour **Combs,** mounted best Paste Stones, **8/9** Real Horn Combs, **11/3**

Per set of three.

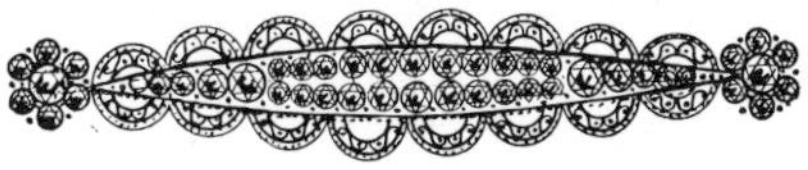

No. F. 3544. Very dainty Paste **Hair Slide**

Price .. **7/6**

ALSO MANY OTHER DESIGNS.

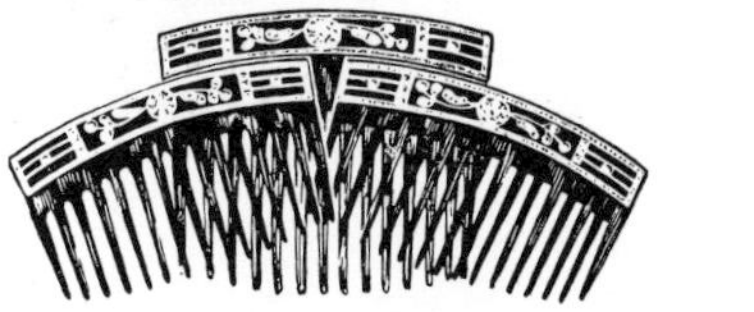

No. F. 3099. **Fancy Combs,** shell colour.
Set fine quality Paste .. .. price **15/9**
Real Horn Combs.. .. .. ,, **23/6**

Per set of three.

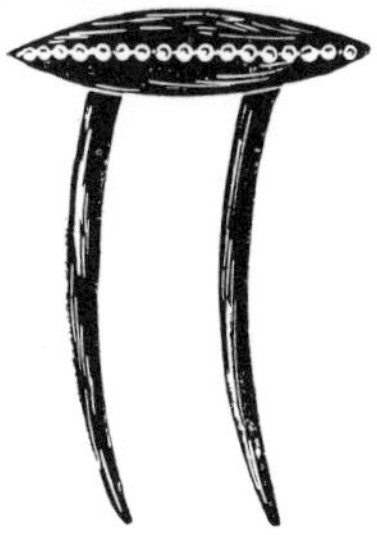

No. F. 71/1.
Shell colour **Prong,**
ne Crystal Mount, **3/11**
Real Horn .. **5/3**

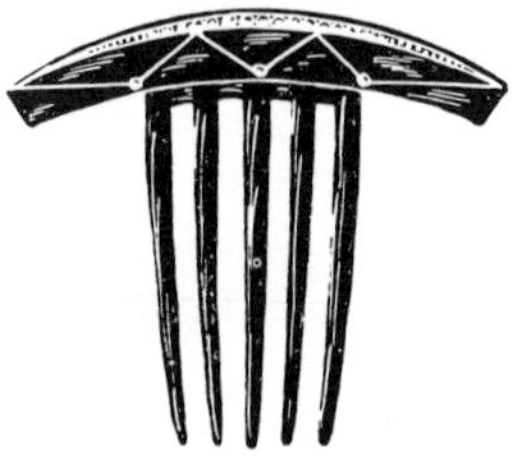

No. F. 71/4.
Shell colour
"Casque" Comb.
Fine Crystal Mount, **6/6**
Real Horn .. **8/6**

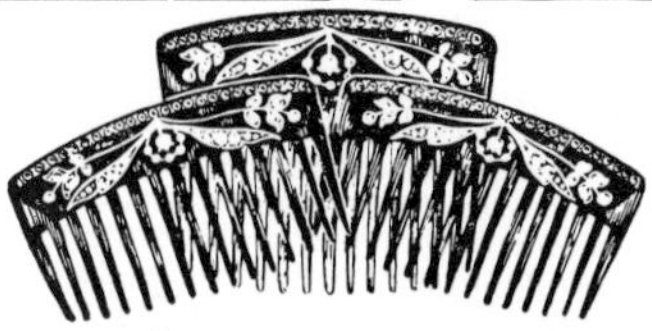

No. F. 3094. **Fancy Combs,** shell colour.
Set fine quality Paste .. price **19/6**
Real Horn Combs .. ,, **27/6**

Per set of three.

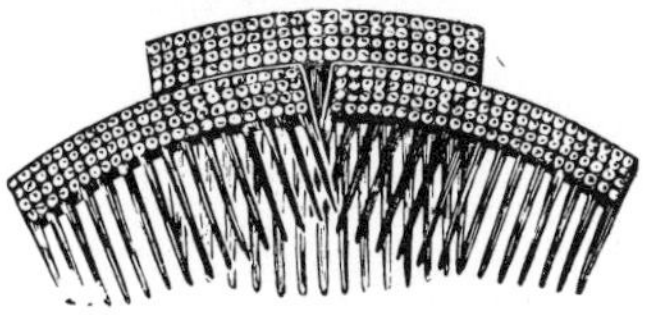

No. F. 76/28. **Fancy Combs,** shell colour.
Fine quality Pas e, securely mounted .. **24/6**
Real Horn Combs **32/6**

Per set of three.

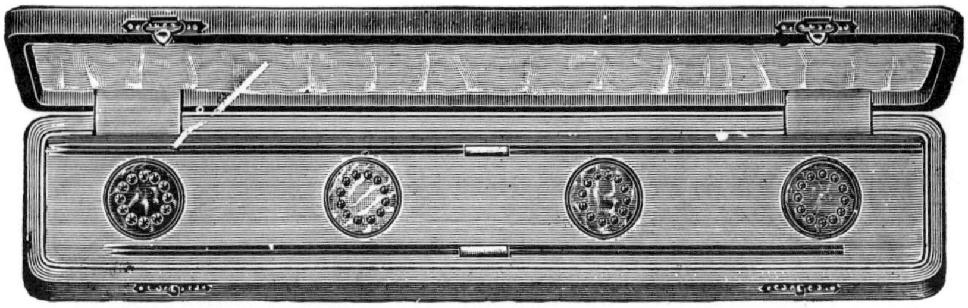

Case containing Four Dainty Screw Top **Hat Pins.** Assorted Colours. Shaded Mother-o'-pearl Set Parisian Brilliants. Price **7/11** complete.

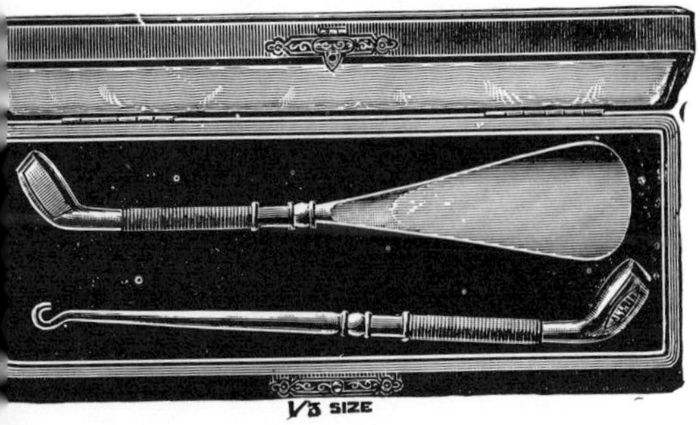

1/3 SIZE

No. F. 10491.
"GOLF" SILVER MOUNTED
Shoe Lift and Button Hook.
Complete in Velvet and Satin Lined Case.
Price **5/11**

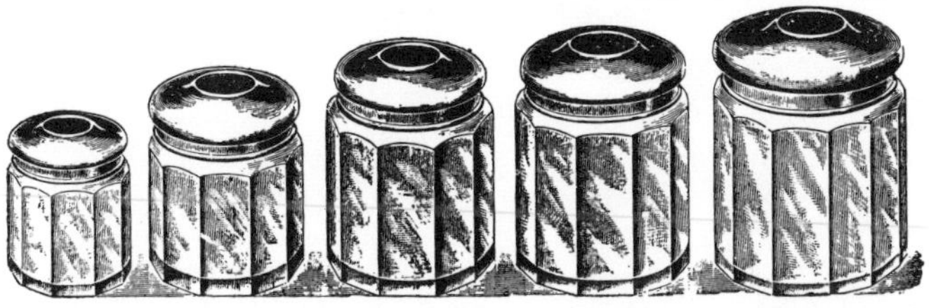

No. F. 361 F. 363 F. 364 F. 395 F. 366

Silver Mounted Hair Tidies.

Prices **3/3** **4/6** **5/6** **6/6** **7/6**

Crystal Glass. Fancy Cut. **Hair Pin Boxes.**

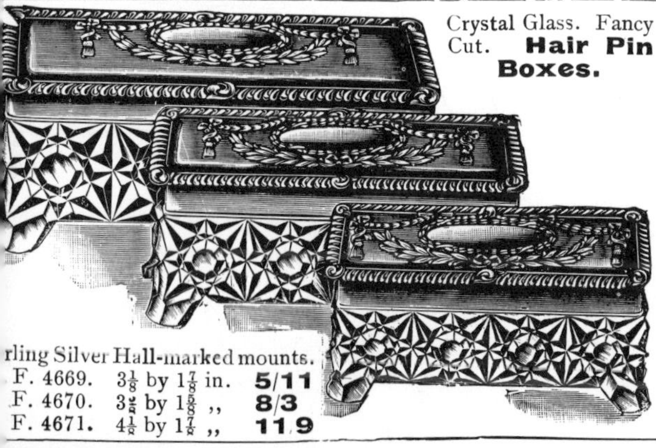

rling Silver Hall-marked mounts.

F. 4669.	$3\frac{1}{8}$ by $1\frac{7}{8}$ in.	**5/11**
F. 4670.	$3\frac{3}{4}$ by $1\frac{5}{8}$,,	**8/3**
F. 4671.	$4\frac{1}{2}$ by $1\frac{7}{8}$,,	**11/9**

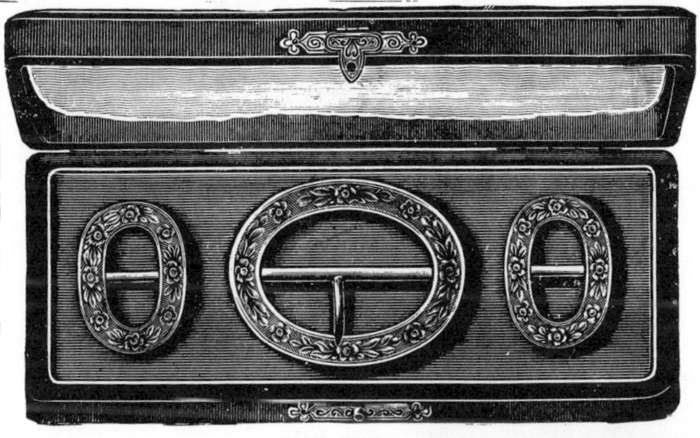

HALF SIZE

No. F. $83\frac{1}{2}$.
Real Enamel on Sterling Silver
Waist Buckle and Shoe Slides.
Complete in Velvet and Satin Lined Case.
Price .. **10/6**

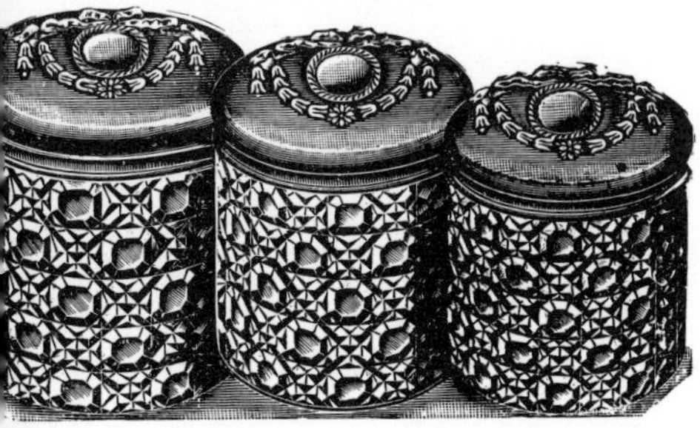

Crystal Glass. Fancy Cut.
Powder Box.
Sterling Silver Mount.

No. F. 4625.	2 by $1\frac{7}{8}$ in.	**3/4½**
,, F. 4624.	$2\frac{3}{4}$ by $2\frac{1}{8}$,,	**4/3**
,, F. 4623.	$2\frac{1}{2}$ by $2\frac{1}{4}$,,	**4/11**
,, F. 4622.	3 by $2\frac{1}{2}$,,	**5/9**
,, F. 4621.	$3\frac{1}{4}$ by $2\frac{3}{4}$,,	**6/9**
,, F. 4620.	$3\frac{1}{2}$ by $3\frac{1}{8}$,,	**8/9**

No. F. 1302/2.
Silver Mounted Hair Brush and Comb.
In Velvet and Satin Lined Leatherette Case
Price **15/6**

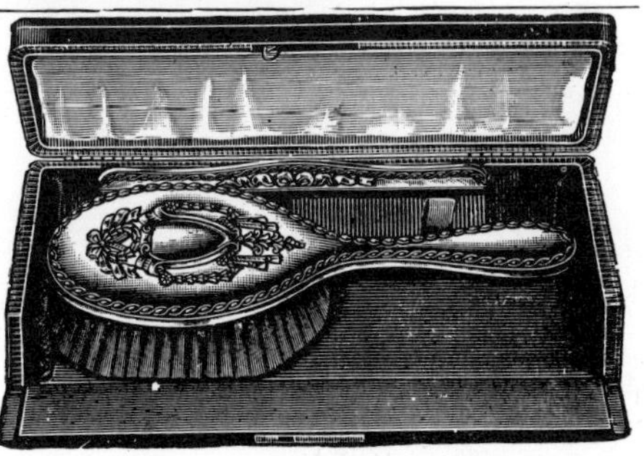

Manicure Sets.

No. F. 318

White Xylo **Manicure** Set, velvet and satin lined case.

2/-

F. 318/1

Special quality, style as above. Superior Finish.

2/6

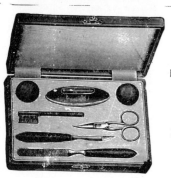

No. F. 3775.

Ebony Manicure Set.

5 3

No. F. 3745.

Ivory

8/3

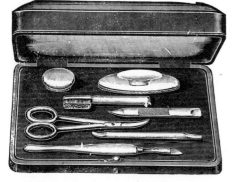

Fine quality Manicure Set.
Leather covered case.
No. F. 333.   Real **Ivory** .. Price **13 3**
 ,, F. 3224.   **Ebony** .. ,, **8 3**

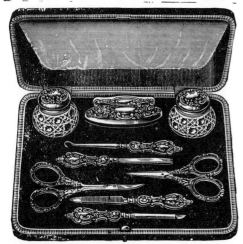

No. F. 879.
Silver-mounted Manicure Set.
Special Value .. **25/6**

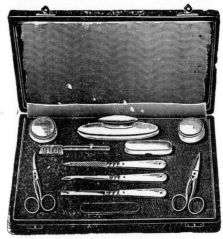

No. F. 321.   **Manicure Set.**
Eleven pieces.   Xylo fittings.
Velvet and satin lined case   Price .. **4/9**

No. F. 327.   **Manicure Set.**
Best quality white Xylo fittings and steel cutlery.
Inside cover fitted with mirror.
Velvet and satin lined case.   Price **15 9**

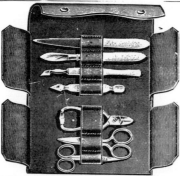

Folding Manicure Set.

Leather case.

F. 2158. Ivory fittings, **15/9**

F. 3313. Ebony **11/6**

F. 2106.
Silver-mounted Manicure Set, Exceptional Value.
12/6

Other Patterns.
15/9
18/9
21/-
30/-

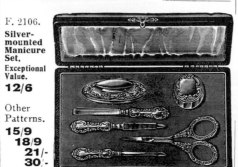

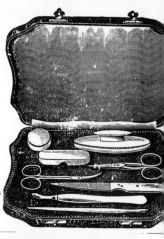

No. F. 348.
Manicure Set.
Splendid quality white Xylo fittings and steel cutlery
6/3

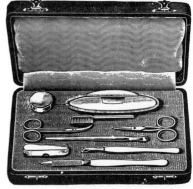

No. F. 336.   **Manicure Set.**
Fine quality Xylo fittings and steel cutlery.   **8/6**

F. 3910.

Manicure Set,

Ivory fittings.

Steel cutlery.

Silk lined leather case.

18/6

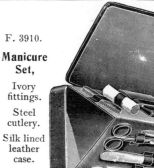

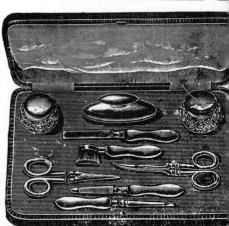

No. F. 909.   **Sterling Silver-mounted Manicure Set.** Complete in Velvet and Satin Lined Leather Case **37/6**

A variety of other Styles and Prices in stock.

PHOTO FRAMES.

No. F. 3672. Photo Frame.
Hall-marked Silver, Cabinet size **3/11**

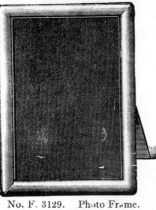

No. F. 3129. Photo Frame.
Hall-marked Silver, Cabinet size **4/6**
F. 3131. Imperial size,
8¼ by 6 in. .. **11/9**

No. F. 3768. Photo Frame.
Silver-mounted, Cabinet size **4/11**

No. F. 3051. Hall-marked Silver
Photo Frame, Cabinet size **7/9**
F. 3063. Imperial size, 8¼ by 6 in. Sight
19/9

Photo Frames. Hall-marked Silver.
F. 3138. Size of sight, 2¼ in. **3/8**
,, 3137. ,, ,, 2⅞ in. **4/9**
,, 3008. ,, ,, 3⅝ in. **6/6**

No. 40629.
Fine Range of Gilt Metal Double Screen
Frames with gilt mat.

C.D.V. Cabinet. Imperial.
2/4½ 2/11 4/11

F. S2968
Brass Curb
Photo Frames
C.D.V. **2/-**
Cabinet **3/3**
Promenade
4/6
Boudoir **5/8**
Imperial **7/6**

Photo Frames. Hall-marked Silver.
No F. 3348. Cabinet size **5/11**
,, 3349. Boudoir ,, **11/9**
,, 3350. Imperial ,, **16/6**

> **Write for our Departmental List Post Free anywhere.**

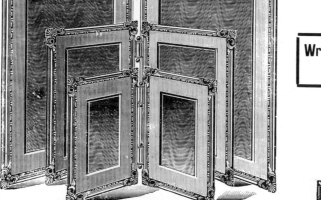

No. F. 38551.
Leather
Photograph Frames.
Persian Calf Finish

In various colours.
Square or Oval Sight.

C.D.V.	Cabinet	Promenade	Boudoir	Imperial
1/-	**1/6**	**2/6**	**2/8**	**2/11½**

Very
handsome
Best quality
Crushed
Morocco
Photo Frame.
No. F. 1477
Cabinet **5/11**
F. 1494
Boudoir **7/11**
F. 1495
Imperial /-

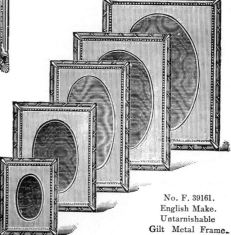

No. F. 39161.
English Make.
Untarnishable
Gilt Metal Frame.

A reproduction of the finest French Gilt. Square or oval sight.

C.D.V.	Cabinet.	Promenade.	Boudoir.	Imperial.
10½d.	**1/-**	**1/10½**	**2/-**	**2/4½**

FANCY LEATHER GOODS.
Ladies' Toilet Cases for Home or Travelling.

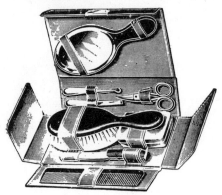

No. F. 5432. **Ladies' Toilet Case.** Seal grain. Fitted with Black Hair Brush, Comb, Mirror, Tooth Brush, Soap Box, and Cutlery .. **8/11**

No. F. 15296. **Ladies' Toilet Case.** Fitted with Hair and Cloth Brush, Comb, Mirror, Tooth Brush and Soap Box. In neat case. **10/-**

No. F. 5434. **Ladies' Toilet Case,** grain, Lined moire. Fitted with Black Hair Brush, Comb, Mirror, Tooth Brush, Box, and Drawer for Trinkets

No. F. 5437. **Ladies' Toilet Case.** Fitted with ebonized hair and cloth brush, comb, mirror, tooth brush, soap box, glove stretchers, scissors, button hooks, etc. Powder grain leather Case. Three sizes. Small **15/6** Medium **18/6** Large **21/6**

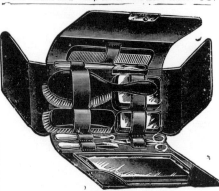

No. F. 5436. **Ladies' Toilet Case.** Fitted with ebonized hair and cloth brush, comb, mirror, soap box, scissors, button hook, etc. Powder grain Folding Case. Price **17/9**

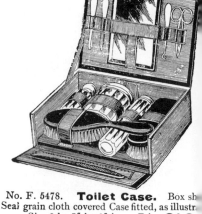

No. F. 5478. **Toilet Case.** Box sh Seal grain cloth covered Case fitted, as illustr Size 9 by 7⅞ by 2⅞ in. Price **21 6**

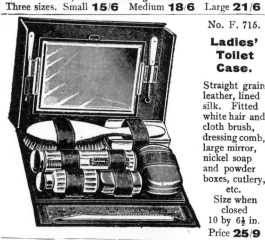

No. F. 715.

Ladies' Toilet Case.

Straight grain leather, lined silk. Fitted white hair and cloth brush, dressing comb, large mirror, nickel soap and powder boxes, cutlery, etc. Size when closed 10 by 6½ in. Price **25/9**

No. F. 15292. **Ladies' Toilet Case.** Fitted with hair and cloth brush, comb, mirror hair curlers, spirit lamp, soap box, tooth brush roller, scissors, button hook, and file, etc. Fine Case for Tourists, covered morocco leather. Price **34/6**

No. F. 5442. **Toilet Case** Long grain Fitted ebony hair brushes. Electro-plated Bottles. Very fine quality. Price **45**

No. F. 5444.

Ladies' Complete Toilet Case.

Long grain roan Case. Lined moire. Best quality fittings as illustration.

Price .. **57/6**

No. F. 15287. Ladies, Brush Case, Long grain leather. Fitted as illustration. Ivory grained fittings .. **13/3**

No. F. 15935. **Ladies' Solid Hide To Case.** Lined moire silk. Fitted with quality ebony hair and cloth brush, mirror, powder box, bottles, scissors, button hook, fi tweezers. Size 16 by 9½ by 4¼ in. Price

Many other Styles in Stock. At the Lowest Possible Prices.

GENT'S TOILET CASES.

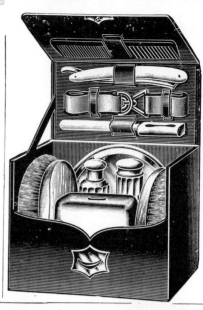

No. F. 5739.

Gent's Toilet Case.

Long Grain Leather, fitted with two Satinwood Hair Brushes, Two Glass Bottles, Nickel Tops, Soap Box, Tooth Brush, Razor and Strop.

Price .. **21/-**

F. 5446. Youth's Toilet Case.

ng Grain Leather, fitted with Hair Brush, Comb, Mirror, Tooth Brush and Soap Box.

Very compact .. **6/3**

No. F. 5449. Gent's Toilet Case.

Seal Grain, fitted with Hair Brush, Comb, Mirror, Tooth Brush, Soap Box, Razor and Strop.

Fine value .. **11/6**

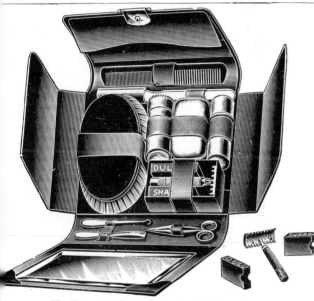

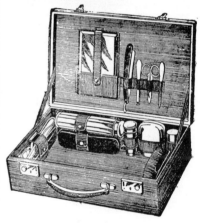

No. F. 5738. Gent's Toilet Case.

Grain Persian Leather, fitted with Hair Brush, comb, Mirror, Soap Box, Shaving Brush, Safety Razor, Etc.
Two sizes .. .. **23/9** and **28/6**

No. F. 15299. Toilet Case.

Fold up shape. Crocodile Grained Leather, fitted with good quality Hair and Cloth Brush, Comb, Mirror, Razor, Strop, Tooth Brush Roller, Soap Box and Cutlery.

Price .. **25/9**

No. F. 5477.
Gent's Seal Grain Leather Attache.
Toilet Case.
Fitted with good quality Hair Brush, Mirror, Razor, Tooth and Nail Brush Roller, Soap Box, Etc. Size 14 in

Price .. **37/9**

F. 346 Gent's Toilet Case.

ceable quality fittings, Military Hair Brush, Brush, Comb, Mirror, Soap Box, Shaving Brush, Razor and Strop, Scissors, Etc.
Solid Hide, Leather Lined Case.

., **43/9** 10 in., **55/-** 11¾ in.. **67/8**

No. F. 5459. Toilet Case.

Seal Grain Roan. Fitted with good quality Hair Brushes, Cloth Brush, Mirror, Comb, Shaving Brush, Soap Box, Strop, Razor, Cutlery, and drawer for studs, etc.

Price .. **44/6**

No. F. 15931. Gent's Solid Hide Toilet Case.

Lined Straight Grain Roan. Fitted with real ebony Hair Brush, Hat and Cloth Brush, Mirror, Comb Three Bottles, Soap Box, Shaving Soap Roller, Razor and Razor Strop, Scissors, Etc.
Size 16 by 9½ by 4¾ in.

Price **70/-**

We have a large stock of Toilet Cases in various styles.   **At the Lowest Possible Prices.**

Attache Writing Cases and Writing Desks.

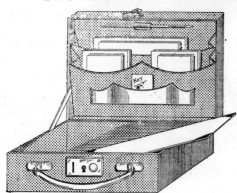

A special line in straight grain.
Attache Case,
Fitted with stationery pockets, nickel lock.
Size 10 by 7 by 3 in.   Price .. **5/6**

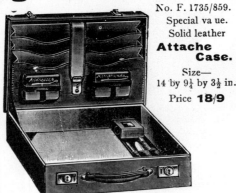

No. F. 1735/859.
Special value.
Solid leather
Attache Case.
Size—
14 by 9¼ by 3½ in.
Price **18/9**

Leather lined, fitted with safety ink, blotter, pen, pencil, paper knife, address and memo books, two nickel locks.
If fitted with cheque book pocket, **21/-**

A Cheap Line.   Sheepskin **Attache Case.**
Tan colour.   Style as above.   Price **15/9**

No. F. 34753
Leather Top **Attache Case.**

Size			
10 in.	..	..	**7/11**
12 in.	..	..	**9/11**
14 in.	..	..	**12/9**

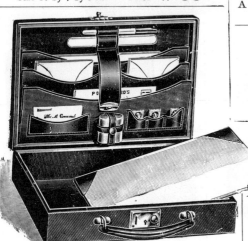

No. F. 34563.
Fine quality straight grain leather
Attache Case.
Size 10 in., **13/6**   12 in., **15/9**   14 in., **18/9**

No. F.O.W.
Polished Wood Writing Desk.
Fitted with Lock and Key.
12 in., **5/9**   14 in., **6/9**
16 in., **7/9**

No. F. 4.   Walnut Polished Writing Desk.
Brass Straps and Mount.   Fitted with
Lock and Key.

Size	..	12 in.	14 in.	16 in.
		10/6	**11/9**	**13/9**

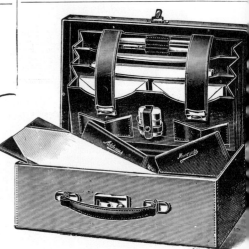

No. F. 622.
Solid leather **Attache Case.**
Very Fine Value.

Size 12 in.	..	..	Price **23/9**
Size 14 in.	..	..	Price **29/6**

No. F. 5977.   Finest quality.   Straight grain leather
Attache Case.
Fitted with cheque book pocket, safety ink, paper knife, pencil, penholder, two books and blotter.   Size 14 in., fitted with two locks as illustration, **26/6**   12 in. fitted with one lock, **22/6**

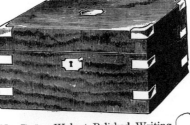

No. F. 5.   Walnut Polished Writing
Desk, Brass Mounts, Lock and Key.
Well built, fitted with Secret Drawer.

Size	..	12 in.	14 in.
		14/6	**16/6**
Size	..	16 in.	18 in.
		18/6	**21/-**
Superior quality—			
Size	..	12 in.	14 in.
		21/-	**23/6**
Size	..	16 in.	18 in.
		25/6	**27/6**

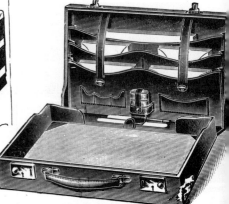

No. F. 6005.   New style.   Finest quality straight grain leather **Attache Case** (when open, back rests as shewn) fitted with safety ink, penholder, paper knife.   English lever lock.   Gilt fitting.
Size 12 in. Price **26/6**   Size 14 in. Price **32**

Finest Value in Writing Cases.

No. F. 6. The "Popular" Writing Case.
Straight Grain Leather.
Size 8½ in. ... **2/6**   Size 9½ in. ... **3/9**

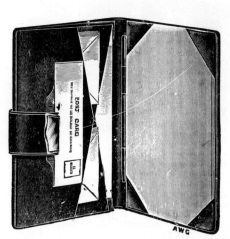

No. F. 3. The "School" Writing Case
Straight Grain Leather.
Size 8¾ in. **1 6**   Size 9¾ **1/11½**

No. F. 7. The "Favourite" Writing Case.
Folding Blotter.   Seal Grain Leather.
Size 8½ in. ... **3 3**   Size 9½ in. ... **4/6**

F. 37827½. The "Holborn" Writing Case.
Fine Quality Roan Leather. Fitted with Safety Ink,
Calendar, Paper Knife. Mounted two Sterling Silver
Corners. Size 8½ in. ... **7/11**   Size 10 in. ... **9/11**

EXCEPTIONAL VALUE.
No. F. 27. Fine Quality Imitation Crocodile **Writing
Case,** Leather Lined. Fitted with Safety Ink, Pen-
holder, Pencil, Capacious Stationery Pockets.
Size 8½ in. ... **7/3**   Size 10 in ... **9/3**

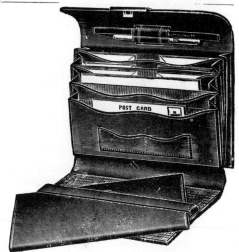

No. F. 17. The "Tourist" Writing Case
Seal Grain Leather. Separate Blotter.
Splendid Value.
Size 8½ in. ... **8/3**   Size 10 in. ... **10/6**

No. F. 34125. Fine Quality Levant Seal.
Fitted with Loose Blotter.
Size 10¾ in. ... **25/9**

F. 34121. Splendid Value. Roan Leather Writing Case.
Lined throughout, Straight Grain Roan. Fitted with
Safety Ink, Pen and Pencil. Size 10¾ in. ... **15/9**

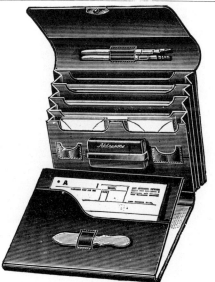

No. F. 1934. Solid Hide Writing Case Lined Roan
Leather. Size 10¾ in. ... **24/6**

A Large Selection of Writing Cases from 1/- each in stock.

High-Class Fancy Leather Goods.

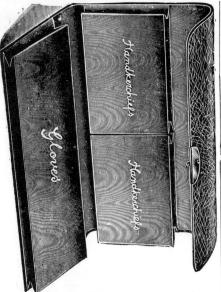

No. F. 5369. Long grain leather
Glove and Handkerchief Combination.
Price .. **7/6**

No. F. 15970. **Jewel Case.**
Grained leatherette with lift-out tray Sunk nickel handle.
Size 6 in., **2/11** 7 in., **3/11** 8 in., **4/11** 9 in., **5/11**
No. F. 15971. Superior quality and finish.
Style as above. Straight grain leather. Without handle.
6 in. .. **3/11** 7 in. .. **4/11** 8 in. .. **5/11**

No. F. 5562.
Glove and Handkerchief Combination.
Long grain leather.
Silver Top Perfume Bottle.
Price .. **8/11**

No. F. 5388. **Jewel Case.**
Long grain roan. Richly lined.
5 in. .. **8/11**
6 in. .. **10/9**
7 in. .. **12/9**

No. F. 5672.
Jewel Case.
Straight grain leather.
Lined velvet and Moirette nickel lock.

5 in.	6 in.	7 in.	8 in.	9 in.
3/11	**4/11**	**6/11**	**8/11**	**10/11**

No. F. 6105.
Handkerchief Case.
Long grain leather.
Fitted with Perfume Bottle Mirror and
Price .. **8/3**

No. F. 5361.
Long grain leather
Handkerchief and Glove Case.
Price **5/6** pair.

No. F. 5625. **Jewel Case.**
Long grain roan leather.
Lined velvet and Moire, Swing Trays.
Best quality. Press spring lock.
Size 7 in., **28/6** in., **33/9**

No. F. 5673. **Jewel Case**
Attaché shape. Straight grain lea
Lined Moirette.
5 in., **8/11** 6, **10/11** 7, **13/3** 8,

If you do not see what you require, Write us stating your wants.

Fancy Leather Goods.
USEFUL ARTICLES FOR GENTLEMEN.

No. F. 6112/7. The "Holborn" Combination Collar & Brush Case. Straight grain leather. Fitted with real ebony hair brush Size 7 in. ... **7/3** No. F. 6125. Balkan seal, **9/9** No. F. 6110. Solid calf, **14/6**

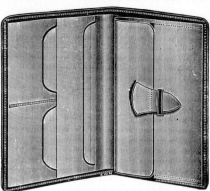

No. F. 507.
Letter Case
Persian Morocco faced Sheep Skin.
5/11

No. F. 610. Style as above. Real Morocco, faced Calf.
8/11

No. F. 611. Style as above. Real Seal, faced Calf, **10/6**

No. F. 6112/8. The 'Holborn' Combination Collar & Brush Case. Straight grain leather, fitted with 2 real ebony hair brushes. Size 8 in., **10/3** No F. 6125. Balkan seal **13/9** No. F. 6110. Solid calf **18/9**

No. F. 5379. Folding Tie Case, straight grain leather. Lined Moire. Price **5/4**

No. F. 3786. Fine grain leather Inket Box. Lined velvet.

No. F. 5741. The Traveller's Shaving Mirror, to hang or stand. In fine seal grain leather case.
No. 1. ... **7/11**   No. 2 ... **13/9**

Cigarette Case.
Covered Frame. No. F. 15340. Real Morocco.
2 sizes, **5/3** and **6/6**

No. F. 15341. Capra Seal Leather, self lined Riveted frame.
2 sizes, **3/6** and **3/11**

F. 5581. Expanding Tie Case, with loops for tie pins, space for studs and needle book. Straight grain leather. Special value. Price **9/9**

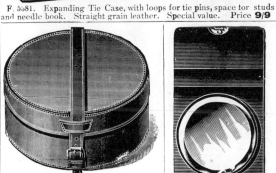

No. F 5076. London Colour Hide Collar Box, round shape. strap and buckle. 5¾in., **3/9** 6½ in., **4/6** 7¼in., **5/3** 8in., **6/-** No. F. 1086. Real Pigskin, lined leather. 7 in. ... **9/9** 8 in. ... **12/9** No. F. 5077. London Colour Hide, horseshoe shape—5 in., **4/9** 6½ in., **5/6** 7¼ in. ... **6/6** 8 in. ... **7/6**

Cigar Case.
Seal grain leather. Strong covered frame 6 by 4⅞ in., **7/11** Many other styles. **2/11 3/11 4/11 10/6 12/6** up to **21/-** each.

No. F. 5463 Walrus grain leather Shaving-paper Tidy and Shaving Mirror. Price **5/9**

ted for studs, gs, tiepins, etc. F. 1 ... **5/6** F. 2 ... **6/9** F. 3 ... **8/9**

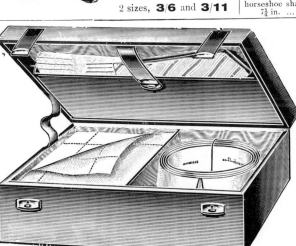

No. F. 6.04. Gentlemen's Combination Collar, Handkerchief and Tie Box. Fine seal grain leather. Price ... **17/9**

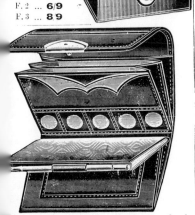

3149. Pocket Book, French morocco, fitted with Bank Note Pocket, **5/-** 3150. Morocco. **6/11** F. 3151. Seal, **8/11**

No. F. 3157.
Letter Case
French Morocco with Bank Note Pocket, 6 in., **2/6** 6½ in., **3/-**

No. F. 3158. Morocco Leather, style as above. 6 in. .. **3/6** 6½ in... **4/-**

F. 3159. Morocco Seal, style as above 6 in. .. **4/11** 6½ in... **5/6**

Z

PURSES. Splendid Value. Large Variety in Stock.

No. F. 3174. Seal Grain Leather Purse.

Nickel fitting. Fitted with centre pocket. Length 4½ in. Price **1/-**

No. F. 1523. Morocco Bag Purse.

Fine Quality. Fitted centre gold pocket. Two sizes. Price **2/-, 2/6**

No. F. 4349. Strong Morocco Purse.

Square shape. Fitted with centre gold pocket. Price **1/9**

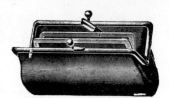

No. F. 4227. Antelope Bag Purse.

Strong gilt frame. Centre division. Three sizes. **1/6, 2/-, 2/6**

No. F. 3160. Seal Grain Leather Purse.

Leather gussets. Strong make. Nickel fittings. Size 4⅜ in. by 2½ in. Price **2/6**

No. F. 4318. Crushed Morocco Leather Purse.

Leather gussets. Centre gold pocket. Flexible sterling silver mount. Three sizes. Price **8/6 9/9 10/9**

A Large Variety of Sterling Silver Mounted Purses in Various Styles.

Prices - **6/6 7/6 10/6 to 21/-**

No. F. 1585. Morocco Leather Purse.

Leather gussets. Centre gold pocket. Stamp pocket. Note tablet. Three sizes. Prices **2/11 3/6 3/11**

No. F. C10281. Real Crocodile Leather Purses.

Back Card Pocket. Leather throughout. Sterling Silver Corners. 3⅞ in. **5/6** 4¼ in. **5/11** 4½ in. **6/6**

Unmounted. **4/6 4/11 5/6**

Gent's Strong Serviceable Purses.

Five sizes.

No. F. 779. **Real Pigskin.**

1/- 1/3 1/6 1/9 2/-

No. F. 784. **Willow Calf.**

1/3 1/6 2/- 2/6 3/-

No. F. 789. **Real Seal.**

1/3 1/6 2/- 2/6 3/-

No. F. 4299. The "Housekeeper" Purse.

Extra strong morocco leather purse. Leather gussets. Calf flaps. Gold and silver pockets. Stamp pockets, etc.

Two sizes. 4¼ by 2½ in. **6/9** 4⅞ by 2⅝ in. **7/6**

No. F. 4230. The 'Shopping' Purse.

Morocco leather. Leather gussets. Large centre pocket. Very Special Value. Price **8/11**

No. F. 4215. Ladies' Puma Purses.

Leather gussets. Centre pocket. Prices **2/9 3/3 3/9**

Gents' Useful Purse.

Fitted with sovereign slide.

Three sizes.

No. F. 744. **Real Pigskin.**

1/6 2/- 2/6 each.

No. F. 747. **Willow Calf.**

2/6 3/- 3/6 each.

No. F. 750. **Real Seal.**

2/6 3/- 3/6 each.

Work Baskets and Work Stands.

WELL BUILT AND RICHLY SATIN LINED. IN VARIOUS COLOURS.

No. F. 381. Satin Lined Workstand.
Buff Willow, Dark Green and
Tuscan Straw.   Price .. **10/6**

No. F. 1106.

Satin Lined
Work Basket.
Buff and Willow
Cream Rush.

Four sizes.

**1/9½ 2/-
2 6 2/11½**

No. F. 2204. Satin Lined Work Basket.
Fine Green and White Cane and White
Straw. Pocket in large size.
Three sizes .. **3 6 4/3 5/6**

No. F. 4154. Cabinet Workstand.
Rush and Buff Willow. 3 sizes.
24/6 30/- 35/9
Cheaper quality, Straw and Willow.
15/9 21/6 27/9

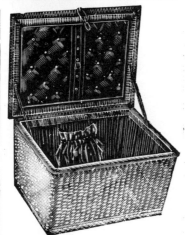

No. F. 474. Satin Lined Work
Basket. Buff Willow and fine Cream
Rush. Three sizes.
5/6 6/11 8/11

No. F. 2257. Fine Quality Work Basket
Three sizes .. **10/6 12/6 15 6**

No. F. 4113. Satin Lined Workstand. Green Enamelled Cane
and fine Cream Rush.
Price **35/9**

No. F. 4001. Satin Lined Workstand.
Buff Willow, fine Green Rush and
Tuscan Straw   Price .. **15/6**

No. F. 2040. Satin Lined Work
Basket. Fine White and Green
Cane. Price .. **10/6**

No. F. 2260. Satin Lined Work Basket.
Green Enamelled Cane and fine Green
Rush. Nickel Handle.
Four sizes.
11/6 12/6 15/6 19/6

No. F. 645. Satin Lined Workstand.
Buff Willow and fine Green Rush.
Three sizes.

17/6 19/6 21/-

No. F. 4127.

Very Useful Work Table.
Fine Cream Rush
and
Havanna Cane.
Satin Lined.
Various Colours.

Price **41/9**

A large selection
of Work Baskets
from 1/- each.

No. F. 4062. Satin Lined Workstand. Enamelled Cane, fine Cream
and Green Rush. Nickel Handle.
Price **49 6**

Z ..

Sewing Companions, Needle Cases, etc.

No. F. 1379 Leather Needle Case. Containing 218 Gold-eyed Needles and pair of scissors. Price **2/-**

No. F. 1143 Leather Needle Case, furnished with useful variety of sewing and art needles, darning and crewel work needles. **1/6**

No. F. 1107 Leather Needle Case. Satin lined, fitted with 278 assorted Gold-eyed Needles. Price ... **2/6**

No. F. 1380 Leather Needle and Scissors Case, silk lined. A useful variety of needles for all classes of work. Sheffield Steel Scissors. **3/6**

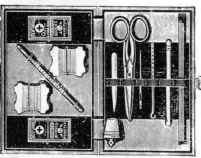

No. F. 1396. Sewing Set. Sheffield Cutlery, good quality Needles, etc. In leather case ... **3/6**

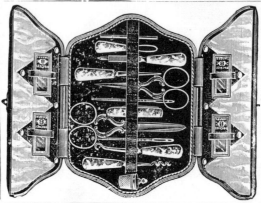

No. F. 1204 Sewing Set. Best quality fittings. Pearl handles. Price **12/6**

No. F. 1603 Sewing Set. Fitted good quality Sheffield Cutlery. French Morocco Case. Price **7/6**

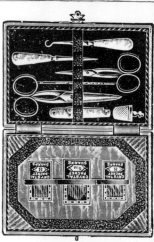

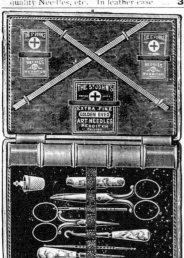

No. F. 1340. Sewing Set. Sheffield cutlery, pearl handle fittings. Strong leatherette case. Price **9/9**

No. F. 3251 Work Box. French Morocco silk lined, with handle, spring lock, fitted with needles, cotton and Sheffield cutlery.
9 in. ... **12/9**
10 in. ... **13/9**

No. F. 1526. Sewing Set. Serviceable quality fittings, Leatherette case. Price ... **4/11½**

N. F. 899. Sheffield Steel **Scissors** Complete in case.
2 pairs ... **1/11½**
3 ,, ... **2/11½**
4 ,, ... **3/11½**

No. F. A311. High-grade Sheffield Steel **Scissors.** Three pairs, **8/9** Four pairs, **12/6** In case.

No. F. 887. Sheffield Steel Scissors.
Complete in case.
2 pairs .. **3/11½**
3 ,, .. **4/11½**
4 ,, .. **5/11**

No. F. A310½. Finest quality Sheffield Steel **Scissors.** For fancy work. In neat case. Three Pairs **12/9**

No. F. C160 Serviceable Quality Sheffield Steel **Scissors.** Fancy Bows as illus. Three Pairs **13 6** Four Pairs **15/6** Plain Bows **7/6 & 10/6**

No. F. A306. Good quality **Scissors** in Folding Case. 3 Pairs **9/6** 4 Pairs **11/6**

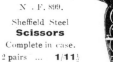

"Cavendish." Finest quality Sheffield Steel **Scissors,** Plain Bows, Highly Polished. 3 Pairs **13/6** 4, **18/6** 6, **30/-** In Case complete.

No. F. A310. Fine quality Sheffield Steel **Scissors.** In Leather Case. 3 Pairs **11/6** 5 Pairs **17/6**

No. F. 165. Three Pairs of Serviceable quality, **Sheffield Steel Scissors.** Complete in Fold-up Case. Price .. **7/11**

Folding Nail Scissors. **1/-** **1/4½** & **1/10½**

No. F. A310½. Three pairs best fine polished Steel **Scissors** Complete in Velvet and Satin-lined Case Price ... **12/9**

Flasks, Spirit Frames and Smokers' Cabinets.

No. F. 2393.
Three Bottle Spirit Frame.
Nickel-plated fittings.
Fancy Glass Bottles.
21/-
Other styles
25 - 29/6
37/6 45/-

No. F. 1733.
Combination Spirit Stand.
Strongly built in oak.
Three Bottles and Glasses.
Drawers for Cards, etc.
Space for Cigars and Cigarettes.

Plain	Half Cut	Full Cut Bottles.
38/9	**45/-**	**57/6**

A cheaper Stand   Price .. **27/6**

No. F. 2708.
High-class Spirit Frame.
Oak or Mahogany, inlaid as illustration.
Best Quality Cut Glass Bottles.
Price **67/6**

No. F. 020E.   Spirit Flask.
Leather covered top, white metal chased cup, screw top.
Height 4½   5   5½   6 in.
Price **2/-   2/3   2/6   2/11**

No. F. 504.   Spirit Flask.
Leather covered top, electro-plated chased cup, screw top.
Height 4½   5½   5¾ in.
Price **4/6   5/-   5/6**

No. F. 2493.
Strong Oak Pipe Rack.
Nickel-plated Mounts.
To take 4 pipes, **2/-** 6, **3/-** 8, **3/9**

No. F. 4 229/3.
Bayonet Top Flask.
Gilt lined.
Nickel-plated cup and top
Imitation Crocodile leather.
Height 5¾ in.   Price **8/11**

No. F. 535.   Spirit Flask.
Leather covered top, silver-plated chased cup, bayonet fastener.
4½ in   5½ in.   5¾ in.
16/6   17/6   19/6

No. F. 2666.   Substantially made **Smokers' Cabinet.**
Well finished Oak Colour Nickel plated Mounts, fitted with Pipe Rack, Tobacco Jar, space for box of Cigars. 14 by 11 by 8 in. **10/-**
No. 2677. Style as above, but fitted with glass panel in door. **10/9**

No. F. 2760.
Useful Combination **Pipe Rack.**
Fitted with Tobacco Jar, Drawer for Cigars, Cigarettes, &c.
Nickel-plated Mounts.
Size 15 by 9½ by 6 in.   Price **9/6**

No. F. 2820.
Fine Value Smokers' Cabinet.
Oak Inlaid, sound construction, well finished, fitted with Pipe Rack, Tobacco Jar, space for box of Cigars.
Size 12 by 11 by 7½ in.   Price **12/6**

No. F. 2525.   **Oak Smokers' Cabinet.** Solidly built, fitted with Pipe Rack, Tobacco Jar, two Drawers Space for box of Cigars.
Size 14 by 13¼ by 6½ in. Price **19/6**

No. F. 2833.   Oak Inlaid **Smokers' Cabinet.**
Well made and finished.
Fitted with Pipe Rack, Tobacco Jar, space for box of Cigars.
15 by 12 by 7½ in. Price **21/-**

No. F. 2830.
Oak Inlaid Smokers' Cabinet.
Fitted with Pipe Rack, Tobacco Jar, 2 Drawers.
Space for Box of Cigars. Two Glass Doors.
Size 15½ by 14½ by 9 in. Price **24/6**

No. F. 2375.
Well made Oak Cigar Box.
Lined cedar wood, nickle plated mounts, fitted with Lock and key, size
Size 11 by 7 by 4½ in.   Price **6/11**
No. F. 2496.   Cigarette Box to match Cigar Box.
8½ by 5½ by 2¾ in.   Price ... **5/6**

F. 2789. Combination **Smokers' and Liqueur Stand.**
Oak, well built and finished. Fitted with two full size Spirit Bottles, two Glasses, Tobacco Jar, Drawer
Size 40 by 19 by 18 in. Price **75/-**

We are only able to illustrate a small portion of our enormous stock.   Send for our Fancy List.

TROUSER AND TIE PRESSES ARE EXCELLENT CIFTS.

Tie Presses.

A useful article. Quite as necessary as a Trouser
No.] Press. In the following grades :—   [Each
1. Polished birch boards, 14 by 6 in. **4/6**
3. Solid moulded oak, top board marquetry
   inlaid, 14 by 6 in. **6/9**
4. Solid mahogany, top board marquetry inlaid
   14 by 6 in. **7/6**
5. Polished birch boards, 17 by 6½ in... .. **5/9**
   The above are fitted with patent automatic stretcher
   which removes creases previous to pressing.

The "Express" Press.

Five-ply birch top & bottom boards, ⅜ in. thick, stained and
polished Walnut or Oak colour. Nickel-plated fittings, patent
drop-down screw bars which fold underneath for convenience
of packing. Size, 28 in. long, 14 in. wide.
Three separating cardboards with each Press. Price **8 9**
Or fitted with Patent Automatic Stretcher, **11/9**

The "National."
The most Popular Press on the market.

Solid Oak top board, moulded edges. Five-ply bottom board
⅜ in. thick, polished or fumed oak, nickel-plated spring steel
top bars 2 in. wide. Patent connected drop-down screw bars
½ in. diam. which fold under Press for convenience of packing.
Fitted with anti-friction ball nuts. Size, 30 in. long, 14 in. wide
Six separating cardboards with each Press   Price **21/**
EXTRAS—If with solid Walnut or Mahogany Top Coards, **3/6**
    If with self-locking Automatic Ratchet Stretcher, **2/6**

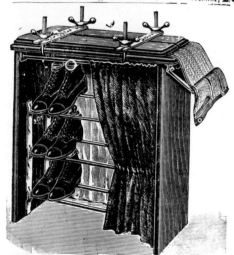

Boot Rack, Trouser Press and Stretcher.

The Boot Rack is srongly made with highly-polished
birch sides, imitation oak walnut or mahogany, and
nickel-plated steel rods. By unscrewing the nuts, for
which a spanner is provided, it can be easily taken to
pieces, and packed into very small compass. Will
accommodate about **12 pairs of Boots**, and forms
a very convenient and rigid stand for the Trouser Press
With each Boot Rack are supplied a pair of curtain
rods and all the necessary fittings for attaching a press.
The National Trouseis Press, with Automatic Stretcher,
  Boot Rack, and Curtains back and front   ... **50/**
The National Trousers Press, with Automatic Stretcher
  and Boot Rack, without Curtains **42/**
Boot Rack only, with polished Table Top and Curtains back
  and front **34/**
Boot Rack only, with Curtain Rods and Fittings for attach-
  ment to press, no Curtains **21/**
  Ditto, in solid Mahogany or Walnut ... extra **6/6**
Boot Rack only, with polished Table Top, no Curtains **25/**
  Ditto, in solid Mahogany or Walnut ... extra **8/6**
Curtains, in Dark Red, Green or Blue ... pair **9/**

GAMAGE'S
SPECIAL
TROUSER PRESS
AND STRETCHER
COMPLETE
Price **10'6**

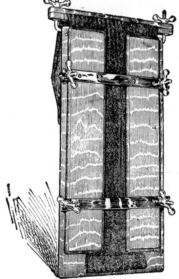

The "Mayfair" New Style of
Press. Built specially for Trousers with
permanent turn-up bottoms. Well finished,
nickel-plated fittings.   Price **12/6**

The "Piccadilly."
Heavier and superior quality, **18/-**

SIZE 24"x 12" WEIGHT ⊥0 LBS
THE AUTOMATIC STRETCHER FOLDS UNDER-
NEATH ..E BOTTOM BOARD OF THE PRESS
WHEN NOT BEING USED.

The "Portmanteau."

Specially designed for the Traveller. It takes
up very little space in Kit Bag or Suit Case,
and will effectively press and stretch from
1 to 4 pairs of Trousers **21/-**
    (Not including the Kit Bag.)
Two Cheaper Lines, complete with Stretcher
The **Tourist, 9/-**   The **Portable, 10/6**

The "Kit Bag"

Combined Trouser Stretcher
and Coat Hanger.

Made in selected oak, with
best nickel-plated fittings.

Size 18 by 15 in.

Weight 2¾ lbs.   Price **10/6**

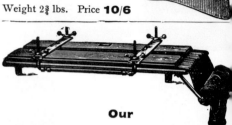

Our
"Challenge" Press and Stretcher

Polished oak finish, Nickel-plated Fittings.
Special value .. **12/6**

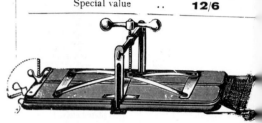

The "Service" Press.
Solid Rubber Feet.
The strongest Press you can purchas

ALMOST A TON PRESSURE OBTAINED
BY A FEW TURNS OF THE SCREW.
WILL TAKE UP TO **12** PAIRS OF TROUSER
Solid figured Oak top boards, moulded edges. Five-ply
bottom board ⅜ in. thick. Polished or fumed oak.
Nickel-plated or Antique Copper-bronzed Fittings.
Fitted with self-locking Automatic Ratchet Stretche
Size of Press, 30 in. long, 14 in. wide, **50/-** complete
Or supplied without Patent Stretcher, **45/-**
Can be fitted with solid Walnut or Mahogany to
boards for **4/-** extra.

Boot Cabinet.

With **3 Drawers and Trouser Press**, complete
A HANDSOME PIECE OF FURNITURE.
Supplied in Oak or Mahogany.   Price **£6 7 6**

Or Cabinet, with polished top, but without
    Trouser Press .. **£5 0 0**

A **Large Selection,** Illustrated in our
Fancy List, sent on request.

POCKET CUTLERY.   Best Make and Finish.

No, F. 4810.
Two-blade Vest Pocket Knife.
Length closed, 3½ in. Stag or white handle.
Price   ..   **1/-**

No. F. 2109. Useful Two-blade
Pocket Knife. Length closed 3½ in.

Ivory or Stag handle   ..   **1/6**
With Pearl handle   ..   **39/**

Genuine Swedish Pocket Knives.

No.	F 3	F. 2	F. 1	F. 9
Size	5¼ in.	6¼ in.	7¼ in.	9 in.
Price	10½d.	1/3	1/6	2/-

No More Broken Finger Nails.
Opens easy by rings at end.
Two blades. Nickel handle.
Price   ..   **1/-**   **1 6**   **2/-**
Sterling silver handles, **7/6** and **8/6**

No. F. 180. Handy Two-blade
Penknife.
SUITABLE FOR LADIES' USE.
Ivory handle   ..   **2/-**
Pearl handle   ..   **3/9**

No. F. 120.
Vest Pocket Knife.
Two blades, and nail trimmer and file combined.
Ivory or stag handles, **2/6**
Pearl handle **4/6**

No. F. A202.
AMERICAN PATTERN.
Flat and compact Vest'
Pocket Knife and Nail File.

Nickel-silver handle
2/9
Ivory handle
3/6
Pearl or Shell handle
5/-
Sterling Silver handle
6/9

No. F. 4045.
Two-blade Knife.
Ivory or Stag handle
Price   ..   **2/3**

No. F. 1288.
The Smoker's Vest Pocket Knife.
Ivory handle   ..   **4/6**

No. F. A204. Fine quality Combination
Smoker's Knife. Two blades, scissors, button hook, cigar piercer, etc.
Length 3 in. Ivory handle   ..   **9/6**

No. 5323½. The Gent's Favourite Vest
Pocket Combination Toilet Knife and
Scissors. As illustrated.
Ivory handle **5/6**
Pearl or shell handle   ..   **8/6**

CAVENDISH BRAND.
Finest quality.
Two-blade Knife.
Ivory or stag handle,
3/11

No. F. A200. Smoker's Combination Knife.
Two blades, cigar piercer, tobacco stopper, button hook, &c.
Chequered horn handle   ..   **7/6**
Genuine ivory   ,,   ..   **8/6**

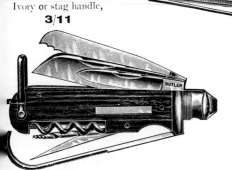

No. F. 2204. Strong Combination Knife.
FOR TOURISTS, CYCLISTS, &C.
Stag handle, **3/11**   Ivory handle, **4/9**

Gamage's Popular Combination Sports Knife.
Stag handle, with shakle and chain complete, **2/6**

No. F. 2104. The "All-round" Combination Knife.
FOR SPORTSMEN.
Length 3½ in.
Stag horn handle, **5/6**   Genuine ivory handle, **7/6**

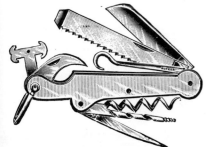

No. F. A219. Strong Useful Combination Knife.
Fitted with strong blade, saw, gimlet and corkscrew. Length 4 in. Nickel handle .. **9/6**

No. F. B. 400. The "GEM." Combination Sports
Knife, with chain complete. Ivory handle, **5/6**

No. F. A223. The "Colonial" Camp Knife.
Fitted with two strong blades, turnscrew, tin-opener, corkscrew, button hook, etc. Length 5 in.
Nickel handle   ..   **18/9**

Suitable Presents for Gentlemen.

Gamage's "Perfection" Razor.
(Has no equal at the Price)

Finest Sheffield Steel. Narrow, medium or wide hollow ground blades. Black handles. We guarantee this Razor for two years. If not satisfactory, and being returned to us in good condition, we undertake to exchange same.   Price **2/6**

Gamage's Famous "Strong Beard" Razor.

Used daily by thousands, and highly recommended to those with heavy beards. Finest Sheffield Steel. Narrow, medium or wide blades. File-cut thumb grip. Black handle. Guaranteed 3 yrs. Price **4/-**

Gamage's "Silver Ring" Razor.

Manufactured in Sheffield from Huntsman's Special Steel. Narrow, medium or wide blades. Black handle. Nothing better made. Guaranteed three years.   Price **5/-**

The Latest In Safety Razor.

The only razor at less than One Guinea that can be stropped without removing the blade. Equal in workmanship and efficiency to any Guinea razor. Complete in handsome case. with special strop in hinged partition & 6 renewal blades, **10/6**

Twin-Plex Rotary Stropper
For Gillette Blades.

Strops both edges at once.

It is guaranteed to last and give perfect service for 10 years.

Full directions sent with each.
Price   ..   **15/-**

The "Clemak" Safety Razor.

Complete with Seven Blades and Stropping Handles.   Price **5/-**

The 'Popular' Case, with 12 Blades, **7/-**
The "Combination" Set, with Stropping Machine and Strop   ..   ..   ..   price **10/-**

Wilkinson's Patent Roller Safety Razor

In Leather Cases. Razor and 3 Blades, **17/6**
Razor and 5 Blades, **24/-**
Razor and 7 Blades, **30/-**
Razor and 7 Blades, **45/-**
Razor and 7 Blades, Stropping Machine, Shaving Brush and Soap. Price **50/-**

"Ever Ready" Safety Razor.

Complete with 12 blades and directions. In real leatherette box.   Gamage's price **4/6**
Advertised price, **5/-**

The 'Gillette' Safety Razor

With 12 New Process Blades.

In neat leather case.

Price   ...   **21/-**

Shaving Stand,

No. F. 500.

5½ in. bevelled glass mirror, polished nickel stand two china bowls and shaving brush.
Price   ..   **7/11**

No. F. 500D.

Style as above, fitted with plain and magnifying glasses.
Price   ..   **10/6**

Shaving Stands in Various Styles.
12/6   14/6   18/9   21/-   25/-

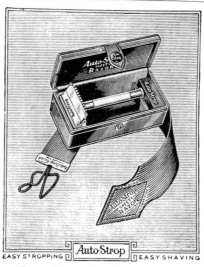

Standard Set (No. 1) **21/-**
The "Tourist" Auto strop Set. Price **27/-**
The "Travelling" Auto Strop. Shaving Set.
Consisting of Auto Strop, Safety Razor Strop, Shaving Brush, Soap, etc. Price **36/-**

The A B C Safety Razor
THE CHEAPEST AND NEATEST ON THE MARKET.
2/6

Complete in box with stropping attachment.
Price **2/6**   Extra Blades **1/3** each.

The "Wilkinson" Patent Roller Safety Razor.
Good quality.   Hollow Ground Blade.
Light, Simple and Clean.   Complete in neat case
Price **6/6**   Extra Blades **3/-** each extra.

SILVER-PLATE DEPARTMENT.

No. F. 8. Tea Set. "Georgian" Pattern.
Silver-Plated on Nickel Silver.
2½ pint size. Price **57/6** set of three pieces.

No. F. 6.
Afternoon Tea Set.
Silver-Plated on best Nickel
Silver. 1½ pint size

Price 42/9
per set of three pieces.

No. F. 5.
Afternoon Tea Set.
"Queen Anne" Pattern. Silver-plated
on Nickel Silver. 1 pint size.
Price **32/6** per set of three pieces.

No. F. 1291.
A Cheap Silver-Plated
Afternoon Tea Set.
"Queen Anne" Pattern.
Three pieces for **18/9**

No. F. 1302/1.
Silver-plated Tea Pot.

Neat Design. 2 pint	.. ..	**10/6**
Sugar Bowl to match	.. ..	**5/9**
Cream Jug to match	.. ..	**4/9**
3 pint Coffee Pot to match	..	**12/9**

. 1190.   **Silver-Plated Tea Set.**

"Queen Anne" Pattern
2½ pint size. Price **38/6**
per set of 3 pieces.

Coffee Pot to match,
3 pint size. Price **24/6**

No. F. 1211.
Silver-plated Tea Pot.

2½ pint size. Hand Engraved	..	**23/9**
Sugar Bowl to match	..	**15/9**
Cream Jug, to match	..	**11/6**
3 pint Coffee Pot to match		**27/6**

No. F. 1310.
Silver-plated Tea Pot.

2½ pint size. Hand-chased..	..	**33/9**
Sugar Bowl to match	..	**21/-**
Cream Jug to match..	..	**16/6**
3 pint Coffee Pot to match ..		**40/-**

No. F. 1276. Fluted
Pattern Silver-
plated Tea Set.

2½ pint Tea Pot ..	**15/9**
Sugar Bowl to match	**8/9**
Cream Jug to match	**7/6**
3 pint Coffee Pot to match	**19/9**

No. F 1425. Silver-Plated Tea Set.
2½ pint size. New design. Pierced mount.
Price **47/6** per set of 3 pieces

F. 1957. Six Tea Knives, imitation ivory handles, Velvet-lined Case. Price **8/11** also at **10/6** & **12/6**

No F. 1134. Six Tea Spoons and Sugar Tongs.

Electro-plate **11/6**
Sterling Silver **27/6**
Complete in velvet-lined Case.
Silver Teas and Tongs, various patterns, from **21/-**

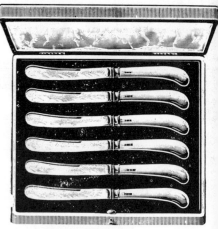

No. F. 1947. Six Silver-handle Tea Knives. Complete in velvet-lined Case. Assorted Styles.
Price **19/6**
Also in Various Patterns: **11/9 14/9 17/6**

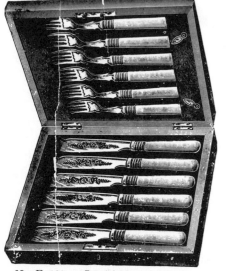

No. F. 130. Special Value. Six Pairs
Fish Knives & Forks.
Silver-plated and Engraved Blades, Ivorine Handles, Walnut Polished Velvet Lined Case. Price **15/6**
Superior qualities, Extra Silver-plated. Various styles of Engraving. Prices :—
18/6 21/- 25/- 27/6 32/6

No. F. 88. **Oak Cabinet.** Fitted with serviceable Sheffield Steel Table Cutlery, and Electro Plated Spoons and Forks.

6 table knives, 6 dessert knives, 1 pair meat carvers, 1 steel, 6 table forks, 6 dessert forks, 6 dessert spoons, 4 table spoons, 6 teaspoons. Imitation Ivory handles.

Quality A **90/-** B **105/-** C **126/-**
Or with Ivory Handles.
£16 10 £18 10 £21

No F. 5058. Joint Carvers and Steel. Sheffield Steel Blade. Point Stag Handles.
Complete in Velvet-lined Case.
Special Value **10/6**
Other Styles.
Superior Quality and Finish.
12/6 15/6 18/6 21/- and **27/6**

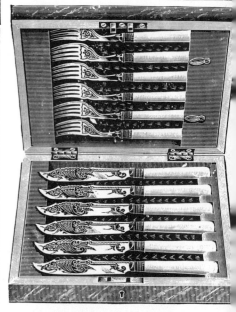

No. 543. **Fish Knives and Forks,**

Six Pairs. Serviceable quality Silver-plate. Neatly Engraved Blades, Grained Ivorine Handles, Hall-marked Silver Mounts, Solid Oak Case. Price .. **27/9**

Case as above, containing 12 Pairs Fish Knives and Forks.
Price ... **47/6**

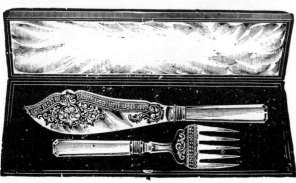

No. F. 4033.
Fish Servers.
Silver-plated
Richly Engraved
Blades.
Complete in Velvet
Lined Case.
Grained Ivorine
Handles
Price **11/9**
Genuine Ivory
Handles
Price **15/9**
Other Styles :—
Ivorine Handles, **12/6**
14/6 18/9 20/- 23/9
Ivory Handles
8/6 25/6 27/6 32/6

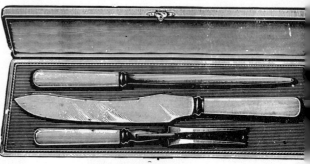

No. F 77. Joint Carvers and Steel.
Hand-forged Blades. Grained Ivorine Handles. Leather Case
Price **15/9**

(Five pieces) Joint Carvers, Poultry Carvers and Steel.
Ivorine Handles. Price **28/6**

Silver-Plate Department.

No. F. 798. Silver-plated on Nickel Silver
Cruet Frame. Cut Glass Bottles.
4 bottle, **12/9**   6 bottle, **18 9**

No. F. 4066. **Cake Basket** "Queen Anne" Fluted Pattern.
Silver-plated on Nickel Silver.   Special value.   Price **10/11**

No. F. 324.
Splendid value
Cruet Frame.
Silver-plated on
Nickel Silver.
Cut Glass Bottles.
Price **17/9**

No. F. 5355. "Connaught" Cut Crystal Glass
Salad Bowl.
Silver-plated on Nickel Silver Mount and Servers.
Price, complete   ...   **17/9**
or with Sterling Silver Mount and Servers ... **56/6**

No. F. 4539. **Cake Stand.** Silver-plated
on Nickel Silver Frame, 4 china plates. Height
16in. **18/9**   No. F. 4537. Different Shape Frame
with two plates. Height 14 in.   Price **14/9**

No. F. 13018. **Salad Bowl and Servers.** Rich Decorated
China. Silver-plated on Nickel Silver Mount, and Servers with China
Handles.   Price ...   **19/9**   Smaller size Bowl ... **16/6**

No. F. L. 1808.
**Egg Frame
and Spoons.**
James I. pattern.
Silver-plated on
nickel silver.
4 cups, **24/6**
6 **35/9**

No. F. L 258/1.   **Egg Frame and
Spoons.** Silver-plated on nickel silver.
4 cups, **12/11**   5, **14/6**   6, **16/6**

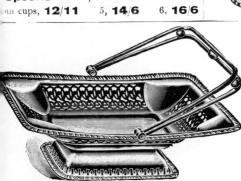

No. F. 391.   **Cake Basket.** Pierced design.
Silver-plated on Nickel Silver.   10½ by 8   Price **14/6**

No. F. 14774.   **Cake Stand.**
Silver-plated on Nickel Silver.   Price **17/6**

Fine Quality Silver-plated Cake Basket.   Saw
Pierced Design.   Size 11 in. by 8½ in.
Price   ..   **25/-**

Silver-Plate Dept., Butter and Jam Dishes.

No. F. 3. Silver-plated on nickel silver cover for 1lb. size **Marmalade Jar.** Price **5/11**

No. F. 87. **Preserve Jar.** Fine Cut Glass. Silver-plated on nickel silver mount and spoon, **3 11** Sterling Silver mount and spoon. Price **11/9**

No. F. 1683. **Double Shell Jelly Frame and Spoons** Fitted with two glass linings. Silver-plated on nickel silver stand and spoons. Price **13/9**

No. F. 14. New Pattern **Preserve Dish.** Silver-plated on nickel silver frame and cover. Price **5/3**

No. F. 13236. Dainty Coloured **Preserve Dish.** Silver-plated on nickel silver frame and spoon, **6/6**

No. F. 2421. **Double Preserve Dish.** Rich decorated china. Silver-plated on Nickel Silver Frame. Price **13/9**

No. F. 2415. **Preserve Stand.** Pretty decorated China Dish. Silver-plated on nickel silver frame, **8/9**

No. F. 144. **Shell Butter Dish and Knife complete.** Price **2/9**

No. F. 5038. **Covered Shell Butter Dish and Knife.** Silver-plated on Nickel Silver. Price **8/9**

No. F. 403. **Butter or Preserve Dish.** Bright Pressed Glass. Silver-plated on Nickel Silver Tray. Including Butter Knife or Jam Spoon. Price **3/**

No. F. 1024. **Glass Butter Dish.** Silver-plated Mounts. Price **6/11**

No. F. 183. **Cut Glass Butter Dish.** Silver-plated on Nickel Silver Mounts. Price **6/11**

No. F. 14069. **Glass Butter Dish** Silver-plated on Nickel Silver Mounts. Price **8/6**

No. F. 107. **Double-Shell Butter Dish** Silver-plated on Nickel Silver. Length 8½ in. Price **12/6**

No. 4675. **Butter Dish.** Revolving Cover. Silver-plated on Nickel Silver. Price **21/-**

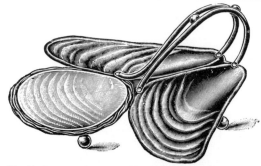

No. F. C 2259. **Lunch Frame** for Biscuit, Butter and Cheese. Silver-plated on Nickel Silver. Price **19/9**

No. F. 4451. **Cheese Dish.** Silver-plated on Nickel Silver. Complete with Glass Lining. Price **17/6**

SILVER-PLATE DEPARTMENT.

No. F. 200.
Cut Crystal Glass Sugar Bowl
Silver-plated on nickel silver
Mounts and Spoon complete.
Price .. **7/6**

No. F. 209. **Toast Rack.**
"Merry Thought" Silver-plated on nickel silver. Price **5/3**

No. F. 2831. Silver-plate **Sugar Scuttle and Scoop.** Price .. **10/6**

No. F. 10. **Toast Rack.**
Silver-plated on nickel silver. Price **9/6**
No. F. 9. Five-bar Toast Rack. Design as above, **6/11**

No. F. 3614. **Toast Rack.**
Silver-plated on nickel silver.
Price **3/11**

No. F. 226.
Sugar Dredger.
Fine Cut Glass. Silver-plated on Nickel-silver mount. Height 6¾ in.
Price **2/6**

"Connaught" **Condiment Set.**
Salt, Pepper, and Mustard. Cut Crystal Glass. Silver-pated mounts, **5/3**
Sterling Silver mounts, **15/9**
Mounted Spoon extra.

No. F. 30.
Crystal Glass Double **Pepper and Salt.**
Silver-plated mounts **2/11**
Sterling Silver mounts **5/3**

No. F. 176.
Sugar Dredger.
Very fine Etched Glass.
Silver-plated on Nickel-silver mount .. **5/9**
Sterling Silver mounted **13/9**

No. F. 46.
Two Cut Glass **Salt Pourers.**
Sterling Silver mounts.
Complete in velvet-lined case ... **7/11**
No. F. 46½s. Above pattern, Cut Glass **Salt, Pepper and Mustard.**
With Sterling Silver mounts and Spoon.
Complete in case .. **18/9**

No. F. 2. Pair Cut Glass **Knife Rests,** Sterling Silver mounts.
Complete in velvet-lined case, **8/3**

No. 750.
Silver-plated **Cruet**
with Salt Pourer.
Fancy Cut Crystal Glass.
Price **9/6**

No. F. 46s. Two Cut Glass **Salt Cellars,**
Sterling Silver mounts and Spoons, in velvet-lined case ... ... price **7/6**

Fo. F. 10342½.
Sterling Silver Swan **Salt Cellar and Spoon.**
Glass lining. Illustration two-thirds actual size.
Price .. **5/-**

F. 125B. Crystal Glass, Double **& Vinegar Bottles.**
Sterling Silver mounts .. **6/11**

No. F. 3419. **Sugar and Cream Frame.** Silver-plated on nickel silver. Price .. **15/9**

No. F. 4844.
Breakfast Cruet
Silver-plated on Nickel-silver Frame. Cut Glass.
Price .. **7/9**

No. F. 639. **Fruit or Salad Bowl.**
Choice Wedgwood China. Silver-plated on nickel silver Frame and Spoon. Price **25/9**

Silver Plate Department   Useful Xmas Gifts

No. F. 2417.
Toddy Glass
And Silver-plated Holder
Suitable for all Hot Liquids.
Price .. **5/6**

No. F. 672.
Toddy Glass.
Silver-plated on nickel
silver holder.
Price .. **2/4**

No. F. 3881.
Syphon Stand.
Silver-plated on Nickel
Silver.
Price .. **11/-**

No. F. 3882.
Syphon Stand.
Silver-plated on Nickel
Silver.
Price .. **11/-**
Other styles,
14/6 17/6 21/-

No. F. 121. Spirit Flask.
Leather covered top, silver-
plated cup, bayonet fastener.
Height 5½   6   6½ in.
Price **10/6 12/6 13/6**

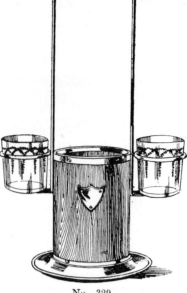

No. 329.
Syphon Stand.
Seasoned Oak and Silver-plated on nickel
silver fittings.
Fitted with two glasses.
Price **22/9**

No. 330.
Style as above. Fitted with 4 good
quality glasses.   Price **27/6**

No. F. 504. Spirit Flask.
Leather covered top,
electro-plated chased
cup, screw top.
Height 4½ 5½ 5¾ in.
Price **4/6 5/- 5/6**

Silver-plated
Nickel Silve
Cut Crystal g
decanter with
goblets.   4

No. F. 2488. **Liqueur Stand.**   Silver-plated on Nickel Silver Mounts.
Crystal Glass.   Price ... **40/-**

No. F. 1032. Silver-plated
Syphon Combination
Including Four Glasses.
Price .. **23/6**

No. F. 2092.
**Whisky or
Brandy and
Soda Stand.**

No. F. 114.
Cut Crystal **Glass Jug.**
Silver-plated on nickel
silver mount.
1½ pint .. **11/6**
2 ,, .. **14/6**

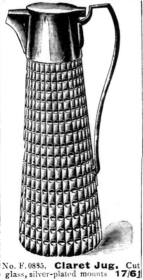

No. F. 0885. **Claret Jug.** Cut
glass, silver-plated mounts **17/6**

No. 1733.
**Combination
Liqueur Stand.**
Three bottles and glasses. Drawer
for Cards, etc.
Space for Cigars, etc.
Plaid bottles **38/9**
Half-cut ,, ... **45/-**
Full .. ,, ... **57/6**

No. F. 1012/B.
Claret Jug. Cut glass, silver-plated mounts **22**
No. F. 1012. Best quality mounts and finish .. **3**

No.. F. 4461.
Ice Pail.
Cut glass, Silver-pla
on Nickel Silver Mou
Price .. **13/9**

SILVER-PLATED VASES AND FLOWER STANDS.

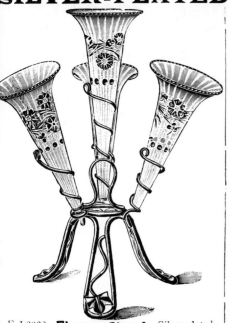

.F. L2362. **Flower Stand.** Silver-plated Nickel Silver. Effective Engraved Glass Vases. Height 12 in.   Price .. **13/6**

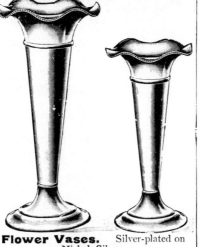

Flower Vases.   Silver-plated on Nickel Silver.
No. F. 1.   Height 5⅝ in. ..   **5/9** pair.
No. F. 2.   ,,   7 in. ..   **7/9**   ,,

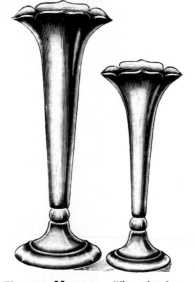

Flower Vases.   Silver-plated on Nickel Silver. No. F. 58. Height 7¾ in. Price **10/9** pair. No. F. 57.   Height 8¾ in.   Price **13/6** pair.

No. F. 2460.   **Flower Stand.**   Silver Plated on Nickel Silver Frame. Cut Glass Tubes. Size 13½ by 8½ by 10½ in. Price **39/9**

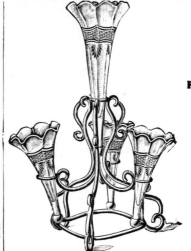

No. F. 2461.

Flower Stand.

Silver Plated on

Nickel Silver.

Cut Glass Tubes.

Height 15½ in.

Price .. **24/9**

No. F. 2459.
Flower Stand.
Silver Plated on
Nickel Silver.
Engraved Glass
Tubes. Height 15½ in.
Price **26/6**

No. F. 1981.

Flower Stand.

Smart Design.
Silver-plated on
nickel silver.

Price .. **37 6**

No. F. 17.
Flower Stand.
Silver-plated on Nickel Silver.
Height 9 in.   Price **11/6**

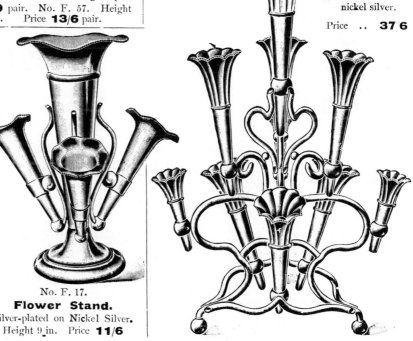

No. F. 2080.   **Flower Stand.**
ilver-plated on nickel   silver.   Price **38 6**

Delicacies for the Festive Xmas Season.

FULL LIST SENT ON APPLICATION.

Christmas Puddings.

THE REAL OLD ENGLISH KIND!

A. W. GAMAGE, LTD., have the pleasure to announce that they are now able to supply for immediate dispatch to friends abroad rich Christmas Puddings, made expressly for them by the famous firm of Messrs. Peek, Frean & Co., Ltd., London. They are made from a famous Old English recipe and are guaranteed to contain only the finest and purest ingredients. As is the rule with all "Gamage" goods, these Puddings cost considerably less than is charged elsewhere.

PRICES :—

Miniature Puddings (in Basins) .. **2/4½** doz. or **3**d. each.

		In Basins.	In Tins for Export
No. 1 size pudding, approx.	1 lb.	**11**d. ea.	**10½**d. ea.
No. 2 ,, ,,	2 lb.	**1/7** ,,	**1/6½** ,,
No. 3 ,, ,,	3 lb.	**2/4½** ,,	**2/3** ,,
No. 4 ,, ,,	4 lb.	**3/1** ,,	**2/11½** ,,
No. 5 ,, ,,	5 lb.	**4/8** ,,	**4/6** ,,

Postage extra.

For cost of postage abroad write for Special Leaflet.

Xmas Mince Meat.

Superior quality. Prepared by Messrs. L. Noel & Co., from a Special Recipe.

1 lb. Glass Jar .. .. Price **7½**d. & **10½**d.
2 lb. ,, ... ,, **1/7½**

Can be had also in 4, 7, and 14 lb. Jars.

TEA.

Sensible Xmas Presents,

The famous Holborn Blend, specially selected leaf. Packed in lead Packets. Highly recommended for Strength, Delicious Flavour, and great Fragrance.

There has never been so good a blend of Tea produced at the price. Per lb. .. .. **1/4½**. Also in ½ lb. packets, **8½**d.

Postage extra except with other goods to value of **10/-** and over when Carriage is paid.

Fancy Tea caddies suitable for above, see page 404.

The A.W.G. Pure Coffee, ground or whole, the finest the world produces .. Price **1/8** per lb. Put up in ½ & 1 lb. tins

Specially recommended for our Coffee Machines and Percolators.

The famous Red, White and Blue Coffee (mixture) per lb tin **1/5½**
½ lb. tin .. **9**d.

Fruits in Syrup and in Jelly.

FOR DESSERT.

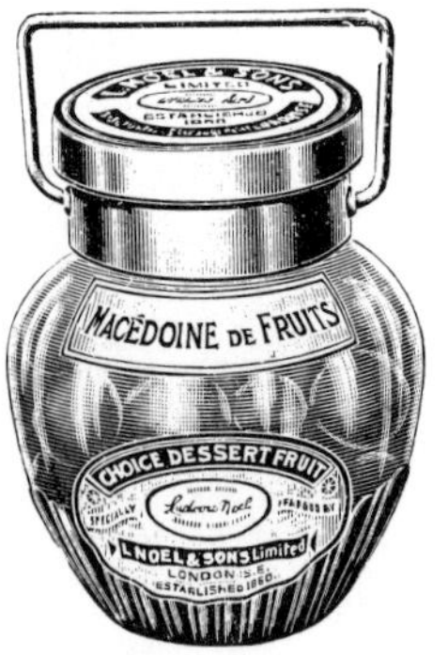

SMALL GLOBE.

	Large In Glass	Small Globes.	1 oz. Squat	2 oz. Bots.
Apricots, whole	2/6	—	—	1/7
,, halves	2/6	1/0½	11d.	1/7
Macedoine, Mixed Fruits	2/11	1/2	11d.	1/7
Peaches, White halves	3/3	1/3	—	—
,, Yellow whole	2/6	—	—	—
halves	2/6	1/0½	11d.	1/7
Pears, White halves	2/6	1/0½	11d.	1/7
Pineapple chunks	1/10	9d.	7½d.	1/2
,, slices (Hawaiian)	2/2	11d.	10d.	1/4½
Raspberries	2/6	1/0½	—	—
Young Stem Ginger	2/9	—	—	—

Denkin's English Dessert Canned Fruits

in heavy syrup, from Lord Shudley's Estate.

Ready for immediate use.		About 1 lb.	2 lb.	3 lb.
Black Currants	doz. **8/3**	**8½**d.	—	—
Raspberries and Red Currants	,, **8/3**	**8½**d.	**11½**d.	—
Loganberries	—	—	**1/-**	—
Golden Plums	,, **5/9**	**6**d.	**8**d.	**10½**d.
Victoria Plums	—	—	**9½**d.	**11½**d.
Damsons	—	**7½**d.	**1/-**	**1/3½**

Wilts United Dairies Diploma, Fruit Salad in glass, very choice **10½**d.

All Goods to value of 10/- post free.

All Goods to value of £2 and over Carriage Paid in the United Kingdom.

Write for special list of Table Delicacies post free.

Heinz Special Xmas Hamper.

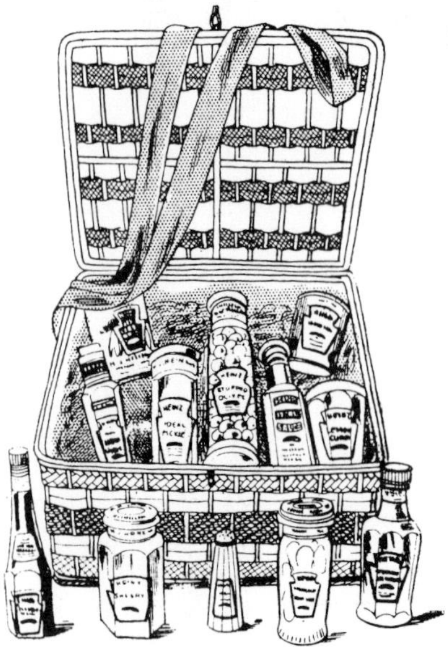

Must not be confused with an ordinary rough hamper. This is beautifully made of fancy basket work in Green and White with silk ribbons, and same is being offered more as an advertisement for our new department. When emptied makes a beautiful work basket.

Size of basket ... 14½ by 12½ by 7.

Contents.

Bottle of Ideal Pickles.
Fancy bottle of Stuffed Olives.
,, glass of Lemon Curd.
Large bottle of Tomato Chutney.
Fancy ,, Ketchup.
,, ,, Ideal Sauce.
,, ,, Stem Ginger.
,, Tin of Spaghetti Italienne.
,, small tin Evaporated, Horse Radish.
,, bottle of Sherry flavoured Calves Foot Jelly.
1 Tin of Pea Soup.
1 Castor of Celery Salt.

The quality is the highest. It is Heinz. The name is sufficient guarantee. Packed complete, **10/-**
Or sent carriage paid, **11/-**

Special Parcels & Hampers put up to Order.

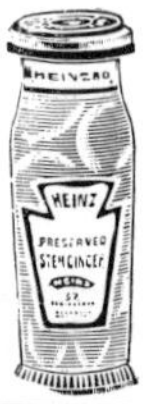

Heinz Famous Spanish Queen Olives.

10 oz. duchess bottle, **1/1** 24 oz. do., **3/-**

Preserved Stem Ginger.

Small bottle, **10½**d. Large bottle, **1/4**

Special Xmas Offer to introduce our New Department

State price and leave to us.

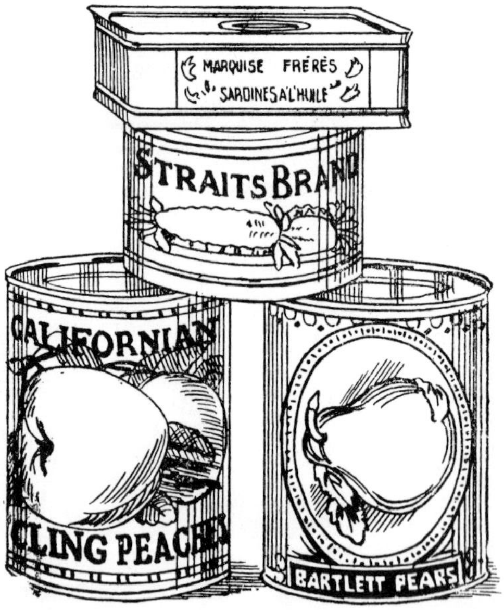

Exceptional care has been taken in the choice of the following, and A. W. Gamage, Ld., thoroughly recommend each article listed. We want you to make use of us. Any of these goods can be packed and sent with your other orders. We are offering you the pick of the World's Markets at exceptionally low prices. Give them a trial. We are sure of repeats.

Sardines,

Marquise Freres, Sardines a l'Huile, 18 oz. tin, patent opener.
10½d. **9/9** doz. tins.

Double Crown **LOBSTER** ½ tins price **1/3**

Salmon,

Disa Brand (Registered). Choicest Red Salmon. Finest selected fish, in one piece. Price **7½**d.

New arrival of Choice Fruits.

IN TINS.

Pineapple Cubes, From Singapore Pines. 1½ lb. tins, **4½**d. 2½ lb. tins, **7½**d. 3 lb. tins, **8½**d.

Apricots, Peasant Brand, packed where grown from selected fruit only, **8½**d. The Olympic Brand, extra choice, **9½**d.

Peaches, Direct from the Sunny Southern Climes. Peasant Brand Californian Cling Peaches, **8½**d. Olympic Brand, choicest extra standard quality, packed from selected fruit only. Californian Cling Peaches, **9½**d. Specially recommended.

Pears, Peasant Brand Bartlett Pears, packed where grown from selected fruit, **10½**d. Olympic Brand, extra choice Californian Bartlett Pears, **11½**d.

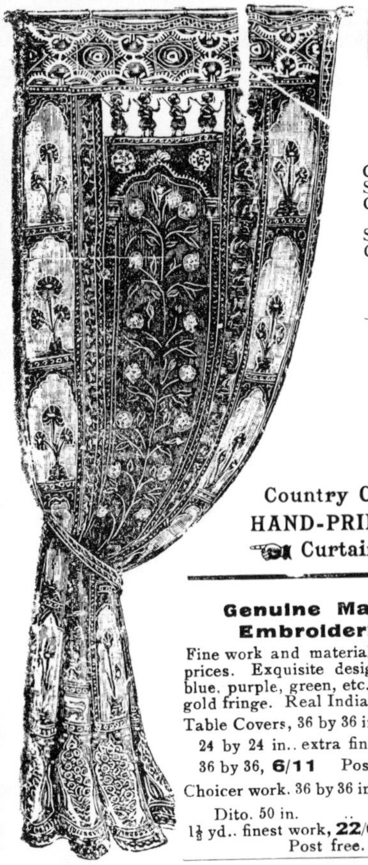

Oriental Embroideries

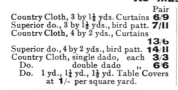

PRICES OF HANDSOME CURTAINS
As illustrated.

	Pair		Pair
Country Cloth, 3 by 1½ yds. Curtains	**6/9**	Furokoobad, Hand-painted. 4 by 2 yds., Curtains ...	**16/11**
Superior do., 3 by 1½ yds., bird patt.	**7/11**	Do. 3 by 1½ yds. ,, ..	**9/11**
Country Cloth, 4 by 2 yds., Curtains	**13/6**	Do. 3 by 2 yds., Spreads ..	**12/11**
Superior do., 4 by 2 yds., bird patt.	**14/11**	Do. 3 by 3 yds. ,, ...	**18/11**
Country Cloth, single dado, each	**3/3**	Do. 2 by 2½ yds. ,, ...	**18/11**
Do. double dado ,,	**6/6**	Do. 1 yard Covers, .. each	**1/3**
Do. 1 yd., 1¼ yd., 1½ yd. Table Covers at **1/-** per square yard.		Do. 1¼ yds. ,, ,,	**1/9**
		Do. 1½ yds. ,, ,,	**2/9**

WE HOLD an enormous Stock of **Beautiful Eastern Embroideries,** obtained from the choice of Novelties imported from TURKEY and INDIA.

JUST THE THING FOR A CHRISTMAS GIFT

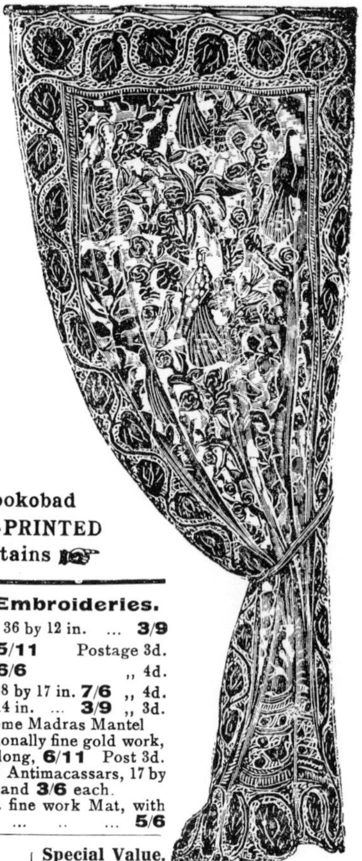

Country Cloth
HAND-PRINTED
Curtains.

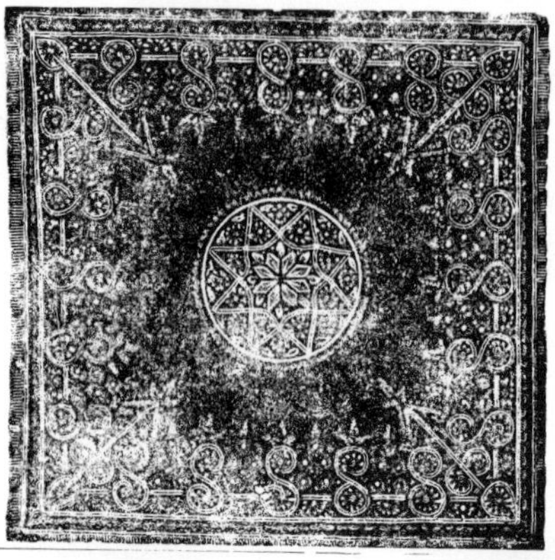

Furookobad
HAND-PRINTED
Curtains

Genuine Madras Embroideries.

Fine work and material at very low prices. Exquisite designs on dark blue, purple, green, etc. cloths, with gold fringe. Real Indian hand work.

Table Covers, 36 by 36 in. ... **5/6**
24 by 24 in.. extra fine work **6/6**
36 by 36, **6/11** Postage 4d.
Choicer work. 36 by 36 in. **7/6** **8/11**
Dito. 50 in. **15/9**
1½ yd.. finest work, **22/6** and **35/6**
Post free.

Madras Embroideries.

Table Centres, 36 by 12 in. ... **3/9**
54 by 12 in., **5/11** Postage 3d.
52 by 13 in., **6/6** ,, 4d.
Extra choice, 68 by 17 in. **7/6** ,, 4d.
Ditto, 36 by 14 in. ... **3/9** ,, 3d.
Very handsome Madras Mantel Border, exceptionally fine gold work, about 3 yds. long, **6/11** Post 3d.
Chair-backs or Antimacassars, 17 by 25, **2/9** and **3/6** each.
17 by 17, extra fine work Mat, with white border **5/6**

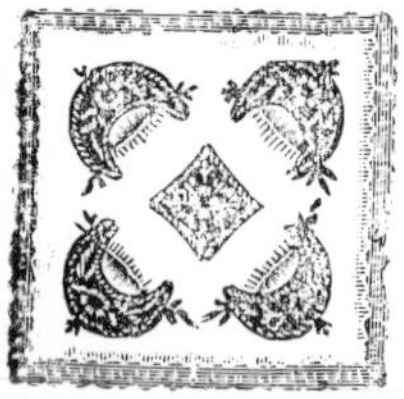

Turkish Embroidered Mats.

very special line, similar to illus ation, in a large variety of colours nd designs. Size 12 by 12 in.

Price **1/4½** Postage 3d

r this size Mat can be had sta aped with scalloped sides. **1 6** Postag

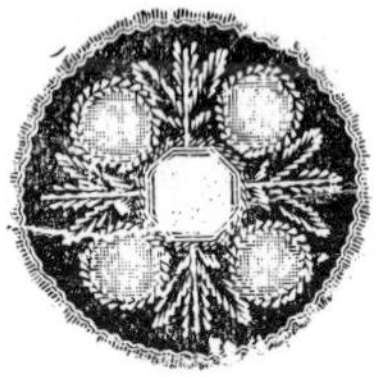

Turkish Embroideries.
Cheap Line. Turkish Mats
About 6 in. diam., various colours, with sequins, tinsel, etc. **4½**d. Post 1d.
Also in square shape, about 6 in. square, **4½**d.
Postage 1d.
Larger size, 10 by 10, **11½**d.
Postage 2d.

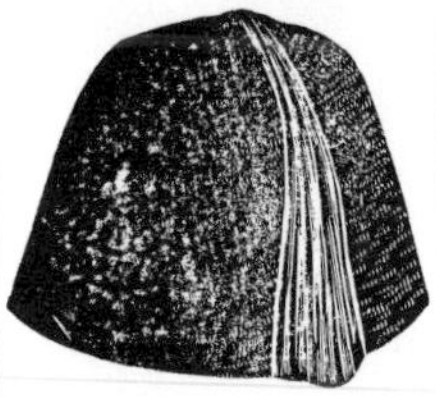

The Turkish Fez,
various sizes,

9½d. and **1/-** Postage 3d.

Belts, 2/9 3/9

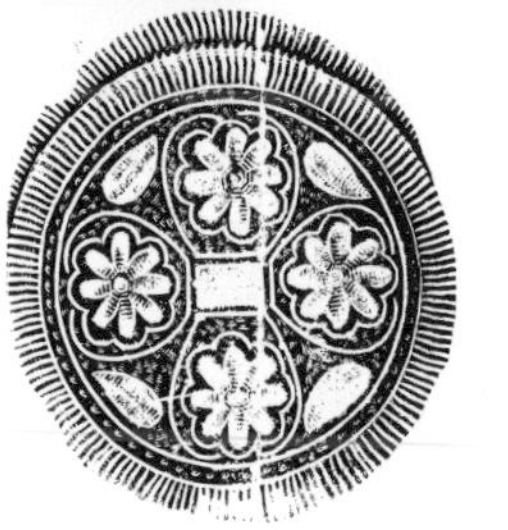

Madras Embroideries.

6 in. round Mats, **6**d. in. square, **6**d. Post 1d
10 in. round or square ... ... **1/-** ,, 1d.
12 in. ,, ,, ... **1/4½** ,, 2d.
16 in. round ... **2/6** 16 in. square, **2/9** .. 3d.

Special Value.

Madras Embroidered Muslin.

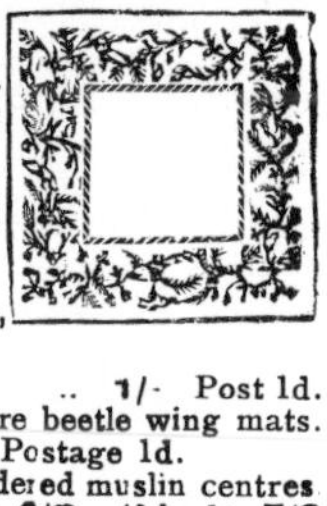

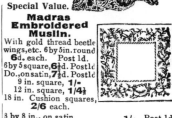

With gold thread beetle wings, etc. 6 by 5 in. round **6**d. each. Post 1d.
6 by 5 square, **6½**d. Post 1d
Do., on satin, **7½**d. Post 1d
9 in. square, **1/-**
12 in. square, **1/4½**
18 in. Cushion squares, **2/6** each.
8 by 8 in., on satin ... .. **1/-** Post 1d.
6 by 6 in. round or square beetle wing mats.
Price **4½**d. Postage 1d.
Beetle wing and embroidered muslin centres
27 by 14, **3/9** 36 by 14, **4/6** 45 by 14, **5/6**
36 by 19, embroidered, **3/11** 34 by 16, tinsel **7/11**
Postage 2d. each.
1 yd square muslin Table Cover, embroidered with beetle wings, **5/6** **5/11** **8/6**
54 in ditto **15/9** 45 in., **11/9** 24 in., **3/11**

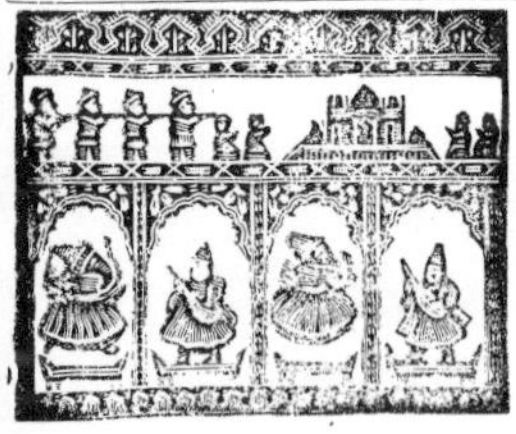

dian and Japanese Dadoes.

In various sizes and designs.

able for bazaars, walls and genera decorating.

an Dadoes, similar to illustration, yds. long by 16 in. deep, **3/6** **6/6**

anese, various colours and designs, 25 yards, by 27 in., **21/6**

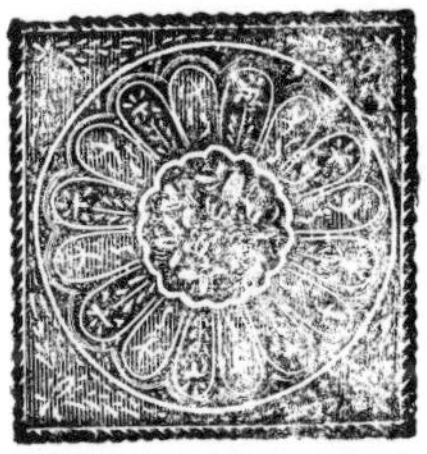

Turkish Embroidered squares and Covers.

Beautifully worked Cushion Squares or Table Centres in a large variety of designs and colours, hand-worked, size 20 by 20 in.
Price **3/6** Postage 3d.

Similar to above, but larger, very handsome Table Cover or Cloth 36 by 36. **15/6** Post free.

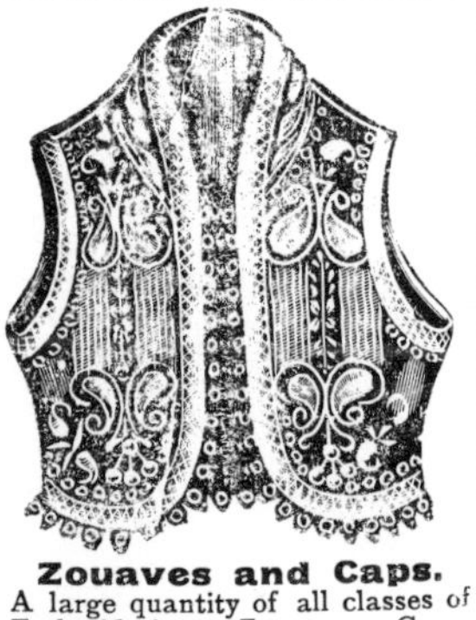

Zouaves and Caps.

A large quantity of all classes of Embroideries, Zouaves, Caps, Belts, etc., are kept in stock, too numerous to mention.
Embroidered Zouaves from **6/9**

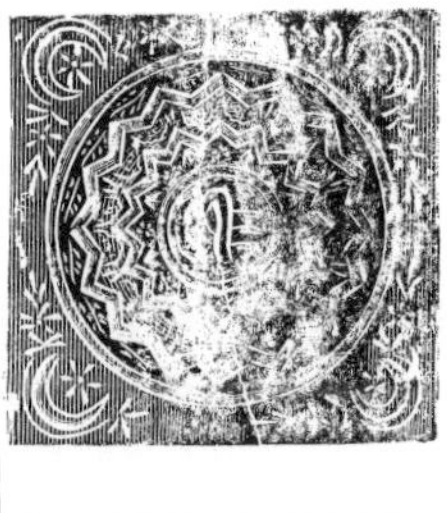

Cushion Squares.

Finest quality, very best work. Turkish Embroideries, large size Cushion Squares. Exceptionally handsome. Various colours.
4/6 **5/6** **6/6** **8/6** **10/6**
Table Covers.
8/6 **11/6** **15/9** **25/6**

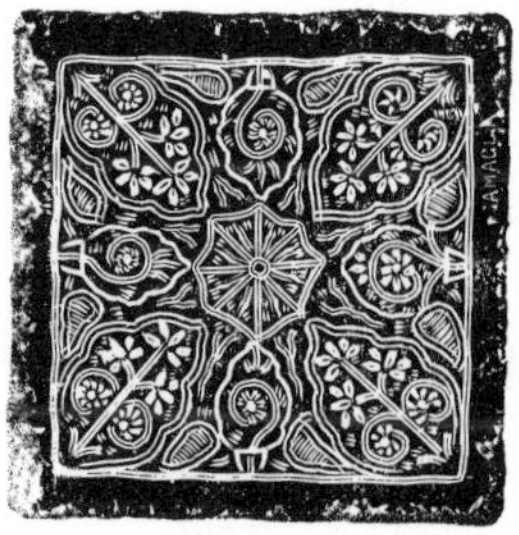

Delhi Squares. Indian cloth, hand printed in colours, all different designs suitable for Cushion Squares or Table Covers, size 24 by 24 in. **9**d. Post 1d.

yd. square Delhi Cover, native cloth, **1/-**
Postage 1½d.

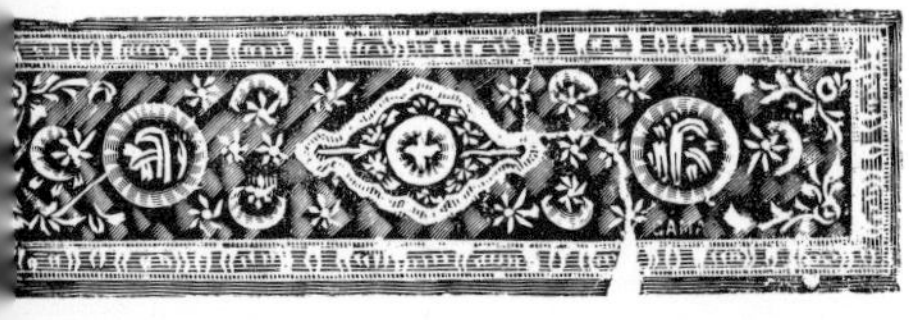

Eastern Embroidered Table Centres or Piano Tops.

Various coloured satin, beautiful designs, gold and silver tinsel, suitable for pianos, sideboards or tables. Handsome Present.

48 by 12 in. **6/11** Extra fine work and longer, 54 by 12 in., **8/6**
Postage 3d.

Turkish Table Centres.

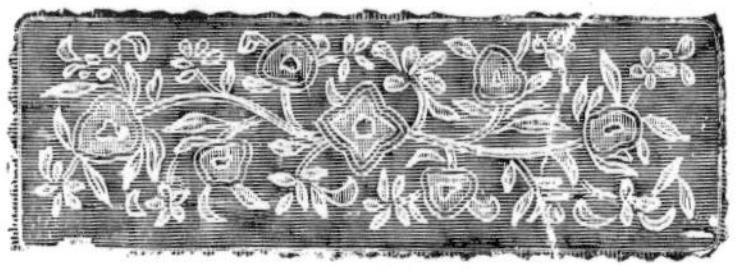

Handsome centre in all colours, beautifully worked, hundreds of different patterns.
22 by 11 in., **2/11** 27 by 12, **3/11**
36 by 12 in., **4/11** Postage 3d.

Better quality Tinsel Work.
17 by 12, **2/6** 27 by 12, **4/11**
2 by 12, **3/3** 36 by 12, **6/11**
23 by 12, **3/11** Post extra

Special Notice. In All Oriental Goods Designs and Exact Sizes cannot be guaranteed, but nearest will be sent.
All Goods to the value of 10/- and over on this page post free.

Damascus Furniture make Acceptable Xmas Gifts.

Kus Kus Fans. Made from Eastern Aromatic Roots. **10½d.** and **1/3**
Post 3d

Folding Tray Stands in good quality Whitewood, **6/11** Carved, **12/6** to **22/6** Carved and Inlaid, **15/6** to **25/6**

Trays suitable on another page.

Chopper pattern Kus Kus revolving Indian Fan.
Price ... **9½d.**
Postage 3d.

Indian Peacock Feather Fans or Screens. Embroider'd with beetle wings, &c. Various shapes.
Price **9½d.**
Postage 3d.

X. 91. Damascus Carved Moucharabia Screen 3-folds. Exceptionally fine work.
4 ft. high, **75/-** 5 ft. **97/6**
6 ft. 5 in. **£8 18 6**
Also large 4-fold Screens, **£9 17 6**

X. 53. Damascus Stool, carved and inlaid, 20½ by 14½ in.
Price **26/6** Packing 1/-

X. 56. Cairo Inlaid Stool, beautifully Carved and Inlaid.
16 in. high, 11 in. wide ... **11/9**
18½ ,, 12½ ,, **16/-**
21½ ,, 15 ,, **19/6**
23 ,, 17 ,, **25/-**
Carriage forward under 20/- value. Crate 1/-

X. 157. Damascus Carved and Inlaid Coffee Stool,
16½ by 11½ in. ... **12/6**
19 by 13 in. ... **15/6**
20½ by 15 in. ... **21/6**
Crate 1/-

X. 362. Damascus Carved and Inlaid Pedestal, 36½ by 15 in.
Price, **30/** each. Crate 1/-

X. 69. Damascus Carved and Inlaid Flower Stand.
23 in. high ... **13/6**
30 ,, ... **27/6**
Crate 1/-

X. 40.
Best Inlaid Stools.
9½ in. wide, 15 in. high **9/6**
10 ,, 17 ,, **12/6**
13 ,, 18 ,, **14/6**
14½ ,, 19½ . **16/9**
Packing 1/-

Bombay Blackwood Teapoy.
X. 245. Carved Occasional Bombay Blackwood Table. 19 by 15 in.
Price **11/6** Crate 1/-

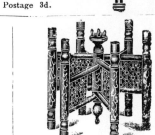

Indian, Damascus and Egyptian Tray Stand.
X. 24. Egyptian, plain wood, 6/
Damascus, plain carved—
18 by 18 in., **12/6** 21 by 21 in., 1
27 by 27 **22/6**
Carved and Inlaid—
12 by 20½ in., **15/6 22/6 25**
Best Inlaid Damascus—
21½ by 20½ in., **30/** 18 by 19 in., 2

X. 60
Algerian Inlaid Stool, b polish, extra fine wor
20½ by 18½ in. ...
20 by 15 in. ...
19 by 14 in. ...
Crates 1/-

X. 1326. Inlaid Folding Chairs. Carved. Price **£5 12 6**
X. 160. Beautiful specimens, Carved and inlaid, **47/6 & 59/6** Crate 1/-

X. 85.
Damascus Carved and Inlaid Folding Chair
Height 44 in.
Price ... **21/6**
Packing, 1/-

X. 75. Damascus Koran or Music Stand.
About inches high
20 23 26 30 32 36
7/6 12/- 14/6 17/6 21/6 23/6
No. 48. Inlaid, in four sizes.
6/9 9/9 12/- 14/6

X. 870. Carved Tea Table with Shelves, foldi
Size about 29 by 18 in. Price **63/-** Crate 1/-
X: 78: Without shelves. Price **52/6**

In all Oriental Goods sizes are appr mate. Designs cannot be guarante but nearest will be sent.

Goods to value of 20/- Carriage p

ESENTS FROM THE EAST. BENARES, MORADABAD, SYRIAN AND POONA BRASS WARE AS XMAS PRESENTS

X. 187.
enares Tumblers.
2½ in. ... **6½d.**
2¾ ,, ... **10½d.**
3 ,, ... **1/-**
4¼ ,, ... **1/3**
Postage 3d. to 5d.

X. 151.
Two-Handled Benares Vase, 11 in. high, very handsome.
Price **6/9** Post 6d.

X. 53.
Benares Brass-work Jug.

3½	4½	6½
1/-	**1/9**	**2/3**
9	10½	12 in.
4 6	**6/-**	**10/6**

New Moradabad Serviette Rings.
1/-
Postage 2d.
Also Cobra Pattern

X. 166.
Benares Peacock Candlestick.
New Design.
Small size, **2/-**
Large size, **3/6**
Post 3d. and 5d

Benares Brass Bottle.
10½ in. high ... **4/6**
15 ,, ... **6/6**
Postage 6d.

X. 156.
10 in. high ... **4/6**
12 ,, ... **6/9**
Massive Handsome Present
Postage 4d. and 6d.

Benares Brass Ware.
Spill Vase.
Size 8 in. high.
3 6
Postage 4d.

X. 157. Benares Tray.
Beautiful work.
9in., **3/6** 12in., **4/9** 15in., **6/-**
in., **7/6** 18in., **8/6** 19in., **11/6**
24in., **15/6** 27in., **22/6**

X. 189. Benares Hand Bell. 7 in. high, beautiful tone
Medium size **2/-**
Small ,, **1/3**
Large .. **3/-**

Benares Jardinieres.
Real Indian Handwork.

3in. across	**1/-**	6¼in. across	**4/9**
3⅛ ,,	**1/3**	6¾ ,,	**5/3**
3¼ ,,	**1/4½**	7 ,,	**5/6**
3½ ,,	**1/9**	7½ ,,	**5/9**
3¾ ,,	**1/11**	7¾ ,,	**6/11**
4¼ ,,	**2/3**	8 ,,	**7/6**
4½ ,,	**2/4½**	8½ ,,	**8/6**
4¾ ,,	**2/6**	8¾ ,,	**9/6**
5 ,,	**2/9**	9 ,,	**10/-**
5¼ ,,	**3/6**	9¾ ,,	**11/9**
5¾ ,,	**3/9**	10 ,,	**12/6**
6 ,,	**3/11**		

Poona Shaped Benares Jardinieres. Raised Work.

3¾	5	6	7	8½ in.
3/6	**4/6**	**6/6**	**9/11**	**14/6**

Also in various other shapes.

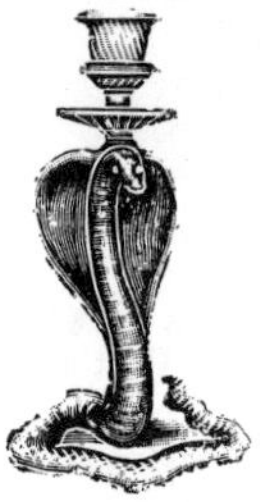

Benares Cobra Candlestick.
Unique Design.
Small ... **1/11**
Medium ... **2/11**
Extra large **6/3**
Post 3d. & 6d.

Benares Scolloped Tray.
5¼ in., **1/-** 12 in., **7/6** 15 in., **9/-**
18 in., **11/6** 20 in., **15/-**
24 in., **21/6** 27 in., **37/6**

Moradabad Trays
In all Sizes and all Prices.

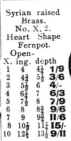

amascus Brass Incense Burner
erced tops, engraved holder in
abic characters. Very choice
astern work. All hand-made.
Approximate sizes.
n. high by 3 in., **8/9**
,, ,, by 4 ,, **10/6**
,, ,, by 4½ ,, **15/-** Post
,, ,, by 5½ ,, **19/6** free.
an also be had in silver inlay
extra cost. Pastilles for
urning, various, **4½d.** per doz.

Poona Bell,
Small **10½d.**
Large, **1/9**
Post 3d.

Ebony Elephant.
Real Tusks.

2	2½	3	3½ in.
1/3	**1/6**	**1/11**	**2/6**
4	4½	5	
2/11	**5/6**	**6/11**	

5½ in. **8/6** 6in. **10/9**
Post 3d. to 9d. extra.

Real Indian Joss Sticks (Incense used in their temples), **2d.** per bundle
Postage 1d.

Genuine Indian Carved Native Figures, of various casts and occupations, on decorated base. Hand-coloured. Size about 4 in. high. Price **9d.** each Post 2d.
A limited quantity only.

Moradabad Ware.
Enamelled Brass Goods of neat and distinct designs.

Syrian rass Finger Bowls
10½d. **1/3** **1/6** **2/-** each
Postage 3d.

Genuine Lucky Kaffir Bangles

1/- **1/6** **2/-** each
In Gold Cased,
3/- and **5/-**
Silver, **7/6** **10/6** **15/6**
Gold, **£2** **£3** & **£5**
These Bangles are handmade in 20 different designs by natives.

STATE SIZE OF GLOVE when ordering by Post.
POST FREE.

Syrian raised Brass.
No. X. 2.
Heart Shape Fernpot.

X.	Open-ing.	depth	
1	4	4½	**1/9**
2	4¾	5½	**3/6**
3	5¾	6	**4/-**
4	6½	7	**6/3**
5	7¾	8	**7/9**
6	8	8¾	**9/6**
7	9	9¾	**11/6**
8	10½	11¼	**15/-**
10	12½	13½	**9/11**

Raised Brass Syrian Fernpots.
No. X. 1.
Straight Shape.

X.	Open-ing.	depth	
1	3½	3¼	**1/3**
2	4	3½	**1/6**
3	4¾	4¼	**2/6**
4	5½	4¾	**3/-**
5	6¾	5¼	**3/11**
6	7¾	6¼	**5/6**
7	8	7	**6/3**
8	9	8	**8/6**

All sizes are approximate.

Benares Gongs.

Gong		Beater.
in. ...	**3/6**	**10½d.**
,, ...	**4/6**	**1/-**
,, ...	**5/6**	**1/6**
to 11½ in.	**6/9**	**1/9**
,, ...	**7/8**	**2/-**
,, ...	**8/11**	**2/-**

X. 210 Moradabad Enamelled Powder Box or Tobacco Jar, with lid, in 3 sizes. Size across top, 3½ in. **4/11** 2½ in. **3/-** 2 in. **2/3** Postage 3d. and 4d.

X. 217 Moradabad Bowls, in 4 sizes.
2¾ in. **9½d.** 3½ in. **1/3**
4 in. **1/9** 4½ in. **1/11**

X. 216 Moradabad Enamelled Tumblers, in 4 sizes, 5 in., **2/6** 4½ in. **2/-** 3½ in. **1/9** 2½ in. **10½d.**
Very Fine Work,
Postage 3d. and 4d.

Moradabad Cups and Saucers **2/6**
Vases, Goblets, Souries, Bowls, etc.
Price **2/3** **2/6** **3/-** **3,6** etc.

X. 10. Brass and Copper Damascus Jugs.
Height

6	8	9½	11½ in.
3/11	**5/6**	**8/6**	**11/6**

X. 142. Benares & Poona Goods. Various shapes.
From Poona ... **1/6**
,, Benares ... **2/6**
Also Benares Elephant
3/-

Dozens of other Brass Novelties too numerous to specify.

In all Oriental Goods sizes and prices are approximate Designs cannot be guaranteed, but nearest will be sent.

All Goods to the value of 10/- and over sent Carriage paid, other than this Carriage Forward.

Xmas Novelties in Silvered Japanese Antimony MAKE ACCEPTABLE PRESENTS.

Pot Pourri Boxes.
No. X. 5258/2. Assorted designs.
3 by 1⅛ in. .. **2/6** each Post 3d.
Smaller and Cheaper Pattern.
No. X. 5294/5 .. .. .. price **1/-** each

Powder Boxes
Dragon Design.
2¼ by 2⅜ in.
2/- ea. Post 3d.

No X. 5258/9.

Puff Boxes.
No. X. 5222/15/16.
Dragon design 3 in. **1/11**
4 in. **3/-** each Post 4d.

Antimony Serviette Rings **6d.** Post 2d.
Dragon and Floral Design.
Heavy design **10½d.**
Special value.

Dragon Tankard.
No. X. 5226/13.
Very handsome and massive.
2⅛ in. high.
Price **1/-**
Post 3d.

Antimony Stamp Boxes.
Various Designs.
No. X. 5266/32. Dragon Design, 2¼ by 2¼ in., **9½d.** 1-way
,, X. 5266/33. ,, ,, 3¼ by 2⅜ in., **1/-** 2-way
,, X. 5266/34. ,, ,, 5 by 2¼ in., **1/6** 3-way
Postage 3d.

Antimony Inkstands.
No. X 5286/25.
4⅞ by 2⅝ in.
Massive finish.
2 pots & penwiper
2/6 and **3/6**
Post 3d.

Various Designs. Other pattern Inkstands, **6½d** & **1/-**

Ducks and Stream Inkstands.
X. 5244/10.
8¼ by 4 by 2 in.
3/- each.
Postage 4d.

Willow Pattern Crumb Scoop.
No X. 5286/27.
12½ in. long. Price **2/6** each. Postage 4d.

No. X. 5284/13.
WISTERIA Pattern.
Oblong.

Pot Pourri Box.
Size 3½ by 2 in.
Price **2/3** each.

Trinket Boxes.
No. X. 5254/16.
Dragon Design.
1½ by 1½ by ⅞ in.
Price **6d.** each. Post 3d.
X. 5278/25. 2 by 1½ by 1 in.
Price **1/-**
X. 5278/22. 3 by 2 by 1¼ in.
Price **1/6** Post 3d.

Ring or Stud Boxes
X. 5248/13 Dragon Design.
2 by 1¼ in.
Price ... **1/6** Post 3d.

No. X. 5286/6. Willow Patt.

Trinket Box.
2 in. diameter.
Price ... **1/-** Post 3d.
X. 5286/2. 2 in. by 1⅛ in. deep
Price ... **1/6** Post 3d.

No. X. 5272.
Chrysanthemum Pattern.

Pot Pourri Jars on Stand.
Size 5 in. high. **3/6** Post 3d.
X. 5272/1. 5¼ in. high. **5/9** ,, 4d.

X. 5258/25. Dragon Design.

Jewel Caskets
Beautifully lined and padded in silk.
Various styles. About 5¼ by 4½ by 3 in.
Price **10/-** and **10/6** each.

Round Boxes
2½ in. diam. Chrysanthemum and Dragon Designs.
Price .. **1/-** each. Post 3d.

No. X. 5258/20.

Dragon Jewel Casket.
Satin Lined.
Size 3 by 3 by 3¼ in. high.
Price .. **5/9** Postage 4d.
3¼ by 3½ by 4 in. .. **3/11**
Chrysanthemum Pattern.

Oval Trinket Boxes.
Dragon Design. Gilt lined. Post
No. X. 5258 11. 2 in. ... **10½**
,, X. 5258 12. 2⅜ in. ... **1/-**
,, X. 5258/13. 3¼ in. ... **1/-**
Satin Lined :—
,, X. 5258/14. 2 in. ... **1/-**
,, X. 5258 15. 2⅜ in. ... **1/-**
X. 5258/16. 3¼ in. ... **2/-**

No. X. 301.

Silvered Antimony Glass Holder suitable
Milk, Drinks, etc. **1/9** Post 3d.

Match Boxes
No. X. 5254/2/3. Dragon Design.
Correct sizes. Ordinary size
Large size ... **1/-** Postage 3d.

No. 5288/47. **Antimony Parrot Inkstand.**
Size 3 in. high. Price **1/3** each. Post 3d.

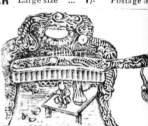

Japanese Antimony
Crumb Brush and Tray
Various designs.
Large size **2/11**
Smaller size,
1/11½
Medium size,
2/4½
Heavy Dragon Design.
with scoop,
2/6 complete.
Post 4d.

Japanese Antimony
Candle Rings
Assorted Patterns. Very effective. **3d.** ea. Post 2d.

Designs and Sizes are approximate in all ORIENTAL GOODS; Nearest will be sent. All Goods to value of 10/- and over carriage paid,

Antimony Tea Caddies
Antique Silver shape. Dragon Design.
5 in. Price **4/9** Postage 6d.
Various other patterns and designs,
wood lined, **7/6** to **15/6**

The Holborn Blend Tea for filling these caddies 1/4½ per lb., also in ½ lb. packets

Antimony **Tea Caddie**
Square shape. Dragon Design.
4½ in. Price **3/11** Post 6d.
Also oval shape & other designs.

For esents.

New Silvered Japanese Antimony Boxes, etc.

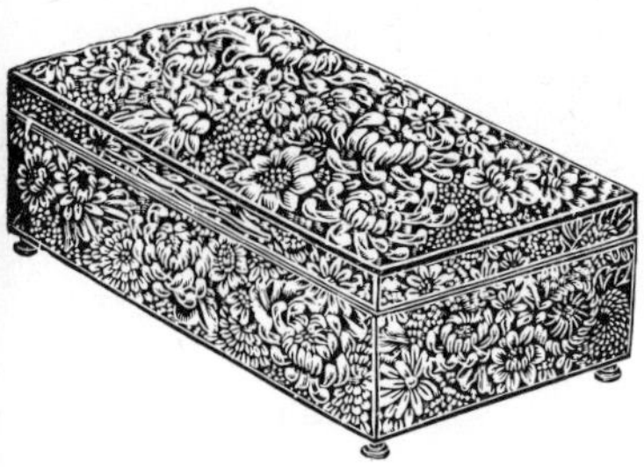

Cigarette Boxes.

Chrysanthemum Design. Post 4d. & 6d each.
X.5272/5. 3¼ by 3¼ by 1½ in. .. **2/-**
X.5272/6. 4 by 3 by 1¼ in. .. **2/6**
X.5272/3. 4¼ by 3⅜ by 2in , wood lined **4/6**
X.5272/4. 7½ by 3¾ by 2¼in. ,, ,, **6/-**
For Cigarettes, Wood-lined Boxes recommended

. X. 374. New Dragon Design **Hat Pin Box.** Size 8½ by 2½ by 3½ in. Satin lined, with lock and key **7/6**
11 by 2½ by 3½ in. ditto ditto .. **9/6**
. X. 528. As above, but unlined, without lock, ½ by 2½ by 2½ .. **5/11** Postage 5d.

. X. 37. Japanese Antimony **Glove Box** Dragon and Elephant Designs. Satin lined, with lock and key. 12 by 4 by 3. **15/6** Post free.

. X. 373. Handsome Satin lined Chrysanthemum and Monogram Design **Trinket Box,** with lock and key Size 4½ by 5½ in. Price **6 11** Post 4d.
. X. 377. As above, but in Dragon Design, 4½ by 3¼ in. Price **4/6** Post 4d.
. X. 522. Peacock Design, 3 by 4 in Price .. **3/11** Post 4d.

. X. 5234. **Cigar Boxes.** Dragon or Iris Design. 9 by 5½ by 3 in. **18/6** Post 6d
. X. 315H. **Cigar Boxes.** Special Line. Size 8 by 4½ in. Wood lined **10/6**

Cigarette Boxes.

No. X. 5222/22. Dragon design. 3¼ by 3¼ by 1½ in., **2/-** Post 4d.
Also in Chrysanthemum Design

No. X. 5286/40.
Willow Pattern **Cigarette Box,** unlined.
Size 3¼ by 3¼ by 1½, to hold 25, Price .. **2/3** Post 4d.
No. X 5286/41.
Size 4 by 3 by 1¼, **2/9** Post 4d.
No. X. 5286/42.
Size 4¼ by 3½ by 2½ to hold 50, lined cedar wood, **4/3** Post 4d.
No. X. 5286/43.
Size 7¼ by 3¾ by 2½, lined cedar wood. Price .. **6/9**

Hairpin Boxes. Dragon Design
No. X. 1H. 3 by 1½, **1/-** Post 3d.
Ditto 4 by 1½, **1/4½** ,, 3d.

Nos. X. 5284 and X. 5284/1. Chrysanthemum Design.
Glove and Handkerchief Boxes
Silk lined. Size of Handkerchief Box, 6¼ by 8 in.
Size of Glove Box, 12 by 3⅛ in. **15/-** ea. Post free

In all Oriental Goods, sizes and designs are approximate, and nearest will be sent. All Goods of value of 10/- and over Carriage Paid.

Cigarette Boxes

X. 5222/23. Dragon Design.
4 by 3 by 1¼ in. **2/6** Post 4d.
4 by 4 by 1¼ in. **3/-** ,, 4d.
No. X. 11H. 4½ by 3½ by ⅞ in.
Wood lined .. **3/-** Post 4d.

No. X. 14H. Very handsome, Dragon Design, wood lined **Cigarette Box,** 4 by 4 in. **3/11** Post 4d.
Order early, only a limited number

Jewel Boxes. Post 4d.
X. 5258/4. Lined Royal Blue Velvet. 3⅞ by 3 by 3¼ in. ... **3/6** each
X. 5292/23. Similar shape, fitted with lock and key. 4 by 3 by 1⅝ in. **4/6**

X. 5284/25. **Hairpin Boxes** 4½ by 1⅜ by 1½ in. Chrysanthemum Design. Price **1/9** Post 3d.

No. X. 53H. Silvered Antimony **Jewel Cabinet.** Dragon Design. Very handsome and exceptionally well made. One long and two short drawers, elegant handles Size 6 by 6 by 6 in. **15/6** Carriage paid.

X. 372. Jewel Cabinet, Velvet lined, drawers with lock and key. Size 6 by 4½ by 4 in. ... **15/-**

Several other patterns at **9/6** Post free over 10/- in value.

No. X. 9266. Japanese Massive Antimony Dragon design **Cigar Box** Cedar and oak lined, as illus. Price **21/-**

Others at **9/6** **18/6** **21/-** **25/6**

An IDEAL GENT'S GIFT.

No. X. 5236.
Cigarette Boxes on feet.
Dragon design, Inlaid Wood Lining.
4¼ by 3⅜ by 2¼, for 50 ... ... **5/-** each
No. X. 5236/1. 7 by 3¾ by 2½, for 100, **8/6** ,,
Postage 6d.
Cigar Box, unlined, 8 by 4⅜ by 3, **11/6**

Bamboo Design Antimony **Cigarette Box.** Wood lined. No. X. 282 3¼ by 4½ in. **3/11**
No. X. 368. 3⅜ by 6½ in. ... **6/6**
,, X. 214. 3¾ by 6 in. Unlined ... **3/9**
Postage 4d. and 5d. extra.

No. X. 517. Hawthorne Design Box. 3 by 2¼ in. Price ... ... **1 6** Post 3d.
Also Cigarette Boxes, same design, various prices

No. X. 5286/14.
Willow Pattern
Hairpin Box.
Size 4½ by 1⅛ in.
Price **1/10½**
Post 3d.

Noveltles in Silvered Japanese Antimony

Make acceptabl[e] Christmas Presen[ts]

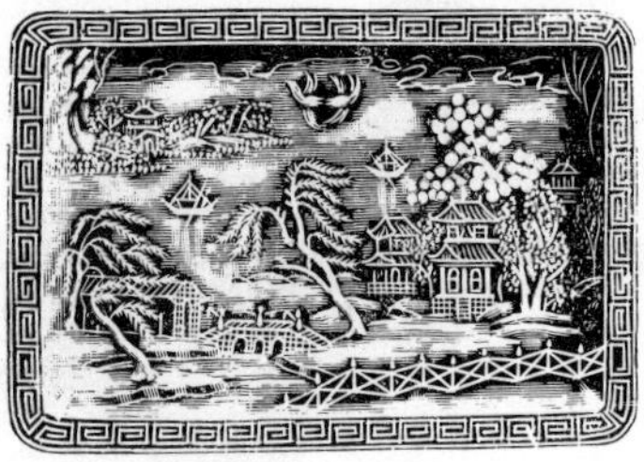

No. X. 5286/55. Willow pattern **Trays,** Size 9⅝ by 6⅞ Price **2**/-. postage 4d.
5286/47. Ditto. 4¾ by 3 Price **4½**d. each
5286/48. Ditto. 6 by 4½ ,, **7½**d. ,,

Round Willow Pattern **Ash Trays,**
5286/46. 5 in. diameter Price **7½**d. each.
5286/45. 4½ in. ,, ,, **6**d. ,,
5286/44. 3½ in. ,, ,, **4½**d. ,,

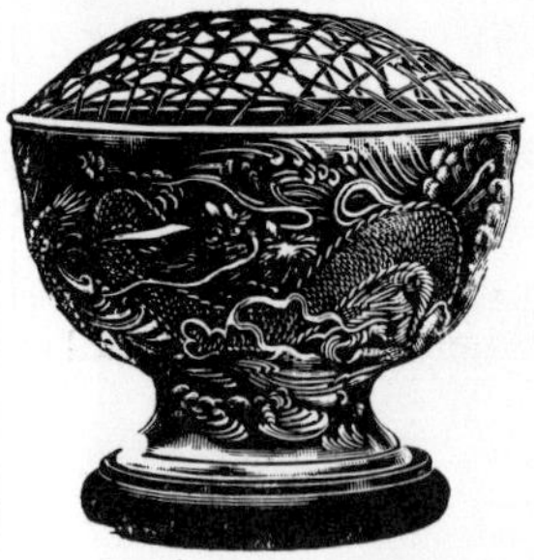

X. 5218 4.
Rose Bowls.
Dragon design

Size	Price ea.
4½ in.	**4 6**
5 ,,	**6/9**
6 ,,	**9/6**
7¼ ,,	**13/6**

Post 6d. & 9d.
Larger sizes, **18/6 21/6** and **30/-**

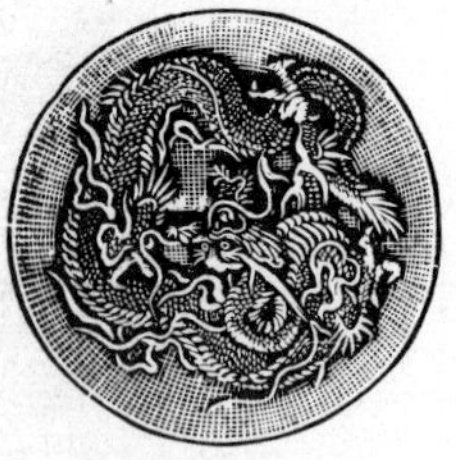

X. 5244/19. **Ash Tray,** Dragon Design.
3½ in. ... **4½**d. 4½ in. ... **6**d.
5½ in. ... **9**d. Post 3d.

Dozens of other various
Ash Trays
1d., **3**d., **4½**d., **6**d., **7½**d., **9**d., **1/3**, **1/6** & **1/9**

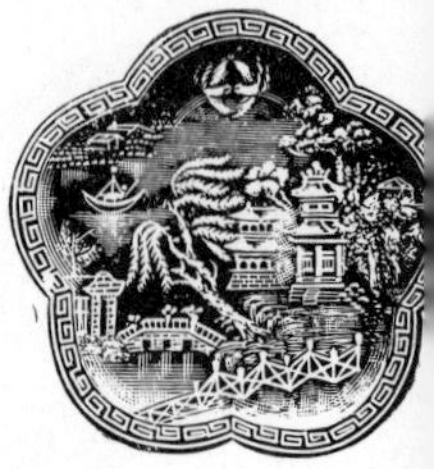

Ash or Pin Tray[s]
Willow Design. Three sha[pes]
3½ in. **4½**d. ea 5 in. **7½**d.
Postage 2d. & 3d.

Rose or Violet Bowl.
Plum Blossom Design.

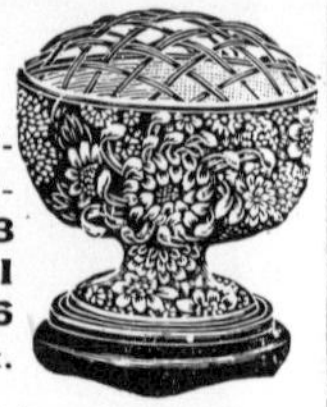

	in. diam.	
X. 5266/36.	2¼	**2/-**
X. 5266/37.	2¾	**3/-**
X. 5266/38.	3½	**4 3**
X. 5266/39.	4	**4/11**
X. 5266/17.	4¾	**5 6**

Postage 3d. to 6d. ex.

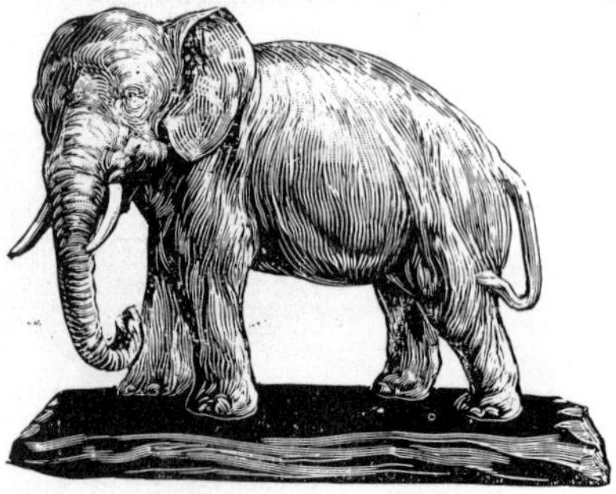

Silvered Antimony Elephants.
WONDERFUL MODELS.

X.	5252/8.	1¼ in. high.	**6**d. each
,,	5252/9.	2½ in. high, without stand ...	**9**d. ,,
,,	5288/19.	4 in. high, on stand ...	**1/6** ,,
,,	5288/20.	3¾ in. high, ...	**2/6** ,,
,,	5288/21.	4½ in. high, ...	**3 6** ,,
,,	5288/22.	5½ in. by 8 in. long ...	**4/6** ,,
,,	5288/23.	7½ in. high, on stand, 9in long	**8/9** ,,
,,	5286/24.	8½ in. high, about 12 in. long	**10/9** ,,
,,	5288/25.	8¾ in. high by 12¼ in. ...	**12/9** ,,

Postage 3d. to 6d. under 10/- value

No.	5288/39.	Tiger on Stand	**2/6** each.
,,	5288/15.	Do. large size	**5/11** ,,

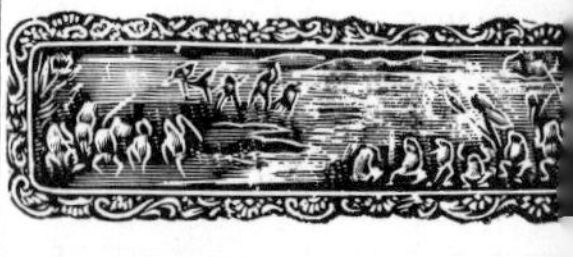

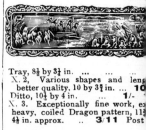

Tray, 8½ by 3½ in. ... ...
X. 2, Various shapes and leng[ths] better quality, 10 by 3½ in. ... **10**
Ditto, 10½ by 4 in. ... **1/-**
X. 3. Exceptionally fine work, e[xtra] heavy, coiled Dragon pattern, 11[…] 4⅛ in. approx. .. **3/11** Post

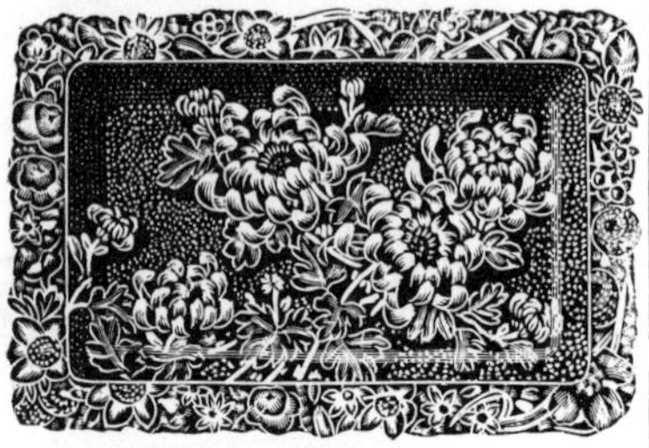

Japanese Antimony
Brush and Comb Tray.
Chrysanthemum Pattern.
No. X 5278/21. 10 by 6½ in. **2/9** Post 4d.
Various other patterns same price.

Finest Selection of
Japanese Antimony Ware.

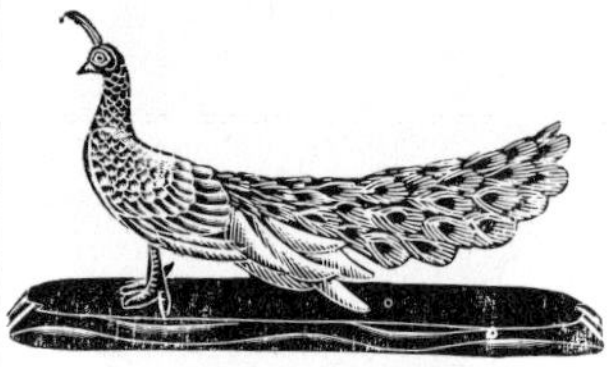

No. X. 53068.
Silvered Japanese Antimony
Peacock on Stand.
Price **5/-** each. Postage 4d.

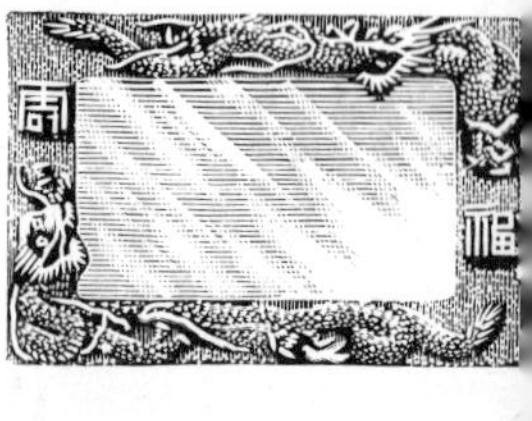

No. X. 5276/30. New Dragon Desi[gn]
Postcard Frame. 6½ by 4
Very choice. Price **1/9** each. Pos[t]

Antimony Card Trays
Price **1/6**, **2/6**, **2/10**, **3/6**, **4/6** […]

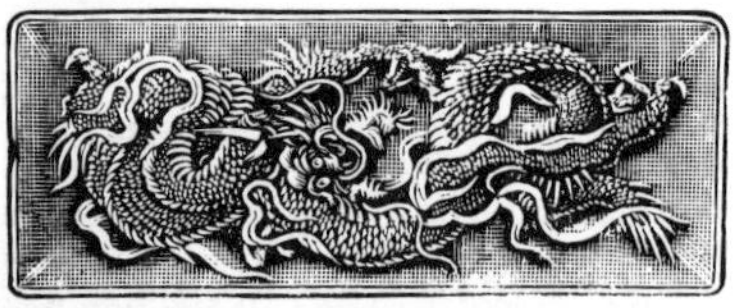

5244/11. **Pen Trays.** Dragon Design.
Size 8¼ by 3 in. Price **9**d. each. Post 3d.
,, 10 by 4 in. ,, **1/3** ,, ,,

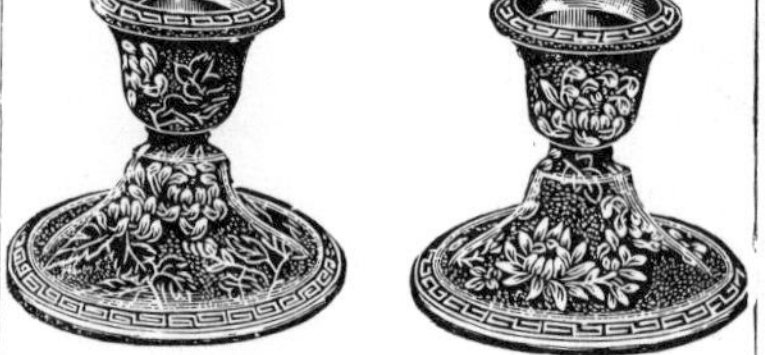

No. 5284/8.
Japanese Antimony **Candle Sticks.**
New Design. 3¼ by 3 in.
Price .. **3/11** pair.
Postage 4d.

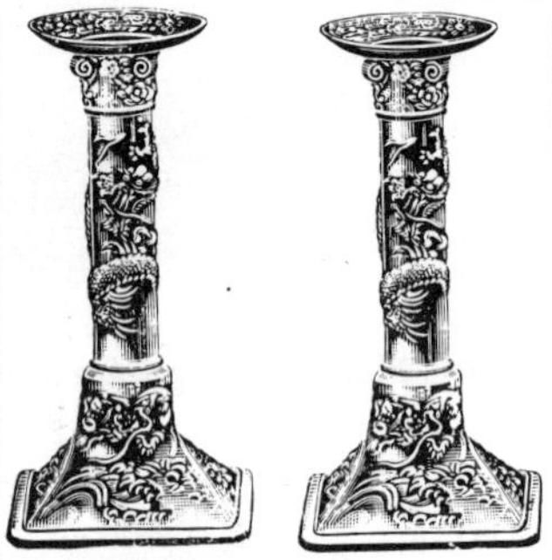

X. 5222/18. **Candlesticks.**
Dragon Design.
7 in. high, price **5/11** pair. 7½ in., **6 11**
Chrysanthemum Design.
8½ ,, ,, ,, **8/11** ,, Post 6d.

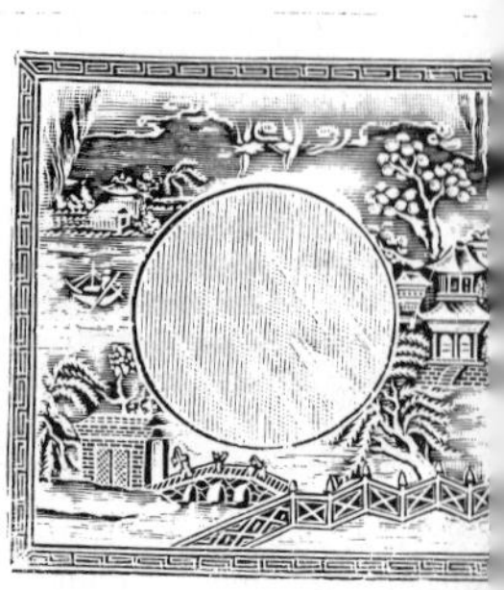

Willow pattern **Photo Fram[es]**
No. X. 5286/62. 3½ by 3½ in. Price
,, X. 5286/63. 4½ by 4½ in. Price
Postage 3d.

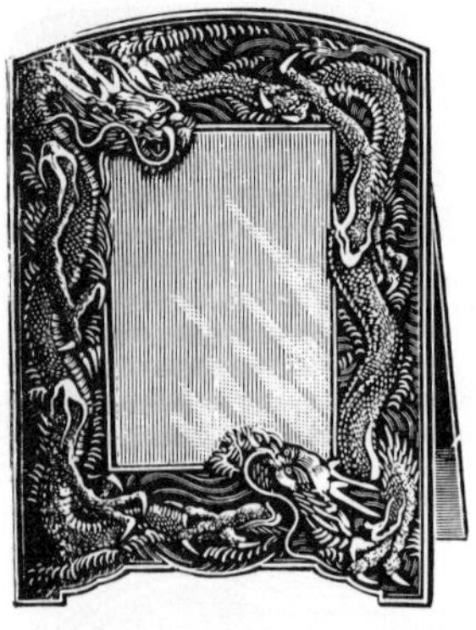

X. 5208/38 **Cabinet Photo Frames.** Dragon Design. 9 by 7 **3/11**

X. 5276.	3 by 2½ in. ...	**4½**d.
,, 1/2.	4¼ by 3 in. ...	**6½**d.
,, 5278/9	4½ by 3½ in. ...	**9½**d.
,, 5222/4.	5½ by 4 in.	**1/3**
,, 5222/6.	6½ by 5 in.	**2/-**

,, 5278/12. Same style, Chrysanthemum decoration, 6¾ by 5 in. **2/-**
,, 5278/13. Ditto, 9 by 6⅓in. ... **3/6**

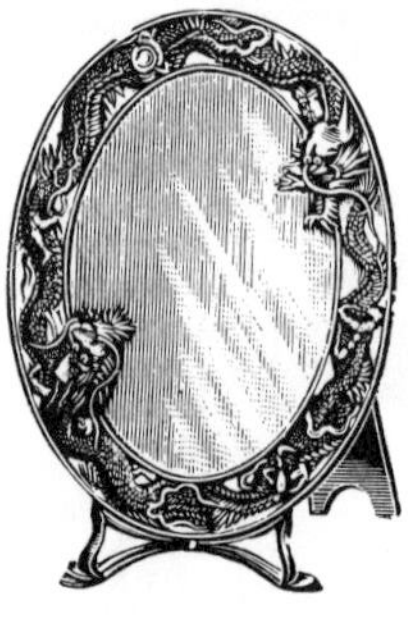

Antimony Frame.
Oval shape. Dragon Design
X. 5276/1. 3½ by 2½ in. Price ... **4½**d.
,, 5276/3. 4½ by 3¼ in. ,, ... **6½**d.
Larger sizes, **1/-** Postage 3d.

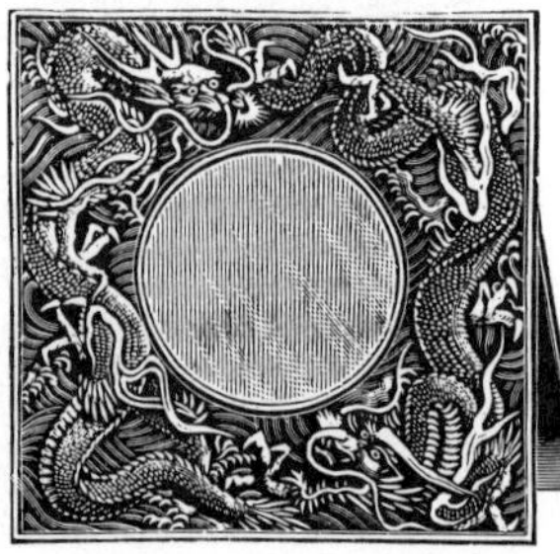

Square shape Photo Frames
X. 5278/8. 3½ in. square ... price **6½**d.
,, /19 4 in. ,, ... ,, **1/-**
X. 5152/1 8 in. ,, (4 in. opening) **4/6**
Postage 3d. and 4d.

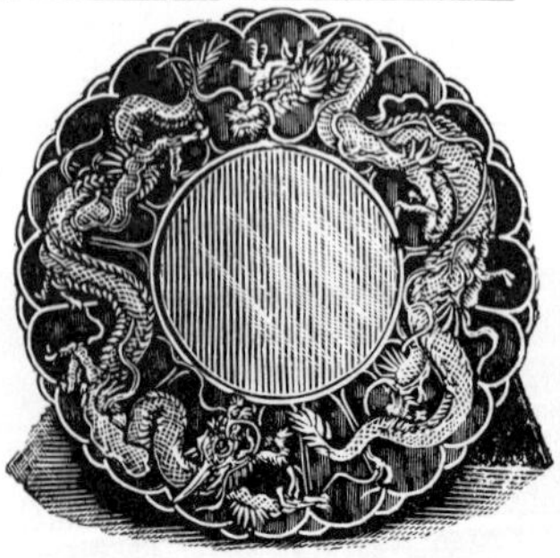

X. 5208/42. **Chrysanthemu[m] Shape Photo Frames.**
Size of opening 4in., 8in. overall **5/-** Pos[t]
X. 5248/12. Fancy Floral 10¾ by 12 in., to photo 7½ by 10 in. ... **13/9** Many other si[zes] tasty designs to these, various shapes and [sizes] from **4½**d., **6**d., **9**d., **1/-**, **1/6** Post 3d. to [...]

Hundreds of other Antimony Novelties. New Designs always arriving.

Japanese Lacquer Work and Indian Sandalwood.

5232. Cherry Lacquer Gold Decorated Glove and **Handkerchief Boxes.** Size of Glove Box, 10½ by 3½ in. Size of Handkerchief Box, 7 by 5½ in. Price **6**½d. each Post 3d.

New Gold Lacquer **Hdkf. and Glove Boxes.** Assorted designs. 7½ by 6 by 2½ in., **4/6** set of 2. 7¾ by 6½ by 3¼ in., **5/3** set of 2. Post 6d.

Cherry and Gold Lacquer **Chests of Drawers.** Casket shape. y 5 by 4 in., 2 drawers, **4/6** Postage v 6 by 5 in., 3 — **6/9** 6d.

cquer Crumb Brushes & Trays Assorted shapes. Size 11 by 9 in. ck & gold **1/-** Cherry & gold, **2/6** d ground, **2/11** Postage 4d.

Round Green and Red **Lacquered Trays.** Good quality (signed). 9½ in. .. **1/11**½ 12 ,, .. **3/6** 15 ,, .. **4/9** Post extra

blong Green and Red quer **Trays** (signed). Good quality.

12 15 18 21 in.
1/6 2/3 3/6 5/3 pair
7/3 pr. 26 in. **9/11** ,,

Round Trays. Special line. Green only. 9½ in. **1/9** pr. 12 ,, **2/6** ,, 15 ,, **3/11** ,,

---

X. 3244/9. New Gold Lacquer **Glove and Handkerchief Boxes.** Assorted designs. Glove box, 11¾ by 3½ in. Handkerchief box, 7¼ by 6¼ in. Price **1/6** each. Postage 4d.

X. 3264 Glove and Handkerchief Boxes. Cherry Lacquer Gold Decorated. Glove box, 12 by 3½ in. **1/-** each Hdkf. box, 7½ by 6¾ in. Post 4d.

Cherry and Gold Lacquer **Tea Caddies.** ½ lb., **1/6** & **1/9** each. 1 lb., **2/3** & **2/9** each. Postage 4d.

Glove and Handkerchief Boxes Beautiful finish. Splendid present. Various designs. Price **2/6** each. Postage 4d

Japanese Fancy Lacquered **Kishu Round Trays.**

| 9½ | 12 | 15 in. diam. |
| **10**½d. | **1/6** | **2/11** pair. |

Special Line. Fancy **Kishu Oblong Waiters.**

11½	15	17	20½ in. long
7	9	10	12 in. wide.
1/-	**1/6**	**2/-**	**3/6** per pair.

5000 Unique Hand Painted Caricature Match Stands.

Having purchased the whole of the Manufacturer's Stock of the above at a big Discount for Cash, we are able to offer them at 10½d. each, usual price being 1/6. These are about 11½ in. high are very true Caricatures, well cut and painted, with metal standard attached to hold box of matches. Messrs. Lloyd George, Winston Churchill and Balfour. Price **10**½d. each. Usual price 1/6 Post 3d. A DISTINCT NOVELTY.

Real Indian Carved Sandalwood Boxes.

X. 512 Glove Box, hand carved and inlaid, with lock and key. Size 11 by 4½ by 2¼ in., **5/9** Post 4d Similar, but all sandalwood, with very deep and choice carving, **8/6**

X. 513 Handkerchief Box, well carved and inlaid, with lock and key. Size 8½ by 6½ by 2¼ in. **5/9** Post 4d Similar to above, but deeper and choicer carving **8/6**

Diamond Shape, Carved and Inlaid **Sandalwood Box** Price **2/-** Post 6d.

In Various Shapes. Stamp and Pin Box. Well carved and Inlaid in quaint Indian designs. Size of Stamp Box, 2¾ by 2½ in. **9**d. Post 2d.

X. 510. Hair Pin Box. 6¾ by 2 by 1⅛ in. **9**d. Post 2d.

X. 507. Needle Boxes, **6**d. each Card Boxes, **1/9** and **2/-** Money Box, **3/-** Post 3d.

X. 511. Pen and Trinket Box, well carved and choicely inlaid. 6 inches long, **1/3** 9 inches long, **1/9** Post 3d.

Indian Carved Fans. Sandalwood. Opening .. 14 in **1/6** ea. Post 2d.

Carved imitation Ivory Fans very neat. Price **1/6** Post 3d.

Grotesque and Novel Jap **Tobacco Jars** In pulp ware. Lifelike heads with real hair and glass eyes. A splendid Xmas present. 6 to 7 in. high. **3/6** each. Postage 4d. Various Heads

Japanese, China & other Novelties. SUITABLE FOR PRESENT

Choicest Selection of **Satsuma Miniature Vases,** embracing many designs. Exquisite examples of Japanese art. Average size about 2⅜ in. high. Price **1/9** each. Postage and packing, 3d.

Superior work and quality of China. Price **2/3** each. Postage & packing, 3d. Do., suitable for any connoisseur. Price **2/9** each. Postage & packing. 3d.

Similar designs in the finest **Imari** Miniature China **1/9** each. Postage 2d.

With all Jap. Vases, etc., the designs being in most cases hand work, vary in pattern thus their uniqueness.

X. 22. Very dainty Miniatures. **Kaga Vases.** As above. 2¼ in. high, Price ... ... **6**d. each. Post 2d

Vases.

Stone Porcelain. Decorated with high reliefs of birds, animals, figures, flowers, etc. Assorted Shapes. 3½ in. high **1/-** 6 ,, ,, **1/3** 6 ,, ,, **1/9** 8½ ,, ,, **4/6** Post 3d. to 6d.

Kameido Tobacco Jar. In various shapes. Size 7½ by 5½ in. Well coloured. **4/9** Post 6d.

A fine range of Jap. Clay Nodding Figures. **4½**d. **6**d. **7½**d. **9½**d. **1/-** and **1/9** Post 4

All Designs and Sizes are approximate and cannot be guaranteed. Nearest will be sent.

Tete-a-Tete Jap Tea Sets, comprises 5½ in. high Teapot, 3½ in. high Jug, 13¾ in. diam. Basin, 2½ in. diam. Cups, 4¾ in. diam. Saucers. Complete Set (including tray) .. .. **2/6** Better quality, **3/11** Post 6d.

Black and White Tea Cup and Saucer. Ordinary size .. **6½**d. Large ,, **7½**d. Coffee Cups and Saucers .. **6½**d. Plates, 5 in. .. **4**d. ,, 6 ,, .. **5½**d. Bread and Butter **1/-** Teapots **1/-** and **1/9** Sugar and Cream— Small size, pair **7½**d. Large size .. **1/-**

Real Kaga Ware Teapots, hand-painted real gold and sepia, can always be matched **2/- 3/3 4/6 5/9** Post 4d. and 9d. Teacups and Saucers, Finest quality, **2/-** Largest size Teacup, **2/6** Plates 4⅜ in. **10½**d. 6 in. **1/-** 8 in. **2/3** Coffee Cups and Saucers **/9** Small size **1/3** Sugar & Cream **/6** pair.

Kaga Panel Tea Plates size 5 in. **4**d. 6 in. **5**d Bread & Butter Plate **1/-** Cups & Saucers, Kaga painted red decoration on white porcelain **7½**d Coffee Cups & Saucers **6½**d. Teapots **1/-** & **1/9** Coffee Pots .. **4/6** Sugar & Creams, small **4½**d. pair Medium **7½**d. ,, Large **1/-** pair

KAMEIDO-YAKI WARE (Stone Porcelain)
Quaint Forms and Grotesque Shapes.
Decorated with Birds, Animals and Flowers in High Relief. RICH COLOURINGS.

Bulb Bowls.
Size 4 in. .. **1/-** each. ,, 5½ in. .. **2/-** ,, Post 6d.

JAPANESE AFTERNOON CHINA TEA SET
Fine quality, dainty decoration, comprising 4 cups and saucers, 4 plates, 1 bread and butter plate, cream jug, covered sugar and large size teapot with strainer. **6/6** complete set. Only a limited number Packing 6d. extra.

Many other Grotesque Novelties which would be suitable for Presents

Genuine **Japanese Cloisonne Vas** complete with black wood stands, exquis designs and work. Small size, about 1⅝ **1/9** ea. Post 2d. Medium, 2⅜ in. **2/9** Post Larger, **3/11** Post 3d. Several other sizes a patterns at various prices.

Individual Breakfast Set. Complete with lac tray, 10 by 14, dainty Japanese china cup. sauce plate. teapot. milk and sugar basin .. **5/** Post and packing, 8d

X. 17. Genuine Kaga Combination Morn Cup, Saucer and Plate, finest Egg-shell Ch Well painted and decorated gold shading. **2/6** Post 4d.

Japanese Crabs, Lobsters, Insects, &c., for attaching to curtains. Very fine specimens. Large size, including crabs, grasshoppers, spiders, &c., **1/-** each. Post 3d. Medium (insects only) **7½**d. Small do. **4½**d. ea. Post 1d. to 3d.

SPECIAL LINE.
Spider, extra fine specimen, 9in. over all, 4 in. body. **6**d. Post 2d Large Japanese Crab, for curtains &c. Large variety **1/-** Post 3d.

Woven Paper Snakes, for Curtains, Ties, & c, Latest design **1/-** Post

Japanese Novelties for Xmas.

Japanese Silk
Hand painted
Balloon Pincushion
9 in. long.
Price ... 1/11

Pincushion in shape of
Jap Lantern.
Price ... 6d.

Jap Pincushion
Tap and
Ball, 4d. each
Extensive
variety.
5d. and 1/-
Postage 3d.

Hand-painted Japanese Fans
steel frames, lacquer handle, silk centres,
views and faces, 6d. Post 2d
Miniature Fans for the hair, 1½d.

Japanese Silk Kimonos with Sashes, for Evening Wear.
In pale blue, mauve, light green, pink, white and cream grounds, with dainty printed floral designs. Price **26/9** each.

Japanese Silk Kimono Jackets to match
Price **12 11** each.

Fine Native Hand Embroidered Kimonos
In antique and modern styles.
53/6 84/- 115/- and **150/-** each.

Jap. Native Cotton Printed Kimonos with Sashes.
For bath gowns and dressing wrappers.
Blue and white. Price **5/6** each.

Washing Dressing Jackets to match.
In blue and white. Price **3 3** each.

Dainty Coloured Printed Kimonos in Cotton Crepe.
For Bazaars or Fancy Wear, with silk collars and cuffs. Price **7/6** each.
Postage 3d. each under 10/- value.

Japanese Antimony.

Japanese Antimony TEDDY BEARS, about 12½ in. high, on Blackwood Stand, as illustration.
Price **7/9½** Usual price 12/6
Ditto, ditto, about 9 in. high on Blackwood Stand.
Price **4/9½** Usual price 8/6
Ditto, ditto, about 7½ in. high on Blackwood Stand.
Price **2/11½** Usual price 4/9
Ditto, ditto, about 3½ in. high on Blackwood Stand.
Price **6½d.** Usual price 1/-
Postage 3d. to 9d. extra.
Limited number only, cannot repeat when sold.

Black and White.
Very Fine Egyptian Silver and Gold Spangled Scarves.

12/6	**15/-**	**17/6**
18/6	**21/-**	**25/6**

Special Line in Silver.
8 6 each.
Postage 3d.
Carriage paid over 20/-

Dainty Ladies' Evening Scarves.
Special Tunis Scarves in numerous colours.
Silver or Gilt Spangled.
Price **5/6** Postage 2d.
Superfine, **8/6**
Very Fine Silk Wraps in various colors.
Price **5/6** Postage 2d.

Made from the rarest and choicest flowers of Japan mixed with Oriental Spices of exceptional fragrance, and retains its perfume for many years
Size of Tin,
4½ by 2¾ by 2¾ in
11½d. per Tin.
Post 4d.

LATEST NOVELTY.
Japanese Mechanical Ebony Figures.
Hand carved, curious and grotesque
Turn the nob and watch the effect
Large size **2 3**
Small size **1 3**
Postage 3d
Dozens of different figures.
A Unique Present.

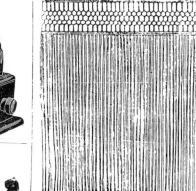

Japanese Tea Cosies.
Hand-painted on silk, handsome fine work.
Size 14 by 9¾ in.
Price **4/6** Postage 3d.
Printed Crepe Cosy.
Full size.
Price **2/11** Post 2d.
Tete-a-Tete Size.
Price **2/9** Post 1d.
Crepe Egg Cosies. **1/-**

Japanese Cherry Blossom.
1/3 per spray. Post 3d.
Pot not included.

Flo al designs in Reeds and Beads
Various colours 3 ft. 6 in. wide by 2 ft. 6 in. deep. **5/6** pair.
Or 3 ft. 6 in. wide by 3 ft. 6 in. deep.
6/11 Carriage forward.
Geometrical Designs. **4 6** and **5/11**
Floral and Fancy Patterns. Various coloured reed grounds interspersed with glass beads 3 ft. 6 in. by 8 ft. 6 in.
12/11 per pair.
Special Line—Best quality, similar in design to above, handsome designs, bead centres, various colours.

3 ft. 6 in. by 8 ft. 6 in.
18/9 pair. Car. for.
The Latest Novelty.
Japanese Curtains in all glass beads, magnificent floral designs.
8 ft. 6 in. by 3 ft. 6 in.
50/- per pair.
Carriage free.

Fine quality Japanese blue and white Pot Pourri Jars. 3½ in. high Price **9**d. Post 3d

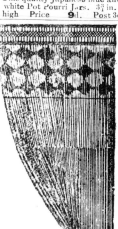

Geometrical Design.

In a combination of red, blue and yellow. In two sizes only.
3ft. 6in by 6ft. 6in.
Price **9/11** pair.

3ft. 6in. by 8ft. 6in
10/11 pair.
Carriage extra.

Japanese Reed and Bead Curtains.
Portiere Shape

FANCY AND FLORAL DESIGNS.

Size 3 ft. 6 in. by 8 ft. 6 in. long

Price **5/11** ea.
Carriage forward.

Better qualities upwards.

ALL GLASS.
22/6 each.

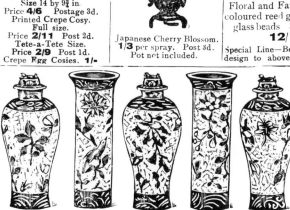

Blue and White Jars and Beakers (Crackle).

4½ in.	..	**3/9** set of 5	10 in.	..	**15/9** set of 5
6 in.	..	**6/9** ,,	12 ,,	..	**25/-** ,,
8 in.	..	**9/9** ,,	14 ,,	..	**42/-** ,,

Packing 6d. under 20 - Carriage 6d. to 1/- extra.

Many other Novelties for Presents.

Fancy Pipes covered with prairie grass **9d.** Post 1½d

Birchbark Canoes with wood stretcher
15 in. **1/9** Post 4d.   12 in. **1/6** Post 3d.   8 in **1/-** Post 3d.
Lighter coloured Bark, 8 in. **1/-** Post 3d.   6 in. **10½d.** Post 3d.
Wood dug-out Canoe   ...   ...   4 in. **3d.** Post 2d.
Also various other sizes.

Novel shape Handkerchief Satchet, made of sweet smelling Prairie grass, which retains its fragrance and scents the handkerchiefs.
Large size, 9 in. square **3/9** Post 3d.   Medium size **2/6**
Small ,, 6 in. ,,   **1.3** ,, 2d

Hundreds of other American Indian novelties comprising hand painted Cornwall wood, which includes vases, bowls, plates, etc. Rustic wood stain articles. American souvenirs, etc. Do not fail to pay a visit to our Indian Exhibits and get a souvenir from America.   **6d.** each.

American Novelty.

Combined picture and match holder Various designs and Indian pictures with model canvas wigwams, etc. on Birch bark frames.   Size 8½ by 5½ ins
Price   **1/-**   Post 2d.
With leather hanger.
With Silver bark frame, bound prairie grass.   Very choice.
Size 7 by 6.   Price **1/6**   Post 3d.

Indian-made pipe rack.
12 by 9 ins. Double Birch bark frame sweet grass binding, leather hanger, two leather pipe rings, rustic match cup fitted with 2 Indian pictures.
Various portraits in colours. **3/6.** Post 3d.
Dozens of other Picture novelties at various prices.

Fringed leather pillow cover, requires 22-in filler.   Smooth finish leather, assorted colors, embossed and oil painted design, unfilled
Very handsome.   Price **18/6.**   Post free.

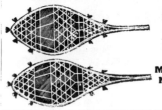

A NOVELTY.
Miniature Snow Shoes.
4 in. long.
Price **7½d.** pair.
Postage 2d.
Made by the North-American Indians.

North American Indian   **Birch Bark Canoe.**

Distinct   **Novelty.**

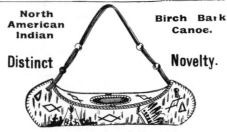

Painted and decorated, bound with sweet smelling prairie grass, suspended with leather thongs and beads. 8½ long Suitable for putting bottle of scent or other present in.
Price **1/6.**   Postage 3d.

Genuine birch bark canoes made by the Indians. Decorated bound with sweet smelling prairie grass. Size 7 ins **6d.**
Size 8 ins **9d.** Post 3d

Birch Bark Canoe Tie-pins. **6d.** Post free.

Real Indian birch bark canoes, various sizes, all styles. Similar to illustration from **1/-** each.

Wall hanger, split seal, embossed and oil painted Indian head design.
Average size 32 by 40 ins
Various well known Indian chief's heads.
Price   ...   **2/-**
Post free.
Very choice work.

CHIEF PAINTED-HORSE

Fancy Work Tidy, made of sweet smelling Prairie grass.   Various colours.
6½ in. long.
Price **1/3**   Post 1d.

Round, sweet smelling Prairie grass Basket.
4½ in. diam. by 2½ in. high
Price   **1/3**
Postage 1½d.

Prairie sweet smelling gr
Basket. Fancy round & squ
shape, 8 in. diam. by 3 in. de
Price **2/6**   Postage 2

X. 9. Birch Bark Indian Wigwans. Made by the Indians of North America. 5 in. high **1/-**
7 in. high, **1/9** Post 2d.
Made in other shapes.

Serviette Ring made of
Prairie grass **6d.** Post 1

American Alliga
Leather Novelt

Match scratch leathe
hanger.   Birch bark
canoe holder.   Indi
papoose ornament.
Various sizes.
Approximate 7¾ by
Price **1/6**   Post

Hundreds of other novelties American alligator leather.
Tie Racks   ..   **4/11**   Pos
Various assorted match
strikers   ..   **1 3**   ,,
Thermometer   ..   **1/3**   ,,
Dozens of other articles mount
on alligator.

Pipe Rack.
Size   ..   9 ins by 12 ins
Cardboard back, birch bark pap
face, leather hanger with bead
Two leather pipe rings, birch bar
canoe match holder, assorted Hia
watha pictures.
Price **2/**
Postage   ..   3d.
Several others at various prices

Russian Novelties.
FOR XMAS

Nest of ... and-painted Dolls. ...taining ... in. high ... e 9½d. ...ost 3d.

Tumbling Figure egg or doll shape will not lie down. Hand-painted. 4 in. high. Price 10½d. Post 3d. Smaller 4½d. 6d. 9d. Post 3d.

The Secret Jar. ...n a set. Price 2/9 Postage 3d.
Nested Balls. 1/- ... 3 in set. 1/9 ... 6 in set.

Nest of 8 carved and hand-painted Dolls. Height from 5½ to ½ in. Price 1/11½ Postage 4d. Larger size, 12 in set, 5/6

Russian hand-painted Mushroom Box, 4½ in. high. Price 1/6 Post 3d.

Nest of 3 Dolls. White wood, decorated by pokerwork. 4 in. high. Price 9½d. set. Post 3d.

2

6in. lacquered ...oon. Price 2d. ... 7½ in. long, ...rved and painted ...ussia wooden ...oons. Price ... each. Post 2d.

Handsomely carved and painted Woodpecker. 4½ in. high. Price . 1/- each. Post 3d. Also in plain wood. Price 9d.

Assorted Figure Boxes, as illustration. Hand-painted. Very quaint. Will open. Can be filled with scent, sweets, etc. Height about 5½ in. Price 1/9 Post 2d.

Pokerwork and hand-painted Doll Box. Height 4 in. 6d. Post 3d. Larger size, 1/3

Hand-painted Mushroom, 4 in. high, containing full range of turned wood novelties, as illustration. Price ... ... 2/6 Post 4d.

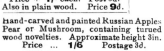

Hand-carved and painted Russian Apples Pear or Mushroom, containing turned wood novelties. Approximate height 3in. Price ... 1/6 Postage 3d.

Handsomely carved & hand-painted wood Vase, 3½ in. high. Various designs. 1/3 ea. Post 3d.

Handsomely carved & hand-painted wood Trinket Box. Various designs. 2½ in. high. 1/- ea. Post 3d

Russian Peasant Made Skittles

Hand-painted & turned flat Skittles Nine and two Balls in Set. Packed in natural bark packet. Price 4/11 Postage 6d.

...d decorated wooden ...with cover. 8½ in. ...gh by 5½ in. dia. ...us Russian Views. ...e 3/11 Post 4d.

X. 3. Handkerchief Box, exquisitely painted, carved, burnt and gilded Various Russian subjects, 8 in. square by 2½ in. 13/6

X. 4. Glove Box, as above, 15 by 3¾ by 2½. 10/6

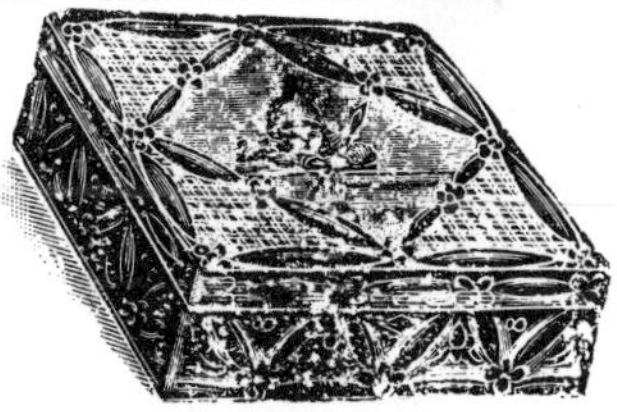

Russian Painted Bowls, fine executed water-colour drawings on wooden Bowls. 3½ in. diam., 10½d. 4 in., 1/3 4½in. 1/9 Postage 3d.

X. 1. Hand painted Oblong Box, various Russian designs. With lock and key. 10½ by 8 by 3½ in. Handkerchiefs, etc. Price 8/6

X. 2. Square size, 7¾ by 7¾ by 3½ in. 6/6 Post 4d.

X. 5.

...tionery box, poker worked and hand painted.

...el shape. Height 4½ in. ...ice 6/6 Postage 3d.

X. 6. Tobacco Boxes, hand-painted and carved. 6¾ by 5 in. 3/11 Post 3d. Ditto, 6¾ by 4½ in. 3/3 Post 3d.

X. 870. Hand painted carved and burnt Jars, fine example of the handiwork of the Russian Peasants. Height 7½ in. Price 8/11 Post 3d. Width 5½ in.

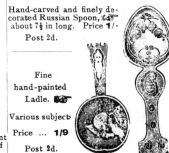

Hand-carved and finely decorated Russian Spoon, about 7½ in long. Price 1/- Post 2d.

Fine hand-painted Ladle. Various subjects Price ... 1/9 Post 2d.

Grotesque Carved Figure Nut Cracker. Hand carved very strong. Height about 11¼ in. Price ... 1/- Post 4d. As above but well painted and decorated, 2/6

...hese RUSSIAN GOODS are made by the Peasants employed by the Moscow Government, Zemstov (Russian Home Industries). Many other fine examples of the patience and ingenuity of the Russian Peasantry can be seen in our **Eastern Bazaar.**

Sizes and Designs are approximate nearest will be sent.

Selection of China Novelties for Xmas Presents.

A   B

C   D   E

Genuine Dutch Porcelain Figures.
A, B, **9**d. pair.   D, **6**d. the pair.
C and E. **4½**d. each.   Postage 2d

Dutch Porcelaine.

Little "Miss Hook of Holland."
Moving Bell figure.
7¾ in. high .. **3/-** Post 4d.
6½ in. inches.   In Porcelain.
Price **2/3** Postage 4d.
5½ in., **1/9** ,, 3d.
Master Hook, 5⅜ in. high.
Price **1/9** Postage 3d.

Dutch Blue and White Windmill.

Many other Novelties in Dutch Blue & White Chir
Price **1/-** each. Postage 3
Large size **1/9**

Blue and White Boxes .. **1** - ea
China Clogs, from .. **6**
Ash Trays **7**
Vases, Vans, Novelties, &
from 3d. to **3 6**

Dutch Milkmaid and Man.
Detachable pails.
Height 4½ in.   Price **1/-** each
Postage 2d.

Blue and White
Dutch China Cow.
Various patterns.
Price **1/6** & **2 3**
Postage 3d.

Dutch Hand-painted Tiles.
n frames.
igned by Artist.
omplete
4 by 8¼in.
2 9
nteriors
1 9 each
Post 4d.
ther sizes
ndscapes
5 by 15,
10 by 18
6/9
10 by 30
8/9

Many other sizes too numerous to mention.

Dutch design Plaques.
Blue and white Dutch Landscape.
9½ in. diam. **6½**d. 11 in. **1/-** 12¼ in. **1/3**
Coloured Dutch Figures or Landscapes.
9½ in. diam. **10½**d. 11 in. **1/3** 12½ in. **1/6**
Post and Packing from 4d. to 6d. extra.

No. X. 10.
Dutch design Vase.
Coloured
Landscape.
Height 8 in.
1/3 each.
Post and Packing 4d.

Bunty Pulls the Strings.

THE LATEST NOVELTY.

Latest Novelty in China Figures Beautifully made
Life. 5¾ in. high, **6½**d. each. 7 in. high, **1/-** ea
Dozens of other China Novelty Figures, Caricat
of Singers, Sportsmen, etc., **6½**d. each. Post 3d

Largest Variety ever known.

Russian Dancing Girl Flower Holder. **1/-** Post

Very attractive series, each model is a study of Grace
Beauty. Fine quality China figures with assort'd two-
effect spangled robes, 6¼ in. high. Six different models

No X 23.
Dutch design
Vases.
Landscape.
9½ in. high.
Blue and White,
or Coloured.
10½d.
Post & Packing 4d.

No. X. 19
Landscape design
9¾ in. high,
in colours.
1/6 each.
Packing & Post 5d.

No. X. 23.
Dutch figured
design, 9½ in. high
Naturally
coloured.
10½d.
Post & Packing 4d.

Grotesque
China Figures.
Dozens of various
Match Stands,
as illustrated.
New ones always
arriving.
6d. each. Post 3d.

X.13 X.14

Something
quite
different.
Almost
human.
Fine quality
China
Figures,
5½ in. high.
A slight turn
of the head
gives each
model a
hundred
realistic
expressions

Hassall's Little Figures.

Ranging from the serious to the comic,
each one is a speaking likeness of someone
we have never seen.
1/3 each. POST FREE.

Many other
types in
Golfers,
Sportsmen,
etc., etc.

**Irresistibly
Funny.**

Movable
Heads and
Hats

**Unique as
Presents.**

No. X. 7   X. 8   X. 9   X. 10   X. 11
Grotesque China Figures, beautifully modelled and colo
Caricatures of your friends. Hundreds o others.
6d. each. Post 3d.

No. X. 1   X. 2   X. 3   X. 4   X. 5.   X 6
Grotesque China Figures. Hundreds of different ones, too
numerous to specify. Always something fresh.
6d. each.   Post 3d.

Epergnes, Flower Stands, Vases, Tea Sets &c.,

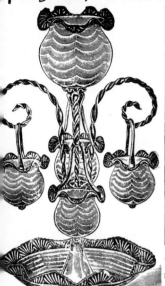

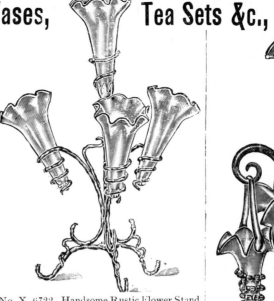

Special Value,

X. 6789. Rustic Flower Stand. 1 tube in clear or green glass, silver-plated and enamelled, 8½ in. high. Price **1/6½**d. Post 4d.
X. 6786. Similar style but longer, made up to 5 tubes, 17in. long by 14½ in. high. Price **10/6** Packing and carriage 9d. ex.

X. 156. Handsome Table Epergne, 18½ in. high, 12 in. a base, with 4 Hanging Baskets In assorted colours **12/11** Packing and Carriage 1/- extra

X. 5839. 21in. high. In all colours, 3 Hanging Baskets **6/11** Cheaper quality, **4/11** Packing and Carriage 1/- extra.

No. X. 6722. Handsome Rustic Flower Stand. 4 tubes, 16½ in. high, with clear or green glass tubes, electro-plated stand **8/6** Packing and Carriage 9d. extra.
No. X. 6742. Similar style, 13½ in. high, 4 tubes Price **7/9** Packing and Carriage 9d.

No. X. 3122.

40 pieces of English China Tea Set.

Decoration—
Red, Blue and Richly Gilded.

Albert shape.

Price .. **18/11**

Packing 1/- Carriage paid.

Rose Bowl.

Iridescent Pearl Glass, on artistic polished brass stand and with grooved top wire net.

Height 9½ inches.

Price **9/11** Post 4d,

Several other glass Rose Bowls, **1/9 2/9 9/6** up to **25/6**, also in Earthenware.

X. 4461. In all colours 21in. high, as illus. 3 branches and 3 hanging buckets **9/11** Cheaper type **7/11** Packing and Carriage 1/- extra.
X. 5821. 14in. high, in all colours. 2-branch **2/11½**d 3 branch **3/11** Postage and packing 3d.
Dark green Epergne similar to above, but perfectly plain, very rich **4/11** Packing and carriage 9d. ex.

Bohemian Crystal Cut-glass Spirit Bottle. Full-cut Hobnail Price **5/9** Half-cut Hobnail, **4/9** Post and packing 6d. extra.

No. X. A1059. Windsor Shape. Decorated with mauve bell flowers and green leafage, gilt edge. Staffordshire China.
40-piece Tea Service **19/11**
29-piece Breakfast Service **19/11** Packing 1/- extra. Carriage paid.

X. 2078. Vase, 8 in. high, Royal Blue Tops, enamelled colours, hand traced Price **3/9** each. Post 6d.

"Dicky" Trinket Set. Litho and gilt. 10 pieces. **5/3** Half shaded and gilt, 10 pieces, **5/3**

Litho do., **6/6**

Packing and Carriage 6d,

Durbar Decoration.

Consisting of dark blue and green tops and bases. Stippled real gold, white centres, with blue and red flower sprays. The whole heavily stippled in real gold.
No. 2. Durbar Art Flower Pot, 8½ in. opening across top.
Price **4/11** Carriage & packing, 9d

No. X. 487/1

Well shaped VASE.

Height, 9½ in.

Price **4/11**

Carriage and Packing 1/- extra.

Vulcan Pot & Pedestal

Height 43 in. 14 in. inside pot.

Very massive; bold design; very work. Exceptional Value.

Plain colours ... **23/6**

Imperial (picked out in various colours) **27/6** Packing 1/- extra.

Afternoon Tea Set, on wicker tray. Fine English China. Enamelled and Printed Colours

Complete with Tray **6/11** Packing 6d.

X. 4474. Flower Pot, glazed top, etched and gilt, enamelled decoration, 9 in. across top Price **7/6** Postage and Packing 9d.
Langley Ware, leadless, glazed, decorated Stoneware.

Splendid Selection of fine quality Vases, Tea Sets, etc. Inspection Invited.

Coffee Machines and Table Heaters make Acceptable Presents.

Demonstrations daily during Xmas Bazaar

The Universal Coffee Percolator.
The ONLY Percolator that Pumps.

Colonial Pattern.

Made of Pure Aluminium.

Any range, stove or gas range.

Colonial Pattern
No. X.

64.	4 cups, 1½ pints	**12/6**
66.	6 ,, 3 ,,	**14/-**
69.	9 ,, 4 ,,	**16/-**
614.	14 ,, 6 ,,	**18/-**

All the working parts made of Pure Aluminium.

Universal Percolator.

Ebonized handle.

Or in High-grade Enamel Ware, Blue outside, all White inside.

No. X.

1104.	4 cups, 1½ pints	**9/6**
1106.	6 ,, 3 ,,	**11/6**
1109.	9 ,, 4 ,,	**13/6**
1114.	14 ,, 6 ,,	**15/-**

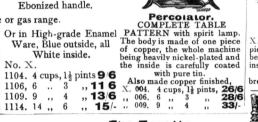

Percolator.
COMPLETE TABLE PATTERN with spirit lamp. The body is made of one piece of copper, the whole machine being heavily nickel-plated and the inside is carefully coated with pure tin.
Also made copper finished,

X. 004.	4 cups, 1½ pints,	**26/6**
,, 006.	6 ,, 3 ,,	**28/6**
,, 009.	9 ,, 4 ,,	**33/-**

The "UNIVERSAL" Tea Samovar.

X. 606 The Body is made of one piece of Copper, the whole Machine being heavily nickel plated, and the inside is coated with Pure Tin
Capacity—2½ pints (averaging 5 breakfast cups or 8 teacups **32/6**

"Ye Mecca" Coffee Machin[e]

A Perfect Cup of Co[ffee] in 2 or 3 mins. Most sim[ple] and economical. Can [be] cleaned very easily. [The] whole of the interior [can] be taken out. Every p[art] can be supplied separa[tely] Lamp gives great he[at] and therefore coffee [can] be made in a few minu[tes.]

After the coffee is re[ady] it can (without be[ing] spoiled) be kept hot [in] the machine by regulat[ing] the lamp (System, La[ng.]

All Polished Brass, Extra Finish. 4-cup s[ize] **11/3**

6-cup size, **12/3** 8-cup size, **13/1[0]**
10-cup ,, **16/6** 12-cup ,, **17/3**

Extra Glass Tops for the above.

2 and 4 cup size, **9d.** 6 or 8-cup size, [1/-]
10 or 12-cup size, **1/3** each. Postage ex[tra]

No. X. 3456.
Russian System Coffee Machine.

Polished brass, well la quered.

4-cup size	..	^c**7/6**
6-cup ,,	..	**9/6**
8-cup ,,	..	**10/6**

Postage 4d. and 6d.

The Teaetta.
Patent No. X. 27958/11.

A cup of well-made tea is at once a delight and a pleasure; but let us not forget that indigestion, with its long train of attending complications, lurks at the bottom of a badly made cup of tea.
By using the "Teaetta," all these drawbacks, doubts and difficulties are at once obviated.
The "Teaetta" is not only useful, it is an ornament as well, makes a most acceptable present, and is an elegant addition to any sideboard.

	Capacity—1 pint.	2 pints.	3 pints.
Handsomely Plated or Copper ...	**22/6**	**31/6**	**42/-**
Best Silver Plated ...	**68/-**	**75/-**	

Carriage paid.

Simplest and most perfect tea maker.
Whistles when water boils.
Turn button and tea is made.
Make it yourself at the table. No more tannin.

"Caffetta" Coffee Maker
No. X. H1387.

Whistles when coffee is ready.
Simple and speedy.
Only methylated spirit used.
Complete instructions.
Plated or Copper.
Size 4 cups **15/6** 6 **21/-** 8 **25/-**
Larger sizes made to order.
Carriage paid.

The "Bocca" Coffee Apparatus.
No. X. H1387.
One of the finest of systems of coffee making ever introduced for table or travelling use. Extracts the whole strength of the coffee. The grounds are separated from the liquid coffee, which pours out perfectly clear.

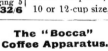

Polished Brass, heavily lacquered.

No.	X. 1	X. 2	X. 3
Capacity	½ 2	1 4	1½ pints 6 cups
H1387	**13/9**	**16/3**	**18/9**

	X. 4	X. 5	X. 6
	2 8	3 10	4 pints 12 cups
	21/6	**24/-**	**26/9**

Polished Copper. Heavily Lacquered.

No.	X. 1	X. 2	X. 3	X. 4	X. 5	X. 6
Capacity	½ 2	1 4	1½ 6	2 8	3 10	4 pint 12 cup
X. 1388	**16/3**	**18/9**	**21/6**	**24/-**	**26/9**	**29/3**
18632	**14/3**	**16/9**	**19/6**	**22/3**	**24/9**	**27/6**

X. 1575 Best Sheffield Silver Plate.
X. 3. 1½ pts 6 cups, **31/6** X. 4. 2 pts. 8 cups, **36/-**

H. 461.
Table Food Warmer.
Polished, lacquered, regulating spirit lamp, wrought iron stand. Round pattern, brass on iron stand ... **10/6**

H. 446 Copper plate on iron stand **11/6**

Table Heaters. Dishes can be kept hot for any length of time, water boiled, etc.

Lang's system of burners.
Lamps can be taken out and used separately.

H. 447/1. With 1 lamp, polished copper, brass mounts	**37/6**
H.447/2 With 2 lamps ditto	**63/-**
H.462/1 With 1 lamp, all brass ...	**29/6**
H.462/2 With 2 lamps ditto	**57/6**
Special Kettles, polished copper, brass mounts ...	**12/6**
All brass ...	**11/9**

The Carlton Table Heater,
Hot Plate and Centre Dish.

Brass Stand, hard soldered throughout, Copper Hot Plate, Copper Centre Dish nickel plated inside with loose lining, bead to dish and cover, N.P. handle. Size of Plate.

	X. 1, 11 by 8 in.	X. 2, 12½ by 9 in.
Entree Dish	10 in.	12 in.
Price complete	**52/6**	**59/6**
Copper with Brass Stand, N.P....	**63/-**	**72/6**
Copper Table Heater Hot Plate ...	**25/6**	**27/-**
Copper with Brass Stand, N.P....	**31/-**	**32/9**

Carriage paid.

New Design Table Heater.

With Sliding Spirit Lamp and Flame Separator. 8 by 14 in. long.

X. 1540/1. Polished Brass, **15/-** complete
X. 1540/2. Polished Copper, **17/6** ,,

No. X. 5122. Patent "Heatorboil" Extending Food Warmer. Polished brass stand, copper top.

12 in. closed	..	17½ in. extended	..	**44/-**
15 in. ,,	..	22 in. ,,	..	**49/6**
18 in. ,,	..	25 in. ,,	..	**57/6**
14 in. ,,	..	35 in. ,,	..	**70/-**

For all other cooking purposes this stove will be found equally efficient and superior. Produces intense heat.

The Universal Spirit Stove

Can be used for all household purposes—making Coffe[e], Tea, Heating Water or Milk, a very convenient stov[e] for Sick Room. Equally good for use with a sma[ll] frying pan for cooking meals in Camp.
Heats a flat iron very quickly.
Made of Brass—Heavily Nickel-plated.

The intense heat generated by this scientific constru[c]tion enables us to offer in this convenient size a stov[e] which will do more work than any other now upon th[e] market, even though 3 times its size.

A quart of water of 500 Fahrenheit will boil furious[ly] in six minutes. Price .. **10/6**

Carriage Paid on all the above to th[e] value of 10/- and over.

To obtain best results use A.W.G. Pure Coffee, 1/8 per lb. (ground or whole) for your Coffee Machine.

Copper and Brass Tea Kettles and Stands.
SUITABLE FOR 'XMAS PRESENTS.

No. X. 18402 and X. 18404.

Tea Kettles, tinned inside,
With regulating Spirit Lamp
(Lang's system).

18402. Capacity about 3 pints,
que brass tarnished, lacquered and
moveable handles. Price **13/9**

18404. Capacity about 3 pints,
que copper tarnished, lacquered
antique brass mountings and
movable handles.
Price ... **14/9**

Kettle on Stand, hammered; powerful
regulating lamp; Kettle with wicker-
covered handle
Capacity about 3 pints.
X. 19834. Brass, polished ... **19/6**
X. 19835. Brass, antique ... **21/-**

No. 17591.

No. X. 17589,91.
Spirit Can with
removable lid,
capacity about
1/5th pint.
17589. Brass fine
polished, lacqd.
2/9 Post 3d.

X17591 Copper,
finely polished,
lacquered with
brass fittings.

For filling spirit stoves. **2/11** Post 3d.

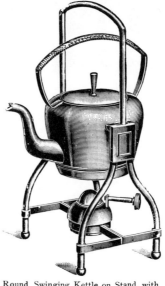

Round Swinging Kettle on Stand, with
powerful regulating lamp Kettle with
wicker-covered handle.
Capacity about 3 pints.
X. 19722. Brass, polished ... **18/6**
„ 19724. Copper, „ ... **21/-**
„ 19837. Brass, antique ... **18/6**

Kettle on Stand, with powerful **regulating**
lamp.
Capacity about 3 pints.
X. 19729. Brass, polished ... **17/6**
„ 19730. Copper „ ... **19/6**

winging Kettle on Stand, mounted on
y, with powerful regulating lamp;
kettle with wicker-covered handle.
Capacity about 3 pints.
. 19725. Brass, polished ... **18/9**
19726. Copper „ **21/6**
19838. Brass, antique, brown
tarnished... ... **19/9**

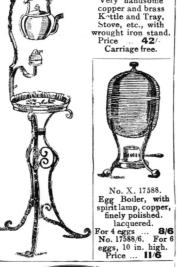

No. X. 16/38.
Very handsome
copper and brass
Kettle and Tray,
Stove, etc., with
wrought iron stand.
Price ... **42/-**
Carriage free.

No. X. 17588.
Egg Boiler, with
spirit lamp, copper,
finely polished,
lacquered.
For 4 eggs ... **8/6**
No. 17588/6. For 6
eggs, 10 in. high.
Price ... **11/6**

X. 19289. Tea Kettle, capacity about 3 pts.
Hammered, with regulating Spirit Lamp.
Retinned inside, antique brass tarnished,
lacquered. **17 6**

X. 17002.
Polished
Egg Boiler,
in brass,
complete
with
spirit lamp.
Boil 4 eggs.
Height
about 9 in.
Useful pre-
sent. **5/9**
Post 3d.

X. 19018/1. New Design. Tea Kettle.
Capacity about 3 pints.

Retinned inside, with regulating Spirit Lamp,
antique brass, tarnished, lacquered, wicker
handle ... **19/6**

X. 5681.

Kettle and
Stand.

Polished
Brass, silver-
plated inside

Capacity
about two
pints. Well
finished.
Price
12/9
Post free.

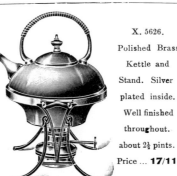

X. 5578.

Spirit Kettle
and Stand.
Very fine
design.
Equisite
work.

Can be had
in polished
Brass,
Copper or
Antique
finish.

Capacity
about three
pints.
Price
28/6

X. 5626.
Polished Brass
Kettle and
Stand. Silver
plated inside.
Well finished
throughout.
about 2½ pints.
Price ... **17/11**

Kettle on
Stand with
Powerful
Regulating
Lamp.
Wicker-
covered
handle.

Capacity about three pints.
Polished Stand.
X. 400/714. Brass polished, **14/9** each.
X. 400/814. Copper „ **16/6** „

Copper and Brass Waiters, Crumb Trays, etc.

ACCEPTABLE GIFTS

Crocodile or Plain Heavy Jug. Hot Water Jugs. Copper and Brass. In hammered or plain copper or brass.

Postage on all Jugs, 4d. & 6d. extra. 10/- and over carriage paid.

X. 1047 or 1055:—

X. 1055.   X. 1047.

	1	2	3	4	6	8	12 pt.
Polished Brass	3/3	4/-	4/11	5/9	8/3	10/3	16/3
,, ,, with lid	5/3	5/11	7/9	9/-	13/11	15/9	23/6
,, or Oxydised Copper	3/9	4/6	5/6	6/2	9/3	11/3	18/-
,, ,, with lid	5/6	6/9	8/3	9/9	13/9	14/6	25/-

X. 1283

HAMMERED JUGS. Polished Brass.

1	2	3	4	6 pt.
3/3	4/-	4/11	5/9	8 3

Polished or Oxydized Copper.

| 3/9 | 4/6 | 5/6 | 6/2 | 9/3 |

1283A. Do. with lid. Brass.

| 5/3 | 5/11 | 7/9 | 9/- | 12/11 |

Polished or Oxydised Copper.

| 5/6 | 6/9 | 8/3 | 9/9 | 13/9 |

X. 748. Patent Hot Water Jug with patent self-closing lid, solid polished brass.

½	¾	1	1¼	1½ pt.
6/-	6/3	6/9	8/6	9/9

Polished Copper.

| 7/9 | 8/6 | 9/9 |

Post 4d. and 6d.

X. 1027. Copper and brass round Waiter. Polished brass—

5	6	8	9	10	12 in.
10¼d.	1/3	1/9	2/2	2/6	3/11

Polished or oxydised copper.

5	6	9	10	12 in.
1/-	1/5	2/-	2/5	2/9	4/6

Postage from 2d. to 6d.

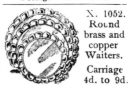

X. 1052. Round brass and copper Waiters. Carriage 4d. to 9d.

	10	12	14 in.
Brass ...	2/9	4/6	6/9
Copper ...	2/11	5/3	7/6

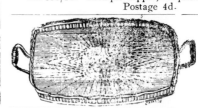

X. 17379/35. High-class finish, brass and copper Trays.

14 in. long, **10/6** 16 in. long, **11/9**
18 in. long, **13/11**

Heavy copper bottoms, heavy brass rims, and dull finish.

X. 17159/33.

Bread Baskets with modern decorations 16½ in. long, 8½ br

| X. 350/13. | Antique brass and lacquered, each | 5/6 |
| X. 350/14. | Antique copper, lacquered ,, | 6/- |

Postage 4d.

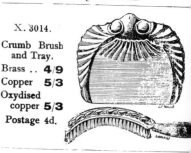

X. 17070. Fan Metal Waiters. Lacquered copper with perforated polished brass and handles. Punched body. Very effective and handsome. **7/3** 16 in., **8/-** 18 in., **10/6**

Antique dark brass Trays, hammered in pattern, light brass mountings, extra heavy

14 in. long .. **6/6** 15 in. long .. **7/9**

Carriage 6d. extra.

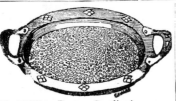

X. 17650 Tray. Oxydised copper finely finished, lacquered with dull brass, handles and wooden stamping.

X. 17650/32, 12½ in. diam. **7/11** Post 6d.
,, 17650/38, 15¼ in. ,, **9/11**

Scoop only, Brass .. **2/11**
Ditto Copper.. **3/6**

X. 3032. Crumb Tray and Scoop. Polished brass, **5/6** Polished copper **6/3**

Postage 4d.
Oxydized copper ... **6/3** complete.

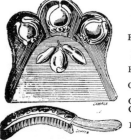

X. 3026. Crumb Brush and Tray Massive Pattern. Brass, **6/6** Copper, **6/9** Oxydised Copper, **6/9** Post 4d.

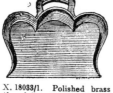

X. 18033/1. Polished brass Crumb Set. Lacquered tray.
Brass, **2/11** ea. Copper, **3/6** ea.
Scoop, **2/11** ea. Copper, **3/6** ea.

Quaint dull copper Waiter, 12 in. diam.
Fitted with brass handles and feet.
8/6
Post 6d.

X. 3014. Crumb Brush and Tray.
Brass .. **4/9**
Copper **5/3**
Oxydised copper **5/3**
Postage 4d.

X. 3020. Crumb Brush and Tray.
Brass, **7/3**
Polished oxydised copper, **7/9**
Very Handsome.
Post 6d.

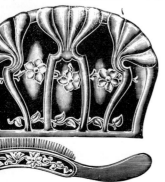

X, 426, SPECIAL VALUE. Crumb Brush and Tray, 12 by 8½ in. Polished brass, price **2/9**
Polished Copper, **2/11** Postage 4d.

X. 1267. Crumb Brush and Tray. Polished Brass, **9/3** Polished Copper, **9/11** Oxydised Silver, **18/3** Post 4d.

X. 3034. Crumb Brush and Tray.

Polished brass	**7/6**	
Polished copper	**7/9**	
Oxydised copper	**7/9**	Post 4d.
Oxydised silver	**13/9**	

Copperoid Crumb Brushes and Trays. Antique finish. Bristle brushes, as illustration.
Price .. **1/9** Post 3

SEASONABLE PRESENTS.

Selection of Cake Stands and Paper Racks.

SUITABLE FOR PRESENTS.

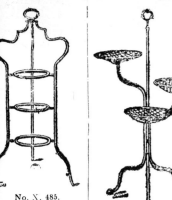

No. X. 485.
Handsome Pattern
Cake Stand.
Made of strong polished
brass tubes, with rings
for glass or pottery
dishes. Height 36 in.
Price **17/3**

X. 402. Cake Stand.
Pretty and useful design,
made of polished brass tubes
and wire dishes, with tubular
edge, height 34 in. **21/- ea.**

X. 5672. Polished Brass
Cake Stand.
27½ in. high.
Well made and finished
throughout **10/11**

No. X. 1496.
Highly burnished, well
and strongly made
Brass Wire Dishes
10/6 each.

No. X. 484.
Magnificent design.
Made of polished brass
tubes and hammered
polished copper trays.
Height 36 in. Price **19/11**

No. X. 1109/2.
**Handsome Brass Table
Cake Stand.**
Complete with fancy China Plates.
2 tiers. Price **8/6** Carriage, etc., 6d.

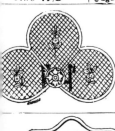

**No. X. 546. Brass
Fire Guard.**
Extra strong. All brass
tube. Polished and lac-
quered Brass Diamond.
Mess Wire Work.
Cast Rose.
Copper Sprays.
Wrought iron hooks.
Size 24 in. wide by 17 in.
high. Price **11/9**

No. X. 1461.
Folding Fire-
guard and
Screen, &c.
Burnished
brass tube
frame, brass
wire square
mesh.
23 in. high.
Central panel,
15 in. wide.
Sides 7 in. wide
Price **13/6**
Post 6d.

A SEASONABLE PRESENT.

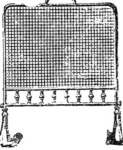

No. X. 1267.
Brass Standing Fire Screen
Well lacquered,
best finish, brass tube,
1⅛ in. diameter,
brass grooved wire square
mesh panel, brass pillars,
size 25 in. high (not
including handle) by 20 in.
wide.
Price **21/-** Crate 1/-

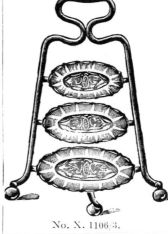

No. X. 1106/3.
**New Design of Brass Table
Cake Stand.**
Fitted with choice China Plates.
Three tiers. Price **15/11**

No. X. 111/3.
Table Cake Stand.
Antique Design.
Made of fine quality brass tubing.
3 tiers. Fitted with fancy China Plates.
Price **17/6**

No. X. 1132.
Paper or Music Rack.
Polished brass tube and brass
grooved wire panels, with polished
oak base and brass feet.
14 by 7 in. ... **9/-** each
16 by 7 in. ... **11/6** ,,
Other patterns **11/- 15/- 15/9**
Carriage forward.

No. X. 1128.
**Handsome Revolving
Paper or Music Stand.**
Brass tube frame, with fancy brass wire panels and polished
oak bottom. Brass legs and feet. Extreme height, 33 in.
Extreme widths, 16 in. by 7 in. **19/6** each.
Larger and better quality stands, **27/6 39/6 45/6**

No. X. 5687.
Polished Brass
Cake Stand.
Strongly and
elegantly made.
32 in. high.
Price .. **14/6**

**No. X. 1116. Choice Double Frame
Brass Table Cake Stand.**
3 tiers. Exceptionally well made and
finished. Complete with plates, **21/-**

**No. X. 1140/3. Adam Design
Brass Table Cake Stand.**
Complete with fancy China Plates.
Two tiers, **12/-** Three tiers, **15/6**

Goods to value of **20/-** and over Carriage paid.

BB

No. X. 26267/1.

Brass Polished Candlesticks.

Antique pattern. With Red Candle. 6¼ in. high. Complete **1 6** Post 3d.

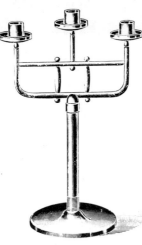

No. X. 19650/3. **Candelabra.**

For 3 Candles. 15 in. high. Antique Brass and Lacquered. Price **8/6** Post 4d.

XMAS RANGE OF

Artistic Brass and Copper
CANDLESTICKS,
Fruit Dishes & Stands,
BISCUIT BARRELS, Etc.

Price

10/6

Post free.

No. X. 19083/1. **Chandelier.**

Brass polished. Tarnished, with seven red candles, and movable arms which can be used at various angles.

Price .. .. **6/6** Post 6d.

No. X. 19650/5 **Candelabra.**

For 5 candles. 15 in. high. Antique Brass, lacquered.

No. X. 1338s.

Brass, with registered grip, **1/10** Polished Copper ... ... **2/3** Postage 4d.

No. 1943

Cand stick antiq copp tarnish lacque 9 in. **3/1** Post

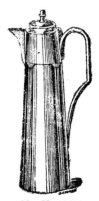

No. X. 18545. Antique Brass, Tarnished. Price .. **7/11**

No. X. 18535. Antique Copper, Tarnished. 13 in. high. Price .. **8/6** Post 6d.

No. X. 17985. Handsome **Fruit Basket.**

Decorated China Centre, Hinged Handle. Brass .. .. **4/6** Post 4d.

No. X. 18435. **Fruit Dish.**

Antique Brass Tarnished. 11½ in. long. 7 in. high. Price .. **8/11** Postage 6d.

No. X. 19877 **Fruit Basket.**

Antique Brass, brown finished. With folding handle, removable glass dish with star. Diam. 8 in. Price .. .. .. **3/11** Post 4d.

No. X. 46110. 5½ in. high. Candlestick. Antique Brass imitation. No. X. 46111. 5½ in. high. Antique Copper imitation. **1/-** each. Post 4d.

No. X. 46112. 5in. high. Candlestick with matchholder. Antique brass imitation. Hammered, **1/11** Post 4d.

No. X. 345/15. **Fruit Dish.**

Antique Brass, brown tarnished, embossed, loose glass top part. 8½ in. diam., 7 in. high. Price .. **7/9** Postage 4d.

No. X. 19637. **Biscuit Barrel.**

Glass with antique brass mountings, stand antique Brass. Price .. **5/6** Post 4d.

No. X. 19891. **Biscuit Barrel.**

Antique Brass, brown finished, folding handle and removable crystal jar. Diam. 4½ in. Total height 10 in. Price ... **4/6** Posttge 4d.

No. X. 345/10. **Fruit Dish**

With removable crystal tray. Brass Polished, Lacquered, Mode Design. 15½ in. diam., 6¼ in. high. Price .. **5/9** Post 4d.

HIGH GLOSS WHITE

TABLE and FLOOR GONGS for XMAS.

X. 064. Burmese Gong and Beater.
5 in. brass, **10/6** Antique copper, **11/6**
7 in. „ **13/9** „ **15/-**
Postage 6d.

The "Bugle" Chime of 4 extra large tubes on oak bracket, loud but sweet
Price **57/6**

Complete octavo of $\frac{7}{8}$ in. nickel-plated tubes, on oak bracket, with beater.
Price **27/6**

No. X. 3254. M.T.
Hanging Gong.
8 in. diameter, mounted on polished oak board.
Complete with beater.
Price **11/6**

X. 5744. Wrought iron and copper Gong Bracket. Patent Sonora Gong.
5¾ by 4 **8/6**
7 „ 5 **9/6**
8 „ 6 **11/6**
Walnut back 6½ by 3 in.
Projection

X. 5742. Polished brass Gong Bracket.
6in. **14/-**
7in. **16/-**
8in. **18/6**
Projection 7 in.
Oak back 11 by 3 in.

Dulcet Gongs.
Most beautiful chimes, mounted on oak frames, with striker complete.
53. Set of 8 gongs, 16½ in. long by 10 in. high.. **52/6** each
52. Set of 5 gongs, 11½ by 10 in. **42/-** each.
51. Set of 4 gongs, 10 by 10 in **33/6** each.
50. Set of 3 gongs, 9 by 10 in. **26/6** each

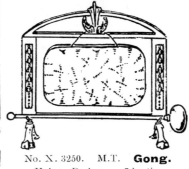

No. X. 3250. M.T. **Gong.**
Unique Design. 7 by 4in.
On fine Quality Brass Stand.
In Brass .. **19/6** } Post free
Antique Silvered finish, **25/-** }

Special Line
This handsome Solid Brass Gong on stand.
Size of Gong, 7 in. dia., 12 in. high over all.
Complete with Beater, **9/11** Post 6d

X 6136. Patent "Sonora" Gong. **10/6**
Polished Brass.
Gong 6 by 4½ in. Height 8 in.

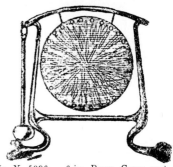

No. X. 5096. 6 in. Brass Gong and cast brass stand. **12/6** Post 6d

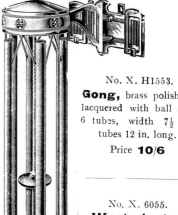

No. X. H1553.
Gong, brass polished. lacquered with ball and 6 tubes, width 7½ in. tubes 12 in. long.
Price **10/6**

No. X. 6055.
Westminster Chimes.
Antique bronzed gongs on fumed oak bracket.
Width 22 in. projection 7 in. .. **28/9**

No. X. 6055.

Dinner Gongs.
Height 10 in., diam. of drum, 5 in.
X. 19711.
Polished Brass.
Price **5/9**
Post 4d.

Height 15 in., diam. of gong, 6½in.
X. 19712.
Polished Brass.
Price **7/11**
Post 4d.

No. X. 19498. **Dinner Gong.**
All brass antique, lacquered.
9¼ in. high. 5½ in diam. of gong.
Price, complete with beater, **7/6**
Post 4d.

No. X. 19659. **Dinner Gong.**
Antique brass plated and mounted on dark oak base. 11 in. high.
Diam. of drum, 6 in. **4/9** Post 3d.

No. X. 19353/2. **Dinner Gong.**
All brass antique.
12 in. high. 9½ in. diam. of gong.
Price **12/9** Post free.

All Goods to value of 10/- and over carriage paid.

B B..

BRASS AND COPPER NOVELTIES for CHRISTMA

No. X. 18119.   Smokers' Set.
Tray 10½ in. diameter, well-made and finished.
Polished Brass, 4/11 Post 6d.
18120 Antique Copper **5/9** „ 6d.

No. X. 2235/56.   **Polished Copper Ash Tray & Match Stand, 6 in. diam., 2/6**

X. 16977/78.   Smoker's Set, new pattern, tray 12½ in. diameter, cigar stand, ash tray, match stand and cigar cutter. 16977, tarnished brass, lacquered **12/6**
16978. Tarnished copper, lacquered **15/9**
Postage 6d.

No. X. 19287.

Smoker Set.
9½ in. diam.
Antique brass
laquered,
3/11 Post 4d.

No. X. 18110.
Height 34 in.
Stand green antique
iron, foot and set
antique brass, tarnished
lacquered, **8/6**

No. X. 18111.
Height 34 in.
Stand green antique
iron, foot and set
antique copper, tarnished, lacquered, with
antique brass mountings
9/6   Post 6d.

X. 2235/45.   **Polished copper Match Stand and Tray, 4 in. diam., 3/-** Post 4d.

No. X. 17450.   Smoker's Set. Modern finish, antique copper, finely oxydized, lacquered, with unique brass mountings and modern stamping, consisting of ash tray, cigar cup, match box and fancy tray, 13½ in. diam. **16/6** Post 6d.

No. X. 18885.
Ash Tray, polished
brass lacquered with
turning bowl. 2½ in. high
3½ in. dia., **1/6** Post 3d.

X. 4698/1.   **Extra heavy Polished Copper Ash Tray 1/6** Postage 2d.

X. 17605/1.
Ash Tray,
brass
tarnished,
lacquered.
Price **1/-**

X. 17606/1.   Copper tarnished, lacquered.
Price ... **1/3**   Post 3d.

No. X. 18300.
Antique Brass tarnished.
Price **2/11**
Post 2d.

X. 470/15.   Wall Match Holder. Antique brass imitation, **1/-** Post 3d.

Brass Log Boxes. Very fine repoussé brass Log Box, wooden lining. Size 20 by 20 by 14 in   Price **19/6**

No. X. 1217.   Ash Tray. Polished Brass or Copper.
4½d. each.   **3/9** doz

X. 2558.   Polished copper Ash Tray.   New Design.
1/6 Post 2d.

No. X. 18626.   Smoker's Set. Brass Tray and Smoker's Sundries on Stand.
Price .. **12/9**   Crate 6d.

Brass Wire Hanging Letter Rack.

Well made and finished.   Does not hold the dust.

No. X. 1 .. **2 3**
No. X. 2 .. **3/3**
Postage 3d.

No. X. 4769/7..
Milk or Hot
Water Glass.
Antique Brass,
Lacquered,
with modern
design.
3½ in. high.
Price ... **1/6**
Post 3d.

No. X. A1457
Art Bronze
Pipe Rack.
To hold 5 pipes
Price **6½d.**
Post 3d.

Solid Polished Brass Hearth or Plate Stand.   Top 10½ in.   Shaped feet.   Splendid value. **6/6** Post 6d

X. 4.   Copperoid Newspaper Rack, antique finish.
Price ... **4/11**   Post 6d.

Antique copper
tarnished
Companion
Stand. Special
Line. 19½ in.
high. Complete
with tongs,
shovel, poker,
brush and stand,
3/9 complete.
Packing 6d.
Solid brass
Companion
Stands—
No. X. 481, **12/9** X. 480, **14/9**
Antique Coppered Bronze—
14/6 and **16/9**

No. X. 169.   Tonguettes. Black and Brass, **2/6** Black and Copper, **2/11** Postage 5d. Special Line in Polished Brass, as above design, **1/11** Post 4d.

No. X. 3
Copperoid Fancy Frame.
Best Silver-plate Mirror.
13 in. **4/6** Post 6d.

No. X. 17059. Art Vase. 8 in. high. Tarnished Copper with Brass mounting.
Price **4/9** Post 4d.

All Goods on this page to value of 10/- & over post free.

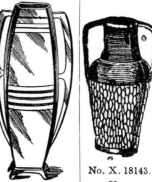

No. X. 18578.   Vase.
Height 11 in.
Brass Tarnished
Lacquered, price **5/9**
Post 4d. each extra.

No. X. 18143.
Vase,
Copper,
9½ in. high,
Price .. **9/6**

Vase.
Antique Brass, Lacquered.

	X. 18541/1	X. 2	X. 3
Height	8¼	10	12 in.
Each	3/9	4/6	5/6

Same antique copper, lacquered, with brass mounts.

	X. 18542/1	X. 2	X. 3
Each	4/	5/-	6/-

Postage 4d. each extra.

XMAS GIFTS.—Useful and Ornamental.

olborn No. 2. Vibrating Shuttle Model.

gh arm Hand Lockstich Machine on wood base,
th ornamental bent cover. Beautifully finished
roughout. A compact and serviceable model.
Complete with all accessories. Price **59/6**
Equal to any sold at £3 7 6

o. 1. Model as above, but with straight shuttle.
Price .. **47/6**
Equal to any machine sold at £2 16 0

e Sophast Sewing Machine. Cheapest on market
ood base. For full particulars, see ordinary list.
Price **32 6**

Seidel & Naumann. No. 9. Sewing Machine.
Price .. **56/-**

idel & Naumann. No. 101. Vibrating Shuttle
Hand Machine. Price **67/6**

Frister & Rossmann. No. 15. Cam Action.
Price .. **56/-**

ster & Rossmann. No. 50. Vibrating Shuttle
Hand Machine. Price **67 6**

All Sewing Machines sent carriage paid in the
United Kingdom.

No. X. 110.
Repoussé
Polished or
Antique Copper
or Brass

Coal Scoop.

Exceptionally
well finished.

Price .. **27/9**

Several other
patterns,
30/- 35/- 46/-

No. X. 2083. Art Bronze Fern Pots.
8 in. outside. 5 in. inside. **2/3** each. ⎫ Post
9 ,, ,, 5 ,, ,, **2/11** ,, ⎬ 6d.
10 ,, ,, 7 ,, ,, **3/11** ,, ⎭ extra.

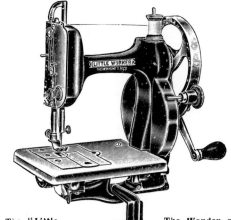
Special Selection of Jardinieres.

No. X. 5691.
Handsome polished.
Brass or Copper Fern Pot.
Repousse Work.
in. across top ... **21/-**

X. 5624. Fern Pot. 8½ in. opening.
Mounted on cast knobs. Pierced top.
In satin brass or oxydised copper
finish. Price **10/6**

No. X. 5621. Fern Pot. 9½ in. opening.
Pierced top on cast feet.
In the new satin brass finish or oxydised
copper. Price **15/6**

No. X. 5429. Jardiniere.
Polished or oxydised copper
or brass hand finished.

8½ in. across top.

Price **6/6** Post 4d.

No. X. 5652 C.
Very massive hand finished
brass or copper Fern Pot.
13½ in. across top.

Price **28/6**

No. X. 5309.
d finished, brass Jardiniere.
RY GRACEFUL DESIGN
Size, 9 in. across top,
Price ... **15/6**

No. X. 16756/0.
Polished brass, lacquered.
7½ in. high, 8 in. diameter, **3/6**

No. X. 16756/2. As above, but in
copper, **4/6** Carriage 6d.

No. X. 17114 0. Polished brass,
lacquered. 6½ in. high, 6½ in.
diameter, **2/6** Post 4d.

SPECIAL VALUE.
No. X. 26644. Fern Pots, hammered.
Brass plated. Antique finish.
No. 1, 4¾ by 5½ 2, 5¾ by 6½ 3, 6 by 8¾ in.
2 6 3 4/6
Postage 3d., 4d. and 6d.
No. X. 26266. Copper plated.
Antique finish. Same prices.

No. X. 687.
In Polished or Oxydised
Copper.
in. 14 in. inside.
7 in. 12 in. inside.
6/11 28/6 each.
Finished Oxydised Silver,
33/6 each.

No. X. 1932. Fine quality cast
polished brass Jardiniere, 3 feet
with rings, pierced top.
Size 6 in. across top, inside
measure ... **15/6**
,, 7½ in. do. do. ... **19/6**
,, 10½ in. do. do. ... **27/9**

Packing 6d. extra on Large Pots. All Goods to the value of 10s. and over Carriage Paid.

ADAMANT METAL WARE.
Rustless Hammered Bodies with Dull Brass Mountings.

| THE LATEST NOVELTY | VERY ARTISTIC. | SUITABLE FOR PRESENTS. | SOMETHING UNIQUE. |

No. X 816. Adamant Plant Pot, 12 in. diam. **9/9**
Quaint. Suitable for modern furnishing.

New Goods always arriving Fresh Shapes and Designs.

Great Variety.

No. X. 813.
Adamant Jardiniere.

6 in.	7 in.	8 in.	10 in. diam.
3/-	3/6	4/3	5/9

If you want the Best Selection of Art Metal Work, We have it.

No. X. 814. **Adamant Plant Pot** (loose lining), size, 10 in. sqr. **18**

Adamant Candlestick, 2/-
No. X. 6½. Ditto, without Match Holder .. **1/-**
Size 10 in. diam. Post 4d.

Adamant.
X. 15. Large Letter Box **5/9**
Size 16 by 8 by 2½ in.
X. 16. Medium ,, ,, **5/3**
Size 12 by 7½ by 2½ in.

No. X. 10.
Adamant Candlestick.
9 in. high .. **2/9**

No. X. 12. **Adamant Waste Paper Tube.** 14 by 8 in. **6/-**

No. X. 6/3960. Table Bell.
New Shape. Antique brass finish
Good melodious tone.

11	4¼ in. high	Price	**1/-**
12	4¼ in. high	,,	**1/6**
13	5¼ in. high	,,	**2/-**
14	5½ in. high	,,	**2/9**

Post 3d.

X. 460/12. Candlestick. Antique iron, with brass mountings, 6½ in. high. **2/3** each.   Post 3d.

New Quaint Fern Stand.
SPECIAL VALUE.
Size, 33 in. high Top.
9 by 5¼ in. deep.
Dull Art Metal work.
Imitation Embossed
Antique Iron.

No. X. 6/4766.
New style of brass **Bell Gong.**
With special beater.
large size 12 in. base 4¾ in.
gong 4¾ in.
Price **8/11**, post 4d.

Small size, 10¾ in. high,
4 in. base. 3¼ in. gong.
Price **5/6**, post 4d.

No. X. 6/3536.
Cow Bell Type Gong.
Brass stand on wood frame.
Complete with beat.

Small size.
Straight 9½ in.   Base 8¼ in.
Gong 5½ in. by 4½ in.
Price **8/6**, postage 4d

Large size.
Height 11 in.   Base 8¼ in.
Gong 8¼ by 5¼ in.
Price **10/9**, post free

X. 460/10.
Candlestick.
Antique Finish,
with imitation
Inlaid
Enamel.
6½ in. high.
Price .. **1/9**
Post 3d.

X. 460/13.
Candlestick,
10 in. high,
embossed
antique iron
imitation,
good value.
3/6 each,
Post 3d.

X. 461/13. New Candlestick, embossed antique iron, imitation, 6¼ in. high, Very quaint, **3/9** Post 3d.

No. X. A1708. **Art Bronze Crumb Scoop.** In various finishes.
Price .. .. .. **1/-**   Postage 4d.

Goods to value of 10/- and over, sent carriage paid.

REPRODUCTIONS IN BRASS FORM UNIQUE PRESENTS

Reproductions of well-known Antique Knockers

Made in Fine Quality Brass in Antique Finish, suitable for Bedroom Doors.

eresting Histories attached to all these Knockers.

These make Unique Christmas Gifts.

Many Dozens of types and styles in all sizes on view. too numerous to specify in Catalogue.

Several other similar patterns Knockers Copies of well known subjects from 1/-

X. 2074. edroom Knocker. anx Cat on fancy ckplate. Size 3½ in. **2/3** Post 3d. 2435. As above on smaller back- e, **1/9** Post 3d.

X. 2065. Bedroom Knocker. Jack Hammer Minehead. Unique. Size 4½ in. **3/11** Post 4d.

X. 1620s. The Lincoln Imp. The most popular pattern made, size 3½ in. **1/3** Post 3d. No. 2068. Similar but larger, size 3½ in , on large backplate. **2/6** Post 4d. Ditto, full size knocker Price **12/6**

X. 2535. Dickens Old Curiosity Shop Knockers, 3½ by 3 in. **3/6** Post 4d. Also Chas. Dickens' Bust Knockers.

X. 2062. Falstaff on fancy backplate Knocker, size 5½ in. **3/6** Post 3d. No. 2362. As above but on smaller back- plate .. **2/3**

X. 2384. The famous Banbury Cross Bedroom Door Knocker, size 5½ in. **5/6** Post 4d.

X. 2386. The Nelson Knocker, size 4 in. **2/3** Post 3d. No. 2372. As above but on fancy back- plate, **4/6** Post 4d.

X. 2122. Brass Caddy Spoon, St. George and the D agon, **1/6** Post 3d. Other patterns **1/- & 1/6**

X. 2421. Brass Caddy Spoon, Lynmouth Tower, **1/6** Post 3d. Smaller size, **1/-**

X. 2415. Brass Caddy Spoon, Lincoln Imp, **1/-** Post 3d. Many other patterns **1/- 1/6** ea.

X. 2051. Durham Sanctuary Knocker, of world-wide repute, a gem for collectors Size 3½ in. **4/6** Post 4d.

X. 2076. The Bat Knocker, a popular pattern. Size 3 by 3½ in. **2/9** Post 3d. Many other patterns from **1/-** each.

X.2524. Nut Crackers, antique finish, back and front of the famous Lincoln Imp, **4/3** Post 4d. 2522. Made in Dickens characters, one side Fagan, reverse Sikes, **4/3** 2523. Pickwick and Mrs. Bardell, **6/-** Post 4d.

X.1280. Antique orass Hat and Coat Hook. St. George and the Dragon, **1 6** Also in Wardrobe Hook **1/-** Post 3d. Many other reproductions same price.

. Brass Dog and ng Pipe Stop, each Post 2d.

X. 23. Brass Pipe Stop, Head of O'Connor, **9**d. Post 2d.

X. 4. Hand and Pipe Brass Pipe Stop **9**d. Post 2d.

X. 39. St. George and the Dragon Pipe Stop, **9**d. Post 2d.

X. 30. Reproduction of the famous Napoleon Pipe Stop **9**d. Post 2d

X. 10. Brass Pipe Stop, Washington, **9**d. Post 2d.

X. 23. Brass Leg Pipe Stop, **9**d. Post 2d.

We are only able to show a few of the many dozen designs of Pipe Stops used years ago, and which are now greatly sought for by collectors, but we have a large variety in our Special Showroom (**OLD LONDON**) well worth a visit.

No. X. 2252.
Complete Set of Six famous Dickens Characters,

Made in Solid Brass, as Ornaments or Pipe Stops, 1½ in. .. **6**/. set of 6, Post 4d. No. 2495. Mounted on Bases, 2½ in. .. **8**/- ,, ,, Same Characters supplied mounted on brass spoons with fancy twisted stem and round stem and round bowl, length of spoon 6½ in. **15/6** set of 6 Post 6d.

All goods on this page to the value of 10/- and over, Post free.

at Boy.   Perker, the Lawyer.   Tony Weller.   Pickwick.   Mrs. Bardel'.   Sam Weller.

Reproductions of Antiques

No. X. 2231.
Old Time Hour Glass with brass frame.
Height 8 in.
Many other patterns at same price.
10 9 Post free.

No. X. 2549.
Quaint Brass Table Bell.
"Queen Elizabeth."

No. 2484. 3 in. high **3/9**
2549. 4 ,, **5/9**
1935. 5 ,, **8/6**
2500. 7 ,, **12/6**

Many other styles and figures, comprising "Nelson," "Dickens," etc., at similar prices.

Visitors are cordially invited to inspect the many interesting articles of both genuine and reproductions of Antiques. With the limited space in this Catalogue we are unable to give anything like an adequate selection of the various goods displayed, which consist of Sundials, Large Repousse Pots, Beer Mugs, Beer Warmers, Trays, Fenders, Companion Stands, Trivets, Hearth Stands, Scoops, Ornaments, Paper Weights, Coal Tongs, Water Clocks, Umbrella Stands, &c.

No. X. 1852.
Brass Snuffer and Tray. Snuffer 7 in., Tray 9½ in. long.
6/- pair complete. Post 4d.
Snuffer without Tray, **4/6**
Also larger and fancier patterns .. .. **9/-** Set.

No. X. 1401.
Brass Door Porter, 18 in. high.
Very useful. **9/3**
Many other quaint patterns—
Punch and Judy, Highlander, Lions, Dogs etc., at various prices.

X. 1771. Old-fashioned Brass Lantern, fitted with Horn—
A fine reproduction.
Size 12 by 6½ in
21/- Carriage paid.
Packing 6d.
Many other quaint shapes from **9/-** to **35 6**

No. X. 1545.
Antique Brass Candelabra (2-light).
Adjustable rise and fall.
16 in high, **23/6** pair.
Also made with 4 lights, **37/6** pair complete.
Many others on view.

No. X. 2233.
Quaint Brass Candlestick.
Fine reproduction.
6 in. high.
10/6 pair. Post 5d.
Many other flat shape and similar style from **4/6** pair.

No. X. 1446.
Solid Brass Candlestick, oval base.
Fine reproduction.
7 in. high.
8/6 pair. Post 5d.

No. 1894. As above, but with square base, **8/6** pair.
Many other sizes, both smaller and larger.

X. 7154. Rare pattern Brass Candlesticks with Bell, 13 in. high
Very massive **23/6** pair
A fine range of the old Twisted Brass Candlesticks in all heights

No. X. 1951.
Brass Toasting Fork with twisted stem,
2/6 Post 4d.
Also made with plain stem.
Ditto, with steel stem, same price.
Other quaint patterns, larger heads,
4/6 Post 4d.

No. X. 2045.
Old-fashioned Brass Candlestick with slide.
18 in. high, **21/-** pair.
Many other sizes.
All prices.

No. X. 2607.
Very fine reproduction of an Oval Brass Jardiniere.
Cast feet and Repoussé work.
Size 12 in. **31/6**
Packing 6d.
No. X. 2083. Round ditto.
Size 8 by 8 in... .. .. **21/-**
No. X. 2083L. Larger size.
Size **42/-**
Packing 6d. extra.
Many other styles and designs.

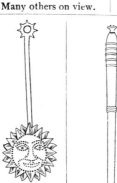

No. X. 2741.
"The Sun" Flat Chestnut Roaster, finely pierced brass,
8/- ea. Post 6d.
Many other pierced Roasters all sizes, from
3/11 to **25/-**
USEFUL OLD TIME GIFTS.

X. 1988. Warming Pan in brass or copper,
Size 10½ by 11 by 12 in. across.
Plain ... **14/6 16/- 17/6** each
Engraved ... **17/6 19/6 21/-** ,,
A Unique Ornament for the Hall.
The Old Time Disinfector, similar to above but with engraved steel handle,
27/6 Carriage paid. Packing 6d.

No. X. 1990C.
Antique Brass Enclosed Chestnut Roaster, round, square, oval or octagonal, or triangular shape,
7/- Post 5d.
Made in horseshoe and lemon shapes.
7/11 each.
Also in very fine Repousse work, with slides and fancy handles, small and large, from
13/6 upwards.

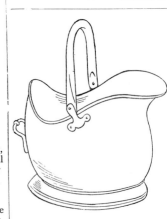

No. X. 2593.
Antique Coal Scuttle, Helmet shape.
In either Brass or Copper.
A fine reproduction in every detail.
21/- each. Carriage paid. Packing 6d.

No. X. 2594. As above, but with hood,
25/6 upwards. Packing 6d.

Children's Chairs, Desks, &c., for Christmas.

No. X. 700. Child's Chair.
Dimensions—Height of back 15 in.
Height from floor to top of seat. 10 in.,
width of seat, 13 in., depth, 12 in.

Upholstered in Cretonne.
Green Rush, **5/6**   Cane, **6 6**

MANY HAPPY HOURS

Will be the result if one
of these Children's Sets
are given this Xmas.

Child's Table and Two Chairs.

Upholstered Seat. Very strong. Just the thing for the younger
children. Painted dark colour. Size of Table, 16½ in. high, top 18¾
by 12¾ in   Chairs 18½ in. high, seat 9½ in , **8 11** Packing 1/-
Upholstered Sofa or Settee to match.   Size 28 by 13½ in .. **15/-**
Packing 6d. extra.   Upholstered Settee .. **19/11**
Larger size Set, Table 16½ by 26¾ by 17 in. high : Chair 10½ by
10 in. seat ; 21¾ in. over all.   Price .. **15/-** set.

**The Children's "Croquet"
Upholstered Chair.**
In various coloured Cretonnes.
Superior Style (as illustration).
14 in. seat, 27 in. high .. **4/9**
11½ „ 24 „ **3 3**
Several other Upholstered Wicker
Chairs in various styles, from **5 6** each.

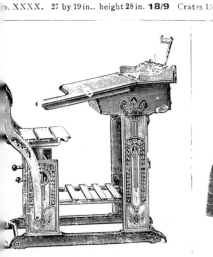

School Desk.

No. X. Made of Ash light finish, thoroughly braced,
strong and durable, fitted with lid, leather lined, and
black bound, size 21 by 13½ in., height 22 in ... **8/11**
No. XX. Similar to above but 22 by 16 in , and ht. 24 in.
Price ... **10 11**
No. XXX. Similar to above, but 24 by 18 in. and 26 in.
high ... **12/9**
No. XXXX. 27 by 19 in.. height 28 in. **18/9** Crates 1/-

Child's Table and Two Chairs:

Extra strong, legs unscrew, finished in many colours. For the elder Children
Size of Table, height 21 in , top 22½ in. by 14 in.   **11/6** Packing 6d.
„ Chairs, „ 21½ in., seat 13½ in...
Made also in Bamboo with Matting Tops and Seats. Table **5/6**. Arm-
chair **5/6** Chair, without arms **4/6** Packing 6d. per set extra.

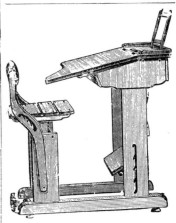

No. X. 485. Desk.
Adjustable Seat and Footrest, with
Receptacle for Books, Covered ink-
well, Book-holder. Polished dark or
light colour
Price **25/6**   Crate **1/-**

A Christmas Novelty.

Many Types of Children's Chairs etc.,
too Numerous to Specify.

No. X. 493. Desk. A good serviceable
desk, polished light or dark colour, adjust-
ble seat and footrest, fitted book receptacle,
covered inkwell, book-rest, carved ends ;
superior quality.

Price .. **30/-**   Crate 1/-

No. X. 6. Child's Oak Bureau. With flap shelf underneath,
pigeon holes, etc. 36 in. high by 22 in. wide by 9 in. deep. Size of
writing space, 19 by 10 in. Price **17/11**   Packing 1/-
No. X. 7. Upholstered seat, revolving chair to match, price **5/6**

No. X. 484. Desk. Folds flat. Can be used
with any chair. Adjustable so that desk can be
used for a child or an adult. Covered inkwell,
pen receptacle. Polished light or dark colour.
Price **16/6** (not including chair).   Packing 1/-

The "Bahfkot" At once a bath and a cot.
BABY'S CHRISTMAS PRESENT.
(Patented and Registered Nos., 285825, 480944).

In use as a Bath.

In use as a Cot

The "BAHFKOT" is a fine, specially waterproofed hammock or cot of best rubber cloth, swung on a light yet very strong frame, at a convenient height from the ordinary nursery chair. A clear idea of the general structure and appearance is given in our illustration. It is superior to the metal bath in that the rubber cloth is perfectly antiseptic, and would not poison an open wound, which it is possible for a metal bath to do. The "Bahfkot" is equipped with receptacles for soap, sponge, flannel, scissors, and the various other articles necessary for baby's toilet. No need to lift it to empty, a protected tap is fitted to draw off. Can be folded up and strapped to bottom of trunk.

INVALUABLE FOR TRAVELLING.

Price ... ... **21/-** Carriage paid.

In rocking position.
No. X. 19.

Kindergarten Chair.
High-class chair in Walnut Finish and with Lever Action.
No. X. 19a. With baluster back, **11/9**
With baluster back and pan. **14/6**
Crate 1/-

The "Kumfee."
No. X. 407. Combination High Chair. Plain turned imitation Bamboo, fully upholstered, including sides, fitted with Adjustable Back for Baby to lie down. Complete, with all the Kindergarten and Pan .. .. .. **21/-** Crate 1/-
Sanitary Leather Upholstery used.

Dont Forget His Majesty the Baby, but get him The "SHURESETE."

"Most Comfortable, most Unique and most Hygienic Adjustable Baby Chair Made"
—*Vide Press.*

The DE LUXE MODEL CHAIR for Baby.

Adjustable Footrest with a combined box to prevent the Baby from sliding out of the Chair. Front part of box is movable in connection with the footrest. Through this movable front part's firm combination with the footrest the box is always closed, rendering same absolutely safe and creating a most comfortable position for the legs. This arrangement prevents the baby from slipping through the chair, and also from pushing against the table. Upholstered in sanitary Leather Cloth, with special detachable concealed Commode, Playboard, Beads, Picture, &c. Mounted on Rubber Wheels.

Price **33 6** Crate 1/-

The Acme of Comfort. Baby's Delight

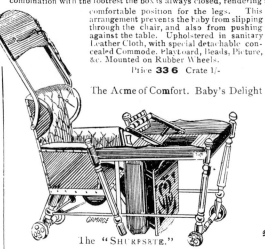

The "SHURESETE."
As a Low or Wheel Chair, showing large Playboard, Picture, Beads, &c.

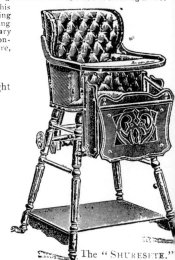

The "SHURESETE."

No. X. 84. As a Wheel Chair.
Kindergarten Chair.
Extra large Playboard, with double set of Beads, Baluster Back, **19/9** With pan **22/6**
Embossed velvet back, **21/9** **24/6**
Well finished in walnut colour.

Comfortable Easy Chair
High Quality.

We particularly call attention to our Easy Chairs.

We make a special feature of this class of work. Comfort, Durability and Design, with moderation in price is our aim.

We are always ready to make special chairs to customers own ideas Chairs can be covered in any material but we price them in Tapestries as we find them in more demand.
Price from **11/9** upwards.
See Furnishing List for Full Range.
No. X. 5. With loose vegetable down cushion, spring edge.
Very Good Chair.
In tapestry, cased hair.
Price ... **45 -**
Packing 2 6

X. 130 Back cotton grounds, gold embroidered linen backs, flush panels, carved fancy toys. 5 ft. 8 in. high, 4 folds as illustration.
Special value **10 11** Carriage forward. Crate 1/-
As above, but better quality with landscape panels.
Price ... **18 9**

Hundreds of other Screens
Prices from **9/11, 10 11, 12 6, 15/6, 18 6 21/6, 25 6, 28/6, 35 6, 38 6 42 -, 45 - 48/6, 53/6, 63/-** and upwards.

Special Value.
SOLID OAK
25 6

The "Harrogate" Rest Chair.
An Exceptionable Xmas Present.

Made in Solid Oak, fumed or golden finish.
Adjustable to three positions, loose cushion back and fixed rest
Beautifully covered in good quality Corduroy Velveteen in various colours.
Extra long seat. Most Restful and Comfortable.
Price .. **25 6**

BUREAUX, for Christmas Presents.

X. 1. Bureaux. In so'id fumed oak. 12 in. deep, 30 in. wide, 42 in high, with pigeon holes, stationery rack, etc. Substantially made and well finished.

Price .. **23/6** Crate 1/- extra.

OPEN.   SHUT.

No. X. 0115. Plain fumed oak **Bureaux,** fitted with three drawers, slides, etc. About 42 in. high, 14¾ in. deep when closed, 27½ in. when open.

Made in 2 ft. 6 in. wide, price **39/6**   Made in 3 ft. 3 in. wide, price **47 6**

No. X. 0115.   Also made in Inlaid fumed oak.

2 ft. 6 in. wide, price **48/6**   3 ft. wide, price **55/6**   Crate 1/-   Carriage paid.

No. X. 199A. Made in solid fumed oak. **Ladies' Bureau,** fitted with stationery box inside. Oxydised mounts. 26 in. wide. 45 in. high. 9¼ in. deep. Writing bed 11 in. by 24 in.

Price .. **19 6** Crate 1/-

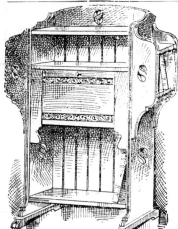

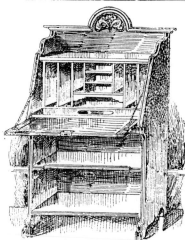

No. X. 0117.
Novel Bureaux.
Made in solid fumed oak throughout. Match lined back.
Size, 5 ft. high by 3 ft. 3 in. wide.
Useful for Study or Boudoir.
Price ... **49/6**
Crate 1/-

X. 098A. **Bureaux Bookcase.** Made in solid fumed oak.
5 ft. 8 in. high, 2 ft. 6 in. wide, fitted with leaded lights. A useful article.
Price **45/-**
Crate 1/-

No. X. 99.
Bureau.
Arch top.
Oak Bureau, moulded front throughout.
Curved back.
52 in. high,
30 in. wide,
10 in. deep.
Writing bed, 18½ by 25½ in.
Price **29/6**
Crate 1/6

"Wunlock" Bureau. Design B. (Patent)

Price **£4 17 6** Carriage paid.

Size—33in. wide, 42in. high, 17½in. deep.   Packing 1/6
Construction—Solid Oak, with Satin Walnut pigeon-holes and linings.
Finish—Good wax polish—any shade.
Design B.S. As above, but Oak everywhere, drawers to pigeon-holes, lined fall, best finish ... **£6 6 0**
Other Patterns similar to above, about 30 by 40 in., from ... **59/3**
The convenience of "One Lock Securing Everything" doubles the valu of The "Wunlock" Bureau.

THE 'Wunlock' Bureau

UNIQUE FEATURES.

(A) **Automatic Locking.**
By simply closing the fall, every drawer is securely fastened.

(B) **The "Wunlock" Arms.**
No slides required, consequently no scratched front.

(C) **The "Wunlock" Interior.**
1. Non-spilling Inkwell.
2. "Ever-ready" Blotter.
3. "Always There" Penholder.
4. Secret Stamp Box.
5. Obliging Cheque Drawer.

A Quintet of Novel Time Savers.

(D) **Invisible Castors.**
Every "Wunlock" Bureau fitted with silent glide Castors.

CONSTRUCTION.

SOLID OAK everywhere, with Cedar drawer linings, and best 3-ply bottoms.

Plain Brass drop handles, or as shown.
Best Wax Finish.
Brown Fumed or Antique.

"Wunlock" Bureau. Design S. (Patent)

Price .. **£3 18 9** Carriage paid.

Size—31in. wide, 42in. high, 17½in. deep.   Packing 1/6.
Construction—Prime Oak, with Satin Walnut pigeon-holes and linings, slot screwed throughout.
Finish—High-grade Wax Polish, any shade, "light fumed," "golden brown," or "antique."
Design S.S. As above, but solid Oak throughout, and with lined fall **£4 13 9**
Every drawer is securely fastened by merely closing the fall.

Useful and Acceptable 'Xmas Presents.

The "Paragon" Bed and Library Table.

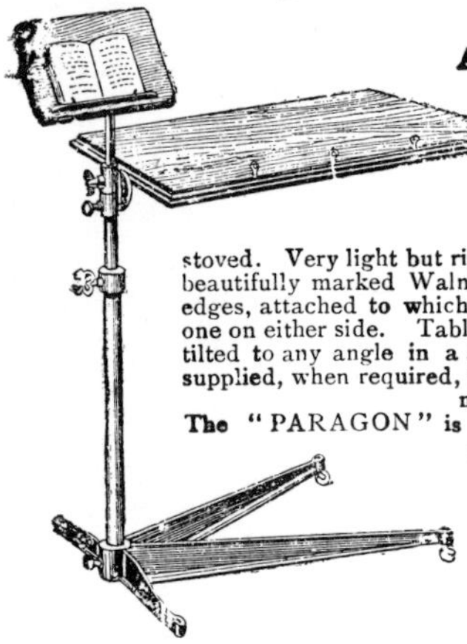

(BRITISH MADE.)

An ideal Table for Hospitals, Asylums, Infirmaries, and other Institutions.

Scientifically constructed of weldless steel tubing, exquisitely jet black enamelled and carefully stoved. Very light but rigid. Table top 24 by 18 ins., made of beautifully marked Walnu finished wood, with moulding round edges, attached to which are two neat collapsible Book Rests, one on either side. Table can be raised or lowered at will and tilted to any angle in a second. A telescopic side table can be supplied, when required, which will be found very convenient for many purposes.

The "PARAGON" is quite indispensable as a Bed Table, and is equally useful as a Reading, Writing, Card Chess, or Work Table, Music Stand, Easel, &c., &c.

Maximum quality. Minimum Cost.

Price ... **23/6**

No. X. 1.	Black Enamelled Stand, and Polished Walnut finished top without Side Table	**23 6**
No. X. 2.	Same as No. 1, but with Side Table, as illustrated	**32/6**
No. X. 3.	Same as No. 1, but with Side Table and Candle Sconce ...	**35/6**

EXTRAS—TO ORDER.

Rod of Stand and Adjusting Set Screws, Plated	**5/-**
Ditto ditto ditto Enamelled Colours	**5/-**
Chess Board Top	**4/6**
Oak Top	**2/6**

A Detachable Telescope Leg, or support, can be supplied for supporting the unsupported end of table, thus giving absolute rigidity and strength for carrying heavy weights, such as Typewriter, &c., &c. Price **4/-** extra,

Crate 1/- Carriage paid.

The "Excelsior" Bed Table.

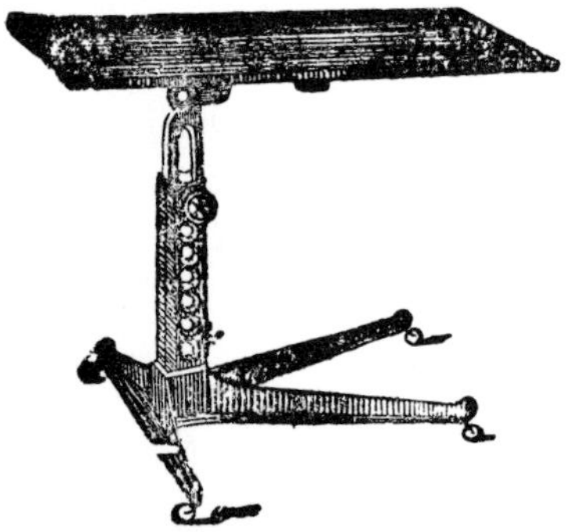

Can be raised or lowered to any angle or position at will. Also swung round when not in use.

Price .. .. **31/6** each.

DESCRIPTION.—The "Excelsior" Table consists of two parts, viz.: the table top and the iron stand. The table top is of wood and built up in several layers so that it shall not warp. The Table is then nicely finished in Walnut, but Oak can be had if desired for 2/6 extra. The Iron Stand is strongly made and mounted on 4 castors, so that the Table can be easily moved from place to place. A steel rod is fitted to the table, and on one side forms a ledge, so that books, &c., will not fall off when the Table is tilted for reading purposes. When the steel rod is swung over to the other side, it falls in the moulding of the Table, and so grips a newspaper that it shall not fall off. A couple of book clips are supplied to hold down the pages of a book when reading.

Sold everywhere at 35/- Our price .. **31/6**

Crates 1/- Carriage paid.

Can be supplied with extra long uprights for high beds for 2/6 extra.

The "OMEGA" Reading and Literary Stand.

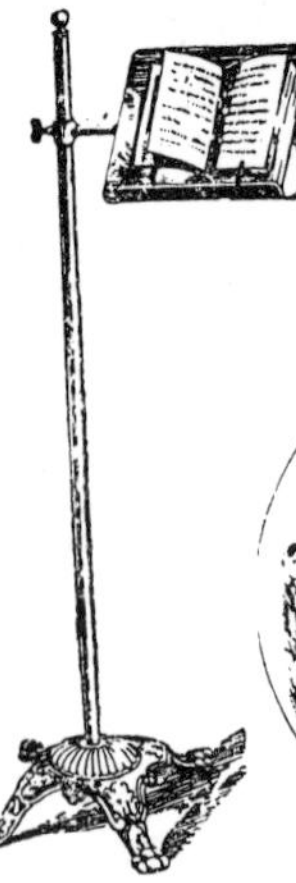

Reading slope can be placed to any height, or at any angle required. The upright brass standard, screws into the iron base, and the whole combination is very rigid.

Indespensible to the Lecture Room, Library, Sick Room, Mission Hall, or Home.

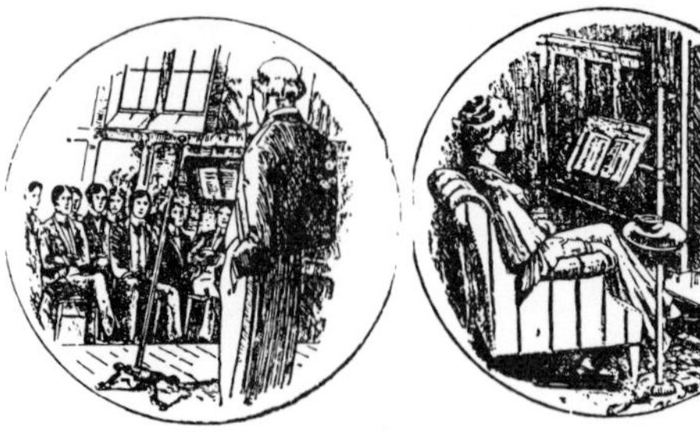

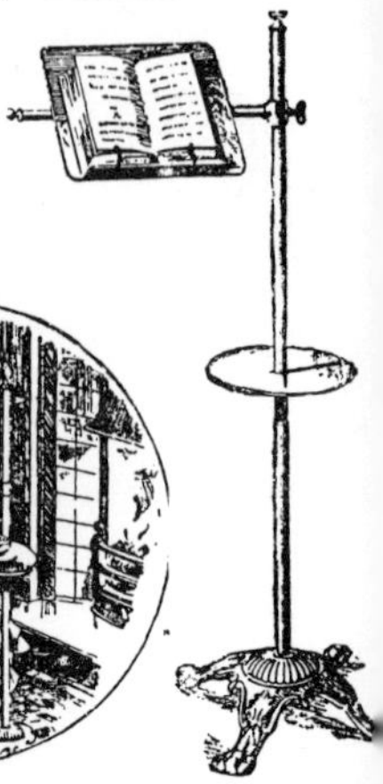

Price **21/-** Packing 6d. Carriage paid. Circular Table 5/- extra.

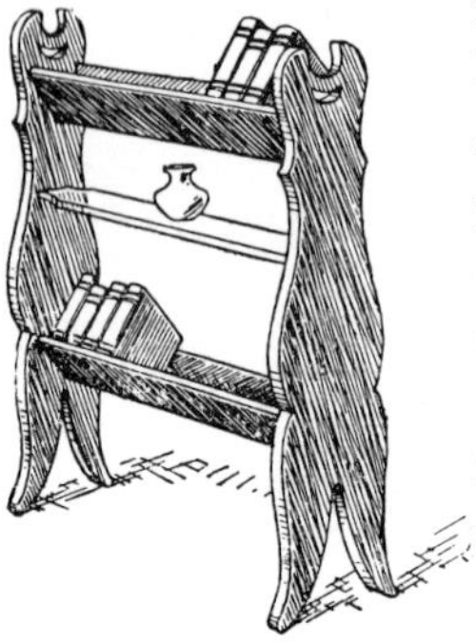

No. X. 503.

Handy Little **Book Trough and Table.**

USEFUL.

Height, 29 in.

Width, 21 in.

Made in solid fumed oak.

Price .. **7/9**

Crate 6d.

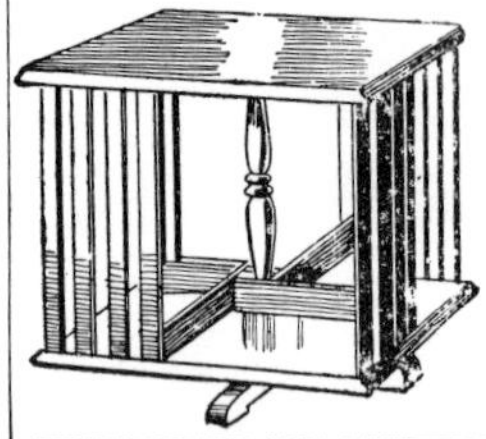

No. X. 222.

Revolving Book Rack

In fumed oak.

13 in. across.

14 in. high.

Price .. **7/**

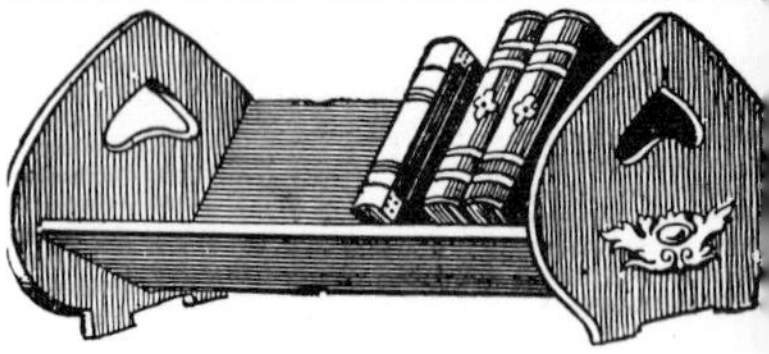

No. X. 268.

Fumed Oak Book Trough.

16 in. long. **3/11**

Or if with copper repousse plates **4/11**

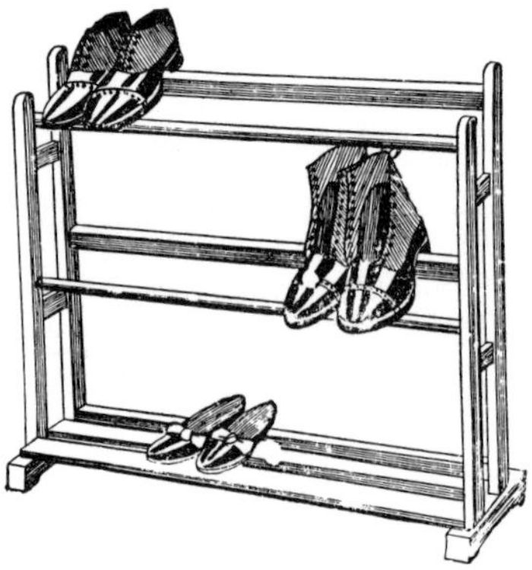

High Quality Boot Rack.

A distinct Novelty. Selling in great numbers. Finely finished in solid Walnut, Mahogany or Oak .. **11/3**

Crate 6d.

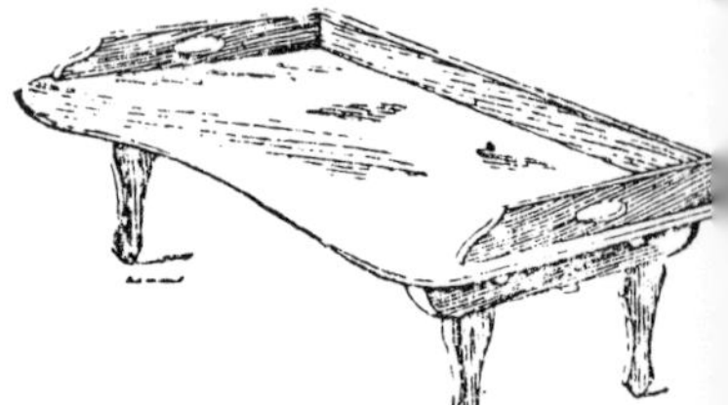

The "Restphul" Bed Table

Solid Oak Bed Table, with folding legs, well finished, light and strong.

Price .. **9/9** Crate 6d.

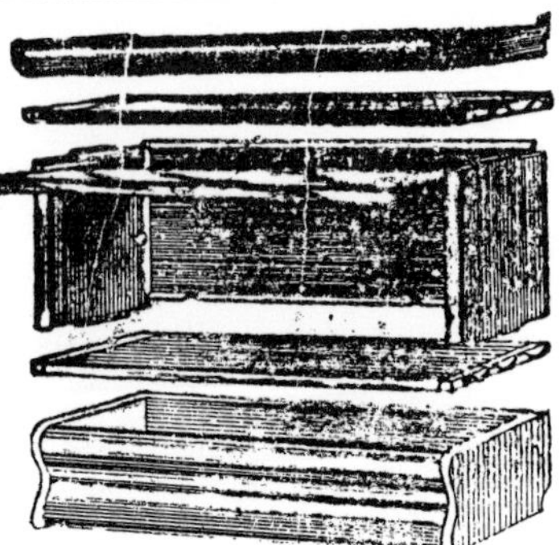

Top.

Section

Base.

Fig. 1.—ILLUSTRATION SHEWING EACH SINGLE PART.

Sectional Ball-Bearing Bookcases.

The above is a long step in advance of any Sectional Book Case, combining the good features of the old with valuable improvements in construction, quality finish, cost, and all the little things that go to make perfection. THE DOORS ARE BALL-BEARING and cannot bind, easily removable always secure. Made in the finest selected quarter sawed Oak, beautifully figured, with back and bottom of 3-ply hard white MAPLE that will not warp. Other Shades to order (same prices). Prices and Sizes.

(For illustrations and full particulars, see Departmental List).

No. X.	Depth.	Height.	s. d.	No. X.	Depth.	Height.	s. d.
9 Top Section	8 in.	-	**8 6**	3 ,, ,,	9¼ in.	10¼ in.	**14 0**
1 Book ,,	8 ,,	9½ in.	**12 6**	4 .. ,,	9¼ ,,	12¼ ,,	**15 0**
2 ,, ,,	8 ,,	11 ,,	**13 6**	13 Base ,,	9¼ ,,	-	**8 6**
12 Base ,,	8 ,,	—	**8 6**	11 Top ,,	12 ,,	—	**10 6**
10 Top ,,	9½ ,,		**8 6**	5 Book ,,	12 ,,	13½ in.	**20 0**
23 Book ,,	9½ ,,	8½ in.	**13 0**	14 Base	12 ..	—	**18 6**

The Sections are made in various sizes (see Special List, showing comparative sizes and dimensions), and at different prices, according to size. For completing the Book Case, top and bottom sections are made.

For Full Particulas and Illustrations depicting the various sizes, see **Special Furnishing List,** *Post Free.*

FINISHED IN GOLDEN OAK.

Beautifully polished, each section is fitted with end plates, oxydized finish, which securely lock making sections rigid, and preventing any fear of wood splitting. Can be taken to pieces when not in use.

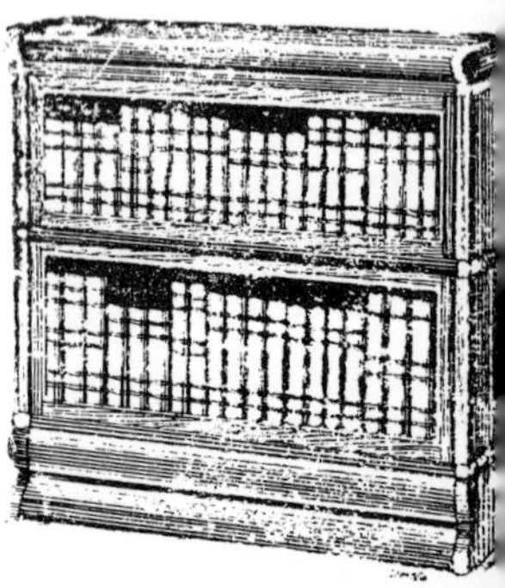

Fig. 3-2 Sect. Case. Suitable for Home

CARPET SWEEPERS for XMAS.

THE WORLD'S FINEST SELECTION AND LARGEST STOCK.
THE MOST ACCEPTABLE XMAS PRESENT.

THE GREAT GROWTH in the use of Carpet Sweepers during recent years, has caused us to make a distinct feature of the **best brands** on the market. The following is believed to be the best selection of patterns known in the trade.

Carpet Sweeper has now become a necessity in every household.

The BENEFIT OF A CARPET SWEEPER

rises from the ease and speed with which it does the work. It causes neither stooping nor backache, and does not permit any dust to escape into the room. The sweeping is done more thoroughly than that done by a broom under the most favourable conditions; and it is less troublesome, inasmuch as the sweepings are taken right out of the carpet into the machine, and so carried completely away.

Bissell's Ball Bearing "Parlour Queen."

Bissell's "Parlour Queen" Carpet Sweeper is all the name implies, and is one of our most highly finished Carpet Sweepers. The case of the "Parlour Queen" is made of Rosewood, beautifully figured and given the highest quality piano polish. All the metal parts are of original design, and well finished in nickel plate. Price **21/-** Carriage paid.

Bissell's Ball Bearing "Elite."

The "Elite" is a new design in Carpet Sweepers and combines elegance and richness in style. The case is entirely new in shape, being oval, thus securing artistic effect and at the same time giving the Sweeper unusual solidity. The woods used in making the case for the "Elite" are of the choicest, being made in Hungarian Ash, Curly Birch Mahoganized, Brazilian Rosewood and Curly Maple in Seal Brown. The bail and metal ends are also specially designed to harmonize with the artistic lines of the case, all the trimmings being nickelled. Price **20/-** Carriage paid.

TOY SIZES.

These are delightfully instructive Toys, which sweep in a miniature way, and retain the sweeping like the real machine.

Practically a bye-product of the Bissell factory, and on that account offered at very low prices.
Baby .. **11½d.**
The Child's .. **1/5½**
The Little Queen, **1/11½**
The Little Jewel, **2/11½**

Carriage Forward.

New Brushes, 3/- New Tyres, 6d. ea.
New Tyre-wheel complete .. **1/-** ,,

Bissell's Ball Bearing 'Grand Rapids."

The most popular Sweeper in the World

The "Grand Rapids" Sweeper is now fitted with ball bearings. It runs so easily, a mere touch propels it, and its efficiency as a dust extractor is greatly increased. This Sweeper is fitted with new pressed steel wheels and improved dust-proof axle tube, which ensure free and easy working. The case is made in six assorted choice cabinet woods.
X. 1. With ball bearings and japanned fittings, **15/-**
X. 2. ,,   ,,   ,, nickel ,, **16/6**
Carriage paid.

Bissell's "Cyco" Bearing 'Universal'

An old Sweeper under a new name.

Formerly known as our regular "Grand Rapids."

Supplied only with "Cyco" bearings and japanned fittings in eight varieties of handsome hardwood. This Sweeper combines the best mechanical equipment with the least expensive quality of finish.
Price **14/-** Carriage paid.

Bissell's "Cyco" Bearing "Superior"

Nickelled Fittings.

The "Superior" has a single automatic dump for each pan, and contains all improvements such as "Cyco" bearings, dust-proof axle tubes, anti-raveler, reversible bail spring, etc. **15/6** Carriage paid.

The 'Standard' Popular Model.

A Strong and Durable Sweeper.

The patterns shown on this page have ample power for medium carpets, but like all non-cyco Sweepers they cannot tackle the heavy piles for which the cyco-bearing movement was created. They are well built, with brushes of pure bristle, and are fully guaranteed.
Price **11/3** Carriage paid.

The "Crown Jewels" Sweeper.
Similar to above, price **10/6**

CARD TABLES for PRESENTS

The "X" Bridge Table.

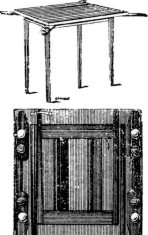

The legs are square and tapered.
The top is made from 3-ply wood screwed on a frame and covered with green felt cloth; the edges are nicely beaded. All folds flat and takes up very little room. The Special Feature of this Table is the Glass Holders and Ash Traps in solid copper at each corner, which fold under the table when not in use.

No. X. 4. In selected Hardwood, stained and polished mahogany, 30 by 24 in., without cups . **9/11**
X. 5. Ditto ditto 30 by 30 in. ,, .. **13/6**
X. 6. Ditto ditto 30 by 30 in., with cups **19/6**
X. 7. In Solid Oak, 30 by 30 in., with cups **21/-**
X. 8. ,, 30 by 30 in., without cups **15/-**

Gamage Card Table. SPECIAL VALUE

No. X. 1. Size 22 in. square top, 28 in. high. Green Cloth Top. Polished walnut colour.
Price **3/11** Carriage paid.

Improved Folding Card Table

SUITABLE FOR CLUBS, CARD PARTIES, BRIDGE PLAYERS, etc.

8/11

Perfectly rigid when open and flat when closed. Legs and Frame Work made of Deal. Top and Folding Pocket made of stout 3-ply boards. Top 24 by 24 in., height 26½ in. Tops are covered in good green felted cloth, firmly glued, and framed with solid walnut trims, all under parts are stained walnut.

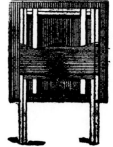

No. B.F., as illustration, 24 by 24 in 26½ in. **8 11**
No. A.P.. suitable for 4 players, stouter and better finished. Top 28 in. square, **11/9** 21 by 21 in., **5/11**

Many other patterns both English and American Card Tables on show.

The "ELPASTO" Replicas of Oil Paintings

are practically indistinguishable, except as to size, from the original pictures. They are reproduced in colours on canvas and are stretched on wooden straine like genuine oil paintings. They are the last word in art—the colours and the brush and canvas marks of the originals are faithfully reproduced. Prices range fro **6/6** upwards. The Pictures can be framed to suit individual taste. Over 200 to choose from.

HARLEM MERE (**Bakhuysen**) Picture **10/-** Frame (Black with dull gold inset) **15/-**

Morland, George.

1763-1804.

English School.

331	Domesticity,	$8\frac{3}{4}$ by 7 in.	**6/6**
332	The Farmyard,	$8\frac{3}{4}$ by 7 in.	**6/6**
333	Blindman's Buff,	$8\frac{3}{4}$ by 7 in.	**6/6**
334	Winter Scene,	$8\frac{3}{4}$ by 7 in.	**6/6**

MRS. SIDDONS (**Gainsborough**) Picture **6/6** Frame (Oak) **6/-**

100	The Syndics, 13 by 9 in.	**Rembrandt**	**7/6**
107	The Halt before the Inn	**Meissonier**	**6/6**
108	After the Bath	**P. Peel**	**6/6**
112	Dante and Beatrice	**Holiday**	**10/-**
141	Fruitfulness	**Rubens**	**20/-**
302	Oak Trees in a Storm (in two sizes)	**A. Calame**	**20/-** and **6/6**
303	The Valley Farm	**J. Constable**	**6/6**
306	The Avenue of Middelharnis	**Hobbema**	**6/6**
309	Behind the Plough	**L. Kemp-Welch**	**6/6**
313	The Mill at Wyk, $11\frac{1}{2}$ by $9\frac{1}{2}$ in.	**J. van Ruisdael**	**7/6**
318	The Day's Labour Done	**F. Arnold**	**6/6**
320	Nearing the Fold	Do.	**6/6**
325	An Autumn Evening in Scotland 22 by 13 in.	**A. de Breanski**	**15/-**

NEWLY ISSUED SUBJECTS.

166	General Booth	10 by 12 in.	**R. de l'Hopital**	6/
167	Bacchus	$9\frac{3}{4}$ by $7\frac{1}{4}$ in.	**Brangwyn**	6/
168	Riverside	13 by $8\frac{1}{2}$ in.	**Cooper**	6/
169	Mignon	$6\frac{1}{4}$ by 8 in.	**G. Buchner**	6/
170	My Model and My Dog	10 by 7 in.	**Herve**	6/
171	The First Pose	$7\frac{3}{4}$ by 10 in.	**Gallelli**	6/
172	Reverie	8 by 10 in.	**Rondel**	6/
173	Village Peace	10 by $7\frac{3}{4}$ in.	**Lucas-Robiquet**	6/
174	Handel	9 by $12\frac{1}{4}$ in.	**Zuber**	7/
175	Farmyard	$10\frac{3}{4}$ by 8 in.	**T. R. Craig**	6/
178	Light of the Bible	7 by $9\frac{1}{2}$ in.	**Bisschop**	6/
179	Fairy of the Forest	$5\frac{1}{4}$ by 10 in	**Sonrel**	6/
180	Hagar	$9\frac{1}{2}$ by $12\frac{1}{4}$ in.	**A. Van de Werff**	7/
182	Family Group	8 by $7\frac{3}{4}$ in.	**Jordaens**	6/

302 Oak Trees in a Storm, **Calame** Picture, **6/6** Frame (Gilt), **7/-**
302A Oak Trees in a Storm, **Calame** Picture, **20/-** Frame (Black with dull gold inset) **25/6**

OWING to lack of space, it is only possible to illustrate but a few of the large range of

PICTURES.

A full list of Titles will be sent on application, with a few illustrations in colour.

Holbein, Hans (The Younger). 1794-1543? **German School.**

139	The Meyer Madonna,	8 by $12\frac{3}{4}$ in.	**6/6**
503	King Henry VIII.	$7\frac{1}{2}$ by 9 in.	**6/6**
531	Lady Jane Seymour	7 by 10 in.	**6/6**
560	Portrait of Morette	$9\frac{1}{2}$ by $11\frac{3}{4}$ in.	**7/6**

327	The Windmill	**John Crome**	**6/6**
336	View of Salisbury	**John Muirhead**	**6/6**
352	Spring in Bohemia	**A. Thamm**	**10/-**
343	A Swabian Garden	Do.	**10/-**
342	'Midst Pines and Heather	**C. Daniel**	**7/6**
500	Lord Philip Wharton	**Van Dyck**	**6/6**
501	Mrs. Siddons (in two sizes)	**Gainsborough**	**7/6** and **6/6**
504	A Black Forest Peasant Girl	**W. Hasemann**	**6/6**
506	Erika	**C. Buchner**	**6/6**

DUTCH INTERIOR, **P. de Hooch.** Picture **7/6** Frame (Black) **5/-**

511	The Cavalier, **Meissonier**		**6/6**
513	The Smoker, Do.		**6/6**
514	The Tailor, **Moroni**		**6/6**
517	The Architect, **Rembrandt**		6
519	Hansel	**F. Schauss**	6
520	Gretel	**F. Schauss**	6
522	The Cellarer, 16 by 13 in.	**Grutzner**	6
523	The Librarian, 16 by 13 in.	Do.	6
524	The Debutante	**R. Pannett**	7
526	Madame Lauzun	**Romney**	7
529	John the Baptist	**Andrea del Sarto**	6
535	Mrs. Siddons	**Lawrence**	6

[STENCILLING.] HOME CRAFTS. [ENAMELLING.

Boxes of Material for Imitating the famous **Japanese Cloisonne Ware.** Most effective work and not difficult. The boxes contain :—

No. 1.—8 Tins of Enamels and Brush .. .. .. **2/3** Post 3d.
No. 2.—14 Tins of Enamels, 1 Plaque, 1 Study, and Brushes **4/3** „ 4d.
No 3.—20 Tins of Enamels, 2 Plaques, 1 Study, and Brushes **6/6** „ 4d.
No. 4.—27 Tins of Enamels, 3 Plaques, 2 Studies and Brushes **9/6** „ 5d.

Separate Tins of Cloisonne Enamel .. .. .. price **3**d., **6**d. and **1/-** per tin.

Lacquers .. .. .. Thinning Medium, **3**d. per tin.

DEMONSTRATIONS DAILY OF ALL HOMECRAFTS during December.

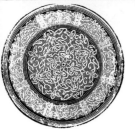

Cloisonne Plaques.
ices .. **3**d., **4**d., **9**d., **1/-**
1/3 **1/6** **2/-** **2/6**
2/9 **3/-** **3/6** **4/6**
Post 1½d., 3d., 4d., 5d., 6d.

Cloisonne Bowl.
No. 2414, **1/3** Post 4d.

Cloisonne Bowl.
No. 2449, **1/-** Post 4d.

Cloisonne Vase.
No. 1405, **1/-** Post 4d.

Cloisonne Jug.
No. 1423, **1/3** Post 4d.

Cloisonne Bowl.
No. 2321, **2/6** Post 5d.

Cloisonne Bowl.
No. 2417, **1/6** Post 4d.

Cloisonne Vase.
No. 2444, **1/3** Post 4d.

STENCIL YOUR 'XMAS GIFTS YOURSELF.

Makes them twice as acceptable besides the pleasure and pastime.

With a very little practice beautiful work may be accomplished by anyone.

We have a large selection of Stencils prices from 5½d. to 3/6.

Separate Colours 4d. & 6d. per tube.

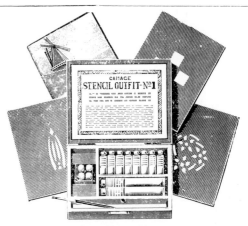

Stencil Outfit No. 1.

This is the smallest of the three outfits, but it is sufficiently complete to easily carry out any of the designs which the purchaser may care to undertake. It contains two stencil brushes, three ready-cut stencils, one stencil paper, a book of instructions, seven small tubes of stencil colours and large tubes of Stencil White and Stencil Medium.

Price .. .. **5/-** Post 3d.

You can 'PHONE your Orders by Ringing 2,700 HOLBORN.

Stencil Outfit No. 3.

This outfit is complete in every detail. In addition to twelve 4-in. tubes of stencil colours, it has large tubes of Stencil White and Stencil Medium, 3 stencil brushes, stencil cutting knife, 1 palette knife, a block of thumb tacks, six blank sheets of stencil paper, six ready-cut stencils, one glass palette on which to mix the stencil colours, a book of instructions and a sheet of stencil transfer patterns. This is without a doubt the most complete outfit on the market to-day.

Price .. .. **11/6** Post 5d.

Stencil Outfit No. 2.

This outfit is larger than No. 1, containing four ready-cut stencils, a book of instructions, two stencil brushes and an assortment of thirteen tubes of stencil colours, together with two large tubes of Stencil White and Stencil Medium, thumb tacks and a palette knife.

Price .. .. **7/6** Post 4d.

Gamage's Pyrography or Poker Work.

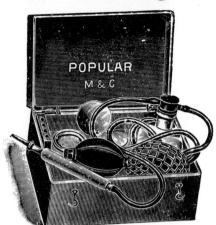

The "Popular" is a dark polished hardwood box, fitted with a strong B quality platinum point, Rubber bellows, nickel spirit lamp. Very good value.
Complete with platinum point No. 286, **12/6** ea.
Extra points, No. 286 . **6/8** each.

The Original No. 2. With a standard A platinum point, best bellows, etc., black cloth covered wood box, inside red. Price **15/11**
Extra points No. 276 .. **8/9** each.

The "Grafton." No. 2 Machine. Fitted with large best bellows, size 5, and one platinum point, No. 266B, bent knife. A practical and compact machine for commencing Relief work, with "Pyro" Flame-top, making spirit lamp unnecessary.
Price .. **23/6** each.

AS an indoor pastime, Poker Work has much to recommend it to those who have spare time and the inclination for an artistic hobby. It offers an endless variety of subjects suitable for decoration in the home, and does not, as in the case with many other arts, require any special talent in its execution.

The "Amateur" is a machine to meet the requirements of those who wish an efficient but inexpensive apparatus. It has a strong platinum point, cork handle, Rubber bellows, and spirit lamp.

The "Amateur" complete with platinum point **10/-** each. Post 4d.

Extra points, No. 265. **4/6** each. Post 1d

The Original No. 3. As No. 2, with nickel spirit lamp, in polished cherry wood box.
Price **15/11**
Extra points .. **8/9** each.

The "Simplex" is so constructed that the Benzoline which is required to keep the Platinum Point red-hot is utilised also for heating the point at first, thereby dispensing with the spirit lamp used with the "Original." The flame is blue and perfectly smokeless. By turning the round vulcanite disc to certain marks, the benzoline gas supplies the lamp, or it may be directed by a little turn into the heated point, and keeps this red-hot. By another little turn, all escape from the bottle is shut off, and this can now safely be packed away in any position.

The "Simplex" with Standard "A" Point (No. 276), complete **22/6** each. Post 6d.

Extra Points for the "Simplex," **8/9** ea. Post 1d.

The "Pyro" is a very handy machine, the flat top taking the place of the spirit lamp.
The "Pyro" complete with standard A point,
No. 276 .. **16/10** Extra points **8/9** each.

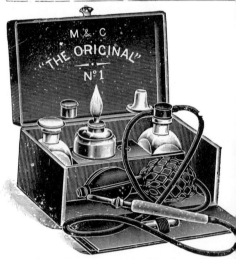

The Original No. 1. with a SPECIAL STRONG QUALITY, Platinum S
(*) Point (No. 277), large best rubber bellows, s 5, &c., cloth covered wood box, **20/6** each.
Extra points .. **12/3** each.

The "Griffin." No. 3 Machine for Relief Burning Fitted with large Red Bell
Complete with knife-shaped, platinum points, No. 30
Price .. **27/6** each.

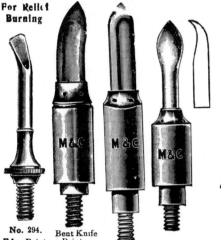

No. 286.	Flat, "B" Medium quality	...	**6 8** each
No. 276.	Flat, Standard "A" quality	...	**8/9** "
No. 277.	Flat, special quality ...	...	**2 3** "
No. 275.	Round. sharp...	...	**8/9** "
No. 290.	Horn shape, "B" quality ...		**6 8** "
No 279.	Horn shape, Standard	...	**8/9** "

GAMAGE'S
PLATINUM
Poker Points
AND
SUNDRIES.

___

All Points are arranged to fit any of our Machines.

No. 287.	French Horn shape ...	...	...	**9 4** each
No. 278.	Extra fine, Flat	...		**8/-** "
No. 284.	Claw shape ...	...	...	**8/-** "
No. 282.	Smoke-diffusing, Flat point	...	**8/9** "
No. 265.	Flat. Small size	...	...	**4 6** "
No. 281.	For producing light or dark shades of a very soft tint. These points are not to touch the wood but are so constructed that they blow hot benzoline gas upon the material and produce light or dark shades, according to slower or more rapid pressure of the bellows. They are particularly useful in portrait and landscape drawings ... ... **8/9** each

Repairs executed at Lowest Prices.

For Relief Burning

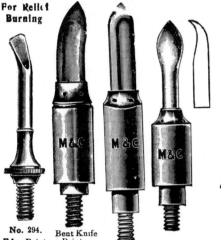

No. 294.
Edge Point for incisive work and burning out back ground
13/3 each.

Bent Knife Point.
No. 300. S.andard **A** qual., **19/3**
No. 266. B quality.
14/11 each.

Knife Point.
No. 292. Standard **A** qual., **19/3**
296. B qual.
14/11 each.

No. 297.
Modelling Point,
13/3 each.

No. 299.
Skew Point, specially for Mosaic and fine work.
10 9 each.

Improved Foot Bellows.

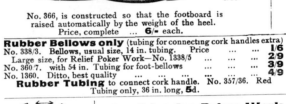

They will now be found a useful help to those who do much Poker-work, leaving them both hands free

No. 366, is constructed so that the footboard is raised automatically by the weight of the heel. Price, complete ... **6/-** each.

Collapsible Stand.
To prevent upsetting the Benzoline Bottle.
No. 49. Stand only, **4½d.** each.

No. 340.
"Pyro" Flame Top.
Price **1/11**
As supplied with the "Pyro" and "Grafton" Machines. It will fit the usual glass bottles sent with our machines

Rubber Bellows only (tubing for connecting cork handles extra)
No. 338/3. Bellows, usual size, 14 in. tubing. Price **1/6**
Large size, for Relief Poker Work—No. 1338/5 ... ... **2/9**
No. 360/7. with 54 in. Tubing for foot-bellows **3/9**
No. 1360. Ditto, best quality **4/9**
Rubber Tubing to connect cork handle. No. 357/36. Red Tubing only, 36 in. long, **5d.**

Sundries for Poker Work

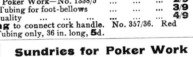

Cork Handle Regulating Tap.
Price ... **10½.**

No. 1604.
New Regulating Union.
Platinum Points that will not heat up properly with a fixed union, will be found to work satisfactorily with this new regulating union. **1/11**

Poker Spectacles. Made of plain glass, and to fit closely over the eyes to protect them from the smoke of the pokered material.
No. 345. Black Leather **4½d.** No. 349. Selvyt velveteen **9d**

Steel Wire Brushes
For brushing off charred surface, No. 347/1, 1 row, **3d**
No. 347/2, 2 rows ... **5d**
No. 347/3, 3 rows ... **7d**

"Mirror" Polish. For obtaining a brighter and more durable gloss after using the "Rapid" Polish.
1 oz. bottles, **9d** each. Post **2d.**
Rapid Polish. A quick and diffective polish for Marqueterie. 4 oz. bottles, **1/6** each

A Guide to Poker Work. By W. D. Thompson. Most practical and up-to-date published.
No. 315. 4th Edition. **1/-**
Post 1d.

NEW SHILLING BOOKS.
Poker Designs
No. 306. Four Sheets.
Selection I.
Price ... ... **1/-** Post 1d.
Selection II.
No. 307. Price **1/-** Post 1d.

DECORATIVE
WOOD WORK No. 1
POKER WORK
AND
Modern Relief Burning
BY
W. D. THOMPSON
ONE SHILLING NETT.

Made of extra steel wire for brushing off the charred surface of the wood, particularly for back grounds and other parts where it is difficult to reach with ordinary wire brushes.
No. 1600. Price ... **10½d.** each.

Steel Wire Scraper.

Marquo Art Stains.
For Marqueterie Pokerwook and Relief Burning.
Colours.
Rosewood, Ebony, Mahogany, Walnut, Satinwood, Oak, Yellow, Blue, Green, Olive Green, Scarlet.
French Polish.
2 oz. Bottle, **5½d.**
Postage **2d.**

Marquo No. 1 Stain Outfit. Handsome polished walnut box fitted with 12 Marquo bottles, and everything necessary for marqueterie staining, etc. Price complete **9/6** each Post 6d,

Marquo No. 3 Art Stain Outfit. Japanned tin box fitted with 6 Marquo bottles Stains and Polish, Chinese Ink, Linseed Oil, Palette and 2 Brushes. Price complete **4/6** Post 4d.

No. 310. **Marqueterie Designs.**
THIRD EDTION.
9 large sheets, 1 being a coloured plate.
Price ... **1/11½d.** Postage **1½d.**
New Shilling Books Marqueterie Designs.
No. 323. Third Series, 4 sheets, **11d.**
No. 317. New Publication. Guide to Marqueterie, Vernis Martin Certosina Work, etc.
By Miss L. V. Fitzgerald Price **11d.** Post 1d.

SIL-VEL WORK
The Modelling on Silk Velvet.

No. 353. Sil-Vel Sheath without Platinum Point. Very practical and easy to fix. **1/6** each

4 SHEETS OF MARQUETERIE DESIGNS
Price One Shilling
[Separate Sheets not sold]
PUBLISHED BY
MOELLER & CONDRUP
LONDON

CC

WOOD CARVING SETS.

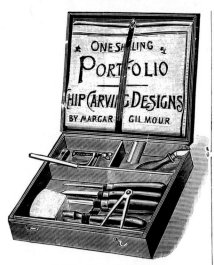

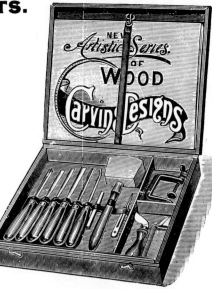

No. 600. Size, 9¾ by 8¾ by 2½ in.
Set of Chip Carving Tools.
Namely: Veiner, V. shaped Parting Tools. Skew Chisel, Carving Knife, Mallet, Punch, Compass, Cramp, Washita Slip and Shilling Portfolio of Chip Carving designs. Price ... **7/9** set. Post 4d

No. 610. Size, 12 by 10 by 2½ in. Complete set of Edged Tools for **Deep Carving.** Namely: Fluter, Gouge, Extra Flat Gouge, Skew Chisel V-shaped Parting Tools, Front Bent Gouge, Carving Knife, Washita Slip 2/6 Album of Carving Designs. Cramp, Mallet, Compass and Punch. Price, **10/9** Postage 6d.

No. 620A. Contains a complete SET OF TWELVE **Edged Tools for Chip and Deep Carving.** Namely: Fluter, Gouge, Extra Flat Gouge, Skew Chisel, V-shaded Parting Tool. Background Bent Gouge, Veiner, Extra Flat Narrow Gouge, ditto Medium, Broad Gouge, Front Bent Gouge, Bent Background Tool, Carving Knife, Two Albums of Designs (published 1/- and 2/- each), Mallet, Compass, Punch, Cramp, Turkey Slip Washita Slip. Price **16/9** per set. Postage extra.

WOOD CARVING TOOLS.
SPECIAL ENGLISH MAKE. **ENDLESS VARIETY**
Tools are shouldered, straw coloured and ground sharp. Price, including handle **9d.** each any shape.

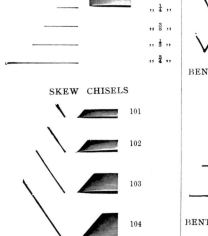

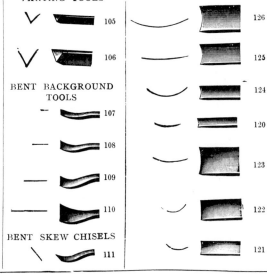

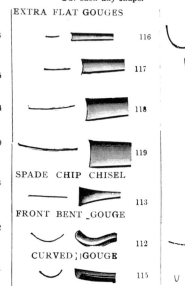

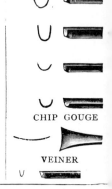

100⅛ in.	
„ ¼ „	
„ ⅜ „	
„ ½ „	
„ ¾ „	

PARTING TOOLS
105
106

BENT BACKGROUND TOOLS
107
108
109
110

BENT SKEW CHISELS
111

SKEW CHISELS
101
102
103
104

GOUGES
126
125
124
120
123
122
121

EXTRA FLAT GOUGES
116
117
118
119

SPADE CHIP CHISEL
113

FRONT BENT GOUGE
112

CURVED GOUGE
115

FLUTERS

CHIP GOUGE

VEINER

Chip Carving Knives.

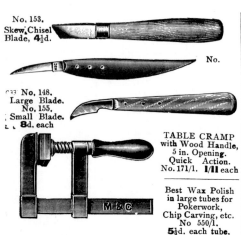

No. 153.
Skew Chisel Blade, 4½d.

No.

No. 148.
Large Blade.
No. 155,
Small Blade.
8d. each

TABLE CRAMP with Wood Handle, 5 in. Opening. Quick Action. No. 171/1. **1/11** each

Best Wax Polish in large tubes for Pokerwork, Chip Carving, etc. No 550/1. **5¾d.** each tube.

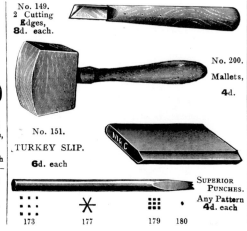

No. 149.
2 Cutting Edges, **8d.** each.

No. 200. Mallets, **4d.**

No. 151.
TURKEY SLIP. **6d.** each

SUPERIOR PUNCHES. Any Pattern **4d.** each

173   177   179   180

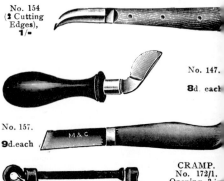

No. 154 (2 Cutting Edges), **1/-**

No. 147. **8d.** each

No. 157. **9d.** each

CRAMP. No. 172/1. Opening, 3 in. **6d.** each
No. 172/2. Opening, 4½ **8d.** each

est Whitewood Articles, for Poker Work, Wood Carving, etc.

Manufactured from Chestnut and Sycamore.

Many of the articles traced for Poker Work (marked P) are now supplied with Coloured Designs free of charge, to convey an idea of the work when finished.

No. 647. 9¾ by 7¼ in.
Cabinet Frame.
P. 1/- K., 1/- W., 10d.

No. 925/2. 9¾ by 11¼ in.
Cabinet Frame.
K., 1/- P., 1/-
S.K., 1/3½ W., 10d.

No. 995/2. Bevelled edges.
Cabinet Frame.
P., 1/6 K., 1/6 W., 1/4

No. 963/2. Bevelled edges.
Cabinet Frame.
W., 1/6 P., 1/8.

No. 936. 13 by 7¼ in. Cabinet
Frame. K. 1/6 P., 1/6 S.K., 1/8½

No. 928/2. 10 by 8 in.
Bevelled opening.
, 1/9 P., 1/9 W., 1/6

No. 527. 3-division
Stamp Box. P., 9½d.
K., 9½d. S.K., 11d.

529. 4 compartments.
Square Stamp Box.
P. 1/- K. 1/- W. 11d.

No. 758. 2 compartments.
Hairpin Box.
P., 8d. K., 8d. S.K., 9d.

No. 1194. 4 by 3 in.
Hairpin Box.
P. 11d., K., 11d. S.K., 1/-

Cabinet Frame.
No. 2509. 6½ by 6½ in.
Opening 3½ in.
K., 1/4½ S.K., 1/7
P., 1/4½

No. 714. 8½ by 2½ in. Pencil Box.
P., 1/- K., 1/- S.K., 1/3

Box with lock and key.
No. 1126. 3½ by 2½ by 1½ in.
Trinket Box. P., 11d. W., 9d.
No. 1127. P., 1/2 W., 1/-

No. 611. 4½ by 3 by 2. S.K. 1/10
,, 613. 7 by 4½ by 3 ,, 2/8
,, 615. 9¼ by 6¼ by 4 ,, 4/-

No. 729. Match-holder.
Swedish size.
P., 7d. K., 7d.
S.K., 8d.

No. 729½. Large size
P., 8d. K., 8d.
S.K., 9d.

No. 728. Match-cover.
Swedish size.
P., 3d. W., 2½d.
K., 3d.

No. 728½. Large size.
P., 4½d. W., 4d.
K., 4½d.

No. 717. Match-holder.
W., 8d. P., 8½d.

No. 929/2. 10¾ by 8 in.
Cabinet Frame.
P., 1/9 W., 1/6

No. 517. Round Flat
Box. K., 5d.
S.K., 7½d. P., 5d.
No. 519. 2⅝ in.
K., 6d. S.K., 1/2
No. 645. 3½ in.
W. 4½d. P. 5d. K. 5d.

636. 5½ by 3½ in. W. 1/- P. 1/3
637. 6⅜ by 10½ ,, ,, 1/3 ,, 1/6
No.638. With lock and key.
9½ by 6½ by 3¾. W. 2/9 P. 3/3

No. 644. Octagona
Stud Box. Hinged lid.
P. 1/3 W. 1/2

Casket. 5½ by 3¾ in.
8071. K., 1/3 S.K., 1/7
8021. P., 1/3
6¾ by 4¾ in. 8073. K., 1/7 S.K., 2/-
No. 8023. P., 1/7

Work Box.
6¾ by 4½ in.
No. 8052.
K. 1/1 S.K. 1/4
8002. P., 1/1
8054. 8½ by 5¾ in.
K. 1/7 K. 2/-
8004. P., 1/7

No. 783. 4½ by 2⅜ by 3¼ in.
Playing-card Box.
P., 1/6 K., 1/6 W., 1/3

Boxes.
No. 631. 5½ by 3¾ by 2½ in. P., 1/3
,, 634. 7¾ by 5 by 2½ in. P., 1/11½

No. 1327. Thermometer
S.K., 1/10 S., 1/8

3715. 11¾ by 7½ in.
Cabinet Frame.
P., 1/9 W., 1/6

No. 786. Bridge Box. 8½ by 5 by 2½ in.
N.P., 2/3 W., 1/10 K., 2/3
No. 1349. 4½ by 4 by 1½ in. Flat Cigar-
ette Box. P., 1/- W., 10½d.

No. 2524. For Cigarettes. 6½ by 4 in.
K., 2/3 N.P., 2/3 W., 2/-

No. 668. Cigar Box. 8½ by 6¼ in.
Cedar lined. 2 divisions.
K., 4/3 N.P., 4/3 W., 3/10

No. 632. Fancy Box.
1 by 4 by 2½ in.
P., 1/8

No. 591. 9½ by 3½ in.
P., 2/3

P—Designed for Poker Work. **K**—Designed for Chip Carving. **S**—Satin Walnut, Plain. **S K**—Satin Walnut, Designed.

CC..

Best Whitewood Articles for Poker Work, Wood Carving, etc.

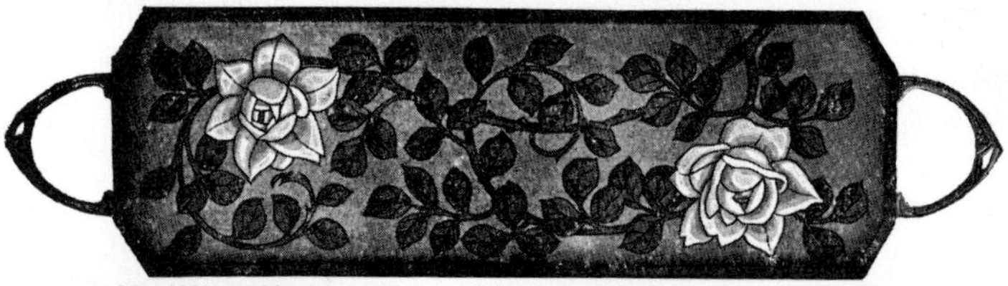

No. 1066. 18 by 6 in. Tray with brass handles. P, **3/6** W, **3/3**

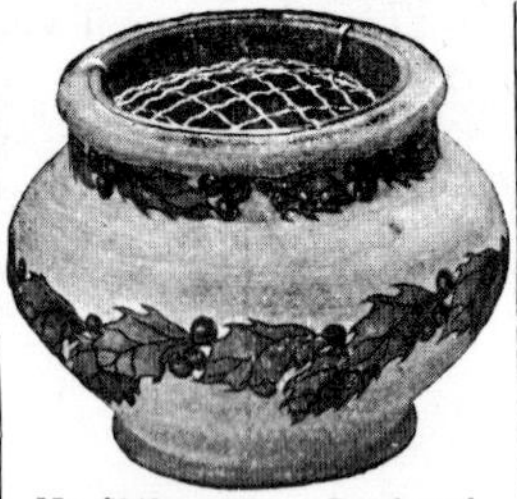

No. 1348. Rose Bowl with metal lining: 6¾ by 5 in.
P, **4/11** W, **3/11**

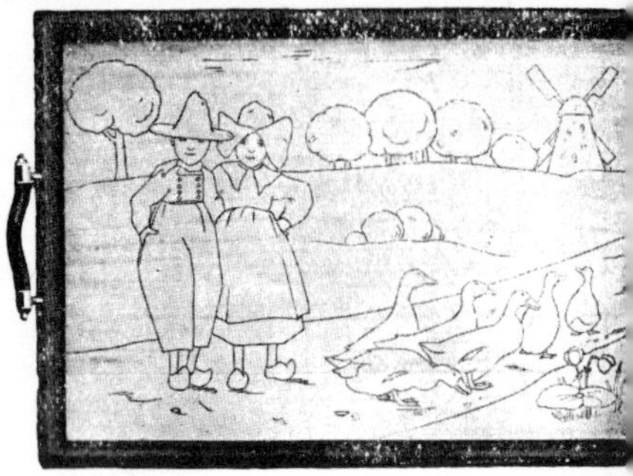

No. 3685. Tea Tray, brown oak rims.
16in. P, **3 3** K. **3 6** SK, **4/3** 20in. P. **4/6** K, **4 9** SK
No. 3888. Best heavy quality, rosewood polished ri
16 in. P. **5 3** K. **5 6** 20 in. P **6/6** K **7/**

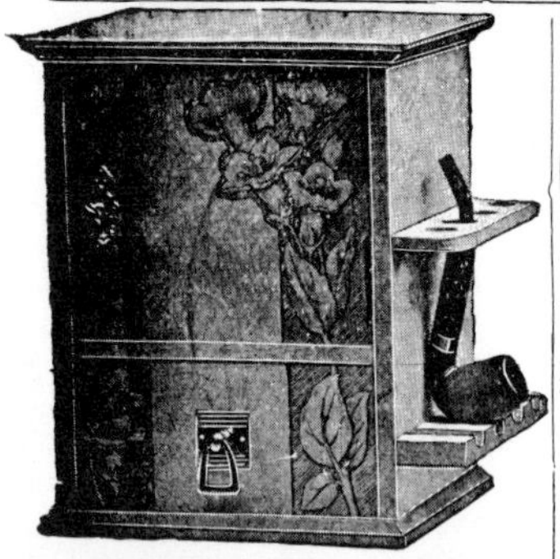

No. 3912. Smoker's Cabinet with drawer
10¼ by 9 by 7 in. P, **5/3** W, **4/9**

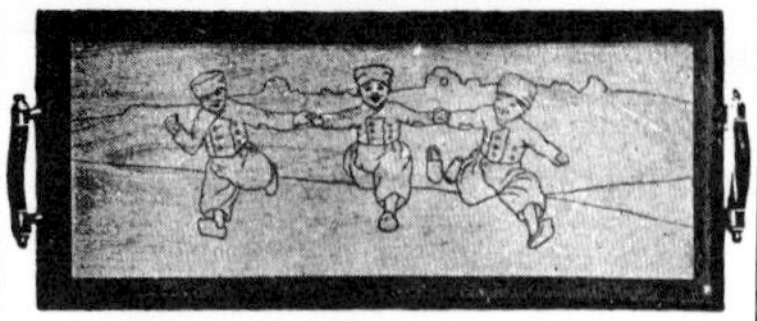

No. 3217. Glass or Card Tray.
13 in. long 15 in. long 17 in. long
P, **1/9** K, **1/11** P, **2/4** K. **2/4** P, **2/9** K. **2/9**

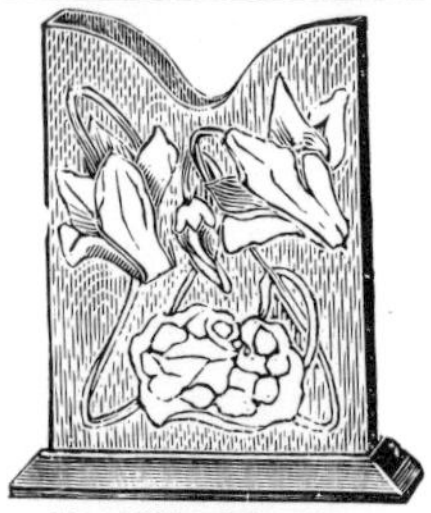

No. 1656. 5 by 4½ in.
Postcard Stand.
P, **10½**d. K, **10½**d. W, **9**d.

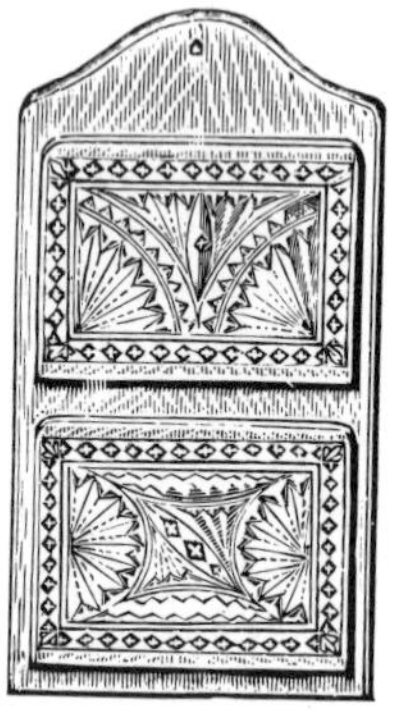

No. 548. Letter Rack
9 by 4¾ in.
K. **1/2** SK **1/4** P, **1/2**

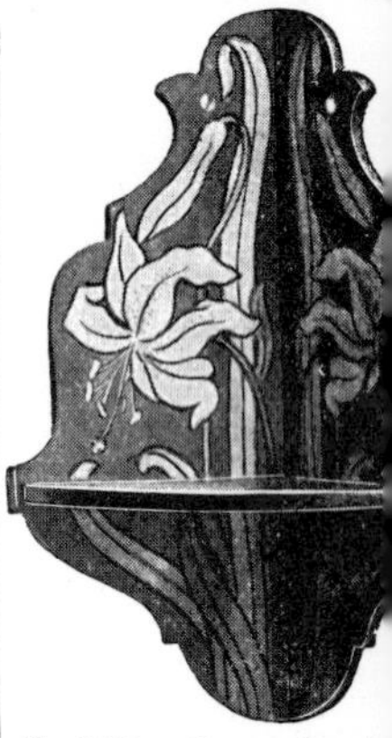

No. 3129. Corner Bracket
15⅝ by 6¼ in. P, **2/-** W, **1/**

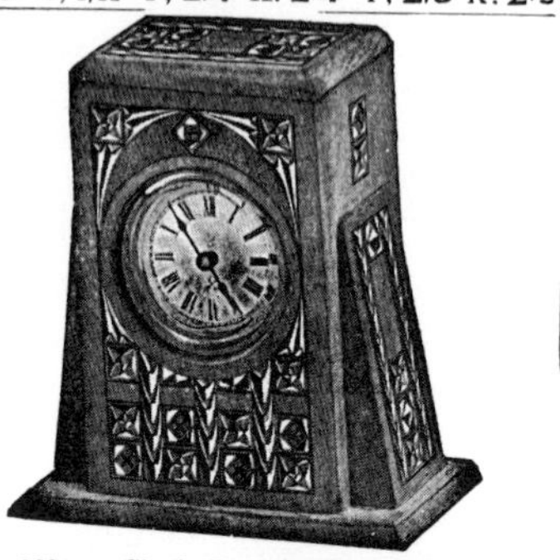

No. 1691. Clock Case WITHOUT Clock.
5¼ by 5¼ by 2¼ in. SK, **2/-** S, **1/10**

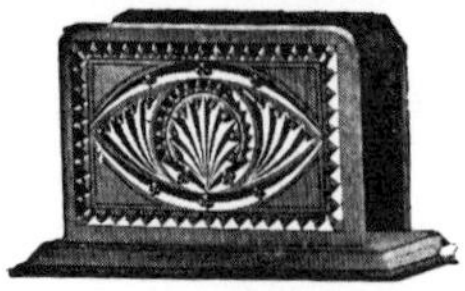

No. 551. Letter Rack.
6¾ by 3½ in.
K. **1/-** SK **1/2** P, **1/2**

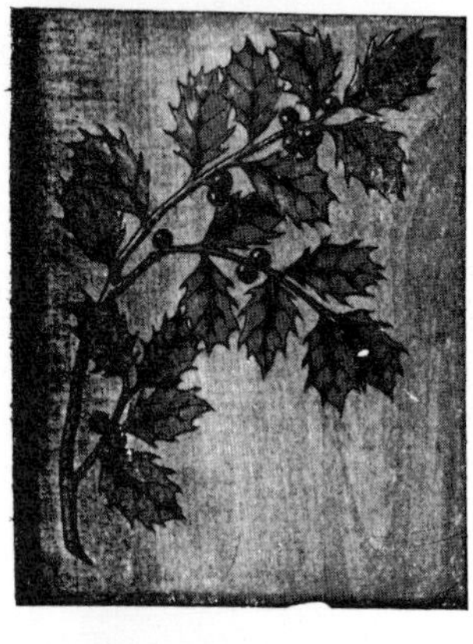

No. 1142½. Blotter Wood, one side.
10 by 7½ in. P, **2/3** K, **2/3**

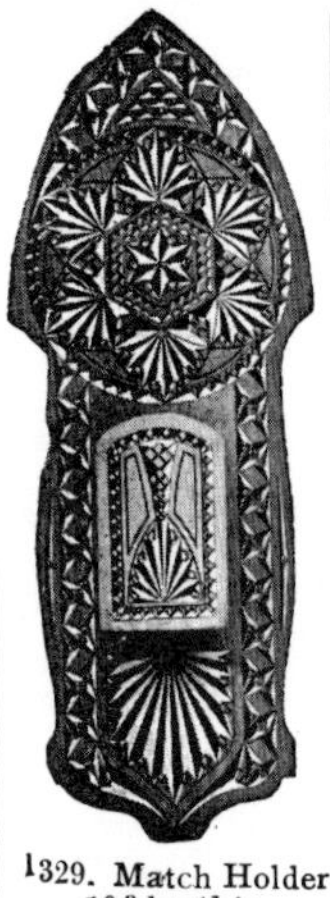

1329. Match Holder.
10⅜ by 4¼ in.
SK, **1/3** S, **1/2**

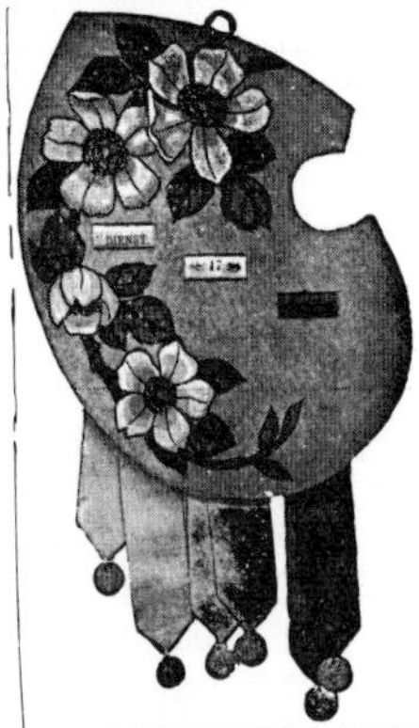

No. 773.
Calendar.
P, **1/4½**
K, **1/4½**
W, **1/2**

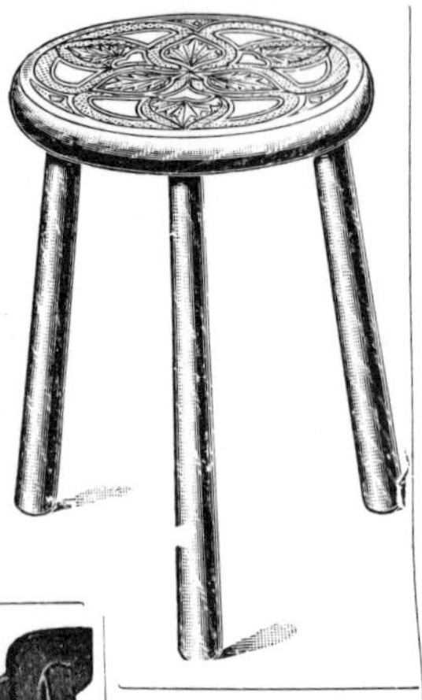

No. 1492.
Round Top
Milking
Stool.
EP, **1/0½**
K, **1/0½**
SK, **1/9**

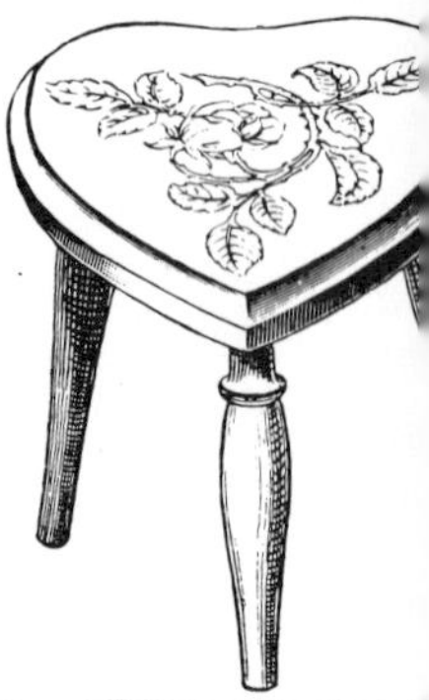

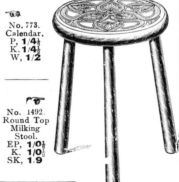

No. 3652.
Milking
Stool.
11¼ by 11¼in.
P, **1/9½**
M, **1/10**
W, **1/6**

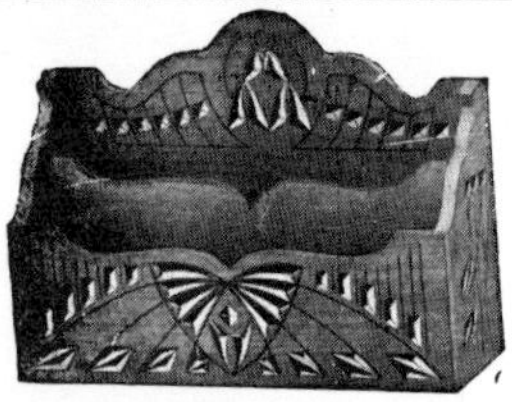

No. 682. Stationery Rack. 7½ by 5¼ in.
P, **1/9** K, **1/6½** SK, **1/10½**

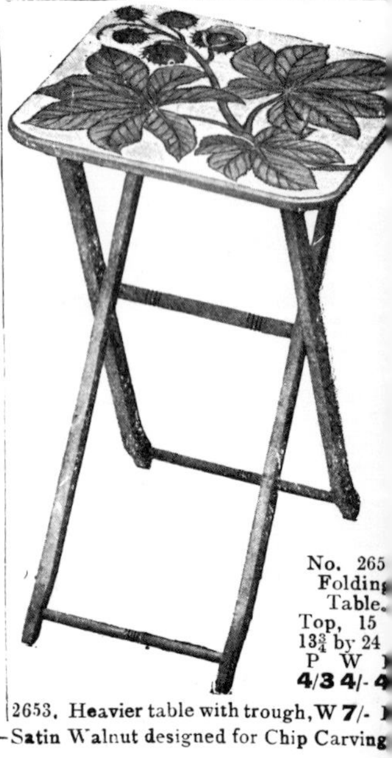

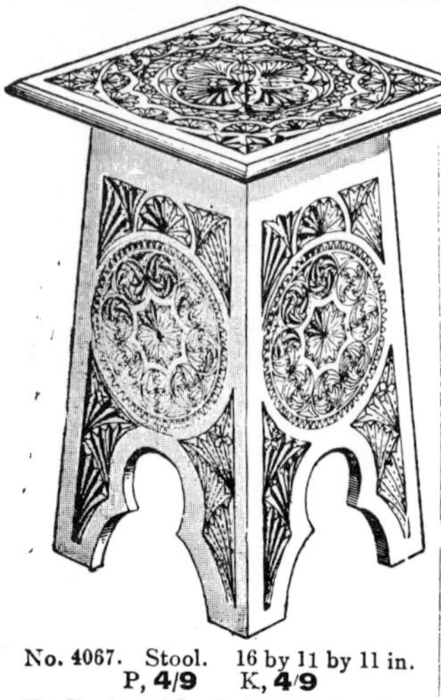

No. 4067. Stool. 16 by 11 by 11 in.
P, **4/9** K, **4/9**

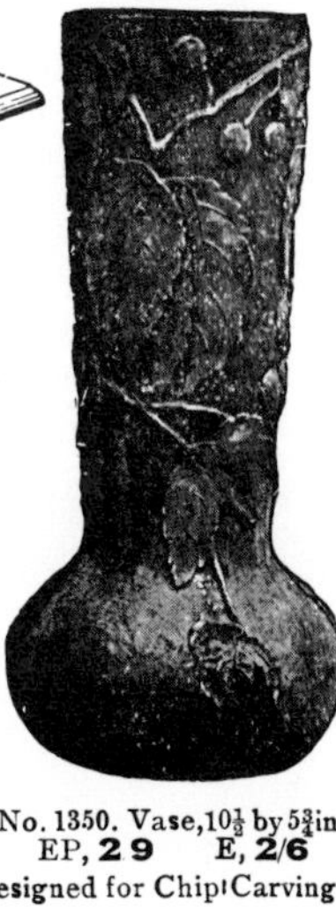

No. 1350. Vase, 10⅓ by 5¾in.
EP, **2 9** E, **2/6**

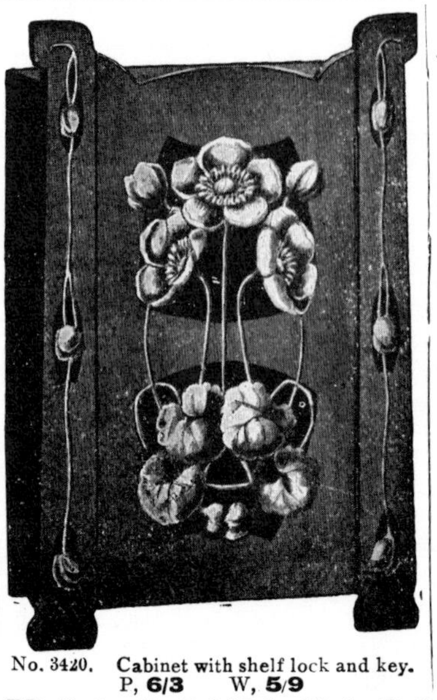

No. 3420. Cabinet with shelf lock and key.
P, **6/3** W, **5/9**

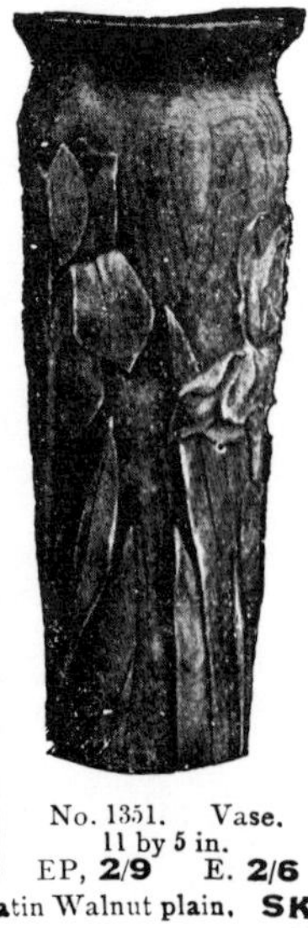

No. 1351. Vase.
11 by 5 in.
EP, **2/9** E. **2/6**

No. 265
Folding
Table.
Top, 15
13¾ by 24
P W
4/3 4/-

2653. Heavier table with trough, W **7/-**

P—Designed for Poker Work, **K**—Designed for Chip Carving. **EP**—Designed for Relief Poker Work, **S**—Satin Walnut plain, **SK**—Satin Walnut designed for Chip Carving

Best White Wood Poker Work Wood Carving, etc.

No. 937. 11 by 8½ in. Cabinet Frame. **P, 1/9 W, 1/6**

No. 1894. Cabinet Frame. **E.P, 1/10½**

No. 980. L ndcape Frame. **P, 1/9 W, 1/7**

No. 1697. Cabinet Frame. **S.K. 2/3 S 2/-**

No. 2876. Cabinet Frame **S.K. 2/6 S, 2/3**

No. 1756. Glove Boxes. 10½ by 3¾ by 2¼ in. Unpolished inside. **K, 1/9 P, 1/9**
No. 812. Polished inside. 12¾ by 4¾ by 2¾ in. **P, 2/3 K, 2/3 W, 2/-**

No. 2217. 6 by 6 by 1½ in. Unpolished inside. **P, 1/9 K, 1/9**

No. 1207. Handkerchief Box. 7½ by 7½ by 2¾ Polished inside. **P, 2/6 K, 2/3 W, 2/-**

Handkerchief Box. 6¾ by 6¾ in. No. 8031. **K, 1/8 S.K, 2/-** „ 8031. **P, 1/8**

Glove Box. 12 by 4¾ by 2¾ in. No. 8032. **P, 1/10** 8082. **K, 1/10 S.K, 2/3**

No. 917. Pipe Rack. **P, 2 6 W, 2/3**

No. 905½. Pipe Rack. 12½ by 5½. **P, 1/2 K, 1/2 S.K, 1/4**

Tea Caddy. Metal lining N . 2503. **S.K, 3/3** .. 1198. **P, 3 6**

No. 653. Inkstand. 5½ by 5 in. **P, 1/10 W. 1/7**

No. 1008. Photo Bracket. 10½ by 10¾ in. **P, 2 8 W, 2/4**

. Hatpin Box. 10¼ by 2¾ by 1¾ in. **K, 1/3 P, 1/3 S.K, 1/5**

No. 1269. 5½ by 4 in. Reliable Clock **P, 4/3 K 4 11 M, 4/3**

No. 5811. 4 by 2¾ by 5. Bee Clock Case. **P, 1/3 M, 1/3 W, 1/-**

No. 814. News Rack. by 8½ in. **P, 4/6 W, 4/-**

No. 2432. Candlestick. 8½ by 7¼ in. **P, 2/9**

No 1241. Calendar with strut. **P, 1/3**

No. 1257. 10¼ in. high. Calendar ... **P, 1 3** No. 1244. Match-holder **P, 1/-**

No. 1242. Match-holder. **P, 1/-** No. 1267. Calendar. **P, 1/3**

No. 938. Cabinet Frame. 13¼ by 8 in. **P, 2/3 W, 1/11½ K, 2/-**

—Designed for Poker Work. **K**—Chip Carving. **M**—Marqueterie. **E.P**—Relief Poker Work. **S**—Satin Walnut, Plain. **S.K**—Satin Walnut, Designed

CHIP CARVING PRACTICE PANELS.

WOOD CARVING DESIGNS.

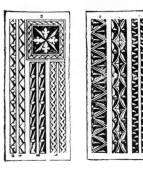

Panel No. 260/3.   Panel No. 260/4.   Panel No. 260/8.

All partly carved for **beginners.**

No. 260. Assorted **5½d**

No. 316.
Guide to Chip Carving.
By W. Jackson-Smith.
THIRD EDITION.

1/- each.

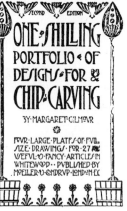

No. 250.
Chip Carving Designs.
SEVENTH EDITION.
4 Large Sheets. **11**d. a Set.

No. 252.
Relief Carving Designs
SIXTH EDITION.
With Working Instruction
9 Large Sheets. **1/11½** a S

THE NEW PEWTER RELIEF MODELLING.

Outfit No. 16.
In cloth **covered** box containing **complete** set of **9** modelling tools, felt pad, linoleum, glass slab, & mounting pins.
Price 6/-

☞ The New Pewter Relief Modelling.

The latest fashionable pastime in Artistic Wood Decoration. Easily executed. Effective results obtained in a very short time. The woodwork articles for ornamentation are supplied with a sheet of metal ready designed, so that it is made easy for the amateur, in that he has an artistic and suitable design ready to commence upon. Full directions for this new handicraft are supplied with every outfit and can also be obtained when purchasing articles to be worked.

Tools & Accessories for Pewter Relief Modelling

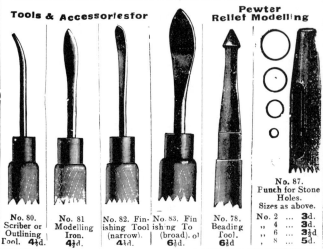

No. 87. Punch for Stone Holes.
Sizes as above.
No. 2 ... **3**d.
,, 4 ... **3**d.
,, 6 ... **3½**d.
,, 8 ... **5**d.

No. 80. Scriber or Outlining Tool. **4½**d.
No. 81 Modelling Iron. **4½**d.
No. 82. Finishing Tool (narrow). **4½**d.
No. 83. Finishing Tool (broad). **6½**d.
No. 78. Beading Tool. **6½**d.

M&C PEWTER MODELLING OUTFIT No 18.

In Cloth-covered Wood Box, containing complete set of Modelling Tools and accessories. Outfit No. 18 ... **14/9** e

Card of 9 Modelling Tools, 3/6

No. 86. Nail Driver. Price ... **4½**d.

No. 84. Embossing Iron. Price **5**d.

No. 85. Piercer or Nail Holes. Price ... **3**d.

No. 99. **Scissors.**
Price **1 6** each

SHEETS OF PEWTER.

Soft and pliable. Thickness. Specially prepared.

No. 67.	Thin Sheets	(0.2 m/m) **3/6**	per sheet	(21 by 15½ in.)
,, 68.	Medium Sheets	(0.3 m/m) **4/3**	,,	(21 by 15½ ,,)
,, 69.	Large Sheets	(0.3 m m) **10/-**	,,	(36 by 34 ,,)

SHEETS OF SILVER.

In Lengths, 4½ in. wide (47 sq. in. to oz.) (0.1 m/m) **4/-** per oz. (Avoir)

Sundry Accessories.

Linoleum, 10 by 8 in.	... ...	**4½**d. ea
Felt, 10 by 8 in.	...	**5**d.
Plate Glass Slabs, 10 by 8 in.	...	**9**d.
Grease Remover, No. 92, in bottles		**6**d
Metal Varnish, No. 93, in bottles		**10**d.
Patina Pewter Coloring, in bottles		**7½**d.
Ivory Filling Material, No. 94 ...		**4**d.
Burnishing Powder, No. 95 ...		**3**d.
Mounting Pins, in boxes ...	...	**3**d.
Hammer, No. 88 ...	...	**7½**d.

No. 98. **For Burnishing**
Price **2½**d each

SILVER MODELLING TOOLS 5½ in. long).

No. 72. Outlining Tool. **7½**d. each.
No. 73. Modelling Iron. **7½**d. each.
No. 74. Finishing Tool. **7½**d. each.

No. 491.
PEWTER MODELLING ACCESSORIES
CONTENTS
No
91 PEWTER PATINA COLOUR
92 GREASE REMOVER
93 METAL VARNISH
94 IVORY FILLING POWDER
95 BURNISHING POWDER

491. Set of Liquids and Powders, in Cardboard Box.
2/6 each.

Ornamental Stones.

FOR DECORATION OF PEWTER MODELLING WORK
Box containing 54 stones of assorted sizes, 3, 5, 7 and 9 m/m, in the following colours viz :

OPAL, EMERALD, AMETHYST, RUBY, SAPPHIRE OR TURQUOISE
Any colour, **6**d. per box.
No. 378. Small Round Coral. 30 Assorted Stones, **1/-** per b
,, 380. ,, Square Green. 24 ,, ,, **1/-** ,,
,, 381. ,, Round Peacock's Eyes
30 Assorted Stones, **1/-** ,,
Particulars of further Assortments on application.

PRACTISE PANELS.

6 by 4 in. Board and sheet of Pewter, ready designed.
No. 2095. Leaf Design. **9**d. each. No. 2096. Fruit design.

Articles for Pewter Relief Modelling.

MP means Stained Wood with Loose Pewter Sheet, designed, and the necessary Coloured Stones.

Cabinet Frame. 1910 MP.
3 9 each   10 by 8 in.

Belt Clasp. 2146 B. **1 8** each.

Cabinet Frame   1937 MP.
2/9 each   9½ by 6¼ in.

Frame. 2174 MP. 10 by 8 in. **3/3**

No. 2172.
MP.
Frame
11 by 6 in.
3/3

Cabinet Frame 1936 MP.
3/6 each   12 by 6¾ in.

Belt Clasp   1973A MP.   **1/9** each

Belt Clasp   2148A M.P.
1/6 each   3½ in.

Serviette Ring
No. 2052 MP.
1/- each.

Cabinet Frame. 2029 MP.
4/= each.   10½ by 8½ in.

1969 C   1971 B   1971 C   1971 D   1969 D   1970 A

Hatpins.   Half natural size.   MP.   **6d.** each

Cabinet Frame   1912 MP.
3/9 each   13 by 7¼ in.

DEMONSTRATION BY LADY EXPERT DURING DECEMBER.

Brooches. MP.

2400 B **10½d.** each   2402 B **10½d.** each   2401 A **1/4½** each

Cabinet Frame. 1909. MP.
3/9 each.   10¼ by 8½ in.

Rose Bowl 1235 MP.
2/11 each   5¾ in.

Rose Bowl   2129 MP.
3/- each   4½ by 4 in.

Box   2021 MP.
2/3 each   3½ by 3½ in.

Trinket Box
1943 MP.
2/3 each
3½ by 3½ in.

Cabinet Frame   2030 MP.
3/11 each   10¾ by 8¾ in.

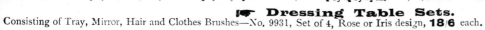

2134 MP.   Blotter 10½ by 8 in.   **3/6**

Blotter.   2063 MP.
1/11 each   6¼ by 3 in.

Pincushion Box   3 in.
2137 MP   **1/6** each

Powder or Trinket Box
Iris or rose design.
2142 MP.   **1/9**   4 by 2 in.

Inkstand   8981 MP.   **3/3**
6¼ by 5 by 2¾ in.

Inkstand. 2048 MP.   **3/3**
4½ by 4½ by 3½ in.

Puff Box 2141 MP.
Iris or rose design.
1/6 each   3 in.

Hand-Mirror.
9932 MP
Iris or rose design.
3/9 each.
11½ by 4½ in.

Hand-glass. 1944 MP.
5/3 each   13⅜ by 6 in.

☞ Dressing Table Sets.
Consisting of Tray, Mirror, Hair and Clothes Brushes—No. 9931, Set of 4, Rose or Iris design, **18/6** each.   No. 241, set of 6, Butterfly design, **25/6**

Articles for "PEWTER RELIEF MODELLING."

MP.—Means Stained Wood with Loose Pewter Sheet, Designed, and the necessary Coloured Stones.

Box. **2133 MP. 4** by 2¾ in.

Price **1/9** each.

No. 1925. MP. Postcards and Stamps.
7¾ by 4¾ in. **4/3** each.

No. 2071. MP. Box. 7½ by 5¼ by 2¾ in.
Price **3/9** each.

No. 2045. MP. 6½ by 4¼ by 3¾ in.
Cigarette Box. **4/9** each.

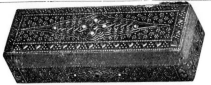

No. 1918. MP. 11¾in. high. Glove Box. **4/6** each

No. 2072. MP. Box, with lock. 9¼ by 6½ by 4 in.
Price **5/11** each.

No. 1985. MP. 10½ by 5½ in. Casket and Shaped
Price **8/9** each.

No. 1919. MP. Handkerchief Box.
6½ by 6¼ in. **4/3** each.

2086 N
9 by
by 1½ in
Pencil
1/11

DEMONSTRATION BY LADY EXPERT DURING DECEMBER.

No. 1913 MP. 9½ by 5 in.
Stationery Rack. **2/.** each.

No. 1924. MP. Postcard
Stand. **2/3** each.

Clock Case, complete with Reliable Clock.
No. 2132. 3½ in. dial. Price **8/6** each.

No. 2168.
Calendar.
7 by 4¾ in.
2/- each.

No. 2130.
Match
Holder.
7¼ by 3½ in.
1/11½

No. 2139.
Matchbox
Holder.
2½ by 1¾ in.
9d. each.

No. 1915.
MP.
Matchbox
Stand.
3½ in. high.
1/9 each.

No. 2015. MP. Letter Rack.
7½ by 4 by 2¾ in. **2/3** each.

No 2064. MP.
Watch Stand.
5¾ by 4in.
1/6 each.

Clock Case, complete with Reliable Clock.
No. 1954. MP. 2 in. dial. 6½ by 4¼ in. **5/6**

No. 2135. MP. Pipe Rack. 12 by 5½ in.
Price **2/3** each.

2136. MP. Perpetual Calendar
9 by 6½ in. **2/9** each.

No. 2159. PM.
7½ by 5 in.
Watch Stand.
2/- each.

1951. MP. Glass Tray. 12 by 4¼ in. **2/9** each.

No. 2054. MP. Ash Tray.
5½ by 1½ in. **2/9** each.

No. 2085.
MP. 11 by 3½
Door Protec
1/3 each

AVIARIES, PARROT CAGES, CANARY AND WILD BIRD CAGES,

as illustrated), are of Best Possible Value, and every care is taken in making and finishing. They are of the Latest Up-to-date designs with all the New Improvements, and have a very attractive appearance. Aviaries can be wired closer for Small Foreign Birds, but must have inside Feeders instead of outside. Special Prices for this class of Cage on application.

No. 32. THE CRYSTAL PALACE Design.

p and body made of best quality Tinned Wire, Wood lined mahogany, outside feeders, seed drawer, glass seed protectors, no sliding Parts.

2 ft. 8 in. by 16 n. ... **21/-**   3 ft. by 16 in. ... **32/-**
Crates 1/3 and 1/6 extra. Carriage free.

962. All Brass top, base beautifully enamelled, cream gold band and richly ornamented, deep etched glass seed plates. A splendid cage.

11 in. by 8 in. ... **8/11**   12 in. by 9 in. ... **9/11**
Packing 10d. extra. Carriage free.

Canary Cage.

Brass, well made, with sanitary detachable base, outside fluted feeders, and ruby glass seed protectors.

0 in. by 7 in. ... **5/6**   11 in. by 8 in. ... **6 6**
Crates 6d. and 7d. extra. Carriage free.

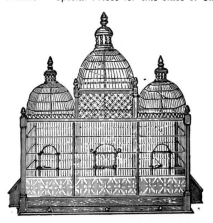

No. 212. THE HOLBORN is a very attractive Aviary. Most suitable for drawing room. Made of best Tinned Wire, woodwork solid mahogany, highly polished, with two sliding partitions, so as the Aviary can be divided into three separate compartments or can be used as one large flight cage.

3 ft. by 16 in., **70/.**   3 ft. 6 in. by 18 in., **86/-**
Crates 1/6 and 1/9 extra. Carriage free.

Parrot Cage. Best London made.

Made in bright tinned wire and bright tinned base, with loose grating, sliding tray for cleaning, brass top and ring, feeders pass into the cage from the outside.

Size   14   18   20 in. square.
11/3   15/3   17/9
Carriage free.

Ditto. New Indestructible Parrot Cage. Made with flat pierced bands through which the upright wires pass and tinned after made. Bottom made detachable so that the cage can be thoroughly cleansed. Richly japanned and ornamented, loose gratings and sliding drawer.

Size   16   18   20 in. square.
22/6   26/9   29/11
Cratage   1/3   1/6   1/9 extra.
Carriage paid.

Please Note.—Cages illustrated on this page are sent CARRIAGE PAID to nearest Station in England or Wales. Elsewhere within the United Kingdom Carriage will be met Half Way. When ordering quote Y Dept. and state the Carriage. For other class of Cages write for the Household List—sent Free of Charge.

No. 35. THE OLYMPIA design. Tinned Wire, woodwork stained mahogany, seed drawer, outside feeders, glass seed protectors.

2 ft. by 14 in., **12/9**
2 ft. 6 in. by 14 in., **18/6**
Crates 1/- & 1/3 Carriage free.

No. 250. Magnificent design with solid brass tubular pillars & bars. Heavy plain brass base, outside sliding feeders, plate glass panels back and front and seed protectors.

Size 9 by 11½ in.
25/-
Packing 1/- extra.
Carriage free.

Canary Cage.

This Cage, being made of solid Brass, has a huge sale.
Fitted with deep seed protectors, sanitary outside feeders, and is well made and highly finished.

11½ in. by 8½ in., **9/3**   12 in. by 9 in., **9/11**
Crate 7d. and 8d. extra. Carriage free

Ditto. Same design as above, and fittings made of Sanitary tinned wire, with richly japanned base.

11½ in. by 8½ in., **5/3**   12½ in. by 9½ in., **5/9**
Crate 7d. and 8d. extra. Carriage free.

Spong's Knife Cleaner.

USEFUL PRESENT.

Best London Manufacture. Highly recommended for sharpness and durability, well made and finished in all details, fitted with a patent constant pressure spindle which regulates the working of the interior which keeps the machine in good working order. A twelve months' guarantee sent with each machine. To hold knives including carver
3, **21/9**   4, **33/6**   5, **46/9**
Carriage free.   Packing 1/- extra.

No. 162A. **Dish Covers.**

Made of best quality block tin with metal handle. Good cover for hard wear.
10, **2/3** 12, **2/9** 14, **3/3** 16, **3/9** 18 in., **4/9**
(Set of 4) 10, 12, 14, 16 in.   **11/6** set.
Ditto, nickel-plated, superior quality.
2/11½ **3/11½** **4/9** **6/6** **8/11**
(Set of 4) 10, 12, 14, 16 in.   **17/9** set.
Carriage and packing free.

Cook's Knife. French shape.

British manufacture of best Sheffield steel with black bone handle, rivetted tang, size of blade 6in. Note our price **9½d.** Elsewhere 1/6½ Post free.

Domestic Scales.

Best London manufacture; makes an excellent Christmas Present.

Complete with a set of best round Weights. Weighing ¼ oz. to 7 lbs. Very useful for all fancy cooking and checking tradesmen.
Our price complete **5/6** Sent carriage forward.

Icing Syringe.

Best Block Tin **11½d.**

Tube extra .. .. **2½d.**
Post free.

The Holborn Roaster.

Latest and Best Method of Cooking.
More Satisfactory than Paper Bags.

No attention required.   Stout Tin Roaster with iron straps round bottom.   The top is fitted with a Tin Dish with perforated bottom to hold the spare fat from the joint cut into pieces, which bastes the meat while cooking.   Will roast to perfection Beef, Mutton, Pork. Fowls, Fish, Turkeys, Geese, etc. Ham and Tongue cooked in Roaster it most delicious.   Will make the toughest meat tender, or an old fowl like chicken. Apple dumplings, &c., steamed in the Roaster retain all the natural flavour, nor e of which is evaporated in the Roaster.
12 by 8½   14 by 11   14 by 12 in.
2/11½   **3/9½**   **4/3½**
Carriage and packing free.

The "Gamage" Food Chopper and Mincing Machine.

The best cheapest and most reliable.   Every part replaceable at a small cost.   Thousands in daily use.

The most reliable and perfect machine sold. British manufacture throughout. No kitchen is perfect without one. This machine being thickly coated with tin is easily cleansed. The 4 discs supplied with the machine are made of steel case-hardened, and accurately ground
both sides.   It will chop all kinds of food, raw and cooked meats, fish, poultry, suet, bread, vegetables and fruits also.   Can be used for preparing various potted meats.   Our price **3/11**
Nickel-plated Sausage Filler to fit machine, extra **1/-**
Carriage extra 7d.

Butter Shapers or Curlers.

A nice Present.

As used by the leading Restaurants Cafes. Hotels, etc.

Used by dipping the curler into a bowl of hot water and drawing the curl along the pat into a bowl of cold water.   Price **7½d.** Post 2d.

PLEASE NOTE.

Goods illustrated on this page otherwise than stated are sent carriage paid to the nearest station in England or Wales elsewhere within the United Kingdom, carriage will be paid halfway, when ordering quote **Y** Dept.

ICING PIPES.

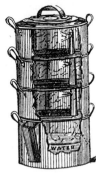

These Pipes fit the Icing Syringe. Are nicely made and nickel-plated. The various designs are absolutely perfect. The principal designs used are as follows :—

No.		No.		No.	
1.	Writer	10.	Large Leaf	18.	Bent Rose
4.	Small Border	11.	Rose	22.	Border
5.	Rope	12	Shell	23.	Hollow
6.	Fine Star	13.	Five Star		Band
7.	Large Star	14.	Ten Star	26.	Grape
8.	Eight Star	15.	Dahlia	28.	Forget-me-
9.	Fancy Band	17.	Small Leaf		not

To Ice Cakes is an excellent pastime.
The ice is very easily made.
Our price 2½d. each. Per doz. assorted **2/3** Post free.

The "Gamage" Steam Cooker.

Over 300 000 in use.   The best and most durable.
Will last years with ordinary care.
The most imitative Cooker on the market.
Do not be misled in buying one less than Gamage's price, otherwise you will be certainly disappointed.

Makes a very suitable and sensible Present.

Cooks more food with less trouble or cost of fuel than by any other method.   It is absolutely the ideal cooking utensil.
Never boil your food; because steaming it preserves the flavour, saves waste in bulk and weight, retains those nourishing juices and important chemical qualities, which, if boiled is in the water to be thrown away. Anyone who has once eaten steamed fish, meat, poultry vegetables, puddings, etc., will never again order them to be boiled.
Cooks entire meal for a family at one time; meat, vegetables and pudding cooked with only one lot of
water, one lot of fuel, oil, gas or coal.
One quality only.   Made of best block tin with copper bottom. OUR PRICE, as advertised.
Complete with Drainer and Full Cook's Timetable including a useful book on Cooking by steam, written by a well-known Lady.
Our price **4/3**
Carriage and packing extra 11½d.

Lightening Mincer

45,000 already sold.

With improved metal handle, not wood. Will cut parsley, mint, onions, and various other vegetables to a fineness in much less time than by the old method.

Our price **6½d.** Post free.

Overhead Clothes Airer.
An Excellent Present.

Flat laths 10 ft. long can be cut to suit smaller rooms Consisting of 4 strong rods, 2 galvanized brackets, 12 yds sashcord. One double, 2 single pulleys, and cleat hook The drier goes close to the ceiling, therefore the cloth are out of the way. It can be fixed in about half an hour without defacing the wall or ceiling, and can be removed at any time in about ten minutes. Price **4/-** Worth 7 Carriage extra. Packed in separate parts for transit

esirable Xmas & New Year Presents.
☞ **The Best and most Useful.**

HALL BRUSH SETS, OAK TRAYS, CRUMB SETS

No. G J. 1332.
Imitation Fumed or Polished Oak.
Size of Panel, 10 by 8½ in.
5/6½ Carriage free.

No. G J. 1324. Imitation Oak, Walnut, Ebony, highly polished, with two good brushes.
Size of panel, 13 by 10¼ in.
6/11 Carriage free.

Imitation Oak or Ebony.
Size of panel, 12 by 6 in.
8/3 Carriage free.

No. 2519. Imitation Rosewood, highly polished, with mirror and three good brushes.
Very acceptable present.
Size of panel, 18 by 9½ in.
12/9 Carriage paid.

No. 2500. Imitation Rosewood.
Highly polished, with mirror and three best brushes.
Size of panel, 14½ by 10 in.
13/6 Carriage free.

No. 2522. A Neat Design.
hly Polished Rosewood or lnut, with three brushes, prising handle, cloth, velvet nd rim. Panel, 12 by 8 in.
15/9 Carriage paid.

No. 2507. Polished Rosewood or Walnut, wood panel, bevelled mirror, with three good quality bristle brushes.
Size of panel, 15 by 10 in.
21/6 Carriage free.

No. 2511. Highly polished Shield, Rosewood or Walnut, with round bevelled mirror let into a brass frame. Best quality.
three brushes.
Size of panel, 18 by 11 in.
23/6 Carriage free.

No. 2524. New Design.
Highly Polished, with mirror fitted in brass rim, with three best quality brushes.
Size of panel, 14¾ by 12¾ in.
25/6 Carriage free.

No. 2504. A Unique Design.
Polished Light and Dark Oak Panel with large oval bevelled mirror, cloth, velvet, and hat brushes.
Size of panel, 12 by 18 in.
32/6 Carriage free.

No. G J 89/13B.
Crumb Brush and Tray, square pattern, finished light or dark Oak colour.
Size 10½ by 8½ in.
Price .. **2/6½**
Post free.

No. G J 5081C.
The Vincient
Crumb Brush and Tray, with best nickel plated corners.
black rims and light centre.
Size 9 by 8¾ in.
Price .. **5/0**
Ditto, with dark Oak rim and base, **5/9**
Post free.

Crumb Brush and Tray.
No. 15. Elegant design, best London made, Fumed Oak, with a real let-in centre.
Curved Rims. **9/11**
Do., Solid Mahogany, highly polished with inlaid centre. **10/6**
Do., solid oak with inlaid centre, highly polished Dark Oak. **5/3**
Postage 4d. extra.

Oblong Oak Tray or Waiter.
No. GW 4131B
These trays have met with a huge succees. The hand grips are let into the rim so as the tray can be used as a Dinner Carrier.
Highly polished dark Oak.
Carriage paid.
a. **5/9½** 20 in. **6/6** 22 in. **7/3** 24 in. **8/3**

The Holborn Tray. Made of selected well-seasoned Oak; will not warp by heat; the rims are straight with Copper or best Plated corners and handles. Highly finished and well made Polished Dark Oak. Size, 16 in., **6/9** Post 5d.
20 in., **8/6** Post 6d. 24 in., **10/9** Post 6d.
Carriage on Sets of three. 11½d.

Oak Tea Tray

THE "LONDON." This Tray is best London made of selected Oak, fumed, with bronzed screwed-on handles.
Thoroughly recommended for good hard wear.
16 in., **3/9** 20 in.. **5/9** 24 in. **8/6** Post 4d., 5d., 6d.

GW 4160. These trays are highly recom-ded, being strongly made, are durable, highly ed with imitation rosewood, polished rims ight Oak base. 16 in. **2/9½** 18 in. **3/3½**
20 in. **3/6½** 22 in. **3/9½** 24 in. **4/6**
Carriage paid on one or more.

with Polished Wood Handle. Price ... **2/9½**

Saw-edge Nickel-plated Bread Knife

Set of Three Knives, Bread, Cake and Butter, with ebonized handles
Price **1/9½**

Best quality Bread Boards, made of best selected wood and will not warp or crack. A Board and Knife make a very nice present. Plain Board with fancy carved border, 12 in., **1/3½**
Do., better quality, with wheat carved boarder, **1/9½**
Do., best qlty. **2/6½**
Do., best carved wheat boarder with word "Bread," **3/3½**
Post paid.

BREAD KNIVES to match the above Boards, carved wood handles, best steel blades. Cheap, **1/0½** Medium, **1/6½** Best, **1/11½**
Extra best quality **2/9½**

LADIES' and GENT'S HAIR BRUSHES, etc., in Ebony and Satinwood

THE "TRIUNE" BRUSH SET.

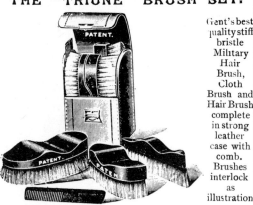

Gent's best quality stiff bristle Military Hair Brush, Cloth Brush and Hair Brush complete in strong leather case with comb. Brushes interlock as illustration

Solid ebony backs, stiff white bristles .. **14/6** per set·
Polished satinwood back, ditto .. .. **10/6** ,,

CLOTH BRUSHES.

Best quality stiff XXX bristles in 3 sizes, mahogany boards and rosewood backs, **5/3 6/- 6/9**
Also other qualities and sizes at **2/9 3/9 4/6**

Very handsome Inlaid Rosewood backs, best black bristle, close set, French polish, high-class finish.
D. 240 .. **4/6**   D. 241 .. **6/-**   D. 242 **8/-**

D. 2/100.   Rosewood back, best black bristles .. **2/3**
D. 4/100.   Ditto, larger **3/3**

1/11  **1/11**

D. 115.   Round-faced mahogany board, rosewood back, pinned, in 2 sizes.
D. 1 .. **1/11**   D. 2 .. **2/3**   Post 2d.

SHAVING BRUSHES.

Pure Badger Hair.

D. 1, **1/6**   D. 2, **1/11**   D. 3, **2/6**   D. 4, **3/-**   D. 5, **3/9**   D. 6, **4/10**
Superior Badger Hair, all picked bristles and best quality bone.
D. 1, **2/-**   D. 2, **2/9**   D. 3, **3/9**   D. 4, **4/11**   D. 5, **5/9**   D. 6, **6/3**

Turn back or pocket Shaving Brushes in nickelled metal. These brushes can be unscrewed and the bristles turned inside the handles, thus making holders so that the brushes, although wet, cannot harm anything in the bag or pocket. In nickel, with union bristles.   D. 0, **1/-**   D. 1, **1/6**   D. 2, **2/-**
In nickel, best badger.   D. 0, **2/6**   D. 1, **3/6**   D. 2, **2/11**

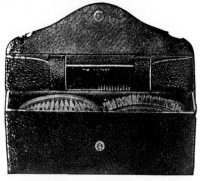

Pocket Brush and Comb Case.

Best quality strong leather case as illustration, contains 2 stiff bristle handle hair brushes and comb.   Can be carried in the pocket.
7 in. by 3 in.   Price **5/6**   Postage 3d.

Solid Ebony Cloth and Hat Brushes.

D. 142.   Best Ebony and pure bristle Cloth Brush, pattern as illus., 9 rows bristles.. **8/11**
143.   Ditto, 10 rows **10/6**

D. 371.   As illustrated, best quality trepanned ebony Cloth Brush, 7 rows, size 7 by 1¾ in. **2/6**
D. 1a.   Solid back, round end, fitted sides, 4¾ by 1⅝ **3/3**
D. 3a.   Ditto, 6 by 1¾ **4/3**
D. 228.   Trepanned Brush, ebony, best quality bristle, 11 rows, 7 by 1¾, very handsome **5/3**

D. 371.   As illustrated, No 1 Quality Hat Brush, size 7 by 1¾ in. **2/6**
D. 228.   8 rows, as above, 7 by 1⅝ in. .. **3/3**
D. 234.   Roached back, 8 rows, 6½ by 1¾ in., **4/3**
Postage 2d.

THE IDEAL COMB FOR LADIES.

Made in Dressing Comb, as illustration, and Rake (all wide teeth).

The latest novelty in GRIPWELL COMBS (Patented).   The feature of Gripwell Combs is the exceptionally heavy construction of the back, which prevents breakage and provides a most comfortable grip.   This had never been considered before in the construction of combs.   The Gripwell Combs are the Ideal Combs for Ladies.

THE DIAMOND GRIPWELL COMB is of the latest and most perfect design.   The shape and substance of the back have been specially studied to make the use of the comb a perfect luxury and comfort.

The finish is of the best; the teeth are carefully grailed and highly polished, thus allowing same to pass freely through the hair.   These Combs are made of finest Vulcanite, the highest grade Para rubber being employed for its manufacture.   Vulcanite is not inflammable like Celluloid, it does not split like horn, it is elastic, strong and springy, it is the best material for Combs.
Price **3/6**

Gent's Military Hair Brushes

Genuine Ebony-back Hair Brushes
London Made.
Complete in stout leather case, with comb.

No. 2.   Roach back, 11 rows good quality bristle, **7/11**
No 3.   Hollow back, 10 rows stiff bristles .. **8/11**
No. 4.   Hollow back, 12 rows stiff bristles.   Special value **10/6**
D.   Ditto, larger size wide set .. **12/-**
D. 6.   Roach back, 11 rows very stiff bristles, heavy brush **18/-**
D 7.   Large size ditto **18/-**
D 8 & 9.   The very finest brushes obtainable, treble X bristles .. **25/6** and **30/-**

Satinwood Military Brushes in Leather Case.

 no — leather case image appears here

D. 5.   13 row unbleached stiff bristles, large size brush, excellent value .. **6/11**
D. 7.   11 row unbleached stiff bristles, superior quality, **7/11**
D. 8.   11 rows best white bristles .. **8/11**
D. 9.   12 rows unbleached extra stiff bristles, our best selling line .. **10/-**

Ladies' and Gent's Hair Brushes

Ladies, Ebony-backed Hair Brushes.
Long Oval, as illustration.
13 rows best white long drawn bristles
Splendid Value.

3/11

Ladies' Broad Oval Satinwood Back.
13 rows long stiff white bristles.

5/11

Ladies' Hair Brush, best quality polished satinwood back, extra stiff bristles, balloon cut, as illustration.   15 rows.

6/-

Ladies' Long Oval, polished satinwood back, long cut bristles, 13 rows.   Splendid value, **4/3½**

Very superior quality Ladies' Ebony Hair Brushes, extra long bristles and very stiff, 12 rows.   No. 555 .. **10/6**

Gent's Handled Hair Brush.   Special value 16 rows, extra wide oval, polished screw back.

2/-

Gent's Broad Oval, very stiff white bristles, 16 rows, polished screw satinwood back, **3/9**

Useful Gifts in Toilet Brushware, Ebony Goods, etc.

TORTOISESHELL=COVERED TOILET BRUSHES, ETC.

— PLAIN, OR —

Inlaid with Sterling Silver and Mother-o'-Pearl.

These elegant Brushes are in every way equal—both in appearance and wear—to the solid tortoiseshell, at half the price.

INLAID STERLING SILVER AND MOTHER-O'-PEARL

Hat Brush.   **Cloth Brush.**

8 rows, **19/6** each.   8 rows, **24/3** each

Size 1½ by 6½ in.

INLAID STERLING SILVER AND MOTHER-O'-PEARL

Hand Mirror.

4 in. by 10½ in.

45/- each.

Solid Genuine Tortoiseshell Ladies'
Hair Brushes from **45/-** each.
at & Cloth Brushes, from **32/-** each
lid backed Tortoiseshell **Mirror, 60/-** each
ressing Combs, **5/6 8/6 10/6**
12/6 16/- each, according to thickness.
Back Combs, 10/6 to **25/-** each.
Side Combs, 8/6 to **20/-** pair.

INLAID STERLING SILVER AND MOTHER-O'-PEARL
Hair Brush
Small, 2½ by 8¾ in., 11 rows of stiff bristles, **32/6**
Large 2¾ by 9¾ in. 13 rows of stiff bristles, **38/9**

REAL TORTOISESHELL COVERED

Hat Brush.   **Cloth Brush.**

1½ by 6¾ in.   1½ by 6¼ in.
11/6 each.   **15/6** each.

Beautifully inlaid mother of pearl and silver and solid tortoiseshell Shoe Lift ... **19/6**
Solid Tortoiseshell plain (not inlaid) ... **14/6**

We carry a Large Stock of Genuine Tortoiseshell Ladies' Hair Brushes Dressing Combs, Back & Side Combs, etc.

Real Tortoiseshell Covered **Hair Brush**
Small, 2½ by 8¾ in 11 rows of stiff bristles. **23/6** each.
Large, 2¾ by 9¾ in, 13 rows of stiff bristles, **28/6**

Real Tortoiseshell Covered **Hand Mirror.**
4 by 10½ in. **36/9** each.

Back View.

Plain, solid tortoiseshell Nail File. 4½ in. long. **4/6** each.

Plain tortoiseshell mounted Hair Tweezers. **3/-**

Pain, solid tortoiseshell Glove Stretcher, 7½ in. long. **17/6**
Solid plain tortoiseshell Button Hooks **6/6**
  ,, inlaid ditto **6/6 8/6**
Scent Bottle Cork Screws, tortoiseshell handles ... **3/-**

USEFUL PRESENTS IN EBONY GOODS.

und Ebony Hand Mirrors

OVAL HAND MIRRORS

in best ebony
No. D. 0, 4½ in. diam., **4/6**
No. D. 1. 4½ in. **5/3**
No. D. 2 5½ in. **5/9**
No. D. 3 5¾ in. **6/6**

Best qual. English made Mirrors.
5 in. **3/6**
5½ in. **4/3**
6½ in. **5/3**
7½ in. **7/3**

In ebony, as illustrated Cheap qua...
5 in. **2/6**
5½ ,, **2/11**
6 ,, **3/3**
6½ ,, **3/10**

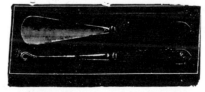

No. F. 3129. Ebony-handled Button Hook and Shoe Lift on Velvet Pad, 7½ in. Per Set **2/3**
No. F. 3130. Ditto, 10 in., set **3/9** Postage 3d.

Solid Ebony Puff Boxes, Flat top, as illustration.
1/6 2/6 5/-
Dome top,
1/8 2/10 5/6

Ebony Brush Trays, is illustration .. **5/11**
Same size Tray, without centre part .. **4/6**

Ebony Pin Boxes, as illustrated. **6/11** Smaller size, **5/9**

Button Hook Shoe Lifts, ebony. No. D. 555, Best qual. 9 in **2/6** 11 in. **2/11** D. 552, Ordinary qual. 9 in. **1/4** 11 in. **1/9** Post 2d.

ZENOBIA
TRUE FLOWER PERFUMES

Lily of the Valley, natural, as supplied to H.M. Queen Alexandra, H.M. Queen of Spain, &c., &c.

2/- 3/6 6/- 10/6 per bottle.

Also Rose Supreme at same prices.

The Popular Zenobia Pea Blossom. Possesses the true fragrance of the real Sweet Pea, **1/6 2/6 3/6 5/-** per bot.

Also Night-scented Stock Carneta Treek-à-Trique, same price

Handsome Gilt Covered Present Presentation Box. In the following Zenobia odours: Sweet Pea, Lily of Valley, Violet, Stock, Parma Carnation, Wallflower

4/6 per case.

Perfumes in Fancy Cases.

We illustrate below a few examples of CORBYN'S best quality Perfumes in fancy cases at very low prices making very acceptable Gifts.

Series No. 1.

Cases of 1, 2 and 3 bottles. Prices **4/6 6/6** and **8/3** Assorted odours as below.

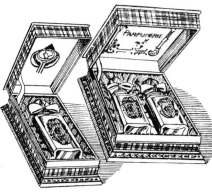

Series No. 2.

Case of 1 bottle .. **3/6**

,, 2 bottles .. **5/6**

Assorted odours.

Jockey Club, Parma Violet, Opoponax, Sweet Pea, White Rose, etc.

Series No. 2.

Series No. 3.

In case of 1 bottle only

SPLENDID VALUE

Assorted odours.

2/9

per bottle.

Potter & Moore Mitcham Lavender Water

In bottles:

1/6 2/6 3/9 6/6 12/-

Post extra.

Handsome Gilt Presentation Box, plain yet attractive, in the following odours:

Sweet Pea, Carnation, Wallflower, Night Scented Stock and Parma Violet.

Price .. **3/6** per box.

French Lavender Water.

GIRAUD'S, Superior quality.

In bottles:

1/3 2/3 3/- 4/11 & 8/6

Post extra.

Courvoisier's
Trefleurs

The new and lasting Trefle Perfume in handsome cases.

Price .. **3/-**

Post 3d.

Concentrated Perfumes without Spirit.

Courvoisier' Viotto, Lily of the Valley and Havanita.

One drop is equal to a teaspoonful of the finest perfume.

In handsome presentation cases, **3/9** ea. Post 1d.

Viotto (Otto of Violet) **Soap**. Fragrant and true colour of Violet perfume, combined with the finest super-fatted Toilet Soap. Price **2/6** per box. Postage 3d.

India-rubber Hot Water Bottles.

Best quality guaranteed English make.
Jug Handle.

Ordinary Handle

10 by 7 ..	**4/1½**
10 ,, 8 ..	**4/2**
12 ,, 6 ..	**4/1**
12 ,, 8 ..	**4/8½**
12 ,, 10 ..	**5/5**
14 ,, 8 ..	**5/3**
14 ,, 10 ..	**5/10**
16 ,, 10 ..	**6/11**

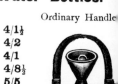

Scarlet Plush Covers for same

1/- 1/3 1/6

Selvyt Covers,

1/6 extra.

Perfumery, Sprays, etc., for Christmas Presents.

E carry a large stock of all the best known Perfumes by the chief makers, Atkinsons, Courvoisier, Giraud Fils, Roger & Callet, Corbyn, etc.

PERFUME SPRAYS

aranteed best English Cut Glass stal, hobnailed pattern PERFUME RAYS, complete with best quality bellows with silk tassels.

Popular patterns, as illustrations.

To hold 2	4	8 oz.
4/6	**6/3**	**8/9**

The old-fashioned hobnail pattern, best English deep cut, very fine finish, and fitted with best quality bellows and silk tassel.

o, Globe shape.

hold
z. Perfume, **7/6**
    ,,   **9/6**
    ,,   **12/6**
    ,,   **14/6**

NEW DESIGNS IN PERFUME SPRAYS.

ree latest patterns as illustration, each complete in box with bellows.

No. D. 1   No. D. 2   No. D. 3

To hold 2 ounces of perfumes.

All one price .. **2/11½** each.

Pocket or Bag Pump Sprays.

A strong nickelled Spray.

Well made and do not readily get out of order.

In two sizes.

10½d. and **1/6** each

Courvoisier's PERFUMES

AN EASTERN BOU-QUET PERFUME.

Courvoisier's Latest Production in Perfume.
OMAR KHAYYAM "The perfume of an Eastern Garden."
2/9, 5/-, 11/6. 21/- and **42/-** per bottle Postage extra.

TRUE VIOLET PERFUME.

VIOTTO
Otto of Violets Perfume.
1/8, 3/2, 6/-, 11/9, 22/6 per bottle.

Courvoisier's New Series of Perfumes for 1913.

SALUT D'AMOUR. LE'MIRACLE. LONDON PRIDE.

These perfumes represent the very highest grade of distinctive odours In artistic stoppered bottles with Mother of Pearl labels.
7/6 per bottle.

COURVOISIER'S well-known All-flower Perfumes in original designs, cut-glass bottles, each in presentation carton, as illustration.

In the following odours: Lilac, Sweet Pea, Carnations, White Heliotrope, White Rose Parma Violet, Wallflower.

Price .. **2/6 4/6 7/6**

Each bottle in presentation carton, making it a very acceptable 'Xmas Present.

"Iroma" Perfume.

The Crown Perfumery Company's New Perfume for 1913. An Original Odour reminiscent of Old English Gardens.

2/6 & 4/6 per bot. Post 3d.

Powder Iroma (in 3 shades), **1/6** per box. Post 2d.

Soap, **2/6** per box of 3 Tablets.

Post 3d.

EAU DE COLOGNE.

Guaranteed Best Quality.
Imported Direct.

Johann Maria Farina

Gegenuber dem Elogius Platz. Genuine and Very Best.

2 oz.	4 oz.	8 oz. bottle.
1/-	**1/10½**	**3/6**

Original case of ½ doz. 4 oz. bottles, **10/9**

In wicker-covered bottles.

Small, **3/-**   Medium, **5/9**   Large, **11/-**

Johann Maria Farina Hausa Platz Eau de Cologne.

In gold necked bottles, as illustration.

A HANDSOME 'XMAS GIFT.

3/9 per bottle.

ATKINSON'S PERFUMES.

Per bottle .. **1/9 2/9 4/10 11/6**

Chypre	Jockey Club	Opoponax
Ess Bouquet	Lily of the	Peau d'Espagne
Heliotrope	Valley	Stephanotis
Jasmin	Moss Rose	Violette de Parme
	White Lilac	Wood Violet

ATKINSON'S White Rose Perfume.

2/- 3/6 6/- 10/6 per bottle.

ATKINSON'S Poinsetta Perfume.

4/6 and **8/6** per bottle.

Special Value in Meerschaum and Amber Cigar and Cigarette Tubes.

The "St. James" Tube.

Meerschaum and real block Amber Mouthpiece. Silver mounted. One mount.

$2\frac{1}{4}$ in.	$2\frac{1}{2}$ in.	3 in.	$3\frac{1}{2}$ in.
2/9	**3/3**	**3/9**	**5/-**

Post free.

The "Piccadilly" Cigarette Tube.

First quality Meerschaum with real block Amber Mouthpiece. Unmounted.

$2\frac{1}{4}$ in.	$2\frac{1}{2}$ in.	3 in.	$3\frac{1}{2}$ in.
2/3	**2/9**	**3/3**	**4/6**

Post free.

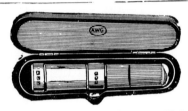

The "Buckingham" Cigarette Tube.

Meerschaum and real block Amber Mouthpiece. Two silver mounts.

$2\frac{1}{4}$ in.	$2\frac{1}{2}$ in.	3 in.	$3\frac{1}{2}$ in.
3/3	**3/9**	**4/3**	**5/6**

Ditto, 9-ct. gold mounts

5/9	**6/3**	**6/9**	**7/3**

Post free.

The "Gamage" Cigar Tube.

Real Meerschaum with genuine Amber Mouthpiece. Silver mounted (two bands). SPECIAL VALUE.

$2\frac{1}{4}$ in.	$2\frac{1}{2}$ in.	3 in.	$3\frac{1}{2}$ in.
4/6	**5/6**	**6/6**	**8/-**

Also 9-ct. Gold mounts, from **10/6**

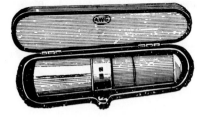

The "Sir Arthur" Cigar Tube.

Real Meerschaum with genuine block Amber Mouthpiece. Silver mounted (one band).

$2\frac{1}{4}$ in.	$2\frac{1}{2}$ in.	3 in.	$3\frac{1}{2}$ in.
3/9	**4/6**	**5/3**	**7/3**

Post free.

SPECIAL FINE QUALITY—The "Montague" Meerschaum Cigar Tube. Block Amber Mouthpiece.

$2\frac{1}{4}$ in.	$2\frac{1}{2}$ in.	3 in.	$3\frac{1}{2}$ in.
3/-	**3/9**	**4/6**	**6/6**

Post free.

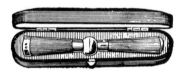

Golf Ball Tube.

The most hygienic tube ever produced.

Containing in centre of ball an absorbent wad, thereby filtering and purifying all smoke before entering the mouth.

In first quality block Amber and solid Silver mounts.

$3\frac{1}{2}$ in., **11/6**	$3\frac{3}{4}$ in., **12/9**	4 in., **15/6**
9-ct. Gold, **21/-**	**24/-**	**27/-**

Post free.

The "Pall Mall" Cigarette Tube.

Ambroid. 9-ct. Gold Mount.

$2\frac{1}{4}$ in.	$2\frac{1}{2}$ in.	3 in.	$3\frac{1}{2}$ in.
4/9	**5/3**	**6/6**	**7/6**

Ambroid. Unmounted.

2/6	**3/3**	**4/-**	**5/6**

First Quality Block Amber.

2 in., **8/6**	$2\frac{1}{2}$ in., **11/9**	3 in., **15/-**

Post free.

The "Madras" Ambroid Cigar Tube.

In Russia Leather Case. 9-ct. Gold Mount.

2 in.	$2\frac{1}{2}$ in.	3 in.	$3\frac{1}{2}$ in.
6/9	**7/9**	**9/6**	**11/9**

Finest Quality Block Amber.

13/6	**19/6**	**24/-**	**31/-**

Also plain without mount.

Ambroid Cigar Tubes in Russian Leather. The "Damascus."

2 in., **3/9**	$2\frac{1}{2}$ in., **4/6**	3 in., **6/6**	$3\frac{1}{2}$ in., **8/6**

Finest Quality Block Amber.

10/6	**16/6**	**21/-**	**27/-**

Post free.

Special Lines in Virginia & Turkish Cigarettes. Packed suitable for Presentation.

THE "CLUB" VIRGINIA CIGARETTE.

THIS is a NEW INTRODUCTION and represents the very highest grade of VIRGINIA CIGARETTES. Beautifully packed in boxes of **50** and **100**

PRICE .. .. **2/6** and **4/10½**

STEFANO'S Celebrated Imported Turkish Cigarettes. We have specially impor ed **a** large parcel of this well-known Cigarette in 3 sizes. Unrivalled.

In Boxes of **100** .. **3/6**
Ditto **50** .. **1/9**
NON PLUS ULTRA.
In Boxes of **100** .. **4/-**
Ditto **50** .. **2/-**
FLEURS D'ORIENT.
Extra large and extra quality.
Per **100** .. **7/6**

HAND-MADE VIRGINIA CIGARETTES.

WE have had specially manufactured and packed for us a supply of Hand-made Virginian Cigarettes — Gold Tipped, Cork 1ipped and plain. They are put up in handsome cabinets of **50**, and after use the inner portion of the cabinet can be removed, leaving a useful receptacle for handkerchiefs or other similar articles.

PRICE only **2/6** per CABINET.
Postage 3d.

GENUINE HAND-MADE VIRGINIA CIGARETTES.

SPECIAL LINE.

CHOICE PANDORA BRAND.

Straight Cut Virginian Cigarettes.

Hand-made by the well-known Cigarette Specialists,

Messrs. R. LOCKYER & Co.

Price .. **3/10½** per box of **100**

Usual retail price 4/9 per box.

Gamage's Value in Briar Pipes, Companions, etc.

"ANCHOR" Brand ROOT Briar Pipes.

SPECIAL NOTICE.—Genuine Old Briar Roots are practically now unobtainable, except at exorbitant prices. We have been fortunate enough to secure the entire stock of First Grade "ANCHOR" Brand genuine Old Seasoned Briar Root Pipes, each Pipe being guaranteed to be upwards of 20 years old. The longer they are smoked the sweeter they become, a sure proof of the age of the Briar Root. We have only the following four patterns in stock and cannot repeat when sold. The prices quoted are **25** per cent. below the makers' list prices. In four patterns only at **2/6** each.

C. 1. Bent Army push mouthpiece. Price **2/6**

C. 2. Bent, screw saddle mouthpiece. Price **2/6**

C. 3. Bent, screw saddle mouthpiece, square bowl .. **2/6**

C. 4. Bent, screw mouthpiece Price **2/6**

Gamage's A.W.G. Briar Pipes.
Hall-marked Silver-mounted Briar. Vulcanite Push-in Mouthpieces.

We have our Pipes manufactured for us from specially selected materiasl. The following illustrations represent only a portion of our varied stock All Pipes stamped "A.W.G." will be exchanged, should the bowl crack or burn, or the mouthpiece crack through any fault in the Pipe.

No. C. 1.

No. C. 2.

No. C. 3.

No. C. 4.

No. C. 5.

No. C. 6.

Pipes are in patterns as above illustrations. When ordering simply state the number. **Picked Briars** very superior quality, best Vulcanite Mouthpieces, thick Silver Hall-marked Band. Very Handsome Pipes, **2/6** each. Also superior quality Briars, thick Hall-marked Silver-mount, best Vulcanite Mouthpieces at **1/6** and **1/-** each.

We have a large selection of Finest Quality LORNE Pouches both plain and covered in various skins.

Size .. No.	C. 4	C. 5	C. 6	Size .. No.	C. 4	C. 5	C. 6
Finest Buckskin Pouch ..	1/11	2/3	2/9	Sealskin, silver H.M. shield	4/-	4/6	5/3
Do. with silver H.M. shield	2/5	2/9	3/3	Velvet Crocodile ..	3/6	4/-	4/9
Kangaroo	2/2	2/6	3/-	Do. with silver H.N. shield	4/-	4/6	5/3
Do. with silver H.M. shield	2/8	3/-	3/6	Finest Antelope	3/9	4/6	5/3
Sealskin	3/6	4/-	4/9	Do. with silver H.M. shield	4/3	5/-	5/9

These Pouches may be had Square or Round,

AS ILLUSTRATIONS.

They are Best Rubber Lined and Splendid value.

old Shields, 9-ct., on any of ove Pouches .. **3/9** extra

Best quality, British Make

Wallet Pouches,

India Rubber Lining with flaps, as illustration. In three sizes.

Light brown pigskin **2/- 2/6 3/-**

Black Morocco.. **2/3 2/9 3/6**

have a very large selection of handsome new Tobacco Jars. llustrate herewith a few, but it is impossible to convey an idea he taking appearance of these goods without inspecting them. llustration, in Princess Gilt Ware, new style, extra wide airtight lid with brass screw clips .. ¼ lb., **3/6**; ½ lb., **4/6**

ghed Gilt Vase-shaped Tobacco Jar, fitted with air-tight lid and brass screw .. .. ¼ lb. size, **2/3**; ½ lb. size, **3/3**

Postage on Jars: ¾ lb., 3d.; ½ lb., 4d.; 1 lb., 5d.

Cavendish Shape. Majolica Ware.
The Cavendish Jar is air-tight, fitted with brass screw clips. Will keep tobacco in condition for any period.

¼-lb. size .. **2/3** ½-lb. size .. **3/3**

Princess Ware.

GAMAGE'S Colonial Tobacco Jar.

Gilt, air-tight, with bronzed screw clips.

¼-lb. size **2/3**

½-lb. size **3/3**

DD

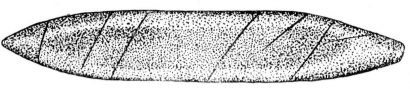

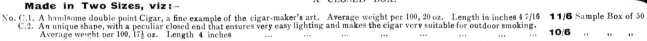

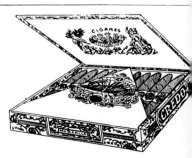

Companion Pipe Sets.

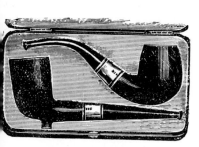

The "M F H."
Hall-marked silver band.

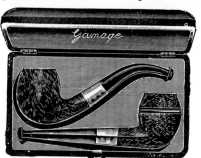

Complete
4/6
Post free.

Best gold-lined case.

The "Lenore"

Complete
4/6
Post free.

The "Fleet."

Every Pipe bearing the name "GAMAGE" is guaranteed Perfect.

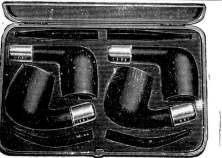

The "Dreadnought." Suitable present. This case contains 4 best quality Briars, with 2 amber and 2 vulcanite mouthpieces. Our price **29/6**
Or 4 vulcanite mouthpieces .. **15/9**

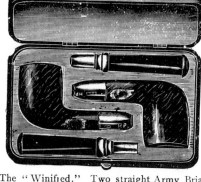

The "Winifred." Two straight Army Briars, real block amber mouthpieces and silver spigots.
Our price **22/6**

Also with vulcanite mouthpieces and silver spigot mounted as illustration .. **10/6**

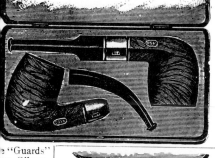

The "Guards" Two Silver-mounted Briars, with vulcanite mouthpieces.
price **10/6**

"Tommy's Favourite." Two straight Army Briars, vulcanite mouthpieces.
price **9/6**

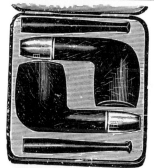

Genuine South African Calabash Pipes. Fine quality Calabash with ambroid mouthpiece, silver.mounted band in best qual case, as illustrated **12/6** to **15/6** Post 2d.
Also with vulcanite mouthpieces, not in case at **3/6** & **4/6**
Silver spigot mounted at **6/9**

No. C. 1016.
4 Pipe Companion, 2 block amber mouthpieces, 2 hand cut vulcanite. Price **41/6** Post free.
Or with 2 ambroid mouthpieces and 2 vulcanite.
Price .. .. **27/6** Post free.

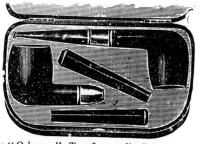

The "Osborne." Two first quality Briars, 2 vulcanite and 1 amber mouthpieces, at our cut price .. **18/9**

Briars in Cases.

An "Anchor Brand" Pipe, Straight or Bent, complete in plush-lined leather case, best quality, silver spigot mount, and picked briar bowls.

Price **3/6**

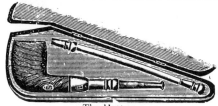

The Hatton.
First quality. Briar amber mouthpiece and Albatross stem. An ideal reading pipe. Our price **14/6**

The "Victoria." Containing 3 London made Briars with 1 amber and 2 vulcanite mouthpieces Our price **24/6**

Also with 2 ambroid mouthpieces and 1 vulcanite. **16/6**

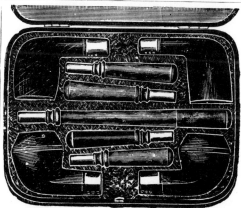

The "Princess." Handsome companion, consisting of 4 silver-mounted pipes, 2 block amber and 2 vulcanite mouthpieces, and 1 amber and vulcanite mouthpiece.
Our price **42/6**
Also 2 ambroid and 2 vulcanite mouthpieces .. **27/6**

DD..

A Present that will be appreciated.

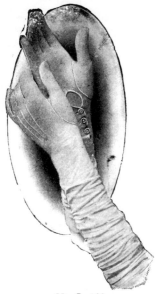

No. L. 109.
Ladies' Mousquitere White Kid Gloves in
12 or 16 button length.   Other lengths to order.
12 button .. **2/11 3/11 4 11 7/6**
16   .. **3/11 4/11 5/11 7/11 9/6**

No. L. 112.

Ladies'
3-button suede
Glove.

Round seam
sewn plain
points.

**Trefousse's
make.**

In Black,
White, Tan
Beavers,
Drab Biscuit,
Grey Slate.

**3/6
3/11
4/6**

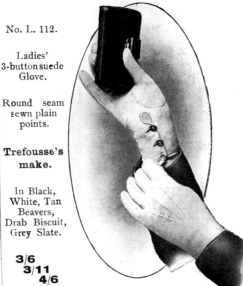
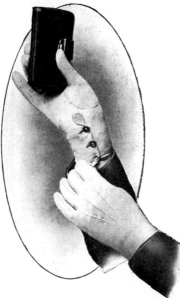

No. L. 115.

Ladies'
Mousquitere
Suede Gloves
in
12 or 16 button
length.

Other lengths
to order.

Buttons
12   16
2/11 3/11
3/11 4/11
4/11 7/6
7/6 9/6

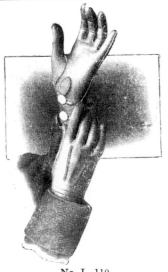

No. L. 110.
Ladies' best quality French Cherette Glove.
Trefousse's own Make.
Pique sewn.   Fine cord points.
2 large pearl buttons.   Tan Beaver.
Slate and white, **5/11** per pair.

No. L. 113.

Ladies'
Pique Suede
Glove.

Embroidered
3-cord point,
made from
specially
selected skin
by
**Trefousse
& Co.**

3 peal buttons

4/6 and **5/6**
per pair.

No. L. 116.
Ladies' 3-button Suede Glove.
Round seam sewn with neat ancy point.
Trefousse's best quality.
In Black, White, Drab Beaver, Slate Grey
4/6 per pair.

No. L. 111.
Ladies' 2-button real Reindeer Pique Sewn Glove.
Bolton thumbs in Tan, Slate, Black and White.
4/11 6/11 per pair.

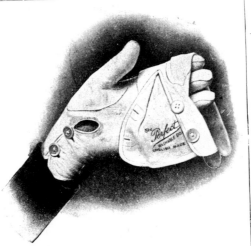

No. L. 114.
Ladies' 2-button Perfect Washable Doeskin in white only
The special dressing of this leather enables the glove
to be washed successfully several times.
2/11 per pair.

No. L. 117.
Nansen
Motoring
Glove.
Natural Hair
Lined.

Ladies' or
Gent's Natural
Gazelle Glove
not a ordinary
lined Glove.

The Hairy
surface of the
skin forming
the inside
lining with
dome or strap
fastening.

With Dome,
7/11
With Strap,
8/11

Useful Xmas Presents for Ladies.

Dent's and Trefousse's Best French Gloves.

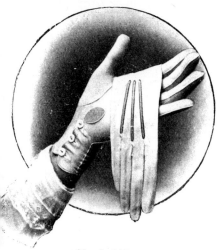

No. L. 100.

utton Kid Gloves, in Tan, Beaver, Biscuit, Slate,
Black, White.   Fine 3-cord Points.
1/11 and **2/6** per pair.

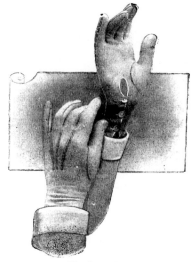

No. L. 103.

Ladies' Fine Kid Glove. 3-dome fastener.
Round seam, plain points.
In Tan, Beaver, Slate, Biscuit, Black, White.
3/6 per pair.

No. L. 106.   Ladies' Pique Sewn Suede Gloves.
Embroidered, 5-cord points.
In Slate, Tan, Beaver, Brown.   **26** per pair.

No. L. 107

Ladies'
3-button
Pique
Sewn
French
Suede
Gloves.

Em-
broidered,
3-cord
Points.

Tan,
Beaver,
Brown,
Slate,
Mole,
Black.

3/6
per pair.

No. L. 101.

ies' 2-dome Nappa Gloves, spear points. Bolton
humbs. In Tan **only**. Strong and serviceable.
2 6 per pair.

No. L. 104.

Ladies' 3-button Fine French Kid Glove.

Trefousse's own Make.

Plain points, medium and long fingers.
In all Colours, Black and White.
4/6 per pair.

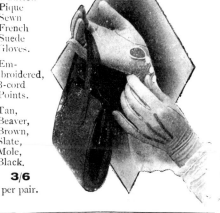

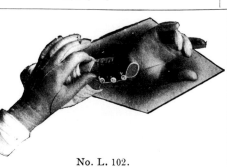

No. L. 102.

Ladies' 3-button fine Luxemburg Kid Gloves.
Plain Points.
In Tan, Beaver, Biscuit, Black, White.
Price .. **2/6** per pair.

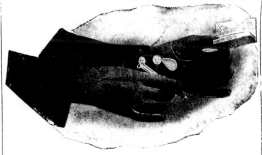

No. L. 105.

Ladies' 2-button Dik Antelope Glove, the ideal Winter
Glove. Soft supple skins. In Tan, Beaver, Brown,
Mole, Slate, Black.   **3/6** per pair.

No. L. 108.   Ladies' heavy Tan Cape p x
seam sewn Glove, 3-button, spear points, Bolton
thumb. Suitable for riding, driving, or heavy
use.   **3/9** per pair.

Xmas Presents in Ladies' Winter Gloves.

Ladies' Medium Brown Cape Winter Glove.

Pique sewn, lined wool, fur lined, half-way brown glove, black or brown fur at wrist.

1 dome strap fastener.   Dent's make, **4/11** pair

Ladies' Tan or Grey Heavy Mocha Gloves

Pique sewn, wool lined, white fur up wrist, beaver coloured fur at top of wrist, 1 dome strap gussetted fastener.

Dent's best make, **6/11** pair.

Also same style in real Gazelle Natural Hair lined Dent's best make, **9 6** pair.

Ladies' Tan Cape Winter Glove.

Pique sewn, lined wool, strap wrist, 1 dome fastener. A Thin Smart Glove.

Dent's best make, **3/11** pair.

Ladies' Tan or Grey Mocha Gloves.

Lined wool, elastic fur wrist.
Dent's Best make, **4/11** pair.

Ladies' Tan Mock Buck Gauntlet Motor Driving Gloves.

Prix seams, full size shaped gauntlets.
Real Natural Lambskin Lining.
Dent's best make **12/6** pair.

Girl's Winter Gloves.

In dark brown Cape Leather, pique sewn, wool lined, fur top wrist, 1 spring fastener.

Dent's best make, in all sizes from 2 to 7.
Price **3/6** pair.

Ladies' Brown Cape Leather Glove.

Pique sewn, elastic gussetted fur wrist, lined segovia wool.

Dent's best make, **3/11** pair.

Ladies' Brown Cape Glove.

Pique sewn, lined wool, fur at wrist, 1 dome fastening.   Dent's best make **4/11** pair.

Boy's Warm Winter Brown Tan Cape Gloves.

Pique sewn, wool lined, 1 dome fastener.

Dent's make, in all sizes from 1 to 7s, **2/6** pr.

Also in strong Mocha, in tan, wool lined, 1 dome fastener, **2/6** pair.

Gent's Winter Lined Gloves. USEFUL PRESENTS.

Gent's Austrian Brown
Kid Glove.
Pique sewn, lined Segovia Wool, 1 dome fastener. Dent's make.
2/6 per pair.

Gent's Strong Tan
Cape Glove.
Prix seams, Bolton thumb, lined with best Segovia Wool, 1 dome fastener, Dent's make.
3/6 per pair.

Gent's Tan
Cape Leather Glove.
Pique sewn, lined throughout with wool, strap wrist. **3/11** per pair.
Also in Grey Swedes, **3/6** per pair.

Gent's Strong
Tan Cape Glove.
Pique sewn, elastic wrist, Bolton thumb, lined white fur. Very warm for winter wear.
Dent's best make. **6/6** per pair.

Gent's Heavy Tan or Grey
Mocha Glove.
Prix seams, Bolton thumb, plain points, 1 horn dome fastener, lined throughout with fur. Very warm for winter wear. Dent's best make.
Price **7/6** per pair.

Gent's Tan
Cape Leather Glove.
Pique sewn, Bolton thumb, lined wool and fur lined at wrists, 1 dome fastener. Dent's best make.
Price .. **4/11** per pair.

Gent's Nansen,
Real Gazelle Gloves.
In Tan or Slate, with the natural Gazelle hair inside forming a warm and indestructible lining, strap roller wrist.

Trefousse's best make. **9/6** per pair.

DENT'S GRIP.
Dent's Celebrated **Grip Glove.** Lined best Segoria Wool.
An unique glove for driving, made from strong Tan Cape Leather, 1 dome fastener. This glove is specially pleated on hand to ensure perfect grip of reins or wheel.
Dent's best make. Price .. **5/11**

Gent's Strong Tan or Grey
Mocha Glove.
Prix seam, Bolton thumb, strap roller, dome fastener, lined wool. Lined natural Gazelle hair at wrist.

Price .. **5/11** per pair.

Xmas Presents in Motor Gloves.

No. L. 10.
Gent's Black Coney Seal Fur Motor Gauntlet Gloves.

Stout fine-grain tan Cape leather palms, piqué sewn, Bolton thumb, elastic grip wrist, large soft gussetted gauntlet, lined best Segovia wool throughout.
Dent's make. As illustration No. L. 10 **14/11** pair.

No. L. 11.
Dent's Tan Cape Driving Gloves.

Lined lamb's wool, Bolton thumbs. Quite the best glove for driving or motoring.
Price .. **6/11**

No. L. 12.
The Skimit for Swiss Sports.

Made from specially prepared snow resisting cloth, elastic grip wrist, and lined best Segovia wool.
The fastener is arranged at back so as not to impede free action.
Gamage's special design in Ladies' or Gent's size.
As illustration No. L. 12 .. **3/11** per pair.
With leather faced palm .. **4/11** per pair.

No. L. 13.
Gent's Silver Grey Fur Gauntlet Motor Gloves.

Stout tan Cape leather palms, Bolton thumb fur lined, elastic wrist, extra large stiff gauntlets.

Dent's make .. **16/11** per pair.

Price and quality cannot be beaten.
As illustration No. L. 13.

No. L. 14.
Ladies' and Gent's Natural Rabbit Fur Glove.

Heavy tan Cape leather palm, Bolton thumb, sac wrist, lined wool; very warm glove.   Price .. **6/11** per pair.

No. L. 15.
Musk-Rat Fur Gloves.

Dark Brown Musk-rat Fur Gloves.   Strong tan Cape palms, 1 dome strap roller fastener, Bolton thumb, lined fur throughout.
A smart glove, very warm and durable.
Dent's best make .. **25/-** per pair.

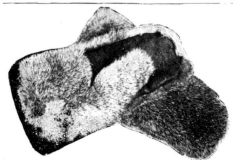

No L. 16.
Gent's Natural Rabbit Fur Canadian or Motor Mitts.

Heavy tan Cape leather palms, Bolton thumb, sac wrist lined best Segovia wool. **Positively the warmest Glove obtainable.** Dent's make. **6/11** per pair

No. L. 17.
Gent's Fine Quality Musquash Fur Motor Gloves.

Piqué sewn, Bolton, elastic wrist, lined wool, full size soft gauntlet. **35/6** pair.

No. L. 18.
Gent's Grey Opossum Fur Motor Gauntlet Gloves.

Gauntlet Gloves.   Heavy tan Cape leather palm and front of gauntlet, piqué sewn Bolton thumb, dome strap wrist fastener, soft gussetted gauntlet, lined best Segovia wool, very warm and durable.

Dent's best make. As illustration No. L. 18.
35/- pair.

IMPORTANT—In ordering please quote number and size.

Useful Presents in Motor Gloves.

Strong Brazil Tan Leather Motor Driving Gloves.

Lined Chamoise leather, strap roller wrist, 5½ in. semi-stiff gauntlet. **9/11** pair.

Gent's Tan or Black Strong Cape Leather Motor Driving Gloves.

No. L. 20.

Strap Wrist, 6 in. semi-stiff Gussetted Gauntlet, Lined Wool ... **5/11** pair.

Gent's Strong Cape Leather Motor Driving Gloves.

No. L. 21

Sac Wrist, 4½ in. stiff Gauntlet, in Tan or Black. Lined and Unlined. Dent's make **7/6** pair.

Gent's Extra Strong Oak Tan Cape Driving Gloves.

No. L, 23.

Elastic wrist, 6 in. semi-stiff Gussetted Gauntlet, Double Palms, lined Wool, Prix Seams. Also in Black. Dent's make. **7/11** pair.

Our Specialite Chauffeur Glove.

No. L. 24.

In Tan or Black, Extra Strong Double Palms, Elastic Wrist, Cane supported Gauntlets, lined Wool. Specially suited for Chauffeur's wear.
Dent's Best Make. **8/3** pair.

Gent's Fine Grain Tan and Black Cape Leather Gauntlet Gloves.

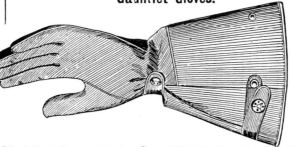

Lined Best Segovia Wool. Semi-stiff Fully Gussetted Gauntlet, 2 Strap Fastenings, in all sizes.
Dent's Best Make. **8/11** pair.

Gent's Oak Tan Leather Driving Gloves

No. L. 27.

Elastic Strap and Dome Fasteners, fully Gussetted Soft Gauntlet, lined Segovia Wool back made from whole piece of leather.
Dent's Best Make. Also in Black. **12/6** pair.

Gent's Black or Tan Strong Cape Driving Gloves.

No. L. 28.

Elastic Wrist. lined best Segovia Wool, extra long Soft Gauntlet, Full Gusset, 1 dome Strap Fastener. Extra smart and durable. **14/11** pair.

The "Holborn" Chrome Gauntlet Motor Gloves.

No. L 29.

Waterproof, Chrome Leather, Lambskin lined, extra large semi-stiff Gauntlet. Unsurpassed for Durability. As sketch No 29
21/- pair.

Important.—In Ordering Please Quote Number and Size.

Xmas Presents for Motorists.

No. L. 1.

Gent's Black Electric Seal Motor Gauntlet Gloves.

Strong tan Cape palm, piqué sewn, elastic grip waste. lined best Segovia wool, gauntlet extra large and soft.

Dent's Best Make.

As illustration No. L. 1. .. **30/-** per pair.

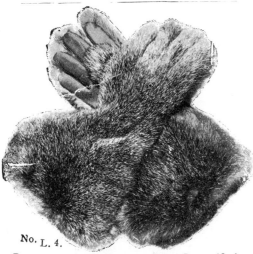

No. L. 4.

Gents' Long Brown Fur Gauntlet Driving Glove.

Lined grey fur, leather palms, elastic wrists.

Dent's best make .. **21/-** pair

No. L. 7.

Ladies' & Gent's Natural Rabbit Fur Motor Gauntlets.

Heavy fine grain Cape leather palm, piqué sewn, Bolton thumb, elastic grip waist, lined best Segovia wool, extra large semi-stiff gauntlet.

Dent's make.

As illustration **No. L. 7.** .. **10/6** per pair.

No. L. 2.

Imitation Persian Astrachan Lamb Motor Gauntlet Gloves.

With strong Black Cape Palms, lined fleece wool, strap and dome at wrist of Gauntlet.

Very warm Gloves. Dent's make.

10/6 per pair.

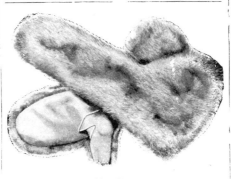

No. L. 5.

Ladies' and Gent's Natural Rabbit Fur Motor Driving Mitts

Fine grain tan Cape leather palms, Bolton thumb elastic wrist, lined best Segovia wool throughout, semi-stiff gauntlet. Dent's Make.

As illustration No. L. 5. **10/6** and **14/11** per pair.

No. L. 8.

Ladies' and Gent's Beaver Gloves.

Short Gauntlet, Sack Wrists.

Leather palm. Lined fur throughout.

18/11 pair. Dent's best make.

No. L. 3.

Black Sheared Fur Motor Gloves.

For Ladies or Gents. Heavy tan Cape palms, Bolton thumb, elastic wrist, piqué sewn, lined best Segovia wool.

Thoroughly dependable.

Dent's best make. As illustration No. L. 3.

Price .. **8/11** pair.

No. L. 6.

Gent's Grey Fur Motor Gloves.

Heavy grey buck palm, piqué sewn, Bolton thumb lined rabbit fur throughout, sac wrist. Dent's make

As illustration No. L. 6. **12/6** per pair.

No. L. 9. ### Gent's Nutria Beaver Motor Gloves.

Semi-soft gauntlet, gussetted wrist, 1 strap dome fastener, piqué sewn, Bolton thumb, wool lined hands, gauntlet lined lamb. In Ladies' or Gent's

As illustration No. L. 9. .. **14/11** per pair.

IMPORTANT—In ordering please quote Number and Size.

GAMAGE'S ZOO. The Largest Zoological Department in London.

Send for Fully-Illustrated List. Post Free. All Live Stock is offered subject to being in Stock and is sent carriage forward.

Parrots, Cockatoos and Parakeets in great Variety.

LEMON-CRESTED COCKATOO.

Lemon-crested Cockatoos, **30/- 35/-**

Bare-eyed Cockatoos, **35/-** ea.
Slender bill Cockatoos **35/-** ,,
Rose Cockatoo ... **21/** ,,
Leadbeater do. ... **42/-** ,,
White Java do ... **35/-** ,,

Cuban Amazon, very rare ... ... **60/-** ,,
Red and Buff Macaw, grand bird, talking, **£7 10 0** ,,

Indian plain Parrots, Young ... ... **7/6** ,,
Rosella Parakeets ... **25/-** ,,
Mealy do. ... **50/-** ,,
Quaker do. ... **7/6** ,,
Moustache do. ... **7/6** ,,
Redrump do. ... **25/-** ,,
Barnards do. ... **50/-** ,,
Travelling Boxes, 6d. each.

GREY PARROT. AMAZON PARROT.
African Grey Talking Parrots
We usually have several talking birds on hand, prices according to bird's ability.
Amazon Parrots.
Young birds, **30/- 35/- 42/- 50/-** each.

Chattering, Lory... **42/-** ea.
Elestus, Lory ... **42/-** ,,
Ringneck Parakeets **7/6** ,,
Tovi do.**10/6 12/6** ,,
Half-moon do. **12/6** ,,
Pennant do. **45/-** ,,
Adelaide do. **50/-** ,,
Blossom Head **10/6 12/6** ,,
Yell. Cheeked Conure**21/-** ,,
Blue Crowned ,, **42/-** ,,
Patagonian ,, **60/-** ,,
Blue Crois., Green, Yellow Budgerigars **7/6** ,,
,, pair **10/6**
Bluewinged Lovebirds **12/6**
Yellow collared Parakeets **80/-** ea.
Many colour **60/-** ,,
Port Lincoln ... **45/-** ,,
Cockatiels ... **10/6** ,,
Grey-headed Lovebirds ... ... pair **3/9**
Grand New Guinea, Lory ... ... **65/-** ,,
Travelling Boxes, 6d. extra.

ROSE-BREASTED COCKATOO.

Beautiful Birds for Cages and Aviaries. Immense Variety.

Senegal Waxbill... **3/6** pr.
St. Helena do. **4/6 5/6** ,,
Orange Cheek do. **3/6** ,,
Golden-breasted do. **4/6** ,,
Grey Java Sparrow **2/9** ,,
Cutthroat ... **3/9** ,,
Spice bird ... **2/9** ,,
Green Singing finch **5/6** ,,
Silverbill ... ... **3/6** ,,

JAVA SPARROW.

Zebra finch... **10/6** pr.
Combassou ... **3/6** ,,
Longtail Whydah **5/6 7/6** ,,
Gouldian Finch, Red ... **35/-** ,,
Do Black ... **25/-** ,,
Masked Finch ... **20/-** ,,
Ruficanda Finch **30/-** ,,
Grass finches ... **18/-** ,,
Pekin Nightingale **7/6** ,,
Red Cheek Bulbul **7/6** ea.
Diamond Sparrows **30/-** pr.
Indigo Bunting ... **20/-** ea.
Nonpareil do. ... **27/6** ,,
Orange Head Ground Thrush **42/-** ,,

Indian Shamahs ... **35/-** ea.
Do. Dyal Bird **35/-** ,,
Do. Barbet ... **35/-** ,,
Palm Tanager **12/6** ,,
Violet do. **8/6** ,,
Pileated Finch ... **5/6** ,,
Black Tanager **10/6** ,,
Australian Water Rail ... **20/-** ,,
Do. Budgerigars **7/6** pr.
Do. do. (yellow) **10/6** ,,
Bearded Tits **12/6** ,,
Bib finches... **3/6** ,,
Double Band finches **25/-** ,,
Hunting Cissas ... **63/-** ,,
Chongola Sparrows **6/6** ea.
Black throated Troupial **27/6** ,,
Jamaica do. **30/-** ,,
Orioles ... **42/-** ,,

RIBBON FINCH.

Senegal Doves ... **12/6** pr.
Scarlet Weavers... **5/6** ea.
Orange Bishop do. **4/6 5/6** ,,
Crimson Crown do. **6/6 7/6** ,,
Masked Weaver... **3/6** pr.
Crested Mynah ... **15/-** ea.
Hill do. ... **42/-** ,,
Australian Piping Crow ... **42/-** ,,
Lovebirds ... **3/9** pr.
Olive finches ... **25/-** ,,
Saffron finches ... **7/6** ,,
Golden-fronted Bulbul ... **50/-** ea.
Bichano finches ... **25/-** pr.
Cuban finches ... **25/-** ,,
Silky Cow Birds **10/6** ea.

Firefinch ... ... **4/6** pr.
Red Avadavats **3/6 4/6** ,,
Green ... ... **5/6** ,,
Cordon Bleu ... **4/6** ,,
White Java Sparrows **10/6** ,,
Bengalese... ... **3/9** ,,
Bk Head Mannikens **2/9** ,,
Wh. do. do. **4/6** ,,
Tricolour do. **4/6** ,,
Lavender finch **5/6 6/6** ,,
Virginia Cardinal **27/6** ea.
Red-crested do. ... **7/6** ,,
Pope Cardinal ... **8/6** ,,
Wh. Java Doves ... **6/6** pr.
Ring Doves ... **3/6** ,,
Diamond Doves... **20/-** ,,
Zebra Doves ... **15/-** ,,
Masked Doves ... **12/6** ,,

Very suitable for Christmas Presents.
Finger-tame Birds.
Unique Pets. Will sit on finger. Quite tame.

Avadavats...	**2/6** ea.	Tigerfinch ...	**3/6** ea.
Waxbill	**2/6** ,,	Orange Cheek	**3/6** ,,
Black Head Nun...	**2/6** ,,	Java Sparrow	**3/6** ,,
Silverbill ...	**2/6** ,,	White Head Nun	**3/6** ,,
Budgerigars ...	**7/6** ,,	Bullfinch ...	**10/6** ,,

Travelling Cages, 4d. and 6d. extra.

WAXBILL.

Travelling Cages .. .. **4d. 6d. 1/- 1/6 extra.**

GOULDIAN FINCH.

Canaries.

We have a large selection of the principal breeds at following prices.

Norwich & Yorkshire.
Guaranteed Cocks in song, **8/6 10/6 12/6 15/-**
Hens, for Breeding and Aviaries, **3/- 3/6 4/- 4/6 5/- 6/-**

Norwich Crests and Crest-breds, Cocks,
12/6 15/- 21/- 25/-
Hens **6/6 7/6 10/6**
Travelling Cages, 6d. extra.

As a **Christmas Present**
a Canary and Cage is very appropriate. We can supply a good singing canary, either Norwich, Yorkshire, or Hartz Mountain Roller, complete with handsome ornamental brass cage, packed free, carriage forward, **15/6**

Hartz Mountain Rollers are specially trained birds with beautiful soft rolling song **8/6 10/6 12/6** Hens same strain, **3/- 4/- 5/-** **St. Andreasberg Rollers** selected birds with beautiful nightingale and bell note, very sweet in song, **12/6 15/- 18/- 21/- 25/-** each. Hens, same strain, **3/6 4/6 5/6** Packed free. Carriage forward.

British Birds.

Bramblefinch ...		**1/-**	**1/6**
	Hens	**6d.**	**9d.**
Bullfinch, Cocks		**3/6**	**4/6**
	Hens	**1/6**	**2/-**
Chaffinch, Cocks		**1/-**	**1/6**
	Hens	**6d.**	**9d.**
Greenfinch, Cocks,		**6d.**	**9d.**
	Hens	**4d.**	**6d.**
Hawfinch, Cocks		**10/6**	**12/6**
	Hens ...	**4/6**	**5/6**
Goldfinch, Cocks ...		**3/6**	**4/6**
	Hens ...	**2/-**	**2/6**
Linnet, Cocks		**1/-**	**1/6**
	Hens		**6d.**
Yellow Hammer, Cocks,	**1/6**	Hens,	**9d.**
Siskin, Cocks...	**3/6**		**4/6**
	Hens ...		**2/-**

Travelling Cages. 6d. extra.

Pigeons

		Pair			Pair
White Fantails	**5/6**	**6/-**	Magpies ...	from	**6/6**
Turbits ...	from	**8/6**	Runts ...	..	**12/6**
Tumblers...	...	**5/6**	Jacobins ...		**7/6**
Pouters ...	...	**7/6**	Dragoons		**6/6**
Short-faced Tumblers	...	**10/6**	Homers ...	...	**5/6**
Carriers ...	,,	**12/6**	Norwich Croppers	..	**10/6**
Show Homers	,,	**7/6**	Pigeons for Shooting or Sport ...		**12/-** dozen

Travelling Boxes, 3d. extra.

GAMAGE'S ZOO. A Xmas Attraction

Everything Alive.   Pets of all kinds.   Singing Canaries.

Write for fully Illustrated List, Stock Catalogue,   Below is a FEW of the Pets to be seen

Small Monkeys, Mongooses, &c.

The Sooty Mangaby

Is a native of the West Coast of Africa. He is a very merry fellow, full of life and always a source of fun and amusement to the owner

The Mangaby is very suitable for a pet, and is easily kept in captivity. His face is black, hence the name "Sooty," with a dirty white chest and side whiskers. He is sometimes called the White Eyelid Monkey, on account of the absence of colour on the eyelids.

SOOTY MANGABY MONKEY ... from	**50/-**
BONNET MONKEY ... ... ,,	**35/-**
SMALL RHESUS ... ... ,,	**35/-**
CALLITHRIX MONKEY ... ... ,,	**45/-**
MONA ... from **42/-** PUTTY NOSED ,,	**63/-**
MOUSTACHE, from **70/-** SQUIRREL ,,	**63/-**
Tame Monkeys, suitable for Pets, always in stock ... ... ,,	**30/-**

The Marmoset.

These interesting little creatures make charming pets, and it is most amusing to watch their funny ways and antics; they are not as big as a squirrel and are fairly hardy. People train them to carry in the pocket or muff.

LION-FACED MARMOSET	**30/-**
WHITE-EARED ditto	**30/-**
PIGMY MARMOSET, rare	**42/-**
RING TAIL LEMURS, each **63/-** or the pair,	**110/-**
MEERCAT ... ... From	**42/-**
PARADOX CAT ... ... ,,	**5/-**
CIVET CAT ... ... ,,	**63/-**
LEOPARD CAT ... ... ,,	**55/-**
GENNET CAT ... ... each	**35/-**
ARMADILLOS ... ... ,,	**63/-**
AMERICAN RACCOON ... ... ,,	**84/-**
FLYING FOXES ... ... ,,	**42/-**
AUSTRALIAN OPOSSUM ... ... ,,	**35/-**

The Grey Indian Mongoos

(Or ICHNEUMON).

The Mongoose is about half the size of a cat, and, in colour is a grizzly grey. It is a native of India and Ceylon. It has a reputation as a great vermin killer, and has been known to destroy whole colonies of rats. It is also kept a great deal in captivity as a pet, in which capacity it thrives remarkably well.

Mongooses (wild)	**21/-, 25/-**	each
,, (tame)..	..**43/-, 50/-, 63/-**	,,

Mongooses are sure rat exterminators.

DOGS.

Approximate prices. We can supply any kind breed, at reasonable prices, on short not

---

If you require a dog, write us. As a Xmas Present a dog or puppy is always acceptable.

Airedale Dogs.

Pedigree, finest guards, good companions. Dogs, from **63/-** : Bitches, **42/-** Puppies, Dogs, **25/-** ; Bitches, **15/-**

Irish Terriers.

Dogs, from **35/-**; Bitches, **20/-** ; Pedigree Dogs, **50/-** Puppies, Dogs, **12/6** ; Bitches, **8/-** ; Pedigree puppies, **25/-**

Fox Terrier (Wire Haired).

Dogs, from, **35/-** ; Bitches, **20/-** Pedigree Dogs, **50/-**

Fox Terrier (Smooth).

Dogs, from, **35/-** ; Bitches, **17/6** Pedigree Dogs, **50/-** ; Puppies, **10/6**

West Highland Terriers (White).

Pedigree Dogs .. .. from **168/-** ,, Puppies .. .. ,, **84/-**

Squirrels.

Common Red Squirrels, Adults, **6/6** each.
American Grey Squirrels **21/-** ea.
Malabar Squirrels, very rare, **35/-** each.
Indian Palm Squirrels, Very rare, **15/-** each.

Carriage forward.   Travelling Boxes, 1/- extra.
Squirrel Cages .. **7/6** and **15/6** each.
With revolving wheel, **12/6**   Crate 1/- extra.

Ferrets.

White and Polecat. Trained for Rabbiting and Ratting, **5/6   6/6   7/6**
Untrained, **3/6** and **4/6**
Prices advance beginning and later part of year.

Guinea Pigs.

Smooth Coated, Young	**3/6**	pair.
,, Adults .. **4/6** and	**5/6**	,,
Rough Coated, Young	**4/6**	,,
,, Adults .. **5/6** and	**6/6**	,,
Abyssinian, prize strain, from ..	**6/6**	,,

Carriage forward.

Fancy Mice.

All colours, **1/-** pair. Suitable cages with glass fronts, **1/4, 2/-, 5/6 15/6**

Japanese Waltzing or Spinning Mouse.

Very amusing. **2/9** Pair. Travelling cage 4d. extra. Suitable cages **2/9** and **3/6**

Dormice.   From **3/9** pair.   Good size and colour, and bushy tails.   Suitable cages, **3/6** and **4/6**

Fancy Tame Rats.

White, Black and White, **1/-**   Suitable Cage, **3/6**

Interesting Pets Always on View.

Pekinese Spaniels.

Pedigree Dogs .. from **£10 10** ,, Puppies .. ,, **5 5**

Schipperkes.

From **70/-**   Puppies from **42/-**

Toy Yorkshire Dogs from **84**

Yorkshire Terriers.

Dogs from **42/-**   Puppies from **30**

Pomeranians.

From **63/-**   Pomeranian Puppies, Whi Chocolate, Black or Sable. A splendid pet. From **42/-** each.

Scotch Terriers.

Pedigree Dogs	from	**63/-**
,, Bitches	,,	**42/-**
,, Puppies, Dogs ..	,,	**35/-**
,, ,, Bitches	,,	**25/-**

Jarboas.

From Egypt. Amusing and interestin Tame. **7/6** each.   Cages **3/6** & **7**

Rabbits.

Blue and Tan	**12/6** pa
Silver Grey, young **5/-** pr. Adults	**10**
Flemish Giants, young ..	**5/-** pa
,, Adults ..	**12/6**
Belgiums, young **4/6** Adults	**8/6**
Belgium Flemish first cross, young	**3/-**
,, ,, Adults	**6/6**
Young pretty Pet Rabbits **1/- 1/6**	
Himalayan, young, **4/-** pair. Adults	**8**
White Polish ,, **6/-** ,,	**12**
Dutch, young, **4/-** pr. Adults, **7/6, 8**	
Angoras (White), young ..	**4/6** p
,, ,, Adults ..	**10/6**
English, young	**4/6** p

Harness Goats.

Trained to cart, and used to harn perfectly quiet and docile. From **42/-**

Hornless Goats.

Trained to harness, from **63/-**   For c and carriages, see Toy List.

All Live Stock is offered subject to being in stock, and is sent Carriage Forward, passenger tra Please state nearest Railway Station,

Useful Christmas Presents in the Drapery Department.

Furs can be
sent on
approval on
receipt of two
satisfactory
London trade
references, or
Cash Deposit to
cover value.

Model S. 921

Model
S. 923

Model S. 922

**Magnificent Real Fisher
Marmot Tie.**

ch Dark Sable Brown Colour, 78 in. long,
n. wide, trimmed **4 Tails and 8 Paws** ,
and lined Rich Dark Satin Merv.
Price **33/9**

ndsome Large size Pillow Muff to
tch, as illustration. Price **35/9**

**Very Handsome Real Fisher
Marmot Wrap.**

Rich Color. New Russian Sable finish.
Trimmed 12 Tails, 2 Heads, 8 Paws, and
lined Satin Merv. Price **52/6**

Large Muff to match, as Illustration.
Bargain price **42/-**

Real Fitch Ties.

Marvellously Cheap.

Sable Dyed Russian Fitch, length 65 in.
trimmed 6 Tails and 8 Paws. All choice
Skins of very fine quality, lined Rich
Brown Satin Merv. Price **18/11**

Fancy Muff to match, as Illustration.
Price **15/11**

Real Russian Hare Ties.

Specially Selected. An
excellent substitute for real Fox.
Rich Silky Black. Similar to
Illustration. Trimmed 2 Tails
and Paws.
2/11, 3/11, 4/11, 6/11 each.
Pillow Muffs to match,
3/11, 4/11, 6/11

Very Handsome
**Real Russian
Black Fur Set.**

Closely resembling real Fox.
Smart Wrap, trimmed Heads,
Tails and Paws, and hand-
some fancy Muff to match.

Sensational Value.

Price
Wrap and Muff **15/11**

Model
S. 925

Model
S. 924

Real Coney Sets.

TIE AND MUFF.

ndsome Tie 58 inches long
12 inch Pillow Muff. Both
d Squirrel Lock Fur.

argain price.
Tie and Muff, **12/9**

o a larger Set real Coney,
68 inches long and Pillow
ff 13 inches wide only lined,
rv Silk.

Price
Tie and Muff **12/9**

**Handsome
Real Coney Fur Coat.**

Guaranteed to be made from
choice Solid Skins of good
quality. Deep Red Collar, Coat
lined Silk throughout. Can be
had with cut away round corners
at bottom as sketch, or with
round square corners.

Length 50 inch. Price **84/-**
,, 52 ,, ,, **87/6**
,, 54 ,, ,, **92/6**
Cheaper quality coats from **59/6**

Bargains in Real Wolf Ties.

Real Wolf Ties, trimmed Tails,
Black only, 80 in. long .. price **10/6**

Real Wolf Ties, Black, trimmed
Tails and lined Silk, 90 in. long **12/11**

Real Wolf Shaped Ties lined Satin,
trimmed Tails, Paws, &c.
Straight in front but shaped to
lay flat round neck .. price **18/11**

(As Illustration.) Real Wolf
Wraps (Black), shaped and trimmed Tails and Paws, back and
front, lined Silk .. price **37/6**

Model 926.

Grey Natural Squirrel Wraps, made of twenty choice skins. Wrap 68 in. long, without tails, trimmed tails and paws and lined grey satin.
Price **29/11**

Handsome Fancy Muff to match (12 skins), **23/9**

Grey Squirrel Wrap, made from 16 skins, all carefully selected, and of good color. Length 56 in. without tails.
Price **18/11**

Model 928.

THE LATEST CRAZE IN FURS.

NATURAL FOX WOLF.

Fancy Tie, exactly as illust. 45 in. long from head to tip of tail.

Lined mole satin merv.

Price **18/11**

Fancy Animal Muffs to match.
18/11   23/9   47/6

Model 927.

Butterfly Style Real Squirrel Ties, all good Skins of clear grey color, lined satin.

A limited supply only.

Price **7/11**

Young Ladies' Squirrel Ties, similar to sketch, dark grey skins, lined satin, **4/11**

Model 930.
Real Coney Fur Set. Coney Tie, 56 in. long, and pillow muff, 12 in. wide, lined Squirrel Lock, all solid skins. Set complete.   Price **8/11**

Real Coney Butterfly Necklets (as Model 931).
A very smart Tie.
Choice solid bright skins.
Price **5/11**

Model 931.
Butterfly Style Real Squirrel Necklets, five whole skins. Trimmed tails and paws. Good grey color. Price **9/11**
Ditto, ditto, larger size skins. Price **11/9**

SPECIAL—Very fine extra large Necklets, made of eight large solid skins, pure grey color.   Price **15/9**

Model 932.
Squirrel Wrap, made of 16 very choice Whole skins. Trimmed paws and tails.
Price **37/6**

Squirrel Wrap, made of 20 fine dark grey whole skins. Trimmed paws and tails.
Price **42/-**

Real Squirrel Muff to match either of above wraps, made from 12 whole skins, large size, and trimmed four heads and eight tails.
Price   ..   **42/-**
Similar muffs, **29/6 35/9**

Model 929.

NATURAL FOX WOLF.

HANDSOME WRAP.

84 in. long from tail to tail.

Lined rich mole satin merv.

Trimmed tails and paws.

Price **47/6**

Model 933.
Handsome Coney Seal Tie, shaped at neck, lined silk. 70 in. long. 5 in. wide. All solid skins.
Price   ..   **12/11**

Very Fine Real Coney Tie, lined clear Squirrel Lock Fur. All choice solid skins. 80 in. long. 7 in. wide.
Price **18/11**

Large Size Coney Muffs. Pillow shape to go with above. Fine quality bright skins.
9/11   10/11 14/11 16/11

Model 935.
Real Bear Stoles shaped. Lined satin. Trimmed tails.
WONDERFUL VALUE.
12/11 16/11 19/11
Muffs to match.
Pillow shape, **16/11**

Model 934.
Real Squirrel Scarves, made from 6 clear solid skins, trimmed 4 tails and with split ends. Lined Fur.   Price **11/9**
Real Squirrel Scarves, lined grey satin, made of 10 dark grey skins, plain ends, tails.   Price **6/11**
Real Squirrel Scarves, made from eight large clear skins. Trimmed tails and paws. Price **9/11**
Real Squirrel Muffs. Pillow or Fancy shape.
14/11 18/11 21/9 25/9

Drapery Department.

USEFUL PRESENTS IN

HABERDASHERY.

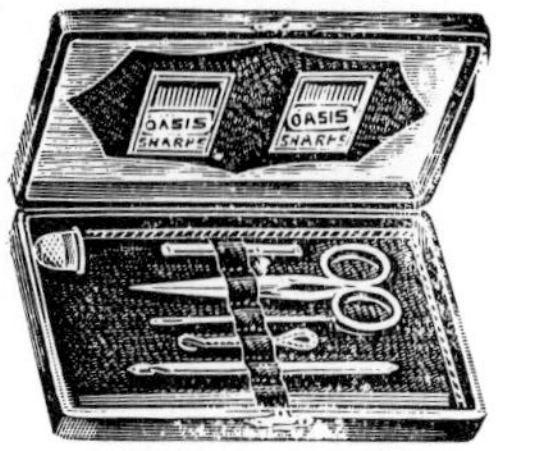

No. S. 701. Haberdashery Companion Case, fitted scissors, knitting pins, crochet hook, thimble, needle-holder, needles, etc. Price **1/11½**

No. S. 702. High-class fancy Needle Case, containing a nice assortment of best needles. Price **1/11½**

No. S. 707. A very nice Needle Case, contains a good assortment of best gilt-eyed English Needles. Price **1/3½**

All articles on this page Post Free

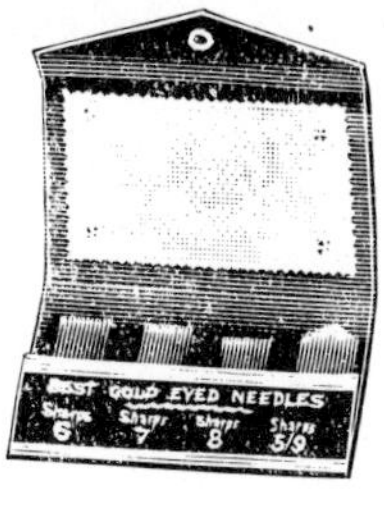

No. S. 703. Compact leather Needle Case, containing best needles. Price **10½d.**

No. S. 704. Good Value. Neat Case containing useful assortment of good English needles. Japanaise design on cover. **5¾d.**

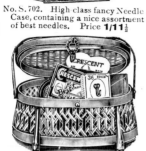

No. S. 705. Imitation leather Case, contains Sheffield scissors, thimble, gilt-eyed needles, knitting pins, crochet hook, etc. Price **1 3½**

No. S. 706. *Japanese Haberdashery Work Basket*, fitted with needles, cottons & other useful articles, **7½d.**

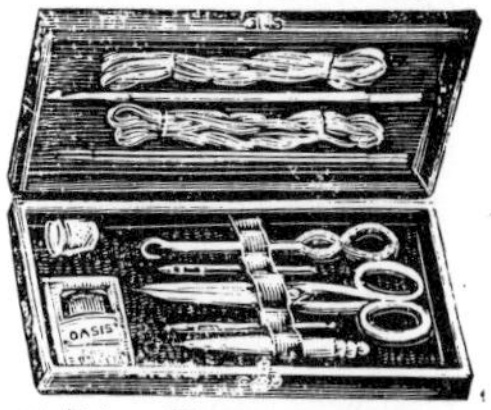

No. S. 708. Fancy Straw Work-Basket, fitted with a good and useful assortment of Haberdashery. Size 6½ by 4½ by 4 in. **1/3**

No. S. 709. Child's Haberdashery Case, containing coloured silks, crochet hooks, knitting pins, button hook thimble, scissors. etc., **1/11**

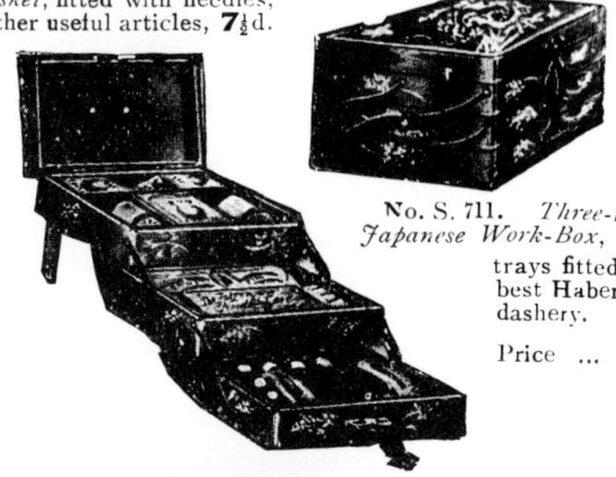

No. S. 711. *Three-tier Japanese Work-Box*, three trays fitted with best Haberdashery.
Price ... **3/3**

No. S. 712. A small Three-fold Needle Case containing a useful assortment of good English Needles.
Price **9½d.**

No. S. 713. Useful Box-case with tray, fitted cottons, silks, knitting pins, scissors, thimble, needles, etc., **3/3**

No. S. 710. *Japanese Lacquer Haberdashery Boxes*, fitted lift-out tray, brass hinges, etc., with a good assortment of best haberdashery.
by 6 by 3 in. **3/11** 9½ by 6½ by 3¼ in. **4/11** 10½ by 7⅜ by 3¾ **5/11**

No. S. 714. Neat Case, contains scissors, thimble, buttonhook, needles, etc., **2/11**

No. S. 715. *Batchelors' Rolls.* Fitted complete as illustration. Price **1/11**

No. S. 716. Fancy straw oblong Basket, lined silk, fitted with good assortmt. of Haberdashery, **1/9**

No. S. 717. Neat leatherette Box-case with lift-out tray, fitted scissors haberdashery, etc. Price **2/4**

No. S. 718. Fancy straw Work Basket, lid lined silk, fitted good assortment of reliable Haberdashery.
Price **2/3**

No. S. 719. *Grand Value.* Case containing 300 needles, a most useful assortment. Price **1/3**

No. S. 720. Real Sued leather Travelling Kit. Each case fitted with a good assortment of Haberdashery. 
Lady's or Gentleman's Case. Price **4/11**

No. S. 721. Imitation Crocodile Needle Case, fitted good assortment English Needles Price **6½d.**

No. S. 725. Well-made Walnut Cabinet, fall-down front. 11¾ by 10⅜ by 6⅞, **23/6** 13¼ by 10⅜ by 6⅞ **26/3**

No. S. 722. London-made Walnut Haberdashery Cabinet, fitted with finest quality Haberdashery.
⅞ by 9⅜ by 5 **11/9** 15¾ by 10¼ by 6⅝ **21/9**

No. S. 723. Sheraton Design. Inlaid Mahogany Cabinet, best Haberdashery. 10⅜ by 7⅞ by 3¼ in. **9/9** 11⅜ by 9¼ by 5, **13/9** 16⅜ by 10⅜ by 5⅝ in., **23/9**

No. S. 724. Hexagonal Fancy Japanese Work-Basket, fitted good assortment of best Haberdashery. 11 by 7 in., **2/11**

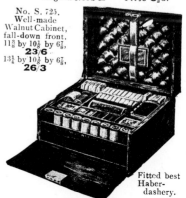

Fitted best Haberdashery.

Ladies' Handkerchief Boxes and Sachets.

DRAPERY DEPARTMENT.

No. S. 704. Fancy Box in dainty colours with pretty coloured photos of beautiful women. containing Six Ladies' Handkerchiefs.
Price ... **2/6**

No. S. 711. Hand-painted Satin Handkerchief Sachet, perfumed and satin lined, containing Six Ladies Hemstitched Handkerchiefs. Size, 8¼ by 6¼ in. Price ... **2/4**

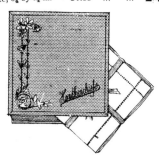

No. S. 707. Pretty Art Box in art moire effect with dainty enamelled metal decoration, containing Six Hemstitched Ladies' Handkerchiefs. Price ... **2/11**

No. S. 715. Art Box in effective colourings with coloured miniatures mounted on panel, containing Six Large Hemmed Handkerchiefs with self fancy borders. Price ... **2/4½**

No. S. 717. Beautiful Hand. painted Sachet, all satin, with band and bows of satin ribbon, containing 6 Hem-stitched Ladies' Handkerchiefs.
Size 10¾ by 8½ in.
Price **4/11**

No, S. 705, Fancy Cloth Covered Box with pretty design of birds and holly, &c., containing 6 Embroidered Hem-stitched Ladies' Handkerchiefs.
Price .. **1/11**

No. S. 712. Very pretty Box with ruched bevelled silk border and coloured country scenery on lid, contains 6 Hemstitched Ladies' Handkerchiefs. Price .. **3/6**

No. S. 709, Pretty Imi Linen Box with coloured pictures of beautiful women mounted on Panel and recessed in lid, containing 6 Hem-stitched Ladies Handkerchiefs.
Price .. **1/11**

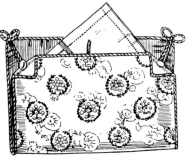

No. S. 716. Handsome Brocaded Silk, lined satin and perfumed Sachet, containing 6 Ladies' Hem-stitched Handkerchiefs. Size 11 by 7½ in. Price .. **3/11**

No. S. 703, Very pretty Box, bordered plush. Size, 9 by 6¾ in., with coloured views, containing 6 Irish Hemstitched Handkerchiefs.
Price .. **2/11**

No. S. 714. Hemstitched, Embroidered and Drawn Thread Sachet, with satin ribbon bow, containing 6 Ladies' Hemstitched Handkerchiefs
Price .. **3/4½**

No. S. 706. Very pretty Box with hand-painted inset pictures of children's faces, containing 6 hem-stitched Linen Ladies' Handkerchiefs.
Price .. **2/11**

No. S. 701. Dainty Hand-painted Handkerchief Sachet, perfumed. 11 by 9 in. Containing 6 Hem-stitched Ladies' Handkerchiefs.
Price **4/11**

No. S. 702. Fancy Box, containing Three Ladies Hem-stitched Handkerchiefs.
Price ... **1/0½**

No. S. 710. Dainty Box with plush band across and gilt and enamel metal mounting in new art colours, containing Six Ladies' Hem-stitched Handkerchiefs
Price ... **2/11**

No. S. 708. Fancy Box, cream Imi morocco with coloured photos of pretty women, containing Six Hem-stitched Ladies' Handkerchiefs. Price ... **1/11**

No. S. 718. Handsome Plush Box with pretty oxydised metal handle and corners. Size 8½ by 6½ in. Containing Six Hem-stitched Ladies' Handkerchiefs. Price **3/11**

All goods on this page post free.

No. 821
Ladies' Hemstitched and Embroidered Handkerchief.
Price **4**d. each, or **6** for **1/6**
Post free.

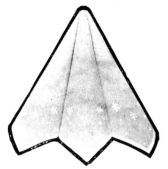

No. 822
Ladies' Embroidered and Hemstitched Handkerchief.
Price **5**d. each, or **6** for **2/6**
Post free.

No. 823
Ladies' Hemstitched and Embroidered Handkerchief.
Price **7½**d. each, or **6** for **3/6**
Post free.

No. 824
Ladies' Hemstitched and Embroidered Handkerchief.
Price **6**d. each, or **6** for **2/1**
Post free.

No. 825
Ladies' Fancy Drawn Thread Linen Handkerchief.
Price **7½**d. each, or **6** for **3/6**
Post free.

No. 826
Ladies' Plain Hemstitched Linen Handkerchief.
Box of **6**, Price **2/6** Post free.

No. 827
Ladies' Fancy Embroidered Handkerchiefs.
6 assorted patterns in box.
Price **1/11½** Post free

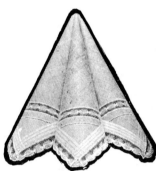

No. 828
Fine Irish Lawn Lace Trimmed Handkerchief.
Price **4½**d. each, or **6** for **2/2**
Post free.

No. 829
Ladies' Irish Lawn Initial and Hemstitched Handkerchief.
White with Pink Sky and Helio Colored Border and Letter.
Price **3½**d. each, **6** for **1/6**
Post free.

No. 830
Ladies' Fancy Drawn Thread Linen Handkerchief.
Price **10½**d. each, or **3** for **2,6**
Post free

No. 831
Ladies' Fancy Drawn Thread Linen Handkerchief.
Price **5½**d. each, or **6** for **2/6**
Post free.

No. 832
Ladies' Pure Irish Linen Initial Handkerchief.
½ in. letter in wreath.
Price **5½**d. each, or **6** for **2/6**
Post free.

No. 833
Ladies' Fine Irish Lawn, Lace Trimmed, Art Embroidered Handkerchiefs.
Price **10½**d. each, or **3** for **2/6**
Post free.

No. 834
Ladies' Fancy Lace Trimmed and Embroidered Handkerchief.
6 patterns assorted in Box.
Price **2/11** box. Post free.

No. 835
Ladies' Irish Linen Veined and Embroidered Handkerchief.
6 assorted patterns in box.
Price **2/11** box. Post free.

No. 836
Ladies' Fine Irish Lawn Lace Trimmed Handkerchief.
Price **7½**d. each, or **6** for **3 6**
Post free.

EE

No. S. 1090. Very handsome Guipure Lace Coat Collar. In Ivory or Paris colour.   Price ... **1/11½** Post free.

No. S. 1016. Pleated and tucked **Net Jabot.** Ivory & Paris colour. Price **1/0½** Post free.

No. S. 1018. Fine Net Vest with Hemstitched Frill. Ivory, Paris or Black.   Price **2/3** Post free.

No. S. 1017. Pretty Lace Jabot. Ivory or Paris colour. Frice **1/11½** Post free.

No. S. 1010. Effective Real Guipure Lace Collar. Ivory or Paris Colour. Price **1/11½** Post free.

No. S. 1015. Fine Guipure Lace Coat Collar. In Ivory or Paris Colour. Price **1/6½** Post free.

No. S. 1001. Pretty Satin Cravat, edged Ninon. In all fashionable colours. Price **1/0½** Post free.

No. S. 1008. Effective Crepe de Chine Artist's Bow. All colours. **1/0½** Post free.

No. S. 1006. Pretty Two-tone Satin Bow. Stocked in 12 different ways. Price **7½d.** Post free.

No. S. 1014. Pleated Lace Frill. Ivory or Paris colour. Price **1/0½** Post free.

No. S. 1011. New Design in Guipure Lace Neckband. Ivory or Paris Colour. Price **7½d.** Post free.

No. S. 1003. **Black Velvet and Coloured Satin Bow,** to be had in 12 different ways. Price **7½d.** Post free

No. S. 1020. Ivory Net Cravat, coloured bow. All latest colours Price **7½d.** Post free.

No. S. 1007. Smart Satin Bow. Can be had in all best colours. Price **7½d.** Post free.

No. S. 1012. Fine Make, Guipure Lace Neckband. Ivory or Paris Colour. Price **1/0½** Post free.

No. S. 1021. Fancy Muslin Collar with Guipure edge. White only. **1/6½** Post free.

No. S. 1023. Very pretty Collar. Fine Spot Net with Guipure edge. In Ivory Colour. Price **1 11½** Post free.

No. S. 1022. Guipure Lace Collar. Ivory or Paris Colour. Price **7½d.**   Post free.

No. S. 1004. **Velvet Cravat with Pearl Drops** In 7 choice colours. Price **1/0½** Post free.

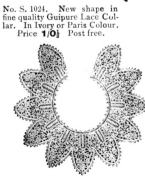

No. S. 1024. New shape in fine quality Guipure Lace Collar. In Ivory or Paris Colour. Price **1/0½** Post free.

No. S. 1002. Dainty Satin Cravat. In all good colours. Price **7½d.** Post free.

No. S. 1025. Effective Guipure Lace Coll. Ivory or Paris Colour. Price **1/0½** Post free.

No. S. 1013. Very pretty Spot Net and Guipure edged Collar. Ivory Colour. Price **1/0½** Post free.

S. 1005. Pretty Satin Cravat, in all prevailing colours. **7½d.** Post free

No. S. 1009. Vandyke Lace Collar in real Guipure. Ivory or Paris Colour. Price **1/6** Post free.

No. S. 1000. Satin and Ninon Cravat. In all fashionable colours. Price **1/0½** Post free.

No. S. 1026. New shape Guipure Lace Collar. Ivory or Paris Colour. Price **1/0½** Post free.

Drapery Department.

Children's Frocks and Pinafores.

Model S. 4064. Infant's Muslin Frock, clear muslin, trimmed embroidery. Price **7/11** Post free.

Model S. 4164. Infant's Embroidered Muslin Frock, trimmed lace. Price **9/11** Post free.

Model S. 3962. Nainsook Pinafore, trimmed lace. Post free.
Sizes 18 20 22 24 in.
Price **2/8 2/11 3/6 3/11**

Model S. 5062. EMBROIDERED MUSLIN FROCK. Sizes 18 20 22 24 in.
Prices **1/11½ 2/6 2/11 3/6**
Post free.

Iodel S. 6822. Infant's Embroidered Muslin Pinafore. Price **1/11½**

Model S. 7062. Embroidered Muslin Pinafore.
Sizes 18 20 22 24 in.
Price **2/8 2/11 3/6 3/11**
Post free.

Model 1362. Embroidered Muslin Pinafore.
18 20 22 24 in.
2/8 2/11 3/6 3/11
Post free.

Model S. 7181. Infant's Muslin Pinafore. Price **2/11**

Model S. 746. Child's Toddling Frock, Cream **Cashmere**, trimmed lace insertion, and silk embroidered, etc. **7/11**

Model S. 5164. Infant's Muslin Frock. Embroidered flouncing, trimmed lace and ribbon. **10/9**

odel S. 191. Child's clear Muslin Frock, trimmed embroidery flouncing, lace and ribbon.
19 in., **9/6** 21 in., **10/6** 23 in. **11/6**

Model S. 7062.
Embroidered Muslin Pinafore
18 in., **2/8**
20 in., **2/11**
22 in., **3/6**
24 in., **3/11**

Model S. 9854.
Infant's Muslin Frock, clear muslin, trimmed embroidery and ribbon.
18 in., **3/11** 20 in. **4/3**

Model S. 091. Child's Muslin Frock. Embroidered Muslin, trimmed ribbon. Sizes 19 21 23 in.
Prices **8/11 9/11 10/11**

LATEST DESIGNS IN MUSLIN APRONS. DRAPERY DEPARTMENT.

Our Aprons are well-known for their shape, perfect fitting skirts, and wide and long Strings.

Model S9055.
White Embroidered
Muslin Apron.
Price **1/6½** Post free.

Model S7165.
Dainty Four o'clock White
Muslin Tea Apron.
Price **1/11½** Post free.

Model S9355.
Princess Style White
Embroidered Muslin Apron.
Price **1/11½** Post free.

Model S0365.
Dainty Four o'clock
White Embroidered Muslin
Tea Apron.
Price **2/11½** Post free.

Model S0655.
Princess Style
White Embroidered
Muslin Apron.
Price **1 11½** Post free.

Model S6055.
White Embroidered
Muslin Apron.
Price **1/6½** Post free.

Model S6155.
White Embroidered
Muslin Apron.
Price **1/9½** Post free.

Model S2365.
Dainty Four o'clock
White Embroidered Muslin
Tea Apron.
Price **3/3** Post free.

Model S0055.
White Embroidered
Muslin Apron.
Price **1/3½** Post free.

Model S2955.
White Embroidered
Muslin Apron.
Price **2/11½** Post free.

Splendid Xmas Presents.—Upholstered Cane Chairs.

The Bachelor's Chair.
Buff Wicker Chair. Seat 20 in. by 20 in.
Upholstered in Cretonne. Price **21/-**

The Gloucester.
Buff and Wicker Chair upholstered in Cretonne.
Seat 18 in. by 18 in. Price **17/9**

The Chiswick.
Buff Wicker Chair upholstered in Cretonne. Seat
18 in. by 18 in. Price **13/3**

The Carlton.
Buff Wicker Chair upholstered in Cretonne.
Depth of seat 23 in. Width of seat 20 in.
Price **22/6**

The Grosvenor.
Buff Wicker Chair upholstered in Cretonne.
Depth of seat 23 in. Width of seat 22 in.
Price .. **24/9**

The Bedford.
Buff Wicker Chair upholstered in Cretonne.
Depth of seat 21 in. Width of Seat 20 in.
Price .. **12/11**

The Hanover.
Buff Wicker Chair. Depth of seat 19 in. Width
of seat 18 in. Price upholstered in Cretonne,
18/6 Upholstered in Taffeta **21/-**

The Burlington.
Buff Wicker Chair upholstered in
Cretonne. Depth of seat 24 in.
Width of seat 21 in.
Price **19/9**

Upholstered Cane Lounge.
Strongly made, very comfortable. Adjustable head and leg rests
Fitted with glass holders in arm rests.

Upholstered in Cretonne	..	..	..	**31/9**
Upholstered in Tapestry	..	..	..	**37/6**

All above Carriage extra outside our delivery Radius.

Cane Chairs for Xmas Presents.

Something Quite New.—The following **Special Lines** are upholstered in P.D. cloth—can be washed with soap and water to take away any stains such as ink or grease.

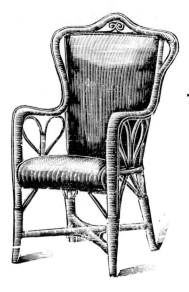

The Clarendon.

Upholstered in P.D. cloth. Seat 18 in. by 18 in.   Price **17/6**

The Chester.

White and coloured Cane Chair upholstered in P.D. cloth. Seat 18 in. by 18 in.   Price **15/6**

Cane Chair. No. 3340. Upholstered in Tapestry. Seat 18 in. by 18 in.   Price **14/6**

Children's Chairs.

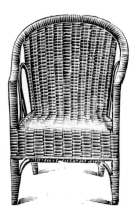

No. 7901. Child's Natural Cane Chair. Price **6/9**

No. 7901A. Child's Natural Cane Chair. Price **7/6**

No. 6901. Child's Natural Cane Chair. Price **7/9**

No. 43. Child's Table. Natural Cane. Price .. **7/11**

No. 846. Child's Chair in Cream Rush. Upholstered in Cretonne. Price .. **5/11**

No. 3. Child's Natural Cane Chair. Price .. **4/9**

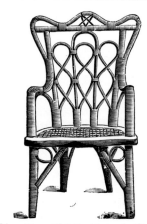

No. 33. Child's Natural Cane Chair. Price **4/11**

No. 9. Child's Natural Cane Chair Price .. **6/9**

All above Carriage extra outside our delivery Radius.

Gamage's Restaurant

Visitors, regular shoppers and business people will appreciate this quiet retreat for

LUNCHEONS, AND LIGHT
AFTERNOON TEAS REFRESHMENTS.

Reasonable Prices HOME COOKING **OPEN ALL DAY**

After a morning's shopping, or an afternoon's trot, here, there and everywhere, Gamage's Restaurant provides a retreat in which one can rest and enjoy home cooking far away from the bustle of the Store above, and the street outside. Gamage's Restaurant is one of this Store's greatest attractions, is approached from the Bag and Trunk Department, and everything being furnished in white presents a cool appearance, extremely cool in Summer, whereas in Winter, while heated, the temperature is so regulated as to be comfortable, at a temperature which does not engender cold or chills.

We dwell on this Restaurant and its accessibility, because so many have been in our Store, and yet have not been in the Restaurant, which has been established nearly four years, and makes a speciality of home cooking, with a varied menu. A charming luncheon can be had for 1/6, and a tea for 9d. Ice Creams and Iced Drinks are served in the Summer from the American Fountain, and warm drinks in the Winter.

It has proved a pleasing retreat for ladies, and is under the management of a lady, and attended to by waitresses. Retiring rooms are provided, and the Restaurant is almost next to the Information Bureau, has a telephone booth fitted therein, from which you can speak either to the City, or over the long distance wires.

Particular stress is laid upon the fact that everything is done to ensure the best from the markets, and everything that is in season is furnished at most reasonable prices.

The aim of the establishment being not so much to make a profit out of the Restaurant as to provide inside the Building a Restaurant in which all our patrons can obtain luncheon à la carte, or afternoon teas.

Gamage's Soda Fountain

The finest American Bar in Europe. Under the care of qualified American attendants. A splendid selection of Winter Drinks, Cool Drinks, Fancy Drinks, Tonics, Ice Creams, etc. Booklet containing full list and prices of all seasonable drinks free on application at the Soda Fountain, where are also to be obtained the finest American and English Confections, being special agents for—

Heide's American Chocolates, Peppermints and Candies, De Villar's Chocolates, Plasmon Chocolate, Allen & Hanbury's Chocolate, Pascall's Maltex, Killengrey's Royal Butter Scotch, Sen-Sen Gum.

Gamage's Toilet Saloon

We feel sure that the many thousands whose business daily carries them to the City need only our mention of this essential feature of a gent's outfitting house to give same a trial. Expert English attendants, together with the most modern hygienic appliances and comfortable surroundings have earned well deserved praise from the Saloon's patrons, numerous as the latter are we feel sure there are many who would appreciate the service our saloon offers did they but know of its location :

In the east building, directly on entering either the Jewellery or Gent's Outfitting and Tobacco Departments.

A. W. GAMAGE, Ltd., HOLBORN, LONDON, E.C.

Catalogue of any Department
POST FREE.

We issue Special Illustrated Catalogues of the following departments, any of which may be obtained free on application.

Drapery.

Sports and Games.

Horticultural, Poultry Appliances,
and Live Stock.

Guns and Fishing Tackle,
Taxidermy, and everything for the Naturalist.

Scouts' Outfits.

Cycles, Cycle Accessories,
Cycle Clothing, &c.

Motor Clothing and Accessories.

Bags and Trunks
and all Travelling Requisites.

Baby Carriages, Cots,
Chairs, and Kindergarten Furniture.

Bees and Bee Appliances.

Toys and Musical Instruments.

Jewellery, Fancy Goods,
Stationery, Books, &c.

Drugs and Toilet Requisites.

Cigars, Tobacco, Pipes, &c.

Fitted Luncheon Baskets, &c.

Photography, Magic Lanterns
and Optical Goods.

Conjuring and Magic.

Household Utensils,
and China and Glass.

Tools, Lamps,
Gas and Electrical Fittings.

Furniture.

Wireless & Mechanical Models.

Tailoring and Outfitting.

Sale Lists (Twice Yearly).

'Xmas Presents List.